THE WELFARE STATE

Transformations of the State

CRC 597

The University of Bremen's Transformations of the State Collaborative Research Centre (TranState) served as the institutional, intellectual, and administrative home for the preparation of this Handbook. Funded by the *Deutsche Forschungsgemeinschaft* (German Research Foundation), TranState is made up of about a hundred researchers from all disciplines of the social sciences and all stages of career development.

TranState defines the multifaceted modern state in four intersecting dimensions: *resources*, or control of the use of force and revenues; *law*, or jurisdiction and the courts; *legitimacy*, or the acceptance of political rule by the populace; *welfare*, or the facilitation of economic growth and social equality. This Handbook focuses on the welfare dimension. Oxford University Press has now asked TranState to serve as home base for another book in the Handbook series, this time taking a wide-angle, multidimensional view of the state and how it has developed under globalization.

THE OXFORD HANDBOOK OF

THE WELFARE STATE

Edited by

FRANCIS G. CASTLES

STEPHAN LEIBFRIED

JANE LEWIS

HERBERT OBINGER

and

CHRISTOPHER PIERSON

OXFORD
UNIVERSITY PRESS

OXFORD
UNIVERSITY PRESS

Great Clarendon Street, Oxford OX2 6DP

Oxford University Press is a department of the University of Oxford.
It furthers the University's objective of excellence in research, scholarship,
and education by publishing worldwide in

Oxford New York

Auckland Cape Town Dar es Salaam Hong Kong Karachi
Kuala Lumpur Madrid Melbourne Mexico City Nairobi
New Delhi Shanghai Taipei Toronto

With offices in

Argentina Austria Brazil Chile Czech Republic France Greece
Guatemala Hungary Italy Japan Poland Portugal Singapore
South Korea Switzerland Thailand Turkey Ukraine Vietnam

Oxford is a registered trade mark of Oxford University Press
in the UK and in certain other countries

Published in the United States
by Oxford University Press Inc., New York

© The several contributors 2010

British Library Cataloguing in Publication Data

Data available

Library of Congress Cataloging in Publication Data

Data available

Typeset by SPI Publisher Services, Pondicherry, India
Printed in Great Britain
on acid-free paper by
CPI Group(UK)Ltd,Croydon,CR0 4YY

ISBN 978–0–19–957939–6

5 7 9 10 8 6

Contents

List of Tables   x
List of Figures   xiii
Select List of Abbreviations   xv
About the Contributors   xix
Preface   xxiii
    STEPHAN LEIBFRIED
Note on the Jacket Illustration   xxvi
    STEPHAN LEIBFRIED

1 Introduction   1
    FRANCIS G. CASTLES, STEPHAN LEIBFRIED, JANE LEWIS,
    HERBERT OBINGER & CHRISTOPHER PIERSON

PART I PHILOSOPHICAL JUSTIFICATIONS AND CRITIQUES OF THE WELFARE STATE

2 Ethics   19
    STUART WHITE
3 Intellectual Roots   32
    CHRIS PIERSON & MATTHIEU LEIMGRUBER
4 Critics and Beyond   45
    DESMOND KING & FIONA ROSS

PART II HISTORY

5 The Emergence of the Western Welfare State   61
    STEIN KUHNLE & ANNE SANDER
6 Post-War Welfare State Development   81
    FRANK NULLMEIER & FRANZ-XAVER KAUFMANN

PART III APPROACHES

7 Research Methods   105
EDWIN AMENTA & ALEXANDER HICKS

8 Public and Private Social Welfare   121
WILLEM ADEMA & PETER WHITEFORD

9 Families versus State and Market   139
MARY DALY

10 Disciplinary Perspectives   152
EINAR ØVERBYE

PART IV INPUTS AND ACTORS

11 Needs and Risks in the Welfare State   169
JAN ZUTAVERN & MARTIN KOHLI

12 Democracy and Capitalism   183
TORBEN IVERSEN

13 Unions and Employers   196
BERNHARD EBBINGHAUS

14 Parties   211
MANFRED G. SCHMIDT

15 Political Institutions   227
ELLEN M. IMMERGUT

16 Public Attitudes   241
STEFAN SVALLFORS

17 Gender   252
ANN SHOLA ORLOFF

18 Religion   265
KEES VAN KERSBERGEN & PHILIP MANOW

19 Migration and Ethnic Minorities   278
STEPHEN CASTLES & CARL-ULRIK SCHIERUP

20 European Union   292
GERDA FALKNER

21 Intergovernmental Organizations   306
KLAUS ARMINGEON

22 Globalization 318
   DUANE SWANK

PART V POLICIES

23 Social Expenditure and Revenues 333
   HERBERT OBINGER & UWE WAGSCHAL
24 Old-Age Pensions 353
   KARL HINRICHS & JULIA F. LYNCH
25 Health 367
   RICHARD FREEMAN & HEINZ ROTHGANG
26 Long-Term Care 378
   AUGUST ÖSTERLE & HEINZ ROTHGANG
27 Work Accident and Sickness Benefits 391
   OLLI KANGAS
28 Disability 406
   MARK PRIESTLEY
29 Unemployment Insurance 420
   OLA SJÖBERG, JOAKIM PALME & EERO CARROLL
30 Labour Market Activation 435
   LANE KENWORTHY
31 Social Assistance 448
   THOMAS BAHLE, MICHAELA PFEIFER & CLAUS WENDT
32 Family Benefits and Services 462
   JONATHAN BRADSHAW & NAOMI FINCH
33 Housing 479
   TONY FAHEY & MICHELLE NORRIS
34 Education 494
   MARIUS R. BUSEMEYER & RITA NIKOLAI

PART VI POLICY OUTCOMES

35 The Social Rights of Citizenship 511
   JOHN D. STEPHENS

36 Inequality and Poverty   526
    PETER SAUNDERS
37 Macroeconomic Outcomes   539
    ISABELA MARES
38 Welfare Retrenchment   552
    JONAH D. LEVY

PART VII WORLDS OF WELFARE

39 Models of the Welfare State   569
    WIL A. ARTS & JOHN GELISSEN

Established Welfare States

40 The Nordic Countries   586
    MIKKO KAUTTO
41 Continental Western Europe   601
    BRUNO PALIER
42 The South European Countries   616
    MAURIZIO FERRERA
43 The English-Speaking Countries   630
    FRANCIS G. CASTLES

Emerging Welfare States

44 Latin America   644
    EVELYNE HUBER & JUAN BOGLIACCINI
45 East Asia   656
    ITO PENG & JOSEPH WONG
46 Eastern Europe and Russia   671
    LINDA. J. COOK

PART VIII PROSPECTS

47 The Sustainability of Western Welfare States   689
    HOWARD GLENNERSTER

48 The Global Future of Welfare States   703
    IAN GOUGH & GÖRAN THERBORN

References   721
Subject Index   821
Name Index   861

List of Tables

5.1 Overview: Establishment of first statutory social security schemes in selected ILO member countries (down to 1945)   71

7.1 Causal research according to methodological approaches   107

7.2 Welfare programme consolidation in early democracies and proto-democracies (1920)   111

8.1 From gross to net social spending (2005)   131

8.2 The income accounting framework   136

9.1 Main family policy reforms at national level since the mid-1990s   144

9.2 Constellation of factors animating state policy towards families   149

10.1 Disciplinary perspectives on the welfare state: Core debates   153

11.1 Socio-economic causes of new social needs and risks   177

11.2 Selected risk and need profiles: Employment   180

11.3 Selected risk and need profiles: Family   181

13.1 Ideal-typical modes of labour relations and their institutional affinities   204

14.1 Policy positions of political parties on expansion of the welfare state versus retrenchment (early 21st century)   214

14.2 The welfare state and the difference between social democratic and secular conservative party composition of government in 21 OECD countries (since the 1950s)   218

14.3 Social policy positions of major families of parties since the mid-1950s   224

15.1 Veto points and veto players in selected OECD countries (1980–2005)   233

20.1 Forms of EU social policy   299

20.2 Impact of European integration on national social spending   301

23.1 Trends in social expenditure (1980–2005)   336

23.2 Programme-related public spending in per cent of GDP (2005)   339

23.3 Levels of taxation in 21 OECD countries (1990–2006)   346

23.4 Taxation trends in 21 OECD countries (1990–2006)   349

23.5 Attitudes towards taxation and the welfare state (1985–2006)   351

24.1 Net replacement rates of public pensions at various earnings
      levels (2004)   358

24.2 Funding and types of pension schemes   364

29.1 Years of introduction of first laws providing for unemployment
      benefits at the national level in eighteen OECD countries   422

29.2 Net replacement rates and coverage in labour force (in per cent)
      in eighteen countries (averages for 1930–39, 1947–70, and
      1975–2005)   424

31.1 Minimum income provisions in selected EU countries (1992–2006)   454

31.2 Guaranteed minimum income levels in OECD countries (2006)   455

32.1 Child well-being in Europe by dimension (c. 2006)   476

33.1 Occupied dwellings by tenure in European Union member states
      in per cent (1990, 2004)   483

33.2 Government housing interventions in European Union member
      states (2004/5)   486

35.1 Average replacement rates by welfare state regime (1950, 1995)   520

35.2 (Quasi-)Social rights indicators of services and gendered policies
      (1970, 1985, 1999)   521

35.3 Results of regression on social rights measures   524

36.1 Social expenditure, income inequality, and poverty rates in OECD
      countries (mid-2000s)   533

37.1 Average unemployment in advanced industrialized political economies:
      Cross-national and temporal trends (1960–75, 1976–95)   549

39.1 Empirical robustness of welfare state models   575

40.1 Key OECD indicators of the role of the state in social policy (1990)   594

40.2 Key OECD indicators of the role of the state in social policy (2005/6) 598

43.1 Liberal regime characteristics according to Esping-Andersen and
      English-speaking family of nation characteristics according to Castles
      and Obinger   637

43.2   Shares and progressivity of cash benefits and household taxes in
       household disposable income in English-speaking and selected other
       OECD countries (mid-2000s)   639

43.3   Measures of the dispersion of components of social expenditure, child
       poverty, and inequality in 18 OECD countries (mid-2000s)   641

46.1   Selected welfare indicators (2005)   677

47.1   Additional spending driven by demography, assuming present policies
       in per cent of expected GDP, excluding education (2004–2050)   694

48.1   Cluster analysis and mean values for welfare regimes of 65 non-OECD
       countries (2000)   712

LIST OF FIGURES

8.1 Public social expenditure by broad social policy area in percentage of GDP (2005)   127

13.1 Trade union density, social expenditure, and bargaining coverage (1980, 2000)   202

23.1 Patterns of social spending in 19 OECD countries (2005)   341

24.1 Typology of pension systems   356

24.2 Public and private pension spending as a percentage of gross domestic product (2003)   359

24.3 Pension spending as a share of total non-health social expenditure (2003)   360

24.4 Household income inequality, population aged 65+ (mid-2000s)   361

27.1 The sequential introduction of social insurance laws in different continents and in the OECD-18, with OECD-18 countries excluded from their continents (since the 1880s)   393

27.2 Generosity (net benefit/net wage) and universalism (insured/labour force) of work accident benefits in 18 OECD countries (1930, 2000)   397

27.3 Generosity (net benefit/net wage) and universalism (insured/labour force) of sickness benefits in 17 OECD countries (1930, 2000)   403

30.1 Employment rates (1989, 2007)   445

31.1 Extent and generosity of social assistance in OECD countries (1992)   452

32.1 Per cent of children living in a lone parent family (2006)   464

32.2 Spending per child in per cent of spending per older person (1980–2003)   468

32.3 Child benefit package for couple with two children one earner by level of earnings (2005). Ranked by average earnings: Per cent extra over a childless couple on the same earnings   470

32.4 Fertility rate 2006 by family spending as a per cent of GDP 2005   472

32.5 Child poverty rates before and after transfers (2006)   475

32.6 Overall child well-being by per cent GDP devoted to family benefits
      and services (2005)   477

34.1 The relationship between public education and social spending
      in per cent of GDP (2005)   497

34.2 Variation of spending on education (2005)   498

34.3 Variation of spending on tertiary education (2005)   499

34.4 Hierarchical cluster analysis of education systems: Ward method,
      Euclidian distance measure (*c.* 2005)   500

SELECT LIST OF ABBREVIATIONS

ADLs	Activities of daily living
AEI	American Enterprise Institute, Washington, DC (1943 ff.; http://www.aei.org)
AFDC	Aid to Families with Dependent Children, USA (1935–1997; now TANF)
ALMP	Active labour market policies (1990s ff.)
ATTAC	The international anti-globalization network ATTAC (1998 ff.; Action pour une Taxe Tobin d'Aide aux Citoyens = Association for the Taxation of Financial Transactions for the Aid of Citizens; http://www.attac.org/)
BRIC	Brazil, Russia, India, & China
CCT	Conditional cash transfer programme
CEE	Central and Eastern European
CEPAL	Comisión Económica para América Latina y el Caribe, Santiago, Chile (= ECLAC; 1948 ff.; http://www.eclac.org/)
CPF	Central Provident Fund, Singapore (1955 ff.; http://mycpf.cpf.gov.sg)
CPS	Centre for Policy Studies, London (1974 ff.; http://www.cps.org.uk/)
CV	Coefficient of variation
CWED	Comparative Welfare Entitlements Dataset (http://www.sp.uconn.edu/~scruggs/wp.htm)
DC	Defined contribution
DRG	Diagnosis related group
ECJ	European Court of Justice, Luxembourg (1952 ff.; http://curia.europa.eu)
ECLAC	Economic Commission for Latin America and the Caribbean, Santiago, Chile (= CEPAL; 1948 ff.; http://www.eclac.org/)
ECM	Error correction models
EFTA	European Free Trade Association, countermovement to founding the EEC [EU] in 1957 (1960 ff.; http://www.efta.int/)
EITC	Earned Income Tax Credit, USA (also EIC; 1975 ff.; in UK: Working Tax Credit)
EPL	Employment protection legislation
ESA	Event structure analysis
ESF	European Social Fund, Brussels (EU; 1957 ff.; http://ec.europa.eu/employment_social/esf/index_en.htm)
EU	European Union as of Maastricht Treaty 1992, Brussels (EEC [European Economic Community] or EC [European Community]; 1957–1992; http://europa.eu/index_en.htm)

EUR The Euro currency (also €; accounting currency 1999–2001; in circulation as of 2002, 2009 in 16 Member States)

Eurostat Statistical Office of the European Communities [European Union], Luxembourg (1953 ff.; http://ec.europa.eu/eurostat)

GATS General Agreement on Trade in Services (1995 ff.; under WTO; see http://www.wto.org/)

GATT General Agreement on Tariffs and Trade (1947 ff.; see now WTO http://www.wto.org/)

GDP Gross domestic product

GNP Gross national product

GP General (medical) practitioner, UK

GPA Global Program on AIDS, UN (but see also WHO; 2001 ff.; http://www.un.org/ga/aids/ungassfactsheets/html/fssgcall_en.htm and http://www.unaids.org/en/default.asp)

HMO Health Maintenance Organization, USA

HRS Health and Retirement Study, USA (http://hrsonline.isr.umich.edu/)

IBRD International Bank for Reconstruction and Development = World Bank (WB), Washington, DC (1946 ff.; with IMF one of the two Bretton Woods institutions founded in 1944; http://www.worldbank.org/)

ICSID International Center for the Settlement of Investment Disputes, Washington, DC (1966 ff.; WB founded arbitration institution devoted to investor-state dispute settlement; http://icsid.worldbank.org/ICSID/)

IDA International Development Association, Washington, DC (1960 ff.; grant-making or interest free credit-providing branch of the WB; via http://www.worldbank.org/)

IEA Institute for Economic Affairs, London (1955 ff.; http://www.iea.org.uk/)

IFC International Finance Corporation, Washington, DC (1956 ff.; member of WB Group, financing investment in private sector in developing countries; http://www.ifc.org/)

IFI International financial institutions

IGO International governmental organizations

ILO International Labour Organization [and Office], Geneva, Switzerland (1919 ff.; http://www.ilo.org/)

IMF International Monetary Fund, Washington, DC (1944 ff. http://www.imf.org/)

INGO International non-governmental organizations

IO Intergovernmental organizations

ISI Import substitution industrialization

ISSP International Social Survey Programme (1984 ff.; http://www.issp.org/)

KMT Kuomintang, China

LDC Less developed country

LDP Liberal Democratic Party, Japan

LIS Luxembourg Income Study, Luxembourg (1983 ff.; http://www.lisproject.org/)

LTC	Long-term care
MIGA	Multilateral Investment Guarantee Agency, Washington, DC (1988 ff.; WB Group; http://www.miga.org/)
MLSG	Minimum Living Standard Guarantee, China (and South Korea)
NDC	Notional defined contribution
NHI	National health insurance
NHS	National Health Service, UK (1948 ff.; http://www.nhs.uk)
NICS	Newly industrialized countries
OECD	Organization for Economic Co-operation and Development, Paris (1961 ff.; dates back to Marshall Plan 1948–1951; http://www.oecd.org)
OMC	Open Method of Coordination, EU (Lisbon Strategy; 2000 ff.)
OPEC	Organization of Petroleum Exporting Countries, Vienna (1960 ff.; http://www.opec.org)
PAYG	Pay as you go
PPP	Purchasing power parity
QCA	Qualitative comparative analysis
SCIP	Social Citizenship Indicators Programme (http://www.snd.gu.se/sv/catalogue/series/55)
SD	Standard deviation
SERPS	State Earnings-Related Pension Scheme, UK (1978–2002; replaced 2002 by State Second Pension)
SHARE	Survey of Health, Ageing and Retirement in Europe (http://www.share-project.org/)
SOCX	Social Expenditure Data Set (OECD; http://www.oecd.org/els/social/expenditure)
SOE	State-owned enterprise
TANF	Temporary Assistance for Needy Families, US (1997 ff.)
TRIPS	Trade-related Aspects of Intellectual Property Rights (1994 ff.; under WTO; see http://www.wto.org/)
TSCS	Time-series cross-section
UN	United Nations, New York (1945 ff.; http://www.un.org)
UNDP	United Nations Development Program, New York etc. (1965 ff.; http://www.undp.org/)
UNESCO	United Nations Educational, Scientific and Cultural Organization, Paris (1946 ff.; http://portal.unesco.org/)
USD	US Dollars (US$)
WB	World Bank; Washington, DC (1946 ff.; see also IBRD; with IMF one of the two Bretton Woods institutions founded in 1944; http://www.worldbank.org/)
WHO	World Health Organization, Geneva, Switzerland (1948 ff.; http://www.who.int/en/)

WTC   Working Tax Credit, UK (2003 ff., predecessor 1999–2003 WFTC with 'F'
         standing for families; see also EITC, USA)
WTO   World Trade Organization, Geneva, Switzerland (1993 ff.; http://www.
         wto.org)
US AID   United States Agency for International Development, Washington, DC
         (1961 ff.; originates with Marshall Plan 1948–1951; http://www.usaid.gov/)

About the Contributors

Willem Adema is Senior Economist in the OECD Social Policy Division, Paris.

Edwin Amenta is Professor of Sociology at the University of California, Irvine.

Klaus Armingeon is Professor of Political Science at the University of Bern and Director of the Institute of Political Science (IPW).

Wil A. Arts is Professor of Modern Sociology at University College Utrecht and Professor Emeritus of General and Theoretical Sociology at Tilburg University.

Thomas Bahle is a Researcher at the Department of European Societies and their Integration at the Mannheim Centre for European Social Research (MZES).

Juan Ariel Bogliaccini is a Doctoral Student at the Political Science Department, University of North Carolina at Chapel Hill.

Jonathan Bradshaw is Professor of Social Policy at the University of York and Member of the Research Committee of the International Social Security Association (ISSA).

Marius R. Busemeyer is a Researcher at the Max Planck Institute for the Study of Societies in Cologne.

Eero Carroll is a Post-doctoral Research Fellow at the Swedish Institute of Social Research (SOFI) at Stockholm University.

Francis G. Castles is Professor Emeritus at the University of Edinburgh and Adjunct Professor of Political Science at the Research School of Social Sciences at Australian National University and at the Centre for Social Policy Research (CeS) in Bremen.

Stephen Castles is Research Professor of Sociology at the University of Sydney and Associate Director of the International Migration Institute (IMI) at the University of Oxford.

Linda J. Cook is Professor of Political Science at Brown University, Providence, RI.

Mary Daly is Professor of Sociology at the School of Sociology, Social Policy and Social Work at Queen's University Belfast.

Bernhard Ebbinghaus is Professor of Sociology and Director of the Mannheim Centre for European Social Research (MZES).

Tony Fahey is Professor of Social Policy and Head of the School of Applied Social Science at University College Dublin.

Gerda Falkner is Director of the Institute for European Integration Research of the Austrian Academy of Sciences in Vienna, and a Professor in the University of Vienna's Department of Government.

Maurizio Ferrera is Professor of Political Science and President of the Graduate School in Social, Economic and Political Studies of the State University of Milan.

Naomi Finch is Lecturer in Social Policy at the University of York.

Richard Freeman is Senior Lecturer in Theory and Method in the Graduate School of Social and Political Science at the University of Edinburgh.

John Gelissen is an Assistant Professor of Methodology and Statistics at Tilburg University.

Howard Glennerster is Professor Emeritus of Social Administration at the London School of Economics and Co-Director of the Centre for Analysis of Social Exclusion (CASE).

Ian Gough is Professorial Research Fellow at CASE, LSE, and Emeritus Professor at the University of Bath.

Alexander Hicks is Winship Distinguished Research Professor at Emory University in Atlanta, Georgia.

Karl Hinrichs is a Senior Research Fellow at the Centre for Social Policy Research (CeS) at the University of Bremen and Professor of Political Science at the Humboldt University Berlin.

Evelyne Huber is Morehead Alumni Professor of Political Science and Chair of the Department of Political Science at the University of North Carolina.

Ellen M. Immergut is Professor of Comparative Politics at the Humboldt University Berlin.

Torben Iversen is the Harold Hitchings Burbank Professor of Political Economy at Harvard University.

Olli Kangas is Head of the Research Department of the Social Insurance Institution of Finland (Kela).

Franz-Xaver Kaufmann is Professor Emeritus of Sociology and Social Policy at the University of Bielefeld.

Mikko Kautto is Head of the Research Department at the Finnish Centre for Pensions.

Lane Kenworthy is Professor of Sociology and Political Science at the University of Arizona.

Desmond King is the Andrew Mellon Professor of American Government and Professorial Fellow at Nuffield College at the University of Oxford.

Martin Kohli is Professor of Sociology at the European University Institute in Florence.

Stein Kuhnle is Professor of Comparative Politics at the University of Bergen and Professor of Comparative Social Policy at the Hertie School of Governance in Berlin.

Stephan Leibfried is Professor of Public Policy at the University of Bremen, Director of the Collaborative Research Centre Transformations of the State (TranState) and member of the History and Institutions unit of the Centre for Social Policy Research (CeS) there.

Matthieu Leimgruber is Lecturer at the University of Geneva and a Research Fellow at the Swiss National Science Foundation.

Jonah D. Levy is Professor of Political Science at the University of California, Berkeley.

Jane Lewis is Professor of Social Policy at the London School of Economics.

Julia F. Lynch is Janice and Julian Bers Assistant Professor in the Social Sciences at the University of Pennsylvania.

Philip Manow is Professor of Political Science (Modern Political Theory) at the University of Heidelberg.

Isabela Mares is an Associate Professor of Political Science at Columbia University.

Rita Nikolai is Head of the Junior Research Group Education and Transitions into the Labour Market (funded by the Federal Department of Education and Research) at the Social Science Research Center Berlin (WZB).

Michelle Norris is a Senior Lecturer at the School of Applied Social Science at University College Dublin.

Frank Nullmeier is Professor of Political Science at the University of Bremen, Principle Investigator at the Collaborative Research Centre Transformations of the State (TranState), and Director of the Centre for Social Policy Research (CeS), heading its Theory and Constitution of the Welfare State unit.

Herbert Obinger is Professor of Comparative Public and Social Policy at the University of Bremen, directs the History and Institutions unit of the Centre for Social Policy Research (CeS) and directs two projects in the Collaborative Research Centre Transformations of the State (TranState).

Ann Shola Orloff is Professor of Sociology, Gender Studies and Political Science at Northwestern University.

August Österle is an Associate Professor at the Institute for Social Policy at the Vienna University of Economics and Business.

Einar Øverbye is Professor of International Social and Health Policy at the Oslo University College.

Bruno Palier is a Senior Researcher at the Centre for Political Research at Sciences Po (CEVIPOF) in Paris.

Joakim Palme is Director of the Institute for Future Studies, Sweden.

Ito Peng is Professor of Sociology and Associate Director of the School of Public Policy and Governance at the University of Toronto.

Michaela Pfeifer is a Researcher at the Department of European Societies and their Integration at the Mannheim Centre for European Social Research (MZES).

Christopher Pierson is Professor of Politics at the University of Nottingham.

Mark Priestley is Professor of Disability Policy at the University of Leeds.

Fiona Ross is Senior Lecturer in the Department of Politics, University of Bristol.

Heinz Rothgang is Head of the Health Economics, Health Policy and Outcomes Research Unit at the Centre for Social Policy Research (CeS) at the University of Bremen and Principle Investigator at the Collaborative Research Centre Transformations of the State (TranState).

Anne Sander is a Research Associate at the Hertie School of Governance in Berlin.

Peter Saunders holds a Research Chair in Social Policy at the Social Policy Research Centre and is a Scientia Professor at the University of New South Wales.

Carl-Ulrik Schierup is Professor and Director of the Institute for Research on Migration, Ethnicity and Society (REMESO) at Linköping University.

Manfred G. Schmidt is Professor of Political Science at the University of Heidelberg.

Ola Sjöberg is an Associate Professor of Sociology at the Swedish Institute of Social Research (SOFI) at Stockholm University.

John D. Stephens is the Gerhard E. Lenski, Jr. Distinguished Professor of Political Science and Sociology and Director of the Center for European Studies at the University of North Carolina.

Stefan Svallfors is Professor of Sociology at Umeå University.

Duane Swank is Professor of Political Science at the Helen Way Klingler College of Arts and Sciences at Marquette University in Milwaukee, Wisconsin.

Göran Therborn is Professor and Chair of Sociology at the University of Cambridge.

Kees van Kersbergen is Professor of Political Science at the Free University (VU) in Amsterdam.

Uwe Wagschal is Professor of Comparative Politics at the University of Freiburg, Germany.

Claus Wendt is Professor of Sociology and Health and Healthcare Systems at the University of Siegen, Germany.

Stuart White is Director of the Public Policy Unit, University Lecturer in Politics and Tutorial Fellow in Politics at Jesus College at the University of Oxford.

Peter Whiteford is Professor at the Social Policy Research Centre at the University of New South Wales and a former OECD officer.

Joseph Wong is an Associate Professor of Political Science at the University of Toronto and holds the Canada Research Chair in Political Science.

Jan Zutavern is a Research Fellow at the European University Institute in Florence, Italy.

Preface

STEPHAN LEIBFRIED

In November of 2006, Dominic Byatt of Oxford University Press approached me about editing a volume on the welfare state for the Oxford Handbook series. He was imagining a 'genuinely agenda-setting book' that would encompass political science, sociology, social policy, and economics. It should be the 'most authoritative survey and critique of work on the welfare state'. A tall order indeed! The welfare state as a subject of study is as colossal as the giants of Want, Disease, Ignorance, Squalor, and Idleness it is charged with eradicating (Beveridge 1942: pt. 7). A colleague and I had just finished assembling and writing an introduction to a reference collection of classic reprints that covered the post-World War II history of welfare state theory, and it weighed in at over 2,000 pages (Leibfried and Mau 2008a, b). There was an abundance of cutting-edge new work on the welfare state, both empirical and theoretical, and it was this that Dominic wanted to see addressed in a Handbook of less than 950 pages . . . Daunting as it was, I took up his challenge. After all, welfare states engage over half of state expenditures in the OECD world—and Beveridge's five giants are still alive and kicking.

My first move was to enlist Frank Castles, who is not only an expert on the welfare states and on the states *in toto* of many nations, large and small, but also a talented editor, known for making the work of scholars from diverse lands available to a wider audience. The two of us then set out to build a compatible but multifaceted team: Jane Lewis, who represents the best of the English social policy and social history tradition and could also, on occasion, remind us that gender matters; Herbert Obinger, one of Germany's leading young scholars in comparative political economy, with whom Frank and I both had a long history of collaboration (see, for example Obinger et al. 2005a); and Chris Pierson, a political theorist with a wide-angle view and an appreciation for the national diversity of welfare state agendas, with whom Frank had successfully co-edited a teaching text on the welfare state (Pierson and Castles 2000, rev. 2006). The five of us come from diverse disciplines, but we share the conviction that an understanding of the development of the welfare state and its contemporary manifestations can only be achieved by considering the similarities and differences among nations. The *Oxford Handbook of the Welfare State*, which we have worked on together for nearly three years, bears the hallmarks of its progenitors: it covers a broad field, and its approach is interdisciplinary and, above all, *comparative*.

A number of staff members from both the Transformations of the State Collaborative Research Centre (TranState) and the Centre for Social Policy Research at the

University of Bremen have played essential roles in bringing this project to fruition. Monika Sniegs of TranState managed the website, the manuscripts, and the editorial team—especially *me*. She and I were aided by our Bremen student assistants Jessica Haase, Stefanie Henneke and Lisa Adler. Peter Boy and Markus Modzelewski set up the website that allowed us and the contributors to stay abreast of each other's progress and bring some consistency and cohesion to the volume. Jana Wagner, Hendrik Steven, Matthias Schuchard, and Melike Wulfgramm turned the forty-eight individual chapter bibliographies into a single, consistent, verified, and much more useful bibliography at the end of the Handbook. Susan Gaines helped with revisions of the introductory material and provided translations of bibliographic entries, and Wolfgang Zimmermann (wozi@wozi.de) designed the jumble of stamps on the dust jacket. Janis Vossiek undertook the time-consuming citation analysis that we relied on in Chapter 1.

On the part of all five editors, I wish to thank the Deutsche Forschungsgemeinschaft (German Research Foundation) and the University of Bremen, which provide funding for TranState and its international collaborations. This book has set the stage for *The Oxford Handbook on Transformations of the State*, which will examine how the evolution from closed to open economies in the decades since World War II has affected the defining characteristics of developed Western nation states (Leibfried and Zürn 2005; Hurrelmann et al. 2008).

We have many other debts of gratitude. Thanks go to Jacobs University Bremen for financing a sabbatical semester for Herbert Obinger. The Hanse Institute for Advanced Studies provided us with a meeting place in northern Germany and made it possible for editors from Australia, the United Kingdom, and Germany to engage in something more than virtual encounters. The Hanse, located in the city of Delmenhorst and directed first by Gerhard Roth and now by Reto Weiler, granted generous fellowships to Frank Castles and Chris Pierson, allowing them to dedicate time to editing and rewriting the articles—no trivial task, given that many of the authors were writing in English as a second language.

We are, of course, grateful to all of the scholars whose contributions made this volume possible, with particular thanks to Bernhard Ebbinghaus, Marius Busemeyer, and Rita Nikolai who stepped in to supply missing chapters at very short notice, and to Maurizio Ferrera and John Stephens, who helped us to revise and improve some of the chapters. Axel West Pedersen also gave generously of his time and expertise in a moment of need. We also wish to thank the Schwaneberger Verlag, which gave us access to their Michel stamp catalogues when we were gathering material for the book cover, as well as the many colleagues who directed us to stamps with welfare state themes, particularly Klaus Petersen, for the Scandinavian stamps, and Barbara Darimont, who researched and hunted down the Chinese stamps for us. Obtaining copyright permissions from postal authorities and artists would have been impossible without the help of Dongmei Liu and Yang-Yifan at the Max Planck Institute for Welfare Law in Munich, and Jianan Xu of the China Post Group's Department of International Cooperation; Claire Moulin-Doos, for the French stamps; Aurelia Ciacchi, for the Italian ones; and Ayumi and Hisashi Fukawa, for the Japanese stamps. Last, but far from least, we would like to thank our editors at Oxford University Press. The commissioning editor, Dominic Byatt, not only generated the idea for this project, but also provided practical support and encouragement as we framed the chapters, solicited authors, and began editing. The copy editor, Tom Chandler, did a phenomenal job of removing the many inconsistencies and glitches that plagued this multi-country, multi-author, and multi-editor behemoth, and did so with great courtesy and good humour.

In recent years, as nations around the world have struggled to contain or shrink their welfare states—at a time when we need, more than ever, to analyse the effects of reform on social rights and equality—academic interest in the welfare state seems to have waned or become more abstract and theoretical in the disciplines that traditionally addressed its nuts and bolts. To varying degrees in different countries, empirical and institutional economists have turned to other issues or have been marginalized, historians have lost interest, sociologists have gone post-modern, legal scholars have found better-funded research topics, and, in Britain, the home of the study of 'social administration', social policy has often had to fight for its place in the academy. The studies described in this volume defy this trend, employing a wide range of approaches, from just about every discipline in the social sciences.

T. H. Marshall noted in 1949 that 'in the twentieth century, citizenship and the capitalist class system have been at war' (1964b: 84). He also noted that 'the wars of religion have been succeeded by the wars of social doctrine' (1964c: 61). These wars rage on. In this volume, we have covered the major lines of conflict since the 1970s and identified many of the challenges for the future—challenges that we hope policy makers and scholars of the welfare state will meet head on. In the twenty-first century, citizenship finds itself at war with both national and *global* capitalist systems, and it is likely to take sustained national and international efforts to level the playing field and keep Beveridge's giants at bay.

NOTE ON THE JACKET ILLUSTRATION

STEPHAN LEIBFRIED

In order to highlight the comparative, international nature of this volume's essays, we wished to illustrate the book jacket with symbols of welfare states from all over the world. The welfare state has been little celebrated on most national icons such as flags, state seals, coins and bank notes, but many nations have issued postage stamps that honour welfare state founders or champion social policies and ideals. This may have to do with the fact that in many countries the post office once served as a state bank, making pension and unemployment payments and issuing revenue stamps to record the payment of contributions. Perhaps tellingly, most of the postal stamps we found with welfare state themes were special commemorative stamps: even in countries whose welfare states developed hand in hand with nationhood—Germany, Australia, New Zealand, and Uruguay—welfare motifs were not among the core national icons selected for regular issue stamps.

While hunting for stamps to adorn the book jacket, I noticed that the welfare motifs used fall into five distinct categories, roughly corresponding to the types of protagonists in welfare state development. *International* welfare motifs have appeared on many nations' stamps, often in recognition of some event, like the World Social Summit in Copenhagen in 1995, or a United Nations special observance, such as the International Women's Year, the Year of Older Persons, or the Year for the Eradication of Poverty. The United Nations also issues its own postal stamps with these themes, as do the International Labour Organization (ILO) and the World Health Organization (WHO). The latter has been especially successful in popularizing its yearly health themes, and its members also tend to issue their own stamps for the WHO's yearly campaigns.

Stamps celebrating the anniversaries of welfare state *institutions* such as social insurance and pension insurance began to appear after World War II. Many nations have issued commemorative stamps in honour of the *founders and architects* of their welfare states. There are German stamps depicting Chancellor Otto von Bismarck, and Uruguayan ones of President José Batlle y Ordoñez, both nineteenth-century nation builders and pioneers of the welfare state—though Batlle's role is now largely forgotten outside of Latin America (cf. Mesa-Lago 1978: 70–112; Papadopulos 1992; see chapter 44). Of the twentieth-century welfare state founders and reformers, President Franklin D. Roosevelt and his Secretary of Labour, Frances Perkins, are both honoured on American stamps. And of the post-World War II reformers and founders, Chancellor Konrad Adenauer appears on German stamps, Prime Minister

Einar Gerhardsen on Norwegian ones, and Tommy Douglas, who founded the Canadian health system, is honoured on Canadian stamps. Interestingly, though we associate the welfare state with these leaders, many of them are also known for nation building or post-World War II economic reconstruction, and the stamps—with the exception of a single Roosevelt stamp—do not specifically recognize their contributions to social policy. Notably missing from the line-up of founders' stamps are William Beveridge—recognized as the father of the National Health Service in the United Kingdom—and New Zealand's first Labour Party Prime Minister, Michael Joseph Savage, who introduced a comprehensive cradle-to-grave welfare state in the 1930s, which served as inspiration for the post-war welfare state reform on the other side of the world (ILO 1949).

Examples of *other individuals* whose work has had far-reaching consequences for welfare state cultures include the German protestant minister, Johann Hinrich Wichern; reformist doctors like Arvo Ylppö, who founded child care clinics in Finland, and Julius Tandler, who introduced industrial hygiene in Austria; agitators for social reform like the unionist Ferdinand Hanusch and the Catholic reformer Karl Freiherr von Vogelsang in Austria; and the American unionist Samuel Gompers, who was instrumental in setting up the ILO. Most of these figures are recognized only in the nations where they worked, but there are a number of Catholic heroes of social welfare, like the Albanian nun, Mother Theresa, who are honoured on stamps around the world.

Non-state instruments of social policy comprise the fifth and most varied category of postage stamp motifs that I identified. There are stamps that pay tribute to children's clinics, hospitals, medical associations, nurses, accident prevention and protection measures, and, of course, the International and national Red Cross. In Finland, even day-care centre anniversaries, women's support groups, and a novel have commemorative stamps. (The novel is Väinö Linna's trilogy *Under the North Star* (1959–62 [2001–3]), which helped set the stage for the introduction and acceptance of a Scandinavian type welfare state in Finland). In China, where near-universal health insurance is now being introduced, there is a series of stamps depicting the barefoot itinerant doctors who have long served the rural poor. Another series indirectly highlights China's default policy of individual savings in lieu of a comprehensive pension system: these stamps celebrate the one-child family planning policy, which has led to an ageing population that can no longer rely on traditional means—family—but has an unbelievably high savings rate that is 50 per cent of GDP. Public awareness campaigns have also made use of postage stamps to call attention to social and health issues such as child and youth welfare, AIDS, cancer, polio, and tuberculosis. Controlling the spread of tuberculosis was one of the first grand successes of public health, and the theme appears frequently on stamps from various countries, but for some reason it completely dominates Finnish stamps between 1946 and the mid 1970s.

In comparing stamps from different nations, I also noticed that they reflected some of the major regional differences in welfare state cultures. Education and housing are prevalent stamp themes in Southeast Asia and China, where social policies emphasize these aspects of welfare more than in twentieth-century Western welfare states (Rieger and Leibfried 2003: 255 ff.). Since the 1990s, the countries of Eastern Europe have produced far fewer welfare state commemorative stamps than any other region of the world, perhaps because welfare provision was part of the communist system that these countries rejected and they have not had time to reconstruct (but see Chapter 46). One does, in fact, find stamps celebrating a return to pre-communist social insurance systems in some Eastern European countries (e.g. Lithuania, 2006). In Latin America and Southern Europe, as well as parts of Eastern Europe, the stamps frequently depict Saint John Bosco or other Catholic Saints who were known for their work with the underprivileged and epitomized the Church's formal and informal contributions to national welfare states. Scandinavia's stamps have a strong focus on the provision of health and other services, whereas stamps from continental Western Europe are more likely to focus on welfare state institutions and funds and on their founders. Worker protection and industrial hygiene was a starting point for many countries' welfare states, and, accordingly, seems to be a common early theme for stamps around the world. Regional treatments of more recently recognized welfare state issues like gender, race, age, or other types of discrimination that might produce unequal life chances are, however, quite varied.

Historically, relations between nation states have played a significant role in the development of many welfare states, and this is also evident in some of the stamps. Both Switzerland and tiny Liechtenstein issued commemorative stamps for the fifty-year anniversary of their pension insurance systems (AHV), as Liechtenstein had adopted it from the Swiss. Uruguay, with its large population of Italian immigrants, has a commemorative stamp for the *Ente Nazionale Assistenza Sociale,* an Italian welfare programme for expatriots around the world. Ireland honoured the centennial of the founding of its pension system—in Britain—with a commemorative stamp in 2008. This created some controversy in Britain, where the centennial was not similarly recognized, and there were outcries of discrimination from the Welsh community, as the founder of the pension system, Prime Minister Lloyd George, was a Welsh statesman. We might note, however, that the British postal system has generally done little to honour the founding of its model welfare state, with the exception of a four-stamp series issued to celebrate the fifty-year anniversary of the National Health Service in 1998 (a 50 pence commemorative coin was also issued for the occasion). Neither William Beveridge, who designed the system, nor Aneurin Bevan—another Welshman—who insured its enactment, are acknowledged with their own stamps. (They are, however, included on a couple of privately issued covers designed to accompany the 1998 NHS stamps.)

A number of public-awareness and health campaigns in the Americas have involved continent-wide actions, wherein the participating nations issue their own stamps around themes such as 'the fight against poverty', 'education for all', and the 'campaign against hunger'. Though the European Union plays a significant role in its member states' welfare policies (see Chapter 23) and might well benefit from public awareness of that role, none of the member states have issued stamps that attest it and the EU itself is not authorized to issue stamps.

My brief sojourn in the world of stamps revealed a colourful, international array of welfare state themes and icons—too many to be included in the jumble portrayed on the book jacket of this Handbook. Stamps with such themes appear to have been on the increase since the 1960s—an increase that, ironically, has continued uninterrupted through the 1990s and 2000s, a period when welfare state expansion in most regions stopped and threats of retrenchment dominated political rhetoric (see Chapter 38). During this period, postal services in some countries were privatized, perhaps weakening the role of stamp imagery as a statement of national sentiment. And yet, the societal consensus that built the effective welfare states of the 1950s and 1960s is still honoured, and the ills of hunger, poverty, discrimination, lack of education, inadequate housing, and ageing societies are maintained in the public eye by the images chosen for postage stamps.

———

Listed below are the country, year of issue, and a brief description for each of the stamps that appear on the cover, spine and inside flaps. The artists and copyright holders are acknowledged at the end of each entry. Every effort was made to identify and contact each of them for permissions; we would be grateful for notification if there are any omissions so that they can be corrected in future printings or editions. We would also like to express our thanks to graphic designer Wolfgang Zimmermann (wozi@wozi.de) for so graciously offering us his advice and expertise.

AUSTRIA 1986: Julius Tandler [1869–1936] industrial hygienist. (Portrait by Otto Zeiler, reproduced here courtesy of Marianne Siegl; stamp © Austria Post)

BELGIUM (1) 1966: celebrating the 75 years of Papal *encyclicals* on social issues that began with the *Rerum Novarum*; (2) 2007: one of a series honouring Belgian scholars, with Philippe Van Parijs and the image from the cover of his book on the basic income philosophy, *Real Freedom for All*, Oxford University Press, 1995. (2, Els Van de Vyvere; all © Belgian Post)

BRAZIL (1) (on the spine) 1981: 60th anniversary of the Ministry of Labour; (2) 1986: a national campaign for the prevention of workplace accidents; (3) 2005: 'Fight against Poverty – Cisterns', emphasizing the role of accessible clean water. (1, Joana Bielschowsky; 2, Jô Oliviera; 3, Fernando Lopes; all © Ministry of Communications)

CHINA (1) 1973: from the 'Barefoot Doctor' series, honouring country doctors; (2) 1983: from a series promoting the one-child family planning policy. (All © China Post Group)

DENMARK 1988: 40 years of the World Health Organization. (Boye Willum Wilumsen; © *Post Danmark A/S*)

FRANCE (1) 1985: honouring Victor Hugo [1802–1885], from the annual series on famous personages; (2) 1989: allegory for equality, celebrating the bicentenary of the French Revolution. (1, Jacques Jubert; 2, Claude Duras and Roger Druet; all © *La Poste*)

GERMANY (1) 1965: honouring Chancellor Otto von Bismarck [1815–1898]; (2) 1989: 100 years of Social Insurance; (3) 1992: honouring Chancellor Konrad Adenauer

[1876-1867] (1, Rudolf Gerhardt; 2, Erwin Poell; 3, Hans Günter Schmitz; all © *Bundesministerium der Finanzen*)

ICELAND 1994: United Nations International Year of the Family (© Iceland Post Ltd.)

ITALY (1) 1998: commemoration of Mother Theresa [1910–1997] and her work in Calcutta; (2) 1990: centenary of Labour Day (1, M. Temo; 2, E. Donnini; all © *Posteitaliane, Filatelia*)

JAPAN 1969: 50th anniversary of the International Labour Organization (© Japan Post)

KOREA 1983: The Day of the Teacher (© Korea Post)

NETHERLANDS 1975: in recognition of International Women's Year (© TNT Post Netherlands)

NEW ZEALAND 1993: 'The Great Depression' from the series 'Emerging Years—1930s' (Ross Jones; © New Zealand Post)

NORWAY 1997: one of a series with Finn Graff's caricatures of Prime Minister Einar Gerhardsen [1897–1987] (© *Posten Norge* AS)

SAN MARINO 2007: the European Union's Year of Equal Opportunities for All (Daniela Longo; © *AASFN*)

SPAIN 2007: 'Education for All' (© *La Sociedad Estatal Correos y Telegrafos S.A.*)

SWEDEN 1976: 'workers' safety' (Olle Kåks; © Sweden Post Stamps)

SWITZERLAND 1998: 50th anniversary of AHV, Switzerland's pension system (Marianne Brügger; © *Die Schweizerische Post*)

UNITED KINGDOM (1) 1998: '1,700,000 prescriptions dispensed every year', from a series celebrating the 50th anniversary of the National Health Service; (2) 1970: from a series commemorating the centenary of Charles Dickens' [1812–1870] death, shows George Cruikshank's frontispiece of the 1838 edition of *Oliver Twist* (All © Royal Mail Group Ltd.)

UNITED NATIONS 1954: 35th anniversary of the International Labour Organisation (© United Nations Postal Administration, New York)

UNITED STATES (1) 1945: one of four in commemoration of President Franklin Delano Roosevelt [1882–1945]; (2) 1980: honouring Frances Perkins [1882–1965]; (3) 1985: 50th anniversary of the Social Security Act; (4) 1998: FDR's New Deal Programs, from the series '1930s Celebrate the Century—Depression, Dust Bowl, and a New Deal' (1, 2 © Smithsonian Institute National Postal Museum; 3, 4 © United States Postal Service)

URUGUAY 2003: centenary of the presidency of the father of the Uruguayan welfare state, José Batlle y Ordoñez [1856–1929] (Alejandro Muntz; © *Correos Uruguayo*)

VATICAN 1960: hospitality and acceptance for migrants (Grassellini; © *Poste Vaticane*)

CHAPTER 1

....

INTRODUCTION

....

FRANCIS G. CASTLES

STEPHAN LEIBFRIED

JANE LEWIS

HERBERT OBINGER

CHRISTOPHER PIERSON

THE SCOPE OF THIS HANDBOOK

....

THE twentieth century is often portrayed as one of extremes (Hobsbawm 1994). Its first half witnessed the rise of totalitarian regimes, two world wars and more than a few genocides. The second half was characterized by the spread of democracy, unprecedented economic wealth and, in consequence, a degree of well-being and a guarantee of social rights arguably unknown in human history. In retrospect, however, this is largely a 'Western' story, since war, starvation, dictatorship, and impoverishment remained the norm throughout the twentieth century and beyond for millions of people living in other parts of the world (Cornia 2004). This bifurcated development has many causes. Unquestionably, though, one of the major reasons for the successful Western trajectory is connected to a mostly European invention of the late nineteenth century, which today is referred to as the welfare state—or *Sozialstaat, l'état providence, verzorgingsstat, estado providencia* or *sociale* or *del bienestar* or *social de derecho, stato sociale* or *del benessere, estado de bem-estar-social, folkhemmet, fukushikokka* (社会福利国家), *shèhuì fúlì guójiā* (Pinyin simplified characters 社会福利国家, traditional characters 社會福利國家)— but which developed to its fullest extent after World War II.

This Oxford Handbook takes stock of the 'state of the welfare state' from a comparative perspective (Amenta 2003), a perspective vital both for demonstrating the huge variability of welfare state forms and trajectories of development as well as providing the basis of a methodology for understanding the factors contributing to that variability—and also for understanding the corridors laid out to bound such variability in the many *Atlantic* and other *Crossings* (Rodgers 1998) of reform ideas in academia and politics. The Handbook is designed to cover all the relevant aspects of the modern welfare state and to summarize the state of the art in contemporary welfare state research. In eight Parts, it sheds light on the philosophical justifications underlying the welfare state, the approaches, methods, and disciplinary perspectives of comparative social policy research, the historical development and driving forces of the welfare state, its past achievements, contemporary challenges, and likely future developments.

Such a comprehensive endeavour inevitably requires an international and interdisciplinary division of labour. This volume consists of forty-eight chapters written by scholars from diverse disciplinary backgrounds. The fact that the welfare state is, in essence, a European invention (Flora 1986–7: vol. 1, xii), which, in addition, has experienced its greatest proliferation and expansion in north-western Europe, explains the strong presence of European scholars in contemporary welfare state research. In contrast to the dominance of American scholars in political science (cf. Goodin and Klingemann 1998) and other social science disciplines, this volume brings together scholars from many countries and achieves an arguably better balance between the English-speaking and continental European worlds of scholarship.[1]

An analysis of the almost 1,900 entries in the Handbook bibliography also reveals a quite different balance amongst the English-speaking nations from that in political science. Although hardly decisive, since Oxford and Cambridge University presses publish in the United States as well as in the United Kingdom, both of these publishers, with more than a hundred citations each, markedly outscore the most strongly represented American university presses, Chicago and Princeton, with twenty and thirty citations respectively. Moreover, UK publishers specializing in social policy topics, like Routledge, Palgrave Macmillan, and Edward Elgar, are referenced more frequently than any American publishers.

The study of the welfare state is not only a much less American dominated topic than political science, but is also probably more bookish and certainly more so than economics, with some 65 per cent of citations in the bibliography referring to books and book chapters and only a little less than 30 per cent to journal articles. American journals are well represented, with the *American Political Science Review*, *World Politics*, and *Comparative Political Studies* most cited, but they are again outscored or rivalled by journals of UK origin, with the *Journal of European Social Policy* and the *Journal of Social Policy* leading the way and journals with an explicit social policy focus being almost exclusively of UK provenance. Finally, though, if our analysis of citations truly represents the state of our knowledge base, it should be noted that contemporary welfare state research is actually a very cross-disciplinary affair, with

---

[1] Perhaps illustrative of this national diversity is that the single most-cited text in the Handbook is by a Danish scholar who teaches in Spain, and that the scholar with the most cited works is an Australian whose most recent teaching post was in Scotland.

only about one-fifth of journal citations being clearly identifiable as having an explicitly social policy focus.

A very important point to emphasize is that the strong UK presence revealed by our citations analysis is one of sources more than of authorship. On the whole, European scholars seeking the broadest audience for their research on welfare state topics go to British-based journals and publishers, with the Oxford and Cambridge presses probably seen as the key to the widest dissemination of new findings. The citations analysis reveals that only about 5 per cent of the sources in this Handbook are to books and articles in languages other than English, but the authorship of work in this area is far more internationally diverse than this statistic suggests. It is this which makes the strong presence of a wide European authorship of this Handbook so vitally important. Although, inevitably, the Handbook has a strong automatic citation bias for English language works and against works available in other languages, and 'only a small sample of the best national literatures on the welfare state...is accessible in English' (Leibfried and Mau 2008b: vxxi), through its more diverse authorship, it taps into this diversity of national literatures more fully than would otherwise be possible.[2] We further wish to point out that, in this volume, we seek also to look beyond even this OECD boundary, identifying recent developments in other parts of the world where the welfare state is of a more recent vintage and is confronted with peculiar challenges (Part VII).

ORIGINS OF THE WELFARE STATE

The origins of the Western welfare state (Part II) date back to the last quarter of the nineteenth century and are closely associated with the deep societal, economic, and political transformations taking place at that time. This *Great Transformation* (Polanyi 1957 [1944]) included industrialization and the rise of capitalism, urbanization, and population growth. On the one hand, these fundamental changes undercut the traditional forms of welfare provision offered by family networks, charity organizations, feudal ties, guilds, municipalities, as well as churches and led, in consequence, to a massive pauperization which was so impressively described by Friedrich Engels in his analysis of the situation of the working class in England (Engels 1975

---

[2] How much of an iceberg phenomenon the English literature on foreign nations is can be most easily demonstrated in the German case. There is a massive analytical project on sources of the founding period of the welfare state from 1867 to 1914 presently comprising 25 volumes (Tennstedt et al. 1978 ff.) and a similarly massive, and now completed, analytical plus source documentation project for the period 1945 to 1994, comprising 11 analytical and 10 documentary volumes (BMA and BA 2001–2009). None of this is available in the English language. Naturally there are also many other German analyses of the welfare state—like Kaufmann's cited in this introduction—which are unavailable in English. However Kaufmann (2010) will remedy this.

[1845]), by Charles Dickens in works such as *Oliver Twist* (1849/50) and *Great Expectations* (1860/1), and in some of the novels of Honoré de Balzac in his series *La comédie humaine* (1896 ff. [1829 ff.]), by Émile Zola (1885) as part of his 1871 to 1893 series *Les Rougon-Macquart. Histoire naturelle et sociale d'une famille sous le Second Empire*, and by Victor Hugo in *Les misérables* (2008 [1882]). On the other hand, the gains in productivity resulting from industrialization provided the resources necessary to cope with the emerging 'social question'. In political terms, the second half of the nineteenth century witnessed the formation of nation states, secularization (with fierce conflicts over jurisdiction in social and educational affairs between the Catholic Church and liberals in continental Europe), an unusually long period of peace, and, finally, the spread of civil rights and mass democracy, putting in place the institutional basis for the political articulation of ever-increasing social needs (Rimlinger 1971; Alber 1982). Political and economic ideas also underwent substantial change, with liberalism developing a strand more ready to accept legislation designed to enable the individual to reach his or her potential and an increasingly wider body of economic theory ready to admit the possibility of raising taxes in order to permit state spending on social programmes (broadly, for national variants on these themes, see Rimlinger 1971: 35ff.[3]). The counter-movement to Polanyi's *Great Transformation* (1944) gave rise to collective organization initially along class lines and fashioned a growing labour movement which itself became an important driver of welfare state consolidation.

While all the nations of Western Europe—and a few European offshoots in North America and the Antipodes—were affected by these fundamental transformations, the political responses to these common challenges and the moral purposes in providing more or less 'welfare' differed in many ways. Thus we find remarkable diversity with respect to the timing of welfare state consolidation, policy goals (whether to provide a safety net for the few, to work towards optimal provision for all, or simply to maintain the status quo), the precise forms of institutional solutions in terms of financing mechanisms, programme type and administration, the public–private mix, the type of intervention (provision of transfers vs. regulatory social policy), and national trajectories of welfare state building, i.e. whether social programmes were enacted from top down (as in the authoritarian monarchies in Europe) or emerged from bottom up (as in the democracies of the New World plus Switzerland). In the United States, which was early in moving towards a democratic suffrage, social provision nevertheless tended to be imposed from above in the hope of forging a nation out of immigrants, mainly via public education (Heidenheimer 1981, 2004; Hega and Hokenmaier 2002; see also Chapter 34).

This diversity can be attributed to significant differences in national political contexts, which have, in their turn, been shaped by different legacies in terms of state and nation building (Rokkan 1999), distinctive national political cultures (particularly in terms of the degree of trust in the state and its capacity to solve

---

[3] For exemplary studies of these developments in one country, in Britain, see Collini (1991) and Daunton (2001, 2002).

problems), differences in societal cleavage patterns, actor-constellations, and the pressure of socio-economic problems. However, even this list of factors explaining the emergence and diversity of the welfare state is far from exhaustive. Peter Baldwin (1990: 36–7) has noted that there is hardly a variable which has not been regarded as influential in this respect: 'Industrialisation, free trade, capitalism, modernisation, socialism, the working class, civil servants, corporatism, reformers, Catholicism, war—rare is the variable that has not been invoked to explain some aspect of its development', to which list might be added the governmental apparatus necessary for the administration of social programmes, particularly at the local level and a whole intragovernmental division of labour which is massively different in unitary and federal states (Obinger et al. 2005a). In fact, there is neither a specific configuration of socio-economic variables triggering welfare state consolidation nor is welfare state building related to a particular group of actors. Rather, the counter-movement against unregulated capitalism consisted of actors from across the entire political spectrum (Polanyi 1957 [1944]: 147).

Looking back at this founding period of the welfare state from the vantage point of the early twenty-first century, what stands out is that these early beginnings of state social policy coincided with what we now recognize as the 'first era of globalization' commencing in the 1870s and brought to an abrupt end with the declaration of war in 1914 (see inter al. James 1996: 1–26, 2001; Bayly 2004; Rieger and Leibfried 2003: 19f.). Creating a social insurance system for blue collar workers in the 1880s was perceived by welfare state founders like Bismarck as providing Germany with a competitive advantage over England through what we might now describe as a programme of social investment aimed at promoting 'endogenous growth'. The British bought into this view, feeling their former position as 'workshop of the world' was profoundly challenged by developments elsewhere in Europe (Hennock 1987, 2007).

It is not surprising then that welfare state theorizing has mainly been inductive (Kaufmann 2001, 2003b) and that the welfare state was almost at the peak of its development by the time that modern welfare state theories identifying the inputs and actors consequential for welfare state growth (see Part IV) were formulated from the 1950s onwards. There is, however, one exception to this rule that theorizing had to await the mature development of the welfare state, and it is, arguably, no coincidence that the first (functionalist) generation of modern welfare state theories strongly built on this tradition of reasoning. Already at the time of its inception, numerous social scientists attributed the emergence of the welfare state to the fundamental changes in society and economy brought about by industrialization. Amongst them, German economist Adolph Wagner, a leading *Kathedersozialist*, argued in 1893 that the far-reaching changes in economy and society would generate increasing levels of state intervention and rising public expenditure. On this basis, he predicted the transformation of the nineteenth-century night watchman state into a '*Cultur- und Wohlfahrtsstaat*' (Wagner 1893, 1911).

Wagner's Law of a 'growing public' sphere (Lindert 2004) turned out to be a powerful prediction. The rise of the welfare state during the course of the twentieth century was impressive as was the concomitant growth and transformation of the public sector. In the nineteenth century, the state had been substantially a warfare state, with military spending amounting to 25 per cent of total public expenditure. Public social expenditure, by contrast, was a residual spending item equivalent to only about 5 per cent of public expenditure or less than 1 per cent of GDP in most nations (Lindert 2004: 171–2; Cusack 2007: 105). By the first decade of the twenty-first century, however, spending priorities had been entirely turned upside down: Today, on average, in the long-standing OECD member states, with average public expenditure of around 40 per cent of GDP, more than half of that total expenditure is absorbed by the welfare state, while the military now occupies a residual position similar to that of the welfare state in the late nineteenth century (see Castles 2006). This empirical shift from the 'warfare' to the 'welfare state' was accompanied by an intellectual climate change in the social sciences and in the wider public discourse only rarely explored in any scholarly depth (see Kaufmann 2003b).

However, this growth in the size of the state, in terms of both spending and the numbers of people it employs, together with its more interventionist role occurred in spurts and assumed quite different trajectories in different countries. Governments may finance social provision, directly provide welfare services as well as cash benefits, and/or regulate provision made by the third or private sectors. Different countries have committed to different roles for the state at different periods in time. A first period of expansion occurred between the two world wars (Rimlinger 1971; Alber 1982). The devastating social repercussions of World War I were a triggering event, but the transformation also had important political sources. Democratization followed the collapse of the imperial empires in Europe. Extensions to the franchise provided underprivileged sections of society with a voice and gave the parties of labour and an emergent Christian presence in party politics access to the corridors of power for the first time. And first efforts to internationalize social policy were already under way with the establishment of International Labour Organization (ILO) in 1919.[4] In many countries, the Great Depression put an end to this first

---

[4] The official rationale for the establishment of such an organization already connected the idea of a sustainable peace with a just and effective international social policy and recognized the need to tame the new global competition. The Versailles Treaty of 28 June 1919 stated in the introduction to Part XIII on 'Labour' 'Whereas the League of Nations has for its object the establishment of universal peace, and such a peace can be established only if it is based upon social justice; And whereas conditions of labour exist involving such injustice, hardship, and privation to large numbers of people as to produce unrest so great that the peace and harmony of the world are imperilled; and an improvement of those conditions is urgently required: as, for example, by the regulation of the hours of work, including the establishment of a maximum working day and week, the regulation of the labour supply, the prevention of unemployment, the provision of an adequate living wage, the protection of the worker against sickness, disease and injury arising out of his employment, the protection of children, young persons and women, provision for old age and injury, protection of the interests of workers when employed in countries other than their own, recognition of the principle of freedom of association, the organisation of vocational and technical education and other measures; Whereas also the failure of any nation to adopt humane conditions of labour is an obstacle in the way of other nations which desire to improve the conditions in their own countries; The HIGH CONTRACTING PARTIES, moved by sentiments of justice and humanity as well as by the desire to secure the permanent peace of the world, agree to the following: ....' (http://avalon.law.yale.edu/imt/partxiii.asp; see Herren 1992)

phase of welfare state expansion. In some of them, like Britain and Australia, this represented merely a conservative turn, but in others the effects were cataclysmic. Against a backdrop of dramatic economic slowdown, some of the countries of continental Europe made major benefit cutbacks, reinforcing political crisis, and, in a number of cases, contributing to the downfall of democratic regimes.[5] In a few countries, however, economic stagnation was an impetus to social policy transformation. In the United States, the crisis was the prelude for welfare state take-off, while, in Scandinavia, the same economic events were the precursor of a move towards a new—and, arguably, more advanced—stage of welfare state development.

POST-WORLD WAR II DEVELOPMENT

World War II once again made the warfare state the first priority, but, like its dreadful Great War predecessor, the end of the war provided the impetus for further social policy expansion. But note, for the first time, it was also a war in which the idea of welfare was presented as part of *casus belli* and as a reason why the war should be seen as a just war. Two of the eight war aims in the Atlantic Charter of 14 August 1941, which Roosevelt and Churchill agreed on in Ship Harbour, Newfoundland, concerned social welfare, specifically 'securing, for all, improved labor standards, economic advancement and social security' (point 5) and 'that all men in all the lands may live out their lives in freedom from fear and want' (point 6). 'Social security' now became the grand international slogan (Kaufmann 2003c). The Beveridge Plan of 1942 is justly famous as one of the founding documents of the modern welfare state, but much less well known is the fact that there were also Nazi counter-plans for a new kind of welfare state after assumed victory (Recker 1985). At this tipping point of European history, the warfare and the welfare state were ideologically fused into one.

The catastrophe of war and the subsequent commitment to establish a new and internationally sanctioned order which would protect peace and security had a major impact on post-war welfare state development. War itself can be 'locomotive of change' enhancing and building new forms of social solidarity (Titmuss 1950; Goodin and Dryzek 1995) and making state intervention and the funding to finance it more acceptable in the ensuing peace (Peacock and Wiseman 1961). Moreover, the need for economic reconstruction after World War II was a profound stimulus to economic growth and provided resources for welfare state expansion on an

---

[5] The fate of the welfare state under Nazism and Fascism is not as well researched as the founding and post-World War II periods. Good national or English language syntheses are largely missing: presently, on Germany, see Mason (1993, 1995), Recker (1985), and Aly (2008); and, on Italy, Cherubini and Piva (1998), De Grazia (1992), and Quine (2002).

unprecedented scale. And the 'Cold War', starting in 1947, if not already in 1945, instigated a competition of economic systems and further supported ambitions to outcompete the Eastern block in terms of welfare performance. This is the period which, in retrospect, has sometimes been described, with a mixture of hindsight and nostalgia, as a 'golden age' both of economic and of welfare state development. War and the economic displacement it caused had once again created enormous social needs to which nations were now better able to respond, given the centralization of tax powers enacted during wartime and the sustained economic growth initiated by post-war reconstruction. Moreover, a commitment to prevent war ever again causing such physical, economic, and social destruction was a driving force for European integration, which was promoted in the initial post-war period as a mechanism for preventing future conflicts through increased economic integration and trade.

Although increased trade integration was the leitmotif of future European economic development, the massive growth of the welfare state during the so-called *trentes glorieuses* (1945–74) took place against the backdrop of relatively closed economies. Since exit options for mobile factors of production were low in the initial period of the post-war settlement, there was considerable room for redistribution and this was exploited by governments of all partisan complexions. 'Liberalism' could then be 'embedded', mostly in a lasting fashion—and even the United States could see itself, at first, as catching up with the European Joneses, and not, as in the period from the 1980s onwards, as standing against the European welfare tide in a kind of principled 'exceptionalism' (see Glazer 1998). The experience of war and depression paved the way for the emergence of a—however brittle in some countries—Keynesian consensus justifying policies that promoted high levels of employment and high tax and expenditures levels, as well as nourishing the notion that government intrusion in economic and social affairs was imperative for stabilizing demand and the business cycle in capitalist economies. Distributional conflicts were mitigated by a comparatively symmetric balance of power between the interest organizations of labour and capital and by exceptionally high rates of economic growth. Partisan competition as well as system competition in a world now divided by an Iron Curtain further fuelled welfare state expansion. Under these circumstances, social benefits were everywhere significantly raised, existing programmes were extended to cover new groups of beneficiaries and entirely new schemes adopted (see Part V describing trajectories of development of expenditures and revenues as well as a wide range of separate social programmes). As a consequence, welfare state coverage as well as spending levels rose dramatically with important impacts on policy outcomes including a decrease in inequality and poverty, the guarantee of social rights and macroeconomic performance (see Part VI).

Despite this massive expansion, however, the institutional differences laid down in the era of welfare state consolidation persisted or were transformed into new ones. Hence, Western nations took different routes to and through welfare state modernity (Therborn 1995*b*; Castles 1998*a*). In contrast to the claims of functionalist accounts in the 1950s, 1960s, and into the mid-1970s, no marked convergence occurred as these countries became wealthier. This holds true for social expenditure and welfare state institutional patterns alike. Thus the United States remained a residual provider of welfare, preserving insurance-based benefits for particular groups deemed to be deserving (in the main older people), and failed to develop major state services (particularly health care)—the latter leading to ever deeper conflict and political impasse around issues of national health reform (Marmor and Oberlander 2009). At the other end of the spectrum, the Scandinavian countries used the full range of tax and insurance-based benefits and public services. In light of these persisting cross-national dissimilarities, welfare state research has devoted a substantial intellectual effort to identifying the character of these variations and their sources. Among the various classifications suggested in the literature, Esping-Andersen's (1990) typology of welfare regimes is unquestionably the most important. The historical origins, achievements and vulnerabilities of these welfare regimes, as well as of other 'families of nations' both within and without the OECD-area, constitute the topic of Part VII.

CRITIQUES AND CHALLENGES

In the 1970s and early 1980s, the 'golden age' of welfare capitalism began to falter, and the 'silver age' began to dawn (Taylor-Gooby 2002; Chapter 6 below). Deteriorating economic performance in the wake of the oil shocks and the failure of many governments to cope with emergent stagflation led to—a renewed—scepticism concerning the role of the state in society and economy. As a consequence, the welfare state was increasingly critiqued from almost every point on the political spectrum. Conservatives complained about ungovernability in general (Crozier et al. 1975), while liberals lamented inefficiencies and paternalism. Certainly, though, the most influential critiques—in terms of real world political consequences—were those articulated by theories of *neoliberalism* and a newly morally engaged conservatism (see Chapter 4 below), the ideas of which gained more and more importance over time. In influential conservative—*New Right*—critiques of American attempts to address the issue of poverty in the post-war era, Charles Murray (1984) launched a powerful attack on the moral hazard of welfare policies, making a case for the abolition of welfare benefits in the US, while Lawrence Mead (1986) also attacked the provision of welfare, but argued for much greater conditionality in their administration—the beginnings of the idea of 'welfare-to-work'. In this account, and in the pincer movement of both economists and political scientists—some inspired by the neoliberal ideas of Hayek (1944; Plickert 2008)[6] and Friedman (2003[1962]) and

---

[6] Hayek was awarded the Nobel Prize in 1974, but the Nobel Committee did a careful balancing act and made him share the award with Gunnar Myrdal, one of the leading architects of the Swedish Social Democratic welfare state. Hayek did allow some minimalist room for state intervention for welfare: '[W]e must, of course, not forget that there are in a modern community a considerable number of

others persuaded by the logic of rational choice theories, which cast doubt on who really benefited from social policies—state intervention was increasingly seen as part of the problem rather than as a tool for overcoming macroeconomic imbalances or for social amelioration (documented and confronted by Goodin 1988). *Post-materialists* argued that a growing welfare state bureaucracy undermined individual autonomy and the institutions of civil society (Beck 1999), while feminists perceived the welfare state as an institution underpinning and freezing traditional gender relations (Fraser 1994*b*), *Marxists*, as they had at previous stages of capitalist development, identified an emergent contradiction, arguing that capitalism had ceased to be viable without the welfare state but that, at the same time, the very growth of the welfare state undermined the logic of capitalist accumulation, producing a so-called 'crisis of crisis management' to cite Gough (1979; see also Offe 1984; O'Connor 1973; Klein 1993).

Arguably, though, the most influential critique—in terms of its real-world political consequences—was that articulated by theories of neoliberalism (see Part I), the ideas of which gained more and more importance over time. An ideological climate change was in the making (Le Grand 1997): commentators and politicians in many countries urged that more attention be paid to the responsibilities as opposed to the rights of individuals, particularly the responsibility to engage in the labour market. Such calls resulted in policies that often tended to the punitive in the United States, while Western Europe developed more enabling 'activation' strategies, albeit that, in the Nordic countries, the welfare state had from the first been built firmly on conditionality and the work/welfare relationship. Two decades of unrelenting intellectual attack along these lines increasingly challenged the optimistic faith in the beneficial effects of big government on which the post-war welfare state consensus had rested. Increasingly the aspiration was to replace states with markets—or, where that was not possible, with 'quasi-markets' (Le Grand 1999). With the first moves being made in the English-speaking countries, neoliberal ideas soon spread across the globe.

This process was accelerated and reinforced by international organizations such as the World Bank and the International Monetary Fund and triggered a major rethinking of the role of the state in economic and social affairs (Deacon et al. 1997), minimally counterbalanced by international social institutions such as the International Labour Organization and the World Health Organization and by UN World Social Summits as in 1995. 'Rolling back the state' to its core functions was more and more seen as offering major comparative advantages in an international political economy which had undergone a fundamental transformation (Scharpf 2000*b*). This transformation had occurred in several stages. The collapse of the Bretton Woods financial system

---

services which are needed, such as sanitary and health measures, and which could not possibly be provided by the market for the obvious reason that no price could be charged to the beneficiaries or, rather, that it is not possible to confine the benefits to those who are willing or able to pay for them' (1980 [1947]: 111). Myrdal (1957) was one of the first scholars to systematically consider the interaction of open or closed economies and welfare-state building. However, he still shared the majority opinion that welfare states could only fully develop in closed economies.

and the economic slow-down resulting from the two oil price shocks in the 1970s began the process. The 1980s witnessed deregulation and internationalization of capital markets and an ever-increasing trade liberalization. The collapse of communism in 1989 was a geopolitical event that seemed to confirm the neoliberal view that public intrusion in economic affairs leads to inefficiencies. The 1990s witnessed the emergence of a truly 'global' economy and could build on significant progress in European integration with the formation of the Single European Market and later European Monetary Union, with a European 'common currency' from 2002. Finally, eastwards enlargement of the EU from 2004 onwards anchored a considerable disparity in wealth across EU member states and created new opportunities to remove business and capital to low wage countries.

Taken together these external changes had far-reaching consequences for advanced welfare states. The deepening of European integration not only imposed constraints on fiscal and monetary policy, which precluded the practice of traditional Keynesian macroeconomic policies at the national level, it also created 'semi-sovereign' welfare states which became embedded in an emerging multilevel social policy regime (Leibfried and P. Pierson 1995). At the same time, it is clear that 'the policy-making capabilities of the Union have not been strengthened nearly as much as capabilities at the level of member states have declined' (Scharpf 1994: 219), thereby precluding a supranational Keynesianism practised at the European level. More generally, the second era of economic globalization setting in since the 1970s increased competition between nation states for footloose capital and intensified pressures on national social standards. Enhanced exit options for capital imposed tighter limits for taxation and redistribution and also led to a newly asymmetric balance of power between labour and capital. It also led to an ideological climate shift contrasting radically with that of the era of nineteenth-century globalization. Now there is a marked tendency to perceive social investment as a dead weight on the economy rather than as a factor providing a boost off the starting blocks in 'a race to the top'. In a nutshell, the transformation of the international political economy decreased the autonomy and sovereignty of the nation state—but did not support the evolution of functionally equivalent higher authorities at the international level.

That economic conditions were no longer as propitious for domestic welfare state development is uncontested. Actual impacts are, however, more open to question. Effects of increasing trade are by no means all negative. Trade is an important source of economic growth which may generate the fiscal resources necessary for the viability of the welfare state in the long run. In this view, the major challenge to mature welfare states is to find an optimal adjustment strategy that is able to reconcile the trinity of economic imperatives generated by globalization—liberalization, flexibilization, deregulation—with solidarity. Retrenchment is not inevitable and its progress is a highly contentious theme of the literature (see discussions in Parts V and VI), with several contributions to this Handbook arguing strongly that the idea that globalization has simply unleashed a 'race to the bottom' in social provision lacks empirical foundation.

In addition to these external challenges, mature welfare states have also been confronted with a set of domestic challenges closely connected to societal modernization and structural economic change. Although they are less frequently the stuff of political debate, it is possible that these other 'unseen' changes are even more important for changes in the character of welfare provision than are changes in the international political economy (P. Pierson 1998). Moreover, they are changes in large part generated by the welfare state itself (Kaufmann 1997). One important challenge results from the transition from industrial to post-industrial economies (Iversen and Cusack 2000). The rise of the tertiary sector in the post-war period created three major problems: first, the productivity of the service sector was lower than that of industry. As a result, both the rate of growth of the economy and of wages has been reduced with negative feedback effects on public revenues. Western governments have experienced growing difficulty in financing generous cash benefits and public services, where a reduction in labour costs tends to threaten the quality of the service, which in turn has electoral consequences. Second, gains in employment in the private service sector can only be achieved at the expense of higher inequality unless the public sector exercises a compensatory function (Scharpf 2000a). Hence, some scholars diagnosed a 'trilemma of the service economy' characterized by a trade-off between employment growth, income equality, and sound state finances (Iversen and Wren 1998).

Structural change in the economy in combination with intensified international regime competition has triggered fundamental changes in labour markets. The pressure to raise productivity levels and the transition towards a post-industrial information society have raised skill requirements. Huge numbers of low-skilled jobs have either been destroyed or else relocated to low-wage economies. Higher flexibility requirements as well as increased labour market-participation by women have led to the spread of atypical employment forms such as part-time work, temporary work, or fixed-term employment. These were forms of employment for which existing welfare states were not well designed. Rising female labour market participation is important in other ways, casting doubt on the assumption that, in families, men would take primary responsibility for earning and women for care. Measures to reconcile paid employment with unpaid family work have been expanded in Western welfare states since the mid-1990s. Given the general desire to increase employment rates, the challenge for the welfare state has been to provide sufficient social services for children and frail elderly people. In some countries, particularly the United States, an externalization to the market is seen as an appropriate solution that is also affordable due to the availability of low wage migrant labour. In addition, societal modernization has undercut the welfare production capacity of families. Divorce rates, the number of births out of wedlock and, hence, the number of lone parent households have increased. The erosion of traditional family forms and changes in the contributions men and more particularly women make to families have generated new social risks and needs. For example, poverty has demographically spilled downwards from elderly people to single parents and families with many children, and the process of family change has increased the demand for social care.

Two other domestic challenges are of relevance. The first is demographic. Life expectation has significantly increased over the past decades and there is much evidence that the welfare state has in part caused what is basically a positive development through its provision of improved health care services, although higher standards of living are clearly the most important factor. Fertility rates have declined rapidly, but this is a trend with many other causes including innovations in contraceptive technology, individualization, and the mounting opportunity costs of family formation, primarily for women. The consequences of these demographic changes— which will fully unfold as the 'baby boomers' retire in the coming decades—are quite clear: the 'greying' of society directly affects the most expensive programmes of the welfare state, i.e. pensions, health and long-term care, and will therefore require greater financial resources in the future. Along with the decline in fertility, this means that the size of the economically active population is diminishing so that the age group of the 20–60-year-olds will have to bear an ever-increasing financial burden.

The second further challenge is the growing ethnic heterogeneity of Western societies. The immediate post-war period was characterized by relatively high levels of ethnic homogeneity in Europe (Therborn 1995b). Labour migration and the influx of refugees have reversed this situation from the 1960s onwards. Migration may have various impacts on the welfare state. It creates new needs resulting from a higher incidence of poverty among immigrants, it requires efforts to improve social inclusion, but may also help to attenuate the demographic pressure of ageing—at least for a transitory period. A more recent debate focuses on the possible impacts of growing ethnic heterogeneity on solidarity and redistribution. The argument is that the ethnically homogeneous nation state provided a set of common values and a political setting—a sort of political community—which was able to achieve legitimacy for a redistributive regime among its members. According to some scholars growing ethnic heterogeneity will reduce this solidarity and drive Europe towards a more American-style social policy (Alesina and Glaeser 2004; but see Banting and Kymlika 2006a and Chapter 19 below).

In sum, the challenges and risk patterns of post-industrial societies today are very different from those of the industrial societies that historically were the main reference point for the era of welfare state construction and consolidation. Old welfare states meet new social risks and the discrepancy between outdated social regulations and new challenges is an important site for welfare state adaptation with a view to finding a new balance between more traditional forms of social compensation and the more recent emphasis on social investment (Armingeon and Bonoli 2006).

As was the case with the external changes, all these domestic challenges affect different national welfare states in different ways (Esping-Andersen 1996a; Scharpf 2000a). To a significant degree, the extent of each nation's vulnerability to these forces of transformation can be related to variations in existing welfare and production regimes and the extent of their coordination with other public policy areas such as education or fiscal policy. Given cross-nationally varying vulnerabilities and records of success, it comes as no surprise that the advanced democracies have responded quite differently to these challenges. Moreover, cross-national differences in the adjustment pathways adopted have been further influenced by the impact of welfare state patterns on political reform capabilities (see Parts V and VI).

A synopsis of the external and domestic challenges to mature welfare states reveals the following picture: the shift to a predominantly service economy and economic globalization entail tighter constraints on public revenues, while societal modernization and changes in the economic structure produce mounting social needs, new risk patterns, and new priorities for social policy intervention, with education and social service provision on top of the list. Moreover, shrinking public revenues and rising pressures on public expenditure constitute a situation of what Paul Pierson (1998) calls 'permanent austerity', which must be managed by nation states whose sovereignty and autonomy have declined significantly in the wake of globalization and European integration, without international authorities able to pick up the slack. Thus, though social policy has already become more inter-, trans-, and supranational in character during recent decades, and all the signs suggest that these are trends which will continue, the instrumentalities of effectiveness still need to be achieved.

THE SHAPE OF THINGS TO COME

These future developments are addressed in the final part of this handbook (Part VIII). Is the welfare state as we have come to know it in the era since World War II sustainable in face of the challenges we have described above? And what of other challenges? In Part VII of the volume, apart from examining the variety of welfare models in OECD countries, we look also to the developing world and examine recent trends of social policy development in East Asia, Latin America, Eastern Europe, and the former Soviet Union. But what of countries in Africa, South Asia, and the Middle East, where social policy institutions remain vestigial and economic and demographic prospects are still more dire? And these are challenges couched in conventional terms of the availability of greater economic resources to finance new roles for a more caring state. What if the real challenge for the medium and long term is that of securing social amelioration and greater social justice in a world in which the possibility of economic growth is constrained by global warming?

This Handbook was written and edited in an unfolding global financial and economic crisis, beginning in March 2008 and getting into full swing in September of that year. In that crisis we saw a climactic change in the role of the state, a change that had been building for some years into the new Millennium: the state was forcibly brought back in, first in slowly freezing privatization or reconsidering nationalization, then in state anti-terrorism activities after 9/11/2001, . . . and then in building public dams against the rising crises after 9/08, dams that were built nationally and to some extent also supranationally at the EU level and coordinated at G8 to G20 levels and by some of the global institutions of the Bretton Woods era. We have seen a political growing together crossing the borderlines of the OECD-world, with BRIC-states taking on a new role, i.e. Brazil, Russia, India, and China. The state issue is at stake amongst other things in creating strong international anti-crisis regulation and in making it stick across the board—a movement which, for the moment, seems to work only against tax havens. Welfare state issues light up here and there like comets in the skies, with some heads of state favouring the introduction of a 'social market economy' in the OECD-world and beyond, while others focus on unemployment or on preventing international big business (and, particularly, banking) breakdown as their major priorities. Still others like Benedict XVI, in a social encyclica on *caritatas in veritate* (2009)—but, for the first time in history, without an original Latin source—dwell with high international visibility on the sins of the recent past and now critique capitalism's unrestrained overindulgence and excesses.

A closer look at what triggered the present crisis points us to the pivotal impact of housing (see Chapter 33 below): to a United States, that has seen home ownership as the bedrock of the American Dream (Jensen 1996, 2003), but has failed to find a way to deliver low cost public housing for its working classes and which relied instead on subsidizing and encouraging private provision, increasingly by any and all means, looking the other way—and, thus, without proper oversight. So, in a sense, we have an incomplete American national welfare state noted in so many contexts in this Handbook combined with an unfit banking system and flabby regulatory oversight as a proximate causal nexus for much that has unfolded since 2008 (Hellwig 2009). Tony Judt once noted: 'European post-1945 history has crystallized into a system of security that provided safety against all collisions, any unexpected turns... Europeans need to realize this epoch has ended. For a variety of reasons broad popular participation in education and prosperity is not a political priority anymore. What comes instead is unclear, what can be preserved is uncertain—but we have left an epochal safe haven' (in Leibfried and Mau 2008b: xi; see also Judt 2005). What Judt notes for Europe holds for the OECD-world in general and also, to some extent, the wider world beyond.

It is likely that all these issues will have to be faced in a new geopolitical context as the United States grapples with its dependence on its main creditor, China. There are many who predict the global transfer of power from the United States to China—but a transfer of that magnitude has never before been achieved peacefully. Hoping for the contrary, we need to forge a new social contract for the twenty-first century and it must be more supranational, more global than ever. To do so we need to be fully informed about the welfare web in which we are already enmeshed. Only, thus, can we make sense of the experiences crystallized in these institutions, its layers upon layers of moral economies—rather than deconstructing them blindly, as we have often done since the 1970s.

PART I

PHILOSOPHICAL JUSTIFICATIONS AND CRITIQUES OF THE WELFARE STATE

CHAPTER 2

....

ETHICS

....

STUART WHITE

INTRODUCTION

....

WHAT we call the 'welfare state' is central to modern democracy. Political scientists debate the causes of its emergence and evolution. Economists debate its consequences for the wider economy. Social policy experts debate the wisdom of specific policies and propose reforms. Amongst this welter of multidisciplinary analysis, political philosophers also have a role. For the welfare state is centrally an expression of certain ethical ideals. It is defended in the name of social justice. It is held to violate other ideals, such as individual liberty. Political debate over the future of welfare states taps directly into these claims and counter-claims. But since these claims are essentially philosophical, they call for the expertise of the political philosopher. The political philosopher cannot say in detail what welfare states should look like. But she can certainly clarify the normative terrain of debate and, in this way, assist democratic citizens in deciding between different welfare state futures.

This chapter seeks to clarify some of the core ethical arguments surrounding welfare states. The analysis focuses on three key values. First, we will consider the concept of *need*; second, we focus on principles of *equality* and, third, we look at arguments surrounding the implications of the welfare state for *liberty*. A final section concludes by noting some new normative issues likely to move to the forefront of debate in the future. The focus here *is* philosophical, rather than on intellectual history or different ideologies of welfare. That said, in the real world of welfare state politics, philosophical argument enters into debates in ways that are shaped and constrained by local institutions and ideological traditions. In what follows, I try to take account of this, drawing on Gøsta Esping-Andersen's influential typology of so-called 'liberal', 'conservative', and 'social democratic' welfare states (Esping-Andersen 1990).

NEEDS

Welfare states are frequently understood as mechanisms for the satisfaction of *basic needs*. For example, when welfare states are discussed in terms of how far they alleviate or prevent poverty, there is an assumption that it is part of the task of the welfare state to prevent people suffering deprivation of their basic needs. Key issues of debate here concern: what are basic needs? How do we conceptualize and (hence) measure them? Do citizens have rights to what they need? Should welfare states aim only at assisting the most needy?

One way to elaborate the idea of basic needs is by drawing on Amartya Sen's influential notion of capabilities (Sen 1992). Sen's analysis starts by defining a person's well-being as constituted by the 'functionings':

> beings and doings [which] . . . can vary from such elementary things as being adequately nourished, being in good health, avoiding escapable morbidity and premature mortality, etc., to more complex achievements such as being happy, having self-respect, taking part in the life of the community, and so on. (Sen 1992: 39)

A person's *capability* is her power to achieve functionings: 'a set of vectors of functionings, reflecting the person's freedom to lead one type of life or another' (Sen 1992: 40). If we can agree on a set of functionings constitutive of a minimally decent life, we can then identify a related set of capabilities. Basic needs can be understood by reference to these capabilities.

Sen argues that the notion of basic capabilities should not be understood purely in terms of functionings linked to biological survival. Human beings are social creatures who have needs *as members of a society*. We have needs related to social status and opportunity for participation in social life. Thus, as Sen notes, Adam Smith pointed out how important the possession of a good linen shirt was to an eighteenth-century artisan (Sen 1987). A good linen shirt might not be a biological necessity. But it was, in the social context, a necessity if he was to meet his need for self-respect and participate in the wider society without ridicule or disapproval. This insight also underpins the claim that 'poverty' needs to be understood in terms of how well off people are relative to the general affluence of their society and not simply in terms of their command of absolute levels of commodities (Sen 1987). As the average level of affluence in a society rises, the cost in commodity terms of maintaining status and participation in society is likely to rise, so that individuals need command over more commodities in absolute terms in order to maintain a given level of capability. Of course, agreement on this conceptual approach to understanding basic needs (and, relatedly, poverty) still leaves open lots of questions about the precise specification of the capabilities and commodity bundles which define a basic needs threshold. There is an innate contestability about the notion of basic needs, and any satisfactory theory will need to identify political processes whereby debates over the content of needs can be fairly (and always provisionally) resolved (Fraser 1989b; Young 1990).

Distinct from the question of what basic needs are is the question of whether, or in what sense, individuals have a moral *right* to their satisfaction. Focusing primarily on the UK, T. H. Marshall famously argued that the welfare state represents a further stage in the development of citizenship rights (Marshall 1964b). Building on civil and political rights, the welfare state realizes 'social rights'. In recent years, however, many welfare states, perhaps especially liberal welfare states, have shifted towards the increased use of 'conditionality' in welfare state programmes, e.g. making cash assistance to the unemployed conditional on tougher work-related requirements. Both critics and supporters of the conditionality movement have argued that this marks a break with the Marshallian philosophy of 'social rights'. There is, moreover, an important current of opinion, across a wide range of welfare state types, which argues for the replacement of many conditional and targeted welfare benefits with an unconditional cash grant or *citizen's income* ideally set at a level sufficient to cover a standard set of basic needs (Van Parijs 1995; Raventós 2007).

In fact, conditionality is not necessarily in conflict with the idea of social rights (White 2000). The key question is just what a social right is a right *to*. Certainly if a social right is a right simply to be *given* resources, then conditionality conflicts with social rights. But social rights might be understood, alternatively, as rights of *reasonable access to* relevant resources. Whether conditionality then conflicts with a given social right depends on whether the specific conditionality rule denies individuals reasonable access to needed resources. For example, if a minimum income is made conditional on taking up a job, and there are a good range of jobs on offer, then the right of reasonable access to a minimum income is not obviously violated.

Justifications of conditionality fall into two categories. On the one hand, there is the *paternalist argument*: conditionality is justified because it is in the best interest of the welfare recipient herself (Mead 1992). Of course, there is a strong presumption against paternalism (in practice, this may be especially strong in nations with liberal welfare states). But some philosophers have argued that the presumption is not absolute (G. Dworkin 1971). Paternalism can be justified, they argue, if the restrictions on liberty are ones that the individuals concerned would consent to as a way of insuring themselves against their own short-sightedness or weakness of will. In such a case, paternalism is 'self-paternalism', and actually represents a way of strengthening the individual's ability to act on her own best judgement, rather than overriding this judgement. It is conceivable that some conditionality policies might be justified in these terms. However, the views of welfare recipients themselves are important in delivering this sort of justification. This brings us back to the need for fair political processes (in this case, ones that give effective voice to the welfare recipients) in determining policies to address basic needs.

The second argument for conditionality is the *fairness argument*. It appeals to the alleged unfairness to others of people taking resources without regard for their behaviour towards society. One version of the argument, relevant to the debate around work-related conditionality, appeals to the principle of *reciprocity* (White 2003). If individuals share in the fruits of their fellow citizens' labours then they have a duty to make a corresponding productive contribution to the society in return, within the limits of their capacity to make such a contribution. If they do not make such a contribution then, the argument runs, they take unfair advantage of and, thus, *exploit* their fellow citizens.

The reciprocity argument can be challenged in at least two ways. First, the demand for reciprocal contribution from welfare recipients should not be divorced from questions about the wider fairness of the economic system. If the structure of opportunity and reward in the economy is fair, then perhaps it is right to say, with John Rawls, that 'all citizens are to do their part in society's cooperative work' (Rawls 2001: 179). The insistence on reciprocal contribution, in this context, captures one aspect of the ideal of a society as a 'fair scheme of social cooperation between free and equal persons' (Rawls 1999, 2001). However, if the economic system has an unjust structure of opportunity and reward, then the insistence on reciprocal contribution from those receiving welfare benefits is questionable. If those receiving welfare benefits tend to be those who have suffered from society's failure to achieve just structures of opportunity and reward, then can we really say that these citizens have the obligation to contribute, as they would have in a just society? Isn't there a risk that the attempt to enforce this supposed obligation will consolidate their unjust disadvantage and so compound background injustice (White 2004a)? The discussions around equality and liberty below, of course, are important in our assessment of how far the existing structure of opportunity and reward is just. A related point is that the justifiability of a given conditionality policy might vary according to the particular kind of welfare state (e.g. liberal or social democratic) it is embedded in, since this could affect the degree of background justice.

A second challenge to the reciprocity argument is that some resources, such as land, are an inheritance from nature or past generations. As they are not the product of our fellow citizens' labours, it is not clear that their distribution should be regulated by the reciprocity principle. According to one philosophical tradition, with roots in many countries of diverse welfare state types, these inherited assets should be seen as the common property of the nation (or, indeed, of humanity), to which all individuals have a rightful claim (Paine 1987). Indeed, if one takes seriously the liberal principle of neutrality, which holds that the state should not discriminate between citizens on the basis of their different conceptions of the good life, then there is a strong presumption in favour of giving each person an equal share of these resources. The value of the relevant assets should revert to the community and should then be distributed as a uniform grant. On this basis some have recently defended the policy of citizen's income or related ideas of universal endowment (Steiner 1994; Van Parijs 1995; but see also van Donselaar 2008, for a critique of this argument). Note, however, that while the effect of a citizen's income might be to help satisfy a standard set of basic needs, this rationale for the policy does not in fact rest on an alleged right to be given, unconditionally, the resources necessary to meet basic needs. It rests on a presumption in favour of equality as a basis for individuating claims to specific resources. It is really an equality-based argument of a kind, rather than a needs-based one.

Returning to the basic needs justification for welfare provision, an obvious question arises: should welfare policies be targeted specifically at those 'in need'? For example, if the state has a commitment to prevent poverty, should it 'target' cash assistance so that it is just sufficient to relieve those who would otherwise be in poverty, but offer no assistance beyond this? One of the features distinguishing liberal welfare states from conservative or social democratic welfare states is the strong reliance on 'means-testing' of this kind (Esping-Andersen 1990). The questions might thus have more immediate salience in a liberal welfare state, although resource scarcity means that no welfare state is ever likely to evade them.

It is difficult to generalize about the rightness or wrongness of needs-based targeting, but we should note the ethical considerations on each side of the debate. On the one hand, means-testing looks like an 'efficient' means of satisfying the community's obligation to secure basic needs: it apparently meets basic needs at minimum cost to the wider society. This, it might be said, is fair to those who are foregoing resources to help the less advantaged. If the rationale for enforcing their contribution is that there is an obligation to help meet basic needs, then how can we legitimately force people to give up more resources than is strictly necessary to satisfy this obligation?

On the other hand, critics argue that the apparent 'efficiency' of means-testing in meeting basic needs is illusory. First, means-tested benefits might come with greater stigma for the benefit recipient. Since, as we have seen, an adequate notion of basic needs must take into account needs for status and respect, means-testing subverts the meeting of basic needs. Second, critics argue that means-tested assistance is subject to a political dynamic which leads to inadequate levels of assistance. Having no direct interest in the provision of means-tested welfare, more affluent citizens vote, over time, for low levels of spending on such welfare, undermining its effectiveness in addressing basic needs. Basic needs might thus be more effectively secured by a welfare state which offers goods and services to a much wider cross-section of the population than simply the most needy. Clearly, in this case, the resolution of the normative question depends on the results of research into the dynamic properties of different types of welfare state (Rothstein 1998).

EQUALITY

Is provision for basic needs the only ethical objective of the welfare state? While the principle of securing basic needs seems to capture what so-called liberal welfare states are primarily aiming at (albeit in a highly targeted way that can be challenged as inadequate) it does not fully capture the apparent ethical motivations behind conservative and social democratic welfare states (or, indeed, all of the policies adopted in liberal welfare states). Take the case of social insurance. While social insurance schemes do have a role in securing basic needs, they typically also seek to dampen down variation in living standards beyond what is necessary to meet basic needs. This function can, perhaps, be understood in terms of an expanded conception of basic needs: perhaps the interest in continuity of living standards is itself a basic need, insofar as it gives people firmer long-term expectations about their material circumstances which, in turn, consolidates their ability to formulate long-term projects (Goodin 1988). However, what if background living standards are themselves unequal? Is it sufficient for a welfare state to increase security in economic expectations taking this inequality as a given? Or, as in social democratic welfare states, should the welfare state seek to bear down on this background inequality itself?

The demand for equality is, of course, highly complex. At the most abstract level, we can distinguish at least three egalitarian objectives:

1. *Strong meritocracy.* Individuals should have equal opportunity, regardless of features such as class background, race, ethnicity, or gender, to develop their natural abilities into marketable talents and to win positions of reward and status on the basis of their talents (White 2006: ch. 3).
2. *Luck egalitarianism.* Individuals should not be disadvantaged in their opportunities to lead good lives by differences in endowments that are a matter of 'brute luck', e.g., the class into which one is born or one's natural ability; but inequalities reflecting different life-style choices are just (Cohen 1989; Dworkin 2000; Barry 2005; White 2006: ch. 4).
3. *Relational equality.* A good society is one in which social relationships are characterized by equality of status and the absence of domination (Anderson 1999).

Strong meritocracy is committed to an ambitious form of 'equality of opportunity'. Equality of opportunity implies an absence of discrimination in employment and related decisions, so that positions go to the applicants with the most job-relevant talent. But for the strong meritocrat, it also requires that individuals have equal opportunity to *develop* talents. This directs our attention to a wide range of social forces which influence talent development. Related to this, it may call for a range of public interventions, via the welfare state, to reshape these social forces: interventions to assist children's development in pre-school years; in the design of the education system; in the distribution of financial assets which might play an important role in determining educational and labour market opportunity (Ackerman and Alstott 1999; Prabhakar 2008).

But is strong meritocracy sufficient for social justice? 'Luck egalitarianism', a philosophical position recently developed out of the work of philosophers such as John Rawls and Ronald Dworkin, argues that it is not (Cohen 1989; Rawls 1999; Dworkin 2000). For even in a strong meritocratic society, resources and life-prospects will be unequally distributed as a result of inequalities in endowments of natural ability over which individuals have no control. Luck egalitarianism calls, therefore, for state action to correct for these further sources of 'brute luck' inequality.[1]

Exactly what this implies for the design of the welfare state is a matter of considerable debate. Dworkin seeks to apply the luck egalitarian intuition, as he understands it, by proposing the thought-experiment of a 'hypothetical insurance market'. Roughly speaking, we are to imagine individuals in an insurance market which has two important characteristics: (a) no individual knows their own endowment of marketable ability (or of what Dworkin calls 'handicaps') until they make an insurance purchase; and (b) each individual has equal purchasing power based on a per capita share of society's external resources. We are also to imagine different insurance companies offering a range of insurance policies, e.g. policies that provide insurance against failing to be at a certain point in the distribution of earnings power. The more generous the insurance cover one chooses to purchase (e.g. the higher the earnings power one insures against failing to have), the more of one's initial share of resources will be paid as an insurance premium. Dworkin argues that we can discern the kind of insurance policies that the 'average' individual would choose to buy. Real-world welfare state programmes should be based on this average insurance package. On this basis, Dworkin has argued for generous subsidies to the low-paid and unemployed (but with work conditions) and for a comprehensive health-care package that would be available to every citizen as of right (Dworkin 2000).

If we start from institutions, rather than theory, it is perhaps the institutions of the social democratic welfare states which seem at first sight to conform to the ambitions of luck egalitarianism. Social democratic welfare states are the most successful at bearing down on inequality in the distribution of income and wealth in a way that arguably limits brute luck inequality in this area. They also practice 'specific egalitarianism' in which specific goods, such as education and health-care, are taken out of the marketplace and provided to all citizens on a strictly egalitarian basis. This can be seen as further insulating the overall distribution of advantage from brute luck. By the same token, from the luck egalitarian point of view, both conservative and liberal welfare states look suspect. The liberal welfare state, by aiming only at assisting the most needy, is unlikely to go far enough in preventing or mitigating brute luck inequality (even if it is successful at securing basic needs). Conservative welfare states appear too concerned with the security of unequal living standards, above a basic needs threshold, without questioning the justifiability of the underlying inequality. Conservative welfare states are also associated with much lower labour force participation by women, and the luck egalitarian (not to mention the strong meritocrat) will view this too as unjust.[2]

---

[1] Disadvantage is a matter of brute luck when it is a result of birth and other kinds of lotteries that are not willingly entered into. It contrasts with what Dworkin calls 'option luck' which is a matter of how deliberate gambles turn out.

[2] It might be objected that the differences in labour force participation largely reflect gender differences in lifestyle choice to which a luck egalitarian should be indifferent. However, this is to ignore the extent to which some choices may be shaped by strong social norms over which no particular

There are, however, two sides to luck egalitarianism. If Smith has a higher income than Jones because she chooses to work more, or because she chooses a higher-paying job, then the resulting inequality is just, assuming that these were also real options for Jones. In this respect, luck egalitarianism tries to incorporate a conception of *personal responsibility* (Cohen 1989). (This perhaps reflects its origins, at least in its present form, in countries which have liberal welfare states.) This complicates the policy implications of luck egalitarianism and might call for some qualification to our earlier assertion that the institutions of the social democratic welfare state come closest, amongst existing welfare states, to meeting the demands of luck egalitarianism.

The emphasis on personal responsibility lends support in principle to policies which discriminate welfare provision based on how far people are responsible for their disadvantage. However, even considered on its own terms, luck egalitarianism demands a cautious appraisal of such policies. Luck egalitarianism holds that in-equalities due to choice are just when choices are made against a background in which brute luck inequalities in endowments have been handled appropriately. Insofar as this is not achieved, the luck egalitarian has reason to be careful about responsibility-discriminating policies. For example, if 'bad choices' correlate with brute luck disadvantage, e.g. unhealthy eating correlates with low earnings potential, then the luck egalitarian might oppose responsibility-sensitive health-care since, given the correlation, this could further disadvantage groups who are uncompensat-ed victims of bad brute luck. There is a related problem of disentangling the contributions of brute luck and personal responsibility in causing disadvantage. Choices reflect preferences. But preferences are shaped by one's social environment, something which is largely a matter of brute luck. So, even under ideal conditions, there is a difficult question of how to separate choice and personal responsibility from the effects of (unchosen) social environment (Roemer 1993).

The emphasis on personal responsibility in luck egalitarianism is a major concern for some political theorists. In an important paper, Elizabeth Anderson argues that luck egalitarianism is at once implausibly harsh in allowing individuals to face the consequences of their lifestyle choices and also demeaning in calling for those with limited skills or disabilities to be given mere financial compensation (Anderson 1999). Although Anderson's criticisms of luck egalitarianism are overstated, her paper draws out helpfully a distinct egalitarian perspective (White 2006: ch. 4). According to Anderson, egalitarianism is not fundamentally a matter of how we *distribute things* but of the *quality of social relationships*. Her account identifies in effect two particularly important features of social relationships: *status* and *power* (see also Young 1990). An egalitarian society is, fundamentally, a society in which individuals relate to one another as equals: they regard one another as having equal civic and political standing (status) and no individual has the capacity to dominate another (power). The ideal, in essence, is something like: 'no master, no slave', a formulation which we cannot reduce to a purely distributive egalitarian principle of

---

individual has control. We will return to this tricky issue of how brute luck can shape the context of choice below.

the form 'Alf and Betty should be equal in the amount of good X each has'. The significance of the distribution of income and wealth, on this view, derives from how it affects status and power relations. According to this *relational egalitarianism*, the welfare state's job is to help secure the conditions for status equality and the absence of domination.

The emphasis on using welfare policies to prevent domination marks a point of commonality with two other philosophical approaches to the welfare state. One is Robert E. Goodin's analysis of the welfare state as, in part, a device for preventing relationships of 'vulnerability' which would otherwise give rise to exploitation (Goodin 1986, 1988). The other is the neo-republican philosophy which sees the task of the state in general as securing freedom as 'non-domination' (Pettit 1997; Skinner 1998). Compared to a pure luck egalitarian approach, these relational perspectives are not concerned with eliminating brute luck inequality for its own sake. They may, however, ground a more sceptical approach to policies of conditionality and responsibility-based discrimination. Relational egalitarians will be worried about the possible threats to equal civic standing in such policies and, not least, about the way such policies could help to create or consolidate relationships of domination. The relational egalitarian perspective has recently become very important in the philosophical defence of citizen's income (Raventós 2007).

LIBERTY

Since the 1980s we have seen a shift towards 'neoliberalism' in many advanced capitalist countries with welfare state retrenchment as a chief goal. The neoliberal case has rested in part on claims about efficiency, but retrenchment is also defended as the recovery of individual liberty (Hayek 1960; Nozick 1974). This shift has been particularly pronounced in those countries with liberal welfare states. In these countries, supporters of the welfare state have been under considerable pressure to respond to a confident liberty-based critique of the welfare state. Is an adequate response to be had?

In the era of the welfare state's emergence the debate was often structured around a dispute between so-called 'negative' and 'positive' conceptions of liberty (Berlin 1969).[3] Negative liberty is the liberty of the individual from interference by others (force and coercion) to act as she wishes or might wish to act. The welfare state, with its structures of coercive 'redistribution', was seen by critics as an assault on negative

---

[3] Berlin (1969) is the most widely noted study of 'negative' and 'positive' liberty, but it should be noted that Berlin's central notion of 'positive liberty' is arguably somewhat different to that discussed here, focusing much more on the overcoming of irrationality within the agent rather than the absence of resource constraints to action.

liberty. However, some revisionist liberals, taking their cue from thinkers such as T. H. Green, argued that negative liberty represents an inadequate understanding of liberty (Green 1991).[4] Liberty, they argued, is the power of self-development. Negative liberty is valuable insofar as it enhances this power, but loses its value when it works to limit it. The use of state coercion to establish a framework in which all citizens are guaranteed the resources necessary for self-development might involve limitations on negative liberty. But these are justified, so it was argued, if they result in more, or all, citizens having the liberty that really matters: the power of self-development. One can see a clear echo of the revisionist liberal ideal of positive liberty in contemporary thinkers such as Amartya Sen and Martha Nussbaum, specifically in their call to focus state policy around the security of a range of basic 'capabilities' (Sen 1992; Nussbaum 1990). Conceptualizing liberty in terms of capability for self-development, or some other set of basic capabilities, in effect ties the notion of liberty closely to the notion of basic needs and thereby makes it amenable for recruitment to the welfare state cause.

One limitation of this approach, however, is that it leaves the welfare state critic free to take their stand on the priority which, so they will claim, ought to be given to negative liberty. Can the case for welfare state policies be made in terms of the very notion of negative liberty to which the critics appeal?

A key insight here is that a lack of income and wealth itself limits negative liberty (Waldron 1993; Cohen 1997: 41–3; Swift 2001). Take one example. I would like to travel from London to Liverpool on the train but I can't afford the ticket. What happens? I get on the train. The ticket inspector discovers I don't have a ticket. I am removed from the train at, say, Slough. My lack of a ticket means that I lack the *legal permission* to be on the train, and that I therefore become *subject to coercive interference*— interference ultimately backed up by the coercive apparatus of the state—in doing what I would like to do. Is this not a curtailment of my negative liberty? Let's approach the point another way. In a society with private ownership of resources, the property rights of others place us under a huge array of prohibitions about what resources we can use and, therefore, what actions we can perform. Money is the device we use to remove some of these prohibitions and so acquire the negative freedom to perform specific actions we wish to perform. It is money that enables me to go into the car showroom and leave with a Porsche, which I can then drive from London to Liverpool. Without the money, I would not have the negative freedom to perform this sequence of actions.

Now, what if we say that all citizens must be free – negatively free – at least to some minimum extent? Then it would seem to follow from what we have just said that all citizens must have some kind of guarantee of (reasonable access to) a minimum income. Going further, we should note that the core commitment of many liberal thinkers is not so much to 'liberty' as to 'equal liberty' (see e.g. Berlin 1969). But whether one accepts a normative commitment to either a sufficiency or equality of

---

[4] This is not to say that Green himself was a supporter of many welfare state measures, merely that he offered a conception of liberty which could be used to help justify them.

negative liberty, one cannot rest content with a free-market distribution of income and wealth since this is almost certainly going to violate either commitment. Some form of state action to regulate the distribution of income and wealth—and, hence, probably some kind of welfare state policy—is going to be necessary to secure a sufficiency or equality of negative freedom.

There are two ways of resisting this line of thought. One emphasizes the difference between being subject to a power of coercive interference and actually experiencing interference. When the homeless person tries to sleep on the lawn of the millionaire's house, she is subject to a power of coercive interference, but nevertheless might not experience actual interference. Perhaps the millionaire is willing to let her sleep there. If freedom is lost only when she experiences actual interference, then her poverty does not necessarily deprive her of various freedoms. And, if she hasn't necessarily lost said freedoms, we do not necessarily need 'redistributive' provisions to help her regain them. Alternatively, one might adopt a 'moralized' definition of negative liberty according to which a coercive interference restricts my freedom to act only when it interferes with something I have a *right* to do (Nozick 1974: 262; Cohen 1988). If the millionaire owns his property justly, then the homeless person has no right to sleep on it (without the owner's permission). The coercive interference which keeps her off the land, and so prevents her sleeping, does not reduce her negative liberty since it is not preventing her doing something she has a right to do. Consequently, one cannot argue that redistributive provision of resources is needed to sustain a negative freedom that would otherwise be lost.

Neither of these responses is convincing. In the first case, it is plausible to retort that freedom *is* constrained by subjection to a power of interference as well as by actual interference (Waldron 2006). The homeless person sleeping on the millionaire's lawn knows that she can be sent packing whenever the millionaire wishes. To be 'at the mercy' of another in this way is itself a constraint on one's freedom. One is dependent on the goodwill of another, and must take care to behave in a way that maintains that goodwill. This is, in fact, the core intuition behind the neo-republican conception of freedom as 'non-domination' which we introduced briefly at the end of the previous section (Pettit 1997; Skinner 1998).

Turning to the moralized definition of liberty, there are two problems. First, the moralized conception of liberty has one strongly counter-intuitive implication. Imagine a justly imprisoned criminal who wants to leave her prison. Do the prison guards restrict her liberty by keeping her in prison? Of course they do. But on the moralized definition of liberty one must apparently hold that there is no restriction of liberty here because the guards are not stopping her from doing something she has a right to do (Cohen 1988). Second, on a moralized conception of freedom, the contours of freedom now depend on answering the prior question of what is just. This means that one cannot do what many critics of the welfare state want to do: to employ freedom as an independent yardstick either to determine what justice is or as an independent value which competes with, and properly limits, the demands of justice (Cohen 1988). If we have good reason to think that justice requires an egalitarian distribution of some kind (see above), then one cannot say something like: 'But equality comes at the price of liberty'. Liberty, on the moralized conception we are discussing, is shaped by the demands of justice, so if justice demands equality, liberty is whatever we are permitted to do within the bounds of equality.

We have seen that the conventional, general critique of welfare state policies in terms of (negative) liberty is, at the very least, overstated. This is not to say, however, that there cannot be valid concerns or criticisms about welfare state policies from this standpoint. There is, in particular, an important cluster of issues around *paternalism, diversity,* and *choice* in welfare provision which also need to be considered. These concerns are as often voiced by what one might call left-libertarian critics of existing welfare states as by right-libertarian or 'neoliberal' critics. Again, the concerns are perhaps especially strong in countries with liberal welfare states, without being wholly confined to them.

The issue of paternalism, already broached above in connection with welfare conditionality, arises when the primary rationale of a policy that restricts the liberty of the individual is to do so *for her/his own good.* Thus, if a state compels individuals to save at certain rates for a future pension, paternalism is (likely to be) involved. Liberal philosophy presents a presumption against paternalism, but, as noted above, the presumption is not absolute. Paternalist measures can arguably be justified, consistent with liberalism, if they are measures which individuals would consent to as a way of securing themselves against their own short-sightedness or weakness of will (G. Dworkin 1971). This approach suggests that paternalism might be justified in cases where the restrictions in question are very widely supported, though this still leaves open a question about how the state should treat minorities who have conscientious (e.g. religious) reasons for not accepting restrictions that are desired by their fellow citizens (e.g. turban-wearing Sikhs who wish to work on building sites without wearing standard helmet protection). The idea of 'soft' or 'libertarian' paternalism offers another way of trying to reconcile paternalism and liberalism (Thaler and Sunstein 2008). This works not by denying choice but by shifting its baseline, e.g. enrolling employees automatically into a pension programme with the option of leaving, rather than giving them the option of joining. Such shifts can produce significant changes in behaviour, of benefit to the individuals concerned, without restricting their freedom.

Welfare state provision is sometimes criticized for confusing equality with unifor-mity. In a society with a plurality of different conceptions of the good life, citizens might reasonably wish that welfare provision be sensitive to difference in religious and similar beliefs. This has led some, such as Paul Hirst, to argue for an 'associ-ational welfarism' in which the state retains its role as primary financer of provision but in which actual provision is devolved to third sector associations such as religious groups and trade unions (Hirst 1994). In Hirst's model, citizens are in effect granted vouchers which they can use to purchase welfare provision from preferred providers. This is one of a range of proposals for increasing 'choice' in public provision by means of market-type mechanisms internal to the welfare state (Le Grand 2003). Critics argue that such mechanisms threaten to exacerbate inequalities in provision. However, much seems to depend here on the precise way in which the 'internal markets' are constructed and on the wider social context in which the mechanisms operate (Le Grand 2007). In one recent study of choice in education, Harry Brighouse shows that, depending on the exact policy design and circumstances, 'school choice' can give greater parental choice at no cost to egalitarian objectives and can even improve outcomes from an egalitarian point of view (Brighouse 2000). Here again we see how the normative analysis of welfare state policy must draw not only on philosophical analysis but on relevant empirical research.

CONCLUSION

Rather than trying to summarize the above discussion, in concluding I shall note some issues we have not had space to address.

One important issue concerns immigration policy and its implications for the welfare state (Barry and Goodin 1992). If the egalitarian concern is to insulate the distribution of advantage from the arbitrariness of the birth lottery, then what could be more arbitrary than nationality of birth? Egalitarianism thus draws one naturally to a policy of open borders. But the opening of borders is likely, in practice, to put extra strain on welfare states (in affluent societies). So egalitarians might face a dilemma of how to reconcile (more) open borders and egalitarian domestic social policies. For example, if a state introduces a generous citizen's income domestically on egalitarian grounds, and complements this with an open borders policy, how sustainable is the basic income policy likely to be? The issue of how to adapt welfare states justly to the demands of greater diversity, touched on briefly above, is one further aspect of the challenges posed by egalitarian immigration policy.

Another important issue not addressed here is that of intergenerational justice (Barry 1991). This issue is of obvious importance in considering pension policy, for example. It is also important in thinking about how the welfare state can be rendered consistent with, if not supportive of, environmental sustainability. Moreover, the issues of global and intergenerational justice come together in various ways which will have implications for welfare states.

The philosophical issues discussed in this chapter largely reflect an agenda of debate shaped by the politics of welfare state retrenchment and reconstruction which began in the 1980s, a period in which welfare state supporters have had to clarify and refine their arguments in the face of the confident intellectual opposition of the New Right. Looking ahead, however, this cluster of issues around global and intergenerational justice is likely to become as important as the classical debates between left and right on the justice of the welfare state.

CHAPTER 3

INTELLECTUAL ROOTS

CHRIS PIERSON
MATTHIEU LEIMGRUBER

INTRODUCTION

THE intellectual roots of welfare state thinking are complex and tangled. The late-breaking and multivalent term 'welfare state' occupies a crowded conceptual terrain (which it shares with, amongst others, social security, *Sozialstaat*, *Wohlfahrtsstaat*, and *Etat providence*) and it covers a wide range of institutions and practices. The defence of the welfare state *tout court* is a relatively late development and those who fashioned the institutions and policies most widely associated with that term—statesmen like Bismarck and civil servants such as Beveridge—were often arguing for something rather (and sometimes quite) different. Although the welfare state project has often come to be identified with the prosecution of normative arguments about 'social justice' (see Chapter 2), in fact its ideational roots (even its normative roots) are much more diverse and contested than this. And although the welfare state comes to be identified (largely after 1945) as, in some sense, the historical project of social democracy, its origins more usually lie with liberal or even conservative forces (and ideas).

The picture is further complicated by uncertainty over exactly what it is that the 'welfare state' (and its cognate terms) connotes. There is some agreement over the inclusion of core social services and insurance programmes (at least for those who would allow an institutionally grounded definition), but should this include provision which is funded and/or regulated by the state but delivered by others? Does it include public education or labour market policy or tax expenditures (to take just three frequently contested examples)? Further confusion arises from the fact that the welfare state emerges, if not quite seamlessly then certainly incrementally, from a mass of existing legal provision and social practice, above all, that dealing with vagrancy, the impoverished elderly and the regulation of labour. It represents both a breach with, and a continuation of, earlier social policies—poor laws, laws of settlement, employers' liability. Pre-existing traditions of amelioration and correction, quintessentially the varying strands of (above all, Christian) 'philanthropy', locally administered poor laws and the much newer 'social science' have played a continuing role (Bridgen and Harris 2007).

Any history of the ideational roots of welfare needs also to recognize that there were (especially in the nineteenth century) emergent forms of knowledge in other areas without which it would be hard to imagine the birth of the modern welfare state. These would include advances in the sciences of disease and infection (Baldwin 1999) and the new actuarial and statistical competences without which there could be no social insurance (Ewald 1986). Policy making under rapidly changing social and political circumstances often involved a lot of 'puzzle-solving' (Heclo 1974) and this process of puzzling and knowledge sharing was, from its very earliest days, not just international but truly transnational (Rodgers 1998). Ideas and projects related to the welfare state emerged from the 1880s onwards across a community of shared but also disputed knowledge and opinion that reached all the way from Berlin to San Francisco (sometimes via Sydney and Wellington) and onwards to Tokyo (Westney 1987).

More than this, the notion of the welfare state presupposed, or indeed coincided with, the full emergence of the modern nation state. It required the development of sufficient bureaucratic capacity to handle the new, highly complex social protection programmes. This is why civil servants, from Theodor Lohmann (in Germany) to Edwin Witte (in the United States) to William Beveridge (in the United Kingdom) and Pierre Laroque (in France), often played such a crucial role in establishing the welfare state on the ground. A new class of national reformers emerged with its own ethos, a secular orientation (though often with a background in 'practical Christianity'), and a commitment to the amelioration of living conditions.

One of the most characteristic of all welfare state developments is welfare 'creep': the incremental growth of welfare programmes, coverage, and budgets. There is an element of 'creep' in the intellectual case for welfare too. Those who once argued for the introduction of workplace insurance for male workers in the dangerous industrial occupations did not anticipate a comprehensive system of social provision for all 'from cradle to grave'. Indeed, the earliest welfare programmes were not generally presented as the founding legislation of a new species of citizenship but focused instead upon workers or ex-workers. Legislation to regulate the hours and working conditions of women and children was often quite explicitly grounded in a recognition that they were not full citizens, and, on precisely these grounds, such provision was often thought inappropriate for their 'independent' male colleagues or parents. Certainly a (partial) transition from the status of pauper (which traditionally entailed the loss of whatever citizenship rights one enjoyed) into citizen can be widely plotted in welfare debates and practices throughout the twentieth century. But this is not straightforward or universal. The idea of 'less eligibility' (the classic rubric of the poor law) never really went away and some of the most important state welfare initiatives were seen as an alternative to citizenship. The insight that citizenship comes to be identified with paid work (in the public sphere) points to an alternative way in which gendered welfare citizenship has been constructed (Bock and Thane 1991; Pateman, 1989). The welfare state is clearly in part about bringing the 'popular' into politics but not always on the basis of citizenship.

Finally, we need to recognize that the intellectual underpinnings of a welfare regime may change across time. The fact that the Scandinavian welfare state was, at its origins, the not very generous product of conservative forces may argue against the view that the origins of welfare states lie in the mobilization of working-class numbers. But it tells us nothing about whether the welfare state became, in due course, the medium through which a redistributive politics or the inception of a 'people's home' was realized. The welfare state only really became the project of social democracy after John Maynard Keynes and after 1945 (or after Ernst Wigforss and somewhat sooner in Sweden). Before that, it was really the intellectual property of others.

Having said all of this, it still is possible to identify certain intellectual trends that made possible or plausible a new kind of social policy that comes to be identified with or as 'the welfare state' (though almost always in retrospect). In this chapter, we review the most important of these trends across a range of national (and international) trajectories. We focus most of our attention upon those formative years in which the case for a welfare state was first set out though we do also consider the ways in which these arguments were changed or embellished as the welfare state became rather more of an established fact (especially after 1945). There were important ideational developments in later periods but these undoubtedly built upon the pattern of what had gone before. While the representatives of labour, more especially those organized in trade unions, were sometimes (though by no means always) happy to support state welfare provision for their members, they often saw social policy as an *alternative* to socialism. So did their opponents. Early welfare measures were very often motivated by an attempt to answer the 'social question' but *without* challenging the prevailing economic and political order.

One of the key insights of historical work on the emergence of the welfare state over the past twenty-five years has been a growing recognition of the social policy activism of the state throughout the nineteenth century. Nonetheless, we are perhaps still justified in describing the period between 1875 and 1914 as marking the 'birth' of the welfare state, above all, because of the intensity of policy innovation compressed into these years. It was also a time in which states' social expenditure budgets grew substantially, albeit from an extremely modest baseline (C. Pierson 1991; Lindert 2004).

In fact, the pattern of ideas that underlay (or overlay) these early developments is complex and varied. It includes (following Freeden 2003) new ideas about citizenship, new expectations of bureaucratic organization, new beliefs about the proper objects (and extended limits) of state power (both national and local), new understandings about what constitutes well-being and human flourishing, new (forms of) knowledge about poverty and deprivation, changing ideas about the role of the 'popular' in politics and of the proper forms of democratic governance more generally, new views about what constitutes social justice, new attitudes to time and to risk and changed expectations about how a modern economy can be organized and how the redistribution of wealth can be both justified and delivered.

GERMANY AND FRANCE

It makes sense to begin our survey with the case of Germany as this is almost universally regarded as the first state to have taken the decisive legislative measures that made it a welfare state or *Sozialstaat*. Traditionally, the founding of Germany's welfare state has been identified with the proclamation of the Imperial Message delivered by Chancellor Bismarck on 17 November 1881 and the associated legislation on sickness insurance (1883), accident insurance (1884), and invalidity and old age insurance (1889). In the traditional account, this raft of social legislation is seen, above all, as part of a strategy to bind workers to the newly unified German state and to steer them away from the appeal of the (outlawed) social democrats (Ritter 1986). It was seen to be built around a long-standing and loosely Hegelian commitment to a corporate social role for the state, a paternalistic concern among the governing elite for the well-being of the general population, and a long-standing practice of support for workers provided through a framework of occupational guilds. It was a strategy prosecuted in the context of rapid industrialization and urbanization—indeed, it was in part an attempt to deal with the challenges this presented in a more rational and economically efficient way—but grounded in a profound scepticism about the *laissez faire* claims of English or Manchester liberalism.

More recently, the role of Bismarck has been somewhat downplayed and the innovations of the 1880s recast as a part of the low politics of inter-party rivalry rather than as the gradual unfolding of a 'grand plan'. In this context, others have emerged as intellectual architects of the German reform process. The *Verein für Socialpolitik*, for example, founded in 1872, gave an informed intellectual focus to calls for state intervention and a moderation of the outcomes that markets (including labour markets) generated. The label that stuck to members of the group, *Katheder-sozialisten*, was not uniformly accurate but they were certainly a key source for ideas of 'market-substituting, income-redistributing social politics', and (in the case of Gustav Schmoller, for example) a considerable influence upon key political and bureaucratic decision makers (Grimmer-Solem 2003). A reduced focus upon Bismarck has exposed the sustained work of a number of less elevated political actors.

Theodor Lohmann, a senior bureaucrat advocating factory legislation (which Bismarck consistently resisted), who maintained his interest when Bismarck had moved on, is in many ways characteristic. More liberal than Bismarck, Lohmann was a Christian reformer who favoured state intervention but who wanted the state where possible to act through its support of voluntary organizations (rather than through straightforward compulsion). He worked tirelessly in bureaucratic and political circles to promote legislation that would deliver on this agenda. His ambition was certainly social amelioration and attachment of the working class to the *Reich* but he argued that this might be best achieved by promoting the interests of individuals within their own organizations, including trade unions (Hennock 2007; Tennstedt and Winter 1994; Stremmel et al. 2006).

In France, the idea of *Etat providence* can be retraced to the 1860s. Its original usage was a critical one and while, in the hands of Napoleon III's favourite social thinker Frederic le Play, it came to stand more positively for the role of the state in supporting mutual institutions, its meaning has always been keenly contested. Traditionally, the French welfare system has been presented as decentralized, non-statist and built around ideas such as *mutualité, solidarisme,* and *subsidiarité* (Ashford 1993). While the first term indicated a clear preference for voluntary organizations set up to provide for their members' needs through self-administered cooperation, the principle of *social solidarity* or *solidarisme* relied heavily on state intervention to sustain mutual self-help. The idea of *subsidiarity* is different again. In the French context, it embraces the idea that mutual insurance should be managed by all contributors—workers, employers and the state—and this at some distance from the central state, a system of 'semiautonomous decision making' (Ashford 1993). Ironically, French experience at the turn of the twentieth century may more properly be understood as a reaction *against* subsidiarity (in so far as this embodied a key role for the church), but, as a more general principle, subsidiarity (the idea that social functions should be carried out at the lowest level consistent with equity and efficiency), was important across continental Europe. And while it has been seen as especially significant in those countries where social Catholicism was dominant, it also had its Protestant and even Calvinist equivalents (as for example in Abraham Kuyper's advocacy of 'sphere sovereignty' in Holland; van Kersbergen and Manow 2009). To this we should add a recurrent interest in support of the family and of children, itself associated with a recurring and widespread fear in France of a declining population (Pedersen 1993).

The emergence of early French social policy was, above all, an exercise in nation-state building (following upon the traumatic experience of the Commune and the defeat by Prussian forces in 1871). And, given the late onset of industrialization in France, the initial reform agenda was not so much one of pacifying workers as achieving a fuller laicization of the state (especially in the fields of public education and social assistance). In fact, the contrast between Germany and France has been overdrawn. Despite its explicit statism, the Bismarckian reforms above all strengthened occupational organizations (*berufliche Genossenschaften*) and municipal institutions (*Ortskassen*), giving the nascent German welfare state a much more decentralized profile than is often supposed. Meanwhile, in 'decentralized' France, proponents of Republican *solidarisme* such as Léon Bourgeois envisioned a strong role for the state in supporting and developing the field of mutual organizations. In both countries, contemporary economists and social scientists discussed welfare reform as a way to foster class *rapprochement* and the integration of the working class into bourgeois society. Seeking to tie workers to the state and to the nation was to be a means to increase the cohesion of both the French Republic and the Wilhelminian Empire (Stone 1985).

BRITAIN AND THE ANTIPODES

If we turn our attention to experience in Britain and the innovative social programme of the great reforming Liberal administration of 1906–11—or indeed if we look to the precocious reform agenda of turn-of-the-century reformers in Australia and New Zealand—it makes sense to give priority to the ideas identified with the 'new' or 'social' liberalism, advocated by philosopher T. H. Green and his followers (Bruce 1968; Freeden 1978, 2003). Of the essence of this new liberal view was the belief that liberty was not primarily about the state's non-interference but rather about its securing the best possible conditions for human flourishing. It was still concerned with the fate of the individual but of an individual living within and dependent upon a wider human community. It was not well served by a state that confined itself to the maintenance of order and the upholding of contracts. The state ought also to embody a sense of the common good. It could and should intervene in the realm of contracts and private property to reallocate life chances in a way which equalized access to 'real' equality of opportunity. Since the real opportunities of individuals were cramped by poor housing, ill health, and inadequate education (and incomes), the state could and should act to address these unnatural disadvantages and it could and should use the resources that (progressive) taxation could command in order to do so. It was these ideas that were taken to justify the modest, though still quite transformative, programme of social reforms of the 1906–11 Liberal Government including the provision of school meals, a schools' medical service, national health insurance, old-age pensions, labour exchanges, and urban planning. Just as crucially, it justified the reformed taxation regime that could pay for these (Thane 1996).

Though clearly important, the new liberalism was just one element in a complex assemblage of ideas. Older themes persisted, including the ubiquitous condemnation of the 'unworthy poor'—the feckless, the idle, and the incompetent—and the advocacy of Christian philanthropy. But these views now took their place alongside the more 'scientific' accounts of the nature of poverty that emerged from social survey work. And some of the remedies were also new: whether it was the casework of the Charity Organization Societies, the community-based work of the Settlement Houses, or the 'expertise' promoted by the Webbs (Harris 2004). The late Victorian idea of progress and (social) evolution also had an impact and, often in association with this, eugenics was, at this time, a 'social science' for both conservatives and progressives. Indeed, before it became so inextricably associated with the extreme right, eugenics was often seen by 'progressive' opinion as embodying a legitimate concern for raising the general quality of the population. Similarly, there were social imperialists on both right and left.

Something of the same admixture of utility and idealism could be found in the yet earlier reforms undertaken in Britain's southernmost colonies, Australia and New Zealand. Although the parentage of Australasian social reform is contested, factory legislation and the regulation of wages and conditions in the colonies were in their time the most advanced in the world. The novel system of compulsory arbitration (which encouraged workers to join trade unions) was widely remarked and admired in both Britain and America, as was the willingness of the state to act as employer of last resort. And New Zealand was one of the first states anywhere to introduce a non-contributory old age pension. The ideas of T. H. Green and his successors were widely read in the reforming environment of turn-of-the-century Australasia and these ideas were promulgated by a small but influential group of emigré academics who had studied in Britain (Sawer 2003). The commitment to a rough-and-ready incarnation of 'real' equality of opportunity was captured in the ubiquitous and not very philosophical Australian notion of the 'fair go'. The fact that so much of the work that was done elsewhere by state redistribution was done in Australia and New Zealand by state regulation had a decisive impact upon the development of welfare states in both these countries (Castles 1985).

THE AMERICAN CASE

The United States has often been seen (in this as in so many other ways) as 'exceptional'; usually, in relation to the welfare state, as exceptionally belated, small, and mean. However, thinking about social policy has a long and rich history in the United States. Already during the late eighteenth century revolutionary era, Thomas Paine, in dialogue with French philosopher and mathematician Marquis de Condorcet, was among the first to reflect on the principles of state-financed old age pensions (Rothschild 1995). Remarkably, by the late nineteenth century, Civil War veterans' pensions constituted one of the largest public pension systems anywhere in the world (Jensen 2003; Skocpol 1992). But this substantial entitlement programme died out with the veterans and their survivors, at least in part because it was seen as part of a political economy of patronage, which it was the mission of early twentieth-century Progressives to eliminate. In its place, in Theda Skocpol's (1992) account, came an attempt to institute a 'maternalist' welfare state. Largely the work of educated and professional women and women's organizations, acting politically but outside the formal democratic structures from which they were still largely excluded, this advocacy led to the initiation of a raft of measures to protect women, both as mothers and workers, and their children, including the establishment of the Children's Bureau in 1912 and the Women's Bureau in 1920. In so far as this mobilization was successful, it tended to focus upon the distinctive position of women, above all as mothers.

Daniel Rodgers (1998) take on this story is rather different. For him, the leitmotif of North American social politics from the late nineteenth century through to the era of rapid economic growth after 1945 is one of transnational (above all, transatlantic) borrowing. Whatever was the salience of liberal individualism in the wider population and culture, for those who drove forward the process of welfare reform in the United States (not always with great success), the point of reference was almost always Europe. And (at least until 1914) not the Europe of the Manchester liberals but rather of pioneering Germany. The American Association for Labor Legislation was thus modelled upon the German *Gesellschaft für Sozialreform* (Moss 1996; Rodgers 1998). The multiple institutional obstacles set by a fragmented federal polity and the mounting strength of private alternatives to statist social policy (Hacker 2002) did indeed slow the development of the United States welfare state and brought only partial results before the famous 1935 Social Security Act. However, this cornerstone of the New Deal in many ways only belatedly recapitulated and brought through ideas and concepts that had been in gestation for decades.

SWEDEN AND THE SCANDINAVIAN MODEL

Scandinavia, and Sweden in particular, has a quite central place in the ideational history of welfare. The idea that there is a 'Swedish model' (or a 'Nordic model' or a 'Scandinavian model') and that it is one that others may want to follow, has been enormously influential (see Chapter 40). The core principle of the model is perhaps best captured in Swedish Prime Minster Per Albin Hansson's idea of the *folkhemmet* (or 'people's home'), a term coined at the end of the 1920s and often taken to embody the aspirations of the long period of Swedish social democratic hegemony from 1932 until 1976. At its simplest, this term captures the idea of a national community which would provide a 'good home' for all its members, one grounded in equality and mutual respect. It signalled a new kind of politics for organized labour, one that abandoned the revolutionary millennialism of orthodox Marxism in favour of a strategy of gradual but real social change (which its advocates always insisted was quite different from an unprincipled reformism). The aspiration was to move towards a classless society by moderating economic inequality while providing standards of public service, equally for all citizens, that would nullify the social consequences of such economic inequalities as remained. Private ownership was to be tolerated and growth encouraged but in a context of high social expenditure, extensive social provision and progressive taxation. Through the 1930s, the economists of the Stockholm School (including Ernst Wigforss and Gunnar Myrdal) pressed the case for deficit financing to be a part of this settlement, famously predating Keynes's *General Theory of Employment, Interest and Money* (1936). Meanwhile, Gunnar and Alva Myrdal were exemplars of the attempt to bring the evidence of social science to bear in support of rational welfare reform, as in their 1934 book *Crisis in the Population Question* (Carlson 1990).

Under the terms of the 1938 Saltsjöbaden agreement, the social democrats formalized an 'historic compromise' with Swedish capital. Capitalist economic growth would be encouraged whilst Social Democratic governments would pursue Keynesian economic policies to sustain full employment and use progressive taxation to reduce economic inequality and promote provision for collective needs, such as education, health, and housing. When in the post-World War II period the defence of welfare institutions and full employment threatened inflation and the loss of international competitiveness, this compromise was complemented by the adoption of the 'Rehn–Meidner' model, which entailed an 'active manpower policy' and a 'solidaristic' wage policy. In this way, it was hoped that welfare provision and a rising standard of living for the working population could be reconciled with continuing non-inflationary economic growth. (For a fuller account, see C. Pierson 1991.)

For a long time, Sweden's social democratic settlement was represented as pragmatic or 'post-ideological'. Critics (and admirers) saw the Swedish Social Democrats as a party that had made its peace with capitalism and settled upon the welfare state as the mechanism through which it could then extract the most effective concessions on the part of its core constituency in the organized working class. However, the party's proposal (in the 1970s) to set up wage-earners funds and the attendant prospect of gradual socialization of the economy, reignited an interest in more radical readings of the Swedish social democratic experience. This reappraisal of thinkers such as Per Albin Hansson, Gunnar Myrdal, and, perhaps above all, Ernst Wigforss revealed an account of the welfare state as a much more radical strategy for the gradual transformation of capitalism through 'democratic class struggle' (Tilton 1990; Korpi 1983).

TRANSNATIONAL SOCIAL POLICY DEVELOPMENT

The welfare state has usually been understood as quintessentially a *national* phenomenon or as a set of uniquely *national* projects. Indeed, it has often been seen to be a part of the process of state- and nation-making itself. And yet, from the very earliest days of welfare state development, we have plenty of evidence of the international transfer of policy ideas. Sometimes this process was intergovernmental. At the turn of the twentieth century, it was widely supposed that German's reform programme was being widely imitated across Northern Europe and even as far away as Japan (Hennock 2007; Streeck and Yamamura 2002). Similarly, New Zealand's precocious pensions reform (of 1898) was the object of study back in the United Kingdom.

As early as 1900, reformers, welfare workers, labour lawyers, insurers, and statisticians from many countries met at the social sections of the World Fairs, corresponded through the International Association for Labour Legislation (1901), the ancestor of the International Labour Organization (ILO), and attended professional congresses that debated the mathematical techniques and methods that would later enable the actual implementation of social insurance programmes (Saunier 2008; Rodgers 1998).

This theme of transnational expertise persists throughout the twentieth century. In later times, it came to be especially associated with the work of international organizations such as the World Bank, the Organization for Economic Co-operation and Development (OECD) and the European Union (EU). In the formative years of welfare, it was most often identified with the expanding role of the ILO. Set up in 1919, the ILO became a key source of technical knowledge and expertise in the inter-war period. Originally dominated by social policy experts from Germany and central Europe, the coming of war, and finally the 1941 exile to Montreal heralded an increased influence for Anglo-Saxon ideas. In London, exiled civil servants and politicians from occupied Europe worked in parallel with the Beveridge Commission, generating parallel reform plans for Belgium (Van Acker), France (Laroque) and the Netherlands (Van Rhijn). Roosevelt's 'Four Freedoms' and the social and economic aspects of the 1941 Atlantic Charter also gave a new force to the idea of *social security* (Rodgers et al. 2009). The imperative to social justice in a post-war world was reiterated and expanded upon in the 1944 Philadelphia Declaration of the ILO as well as the 1948 United Nations (UN) Declaration of Human Rights Convention. From this point on, international agencies including the UN and ILO were to have a key role in the setting of benchmarks; as, for example, in the 1952 ILO Convention 102 on Social Security (Minimum Standards).

WELFARE THINKING AFTER 1945

Many traditional accounts of welfare state development have tended to see 1945 as a decisive date, perhaps even the decisive date in the emergence of the modern welfare state. The very term 'welfare state' is widely associated with Archbishop Temple's wartime contrast between the *power state* of Nazi Germany and the *welfare state* which was to be the ambition and promise of post-war Allied reconstruction (C. Pierson 1991). In the British context (and beyond) the key figure here—both as man of substance and potent myth—is William Beveridge. Certainly, the Beveridge Report (*Social Insurance and Allied Services*, 1942) was widely represented (and sometimes read) as the blueprint of a universalist, inclusive and comprehensive welfare state. Despite his patrician tones, Beveridge was a very popular and effective spokesman for his own report. But his reputation owes quite as much to those who came (soon) after him and interpreted both the report and the reforms it had promoted in world-historical terms. Perhaps the most influential of all these sources is T. H. Marshall and his celebrated lecture on 'Citizenship and Social Class' (Marshall 1963). Writing as Labour's new post-war social regime was being put in place, Marshall offered an historic account of the emergence of the welfare state which focused upon the idea of social citizenship as the latest (and highest) stage in a long-standing (and largely English) trajectory in which the winning of a series of legal and then political rights had been the basis of a transformation of the population from subjects to citizens. In fact, for all its Whiggishness, Marshall's was never a straightforward story of the unshackled triumph of social citizenship. He stressed that there was always a potential clash between citizenship equality and market-generated inequality. He also insisted that citizenship always involved duties (including a duty to work) as well as rights. But undoubtedly, he captured a sense that we had 'moved on' and that the coming of a new welfare state settlement was probably irreversible.

As in Britain, the development of the welfare state in continental Europe was also related to the imperatives of post-war social and economic reconstruction. Electoral successes for parties of the left, either on their own or in coalition, seemed briefly to betoken a new beginning for social policy and the prospect of a comprehensive and integrated welfare state which might truly provide for its citizens 'from cradle to grave'. Of course, these expectations were to be disappointed. Many of the reforms built upon what had existed in the interwar period and, especially given the financial constraints within which programmes were introduced, the preceding order of conditional payments, user charges, and means-tested assistance lingered on into the brave new world.

In Germany, the story of the welfare state after Bismarck is inevitably subsumed in that country's more general and catastrophic history in the first half of the twentieth century. Yet, despite the shocks brought by the demise of the Weimar Republic, the economic meltdown of the 1920s and the destructive reign of the Third Reich, German social programmes showed great resilience. They survived both the Nazi era and the attempt of the various wartime allies to reform them in the immediate aftermath of 1945. During the 1950s and 1960s, a restored Bismarckian welfare order, buttressed by the pensions reform of 1957, became associated with the idea of a 'social market economy'. As the brain child of 'ordo-liberal' economists and civil servants such as Walter Eucken, Alfred Müller-Armack, and Ludwig Erhard, the foundations of the *Soziale Marktwirtschaft* were set under the guidance of Germany's brand of Christian democracy and in coalition with social democrats. During the period of the

Wirtschaftswunder ('economic miracle'), the idea of social welfare became reattached to ideas of social solidarity and subsidiarity.

Meanwhile in France, the immediate post-war period saw an attempt to rationalize fragmented pre-war social institutions within a new and universalist structure. However, the far-reaching *Plan de Sécurité Sociale* designed by the 'French Beveridge', the Gaullist Pierre Laroque, did not lead to a complete transformation of existing programmes. Centred around a clear opposition to public assistance and with a focus on securing and generalizing new social insurance rights for the whole population, the *Sécurité Sociale* was composed of both a basic *régime général* and diversified occupational structures. Financed through extensive payroll contributions (in opposition to the tax-based Beveridgian model), the 'extension through diversity' of the *Sécurité Sociale* was also based on a complex set of tripartite management procedures including the state, employers' federations, and trade unions (Palier 2002). Though Beveridgian in appearance, the post-war French welfare state had clearly Bismarckian traits.

In general, these experiences point us towards three important features of the ideational fate of welfare in the post-war period. The first was that the welfare state came to be seen increasingly as the political project of social democracy (though it was also very much the political *practice* of Christian democracy). Of course, the legitimist parties of the left (the social democratic parties that had issued from the split with the communists around 1922) had always been parties of social reform. But they had always maintained (to some extent still retained) the idea of the social ownership of the economy (in however long a term and by howsoever constitutional means) as their real *raison d'être*. Increasingly after 1945, they came to argue first, that the welfare state was the means of prosecuting such a strategy and, subsequently, that perhaps the welfare state was itself the name for this transitional society which was 'not quite yet socialism, but certainly no longer capitalism' (Crosland 1964). A second and closely related change was the claim that the nature of the economy and the tools of (state) economic management had altered decisively. It was the triumph of Keynesianism (or its functional equivalents and its bastard offspring) and the expectation that governments could now run an economy at full employment, control the investment function without taking formal ownership, and steer the distributional outcomes of a market economy through a skilful mixture of taxes and benefits, that were said to have transformed the post-war political landscape. The popular descriptor, *Keynesian welfare state*, gave effective expression to this change. Thirdly, this was taken increasingly to be the uncontested terrain on which legitimate parties (from centre-right to centre-left) were agreed.

What distinguished the post-war welfare state (in the eyes of its advocates) was that it would make a virtue of public provision, that it would subordinate the logic of charity to the logic of citizenship, and that it would explicitly seek to redistribute both income and life chances in the interests of those who were least favoured by unmediated market outcomes. Public administration would yield greater efficiency and uniformity of provision (compared with the patchy and disorderly regime of semi-voluntary services). To adopt a later terminology, large areas of social provision would be 'de-commodified'—that is, taken outside the realm of the market (Esping-Andersen 1985a). With everyone (who wanted one) in a job, the remaining work of income redistribution would come through progressive taxation (rather than transfers), whilst social equality would be enhanced (and class divisions attenuated) by the provision of improving public services (financed by economic growth).

Here we can note just one final feature of the post-war welfare order. Increasingly (in the 1950s and 1960s), social policy (including labour market policy) was presented as a technical problem, one that could be sorted out in the context of a consensus over (a) the way in which the economy should be run, (b) the desirability of an expanding welfare state. For a time, it appeared that there was a broad-based political consensus over the welfare state settlement, one from which only unreconstructed Marxists and unreconciled Hayekians were excluded (though with just a little more hindsight both the depth and the duration of this 'consensus' has been increasingly contested; see C. Pierson 1991). In 1974, at the very moment when the post-war order was beginning to falter, both the Swedish social democrat Gunnar Myrdal and the much-travelled Professor Friedrich von Hayek shared the Nobel Memorial Prize in Economics. This joint award served to signal both the zenith of the post-1945 intellectual justifications of a flowering welfare state and the beginnings of a new and much more critical era. As the critical voices became ever louder, it appeared as if defenders of the established social policy regime had forgotten about the moral economy of welfare (which had been so powerful and so important for thinkers like Marshall). But, in fact, the politics of welfare is always strongly moralized. When the politics of social democracy was 'reinvented' in the 1990s under the rubric of the 'Third Way', and the idea of the welfare state eclipsed by the logic of the *social investment* state, the idea that welfare rights were matched by a set of individual welfare *responsibilities* was brought into centre stage (Giddens 1998). But this move was itself a response to the drastic re-moralization of welfare that had been realized (at least rhetorically) by the intellectual forces of the new right from the 1970s onwards.

CHAPTER 4

··

CRITICS AND BEYOND

··

DESMOND KING

FIONA ROSS

INTRODUCTION

··

FROM its origins, the welfare state has been periodically declared to be in crisis and critics have stood poised with various theories of why this is the case (Heclo 1981; van Kersbergen 2000; Jaeger and Kvist 2003). Welfare states were never as undisputed as implied by the term 'consensus' and it is important not to confuse the post-war era of state building, a shared project between a particular brand of paternalistic conservatism/Christian democracy (concerned with maintaining social stability) and social democracy, with a principled, egalitarian common ideal. Moreover, influential critics of the welfare state have not been confined to the political right. Some of the most piercing critiques driving restructuring have been delivered by social democrats.

This chapter explores how the welfare state's critics, their ideas and advocacy have contributed to institutional change, and most importantly, the substance of that transformation across affluent societies. First we review neoliberal critiques of the welfare state advocated by Friedrich von Hayek and Milton Friedman. These ideas have been deployed directly against Keynesianism and the national welfare state from its earliest days and have influenced the thinking and agenda of the first wave of ideologically driven retrenchers, notably Britain's Margaret Thatcher and Ronald Reagan in the United States (see King 1987). Next, we explore the thinking and impact of conservative critics, Charles Murray and Lawrence Mead. Though their critiques were developed in the context of the United States and a particular 'welfare' programme, AFDC/TANF (Aid to Families with Dependent Children, which later became Temporary Assistance for Needy Families), their damning indictment of the relationships between benefits and behaviour has not been confined to America. Third, we review social democratic critiques, collectively referred to as the Third Way. These ideas have influenced the reformulation of the welfare state *once Keynesianism had collapsed* following the oil crises of the 1970s and the subsequent economic and political turmoil. They were not part of initial disturbances to the welfare state and did not inspire the early retrenchments delivered by leftist leaders, notably in the Antipodes. For example, the monetarist ideas of Roger Douglas, New Zealand's Minister of Finance between 1984 and 1989, can be accredited to neoclassical Treasury and Reserve Bank economists who, together with the Business Roundtable, played a direct role in developing policy initiatives throughout the reform period (Gregory 1998: 4–7), not to ideological shifts within the left at this time. With the ideational transformation of social democracy, the importance (although not the precise position) of the market became uncontested across the political spectrum.

AUTHORS AND AGENTS OF PARADIGM CHANGE

Neoliberal Critiques

The ideas of two exponents of classical liberalism, Friedrich von Hayek and his follower, Milton Friedman, are attributed with radically changing the welfare state in the English-speaking countries and beyond (see King 1987). Warning of the inherent dangers of an interventionist state, Hayek (Keynes's principal intellectual rival from the 1930s onwards) launched his influential critique *before* the institutionalization of the welfare state. In his hugely significant work, *The Road to Serfdom* (1944), Hayek argued that the state had neither the information nor the managerial capacity to effectively control the economy (Feser 2006; Steele 2007). Given these deficiencies, attempts at economic planning would fail. Under such circumstances, the state's corrective action (and one likely to be driven by public demand), would be to exert ever stronger leadership as a means of delivering desired outcomes. The result of this process would be the road to serfdom, understood as the rise of authoritarian, totalitarian states (e.g. Nazi Germany), and a depletion of liberty (Nash 1976, 2004; Feser 2006; Steele 2007). According to Hayek, the state should be limited by a strict rule of law (Feser points out that Hayek rejected extreme laissez-faire ideas, favouring a basic safety net). The pursuit of individual interests would lead to the greater good. Keynesianism, to Hayek's mind, was a solution to political turmoil not a recipe for economic well-being. On the contrary, government deficits would inevitably produce inflation and state interventionism would suppress individualism, liberty, innovation, responsibility, and risk-taking. By freeing the entrepreneurial few to work their magic and relieving them of taxation and regulation, the masses would benefit through trickle down effects (Taylor 2007).

Most scholarly works have not envisioned institutional change as a product of a direct clash between competitive ideas at any given moment in time: policymakers' vision is circumscribed by dominant paradigms, the lens through which they construct their understanding of policy problems and solutions (see Blyth 2001; Cox 2001). Yet Hayek's ideas did not simply disappear from the political landscape as the Keynesian agenda was institutionalized, only to be reawakened with the election of two disciples of his work, Margaret Thatcher and Ronald Reagan, when the status quo began to crumble in the midst of the OPEC crises (King 1987; Cockett 1995). On the contrary, their force and followership were gathering momentum throughout the post-war period and, as Feser (2006: 1) argues, 'The Road to Serfdom (1944) was a key text of the emerging New Right, a movement whose influence *ultimately made possible* [emphasis added] the elections of Margaret Thatcher, Ronald Reagan, and George W. Bush.' In 1947, Hayek created the Mont Pelerin Society, an international forum for free-market thought which developed into an active community for spreading the free-market creed. On Hayek's advice, Anthony Fisher launched the Institute for Economic Affairs (IEA) in 1955 in Britain as a research institute for the diffusion of classical liberalism, the organization accredited with informing Thatcherism (Nash 1976, 2004; Cockett 1995). Fisher continued founding similar institutes throughout North America and, in 1981, launched the Atlas Economic Research Foundation, supporting a further 150 neoliberal think tanks globally (Cockett 1995).

By the 1950s, Hayek's ideas, though marginalized in academic circles, were supported by a growing organizational structure, with adherents inside Britain, the United States, and beyond. In 1962, Milton Friedman published *Capitalism and Freedom*, arguing that as government grows, freedoms (political and economic) diminish. Within two years, he was providing informal economic advice to Republican presidential nominee, Barry Goldwater, a service he continued to offer Presidents Nixon and Reagan, subsequently joining Reagan's Economic Policy Advisory Board in 1981 (Judis 1988). The significance of the revival of classical liberalism as a credible alternative to Keynesianism was evidenced by Hayek's award of the Nobel Prize in Economics in 1974 (albeit alongside left-wing economist, Gunnar Myrdal). Milton Friedman was bestowed with the same honour in 1976.

Throughout the 1970s, the ideas of Hayek and Friedman attracted institutional sponsorship by a number of powerful, well-funded think tanks and institutes. Most prominent among these in the United States was the American Enterprise Institute (AEI), founded in 1943, and the Heritage Foundation launched three decades later in 1973. AEI provided a direct pipeline of advisers to the new Reagan administration in 1981 (as well as to the administration of President George W. Bush) (Judis 1988: 139–40). Journalists were also increasingly active in endorsing the neoliberal creed, perhaps most famously Irving Kristol who co-founded *The Public Interest* in 1965 and, from 1972 preached the virtues of neoliberalism in his monthly column in the *Wall Street*

Journal (see Judis 1988 for an overview). In Britain, Sir Keith Joseph founded the Centre for Policy Studies (CPS) in 1974, charged with the explicit goal of 'converting the Tory Party to economic liberalism' (www.cps.org.uk; see Cockett 1995). Margaret Thatcher, of course, served as Deputy Chairman.

With carefully engineered assistance from these research institutes and think tanks, the New Right sponsored the rise of the Reagan and Thatcher administrations, prioritizing the goal of freeing the market above social planning and decoupling the values of equality and justice, particularly distributive justice. The causes of poverty were deemed to flow, in large measure, from individual behaviours and thus could not be corrected by the state. Consequently, the welfare state stood accused of incurring high economic costs in pursuit of a flawed mission. In June 1974, Keith Joseph summarized state interventionism as: 'thirty years of good intentions; thirty years of disappointment' (www.cps.org.uk). Aside from taxation, most problematic in this regard were cash benefits that rewarded sloth and undermined the most fundamental of capitalist values (Taylor 2007).

The impact of these ideas, however, was neither confined to the English-speaking countries, nor to actors on the political right. In Sweden, where Keynesian ideas were more embedded than in Britain or America, the influence of neoliberalism was promoted by right-wing think tanks but with critical legitimization by the social democratic economist Assar Lindbeck (Blyth 2001). Driving the revival of neoliberalism with a Swedish flavour, were the Centre for Business and Policy Studies, founded in 1948 by Swedish business, and, three decades later in 1978, Timbro, designed, 'to originate, promote and disseminate ideas and issues supporting the principles of free markets, free enterprise, individual liberty and a free society' (www.timbro.se/innerhall/?art=about-timbro). The influence of these organizations stemmed not only from their financial strength, but also from their ability to draw upon a transformation in the thinking of academic economists, endorsing their agenda with expert authority.

Most important in this regard was the shift in the ideas of Keynesian economist Assar Lindbeck, who, by the beginning of the 1980s, was growing increasingly interested in monetarism and its capital-friendly implications (Blyth 2001). Though Lindbeck exercised restraint in the extent to which he embraced neoliberalism, he moved the debate in Sweden by arguing that welfare state growth generated reduced returns and imposed increased economic costs. Blyth (2001: 17) summarizes: 'Once Lindbeck had shifted the discipline as a whole shifted, and what was once unthinkable was fast on its way to becoming a new orthodoxy.' By the end of the 1980s, the impact of the Centre for Business and Policy Studies was evident on the Social Democratic Party as well as on the political right (Blyth 2001: 18–19). Larsen and Goul Andersen (2009) similarly note the significant impact of Lindbeck's and Snower's insider–outsider theory (that the protected position of labour market insiders/the permanently employed renders them highly resistant to competition from outsiders/the unemployed irrespective of potentially lower wage costs) on a new generation of Danish economists whose changed ideas helped transform the ideological foundations of their welfare state.

The picture that emerges from the neoliberal critique of the welfare state is one of ideational challenge to Keynesianism over a period of time: to use Blyth's terminology, for neoliberals ideas served as 'weapons'. They were strategically peddled by agents and think tanks through an increasingly organized and well-funded plan for their promotion. Their substance and significance did not passively emerge with the collapse of Keynesianism.

Although neoliberal ideas had a revolutionary impact in challenging the Keynesian status quo and institutionalizing the primacy of the market cross-nationally, initially they had less success in dismantling the welfare state (Gamble 1994; but see Korpi and Palme 2003: 441). However, with the passage of time, neoliberal aspects of the welfare state agenda, even if melded into other discourses and induced by different actors, have clearly taken effect.

Conservative Critiques

If Hayek saw the interventionist state as a 'Road to Serfdom', traditional conservatives viewed it as a road to social stability. If Hayek saw markets as a road to freedom, conservatives viewed them as potentially detrimental to social values, particularly collective responsibility. If neoliberals feared the economic liabilities of state intervention, conservatives feared the moral hazards. If neoliberals believed there was no such thing as society, as Margaret Thatcher infamously stated, conservatives believed it to be morally prior to the individual. If neoliberals were (relatively) happy to throw cash at the poor (albeit less of it), conservatives demanded a tight link between benefits and work obligations with strict regulation of claimants.

The welfare state for many conservatives, and particularly European Christian democrats who have traditionally been more concerned with society than market freedoms, has served as a vital safety valve, dampening the potential for social disruption and providing all citizens with a sense of membership and obligation to the community (Barry 1997; Willetts 2003; Taylor 2007). Conservatives were not necessarily locked in, on a cognitive level, to the welfare state as a social democratic project; rather they viewed the welfare state as an instrument of conservatism (see Willetts 2003). Uncontrolled markets isolate individuals and destroy the social order.

Generalizing about conservative critiques of the welfare state is a tenuous exercise. First, conservatism, particularly in the two-party systems of the English-speaking democracies, tends to be something of a catch-all category for anyone and everyone right-of-centre. In much of continental Europe by contrast, the multiparty systems accommodate distinctions between Christian democracy, economic liberals, and secular conservatives. Norman Barry (1997: 345) describes conservative critiques as 'an unstable amalgam of moral and efficiency considerations'. With forceful neoliberal critiques of the welfare state gathering momentum over the post-war decades and transforming parties of the right (as we saw in the case of the CPS in Britain), identifying a distinctive conservative welfare state critique is something of a theoretical exercise: with the rise of market liberalism there has been a blurring of ideological boundaries on the right (Barry 1997; Taylor 2007).

That said, there are a number of features of the welfare state that have proved most problematic for conservatives. First, its compulsory and centralizing tendencies crowd out civil society and the private sector. Ideally, the market, state, and civil society should coexist as partners in the provision of welfare. Pluralistic service provision across domains should ensure a vibrant community, encourage enterprise and tame the state's capacity for coercion (Taylor 2007). Second, the size of the welfare state, though not necessarily a problem in principle, had grown, conservatives charged, to the point of stifling private business, discouraging individual responsibility, and suffocating civil society. Its passive benefit system was damaging the social compact, as well as welfare recipients who were becoming isolated from mainstream society and suffering from a welfare-created dependency culture. The cost of the mature welfare state is not irrelevant in conservative critiques, but it is secondary to the social consequences. Strictly conservative critiques of the welfare state have focused on restructuring passive benefit systems rather than retrenching the welfare state.

The two most prominent conservative critics of the welfare state emerged during the mid-1980s in the United States: Charles Murray (1984) and Lawrence Mead (1986). Despite their critiques being targeted at a very specific federal entitlement (AFDC), and an acknowledgement that poverty in Europe may have structural origins in light of labour market inflexibilities (see Barry 1997: 340), their ideas, and particularly those of Mead, have travelled far. Both argued that the system itself induces dependency, and, worse, intergenerational dependency. Benefits do not alleviate poverty, they create it by changing the behaviour of the poor, either as rational utility maximizers (Murray) or due to a lack of efficacy, experience, and aspiration (Mead). As Mead (1997a: 12) argues, 'more important than any economic factor as a cause of poverty . . . is what used to be called the culture of poverty' (cited in King 1999: 235).

According to Mead (1992, 1996), the conservative welfare agenda represents a 'new paternalism'. Benefits need to come with strict work requirements, the behaviours of the poor require regulation and thus the state must assume responsibility for assisting and monitoring the needy. To this end, individuals will sacrifice some liberties, but for the individual and collective good. The state must, therefore, intervene more in the lives of the poor (preferably at the lowest unit of government): it must demand and impose the desired morality, specifically the value of work and personal responsibility (see Barry 1997). The recent notion of 'nudge' behaviouralism (that imperfect human beings can improve their choices without sacrificing liberty if given a gentle nudge from a libertarian but paternalistic regulator), builds directly on this proposition (Thaler and Sunstein 2008).

These ends can be achieved through rigorous workfare programmes. King (1999: 235) summarizes Mead's argument: 'This work requirement will break the dependency culture, foster self-esteem, and equip recipients to enter the world of work permanently and thereby become self-sufficient functioning individuals.' King (1999:

236) elaborates: 'full participation in the labour market is deemed to constitute a key source of self-esteem, worth and entitlement to equal membership of the polity.' As Mead (1996: 589) contends, 'Welfare is changing from a subsidy into a regime . . . The emerging paternalism is justified by antigovernment rhetoric, but its real agenda is state-building.'

State building in this manner does not come cheap. Charles Murray offers a more low-cost (neoliberal) solution to the problem: dismantle welfare (Murray 1984: 228; King 1999: 228). He is less concerned with traditional conservative critiques of this solution; notably deeper poverty, individual alienation, and social disquiet.

The transformation of AFDC in 1996 into a fully-fledged system of workfare (TANF) very much reflected Mead's paternalistic conservatism. Benefits were cut, but the legislation was fundamentally about regulating the poor and seeking to change their behaviours with regard to the labour market and personal choices (including benefit time limits, marriage initiatives, and family caps). These ideas benefited from strong support from the religious right, particularly during the 1980s. However, Mead's credibility also derived from his voice as 'one of the most significant sources of expertise in welfare policy choices' (King 1999: 236). The poor, by contrast, were never invited to join the debate.

The influence of distinctly conservative critiques of the welfare state has not been limited to the United States, although in many places these ideas have become something of a melange, fused with strands of neoliberalism and reformed social democracy. In Britain, American conservative critiques clearly influenced the attitudes of the Thatcher/Major governments in the 1990s regarding the conditionality of benefits and contractualist welfare-to-work programmes (see Lewis 2001: 159). Although considerably less punitive than American variants of workfare, King and Wickham-Jones (1999) and Deacon (2000) have documented the direct impact of American reforms on New Labour's welfare-to-work agenda.

The conservative critique of passive benefits and the centrality of conditionality reconnecting rights and responsibilities are also evident in Scandinavia, particularly Denmark, Sweden, and Norway (Goul Andersen 2000; Larsen and Goul Andersen 2009). Although the Scandinavian welfare states constitute the quintessential work societies and have a history of conditionality and active labour market policy (see Lewis 2001: 163), the shift from the right to work to the duty to do so in the bottom tier of the benefit system with time limits and impaired work conditions (enforced by sanctions) has been stark (Goul Andersen 2000; Kildal 2001). A discourse of 'dependency culture' and 'concern for the work ethic and the dissolution of personal responsibility' has gained influence in Norway (Kildal 2001: 13), where a stronger economy has lent credence to arguments concerning the personalization of poverty. In Sweden, the shift rightwards remained notably more neoliberal up to the late 1980s, with conservative ideas permeating mainstream discourse only during the 1990s (Boreus 1997: 276). Although these ideas have been diffused by international organizations such as the EU and OECD, as well as a change in the thinking of dominant economists, rather than a direct import from American critics of the welfare state, their conservative (and market liberal) influence is nonetheless real.

As Kildal (2001: 15-16) notes, 'a welfare policy that obliges needy citizens to participate in second-rate inferior work is not based on the equal status of all citizens but
rather on an idea of the unequal status of citizens'. She continues: 'the new policy is
less concerned with mutual recognition than with mutual obligations, less concerned
with justice than with personal morality' (Kildal 2001: 16).

This is certainly not to argue that social democratic welfare states have become
politically conservative (see Lindbom 2008; Pontusson 2010). The Nordic welfare
states remain radically different from those of the English-speaking countries in style
and substance. Rather it is to note that social democratic statism can easily slip into a
more authoritarian and moralistic statism when the fine balance of ideas change. An
increasingly distinctive blend of conservative, neoliberal, and social democratic ideas
have defined new social democratic critiques of the welfare state under the rubric of
the Third Way. The social democratic critique of the welfare state emerged *after* the
collapse of Keynesianism; it did not contribute to the erosion of traditional welfare
institutions, although, subsequently, it has exerted a significant influence on restructuring in Europe.

Social Democratic Critiques

If neoliberals complained that the welfare state was a fundamentally repressive
institution, fostering economic and political illiberalism, and conservatives complained that the welfare state induced moral hazards, social democrats complained
that the Keynesian welfare state was simply no longer viable in an era of post-Fordism
and globalization. Although conservatives and neoliberals also accepted the impact
of post-industrialism and globalization on the welfare state, in their critiques these
trends simply exacerbated extant problems (and created additional ones). For social
democrats, the left *had* to embrace the market or confront obscurity, particularly
given the decline of their traditional electoral coalition in the face of post-industrialism, and the resultant need to attract new middle class voters (Kitschelt 1999).
Embracing the logic of structural dependency theses (Wickham-Jones 2003: 36),
social democrats perceived themselves to be politically and economically compelled
to look 'beyond left and right' in search of policy solutions and electoral credibility.

If well-prepared neoliberal ideas served as 'weapons in distributional struggles', for
the left, market ideas and later the Third Way provided 'institutional blueprints
during periods of uncertainty', to apply Blyth's (2001) framework. Of course there
were always radical critics on the left, notably neomarxists who argued that the
welfare state was an instrument of capitalism and served to contain class conflict
(Gough 1979; Offe 1984). Radical streams of feminism also charged that it institutionalized patriarchal and repressive social relationships (see Taylor 2007). However,
it was only during the 1990s that a principled rejection of the traditional welfare state
began to emerge from the mainstream left.

The concept of the Third Way as a political label first started circulating in the early
1990s within the Democratic Party in the United States (see King and Wickham-Jones

1999; Deacon 2000). The initial concept functioned as a reframing tool in response to three successive Democratic losses in Presidential elections (1980, 1984, and 1988) and the scars the party bore from the anti-liberal mood that had become entrenched during the Reagan–Bush years. Attempting to distance himself from old Democratic social liberalism, Clinton marked out a middle way between the severity of the Reagan–Bush neoliberalism-cum-conservatism and the 'bleeding heart' liberalism of the Great Society that, in the 'New' Democratic critique, had undervalued work, responsibility and community.

Following the electoral success of Clinton in 1992, and his re-election in 1996, the British left seemed to have found a political solution to its eighteen years on the opposition benches. At first, the Third Way appeared to be little more than a political and electoral strategy, with the left lurching sharply to the neoliberal right in search of middle-class voters and support from business. Disassociating itself from its past, New Labour issued proclamations such as, 'no return to past failures' and 'the function of modern government is not to second-guess the market' (Blair cited in Hay and Watson 2003: 297).

By the turn of the Millennium, however, the British Labour Party and parties of the left in selective parts of Europe (the Netherlands, Germany, and Scandinavia) proceeded to develop the Third Way (new middle or purple coalition) into a more explicit critique of the welfare state. Though questions remain regarding its cohesion and impact as a distinctive pan-European social democratic approach (see Bonoli and Powell 2002; Lewis and Surender 2004), the doctrine has marked a break in social democratic thinking in one overarching respect: not only were traditional welfare arrangements deemed to be no longer *viable*, they were now deemed to be no longer *desirable*. Ross (2008) summarizes this general reworking of social democratic ideas as specified in the Blair–Schroeder Document (1999):

> social justice had been wrongly equated with equality of result, undermining personal responsibility and the work ethic; social justice had been wrongly equated with higher levels of public spending without due consideration for economic and social trade-offs; social democracy had wrongly assumed that the state could compensate for market failures, resulting in bloated government and the suppression of individual goals and values; social democracy had wrongly promoted social rights without due consideration for responsibilities, producing a lack of reciprocity; and social democracy had wrongly dismissed the effectiveness of the market. (Ross 2008: 369)

The lead exponent of these ideas in the British context has been the popularizer Anthony Giddens (1998, 2000, 2001). For Giddens (1998), welfare state change is not simply an economic necessity in a globalized world: it is about a tectonic shift in the foundations of society. It is about development, lifestyle, and risk. The welfare state is a critical part of this transformation because it stands at the centre of what Ulrich Beck (1992), the German exponent of the Third Way, calls the 'Risk Society'. In Giddens' view, the welfare state's emphasis on protecting individuals against insecurity has induced an unhealthy preoccupation with cosseting them against risk. In the Third Way, risk must be embraced; it is the essence of the entrepreneurial, creative, and vital society. To this end, benefits should be conditional upon responsibilities; individuals cannot simply opt out of the risk society and be passively supported by the state. They must be encouraged, supported, and if necessary required to partake in it, as full members of its community. Individuals help secure their own well-being by embracing new challenges with flexibility. The role of the state is to coordinate welfare activities not deliver them. The state does have an obligation to ensure an adequately skilled and healthy workforce as the foundation for economic competitiveness and social justice (read as social inclusion, not equality of result), but it does not have the traditionally social democratic role of ensuring full employment. Though social democrats have always stressed the importance of work (Huber and Stephens 1998; Lewis 2001), the Third Way is more concerned with the individual's obligation to actively seek employment (see King 1995) than the state's obligation to provide jobs.

Despite the primacy of the market, the Third Way is not simply toned-down neoliberalism. In Giddens's (1998) analysis, one of the most fundamental differences between the new social democracy and neoliberalism is that the former secures social inclusion while the latter reinforces social exclusion. In Hutton's (1995) view, neoliberalism commodifies individuals, breeds economic insecurity, and destroys society. The Third Way's stakeholder capitalism, by contrast, replaces short-term contracts with long-term compacts founded on relationships of trust (see Taylor 2007). Green-Pedersen et al. (2001: 321) argue that unlike neoliberalism, 'the "third way" does not just aim at job creation; it wants to create good jobs, i.e. well-paid jobs based on high levels of skills' (see also Lister 2003b; Lewis 2006b). On a somewhat less positive note, Ralf Dahrendorf (1999) observes that starkly absent from the Third Way equation is a (neoliberal) sense of liberty. In Dahrendorf's (1999: 16) analysis, the Third Way has a strong 'authoritarian streak'. Indeed, in reaching beyond left and right, the new social democracy incorporates conservative and distinctively Scandinavian social democratic ideas about the enabling and paternalistic state alongside market-liberal influences.

There are variations, of course, in the appeal, application, and institutionalization of Third Way ideas across affluent societies (Clasen and Clegg 2004; Lewis and Surender 2004). The term itself has 'fizzled out' even in Britain (Gordon Brown simply refers to 'pragmatism'), although the logic of the Third Way project continues to underpin social democratic choices (Wickham-Jones 2003: 34). Indeed, despite the shallow appeal of Third Way discourse and ancillary concepts such as 'stakeholders', there are overriding similarities in the substance of its policy prescriptions across Europe (Green-Pedersen et al. 2001; Ross 2008). The pro-market, welfare-to-work aspects of the Third Way agenda have been heavily diffused and promoted by international actors, including the European Commission, and national think tanks, such as the Institute for Public Policy Research in Britain. Another critical influence in driving social democratic change cross-nationally has been the thorough conversion of social democratic economists to market ideas, leaving no alternative source of domestic economic advice. Just as Mark Blyth (2001) and Larsen and Goul Andersen (2009) have emphasized the decisive role Assar Lindbeck and younger economists played in driving change in Sweden and Denmark respectively, Green-Pedersen et al. (2001: 311) note the similar impact of social democratic economists in the Netherlands (and Denmark).

Perhaps more important than the precise blend and administration of Third Way practices across affluent societies is the fact that market orthodoxy, though not pure neoliberalism, has triumphed. The primacy of market mechanisms is now ideationally unchallenged across the political spectrum. This is not to suggest that parties and countries do not differ from each other (see Iversen and Stephens 2008). It is to suggest, however, that for the time being, the market reigns supreme. In the historical battle between capital and citizens, the former has emerged victorious (Torfing 1999).

CONCLUSIONS

Despite their comparatively weak structural pressures, critiques of the welfare state have largely emerged from within the English-speaking world where the post-war settlement was never as widely accepted or deeply institutionalized as elsewhere. A number of studies have discussed the structural feasibility of traditionally social democratic solutions in an era of globalization (see Huber and Stephens 2001a). Our focus on ideas discloses more about policymakers' sense of appropriateness than theoretical feasibility. Indeed, ideas are important to understanding change precisely because they are less stable than institutions: this is exactly why ideas create the momentum for institutional disturbance rather than simple lock-in. Neoliberal challenges to Keynesianism were circulating widely at the foundation of the welfare state in Britain and America. Neo-conservative critiques were articulated at least two decades later in America and levelled against a very specific welfare programme (AFDC). Third Way critiques of the Keynesian welfare state, again diffusing from America and Britain in the early to mid-1990s, were more a reaction to the vacuum created by the collapse of Keynesianism following the oil crises of the 1970s and the resultant political damage incurred by parties of the left than a long-term challenge to the principle of the welfare state itself. As Third Way ideas have been formulated into a more coherent doctrine over the last decade, they have gained influence in guiding welfare restructuring across Europe even if their frames and discourse have petered out.

Our focus on the critics has emphasized the endogenous undercurrents disrupting welfare states as well as the path-shaping capacity of new ideas. Simmering ideational pressures have been chipping away at the foundations of the welfare state for decades. Political agendas are more than an amalgam of functional needs, vested interests, institutional habits and public opinion. Ideas and their political advocacy are not simply constraints in the welfare restructuring process, buttressing the status quo and locking-in, cognitively, popular welfare institutions. They are also driving the reform process.

Scholars who assign an important causal role to ideas base their explanatory claims on the premise that the failure of the status quo cannot explain the substance of the emergent consensus (Blyth 2001; Cox 2001; Beland and Hacker 2004; Larsen and Goul Andersen 2009). But the above analysis also demonstrates that ideas have helped create the conditions for institutional restructuring. Certainly neoliberal ideas have driven a 'silent revolution' (Hacker 2004a: 244), de-stabilizing regimes from within. Critics have been articulating and selling their vision of market liberalism within universities, think tanks, and to political leaders on the right from the earliest days of the welfare state. They have not simply defined the direction of change when the status quo collapsed (Hacker 2004a: 244). The revolution in market-liberal ideas has been a well-prepared one. Indeed, the very assumption of an ideational 'consensus' has possibly obscured more than it has illuminated regarding tensions and tremors in the foundations of national welfare states (see Wincott 2003).

We must entertain the possibility that in decades to come the social democratic welfare state may resemble an anomalous moment of normative and pragmatic collectivism in industrial societies. In the scope of history, the decades of the national Keynesian welfare state may be read as the punctuation in the long-term equilibrium of market dominance. The privatization of risk management is congruent with the individualization of social needs (see Hacker 2004a) and, once 'hollowed out' (Jessop 1994), with policy provision fragmented between state, market, and civil society and towards less controllable actors within each arena (Europe, and private contractors), it is difficult for the state to regain control over the provision and substance of social policy. Once responsibility for social risks has been privatized, the institutional and political barriers to recollectivization are considerable. Ideationally, the privatization of risk imposes cognitive barriers on the appropriateness and feasibility of a range of potential alternatives. Beland and Hacker (2004: 43) have argued convincingly that, '[b]y fostering vested interests, shaping public expectations, and embedding institutions, the spread of private social provision (usually in response to indirect state encouragement) may constrain the scope for government programmes even if political conditions are otherwise permissive. Thus, while institutional theorists are correct that state actors often enjoy relative autonomy, attention to private social policies indicates some of the real limits of state autonomy.' Add to this the functionalist and legal imperatives (e.g. employment policy), as well as ideational pressures, of European integration, and the facilitative conditions for cross-national lock-in to a (broadly) shared paradigm seem overwhelming even if national departures over policy details preclude the emergence of a unitary European social policy (Leibfried 2000). It is not insignificant that the new member states of the former communist countries have decisively endorsed market liberalism.

Yet we are unlikely to be witnessing the 'end of history'. The current diagnosis of the relationship between economic growth and social security will face credible challenge: the present does not represent a permanent reconciliation between capital and citizens. As Fitzpatrick (2003: 3) asks with insight, 'If the resurgence of market capitalism was and is inevitable, then what are the laws of history which will make the future an endless reflection of the present?' Ideas can serve as cognitive locks but they also become stale across time, as new challenges emerge and fresh visions for society develop in reaction to the status quo. Likewise, the very trends produced by market capitalism are likely to generate new needs, coalitions and demands for change. King and Rueda (2008), for example, have documented the surge in low-cost labour resulting from the spread of market orthodoxy. The construction of the welfare state, of course, was very much part of the state-building process and social policy may again be called upon to reconstruct social relationships. Politically, we now have a veritable growth industry in organizations whose sole purpose it is to devise and advocate new ideas, from think tanks, to academia, to independent experts and policy advisors. Although the most powerful of these advocacy organizations have been sponsored by pro-market business interests, cracks will emerge in the market-dominant paradigm as the social and economic costs of these ideas take their toll or a 'big bang' unifying event again serves to elevate social justice above market price on the European agenda. These actors will seek to conduct their own 'silent revolution' from within and be poised to diagnose the inherent problems with the status quo and supply a credible alternative when post-industrial societies confront the crisis of market orthodoxy.

PART II

HISTORY

CHAPTER 5

....

THE EMERGENCE OF THE WESTERN WELFARE STATE

....

STEIN KUHNLE

ANNE SANDER

INTRODUCTION

....

THIS chapter seeks to provide a perspective on the early origins of the welfare state by focusing on the emergence of the institutions of social insurance in the countries of the European cultural complex including the European (British) settler nations. This take on the welfare state is a relatively narrow one in that it neglects other areas of emerging governmental responsibility for societal well-being such as health and education and pays only passing attention to non-state and sub-state welfare arrangements or to the complex public–private mixed responsibilities which have developed in all countries. Such a narrow perspective is necessitated by considerations of space, but is also historically justifiable. The last two decades of the nineteenth century mark the 'take-off of the modern welfare state' (Flora and Alber 1981). These founding years and the decades thereafter are very much associated with the emergence and growth of social insurance-like policies.

In what follows, we look at the early period of social insurance and protection developments until the end of World War II, and point to variations in timing, risk perceptions, and principles of social security across Western states. Industrial, urban, and capitalist developments, with their inherent, unprecedented social problems, spurred political demands for change of regimes and of social rights. Changes in social structure, population movements, growth of wage labour, and new kinds of social insecurity were clearly conducive to a 'new thinking' about the social role of the state. The key question was whether the state should take a more active social role and, if so, in what way? On entering the twentieth century, social policy and welfare emerged to become a crucial issue on the political agenda and while some commonalities can be observed in the emergence of Western welfare states, there were also significant variations. The foundations for a divide between a social insurance model premised on an application of relatively pure insurance principles (continental Europe) and a social citizenship model premised on universal tax-based, provision (Scandinavia, Britain, Canada, New Zealand) was, although not necessarily intentionally, established in this early period.

We start with an overall picture of early collective solutions to social problems. We then look at the political innovation of social insurance in the 1880s. Why was imperial, authoritarian Germany a social insurance front-runner rather than the more democratic United States and both more democratic and earlier and more industrialized England? And to what extent—or for how long—was it a forerunner? What social insurance risks had priority for policy making and legislation, and should insurance be voluntary or compulsory? Which groups should be covered and what should be the basis for entitlement to benefits—labour market status (workers, employees), industry or occupation, citizenship, or need—to be decided by an income and/or means test? Why did the authorities in different countries react differently to the new challenge of social policy once the idea of social insurance had been emphatically put on the political agenda towards the end of the nineteenth century? The first part of the chapter covers the period until about the end of World War I. The second major section covers the phase of consolidation, expansion, and geographical diffusion of social insurance and protection legislation after World War I. We end with a brief look at the World War II experience.

EARLY COLLECTIVE SOLUTIONS TO SOCIAL PROBLEMS AND CHANGING IDEAS OF PUBLIC INTERVENTION

Poverty has existed in some form or other since time immemorial, but has not always or everywhere been perceived as a 'social' problem. The relief of poverty has always been considered a Christian duty, but social aspects of poverty were not emphasized until the sixteenth century (Marsh 1980). The British Act Concerning Punishment of Beggars and Vagabonds from 1531 tried to differentiate between the 'deserving' and 'undeserving' poor, a distinction which was dominant in many national laws for hundreds of years, and is still not everywhere completely obsolete in practice. Until the end of the Middle Ages, poverty had been a matter of only local concern. This began to change with the development of nation states. The famous Elizabethan Act for the Relief of the Poor of 1601 established a national system—to be administered by parishes—for the relief of destitute children, the disabled and infirm, the unemployed and the work-shy. The Prussian *Landrecht* of 1794 gave the state a clear patriarchal responsibility for the poor, but it was delegated to local communities to provide social care (Dorwart 1971). France never created a legal right to poor relief: 'In France, the feeling was still [mid-nineteenth century] that the poor had to be threatened with the possibility of starvation to be kept industrious' (Rimlinger 1971: 46).

As modern nation states began to develop, the problem of the poor became one of national significance, but, generally, it was still left to local authorities to implement national laws on poor relief, vagrancy, and begging (Rimlinger 1971). And, it should be noted, this was a relief of the poor within a framework of repression. During the nineteenth century, persistent problems of poverty and problems related to poverty, plus population growth, urbanization, and spread of industrialization, all contributed to the increasing salience of social problems in many European countries. The two traditional methods of dealing with social problems, philanthropy and poor laws, were increasingly seen by authorities and people alike as being inadequate (Marsh 1980: 5). Poor laws were reformed in many countries, and during the second half of the nineteenth century two sets of forces were set in motion which slowly, but persistently and radically, came to change the role and responsibility of the national state for the welfare of its citizens. One derived from the changes attendant on the Industrial Revolution, the other revolved around the radical new conception of rights of the individual emanating from the American and French Revolutions (Rimlinger 1971: 2–3).

The experience of industrialization sustainably altered the debate on the nature of social contingency and perceptions of poverty. Old age or sickness had of course been perceived as a threat to the well-being of individuals from time immemorial. Now, however, a new-found understanding of unemployment and of the operation of the business cycle made for a rethinking of the whole notion of welfare (Briggs 1961), with the focus changing to provisions that addressed the most significant social deficits with the most evident social consequences. The evolving 'social question' accompanying industrialization served as an important spur for the crystallization of the notion of social rights, as workers started to perceive themselves as one class and as the labour movement gained increasing importance. Focusing on the question of how economic progress could be secured in face of the political and moral threat imposed by the condition of the working class, the solution was increasingly seen as some kind of state action. Prior decades had seen the spread of democracy and political rights. Directly or indirectly, these now smoothed the way for social rights.

THE BREAKTHROUGH OF SOCIAL INSURANCE

The take-off period of the modern welfare state followed what Rimlinger (1971) labelled 'the liberal break', a break between the old, pre-industrial concept of dependence and protection and the emerging modern concept of social protection induced by industrialization and democratization. From the end of the eighteenth to the end of the nineteenth century, ideals of liberalism, of principles of individual freedom, equality, and self-help, dominated social policy thinking. The erosion of liberal principles was prompted by rapid social transformation and growing political mobilization of workers and demands for democratization.

Surprisingly, one might claim, a radical new social policy solution, the idea and principle of social insurance, was first legislated on *a grand scale* in authoritarian, imperial Germany, not in the more industrial and democratic, but liberal, England. The idea of social insurance built on Prussian experience in the period from the 1840s onwards (Hennock 2007). At the time of the legislation, Germany was neither the most industrialized nor—by far—the most democratized European country. But it was rapidly industrializing towards the end of the nineteenth century. Announced in the Imperial Decree of 1881, Bismarck's programme for sickness (1883), accident (1884), old age and invalidity insurance (1889) was implemented in the course of only six years. The new policy was radical in several senses, but most importantly in the way that individual citizens (initially, largely industrial workers) were to be compulsorily insured and become entitled to social benefits as a matter of right rather than provided with poor relief benefits on the basis of discretionary needs and means tests. Thus, the new policy also reached beyond the very poorest strata of society and can, at least in hindsight, be seen as the 'natural' beginning of an institutional framework which gradually came to expand and to incorporate all or nearly all citizens—or residents—of nation states into national 'welfare regimes', which again could—and came to—be differentially constituted in developed nation states in terms of principles of coverage, organization, financing, and redistribution.

Social insurance and 'social security' came to embody an entirely new conception of social protection in the history of nation states. Prior to this time, central governments had two main functions. Primarily, they were still concerned with protecting their populations from foreign intrusion and violence as well as from domestic criminality. Secondarily, and already with a more modernizing focus, state capacity was used to invest in and build infrastructure for transport and communications to promote economic development—public goods provision which, according to the theory of Adam Smith a hundred years earlier, could not be expected or induced from private interests. Now, with the development of social insurance, the state became involved in social protection on an unprecedented scale, dealing with various categories of economic insecurity and providing services and income on the basis of individual rights (Marshall 1964a).

Social insurance was the core element of an emerging new role of the state, but governments also increasingly began to take an interest in many other social issues, such as public education; public health; health and hygiene conditions at the workplace; worker protection; factory inspection and protection against child labour; length of working hours; and relations between employers and workers. State responsibility for the well-being of citizens other than through cash benefits had started to develop already before major social insurance initiatives, as exemplified for instance by the first national Factory Act in England (1802) and by the Prussian law (1839) restricting child and juvenile employment. Statistical offices developed and expanded all over Europe during the latter half of the nineteenth century, thus strengthening state capacity to collect information on and monitor developments in many sectors of society, and thus improving the basis for public policy making (Landes 1972). Which, if any, social policy issues could be acted upon by governments depended quite largely on these and other kinds of 'state capacity' (Rueschemeyer and Skocpol 1996; Kuhnle 1996).

This was also a period in which new economic theories were developed and a new knowledge-based discourse on the possible social policy role of the state was emerging. Sociologists and social scientists—although few in numbers—were at the end of the nineteenth and the beginning of the twentieth centuries seriously concerned with the 'social question' and influential in public debates (Rueschemeyer and Skocpol 1996). Social policy knowledge began to be circulated internationally not only through governments and professional bureaucracies, but also through civil society associations such as *Verein für Socialpolitik* (established in 1873). Associations with similar aims for informed discourse were established in many countries in the 1880s, e.g. the Fabian Society in Great Britain and associations for national economists in Scandinavian countries.

But Was the Innovation German?

Although the German social insurance programme of the 1880s stands out as a path-breaking event and as an example of a critical juncture in terms of *national* social policy development, Germany was not the first country to embrace the idea of social insurance. Many smaller, limited insurance schemes had been established prior to the 1880s (Alber 1982; Perrin 1969).

Bismarck's social insurance legislation was a top-down decision, generally understood as an attempt to build worker loyalty towards the imperial regime after having repressed the freedom of organization, assembly, and expression of a growing, radical socialist movement and party (Rimlinger 1971; Wehler 1985). The idea of social protection to secure the loyalty of the workers to the state was supposedly one Bismarck picked up from Napoleon III when he was Prussian ambassador to Paris in the early 1860s, although France itself later lagged behind other industrial countries in the development of social rights (Rimlinger 1971: 61 and Table 5.1 below). However Bismarckian social policy was not only about pacifying working class protest, but also a contribution to state and nation-building (Manow 2005). The German legislation was a radical break with liberalism also in the sense that it instituted the principle of state-controlled, contributory, and *compulsory* insurance, ideas still too radical in other national political contexts, where the principles of liberalism had a stronger foothold. But that the precedent for a new role of the nation state had now been established soon became obvious, and a new social policy discourse on the welfare responsibility of the state spread across European countries and even across the Atlantic and to the Antipodes. International congresses on issues of accident and social insurance were held and national governments in many countries instigated research, studies, and reports. In the period from 1884 to 1888, for example, and with clear references to German social insurance legislation, the governments of Denmark, Sweden, Norway, and Finland all established public commissions to investigate what could be done on the 'social question' in their own countries and what lessons could be drawn from the German example (Kuhnle 1981).

Yet working-class mobilization was not the only direct or indirect factor that played a crucial role and had a significant impact on social policy development. As Manow and van Kersbergen (2006, 2009) emphasize, the impact of religious ideas is often unjustifiably underestimated in welfare state research. With the German *Kulturkampf* (1871–8), the struggle for power between the Roman Catholic Church and the Prussian state escalated. This struggle took place in other countries also, leading to the emergence or strengthening of Christian Democratic parties and trade unions throughout Western Europe. This conflict contributed to a greater state intrusion into social policy and education in an attempt to lessen the temporal power of the Church and its frequently dominant role in welfare provision. Contrasting church–state conflicts and constellations have 'led to different coalitions between lower and middle classes [and] [t]his, in turn, led to distinct institutional paths of welfare state development in the West' (Manow and van Kersbergen 2006: 1).

Why Germany, not England or the United States?

Flora and Alber (1981) note that the propensity to introduce social insurance early was considerably greater in the constitutional-dualistic monarchies (Austria, Denmark, Germany, Sweden) than in parliamentary democracies and that this is even more remarkable given differences in socio-economic development. England was both more democratic and industrialized than Germany at the time. The 'social lead' taken by non-parliamentary regimes is hypothesized to be partly an effect of a greater need for such regimes to pacify a growing and hostile labour movement, partly an effect of stronger state bureaucracies and partly of the domination of landed interests that could shift the costs of social expenditures to the urban upper and middle classes. Parliamentary democracies generally adopted social security somewhat later, often as a consequence of the extension of suffrage, but with higher levels of population coverage and adequacy of protection. These findings demonstrate that the emergence of welfare states is not just a matter of progressive development: neither the logic of industrialism nor the strength of the working class are by themselves sufficient explanations. Social policies were introduced with different motivations in different places and the various factors have carried different weight in different periods.

In an alternative comparative (and temporal) perspective, Britain is hailed as a pioneer in launching a 'modern welfare state' (Orloff and Skocpol 1984), since Britain had before World War I already instituted workers' compensation (1897), old age pensions (1908), health insurance (1911), and the world's first compulsory unemployment insurance (1911)—in sharp contrast to the United States, which by that time had quite extensive Civil War pensions covering a large proportion of elderly Americans, but which failed to institute modern pensions and social insurance during the Progressive Era. And, in fact, already by 1911 Britain had surpassed Germany as a welfare state leader with more risks and larger parts of the population covered (Flora and Alber 1981: 55). The contrast between Britain and the United States is explained by the existence of a strong civil service and competing, programmatically oriented political parties in Britain.

It is less easy to explain why Britain lagged German developments by twenty to thirty years, since both a strong state administration and party competition were well established in Britain by the 1880s, although the Labour Party was founded as late as 1900, thirty-one years after Bebel and Liebknecht founded the Social Democratic Workers' Party of Germany. However, British local government structures, necessary for implementation of public policies, were not very comprehensive by the early 1880s. Differences in timing, principles, and scope of early state social insurance or security legislation must, among other factors, be sought in the experience of different institutions, e.g. the Prussian health funds (*Krankenkassen*) vs. the friendly societies (Hennock 2007), that were active in the United Kingdom, New Zealand, and Australia. Friendly societies were successful voluntary working-class associations with a huge membership. Their growth can be regarded as an outcome of early and gradual industrialization (or efficient capitalist agriculture in the cases of Australia and New Zealand). The prevalence of alternative welfare providers at the time of the birth of national social insurance helps to explain the paradox of the relative lateness of welfare state development in more affluent and more democratic nations.

When Bismarck's idea of compulsory social insurance came on the political agenda, Britain and its settler nations had a fairly well-functioning, non-state alternative in place, thus the governmental urge to legislate and the 'objective' problem pressure were less than in Germany. In fact, the largest organized opposition to the British Old Age Pension Act in 1908, introducing non-contributory pensions, came from the friendly societies (Rimlinger 1971: 59). In Prussia, the history of compulsory insurance followed both logically and chronologically from the decline of the guild (Hennock, 2007: 331). That Britain, as other parliamentary democracies, did later develop comprehensive and even compulsory social insurance is due to other factors, including the parties' need to appeal to new groups of voters in combination with the increasing financial feasibility of state social initiatives. It was a Liberal government which, after the landslide electoral victory of 1906, introduced in 1908 a means-tested old age pension scheme payable from general taxation. This was followed by the National Insurance Act of 1911, which, in introducing compulsory sickness and unemployment insurance, in a matter of few years brought Britain to a par with Denmark at the top of the league of embryonic welfare states. The 1908 law was an attempt to provide a basic income to 'deserving' old people free from the taint of the Poor Law. This is analogous to the idea behind the old age assistance laws introduced in Denmark (1891) and New Zealand (1898). The motivation for the National Insurance Act of 1911 was different in that its purpose was to provide health and unemployment insurance mainly to those active in the workforce with the aim of improving national efficiency and economic strength (Rimlinger 1971: 59-60). The British pension law was amended as a Widows, Orphans, and Old Age Contributory Pensions Act in 1925.

Small, Pioneering Nations in the Shadow of Big Nations

Comparative political research in the early post-World War II period was dominated by large nation comparisons, reflecting the largely unwarranted assumption that big nations make innovations which are then taken up by (diffused to) their smaller brothers. Comparative studies of historical (and current) developments in the welfare state offer a correction to this view.

Briggs (1961: 147) has argued that 'German social insurance stimulated foreign imitation. Denmark, for example, copied all three German pension schemes between 1891 and 1898'. Again, it is a question of (time) perspective, tracing of policy ideas, and level of analysis. The Danish government and parliament had been concerned with various social policy options since the 1860s—the legislation that occurred in the 1890s rested on pre-Bismarckian initiatives and studies (Kuhnle 1996). Briggs's assertion also must be contested on the grounds that none of the three laws introduced in Denmark in the 1890s built on German principles of social insurance. The Danish old age pension law of 1891 was a non-contributory scheme which instituted (local) means-tested pensions to 'deserving' people over 60 years of age who had not received poor relief in the previous ten years. The Danish law bore no resemblance to the German contributory income-maintenance scheme of 1889, but the *timing* of social legislation in Denmark, as in the other Nordic countries in the 1890s, may be said to have been influenced by the German legislation. The Danish old age pension law was not the first of its kind, Iceland—part of Denmark until full independence in 1944—introduced a similar law in 1890. And, on the other side of the globe, another small nation, New Zealand, introduced a means-tested old age assistance law in 1898. Australia, small in terms of population, passed a non-contributory national pension scheme in 1908, superseding earlier (but quite similar) colonial schemes that had been introduced in New South Wales (1900), Victoria (1901), and Queensland (1908). Thus, a number of small Western nations were pioneering quite extensive means-tested old age assistance schemes from earlier on along principles other than those in the German legislation.

Denmark—before the Social Democratic Party had come close to governmental power—already had the world's most extensive coverage of social risks by 1907—with, in addition to the old age assistance law, legislation covering workmen's compensation (1898), subsidized voluntary sickness insurance (1892), and subsidized voluntary unemployment insurance (1907). The *first universal contributory old age pension* scheme, combined with old age assistance, such that all citizens above pension-age could claim a pension (Palme 1990)—anticipating a universal citizenship-based pension scheme (introduced in 1946)—was introduced by a Liberal government in Sweden in 1913, putting Sweden on a par with the United Kingdom in terms of the proportion of the population covered by social security schemes in the period before the outbreak of World War I (Flora and Alber 1981). Although all Nordic governments in the 1880s were positively inspired by German social insurance legislation to act politically, to do *something*, on the social question, only Norway is an example of imitation of German legislation. The explanation of both the contents and sequence of the early legislation (1890s–1910s) in the Nordic countries must rather be sought in 'path dependency' and—to some extent—in sheer coincidental, unplanned sequential tabling of legislative proposals (Kuhnle 1996). The text of the Norwegian industrial accident insurance law of 1894 closely followed the German text of 1884, and Norway was, with a Conservative government and Liberal parliamentary votes, the only Nordic country in the 1890s to introduce a fully compulsory law.

Opting also for compulsory sickness insurance in 1909, Norway was, in general, more prone than her neighbours to endorse the 'German' principle of compulsory insurance. Denmark and Sweden opted for subsidized voluntary insurance in their first laws. This can, at least partly, be explained by the fact that the relative share of workers covered by voluntary insurance was much lower in Norway than in Denmark and Sweden, so there was a more acute need to enact a programme that would quickly provide coverage for a relatively broad sector of the population (Kuhnle 1981). Here again, we see that the pre-existence and relative importance of alternative welfare providers played a role in shaping the emerging welfare states. France pioneered the introduction of subsidized voluntary *unemployment* insurance at a *national* level in 1905, with Norway following suit in 1906.

What Risks Were Given Political Priority?

Flora and Alber (1981) found in their historical comparison of twelve European countries that social insurance for industrial accidents tended to be introduced first, unemployment insurance last, and the other two systems in between. This trend is also evident on the global scale, as Table 5.1 indicates. Altogether thirty-two countries in the world had introduced some kind of legislation on insurance or compensation for industrial accidents or occupational hazards by the end of World War I, eighteen countries had introduced some kind of sickness insurance or benefit scheme, with Germany (1883), Norway (1909), the United Kingdom (1911), and the Netherlands (1913) as the pioneers of compulsory schemes. Some kind of old age, disability, or survivors' insurance or assistance scheme was in place in thirteen countries, and only seven countries had introduced unemployment benefit schemes. But the sequence of introduction of legislation differed both in Europe and in the broader comparison, as also exemplified by the only two countries which had passed laws on all four risks by 1918. The United Kingdom (including Ireland) manifested the sequence Accidents / Old age / Sickness / Unemployment, while the Danish sequence was Old age / Sickness / Accidents / Unemployment. No country introduced a scheme for unemployment insurance as its first social insurance law, but Finland and Norway exceptionally introduced measures of unemployment protection as their second laws. Not counting the limited (seafarer's) old age pension scheme of 1885, France is also a member of this group. Germany lagged behind many countries with its first law on unemployment in 1927.

Consolidation, Expansion, Diffusion, and War

As has been shown above, the factors explaining the timing of policy innovation prior to World War I have different explanatory weights across countries and time, depending upon, among other things, social cleavages, the history and characteristics of the state, the prevalence of non-state welfare provision, and political party and government constellations. Obviously, parties also at times change political preferences and strategies. Table 5.1 shows that around fifty social insurance laws had been passed before any labour or social democratic party for the first time formed a majority *national* government (Australia in 1910). Suffrage was radically extended throughout Western nations during the early decades of the twentieth century, such that universal manhood suffrage was generally in place by 1920 and in many countries also full or near universal woman suffrage. The party-political basis for voter mobilization and participation had significantly changed since the early phase of social insurance evolution, when governments and parliaments were dominated by conservative and, gradually, liberal political forces. World War I had a radicalizing effect on post-war (social) politics making for a generally much stronger role of government in social matters. During the interwar period, the rising impact of labour and social democratic parties and their participation and leading positions in governments were conducive to more active expansion of social security coverage in the Scandinavian countries (partly 1920s, particularly 1930s) and in New Zealand (after 1935).

In the interwar period, state social insurance and protection was extended in three ways: in terms of the scope of risks, in terms of the coverage of population, and through an increase in compulsory provision (Flora and Alber 1981; Table 5.1).

Table 5.1 Overview: Establishment of first statutory social security schemes in selected ILO member countries (down to 1945)[a]

Member State	Sickness or Maternity Benefit Scheme	Old age, Invalidity, and Survivors' Pension	Accident Insurance; Occupational Hazards	Unemployment Benefit Scheme	Family Allowance Scheme
Argentina	1934 (maternity insurance)	1919 (railway workers' scheme)	1915 (flat-rate invalidity and survivors' benefit)	—	—
Australia[b]	1912 (cash maternity benefit)	1908 (non-contributory invalidity and old age benefit)	1900 (Southern Australia)	1944	1941
Austria	1854 (miners' scheme)	1854 (miners' scheme)	1888	1920	1948
Belgium	1844 (seafarers' scheme)	1884 (seafarers' scheme)	1903	1920 (subsidized, voluntary)	1930
Brazil	1931 (limited to particular groups of workers)	1923 (railway workers' scheme)	1919 (flat-rate invalidity and survivors' benefit)	—	1941
Bulgaria	1924	1924 (invalidity and old age)	1924	1925	1942
Canada	1935 (medical care; Alberta only)	1927 (non-contributory old age)	1902 (British Columbia only)	1940	1944
Chile	1924	1924 (invalidity and old age)	1916	1937 (salaried employees scheme)	1937
Costa Rica	1941	1941	1925	—	—
Cuba	1934 (maternity insurance)	1923 (employees in land transport undertakings)	1916	—	—
Czechoslovakia[c]	1888 (Bohemia, Moravia, Silesia only)	1889 (miners' scheme)	1888	1921 (subsidized, voluntary)	1945

(continued)

Table 5.1 Continued

Member State	Sickness or Maternity Benefit Scheme	Old age, Invalidity, and Survivors' Pension	Accident Insurance; Occupational Hazards	Unemployment Benefit Scheme	Family Allowance Scheme
Denmark	1892 (subsidized, voluntary)	1891 (non-contributory old age)	1898	1907 (subsidized, voluntary)	—
Ecuador	1935	1928 (bank employees; invalidity and old age)	1921	—	—
Finland[d]	—	1937	1895	1917 (subsidized, voluntary)	1943
France	1928	1885 (seafarers' scheme) 1910	1898	1905	1932
Germany	1883	1889 (invalidity and old age)	1884	1927	—
Greece	1926	1922 (seafarers' scheme)	1914	1945	—
Hungary	1907	1925 (miners' scheme)	1900 (agricultural scheme)	—	1938
Iceland[e]	1936	1890 (non-contributory old age)	1903 (fishermen on decked vessels)	1936	—
Ireland[f]	1911 (cash benefit & medical ass.)	1908 (non-contributory old age)	1897	1911	1944
Italy	1910 (maternity insurance)	1861 (seafarers' scheme)	1898	1919	1936
Japan	1922	1941	1905 (miners' scheme)	—	—
Luxembourg	1901	1911 (wage-earners' scheme)	1902	1921 (non-contributory)	—
Mexico	1942	1942	1931	—	—

Member State	Sickness or Maternity Benefit Scheme	Old age, Invalidity, and Survivors' Pension	Accident Insurance; Occupational Hazards	Unemployment Benefit Scheme	Family Allowance Scheme
Netherlands	1913 (cash benefit & medical ass.)	1913	1901	1916 (subsidized, voluntary)	1939
New Zealand	1938	1898 (non-contributory old age)	1900	1930	1926
Norway[g]	1909	1936	1894	1906 (subsidized, voluntary)	1946
Panama	1941	1941	1916	–	–
Paraguay	1943	1924 (railway workers' scheme)	1927	–	–
Peru	1936 (wage-earners' scheme)	1936 (wage-earners' scheme)	1911	–	–
Poland[h]	1889 (West and Upper Silesia only)	1889 (invalidity and old age)	1883	1924	–
Portugal	1919	1919	1913	–	1942
Romania	1912	1912	1912	–	1944
Republic of South Africa	–	1928 (non-contributory old age)	1914	1937	1947
Spain	1929 (maternity insurance)	1919 (old age benefit)	1922	1919 (subsidized, voluntary)	1938
Sweden	1891 (cash benefit & medical ass.)	1913 (invalidity and old age)	1901	1934 (subsidized, voluntary)	1947
Switzerland	1911 (Federal Act)	1916 (invalidity and old age; Glaris only)	1911	1924 (subsidized, voluntary)	–
USSR	1922	1922	1922	1922	1944
United Kingdom	1911	1908 (non-contributory old age)	1897	1911	1945

(continued)

Table 5.1 Continued

Member State	Sickness or Maternity Benefit Scheme	Old age, Invalidity, and Survivors' Pension	Accident Insurance; Occupational Hazards	Unemployment Benefit Scheme	Family Allowance Scheme
United States	–	1935[i] (old age benefit)	1908	1935	–
Uruguay	–	1919 (limited to particular groups of workers)	1920	1944 (meat canning industry)	1943
Viet-Nam	1944 (cash benefit & medical ass.)	–	1943 (flat-rate invalidity and survivors benefit)	–	1944
Yugoslavia[j]	1888 (Dalmatia, Slovenia only)	1889 (Dalmatia, Slovenia only; miners' scheme)	1887	1927	–

Notes: [a] Member countries that had introduced at least three out of five pillars by 1945.
[b] Commonwealth of Australia (federal state) after 1901, separate (British) colonies before that.
[c] Part of Austria/Austro-Hungarian Empire until 1918. Inherited Austrian law.
[d] Part of Russian Empire until 1919.
[e] Under Act of Union with Denmark from 1918 to 1943. Danish dependency before that.
[f] Under British rule until 1921.
[g] Part of Kingdom of Sweden–Norway until 1905.
[h] Part of Austro-Hungarian Empire until 1918. Inherited Austrian law.
[i] Civil War Pensions for veterans were implemented as early as 1862, including additional provisions for widows and dependants as of 1873.
[j] Kingdom of Yugoslavia as of 1929. Before that Kingdom of Serbs, Croats, and Slovenes, established in 1918 by the union of the State of Slovenes, Croats, and Serbs and the Kingdom of Serbia. Partly under rule of Austro-Hungarian Empire.

Source: Authors' own based on Perrin 1969: 285–7.

For example, industrial accident/occupational injury insurance as well as pension insurance were gradually expanded to cover more groups of workers and employees and also to cover family dependants. Germany was first to introduce survivors' pension benefits in 1911 and most Western countries followed suit in the 1930s. Norway pioneered the provision of medical benefits for family members in its first sickness insurance law of 1909 and most countries extended their laws to include family members after 1930. New Zealand became the first country to develop a scheme for family allowances—in the mid-1920s, thus extending the concept of social risks to be dealt with by the state. Such laws were passed in many countries during the 1930s, in World War II, and immediately thereafter.

While before World War I social security was almost entirely a concern of governments of European and European settler nations, the idea and practice of social security spread during the interwar period to other regions of the world, most visibly to North, Central, and Latin America. This was often with the help of the International Labour Organization (ILO), established in 1919 (see further below).

Social Security Principles Gaining Ground

The spread of social insurance and welfare statism both in terms of countries covered and concerning the scope of provisions and its beneficiaries increasingly became part of social and economic policy in the aftermath of World War I. While previous decades had seen rather cautious experimentation with various schemes of social insurance, social security principles were now gaining ground, developing rapidly in most European countries and European settler nations and also spreading to the European periphery and beyond Europe (see Table 5.1).

The function originally assigned to welfare was that of offering relief to the poorest which was then integrated into the insurance principle whose 'essential advantage ... lay in its affirmation of the right of insured persons to protection against specified risks' (Perrin 1969: 253). This focus on the integration of the proletariat and the notion of social security as a solution to class antagonism was prominent in debates about citizens' social rights which became the key rationale for the growing labour movement. The welfare state as a state particularly for the working class, and closely linked to a demand for social rights as inherent as aspects of democracy, was increasingly associated with 'social democracy' (Briggs 1961: 222). The changing notions of welfare and social security had already become evident before World War I. Social policy considerations shaped election campaigns in some countries and played a part in the election of the world's first Labour Government in Australia in the first decade of the twentieth century. The role of the state as a provider and protector of social rights became evident in the legislation of many Western European countries before and increasingly after World War I (Briggs 1961). But, as Baldwin (1990) has shown, the 'laborist social interpretation' of social and welfare reforms required support from other quarters. Both in Britain and Scandinavia, solidaristic risk-sharing measures also strongly reflected the interests of the middle classes and, in Scandinavia in particular, the interests of the politically emerging agrarian middle classes (see also Kangas 1991).

But not all countries that had started out as pioneers of welfare state development continued on this path—Germany and Australia being the most prominent examples of erstwhile leaders whose later performance faltered in various ways. Nor did the implementation of social security principles always take the social insurance form. Most notably, the United States—widely labelled as a laggard in welfare state development and politically criticized for not having (even until today) introduced comprehensive health insurance—did not adopt policies along European lines (Skocpol 1995). The focus in the United States rather was on separating welfare and social security, with an early introduction of provision for children, widows, and War Veterans, but lagging behind in implementing a national social insurance scheme. It was not until the Great Depression that President Roosevelt and reformers tried to implement more comprehensive measures in the New Deal. The 1935 Social Security Act, introducing contributory old age insurance on a national basis and compulsory unemployment insurance, was, of course, the centrepiece of these struggles.

The reasons for the unequal rise of social security principles are numerous and have initiated broad scholarly discussion. Historical comparative analyses over the years offer different theoretical explanations. Particular significance has been attributed to the social democratic hypothesis which has repeatedly been amended and transformed to focus not only on left-wing parties in power but also on the impact of farmer–labour coalitions (as in the case of Sweden and Finland) or Christian Democratic rule (Amenta 2003; van Kersbergen 1995). While in Europe, trade unions had been able to or had strived to transform their claims into policy through their respective parties, which in turn led to a continuous expansion of welfare as these parties gained power (Korpi 1983; Esping-Andersen 1985a), in other countries, such as the United States, welfare was rather considered as the 'operational expression of social citizenship' (Mead 1997b: 249).

Expansion of Risks and Population Groups Covered

Before the outbreak of World War I, most countries in Europe had introduced at least two of the four pillars in the core fields of insurance; beyond Europe at this time, only Australia had three schemes, and New Zealand two schemes.

In the interwar period, a fifth type of core social security scheme came on the political agenda, namely family allowances, with New Zealand, Belgium, and France taking the lead. Among the lead countries, social security was extended to cover new risks, unemployment in particular, and larger population groups, although once again expansion did not conform to a uniform pattern. Denmark and the United Kingdom were most expansive as to population coverage. Expansion was most visible in countries where socialist or social democratic parties had the greatest electoral support and governmental authority. The weakest expansion occurred under fascist auspices in Italy, Austria, and Germany (Alber 1979).

For Western democratic states, the era beginning with the Great Depression until the aftermath of World War II was characterized by reforms and policy developments which pointed in the *direction* of universalistic welfare states. More and more population groups, including family dependants, were (compulsorily) covered. Also, governments dealt with a broader scope of social risks. However, the depression years also posed a major challenge to governments with unemployment and social hardships on the rise. It is therefore not surprising that the 1930s saw the greatest variation and heterogeneity of social insurance schemes. While some countries witnessed the first retrenchment of provision, others (such as Norway) joined the league of pioneering welfare states (Alber 1982: 153).

Alber finds particularly strong expansion in countries with strong leftist parties and in periods following times of hardship (World War I, the Great Depression). Even countries with similar backgrounds and prior welfare state development took divergent paths. While the difficulties in coping with unemployment and poverty led to stagnation in welfare expansion in Australia (Castles and Uhr 2005), the post-1920 years in New Zealand were characterized by a number of major welfare innovations such as the introduction of the world's first family allowance scheme. Following a halt in policy innovation during the economic crisis, New Zealand Labour gained a landslide electoral success in 1935 based on their plans for social reform leaving the new government to be judged by some as 'the strongest that has ever existed in the English speaking world' (Castles 1985: 26). The 1938 Social Security Act implemented a comprehensive and unified welfare scheme which the ILO judged as having had an important influence on legislation in other countries. Yet, when the Australian government attempted to reform its own (largely individualistic) health scheme in the early 1940s modelling its plans on those in New Zealand, it met with strong opposition and defeat at the hands of the Constitutional Court.

Even countries with rather different concepts of equality and welfare from those in European and the Antipodean settler states shifted towards a more social democratic philosophy of insuring social risks under the pressure of economic crisis. In the United States and Canada, reformist forces tried to introduce comprehensive social security schemes and moved towards greater state intervention in their New Deal policies, which, in Canada, resulted in a strengthened role for the federal government and the introduction of federal unemployment insurance in 1940.

The Idea of Social Citizenship

In most Western countries, in the period after World War I, social security principles had become an integral part of party politics and government policies. Welfare was increasingly regarded as guaranteeing more than just a minimum of economic security, perhaps offering some sort of protection 'from cradle to grave'. But allocating costs and reallocating risks, along with the distributional implications of both, remained fiercely contested terrain. There was still a battle over society's capacity and willingness to treat all of its citizens equally. As Baldwin puts it: 'the battles behind the welfare state lay bare the structure and conflicts of modern society...As economic producers or as members of different classes, individuals were still treated unalike by the market and by inherited hierarchies. But as creatures subject to risk, they could stand equal' (Baldwin 1990: 1–2). Pioneering welfare schemes like Bismarck's were a long way from realizing such equality. Beveridgean ideas may have come somewhat closer. But much of the case for social insurance remained economic. Social insurance could be employed to maintain social stability and thereby secure economic outputs.

The shift in focus from social *welfare* to social *justice* is seen by many scholars as a logical consequence of democratization and the emergence of social rights from the prior institutionalization of political rights (Flora and Alber 1981). Famously, T. H. Marshall (1963) saw this process in terms of the development of social citizenship: as progress in the assignment of rights to citizens, from civil to political to social rights (for a discussion of social rights of citizenship, see Chapter 35). But the degree to which citizenship is intrinsic to the welfare state has always been contested. In practice, the degree of equality aimed at and achieved through social security schemes differs significantly across nations and through time.

The Internationalization of Social Security and Diffusion beyond Europe and the New World: The Role of the ILO

The dawning of a 'new age' of social security was also marked by the establishment of the International Labour Organization (ILO) in 1919 and thus the spread of the idea of minimum social standards on an international scale. Created as part of the Treaty of Versailles, the organization reflected the belief that through social justice universal peace could be accomplished. The most important rationale behind the ILO was the experience of World War I, promoting from the very beginning the diffusion, expansion, and consolidation of social insurance schemes. Much of the spread of welfare provision beyond the West during this time period has to be ascribed to the ILO and the legislative examples it gave (Perrin 1969).

The interwar period was one in which social insurance and social security not only expanded to cover all major risks and more population groups in European countries but also became a worldwide phenomenon. The ILO came to play not only an important role as catalyser for social insurance and as promoter of international best practice, but also as a storehouse for statistics, documentation, and national social and labour legislation. It passed a large number of norm-setting conventions and recommendations in all fields of social insurance, and undoubtedly had an impact upon the growth of social security at a time when its expansion was potentially threatened by world economic developments.

Table 5.1 demonstrates that by the end of World War II social insurance had developed well beyond the borders of Western Europe and the European settler nations. Some Eastern European countries had inherited Austrian law as part of the Austro-Hungarian Empire before 1918. In Latin America, social insurance also took off, starting initially with limited provision covering specific groups, e.g. bankers in Ecuador, railway workers in Argentina, with Chile being among the few countries worldwide which had introduced all five pillars by 1937. In Asia, Japan was the forerunner in the field of social security.

THE WARTIME IMPACT

Following the Great Depression and its significant impact on social policy in a number of countries, the preparations for and the eventual outbreak of World War II marked a further stage in the development of what then came to be modern welfare states after 1945. In fact, the question of what impact warfare has had on welfare and whether war initiated a break in ongoing developments or rather represented continuity has provoked a number of debates. Goodin and Dryzek (1995) have argued that wartime experiences shaped the post-war trajectory of social development by creating a sense of solidarity manifested in subsequent (post-war) generosity of spending, while Peacock and Wiseman (1961) have suggested that wartime increases in government expenditure increase the threshold of 'tolerable taxation' for welfare purposes thereafter.

The wartime experience also illustrates more malign impacts on the ideology of the welfare state. Social policy, as Titmuss (1974b) emphasized, is neither ideology free and nor does it always imply welfare for all. The development of German social policy in the Nazi years is a case in point. The Weimar years in Germany had seen the further expansion and elaboration of ideas of social citizenship, but this conception was now replaced by that of a citizen defined in racial terms, with eugenic principles (widely current at the time in European thinking) and later euthanasia enlisted as a justification for and a means of shaping the Nazi-type Aryan family.

World War II also significantly shaped visions and plans for post-war welfare state development, although the extent to which Beveridge's famous 1942 Report on *Social Insurance and Allied Services* was actually responsible for the establishment in Britain of what, by 1950, could be seen as the world's most comprehensive welfare state is disputed. With his recommendations, Beveridge explicitly urged the government to fight the five 'Giant Evils of Want, Disease, Ignorance, Squalor and Idleness' to secure peace by providing 'security from cradle to grave'. Both Marshall (1964a) and Titmuss (1950, 1976a) point to the wartime experience as a basis for a spirit of national solidarity and increased social policy efforts in the direction of universal social provision irrespective of class and status. This perspective is contested.

Revisionist historians have argued that there is little evidence that the war induced heightened government awareness of social welfare as a tool of national efficiency or of enhanced social solidarity and it is argued that Titmuss exaggerated the impact of the war on subsequent policy development (Harris 1981; Mommsen 1981; Welshman 1998). Less disputable is the Norwegian case. All Norwegian political parties from the Communists to the Conservatives came out of five years' of German occupation with a commitment to a unique joint political programme before the parliamentary elections of 1945. Inspired by the Beveridge Report and the platform and record of the Social Democrats and the trade union federation (LO) in neutral Sweden, they promised to build a universal national 'people's social security system'. Thus, the impact of wartime experience is likely to have varied not only according to pre-war social policy history, but also on the basis of whether countries were active participants in the war, subject to foreign occupation, materially and physically devastated, and/or carried huge human losses. The United States was the only big industrial economy of the world that had not been debilitated by the war. Arguably because its economy was so strong, the urge to nurture and expand ideas of a welfare state was not as prevalent there as in Europe (Brinkley 1996).

The concept of the welfare state itself came into common usage—and, with the exception of the United States, mostly in a positive sense in Britain and subsequently across Europe—from the late 1940s onwards. A new chapter in Western social policy had begun.

CHAPTER 6

....

POST-WAR WELFARE STATE DEVELOPMENT

....

FRANK NULLMEIER

FRANZ-XAVER KAUFMANN

INTRODUCTION

....

MOST comparative research on welfare states relates to national differences and similarities, i.e. to the spatial perspective. This chapter instead focuses on the question of how one may generalize about changes in the temporal trajectories of welfare states.

The bulk of the welfare state literature divides the post-war era into two periods: a phase of expansion and one of retrenchment. In this view, a period characterized by the formidable growth of social security systems—in which the welfare state firmly established itself as a core institution of Western societies—has been followed by a phase of expenditure cuts and deteriorating social benefits. This two-phase periodization of post-war developments—with an expansion period from 1945 to the oil crisis of 1973 and a subsequent retrenchment phase that has already endured more than three decades—is largely uncontroversial today. No alternative to this periodization has gained comparable academic recognition. And while a number of related terms—such as restructuring, recalibration, phase of permanent austerity, and structural adjustment—have been put forward, the term 'retrenchment' has prevailed in the literature.

The same periodization is captured in the expression 'Golden Age of the welfare state' (C. Pierson 1991; Esping-Andersen 1996*b*) and—less frequently—'Silver Age' (Taylor-Gooby 2002; Ferrera 2008). This terminology does not necessarily imply the notion of a decline, as the classical usage in Hesiod's myth of origin indicates (*Works and Days*, lines 109–201; Hesiod distinguishes five ages, gives the 'bronze' label to the third and fourth age, and rates the *fourth* age as the 'apex of civilization'). Yet the terminology of gold and silver certainly has a strong connotation of decline, and it suggests regret about the loss of a highly valued, harmonious past. The terminology is thus inextricably retrospective: the present is primarily assessed in light of the past, and the whole periodization is dominated by this retrospective orientation. There is currently no readily available equivalent to the older terminology of progress and modernization with its openness towards the future.

Ironically, the work of Paul Pierson (1994) has greatly contributed to the popularity of that term 'retrenchment' and its use as a label for the current historical period, even though Pierson *himself* aimed to show that the cuts implemented by the governments of Ronald Reagan and Margaret Thatcher (1981–9 and 1979–90, respectively) were more limited, and hence that the alleged 'crisis' of the welfare state in the wake of their social policy changes was much less pronounced, than many observers at the time assumed. Pierson rather suggested that welfare states were surprisingly resilient, flexible, and successful in adapting to sometimes drastic changes in economic conditions. Since the mid-1990s, however, only the *extent* of retrenchment has seemed controversial.

A presupposition for speaking about welfare state development in a transnational or even international perspective is that the 'nature of the animal' is known. Social policy researchers have spent considerable energy on the definition of welfare state regimes, the development of welfare state typologies and the appropriate classification of individual countries and policies. Efforts to define and justify periods of welfare state development have, by contrast, been few and far between. Social policy and welfare state are notions, however, whose content varies not only from nation to nation but also from time to time. To grasp and to assess changes in welfare state development is therefore a complex endeavour, and most attempts at periodization do not meet the nature of the challenge.

The next section of this chapter probes the validity of the dominant approaches to periodization in several respects and shows their shortcomings. A further section then proposes a systematic discussion of measurement concepts used in comparative welfare state research and examines how the use of periodization criteria gleaned from this literature influences our understanding of welfare state development since 1945.

PERIODIZATIONS

Periodizations are *interpretations* of history that entail a number of crucial assumptions. By distinguishing and delimiting periods or epochs, they mark the beginning of something new or different, the crossing of thresholds, the discontinuities and ruptures of historical processes and developments. The proclamation of a new period or epoch is never an 'innocent' act or a merely practical decision for researchers, but rather implies a whole set of interpretive frames in which the suggested periodization is grounded while at the same time hiding or marginalizing aspects of social and political reality on which *alternative* periodizations might be based. Thus period-izations are often used for political purposes, to promote a particular perception of growth, change, adjustment, or retrenchment.

The dominant periodization of welfare state developments is remarkable both for its widespread acceptance in the field of social policy research itself and for its lack of congruence with periodizations developed or favoured by historians. In the field of historiography, the terminology of a 'long nineteenth century' (roughly from 1770 to 1914/18) and a 'short twentieth century' (1914/18 to 1989/91) has come to prevail (Hobsbawm 1994). In this broad periodization, World War II marks the end of a first and the beginning of a second sub-period of the 'short' twentieth century rather than a fundamental rupture. Unlike a calendar-based, 'content-free' approach (Osterham-mel 2009: 87), this periodization highlights key events (the American and French Revolutions, World War I, the demise of socialism) as well as the cultural, social, and political shifts indicated by those events.

Neither the years 1914/18 nor the years 1989/91 are, however, crucial dates with regard to the shifts highlighted by the expansion and retrenchment periodization of welfare state development. And a glance at finer grained periodizations reveals even more differences between social policy research and historians: Tony Judt's *History of Europe since 1945* (2005) also starts with the year 1945 but distinguishes four rather than two sub-periods of the post-war era (1945–53, 1953–71, 1971–89, 1989–2005). Most conspicuously, the year 1989 is not viewed as a particularly important historical juncture in social policy research with its focus on quantitative indicators of expan-sion and retrenchment, and on the size and generosity of social security systems. In any case, the currently hegemonic interpretation of welfare state development has to be anchored more strongly in comparative research and its empirical findings, the criteria of periodization have to be better justified and the implicit framings of this periodization have to be made more transparent.

Why 1945 as the Starting Point of a New Phase?

The end of World War II is an obvious historical juncture in the context of social policy research. It coincides with the years of economic recovery from the Great Depression and with the major social policy reforms inspired by Lord Beveridge's (1942) universalistic reform model that were implemented in Great Britain until 1950. Thus 1945 and the early post-war years may be characterized as the period in which the welfare state became firmly entrenched.

Yet with a view to the institutional dimension of the welfare state and the passage of social insurance legislation, this seems less convincing, especially for the

Bismarckian social security systems. In fact, this periodization does not even do justice to the history of the American and Scandinavian welfare states, which experienced massive changes and institutional expansion in the 1930s. If the focus is on institutional innovations, the post-war era appears to be the *end* of a phase in which the core set of social insurances was established in most continental European and Anglo-Saxon countries—insurances related to the risks of old age and retirement, sickness, industrial accidents, and unemployment. These insurances were usually introduced—and first expansions were implemented—prior to 1950. On the basis of the institutional innovation criterion, then, one would rather have to take the year 1950 as the end of a phase of institutional emergence—a phase which may itself be divided into three sub-periods: 'Introductory phase' from early German legislation until 1914; 'phase of extension' between the two world wars; 'phase of completion' in the post-war years, followed by a 'phase of consolidation' and stepwise quantitative expansion of social benefits (Flora and Alber 1981: 54). However, the implied shift in the *interpretation* of the early post-war years is even more important than the question whether 1945 or 1950 is the more appropriate cut-off point as such: the first periodization interprets the early post-war years as the *beginning* of the welfare state's Golden Age, a long expansion phase starting in 1945, while the second highlights the *end* of a previous innovation 'cycle' in 1950.

The post-war era appears in yet another light if the development of *social expenditures* is used as the sole indicator for the growth of the welfare state. According to Christopher Pierson (1998: 108–35), the whole period between 1918/20 and 1973/5 may, then, be seen as a phase of growth and expansion. Based on the expenditure criterion, the year 1945 (or 1950) does not mark a rupture or discontinuity. Even if social insurance coverage is used as an additional indicator, the data suggest a more or less uninterrupted growth trend from roughly 1910 to the 1970s (Flora and Alber 1981: 49, 55).

Despite these considerations and pieces of evidence, it seems appropriate to view 1945 as an important historical juncture. The post-war era should be understood as a phase in its own right because an understanding of social policy and the welfare state based on the notion of social rights as key elements of universal human rights, on par with liberal and democratic rights, only began to emerge during World War II (Kaufmann 2003c). The acknowledgement of social rights as universal human rights may be dated to the years between 1941 and 1948, and it was part of allied and international efforts to design a political order for the post-war era. Even before the United States entered the war, talks in August 1941 between Franklin D. Roosevelt and Winston Churchill resulted in the following important social policy-related message (points 5 and 6 of the declaration that was later called the Atlantic Charter):

> Fifth, they desire to bring about the fullest collaboration between all nations in the economic field with the object of securing, for all, improved labour standards, economic advancement and social security. Sixth, after the final destruction of the Nazi tyranny, they hope to see established a peace which will afford to all

nations the means of dwelling in safety within their own boundaries, and which will afford assurance that all the men in all lands may live out their lives in freedom from fear and want.

The last couple of lines refer to two of the 'four (essential human) freedoms' outlined in Roosevelt's January 1941 State of the Union Address. The principle of universal social rights is here embedded in the notion of freedom from want: 'The third is freedom from want—which, translated into universal terms, means economic understandings which will secure to every nation a healthy peacetime life for its inhabitants—everywhere in the world'. In the Philadelphia Declaration (1944) of the International Labour Organization, the principle of universal social security was further strengthened (Lee 1994) but it wasn't until the Universal Declaration of Human Rights, passed by the General Assembly of the United Nations in 1948, that an explicit catalogue of universal social rights was proposed (in Articles 23 to 28: right to work, free choice of employment, rest and leisure, a standard of living adequate for the health and well-being of self and family, education, and participation in cultural life). This catalogue is prefaced by article 22, which stipulates—in a somewhat conditional form—the basic entitlement to the social rights that are specified in the following articles: 'Everyone, as a member of society, has the right to social security and is entitled to realization, through national effort and international co-operation and in accordance with the organization and resources of each State, of the economic, social and cultural rights indispensable for his dignity and the free development of his personality.' This integration of social policy entitlements into the concept of universal rights was mirrored in the academic sphere by T. H. Marshall's (1964b) threefold concept of liberal, political, and social citizenship rights.

Whereas the international paradigm for social policy before World War II remained selective, especially with respect to industrial workers and the poor, but also with respect to the risks covered, the new international paradigm was universal, providing coverage for the entire population. It joined with the claim for equality of everyone, irrespective of race, religion, and gender. And it extended the scope from policies of workers' protection towards a broad concept of individual welfare. This shift is expressed by the change of leading terms from 'social insurance' to 'social security' and from 'social policy' to 'welfare state'.

This shift of paradigm in social policy was part of a much broader shift in the area of international law. Until World War II, including the regime of the League of Nations, international law was seen exclusively as an affair of governments, not of peoples. But in the light of the fascist consequences of the Great Depression an international elite consensus was reached about a nexus between social order at the national level and international peace. Therefore the vision of an international responsibility for the well-being of nations and their people emerged: Welfare Internationalism. The 'Economic and Social Council' became a main organ of the UN, and the ILO, created under the auspices of the League of Nations, now became the instrument not only for international regulations but also for practical initiatives and assistance for social policy development, especially in the third world.

Why not 1989?

The history of the welfare state is usually written without an emphasis on the epochal changes of 1989. The standard periodization distinguishes an expansion phase from the early post-war years to the 1970s and an ensuing retrenchment phase. This view betrays the literature's focus on Western advanced industrial economies. For the *Eastern European* countries, the political regime change of 1989 also entailed the demise of a socialist welfare state model. This model had built on a full employment guarantee and provided—through a combination of firm-level and state-level security systems—universal benefits covering the risks of sickness and old age as well as family-related services, all of this embedded in an economic planning system that used the education and vocational training sector to manage the labour supply. The revolutions and political changes in the wake of 1989 not only replaced planned economies with (initially often strongly deregulated) market economies; it also replaced communist dictatorial regimes with (semi-)presidential and parliamentary democracies. The newly introduced democratic regimes were immediately faced with a transitional recession, and hence with a challenging economic situation. In short, the restructuring of social security systems after 1990 was but one element of a far-reaching institutional reorganization, and moreover, these restructuring efforts were undertaken in parallel with a first round of retrenchment measures. The 1980s had already brought an economic slowdown to Eastern Europe, which was exacerbated by the post-1990 recession; the subsequent phase of recovery and strong economic growth came to an abrupt end with the financial crisis of 2008, which jeopardized efforts of social policy consolidation in these countries. Only when the stagnation phase of the 1980s is added to the picture, can their trajectories be reconciled with the general retrenchment hypothesis and the claim that the years between 1973 and 1980 represent a critical juncture. However, it would be much more appropriate to consider institutional changes in the demarcation of phases of social policy development; 1989/90, then, clearly emerges as a major rupture in Eastern Europe. Since the transition states were strongly oriented towards reform models that appeared to epitomize the retrenchment trend in Western and Northern European countries, the demise of socialism might indeed be viewed as no more than a somewhat belated alignment of Eastern Europe with that trend. Such an interpretation does not deny the differences between the Western and the socialist welfare state models, but it rates the year 1989 as a less relevant juncture in terms of social policy development. According to this interpretation, the previously socialist welfare states, as different as they might initially have been from their Western equivalents, merely followed the path of the Western countries under the influence of imported ideas and reform concepts in the years after 1989.

However, from an ideological perspective the breakdown of the socialist regimes weakened the political status of the Western European welfare state. Instead of representing a kind of third way between state socialism and unrestrained capitalism, it is now the only alternative to the latter.

Sub-Periods

In order to factor in the status of 1989 as a meaningful if hardly decisive historical juncture in the context of welfare state development, one might resort to a distinction of major phases and shorter sub-periods. Such hierarchical periodizations are widely used. Here we only discuss the possibility of dividing the expansion and retrenchment phases into three sub-periods, respectively (expansion: 1945–50, 1950–60 and 1960–73; retrenchment: 1973–9, 1980–89/90 and 1990–today).

As indicated above, British welfare state reforms stand out in interpretations of the early post-war years (1945–50). But far-reaching reforms—in the context of a social insurance tradition—were also implemented in France, and major reforms of the social security systems of Belgium, Sweden, and Switzerland deserve to be mentioned as well. By contrast, coping with the consequences of their military defeat and the re-establishment of their pre-war social security systems dominated the political agenda in the countries that had experienced fascist and national-socialist regimes—Italy, Japan, Austria, and Germany. Yet Christopher Pierson's (1998: 113) suggestion to characterize this sub-period as a phase of 'reconstruction' appears unconvincing, for the element of innovation was more prominent in these years than mere reconstruction efforts: policy reforms were frequently grounded in the new understanding of social security as a universal right, and so the extension of social security systems to the entire labour force and/or the citizenry at large became a key objective in this period, albeit pursued to varying extents and implemented with varying success.

The years between 1950 and 1960 have been characterized as a phase of 'relative stagnation' (C. Pierson 1998: 132). This assessment is based on the GDP share of social expenditures. However, against the backdrop of massive economic growth and virtual full employment (as well as a low population share of persons over 65), below-average social expenditure growth has to be viewed as a weak indicator for welfare state development. The high employment rate—which reduced the pressure to offer or rely on social benefits—combined with fundamental old-age security reforms, as in Sweden and Germany, are much more telling. Moreover, data on replacement rates (Korpi and Palme 2007) indicate that levels of social policy generosity were already close to their peak values in 1960—for instance, in two out of three branches of the German social security system. There is widespread agreement that the years between 1960 and 1973 represent the major expansion phase of the welfare state (C. Pierson 1998), as indicated by social expenditure growth rates considerably above the long-term average. If the term 'Golden Age' makes sense at all, then it is for this period of roughly fifteen years. However, this was primarily an expansion of benefit levels and coverage. Otherwise, the 1960s are not known as years of social policy innovation. The inputs and demands of the new social movements, from the civil rights movement to the women's movement, had not yet begun to impact social policy. Even important reforms such as the introduction of Medicaid and Medicare in the United States remained limited, and they represented no more than a catch-up with policy developments that had been missed or blocked politically in the 1940s (Hacker 2002). Hence golden years of social policy may well coincide with a dearth of policy innovations and of policy deliberation on the long-term stabilization of the welfare state.

Huber and Stephens (2001a) divide the retrenchment phase into three sub-periods: 1973–9, 1980–90, and 1990–2000. This periodization is justified by a substantive interpretation of these periods – the 1970s as a phase of 'fumbling' in which new challenges emerging between the first and second oil crisis were still tackled along conventional lines; the 1980s as a phase in which policymakers recognized that problems in the social policy field were not merely cyclical but required structural adjustment measures; and finally, the 1990s as a phase characterized by the opening of the Berlin Wall, the demise of state socialism, and EU market and monetary integration. While the 1970s were dominated by piecemeal attempts to respond to the apparent slack of a post-war social policy model that continued to be perceived as broadly successful, political conflicts in the 1980s touched upon the very survival of the welfare state, whose legitimacy was massively questioned by the neoconservative governments in Great Britain and the United States. That even radical retrenchment does not necessarily hollow out the welfare state as a whole was an insight of the 1990s – a phase of welfare state development in which the role of economic internationalization came to the fore. However, sub-periodizations referring to the post-1980 phase remain quite anaemic. Taylor-Gooby therefore speaks of the 'interregnum of the 1980s and 1990s' (Taylor-Gooby 2002: 598), thus underlining the vague contours, ambivalent character, and overall immobility of social policy making in those years.

Region-Specific Phases of Welfare State Development?

Our considerations regarding the meaning of 1989 for welfare state development in the Eastern European countries also suggest an entirely different approach to periodization. For it remains to be asked whether periodizations along a single dimension may ever be plausibly applied to all countries and world regions. Isn't it necessary to differentiate groups or 'families' of countries according to type of welfare state or level of economic development and OECD membership status, or lack thereof? In short, is there a universal development trend that merely unfolds in a more or less delayed fashion in various parts of the world, or should we indeed consider region-specific approaches to periodization?

Considerable evidence for the plausibility of region-specific approaches may be gleaned from welfare state development in East and South-East Asia (Korea, Malaysia, Philippines, Singapore, Taiwan and Thailand). In these countries, the time from 1945 to the late 1990s appears to have been a single, uninterrupted phase of welfare state expansion. After a slow beginning characterized by rather modest levels of social policy generosity, democratization processes starting in the 1980s ushered in a marked expansion of social programmes (Haggard and Kaufman 2008). Moreover, the oil crisis of 1973/4 and the end of the Bretton Woods system did not result in economic downturns. Thus a more appropriate periodization might divide the long and ongoing welfare state expansion phase of these countries into two sub-periods:

a first phase of restrained and a second one of accelerated welfare state development since approximately 1980. In China, the expansion of social security systems began even later, as exemplified by the reform of old-age security in 1997 (Barr and Diamond 2008). The situation in Latin America is more complicated. Up to 1980, social security systems with limited coverage, privileging the manufacturing sector and public servants while neglecting the rural population, were established on that continent. Hence, despite considerable social expenditure levels, the traditional social inequality in these countries was essentially reproduced by their welfare states. In the 1980s, Latin America was faced with a twofold challenge—democratization processes and economic crisis—which triggered rather different developments in the individual countries and a back and forth movement between market-oriented reforms and moves towards universal access to social security. These developments were initially often dominated by privatization efforts while, in recent years, there have been greater political efforts to fight poverty and implement a basic tier of social security programmes. This is relatively congruent with the two-phase periodization of the OECD. However, one would have to interpret the democratic reinvention of the welfare state and the recent wave of social-reform oriented governments as a step in the direction of a new expansion phase of the welfare state (Segura-Ubiergo 2007; Haggard and Kaufman 2008).

Policy-Specific Developments?

The terms 'social policy' and 'welfare state' refer to a number of policy fields. Which policies are subsumed under these headings varies over time and in line with nationally specific traditions. Hence there is undoubtedly a semantic core of the two terms (old-age security, health, poverty relief, long-term care, unemployment, etc., are usually considered to be the major elements of social policy making and the welfare state), but a number of other sub-fields such as housing, education, and labour legislation are sometimes included in the national definitions and understandings of these terms and sometimes not. Such different understandings may lead to very different assessments of welfare state change. In the Bismarckian welfare state, the risks traditionally covered by social insurances are the main reference points for every discussion of welfare state development. Against this backdrop, the growing attention of social policymakers to education and child-care policy over the last ten years is perceived as an *expansion* of the traditional scope and meaning of social policy making and the welfare state. Given these different understandings of individual policy fields, the expectation that 'one-size-fits-all' periodizations are plausible across different areas of social policy is rather questionable.

The assumption of a coherent logic of development across social policy areas is, however, prominent in the discussion of welfare state regimes. Such typologies are currently attacked with the argument that the internal homogeneity of developments in different branches of national social security systems is much lower than Esping-Andersen assumed in his seminal contribution (Scruggs and Allen 2006a). Hence such classifications arguably do not do justice to internal differentiations between social policy areas or sub-fields. This argument may also be made for efforts at periodization. Thus a one-size-fits-all periodization would seem to neglect the differential dynamics of social policy developments. For instance, the Social Citizenship Indicators Programme (SCIP) data show that the turning point in the development of replacement rates in the area of pension policy usually occurred later than in the area of sickness payments and even much later than in the case of unemployment insurance (Korpi and Palme 2007).

The question whether all programmes in a country belong to one and the same type of welfare state regime, and whether shifts in different programmes may be described with one and the same periodization scheme, relates to the internal coherence of welfare state arrangements and to the complementarity of individual programmes. As in the debate on varieties of capitalism, one has to ask whether the overall constellation is coherent, and hence may be viewed as an equilibrium of different social programmes and institutional arrangements. The ongoing debate about Esping-Andersen's *Three Worlds of Welfare Capitalism* since the book's publication two decades ago and considerable evidence of 'partial shifts' between regime types in different branches of social security systems illustrate that such complementarities and elective affinities are probably not as widespread as is frequently assumed. On the other hand, there are attempts to identify complementarities not so much between areas of social policy but rather between social policy and industrial relations, between social policy and production regimes, between social policy and political-institutional features such as electoral systems, between social policy and vocational training—and also between social and foreign as well as security policy. Such evidence suggests that national welfare state developments have been hitherto rather idiosyncratic. It is only under the auspices of growing coordination within the EU that transnational influences become effective (Kaufmann 2003*a*).

Exemplary Reforms as Markers of Welfare State Development?

The complexity of social policy developments in a variety of sub-fields and the permanent changes in terms of privileged instruments, benefit levels, and eligibility criteria are hardly noticed and assessed in all their details by the public. The problems faced by social policy researchers who attempt to produce adequate overviews of the social policy benefit levels of entire societies—overviews that generalize across sub-fields while doing justice to idiosyncratic developments in each of them—mirrors the difficulties faced by citizens and political elites in their attempt to grasp the contours of welfare state development at given points in time. In fact, public perceptions of the welfare state are typically grounded in perceptions of specific pieces of legislation, reform initiatives and areas of social policy that appear to constitute major events and therefore achieve a paradigmatic status, thus hiding the contours and effects of other programmes. The 'true nature' of the welfare state in a given country is, then, not so much a function of measuring benefit levels but of everyday public assessments of exemplary reforms. More than anything else, innovative pieces of social policy legislation have this event character. Parliamentary decisions in favour of a bill or the implementation of new legislation thus signal 'reform' events that may determine public assessments of entire phases of welfare state development. Such reforms—rather than turning points in the development of benefit levels—represent the historical junctures that structure temporal processes. For instance, consider reforms of old-age security in Sweden and Germany during the late 1950s, the 1996 welfare reform in the United States, the establishment of the NHS in post-war Britain, or the privatization of old-age security in Chile in 1981 (Müller 2003), and perhaps also the subsequent introduction of a basic pension (Barr and Diamond 2008) in 2008. An approach that focuses on paradigmatic shifts, reforms, and events is also more conducive to an explanation of the shocks created by the radical market reforms under Reagan and Thatcher—after all, despite continued social expenditure growth, it is hard to overlook the fact that social policy developments entered a new path in the 1980s.

The danger entailed in such an approach is undoubtedly that one might capture the 'image' of reforms rather than their reality and effects. Moreover, precisely those fields of social policy might be neglected by academic researchers that also receive little public attention. Still, these images very much determine broader understandings of social policy epochs. They are themselves part of social policy-related processes and greatly contribute to the framing of the material effects of social security systems. A focus on widely perceived reforms also takes into account that greater weight has to be given to ruptures with regard to structural features, changes of basic principles and the reformulation of basic norms in the analysis of welfare state development than to mere shifts in benefit levels—only the former are evidence for 'deeper' shifts. The threefold typology of Peter Hall (1993) has gained an almost canonical status in the analysis of policy change, as it offers a heuristic for the distinction between structural changes and mere adaptations of existing programmes (first order change: incrementalist adaptation; second order change: new instruments; third order change: policy paradigm shift). Perhaps, however, this typology should be modified for the analysis of welfare state development: changes that usher in a departure from the institutional and ideological foundations of an established path *and* are accompanied by major shifts in coverage, replacement rates and levels of social expenditure are particularly appropriate markers for the beginning of new periods of welfare state development.

THE MEASUREMENT OF 65 YEARS OF WELFARE STATE DEVELOPMENT

In sum, the attempts to describe temporal changes in the development of welfare states by comprehensive periodizations are not entirely convincing. We need more differentiated approaches which take into account the complex character of welfare state developments.

In the following we therefore examine more closely the different criteria and measurement procedures on which the described periodizations are based. Six different types of periodization, each based on a specific set of criteria, may be distinguished. Periodizations may draw on:

1. the macro level of context factors—the economic, social, and political challenges of social policy making;
2. social expenditure trends;
3. the internal structure of social programmes, the generosity of social benefits, coverage, access, etc.
4. the distribution of welfare production between state, market, family, and civil society, as well as governance types of social policy; the outcome of social policy interventions (e.g. poverty rates and measures of inequality);
5. the public legitimation of social policy and the welfare state.

Challenges and Contextual Factors

A first type of periodization refers to the economic, social, and political challenges that constitute the backdrop of welfare state development. This approach to periodization assumes that changes in these conditions translate into risk structures on the one hand, and changing opportunity structures on the other. It largely corresponds with the functionalist explanation of welfare state development. Such periodizations do not highlight the development of social policy itself (even though they usually draw on social expenditure data as indicators of welfare state development) but rather focus on external factors. In this perspective, the Golden Age of welfare state development was brought about by highly favourable external conditions. All periodizations that refer to phases of economic development such as industrialization, deindustrialization, and the rise of post-industrialism, use economic growth rates, Kondratiev cycles, and product innovations as criteria, point out the role of economic globalization as a driving force of welfare state development, or highlight events such as the end of the Bretton Woods system and the oil crisis of 1973/4 and propagate a periodization of welfare state history that is oriented to external factors. The same holds true for references to changes in class and family structures, demographic shifts or new gender relations. Likewise, references to political regime changes, waves of democratization, constitutional reforms, or new levels of political mobilization are a—politics-centred—variant of this approach to periodization. In all the described versions, these periodizations imply that there is a direct relationship between contextual factors and welfare state changes, and hence that functional requirements trigger quasi-automatic mechanisms of adaptation whenever social policy arrangements and their contexts are out of sync. In the expansion phase of the welfare state, against the backdrop of an enormous GDP growth between 1950 and 1975, references to industrialization processes were thus highlighted in periodization schemes and explanatory models (Rimlinger 1971; Wilensky 1975). More complex models that built on Stein Rokkan's version of modernization theory mostly added political factors (introduction of universal voting rights, democratization of political systems; see Flora and Alber 1981). Moreover, despite the criticism levelled against functional explanations from the perspective of the power resources approach, there was also a wave of approaches (based on capitalism theory) that credited economic factors with the power to determine opportunities of social policy making. Three core periodization concepts stem from these lines of thought, and they also entail three versions of the retrenchment hypothesis:

1. The hypothesis of an early onset of the retrenchment phase: it was the oil crisis of 1973/4, together with shifts in international trade relations and the demise of the Bretton Woods system of fixed exchange rates in 1971, that severely restricted opportunities for social policy making at the national level and put pressure on the welfare state.

2. The globalization hypothesis: according to this second view, the above-mentioned developments in the early 1970s marked no more than the initial phase of economic globalization, which gained steam in the 1980s and 1990s and increased the exit options of (financial) capital; the possibility to search worldwide for the most competitive investment locations, in turn, increased the power of corporations, and generous social policy came to be viewed as a threat to national competitiveness. Not all versions of this hypothesis imply the 'race to the bottom' argument, but they all tend to assume that continued welfare state expansion is no longer possible given the internationalization of markets and investment opportunities, and that the new phase of welfare state development characterized by retrenchment was ushered in during the 1980s.

3. The postindustrialism hypothesis: according to this third view, technological changes, the rise of the service economy and the knowledge society as well as the social developments fostered by the restructuring of labour markets are more important than globalization itself. Lower economic growth rates coincide with less job security and increased flexibility, greater qualification requirements, the disappearance of the working class due to deindustrialization processes, increased female labour force participation and a shift in the gender division of labour. These shifts create 'new social risks', and attempts beginning in the 1980s to deal with those risks mark the transition from the 'industrial welfare state' to the 'postindustrial welfare state' (Taylor-Gooby 2004).

The Development of Social Expenditures

Older versions of the functionalist paradigm were closely linked with a measurement concept of the welfare state that viewed the development of social expenditures as a particularly good indicator for the performance of social security systems. Since this assumption seemed entirely adequate with a view to the expansion phase, the notions of a welfare state crisis and of retrenchment tended to go hand in hand with the expectation of dwindling social expenditure levels. And while Esping-Andersen's *Three Worlds of Welfare Capitalism* fostered a shift from welfare state research that remained focused on social expenditure ratios (Wilensky 1975; Flora 1986–87) to multidimensional research that also took the nature of social programmes into consideration, Paul Pierson's influential retrenchment analysis (1994) greatly contributed to a shift back to the traditional focus on government social spending (as a share of GDP) in academic debates. His study of this new phase did *not* use the complex set of measurement instruments developed by Esping-Andersen, and so did not capture shifts in terms of social rights. His proclamation of a new phase rather encouraged attempts to fine-tune the analysis of social expenditures. With a view to the plethora of studies in this vein, one may, however, conclude that there is no evidence for the retrenchment hypothesis based on public expenditure data alone (Castles 2007b). Not social expenditures but rather expenditures for other core responsibilities of the state declined in the 1980s and 1990s. A comparison of twenty-one OECD states between 1980 and 2002 reveals a quite pronounced upwards trend of social expenditure levels as percentages of GDP (and likewise for welfare state funding; Starke et al. 2008). This development is not merely a function of demographic shifts, as we do not only observe a rise of expenditures for old-age security (on average, from 6.7 to 8.3 per cent of GDP), but also growing expenditures for health, unemployment and family benefits. This evidence indicates that the race to the bottom variant of the globalization hypothesis has been falsified if social expenditures are accepted as the primary indicator for welfare state development and retrenchment. However, if this indicator is employed, the two-phase periodization of welfare state development is no longer tenable. The comparison of social expenditures highlights continuities and downplays potential ruptures.

Benefit Levels and Other Programme Characteristics

Even early research on welfare state development had already used other indicators alongside social expenditure levels such as, for instance, coverage. Drawing on a dataset compiled by Walter Korpi on the programme characteristics of social insurances, Esping-Andersen (1990) then presented a theoretically sound and particularly successful concept for the measurement of welfare state *quality* (focusing on decommodification, social stratification, state-market-family relations). His quality standards were derived from a comparison of different social policy traditions in Europe, and the approach corresponded with the power-resources and conflict-based explanation of welfare state development. Meanwhile the dataset (SCIP) has been developed further and has become publicly accessible (Korpi and Palme 2007). The data of the SCIP project for eighteen OECD welfare states make it possible to reconstruct the development of social rights and benefit levels in five social policy sub-fields since 1930 in five-year steps. Most importantly, average replacement rates for the different branches of social security systems offer a basis for research into the beginning of the retrenchment phase: the year with the highest replacement rate can be viewed as the end point of the expansion phase. That there *has* been retrenchment—a claim that is not corroborated by the analysis of social expenditures alone—is illustrated by the fact that the bulk of the measurement values for 1995 (forty-six out of fifty-four values for eighteen countries and three types of insurance benefits—sickness payments, unemployment insurance, pensions; see Table 35.1 in Chapter 35 of this volume) are below each country's peak levels of the average replacement rate for the respective programme area. Only two of the peak years are before 1970 and twenty-three (42.6 per cent) are in the 1970s (i.e. 1970, 1975, or 1980). In all the other cases, the 1970s still have to be viewed as part of the expansion phase. This is particularly true for the Nordic countries in the areas of sickness benefits and pensions, for the Christian Democratic/continental European welfare states in the area of unemployment insurance (with the exception of Germany and Italy), and for the liberal welfare states in the area of pensions. This measurement concept—based on a combination of programme structures and benefit levels—thus allows us to corroborate the hypothesis of welfare state retrenchment, even though the turning point between the expansion and retrenchment phases apparently occurred later than expected, in the 1980s.

The datasets of the SCIP project and the highly complex measurement instruments of Huber and Stephens (2001a)—which combine various social expenditure indicators with Esping-Andersen's and other programme-related indicators—enable a very comprehensive perspective on welfare state development. Still, three deficits remain if the ultimate objective is a 'complete' measurement of welfare state development. First, these measurement concepts do not sufficiently take into account those social benefits that are granted or produced by firms or private actors (with state support)—extant measurement concepts assume the direct provision of social benefits and neglect indirect effects, which are usually fostered by tax incentives. And as soon as tax policy is included, core elements of income tax policy would have to be interpreted as elements of social policy. Secondly, important policy fields that are viewed as core elements of social policy in relevant European countries are not sufficiently covered by available time-series data. This is true for a number of social services, labour legislation and workplace safety regulations. It is also true—to a lesser extent—for the education sector. Thirdly, these measurement concepts are still very much grounded in an understanding of the welfare state as a social insurance state, and so they cannot sufficiently capture changes of the internal logic of social programmes—for instance, changes that are referred to with labels such as activation, increased social control, or social investment. One could undoubtedly attempt to classify individual programmes and related expenditures as activating or social investment oriented and examine the development of expenditure profiles along those lines, thus merely adapting and expanding the conventional approach to the measurement of welfare state development. This would, however, allow no more than a *post hoc* reconstruction of programmatic changes.

A more comprehensive measurement of social policy developments could have revealed that social policy in East Asia during the early post-war years had a very specific character that was, in fact, close to what is called a social investment strategy today. The economic strategy of export-oriented industrialization was premised on low wage costs, but also on skilled workers. Therefore wages were not burdened by social insurance contributions, and only limited social benefits were granted. By contrast, the state was much more active in the areas of primary and secondary education and vocational training (Haggard and Kaufman 2008). The concept of the social investment state, as propagated for Europe by Anthony Giddens (1994: 89), also highlights another investment-oriented feature of welfare production in Asian economies: investment in social capital via support for networks of family members and friends as an instrument of economic and social policy. The combination of these two investment-oriented elements, namely, investments in human and in social capital, in East Asia has thus become a model for those in Europe who call for a shift from the traditional welfare state to a social investment state (Giddens 1998) and a child-centred social investment strategy (Kaufmann 1990: 64–7, 172–8; Esping-Andersen 2002) that puts the education and participation of children and youth front and centre in social policy. These new concepts first characterized Third Way social policy in Great Britain and Canada (Lister 2004) and now have been emulated by many OECD states. Thus education and family policy, child care, and measures aimed at the compatibility of employment and family move towards the centre, and the meaning of the term 'welfare state' has become more encompassing than the traditional understanding of 'social insurance state'. This, in turn, may be viewed as a key indicator for a new phase of welfare state development that started during the 1990s in most OECD countries—and which is not immediately revealed even by a programme-centred measurement of social policy developments along the lines suggested above.

Welfare Production and Welfare Governance

Changes in the combination of state, market and firm-based, or associative and family-based forms of welfare production (defined as the sum of all transactions that create benefits for third parties; Kaufmann 2001) play a key role in our understanding of the welfare state. The expansion phase is widely viewed as a phase of intensive nationalization of social services, accompanied by the marginalization notably of family-based forms of social service provision. Privatization and the withdrawal of the state, the prioritization of the market and the creation of fields of private welfare production by competitive businesses (welfare markets) are, by contrast, character-istics of the retrenchment phase. However, it seems difficult to adequately capture all forms of welfare production and to compare the respective shares of markets, the state, families, networks, and civil society in the overall volume of welfare production over time. That the familiar periodization of the 1980s and 1990s as decades of privatization need not be plausible is illustrated by the findings of Howard (1997) and Hacker (2002). They challenge the traditional understanding of the American welfare state, which appears much more extensive than is usually assumed if firm-based and private security systems supported by tax credits and other taxation instruments are considered. Hacker (2002), moreover, shows that the introduction of the Social Security Act fostered an expansion of private welfare production in the form of firm-based and private insurance solutions, and hence that the expansion of the *private* welfare sector in the United States (also) peaked during the 1940s.

The organization of the welfare state is, however, not only characterized by its role in direct welfare production but also by the tier of government that is responsible for deliberation and decision making in the social policy field. On the one hand, social policy has still not become a field that is subject to the mechanisms of multi-level governance. The authority of international organizations and supranational regional organizations such as the EU to make collectively binding decisions remains very limited. On the other hand, however, policy is increasingly formulated in the context of international networks and exchanges in which conceptual developments, recommendations and decisions, as well as the resources of international organizations, have begun to play a certain role. As indicated, the 1940s were already characterized by an internationalization of social policy ideas. There are institutional precursors of internationalized social policy regimes. After 1945, the Bretton Woods economic and monetary regime came to define the context of social policy making; after 1971— culminating in the Washington Consensus—it was the increasingly market liberal economic policy of the International Monetary Fund (IMF) and the World Bank that played this role. Over the last couple of years, the strict retrenchment orientation at the international level has somewhat abated. Perhaps the year 2000 may be qualified as a turning point and the beginning of a new phase of welfare state development, because even the IMF and the World Bank have now begun to recognize social development as an objective of all types of support programmes, as the signing of the millennium goals indicates. Social policy has thus become part of the policy-making activities even of those international organizations that are not—like the ILO— primarily dealing with social policy issues (Deacon 2007). Early steps in the direction of internationalized social policy making in the immediate post-war years are, in other words, continued in the form of a new welfare internationalism. Still, the dominance of national actors and institutions in the social policy field has not yet been overcome, not even in the EU. The EU's regulatory social policy in the areas of labour law, workplace safety, gender equality and anti-discrimination is successful because it helps enforce stricter standards. With regard to social insurance and issues of redistribution, however, the greater or lesser effects of Open Method of Coordination processes are essentially determined by specific national political constellations (Ferrera 2008).

Outcomes: The Results of Social Policy Activities

A fifth approach to periodization, which focuses on the outcomes of welfare state programmes, is less common. Different phases in the development of social security systems may also be distinguished on the basis of their impact or effectiveness, that is, through consideration of the extent to which they have created or transformed social realities. Hence one might, for instance, distinguish the age of relative equality and middle-class orientation from a period characterized by the shrinking of the middle class and growing inequality. This approach, then, is close to impact studies, especially studies of the distributional effects of welfare state programmes.

Esping-Andersen's measurement concept of social stratification is not an outcome measure in that sense because it considers no more than the entrenchment of equality as a social policy *norm* in individual programmes. If the equality criterion is applied to historical time series, the retrenchment hypothesis may, however, be further corroborated: Scruggs and Allan's replication and update of Esping-Andersen's analysis of social stratification yields evidence for an OECD-wide trend between 1980 and 2000/02 'to gradually "residualize" the welfare state' (2008: 664). The described trend combines the ongoing universalization of social insurance programmes with a growing number of targeted programmes and rising inequality in social security programmes (a decrease of benefit equality). Research on pension policy, for example, indicates a general tendency to shift risks to the beneficiaries through shifts from defined benefit to defined contribution approaches, whether these are private or public (see e.g. Hacker 2006).

On the basis of the Luxembourg Income Study and with a view to the unequivocal outcome indicator of relative poverty, Scruggs and Allan (2006*b*) conclude that poverty grew between the mid-1980s and approximately 2000 in the OECD countries, and sometimes markedly. The OECD study *Growing Unequal* (2008*a*) corroborates this rise of the poverty rate and of income inequality over the last twenty years (mid-1980s to mid-2000s) for thirty countries, and with few exceptions. As social expenditures have been growing at the same time, this finding not only demonstrates the widespread ineffectiveness but also the inefficiency of social policy if its success is measured against the standard of a moderate reduction of income inequality and the avoidance of income poverty. Yet there are no complete time-series data for the entire post-1945 period, and hence only the negative trend since 1980 can be used for periodization purposes.

However, the measurement of welfare state outcomes cannot focus exclusively on income distributions. If, for instance, the area of old-age pensions is considered, it has to be kept in mind that the expansion of the welfare state through the creation of comprehensive old-age security systems institutionalized a whole new phase of the life cycle—with massive consequences for the life-world of citizens. The post-1945 welfare state contributed to a standardization of life cycles and enabled older people to enjoy poverty-free lives to an extent previously unknown. It created a new gender division of labour and family relationships that were no longer dictated by economic necessity. And it contributed to the development of a middle-class society, even though it could not prevent the reversal of this trend due to changing labour market conditions, the increasing fragmentation of societies and the growth of an underclass. Palier and Martin (2008: 17) speak of a general trend towards dualization in the Bismarckian countries: 'The recent trend would deepen the divisions towards a more cleft world: a dual labour market, a dual welfare system and a society divided between insiders and outsiders.'

Finally, one might also consider the set of social policy institutions itself as an outcome—the bureaucracies that administer and pay out social benefits, as well as the sector of professionals working in health care or other social service areas. As shown by Paul Pierson (1994), the welfare state creates its own apparatus and support base—which does not, however, mean that it is necessarily protected against cuts and retrenchment. With a view to social structures as well as organizational and institutional aspects, it would seem that the modern welfare state is primarily dealing with the consequences and requirements of its own emergence and reproduction; social policy has largely become a kind of second-order operation focusing on internal problems, and hence at least temporarily losing its contact with actual social risks and problems. As such, the retrenchment phase may also be interpreted as a consolidation phase of a rapidly developed and complex apparatus, or—more negatively—as a phase of increasing 'introspection'.

Transformations of Welfare State Legitimacy

In our discussion of the question of whether 1945 represents an important historical juncture in the context of welfare state development, we have already hinted at the role of ideas and frames in the periodization of social policy trajectories. Compared with a type of policy that tackled the 'social question' with a hodgepodge of issue-specific instruments and benefits, the post-war understanding of social policy—grounded, as it was, in the notion of basic social rights expressed in the 1948 Universal Declaration of Human Rights—represents an ideological breakthrough. An ideational approach is most apparent in literature that examines the religious roots and motivations of social policy. For instance, Rieger and Leibfried (2003) compare cultures in order to shed light on the moral foundations of social policy. Drawing on Weber's systematic categories and his sociology of religion, they contrast the Western with the East Asian paths of welfare state development. The different religious roots of these two paths are viewed as causes for the strength or weakness of social policy activities in the face of global economic trends. Research that concentrates on Western Europe (Kersbergen and Manow 2009) highlights the denominational cleavage between Catholicism, Lutheran Protestantism, and Calvinism, and suggests that religious thought patterns and motives continue to be relevant, at least implicitly. These might not least help to tackle problems with Esping-Andersen's welfare state typology. Otherwise, the prominence of the *Three Worlds of Welfare Capitalism* is also due to the fact that it links the analysis of social policy-related data with an examination of each country's welfare state conception and its ideological foundations. This is why his political labels for the welfare state types (social democratic, conservative, liberal) have proved adequate. But it is not only Esping-Andersen's typology that is linked with an ideational approach. The retrenchment hypothesis, too, is grounded in the perception of changes at the level of ideas (see Chapter 4). Even during their rise to power, before retrenchment measures were implemented, neoliberal and anti-welfare state parties had helped spread the idea that the welfare state was faced with a legitimacy crisis.

However, we still lack data that would allow us to understand the public justifications of the welfare state and of social policy—in party manifestos and government documents, parliamentary debates and the mass media—in a comparative fashion, for different countries and over longer stretches of time. Closest to this is the Party Manifesto Project which, however, concentrates on shifts on the left–right axis, contains no more than a few social policy-related items and does not permit a finer grained analysis of legitimation criteria for different social policy areas (Budge et al. 2001; Klingemann et al. 2006). Otherwise, more narrowly circumscribed studies of the ideological foundations or development of specific welfare state concepts dominate (on the Third Way: White 2004b; on the Nordic welfare states: Kildal and Kuhnle 2005; more broadly: Taylor-Gooby 2005a). Longer time series are, however, lacking completely. Research combining the history of ideas and concepts on the one hand, and social policy research on the other—drawing on methods of quantitative textual analysis—is therefore desirable. There is considerable evidence for the hypothesis that there have indeed been important shifts regarding the ideas and normative benchmarks used in the (de-)legitimation of the welfare state (while nationally specific traditions also remain present). These shifts, too, might be interpreted as evidence for the retrenchment hypothesis or inspire further reflection on sub-periodizations.

FUTURE TRENDS

The global financial crisis of 2008/9 might have a huge impact on welfare state development and usher in a new period. Based on a theoretical approach that highlights economic context factors, this expectation seems particularly plausible, given that the crisis represents no less than the most severe recession of the post-war era. Social expenditures are most likely to grow as a consequence, at least in the short term, as GDP is shrinking massively; swift expenditure cuts of a comparable size are unlikely to be implemented and might be explicitly ruled out as cyclical programmes—long considered obsolete—experience a revival. This 'emergency Keynesianism' increases the state share of welfare production and delegitimates market liberal concepts of welfare state retrenchment. Whether social benefit levels will ultimately be stabilized in the face of shrinking contributions and tax revenues, rising debt and the related fiscal crisis of the welfare state, or whether social benefits might even be further expanded (as in the cyclical programmes implemented by many countries in the first half of 2009), will greatly depend on political constellations—these, in turn, also depend on economic developments and their framing in public debates. As much as we know about the effects and roles of different political institutions, ideas and actors in the context of welfare state development in individual countries, regions and policy areas, events such as the current financial crisis raise the question of whether economic developments have acted like a railway switchman and forced social policy and welfare state development onto fixed tracks, or whether cultural values, institutional inertia and political traditions do matter in the determination of long-term developments of the welfare state.

PART III

APPROACHES

···

RESEARCH
METHODS

···

EDWIN AMENTA

ALEXANDER HICKS

INTRODUCTION

···

THE literature on welfare states and social policy has benefited from a wide-ranging debate across theoretical perspectives and methodological approaches. Scholars from different theoretical points of view have sought to examine claims across a vast stretch of empirical terrain. They have sought to develop and appraise hypotheses with methods ranging from the detailed examination of a policy sequence in one country to pooled cross-sectional and time-series analyses of social spending across all capitalist democracies. In this chapter we review some of these methodological approaches and address some of their achievements and drawbacks.

In this literature there has often been agreement over what is to be explained. The main focus has been on social spending, either overall or broken down into various types, such as transfers and services, or different functions, such as for health or old age. Social spending has been understood mainly in terms of its 'effort' or its amount as a percentage of economic activity (Wilensky 1975), with some attention to per capita spending (Pontusson 2005) and per-household income replacement rates (Allan and Scruggs 2004). There has also been attention to the adoption of major social programmes in the first half of the twentieth century (Collier and Messick 1975; Hicks 1999). Moreover, scholars in this area have sought to make sense of social policy 'regimes,' or overarching configurations of social policy (Esping-Andersen 1990; Castles 1997). In addition, scholars have sought to understand the retrenchment of social policy since the 1980s, in terms of both alterations in programmes and reductions of spending (P. Pierson 1994; Hicks 1999; Swank 2002; Allan and Scruggs 2004). In the new century, scholarship has often broken past these bounds to examine more detailed questions and to examine programmes outside the usual definitions of social policy.

A wide variety of theories and hypotheses about social policy and welfare states have been developed and appraised. Theories have focused on modernization (Wilensky 1975), class struggle (Korpi 1983), political partisanship (Castles 1989), political institutions like states and party systems (Skocpol 1992; P. Pierson 1994), interest groups (Pampel and Williamson 1989), social movements (Amenta et al. 2005), cultural, world-societal influence (Strang and Chang 1993), and gender (Orloff 1993b; for reviews, see Amenta 2003; Hicks and Esping-Andersen 2005). In most instances, researchers have devised a similarly extensive range of empirical appraisals of theoretical claims. In scholarship on welfare states, there has been an unusual and fruitful dialogue between quantitative and qualitative historical research (Amenta 2003; P. Pierson 2007).

In our review of methods in the study of welfare states, we focus on what Amenta (2003) has termed 'causal research'. This sort of scholarship deploys self-conscious research methods to appraise theory and hypotheses in some significant way (Gerring 2007), or develops theoretical claims that are transportable in some fashion, such as in setting scope conditions on hypotheses (George and Bennett 2005), or both. The welfare state area as a whole has benefited from researchers addressing similar subject matter empirically from a variety of methodological approaches and often synthesizing approaches (Hicks 1999; Huber and Stephens 2001a). The literature has been shaped by its focus on decisions made by states, the adoption of specific policies, or long-standing lines of state action (including individual programmes) that typically have consequences that are often easily measurable, such as the amount of spending devoted to individual programmes. It has led to historical inquiry regarding the adoptions and contractions of these policies and programmes and to quantitative and formal qualitative assessments of spending outputs. Given concern with outputs at the state level, the universe of plausible cases for examination has typically consisted of nations states. Given limited numbers of these, studies have mainly been of observational rather than experimental data employing convenience samples shaped by data availability.

In what follows we address these approaches. We do not provide an exhaustive review of all possible research but focus on examples, often from our own work. The latter spans in-depth historical analyses of a single country case to historical analyses of a few countries to Boolean QCA analyses across medium-N samples of countries and sub-national polities to cross-sectional and pooled cross-sectional and time-series analyses of countries and sub-national polities. We do this to show the variety of methodological work in the area and to highlight the advantages and disadvantages of different approaches. We conclude with suggestions for synthesizing, triangulating, and combining methods in order to minimize the disadvantages and maximize the advantages of different approaches.

APPROACHES TO CAUSAL RESEARCH

To situate different research approaches, we make broad distinctions between comparative and historical work. By *comparative* studies we refer to studies that address the experiences of two or more country cases (Rueschemeyer 2003), not one-country studies that make over-time comparisons or that simply situate empirical questions in a comparative context, and that make significant macro-level comparisons in the aid of causal inference. By *historical* studies we mean ones that include significant over-time variation in potential causes and place a premium on a deep knowledge of cases, path-dependent arguments, and a reliance on primary research (Amenta 2003). However, the main criterion for studies to fit our focus is that studies must take causality seriously in a double sense: to attempt to explain important welfare state developments by the appraisal of alternative hypotheses; to appraise, modify, or produce something at least partly theoretically transportable—a line of causal argumentation conceptualized so as to apply to cases or time-periods deemed analytically similar to those already studied (See Table 7.1).

Each of the categories includes both qualitative and quantitative studies. For instance, historical research may include primary document analyses of the development of policy in one country or quantitative time-series analyses of spending in a country or formal qualitative event structure analyses of policy adoption. Similarly, comparative and historical research may mean the qualitative analysis of the adoption of policy across a small-N sample of countries selected in a most-similar systems design or quantitative analyses of pooled time-series and cross-sections of social spending among capitalist democracies or event history analyses of programme-adoption across the world. Some methodological techniques may fall into more than

Table 7.1 Causal research according to methodological approaches

	Comparative Approach	
Historical Approach	No	Yes
No	Neither: Cross-sectional Quantitative Analyses of Within-Country Subunits; Medium- and Small-N Analyses across Subunits (1)	Comparative Only: Cross-National Small-N Analyses of Particular Periods, Formal Qualitative (QCA) or Cross-Sectional Quantitative Analyses across Countries (2)
Yes	Historical Only: Analytical Historical Case Studies; Time-Series Analyses of one Country (3)	Comparative and Historical: Small-N Comparative and Historical Analyses; Panel, and Pooled Time-Series Cross-Sectional Analysis (4)

one of the boxes; standard OLS cross-sectional regression can be used across countries, sub-national polities, or individuals, for instance. We discuss technique in terms of the methodological approach and the cell of Table 7.1 with which a technique is most closely associated.

Some studies may be comparative or historical, or both, but if they are not causal they fall outside the bounds of this review. These include the comparative studies that Skocpol and Somers (1980) refer to as 'contrast of contexts' and those that Charles Tilly (1984) refers to as 'individualizing comparisons', as well as historical case studies that employ social science concepts to interpret events, but fail to appraise alternative hypotheses or to develop theory seriously.

NEITHER HISTORICAL NOR COMPARATIVE CAUSAL STUDIES

It is possible, however, for a study to be neither historical nor cross-nationally comparative in the sense defined here, but still causal. The most notable examples are within-country analyses, using either large-N statistical techniques or formal qualitative ones analysing policy differences in federal polities across individual subunits (Amenta and Halfman 2000), small-N qualitative analyses across similar units, and studies of individuals (e.g., citizens, voters) analysed through survey data (Goodin et al. 1999). (See cell 1, Table 7.1.)

The main advantage in examining one country at one point in time is that many potential causes at the macro-political and macro-social level are held constant. In studies of sub-national polities, long-term conditions such as the overall political system and language are typically the same. So, too, are more short-term systemic conditions, such as the national political regime, state of the economy, and so on. An additional advantage is that the process by which data are collected is often similar across cases, as when national government agencies gather information about pro- grammes administered at the sub-national level. These studies also often can yield tests of hypotheses that are sometimes difficult to examine cross-nationally, in that there may be more variation on some important causal conditions in subunits in one polity than across country-level polities. In the United States in the middle of the twentieth century, for instance, there was substantial variation among states in democratic political institutions, with some polities and areas of the country greatly restricting such basics as voting rights, and others extending these practices widely (Mayhew 1986; Amenta and Halfmann 2000).

However, the main advantages of such studies for adequate explanations of a given case also serve as a disadvantage in developing portable theory. The arguments may be closely bound to specific macro-social and macro-political conditions in ways that are not easily understood and thus often make it difficult to sift out what is truly transportable in theoretical claims and what is specific to the case at hand. One critic (P. Pierson 2007) of quantitative political science research in American politics argues that it makes extensive general claims that are rarely formulated with explicit scope conditions or tested beyond the borders of the United States.

COMPARATIVE STUDIES

Strictly comparative studies (see cell 2, Table 7.1) encompass some small-N comparative studies and many early cross-national quantitative studies of social policy expenditures and policy adoptions. Small-N comparative studies also often are at least implicitly historical in approach; but some focus on delimited time-periods and in their argumentation deploy Mill's or similar non-dynamic methods of demonstration across comparative cross-sections. We refer to this as informal systematic comparison. In the comparative category we also place cross-national QCA studies (Ragin 1987; Hicks et al. 1995). Strictly speaking, however, QCA may be deployed on any sort of cross-section, including within-country polities (Amenta et al. 2005) and can also be used in ways that take time into account (Caren and Panofsky 2005).

Systematic Comparison

The most rudimentary of systematic comparative methods utilized in sociology is 'systematic comparison'. This method typically involves the identification of very strong and simple empirical patterns of traits across nations. The standard sorts of systematic comparisons tend to use Mill's methods of agreement and difference (Skocpol and Somers 1980), despite Mill's own warnings about the mechanical use of his methods on the observational data typical of the social sciences and central to research on welfare states. An instance of such a strong pattern can be found in Hicks (1999: 37), in the association between economic development and early welfare state 'consolidation'. With development measured as per capita real income over $2000 in 1913 (in 1980 dollars) and early welfare state consolidation meaning the adoption of at least three of the four major types of social insurance programmes—workers compensation, old age pensions, health care, and unemployment compensation—by 1920, Hicks finds that non-developed cases are always cases of no welfare consolidation. This pattern suggests that development is a necessary condition for welfare state consolidation. For association to be regarded as supportive of a proposition investigated by means of systematic comparisons, the pattern must be very strong and simple enough for detection by means of eyeballing. Here 'strong' means without, or almost without, exception, suggesting simple logical relations such as

'A is a sufficient condition for B', 'A is a necessary condition for B', or 'A is a sufficient and necessary condition for B'. The cases in which systematic comparisons can yield such clear results are rare, however. Moreover, theoretical claims usually are more complex, and only rarely will one-factor theories provide much analytical leverage.

Crisp- and Fuzzy-Set Qualitative Comparative Analysis

These circumstances promoted the development of qualitative comparative analysis (QCA), which extends and goes well beyond systematic comparison. Relying on set logic, QCA makes it possible to isolate conditions that are necessary and/or sufficient for specific outcomes (Ragin 1987, 2008). The goals and logics of using these analyses are somewhat different from those of social science research in which the explanation of variance is stressed. By using these methods, one selects a dependent variable and seeks to test or devise an explanation for it. Crisp-set QCA limits analysis to strictly dichotomous qualitative dependent and explanatory variables (for which elements are in a set with a probability of either 1.0 or 0.0). Instead of focusing on how much a given measure adds to explained variance, crisp- and fuzzy-set QCA both address conjunctural causation—the likelihood that two or more conditions must occur simultaneously to produce a result. They also address the possibility of multiple causation—that more than one conjunctural causal path will lead to a result. QCA can generate solutions that are accompanied by quantitative assessments of the strength of results, including statistical significance testing. QCA not only identifies conjunctions of causal factors; it focuses on the likelihood that given conjunctions of causal factors generate a given outcome.

Most extant work has been done through crisp-set analyses, and advancing beyond the example above can show QCA's value. Say we hypothesize that union strength, left-party strength, and Catholicism are all potent causes of welfare programme consolidation in 1920 and construct dichotomous measures of each of these variables (see Table 7.2); a visual assessment of the table suggests an imprecise pattern—yet applying the QCA algorithms produces this tidy solution:

Welfare Consolidation = [Early Union Strength AND Early Strong Left]
OR [Early Union Strength AND Catholicism]

In this instance, early union strength is a necessary condition of both solutions. To produce welfare consolidation, however, also needed is a strong left party or a Catholic country. If unions are strong in a Catholic country, a coalition will form to generate ample welfare programme legislation, even in the absence of a strong left party.

Fuzzy-set QCA (fsQCA) allows elements to have probabilities of inclusion in a set that vary from zero to one and offers several advantages over crisp-set QCA. FsQCA can address theoretical instances where cases do not completely fit a set and more mundanely can exploit the information in datasets that is lost when measures are reduced to dichotomies for crisp sets. In addition, fsQCA provides more estimates of

Table 7.2 Welfare programme consolidation in early democracies and proto-democracies (1920)

	No Welfare Consolidation; Non-Catholic	No Welfare Consolidation; Catholic	Welfare Consolidation; Non-Catholic	Welfare Consolidation; Catholic
Early Union Strength; Early Strong Left			Australia, Denmark, Sweden	Austria, Belgium, Germany
Early Union Strength; No Early Strong Left				Netherlands
No Early Union Strength: Strong Left	Canada, Norway, United States	France, Switzerland		
No Early Union Strength; No Strong Left				

the coverage of any given solution (the degree to which the solution or solutions overlap with the outcome set). It can better identify the consistency of the solution, meaning the degree to which cases with a given combination of causal conditions constitute a subset of the cases with the outcome. To date, however, the more precise fuzzy form of analysis has been seen only in research at the margins of welfare state research, such as analyses of the poor employment growth (Epstein et al. 2008) and the newspaper mentions of social movement organizations (Amenta et al. 2009).

The analytical advantages of QCA, crisp and fuzzy, are many. It allows scholars to address directly unusual circumstances that are often lost in less sophisticated analyses seeking to explain all variance, whether important and theoretically relevant or not, in a measure. Further, QCA encourages more complex theorizing and testing than quantitative techniques usually offer. It is far easier to think in terms of multiple conjunctural causes when there are means to analyse how well they fit relevant data. Finally, QCA seems advantageous in circumstances, common to welfare state research, where the number of (country) cases is too few for extended statistical analyses, but too many to permit conclusions based on inspection.

However, there are drawbacks to QCA. The many contending theoretical claims in welfare state research often lead to the simultaneous analyses of many measures. With QCA in any form, the number of potential explanatory measures (n) is highly limited; the number of combinations of these measures (2^n) quickly balloons beyond interpretive boundaries. An analysis of 10 causal measures will, for instance, yield 1024 combinations. (As we will show below, standard cross-national and time-series analyses suffer from more standard 'degrees of freedom' problems.) Also, analysing datasets with QCA does not obviate the need of scholars to have a deep knowledge of cases. QCA in welfare state research typically must rely on observational datasets. Without a deep historical knowledge of the cases at hand, a researcher may miss the causal connections between concepts and measures vitiating findings. In crisp-set QCA, designing the 'truth table', a necessary preliminary for analysis, is a task with steep knowledge requirements (Ragin 1987). Decisions about break points and degree of membership in categories of fuzzy sets also depend on such substantive knowledge (Ragin 2008). (For the most complete discussions and software, see Ragin 2008; Longest and Vaisey 2008.)

Cross-Country Statistical Analyses

Where the number of available country cases is large enough for the operation of statistical inference, social scientists often employ it, even though cases and their variable traits are not typically randomly distributed. However, the analyses of data lacking explicit temporal dimensions can still be revealing. Operationally, causal claim can be bolstered if associations are not statistically spurious, changes in explanatory variables precede changes in the outcome variable and the explanation relies on an overarching theoretical argument or a specification of plausible mechanisms translating changes in explanatory variables into changes in outcome ones. The typical tool used in comparative statistical analyses of welfare states is OLS multivariate regression (Cutright 1965; Cameron 1978; Myles 1984; Hicks and Swank 1984; Pampel and Williamson 1989; see also the panel analyses of Hicks and Kenworthy 1998, 2003).

These sorts of regression analyses were influential and important in adjudicating debates and advancing knowledge in the early years of research on welfare states, establishing some basic points about welfare state development in the expansionary immediate post-World War II period. Researchers were able to show fairly conclusively that the level of economic development was crucial to the explanation of welfare state effort at all income levels (Cutright 1965; Wilensky 1975) and among poorer countries (Collier and Messick 1975). However, economic development level did little to explain variations in welfare state development among the rich capitalist democracies (Myles 1984; Hicks and Swank 1984), where political factors apparently offered better explanatory leverage (Castles 1982b; Myles 1984).

An advantage of this sort of research, as with all quantitative work, is the ability to examine concurrently large ranges of theoretically indicated hypotheses against alternatives. However, simple cross-sectional analysis has largely been abandoned by scholars, because of the relative inability to appraise large numbers of measures due to degrees of freedom issues across selective and theoretically important groups like rich capitalist democracies. Further, simple cross-sectional regression cannot exploit case-based knowledge or yield conjunctural findings as well as can formal qualitative methods like QCA. For the most part, scholars other than those in the first generation of researchers have concentrated their attention on the numerous data points and historical specificity provided by pooled cross-section and time-series analyses (treated below).

HISTORICAL STUDIES

Several types of single-country case studies are considered 'historical' in our analysis of causal research (see cell 3 of Table 7.1). We address, first, historical narrative work that gains empirical leverage by examining causal propositions by considering historical developments and sequences. The second main type includes quantitative time-series analyses of datasets within one country. A third type includes event structure analyses, which typically examine sequences of events within one unit, often a country (Griffin 1993; Isaac et al. 1994).

Historical Studies Proper

Historical causal studies deploy a scholar's deep historical knowledge, documentary research, and the examination of specific episodes of change to appraise current hypotheses or develop new ones. Historical knowledge makes it possible to identify key instances of relevant variables and events, and allows the detailed examination of causal mechanisms. These analyses typically focus on reasons behind key events such as policymaker goals behind major changes in policy (Skocpol 1992; Castles 1989). Often scholars can identify through documentary evidence what different key actors were proposing and what was likely to occur in terms of policy had some historical event or intervention not taken place. Often these empirical demonstrations of pro-positions are used to generate portable explanations, historical instances of what Strauss (1987) called 'grounded research' (see also Eckstein 1975).

Scholars have claimed that there are several standard disadvantages attached to this sort of research. In the standard view, because they provide an N of one, historical studies are seen as limited to the development of hypotheses or a means to reject specific general hypotheses (Rueschemeyer 2003; King et al. 1994). Also, as mentioned in the discussion of within-country analyses, many of the aspects of the context seemingly 'controlled for' in these studies may be relevant contextual causal factors, yet taken for granted and left un-theorized.

However, scholars have recently noted many advantages of the historical ap-proach. One of these is its ability to examine theoretical mechanisms and the details of causal arguments. This sort of analysis is frequently referred to as 'process tracing' (George and Bennett 2005; Gerring 2007). If, for instance, a partisanship theory expects key programmes to be adopted under specific types of regimes or to be championed by specific sorts of actors, a historical scholar can examine just how much these conditions mattered in a given episode of policy making. Similarly, if a theory anticipates legislative or other key action to take a specific sequence, a scholar with deep knowledge of the case can probe these theoretical mechanisms with subtlety. In addition, the disadvantages surrounding contextual similarity are miti-gated to some extent by the fact that in historical studies relatively long time-periods may exhibit variation of contextual conditions. Moreover, most such studies make comparisons across policy areas and programmes, as well as across periods of activity, inactivity, and retrenchment, and these sources of variation make possible further hypothesis testing (Amenta 1998). Most of these methodological moves expand the number of observations beyond 'N equals 1' (King et al. 1994).

There are advantages that go beyond simply exploiting the various types of historical information in a country case. In addition, historical one-country research can generate and appraise more sophisticated theoretical claims that take into account time order sequences (P. Pierson 2000) and configurational and multiple causes (Ragin 2008). Social scientists working on a case through primary materials can avoid the biases of reliance on secondary research, as in most qualitative comparative historical analyses (Lustick 1996). Historical scholars may also contribute to quantitative research by identifying new sources of data and can often build more valid indicators than can scholars mining data from standard sources. Most of all, historical studies are often asking the kinds of big questions that are simultaneously theoretical and historical (P. Pierson and Skocpol 2002), such as why the United States did not develop a welfare state on the European model when some theories would expect that to have happened. These questions are of both public and social science interest and cannot be addressed simply by way of expanding observations. A deep causal understanding of one case, analysed social scientifically, may provide the best building block for further theoretical argumentation (Mahoney 2000).

Event Structure Analysis

Another means to analyse data over time is event structure analysis (ESA), a formal qualitative tool that forces scholars to be explicit about their counterfactual reasoning. ESAs are designed to provide narrative causal accounts of particular sequences of events (Griffin 1993), culminating in an event of importance. These may include those leading to the enactment of social programmes (Isaac et al. 1994). In providing specific interpretations and causal accounts of key events, these analyses provide aid in the development of theory that is historical in a specific social science sense. That is, these analyses are based on the historical institutionalist insight that *when* something happens in a sequence may be causally important as to why something happens (P. Pierson and Skocpol 2002; Mahoney 2000). Specifically, the standard event structure analysis uses the ETHNO programme developed by Heise (1989). This programme induces a researcher to answer a series of questions regarding a specific causal account, forcing consistent reasoning and allowing for the possibility of replication. It is a kind of process tracing that has been specified to the inductive development of causal accounts. Although the models developed from such analyses are most valid as a causal interpretation of a case, the most useful result is one in which a series of potentially portable middle-range and time-ordered theoretical claims are developed.

Although ESA is a promising tool, its use in social policy analysis is still only emerging, and it must overcome a few hurdles. For the most part, event structure analyses require valid and reasonably complete factual accounts of key events or the means to reconstruct them. Only a deep knowledge of the case materials can aid in understanding where timing might and might not matter and in addressing the many counterfactual questions inherent in this type of formal qualitative historical research. Although these analyses are replicable, it is likely that different scholars will answer the questions about causality differently even for the same case rendering rigour and persuasiveness especially important. But used appropriately ESA can aid in both the causal interpretation of specific cases and the development of more comparative causal hypotheses that address time order explicitly.

Time-Series Analysis

Another key type of historical research concerns quantitative analyses over time within one country, or the statistical analysis of times-series data (Janoski 1992). Within- country across-unit designs that pool cross-sections and time-series data are non-comparative, but they remain historical in the sense used here (Amenta et al. 2005). Although these studies are not necessarily historical in the sense that the author has a deep knowledge of the cases at hand, they often make important claims about the importance of the working of over-time processes within structurally determined time-periods (Isaac and Griffin 1989).

Time-series studies are characteristically studies that employ multivariate statistical techniques, and that thus have the standard advantage of being able to examine several hypotheses simultaneously. Estimation employing the core statistical procedure, termed 'generalized differences', can entail problems in particular circumstances, but solutions for these are available (see Ostrom 1978 on inefficiency; see Gujarati 2003 on lagged dependent variables and inconsistency; Greene 2000). These analyses, however, also require some historical knowledge: mainly in delimiting the time-periods for analysis, and identifying the beginning and end of a homogeneous process such as an era of expansion or retrenchment.

However, time-series analyses have not only some of the standard analytical disadvantages of one-country research, they also miss the benefits of strictly historical work. The questions addressed in time-series analyses are usually at one remove from the policy-making decisions at the centre of historical work and usually address important but limited aggregates such as spending. These analyses also typically suffer from a small-N problem, as identifying coherent time-delimited processes also limits the number of cases for statistical manipulation, though sometimes sub-national polities can be deployed to augment the number of observations (Amenta et al. 2005). Also, however, these analyses have difficulty in addressing time-invariant explanations and factors, such as political institutions and structure of labour movements. For these reasons, scholars often seek to bring across-country evidence to bear, such as devising methods to compare and analyse time-series parameters across countries (Western 1998), using these parameters as descriptive evidence to be explained. More generally, scholars have sought to harness the potential advantages of this research to designs that pool time-series across countries, which we address below.

COMPARATIVE AND HISTORICAL RESEARCH

As with the previous modes of research, comparative and historical (cell 4, Table 7.1), research includes both qualitative and quantitative studies and approaches. Notably, we include here historical analyses of several country cases and the statistical analysis of a cross-section of country cases deepened by the examination of time-series data for each. On the qualitative side, we have what might be termed 'classical comparative and historical research'. On the quantitative side of comparative and historical research there are, most notably, pooled data analyses of cross-sections and time-series. These are typically also carried out across capitalist democracies, usually, however, seeking complete coverage of cross-sections, and focused on the post-World War II period.

Classical Comparative and Historical Research

Classical comparative and historical research at its most systematic is often conducted like comparative research, for example employing systematic comparison by means of the Millsian method of agreement and difference. It typically employs 'most similar systems' designs (Przeworski and Teune 1970), in which characteristics are 'controlled for', or become part of the scope condition of the claims, such as advanced capitalist democracies, or liberal welfare state regimes (see also Gerring 2007). Many key qualitative works make small-N comparisons across long stretches of time in order to appraise and develop hypotheses about some aspect of social policy (Heclo 1974; Baldwin 1990; Steinmo 1993; Immergut 1992a; Orloff 1993a; P. Pierson 1994; Amenta 1998). Classical comparative and historical researchers have been able to address a wide range of theoretically and historically important questions: why did social policy take off when it did and why did it become so prevalent? Why did some countries lead and why did some others fall behind in different phases of the development of social policy? Why did some states adopt distinctive forms of social policy? By situating the experiences of different countries against the group portraits, these researches brought to light historical anomalies and puzzles to solve.

Comparative historical research has provided most of what we know regarding the early adoption of social policies among the more economically developed countries. It has also helped to address debates between political institutional approaches based in Weberian and Tocquevillian theory and focusing on the structures of political institutions and political organizational approaches based in Marxian theory and focusing on the political organization of social groups, notably the labour movement (see review in Amenta 2003). From a focus on left-wing or social democratic party rule, scholars have moved on to consideration of the role of the right-wing parties (Castles 1985), farmer-labour political coalitions (Esping-Andersen 1990), expert-labour alliances (Orloff 1993a), and Christian democratic rule (Huber and Stephens 2001a). Comparative and historical scholars have also gone on to build more theoretically synthetic or configurational arguments, combining the structural strengths of institutional claims with the strengths of claims based on political identities and action (Skocpol 1992; Amenta 1998; Hicks 1999; Huber and Stephens 2001*a*).

Classical comparative and historical research has most of the advantages of historical research on one country, mentioned above. It also has the additional advantage of being able to compare similar trajectories of countries and to pinpoint and explain divergences in policy development (Rueschemeyer 2003). This method has some of the well-known disadvantages in appraising hypotheses also discussed in the treatment of historical qualitative work. And despite the addition of cases, classical comparative and historical research, with its steep informational requirements, rarely addresses complete populations of theoretically relevant cases. Thus researchers must rely on secondary research and its attendant biases (Lustick 1996). Quite possibly this research works best in most similar systems designs such as across 'social democratic' welfare states or 'English-speaking' countries where it is possible for researchers to engage in small-N designs without having to rely as greatly on secondary research.

Classic comparative and historical scholars have also been free to rethink what social policy meant and to deepen the concept. Comparative and historical scholars have been able as well to appraise theoretical arguments by addressing social programmes other than the ones prominent in quantitative work. Among the possibilities were veterans' benefits (Skocpol 1992), education (Heidenheimer 1981), taxation policy (Steinmo 1993), housing policy (P. Pierson 1994; Castles 1998*b*; Bonastia 2000), economic policy (Hall 1986; Weir 1992), and work programmes (Amenta 1998). In this process, comparative and historical scholars have devised new questions and have opened up new research agendas, helping to develop and refine theoretical argumentation (see review in Amenta 2003). Another way to develop the research agenda and advance theory has been to split the concept by taking the developmental *phase* of social policy seriously, entertaining the possibility that different phases of social policy have different determinants, as in the case of the retrenchment of social policy (P. Pierson 1994), which is a more difficult process than adopting one and depends crucially on processes set in motion by the nature of the policy in question. This argument has been deemed appropriate to explain social policy developments since the 1980s (see also Huber and Stephens 2001*a*; Swank 2002). By this time most systems of social spending had been completed and expanded—had become 'institutionalized'—and bids to cut them back were taken up in force by many political regimes.

In addition to the conceptual 'splitting'—with its attention to possibilities of causal heterogeneity across blocks of time or sets of cross-sections—classical comparative and historical research has been at the centre of broader conceptualizations of social policy or ideal types that characterize policies as wholes. Building on previous models of social policy, Esping-Andersen's (1990) 'welfare state regimes' address social policy's influence on labour-market relations. New conceptualizations of social policy have also been provided by feminist scholars (see Chapter 17), many of whom work in a comparative and historical mode (Skocpol 1992; O'Connor et al.

1999). The main responses have been to modify Esping-Andersen's types or to replace them with gender-based policy regimes.

In short, classical comparative and historical research has many of the benefits of historical studies proper, with the added advantage of throwing a case into relief vis-à-vis one or more largely similar cases. This makes it possible to ask new and specific questions in analysing diverging trajectories in social policy. These analyses can be used to appraise theories and arguments and to ascertain how far they extend to different processes and outcomes outside a particular domain of welfare state research, as well as to create or enrich theory for appraisal across other cases. However, typically the arguments cannot be appraised fully with the cases at hand. Knowledge requirements are steep for these analyses and adding cases without the requisite background can lead to a thinning of analyses, issues of validity, and the loss of the advantages associated with historical research proper. Nonetheless, these analyses have played a central role in driving the agenda of research on welfare states (see Amenta 2003).

Statistical Analyses of Pooled Cross-Sections and Time-Series

The analysis of pooled cross-sectional and times-series data has been the method of choice of most sophisticated quantitative analyses of social policy over the last 20 years (see Hicks 1999; Huber and Stephens 2001a; Iversen and Cusack 2000). Pooled data involves measures arrayed across both time and space, and analysing these data helps to overcome some of the shortcomings of cross-sectional and time-series analyses separately. Pooled analyses can address variables acting over time, such as changes in partisan regimes, as well as temporally inert, structural variables, like policy regimes or political structural arrangements.

Pooled data analyses also solve small-N problems entailed by analyses of time-series of limited per-nation length and cross-sectional domains of limited numbers of nations (e.g. the approximately twenty advanced capitalist democracies). The solution is pooling time-series and cross-sections. In addition, pooling helps to illuminate stable differences among countries—as did early cross-sectional research—in addition to exploring the dynamic processes and changes in social spending efforts, the emphasis of time-series analyses. Key to this enterprise has been the excellent and voluminous data collected in the post-war period on these countries by various international organizations, especially the Organization for Economic Co-operation and Development (OECD) and the International Labour Organization (ILO). These data have been augmented by individual scholars (e.g. Huber and Stephens 2001a; Swank 2002). Although there are several problems with the estimation of these models, including over-time and spatial auto-regression, heterogeneous regression intercepts and slopes over time and/or space, and heterogeneous error variances across time and/or place, many means of addressing these estimation challenges are available (see Hicks 1993; Beck 2007; Plümper and Tröger 2004; Hicks and Freeman 2009).

Although data and analysis of welfare states have been largely confined to twenty or so long-standing, OECD democracies, impressive efforts have been made to extend data to Latin America (Huber et al. 2006; Brooks 2009) and beyond to East Asia and Eastern Europe (Haggard and Kaufman 2008). Moreover, studies have begun to address the complexities of transnational as well as sub-national federal contexts (Amenta and Halfman 2000; Obinger et al. 2005b).

In short, pooled regression analyses across rich democracies in post-World War II period have helped to answer many questions and to resolve debates about spending efforts in the periods of welfare state growth and retrenchment. Moreover, resolution of kindred debates is extending beyond the rich long-standing democracies to new parts of the world and transnational contexts.

To analyse statistically the adoption of programmes, as well as legislation regarding retrenchment, similar data have been used to predict nominal or qualitative outcomes, involving techniques falling under the rubric of 'event history analysis' (Usui 1994; Hicks 1999; Hicks and Zorn 2005; for overviews and technical treatments, see Allison 1974; Box-Steffensmeier and Jones 2004; Kleinbaum and Klein 2005a, 2005b). These analyses are often undertaken across all countries, notably addressing the issue of the adoption of policies outside the domain of rich capitalist democracies, filling gaps in knowledge. However, given their wide reach, these analyses are often beset with even greater problems of missing data in respect of potentially relevant measures.

CONCLUSION

Research on welfare states and social policy has addressed all manner of methods. Variability in the availability of forms of data has led to a kind of division of labour. Hard and systematic data suitable for quantitative studies existed only for the post-World War II periods of expansion and retrenchment, while less complete information of this sort was available for the periods of adoption, consolidation, and completion (Hicks 1999). Quantitative comparative researchers mainly analysed data from the 1960s and beyond, and comparative and historical researchers took charge of the first half of the century. There has been a great deal of interesting work as well, however, on the 'off-diagonal' cases, and these studies were often sites of innovation and spurs to analysis of the other variety (see Amenta 2003). Paul Pierson (1994), for instance, opened a new line of thinking and research on retrenchment, providing hypotheses later addressed by quantitative researchers. The quantitative paper by Collier and Messick (1975) cast doubt on the modernization thesis with respect to the adoption of social policy and spurred comparative and historical work, and work by Hicks et al. (1995) applied QCA analyses to policy adoption in the first half of the twentieth century.

The development of the area was accelerated by the open-minded methodological outlook of many prominent researchers. Few quantitative researchers derided the work of comparative and historical researchers as lacking in rigour. Few comparative and historical researchers saw the work of the quantitative scholars as simplistic and lacking in depth and validity. The tone was set early on, with Gaston Rimlinger (1971) employing the gold standard of quantitative studies, social spending 'effort', to situate his path-breaking comparative and historical investigations. The willingness and ability of researchers to work in different modes was key. Francis Castles, Gøsta Esping-Andersen, Alexander Hicks, Evelyne Huber, Torben Iversen, John Stephens, Theda Skocpol, and Duane Swank comprise some of the scholars proficient in one type of methodology, but willing or driven sometimes to employ others.

Given the various strengths and weaknesses of the different methodological approaches, as indicated above, it is useful for scholars to employ more than one. Scholars of social policy have combined methods and triangulated them, reaping advantages, while minimizing the disadvantages of any single approach. Studies have been able to address large questions about differences in timing or trajectories or outcomes in social policy, by examining a few cases or one case in a comparative context, by developing and tentatively appraising relatively complex arguments and by sometimes employing multiple and conjunctural causation, sometimes involving mechanisms of process. Standard quantitative techniques have difficulty in assessing these more complex questions, much as standard comparative and historical work can provide only rudimentary tests of more general hypotheses.

There have been many examples of syntheses and triangulation of methods in the welfare state literature. Evelyne Huber and John Stephens (2001a) address the rise of welfare states and efforts at retrenchment over the last decades with pooled time-series and cross-sectional regression analyses and detailed case histories of different types of highly developed welfare states in examining the development of social policy over long periods. The latter technique is used in order to get around the short-term biases in regression analyses and to closely examine critical periods of policy change. Other examples include work by scholars who employ different techniques on the same subject matter across different works (Skocpol 1992; Skocpol et al. 1993; Pampel and Williamson 1989; Amenta 1998; Amenta and Halfmann 2000).

These scholars have understood that different approaches had advantages and disadvantages, and exploited the advantages of each to allow greater progress than could be achieved by one or another approach. This outlook has helped advance the field tremendously. Preserving this outlook should bring still greater advances in the future, as both qualitative and quantitative approaches increase in sophistication.

CHAPTER 8

PUBLIC AND PRIVATE SOCIAL WELFARE

WILLEM ADEMA

PETER WHITEFORD

INTRODUCTION

IT has long been recognized that the objectives of the welfare state can be achieved through a range of different instruments. Titmuss (1976*b*) identified several different kinds of distributive mechanisms, arguing that it was not possible to understand the impact of social policy without taking these alternative approaches fully into account. He referred to the 'social division of welfare', including three main types of welfare: social welfare (the social services including cash benefits); fiscal welfare (welfare distributed directly or indirectly through the tax system); and occupational welfare (welfare provided as part of employment). This classification could be extended to include legal welfare (redistribution through the courts), and benefits and services provided by the voluntary sector and the informal sector (Rose 1981) as well as self-provision, but the main underlying idea was to look beyond conventional definitions of the welfare state, to identify the different patterns of redistribution provided through

Authors' note: the authors are indebted to Maxime Ladaique for statistical support. The views expressed in this chapter cannot be attributed to the OECD or its member governments; they are the responsibility of the authors alone.

alternative mechanisms, and to explain that different kinds of programmes (e.g. assistance provided either through tax credits or as cash transfers) can have similar effects in some cases, or offsetting effects in others (Sinfield 1978).

Despite this long-standing recognition of the 'social division of welfare' and further studies exploring the details of these provisions (Rein and Rainwater 1986; Hacker 2002, 2004a; Gilbert 2005), it remains the case that most analyses of social expenditure continue to be based on gross (before tax) public expenditure data. 'The prevailing wisdom is easy to summarize. The size of welfare states is measured in the literature by the share of gross domestic product (GDP) devoted to public social spending, which is sometimes referred to as a nation's welfare state effort' (Howard 2003).

However, a narrow focus on gross public spending can be misleading as this ignores the important role of the tax system, through which governments can: (1) claw back financial support through direct and indirect taxation of benefit income; (2) directly provide support to households (e.g. child tax credits); and (3) encourage individuals and companies to provide social support (e.g. through favourable tax treatment of private pension contributions and earnings on private fund assets or private health insurance coverage). Accounting for the impact of the tax system on budgetary allocations with a social purpose leads to indicators of net (after tax) public social expenditure.

The conventional emphasis on direct public spending also ignores other forms of public intervention, for example, when governments mandate employers to provide pension coverage or sickness insurance, or when governments regulate the conditions of private health insurance coverage (for example, by forbidding risk-related premiums). Furthermore, the private sector including individuals can also provide social benefits voluntarily which top-up government regulated provisions. Frequently these benefits are related to collective labour agreements and/or are subject to favourable tax treatment.

Overall, a comprehensive assessment of total welfare provisions means that it is necessary to capture the additions to and subtractions from public spending that are effected through the tax system, as well as the additional support provided through mandatory or voluntary private social spending. Such a comprehensive approach facilitates measuring the total share of an economy's domestic production that recipients of social benefits draw on: net total social expenditure (Adema and Einerhand 1998; Adema and Ladaique 2005, 2009; OECD 2007k).

Analysis of net total (public and private) social expenditure is of growing importance from a policy perspective (Pearson and Martin 2005). Some countries are searching for alternative means of securing social support other than through the public delivery system. For example, in the 1990s policy initiatives concerning the provision of sickness payments in the Netherlands and some Nordic countries involved a shift from public to private provision. In such cases, governments determine benefit entitlements but leave the provision to the private sector.

In addition, many reforms to pension systems, for example, involve changing pension structures or parameters to make them more similar to private sector provisions, either through the replacement or supplementation of defined benefit pension systems with defined contribution systems or 'notional defined contribution' systems (Queisser et al. 2007). Part of the rationale for these reforms is that economic incentives are better enhanced under systems that more closely mimic private sector arrangements (Disney 2004). However, the main concern with these reform proposals is that they will have undesirable distributional outcomes, and the general argument is that universal social support systems that are tax-financed are more redistributive than the combination of private provision and targeted public income support (Korpi and Palme 1998).

This chapter contributes to the discussion of public and private social provisions by drawing together the most up-to-date information on these different ways of providing social benefits. It presents the most recent estimates of net social expenditure, with new estimates taking the analysis up to 2005. The chapter shows that conventional estimates of gross public spending differ significantly from estimates of net public spending and net total social expenditure, with the results that countries are incorrectly ranked in terms of total social welfare effort and differences between countries are incorrectly measured.

Just as importantly, the fact that total social welfare support is incorrectly measured implies that the outcomes of welfare state support may also be incorrectly measured. Thus, apart from identifying the impact of this broader framework on estimates of the size of the welfare state in different countries, the main objectives of the chapter are to consider the implications of this more comprehensive definition of welfare state effort for analysis of the distributional impact of the welfare state and for an assessment of the efficiency and incentive effects of different welfare state arrangements.

WHAT IS SOCIAL SPENDING?

The OECD (2008g) defines social expenditure as follows:

> The provision by public and private institutions of benefits to, and financial contributions targeted at, households and individuals in order to provide support during circumstances which adversely affect their welfare, provided that the provision of the benefits and financial contributions constitutes neither a direct payment for a particular good or service nor an individual contract or transfer.[1]

---

[1] This social expenditure definition only covers benefits provided by institutions, not transfers among households even though they may be of a social nature. Also, social expenditure does not include remuneration for work, as it does not include payments in return for the simultaneous provision of services of equivalent value. Employer costs such as allowances towards transport, holiday pay, or severance payments before the standard retirement are therefore not included here.

Spending on social purposes towards circumstances that adversely affect welfare include *old-age*—pensions, and home-help and residential services for the elderly; *survivors*—pensions and funeral payments; *incapacity-related benefits*—disability benefits and services, employee sickness payments; *health*—spending on in- and out-patient care, medical goods, and prevention; *family*—child allowances and credits, childcare support, income support during leave, sole parent payments; *active labour market policies*—employment services, training, youth measures, subsidized employment, employment measures for the disabled; *unemployment*—unemployment compensation, early retirement for labour market reasons; *housing*—housing allowances and rent subsidies; and, *other contingencies*, other support measures as non-categorical cash benefits to low-income households, or support programmes for substance abusers, legal aid, etc.[2] There is no international agreement on whether marriage support is a social policy objective or not, and fiscal support towards married couples is not included, though such support can be substantial, and in some countries married couples are viewed as the appropriate basic economic unit for taxation (OECD 2006a).

As noted, social benefits to households and individuals can be publicly or privately provided. They are considered 'public' when relevant financial flows are controlled by general government (that is central, state, and local governments, including social security funds). Thus, benefits (partly) financed out of social security contributions paid by employers to social security funds are within the public sphere. Also in line with the National Accounts (SNA 1993: para 8.63), the *OECD Social Expenditure database* (SOCX) records pensions paid to former civil servants through autonomous funds as a private spending item in Australia (partially[3]), Canada, Denmark, the Netherlands, Sweden, and the United Kingdom.

All social benefits *not* provided by general government are considered 'private'. Private social benefits can be categorized in two broad groups:

1. Mandatory private social benefits, including legally stipulated employment-related incapacity-related cash transfers, such as sickness, disability and occupational injury benefits (recorded in Australia, Austria, Denmark, Finland, Germany, Iceland, Korea, the Netherlands, Norway, Slovak Republic, Sweden, the United Kingdom, and the United States in some of the separate states); mandatory employer-provided retirement allowances (severance payments towards retirement, e.g. Italy and Korea); and pensions derived from mandatory (individual and/or employer) contributions, e.g. Switzerland).

---

[2] Although data is broadly compatible and generally reclassifiable, the categorization of social support differs across international organizations. For example, the European System of Social Protection Statistics uses 7 functions (Eurostat 1996) while the Social Security Inquiry uses 11 functions (ILO 2005).

[3] The Australian pension arrangements for former civil servants constitute a hybrid of public and private components. The relevant pension payment is a defined benefit scheme which is guaranteed by the government and thus classified as public. In contrast, the lump-sum payment which many civil servants take on retirement is based on their compulsory contributions and interest rates; relevant spending is grouped under mandatory private social expenditure for Australia.

2. Voluntary private social expenditure, as, for example, social services provided by NGOs, employer-provided (perhaps on basis of a collective agreement) income support during child-related leave or sickness, and pensions derived from employer contributions (in many OECD countries) or fiscally advantaged individual contributions (Individual Retirement Accounts in the United States).

Expenditure programmes are considered 'social' if participation is compulsory, or if entitlements involve interpersonal redistribution of resources. Public social services, social insurance, and social assistance benefits are either financed through general taxation or social security contributions, and therefore involve the redistribution of resources across the population in general or within population groups (e.g. all members of a sickness insurance fund). Many private benefits are provided under the influence of government actions. Indeed, inter-personal redistribution in private programmes is often induced by government legislation (e.g. through forcing insurance companies to have one price for the same policy for both sick and healthy people), or, as in many OECD countries, through favourable tax treatment to stimulate take-up of private pensions. Governments sometimes also influence the collective bargaining process that may lead to employer-provided support for workers during sickness or child-related leave periods or for childcare support (OECD 2007b). Government intervention introduces and/or enhances redistribution among population groups participating in private programmes which leads to a high degree of similarity between legally-stipulated private arrangements and tax-advantaged plans.

What Is not Included in these International Comparisons?

There are various programmes and policies that may well perform a social function but are nonetheless not included in comprehensive international comparisons of social effort. For example, life insurance saving and/or general saving are not included, although such programmes can be tax-advantaged and be used towards retirement, survivor, and/or accident insurance. However, the extent to which this is the case or whether life insurance policies are merely used in association with home-ownership and mortgages is not known.

International comparisons of housing support (see Chapter 33) are also not without difficulty. Data are available on residential support for the elderly and disabled and on rent subsidies for low-income households, but information on mortgage relief for low-income households, while similar in nature, is not available on a cross-national basis.

Additionally, local governments and private agents as non-government organizations and employers may have limited incentives to report their social support outlays to central government or another central recording unit. Hence, the quality of data on spending by such agencies is relatively low. For example, it is unclear to what extent employers provide additional income support during parental leave periods. Over the years the quality and comparability of spending data on some (local and/or non-commercial) social services, such as childcare and early years supports, has improved notably, but much remains to be done to further improve the quality of data on social and health services. Moreover, if good overall expenditure data is available it is not always possible to identify relevant sub-components. For example, expenditure data on pensions paid by private pension funds in Switzerland is available, but it is not known to what extent such payments are based on past mandatory and/or voluntary pension contributions, so a full disaggregation cannot be made.

SOCIAL SUPPORT ACROSS COUNTRIES

In 2005, gross public social expenditure—the conventional measure of 'welfare state effort' in international comparison—averaged 20.5 per cent of GDP across OECD countries (Figure 8.1), and 23.3 per cent among the nineteen countries that belonged to both the EU and the OECD. Social spending to GDP ratios vary from highs of 29 per cent in France and Sweden to lows of around 7 per cent in Korea and Mexico. On average across the OECD, the public social spending to GDP ratio increased from 16 to just over 20 per cent over the 1980 to 2005 period. Public social spending to GDP ratios increased most significantly in the early 1980s, early 1990s and, again at the beginning of this millennium. Public spending to GDP ratios can be expected to increase again in 2009 following the economic slowdown.

In general, spending on cash benefits (11.6 per cent of GDP) is about 40 per cent higher than spending on health and social services (8.4 per cent of GDP). Public pension transfers to the retired population and survivors (7.2 per cent of GDP) and public spending on health care services (6.2 per cent of GDP) are the largest spending items, but with a standard deviation of 1.2 on health spending and of 3.4 for pension transfers, the variation in pension spending is much larger. Indeed, public spending on old age and survivor pensions account for less than 4 per cent of GDP in Australia, Iceland, Ireland, Korea, Mexico, and Turkey, but more than 10 per cent of GDP in Germany, Greece, Poland, and Portugal, over 12 per cent in Austria and France, and is highest in Italy at 14 per cent. By comparison, public spending on income transfers to the working-age population is on average considerably lower across the OECD at just over 4.4 per cent of GDP in 2005, of which spending on unemployment benefits was 1 per cent of GDP.

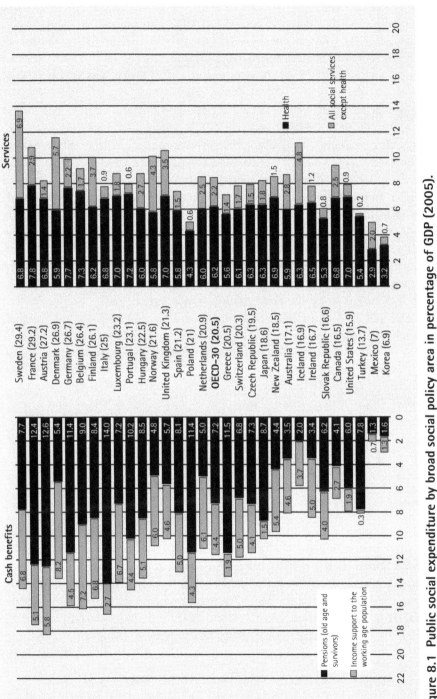

Figure 8.1 Public social expenditure by broad social policy area in percentage of GDP (2005).

Note: Countries are ranked by decreasing order of public social expenditure as a percentage of GDP. Spending on Active Labour Market Programmes (ALMPs) cannot be disaggregated by cash services fiscal support; but the aggregate is included in total public spending (shown in brackets). 2004 data for Portugal.

Source: OECD 2008a.

The importance of private social protection arrangements varies considerably across countries: at over 10 per cent of GDP gross private spending was highest in the US in 2005, and at about 7–8 per cent of GDP also high in the Netherlands, Switzerland, and the UK. On average across the OECD and the EU-15, the role of private social spending is more restricted at around 2.75 per cent of GDP, with its role being most limited in Eastern European countries, Mexico, and Turkey (OECD 2008g).

Unlike public spending trends, private social expenditure to GDP trends do not seem to be responsive to the business cycle, but have increased at a steady pace since 1980. This also confounds the notion that private protection is simply replacing public coverage (Caminada and Goudswaard 2005), or vice versa. Certainly, reductions in the generosity of public incapacity-related income support and increased employer's responsibility for the provision of sickness benefits in the Netherlands and some Nordic countries contributed to an increase in private spending during the 1990s, but the overall impact was limited. Instead, the ageing of populations, the increased prosperity which allowed increased coverage of private pension saving, and the maturing of private pension programmes contribute to a steady increase in private spending. The high and increasing level of private spending in the United States is also explained by the large role of private social health coverage, in the absence of a public health insurance system with universal coverage for workers. In 2005, voluntary private social health expenditure amounted to nearly 6 per cent of GDP, making the total United States health care system the most expensive in the OECD.

THE EFFECTS OF THE TAX SYSTEM
ON SOCIAL EFFORT

The tax system plays an important role in social policy. Taxation (including social security contributions) is used to finance social support, and the manner in which this is done influences the redistributive effects of tax/benefit systems (see below). However, tax systems are also used to claw back social support by taxing transfers payments to and consumption by benefit recipients. The extent to which this occurs varies hugely across countries, and therefore affects international comparisons of social support.[4] For example, depending on household composition and the

---

[4] There is a wide range of measurement and methodological issues involved in the estimation of the magnitude of the effect of the tax system on social effort. In general, the quality of estimates of the size of taxation of benefit income and fiscal support for economic agents (as with private social spending) is considered lower than the quality of information on social spending by central government. Adema and Ladaique (2005, 2009) discuss relevant methodological and measurement issues in detail.

presence of dependents, a claimant of unemployment insurance benefits in Sweden can pay about one-third of her benefit income in tax, while unemployment benefit income is tax-free in several OECD countries, including Austria, the Czech Republic, Germany, Japan, Korea, and the Slovak Republic.

Apart from variation across countries, different benefits are also taxed differently. Child benefits, social assistance, and housing support are generally not taxed across the OECD; pensions and income support payments during periods of child-related leave, sickness, and invalidity are generally part of taxable income, although often taxed at a reduced rate (OECD 2007j).

At around 4 per cent of GDP, direct taxation of benefit income is particularly high in some high-spending welfare states such as Denmark and Sweden, while the OECD average is at 1.2 per cent. Direct tax on public benefit income is less than 0.5 per cent of GDP in Australia, Canada, the Czech Republic, Ireland, Japan, Mexico, Portugal, the Slovak Republic, the United Kingdom, and the United States. As the role of private social spending is generally limited, the 'income tax over private spending to GDP ratio' tends to be small. With the substantial role of private pensions, direct tax paid over private transfers is highest in the Netherlands at 1.3 per cent of GDP and at 0.5 per cent of GDP also substantial in Canada, the United Kingdom, and the United States, with 'tax-to-private-spending ratios' being highest in Iceland and Sweden.

Taxation of consumption out of benefit income is lowest in non-European OECD countries, since indirect tax rates are lower. Indirect taxation levied on consumption of benefit income is less than 0.5 per cent of GDP in Korea, Mexico, and the United States. The OECD average is close to 1.7 per cent of GDP, but indirect tax paid over public benefit income was 2.5 per cent of GDP or more in Austria, Denmark, Finland, France, and Luxembourg. In non-European countries where indirect taxation is relatively limited, gross spending levels can also be relatively low to generate the same net income level for benefit recipients in countries with high indirect tax rates.

The tax system can be used to directly provide social support to clients, and this delivery channel is often used to support families with children in both European and non-European OECD countries. Such fiscal support is often similar to cash support, and sometimes fiscal and cash transfers are part of one the same financial support programme. For example, in Germany in 2005, tax relief for children amounted to EUR 36.5 billion of which EUR 19.4 was off-set against tax liabilities and EUR 17.1 billion paid out in transfer income. Similarly, in 2005, the cost of the Earned Income Tax Credit in the United States amounted to USD 36.9 billion, of which USD 4.9 billion off-setting tax liabilities of clients and USD 32.0 billion in cash payments. In many OECD countries, support for families with children is also embedded in the tax unit. Again support for married couples is not considered as social across the OECD, but fiscal support towards children is, and, for example, favourable tax treatment through a variety of fiscal measures (including the 'Quotient Familial') in France amounted to EUR 13.3 billion in 2005. In all, public spending on family benefits was just over 2 per cent of GDP on average in 2005, of which on average about 10 per cent was delivered through tax systems across the OECD. The role of the tax system in providing family support was most pronounced in France, Germany, and the United States with fiscal benefits towards families amounting to just below 1 per cent of GDP.

The tax system is also used to encourage and subsidize the take-up of private social protection arrangements. In countries where private pension coverage is substantial, the value of relevant tax breaks is also considerable (Adema and Einerhand 1998).[5] Otherwise, tax breaks for current private protection arrangements include favourable treatment of contributions to and income of NGOs, but most substantially include fiscal support towards private health plans in Germany and, most importantly, the United States. In general, tax breaks are least important in countries with relatively high direct tax levies: Denmark, Finland, Iceland and Sweden, and most important at about 1.5 per cent of GDP in Germany and the United States.

THE EFFECT OF TAXATION AND PRIVATE SPENDING ON LEVELS OF SOCIAL EFFORT ACROSS COUNTRIES

In the United States (and also Mexico and Korea), gross public spending is actually lower than net public spending, because they tax benefit income at very low rates, but they use their tax system to deliver social support directly or to subsidize indirectly its private provision. However, in most countries, governments claw back more money through direct and indirect taxation of public transfer income than they award in tax advantages for social purposes (Table 8.1). Thus, across OECD countries net public social expenditure to GDP ratios are on average 2.4 percentage points below gross social spending to GDP ratios; this difference is highest in Denmark and Sweden at around 7 per cent of GDP.

Summing together all public and private social benefits and differences in relevant average tax rates facilitates the identification of the proportion of an economy's domestic production to which recipients of social benefits can lay claim: *net total (public and private) social expenditure*. This proportion is highest at 29 per cent of GDP in France, followed closely by Belgium, and Germany at 27 per cent of GDP. Recipients of social benefits in Austria, Italy, the Netherlands, Sweden, the United Kingdom, and the United States all claim between 23 and 26 per cent of the economy's domestic production. The similarity of net spending levels is driven by including private social spending, particularly in the US, *and* the relatively high level

---

[5] Tax breaks for pensions include tax exemptions for contributions to private pensions, and tax relief for investment income of capitalized pension funds. Because of the complexities of calculating the value of these tax reliefs that are given at three different stages over the saving-period, there is no cross-nationally comparable data set available on the value of tax breaks towards pensions.

Table 8.1 From gross to net social spending (2005)

	Social expenditure in percentage of GDP at market prices, 2005[a]																										
	Australia	Austria	Belgium	Canada	Czech Republic	Denmark	Finland	France	Germany	Iceland	Ireland	Italy	Japan	Korea	Luxembourg	Mexico	Netherlands	New Zealand	Norway	Poland	Portugal	Slovak Republic	Spain	Sweden	United Kingdom	United States	OECD-26
1G Gross public social expenditure	17.1	27.2	26.4	16.5	19.5	26.9	24.0	29.2	26.7	16.9	16.7	25.0	17.7	6.9	23.2	7.0	20.9	18.5	21.6	21.0	22.9	16.6	21.2	29.4	21.3	15.9	20.6
- Direct taxes and social contributions	0.2	2.4	1.4	0.3	0.0	4.0	2.6	1.4	1.4	0.7	0.2	1.9	0.2	0.0	0.8	0.0	2.3	1.3	1.8	1.5	0.8	0.0	1.2	4.0	0.2	0.5	1.2
- Indirect taxes (on cash benefits)	0.8	2.6	2.3	0.7	2.0	2.7	2.6	2.5	1.9	1.1	1.8	1.8	0.6	0.4	3.0	0.1	1.6	1.3	2.1	2.4	2.3	1.8	1.6	2.3	1.4	0.3	1.7
+ Net TBSPs (not including pensions)	0.4	0.0	0.4	1.1	0.5	0.0	0.0	0.9	1.7	0.0	0.4	0.2	0.7	0.5	0.0	1.4	0.7	0.1	0.1	0.1	0.8	0.1	0.4	0.0	0.4	2.0	0.5
1N Net current public soc. exp.	16.5	22.2	23.1	16.6	18.0	20.2	18.8	26.2	25.1	15.1	15.2	21.5	17.6	7.0	19.4	8.2	17.7	16.0	17.9	17.2	20.8	14.9	18.9	23.1	20.1	17.1	18.2
2G Gross mandatory private soc. exp.	1.1	0.9	0.0	0.0	0.2	0.2	0.0	0.4	1.1	1.5	0.0	1.5	0.7	0.6	0.2	0.0	0.7	0.0	1.3	0.0	0.4	0.2	0.0	0.4	0.8	0.3	0.5
- Direct taxes and social contributions	0.1	0.3	0.0	0.0	0.0	0.1	0.0	0.0	0.4	0.2	0.0	0.2	0.0	0.0	0.0	0.0	0.2	0.0	0.3	0.0	0.0	0.0	0.0	0.1	0.0	0.0	0.0
- Indirect taxes	0.1	0.1	0.0	0.0	0.0	0.0	0.0	0.0	0.1	0.3	0.0	0.2	0.0	0.1	0.0	0.0	0.1	0.0	0.2	0.0	0.1	0.0	0.0	0.1	0.1	0.0	0.0
2N Net current mand. private soc. exp.	0.8	0.5	0.0	0.0	0.2	0.1	0.0	0.3	0.6	1.0	0.0	1.2	0.7	0.5	0.2	0.0	0.4	0.0	0.7	0.0	0.3	0.2	0.0	0.2	0.7	0.3	0.3
3G Gross voluntary private soc. exp.	2.6	1.0	4.5	5.5	0.1	2.4	1.1	2.6	1.9	3.4	1.3	0.6	2.8	1.8	0.9	0.2	7.6	0.4	0.8	0.0	0.4	0.8	0.5	2.4	6.3	9.8	2.4
- Direct taxes and social contributions	0.2	0.1	0.3	0.8	0.0	0.8	0.2	0.0	0.2	0.5	0.1	0.0	0.1	0.0	0.0	0.0	1.4	0.0	0.2	0.0	0.0	0.0	0.0	0.5	0.4	0.5	0.0

(continued)

Table 8.1 Continued

Social expenditure in percentage of GDP at market prices, 2005[a]

	Australia	Austria	Belgium	Canada	Czech Republic	Denmark	Finland	France	Germany	Iceland	Ireland	Italy	Japan	Korea	Luxembourg	Mexico	Netherlands	New Zealand	Norway	Poland	Portugal	Slovak Republic	Spain	Sweden	United Kingdom	United States	OECD-26
– Indirect taxes	0.2	0.1	0.6	0.4	0.0	0.4	0.2	0.1	0.1	0.6	0.2	0.0	0.2	0.0	0.1	0.0	0.8	0.0	0.1	0.0	0.0	0.1	0.0	0.4	0.6	0.2	0.0
3N Net current vol. private soc. exp.	2.2	0.8	3.6	4.4	0.1	1.2	0.7	2.5	1.6	2.3	1.1	0.5	2.5	1.8	0.7	0.2	5.5	0.4	0.5	0.0	0.4	0.7	0.5	1.5	5.2	9.1	1.9
4N Net current private soc. exp. [2N+3N]	3.1	1.4	3.6	4.4	0.3	1.3	0.7	2.8	2.2	3.3	1.1	1.7	3.2	2.4	0.9	0.2	5.9	0.4	1.2	0.0	0.8	0.9	0.5	1.7	5.9	9.4	0.0
5N Net total social expenditure[b]	19.3	23.5	26.8	20.7	18.2	21.6	19.5	29.0	27.0	18.4	16.1	23.1	20.7	9.4	20.3	8.4	23.3	16.4	19.1	17.2	21.4	15.7	19.1	24.8	25.9	25.3	20.4
Memorandum item																											
TBSPs towards pensions[c]	1.9	0.1	0.2	1.7	0.1	–	0.1	0.0	0.9	1.0	1.4	0.0	0.6	–	–	0.1	–	–	0.6	0.6	0.1	0.2	0.3	0.0	1.2	0.8	0.0
Average indirect tax rate	9.8	16.2	15.1	10.7	17.3	25.9	20.8	14.9	13.0	21.6	21.0	12.1	6.6	12.6	22.3	6.3	17.2	15.3	22.5	16.7	16.8	17.0	13.0	20.5	13.3	4.3	15.5

Notes:

a) Social expenditure data for Portugal 2005 concern estimates; – cell with no information.

b) In order to avoid double counting, the value of TBSPs towards 'current' private social benefits has been ignored for the calculation of net total social expenditure.

c) Because of conceptual issues and gaps in data availability, tax breaks towards old-age pensions are shown in the table as a memorandum item.

Source: Adema and Ladaique 2009: 48.

of direct and indirect taxation on income transfers in European countries vis-à-vis non-European countries.

In some countries, spending levels are contained because of the strong element of targeting in the distribution of social support. With at least 15 per cent of public social spending awarded subject to income-testing (Adema and Ladaique 2009), social protection systems in Ireland, New Zealand, Canada, and particularly in Australia (at 40 per cent of all public social spending), contain a strong element of targeting to low-income households. In these countries, public spending is around 3 percentage points below the OECD average, which in Australia and Canada at least is compensated through private pension systems (this may play a significant role in Ireland as well (Adema and Einerhand 1998), but reliable spending data are not available for recent years).

Low public social spending countries (around 20 per cent of GDP or less) levy little direct tax on benefit income (Australia, the Czech Republic, Canada, Ireland, Japan, Korea, Mexico, Portugal, the Slovak Republic, and the United States), but the opposite does not always hold true. In particular France and Germany are high social spending countries with a relatively limited direct tax burden (around 1 per cent of GDP) compared to most other European countries, which contributes to these two countries having the highest level of net total social expenditure as a percentage of GDP. Of the five countries with the highest level of direct and indirect taxation of benefit income (Austria, Denmark, Finland, Norway, and Sweden), the Scandinavian tax/benefit systems generate strong redistribution of public resources through tax-financing of social services for the elderly and the working population (Figure 8.1). By contrast the Austrian system, with its strong emphasis on transfers for those in retirement (rather than service support), is less redistributive in nature.

DIFFERENCES IN THE IMPACT OF PRIVATE AND PUBLIC SOCIAL SPENDING: EFFICIENCY AND EQUITY IMPLICATIONS

Given this apparent complementarity between public and private spending, do differences in public and private provision matter? This question comes to the heart of other major debates about the effects of welfare state provisions. On the one side, there are arguments that high levels of welfare state spending (and taxing to finance this spending) create inefficiencies that reduce work effort and saving. On the other side, there are arguments that high levels of welfare state spending are associated with lower levels of inequality and poverty, and that even if this reduces incentives to work and save—propositions that are seen as debatable—that this may well be a price worth paying for these better distributional outcomes.

However, the discussion above shows that the conventional measures of welfare state effort are seriously misleading—total net public and private social expenditure shows much less dispersion than gross public spending, tax effects, or private social spending. If welfare state effort is mismeasured is it possible that welfare state effects and outcomes are also mismeasured? Do variations in the mix of public and private provision matter as much for incentives and equity as they do for measured levels of spending?

The literature on the incentive effects of welfare states is vast, but one view is that of Schuknecht and Tanzi (2005: 9), who argue that

> high levels of public spending create inefficiencies on the tax side—because they require higher tax rates—and on the expenditure side—because they require large bureaucracies, and because, from the individual citizen's point of view, government services often have a zero (or at least a very low) price thus stimulating greater demand for them. Finally, high public spending may lead to macroeconomic difficulties when it is partly financed by fiscal deficits.

In contrast, Lindert (2005: 1) argues that

> OECD experience since 1980 does not show any negative effect of larger tax-financed transfers on national product. There are good reasons for this 'free lunch puzzle.' High budget welfare states feature a tax mix that is more pro-growth than the tax mixes of low budget America, Japan, and Switzerland. The high-budget states also have more efficient health care, better support for child care and women's careers, and other features that mitigate the negative incentives on transfer recipients.

It is sometimes argued that private provisions can have better implications for incentives to work and save than public provisions (Disney 2004), leading to government interest in reforming public provisions to make them more like private provisions, most notably in regard to pensions, but also sickness coverage. However, Disney also points out that contributions to public pension programmes differ from other taxes levied on households to the extent that participants perceive contributions as giving them a claim to future pension benefits.

> To the extent that pension contributions are perceived as giving individuals rights to future pensions, the behavioural reaction of programme participants to contributions will differ from their reactions to other taxes. In fact, they might regard pension contributions as providing an opportunity for retirement saving, in which case contributions should not be deducted from households' earnings, and should not be included in the tax wedge. An issue for programme design therefore arises: if pension programmes can be designed explicitly to look like retirement saving programmes, the potentially adverse impact of higher pension contributions on employment might be alleviated. (Disney 2004: 270)

Disney shows that the diversity of programme design can be illustrated by comparing two types of programme. At one extreme the Swedish public pension reform in 1998 and the Italian pension reform in 1995 tried to make their public pension programmes look more like a private retirement saving system by linking individual pension entitlements very closely and explicitly to actual contributions paid. At the other extreme, Australian public pensions are income-tested and financed out of general taxation, and participants seem to have no expectation of receiving specific benefits in return for their tax payments during the working lifetime. Disney argues that these design features, as well as the overall costs of the programme, matter for incentives. He estimates what he calls the redistributive and actuarial shares of public pension provision, finding that there appears to be a trade-off between the level of contributions (spending) and the degree of redistribution. For a sample of twenty-two countries he finds that the effective contribution rates in the 1990s range between 15 per cent in Australia and 58 per cent in Greece, with Australia having the lowest effective contribution rate and the highest redistributive share, around 38 per cent of the effective contribution rate. In contrast, countries like Portugal, Luxembourg, and Greece have much higher contribution rates but very limited redistribution (effective tax rates of around 5 per cent).

Disney's results reveal robust evidence that when public pension programme contributions are broken down into a tax component and a savings component, the tax component of the payroll contribution reduces economic activity rates among women while a higher retirement saving component has the opposite effect. He finds little evidence that average tax rates, however constructed, have any adverse impact on the economic activity rates of men.

Disney's (2004) results can be seen as confirming Lindert's (2005) arguments—the design of welfare states matters for outcomes. These arguments can be put another way: the reason why some high spending welfare states have less adverse implications for incentives than expected is that they are structured like private provision—there is a stronger association between what people put into the welfare state and what they get out from the welfare state than in some low spending but more progressive countries. In effect, high spending welfare states incorporate private spending design features within their public systems. Lower spending welfare states tend to separate public and private provision.

What are the implications of these arguments for equity outcomes? As with studies of the incentive effects of welfare states, there is a vast literature analysing the distributional outcomes of welfare state design. One of the best known of recent studies is that of Korpi and Palme, who argue that welfare states that provide high income earners with clearly earnings-related benefits within encompassing social insurance institutions reduce inequality and poverty more efficiently than by flat-rate or targeted benefits. They note:

> The traditional arguments in favor of low-income targeting and flat-rate benefits have focused exclusively on the distribution of the money actually transferred and have overlooked three basic circumstances. One is that the size of redistributive budgets is not necessarily fixed but tends to depend on the type of welfare state institutions in a country. A second factor is that there tends to be a tradeoff between the extent of low-income targeting and the size of redistributive budgets. The third circumstance of importance here is that ... the outcomes of market-dominated distribution tend to be even more unequal than those found in earnings-related social insurance programs. Recognition of these factors helps us understand what we can call the Paradox of Redistribution: *The more we target benefits at the poor only and the more concerned we are with creating equality via equal public transfers to all, the less likely we are to reduce poverty and inequality.* (Emphasis in original, 1998: 36)

Relatively few studies have considered the implication of private social provision for distributional outcomes; exceptions include Caminada and Goudswaard (2005) and Castles and Obinger (2007). Both of these studies use cross-country regression analysis to consider the relationship between variables such as private social spending, taxes paid on benefits and distributional outcomes. Caminada and Goudswaard, for example, find

> a negative relationship between net public social expenditure and income inequality, and a positive relationship between net private social expenditure and income inequality. The impact of total expenditures (public and private) on income inequality across 16 wealthy countries appears to be statistically trivial. As a result, changes in the public/private mix in the provision of social protection may indeed affect the redistributive impact of the welfare state. (2005: 187)

The problem with the conclusions of both Caminada and Goudswaard (2005) and Castles and Obinger (2007) is that like much of the social policy literature they do not actually take account of the implications of private welfare provision for distributional outcomes. Put another way, their measure of distributional impacts is not necessarily accurate.

Consider Table 8.2 which sets out the standard accounting framework used to analyse the redistributive effects of the welfare state (OECD 2008a). In the framework,

Table 8.2 The income accounting framework

Income component	Adjustment	Equivalized income component
Wages and salaries + Self-employment income + Property income =		
1. Factor income + Occupational and private pensions =	equivalence scales	= Equivalent factor income
2. Market income + Social security cash benefits (universal, income-related, contributory) + Private transfers + Other cash income =	equivalence scales	= Equivalent market income
3. Gross income - Income tax (and employee social security contributions) =	equivalence scales	= Equivalent gross income
4. Cash disposable income	equivalence scales	= Equivalent cash disposable income

Source: Adapted from O'Higgins et al. 1990: 30–1.

income from wages and salaries, self-employment, and property sum to 'factor in-come'; factor income plus occupational and private pensions gives 'market income'; market income plus public and private transfers, as well as other types of cash income, produces 'gross income'; finally, gross income minus personal income taxes and workers' social security contributions gives 'cash disposable income'. This last concept, when adjusted to reflect differences in household needs through an equivalence scale, gives 'equivalized disposable income'—the main measure of household well-being used in virtually all studies of income redistribution. The approach set out in the table is an accounting framework that allows different components of income to be related to each other and suitable aggregates to be derived, but this framework is both linear and static.

The framework can be used to construct a number of measures of the redistributive impact of social security and taxation policies. With micro-data, the framework can be applied to each household's income to produce the four income measures identified in Table 8.2. These unit records can then be aggregated and analysed to produce measures of distribution and redistribution across the population as a whole. In particular, the degree of redistribution effected by taxes or social security transfers can be calculated by comparing income shares or other measures such as Gini coefficients at different stages in the process outlined in the table. For example, the impact of cash transfers can be evaluated by comparing the difference between measures of inequality or poverty on the basis of market income (Stage 2) and on the basis of gross income (Stage 3), while the effects of taxes can be calculated by comparing measures of gross and disposable incomes (Stage 4).

There are a number of significant components of income missing from this framework. What are included are the direct cash benefits of government spending and some of the taxes used to finance government spending (income taxes and employee payroll taxes). The taxes paid on welfare payments are included as part of observed direct taxes, while some tax expenditures (for example, payments for children through the tax system) are also included if not measured separately.

But the standard framework does not include employer social security contributions—which are insignificant or non-existent in Australia, Denmark, and New Zealand but account for more than 25 per cent of total tax revenue in France and the Czech Republic. Given that these contributions actually pay for a large part of social security spending in many countries, an assessment of their distributional impact is warranted.

The incidence of employer contributions is subject to debate, but one straightforward approach is to assume they are incident on wages. At the first stage this would appear to imply that employer contributions should be added at all stages of the framework. Inclusion of employer social security contributions in factor and market income and household taxes would change both factor market-income inequality and therefore measures of the effectiveness of different tax-transfer systems (Mitchell 1991), since the difference between factor incomes and disposable incomes would be greater than conventionally measured.

But should all taxes financing social benefits be included as taxes that reduce disposable incomes? The argument of Disney (2004) about the incentive effects of different pension systems is equally relevant here. If parts of the contributions towards public provisions are not taxes but are seen as equivalent to private savings should they be deducted from incomes?

There is a related complication. The standard framework includes private and occupational pensions in the market income of households. But apparently nobody pays for them—neither employees nor employers. The standard approach (and the SNA conventions) treats contributions to government pensions as a tax that finances the retirement pensions paid out in the same year, while contributions to private pensions are effectively treated as a form of private consumption, and employer contributions to (public and) private pensions are simply outside the scope of household surveys.

Similarly, publicly funded sickness benefits are treated as a part of the redistributive activity of the welfare state, while employer-provided sickness pay is treated as part of the wage package. While health care spending is not usually taken into account in the standard analysis of the impact of cash transfers, similar issues arise. Fiscal incidence studies of the broader impact of the welfare state normally include government spending, but in a number of countries—most notably the United States—occupationally funded health care is nearly as important as government spending.

These factors affect international comparisons of income distribution in several ways that parallel the effects on measures of welfare effort and on incentive effects. For example, countries with earnings-related social security systems will look more equal because a higher proportion of the savings that well-off individuals make for retirement are made through taxes. Conversely, where flat-rate or means-tested benefits are provided, a higher proportion of savings for retirement are made through occupational and private pension contributions, which are not usually taken into account. (These biases can be addressed in several ways. For example, the United Kingdom *Households below Average Income* statistics subtract occupational pension contributions from disposable income, on the basis that these contributions do not enhance current living standards.) As far as we are aware there are no studies that model the impact of the benefits and the costs of occupational welfare on income distribution. Overcoming this bias requires broadening the framework used to assess household well-being and distributive outcomes.

In summary, just as conventional measures of public spending are incomplete measures of welfare state effort, the incentive and distributional effects of private and occupational welfare are usually not included in assessments of welfare state outcomes. Different social security systems produce different distributions of public and private pension rights, and the incomplete treatment of this redistributive activity may bias cross-country comparisons of income distribution. The implication of this is that just as comprehensive measures of welfare state effort suggest greater similarities in real spending levels, real outcomes will be more similar than conventionally measured.

....

CHAPTER 9

FAMILIES VERSUS STATE AND MARKET

....

MARY DALY

INTRODUCTION

....

THE organization of family life and the relationship between the family, the state, and the market vary profoundly within and across national settings. In some countries, the particularity of family is uppermost with family seen as distinct from the state and public life. More liberal perspectives privilege family privacy and generally eschew intervention in the family but, rather than setting up an elaborate architecture for this purpose, the preference is to leave family to its own devices. In yet another framing of the relationship, family is more diffuse, not locked away in its own domain, but interlinking closely with a host of institutions. These are patterns set by history. Until relatively recently, governments were able to take for granted the existence of the traditional family, in terms of both its form and the gendered contributions of earnings and care made by the husband/father and the wife/mother. However, during the last thirty years family change has become a major factor driving policy change. This piece focuses mainly on the responses of states and in particular on how philosophies and practices are institutionalized in social policies in different countries and how social policies are acting as change agents in relation to family functioning and family relationships.

The primary objective is to understand family as an object of on the one hand state policy and on the other hand market functioning in a range of countries today.

This is accomplished through an analysis of the expansion and reform of family-related policies over the last ten years and a consideration of how these are to be explained, especially in light of the classical approaches to the family. The empirical line of analysis is to identify emerging policy approaches to the inter-relations between family, state, and market, in their own right as they evolve in particular countries and in light, of a seeming consensus on the part of the European Union (EU) and the Organization for Economic Co-operation and Development (OECD) about the appropriate focus and orientation of family and work life today. Comparison is to the fore. A case can be made for over-sampling the so-called 'liberal', non-European countries given both the literature's strong European focus and liberalism's towering influence in the age of globalization. Hence, Australia and United States are included along with France, Germany, Sweden, and the United Kingdom. Most of the variation in policy approaches to the family is actually accounted for by these six countries.

The chapter proceeds in four steps. The first introduces the field, outlining the main features of family policy as it has developed over time and the insights of scholarship. Following this, the piece moves on to consider the main contours of current reform, especially in light of the model of family policy being promoted by the EU and the OECD. The third section considers explanatory factors and the utility of the main approaches to understanding family policy. A conclusion brings the piece to a close.

UNDERSTANDING FAMILY, STATE, AND MARKET INTER-RELATIONS

Generalizing somewhat from Bahle (2009), one can identify two contexts in the history of engagement between states, markets, and families. The first was of industrialization and nation building wherein the state and political interests, from the late nineteenth century on, endeavoured to respond to the needs and problems thrown up by the shift from agricultural to industrial production and the expansion of the state into society. The settlement that underpinned the early welfare state was that between capital and labour, but this was predicated on a second settlement at the level of the household between men as earners and women as carers. With the male breadwinner family as the orienting image, early social policies assumed the existence of a family wage, and provided subsidies for both marriage and the dependants of the breadwinner (Crouch 1999). The dynamic in the second period, commencing in the 1970s, lay in the expansion of the service economy and, associated with this and other factors, the large-scale movement of women into the labour market. This turned the focus on the nature of family-related roles and functions and the interface between family and market. Gender politics sat alongside class politics as shaping influences in this period when services substituting for maternal care-giving and financial support for families grew rapidly, as did state interest in the care of children.

In the classical post-war literature, the family's intersection with the state and the market has tended to be conceptualized in rather static functionalist (Parsons 1967) and economic terms (Becker 1981). I want to pursue a broader understanding of family, one that interrelates economic, sociological, ideological, and political aspects. My conceptualization of the family views the interrelations between the family, state, and market in the following terms: looked at economically the main functions of the family relate to income redistribution, labour supply, and consumption; looked at sociologically the family is a form of social organization that provides for care needs, arranges intergenerational and gender relations, and through these and other means plays a key role in the social organization of life; as an ideological entity the family affects continuity and change in value systems; looked at politically the family is a site of social control and a source of social order.

Scholarship on family policy is one of the richest seams of knowledge on the interrelations between state, market, and family. A literature that has taken time to grow, in many ways mirroring the gradually increasing legitimacy of family as object of attention on the part of the state, it has been rather narrow. An abiding interest has been in identifying institutional features of state policies towards families. This scholarship has been largely focused on the specific, frequently technical, features of provision (Bieback 1992; Wingen 1997). Attention has centred on types of policy instrument (cash benefits, tax allowances, leave, and services), administrative arrangements, and on how policy has engaged with the social conventions governing family life and behaviours (marriage, parenthood, childhood, generational interrelationships). Over time this literature became increasingly comparative, marrying an interest in variations in institutional provision with the study of political motivations for state–family engagement as they varied by national setting. The role of family policy in underpinning political and economic arrangements has been a seam of cross-national comparison (Wennemo 1994; Gauthier 1996; Kaufmann et al. 2002). In a framing that picked up on the fact that states did not always target the family directly, the differentiation between countries in terms of whether they operate an explicit or implicit approach to family proved enduring (Kamerman and Kahn 1978).

However, scholarship on the welfare state was slow to recognize the import of family, viewing the state–market nexus as the major source of political activity. This was partly because family was seen to animate a different bundle of concerns, more about gender, health, and well-being than about welfare as the 'hard' object of class politics. There was a certain 'taken-for-granted' status about the family in welfare state scholarship as evidenced in the earlier work of Gøsta Esping-Andersen (1990) in which family was little more than the context in which state–market relations played out. It was feminist scholarship that did most to bring the family into the comparative welfare state fold (e.g. Lewis 1992; O'Connor et al. 1999; Daly and Rake 2003). This work pointed out how all states operate with a set of preferences about family functions and gender roles and that such preferences not only shaped what might be called 'welfare relations' but were also the stuff of economic and employment organization. Such concerns have found their way to the heart of recent policy, and scholarship reflects this, demonstrating that family provides a lynchpin in the functioning of states and markets and that the degree to which social policy seeks to familialize or defamilialize people and activities is a crucial feature of political and economic systems (Esping-Andersen 1999; Leitner 2003).

What factors motivate state engagement with the family? Four classic concerns have been identified: demographic change; horizontal redistribution between those with children and those without; poverty alleviation; gender equality (Wennemo 1994; Gauthier 1996). The strength of particular underlying motivations and the diversity of national philosophical orientations towards the family have led to a number of distinct models of family–state–market relations in Europe historically.

A first approach, exemplified by France, was pro-family and pro-natalist in orientation. The family had value as a political and moral entity and so there was legitimacy for state policy to secure the material and moral functioning of the home (Lenoir 1991). The links between fertility, family, and national interest have been of concern across the political spectrum ever since France first experienced a transition from high to low fertility in the late nineteenth century. The future of the nation became interlinked with the vibrancy of the family (Revillard 2006). Familialism, an ideology that promotes family as a way of life and as a force for social integration, was deeply embedded historically in the national culture, and the state assumed a role as a defender and protector of families, prodded along by a highly effective lobby of pro-family organizations (Lenoir 1991). As it developed, France's policy framework tended towards generous and broad-based (including both financial assistance and childcare services) support for families (Pedersen 1993). Given both the strong support of family as a way of life and pro-natalism, the dominant depiction of women was as mothers rather than workers, although this changed over time.

The second approach, typified by (West) Germany, was more selective about the kind of support given to families, although there too family had high social value and constituted a legitimate ground for political action. Indeed, the claims of the family were elevated and placed above those of other institutions or social categories by the principle of subsidiarity—which decrees that, while the purpose of state support is to enhance family well-being and functioning, such state action should not undermine the autonomy of the family. Internal family relations were viewed as differentiated, with strong preference for the male breadwinner/female homemaker family model. The mother at home symbolized the appropriate moral order. This together with the widespread belief that young children should be cared for at home made for a robust gender division of labour. It was a widely held belief, and one slow to recede, that families should be compensated for child rearing. Hence, the (West) German welfare state tended to organize its support of families in the form of income supplements rather than services.

The third model was egalitarian, wherein the objective of the state was to support employment on the part of both female and male parents and to give families access to high quality childcare and other services. This model, found in the Scandinavian countries, did not operate with a strong concept of family as a collective or even separate institution (Ellingsaeter and Leira 2006). Indeed, it tended to airbrush away the family in seeking to foreground conditions for the well-being and gainful activity of all. Women's role and identity was written into the institutions of state and market as was a more general principle of individual independence and autonomy. Family membership might be a source of emotional stability and identity, but family as an economic and social unit was much less prominent as compared with other parts of Europe.

Finally, there are countries such as the United Kingdom (and Australia and the United States) where, rather than generic family support, policy draws mainly from an anti-poverty and economic functioning orientation. State intervention in family lacked strong legitimacy in these countries, apart from in preventing or managing social ills. The value placed on independence and self-sufficiency, on the part of both individuals and families, tended to downgrade state intervention for the purposes of generic family support. This rendered family policy relatively underdeveloped; where it existed it was oriented mainly to the prevention of poverty and 'crises' occasioned by familial dysfunction. Policy stayed well away from the social recognition of the family as practised by French and German policy (O'Connor et al. 1999).

How are things changing?

CURRENT ORTHODOXIES AND REFORMS

As we have seen, family policy can have diverse goals just as there are different interpretations of the relationship between family policy and family life. The last five to ten years have started to undo the diversity. Of significance here was the interest shown by key international actors in matters of family and family policy. The EU and the OECD have been especially active. While there are divergences between the policy approaches of the two organizations and even within them,[1] some broad parameters unite them. A key concern is the formation of 'flexible' labour markets and households for a globalized economy (Mahon 2006: 174). Mindful that the approach of the two organizations can only be covered in a very general way here, one can identify a number of commonalities. They both put the accent on:

- the distribution of employment and family in the lives of both mothers and fathers and the need for social and economic policy to incentivize employment on the part of mothers and more involvement in caring on the part of fathers;
- increased provision of out-of-home care and early education of children;
- balance between work and family life (the so-called reconciliation of work and family life);
- promotion of children's education and well-being.

---

[1] Mahon (2006), for example, shows that two quite different frames are to be found within the respective OECD directorates on employment and education.

In effect, in a move away from implicit family policy, countries are being pushed to develop strategies around the family. These strategies relate first and foremost to the family as an economic unit but they impinge also on the organization of family life (touching on gender and generational relationships). Of the two, the EU has gone furthest—setting targets (on both childcare and female employment) and introducing laws compelling employment leaves for the purpose of childcare (Lewis 2006a).

Against this general backdrop, Table 9.1 sets out the main issues and thrust of reforms in the six countries since the mid-1990s. In terms of (lacking) volume and extent of reform, the United States stands apart from the other six countries in having seen little or no change. In this and other ways, it makes up 'the rump' in the present comparative analysis. The only agenda around family policy reform in the United States is to reduce dependency on (already comparatively ungenerous) public funds. This is especially the case for lone mothers, who represent one of the last vestiges of 'maternalism' in the American welfare state (Orloff 2005b). The thrust of any reform that is underway is to privatize further the care/employment interface.

Sweden, too, has seen less reform than the other countries, perhaps because Sweden already has gone beyond the international norm. The Swedes are sticking to their model—changes made over the last ten years are qualitative in nature, rolling out the model further rather than changing it. Men's family roles have been a primary concern, with part of the care leave designated specifically for men (the 'daddy

Table 9.1 Main family policy reforms at national level since the mid-1990s

Australia	Compelling part-time employment among lone parent welfare claimants once their children reach 6 years, restructuring of family allowances as tax credits, introduction of childcare tax benefit, stronger support for male breadwinner couples and generally for families with children, welfare to work measures for low-income parents in receipt of government support, introduction of a lump-sum maternity payment
France	Extension of parental leave, shifting some financial support for the care of children from funding for crèches to direct payments to parents, increase in the range of childcare types publicly supported, streamlining of the childcare allowances and introduction of one that promotes 'freedom of choice' for parents
Germany	Expansion of out of home childcare for the under 3s, children over 3 years given an entitlement to a childcare place, parental leave reformed to encourage mothers' employment, a period of 'daddy leave' introduced into the parental leave
Sweden	Extension of designated leaves for fathers, extension of rights for children, expansion in childcare provision and capping of fees, decentralization and then recentralization in the administration of early childhood education and care
UK	Expansion of childcare and early education, increased income support to families with children, right to free part-time nursery care for 3 and 4 year olds, welfare to work measures for benefit recipients, especially lone mothers, extension of employment leaves with a focus on maternity, some switching from cash support to tax credits
USA	Increase in employment among lone parent benefit claimants

month') and a general strengthening of fathers' rights. Another trend is towards further individualization, for example children's access to day-care and their capacity for independent agency are both being strengthened by legal and policy changes. There have also been some changes in the governance of early childhood education and care, with first decentralization and then moves towards recentralization. Overall, the reforms continue the strong thrust in Sweden towards welfare within a model committed to individualization in the service of gender equality, equity, and high levels of employment.

The other four countries have all been reforming actively. The United Kingdom has probably undertaken the most extensive reform programme. It is rapidly moving away from its non-interventionist instinct. It is expanding provision for childcare and children's early learning, promoting employment for lone mothers and all those in 'workless households', extending employment leaves for both parents but for mothers especially, and introducing measures around employment flexibility so as to better balance work and family life (Lewis and Campbell 2007). As well as increasing the amount of financial support to families, the main burden of support for children has been shifted from the social security to the tax system (thereby tying income support more closely to employment and earning). These are in many ways steps in a new direction for the United Kingdom—the state is showing itself to be prepared to move beyond the threshold of the family home in the interests of generalizing the model of the working family. In New Labour's 'reconstructing Britain' project, family, traditionally left to its own resources, has been mobilized to effect a change in practices around employment and personal behaviours. In the process the labour market is foregrounded as a source of support, the family is purged of some of its economic 'bad habits' and the state's supportive role is diminished.

In Germany a language of choice in relation to motherhood and family has been introduced, especially since 2000. As earlier noted, Germany had a strong concept of family life historically and, more than anywhere else, its social policy idealized the male breadwinner model as the superior form of family arrangement. This is changing. While the principle of subsidiarity restricts the public authorities' room for manoeuvre, Germany is now more strongly encouraging out-of-home care for children and employment on the part of mothers. Parental leave was individualized in 2000 and was reformed again in 2008 to make it earnings-related (rather than flat-rate) and render it more compatible with simultaneous part-time employment on the part of the leave taker. Childcare was moved from being a marginal issue to a core policy concern—children were given an entitlement to a childcare place in 1996 and the last two governments have shown leadership if not entrepreneurship in the cause of out-of-home provision of care for young children. While paternity leave has been avoided, the parental leave system has been reformed to encourage the second partner to avail of it. Employment issues also informed the changes in Germany but these are mixed with a desire to increase women's options and sense of choice, especially in the context of a dramatically low birth rate.

In France, the thrust of reform over the *longue durée* has been of greater economic and social instrumentalism in policy. Economic and employment creation goals have infiltrated a policy space that was historically about supporting and promoting family as a prized location and way of life. The centre of gravity has shifted away from the family as a 'sacred space' towards family as service provider or consumer. Natalism is now the longest thread in French family policy—it survives where familialism declines. Parents are allowed greater flexibility (aka 'libre choix') about how they manage childcare. Cash benefits to allow parents to hire an informal carer or care for their children themselves and an extension of coverage of parental leave benefits encouraging mothers to stay at home for longer have been prominent in policy reform. The rate of increase in public expenditure on allowances and leaves has exceeded that on crèches and institutional care (Martin and Le Bihan 2009: 63). Whereas the pedagogical development of children informed earlier rounds of reform, the changes undertaken since the 1990s have lent early childcare and education a stronger 'reconciliation' character, especially that for children aged over three years (Bahle 2009). Attention focuses more closely on the behaviour of parents and less on children as a population sector with entitlement. One result is more stratification by social class as regards the early childcare experience of children (Martin and Le Bihan 2009). Overall, family policy in France, so distinct historically, has undergone a process of 'mainstreaming' whereby it becomes another instrument to serve economic and social goals and French family-related policy goals come to resemble more and more those of other countries.

Against the direction endorsed by the EU and OECD, Australia is on a neo-familial route (similar to France in some respects but quite different to the United Kingdom). The marriage of a conservative social and gender philosophy with a neoliberal approach has resulted in an increasing reliance on a traditional form of family on the one hand and marketized mechanisms of childcare on the other. The thrust of reform under the Howard government was towards the male breadwinner family (Brennan 2007). Little was done to ease mothers' entry to the labour market, to expand fathers' involvement in their children's lives, or to reconcile work and family life. The protection and promotion of the 'choice' to be a stay-at-home mother was an important reforming principle, although not necessarily for lone mothers or indeed for low-income parents in receipt of benefits (who from 2006 were targeted with welfare to work programmes). Instead of paid maternity leave, a universal lump sum payment or grant to all new mothers regardless of employment history or status was introduced and tax allowances were restructured to favour single-income couples (although this has been eased somewhat over time). In addition, while expenditure on childcare has significantly increased as have the numbers of children using formal childcare, some of the collectivism in childcare which predated the Howard government has been undone, with subsidies for childcare provision opened up to for-profit providers, and subsidized childcare made available to all families (regardless of workforce status). Viewed through European eyes, Australia looks as if it has turned its face towards the past, but this turn has involved an activist stance by the state—expenditure on cash benefits to families is now amongst the highest in the OECD with much of the money going to single-parent households. There are some signs that a more family-friendly labour market stance is being taken by the Labor Government elected in 2007, although these fragile shoots may well be vulnerable to the 'rough winds' of economic crisis management.

What underlies these changes?

EXPLAINING CHANGE

Looking across countries, it is possible, and necessary, to identify a number of perspectives that help explain the changes underway.

One factor, widespread across countries, is economic and especially labour market developments. The needs of the market, and the labour market in particular, elevate policy's role in shaping the labour supply of family members and indeed employment availability more broadly. In effect, the underlying thrust is to integrate more closely family policy with employment policy and with more broadly economic objectives. While economic and labour market considerations are a key factor shaping family policy changes everywhere, the focus varies. In Germany and the United Kingdom labour market participation on the part of parents is being incentivized. State support in these countries and especially the United Kingdom is increasingly for the 'all working family'. As part of this, states are pushing an increase in the supply of out-of-home care for young children. There is also another set of employment-related concerns—employment creation. At least part of the reason for the reform of family support in France has been employment creation—parents are given greater choice about how they manage their childcare so as to incentivize the employment of child carers, thereby increasing employment rates. These and other developments suggest that the nomenclature of 'family policy' is outmoded; now in the interests of accuracy it seems that we should speak of 'work/family policy'. The effects extend widely—the very nature of family life can actually be altered by the desire to make family more compatible with employment.

Ideological factors are also at play. Political philosophy has always been influential in family-related matters. In fact, the strength of organized religion or the degree to which religious beliefs and morals galvanized politics is one of the classic explanations of family policy, especially from a historical perspective (Bahle 2008). Church–state relations, in particular the power of Catholic-oriented and conservative parties, were associated with a more elaborated family policy (as well as one oriented to the traditional two-parent, one-income family). Recent changes in family-related provisions give ground to question whether the observed historical relationship between political party and family policy (Morgan 2006) still prevails. It is difficult now to know a party's stance on the family by its positioning on the left–right spectrum. For example, there have been few differences between the Social Democrat-led coalition in Germany and the Christian

Democrat-led coalition, and if anything the latter prosecuted a more intensive move away from the traditional family. *A priori* the Australian case provides the strongest basis for an argument of political philosophy—there the conservative Howard government stuck close to a traditional, roll the clock back, kind of position. Explanation for what is happening in the other countries demands that we appreciate that political philosophies are modernizing. The Third Way philosophy that has taken hold in the United Kingdom and to a lesser extent Germany, for example, justifies intervention in the family in the interests of activation, self-sufficiency, and social inclusion (as economic inclusion especially) (Daly 2004). The changed political culture is also driving some of the focus on children and childcare—the utilitarian functions of social policy in developing future human capital are to the fore. Childhood has become politicized and children a potential asset to be 'harvested' in the future, provided the long-term and life course effects of childhood poverty and deprivation are addressed (Jenson 2006). But there are other ideological currents in play as well.

The role and influence of the international organizations must be factored into the explanation too. However, it would be wrong to imply that the process of change is one whereby the international organizations dictate and national policy responds. There are at least two arguments against this interpretation. Diversity is one powerful counter-argument—no country has the same reform agenda. Secondly, national and international reform processes are closest when there are pre-existing 'affinities' between them—that is, when reform also has a national impetus. The United Kingdom is an exemplar case here. The strong liberal undercurrents in the international agenda find fertile soil there. The expansion of childcare appeals because it is an opportunity to grow the childcare market sector (true also for Australia and France) and employment for lone mothers feeds the thrust towards activation and self-sufficiency. Equally, some of the traditional social class fault lines are being endorsed by reform. In the United Kingdom there has been significant investment in family support services for the purpose of improving family functioning and stabilizing family and community relations in poor neighbourhoods. In fact, early education and socialization, especially of children from low-income backgrounds, are not promoted in the United Kingdom (and we might add Australia) on grounds of child well-being per se, but because they serve to integrate children into state-controlled programmes and/or foster human capital accumulation (Bahle 2009).

There is also the possibility that reforms are, in part anyway, a response to societal considerations and problems. The idea of new social risks has a considerable remit. Typically juxtaposed to the classic welfare state which interpreted risk mainly in terms of men being unable to earn an income from the labour market (or for women the absence of a male breadwinner), the post-industrial welfare state is faced with a different set of risks, many of which arise in private life (Bonoli 2006a). There is a real correspondence between the risks highlighted by this literature and the objects of reform as they are proceeding in the six countries studied here: the integration of the marginalized into the labour market, coverage of the risks associated with increasing family instability, dealing with the consequences of the movement of women in large numbers into the labour market, managing intergenerational relations, and in particular balancing the needs and entitlements of the younger vis-à-vis those of the older generations. Although it is not theorized as such, the literature on social risks can be expanded to think in terms of risks around social integration. Family is changing as are the values relating to it and family policy is as much a response to these as it is to changes occurring either in the market or the state. If we locate today's welfare state in its social context, we entertain the possibility that reform in family policy is in many ways a response to 'new' social problems that are not directly related to economic issues but to factors like people's commitment to family (values) and how changing cultural norms and lifestyles affect people's wish to pursue a family-based life (Kaufmann et al. 2002; Bahle 2008). This is a key way of filtering issues around demography and declining birthrates. Although they may not owe their origins completely to them, greater support for families with children and concerns around work/life balance have a concern about women's and men's willingness to bear and raise children. Hence, state policies might be understood as an attempt to re-embed individuals in family life and to elevate family as a form of social integration. This has gender implications. It is obvious from the foregoing analysis that gender relations are being continuously refashioned, especially as regards how mothers and fathers perform their family-related roles and combine them with employment. There is a move to gender neutrality in most of the countries, apart from perhaps Australia.

   All of this leads to one major conclusion. Family policy is a complex field, a highly contested (politically and morally) domain of policy. Hence, it is important to recognize that a constellation of factors is involved of a kind sketched in Table 9.2. Explanations must, therefore, reach across disciplines and interests rather than focusing on politics, or economics, or social exigencies, or norms and ideologies in isolation.

Table 9.2 Constellation of factors animating state policy towards families

Economic:	Market demand/supply/profits re services Human capital development
Ideological/cultural:	View of children's role, needs, contribution to society Philosophical orientation towards the family Ideology around welfare
Political:	Social class tensions/orientations, biases Engagement of political actors, including international organizations
Social:	New social risks Social integration Demographic renewal Gender-related norms and practices

CONCLUSION

Societies approach the relationship between family, state, and market in rather different ways as the six countries studied demonstrate. A range of factors have conditioned this set of interrelations historically; the homogenizing tendency of economic growth and development being reined in by the specificities of political philosophy and politics at nation state level. It has generally been accepted that family policy unfolded in two major rounds or periods (the first associated with industrial expansion in the post-war period and the second from the 1970s on). I suggest that we have embarked on a third age of family policy. This is marked by a number of features. First the family is opened up—it is no longer private in the way that it once was as the state and the market compete to undertake some of its activities. Second, greater intervention especially on the part of the state makes for more micro-management of family life and cuts down on family autonomy. The roles of mother and father are more externally defined than they ever were. Third, the distinctiveness of family policy across countries is being eroded. While no country has exactly the same reform programme and none is following exactly the approach endorsed by the EU and OECD, they have in common a proclivity to 'mix and match'. The result is a hybridization of existing systems, although Sweden and the United States are unique in that their relatively long-standing approaches to the family remain more or less unchanged, although outcomes have changed (see Chapter 32).

At the present time, there are a number of impulses for reform, drawing from a mix of economic, political, and social concerns. They relate essentially to employment and economic self-sufficiency, a bundle of issues centring on 'work–life balance' (which is rooted in concerns about demographic decline, the quality of family life and both employment and family as contributing to social integration) and gender equality. The significance of each varies. Of the three, gender equality is weakest as a driver of contemporary reform, apart from in Sweden. The strongest reform dynamic is centred on encouraging employment on the one hand but finding a balance between that and family life on the other. It is worth taking a little time to consider why there are seemingly contradictory responses. I suggest that this is because, stripped down to basics, there are now only two competing ideologies on family (unlike the past, where in Western Europe alone there were at least five perspectives (Bahle 2008)). The first is that family is little more than a household. This approach views family primarily as an economic arrangement, the functions of which can be as, if not more, efficiently carried out by other organizations as economic and other expediencies dictate. The opposing view is that family constitutes a sphere of life and a set of relations that are both unique and valuable in their own right (the view that informed policy historically in France and Germany). If the former sees family as little more than a collection of individuals and pushes reform in the direction of individualization, the latter is family centred and recognizes family as a social institution meriting public support. Two commonalities should be noted: both have a functional reliance on families to achieve particular ends; neither is particularly interested in gender equality (hence Sweden is not the guiding ideal). All the countries studied here have something of both, even the liberal ones. Hence, one sees the simultaneous expansion of a family orientation in employment policy (and the increasing use of income support and tax policy to encourage employment) and of policy to balance work and family life (more childcare, more flexibility, more economic support for the care of children, more generous parental leaves). It is at least worth entertaining the possibility that work–family reconciliation is in some ways a resurrection of the second view, the social integration function of the family. This social integration concern is, I venture to suggest, acting as a brake on individualization. The particularity of family and of family policy—moral overtones, political complexity, societal import—continues, as does the 'pull' of historical factors.

There are a number of implications in all of this for how to understand the relations between families, states, and markets. I suggest that the interlinkages should be conceptualized as lying at the intersection of five axes or balances:

• *demography* and *life course* (reproduction rates and family-related roles and practices);
• *employment* (labour supply, conditions of employment);
• *care* (the supply and cost of caring labour, the meaning and practice of parenthood, quality of children's lives and opportunities, generational relations, the distribution of care);
• *income* (sufficiency, access, equality);
• *social integration* (management of social risks).

These cut across the classic divides in the field between economics and politics or social and demographic factors and they locate the family in society as well as in polity and economy. As well as giving a range of categories of analysis, seeing policy as having to field these diverse dimensions also helps to explain the ambivalence that seems to characterize national policies. Australia, while encouraging mothers to be home-based, is also expanding childcare provision outside the home. France continues to support women as mothers and as workers, but the long history of high quality formal childcare provision has given way to the promotion of family-based care, intended primarily as an employment rather than a family policy. There has been no attempt to promote care by fathers. In Germany too, reform is Janus-faced—rather than trenchantly undoing the male breadwinner model, it is 'softening' some of its edges. And even the United Kingdom, which has fervently embraced a work activation agenda, has further strengthened some of the maternalist elements by increasing the support of the carer independently of her market status (Campbell 2008).

When it comes to explanations, we need to think in terms of an explanatory constellation rather than a single factor. Economic, political, ideological/cultural, and social factors all have relevance (see Table 9.2). It is worth emphasizing, by way of concluding, that sociological processes have to be considered along with the more conventional (to the field) other three sets of factors. What we are seeing across countries now is no less than a new way of organizing everyday family life in which states as well as international organizations and markets are more prepared to get involved for the purpose of reconfiguring the family's place in society and aspects of its 'internal' organization.

....

CHAPTER 10

DISCIPLINARY PERSPECTIVES

....

EINAR ØVERBYE

INTRODUCTION: HOW TO TOUCH AN ELEPHANT

....

WHEN three blind men were to describe an elephant, legend has it that the one who touched the hide perceived the elephant as a wall, the one who touched a foot believed it to be a tree, and the one who touched the trunk thought it was a snake. Similarly, different disciplines see different things when they use the concept 'welfare state', depending on how some aspect of the welfare state fits with ongoing debates within the discipline. Table 10.1 presents a simplified account of how different aspects of the welfare state link up with core debates within seven disciplines. This chapter elaborates these linkages to core disciplinary debates.

The questions in Table 10.1 are crude starting points. In practice, welfare state debates within disciplines overlap, because the disciplines themselves overlap. There are also cross-cutting questions across disciplines.[1] One cross-cutting question asks

---

[1] A discipline can be defined as a separate branch of knowledge. It is debatable if social policy, social administration, and social work are sufficiently coherent to constitute disciplines, or if they should rather be regarded as disciplinary hybrids, or as sub-themes within sociology, political science and (possibly) psychology. Then again the demarcation criteria necessary to delineate separate disciplines are not clear. The pragmatic argument applied here is that these themes are sufficiently distinct that the disciplinary label can be used. Social policy, social administration, and social work are disciplines 'inside' the welfare state, in the sense that most of their subject matter is tied to questions inherent to the welfare state. While the older and more established disciplines of sociology, economics, political science, and law are disciplines whose main subject matter is not directly tied to the welfare state as such—they are 'outside' disciplines looking in.

Table 10.1 Disciplinary perspectives on the welfare state: Core debates

Sociology	Does the welfare state enhance social integration, or does it undermine social integration?
Economics	Does the welfare state enhance economic efficiency, or is it a drag on economic efficiency?
Political science	Is the welfare state a result of conflict politics or consensus politics?
Social policy	Does the welfare state redistribute to the poor, or is it mainly of benefit to the better off?
Social administration	Is a publicly or privately managed welfare state best able to provide cost-effective welfare benefits and services of an acceptable quality?
Social work	Does the welfare state enable and empower marginal citizens, or is it a means to control and discipline them?
Legal studies	Does the welfare state represent a strengthening and broadening of the rule of law, or rather a weakening of the rule of law and a return to arbitrary rule?

whether some welfare state designs (aka welfare regimes, aka families of welfare nations) differ from others (Esping-Andersen 1990; Castles 1993)—are some welfare state designs more economically efficient than others, for example? Another cross-cutting question concerns the differential weight that should be given to structural (institutional) and agency (actor) factors when studying a particular aspect of the welfare state. The battle between agency and structural approaches is also the grand underlying theme in the historical study of welfare state developments. How much is due to the ideological and idiosyncratic ideas of the people in charge and how much can be traced to the layers upon layers of structurizing factors reaching down into the darkness of the past? Yet another cross-cutting theme is whether welfare states in democracies differ from welfare states in autocracies, including whether the notion of an autocratic welfare state is a contradiction in terms.

The last question points to an ambiguity in the welfare state concept. For some, the term 'welfare state' connotes a set of interconnected legal, political, and social rights (Marshall 1964*b*). For others, it is just a convenient shorthand for the many welfare programmes that can be found in most states or at least in most states with high average incomes (Barr 1992). The former usually define a democratic decision-making system (political rights) as an integral part of a welfare state. The latter decouple the political decision-making system and the welfare state. They may even decouple the rule-of-law principle and the welfare state. This ambiguity makes it a complex task to review disciplinary perspectives on the welfare state. For example, from the perspective of legal studies, welfare states are necessarily embedded in a rule-of-law legal structure. If not, legal studies would hardly have any starting point for an analysis. In contrast, at least some political scientists would have no qualms about analysing the 'welfare state' of an autocratic regime based on the arbitrary day-to-day decisions of an absolute ruler—provided the regime provided some modicum of health and social benefits to at least some of its subjects. Different conceptualizations of what a welfare state is about mean that some study apples while others study oranges or even more distantly related fruits. Add fuzzy disciplinary borders and different welfare state concepts within disciplines, and it is easy to understand why reviews of disciplinary approaches to the welfare state are seldom written.

With these caveats in mind, a brief presentation of some major strands in the disciplinary debates on the welfare state follows, starting out with the three classical social science disciplines: sociology, economics, and political science.

SOCIOLOGY, ECONOMICS, AND POLITICAL SCIENCE

As a necessary oversimplification to be able to say anything at all, it is assumed that the core theme in sociology is the study of the conditions for social integration in a society (or if one prefers a normative framing of the question: how to maintain or enhance social integration). The core theme in economics is the study of the conditions for efficient allocation of limited resources (normatively framed: how to maintain or enhance economic efficiency). And the core theme of political science is the study of how political power is wielded in a territory (normatively framed: how to use power wisely).

Sociology

Modern sociology is a diverse enterprise, but its main—and oldest—theme is the study of social integration. This was the theme of Durkheim's *Suicide* [1897] (1992); arguably the book that launched the sociological enterprise. This book simultaneously launched the sociological study of welfare arrangements. In the last chapter of *Suicide*, Durkheim suggests that, in order to enhance social integration, it is necessary to strengthen 'the occupational group or corporation'. The practical instrument for making this happen is to ensure that such groups or corporations preside over 'companies of insurance, benevolent aid and pensions'. In Durkheim's preface to the second edition of his equally influential *The Division of Labour in Society* (1984 [1902]) this suggestion is elaborated and the state is brought in. Here, Durkheim suggests that the state should use regulation policies (tax subsidies etc) to stimulate occupational groups to take responsibility over insurance, benevolent aid, and pensions. In short, Durkheim conceptualizes the welfare state as a means of patching up social integration in societies where industrialization and accompanying cultural change threaten to weaken social ties. Lines can be drawn from Durkheim's suggestion to Parsons's (1971) approach to welfare issues in his structural–functionalist vision of society. Here, welfare arrangements emerge as one of the feedback mechanisms required to re-establish social integration in systems upset by external disturbances (disturbances that can be summed up by the umbrella term 'modernization').

Lines can also be drawn to Wilensky's (1975) analysis of the relationship between economic growth (a crude indicator of 'modernization') and welfare state expansion. The equation of welfare with modernization has spurred the grand convergence debate, the issue being the extent to which states faced with similar economic, social, and demographic challenges respond in ways that make their welfare arrangements more similar across time. The convergence debate can be perceived as a structure-versus-agency debate: to what extent are political elites constrained in their welfare policy choices by similar historical–structural challenges and to what extent do they have room to pursue their own idiosyncratic welfare policies? The line from Durkheim can be drawn further to the more recent preoccupation with whether welfare policies—in particular labour market activation of various types—enhance social citizenship, that is with their capacity to combat social exclusion (Room 1995). Yet another twist on the social integration theme arises from the study of an eventual relationship between ethnic/cultural homogeneity and welfare state developments. For example, Quadagno (1988b) argues that the rather lean United States welfare state is the result of a high degree of ethnic fragmentation, which impacted on American welfare-political developments at critical historical junctures. A related example is the surge in interest in the possible welfare state consequences of the trend towards more ethnically heterogeneous (multicultural) European societies (Alesina and Glaeser 2004). The empirical findings of such studies differ; the point being emphasized here is only that a common underlying theme concerns the conditions for, or effects of, social integration.

Incidentally, Durkheim (1984[1902]) was of the opinion that the state should *not* have a direct role in welfare provision. Durkheim wanted to strengthen the intermediaries between the state and individuals rather than the state itself. His recommendation was for the state to steer 'from the second line' by stimulating corporatist welfare arrangements, not to run the show. (This 'steering by stimulating intermediaries approach' is recognizable today in the French tradition of stimulating mutual societies and the like (*mutualités*), and represents a less state-centred social protection approach than the otherwise rather similar German *Sozialstaat* tradition.) This state-sceptical stance is mirrored in another sociological tradition similarly preoccupied with social integration, but with quite another take on welfare state expansion. Here, scholars worry that the assumption by the state of ever-more welfare tasks by the state will weaken, rather than enhance, social integration. An example concerns the debate on the 'substitution issue', investigating whether the welfare state weakens, rather than strengthens, the family and other intermediate collectives between individual and state (Lingsom 1997). Another ongoing debate concerns whether the welfare state fosters the creation of a separate underclass, not integrated in society (Murray 1984).

The sociological study of the welfare state branches out into sub-discourses partly in conflict with each other, but the common underlying theme of social integration is recognizable. Even power resource theory, arguably the most hard-nosed sociological tradition in the study of the welfare state (it is about different material interests, in particular those of labour and capital, mobilizing their various resources and then slugging it out in the democratic class struggle), shares a vision that the end result of an eventual welfare policy victory on the part of the less privileged classes will be a more well-integrated society (Korpi 1983). The 'institutional/universal' (i.e. all-encompassing) welfare state designs resulting from these class wars (if the assumed representatives of the underprivileged win, that is) are supposed to unite the middle classes and the downtrodden, in a material as well as a social sense (Rothstein 1998). Even in the hard-core sociological traditions guided by material interest concerns, the theme of social integration is never far away.

Economics

A worry that welfare arrangements may serve as a disincentive to thrift is older than the welfare state. Whether or not this worry is well founded, how large eventual negative efficiency effects may be or whether negative effects may be eventually offset by even larger (and usually more subtle) positive efficiency effects, is the core theme in the economic debate on the welfare state. The basic underlying question is about economic efficiency, be it on a micro or macro level. It is a debate with many twists and turns. The disincentive argument is simple and straightforward: if people get paid for doing nothing, it may reduce their motive to do something. The counter-arguments are usually more subtle, for example the notion that unemployment insurance acts as a Keynesian automatic stabilizer, since expenditures go up (and stimulate demand) in hard times and decrease (and make public spending contract) in good times. Another counter-argument holds that unemployment benefits allow the unemployed to search longer for optimal work, securing a better (more efficient) fit between the buyers and sellers of labour.

These are only two of a series of arguments that can be made about possible underlying positive efficiency effects of welfare schemes. The welfare state—by dampening social conflicts—may also create a more stable and predictable environment for investors, attracting capital satisfied with modest but safe returns. Some even see a large welfare state as a way to get interest groups to accept open markets by offering them social protection if they should end up as losers (Rodrik 1998). Within this line of thought, the welfare state is conceptualized as a *credible commitment device* through which anticipated winners of economic globalization dampen resistance among anticipated losers. These different views can be tied to the convergence debate: if the welfare state is mainly a drag on efficiency, economic globalization is likely to result in convergence towards the bottom, as large welfare states are out-competed by smaller welfare states. But if some welfare state designs enhance economic efficiency, other countries are likely to imitate them, resulting in convergence towards some welfare state designs rather than to others.

More direct crossovers between economics and sociology also exist: some economists mirror pessimistic-type sociological arguments in assuming that welfare policies lead towards the learning of dysfunctional norms, making negative incentive effects worse across time, while others link in with optimistic-type sociological arguments, claiming that safety-nets encourage risk-taking behaviour and thereby actually boost an entrepreneurial culture. The positive-versus-negative economic effects debate also comes in political economy versions. Some political economists portray welfare state expansion as the result of rent-seeking behaviour by vested interests, which is assumed to proliferate and grow stronger the longer the growth of such interests is uninterrupted by war or similar social tumult (Olson 1982). Others see the welfare state as a rational response to market failures in private insurance markets, since the state is not subject to adverse selection and interdependent risk problems when providing social protection. Here, welfare policies emerge as an efficient way in which the majority can obtain insurance against social risks (Barr 1992). Political economists writing within a rent-seeking framework tend to regard welfare policies as a game with winners and losers and, hence, have a conflict view of the political process (Browning 1975). The conflict perspective corresponds to the 'democratic class struggle' approach favoured by sociologists writing within the power resource tradition summarized previously above. On the other hand, those who argue that the welfare state is a rational way of providing insurance (and is thus in the enlightened self-interest of all) assume (at least implicitly) a long-run harmonious view of politics. Arguably, there is a correspondence between such views and neo-functionalist approaches in the sociological study of the welfare state. For example, a majority demand for insurance against social risks may represent the homeostatic variable; 'modernization' represents various disturbances that weaken existing insurance institutions and introduce new risks; competition between political elites represents the correction mechanism which restores equilibrium; and various welfare policies are among the means used to accomplish this feat (Stinchcombe 1985). This conflict-or-consensus difference also provides a crossover to the questions with which political scientists are concerned.

Political Science

Are welfare arrangements brought into being by political actors wielding their power to suppress the interest and/or political ideals of others? Or are welfare arrangements outcomes of a never-ending debate about ideas, where opponents use the power of persuasion and enlightened debate to approach a state of affairs closer to the common good? Whether or not the welfare state is a product of conflict or consensus is tied to the issue of whether welfare arrangements are in the enlightened self-interest of all or the result of rent-seeking on the part of various interest groups (see above). But it is also tied to the politics of ideas, including political ideologies. The Bismarckian social insurance legislation of the 1880s, arguably the first act in the drama of the modern welfare state, displayed ideological ambiguity on both the left and the right—an ambiguity that persists to this day. These policy measures provided the German urban industrial working class with protection against social risks such as work accidents, sickness, disability, unemployment, and old age. The measures were the result of a compromise between what can loosely be labelled a conservative and liberal ideological faction within the ruling strata (Briggs 1961). Conservatives were concerned with political integration and national consensus-building, while liberals were inclined to limit the reach of social protection to the poor and let the rest care for themselves through voluntary associations and/or the market. Mirroring the ideological split on the right was that on the left between (a) a reformist branch, dominated by different brands of social-democratic parties, who have tended to go along with welfare reforms and often initiated ambitious reforms themselves, and (b) a revolutionary branch, regarding welfare policies as a means of pacifying the working class, to be resisted in order to bring on the revolution. As versions of the Bismarckian social legislation spread to more countries, these ideological schisms were also exported and in various ways interacted with local political differences. Ideological ambivalence among parties of both left and right has allowed for a wide scope of local/situational adaptations when political elites have manoeuvred within the welfare-political field. Due to different political configurations, the answer to the grand question (is the welfare state an outcome of conflict politics or consensus politics?) is that 'it depends'. In some countries, the expansion of welfare arrangements has been a rather peaceful affair, marked by cross-party consensus. In others, it has been marked by virulent political conflicts. It may even be argued that many of the revolutions that took place during the twentieth century occurred when ruling elites were too slow, or unable, to respond to popular demands for social protection (broadly defined).

During the 1970s and 1980s, the neo-institutionalist revival impacted heavily on political science. This led to a shifting emphasis within welfare studies. The neo-institutionalists built on the 'cognitive turn' that took place in psychology in the same period (Powell and Dimaggio 1991). They argue that how people cognitively perceive their interests is heavily constrained by the institutional settings within which they find themselves. Political scientists started to ask questions such as: how does the structure of the state (e.g. unitary versus federal) impact on the power plays (or consensus deliberations) that differently placed local, regional and central elites engage in with regard to welfare politics? How does the structure of industrial relations (e.g. industry or crafts-based unions) impact on how workers perceive their welfare interests and/or formulate their ideals? How does the institutional structure of previous welfare legislation (e.g. universal versus residual/means-tested welfare arrangements) impact on how interest groups, bureaucrats, as well as new leaders, perceive the solutions to new welfare challenges (such as the increasing risk of precarious employment, or the risk of single parenthood)? Neo-institutionalists often assume welfare policies to be *path-dependent*, meaning that the scope for incoming political elites to alter welfare policies is constrained by the existing institutional landscape. Re-enter the debate concerning the relative importance of structures (existing institutions) versus conscious agency (flesh-and-blood politicians) in shaping the future welfare state.

During the 1990s and 2000s, the shift from welfare expansion to welfare retrenchment led to yet another disciplinary reorientation. Rather than seeking to explain why welfare arrangements were ever expanding, the question became one of explaining how retrenchment might come about. Paul Pierson's (2000) concepts of 'credit-claiming' and 'blame avoidance' were conceptual innovations aimed at capturing the new political reality. Pierson claimed that the politics of welfare retrenchment is characterized by political elites trying to shift the blame for unpopular cutbacks to others (be they political opponents or political elites at different government levels), while the earlier expansionist phase was often characterized by a scramble to claim the credit for new welfare initiatives. These concepts have a somewhat Machiavellian air, assuming that, in their quest to maintain or to acquire power, political elites are generally in a position to manipulate voter perceptions. Cutbacks can also be analysed as a consensus-building process, in which elites investigate each other's willingness to stick to common cutback proposals, and/or to cognitively frame cutbacks in the same way vis-à-vis voters (Overbye 2008).

The diverse disciplinary debates within political science differently emphasize the role of interests, ideas (including ideologies), existing institutional arrangements, cognitive structures, and rhetorical-strategic considerations when explaining welfare-political change. But an underlying theme is, arguably, the extent to which changes reflect irresolvable conflicts or consensus, together with the extent to which eventual outcomes are the product of real or manipulated agreement.

SOCIAL POLICY, SOCIAL ADMINISTRATION, AND SOCIAL WORK

The shorthand definition of a discipline is 'a separate branch of knowledge'. Sociology, economics, and political science are well-established disciplines. Sociology and economics may also claim distinct epistemological outlooks in the study of human behaviour, somewhat cartoonishly summed up as the difference between *homo sociologicus* (ruled by norms) and *homo economicus* (ruled by incentives). Political science is a less coherent discipline, as political scientists often pragmatically borrow theories from economics, sociology, and other sciences (such as psychology) when they have a bearing on the issue at hand. Social policy, social work, and social administration are similarly concerned with a set of problems, and pragmatically borrow insights from other social science disciplines, usually without fussing too much about deeper epistemological consistency (begging the question of whether such a thing can exist in the social sciences in the first place). Unlike political science however, they are not always taught separately. In the United States they are often taught together under the heading of social welfare, and in Europe institutional dividing lines differ from one country to another. Nonetheless, their subject-matters are sufficiently different to warrant separate treatment here.

Yet again to oversimplify, it is assumed here that the main disciplinary debate in social policy concerns problems relating to the outcomes of welfare state policies. Social administration is concerned with problems related to the management and delivery of welfare benefits and services. And social work is concerned with how people who experience social problems can be guided to solve them, and the extent to which welfare state institutions and provision are a help or a hindrance in this respect.

Social Policy

The founding texts of social policy are arguably the writings of Richard Titmuss and, in particular, his essay 'the social division of welfare' (1976b [1955]). Titmuss was concerned with policy outcomes and, in particular, whether social policies redistribute from the better-off to the poor. To what extent the welfare state redistributes to the poor has been a major question in social policy ever since. This provides a crossover to the sociological study of the welfare state, since many sociologists are equally concerned with social inequality and social integration (not least because social inequality is often considered as a crude proxy indicator of weakness in the fabric of social cohesion).

Titmuss differentiated between residual, achievement-oriented, and institutional/universal welfare policies; roughly corresponding to Esping-Andersen's (1990) later differentiation between Anglo-American (liberal), continental-European (conservative), and Scandinavian (social democratic) welfare states. Titmuss assumed that institutional/universal (all-encompassing) welfare arrangements would be more redistributive than residual (means-tested) and achievement-oriented (contributory insurance) welfare arrangements. He was among the first scholars to broaden the policy focus to consider also the redistributional impact of indirect social policies such as fiscal welfare (tax subsidies) and occupational welfare (health care and pensions provided by employers and/or trade unions, but regulated and eventually tax subsidized by the state). Some scholars have pushed the boundaries of what should be considered part of the welfare state even further, arguing that institutional arrangements such as compulsory arbitration, high customs barriers, immigration controls, and subsidized home ownership can in certain contexts be considered near substitutes for a tax-and-spend welfare state (Castles 1988).

Arguably the most debated social policy controversy concerns whether institutional/universal welfare arrangements redistribute more to the poor than residual/means-tested welfare arrangements. Following in the footsteps of Titmuss, an influential view holds that universal welfare arrangements can bring together the welfare interests of the poor and the middle classes, allowing the latter to ride along on the coattails on the former (Baldwin 1990; Korpi and Palme 1998). The issue is contested, however. Goodin and Le Grand (1987) suspect that the middle classes rather than the poor are the main beneficiaries of universal welfare services. Tullock (1983) claims that, if universal welfare arrangements redistribute more to the poor, it must be because higher/middle income groups are unable to 'see through the universalist veil' and discover that more money is taken away from them than in a residual welfare state. He doubts if higher/middle income groups are really unable to understand this (at least in the long run). This ongoing social policy debate has a rough political economy parallel in the different predictions of the Meltzer–Richard hypothesis and Director's Law-hypothesis (Mueller 1989). The Meltzer–Richard hypothesis assumes that redistribution in a democracy will usually go from people earning above the median to those earning below the median. This corresponds with a hypothesis that the poor are in alliance with the lower-middle classes. Director's Law, however, assumes that redistribution from both tails of a distribution to the middle is more stable than redistribution from one of the tails. This corresponds with a hypothesis that the middle classes benefit at the expense of both the rich and poor.

This empirical debate is not settled. However one may question whether the taken-for-granted assumption in all such studies that *redistribution* is the primary purpose of the welfare state is really accurate. If one instead assumes that social *investment* (in education, health, and so forth) is the main purpose of many welfare policies, it is not obvious that the most redistributive policy is simultaneously the one providing the highest investment returns. Similarly, if *insurance* (against unemployment, disability, etc.) is the primary purpose of many welfare policies, strong occupational groups may perhaps be quite satisfied if ruling politicians limit social protection to their particular groups, excluding other (poorer) groups. Social policy studies assuming that redistribution is the main (or even only) purpose of the welfare state often overlook the fact that the actual welfare objectives of governments can be diverse, complex, and internally in conflict.

A less discussed but probably more important global social policy issue than redistribution per se is the *insider/outsider* schism. Most countries have social insurance programmes inspired by the initial Bismarckian social insurance legislation. Public servants as well as full-time urban industrial workers in large firms are covered by pension, work accident, disability, and health care schemes almost everywhere. But they often comprise small groups; from roughly two-thirds of the formal labour force in most Latin American countries to less than 10 per cent in some Asian and African countries (Ginneken 2003). These welfare schemes may serve as beacons showing yet-excluded groups the promised land, but they may also be privileges for powerful, entrenched groups that tie up tax revenues that could alternatively be used for targeted social assistance aimed at the truly poor and destitute. The redistributional tendency in an insider/outsider welfare state is often regressive, redistributing from a majority to an above-the-median minority. But then again the political purpose of such welfare arrangements may perhaps not be redistribution at all, but rather to provide 'insider' groups with insurance against social risks. The insider/outsider schism is not easy to overcome, since 'privileged' social insurance schemes do provide people with incentives to work in the formal sector, while a shift to (more redistributive) social assistance would make it even more lucrative to remain in the informal sector. Here we encounter a version of the redistribution-versus-incentive problem with which economists are concerned (see above). The insider/outsider schism particularly characterizes countries of the Southern European welfare regime (see Leibfried 2001 and Chapter 42 below). A key aspect of these countries' social policies is that, strong insider groups have had access to generous welfare programmes, while less-strong outsider groups largely had to rely on the (extended) family or charity. In recent years, the insider/outsider schism has become less pronounced in Southern Europe, but a case can be made that this is the welfare state design that best captures what the 'typical welfare state' looks like in the world at large, including most Asian, Middle East, African, and Latin-American countries (Ginneken 2003).

Social Administration

The central issue in social administration concerns how to manage the welfare state, including how to provide cost-effective welfare benefits and services of an acceptable quality. Social administration is related to social policy but also seeks inspiration in public management and organization theory (two applied branches of political science). Social administration focuses attention on the many administrative intermediaries between governments and welfare claimants—including the tensions between welfare state administrators at various government levels and the myriads of professions and semi-professions that serve different claimant groups.

The increased cost-pressure brought about by economic globalization plus an ageing population has led to a flurry of reorganization initiatives, known under the umbrella term of New Public Management (Minogue 1998). The advantages and disadvantages of this new toolbox of management ideas, set against traditional (Weberian) bureaucratic management, has become the intense core debate within the earlier somewhat sleepy backwater of social administration studies. New management ideas include the introduction of *purchaser–provider* models within public welfare services, *outsourcing* of welfare service provision to private welfare providers, and giving claimants a stronger *voice* or better *exit options* if they are dissatisfied (Le Grand 2007). More use of *targets and performance measures* is yet another new management device, as well as *decentralization of decision-making authority* to middle-level managers (including, in some countries, regional or local authorities). These reforms try to make separate welfare agencies more efficient in carrying out their core tasks and to handle the ever-present tension between accountability and professional autonomy within each welfare agency (Bruijn 2007). A second wave of management reforms has been concerned with how to ensure sufficient cooperation and coordination across welfare agencies (Christensen and Laegereid 2007),

The renewed interest in coordination includes finding solutions through *governance* (network management) between agencies rather than top-down management and to let *public–private partnerships* replace hierarchical public control. In sum, a whole smorgasbord of new, and often contradictory, management ideas are now transforming the welfare state from within. The reorganization drive is not only seen in OECD countries, but also in many middle and low income countries, where public welfare services (including health services) often have a bad reputation due to administrative inefficiencies, poor quality, and/or 'informal user-fees'. Is the end result a welfare state that provides higher-quality services in a more cost-efficient manner? That is the core empirical question. Related questions concern the relationship between new management designs and topics such as social integration, the use and abuse of power, claimant empowerment, and redistribution effects, illustrating the many overlapping debates between social administration and other disciplines.

Social Work

To a larger extent than the other disciplines reviewed here, social work applies an explicit bottom-up perspective when studying the welfare state. Social work is partly a discipline but also a profession, i.e. an occupation that demands a special education. Its roots are not only among state welfare bureaucracies but also among charitable societies (among the intermediaries between state and individual, to use Durkheim's vocabulary). Charitable societies were often in opposition to the sometimes harsh practices of the old Poor Laws, and wary of the social stigma connected to applying for welfare benefits and services. An awareness of the tension between the roles of helper and controller (including gatekeeper) dates back to the origins of social work. Among the founders of the discipline the 'scientific philanthropy' perspective of Richmond emphasized the role as helper, while Addams's interest in the structural setting for offering assistance also included an awareness of the controlling aspects of welfare policies (Johnson and Yanca 2004).

The core welfare state debate in social work concerns how (if at all) welfare benefits and services can be designed and delivered in ways that empower and enable marginal citizens. Titmuss's works, as well as Goffman's essay on stigma (1990), are important founding texts in this regard. Social work even has an ambivalent stance towards its own professional role. Is not a professional helper, by implicitly claiming to have more insight that the user of welfare services, also someone who may intimidate the marginalized by making their definition of the situation (and own voice) appear inferior?

Partly due to economic globalization, and partly due to ageing populations, welfare benefits and services are everywhere being redesigned to ensure that 'work is the first option'. So-called labour market activation can be implemented by 'nice' as well as 'not-so-nice' policy measures (Lødemel and Trickey 2000). Not-so-nice measures include benefit cuts, shorter benefit periods, harsher eligibility criteria, or tying benefits to low-paid public works (workfare). These are often regarded with suspicion from a bottom-up social work perspective, as they fairly explicitly serve to discipline potential welfare clients and bring down benefit rates. Nicer activation measures include free or subsidized retraining efforts, softer means testing (or doing away with means testing altogether) to prevent poverty traps, and attempts to involve the user in his/her activation process, to make him/her internalize the activation goals. Nicer activation measures sometimes also meet a suspicious stare from bottom-up social work scholars, in particular those inspired by Foucauldian notions of 'pastoral power' (Villandsen 2007). Pastoral power derives from the desire of professionals to make their clients see the light, to make them accept and internalize what it is that the professionals deem good, in contrast to what the clients themselves may perceive as good, including how they would express the notion of 'good' in the first place. The sensitivity of social work to the potential abuses of professional power—including pastoral power—heightens its disciplinary sensitivity concerning the possible darker aspects of the welfare state. In contrast to this dark view, however, a pragmatic stance might surmise that exposure to pastoral power is perhaps better than the alternative, at least if the alternative is the not-so-nice activation measures or nothing at all.

A related social work issue concerns whether some welfare state designs are more empowering than others. Here, the discussion between the proponents of universal and residual welfare policies resurfaces. Titmuss presumed that universal welfare state designs stigmatize claimants to a lesser extent than residual welfare state designs, while Pinker (1971), for example, assumes that it is primarily the perception of the claimant group (e.g. old-age pensioners versus young unemployed males) rather than the design of welfare arrangements as such, that is the crucial factor in explaining eventual stigma. This empirical debate is far from settled. Stigma is a sociological concept, yet again illustrating how the debates criss-cross disciplinary boundaries and that similar debates are taken up, in different ways, across disciplines.

LEGAL STUDIES

Like sociology, economics, and political science, law (legal studies) is a well-established discipline. Law is a normative science, concerned with creating a predictable environment for human interaction. The antithesis to the rule of law is arbitrary rule, implying that the state-sanctioned decisions of today have no consequences for what will be the state-sanctioned decisions of tomorrow. If rules are arbitrary, there is no need to justify a break with established practice, other than simply registering that the ruler has apparently changed his/her idiosyncratic taste. If ruled by law, a break with established practice will need some explicit justification. It will not be sufficient simply to register an implicit 'changed taste' among the rulers, including a 'changed taste' among those who make decisions on behalf of rulers, such as (in a welfare state context) public welfare administrators and professional welfare deliverers.

The core question within a legal approach to the welfare state is the extent to which the welfare state represents a strengthening or a weakening of the rule of law. It is fruitful in this regard to draw a distinction between material rights (the right to certain benefits and/or services), and procedural rights (the right to be treated in a certain way if applying for a welfare benefit and service, including a right to proper procedures and the right to complain a perceived wrong decision) (Kjoenstad and Syse 2008). When specifying the exact meaning of *material* welfare rights, legal scholars sometimes clash with economists. Economists usually regard *macro-economic flexibility* as a good thing. That is: a government should not 'tie itself totally to the mast' when fulfilling a very expensive future fiscal promise (for example a public pension promise). Economists will often advise a government to keep a fairly wide scope for future fiscal manoeuvre to ensure there is money enough available for whatever tasks future governments deem most important (perhaps public schools rather than public pensions?). This however may clash with a legal concern that today's citizens should be allowed to live in a maximally predictable welfare environment, implying that welfare benefits such as public pensions should be promised in ways that are legally binding even on future governments. To the extent that such flexibility is increased, this might be perceived at least by some legal scholars as a shift back towards arbitrary rule.

Similarly, legal scholars sometimes clash with welfare state professionals (including social workers) when it comes to specifying the exact content of *procedural* welfare rights. Welfare state professionals usually appreciate having a high degree of professional *discretion* in their dealings with claimants. That way, they can use their professional competence to the max without being hindered by formal procedures. However, legal scholars again tend to emphasize the desirability of predictability as regards what welfare claimants may expect when dealing with professionals. This tension is further heightened by the increased emphasis on activation of welfare claimants. Labour market activation is probably easier to achieve in a flexible legal environment, where professionals and claimants can tailor-make whatever activation measures suit claimants. But too much procedural flexibility can make it difficult for a claimant to anticipate which (if any) aspects of his/her treatment is an unquestionable right and how much is up to the discretion of the professional. Professional discretion can also make it difficult for a claimant to appeal a perceived 'wrong' procedure or 'wrong' outcome, since the more flexibility that is allowed in the meeting between claimant and professional, the more difficult it becomes to document and operationalize what it is that 'wrong' signifies in particular cases. Again, some legal scholars may interpret flexibility in this regard as a change towards arbitrary rule. These issues become even more contested when we remember that the welfare state is not only about distribution of benefits and services, but also about *protective coercion*, such as deciding when to protect people with psychiatric disorders against themselves, and when to protect children against their parents. Such questions illustrate that not only are there fuzzy borders and overlapping debates between disciplines: there are also disciplinary antagonisms and quarrels to be aware of.

The Elephant Revisited

This chapter has offered a rough guide to disciplinary debates on the welfare state, including a brief review of crossovers and antagonisms between disciplines. Studying something from a disciplinary perspective is often necessary to add depth to a study. But, just as often, depth requires knowledge about what is going on outside one's own discipline. An awareness of alternative disciplinary approaches is helpful if one is to come to grips with more than the trunk, hide, or foot of the amorphous, multifaceted, and normatively ambiguous animal representing the welfare state.

PART IV

INPUTS AND ACTORS

CHAPTER 11

....

NEEDS AND RISKS IN THE WELFARE STATE

....

JAN ZUTAVERN

MARTIN KOHLI

INTRODUCTION

....

WELFARE states exist to meet the needs of their citizens. While this is only one of the welfare state's many raisons d'être, it would seem odd to defend a welfare state that did not at least also do that: satisfy needs. Evoking needs is an essential way of staking claims to the welfare state, and responding to them a key justification of its existence. This applies equally to risks. Compulsory protection from typical risks is one of the major means through which welfare states have addressed needs. Throughout this chapter we will refer to risks as the likelihood that a need does or does not arise, where that likelihood can be calculated and influenced by human action (Zinn 2008). It should be kept in mind, however, that, particularly with regard to individual control, the notions of need and risk may have different, even opposing meanings.

To the welfare state scholar, the relation between needs and the welfare state raises two questions: first, which needs must welfare states attend to in order to preserve their legitimacy and, second, which needs do welfare states effectively address, and how well do they do it? Explicit and systematic usage of the concept of needs in the literature has been largely confined to the former, normative perspective. Different conceptions of needs and the question of their appropriateness in establishing legitimate grounds for social policy intervention have been at the centre of normative debates ever since the modern welfare state was born. Empirical welfare state research, on the other hand, has generally not considered concepts of needs to be of much analytical use. Although the notion is regularly evoked in empirical inquiries, it remains conceptually underdeveloped and often unconnected to theories and empirical findings.

Our first objective in this chapter, therefore, is to sound out what empirical-analytical research can learn from normative scholarship for the explanation of welfare state responses to needs and risks. As we will see, normative conceptual distinctions are relevant also for positive theories. But do needs and risks still matter empirically? Hasn't the expansion of the welfare state in the West (here our discussion is limited to the OECD countries) mothballed needs along with the fragmented social policies of the pre-modern Poor Law era? And hasn't the transition to a post-Fordist society multiplied and individualized risk to the point at which social insurance has lost its effectiveness? Answering these questions is our second objective. Taking note of the recent literature, the answer is a clear no. On the one hand, old labour market and life-course related needs and risks are far from disappearing. On the other, the very maturation of the welfare state has propelled a number of new needs and risks onto the policy agenda. What they are and how they vary between welfare states is the third issue we address.

CONCEPTUALIZING NEEDS AND RISKS

In common parlance, needs are ubiquitous. Plants need water, firms need capital, governments need support, and sometimes all we need is love. The needs that fall within the purview of the welfare state are the needs of individual citizens. Since their resources are limited, welfare states have to be selective in the needs that they provide for. According to a widely held view, welfare states respond to the needs of those individuals who, owing to their organizational strength and political resources, prevail in the struggle for influence over governments. But how, then, did welfare states ever come to attend to the destitute and socially marginalized, who lack such political clout? Somehow, needs seem to make demands on the welfare state that are in part independent of the individual who claims the need. What you want the welfare state to do for you, e.g. if you are about to lose your job, is entirely your matter. What you need it to do in that situation is not. Assessing a particular condition in the metric of needs—and the same applies to risks—withdraws that evaluation from the sphere of the subject. This implies that welfare state responses to needs are not entirely contingent upon preferences and the conflicts that ensue from them. Rather, they are always also the result of a (more or less) public—and (more or less) rational—evaluation of what people 'really' need, and of the risks they effectively face. Such a partial liberation of justifications and causes for social policy from subjective fiat does not, however, by itself direct us to an unambiguous normative or positive standard, on the basis of which we could evaluate different needs and their consequences for policy. It is the diversity of such standards that has been the bread and butter of normative debates (see Chapter 2). The most fundamental opposition is between proponents of absolute and of relative conceptions of needs.

Advocates of absolute concepts argue that there exists a set of 'basic' needs that are so fundamental that their satisfaction becomes a pre-condition for anything else human beings may want to achieve (e.g. Goodin 1985; Alkire 2002). This essential nature of basic needs confronts the welfare state with a strong moral obligation to provide whatever it takes to satisfy them where other social institutions fail to do so. Ultimately, proponents of such absolute conceptions of needs have to prove that there exists a list charting basic needs that finds sufficiently widespread approval to represent an 'overlapping consensus' (Nussbaum 2000), but remains specific enough to serve as practical policy guidance. Doyal and Gough (1991) have addressed this problem by proposing a hierarchical model of universal goals (avoidance of serious harm, participation in a chosen form of life), basic needs (health, autonomy) and those universal characteristics of satisfiers required to meet basic needs (e.g. adequate nutrition, security). Their model is an attempt systematically to link basic needs to specific, variable, and practically relevant forms of satisfaction. Ultimately, the model stands or falls with the acceptability of universal standards for assessing the adequacy of specific satisfiers for basic needs. Scholars have expressed strong doubts whether Doyal and Gough's bid is successful (Soper 1993). And it is indeed questionable whether standards for the evaluation of needs can ever be 'fundamental', in the sense that they unambiguously and completely rank all possible, culturally specific interpretations of needs (Sen 2000; Fraser 1989a). Despite the theoretical hurdles that absolute conceptions of needs face, they have found important applications in the form of practical standards for policy intervention such as the Human Development Index or the official poverty lines of the United States. No matter how incomplete such absolute standards are, their normative weight makes them a powerful foundation of social policy and thus a crucial object of research.

Whereas absolute concepts focus on what is 'essential' about human needs, relative notions of needs draw attention to the variety of ways in which any basic need can be satisfied. Proponents of relative concepts put their finger on the practical manifestations of basic needs and the conditions of their satisfaction. While concepts of absolute needs motion us towards those needs that any society has to satisfy in one way or another, relative needs explicate the dimensions in which forms of satisfaction vary. Rather than being mutually exclusive, the two concepts thus allow us to build a bridge between the—necessarily open—normative conceptions of needs and the empirical question of how societies, and welfare states in particular, meet needs. A first source of variation in needs satisfaction is spatial and temporal differences in the physical, economic, and cultural constraints and resources for satisfying basic needs. One way of evaluating the constraints and opportunities that determine what exactly individuals need is to assess empirically how basic needs are 'normally' satisfied inside a given reference group. Where members of that group lack such 'normal' means, the satisfaction of basic needs is likely to be curtailed. This interpretation of group-specific social standards underlies several statistical measures such as 'normal' baskets of goods or relative poverty thresholds. In contrast to absolute measures, which define *a priori* or normatively what constitutes 'adequate' satisfaction of basic needs, such relative indicators rely on an empirical determination of 'typical' levels of satisfaction to which they may add a relative threshold, e.g. 50 per cent of median income (Boarini and Mira d'Ercole 2006).

But reference groups are not only an indication for potentially successful needs satisfaction. They also define what is required in order to be accepted as a full member of a given community (Sen 1983; Goodin 1990b). Cultural practices and standards constitute the things, beings, and doings that members of a community are generally able and expected to achieve. By implication, this kind of relativity only applies to those basic needs for which inter-individual comparisons are a constitutive element. These are generally all participatory basic needs, such as the need for social recognition or the need for a cultural identity. This conception finds important practical application in measures of inequality (Atkinson and Bourguignon 2000; Förster and Mira d'Ercole 2005), relative deprivation (Townsend 1979; Boarini and Mira d'Ercole 2006), or social exclusion (Atkinson and Davoudi 2000; Hills et al. 2002). The reverse of the need for identification and participation is the need for distinction. Differentiation is needed to assure communities of their identity and individuals of their personal achievements. Satisfaction of the need for distinction is inversely related to other individuals' achievements or group specific status endowments; in other words, satisfiers for distinction are 'positional goods'. By implication, participatory and differentiation needs conflict where they demand the same satisfiers. Measures aimed at extending participation through e.g. progressive taxation or equal opportunity policies thus withdraw from individuals some of the means for ascertaining their distinctiveness. Welfare states vary considerably with respect to the relative weights they attach to the two needs and the characteristics—occupation, employment status, gender, age—that they select as the basis for legitimate distinction.

In sum, different conceptions of needs draw attention to different types of analytical problems. First, the values on which notions of basic needs rest point to the potential breadth of needs that welfare states may be confronted with. Even the most parsimonious concepts add to the 'classical' domains of welfare state provisioning a series of needs and related risks—e.g. health, education, emotional care, physical security, or salutary environments—in the satisfaction of which the state is already involved, but which are rarely considered in conjunction by policy-makers and researchers alike. Secondly, a perspective on the different environmental conditions under which basic needs are satisfied reminds us of the relative importance of and interaction between global, national, and local contexts, and of the specific constraints they impose on needs satisfaction. Thirdly, concepts of relative needs grounded in inter-individual comparisons stress the trade-offs and potential conflicts involved in the satisfaction of needs, both between different social groups and for the individual as a member of various reference groups. Stated as political claims, needs call for different forms of social policy at various levels of intervention. Where they underlie specific policy instruments such as poverty thresholds, means tests, or insurance principles, they act as powerful filters for the way welfare states respond to changes in their socio-economic environments. The confrontation of needs claims with policy instruments, finally, draws attention to the critical question of who has authority to define needs or risks and adequate satisfaction or protection. In the next section, we show how welfare state theories have treated needs and risks, and make some suggestions as to how they can do so more systematically.

NEEDS, RISKS, AND THEORIES
OF THE WELFARE STATE

Most historiographies of post-war welfare state theorizing distinguish between functionalist, political, and institutionalist families of explanations (Myles and Quadagno 2002; C. Pierson 1991). All three implicitly use the notion of needs. Nonetheless, we argue that there is room for a more systematic conceptualization of needs in all of them. For functionalists, social policies are the unmediated response to social and economic pressures. Potentially intervening forces such as the political organization of social demands or governmental institutions are assumed to be either neutral towards or fully determined by socio-economic change. Welfare states do what they *need* to do in the face of socio-economic challenges. Their response is triggered whenever transformations of socio-economic conditions for economic production and social reproduction cross a threshold beyond which existing forms of needs satisfaction lose their effectiveness. Functionalist explanations, then, stand or fall with their specification of the needs they assume to be the responsibility of the welfare state. Wilensky's classical argument that industrialization and demographic change caused welfare state expansion by creating new needs, especially among the elderly, may serve as a case in point (Wilensky 1975). By failing to distinguish between an expansionary pull, that is due to slackening economic constraints on the satisfaction of basic material needs of the elderly, and an expansionary push, resulting from political demands for and a policy commitment to reducing age-related inequalities by enabling the retired to participate more fully in social life or maintain their achieved status, Wilensky misses the far-reaching practical consequences of these different needs conceptions for policy design. No matter what one thinks about the persuasiveness of functionalist explanations as such, functionalists need to be specific about needs if they are to accommodate empirical variations in welfare provision.

Once we raise the question of which needs welfare states are committed to, we also want to know what causes variations in need satisfaction. One way of addressing this question is to examine variations in the social and economic changes that give rise to needs and risks. To the extent that processes such as (de-)industrialization and demographic change not only have advanced to different degrees in different countries, but also have distinct national manifestations, they could be an effective source of variations. However, the consequences of social and economic transformations for human needing must be articulated as problems for the welfare state if they are to trigger policy changes. As long as these political sources of variation are not taken into account, the explanatory force of even the most sophisticated accounts of socio-economic change will remain limited.

Thus, political and institutional approaches to welfare state theory have argued that 'politics matters' by showing how variations in organizational capacities, institutionalized procedures for decision making and administrative practices selectively channel and process social demands and grievances. First of all, such a perspective vigorously veers to political preferences based on wants and desires. Social policy outcomes become the result of institutionally mediated power struggles between organized interests ('power resource' approach, e.g. Korpi 1983; Huber and Stephens 2001a). But for determining the interests that actors are presumed to pursue, power-based accounts tend to rely in part on the notion of needs. If we assume actors to be rational in setting their (political) goals, it is rather implausible that they would want something which they do not also need. Since we can assess needs without having to rely exclusively on the subjects that bear them, they allow us to formulate preference-based hypotheses independent of the aims expressed by political actors. Awareness of the different normative conceptions of needs should help us to appreciate the potential tensions that actors face when trying to satisfy conflicting needs. Normative theories also remind us that there is no principle that would allow the researcher to unambiguously rank the potential needs of any given actor. Acknowledging this inherent ambiguity of needs, several authors have made a case for abandoning objective assessments of needs altogether. They argue that we should instead focus entirely on the actual political contestations through which needs are defined as real and legitimate (Stone 2002; Fraser 1989b; Robertson 1998).

One powerful player in such contestations is the welfare state itself. Most social policy instruments are founded upon or entail a specific conception of recipients' needs or risks. As rules for policy implementation, they influence the chance of any need or risk finding public recognition. At the level of policy design, such rule-based legacies of needs satisfaction and risk protection are often fiercely guarded by current beneficiaries to the disadvantage of new, insufficiently articulated and poorly organized needs and risks (P. Pierson 2006). At the level of implementation, they circumscribe the discretion of street-level bureaucrats in defining the range of needs and risks to which they will respond. By posing the question of which needs and risks benefit from discretion or rules respectively, the recent trend towards the decentralization and individualization of social benefits and services has opened up a research agenda of increasing importance.

Finally, different conceptions of needs are part and parcel of basic welfare regime variations, e.g. as conceived prominently by Esping-Andersen (1990). It is, however, not only liberal welfare states that are 'needs-based', as Esping-Andersen's narrow notion of needs leads him to argue. Liberal welfare states do, indeed, target much of their social policy towards individuals who face constraints in satisfying their basic (non-comparative) needs, which allow for autonomy of agency and avoid interventions that might curtail the fruits of individual achievement. Scandinavian welfare states, on the other hand, have gone furthest in meeting needs of participation in the national community and, thus, in inequality reduction across various social groups, whereas welfare states on the European continent have traditionally placed more emphasis on distinctions based on seniority and occupational membership.

In other words, social policy variations are due to an important extent to the institutionalization of different forms of need satisfaction and risk protection. Such variations may persist even where the socio-economic conditions responsible for the emergence of needs and risk profiles have been transformed and new needs or risks are competing for political attention. It is precisely this question of the relation between new and old needs or risks that has gained prominence in recent welfare state scholarship. In the next section, we turn to the empirical literature to portray the major challenges facing welfare states today.

SOCIO-ECONOMIC CHALLENGES, NEEDS, RISKS, AND WELFARE STATES

Although welfare states are inherently political achievements, the impetus for their development often lies in the disruptive force that large, macro-historical transformations have levelled against extant social orders. National variations notwithstanding, it was the watermark of first-generation welfare states to have institutionalized a model of social provisioning closely articulated with the functional exigencies of industrializing societies. The model relied on a gendered division of work based on male full-time and continuous employment and female care work inside the family, sustained by economic growth and high labour demand. The welfare state's key contribution was the mobilization of solidarity in those 'legitimate' circumstances in the life of a worker in which the successful commodification of his labour power could no longer be expected. It thereby helped to institutionalize a 'Fordist' life course consisting of three main stages—education, employment, retirement (Kohli 2007; Mayer 2001)—providing financial support for its first and especially last phase and protecting its middle phase against unforeseen or short-term vulnerabilities (sickness, accidents, disability, short-term unemployment).

Today, this model is showing clear signs of wear. The social and economic conditions that sustained its performance have receded. New needs and risks are joining old ones, as a result of structural and cultural changes and of welfare state institutions protected by their old constituencies. The key developments to which the literature has attributed the emergence of new needs and risks are the tertiarization, feminization, and flexibilization of the labour force, increasingly unstable families, and declining fertility rates that combine with higher longevity to tilt the age structure of societies upwards. As the data for selected OECD countries in Table 11.1 illustrates, the onset and speed at which these processes have advanced differ considerably. Critical for welfare state responses has been a society's progression prior to the tightening of economic conditions at around the time of the first oil crisis. By then, in countries such as the United States and the Netherlands, less than a quarter of the working-age population was still employed in the primary and secondary sectors. Accordingly, further losses have been rather low and more than compensated for by a vigorous expansion of the service sector. Other countries such as Germany, Italy, and Japan have only recently reached comparable levels, and thus have had to cope with the bulk of pressure for adaptation under conditions of low economic growth and austerity.

While it would seem that the loss of employment in the primary and secondary sectors has been (over-)compensated for by the growth of the tertiary sector—the German and United Kingdom service sectors are the only ones that, in aggregate terms, have been unable to absorb all employment made redundant in agriculture and manufacturing—the picture changes when we consider rising female labour force participation during this period. The Netherlands and Spain have witnessed the largest expansion of female employment since the early 1980s, followed by Australia and Germany. With respect to tertiarization, the service-heavy economies of the United States and the Netherlands have been joined by Australia, the United Kingdom, Sweden, and Denmark, in part as a correlate to high levels of female labour force participation concentrated in both public and private services. The Netherlands, France, and the United Kingdom stand out for their landslide flexibilization of family relations—a change that had already largely occurred in the Nordic countries as well as the United States as early as the 1970s. Japan combines a substantial increase in family disruptions with extremely low levels of children born out of wedlock. Tradition has persisted most strongly in Italy, for which the main challenge in this respect still lies ahead. In comparison to the World War II birth cohort, when only Germany was clearly below the replacement level, the fertility of women born around the time of the first oil crisis has decreased everywhere,[1] with the highest relative declines recorded in Australia, Italy, Japan, and Spain—countries in which life expectancy at birth is now among the highest in the world.

The data reported here largely confirm the welfare regime variations of socio-economic change described in the literature (e.g. Goodin et al. 1999), with the Nordic and English-speaking societies leading the shift to post-industrialism, while Japan, continental, and especially Southern Europe are trailing. Nonetheless, the diachronic perspective reveals significant country differences within regimes (compare e.g. the

---

[1] The cohort perspective given here yields higher values than the current period Total Fertility Rate (TFR) but is close to the current period TFR adjusted for tempo effects (as calculated by the Vienna Institute of Demography, see www.populationeurope.org).

Table 11.1 Socio–economic causes of new social needs and risks

	Sectoral employment			Female LFP rate		Total divorce rate (periods)		Births out of wedlock		Total fertility rate (cohorts)		Live expectancy at birth (years)			
	losses 1st + 2nd	gains 3rd	level 3rd									Women		Men	
	Δ 1969–2006	Δ 1969–2006	Ø 2002–2006	Ø 1982–1986	Ø 2002–2006	1970	2000	1980	2004	Co. 1941–1945	Co. 1971–1975	Ø 1969–1973	Ø 2002–2004	Ø 1969–1973	Ø 2002–2004
Australia	−12.4	16.4	52.7	54.1	68.3	11.0	46.0	12.4	32.2	2.58	1.96	74.9	83.0	68.1	78.1
Denmark	−16.0	19.2	54.2	74.9	76.4	26.2	37.5	33.2	45.4	2.21	1.96	76.0	80.1	70.7	75.5
France	−16.5	17.0	45.2	56.1	64.0	9.9	40.9	11.4	46.4	2.31	2.18	75.9	83.5	68.3	76.4
Germany	−17.5	16.3	43.0	52.6	66.6	18.1	44.3	11.9	27.9	1.83	1.62	73.8	81.8	67.7	76.4
Italy	−13.4	16.2	36.1	40.7	50.0	2.8	12.5	4.3	14.9	2.08	1.48	74.9	83.3	69.0	77.5
Japan	−13.8	16.2	46.1	57.0	64.8	9.3	33.1	0.8	2.0	2.06	1.45	75.4	85.5	70.0	78.6
Netherl.	−9.6	26.2	57.1	40.6	68.3	8.3	39.3	4.1	32.5	2.11	2.00	74.7	81.7	71.0	76.8
Spain	−17.3	23.1	39.1	34.9	57.8		.	3.9	23.4	2.49	1.60	74.8	83.6	69.2	76.8
Sweden	−17.0	18.9	53.9	79.3	78.0	29.9	53.9	39.7	55.4	2.00	1.70	77.2	82.6	72.0	78.2
UK	−18.0	16.7	52.5	63.4	70.7	13.4	52.7	11.5	42.3	2.04	1.78	75.0	80.8	68.8	76.5
USA	−9.1	18.5	53.7	64.7	71.8	32.8	50.6	18.4	35.7	2.53	2.10	74.9	80.2	67.3	74.9

Notes: Data on employment are percentages. We report 5-year averages (Ø) except where data is not available. Δ is the sum of yearly changes through the indicated time period.

Sources and definitions: Sectoral employment = civilian employment in percent of the working age population (15–64); female labor force participation rate is in percent of the female working age population (15–64), missing: Denmark: 1982, UK: 1982–3; see OECD 2009e. Total divorce rates = sum of the divorce rates by duration of marriage for the respective year; OECD 2002a: Tab. GE5.1. Births out of wedlock are as a percentage of all births; OECD 2007b: Tab. 2.2. Total fertility rates for the cohort born 1941–45 are completed, for the cohort born 1971–5 projected; D'Addio and Mira D'Ercole 2005: Tab.2. Life expectancy at birth in years is from OECD 2008f; data for Italy and the UK refer to 1971, data for Spain refer to 1970.

high rate of change in Spain with the low rate in Italy), as well as within-country contrasts between labour market and family-related change.

What is the significance of these social and economic transformations for the welfare state? Insofar as they do, indeed, mark a departure from the conditions that sustained the 'old' Fordist model of provisioning, they not only give rise to new social needs and risks, but also undermine the viability and effectiveness of existing welfare arrangements (Esping-Andersen 1999; Taylor-Gooby 2004; Bonoli 2005). The unwinding of agricultural and industrial employment entails a devaluation of sector-specific skills (Iversen and Cusack 2000) and thus the risk of frictional and structural unemployment. In contrast to this transitional phenomenon, the growth of the service sector has brought with it a number of risks that are likely to persist. Unstable employment and wages that are no longer poverty-proof can be attributed to the polarization of skill requirements and wages in tertiary employment. The consequences are working poverty and rising inequality. Welfare states and social partners that intervene with protective labour regulations to stabilize employment biographies and wages pay the price of lower employment levels and higher and longer unemployment (Iversen and Wren 1998; Kenworthy 2003).

As women are entering the labour market under conditions that are still likely to be more adverse than those of their male colleagues, they also face a dilemma at home. A largely undiminished desire for children (OECD 2007b) and a preference for 'intimacy at a small distance' between parents and adult children make it difficult for women to dissociate themselves from care work inside the family, which still falls predominantly on their, rather than on their male partners', shoulders. Women's choice, then, is between the stress of balancing employment aspirations with care for children or the elderly and the stress of having to forego one or the other (Hakim 2000; Lewis and Huerta 2008). Divorce significantly increases the risk of material and social deprivation. But while a more fragile solidarity between partners may have indeed diminished the ability of families to stabilize unsteady employment biographies and provide effective poverty safeguards, supporting ties across family generations remain strong (Kohli et al. 2010). Through a net flow of transfers from parents to their adult children, the fruits of the industrial welfare state are partly handed down to post-industrial generations (Albertini et al. 2006).

Country-specific risk profiles (see Tables 11.2 and 11.3) again largely conform to regime variations, but exhibit some significant nuances. Sweden stands out for its low labour market related risk scores and the virtual absence of any child penalty for female employment. Denmark registers comparable or slightly higher risk levels, but is conspicuous for its low levels of part-time work among mothers with two or more children. Employment-related risk levels are relatively low also in the United States,[2] with the unsurprising exception of low-wage work—almost a quarter of full-time dependent workers in the United States bring home less than two-thirds of full-time median earnings. While the United Kingdom diverges from the liberal

---

[2] It should be noted, however, that a low share of fixed-term employment can also indicate a low degree of employment protection, in other words, an easy pattern of 'hire and fire'.

pattern with a relatively high average incidence of long-term unemployment (which has, however, decreased significantly since its peak in the mid-1990s), Australians are more likely than Anglo-Saxons in the Northern hemisphere to work in temporary or low-skill jobs, and Australian mothers are more likely to withdraw from the labour market, on a par with the Mediterranean countries.

On the European continent, the risk profiles of the Netherlands, France, and Germany largely resemble each other. Beyond similarities, labour market risks in the Netherlands are marked by the well-known prevalence of part-time employment. Four out of five Dutch mothers with two and more children work part-time. The German labour market, on the other hand, is characterized by a significant child penalty for working mothers. It also has a below-average employment ratio of low-skilled people, reflecting, in part, the relatively high level of education of the young adult population. In Italy, by contrast, a quarter of the population between 15 and 64 were low-skilled employees in 2003; this figure is topped only in Spain, which registers the same high proportion of young adults not completing a higher education (40 per cent of the 25–34 age group). The two Southern European countries also have had the highest proportion of long-term unemployment. Employers in Spain, moreover, make particularly heavy use of temporary contracts.

With respect to family transformation, a contrast between the data from Tables 11.1 and 11.3 shows that the high rates of divorce and out-of-wedlock births in the Nordic and liberal welfare states do, indeed, translate into higher shares of children growing up with single mothers. In Southern Europe, on the other hand, single parent families continue to be a marginal phenomenon. Whereas their level in Italy has fluctuated within a narrow band, it is growing in Spain. Demographic change has been most pronounced in Italy and Japan. The ageing process has been slower in the United States, the United Kingdom, France, and Scandinavia, but different levels in the early 1970s have led to significant risk variations also here. While material provision for the elderly in Northern Europe has limited their poverty risks, Italy and above all Japan face, together with Australia and the US, the highest levels of relative poverty in old age. The largest numbers of children growing up in income-poor households live in the United Kingdom and the United States.

The bigger picture, then, is one of an increasing incidence of risky life circumstances that either have become problematic or more prevalent in post-industrial societies. They thus present new challenges to the industrial model of social provisioning. While 'old' industrial needs and risks have not disappeared (Scarbrough 2000)—and their successful coverage may indeed foster provision also against new risks, e.g. through intergenerational transfers—welfare states face potential pressures for adaptation. These pressures, however, are of a political nature. Without the articulation of new needs, either by those who bear them or by their advocates in the policy arena, social and economic transformations and the corresponding risk profiles will not effectuate policy change.

Besides considerable cross-regime and cross-country variations in the onset and progression of such transformations (Bonoli 2007), scholars have looked to the specific constellations of risk groups and their organizational capacities, and to the existing

Table 11.2 Selected risk and need profiles: Employment

	Unemployment				Employment						Low skill employment	
	Total		% >1 year		% part-time		% fixed term		% low wage			
	Ø 1983–87	Ø 2002–06	Ø 1983–87	Ø 2002–06	Ø 1983–87	Ø 2002–06	1983	1998	1983	2004	1992	2003
Australia	8.8	5.7	28.5	19.9	20.2	24.4	15.6	26.4	14.6	14.5	27.2	23.2
Denmark	7.8	4.8	33.0	21.7	20.3	16.9	12.5	10.1		10.7	25.3	11.0
France	9.8	8.8	42.4	39.8	11.7	13.4	3.3	13.9			27.2	21.2
Germany	7.0	10.0	46.1	52.2	11.5	20.4	10	12.3	14.3[a]	16.9	9.4	8.5
Italy	10.7	8.1	64.3	54.4	8.1	13.6	6.6	8.5	18.5		38.8	26.5
Japan	2.8	5.0	15.7	32.9	16.5	18.0	10.3	10.8		14.3		10.7
Netherl.	12.6	4.4	51.6	34.7	21.5	34.9	5.8	12.7	10.4	14.8[b]	21.3	20.1
Spain	19.9	10.3	56.5	35.9	5.0	9.3	15.7	32.9		16.2[c]	37.2	32.5
Sweden	3.2	6.5	12.1	17.6	16.8	13.9	12	12.9		6.4	24.8	11.6
UK	11.3	5.0	47.7	22.3	19.7	23.6	5.5	7.1	18.8	20.8	17.9	8.6
USA	7.6	5.5	10.4	11.0	14.9	13.0	5.5	3.2	20.4	23.9	8.3	7.5

Notes: [a] 1984; [b] 1999; [c] 2003: see Table 11.1.

Sources and definitions: Total unemployment = unemployment as a percentage of the labour force; long-term unemployment = unemployment spells >1 year as a percentage of total unemployment; part-time employment = civilian employees usually working under 30h per week as a percentage of total civilian employment; OECD 2009e. Fixed-term employment as a percentage of total employment is from Kalleberg 2006: Table 5.2. Low wage employment = percentage of full-time workers earning less than two-thirds of full-time median earnings; OECD 2009f. Low-skill employment = percentage of the working age population (25–64) in employment that has not completed an upper secondary education or higher (data not entirely comparable over time); own calculations based on data from OECD 1994d, 2005c.

Table 11.3 Selected risk and need profiles: Family

	Working mothers with 2+ children		Lack of higher skills (25–34)	Children in single mother households		Old age 'dependency' ratio		Dependent poor (<50% med.inc.)	
	Empl. rate	% part-time						<17	66+
	2000		2003	mid-1980s	ca. 2000	1973	2007	ca. 2000	
Australia	43.2	63.1	25	8.4	17.8	13.4	19.5	3.0	2.8
Denmark	77.2	16.2	14	12.0	14.3	20.1	23.4	0.7	0.8
France	58.8	31.8	20	6.7	11.5	21.2	25.2	1.8	1.7
Germany	56.3	60.2	15	8.4	12.5	21.8	30.5	2.0	1.6
Italy	42.4	34.4	40[a]	4.2	4.9	16.2[c]	29.8	2.8	2.6
Japan			6			11.0	33.1	2.6	4.5
Netherl.	63.3	82.7	24[a]	7.8	9.0	16.6	21.7	2.0	0.2
Spain	43.3	15.3	40	3.8[b]	6.9	16.2	24.2	2.9[d]	1.8[d]
Sweden	81.8	22.2	9	13.5	17.8	22.4	26.5	0.8	1.3
UK	62.3	62.8	29	12.9	21.7	21.8	24.2	4.1	2.0
USA	64.7	23.6	13	18.8	19.5	16.0	18.7	5.7	2.9

Notes: [a]2002; [b]1980; [c]1971; [d]1995: see Table 11.1.

Sources and definitions: Working mothers = employment rate of women with 2 or more children <15 and shares working part-time (see Table 11.2); OECD 2002b: Tables 2.4 and 2.5. Lack of higher skills = percentage of the population aged 25–34 that has not completed an upper secondary education or higher; OECD 2005c: Table A1.2a. Children in single mother households = percentage of all children <18 living in a single mother household; Luxembourg Income Study Inequality and Poverty Key Figures. Old age dependency ratio = population 65+ as a percentage of population 15–64; OECD 2009e. Dependent poor = share of children (<17) and the elderly (66+), respectively, with an equivalized disposable income below 50 per cent of the median for the entire population, as a percentage of total population; own calculation based on data from Förster and Mira D'Ercole 2005: Annex Table A6, A7.

policy schemes that determine how welfare states have responded to these risks (Armingeon and Bonoli 2006). Their conclusions tend to be pessimistic. The population affected by new social risks—children and young people, single mothers, low-skilled and low-wage service workers, long-term unemployed—is less likely to be politically active, and to be present in political organizations. Even where new needs find political recognition, they face well-organized opposing interests in zero-sum games that leave little room for political exchange. This lack of political clout has caused some scholars to caution against too much optimism about those strategies of policy 'recalibration' on which welfare states have already embarked. Policies for the 'activation' of benefit recipients and the 'de-familialization' of working-age women in particular are bound to walk a tightrope between meeting the multiple needs of affected individuals and the political demands of those whose solidarity is called upon (Dean 2003; Taylor-Gooby 2006; Leitner and Lessenich 2007).

In short, the policy challenge confronting post-industrial societies arises from the coexistence of new social needs and risk profiles with those enduring 'Fordist' needs that continue to lend strong support to traditional welfare state institutions. Rather than ushering in a wholesale restructuring of the welfare state, this growing heterogeneity pressures existing policy arrangements to adapt to a larger variety of risk situations. Tight financial limits and increasingly fragile political resources for the legitimation of state interventions imply that such a differentiation of policies will have to draw on increasingly diverse forms of private social provision. However, grievances voiced outside established policy arenas are unlikely to reach policymakers through institutionalized channels for the aggregation of class- or milieu-specific interests. The governance of post-industrial welfare states will thus require a higher sensitivity to unvoiced but experienced needs if it is to retain its legitimacy and effectiveness in addressing social problems. For welfare state scholarship, the agenda comprises both a careful analysis of the socio-economic developments that cause new needs and risk profiles and an assessment of how the latter will be voiced and mobilized. The precondition for both tasks is a theoretically grounded, nuanced conceptualization of needs and risks.

CHAPTER 12

DEMOCRACY AND CAPITALISM

TORBEN IVERSEN

INTRODUCTION

THE welfare state is at the centre of a long-standing debate in political economy about the relationship between capitalism and democracy. A standard view holds that democracy compensates for inequalities in the distribution of property and income by the extension of the welfare state. But this view raises a number of empirical and theoretical puzzles that are at the core of a large and diverse political economy literature on democracy and capitalism. The purpose of this chapter is to identify these puzzles and how they have been addressed in the literature. My focus is on broad theoretical questions and puzzles in political economy as they relate to research on redistribution and the welfare state.

First, if democracy empowers those who are at the lower half of the income distribution, why don't the poor soak the rich? Second, and related, if the welfare state is all about 'politics against markets' (the title of Esping-Andersen's first book) how can capitalism be a viable economic system under democracy? Third, if democracy 'compensates' for economic inequality how can we explain that countries with relatively egalitarian labour markets also redistribute a lot (think Sweden) while countries with relatively inegalitarian labour markets redistribute little (think the United States)?

This essay discusses three different approaches to the study of democratic redistribution, and then considers the recent literature on capitalism as an economic system and how economic and democratic institutions relate to one another as well as to the welfare state. The first approach assumes that democratic politics is structured around a single left–right redistributive dimension. The central issue in this literature is whether 'Who Governs' matters, and if so, in what ways. These are key questions for political economy because it goes to the heart of whether democratic politics makes a difference: do the poor ever get a chance to try to soak the rich, and how successful are they when they do?

The main weakness of this approach is that it does not explain why politicians should limit themselves to pursuing redistribution in a single policy dimension. Where there is no such limitation, opportunities to form distributive coalitions abound. Work that puts coalitional politics at the centre of its analysis paints a richer and more realistic picture of the politics of redistribution. But the cost may be theoretical intractability, and much of the coalitional literature falls into the trap of *post hoc* description. I will discuss two recent attempts to move beyond such description.

The third approach explains distributive politics as a function of the specific design of democratic institutions—including electoral rules and federalism. The strategy here is to substitute *ad hoc* model assumptions, such as unidimensionality, with ones that are rooted in careful observation of actual institutional designs. This approach moves beyond the partisan literature by explicitly considering how economic preferences are aggregated into policies, at the same time as it avoids the chaotic world of unconstrained coalitional politics. I argue that this combination has produced a vibrant research programme that helps answer the three key questions identified above: under what circumstances the poor will soak the rich, how capitalism is a viable economic system under democracy, and why equality and redistribution tend to go hand in hand.

The 'varieties of capitalism' approach, in particular, illuminates the relationship between redistributive politics and economic performance and helps explain why there is no necessary contradiction between the welfare state and the market. This work also helps make sense of the observed institutional diversity of modern capitalism, and why such diversity persists in the face of global market integration. But work in this tradition has thus far produced few insights into the relationship between economic and political institutions, and it has little to say about the political origins of economic institutions—focusing instead on economic-organizational efficiency as a cause.

Some of the most recent literature on democracy and capitalism seeks to endogenize institutions, including the institution of democracy itself, by modelling these as a function of class interests. The move is tempting, and probably desirable, but it does come at a cost because without institutional constraints difficult issues of multidimensionality and preference aggregation re-emerge. In the concluding section, I suggest that there is a new structuralist turn in political economy where the parameters for our models of institutional design are derived from the specific historical conditions that have shaped capitalism in different parts of the world. These origins may in turn help account for current patterns of distribution and redistribution.

DEMOCRACY AND PARTISANSHIP

There are two standard approaches in political economy to explaining variance in distribution and redistribution. One originates in Meltzer and Richard's (1981) hugely influential model of redistribution, which has been the workhorse in the political economy for the past two decades. The model is built on the intuitively simple idea that, since the median voter tends to have below-average income (assuming a typical right-skewed distribution of income and high turnout), she has an interest in redistribution. With a proportional tax and flat rate benefit, and assuming that there are efficiency costs of taxation, Downs's median voter theorem can be applied to predict the extent of redistribution. The equilibrium is reached when the benefit to the median voter of additional spending is exactly outweighed by the work disincentives (or other inefficiencies) produced by such spending. This implies two key comparative statics: spending is higher (a) the greater the skew in the distribution of income, and (b) the greater the number of poor people who vote.

The latter suggests that an expansion of the franchise to the poor, or higher voter turnout among the poor, will shift the decisive voter to the left and therefore raise support for redistribution. Assuming that the median voter's policy preference is implemented, democratization will therefore lead to redistribution. There is some support for this proposition (see esp. Rodrik 1999, Ansell 2008a on democracy; Franzese 2002: ch. 2 on turnout), but the evidence that democracy increases redistribution is far from conclusive (see esp. Ross 2006). Even if democracy increases redistribution, it seems clear that the bulk of variance in redistribution is *within* rather than between regime types.

The other implication—that inegalitarian societies redistribute more than egalitarian ones—has been soundly rejected by the data (see Lindert 1996; Moene and Wallerstein 2001; Iversen and Soskice 2009). Indeed, the pattern among democracies appears to be precisely the opposite. As noted in the example above, a country with a flat income structure such as Sweden redistributes much more than a country like the United States with a very inegalitarian distribution of income. This is sometimes referred to as the 'Robin Hood paradox', and it is a puzzle that informs much contemporary scholarship.

The other main approach to the study of capitalism and democracy focuses on the role of political power, especially the organizational and political strength of labour. If capitalism is about class conflict, then the organization and relative political strength of classes should affect policies and economic outcomes. *Power resources theory* focuses on the size and structure of the welfare state, explaining it as a function of the historical strength of the political left, mediated by alliances with agrarian interests and the middle classes (Korpi 1983; Esping-Andersen 1990; Huber and Stephens 2001a).

One key attraction of power resources theory is that it can potentially account for the Robin Hood paradox. If centre-left governments *simultaneously* promote pre-fisc income equality (especially through investment in education) *and* redistribution (especially through transfers) the two will tend to go together. A complementary logic is that if strong left governments are associated with strong unions, and if the latter promote equality in wages while the former increase redistribution, redistribution will again be a complement to equality; not a substitute as implied by the Meltzer-Richard model. This insight is nicely explained in Bradley et al. (2003), which shows that unions are key in explaining wage distribution while left governments are essential in explaining redistribution (see also Hicks and Swank 1992; Cusack 1997; Allan and Scruggs 2004; Pontusson 2005; Castles and Obinger 2007).

But while partisanship seems clearly to matter, power resource theory provides no explanation for why the left is strong in some countries and weak in others. This variation is only weakly related to unionization (see Iversen and Soskice 2006), and unionization is itself in need of explanation. Moreover, if we use a simple left–right conception of politics, there are strong theoretical reasons to expect governments to be centrist. Although Downs applied his argument only to majoritarian two-party systems, the median-voter theorem also applies to unidimensional models of legislative politics in multiparty systems. Essentially, no proposal or coalition can get majority support that deviates from the position of the median legislator (Laver and Schofield 1990). Power resource theory does not explain why the median-voter theorem is systematically violated, and paradoxically therefore offers no account of why partisanship should matter. An important puzzle is therefore why there are stable cross-national differences in government partisanship (see Powell 2002; Iversen and Soskice 2006).

Rather surprisingly, most of the literature also fails to distinguish between the preferences of parties and the preferences of voters. Observed policy differences between left and right governments could be due to either. There are methodological fixes to this problem, but we also need a theory of voter preferences. This is particularly important because voters have an incentive to be 'rationally ignorant' as argued by Downs many years ago. The lack of political information among ordinary voters has been thoroughly documented since the publication of 'The American Voter' in 1960 (Campbell et al. 1960; see Lewis-Beck et al. 2008 for an update), and the consequences for partisan politics and redistribution are amply illustrated in a recent book by Bartels (2008). Bartels shows that ordinary people routinely vote against their own distributive interests, *even* when they are motivated by these interests.

Yet, against both theory and evidence, the standard political economy approach to redistribution and the welfare state assumes that people are fully informed about their interests and how these are affected by public policies. A major research agenda is therefore to endogenize the acquisition of political knowledge in models of redistribution. I suspect that this involves much closer attention to the role of informal networks and the social incentives these provide their members to be informed. There is a burgeoning literature on social capital and the welfare state (see Rothstein 2001; Rothstein and Stolle 2003), but it does not speak to the political knowledge issues and is not well integrated with standard political economy perspectives to redistribution.

WORLDS OF WELFARE CAPITALISM
AND COALITIONAL POLITICS

Distributive politics is inherently multidimensional because a pie can be divided along as many dimensions as there are political agents vying for a piece. It is therefore hard to understand why politicians should constrain themselves to contest a single policy instrument such as the proportional tax/flat-rate benefit in the Meltzer-Richard model. And when alternative tax-benefit schedules are considered the results change in fundamental ways. In Snyder and Kramer (1988), for example, the choice is over different—linear and non-linear—tax schedules, and the majority choice is no longer redistribution that benefits the poor. The Snyder-Kramer model is itself in fact restricted to one dimension (because it limits the choice to single-parameter schedules subject to an exogenously given revenue target), but it clearly demonstrates the sensitivity of results to the assumptions made about the structure of taxes and benefits.[1]

One of the first to recognize the importance of multidimensional distributive politics was Esping-Andersen (1990). Each of his three different 'worlds' of welfare capitalism is associated with a distinct tax-benefit structure. In the most redistributive (social democratic) type, progressive taxation is coupled with flat rate benefits; in the 'liberal' type means-tested benefits are targeted to the poor; while in the 'conservative' type benefits are tied to income and occupation. Castles (1998a) separates out a distinct Southern European cluster, but it may be converging to the continental European pattern (Castles and Obinger 2008). Esping-Andersen's three main types have been highly resistant to change.

Esping-Andersen makes the plausible (and interesting) argument that the structure of benefits is associated with, and perhaps causes, different social divisions and political patterns: the poor against the middle class in the means-tested, insiders versus outsiders in the conservative, and public against private sector in the social democratic. To explain redistributive politics, political economy therefore has to endogenize the structure of benefits. Clearly this task can be accomplished neither with a median voter model, nor with a simple left–right partisan model. Esping-Andersen instead suggests that the answer lies in historically unique class coalitions: red–green coalitions in Scandinavia, resulting in universalism; state–corporatist coalitions in continental Europe; and alliances between middle-class and higher income groups in liberal countries. Echoing the recent literature on path dependence (P. Pierson 2000), Esping-Andersen then suggests that the structure of the benefit system reproduces the political support for each type.

But neither the origins of Esping-Andersen's three worlds, nor their stability, can be said to be *explained* in any conventional scientific sense since there is no argument

---

[1] The winner in the Snyder-Kramer model is the middle class—a result that is echoed in the multidimensional model (using probabilistic voting) by Dixit and Londregan (1996).

to preclude alternative outcomes. For example, why would it not be possible for liberal welfare states to expand redistribution towards the middle class? Or why does the middle class not try to exclude the poor from sharing in the generous benefits of the social democratic model? Or why can outsiders not offer a deal to a sub-set of insiders in the conservative model that would cause the original coalition to break up? Without any explicit theory of coalitions, much of Esping-Andersen's analysis comes across as *post hoc* description.

What Esping-Andersen understood intuitively is that social policy is multidimensional and multidimensionality implies coalitional politics and distinct outcomes. But to move beyond *post hoc* description we need a theory of why distributive politics takes on particular forms at particular times.

Modelling multidimensional coalitional politics is at the centre of several new attempts to understand distribution in democracies. In Roemer's (1998) model, people have intrinsic preferences on some ascriptive dimension, such as race or religion, in addition to preferences over redistribution. If the redistributive dimension was the only one that mattered, the analysis would essentially collapse to a Meltzer-Richard model. When a second dimension is introduced, however, the right party can appeal to poor religious (or racist) voters, and the left party is forced to respond by attracting more wealthy anti-clerical or anti-racist voters. As this 'exchange' of voters takes place, the two constituencies will tend to become more similar in terms of income. The original pro-welfare coalition is thus broken apart by appeals to commonalities on another, non-economic, dimension. As Riker (1986) recognized informally many years ago, the (re-)bundling of issues is a critical component of coalitional politics, and it helps explain why the poor don't soak the rich.[2]

Alesina and Glaeser (2004) make a related argument for why racial politics may undermine redistribution. If people feel altruistic only towards people of their own race, they will not redistribute to a minority that constitutes a disproportionate share of the poor. Of course, if solidarity with the poor is a 'taste' then we need a theory of why people acquire this taste, and Alesina and Glaeser go on to argue that elites that oppose redistribution can use the 'race card' to undermine support for redistribution. This is similar to the logic in Roemer's model.

Austen-Smith and Wallerstein (2006) provide a quite different story about the importance of race. In their model people have 'race-blind' preferences and are simply trying to maximize their net income. But the mere existence of a second dimension (here affirmative action) can cause a legislative coalition in favour of redistribution to break up. The reason (loosely speaking) is that the rich in the majority can offer a bargain to the minority that strengthens affirmative action but reduces redistribution to the poor. Of course, other coalitions are also feasible, but

---

[2] The model is in fact more complicated because, once again, there is no equilibrium with majority voting in a multidimensional space. Roemer solves this problem in two alternative ways. In the first formulation one party gets to select its platform before the other party, producing a Stackelberg equilibrium. In another, different factions of both parties must all agree to the policy platform, and this reduces the feasible policy space to a single point.

none can be put in place that would generate as much redistribution as if bargaining took place in a single redistributive policy dimension. The net result is thus less redistribution.

The Roemer and Austen-Smith models are mathematically complex, but they do point to a powerful logic that applies generally to any context in which a redistributive dimension is complemented by a second or third dimension. This may explain why countries with a higher dimensionality of the policy space also tend to have less redistribution. Yet, apart from some attempts to gauge the effects of ethnic-linguistic fractionalization on spending, no systematic comparative test of the effect of multi-dimensionality on redistribution has to my knowledge been carried out.

For welfare state research the challenge is not merely to explain the *level* of redistribution but also the different *forms* that welfare states take. As explained in the next section, the differentiation between the liberal and social democratic variants can potentially be accounted for in a simple three-class model where the incentives to form particular coalitions are a function of political institutions. The structure of political parties may also matter. In a new book, Manow and Van Kersbergen (2009) argue that European Christian democratic parties are cross-class parties that have to satisfy very different constituencies and consequently adopt an insurance-based social model where social protection is generous but redistribution is modest (by tying benefits to income and past contributions). This is very similar to Esping-Andersen's description of the Christian democratic welfare state, but there is now a testable model that roots this type in a particular coalitional politics induced by the structure of the party system. In Manow and Van Kersbergen's formulation, the three worlds of welfare capitalism emerge as distinct cross-class compromises resulting from the interaction of electoral systems and Christian democracy. This suggests the importance of paying close attention to the role of political institutions, which are largely ignored in Esping-Andersen's work.

Democratic Institutions

In the view of many scholars, focusing on the role of institutions strikes an attractive middle ground between historical research and 'thick description', on the one hand, and abstract formal models of distributive politics, on the other. Instead of what sometimes appear as restrictive and *ad hoc* model assumptions, the constraints on political behaviour are derived from observed characteristics of political and economic institutions. And instead of *post hoc* descriptions of behaviour, outcomes are predicted from the interaction of purposeful behaviour and institutional constraints.[3] This approach has been highly successful in explaining cross-national

---

[3] 'Institutions' defined broadly as the 'rules of the game' (North 1990).

differences in economic policies and outcomes. In this section, I pick some prominent examples that either focus on democratic institutions (this section) or economic institutions (the next section).[4]

I begin with a discussion of the role of the electoral system because it is a feature of democracies that varies a great deal *and* co-varies closely with government spending, redistribution, and income equality (Persson and Tabellini 2003). This co-variation has become the focus of intense scrutiny in recent work in comparative political economy.

Persson and Tabellini explain the association with reference to the incentives of politicians to either concentrate benefits on pivotal electoral districts or spread them out on broadly defined groups or classes. In single member plurality systems, they argue, if middle-class swing voters are concentrated in particular districts, parties have an incentive to completely ignore other districts that are ideologically predisposed in one way or the other. These districts are 'safe' and therefore not worth fighting over. Money instead flows to swing votes in middle class districts. In proportional representation (PR) systems where all candidates are elected on national lists, by contrast, there are no safe districts so politicians cannot ignore the loss of support among other groups if all transfers are concentrated on the middle class. The result is greater dispersion of spending across classes or more spending on broad public goods. The analogy to universalism in Esping-Andersen's discussion of the social democratic welfare state is obvious, although the notion of geographically targeted spending in single member district systems has no obvious correspondence in Esping-Andersen's typology.

One problem with the Persson-Tabellini account is that PR systems tend to spend more on *both* transfers and public goods. To explain this Persson and Tabellini point to a 'second-order effect' of PR, namely that PR systems tend to have more parties and be ruled by multi-party governments. If each party wants to spend on its own group (so that the space is multidimensional) this can lead to a common pool problem with excessive spending (see also Bawn and Rosenbluth 2006; Crepaz 1998).

But the more important consequence of having multiparty systems may be that they lead to a distinct form of coalitional politics (assuming that no single party has an absolute majority). In Milesi-Ferretti et al. (2002), for example, there are three candidates representing either 'districts' or classes, and governments are formed through a coalition between two candidates. As in the Persson-Tabellini model, majoritarian electoral systems with single member districts encourage geographically targeted spending, but this bias is reinforced by coalition bargaining because voters in each district will vote for politicians with extreme preferences for targeted spending towards their district—a logic that may also apply to federalist systems. In PR systems, on the other hand, classes will elect leaders who only care about transfers to the class they represent, neglecting local public goods. Even though the mix of spending is inefficient in both systems, the model helps explain why spending takes such different forms in different countries.

---

[4] These examples are meant to be illustrative. I do not pretend to offer an exhaustive discussion of the institutionalist literature (see also Chapter 15).

The redistributive consequences of the Persson-Tabellini and Milesi-Ferretti et al. models are ambiguous. In the Iversen and Soskice (2006) class coalition model, on the other hand, they are at the core of the institutional argument. In this model, class parties either form coalitions with each other (as in multiparty PR), or they are themselves coalitions of classes (as in two-party majority rule). In the former case the parties representing the poor and the middle class have an incentive to ally to tax the rich (as opposed to the middle and the rich taxing the poor), and this leads to a centre–left partisan bias. In two-party majoritarian systems, on the other hand, parties are themselves coalitions and, while both will appeal to the middle class, the median voter will worry about post-election deviations from this platform. Assuming that the right cannot engage in regressive redistribution, incomplete platform commitment puts the median voter at risk and gives the centre-right an electoral advantage. The implication is that partisanship and redistribution systematically co-vary with electoral system. Unlike power resource theory, which treats partisanship as an exogenous variable, redistribution in the Iversen-Soskice model is a function of partisan coalitions induced by the electoral system. And unlike the Meltzer-Richard model, the possibility of partisanship emerges because spending can be targeted and therefore is multidimensional.

Another democratic institution that has generated intense scholarly scrutiny is federalism. Much of the research in this area originates with Brennan and Buchanan's (1980) argument that competition between local governments for mobile sources of revenue undermines the ability of governments to impose 'excessive' taxation. Coupled with the potential ability of states to secede, which restricts the ability of central governments to exploit member states, federalism may also constitute a credible commitment to property rights—what Weingast (1995) calls 'market-preserving federalism'. Viewed from the left, this logic suggests that federalism may undermine the welfare state and lead to under-provision of social welfare, or even a 'race to the bottom' (P. Pierson 1995).

A related argument is that federalism makes it harder to pass new legislation because it has to be agreed to at different levels of government and in two legislative assemblies at the federal level (Scharpf 1988). The implication is a status quo bias, which has been argued to slow down the expansion of the welfare state (Cameron 1978; Castles 1998a; Huber and Stephens 2001a). But while federalism does appear to be associated with smaller governments, there is in fact a striking amount of variance across federalist states (Obinger et al. 2005a; Castles et al. 2005). Swiss and US federalism seems to produce tax competition and low spending, whereas German or Austrian federalism is linked to cross-regional coordination and redistribution.

To account for this variation, Rodden (2003) has proposed to distinguish between federalist systems with different fiscal institutions. If local spending is locally financed, tax competition puts a damper on spending, but if local spending is financed through central or intergovernmental grants local politicians have little incentive to contain spending. Revenue sharing may be seen as a source of common pool problems, or it may be seen as a method to reduce the power of those with mobile assets and empowering (central) governments to pursue redistribution.

Whatever the normative perspective, if there are two different types of federalism, then a key issue is why some governments adopted one form rather than the other (Wibbels 2003). Obinger et al. (2005*a*) suggest that the answer is found in the original distribution of jurisdictions across government levels. Only in countries such as Austria and Germany where the federal government initially assumed large social policy responsibilities, and where federal institutions facilitated coordination and revenue-sharing did federalism permit significant welfare state expansion.

By anchoring model assumptions in the rich details of actual political institutions, the new institutionalist literature enables the coupling of formal reasoning with the realism of inductive research. It reduces the indeterminism of democratic policy making and suggests promising ways to endogenize partisanship, coalition formation, and styles of policy making. Our understanding of redistribution and welfare has been greatly advanced in the process. But by highlighting the critical importance of institutional detail one cannot help but wonder if the real task is not the explanation of the institutions themselves. I return to this question below. But first I turn to another successful branch of institutionalism that focuses on modern capitalism as an economic system with distinct implications for distribution and the welfare state.

VARIETIES OF CAPITALISM

As noted above, it is common to portray democratic capitalism as a system where markets allocate income according to efficiency while governments redistribute income according to political demand. This suggests a convenient intellectual division of labour between economists and political scientists, but this view is based on a neoclassical view of the economy that few today believe in. Instead, the dominant approach to the study of capitalism as an economic system builds on new institutional economics and is known as the 'varieties of capitalism' (or VoC) approach (Hall and Soskice 2001*b*). Just as democracy has been shown to divide into institutional sub-species, so has capitalism. As I discuss at the end of this section, there is in fact a close empirical association between political and economic institutions, although the reasons for this association are only beginning to be understood.

The VoC approach assumes that economic institutions are designed to help firms and other economic agents make the best use of their productive assets (Hall and Soskice 2001*b*). As argued by Williamson (1985), North (1990), and others, when an economy is characterized by heavy investment in co-specific assets, economic agents are exposed to risks that make market exchange problematic.[5] A precondition for such an economy to work efficiently is therefore a dense network of institutions that

---

[5] Polanyi (1944) is an important precursor for many of these arguments.

provide information, offer insurance against risk, and permit continuous bargaining and impartial enforcement of agreements.

Another central feature of the VoC approach is the idea of institutional complementarities where the effectiveness of one institution depends on the design of another. A precursor for this idea is Lange and Garrett's (1985) congruence model where redistributive policies only produce good economic performance where unions are centrally organized. The VoC approach takes the idea much farther and argues that *all* major institutions of capitalism are complementary to each other: the industrial relations system, the financial and corporate governance system, the training system, and the innovation system.

The VoC argument suggests a very different explanation for the welfare state than power resources theory. Mares (2003), for example, argues that companies and industries that are highly exposed to risk will favour a social insurance system where cost and risk are shared, leading employers to push for universalistic unemployment and accident insurance. Although low-risk firms will oppose such spending, it is remarkable that universalism has been promoted by groups of employers since the literature associates it so closely with policies imposed on employers by unions and left governments. Estévez-Abe et al. (2001) and Iversen (2005) further argue that social protection (including job protection, unemployment benefits, income protection, and a host of related policies such as active labour market programmes and industry subsidies) encourages workers to acquire specific skills, which in turn enhances the ability of firms to compete in international markets. The welfare state is thus linked to the economy in a manner that creates beneficial complementarities. This may help explain the lack of evidence for the deleterious effects of social spending on growth (see Lindert 1996; Pontusson 2005), and why globalization has not spelled the end to the welfare state. In some institutional settings generous social spending may indeed impede performance, but the point of the VoC story about the welfare state is that such spending tends to occur only in settings where it complements the operation of the production system (Iversen 2005).

A still under-explored topic in the VoC literature is the relationship between economic and political institutions. It is striking, for example, that the division into liberal and coordinated market economies is almost perfectly collinear with the division into PR and majoritarian electoral systems. One possible explanation, which echoes Katzenstein's (1985) work on corporatism, is that PR promotes the representation of economic agents with co-specific assets in the legislature and its committees. Such representation facilitates compromise over regulatory policies in which there is a strong element of common interest. Since co-specific investments are less prevalent in liberal market economies the right has a strong interest in preventing the redistribution that is associated with PR (as described in the previous section). Majoritarian systems instead encourage parties to elect strong leaders in order to convince the median voter that they are not beholden to special interests or to 'excessive' redistribution (see Cusack et al. 2007; Iversen and Soskice 2009).

These conjectures will have to be corroborated through historical research since the institutional configurations we observe today are the result of developments in the late nineteenth and early twentieth centuries. This observation in fact applies to the entire institutionalist approach to political economy. The more successful political economy is in explaining economic policies and outcomes with reference to the institutional design, the more pressing it is to explain why one design was chosen rather than another (Thelen 1999; P. Pierson 2000). But the question then is how we can approach this task without being overwhelmed by the complexity of institution-free politics. In the concluding section I ask whether the answer may lie in a new form of structuralism.

Conclusion: Towards a New Structuralism?

A decade ago nearly all comparative political economists would have called themselves institutionalists. Today an increasing number of scholars are convinced that the only way forward is by going back—back to the origins of institutions and the socioeconomic and political conditions that gave rise to them. The questions that are being asked by these scholars are fundamental: Under which structural-economic conditions do autocracies commit to democracy and redistribution (Acemoglu and Robinson 2005; Boix 2003)? What are the origins of modern skill systems and the labour market and social systems with which they are associated (Thelen 2004; Iversen and Soskice 2009)? What accounts for differences in the structure of social programmes (Mares 2003; Swenson 2002). What are the origins of more or less distributive forms of federalism (Wibbels 2003; Castles et al. 2005)? And what accounts for electoral institutions that are closely associated with left governments and redistribution (Boix 1999; Cusack et al. 2007)?

In a recent article, Rogowski and Macray (2008) conjecture that many of the institutional effects that have been documented in painstaking detail by decades of institutional research are in fact epiphenomenal to the structural conditions and interests, especially economic inequality, that gave rise to them. If this is true, it puts a premium on understanding the 'pre-strategic' policy-preferences of agents and the circumstances that determine how they are 'aggregated'. New structuralism (to distinguish it from Marxist structuralism, structural functionalism, and other uses of the term) seeks to explain the design of democratic and social institutions, and the coalitions that underpin them, with reference to the structural conditions in the early formation of markets and states.

Examples include Acemoglu and Robinson's (2005) focus on the distribution of income and the size of the middle class in explaining emergence of democracy; or Iversen and Soskice's (2009) emphasis on the organization of capitalism at the dawn of the industrial revolution in explaining distinct electoral and social systems. Martin and Swank (2008), switching the focus of the causal story, instead suggest that the early structure of party systems shaped the subsequent organization of capitalist production. In a similar vein, Obinger et al. (2005*a*) suggests that the interaction of early democratization and the role of the central government in social policy formation determined the form that federalism would later take, including its distributive consequences.

These examples do not add up to a single coherent approach to the study of capitalism and democracy. They do however highlight the importance of understanding the historical origins of the economic, political, and social institutions that shape distributive politics. The recent historical turn in political economy highlights the importance of identifying the structural attributes of economies and states, and the agents that populate them, in order to build models of institutional design that have explanatory as well as descriptive power. Similarly to the institutionalist project that has matured over the past four decades, the success of the new structuralism will depend on combining carefully identified historical constraints with rigorous theorizing. But by treating institutions as causal bridges to the past, as opposed to simply a point of departure, we may gain a deeper understanding of the pattern of distribution and redistribution that is observed in contemporary democracies.

....

CHAPTER 13

UNIONS AND EMPLOYERS

....

BERNHARD EBBINGHAUS

INTRODUCTION

....

FROM the time of early industrialization onwards, the *capital–labour* conflict has shaped the development of social and industrial citizenship rights. Organized capital and labour, that is employer (or business) associations and trade unions, organize the collective interests of the two sides of the employment relationship. These 'social partners' directly regulate employment conditions via collective bargaining, but they also influence social policy making, are sometimes involved in its administration, and provide some occupational welfare functions. As major collective actors in both the industrial relations arena and the social policy sphere, they directly affect through collectively negotiated wages the primary distribution of market income and influence the politics of post-tax, post-transfer redistribution.

Research in this area has often reflected a skewed division of labour: the study of organized capital and labour has remained largely the main object of research in industrial relations and political economy, while social policy analyses have concentrated on the welfare *state*, less on firm-provided or collectively negotiated welfare corporatism. Power resources theory in welfare research, corporatist theory in industrial relations, and more recently the 'varieties of capitalism' approach emphasize the labour movement, the social partners, or the firm. While the 'new politics' perspective and the globalization thesis de-emphasize the old social partners' influence in periods of welfare state restructuring, other observers see an increased scope for new social pacts and more private occupational welfare arrangements.

Whether and to what degree unions and employers play a significant role in welfare capitalism will be the leading question of this chapter. First, it will map the main theoretical perspectives which focus directly or indirectly on the role of employers and unions in welfare state development. Second, it will investigate the conditions under which collective interests become organized and mobilized, how well worker and employer interests have been organized and integrated into the overall political economy. Third, it examines differences in the degree to which welfare states share public space, that is, the influence that social partners have on policy making and implementation in different countries. Fourth, it looks at selected policy fields (wage bargaining, labour market policy, pension policy, and health care) and shows how the interests of labour and capital are differentially affected and have varying influence across advanced economies. A final comparison of the developing societies and new market economies indicates that in these countries, corporatist intermediation is more fragile than in advanced economies, and organized labour and capital have less influence on employment conditions and social protection.

THEORIES OF UNION AND EMPLOYER IMPACT

The organized interests of capital and labour assume different importance in the main theories of welfare state development. The mobilization and representation of these interests figure prominently as the independent variable in the power resources, corporatist theory, and 'varieties of capitalism' approaches, explaining cross-national differences in regimes. The influence of these interest groups remains more indirect in other approaches, including functionalism, the state-centred and institutionalist approaches, and the globalization thesis.

According to *modernization* theory (Wilensky and Lebeaux 1958), industrialization increases the pressure on nation states to provide income support against social risks. Although the social question and working-class mobilization were inherent to the 'logic of industrialization' thesis, employers and worker organizations were conceptualized as rather passive actors. Closely related, the pluralist school of industrial relations (Kerr et al. 1960) assumed that collective bargaining would institutionalize 'class conflict' and that industrial conflicts would largely 'wither away' (Ross and Hartman 1960). The resurgence of class conflict in the late 1960s, led to strands of conflict-oriented theory that took issue with these functionalist approaches.

Power resources theory looks at the influence of interests groups—notably organized labour and employers—in advancing or hindering social policy development (Korpi 1983). Comparative studies investigated the post-war welfare reforms resulting from labour's power resources, both left parties' electoral success and the strength of union movements (Korpi 1983). Most notably, Esping-Andersen (1990) traced three political ideologies—liberal, social democratic, and conservative conceptions—to distinct political movements, while acknowledging the legacy of state traditions. Many quantitative studies of welfare state development showed a strong correlation between social expenditure and labour movement strength. The latter is measured by either union density or left party election results, two highly correlated variables that cannot be tested at the same time (Huber and Stephens 2001a). Historical studies stressing the result of cross-class alliances between blue-collar workers, white-collar urban middle class, and rural small-scale-farmers interests (Baldwin 1990) amended the social democracy thesis.

Corporatist theory understood Keynesian post-war welfare states as part of an implicit 'social pact' between organized capital and labour: extended social rights and full employment policies were exchanged for the acceptance of the social market economy (Crouch 1993). Social protection became an important buffer against the volatility of a globalized market, thereby helping to maintain the social consensus, particularly in small European states (Katzenstein 1985). The preconditions for corporatism are centralized interest associations with quasi-public functions for both organized capital and labour. Policy concertation with social partners, their involvement in social security administration, and negotiated tripartite social pacts have evolved considerably since the heyday of neo-corporatism in the 1960s (Berger and Compston 2002). Since the mid-1970s, both welfare states and corporatism have come under pressure, leading some observers to proclaim their 'end' (Lash and Urry 1987) with the turn toward supply-side monetarism, labour market deregulation, and bargaining decentralization. However, social pacts on pay moderation as well as reforms of employment and social policies have occurred as part of a strategy of 'competitive corporatism' in recent years (Rhodes 2001).

By bringing capital back in, the *varieties of capitalism* approach (Hall and Soskice 2001a) juxtaposes liberal and coordinated market economies, focusing on the microfoundations of firms' (non-)cooperative relations. Of particular interest here are the linkages between welfare states and labour relations (Ebbinghaus and Manow 2001). In particular, comparative historical studies have discovered that employers were far from always being opposed to social policies (Mares 2003; Swenson 2002)—for instance, US health insurance is a fringe benefit provided by corporate welfare policies (Hacker 2002; Martin 2000). A key claim is that 'institutional complementarities' can lead to comparative advantages, for example, early retirement policies help firms restructure their personnel in socially acceptable ways (Ebbinghaus 2006). Equally, the interaction of unemployment protection, employment regulations, and wage bargaining institutions maintain firm-based or occupational skills in coordinated market economies (Estévez-Abe et al. 2001). However, there is also the danger of a functionalist fallacy in assuming but not proving that business interests were indeed crucial in affecting social policy making.

State-centred theories focus on the strategies used by political elites to maintain their position, thereby de-emphasizing the role of organized interests (Heclo 1974). Most prominently, Bismarck's social policies are seen as reforms 'from above', as part of an authoritarian paternalist strategy to insure against the social risks, while suppressing the political and economic mobilization of the workers' movement (Flora and Alber 1981). The British development of civil, political, and social citizenship rights (Marshall

1964*b*) was understood as a long-term gradual process, while the development of industrial citizenship remained something of a footnote. In the voluntarist tradition, the state should not intervene in industrial relations, though anti-union policies under the Thatcher government in the United Kingdom and the Reagan administration in the United States shifted the power balance toward employers in the 1980s. In Anglophone pluralist systems, employer interests have, in any case, always had favourable access and plentiful resources for lobbying governmental authorities.

Institutional theories postulate that political systems provide 'veto points' for interest groups to influence policy making (Immergut 1990), if not to block major changes to the status quo. Particular institutional arrangements account for cross-national variations in the political capacity of governments to unilaterally intervene in both the public sphere of welfare and the regulation of occupational welfare, including federalist second chambers, coalition governments, popular referenda or constitutional courts. Interest groups can use these veto points by persuading political parties or other political actors to intervene on their behalf. In consociational democracies such veto points can provide ample opportunities for organized interests to block reforms, while in majoritarian political systems this is not possible. More formally, the *veto player* theorem (Tsebelis 2002) postulates that individual or collective actors might be pivotal in altering the status quo. Of particular importance is the coherence of collective actors and their congruence on policy positions, often mapped in a two-dimensional policy space. These theories have focused on constitutional or partisan veto players, and neither organized capital, nor unions have yet been at the centre of this research agenda. But unions can have 'veto power' through political exchange. Through the use of the strike weapon or by obstructing implementation, governments may be compelled to make deals with the social partners to overcome reform blockage (Ebbinghaus and Hassel 2000; Schludi 2005).

Finally, the *globalization* and Europeanization theses focus their analysis of welfare state restructuring on transnational economic processes and supranational political coordination. Mirroring modernization theory's endogenous convergence postulate, the globalization thesis assumes that convergence occurs for *exogenous* reasons: global competition in capital, producer, and labour markets puts pressure on domestic actors to lower labour costs and provide firms in search of investment possibilities with the opportunity for 'regime shopping'. These economic forces supposedly empower 'footloose' capital, challenge the coordination of national employer associations to take wages out of competition, and severely limit the capacity of unions to raise wages and improve working conditions above competitive levels. However, the globalization thesis (Fligstein 2002) as well as the European 'social dumping' thesis (Alber and Standing 2000) have been shown to be somewhat questionable in light of evidence relating to weakness of economic competition, the relative lack of cross-border relocations, and a less clear impact on social spending. A counter argument is that welfare states could buffer the consequences of international economic pressures and thereby legitimate substantial social policy intervention in open economies (Garrett and Mitchell 2001; Rieger and Leibfried 2003), although this thesis remains disputed.

The Organization of Capital and Labour

The organization of collective interests is the precondition of becoming influential in the industrial relations and social policy arena. In order to negotiate employment conditions and influence policy making effectively, the interests of workers need to be collectively organized in trade unions and through workplace representatives (or works' councillors). Similarly, most employers will have to rely on their associations to engage in collective bargaining and advance their interests in the public realm. Pluralist theory assumes that all interest groups will be similarly capable of organizing as pressure groups and thus compete equally. However, this view was challenged by the post-war rise of corporatism as empirical reality and theoretical paradigm (Schmitter and Lehmbruch 1981).

Olson (1965) pointed to the 'free-rider' problem faced by voluntary membership organizations: rational (self-interested) actors—whether workers or employers— have little interest in undertaking the collective action required to procure 'public goods' such as higher wages or limited wage competition because it is often very difficult to exclude non-members from enjoying the fruits of such collective action. While small groups can overcome this problem easily, larger voluntary organizations need to enforce negative sanctions on non-members (for example, by enforcing the 'closed shop' that requires employees to unionize) or use selective incentives (such as strike insurance for members only) to make membership pay. Arguably, though, social norms and ideological orientations may alter the cost-benefit calculation. Offe and Wiesenthal argue (1980) that capital's capacity to organize is structurally higher than that of labour. Employers as a smaller group with more narrow instrumental interests, plentiful (financial) resources, and structural economic power can pursue their interests more autonomously, while workers are a larger heterogeneous group with diffuse political and economic interests. By and large workers have to rely on collective action to compensate for lack of individual bargaining power, particularly if the welfare state does not provide sufficient non-work benefits. Comparative studies of business and employers' associations in OECD countries (Streeck 1991; Traxler 1993) have challenged this two-logic thesis, showing that even though employer associations are more concentrated and better organized than trade unions, producer coalitions are more fragmented and narrower, given the competitive pressures within each sector.

Trade unions are collective associations for advancing the interests of employees at their workplace and in society; the membership base shapes their organization, resources, and orientation (Ebbinghaus and Visser 2000). In principle, trade unions allied with political parties and cooperative self-help associations formed part of a single labour movement. However, political, religious, and ethnic cleavages often strained the relationship between unions and parties, leading to splits in the labour movement nationally and internationally such as between reformist and radical, unitary and Christian, national and regionalist movements. Pronounced organizational differences emerged also in respect to occupational status and economic sector. Overcoming the craft unionism that characterized the Anglophone market economies, industrial unionism has become dominant in most Nordic or continental European movements. Traditional status differences, partly promoted by stratifying social policies, often led to separate organizations for white-collar employees, professionals, and civil servants. These ideological and functional fragmentations also hampered the international organization of the trade union movement, but since the 1990s greater unity has been achieved, most notably within the European Trade Union Confederation (ETUC). The role of unions in the workplace can also take different forms (Rogers and Streeck 1995): if they have sufficient membership, local unions may be the unitary representative structure as in liberal market economies, Japanese or Nordic workplaces, while unions can coexist with and partly profit from statutory workplace representation in continental Europe (e.g. German codetermination).

Organized capital assumes different forms and functions, depending on historical and national circumstances. The interests of business are often (but not always) differentiated in separate organizations: employer associations, trade associations, and Chambers (Schmitter and Streeck 1999). Employer associations organize the employers' interests vis-à-vis unions as collective bargaining partners and the state as regulator of employment relations. Internal differentiation occurs between private and public employers, manufacturing and service sectors, or large and smaller firms (van Waarden 1995). Only a few countries, most prominently Germany and Sweden, maintain independent employer associations while, in most others, peak business associations have assumed the representation of employer and producer interests. Chambers of commerce and of artisans coordinate particularly small and medium-sized firms at the local and regional level. In continental Europe, membership is often mandatory, assuming a self-regulatory quasi-public function, for instance, in regulating dual vocational training in Germany (Thelen 2004). While employer associations regulate employment conditions through collective bargaining, they also lobby policymakers on matters relating to employment law and social policy legislation. Business associations have also become increasingly involved in social policy debates. Employer interests, too, have been organized at the international level since the founding of the ILO, and at the European level since the first days of the European economic integration process (*BusinessEurope*). Moreover, large firms, in particular multinational corporations, often have the resources to negotiate with unions and the lobbying capacity to influence policymakers at national and even international level (e.g. the European Round Table of large companies that promoted the European single market).

Union strength is commonly measured by union density, i.e. the share of organized workers among the dependent employed, which varies quite considerably across capitalist economies (Ebbinghaus and Visser 2000). Union density is loosely correlated to the size of social spending as suggested by the power resources thesis, though there are also some outliers (see Figure 13.1). The Nordic union movements are exceptionally well organized and profit from universal welfare states, thanks partly to the union-run unemployment insurance funds that provide a selective

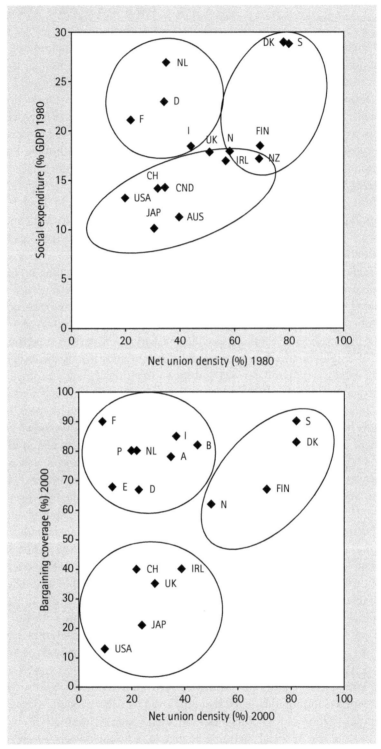

Figure 13.1 Trade union density, social expenditure, and bargaining coverage (1980, 2000)

Sources: OECD 2008*g*; Ebbinghaus and Visser 2000; Visser 2003.

incentive for membership (except in post-war Norway). The continental European unions have a lower and more varied level of membership organization (Belgian unions profit again from their involvement in unemployment benefit provision). However, they profit from relatively extensive collective bargaining coverage thanks to strong employer organizations or state intervention on their behalf. Labour unions in liberal market economies have a lower (and declining) union density. Moreover collective bargaining is more limited due to decentralization (except in Australia and New Zealand) and the same holds for the company-based unionism in Japan (Visser 2003).

While strong unions and encompassing bargaining coverage can provide collective protection of workers with respect to employment conditions and some social benefits, workers and their organizations also profit from state intervention. Extensive labour market regulation via legislation and generous social protection for the core workforce provide favourable institutional support to organized labour. Although a higher level of union density may explain the somewhat higher level of social expenditure in the United Kingdom (and Ireland) compared to the United States, it is the combination of deregulated labour markets and meagre public welfare provision that reinforces the linkage between liberal welfare states and voluntarist labour relations. In the Nordic countries, strong labour movements have been crucial in expanding the welfare state, but, at the same time, universalist social policies combined with a strong role for unions in unemployment insurance and labour market policy have helped to maintain union power. In continental Europe, the institutionalized role of the social partnership in social insurance and employment relations independent of their organizational strength has constituted a stronghold for organized labour and their defence of acquired social rights, but may, simultaneously, lessen their mobilization capacity.

Borrowing from corporatist theory (Crouch 1993), cross-national variations in industrial relations can be summarized in terms of four models: contentious relations, pluralist bargaining, and neo-corporatism with stronger or weaker unions (see Table 13.1). The contentious relations model is characterized by class conflict, non-cooperation, and deficits in self-organization: for this reason, social mobilization in countries where this model dominates often provokes state intervention. Historically, pluralistic bargaining arose when employers, supported by political and legal changes, altered their strategy to 'the development of procedures for conducting conflicts with labour in such a way that mutually damaging action is avoided' (Crouch 1993: 36). However, voluntary bargaining still suffers from short-termism and particularistic interest representation, while the state remains reluctant to intervene in material bargaining issues. Finally, corporatist interest intermediation is based on long-term common 'positive sum' interests among all stakeholders, presuming relatively centralized and encompassing organizations as well as institutionalized support by the state as in Nordic countries. However, continental European unions have much lower membership and have been, at least historically, more politically divided (Ebbinghaus and Visser 2000), while their social partnership models have depended on and reproduced the conservative welfare state.

Table 13.1 Ideal–typical modes of labour relations and their institutional affinities

Modes (Prime examples)	Contentious (France, Italy)	Pluralist (United Kingdom, USA)	Neo-Corporatist (Sweden, Denmark)	Social partnership (Germany, Benelux)
Labour	Fragmented	Particularistic	Strong, centralized, encompassing	Encompassing but weaker unions
Capital	Paternalist vs. large/state firms	Large firms, weak/no peak	Strong, centralized	Strong, centralized
Perspective	Antagonistic class conflict	Short-term group interests	Long-term common interests	Long-term common interests
Role of the state	State intervention	Non-interventionist	Enabling/cooperative	Enabling/cooperative
Mode of change	Waves of protests	Economic stop-and-go	Consensual	Consensual
Welfare regime	Southern	Liberal/residual	Universalist	Conservative
Market economy	(State-)coordinated	Non-coordinated	(Centrally) coordinated	(Sector-)coordinated

Sources: Crouch 1993; see also Ebbinghaus 2006.

Social Governance: Sharing Public Space with the Social Partners

Welfare states vary in the extent and forms in which they 'share' public space: the responsibilities for wage policy, employment regulation, and social protection are differently distributed between the state, the social partners, and individual employers and workers. The influence exerted by organized interests and the ways in which state and social partners share responsibility vary considerably. We can distinguish five different forms of social governance: unilateral state intervention, institutionalized consultation of or lobbying by interest groups, voluntary social concertation, delegated self-administration, and autonomous self-regulation.

Unilateral state intervention occurs when governments are not bound—either by rules or traditions—to consult the social partners and when they are not needed for implementation. However, government responsibilities in social and employment policies are often divided across different ministries, providing the social partners with differential access to government. Depending on the institutional *veto points* in the political decision-making process (Immergut 1990), interest groups can use political pressure to block such unilateral policies, in particular when unions or employer organizations have close ties to powerful political parties (van Waarden 1995). Certainly, unions may gain other, non-institutionalized veto power, for instance, when they succeed in blocking unilateral state intervention through mass protest or even general strikes (Ebbinghaus and Hassel 2000). For pragmatic reasons, governments may consult or even negotiate with the social partners, in particular with unions, to avoid political and social conflicts over state interventions.

Consultation preserves maximum authority for the state, while obtaining the advantage of gaining information from interest groups about their preferences and strategies. The government (or parliament) may wish to confer with the social partners or may be legally obligated to consult an advisory council, but policymakers are free to diverge from the opinions so given. Formal consultation for example exists in the European Social and Economic Council that represents very heterogeneous interests at EU-level.

Concertation entails an agreement between government and social partners, involving some concessions on both sides. It occurs when employers and unions are involved in policy formulation and implementation, including the content of legislation and tripartite agreements. While consultation is legally prescribed or informal but routinely practised, concertation occurs primarily on an *ad hoc* basis and depends on the voluntary agreement of all sides, thus being far more conditional. The rise of concertation since the 1990s was linked to particular challenges as European countries faced the issues raised by European Monetary Union and welfare state reform (Siegel 2005).

In the case of *self-administration*, the 'principal' delegates some (though not all) decision-making authority and implementation power to an 'agent'. Depending on the authority delegated and resources provided, the agency may be more or less autonomous of the state. Moreover, the influence of the social partners depends on the agency's rules of representation (nominated or elected), the composition (bipartite or tripartite), and the decision-making rules (qualified or simple majority). Their influence is relatively limited when self-administration is decentralized, representatives are elected from open lists, composition is tripartite (with independent experts), and no minority veto exists. In contrast, their power tends to be greater when self-administration is centralized, they can nominate representatives, composition is bipartite (without state involvement), and each side has a veto right.

Finally, *self-regulation* results from voluntary agreement between the collective bargaining partners without state interference. The state can only indirectly influence the outcome of the 'autonomous' decision of the social partners by refusing extension of collective agreements, by making state subsidies or tax concessions conditional, or by intervening as an exceptional measure (but thereby damaging subsidiarity). Although free collective bargaining is a prime example, the social partners may also negotiate occupational welfare outside the public welfare system (Shalev 1996; Trampusch 2007).

THE INFLUENCE OF EMPLOYERS AND UNIONS
IN SOCIAL POLICY AREAS

Collective Bargaining

In accordance with their central role in labour relations, employers directly or through their associations negotiate with trade unions (or workplace representatives) on employment conditions. Collective bargaining was institutionalized around the foundation of the tripartite International Labour Organization (ILO) in 1919. The rights to organize in independent voluntary organizations, of collective action (strike or lockout), and the legal status of collective agreements are enshrined in several ILO conventions, European Union declarations, and national legislation. Collective negotiations on wage and employment conditions have a substantial impact on the market incomes of the dependent workforce. However, there are important variations as to the degree of state intervention in collective bargaining through extension (*erga omnes*—towards all employees) of collective agreements, forced arbitration in case of labour disputes, or limits on the right to strike (Traxler 1999). In addition to providing a procedural framework, the legislator also intervenes in setting employment conditions via labour law, setting reservation wages through non-work benefits (e.g. unemployment assistance), and in some countries by legislating minimum wages.

Employers and workers co-finance via social insurance contributions to a varying degree or provide direct social benefits as occupational welfare. Overall, social contributions reduce net wages for workers and increase non-wage labour costs, independent of the divisions between the two sides. An increase in social contributions will have two negative effects for labour: it reduces the bargaining scope and the net wages of workers, and it raises overall labour costs to the detriment of employment and competitiveness. Thus, wage negotiations and social policy reforms have to be seen as interdependent (Ebbinghaus and Hassel 2000). In the past, unions and employers negotiated corporatist income policies by increasing the deferred wage, for instance by extending early retirement benefits (Ebbinghaus 2006). Welfare state expansion during the high days of corporatist income policies suggests an implicit and sometimes explicit *political exchange* between wage moderation and social rights. However, today's international economic competition and limits on welfare state spending no longer permit such an exchange.

Labour Market Policy

Given its interventionist impact on the labour market, unemployment insurance was the last of the four classic social risks to be introduced in most European welfare states. France and the Benelux countries were early in subsidizing voluntary unemployment insurance at the communal level. Following Britain's first unemployment insurance, most advanced economies introduced mandatory public unemployment insurance. Some Continental schemes were co-financed and self-administered by employers and workers, while the Scandinavian union-run unemployment funds are state-subsidized, but provide a perceived selective incentive for union membership (Rothstein 1992). In addition, employment services for the jobless have developed from communal or union self-help into public labour offices. In most countries, these remained separated from unemployment insurance, but in Germany both active and passive labour market policies are organized in one tripartite organization. Although tripartite self-administration is common for public employment services, the state also assumes a more dominant role through its increased financial involvement and the shift from passive towards active labour market policies since the 1990s. The more the state subsidizes or exclusively finances unemployment insurance, the less influence the social partners have.

In most countries, we see a trend towards decentralizing active labour market policy. The United Kingdom embarked on deregulation, Swedish employers and the Conservative government induced de-corporatization, the Dutch and German governments have limited the influence of social partners, and in France employers have also pushed for a reform of social governance. However, since the success of labour market reforms depends on collective bargaining, governments need the cooperation of unions and employers, as was evident in the introduction of 'flexicurity' in Denmark and the Netherlands. In Germany, concerted action on labour market reforms was more difficult to acheive, with the Alliance of Jobs talks being overshadowed by the Hartz reforms of long-term unemployment assistance which the unions were protesting against. To the degree that the social partners represent 'insider' interests, the government has to bring in the interest of 'outsiders'. For example, the Irish tripartite concertation process also included advocacy groups to voice the interests of those excluded from employment.

Pension Policy

Both employers and unions have a manifest interest in old age pensions. Mandatory old age insurance can take wages out of competition by forcing all employers to contribute and by spreading social risks more widely. Contributions toward pensions are 'deferred' social wages. The more pension schemes are subsidized by the state, the more firms with voluntary pensions on a defined benefit basis would be relieved (Swenson 2002). A further rationale for employers arises from opportunities to use public or collective schemes to shed older workers in a socially acceptable way prior to and at mandatory retirement age (Ebbinghaus 2006). Cross-national differences in social partner involvement reflect historical variations in the development of welfare states, commonly exemplified by Bismarckian social insurance and the Beveridge-type welfare state (Flora and Heidenheimer 1981). Where old age pensions were introduced as social insurance for industrial workers, benefits tended to be financed and self-administered by both the employer and the employees. On the other hand, in Beveridge-type welfare states, voluntary self-help was supplanted by state-provided social benefits to all citizens, financed by general or payroll taxes and administered by public agencies.

Concertation *and* social conflict have been present in pension reform throughout Europe: while strikes against the Italian pension reform in 1994 and the French government in 1995 indicate that unions remain able to muster a political strike, concerted reforms were undertaken in Italy in 1995 and in France in 1993 that prevented such mobilization (Ebbinghaus and Hassel 2000). Bringing the trade unions into reform coalitions usually entails phased-in reforms and *quid pro quo* side-payments (Bonoli 2000*a*). Following recent reforms that foster private pensions, unions might be able to enhance their bargaining role in negotiating occupational pensions as in the Netherlands. The state can use regulatory power and 'incentives' through taxation policy to influence private pensions and intervene in self-regulation. Thus, while shared responsibilities make reforms more difficult, particularly in implementation, the state still has considerable authority over important parameters with respect to the public pension system, and it can influence occupational pension development by using regulatory frameworks.

Health Care

The role of employers and unions in health care is related to the type of system (Rothgang et al. 2005). In national health service systems such as in Great Britain and Scandinavia, where health care is tax funded and hospitals are often publicly owned, private sector employers tend not to be directly involved, and public sector unions and professional associations play a role in negotiating employment conditions. In contrast, in social health insurance schemes such as in Germany or France, employers and workers are the major contributors to funding and, as such, their representatives are part of self-administration. When negotiating with medical associations, therefore, both employee and employer representatives have an interest in stable contribution rates. Even German employers critical of increasing health care costs were never advocates of privatization (Giaimo and Manow 1999). However, the Clinton health care plan of 1993/4 was not only opposed by health care providers and insurers, but also by business interests.

ORGANIZING PROBLEMS IN DEVELOPING COUNTRIES

Our knowledge of trade unions and employer organizations as well as of their impact on welfare state development is less advanced for the large set of countries outside the traditional OECD advanced economies (Mares and Carnes 2009). In many non-democratic countries, fundamental rights to organize have been denied to workers (and sometimes to employers too). Today, the ILO conventions on the freedom of association (No. 87 of 1948) and the right to collective bargaining (No. 98 of 1949) have been ratified worldwide by 150 and 160 countries respectively, though many developing countries joined late or have suspended such rights for some time.

With the democratic wave following the end of the Cold War and fall of communism in the East, transition economies in Central and Eastern Europe have led to the organization of free trade unions, the right to strike and collective bargaining. For those ten plus two new member states joining the European Union in 2004 and 2007 respectively, the *acquis communitaire* included fundamental civil, political, and social rights. However, in these transition economies, unions are fragmented and union density is relatively low, with just a few exceptions (Avdagic 2005; Visser 2003). The development of social policy remains a mixture of public policies to provide minimum income for older people and the unemployed as well as some privately funded pensions as advocated by international organizations such as the World Bank.

Latin American countries have had a longer tradition of trade unions and employer associations, with some countries already belonging to the ILO during the interwar period. However, the suspension of civil and social rights during periods of authoritarian rule often interrupted more democratic spells (Segura-Ubiergo 2007). In the past, state corporatist, populist, and clientelist state–union relations coexisted with import-substituting industrialization, though recent democratization and market liberalization have led to a further decline in union membership (Visser 2003). The development of the welfare state has been advanced not so much by mass mobilization in democratic times as by authoritarian measures to stabilize the income of particular social groups, in some cases also relying on private funded pensions (Haggard and Kaufman 2008; Mares and Carnes 2009).

The development of trade unions has been delayed or suppressed in many parts of the world. In Africa and the Middle East, the postcolonial countries were slow in ratifying ILO conventions or in responding to international campaigns for worker rights aimed at multinational firms operating in these countries. Most notably, South Africa ratified the two ILO conventions only in 1996 after the end of apartheid and the return to democracy. With the exception of its more prosperous countries, unionization rates are lowest worldwide throughout much of Africa (Visser 2003). Social protection has been mainly focused on providing basic health and education, partly provided by international aid.

Labour relations in Asia have suffered from decentralized bargaining, paternalist employers, and weak union movements (Benson and Zhu 2008). India has signed many ILO conventions, but despite its mass democracy it has not recognized the ILO conventions on organizational and collective bargaining rights. Despite its opening to world markets, China has also not signed these conventions and severely limits these rights. The new tiger economies in Asia are also known for their limits on organization and workers' right to strike, while business interests have substantial influence on government policies. 'Studies of the union situation in East and

South-East Asia agree on the weak structure of industrial relations, the extreme decentralization of collective bargaining' (Visser 2003: 384). Some fast growing Asian economies increasingly need social protection beyond what companies are willing to provide and future ageing further challenges public policy in East Asia.

OUTLOOK

Comparative research on industrial relations and welfare states often has been separated, although unions and employers play an important role in shaping market income and influencing social redistribution. While earlier studies on the development of welfare states emphasized the logic of industrialism and the mobilization of labour in advancing social and industrial citizenship rights, more recent studies on welfare state restructuring de-emphasize the role of unions and rediscover the role of employers in modern economies. A more balanced and moderate view of the actual role of employers and unions will be necessary to better understand the ongoing changes and challenges in the organization of capital and labour interests, the changing shift in responsibility between state and non-state actors, and subsequent repercussions for income inequality and social security.

The decline in membership in most trade union movements in advanced economies will hamper the defence of social rights and the capacity to find socially acceptable adjustments to socio-demographic challenges and world economic pressures. Employer associations have also been affected by the common trend toward decentralization and deregulation partly advocated by these organizations. Multinational companies have gained in importance relative to more cooperative strategies among employers, moving from negotiated collective agreements on employment conditions to more union-free strategies of 'corporate social responsibility'. The continued problems in organizing workers' interests in developing countries have only increased the pressures on working and living conditions for workers, given the increased global competition between countries with different labour standards, wage levels, and social security. The rather limited role unions and employers play in these societies has led to lacunae in research on the variations among and conditions for organized interest capacity in influencing working conditions and social security beyond the thus far advanced welfare states.

CHAPTER 14

....

PARTIES

....

MANFRED G. SCHMIDT

PARTISAN THEORY AND THE WELFARE STATE
....

THE role of political parties in shaping the welfare state is the topic of a voluminous body of literature written chiefly by political scientists, social historians, and sociologists. The major part of this literature centres attention on economically advanced democracies, and accordingly, the present chapter focuses on these countries.

The theoretical core of the literature on the relationship between the welfare state and political parties consists of the 'parties do matter' view or 'partisan theory' (Hibbs 1992: 361; Hibbs 1987) of public policy. According to this school of thought, political parties and, above all, the party composition of governments are major determinants of the timing, substance, expansion and retrenchment of the welfare state (Hibbs 1977; Tufte 1978; Castles 1982a; Rose 1984; Schmidt 1982a, 1996; Huber and Stephens 2001a; Zohlnhöfer 2009).

The view that political parties make a difference in social policy is derived from an actor-centred institutional theory of democratic political markets. In these markets the demos plays a role similar to that of the consumer in theories of consumer sovereignty, with politicians and governments delivering policies in exchange for specific or generalized political demand and the support of the demos, subject to imperatives of the electoral calendar and the institutional constraints of the policy process (Budge and Keman 1993). In contrast to standard market-based theories, partisan theory regards democratic markets as contingent upon institutional and cultural circumstances varying from country to country. Partisan theory is, therefore, inherently comparative.

Partisan theory predicts significant covariation between measures of the party composition of governments and indicators of the welfare state (such as gross or net social expenditure as a percentage of GDP, levels of social rights, or welfare state regimes). Furthermore, it presumes that this covariation mirrors probabilistic or causal relationships between the welfare state and the party complexion of government. Standard measures of the latter concept include rightist and leftist parties' participation in government and short-term and long-term cabinet seat shares of various political-ideological families of parties, whether of liberal, secular-conservative, centrist-religious, or leftist complexion.

In explaining differences in the welfare state, partisan theory relies mainly on nine key propositions concerning linkages between social constituencies, parties and social policy:

(1) Political parties have multiple goals. Their foremost objectives are office-seeking and the pursuit of policy goals.
(2) The social constituencies of parties have distinctive social policy preferences.
(3) The social policy orientation of parties mirror the distinctive preferences of their social constituencies and differ from the policy orientations of competitors.
(4) Incumbent parties choose social policies which promise to be compatible with office-seeking and broader policy goals.
(5) Governments are capable of implementing the policies adopted.
(6) Implementation of these policies results in distinctive welfare state outputs and outcomes and leads to clear partisan differences in public policy.
(7) This further implies that significant change in the party composition of government is associated with—and, by inference, causally related to—changes in social policy choices, outputs and outcomes.
(8) The extent to which party differences matter in social policy is contingent upon a wide variety of factors. Particularly large party effects are generated for instance where the government has a large majority, where a coalition government is relatively homogeneous, where a relatively small number of veto players exists, where the opposition parties are divided, and where there is a substantial room to manoeuvre for domestic policy.
(9) Advanced partisan theory adds to standard partisan theory the distinction between short-term impacts and the long-term legacies of parties. Partisan effects comprise not only contemporaneous short-term impacts (measured by a party A's cabinet seats share at a particular time-point or over a shorter period), but also the long-term legacy of party A on policy positions in that society.

WHEN AND HOW POLITICAL PARTIES MATTER

The propositions of the 'parties do matter' view are not uncontroversial. Some critics premise their arguments on the narrowly circumscribed steering capacities of governments and/or the low degree of manoeuvrability of market economies and liberal societies. Examples include earlier functionalist accounts of welfare state development (Wilensky 1975), theories of autopoietic social systems (Luhmann 1981) and the 'race to the bottom' view in the literature on globalization (see Chapter 22 in this volume). Historical institutionalist approaches want to nuance the findings of partisan theory by suggesting a recent change away from strong partisan effects either as a consequence of a 'new politics of the welfare state' (see section below on party differences in periods of retrenchment) or because of converging social policy positions of contemporary parties (Seeleib-Kaiser et al. 2008).

Although conceding the multi-causal determination of all policy outcomes and the specific 'dependent variable problems' of measuring social policy outcomes (Clasen and Siegel 2007), the evidence of a wide variety of studies is that the 'parties matter' hypothesis passes the empirical test reasonably well. Two types of studies have provided particularly valuable testimony in favour of partisan theory: first, comparisons of the social policy positions held by political parties, and, second, studies of the impact of parties on the welfare state.

Policy Positions: Political Parties and the Welfare State

Policy positions of political parties have been estimated mainly from party programmes, as in Thomas (1976), party manifesto data (Volkens et al. 2007) and expert judgements on policy positions of political parties (Benoit and Laver 2006).

These studies furnish proof of partisan differences in a wide variety of policy areas, including the welfare state. Particularly useful for identifying the role of parties in shaping the welfare state is a key variable from the policy positions literature: a party's position vis-à-vis the choice in the trade-off between taxes and public services. Because the social budget in OECD countries comprises up to two thirds of total public expenditure, the taxation-services variable in Benoit and Laver (2006) may be regarded as a proxy of the parties' position vis-à-vis expanding the welfare state (at the cost of raising taxes and/or social insurance contributions) or welfare state retrenchment in order to lower taxes and/or social insurance contributions (see Table 14.1).

The Benoit and Laver data indicate significant differences as well as remarkable commonalities in the social policy positions of parties. The major findings of a re-analysis of these data within a party families framework can be summarized as follows (see Table 14.1):

- Radical socialist and communist parties have very strong preferences for expanding the welfare state regardless of the cost involved.
- Pronounced pro-welfare commitments, albeit less extreme, characterize the family of the social democratic parties.
- Public social protection and an acceptance of high levels of taxation are also trade marks of most centre parties, and, above all, of Christian democratic parties.

Table 14.1 Policy positions of political parties on expansion of the welfare state versus retrenchment (early 21st century)

Scale from 'promotes raising taxes to increase public services' (1) to 'promotes cutting public services to cut taxes' (20)

Country	Pair of largest leftist party and largest centre or rightist party	Position of the largest party of the left	Position of the largest centre or rightist party	Party difference (left minus right or centre)
Australia	Australian Labor Party vs. Liberal Party	8.7	12.9	−4.2
Austria	Sozialdemokratische Partei Österreichs vs. Österreichische Volkspartei	7.5	14.7	−7.2
Belgium	Cartel Sociaal Progressief Alternatief-Spirit vs. Centre Démocrate Humaniste	7.3	14.3	−7.0
Britain	Labour Party vs. Conservative Party	8.1	15.3	−7.2
Canada	Liberal Party vs. Progressive Conservative Party	11.2	14.2	−3.0
Denmark	Socialdemokratiet vs. Venstre, Danmarks liberale parti	7.4	14.8	−7.4
Finland	Suomen Sosialidemokraattinen Puolue vs. Suomen Keskusta	8.4	9.5	−1.1
France	Parti Socialist vs. Rassemblement pour la République	7.1	14.3	−7.2
Germany	Sozialdemokratische Partei Deutschlands vs. Christlich Demokratische Union and Christian Social Union	9.3	14.4	−5.1
Greece	PASOK vs. Nea Dimokratia	10.9	14.8	−3.9
Ireland	Labour Party vs. Fianna Fail	6.6	13.8	−7.2
Italy	Democratici di sinistra vs. Forza Italia	6.7	17.5	−10.8
Japan	Communist Party vs. Liberal Democratic Party	8.7	10.1	−1.4
Netherlands	Partij van de Arbeid vs. Christen Democratisch Appel	8.1	13.3	−5.2
New Zealand	Labour Party vs. National Party	8.6	14.7	−6.1

Scale from 'promotes raising taxes to increase public services' (1) to 'promotes cutting public services to cut taxes' (20)

Country	Pair of largest leftist party and largest centre or rightist party	Position of the largest party of the left	Position of the largest centre or rightist party	Party difference (left minus right or centre)
Norway	Det Norske Arbeiderparti vs. Fremskrittspartiet	6.6	15.3	−8.7
Portugal	Partido Socialista vs. Partido Social Democrata	8.6	14.5	−5.9
Spain	Partido Socialista Obrero Español vs. Partido Popular	7.4	16.7	−9.3
Sweden	Sveriges Socialdemokratiska Arbetarepartiet vs. Moderata Samlingspartiet	7.1	17.7	−10.6
Switzerland	Sozialdemokratische Partei der Schweiz vs. Schweizerische Volkspartei	4.3	18.0	−13.7
United States	Democratic Party vs. Republican Party	6.3	16.8	−10.5
N = 21	Mean	7.9	13.7	−6.2

Source: Calculated from Benoit and Laver 2006: Appendix B.

- Nationalist-populist parties (except for the Swiss People's Party) and most green parties also favour increasing welfare state services rather than lower taxation.
- In contrast, liberal and secular conservative parties quite consistently opt for lower taxation and cuts in public services. Moreover, members of these party families are more likely than others to favour of welfare state retrenchment or cost-saving welfare state recalibration.

Partisan Effects on the Welfare State: Findings from Comparative Studies and Country Studies

The policy positions reported in Benoit and Laver (2006) and in Laver and Hunt's (1992) predecessor study, point to significant party differences in welfare state policies. A wide variety of comparative studies of the welfare state have also identified significant partisan effects. Examples include Huber and Stephens (2001a) as well as Schmidt (1997, 2005). Comparisons of the welfare states in West European democracies, such as Alber (1982, 1983), Flora (1986–7), and Merkel (1993), have also identified partisan effects, albeit weaker and less stable ones than those revealed by comparative studies across the OECD area, including the non-European welfare states in the United States, Japan, Australia, and New Zealand. In the latter group of countries, the course of social policy has deviated from the path of most West European nations—for example through late and incomplete development, as in America, the rise of a peculiar type of social policy, as Australia's 'wage earners' welfare state' (Castles 1985), lower levels of public social protection than in Western Europe, more reliance on voluntary or mandatory private social policy, and slower rates of growth of social expenditure (Obinger and Wagschal 2000; Castles and Obinger 2007).

These differences between West European and non-European welfare states are at least partly attributable to differences in the party composition of government. Strong pro-welfare state parties of social democratic and/or Christian democratic type have been the major parties in power in Western Europe. In contrast, the United States, Australia, New Zealand, and Japan are countries in which non-leftist parties and, above all, market-oriented conservative parties have played a far more important role in shaping the timing and substance of public policy. This constellation of forces has been conducive to the slow or moderate growth of less ambitious, more parsimonious, and more liberal welfare states (Obinger and Wagschal 2000).

Comparative research designs which include non-European advanced democracies are therefore more likely to identify strong partisan effects on the welfare state than smaller, more homogeneous research designs, such as those focusing exclusively on West European nations. In a similar vein, comparisons across European and non-European democracies are also more likely to identify stronger effects of extra-parliamentary power resources, such as trade union strength, power of labour, or left vote, to mention just a few of the variables considered relevant in the wider welfare state determinants literature (Schmidt 1982a, 1982b; Esping-Andersen 1990; Hicks and Swank 1992; Castles 1998a; Korpi 2006).

That parties matter in welfare state development has also been a central finding of studies by Castles (1982a, 1982b, 1998a, 2007a). This work has focused on social expenditure outcomes for various periods from the 1960s onwards and, in its earlier iterations emphasized the causal impact of parties of the right. According to Castles, two potentially seperable partisan forces lead towards a high level of social protection. One is the impact of a strong leftist incumbent party. The other is the political weakness of the 'major party of the right'. While a strong major party of the right and, above all, a government dominated by a major party of the right, is a major barrier against massive expansion of the welfare state, a weak party of the right in government or the absence of a rightist party is an extraordinarily favourable condition of a second road to an expansionary welfare state (Castles 1982b: 58–60, 1998a).

Castles's work clearly demonstrates lasting partisan effects, but his classification of parties, which identifies the Christian democratic parties of the Benelux-nations as centrist parties, but their counterparts in Austria, Germany, Switzerland, and Italy as major parties of the right, and hence, as major barriers to a strong and expansive welfare state (for details see Castles 1982b: 58–60), is questionable. Detailed country studies, such as those of Hockerts (1980), Tálos (1981), Ferrera (1986), Alber (1989), van Kersbergen (1995), and Schmidt (2005), have shown that the Christian democratic parties of West Germany, Austria, and Italy have been major proponents of a strong welfare state. These parties have indeed constituted 'a functional equivalent or alternative to social democracy for expanding the welfare state' (van Kersbergen and Manow 2008: 529).[1]

By focusing on a wider variety of political-ideological families of political parties or *'familles spirituelles'* (von Beyme 1985: 3), recent studies have provided more valid measures of the partisan complexion of government than earlier uni- or two-dimensional indicators. For example, the extent to which parties of leftist, centre, liberal, and market-oriented secular-conservative persuasion have participated in government, measured mainly by duration in office and/or cabinet seat shares of the various parties, have turned out to be particularly suitable measures in the comparative study of welfare states (Schmidt 1996, 2001; see also Huber and Stephens 2001a).

These studies suggest that the central measure of partisan complexion of governments in the comparative analysis of the welfare state no longer resides in the distinction between leftist and rightist parties. Rather, it is the difference between the long-term cabinet seats share of social democratic parties on the one hand and market-oriented secular-conservative parties on the other which matters most. Incumbent social democratic parties normally adopt a pronounced state-centred policy stance and strive for high levels of public social protection and egalitarian outcomes. In terms of fiscal resources, these parties rely mainly on voluminous social budgets financed from social insurance contributions and/or tax revenue, while private mandatory or voluntary social policies play only a small, if not totally insignificant role. Unlike social democratic parties, secular-conservative parties choose a pronounced market-friendly policy stance, aim at social budgets of moderate size and place far more emphasis on private mandatory social policy and company-based voluntary social protection (Seeleib-Kaiser 2001).

Social democratic governments and secular conservative parties in office often prove to be highly significant predictors of trends and structures of the welfare state. Statistically even more significant is the differences between the long term cabinet seat shares of social democratic parties on the one hand and of secular conservative parties on the other (Schmidt 2007: 171–3). Table 14.2 arrays data on bivariate relationships between this measure and various indicators of the welfare state effort in democratic OECD-countries,[2] including

- the share of total public social expenditure as a percentage of GDP in the early 21st century (OECD 2007*l*),
- the change of this share since the 1960s (Schmidt 2005, OECD 2007*l*),

[1] For the changing positions of these parties in periods of welfare state retrenchment see the later discussion of party differences in periods of retrenchment.

[2] For multivariate extensions, see e.g. Hicks and Swank 1992; Huber and Stephens 2001a; Schmidt 1997, 2001; and Swank 2002. Since much of the multivariate literature has concerned itself with convergence or non-convergence of party positions under circumstances of globalization, see also the literature summarized in Chapter 22 below.

Table 14.2 The welfare state and the difference between social democratic and secular conservative party composition of government in 21 OECD countries (since the 1950s)

State	Difference between cabinet seat share of social democratic parties and secular conservative parties 1950–2003	Total public social expenditure (% GDP) in 2003 (OECD 2007k)	Change in the social budget (% GDP) 1960–2003 (percentage point change) (Schmidt 2005; OECD 2007k)	Net publicly mandated social expenditure % GDP 2003 (OECD 2007k: 41)	Index of Decommodification in early 1980s (Esping-Andersen 1990: 53)	Scruggs Indicator of income replacement rate and programme coverage 2002 (Scruggs 2006b: 361)	Meyer's Index of Social Democracy 1996–2003 (Meyer 2007: 213)
Australia	−41	17.0	10.2	20.6	13.0	0.99	11
Austria	53	26.0	9.6	23.9	31.1	2.20	20
Belgium	31	26.0	12.0	26.0	32.4	2.35	16
Canada	−29	17.0	8.7	19.5	22.0	2.14	13
Denmark	39	27.0	15.2	23.8	38.1	2.23	24
Finland	19	22.0	14.5	22.7	29.2	2.21	23
France	−9	28.0	14.4	29.8	27.5	2.09	16
Germany	28	27.0	9.8	29.5	27.7	2.09	17
Greece	−8	21.0	15.2				
Ireland	−58	15.0	6.9	15.6	23.3	1.72	8
Italy	21	24.0	10.9	25.3	24.1	2.11	13
Japan	−94	17.0	13.0	19.7	22.3	1.57	17
Netherlands	21	20.0	9.4	20.6	32.4	2.33	20
New Zealand	−38	18.0	7.3	17.2	17.1	1.40	13
Norway	55	25.0	17.2	23.8	38.3	2.82	23

State	Difference between cabinet seat share of social democratic parties and secular conservative parties 1950–2003	Total public social expenditure (% GDP) in 2003 (OECD 2007k)	Change in the social budget (% GDP) 1960–2003 (percentage point change) (Schmidt 2005; OECD 2007k)	Net publicly mandated social expenditure % GDP 2003 (OECD 2007k: 41)	Index of Decommodification in early 1980s (Esping-Andersen 1990: 53)	Scruggs Indicator of income replacement rate and programme coverage 2002 (Scruggs 2006b: 361)	Meyer's Index of Social Democracy 1996–2003 (Meyer 2007: 213)
Portugal	29	23.0	18.0	23.2			11
Spain	21	20.0	16.1	19.6			11
Sweden	74	31.0	21.0	29.2	39.1	2.39	25
Switzerland	10	20.0	15.5		29.8	1.58	17
United Kingdom	-28	20.0	10.8	22.8	23.4	1.45	10
USA	-57	16.0	9.1	18.9	14.2	1.51	3
Mean	2	22.2	12.1	22.7	26.9	1.95	15.6
Coefficient of correlation		r = 0.81[b]	r = 0.54[a]	r = 0.64[b]	r = 0.83[b]	r = 0.77[b]	r_s = 0.64[b]

Notes: Data on party composition of government was calculated from Schmidt (2008).
Coefficient of correlations are Pearson's r or Spearman's r_s for the correlation of the respective column variable with the party composition of government data (see column 2) between 1950 and the year of measurement of the dependent variable. The percentage point change in the social budget as a percentage of GDP from 1960 to 2003 was correlated with the party composition of government in this period.
[a] = significance level 0.05, [b] = significance level 0.01.

- indicators of net social expenditure (OECD 2007*l*),
- decommodification scores (Esping-Andersen 1990),
- Scruggs's indicator of social rights in the early twenty-first century (Scruggs 2006), and
- Meyer's measure of 'social democracy' (2007).

Contagion Processes and Co-Governing Opposition Parties

Incumbent parties normally play a major role in shaping public policy in general and social policy in particular. However, opposition party effects also need to be considered. Two mechanisms are relevant within this context: the first is generated by contagion from competitors. Processes of this type have been at the centre of research on contagion of bourgeois parties from the left, or, conversely, contagion of leftist parties from liberal or conservative parties (see e.g. Hicks and Swank 1992), or mutual contagion of Christian democratic and social democratic parties (Seeleib-Kaiser et al. 2008).

The second mechanism consists of co-governing opposition parties. This occurs mainly when counter-majoritarian institutions provide the opposition parties with influential cooperation rights or outright veto positions. Patterns of this variety prevail above all in federal states with symmetric bicameralism, such as in the Federal Republic of Germany (Schmidt 1995). Particularly powerful co-governing effects are generated by divided majorities in the upper and lower houses of parliament or, in the German context, divided majorities between the Bundestag (parliament) and the Bundesrat, the representative council of the state governments. Under these circumstances, opposition parties may have a very strong impact on legislation. Major examples can be found in legislation on Germany's welfare state. They include a literal social policy race between the social-liberal government and the Christian democratic opposition party in 1972 (Hockerts 2006), co-government of the social democratic opposition party on legislation on German unification (Ritter 2006), and co-governance of the Christian democratic opposition parties in the labour market reforms of the second red–green government (2002–2005).

CAVEATS

The hypothesis of partisan influences is an important analytical instrument for a better understanding of the determinants of the welfare state and, compared with many other hypotheses in the literature, relatively successful in explaining policy outputs and outcomes. There are, however, certain caveats. The first is that party composition of government is but one variable among a wide variety of determinants of the welfare state and that partisan theory is one approach among others to the comparative study of social policy outputs (see e.g. Obinger et al. 2003; Schmidt et al. 2007; Leibfried and Mau 2008b; and the chapters in this Handbook).

Another caveat concerns cross-national differences in political manoeuvrability. Not all areas of social and economic life in a constitutional democracy are amenable to political manipulation. For example, unitary states with few veto points, such as Sweden and the United Kingdom before devolution, are, in principle, more amenable to partisan manipulation of public policy than states like the USA, Germany, and Switzerland, where government is constrained by counter-majoritarian powers such as federalism, a powerful constitutional court, and an autonomous central bank.

A further caveat concerns the asymmetric applicability of partisan theory to the functioning of majoritarian democracies on the one hand and non-majoritarian democracies on the other. Partisan theory is normally fully applicable to majoritarian democracies, such as Britain, Greece, and Sweden. In these countries, policymakers capitalize on a fairly large degree of political manoeuvrability. However, in non-majoritarian democracies, policymakers often lack freedom of manoeuvre. Consider two non-majoritarian cases: first, an all-inclusive coalition, such as Switzerland during World War II and for most of the period from 1959 until the present day, and second, a democracy, in which the major opposition party is *de facto*, via the second chamber of parliament, co-governing, such as Germany in most of the period of the red–green government (1998–2005). In neither case was there leeway for policy making of the kind that standard partisan theory suggests: that is solo runs of the incumbent party *A*, followed, after a change in power, by solo runs of the former opposition party *B*. The only freedom of choice available in these cases was between bargaining, exit, and blockade of the decision-making process. When bargaining prevails, policy tends to be premised on the lowest common denominator of the coalition partners. That denominator tends to generate policies of continuity rather than discontinuity and is normally associated with limited short-term elasticity in policy making. Because policies result under these circumstances from extended compromise-seeking, it is almost impossible for the voters to attribute the output to the individual players. That, however, means interruption or blockade of the causality that partisan theory postulates in respect of the relationship between voters' preferences, policy choices and policy outputs.

Party Differences in Periods of Welfare State Retrenchment and in the Context of Globalization

The 'new politics of the welfare state' literature (P. Pierson 1994, 2001a) suggests a further major caveat to partisan theory. Proponents of this thesis argue that the very success of the post-1945 welfare state has produced a transformed institutional context conditioning the context of further welfare state development. The key element of this transformation has been the emergence of powerful programme-specific constituencies of welfare state clients and professional organizations with strong interests in preserving the welfare state status quo. It is these interests that serve as the main sources of political protests against any proposed retrenchment of the welfare state. The 'new politics' literature also argues that the politics of cut-backs in social legislation differ from the politics of expansion of the welfare state. While welfare state expansion usually generated a highly popular politics of credit claiming for the extension of social rights and higher benefits, welfare state retrenchment normally affronts voters in general and welfare state clients and organized interests in particular. Hence, blame avoidance rather than credit claiming becomes the watchword for those opting for retrenchment or recalibration of social policy. A further claim of the 'new politics' thesis is that, within the novel context of welfare state retrenchment and welfare defence, the room for manoeuvre available to parties becomes considerably smaller.

Processes of Europeanization and globalization are also commonly regarded as trends which set further limits to partisan effects on the welfare state. However, the relative magnitude of the adaptation requirements produced by Europeanization and globalization is contested. One school of thought argues that adaptation requirements are strong and ultimately result in policy convergence. An alternative view suggests that the timing and magnitude of adaptation vary with, and depend upon, nation state-based institutions and actor constellations (Castles 2007a; Zohlnhöfer 2009).

While partisan effects on the welfare state may have become weaker in the age of welfare state retrenchment and globalization, they have by no means disappeared (Siegel 2002; Castles 2007a; Obinger and Tálos 2006; Rueda 2008). For example, party differences continue to exist in the timing and substance of adaptation processes in response to external change. A comparison of Germany, Britain, Denmark, and the Netherlands shows that social democratic parties respond with longer time lags to external adaptation requirements, because such changes demand from these parties particularly electorally risky changes in public policies (Zohlnhöfer 2009). Moreover, the type of adaptation to globalization varies with the party composition of government. A wider variety of social democratic governments nowadays favours investment in human capital and, thus, investment in the supply side of the economy rather than demand-side-oriented state intervention, such as in the 1960s and 1970s (Boix 1998; Zohlnhöfer 2009).

Persistent partisan effects have also been identified in studies of social rights. In contrast to claims that partisanship has little impact on welfare state commitment, Allan and Scruggs (2004: 496) have shown that 'traditional partisanship continues to have a considerable effect on welfare state entitlements in the era of retrenchment'. Nygard's study of the Nordic countries supports this view: 'social democratic and left-wing parties remain the foremost defenders of the "Nordic Welfare Model", whereas the right has become more hesitant toward welfare state expansion' (Nygard 2006: 356). Korpi and Palme's comparison of eighteen OECD countries in 1975–95, to cite a third instance, also identifies partisan effects on welfare state retrenchment: 'The risk for major cuts has been significantly lower with left party representation in cabinets, while the opposite holds true for secular conservative-centrist governments' (Korpi and Palme 2003: 441). While confessional parties, such as Christian democratic parties, were often responsible for massive welfare state expansion in the past, in periods of austerity and welfare state regress, they have been positioned in the middle between leftist governments and governments of the secular centre-right (Korpi and Palme 2003).

Partisan effects may also interact with other variables, such as veto players or veto positions (Starke 2008) and types of the welfare state (Siegel 2002). For example, welfare states of the corporatist type and centre parties may prove to be more resilient to major cuts than either liberal and social democratic welfare states. This is indeed a major finding of a comparative study of fiscal consolidation, including consolidation of social budgets, in the OECD since 1990 (Wagschal and Wenzelburger 2008). This study notes that spending cuts in liberal welfare states, such as New Zealand, were justified in terms of a pro-market ideology, while policymakers in the social democratic welfare states related their cuts in social spending to the exigencies of coping with a fiscal crisis of the state. In contrast, conservative regimes experienced a more limited fiscal consolidation because social insurance, a key institutional feature of the conservative welfare state, induced a strongly path-dependent development of social rights and social expenditure.

The Wagschal–Wenzelberger study also identifies two other partisan effects. Both are indirect in nature and impact on the two key predictors of fiscal consolidation: fiscal stress and welfare state type. Fiscal stress has many causes, but one is clearly the preference of leftist parties in office for ambitious social spending. Welfare state regimes are also impregnated by partisan effects (Esping-Andersen 1990). 'Social democratic welfare states' incorporate social democratic policy effects, 'liberal welfare states' are inconceivable without the impact of secular centre-rightist parties, and 'conservative welfare states' clearly mirror the long-term impact of two pro-welfare parties, one of social democratic complexion, the other of Christian democratic origin.

FAMILIES OF PARTIES AND THE WELFARE STATE

Overall, the review of the literature and the analysis of the available data on parties and social policy suggest that partisan theory remains a valuable tool in the comparative study of the welfare state in economically advanced democratic states and Table 14.3 summarizes important differences between the various party families in the countries analysed here. Partisan effects were at their strongest in periods of welfare state expansion and were in that period crystallized into distinctive welfare state regimes. Nevertheless, partisan effects are also discernible in a wide variety of cases of welfare state retrenchment. The acceptance of retrenchment, for example, is significantly lower on the part of the leftist parties and is absent from the agenda of radical socialist and communist parties. In contrast, secular conservative and liberal governments are far more likely to consider cuts in social transfers and services in order to consolidate budgets or cut taxes.

Large party differences also characterize the distribution of labour between the state and the market as well as the public–private mix in the production of welfare. Parties of the left favour state-centred policy stances and accept private social policy

Table 14.3 Social policy positions of major families of parties since the mid-1950s

Issue / Family of political party	Promoter or opponent of ambitious social protection	Prefered source of financing the welfare state	Position towards public–private mix in social security	Position towards decommodification	Promoter or opponent of welfare state retrenchment	Other welfare state topics
1. Radical socialist or communist parties	Promoter	(Progressive) taxes on income and wealth	Promotes state-centred varieties	Strong promoter	Opponent	Promotes guarantee of job security and protectionist foreign economic policy
2. Social democratic parties	Promoter	Taxes and social insurance contributions	Promotes state-centred varieties; private social policy conceivable as third or fourth pillar of social security	Strong Promoter	Mainly opponent, promoter only under exceptional circumstances	Favours extensive employment and job protection policies, favours (in most countries) investment in education
3. Religious centre parties	Promoter (especially in periods of higher economic growth)	Social insurance contributions and (voluntary and mandatory) private funds	In favour of a balanced public–private mix	Promoter for social insurance members	Partly promoter, partly opponent	Promoter of subsidiarity and upper limits for social policy
4. Nationalist-populist parties	Promoter	Taxes	In favour of state-centred varieties	Promoter (for national labour)	Mainly opponent	Favour social protection and protectionist foreign economic policy
5. Agrarian parties	Promoter—if costs are externalized	Taxation mainly of urban tax payers	Indifferent—if externalization of costs feasible	Promoter	Opponent	Favour social protection and protectionist foreign economic policy

Issue / Family of political party	Promoter or opponent of ambitious social protection	Prefered source of financing the welfare state	Position towards public–private mix in social security	Position towards decommodification	Promoter or opponent of welfare state retrenchment	Other welfare state topics
6. Secular conservative parties	Opponent	(Voluntary and mandatory) private funds and tax-based liberal welfare state regime	Promote strong private social policy and a parsimonious welfare state	Opponent	Promoter	Oppose trade unions and rigid job protection
7. Liberal parties	Opponent	Promoter of private, capital-funded social security arrangements	Promote strong private social policy and a parsimonious welfare state	Opponent	Promoter	Oppose trade unions; favour equal opportunity policy
8. Green parties	Partly in favour, party against	Taxation	Promote generous social protection; accept moderate role of private social policy	Promoter of basic social income	Indifferent	Promote permissive social policy; favour marginal groups and anti-discrimination

Note on Sources: The policy positions in Table 14.3 are based on the literature cited in the references and Schmidt (2005).

only to a limited degree. In contrast, centre parties, liberal parties and above all secular conservative parties opt for market-friendly social policy choices and provide considerable leeway for action for voluntary private social policy. This is a major cause of the divide between the Scandinavian world of welfare capitalism and the world of 'liberal capitalism' (Hall and Soskice 2001a) in the English-speaking family of nations.

Significant party differences also exist in the sources of financing the social budget. Radical parties of the left favour tax-based funding and highly progressive taxation. More moderate parties of the left, such as social democratic parties, emphasize a combination of social insurance contributions and tax-based funding, while centre parties tend to prefer social insurance contributions of labour and capital on the one hand and relatively high levels of mandatory private and voluntary social expenditure on the other. Finally, a strong preference for private social policy is a trademark of the liberal family of parties and most secular-conservative parties. However, both ot these latter groups of parties prefer taxes to contributions as the major source of financing for the programmes of the 'liberal welfare state regime'.

Two families of political parties have been largely neglected in the study of partisan effects on the welfare state: agrarian parties and nationalist-populist parties. Agrarian parties may turn out to be particularly strong pro-welfare actors, above all within the context of a red–green coalition with social democratic alliance partners (Manow 2007), and normally opt for financing the welfare state mainly through taxation of the urban population. Nationalist-populist parties also tend to favour taxes as the major source of the social budget, because they expect that tax-based welfare state provision makes the state, and national-populist governments in particular, more visible and more popular.

CONCLUSION

The patterns of the relationship between political parties and the welfare state are clear-cut: a wide range of minor and major partisan effects have influenced the structure, expansion, and retrenchment of the welfare state. This does not preclude major changes in policy positions of political parties, as for instance the shift to New Labour in Britain in the 1990s. But major changes in policy positions of parties are relatively uncommon and most of them are more gradual than proponents of convergence theories predict. The remarkable continuity in social policy position of parties documented in Laver and Hunt (1992) and Benoit and Laver (2006) supports this view. The remaining discontinuities in policy positions should not disguise the basic pattern in the relationship between political parties and the welfare state. For the countries discussed here, that is economically advanced Western democracies, the basic pattern consists of political parties that impact significantly on the shape of public policy in general and on the welfare state in particular.

CHAPTER 15

POLITICAL INSTITUTIONS

ELLEN M. IMMERGUT

INTRODUCTION

As all of the entries in this Handbook testify, welfare state comparisons aim to answer particular puzzles. Thus, a specific question determines the range of cases chosen, the time-frame of the study, and the welfare state outcomes that will serve as the dependent variable. So, too, is it the case with states and political institutions. How they are defined and measured, what one chooses as the independent and dependent variables of a study, and the methodologies that one wishes to use, all stem from the particular questions about the welfare state that are being posed. This entry sketches the changing research questions that have motivated research on the impact of state structures and political institutions on welfare states over the last decades. It will pay particular attention to how researchers operationalize political institutions and state structures in both quantitative and qualitative analyses. It begins with the state-centred approach, moves on to the new institutionalism, and ends with new directions in institutionalist research. Indeed, as we will see, there has been a movement from broad, comparative-historical studies of state structures to a more narrow focus on the impact of particular political institutions. The future potential of this line of research, however, may well depend upon a reopening and broadening of research on states and political institutions to consider the transnational, comparative-historical questions with which this strand of research on the welfare state began.

THE STATE-CENTRED APPROACH

Contemporary theories about the role played by state structures and political institutions in the emergence, growth and (possible) decline of welfare states cannot be understood without reference to the larger debates that prompted interest in the study of the welfare state in the post-war period. Starting in the late 1970s, interest in the role of the *state* in the development of welfare states was connected to a general resurgence of interest in the state, which was a response both to pluralist theories of politics and political development, and to Marxist theories of the state. The pluralist view of politics assumed that (in an open political system), interest groups would form spontaneously as citizens felt disturbed by recurring problems, and that these groups would pressure government to enact policies to solve these problems. Responding to continued interest group struggle, governments would gradually improve these policies, such that all of the activities of government could be explained in terms of a balance of interest group pressures—including pressures from unorganized or 'potential' interests. For the welfare state, the implication was that social policies were simply a response to social need, as political rights could be used to pressure governments to respond to social imperatives. In a surprising twist on this argument, however, convergence theory argued that all governments—whether democratic or authoritarian—would need to address these functionalist needs, and that, therefore, welfare state spending could be predicted from the resources available for social spending (size of Gross National Product) and social need (per cent of the population over 65 years of age), as well as the age of the social security system (Wilensky 1975). Thus, the pluralist view, in both its interest group and functionalist variants saw social need and economic development as the determinant of welfare state generosity.

With the resurgence of interest in Marxist theory at the end of the 1960s and early 1970s, a second type of functionalism emerged. Marxist functionalism posited that the capitalist state served the function of supporting the capitalist system. However, exactly how actors within the state were to be regarded—as representatives of the capitalists or as neutral managers—was the subject of heated debate, as well as the process by which civil servants and politicians would know which policies to introduce to serve the aims of capital. The welfare state was an important part of this debate, as welfare state policies could be interpreted either as proof that democratic politics could remedy the inequalities of capitalism or as a sign that capitalism was capable of surface reforms that nevertheless did not threaten the basis of the capitalist system itself. Indeed, some authors viewed the welfare state as a product of cross-class coalitions that rationalized capitalism in the short term, but would eventually undermine both the conditions for capitalist accumulation and legitimation (Block 1984; Gough 1979; Offe 1984).

One response to these bold declarations of both pluralist and Marxist functionalism was a debate on 'Do politics matter?', which focused on the role of left parties and partisan politics, as well as corporatist patterns of interest-group intermediation (Castles 1982a; Schmidt 1996; Wilensky 1981; see also Chapter 14 above), factors whose impact is more apparent if the range of comparison is reduced to the 'rich democracies' (Wilensky 2002). A second response was the development of 'conflict theory', a Weberian alternative to both Marxist and pluralist views of politics, which saw the development of states and social policies as the product of political contestation, including contestation by social classes. In contrast to the debate with convergence theory, which took the form of quantitative, large-N tests and assumed continuous relationships between causal variables, conflict theory focused on the importance of specific national or regional trajectories, and on the role of historically particular configurations of states and social structures in explaining both political development and the emergence of the welfare state. Comparative case studies were critical to refuting the view of welfare states as a response to democracy and/or social need, as in authoritarian nations social rights were introduced as an *alternative* to political rights (Flora and Alber 1981).

Conflict theory challenged pluralism by pointing out that pluralist politics played out on an uneven playing field, one structured in particular by the independent and powerful role played by states. From their engagement with Marxism, conflict theorists developed a series of class-centred views on the politics of the welfare state, but, at the same time, also an appreciation of the relative autonomy of the state. Coalitions between classes and political parties or between workers and employers in different economic sectors—i.e. class-based interests and class-based politics, also called the 'democratic class struggle'—were important for explaining differences in the development of the welfare states (Esping-Andersen 1990; Korpi 1983; Stephens 1979). Once in place, however, these policies affected the mobilization of class-based interests by providing class actors with political and ideational resources, such as a belief in entitlement to social rights (Esping-Andersen and Korpi 1984). At the same time, however, studies of capitalist states rediscovered the 'fiscal interests' of the state so stressed by Schumpeter (Myles 1984) and the role of a relatively autonomous state in stabilizing market conditions for open economies (Cameron 1978; Stephens 1979). Thus, this engagement with class theory also produced an interest in state structures and actors, in sequences of political development, as well as in the feedback effects of public policies.

Perhaps nowhere was this view more directly and clearly stated than in Skocpol's introduction to the book, *Bringing the State Back In* (1985). Here, Skocpol pointed to a range of work in political science and sociology that was influenced by Max Weber and Otto Hintze's view of states as organizations controlling territory and engaged in transnational conflicts and relationships:

> [T]hinking of states as organizations controlling territories leads us away from basic features common to all polities and toward consideration of the various ways in which state structures and actions are conditioned by historically changing transnational contexts. These contexts impinge on individual states through geopolitical relations of interstate domination and competition, through the international communication of ideals and models of public policy, and through world economic patterns of trade, division of productive activities, investment flows, and international finance. States necessarily stand at the intersections between domestic

> socio-political orders and the transnational relations within which they must
> maneuver for survival and advantage in relation to other states. (1985: 8)

Thus, one could view states as actors and as structures peopled with officials whose
interests, ideas, and capacities were dependent upon the organization and international position of the state. Moreover, states did not just assert 'relative' autonomy,
but (as in the Tocquevillian view) influenced the organization, goals, and resources of
social actors, whether these be viewed as classes, groups, or strata. As an example
of the more concrete implications of this perspective, Skocpol turned to the work of
Heclo (1974), which claimed that pension policy in Britain and Sweden had been
shaped by civil servants 'puzzling' over problems of income security in old age, and
as such by 'autonomous' state actors, rather than as a result of interest-group
bargaining or class conflict more broadly understood.

On a more structural level, Huntington's (1971) analysis of how the particular
pattern of political development in the United States had left in place a 'Tudor' state
of courts and parties rather than a centralized, bureaucratic state along Weberian
lines provides a good example of how state structure can influence policy development. As a consequence of this earlier phase in political development, Roosevelt
could only count on sufficient state capacities for massive government intervention
in the agricultural area, and this is where his 'New Deal' of the 1930s began.
The particular pattern for political development had repercussions as well for the
development of political parties, which jumped into the breach of weak bureaucracy
to create a spoils system, bending American social policy in the late nineteenth
century to the will of electoral machines in the area of civil war pensions (Skocpol
1992). Consequently, this policy legacy worked as a brake on further development of
the United States welfare state during the interwar period, a time when many
European states introduced social insurance on a widespread basis (Orloff and
Skocpol 1984). State structures and policy legacies also affected the development of
intellectual ideas about policy, the formation of interest group demands, and the
development of policy coalitions, for example, in the spread of Keynesian ideas and
policies during the Great Depression (Weir and Skocpol 1985).

THE NEW INSTITUTIONALISM
AND THE WELFARE STATE

March and Olsen (1984) incorporated the 'state-centred' approach into their watershed article pointing to the development of a 'new institutionalism' in political
science. This was the beginning of a shift in emphasis away from the state to one
focusing more on political institutions, and as such, a shift away from a broader
sociological analysis of the state to a narrower concern with the impact of democratic

political institutions on public policies. At the same time, in moving away from the state *qua* state, institutionalist perspectives on politics focused more strongly on questions of agency, identities, and interpretation than had the previous 'state-centred' approach (Immergut 2005).

Institutions as Ideal Types

One approach to considering the impact of political institutions on public policies and government expenditures is based on grouping political systems into basic types. The most influential of these typologies is Lijphardt's distinction between majoritarian versus consensus democracies (Lijphart 1999). Majoritarian democracies are characterized by institutions that allow a single party to obtain majority political representation and to use this majority power to enact policies; consensus democracies, by contrast, are characterized by sets of institutions that allow minorities to obtain political representation and wield political power, and thus impede majorities from neglecting their preferences and interests. Consequently, in consensus democracies, governments must take broad sets of preferences and interests into account, which, according to Lijphart, has resulted in more encompassing welfare states in these democracies (1999: 294). The specific institutions that define consensus democracy can be divided into those that fragment executive power (which Lijphart calls the 'executive-parties' dimension), and those that provide decision-making rights to centres of power alternative to the national-level government ('federalism–unitarism' dimension).

A competing typology for understanding the impact of institutions on policy outcomes has been developed by Persson and Tabellini (1999). They base their typology on two independent variables: the type of electoral system (proportional or majoritarian) and the type of regime (presidential or parliamentary). Persson and Tabellini go further than Lijphart in explaining just exactly how the political system favours particular policy outcomes, because they focus on the micro-incentives of the political system. They argue that the key to winning elections in proportional representation systems is winning greater proportions of votes. But in single-member electoral systems, the key is to maximize the number of districts. Consequently, politicians in single-member district systems should favour distributive policies—that is policies in which voters receive more than they have contributed in taxes, and that are concentrated in one district. Entitlement programmes on the other hand, cannot be focused on particular electoral districts, and are hence more attractive to politicians running for office in proportional representation systems. In addition, Persson and Tabellini argue that as presidential systems provide voters with a clear person to blame for tax increases, presidents will tend to veto tax increases, whereas the diffuse responsibility of a parliamentary system will tend to allow more tax increases. Putting the two factors together, they argue that the size of government should be largest when the two factors come together; in other words in a parliamentary system based on proportional representation.

Political Configurations

Typologies provide us with a useful heuristic for identifying the key features of a political system, and to connect these to particular political patterns. However, they are highly vulnerable to the misspecification of cases, and are inherently static, as full-scale constitutional change occurs only rarely. Consequently, some scholars have argued that one should view political institutions as dynamic 'political configurations', which change with political majorities and political preferences. Tsebelis (1995) understands political configurations in terms of 'veto-players'. For Tsebelis, a veto player is any political actor that must agree for legislation to be passed. Veto players may be partisan or institutional. Partisan veto players are the parties in government. Institutional veto players are any institutions, such as second chambers, that must agree to legislation. However, not all veto players are equal. Amongst the partisan veto players, only the two with most diverging—i.e. most distant—positions on an issue are relevant. The reason is that if the two most distant political parties can come to agreement on a piece of legislation, all 'intermediate' parties should also agree to a given proposal. Similarly, an institutional veto player is only relevant to the extent that it has a different position from the government, otherwise, it is considered to be 'absorbed'. For example, if the United States Presidency, House, and Senate are all controlled by one party, we do not expect these three 'potential' institutional veto players to block one another's decisions, and hence, in this configuration there are no relevant institutional veto players. Veto players analysis aims to explain differences in the abilities of governments to pass specific laws, and thus to predict the likelihood of policy change.

Similarly, Immergut (1992b) focuses on institutional veto points created from the interaction of constitutional rules and political results. Veto points are essentially the institutional veto players seen from a different angle. As in the case of institutional veto players, what counts is whether a political arena is constitutionally qualified to veto a proposal, and whether the majority in this area differs from that of the government. Thus, veto points analysis also makes a distinction between 'potential' and relevant veto points. Potential veto points are second chambers, constitutional courts, and referenda. In addition, when governments lack a parliamentary majority, the first chamber of the parliament is a veto point. (For an overview of veto points and veto players in selected OECD countries, see Table 15.1.) As the table makes clear, the combination of electoral results and constitutional rules in creating veto points means that the number and locations of veto points in a particular political system change as the political configuration changes. Moreover, veto points by themselves do not veto anything; instead, they are used by opponents of legislation to block the legislation. Thus, veto points analysis is dynamic and depends upon political majorities and political preferences, including those of interest groups.

Several studies of the development of the welfare state have shown that constitutional veto points matter for interests that wish to block greater governmental intervention in health and other social policy areas. At the same time, however, these authors point to other variables that must be considered as well, such as the

Table 15.1 Veto points and Veto players in selected OECD countries (1980–2005)

Country	Potential Institutional Veto Points[a]	Institutional Veto Points After Absorption[b]	Typical Governments	Institutional Veto Points		Partisan Veto Players		Max. Policy Distance between Governmental Parties[c]	
				Range	Average	Range	Average	Range	Average
Australia	Bicameralism High Court Federalism Referendum	Senate, High Court	Single or Two-Party Majority	1–2	1.92	1–2	1.5	0–14.5	3.5
Austria	Constitutional Court Federalism	Constitutional Court	Single or Multi-Party Majority	0–1	0.56	1–2	1.85	0–36.3	21.4
Belgium	Bicameralism Federalism	None	Multi-Party Surplus Majority	0	0	4–6	4.58	11.5–55.6	26.3
Canada	Supreme Court Federalism SMDs	Joint Decision Making[d]	mainly Single-Party Majority	0–2	1.6	1	1	0	0
Denmark	Referendum	Parliament	Multi-Party Minority	0–1	0.94	1–4	2.64	0–50.5	17.4
Finland	President (pre-1999)	President (pre-1999), Parliament	Multi-Party Surplus Majority	0–2	1.29	3–5	4.12	8.9–79.0	39.5
France	President Bicameralism Constitutional Court Referendum SMD's	President, Constitutional Court	Single and Multi-Party Majority	1–2	1.34	1–3	2.07	0–32.9	14.1
Germany	Bicameralism Constitutional Court Federalism	Second Chamber Constitutional Court	Multi-Party Majority	0–2	1.70	2–3	2.56	1.3–28.3	17.3
Greece	None	None	Mainly Single-Party Majority	0	0	1–3	1.04	0–58.7	1.4
Ireland	Supreme Court Referendum	Parliament, Referendum	Single or Multi-Party Majority (Minority)	0–2	0.95	1–3	1.78	0–54.1	15.9

(continued)

Table 15.1 Continued

Country	Potential Institutional Veto Points[a]	Institutional Veto Points After Absorption[b]	Typical Governments	Institutional Veto Points		Partisan Veto Players		Max. Policy Distance between Governmental Parties[c]	
				Range	Average	Range	Average	Range	Average
Italy	Bicameralism	Chamber of Deputies, Senate	Multi-Party Minority/Majority	0–2	0.24	1–8	5.12	0–41.5	20.7
Japan	Bicameralism	House of Representatives	Until 1993 Single-Party Majority, then mainly Multi-Party Majority	0–1	0.14	1–7	1.95	0–29.3	5.32
Luxembourg	Council of State Constitutional Court	None	Multi-Party Majority	0	0	2	2	2.7–21.6	11.6
Netherlands	Bicameralism	First Chamber, Second Chamber	Multi-Party Majority (Minority)	0–2	0.03	2–3	2.43	2.8–32.7	18.7
New Zealand	Pre-1993 SMDs	House of Representatives	Pre-1993 Single-Party Majority, then Single- or Multi-Party Minority	0–1	0.38	1–2	1.30	0–29.63	4.79
Portugal	President Constitutional Court Referendum	President, Parliament, Constitutional Court	Single or Multi-Party Majority (Minority)	1–3	1.86	0–3	1.44	0–15.0	2.3
Spain	Constitutional Court	Lower House of Parliament	Single-Party Majority/Minority	0–1	0.45	1	1	0	0
Sweden	None except Parliament	Parliament	Single-Party Minority or Multi-Party Minority/Majority	0–1	0.94	1–4	1.52	0–44.4	7.8

Country	Potential Institutional Veto Points[a]	Institutional Veto Points After Absorption[b]	Typical Governments	Institutional Veto Points		Partisan Veto Players		Max. Policy Distance between Governmental Parties[c]	
				Range	Average	Range	Average	Range	Average
Switzerland	Collegial Executive Bicameralism Federal Court Federalism Referendum	Referendum	4-Party Surplus Majority	1	1	4	4	20.5–80.1	51.7
UK	SMDs	None	Single Party	0	0	1	1	0	0
USA	President Bicameralism Supreme Court Federalism SMDs	President, House of Representatives, Senate	Single Party	1–4	3.69	1	1	0	0

Sources: Country chapters and country data found in: Immergut et al. 2007; Klingemann et al. 2006; Obinger et al. 2005.

Notes: [a] This column lists only the institutions mentioned by Huber, Ragin, and Stephens 1993, and does not include the first chamber of parliaments, as they are only a veto point when governments lack a majority in this chamber. As Huber, Ragin, and Stephen's coding of the veto points includes single member districts, this institutional feature is included here as well, although perhaps the electoral system should be considered as part of the system of political competition rather than as a veto point. Largely following Huber, Ragin & Stephen's coding decisions, referenda are listed only when regularly used to veto laws, which is also in line with the discussion in Tsebelis 1995. When governments can control the calling of referenda, however, they are absorbed, thus leaving Switzerland as the only country with the referendum as an active veto point, in line with Huber, Ragin and Stephen's coding as well. In place of Huber, Ragin, and Stephen's later work including judicial review, we mention only courts that actually regularly veto laws, and thus focus more directly on constitutional courts than judicial review in general.
[b] This column is based on Immergut et al. 2007, which considers the majorities for each political configuration in order to determine whether a veto point is open or closed at a particular point in time. The procedures here are the same as used by Tsebelis 1995, except for the consideration of first chambers of parliament as veto points under minority governments. The partisan veto players are coded following Tsebelis 1995.
[c] Difference between the two most distant parties in government; based on the Manifesto Research Group's coding of the left–right positions of parties (Klingemann et al. 2006).
[d] See Canada chapter in Obinger et al. 2005.

type of political parties (Maioni 1998; Obinger 1998), feedback effects over time (Hacker 1998), and to diffusion effects (Brooks 2009), all of which will be discussed in more depth below. Moreover, the impact of veto points has varied over time and across policy areas, indicating the importance of historical contingency and other more complex patterns of contextual causality (Tuohy 1999). Geographic context may also be important. Studies of Latin American pension politics show support for the veto points approach: pension privatization has been more difficult where veto points facilitate interest group or partisan opposition to privatization (Brooks 2002; Kay 1999). However, in Western Europe, politicians have actually been successful in introducing pension reforms in systems with strong veto points and many veto players (Bonoli 2000a; Immergut et al. 2007). One reason for this may be that when governments cannot force change through the political decision-making process, they must generate societal consensus for reforms, which may be more effective than a pattern of top-down decision making followed by public protests (Baccaro 2002; Natali and Rhodes 2004; Schludi 2005). Consensus generation may be more important in mature democracies, however; hence the greater applicability of veto points theory to Western Europe in the interwar and immediate post-war periods, and to Latin America today.

Multivariate Analysis

Quantitative efforts to test the impact of state structures and political institutions on welfare state outcomes have been highly influenced by the work of Huber, Ragin, and Stephens (Huber et al. 1993). Previous efforts to operationalize state structure had been limited to state administrative capacities, defined as state centralization, the age of social security programmes, the budgetary weight of government personnel, and traditions of bureaucratic patrimonialism (Hicks and Swank 1992; Pampel and Williamson 1989; Wilensky 1981, 1975). Instead, Huber et al. focus on the impact of institutions on political decision making, and therefore on the ability of societal actors to press their claims upon the state. Drawing both on the distinction between majoritarian and consensus democracy, as well as veto points analysis, they combine institutional rigidities providing barriers to government action (federalism, presidentialism, bicameralism, referenda) or parliamentary representation (single-member districts) into an index of constitutional structure. Controlling for partisanship, they find that these institutional impediments do indeed slow the growth of social expenditures in the expansion phase of the welfare state, but exert only a moderate impact on retrenchment efforts (Huber and Stephens 2001a). Schmidt, too, has investigated the impact of institutional veto points and partisanship on social expenditures (even expanding the list of institutional veto players to include central banks and membership in the EU) and finds them to be significant as brakes to both welfare state expansion and retrenchment (2002a). Some scholars include unions and employers' associations as a 'veto point,' as their role in social insurance administration may place them in a position to veto policies (Ebbinghaus and Hassel 2000). In my view, however, it is preferable to consider only political institutions as veto points, and to analyse the extremely important role of social interests and economic processes (e.g. economic integration) as separate variables. Armingeon (2002) separates sources of policy blockage into several dimensions, arguing that one must consider the effects of counter-majoritarian institutions (veto points or institutional veto players) separately from those of consociationalism (coalition government or partisan veto players), as veto points prevent the growth of social expenditures in the first place, whereas consociational institutions are helpful for negotiating welfare state cutbacks. (See also the discussion of competitive versus consensual veto points in Birchfield and Crepaz 1998).

The impact of institutions may have cumulative effects over time, which Swank terms 'second-order' effects (2002). 'Inclusive' electoral institutions such as proportional representation (and the associated higher effective number of political parties) were important for the original expansion of the welfare state, and are thus associated with welfare states that enjoy high levels of popular support. At the same time, proportional representation allows contemporary defenders of the welfare state more opportunities for political impact. Similarly, institutional veto points affect current retrenchment politics both directly and indirectly. Their direct effect is to allow opponents of programme cuts to block retrenchment; but as their past impact has been to block the development of an expansive welfare state in the first place, they are also associated with more 'liberal' welfare states that enjoy less favourable public support and are hence easier to cut back (2002: 56-8). Thus, institutions have a long-term impact on political coalitions, and even on norms and values favouring public commitment to the welfare state.

Single Institutions and Institutional Origins

After a period of focus on the politics of retrenchment and the new politics of the welfare state, one can now observe a movement back to a focus on the origins and development of the welfare state, as well as on the origins of individual political institutions themselves (cf. the discussion in Chapter 12 above). One current focus is on federalism. As any study of federalism shows, the label of federalism must be further clarified to set out exactly the impact of federal institutions on political and administrative decision making. One important feature of federalist polities is the widespread use of powerful second chambers (strong bicameralism), as well as constitutional courts and (less commonly) referenda, which is where the blocking effect on political decision making arises (Obinger et al. 2005a). A second critical aspect is 'fiscal federalism', the extent to which jurisdictions enjoy fiscal independence and are subject to fiscal competition, and indeed the exact nature of revenue raising and revenue sharing arrangements (Rodden 2006). It is only where fiscal federalism results in direct tax responsibility in a system of tax competition and/or political blockages are active that federalism exerts a negative influence on welfare states. Moreover, the effects of fiscal arrangements and institutional veto points depend, as previously discussed, on party politics, coalitions, and feedbacks between previous policies and current political interests—in short, on political context. In addition, political and interest-group strategies can be found that bypass federal constraints on welfare state expansion or blockages to welfare state reform (Hacker 2002; Maioni 1998; Obinger et al. 2005a). Finally, federalism (again in conjunction with specific party systems) may not only have an impact on the welfare state, but on the constellations of interests and their organization, thus affecting the politics of the welfare state by changing the constellation of political actors (Martin and Swank 2008).

Electoral Systems

Although included in earlier quantitative studies of the emergence and generosity of welfare states (Huber et al. 1993), electoral systems are re-emerging as a focus of analysis. Cusack, Estévez-Abe, Iversen, and Soskice have all pointed to the link between proportional representation, coordinated market economies and social policies (Cusack et al. 2007; Estévez-Abe et al. 2001). They argue that proportional representation allows interests favouring a generous social wage, incentives for human capital formation, and substantial employment protection to achieve better political representation. Critical to their argument is that proportional electoral systems allow the representation of more interests, and that therefore alliances between middle class and working class voters favouring redistribution on terms favourable to the middle class emerge more readily than in majoritarian systems. Similarly, Lynch (2006) argues that the ability of policymakers to modernize systems of occupational welfare to include all citizens, and to cover risks of the entire life-cycle more equally, depends upon the rules of the electoral game—whether politicians make programmatic or clientelistic appeals to voters—and on programme structures (fragmented or consolidated). Kersbergen and Manow combine the analysis of electoral systems with social cleavages to explain the development of different types of welfare states (van Kersbergen and Manow 2009). Proportional representation combined with the rural–urban cleavage in the Scandinavian countries made agricultural interests central as a coalition partner, and, hence, were responsible for the universal welfare states of the so-called 'social democratic' world of welfare. Proportional representation combined with the state–church cleavage in continental Europe produced the Christian democratic or 'conservative' welfare state, with its emphasis on subsidiarity and status-conserving benefits. Majoritarian electoral systems, by contrast, resulted in less redistribution, and hence, 'liberal' welfare states.

Presidentialism and Regimes

Empirical work is just taking off on other institutions that may be important for broadening the perspective of welfare state research to the supra-national politics of the EU and to include newer democracies, such as those in Latin America and

Eastern Europe. Given the literature on presidential versus parliamentary political systems, the treatment of the presidency is an important issue for understanding the impact of institutions on social policies (Huber et al. 1993; Huber and Stephens 2001a). Further, Huber et al.'s recent work on social spending in Latin America (2008) demonstrates that for this region, regime—whether democratic or authoritarian—is critical for welfare state spending. Given increasing evidence of the persistence of autocratic regimes, more attention to political regime would be important for moving the agenda of welfare state research beyond its initial geographic focus on Western Europe and the OECD nations. Similarly, in light of the prominent role of judicial politics in the European Union and the increasing interest in cosmopolitan rights of citizenship as a solution to problems of migration and inclusion, the impact of courts on social policies would appear to be a promising research frontier.

Broader Views of Institutional Effects

Recent work on institutional effects on the welfare state has broadened the view of institutions from formal political institutions to the more encompassing state capacities, policy legacies, and societal mobilization previously emphasized by the state-centred approach—in short, to the welfare state as an institution in its own right. One important line of research looks at the feedback effects of institutions over time. Not only do welfare state institutions create their own supporters, as suggested by the 'new politics' approach, attention to the time dimension can demonstrate the impact of sequences of events on welfare state politics, which may be very difficult to capture in variable approaches (P. Pierson 2004). Previous political decisions may create watersheds in welfare state development—such as the focus on occupational welfare in the United States after the failure to expand the universal welfare state after World War II—which then generate new sets of actors and interests as private insurers, unions, and employers adjust to the new institutional realities (Hacker 1998). Moreover, institutional change may occur through 'non-legislative' means—an awkward term meant to suggest that non-political means of changing policies may be highly political even though not presented as political decisions. These 'means' include increasing government deficits to the point that future welfare state expansion is precluded (Paul Pierson's 'systematic retrenchment' 1994) or privatizing risk and allowing policy 'drift' (Hacker 2004a).

Previous policies affect state administrative capacities, and thus the basis for both welfare state expansion and recalibration, including policies that depend not just on government but on support from societal actors, such as in the case of activation and training policies (Martin and Thelen 2007). Feedback effects may not only influence actors' degrees of political mobilization and perceptions of their own interests, but may generate beliefs about the normative justifications for the institutions (Rothstein 1998). Further, by classifying citizens, welfare states do not just respond to social stratification but, in fact, effect stratification through their categories. Older work on the welfare state recognized the importance of status categories in continental

European welfare states with their distinctions between workers, salaried employees, and civil servants (Kocka 1981). Newer work has turned to the impact of welfare states in demarcating 'self' and 'other' in issues of race and ethnicity, as well as gender (Lieberman 2005; Naumann 2005). Thus, welfare state politics and policies do not just affect the organization of interests and their expression in politics, but can even reframe societal categories and reconfigure the categories of political conflict.

Conclusions

From this survey of the impact of state structures and political institutions on the welfare state, we see that institutions have had a significant impact on welfare state structures and outcomes. Institutional veto points have provided leverage over political decision making to actors opposed to expansion of social rights for various reasons, and are hence associated with more restricted welfare states and lower levels of government expenditures. By allowing interests opposed to government intervention with opportunities for blocking policies, veto points have had a significant impact on the public–private mix in social provision. Partisan veto players, on the other hand, have proved to be more significant for the politics of welfare state retrenchment, notably *not* by blocking legislation, but instead by helping to generate societal consensus for policy change.

Institutional effects are interaction effects, however, and thus cannot be predicted without attention to the preferences of political actors. Moreover, as institutions and political decisions made within those institutions affect the constellation of organized actors, the preferences of citizens, and the capacities of states, institutional effects must be studied over time and with sensitivity to the fact that such effects change over time. In addition, institutional analysis must consider the problem of 'endogeneity'. Institutions emerge in specific social contexts. Therefore, one cannot consider the impact of institutions on welfare state outcomes without also considering whether particular institutions were chosen with those welfare state outcomes in mind. Finally, recent research demonstrates that geographic dispersion may be as important as the time dimension. New research on the welfare state is thus headed for greater cross-regional comparison and the engagement with transnational patterns and processes with which the state-centred approach began.

CHAPTER 16

....

PUBLIC ATTITUDES

....

STEFAN SVALLFORS

INTRODUCTION

....

WHY should welfare state research care about the state of public opinion? Given that attitudes are often diffuse, ambivalent, or downright contradictory, why should researchers even bother about trying to analyse and explain them? One reason, as Joseph Schumpeter once put it, is that 'attitudes are coins that do not readily melt' (Schumpeter 1942: 12). That is, established viewpoints, normative expectations, concepts of justice, etc., are often very hard to change, and in this way, attitudes often function as a counterweight to abrupt policy changes. Policy reformers need to deal with a set of normative orientations and expectations that have been established by previous politics and policies, and this often hinders or derails processes of change. Conversely, existing attitudes may also be a resource and part of the opportunity structure for actors bent on challenging the institutionalized status quo and effectuating political change.

A second reason is that sustained analyses of attitudes make it harder to confuse elite opinions and strategies with the views of the larger public. Elites often claim to be speaking on behalf of majorities or larger groups, and this kind of research helps us to judge whether that is true or not. This is linked to the question of whether existing social arrangements are legitimate or not. Are they accepted only because people see no alternatives or think that action is futile, or are they normatively grounded? Are institutions considered to be fundamentally just or not?

This kind of research also asks us to judge public policies not only by their distributive effects or by their economic efficiency, but by their normative effects

Author's Note: This research has been funded by the Swedish Research Council and the Swedish Council for Social and Working Life Research. Thanks to Linda Berg, Clem Brooks, Jonas Edlund, Mikael Hjerm, Staffan Kumlin, Wim van Oorschot, Maria Oskarson, Maria Pettersson, Annette Schnabel, and Joe Soss for helpful comments.

on mass publics. Do these policies tend to foster egoism, narrow-mindedness, and exclusion, or do they tend to nurture civic-mindedness, tolerance, and concern for others? These seem to be fairly fundamental questions for a democratic polity.

In order to address issues of attitudinal formation and change, a comparative perspective is particularly fruitful. By comparing attitudes in different institutional settings we hope to shed light on causes and processes behind attitudinal patterns. At a general level, such an institutional analysis involves comparing actors located in spatially different settings, and using elements of the institutional environment in which they are located to explain differences and similarities.

The field was for a long time marred by lack of data. While reasonably good data had been available for a considerable time for such issues as social mobility, income distribution, and economic indicators of all sorts, even by the late 1980s the situation was substantially less good when it came to comparing attitudes across countries. This state of affairs has now completely changed, with the establishment and growth of data production collaborations such as the *European Social Survey*, the *International Social Survey Program*, and the *World Values Survey*. The field is now 'data-rich' compared with the recent past, though there are deficiencies concerning the availability of time-series and comparative data of sufficient specificity that will be explored subsequently. However, advanced analyses, explanations, and interpretations still lag behind.

In this chapter, I aim to take stock of comparative research in the field as far as it relates to attitudes towards welfare policies and the (re)distribution of resources and life chances—what will be referred to as comparative welfare attitudes.[1] I start out with what I see as the first generation of comparative welfare attitude research, in which national surveys on the topic were established and could be compared. I then move on to survey the turn towards explicitly comparative studies, and in particular the extensive research on the link between welfare regimes and attitudinal patterns. The next section presents recent developments in attitude studies beyond the welfare regimes framework. Finally, a section preceding the conclusion highlights important challenges for the future.

FIRST GENERATION: NATIONAL
SURVEYS COMPILED

Although election studies and other general surveys had occasionally looked at welfare attitudes from the 1950s onwards, more extensive and systematic research

---

[1] The terminology used for the *explanandum* will vary somewhat in the chapter, reflecting the different emphasis and focus of particular analysts. The chapter mainly focuses on (implicitly or explicitly) country-comparative work, as it relates to citizens' views about what government should or should not do. For a summary of the field with a slightly different focus, putting more emphasis on welfare state evaluations (see Kumlin 2007).

did not take hold until the 1970s. It took both the maturation of extensive welfare states, and their political questioning in the wake of the economic problems of the 1970s, to make public opinion about the welfare state a salient research issue. This first generation of scholars in the field had to make do with compiling, re-analysing, and comparing national surveys on welfare attitudes, a procedure which made their conclusions intrinsically fragile.

One of the earliest attempts to compile and re-analyse existing surveys was made by Richard Coughlin (1979, 1980). Coughlin compared attitude data from eight rich countries using existing national surveys. Another influential series of re-analyses of existing survey data was carried out by Peter Taylor-Gooby, who used British surveys to describe patterns and pinpoint ambivalences in welfare attitudes (Taylor-Gooby 1982, 1983, 1985).

These first attempts at probing the patterns of welfare attitudes were soon followed by a wave of national surveys, in which different aspects of attitudes to welfare were investigated. In the 1980s, national surveys were conducted and analysed in a host of advanced capitalist countries, including the United States (Cook and Barrett 1992), Germany (Roller 1992), Sweden (Svallfors 1989), and Britain (Saunders 1990).

Although conclusions emanated from different data sets and various comparisons, and differed in substance and emphasis, a set of common key findings from these early works may be summarized in five short points:

1. Overall, attitudes were strongly supportive of an encompassing welfare state. In contrast to sweeping statements in the public debate about generational processes leading younger age groups away from support for welfare policies, or about increasing resistance to bureaucratic-administrative intrusions, the early research in general showed the welfare state to be quite popular. Encompassing welfare policies, which are collectively financed and publicly organized, proved to have overall support from the citizens of the advanced capitalist economies.

2. At the same time, a clear difference in support for universal and selective programmes was found. Universal encompassing programmes such as pensions and health care received strong support, while more targeted or selective programmes such as unemployment benefits and social assistance received much lower support. This pattern essentially applied in most, if not all, advanced capitalist democracies.

3. A clear difference was also documented between general and specific support for the welfare state. General support, in the form of attitudes towards objects such as 'the public sector' or 'social reforms', proved to be more dependent on changes in the public discourse and general ideological dispositions, and public support was therefore more volatile at this level. Specific support for concrete welfare policy programmes, on the other hand, was shown to be more stable because rooted in everyday life experiences.

4. The clear support for welfare policies coexisted with considerable ambivalence regarding several aspects of welfare policies. Quite widespread suspicions about welfare abuse and cheating, for example, and concerns about bureaucracy and

inefficiencies in the public sector were important qualifications to the overall support for the redistributive and risk-reducing aspects of welfare policies.

5. The early research also confirmed the continuing importance of class and 'class-related' factors (such as income and education) as the most important factors shaping welfare attitudes—in contrast to widespread arguments concerning the influence of sector-related cleavages on popular views of the welfare state (Dunleavy 1980; Saunders 1986: ch. 8).

Although these first generation analyses were severely constrained by the non-existence of truly comparative data, they form an important backdrop to later developments in the field. Simply by making welfare attitudes a topic for systematic social scientific research, instead of the object of political and speculative projections, they laid the ground for subsequent extensions and improvements.[2]

THE COMPARATIVE TURN: WELFARE REGIMES AND PUBLIC OPINION

From the 1990s onwards, research on welfare attitudes took an explicitly comparative turn. The precondition for this was the establishment, consolidation, and increasing sophistication of comparative datasets. Data collected (in order of appearance) through the *Eurobarometer*, the *European* (later *World*) *Values Surveys*, the *International Social Survey Program*, and the *European Social Survey* have formed the basis for systematic research concerning the shaping influence of political and institutional factors on welfare attitudes and about the interplay of institutional and attitudinal change.

Perhaps the most important single enterprise in the first round of systematic comparison of welfare attitudes was found in the Beliefs in Government (BiG) project, headed by Max Kaase and Kenneth Newton (for a summary see Kaase and Newton 1995). In these five volumes, the research team aimed to take stock of what could be learned from the first rounds of genuinely comparative attitude research. In particular, the volume on the 'Scope of Government' added a host of valuable analyses of citizens' orientations towards government activities and spending (Borre and Scarbrough 1995). In making a distinction between attitudes towards the *range* of government activities and towards the *degree* of government involvement, these analyses questioned the 'government overload' hypothesis of the time, according to which voters' insatiable requests for ever more government intervention

---

[2] Of course, important single-country studies continued to flourish over the course of the 1990s and 2000s, often focusing on change in welfare attitudes over time—and often finding very little change. For a selection of analyses based on single-country surveys, see Jenssen and Martinussen 1994; Svallfors 1996; van Oorschot 1998; Blomberg-Kroll 1999; the individual chapters in Svallfors and Taylor-Gooby 1999; Andress et al. 2001; Arriba et al. 2006; Staerklé et al. 2007.

led to an overload in government budgets and capacities. What was clear from this research was that it was simply not the case that voters asked for more and more extensions of government responsibilities: on the whole such demands were quite stable over time.

The comparative analyses in the BiG project were still severely constrained by problems of data availability. As readily admitted by the editors, many aspects of comparative welfare attitudes could simply not be tapped with the existing data. Time-series were still too short and the range of countries still too restricted to allow more wide-ranging conclusions. Furthermore, it was apparent that the BiG project was still well short of establishing any coherent theoretical framework with which to understand the patterning of attitudes towards state intervention and redistribution. The many interesting analyses it included were not driven by a joint set of analytical concepts and perspectives.

What gradually emerged as something of a master frame for comparative inquiries was the 'worlds of welfare' categorization famously introduced by Esping-Andersen (see Chapter 39 below). A number of studies analysed whether attitude patterns and conflict patterns corresponded to the typology he suggested, and what might explain instances of non-correspondence. Amongst the earliest studies in this genre were Svallfors (1993 and 1997), which compared attitudes to redistribution in different Western countries, using Esping-Andersen's worlds of welfare as a frame for country selection and analysis. These studies were followed by many others (Bean and Papadakis 1998; Evans 1998; Edlund 1999a, 1999b; Matheson and Wearing 1999; Bonoli 2000b; GelisSen 2000; Andress and Heien 2001; Arts and Gelissen 2001; Svallfors 2003; Jæger 2006; Larsen 2006, 2008).

The main findings of this 'comparing-attitudes-in-regimes-industry' are not completely clear-cut, since both conceptual and empirical problems beset the analyses (see further below). But there seems to be agreement on the following set of findings: we do, indeed, find substantial differences among countries in overall public support for the welfare state, corresponding roughly to welfare policy commitment. Support for equality, redistribution, and state intervention is strongest in the social democratic regime, weaker in the conservative regime, and weakest in the liberal regime. However, we do not find any clear regime clustering of countries. Differences and similarities between countries show interpretable patterns, but they are too complex to be summarized as 'worlds of welfare attitudes'.

Furthermore, we find general similarities across countries in the impact of different social cleavages: categorical differences along class, gender, or labour market status lines show similar patterns across welfare regimes. Where we do find interesting differences between countries in the size and pattern of categorical attitude differences, they do not at all conform to the model suggested in the closing chapter of Esping-Andersen's treatise. Instead, categorical differences seem to follow the historical articulation of particular social cleavages in different contexts. For example, class differences are especially pronounced in Sweden and some other countries of North-Western Europe, reflecting the comparatively high salience of distributive and class-related issues in the political programmes and practices of these countries.

A particularly innovative argument, extending the regime framework in important ways, has been presented in work by Steffen Mau (2003, 2004). Mau extends the
policy regime argument into a discussion of ways in which we might expect norms of
reciprocity to vary between different institutional set-ups. According to Mau, different welfare systems inculcate different norms of reciprocity and hence create different 'moral economies' of the welfare state: while targeted systems tend to demand
of citizens that welfare recipients should be docile and grateful and do their best
to move away from their current 'needy' status, a universal system gives rise to
questions about how the larger collectivity is able to solve its problems of security
and sustenance.

Even though many things about comparative welfare attitudes have been learned
from the comparisons of welfare regimes, this whole line of inquiry has by now
reached an impasse. At present, we could expect little new to be learned from yet
another comparison of welfare attitudes in 'x worlds of welfare capitalism'. In reaching this impasse, a number of conceptual and empirical problems with the analytical
framework have emerged.

One of these problems is specifically related to the regime concept itself. What
really are 'welfare regimes'? Are they country clusters or are they ideal types to
which countries approximate more or less well? Are regimes constellations of
institutions, constellations of distributive outcomes, or constellations of political
actors *and* political institutions? None of this is entirely clear from reading Esping-
Andersen's founding monograph, and different authors have taken different directions in trying to indicate and compare welfare regimes (cf. Castles and Mitchell
1992; Korpi and Palme 1998; Huber and Stephens 2001*b*). If a loose fit is found
between country clusters and some particular outcome (such as, in this case,
welfare attitudes), is this an indication of a loose coupling of institutions and
attitudes or of the fact that countries do not 'fit' the welfare regime (cf. Scruggs
and Allan 2008)?

Another more general problem is how welfare state support should best be
measured in relation to welfare regimes. Studies vary widely in the kind of indicators
they use for attitudinal support, often without much explicit argument as to why a
particular measure was chosen. Analysts vary regarding whether they choose manifest summary measures composed of multiple individual indicators (for example,
Svallfors 2003), some kind of latent constructs (for example, Andress and Heien
2001), or some kind of 'global' single-item measure (for example, Jæger 2006). They
also differ as to whether they try to measure support for specific welfare policies or
attitudes to (re)distribution in more general terms. All in all, this particular 'dependent variable problem' has made comparisons between different analyses difficult
and the accumulation of findings painstakingly slow.

To add to this 'dependent variable problem', there also seems to be an 'independent variable problem'. Some analysts use dubious measures of social cleavages—
class, in particular—and some tend to 'explain' welfare state attitudes with other
attitudes or party choice. All in all, this often creates considerable confusion about
the structuring of welfare attitudes in different policy regimes.

Notwithstanding all these problems, important things have been learned by comparing attitudes in different policy regimes and, as the next section will show, institutional analyses are still highly useful in elucidating the mechanisms behind the formation of welfare state attitudes.

RECENT DIRECTIONS: BEYOND THE WELFARE REGIME FRAMEWORK

Recent comparative scholarship has taken a number of significant steps to widen the perspective beyond comparing welfare regimes. One such important extension has been to broaden the conception of regimes to include the production regimes and political power constellations of various advanced political economies. By including features such as the social organization of markets and the mobilization/articulation of political actors, analysts have been able to show that welfare attitudes are structured by these factors.

One strand of research focuses on the 'skill specificity' of individuals and workforces and argues that this factor has an impact on redistributive attitudes: workers with more industry- or occupation-specific skills tend to ask for more protection and redistribution from the state than workers with more general skills. In countries with a more specific skill profile, demand for state intervention, therefore, tends to be higher than in countries where general skills are more prevalent (Iversen and Soskice 2001; see also the critique by Kitschelt and Rehm 2006; Tåhlin 2008).

Others ask more broadly how risk profiles differ between different political economies and how such risk profiles may affect attitudes to welfare policies (Svallfors 2004; Cusack et al. 2006). The matrix of risks and resources that make up the class and stratification system affect the interests of individuals who are differently placed in this matrix and this affects their attitudes towards redistribution. Regardless of whether skill specificity or class-based risks and resources are seen as the key mechanisms, all these analyses tend to focus on the organization of markets and the distribution of marketable capacities as the key to welfare state support and opposition.

A different but complementary new strand is found among analyses that focus on the feedback effects of the organization of welfare policies and institutions. In these analyses, it is argued that the organizational and distributional effects of welfare policies create feedback effects on mass publics, affecting their interests in, their interpretations of, and norms about policies and polities (P. Pierson 1993; Soss 1999; Mettler and Soss 2004; Soss 2005; Soss et al. 2007; Svallfors 2007). As Mettler and Soss articulate this view, public policies 'influence the ways individuals understand their rights and responsibilities as members of a political community' (2004: 61).[3] In probing such feedback effects, researchers have used both extensive comparative approaches (Svallfors 2007) and intensive nation-specific case studies (Soss 1999; Kumlin 2004; Soss and Schram 2007) to show how and why individuals' understandings and orientations are affected by public policies.

An important methodological extension of the field is found in the attempts to quantify various dimensions of welfare states, or the wider socio-political environment, and the increasing use of multilevel methods then to analyse the impact of these factors on individuals' welfare attitudes (Blekesaune and Quadagno 2003; Jæger 2006; Kumlin and Svallfors 2007). Such hierarchical modelling has been used to show, for example, the impact of different dimensions of welfare regimes on attitudes (Jæger 2006) and to explain the varying magnitudes of class differences in attitudes across different countries (Kumlin and Svallfors 2007).

Such quantification and hierarchical modelling exercises often started out as critiques of the oversimplification and crudeness of letting countries 'represent' welfare regimes. However, they carry their own dangers. One is that underspecified individual-level models may lead to a 'wild goose chase' at the country level, if and when effects of macro-variables are only the reflection of omitted individual-level variables. Another unfortunate side-effect is that analysts often assume a linear additive model in the relationship between various macro-level factors. Since the units at the higher level (countries) are too few to allow extensive modelling of interactions, researchers (without much discussion) tend to assume that the effects of a particular macro-variable are the same regardless of countries' values on other dimensions. This is a highly questionable assumption, and one from which the regime concept was quite explicitly intended to move away. The fact that it is now tacitly reintroduced points to the often problematic circularity of social scientific arguments.

If a broadening of the regime concept, a focus on feedback effects, and a more advanced multilevel approach have in conjunction offered insights into the *formation* of welfare attitudes, new light has also been cast on the *effects* of such attitudes on policy development. A key publication in this regard is Brooks and Manza (2007), which uses aggregated International Social Survey Programme (ISSP) data in order to study the relative impact of attitudes on subsequent policy development. The authors of this study find this impact to be substantial, and clearly dwarfing other well-established factors behind welfare state change. So long-term feedback processes between attitudinal and institutional change appear to go in both directions and to be mutually reinforcing. Although the policy-effect strand of research is still sparse

---

[3] Hence, the policy-feedback research track is clearly connected to the notion of a moral economy of welfare states (Kohli 1987; Svallfors 1996; Mau 2003). Moral economy refers to the system of mutual expectations and reciprocity norms binding rulers and populations and groups within the population. It serves to highlight the point that reciprocity, rather than basic self-interest, seems to be a guiding orientation among groups and within communities (Gintis et al. 2004; Mau 2004).

compared to research on the causes of attitude formation, there seems an obvious case for extending it across time and countries.

In general, research on welfare attitudes beyond the comparative regime framework branches out in two slightly different directions. One is a strict political economy approach, where welfare attitudes are seen as basically reflecting the calculated self-interest of individuals (e.g. Iversen and Soskice 2001; Cusack et al. 2006). The other main strand is a political-sociological approach, where welfare attitudes are seen as reflecting not only self-interest, but also broader considerations about social justice, social rights, and reciprocity (e.g. Mau 2003; Brooks and Manza 2007; Svallfors 2007). In coming years, we may expect to see a variety of exciting and competing analyses that take these two lines of inquiry somewhat further.

WHAT ARE WE MISSING (MOST)?

Before closing, something should be said about things which are still missing in this area of research and the most important challenges that remain for the future. Lacunae are obvious in respect of data, methods, and analytical issues.

Regarding data, one obvious weakness of the field in is the dearth of longitudinal data. As noted above, there are now several cross-national time-series, but they are all cross-sectional. Panel data, in contrast to cross-sectional data, allow the establishment of the time order of events, making it possible for the analyst to establish causal effects. Existing longitudinal *national* data sets that contain attitudinal data tend to be either too short-term or too sparse to be really useful. Moves to redress these data lacunae would add a new dimension to research in this field.

The field also lacks comparative data that cover a large enough span of countries, and yet are sufficiently institutionally specific. Such data tend to be posed at a fairly general level, possibly concealing important variations between different institutional settings. There is a dearth of data specific enough to reveal variations in attitudes between different institutional and cultural environments, and yet comparable across countries. A new module that probes welfare attitudes for the European Social Survey, fielded for the first time in 2008/9, will add considerable leverage in this respect,[4] but there is clearly a need for further data extensions of this kind.

Regarding *methods*, there is clearly a need for innovative combinations of approaches. Although most would agree that combining methods is in principle a good strategy, very little actual cooperation is taking place. In particular, there is a need to complement wide-but-thin survey data with more intensive experimental, interview-based and/or ethnographic data, in order to study processes and mechanisms in

---

[4] The proposal is found at http://www.europeansocialsurvey.org/index.php?option=com_content&task=view&id=219&Itemid=308

more detail. There is also a need for comparative studies that combine analyses of survey data from mass publics with studies of the elite level and the mass media debate/reporting on welfare state related issues.

At the very least, such combinatory approaches could assist us in teasing out the complex relation between public discourse, political articulation, and the dynamics of attitude formation. The ambivalence displayed in the attitudes of mass publics is often used by political actors in order to highlight certain dimensions and traits of the welfare state while leaving other aspects in the dark. Comparative work using combinations of survey data, mass media studies, and elite studies could help to analyse how such political articulation is played out in different institutional contexts and with what attitudinal effects.

On a more technical note, the statistical methods that are typically used are not always ideal for the purpose. The multilevel methods that are now increasingly established as virtually standard in the field were really developed with quite different nested data structures in mind; for example, for cases in which a large number of schools or other organizations are sampled, and then individuals are sampled within these higher-level units. In cross-national comparative survey research, what we have are higher-order units—countries—that are relatively few and chosen on strategic or simple availability grounds. We therefore frequently tend to push these methods beyond what they were originally intended to do, and there is clearly a need for methodological innovation that takes the data structure encountered in research on attitudes far more seriously than at present.

Regarding *theory and analysis*, it has to be said that the ratio between theoretically and methodologically advanced comparative analyses and papers simply parading league tables is depressingly small (cf. Jowell 1998: 168). To put it in a slightly more positive way, comparative research in this field is relatively strong on description and relatively weak on analysis and explanation.

One issue which clearly needs further theoretical and analytical consideration is the role of *norms* and *interests* as explanatory mechanisms. As already noted, political-economy approaches tend to rely heavily on interests as explanatory mechanisms, while political-sociological approaches also consider normative explanations. There seems to be broad agreement that both norms and interests are affected by institutional arrangements and policy feedbacks, but at present there is no consensus or even clear conception on how they work as mechanisms in creating attitudes towards welfare policies.

Another point of analytical contention and confusion is the relative importance of the *past*, the *present*, and the *future* in forming attitudes. Currently, it seems we know little about the relative importance of individual biographies, current circumstances, and future expectations in shaping welfare attitudes. To take an example from the research on class and attitudes, we know that class background, current class position, and anticipated future class mobility all affect attitudes to some extent (Svallfors 2006). But we know very little about the relative importance of these three factors, about whether and why different individuals are affected differently by them, or if findings in these respects extend to other social cleavages.

Conclusion

The field of comparative welfare attitudes has moved on considerably since the early analyses of the 1970s and 80s. It has become explicitly rather than implicitly comparative, using country variation as a key analytical tool. It has moved from comparing compiled single-country studies, first to a comparison of welfare regimes and then on to the analysis of feedback-effects and other explanatory institutional mechanisms. It has become increasingly methodologically sophisticated and it has made the transition from data poverty to relative data abundance, although there are still certain kinds of data we are missing. Important issues are still unresolved—as always in research—but we can expect the field to stay lively and productive. Compared to many other fields of survey-based political sociology, comparative welfare attitude research is more truly international and less obviously dominated by American scholars, which will allow a fruitful mixture of analytical starting-points and issues to continue to flourish. The 'coins that do not readily melt' will remain objects of scholarly attention and innovation for a very long time to come.

CHAPTER 17

....

GENDER

....

ANN SHOLA ORLOFF

INTRODUCTION

....

CAN welfare states promote gender equality? Gender analysts of welfare states investigate this question and the broader set of issues around the mutually constitutive relationship between systems of social provision and regulation and gender. The comparative study of gender and welfare states has, since about 1990, been favoured by the occurrence of two intellectual 'big bangs'—gender studies and regime analysis. It has been powered by the engagement of the two constituencies created by these explosions of innovation and the partial integration of their respective insights in scholarship on gender, politics, and policy.[1] First, many feminist scholars served as ambassadors of gender studies, which encompassed a series of dazzling intellectual developments that moved across disciplines and challenged the masculinist assumptions that reigned in the academy as elsewhere. They reclaimed the term 'gender' from dusty linguistic usage, and deployed it, as Haraway (1991: 131) explained, 'to contest the naturalization of sexual difference in multiple arenas of struggle. Feminist theory and practice around gender seek to explain and change . . . systems of sexual difference whereby "men" and "women" are socially constituted and positioned in relations of hierarchy'. Gender is not an attribute of individuals but a social relationship, historically varying, and encompassing elements of labour, power, emotion, and language; it crosses individual subjectivities, institutions, culture, and language

---

[1] By 'feminist' scholarship, I mean studies of gender that contest gendered hierarchies. 'Mainstream' scholarship refers to research that does not thematize gender and accepts masculinist premises about actors, politics, and work; this term should not be taken to imply that the work falling under this rubric is in other ways unified.

(see e.g. Scott 1988, Connell 1987). Path-breaking work in the 1970s and 1980s established that gender is (in part) constituted by systems of social provision and regulation, and in turn, shapes them (for reviews, see O'Connor 1996; Orloff 1996).

To achieve recognition that 'gender matters', feminists have had to engage in a multifaceted critique, including not only analytic concepts and theories specific to the study of social policy but also the social theories, methodologies, and epistemological presumptions underpinning this and other areas of political study (see e.g. Butler and Scott 1992; Orloff 2005a). Indeed, so fundamental has been the feminist challenge, gender studies can arguably be said to represent a paradigmatic change of the Kuhnian variety. Feminist scholars have moved to bring the contingent practice of politics back into grounded fields of action and social change and away from the reification and abstractions that had come to dominate models of politics focused on 'big' structures and systems (Adams et al. 2005). Rather than developing a new totalizing theory, they seek to understand men's and women's diverse gendered dispositions, capacities, resources, goals, and modes of problem solving deployed in gendered political action. Conceptual innovations and reconceptualizations of foundational terms have been especially prominent in the comparative scholarship on welfare states, starting with gender, and including care, autonomy, citizenship, (in)dependence, political agency, and equality. It is impossible to see—much less to describe and understand—the mutually constitutive relation between gender and welfare states without these conceptual and theoretical innovations.

Second, studies of systems of social provision and regulation moved from essentially linear analytic modes—were welfare states more or less generous, for example—to configurational analyses of 'regime types' or 'worlds of welfare capitalism' in which variation was conceptualized as qualitative and multi-dimensional, resulting in clusters of countries with similar characteristics; these shifts were often also historicizing—emphasizing conjunctures, sequencing, turning points, and path dependency (Orloff 2005a). Or at least that is one way to understand Esping-Andersen's development of the insights of Titmuss, Korpi, and others, alongside his own compelling—if not exactly Kuhnian paradigm-shifting—insights into the character of comparative variation, which appeared in the influential *Three Worlds of Welfare Capitalism* (1990). Taking a basically Marshallian understanding of 'politics versus markets', Esping-Andersen also promoted the concept of 'decommodification' to capture the potentially emancipatory political effects of welfare states for working classes.

Falsely universalizing (implicitly masculinist) analytic frames undergirded almost all comparative studies of welfare states, including Esping-Andersen's, occluding the gendered underpinnings of systems of social provision and the specific situations of women. Yet something about Esping-Andersen's analysis brought greater engagement between feminist and mainstream scholars of welfare states. Perhaps it was his foray into analysis of how changing 'labour-market regimes' and shifts from industries to services affected women and gender, or his revitalization of an emancipatory yet still gender-blind concept of social citizenship rights. This took him squarely onto the intellectual terrain that had been tilled by feminists without acknowledging that work. This circumstance simultaneously provoked women scholars and stimulated their creative reappropriations of the regime concept, expansions of notions of social citizenship rights, and investigations of care services and shifting post-industrial employment patterns, leading to a revisioning of welfare states as core institutions of the gender order (see e.g. Lewis 1992; Orloff 1993*b*; O'Connor et al. 1999).

In contrast to other subfields of political science and sociology, gendered insights have to some extent been incorporated into mainstream comparative scholarship on welfare states (see e.g. Korpi 2000; Huber and Stephens 2000*a*; Esping-Andersen 1999; Esping-Andersen et al. 2002). Historical institutionalism and other modes of historical social science, approaches sharing constructionist proclivities with feminist analysis, are prominent in comparative studies of welfare states (Orloff 2005*a*). Both promote analyses that are time and place specific rather than seeking general laws, both take a denaturalizing and contingent view of political identities and goals, and both share at least some attachment to egalitarian, or even emancipatory, politics. The arguments between feminists and mainstream scholars over the course of the last two decades have been productive, powering the development of key themes and concepts pioneered by gender scholars, including defamilialization, the significance of unpaid care work in families and the difficulties of work–family 'reconciliation', gendered welfare state institutions, the relation between fertility and women's employment, and the partisan correlates of different family and gender policy models. Yet there has rarely been full 'gender mainstreaming', for the mainstream still resists the deeper implications of feminist work, and has difficulties assimilating concepts of interdependency, care, and gendered power.

Feminists begin their critical project with the very definition of the 'welfare state'. Masculinist paradigms centred on pensions and social insurance, following their conception of politics as shaped by economic developmental or class interests. Gender analysts, having given up assumptions about class conflict as the 'motor of history', have a more pluralistic notion of which social policy institutions are 'core'. They point to the significance for gender and women's welfare of state activities such as family and employment law, the reproduction of nations and 'races' (Williams 1995), housing, and the regulation of those who receive benefits. The geographic and socio-political limits of 'welfare states' are contested, but I here concentrate on the comparative literature on the rich democracies, in which the relations among gender, policy, and politics have been most extensively examined.

Conceptualizing Gender for Welfare State Analysis

'Gender' represents the key theoretical and conceptual innovation of feminist scholarship, including that focused on systems of social provision and regulation. Because 'domesticating' intellectual and political trends continually threaten to undermine the central insights of gender analysis, I want to highlight precisely what makes gender so potentially unsettling for analyses of politics, including the politics of welfare provision, by contrasting it with mainstream understandings.

Mainstream analysts of social policy increasingly attend to certain aspects of gender relations. Most focus on women's individual 'differences' from men, in preferences, lifetime labour patterns, and associated social rights (e.g. Esping-Andersen et al. 2002: ch. 3; Gilbert 2008; Hakim 2000). Hakim, under the rubric of 'preference theory', marshals empirical evidence for the heterogeneous 'lifestyle preferences' of women, arguing that they can be grouped by their orientation to work and family as home-centred, adaptive, or work-centred. Home-centred and career-centred women pursue their preferences whatever the policy context, but social policies have some impact on the large majority who are 'adaptive' women. This perspective has been influential in European policy discussions of work/family 'reconciliation', as policymakers seek to activate the 'adaptive' group, presumably without the need to question the gendered division of labour that this idea of preferences tends to take for granted.

Claims for the power of preference—by Hakim, Esping-Andersen, or mainstream economists—have been questioned on at least three fronts. First, these approaches conceptualize gender as an individual attribute and ignore the relational character of gender. Second, there is considerable evidence, to be detailed below, that gendered hierarchies and inequalities, which shape men's and women's preferences, practices, and opportunities, survive. But perhaps the most important question—where do these preferences come from?—is not even asked. Feminists have contributed to a rich literature, in which agency—including preferences, desires, and identities—and structure are mutually constitutive. On this view, knowledge, subjectivity, and political agency are both constrained *and enabled* by existing gendered categories (Butler 1990; Adams et al. 2005; Zerilli 2005). Gendered identities and agency—including orientations to family and employment—are not pre-political, or 'natural'. Rather, welfare provision, alongside other political and social institutions, is involved in shaping gendered divisions of labour and the preferences, needs, and desires that sustain it (see e.g. Morgan 2006; Haney 2002).

Feminists have, through their creative appropriations of diverse social and political thinking produced theories that contest sexual hierarchies—and it is worth underlining that this marks the key difference between feminist and non-critical approaches to gender. For feminists, gender is not only about the 'differences' that concern 'preference' theory but also their construction and maintenance through systems of power, one of which is the welfare state itself. This does not always mean masculine domination, but includes possible local reversals (Connell 1987), 'undoings' of gender (Butler 2004), or radical inaugurations of new political forms (Zerilli 2005). Control of states is a key stake in gendered power struggles given states' monopoly over the collective means of coercion, and their constitution and regulation of the (gendered) categories of political participation and citizenship rights (Connell 1987; Orloff 1993b; O'Connor et al. 1999).[2]

Early feminist interventions around social provision started from premises about the uniformity and fixity of the category of women. The key difference was between women and men, with policies reinforcing that binary division and politics reflecting women's and men's distinctive and competing interests. Both premises have been extensively critiqued (see e.g. Zerilli 2005; Butler 1990). Social policies and politics are now investigated in terms of 'multiple differences' among women (and men), based on other dimensions of power, difference, and inequality like 'race', class, ethnicity, sexuality, religion. Moreover, the position of men is increasingly problematized. The notion of the fixity of gender categories has been replaced by more fluid conceptions of gender, reflected in the phrases 'doing' or performing gender (rather than 'being' a gender), a transformation from gender to gendering (West and Zimmerman 1987; Butler 1990, 2004). This allows for an investigation of the processes of gendering, regendering, or degendering in which welfare states are central influences.

GENDER AND WELFARE STATES: EVIDENCE FOR MUTUAL INFLUENCE

In this section, I will focus on two clusters of empirical research which illustrate the mutual influence of gender relations and systems of social provision and regulation, and which have been the foci of a considerable amount of feminist research. First, I review work on welfare states and the gendered division of labour, employment, and caring labour (paid and unpaid). Second, I assess the politics of gendered welfare states, including regimes, partisanship, political agency, and citizenship.

Gendered Labour, Care, and Welfare States

Care is central to many feminist understandings of gender, reflecting a long-standing feminist concern with the gendered division of labour, unpaid work, domestic labour, and social reproduction as central to women's oppression. Mainstream researchers address care principally as a question of women's differences from men, and as a barrier to employment. In contrast, gender analysis considers care as a socially necessary activity, which is not always recognized as such. Care is predominantly women's

---

[2] States are implicated in intimate violence because by defining some matters as 'private' and properly outside the states' regulatory and police powers, men have been left free to act as they saw fit—and too many acted violently (Brush 2002; see Weldon 2002 for a cross-national survey of policies to combat domestic violence).

work, not a 'naturally' feminine emanation of familial love (England 2005). Doing care is the source of many of women's economic and political disadvantages, but also offers distinctive identifications, resources, and ethical commitments. Moreover, care is a relationship characterized by interdependence and connection, power, and conflict (Daly and Lewis 2000: 283). Understanding the social organization of care forces thinking across the divides between economy and family, public and private, paid and unpaid work, emotion and commodity, culture and state social policy, state provision of services and indirect support for caring in households (Jenson 1997; Daly and Lewis 2000; England 2005).

Gender analysts of welfare states have stressed the linkages among specific gendered divisions of labour, models of family life, and social policy. For much of the post-World War II era, the dominant model supported by policy has been the nuclear family with breadwinning man and his wife, who performed the domestic and care labour, even if she was also employed. This arrangement is often called 'traditional' although its full realization—particularly with widespread housewifery even among the working classes—was limited to the 'Golden Age' between World War II and the early 1970s. Welfare states also sustained men's advantaged position in labour markets, and did not ameliorate fully the economic and other vulnerabilities that attached to women's caregiving. We are now witnessing an ongoing 'farewell to maternalism' (Orloff 2006) and shift to policies that support the 'adult worker family', with both men and women expected to be in paid employment (Lewis 2001). The increasing participation of women in the labour force and decline of the breadwinner household have transformed the organization of care across households, markets, and welfare states. Non-familial care services, both marketized and public, have developed, but women still do a disproportionate amount of unpaid care and domestic labour. This leaves the heart of the gendered division of labour undisturbed, particularly among heterosexual couples. Taking time to care imposes significant costs on caregivers, unless social policy reduces them. 'Crises of care' have emerged, as rising demands for care outstrip the supply of familial caregivers; the twin problems of care—for caregivers and for those who are cared for—present demands for social policymakers (Knijn and Kremer 1997). Allowing for (paid) workers to have time to care is one challenge, while finding new supplies of care workers is another, to which some states have responded by encouraging immigration.

Women have entered employment for many reasons, and governments, particularly within the European Union, are more interested in women's activation, partly to offset problems associated with an ageing labour force and declining fertility among non-immigrant populations (the 'racial' underpinnings of which can only be noted here). Across the developed world, mothers' participation rates are lower than fathers', unless there are state- or market-provided care services and/or other means of 'reconciling' employment and family work. Even when mothers' participation rates equal fathers', as in the Nordic countries, employment patterns differ, with women taking more parental leave and working reduced hours (Ellingsaeter and Leira 2006). Social and employment policies affect gendered employment patterns, as women are drawn into the labour force by differing combinations of service-sector employment (private or public), flexible labour markets, anti-discrimination laws, and/or part-time work; these explain women's relatively high employment rates in the Nordic countries, North America, the United Kingdom, and Australia, relatively lower rates in much of continental Europe and Japan, and increasing levels where policy has shifted, as in the Netherlands (Daly 2000; Estévez-Abe 2005; O'Connor et al. 1999).

The availability of public childcare services is significant for mothers' employment, and is related to gendered divides between public and private and to gendered ideologies about mothering and its potential compatibility with paid employment, which may differ across groups of women. The Nordic countries have defined the provision of care as a public activity, linked to children's well-being and gender equality, both understood to imply mothers' employment. In contrast, until very recently, the care of children has been understood to be the province of the family in the United Kingdom, most of the continental European countries, and Japan, while in North America, care is considered best left to private 'choice', reflecting politically dominant liberalism (O'Connor et al. 1999). In the United States, state provision has been all but ruled out, yet mothers have been able to find private care services, albeit of uneven quality (Orloff 2006). Elder-care has also been examined vis-à-vis the private/public rubric, but patterns differ somewhat from childcare; the Nordic countries are consistent in offering public services for both, the United States for neither, while other countries have a varying mix (Antonnen and Sipilä 1996). Care services and policies, in Europe especially, have been changing rapidly in the 2000s, with the expansion of elder- and childcare services, payments for informal care, and paid leaves. These shifts reveal the construction and transformation of public–private divides as a critical moment in the gendering of welfare, fixing (temporarily) which needs may be addressed through public social policy, and which are to be left to the family, charity, or the market (Lewis 1992; O'Connor et al. 1999).

Women more than men shape their employment behaviour around the requisites of caregiving (and, to a lesser extent, domestic work). However, taking time out of the labour force to do unpaid care and cleaning work in families—even when it does not add up to full-time and lifelong housewifery—imposes costs on caregivers, notably lifelong lower incomes and pension entitlements, economic dependency, and vulnerability to poverty (England 2005; Hobson 1990; Joshi et al. 1999). Employment reduces women's vulnerability and dependency but does not eliminate it: mothers suffer a 'motherhood wage penalty' and a 'long-term gender earnings gap' in most countries (Misra et al. 2007; Waldfogel 1997). Some of these economic disadvantages occur due to women's time spent out of the labour force or working part-time, but there is still a residual [wage] penalty for being a mother due to effects of motherhood on productivity and discrimination by employers against mothers in hiring and promotion; moreover, *paid* care work—disproportionately done by women, is worse paid, all else equal, than other types of work (England 2005). Continental European women report the highest gaps, North American women report intermediate levels, and Nordic mothers' wages are closest to men's wages, at least partly due to policies supporting mothers' employment (Misra et al. 2007).

The relatively higher poverty rates of lone mothers (even if employed) and elderly widows in most rich democracies attests to the continuing vulnerability of caregivers if they find themselves without access to men's incomes. As Hobson (1990) points out in her ingenious application of Hirschmann's 'exit, voice, loyalty' framework to women's situation in marriage, the conditions of lone mothers—importantly shaped by citizenship rights—affect married mothers as well, for they reflect something of what their 'exit options' would be; the better the situation for solo mothers, she argues, the more power partnered women have. Solo mothers have served as a 'test case' of the extent to which welfare states address women's economic vulnerabilities; their poverty is alleviated—to a limited extent—only by generous welfare programmes (e.g. in the Netherlands prior to mid-1990s welfare reforms) or employment supported by care services (e.g. in France), and in best-case scenarios, a combination of these (e.g. in the Nordic countries) (Christopher 2002; Kilkey and Bradshaw 1999). Thus, where welfare is not generous and employment support is left to market sources, solo mothers' relative poverty remains high (as in the English-speaking countries and Germany).

The social organization of care affects also the quality of women's employment as reflected in women's access to positions of authority and other traditionally masculine occupations (which are advantaged relative to feminine ones (Charles and Grusky 2004). Gendered occupational segregation, both horizontal and vertical, occurs across the developed countries, but varies in extent and character. Notably, countries identi-fied as 'gender-egalitarian' in terms of lower gender gaps in wages and poverty feature higher-than-average levels of occupational segregation. Mandel and Semyonov (2006) identify a 'welfare state paradox', in which well-developed welfare states increase women's labour force participation—by offering extensive services and leave—but simultaneously hinder women's access to desirable (masculine) jobs. They argue that employers will rationally discriminate against women in hiring for 'masculine' jobs, since women are far more likely to take leave and short hours provisions than are men. Defenders of the Nordic model argue that critics ignore the gender-equalizing effects of drawing most women into the workforce, the relatively good conditions of female-dominated public sector employment and relatively low gender wage gaps (Korpi 2000; Shalev 2008). They note that horizontal segregation of jobs—that is, gender differentiation of labour—seems to be acceptable to democratic publics (Charles and Grusky 2004); here is an instance of 'preferences' shaped by the gendered division of labour and social policies. The Nordic model is defended for its beneficial effects on working-class women, but gendered inequalities do remain: women's access to elite positions, especially in the private sector, is limited, and occupational segregation is associated with some wage penalty. In contrast, in the United States, where wage gaps and solo mothers' poverty are relatively high, there are few policies geared to employed mothers' care needs, but sex segregation of occupations has been declining since the 1960s and 'gendered authority gaps' are lower than in Scandinavia. The relative gender-neutrality of liberal regimes or market economies seems to be favourable to women with high skills who are willing to pursue a masculinized employment pattern (Shalev 2008; Estévez-Abe 2005; Orloff 2006).

Social policies recognize and offer institutionalized support to some models of caregiving and family organization while sanctioning others, complementing the role of culture in shaping care practices (Kremer 2007). Given the changing landscape of gender across families, markets, and states—including the decline of the male breadwinner and full-time maternal care as ideal and reality, and new demands for care, it is not surprising that significant debate has arisen around which models or ideals of gender, family, and care will be promoted by social policy (Knijn and Kremer 1997; Mahon 2002; Lewis 2001). Mothers' employment is widely accepted, but many of the models in play simply modify the gendered division of labour to accommodate paid work with women's continuing responsibility for care work, as in 'reconciliation' measures—part-time work and/or long maternity leaves—that produce something like a 'one and a half' worker model, as in the Netherlands (see e.g. Mutari and Figart 2001). The ideal of the caregiving woman is also upheld in models of surrogate mothers' care (e.g. by nannies) and intergenerational care (Kremer 2007); these have been important across continental Europe (with the partial exception of France, where this combines with professional children's education and care services (Morgan 2006)).

Models inspired by gender egalitarianism, such as dual-earner/dual carer, focus on professional care and parental sharing, which allow mothers' employment but pose a challenge to ideologies of gender difference (Sainsbury 1996; Crompton 1999; Kremer 2007; Gornick and Meyers 2003, 2009). Sweden, Finland, Iceland, and Norway have adopted the ideal of parental sharing alongside professional care services, and feature policy initiatives to increase men's caregiving work, such as parental leaves designed to encourage their participation, at best only partially successful—Denmark alone of the Nordic states has reversed the trend toward 'daddy leave' although public services are prominent (Hobson 2002; Ellingsaeter and Leira 2006). Finally, an emphasis on 'choice' might allow for pluralism among heterogeneous populations as to which models of care and gender they prefer—this is the vision of both neoliberals and advocates of the 'Third Way' who dominate discussions in the English-speaking world (Mahon 2002). In these cases, the extent of marketization and public subsidization determines whether choices are realizable, and how care quality and gender equality will fare (Orloff 2009). Some women's care sector jobs are professionalized, or at least unionized and relatively well-paid, but others are classic 'bad jobs', and a 'racial' and ethnic dimension of care work is foregrounded in many studies of paid care (Glenn 1992; Lutz 2008). Moreover, caregivers from developing countries or poorer regions within the developed world migrate to the global North or its better-off regions to work for pay providing care to the households of employed women (and men!)—in their homes or in service sector jobs; such migrants delegate their care responsibilities to kin (Lutz 2008; Parrenas 2005). Significant empirical and normative debate concerns the use of immigrant labour for tasks that used to be carried out largely by housewives, focusing on whether such arrangements are inherently exploitative or can be made into 'good jobs'.

Gendered care and employment arrangements have implications for the quality and quantity of care (Morgan 2005; Himmelweit 2007). The principal care crisis in most of continental Europe stems from a lack of public or market services. Analysts agree that in the Nordic countries the quality of public care services is high and the working conditions of care workers are good; the only critique stems from questions of fiscal sustainability, since costs are also high—yet it is basically a political question as to whether subsidizing care is desirable. In the United States, the provision of care is plentiful—but mainly marketized and unregulated, leading to stratification in the quality of care. The choice, then, is a high level of public subsidy to overcome the problems or tolerating inadequate or poor-quality care services. This is a question of politics.

Gender, Politics, and Social Policies

'Politics matters' to gender. The policy regime approach offers a way to simplify descriptions of the complicated patterns of variation through focusing on more or less coherent clusters of countries, 'gendered welfare regimes', characterized by the logic of the male breadwinner, models of motherhood, or the extent to which the personal autonomy of women as well as of men is supported (Lewis 1992, 2001; Orloff 1993b; Leira 1992; Sainsbury 1996; Bergqvist et al. 1999). Regime analyses have been important for understanding the topography of variation in welfare states, yet the typology-based analyses these have often spawned have probably reached the point of diminishing returns. Deepening knowledge of the relations between politics and gender, we might pursue somewhat different strategies: continue to work with the regime concept, with a focus on the articulation of policies and shorn of typologizing as a principal concern, as O'Connor et al. (1999) suggest. Regime types can be seen as distinctive political-institutional opportunity structures, producing historically and nationally specific sets of interests, goals, identities, coalitions, administrative capacities, and definitions of problems and categories that influence social politics in path-dependent ways—policy creates politics. By examining the *articulation* of different policies, more accurate pictures of the effects of systems of social provision emerge. Single logics, or multiple and possibly competing logics, are institutionalized in different parts or levels of states. Alternatively, one might disaggregate the regime concept—into driving forces, mediating institutions, and outcomes—to investigate specific components in a causal analysis.

Korpi (2000) links the predominance of different political parties in the post-war years with different 'family policy models' that reflect ideals about care arrangements, family types (dual-earner or 'traditional'), and preferred institutions for delivering support—states, families, or markets. Social democratic parties, sometimes helped along by affiliated women's movements, have embraced the model of dual-earner families, and women's equality via employment (especially public jobs) and public care services (see also Huber and Stephens 2000a; Hobson and Lindholm 1997). Left partisan predominance is consistently associated with high spending welfare states and large state sectors, public services, generous and decommodifying benefits linked to low rates of poverty for solo mothers and single elderly women, and relatively egalitarian income distributions. In countries dominated by social democratic parties, universal coverage, individual entitlement to benefits, and redistributive structures are particularly advantageous for many women (Sainsbury 1996).

Many welfare state researchers assume that the left is more favourable to gender equality measures than is the right, but this depends partly on how 'equality' is defined. Is it tied to combating poverty and supporting a large public sector, which provides services allowing women more easily to enter employment and jobs for women? This definition sticks with an essentially socialist perspective on 'the woman question', linking women's emancipation to class struggle. Left–right partisan cleavages do map onto gender politics, but there are more diverse and expansive definitions of gender equality or women's emancipation, stressing participation and political freedom, equal opportunity and entrepreneurship, or the creation of autonomous women's spaces (see e.g. Zerilli 2005; Fraser 1994a). Feminist social policy researchers, too, have been more willing to grant the advantages of the social-democratic model, perhaps leading to an underappreciation of the pathways by which liberalism is connected to gender equality, as with equal-opportunity legal and regulatory frameworks (Orloff 2006, 2009).

Conversely, the dominance of the political right has been associated with policies less encouraging for gender equality. The distinctions between secular and religious right parties, or liberal and conservative regimes, have emerged as quite significant for gender. Religious parties have been the principal exponents of subsidiarity and 'traditional' gender ideology in the form of 'familism', which is compatible with state spending, but supports families in forms that reinforce breadwinner/caregiver models and block autonomy-enhancing provision (see e.g. Saraceno 1997; Korpi 2000). Morgan (2006) argues that the way in which religion was incorporated into modern politics in the nineteenth century is key to explaining later support for maternal employment policies, potentially significant for feminist politics. In Sweden and France, religious forces were early subordinated to secular ones and played less of a role in shaping family and social policy than in continental Europe; an activist role for the state in welfare and education was accepted. Religious forces, unsubordinated to the state, were stronger in the Netherlands, leading to institutionalized support for welfare provision by the religious pillars, and the United States, where private welfare provision prevailed.

Secular right parties are mainly concerned to restrict state spending and public services. In the 1980s, Margaret Thatcher and Ronald Reagan were the most prominent proponents of retrenching welfare states. But neoliberals are not necessarily hostile to women's employment, and have been uninterested in offering alternatives to commodification; leaving family support to the market has undercut 'traditional' families as women are drawn into employment and men's prerogatives are unprotected by states, as in the United States (Orloff 2006). They do not favour social spending and state services to support women's employment, but prefer tax breaks. Regulatory measures, such as anti-discrimination legislation, have had more contradictory fates under secular right parties' dominance, although opposition to regulation is now part of the neoliberal mantra.

Innovative analyses in the 1990s revealed the role of women and men as political actors pursuing gendered goals (Skocpol 1992; Pedersen 1993; Koven and Michel 1993). Social policy concerns far more than questions of class, and varies by much more than relative generosity or extent of decommodification. Instead, gender joins class, nation, 'race', religion, and other dimensions of power, difference, and inequality to shape politics in historically contingent and variable ways. For example, we see state officials' stakes in the production and regulation of nations or 'races', citizens and soldiers (what some call 'biopolitics' and which inevitably involves women's reproductive capacities in some way); men's concerns to gain or maintain family-supporting wages; women's interests in combating the economic dependency and poverty linked to their caregiving. Gendered actors may be identified with social movements—women's equality movements, 'maternalists', or anti-feminist groups, or with political parties and state administrations, such as 'femocrats', women in specialized gender equality units. With the expansion of supranational organizations, feminist and other groups have made strategic and tactical use of openings—such as the mandate for gender mainstreaming—at different levels of policy making to press their demands (see e.g. Walby 2004).

Citizenship has long been understood in exclusively masculine terms, linked to a particular conception of political subjects: as rational, autonomous, unburdened by care, impervious to invasions of bodily integrity. If, as gender scholars contend, the need for care is inevitable, given humans' dependence in infancy and old age, and often in between, we must reassess conceptions of citizens and of political action. Women gained social rights before enfranchised men conceded the suffrage, and rights related to women's bodily self-determination are still contested. Women have also often differed from men in the kinds of citizenship rights they have demanded from welfare states; while working-class men may indeed aspire to 'decommodification'—at least when unemployment is not the pre-eminent threat, many women have found that the right to formal, paid work may provide new resources and organizational capacities. Men's citizenship rights have been linked historically to military service and paid employment, and social citizenship rights are often complemented by special benefits for soldiers and veterans, mostly men (Skocpol 1992). Women citizens and feminist scholars have tried to expand the notion of social and political participation that undergirds citizenship rights to include mothering and care work, whether or not it is paid (Knijn and Kremer 1997; Lister 2003a). Drawing on the experiences of women's political action and an understanding of interdependency as the basic human condition, new citizenship rights essential to emancipation have been enunciated by gender scholars: capacities to form autonomous households (Orloff 1993b); rights to time, to care, and to be cared for (Knijn and Kremer 1997), or 'body rights' (Shaver 1994).

Women's presence in politics has revolutionized policy. In the early twentieth century, 'maternalists' entered politics on the basis of 'difference', made claims to citizenship based on their capacities to mother, and idealized a maternalist state that could care for its citizens, especially mothers and their children (Skocpol 1992; Koven and Michel 1993). Today, women's movements for gender equality press for policies to support women's employment, particularly anti-discrimination and affirmative action, parental leave, and childcare services (O'Connor et al. 1999: ch. 3), and higher proportions of women 'holding key positions in governmental and political organizations' positively influence social spending and the adoption of equality policies (Bolzendahl 2009). However, claims based on motherhood have not been abandoned but modified to accommodate women's wage-earning activities. Anti-feminist groups promote ideals of 'traditional' gender institutions in marriage, sexuality, and reproduction as more congruent with women's 'need' for protection. When women's groups and voting blocs are divided, as in Italy between socialist/secular and Catholic orientations, or anti-feminist movements are well-mobilized, the adoption of policies seen as promoting or supporting women's employment and public care provision, key planks of women's equality movements' programmes, has been blocked. Yet as full-time housewifery declines, one may question how long anti-feminist traditionalism will last, especially as it runs foul of neoliberal mandates for women's activation or instrumentalist concerns with declining fertility. Even as feminism may have declined as a set of organized movements, many tenets of gender equality have been institutionalized, and new forms of feminist mobilization, linked to the continuing dilemmas of care and domestic work, economic and political participation, and aimed at restructuring systems of social provision and regulation, have emerged.

The transformation of mainstream scholarship by the full integration of gender analysis is necessary to understand the development of welfare states and capitalism as well as gender. Gender has been at the centre of transformations of welfare states, families, and capitalist economies. Social politics increasingly features issues related to gender: fertility, immigration, labour supply, the supply of care workers and services, taxes, and mothers' employment; gender equality in households, employment, and polity. Women's citizenship, political standing, and capacity to claim social benefits are increasingly based on employment or employment plus parenthood, and this implies that feminist politics is also being transformed, perhaps by bidding 'farewell to maternalism' (Orloff 2009). Gendered insights—particularly around power and politics—radicalize and transform the comparative study of welfare states, a necessary component of projects to ensure that systems of social provision promote equality and care—in other words, welfare, broadly understood.

CHAPTER 18

....

RELIGION

....

KEES VAN KERSBERGEN

PHILIP MANOW

INTRODUCTION

....

RELIGION has played an important role in the development of modern welfare states, but how it has played that role has not always been understood properly or appreciated particularly well. This chapter provides an overview of how past research in comparative social science has dealt with the relationship between religion and the welfare state, evaluates the theoretical approaches and the empirical findings, and provides an alternative view that generates questions for further research. We focus in particular on the experience in Europe and the settler colonies. It is only here that we can draw on a wider research literature on this important topic that has still to be explored more fully and systematically for other regions. Moreover, it was Christianity that developed into a form of 'organized religion', with churches as 'interest groups' (Warner 2000), Christian democracy as an extraordinarily strong political actor, and a rich religious associational landscape that was and still is prominently involved in the provision of social services, poor relief, and social protection. Finally, it was in Europe, North America, and the Antipodes that the welfare state emerged early and matured into a comprehensive system of social protection. Of course, our regional focus does not imply that the impact of religion on the welfare state is confined to the Western world.

For mainstream theories the impact of religion or religiously inspired social and political movements on the welfare state has always remained a puzzle. For the functionalist theories of modernization, the role of religion was considered to be vanishing in consequence of modernization and its main correlate, secularization.

Institutionalist explanations focused on state and nation building and their impact on welfare state development, on the development of state capacity, bureaucratic policy learning, or on inter-state competition, policy diffusion, and international learning, none of which seemed to have much to do with religion. The conflict-theoretical approaches, especially the power resources approach, proposed a positive linear relationship between the power of the (social democratic) labour movement and welfare capitalism. Here, religion or religious social political movements were perceived as simply delaying or distorting the normal social democratization of capitalism.

The questions whether, to what extent, under what conditions, and how religion has influenced welfare state development, however, were rarely addressed (but see Heidenheimer 1983; Castles 1994*a*; Kaufmann 1988) and then only tentatively answered. But why should welfare state researchers pay attention to religion at all? Could it not be a straightforward historical fact that religion's role has been minimal and that scholars were quite right in their neglect of the topic? We argue that, in the light of the long-lasting debate on religion's impact on modern capitalism (Weber 2001), it would be quite odd *not* to address its potential impact on welfare state development, in particular because all major branches of Christianity stress, in one way or another, the privileged position of the poor, the Christian duty of neighbourly love, charity, good Samaritanism, and good works (Troeltsch 1931). Basically, the study of *religion as a cultural force* in modern societies is still poised between the positions that Max Weber and Ernst Troeltsch formulated almost 100 years ago (Heidenheimer 1983)—i.e. between the emphasis on the importance of a religiously based (Protestant) work ethic, which ascribed responsibility for one's economic and social fate to the individual, and the emphasis on the role of religious doctrines, which held the family, the church, voluntary self-help organizations, or the nation state responsible for looking after and protecting those in need of care and protection. The study of the religious obligation towards the poor and destitute or otherwise needy is relevant, in the context not only of Western Europe and the impact upon it of the various Christian denominations, but also of the settler colonies, which were strongly influenced by reformed Protestantism with its profoundly liberal, individualistic, state-sceptic leanings. It is also important for the analysis of the emerging Latin American welfare states, if we look at the struggle between Catholicism and Pentecostal Protestantism for 'religious market shares' and the impact of that struggle on the position of the Latin American Catholic Church in questions of social policy (see Gill 1998). For the emerging East Asian welfare states the debate revolves around the possible impact of Confucianism (Rieger and Leibfried 2003: ch. 5); in the Islamic world the role of Zakāt, which obliges every Muslim to give to the poor, is of central importance for the division of labour between the welfare *state* and religious charitable organizations.

Another reason why religion should receive more attention is that power resources theory was wrong in its proposition of a linear relationship between the power of a social democratic labour movement and the welfare state. It also wrongly supposed that religion had only a delaying influence on welfare state development. Social democrats had little if anything to do with the pioneering experiments in social policy (say, the Bismarckian social insurance laws of the 1880s), nor were they of much importance in many other nations on the European continent that built up generous, encompassing welfare states (see Chapter 41 below), either during the early phases of welfare state development or during the stage of further expansion after World War II. For example, in Italy powerful social and political movements inspired by religion—in particular Christian democracy—have not only been actively involved in the construction of the welfare state, but have been pivotal in determining its character and quality. Moreover, in many countries on the European continent an aggressive anti-clericalism of liberal nation-building elites motivated much of the early legislation in education and social policy in the late nineteenth and early twentieth century, which left its imprint on the institutional legacy of this period (Gould 1999). Here, the state–church conflict over education often superseded the capital–labour conflict in terms of intensity, mobilization, and political salience (Berger 1987). Against the background of the continental experience it becomes clear that the peculiarity of the Scandinavian development has to do with *the absence* of a religious cleavage in homogeneously Protestant societies with Lutheran state churches. The Scandinavian state churches never felt existentially threatened when the nation state started to take over most of the charitable and educational functions that the church had fulfilled previously (van Kersbergen and Manow 2009). In this perspective, religion does not appear as a cultural reservoir of deeply rooted values that translate into different kinds of welfare statism, but as a contentious political and social cleavage that mobilized churches, religious parties and Catholic voters against liberal (secular) state building elites. All this warrants a renewed attempt to understand the role of religion in welfare state development.

RELIGION AS A CULTURAL AND POLITICAL FORCE

We distinguish two approaches. The first is 'ideational', tracing the impact of religious doctrines on principles of social policies. The second is 'political', tracing the impact of the religious cleavage via parties and systems of interest mediation on the institutional setup of the welfare state. In the first case one would ask how the fundamental tenets of a faith have been translated into modern ideas on social justice (cf. Leibfried and Rieger 1997). This can then be specified by inquiring how and to what extent different religions or denominations have developed specific social doctrines that can be argued to have contributed (or not) to the ethical foundation of various types of welfare state regimes (Gorski 2003; Manow 2004).

Different constellations of values might lead to different logics of risk redistribution underpinning different types of regimes. Focusing on the West, one notices a striking isomorphism between regime types and countries' denominational complexions:

> corporate-conservative welfare states were most likely to emerge in predominantly Catholic societies, such as France and Italy...liberal welfare states emerged only in areas heavily influenced by Reformed Protestantism (that is, England and its settler colonies)...[and] that social-democratic welfare states emerged only in the homogeneously Lutheran countries of Scandinavia. (Gorski 2003: 163)

This suggests that varying ethical principles give rise to different institutional forms of distribution, redistribution, and social protection and ultimately translate into distinctive economic and social outcomes. Precisely because of the different values involved, it makes sense to study religion (and not just liberalism or social democracy) as a cultural force, shaping the values, norms, beliefs, and attitudes of the cultural, social, and political community that supports a welfare state regime (see Van Oorschot et al. 2008).

As well as citizens' varying attitudes towards social solidarity, their feeling of security too and therefore their *demand* for social protection might be influenced by religion. Scholars have started to investigate to what extent religion and the welfare state are substitutes, such that the expansion (or decline) of the one (welfare state) occurs at the expense (or to the benefit) of the other (religion). The basic argument, echoing modernization theory, is that religion offers security, and that the demand for security and spiritual orientation during episodes of need and suffering diminishes when the welfare state protects against existential risks (Gill and Lundsgaarde 2004; Hungerman 2005; Scheve and Stasavage 2006; Gruber and Hungerman 2007; Norris and Inglehart 2004). Conversely, where the welfare state's function of offering individuals social security is in decline in times of retrenchment, religion may fill the void. In the wake of privatization this might also lead to reassigning welfare tasks from the state to the churches and charitable organizations that step in where the state retreats from the obligations it once had (Bäckström and Davie 2009). Immigration may also increase public awareness of the moral and religious foundations of social solidarity, for instance in Scandinavia, where formerly homogeneous societies with their generous levels of protection and service provision now host a substantial Islamic community that has contributed to a rising level of ethnic and religious heterogeneity.

Looking at values, attitudes, and social norms, one observes a fundamental difference between a profoundly state-sceptic reformed Protestantism and its liberal leanings on the one hand, and a much more intervention-friendly and state-oriented Lutheranism on the other. The former has been influential in Switzerland, the Netherlands, the United Kingdom, and the settler-colonies, while the latter has had a strong impact in Scandinavia through the Lutheran state churches. In the light of the profound differences between the distinct strands of Protestantism, it is not surprising that in simple juxtapositions of Protestantism and Catholicism it was always Catholicism, not Protestantism, that seemed to have a distinct impact on welfare state development and on its institutional set-up (Castles 1994a). However, once we distinguish between Protestantism's different strands, the retarding and restricting influence of the Protestant sects on welfare state development becomes apparent (Manow 2004).

But one could also focus more directly on social and political movements, particularly Christian democracy and the many organizations within the Catholic milieu, so as to study how religion has shaped programmes of social reform and ultimately how parties (and social organizations) influenced social policy formation and outcomes. This was how the power resources approach amended its basic theoretical framework to adjust for the impact of religion. Initially, its protagonists had exclusively stressed the causal impact of socialist working class mobilization on social policy (Korpi 1983; Esping-Andersen 1985a). They supposed that it was only the working class and its socialist organizations that had been driving the 'social democratization' of capitalism via the welfare state. The fact that (social) Catholicism also promoted welfare state development presented a conundrum for the approach (see Stephens 1979: 100).

However, the 'parties matter' literature (Castles 1982a) showed that Christian democracy was not only a political force with a programme that 'might encourage welfare spending', but was also 'functionally equivalent' to social democracy for welfare state expansion (Schmidt 1982a, 1996). Wilensky (1981) identified a common ideological ground between the two movements and even made the case that historically Catholicism's impact on the welfare state had been more profound than left power. Catholic social doctrine called for a correction of the most abhorrent societal effects of the capitalist order. The Catholic principle of subsidiarity, moreover, posited that in the last instance the state had a duty to intervene to correct for morally unacceptable market outcomes (van Kersbergen 1995). At the centre of the doctrine was not the type of workers' social *rights* and *emancipation* argument that one finds in social democratic ideology, but rather the conviction that people have the Christian *obligation* to help the poor and that social policy can help protect a stable and fair social *order*.

However, it was not only the moral obligations defined in social doctrine and the preoccupation with the problem of social order that determined the pro-welfare stance of religious political parties. The logic of electoral competition and political mobilization also compelled Christian democratic parties to adopt a positive stance on social policy (Huber and Stephens 2001a). These parties operated in the political centre, were seeking the working class vote, and hoped to cooperate with the Catholic unions. Social policies promised to secure the support of the Catholic working class and foster Catholic unity. However, this implied that one of the essential tenets of the power resources model had to be relaxed. The political identity attached to wage labour in capitalism was not inherently social democratic, because apparently workers could be mobilized and organized as Catholics too.

Research started to focus on the differential impact of political movements and parties (including religious ones) on welfare state development. Moreover, as Esping-Andersen (1990) argued, political parties are not so much interested in promoting social spending as such, but more in employing social policies for attaining social and economic goals and in exploiting them for purposes of political mobilization. This implied a radical re-specification of the welfare state: the quantitative 'welfare effort' and social spending conception was substituted by a more qualitative notion. The new approach was much more sensitive to the (potential) social, economic, and political consequences of different types of welfare states, arguably the aspects of social policy that mattered most for political parties, voters, and welfare beneficiaries. Esping-Andersen (1990) identified three kinds of welfare regimes (configurations of market, state, and family) that nations adopt in their pursuit of work and welfare. The new conceptualization of regime types facilitated an improved understanding of the impact of politics on social policies and their effects. It clarified that Christian democracy did not simply promote social spending like social democracy did, but rather that the movement fostered a distinctive welfare state regime, catering to its own political clientele and reinforcing its own resources for power mobilization (Huber et al. 1993; Huber and Stephens 2001a; van Kersbergen 1995).

The Christian democratic welfare regime was shown to work in a much more passive (reactive) policy style and to be cash transfer rather than service oriented. The regime stresses income replacement and job protection, but pays little attention to employment creation. Compared to the liberal version, the Christian democratic welfare regime privileges families over individuals and fosters the so-called breadwinner-carer model. The administration and implementation of the major welfare programmes is fragmented, decentralized, and usually delegated to semi-public agencies that carry out state functions. Unlike the social democratic regime, which promotes equality, the Christian democratic tax-benefit system tends to reproduce the social status (income level, occupational standing) of male breadwinners in the social security system and to inhibit the labour market participation of women, with the main obstacle for married women being the joint taxation of income.

Re-Specifying the Link between Religion and the Welfare State

The theoretical adjustments and refinements to account for Christian democracy's social policy influence produced its own set of anomalies.

(1) The power-resources-cum-Christian-democracy explanation neglected or denied the possibility that Protestantism, in any variant, had played a role in welfare state development. This contrasted with earlier modernization studies. Peter Flora had already claimed that religion had influenced welfare state development, but he had emphasized structural aspects and the *longue durée*. Modernization theory stressed the importance of the decline of religion and the rise of the secular nation

state that took over the church's role in social provision. Protestantism qualitatively changed church–state relationships and facilitated the early transformation of traditional societies into mass democracies, especially in countries where religion had promoted literacy in society's lower strata and made their political inclusion possible (Flora 1983: 22).

In nations in which the Reformation had a lasting impact and in which state–church relations developed gradually, the conditions for collective welfare services were argued to be most favourable, the more so as the decline of religion was believed to facilitate the growing political salience of class. The conflict between state and church in those nations where Catholicism continued to shape culture and politics inhibited or at least retarded the emergence of a welfare state. Religion was taken to explain the difference in *timing* and variation in the *quality* of the welfare states. The ideal type of the welfare state that modernization theorists had in mind was a historical combination of universalism and statism and was found in Scandinavia, where the physical distance from Rome was greatest. In other words, the 'Protestant welfare state' which modernization theory had identified was later rediscovered as the 'social democratic welfare state'.

(2) The amended theses of the power resources model are hard to square with historical facts. For instance, it was liberalism and anti-clericalism rather than Catholicism or Christian democracy that prevailed in the formative period of the Italian and French welfare states (see Lynch 2009; Manow and Palier 2009). In France and Italy much of the early social legislation had an anti-clerical momentum, because the aim of the liberal state-building elites was to establish central state responsibilities in a domain for which the church had always claimed exclusive competency.

Moreover, the emphasis on the strong impact of Catholic social doctrine always sat uneasily with the power resources approach's neo-Marxian emphasis on interest and class. To resort to ideas once an interest-based explanation has reached its limits looks more like a quick theory fix than a convincing and coherent explanation (Iversen 2006). Moreover, the literature's negligence of how the state–church conflict had played out in another important policy domain with central importance for early welfare state development adds to the picture: it was over the question of public (i.e. secular) versus private (i.e. confessional) schools that the religious cleavage became most virulent in Western Europe at the end of the nineteenth and the beginning of the twentieth century. The basic compromise between nation state and church on the school question often prefigured the type of solution that the state and the church found in respect of the 'labour question'. It is therefore important to take into account not only the consequences of the capital–labour conflict that resulted from the Industrial Revolution, but also the consequences of the state–church conflict over education and social policy that resulted from (nation-)state building. The religious cleavage is crucial because it is only in those countries where in the last quarter of the nineteenth century bitter state–church conflicts were waged that parties of religious defence (Catholic parties, Christian democracy) emerged. These parties later on became central political actors that mobilized workers and the middle class *not* along class lines, but along cross-cutting lines of denominational belonging.

(3) It is this history of state–church conflicts that explains certain features of contemporary welfare states that in the conventional 'three regime' model remain unexplained. In particular it is hard to reconcile the comprehensive public pre-school programme and generally un-Catholic family policy in France and Belgium, and to some extent in Italy, with the familiar picture of continental societies that cling to an outdated, Catholic, traditional family model in which the woman is responsible for care-giving and child-rearing and the man is the family's sole breadwinner. We can only understand this anomaly in some continental welfare states if we account for their history of state–church conflicts over the role of the church in education (see Morgan 2009). France, Belgium, and Italy are examples of countries in which the nation state successfully crowded the church out of the education system in the first quarter of the twentieth century.

THE RELIGIOUS CLEAVAGE AND THE HISTORY OF POLITICAL CLASS-COALITIONS

A better account of religion's political impact on the welfare state would need to start from the Rokkanian notion of social cleavages and their political expression in the OECD party systems.[1] We start from the observation that Esping-Andersen's original three-regime heuristic puts much emphasis on a class-coalitional perspective. Did the middle class become a part of the pro-welfare state coalition or did it remain outside? While stressing the importance of a broad political coalition that would include the middle class, Esping-Andersen himself did not offer a convincing explanation *why* the middle class sometimes aligned its interests with social democracy and sometimes not. Soskice and Iversen (2006) have provided us with just such a reason. They emphasize the importance of electoral rules. A majoritarian electoral system leads to a two-party system with a centre-left and a centre-right party, while a proportional electoral system results in a higher effective number of parties. Different party systems trigger different voting behaviour of the middle class. In Soskice and Iversen's simple framework, the electorate comprises three groups or classes: the lower class, the middle class, and the upper class. In a majoritarian system with two parties the lower class votes for the centre-left, the rich for the centre-right party. But how does the middle class decide?

The middle class fears—if the left governs—that the government will tax both the upper and the middle class for the exclusive benefit of the lower class. If a right party governs, the middle and upper class will not be taxed, and, as a consequence, redistribution will be marginal. In this two-party setting the middle class has the choice either to receive no benefits but to be taxed, if the left governs, or to receive no

---

[1] This section is based on Manow and van Kersbergen (2009). The interested reader is referred to this work for a more detailed analysis and for more extensive referencing.

benefits but then also not to be taxed, if the right should govern. Obviously, it would choose not to be taxed. However, in a multiparty system, the middle class's choice is different. Forming a coalition, left and middle-class parties together can tax the rich and credibly commit to divide the revenue. The likelihood then is that in multiparty systems the left will be in government more often, redistribution will be higher, and the welfare state more generous. In majoritarian systems, the middle class will more frequently vote for the centre-right party, governments will more often have a conservative composition, the welfare state will remain residual, and redistribution will be marginal.

This is an extremely smart explanation for the well-known empirical regularity that the left governs more often in countries with proportional representation (PR) than in countries with a majoritarian political system (see Soskice and Iversen 2006: 116, table 1). It thereby plausibly explains the difference between the liberal-residual welfare state in the Anglo-Saxon countries and the generous welfare state in continental Europe or in Scandinavia. However, this approach fails to account for the substantial differences between the equally generous, yet profoundly different Scandinavian and continental welfare states. It is here that the importance of the religious cleavage comes into play.

Majoritarian electoral rules are generally associated with two-party systems. In such two-party systems the labour–capital or left–right cleavage dominates politics. All other cleavages, including the religious conflict, even if they continue to be politically salient, remain latent or are 'incorporated' in the basic left–right cleavage. Here the basic mechanism applies: under majoritarian rules, two parties predominantly represent the economic cleavage and within this setting the middle class more often votes for conservative parties. The welfare state remains residual.

In PR systems, in contrast, a larger effective number of parties allows for the political representation of more than the dominant labour–capital cleavage. Which kind of additional cleavages are represented in the party system depends on the cleavage structure of the country in question. Here the distinction between the Nordic and the continental countries and their welfare states achieves particular relevance. In Northern Europe a religious cleavage did not become politicized along party lines because these societies were not religiously heterogeneous; nor did the 'national revolution' lead to strong state–church conflicts. In marked contrast to the Catholic Church in Southern Europe, the Northern Lutheran state churches did not feel fundamentally threatened when the new nation state started to take over those responsibilities that previously had fallen under the responsibility of the church. Anti-clericalism never became a strong political current in Scandinavia. Instead, it was the cleavage between agrarian and industrial interests that became politicized along party lines because the agrarian sector was still very strong at the moment of mass democratization in late industrializing Scandinavia. Only in Europe's North did strong parties of agrarian defence emerge and receive a substantial share of the votes over the entire post-war period. The strong position of the agrarian parties explains why almost all accounts of the historical development of the Nordic welfare state stress the importance of red–green coalitions for the formation and the subsequent expansion of the welfare state (see Baldwin 1990; Esping-Andersen 1990: 30).

The political space occupied by agrarian parties in the North is occupied by Christian democratic parties on the European continent. These parties have their roots in political Catholicism and are the offspring of the fierce state–church conflicts of the late nineteenth and early twentieth century (see Kalyvas 1996). In the religiously mixed or homogeneously Catholic countries it is the state–church conflict, which—in addition to the left–right cleavage—is prominently represented in the party system. Parties of *religious*, not agrarian, defence therefore developed in continental Europe. And these parties became social democracy's most important ally in the major welfare state building enterprise that took place after World War II.

This history of political class coalitions explains why we find liberal welfare states in countries with a majoritarian electoral system (an exemplary case being the United Kingdom). But it also explains the political coalition behind the generous social democratic welfare state in the North of Europe as the result of a coalition between social democratic parties and parties of agrarian defence. One important precondition for the emergence of red–green coalitions has been *the absence* of a strong religious cleavage, so that parties of religious defence are all but absent from the Scandinavian party systems. On Europe's continent, in turn, we find welfare states that are the product of a coalition between social and Christian democracy (a red–black coalition), if the welfare state was not the product of Christian democracy alone, as for instance in a country like Italy, where the left was too weak and divided to exert much influence on public policy. In these continental countries the second cleavage represented in the party systems, besides the dominant left–right or labour–capital cleavage, has been the religious cleavage.

To summarize: we think that Iversen and Soskice are perfectly right in stressing the importance of a coalition between lower and middle classes, yet by taking into account the impact of different cleavage structures in Nordic and continental countries on emerging party systems one can identify *which type* of middle class party entered into a coalition with social democracy. This insight allows us to explain the types of welfare states to which these political class coalitions have led. Similarly, the variation in Christian democracy on the European continent—sometimes being hegemonic as in the case of the Italian Democrazia Cristiana, sometimes having vanished over the course of the post-war years as in France—allows us to address more systematically the question of the considerable within-type variation in continental Christian democratic welfare states.

IMPLICATIONS AND FURTHER RESEARCH

The welfare state literature has largely neglected the role of religion (particularly Protestantism) and religious cleavages, the impact of parties of religious defence and the legacies of fierce state–church conflicts. Where addressed at all, the influence of religion was perceived as being largely restricted to political Catholicism, and here most of the emphasis was put on the influence of Catholic social doctrine. We are not arguing that social doctrines are irrelevant, but hold that the parties of religious defence, which were the central political actors that translated religious concerns into the realm of democratic politics, have been more important. In those party systems in which parties of religious defence are present, they backed a specific type of cross-class compromise, which became manifest in a specific type of redistributive regime.

This does not imply that the impact of religion on welfare state development is restricted to working solely through this party-political-cum-electoral-system channel. In this respect France and Ireland are interesting, yet at first glance puzzling cases. Both countries lack a Christian democratic party, although religion always was of the highest political salience. Both also employ electoral systems different from the PR standard that prevails in most other European countries (except Britain). However, the French welfare state resembles in most respects its continental homologues (Palier 2002), whereas the Irish combines traits typical for the continental and characteristics that belong to the Beveridge type (Cousins 1997). At closer inspection the French case underlines the importance of parties in the translation of the religious cleavage into politics and policies, while the Irish case in one important aspect qualifies the argument about the interplay of electoral rules and church–state conflicts in Catholic Europe. In France, it was the Christian democratic Popular Republican Movement—which developed into a powerful governing party under the Fourth Republic's PR electoral System, but dissolved in 1967—that was responsible for the enduring 'Bismarkian' nature of the French welfare state (Manow and Palier 2009). The Irish case, on the other hand, is one of a uni-dimensional policy space in which neither the left–right cleavage nor the church–state cleavage dominates (Laver and Hunt 1992). Rather, the two major parties—Fine Gael and Fianna Fáil—represent the pro- and anti-Treaty factions that formed in the wake of Irish Independence and of the Irish civil war (1922/3). Since the independence movement itself had a strong religious dimension, the very special brand of Irish Catholic Nationalism and nationalist Catholicism prevented a state–church conflict from emerging (Martin 1978). The Irish case indicates that the nation state and the Catholic Church were not antagonists everywhere and at all times.

It is important to emphasize that religious parties were never simple *porte-paroles* of religious doctrines, but were above all interested in maximizing votes, seats, or office. Parties need to attract an electorate and have to satisfy specific societal interests if they want to be elected. A welfare state regime represents a political compromise between different electoral and societal groups, and this is particularly true for PR electoral systems in which coalition government (or minority government) is the rule and one-party rule the exception. Specifically, we have argued that a compromise between farmers' and workers' interests supports the welfare state in Scandinavia, whereas the continental welfare state is the institutional expression of an (inter- and intra-party) compromise between workers and the Catholic middle class. In order to understand which kind of political class-compromises were struck in the different European countries, future research might want to study systematically the presence or absence of different societal cleavage lines. Our perspective directs attention to the different logics of redistributive politics in different party system settings.

Our reassessment of the impact of religion on Western welfare state development is an invitation for a renewed debate on the causal sequences behind the different institutional setups of contemporary welfare states. It implies that the threefold categorization between social democratic, conservative, and liberal welfare states may hide rather than elucidate the causal factors in the development of the various welfare state regimes as we know them today. Our approach may also have consequences for analyses of institutional sclerosis and welfare state reform. Since the early 2000s, the literature on the Christian democratic welfare state has been focusing on the puzzle of why and how the 'frozen welfare state landscapes' (Esping-Andersen 1996c: 24), characterized by the welfare-without-work syndrome where reform was thought to be almost impossible, are nevertheless changing. The questions have been how and under which conditions welfare state reform is possible and who is actually doing this? Do Christian democratic parties still play a crucial role in the reform of the welfare regimes to which they are historically attached and may still be politically committed? Or is it the case that the role of Christian democracy is diminishing further, because more generally party political struggles matter less and less in welfare-state reform? Are we witnessing the end of the impact of religion on the welfare state? Ageing populations, sluggish economic growth, long-term unemployment, changing family structures and gender roles, the transformation of life-cycle patterns, post-industrial labour markets, the rise of new risks and needs, as well as international pressures not only seem to bring an end to a golden political age of expansion, but also appear to narrow down the room to manoeuvre for pro-welfare political actors, including religious ones. Or does the retreat of the welfare state offer new opportunities for non-political religious (church) groups and actors to take up the welfare role that they so dramatically lost in the modern period? Such questions will be high on the research agenda in the coming decade.

Research is also needed into the role of non-Christian religions and their political, economic, and social impact. It is evident that the question of the relationship between Islam, modernization, charity, social policy, and the welfare state is likely to become the focus of a future generation of research, if only because—like Christianity—Islam, too, asks the faithful to help the poor. More specifically, and parallel to the rapidly developing research agenda on whether, how, and to what extent religion and the welfare state are substitutes, we need further research on the hypothesis that the state's retreat or structural weakness in the Middle East created a social policy void in which Islamic charities and movements (say Hamas in the Palestinian territories, Hizbullah in Lebanon, or the Islamic charitable institutions in Egypt; see Pioppi 2004) have stepped in to provide the missing social services (including health care and education), adding to the political appeal and strength of the Islamic opposition. One interesting direction for further research concerns the findings of the studies of White (2002) and Clark (2005). Clark found that Islamic charities in countries like Egypt, Yemen, and Jordan are not cross-class organizations, but primarily horizontal middle-class organizations, catering for the middle class itself and much less for the poor; they are gradually developing a middle-class political outlook and a diffuse support for, and a will to cooperate, with the regime. White, in contrast, found that charities in Turkey tend to develop into vertical, clientelistic organizations in a system of social policy patronage that primarily benefits the national Islamic party. Both experiences to some extent echo, but also contrast with, the Western experience: here is a notable opportunity to expand a revised research agenda to other settings.

CHAPTER 19

....

MIGRATION AND ETHNIC MINORITIES

....

STEPHEN CASTLES
CARL-ULRIK SCHIERUP

INTRODUCTION

....

IMMIGRATION and growing ethnic diversity are important—but often neglected—factors in the evolution of welfare systems in Europe and North America. Public welfare systems emerged in the nineteenth and twentieth centuries as mechanisms to consolidate nation states and to reduce class conflict. However, European nation states were imagined as ethno-culturally homogeneous; histories of (often forced) incorporation of territorial minorities and of reliance on foreign labour were largely ignored by scholars. In North America, by contrast, immigrants were too numerous to ignore. There the strategy for controlling difference was assimilation into a new American people through a vast 'melting pot', although this never applied to African-Americans. In both these variants of the 'methodological nationalism' (Wimmer and Glick Schiller 2003) that dominated Western social science there was no room for analysing the significance of ethnic diversity for welfare systems. Social policy was for citizens, and was linked to the notion of solidarity to encourage the sacrifices of warrior-citizens—hence the expansion of welfare linked to the two World Wars. This helps to explain the blindness of much welfare state theory to the implications of ethnic diversity to this very day (e.g. Myles and Saint-Arnaud 2006: 340).

Yet Western societies have always been marked by diversity, both of historical territorial minorities and of successive waves of immigrants. Populations could be imagined as homogeneous in 1945, but they certainly could not by the end of the twentieth century. By 2005, the foreign-*resident* population of European OECD countries was over 24 million (5 per cent of the total population). The foreign-*born* population (i.e. including naturalized persons) was 39 million (over 8 per cent of the total) (figures from OECD 2007g). Including migrants' descendants with the citizenship of the country of residence, Western European countries have minority populations of 5–15 per cent. In the USA, the foreign-born population increased to 35.7 million in 2005 (12.4 per cent of the total). The official classification by 'race' indicated that 14.5 per cent of US residents were Hispanic, 12.1 per cent African-American, 4.4 per cent Asian and 6 per cent 'some other race' (US Census Bureau 2005). In Canada, the 2001 Census showed that foreign-born persons made up 18 per cent of the total population (Statistics Canada 2007). Australia is the most diverse of all developed immigration countries—22 per cent of the population are immigrants and about 20 per cent of the remainder have at least one immigrant parent—but will not be discussed further here.

Three further factors indicate the significance of recent migration for welfare systems. First, migrants and their descendants have their roots in increasingly distant and different societies. Up to the 1960s, most migrants to Western Europe and North America came from Europe; by the 1990s, migrants and asylum seekers were coming from all over the world (S. Castles and Miller 2009). In the United States in 2005, 53 per cent of the foreign-born were from Latin America, 27 per cent from Asia and only 14 per cent from Europe. Second, migrants and minorities are highly concentrated in cities, and within these in specific neighbourhoods—often those most lacking in good housing stock and public amenities. Third, although ethnic minority members are to be found right across the social spectrum, they are over-represented in manual occupations, amongst the unemployed, and amongst people below the poverty line (Schierup et al. 2006).

In this chapter, we will focus on two categories of people: *immigrants*, defined as foreign-born persons who have migrated to European or North American countries; and *ethnic minorities*, which includes the previous category but also embraces their descendants, who may or may not have been born in their country of residence, but who are categorized as different from the majority population through appearance, religious practices, language use, and customs. It is important to note that we are talking about fairly recent immigrants and their descendants here, not about historical minorities or indigenous peoples—to cover these categories too would be impossible in this short account. Two further limitations should be noted. First although many migrants to Western Europe and North America are highly skilled (in fact the skills profiles of immigrants tend to be higher than those of the destination-country populations), this article concentrates on the situation of lower-skilled migrants. Second, although it would be valuable to look at the situation of immigrants with regard to social policy in other destination regions—such as Oceania, East and South-East Asia, and the Gulf states—it is impossible to do so here.

The chapter is divided into two major parts. In the first part we briefly review three current research perspectives on ethnic diversity and the welfare state, each of them of importance for overcoming the general neglect of this issue, essential for both the present and future of North Atlantic societies. In the second part, discussing what we refer to as tendencies towards Americanization of European welfare states, we argue that there is a need for transcending the scope of current approaches through linking issues of migration and diversity to a dynamic political-economic research perspective on neoliberal transformation.

THE STATE OF RESEARCH ON MIGRATION, DIVERSITY, AND THE WELFARE STATE

The lack of frames of reference for analysing migration and ethnic diversity among mainstream approaches to the understanding of the welfare state is still conspicuous, and blunts their analytical power. This shortcoming was notable at a historical juncture when ethnically segmented labour markets and the racialization of access to social citizenship increasingly came to shape the institutions and practices of the welfare state, but has been partly redressed during recent decades. In the following we briefly review three of the more important current approaches:

1. a more general approach endeavouring to link an understanding of racism and discrimination to the analysis of citizenship and social exclusion–inclusion;
2. a growing body of specialized research focused on the analysis of international migration, gender, and changing institutional contingencies of care work;
3. a comprehensive scholarly research and debate on multiculturalism, citizenship, and the welfare state.

Migration, Citizenship, and Racialized Exclusion

Growing deprivation among immigrants and new ethnic minorities across Western Europe and North America since the beginning of the 1980s has caused social scientists to focus on social citizenship and ethnically differentiated patterns of inclusion and inclusion. Some argue that strong welfare states tend to serve as closure mechanisms that exclude newcomers (Bommes and Halfmann 1998), while others believe that welfare entitlements actually helped change labour migration into family settlement, notably in Western Europe after 1973 (S. Castles and Miller 2009).

There is certainly ample evidence for the progressive inclusion of migrants and ethnic minorities into frameworks of social citizenship and institutionalized welfare provision in Europe (e.g. Guiraudon 1998). However, it is important to distinguish

between formal and substantial rights. In certain countries immigrants and minorities have been excluded from full eligibility to welfare benefits and services
(sometimes temporarily). In some cases (e.g. Germany in the 1960s and 1970s),
special services (often inferior in quality) have been provided. Immigrants and
minorities have special needs (related to language, custom, religion, or education),
and welfare systems have responded to these to varying degrees. Differentiation of
provision on grounds of politically defined entry categories (e.g. worker/asylum
seeker, regular/irregular) is common (Sainsbury 2006). Finally, rights of citizenship
are not irreversible, as is currently demonstrated through exclusionary effects of the
securitization of immigration control, the institutionalization of new temporary
migrant labour systems, the 'normalization' of irregularity and informal migrant
labour, and increasingly restrictive access to citizenship for migrants across Europe
and North America.

An important study of migration, ethnic relations, and access to welfare is Faist's
(1995) *Social Citizenship for Whom?* Faist asks whether an 'underclass', marked by
multiple and durable deprivation, could be seen emerging among the offspring of
Turkish and Mexican immigrants in Germany and the United States. His study
juxtaposed Germany's highly regulated welfare state with the market-driven United
States variant. What emerges are two markedly contrasting patterns of racialized
exclusion and 'second class citizenship'. In Germany the dominant pattern of exclusion was migrant exclusion resting on *redundancy* related to high labour market
entry thresholds and ethnic discrimination, in spite of access to education and social
benefits within a still fairly generous welfare state. This contrasted with the proliferation of the racialized *working poor* in the United States due to a bifurcated post-
Fordist economy and neoliberal work-first policies.

The contrast between European patterns of exclusion of racialized minorities from
the labour market and United States patterns of exploitation of the racialized working
poor seems to emerge as a general transatlantic split (e.g. Kloosterman 1999). Thus,
until recently, research on migrant incorporation in the 'old' immigration countries of
North-Western Europe focused mainly on unemployment as the dominant source of
exclusion from social citizenship. However, research on the 'new migration', transforming the previous emigration countries of Southern Europe into *countries of immigration* from the early 1980s (e.g. Anthias and Lazaridis 1999), reveals a more complex
pattern. Here unemployment among immigrants has remained lower than among
nationals, and a large category of the working poor has been produced through a
combination of irregular migration, a frequently changing migration policy, informal
employment and exclusion from the core labour market. The barring of immigrants
from access to citizenship and welfare plays a key part here.

Since 2000, scholars in Northern Europe have paid increased attention to the
racialized new working poor, analysing an upswing in irregular migration, the
growth of migrant domestic labour, and migrant and ethnic minority employment
within an expanding low-wage service economy. Various categories of exclusion
are mutually interdependent and embedded in complex and changing ethnic divisions of labour. Chronic social disadvantage and welfare dependency are potential

'incubators' of working activities that are 'precarious and underpaid and systematically performed by women, immigrants, and disadvantaged minorities' (Mingione
1996: 382). The growth of such jobs in turn puts pressure on welfare institutions.
Specific configurations of racialized exclusion are forged in local and *national
institutional settings* as they are exposed to global pressures (Schierup et al. 2006).

Migrant Labour in the Welfare Sector

Social policy researchers still mostly fail to pay adequate attention to the role of
migration in providing a workforce to staff the lower echelons of hard-pressed health,
welfare, and care services in ageing societies (e.g. Esping-Andersen 2003). Moreover,
through caring, cleaning, and cooking in middle-class households, migrant domestic
workers allow local women to enter privileged segments of the labour market.
Feminist migration researchers have redressed the neglect through studies focusing
on the emergence of a heavily gendered 'service caste' (Andall 2003). Proliferating
markets for domestic service workers are characterized by complex hierarchies of
employers and work tasks, formal and informal modes of employment, and differ-
entially-treated racialized segments (e.g. Cox 2006). Indeed the reinvention of domestic work after it had seemed on the verge of extinction in Western Europe and
North America is based above all on the availability of migrant women, who are
especially exploitable due to the intersection of criteria of gender, ethnicity, and legal
status (Wichterich 2000). These racialized hierarchies are reproduced by formal-
sector recruitment agencies, which sort workers into slots according to stereotyped
images of 'origin', 'culture', 'race', or 'ethnic' disposition. But they are also moulded
through covert agencies and social networks embedded in an underground economy
fed by undocumented immigration from Africa, Asia, Latin America, and Central
and Eastern Europe. The restructuring of the welfare sector in developed countries
has been heavily reliant on the emergence of such gendered transnational care chains.

One essential common denominator for the precariousness and exploitability of
this labour force, as Bridget Anderson (2007) argues, is the construction of domestic
servants as disadvantaged immigrant or racialized minorities through state policies
and public discourse. This implies exclusion from formal or substantial citizenship
and directs the survival strategies of such women towards informal domestic service.
In effect, it may be the predominantly informal character of domestic services, argue
Cox and Watt (2002), which continues to make this important factor for welfare state
and labour market transformation 'invisible' to mainstream quantitatively orientated
social policy research as well as to mainstream gender equality policies. Yet domestic
service workers are not equally 'invisible' everywhere. In Italy, according to Andall
(Andall 2003), a large migrant labour force of domestic servants is essential for the
familistic conservative welfare system; here these workers are among the most
organized migrants (in Catholic labour unions).

Currently a systematic comparative perspective on migrant domestic service and
welfare state transformation is emerging (Lutz 2008): the market for domestic

services is expanding everywhere, but the extent and forms of employment vary, depending on the specific intersection of *gender regimes*, *care regimes*, and *migration regimes*. For Southern Europe and Turkey researchers record a 'continuity in discontinuity' through a shift from limited exploitation of 'live out' native domestics to expanded exploitation of 'live-in' migrant women (Akalin 2007). However, domestic servants had, until recently, become extremely rare in other parts of Europe—most notably in the Nordic countries due to the availability of publicly organized care. This is now changing, but different national employment models have a decisive impact on the actual *extent* to which migrant domestic services become a preferred alternative and the actual practices involved. Among the most illuminating comparative studies on migration and welfare regime change across Europe is that of Williams and Gavanas (2008) comparing the intersection of child care regimes and migration regimes in the United Kingdom, Sweden, and Spain and Simonazzi's (2009) survey of changing elderly care regimes in the direction of home care, private provision, and cash transfers.

Another substantial body of research focuses on the migration of nurses (e.g. Buchan 2006): one instance of a 'global hunt for talent', which exposes persistent structural, institutional, and organizational problems at both ends of the migratory chain. Nurses—often highly qualified—from disadvantaged regions of the world, replace local nurses in Western Europe and North America as these advance professionally or obtain more attractive jobs. However, maintains Kingma (2007), this may lead to the reproduction of existing inadequacies in health care services and create a vulnerable female migrant workforce, rather than resolving basic organizational problems or the nursing shortage. At the same time, according to Kline (2003), the emigration of qualified nurses leads to a serious skill drain and deterioration of health services in the migrants' communities of origin. This is most acute in Africa, but appears also to threaten the quality of public health services in new member states of the European Union (EU) (e.g. Võrk et al. 2004).

DIVERSITY, MULTICULTURALISM, AND THE WELFARE STATE

During the 1970s many immigration countries had moved towards policies designed to recognize the cultural identities and social rights of minorities, as well as the role of the state in combating discrimination and racism. In some cases there were explicit multicultural policies (e.g. Australia, Canada, the United Kingdom); in others, terms such as 'immigrant policy' (Sweden) or 'minorities policy' (Netherlands) were used; in yet others the notion of 'integration of foreign fellow citizens' (Germany) was applied. France was an apparent anomaly, with its Republican approach, which mandated prohibition of identity symbols (such as the Islamic headscarf), rejection of ethnic monitoring, and non-recognition of immigrant cultures and communities, but even here there were surrogate minority policies under the euphemistic label of 'policy of the city'. In the course of the 1990s this trend has been reversed. Political discourse and media debate (e.g. Goodhart 2004) has focused on an alleged conflict between solidarity and diversity, claims also supported by some influential research-ers arguing that strong multiculturalism combined with a strong welfare state had contributed to the failure of immigrant integration (e.g. Koopmans 2003) and the growth of radical right populist movements. From the early 2000s, the stress in European political discourse was no longer on the recognition of minority cultures, but on integration, social cohesion, and 'national values'. In Britain, for example, a citizenship test was introduced to promote knowledge of British society and values. The Dutch Government also made sharp changes in policy, while France, Germany, Sweden, and other countries moved in similar directions (S. Castles and Miller 2009). However, it is important to note that multiculturalist *discourses* have often declined more than actual multicultural *policies*: measures to recognize the social and cultural needs of immigrants and minorities have often changed little, even as public dis-course has shifted.

Claims that diversity is damaging to welfare are often based on the United States as the 'paradigmatic case'. In a much-cited work Alesina and collaborators set out to examine why the United States does not have a strong welfare state. They find that: 'Within the United States, race is the single most important predictor of support for welfare. America's troubled race relations are clearly a major reason for the absence of an American welfare state' (Alesina et al. 2001: 189). They do identify other factors, such as the historical continuity of political arrangements designed to protect property and Americans' belief in opportunities for upward mobility. However, they emphasize that 'racial heterogeneity, both directly and indirectly through political institutions, can explain the bulk of the unexplained portion of the gap between the United States and Europe in welfare spending' (Alesina and Glaeser 2004: 133). Alesina et al. argue that the majority of the United States population are against redistribution, because it would mean transferring resources to black people.

Alesina et al. compare the United States and Europe, arguing that 'European countries are racially very homogeneous and . . . have a large measure of social spending' (Alesina et al. 2001: 232). The implication is that if European countries became more heterogeneous, then support for the welfare state would decline. The Alesina approach has been criticized on methodological grounds. The negative correlation between diversity and social spending shown through multi-country regressions seems to be strongly influenced by the weight of the United States, as an outlier in both respects (Banting and Kymlicka 2006a). Moreover, Alesina et al. assume that the strength of the political left is simply a reflection of racial diversity, and therefore omit this from their regressions. When Taylor-Gooby added this factor, racial diversity was shown to have no significant effect on social spending in Europe (Taylor-Gooby 2005b). In addition, Alesina et al. do not address the differences between long-standing white-on-black racism in the United States and the ethnic diversity that has emerged from recent immigration in Europe. Nor is it clear how they arrive at the idea that Europe (with its large immigrant and ethnic minority populations) is so much more homogeneous than the United States.

A recent attempt to provide an empirical basis for this debate is that of Banting et al. (2006). They look at two distinct but related issues. The first is the fear that ethno-linguistic or racial diversity weakens the welfare state by reducing trust and solidarity ('the heterogeneity/redistribution trade-off hypothesis'). The second is the fear that the adoption of multiculturalism policies to recognize and accommodate ethnic groups generates political dynamics that undermine welfare states ('the recognition/redistribution trade-off hypothesis'). These authors examine the links between ethnic diversity and multicultural policies, and social spending, redistribution and social outcomes. Their regressions show that: 'There is no systematic pattern of countries that have adopted strong multiculturalism policies seeing erosion in their welfare states relative to countries that have resisted such programmes.' They therefore conclude that there is no evidence for the recognition/redistribution trade-off. Similarly, they find little evidence for the heterogeneity/redistribution trade-off. They also note 'preliminary evidence' that the adoption of multicultural policies could mitigate the negative effect of rapid growth in immigration-based heterogeneity on social spending (Banting et al. 2006: 83).

Migration and Transformation of European Welfare States

Some analysts who believe that diversity undermines the welfare state shrug off empirical findings like those of Banting and Kymlicka (2006a), and argue that the 'corroding effects' are likely to be indirect and long-term. In this view diversity could affect support for the welfare state in two main ways: first through the emergence of a climate of public opinion hostile to welfare transfers to immigrants and ethnic minorities; and second through the growth of extreme-right populist racist parties.

Van Oorshot (2006) provides evidence for the first issue. He shows through an analysis of the 1999/2000 European Values Study data that Europeans in twenty-three countries largely share a common 'deservingness culture': elderly people are seen as most deserving, closely followed by the sick and disabled, unemployed people are seen as less deserving, and immigrants are rated as least deserving of all. The majority of Europeans are highly unwilling to support welfare transfers to immigrants; Van Oorschot refers to the work of Alesina and Glaeser (2004), arguing that:

> if in Europe welfare should become negatively associated with 'immigrants', as it is with 'blacks' in the USA, the legitimacy of the total welfare system might be affected, with as a likely longer-term outcome, a reduction of the level of generosity. (van Oorschot 2006: 38)

However, another study of public opinion in Europe, using the data from a number of large surveys, comes to very different conclusions. Addressing the alleged solidarity–diversity contradiction, Crepaz (2006) examines public support for multiculturalist attitudes and the impact on public opinion of multicultural polices. He finds widespread support for multiculturalism amongst the citizens of developed societies. For instance, there is strong backing for the teaching of mutual respect, promoting different cultures, and working for equality of diverse groups. Many people believe that multiculturalism makes society stronger. On the other hand, only 30–40 per cent of respondents in most countries support maintenance of distinct customs and traditions by immigrants. Crepaz finds that there is no link between the existence of multicultural policies and support for redistributive welfare policies. Interestingly, his study shows a positive effect of multicultural policies on trust—a finding which contradicts an increasingly dominant view among European policymakers. Crepaz concludes that these findings indicate 'benign interactions between minorities and the dominant members of society' and that 'this can only bode well for the public support of the welfare state' (Crepaz 2006: 116–17).

Such contradictory findings indicate the need for further empirical research on the topic. For instance it would be useful to analyse whether solidarity with immigrants is affected by the the structure of particular welfare states—especially the issue of whether benefits and services are financed through taxes or 'earned' through social insurance payments by employees.

The second theme, the growth of extreme right racist political organizations, is also open to diverging interpretations. Labour Party politicians in Britain have frequently argued that policies seen as too favourable to minorities could open the door for electoral success by right-wing groups like the British National Party. In several European countries—notably France, Austria, Italy, and the Netherlands—extreme right groups have made considerable gains through anti-immigrant propaganda. Such right-wing parties have their traditional basis amongst small business people, who also support anti-welfare state positions. On the other hand, some new right parties seek to attract working-class support through welfare-chauvinist slogans based on the idea of national preference in both job and benefit allocation (Myles and Saint-Arnaud 2006). Such contradictions help explain the frequent conflicts and splits affecting extreme right groups.

The key question here is whether anti-immigrant and anti-minority mobilization by the extreme right has the potential to undermine popular support for the welfare state. Findings from the empirical evidence reviewed by both Banting et al. (2006) and by Crepaz (2006) cast doubt on whether this has so far happened to an appreciable extent, since support both for multicultural policies (as opposed to multiculturalist discourse in some places) and the welfare state seems to remain robust. However, as Myles and Saint-Arnaud point out (2006), 'this does not settle the issue for the future . . . (W)elfare state practices tend to be institutionally "sticky", are subject to multiple competing forces, and tend to change through the accretion of many small reforms that take time to evolve.' The issue is whether immigration, diversity, and multiculturalism could in the long run have negative effects for European welfare states and for their popular support.

This is in the theme of our 2006 book (Schierup et al. 2006). We argue that inclusionary European welfare states helped set the conditions under which migration and minority formation took place from the 1950s to the 1970s. From the 1980s, however, the neoliberal ascendancy brought about major changes in welfare states. Migrants and minorities often bore the brunt of such changes, but in addition the existence of sizeable, often marginalized minorities arising from recent immigration was a crucial factor in neoliberal 'reforms'. The racialization of exclusion and poverty has been crucial in the shift away from welfare universalism and social redistribution. Racialized ethnicity has complemented hierarchies based on gender, class, and location in the neoliberalization of European societies. The presence of immigrants and minorities has helped legitimate the restructuring of welfare states and has played an important role in strategies to divide the 'deserving' from the 'undeserving' poor. The socio-economic disadvantage and differing cultures of ethnic minority members have helped justify a shift from universal welfare systems to residual approaches, while disciplining the excluded through workfare regimes. Informalization of economies and labour markets have been instrumental in making increasingly feasible the exploitation of racialized labour excluded from the regulated core labour market and social security provisions.

Racialization of Welfare: Some Examples

Central to our analysis is that the United States remains a crucial model for understanding European developments in general and the relationship between migration, ethnic diversity, and changing welfare states in particular.

On the one hand, United States anti-discrimination policies and doctrines of 'diversity management' have come to enjoy a global moral and political hegemony (Bonnett 2006) and serve as a model for European Commission directives on combating discrimination in member states. On the other hand, intersecting changes in production, welfare, and migration regimes have generated an unprecedented commodification of labour in the United States, with migrants and ethnic minorities as the most exposed victims of social precarity. Since the 1980s the tension between explicit policies of equity and racializing practices, embedded in pragmatic governance and politics of class, has become increasingly acute. A liberal inclination to market solutions, fragmented political institutions, and the relative weakness of multicultural consensus building processes have blocked the formation of broad class alliances and the extension of social citizenship (e.g. Wilson 1999). A cocktail of neoliberalism, 'welfare chauvinism' (Banting 2000: 21 ff.), restriction of migrants' access to social citizenship, and racial discourses, have cemented the function of migrants as a flexible reserve army of labour. This can be seen as part and parcel of a wider 'war against labour' (Piven and Cloward 1997) integral to the strategies of United States capital in the 1980s and 1990s. Millions of undocumented workers are permitted only minimal claims on the welfare system. They function as a wage-depressing 'reserve army', putting 'legal' migrants and indigenous blue collar workers under pressure. But even legal immigrants are often deprived of what is left of social citizenship in the United States. Access to citizenship via birthright partially releases the 'second generation' from the state of unfree labour. But the neoliberal under-mining of public welfare provision for the poor has deprived racialized groups of a safety net that used to provide leeway for rejecting the most degraded jobs.

Following a succinct statement by Banting (2000: 19), the United States could, in this perspective, be seen as the 'quintessential case of overt tension where the politics of race have shaped social policy . . . and constrained the capacity of welfare advocates to build stable political coalitions'. Yet if, in contrast to Banting (see also Banting and Kymlicka 2006a, b), we see the United States as trendsetting rather than exceptional in a global wide neoliberal transformation, an assessment of the relative impact of processes of 'Americanization' would be essential for understanding the importance of migration and diversity in the current political economy of changing European welfare states.

Within Europe, national situations and political approaches vary considerably. In each country, differing historical experiences of class struggle, territorial expansion, and colonialism have influenced welfare ideologies and policies. These differences have helped shape the way migrants and minorities have become incorporated into societies. Yet all the varying approaches have been exposed to change through neoliberal practices, as well as through trends towards Europeanization of economic and social policies. Recent transformations have been accompanied by Islamophobia, populist anti-immigration movements, a growing preoccupation with 'terrorism', and the accelerated securitization of migration and asylum policies combined with new racialized divisions in the labour market and in terms of access to social citizenship. Here we will look very briefly at the United Kingdom, Italy, and Sweden as examples (for more detail see Schierup et al. 2006).

In the United Kingdom, over half a century of immigration has resulted in a highly diverse population, which is differentiated on the basis of ethnicity, religion, legal status, gender, generation, and class. A policy of state intervention to maintain good 'race relations' and to prevent discrimination has been linked to a policy of strict entry control, which categorizes groups on the basis of complex and opaque criteria. The situation of immigrants and minorities has been closely bound up with the neoliberalization of the economy, and the shift of the welfare state away from social solidarity and towards individual case-management of exclusion and impov-erishment. Formal possession of British citizenship has never been a guarantee of social inclusion, while the current ideological shift from multiculturalism to 'social cohesion' indicates that recognition of belonging to the nation remains conditional for people seen as culturally alien by the majority group. During the economic boom period from 1997 to 2008, the Labour Government combined a policy designed to bring in large numbers of highly skilled and lower-skilled labour migrants (the latter mainly from EU-Accession States in Eastern and Central Europe after 2004), with a strong rhetoric of hostility to 'unwanted migrants'. The latter referred to irregular labour migrants (even though their labour was vital to low-wage sectors of the economy) and asylum seekers. Legislation on immigration and asylum was rewritten repeatedly (five new laws between 1993 and 2006), imposing ever-more restrictive rules on the entry of asylum seekers and reducing their welfare rights to the point of destitution if they fell foul of complex bureaucratic procedures. Highly skilled migrants by contrast enjoyed full inclusion in the welfare state.

For Italy, the golden days of the 'second economic miracle' have been fading, and reliance on docile and socially excluded irregular migrant labour also seems to be coming to an end. Italy cannot hope to grapple with its looming 'demographic crisis' solely through relying on a global reserve army of cheap domestic servants. At the current critical juncture, where well-worn strategies of informality and clientilism in economic management and governance increasingly prove their inadequacy, the inherent tensions of a racialized dual labour market and exclusivist welfare state and citizenship regime have burst into heated public unrest, typified by the anti-immigrant polemics and actions of the centre-right coalition. Nativist populism and street-level racist violence are increasingly confronted with the mobilization of migrants and new ethnic minorities protesting against harassment and appealing for the dead promises of a liberal constitution to come to life.

In most dimensions of the migration–welfare nexus, Sweden is the mirror opposite of Italy. The specific labour–capital compact on which the Swedish welfare state rested did not allow the use of migration as a vehicle for wage depreciation and the recommodification of labour, as in the United States, Italy, and Britain. Yet Swedish policies are loaded with inherent tensions and paradoxes (Ålund and Schierup 1991). These came abruptly into the open in the economic recession of the early 1990s, which was accompanied by disruption of the industrial compact geared to the maintenance of full employment, through income policies with an indubitable neoliberal twist. These were matched by a gradual shift of the emblematic active labour market policy towards disciplinary neo-American 'workfare' practices. However, this crisis also marked the end of the resistance of the social partners to any effective legislation against discrimination. Since the late 1990s Sweden has introduced new discourses, legislation, and practices of diversity and anti-discrimination that closely match the United States matrix on which they are modelled. However, given parallel neoliberal trends in economics, welfare, and labour market regulation, anti-discrimination legislation and diversity management have come to operate under social circumstances that, step by step, are becoming more similar to structurally grounded forms of poverty and racialized exclusion in liberal welfare states like the United States or the United Kingdom. Existing ethnic divisions have become exacerbated by EU regulations on posted immigrant workers from other member states (in particular pertaining to the new EU member states in Eastern Europe), which have meant a heavy blow to the system of collective agreements regulating wages and working conditions. Recent legislation (2008) has fundamentally changed Swedish policies concerning the import of labour and brought it far along a road of 'Americanization'. It has put an end to a traditional gatekeeper position of the labour unions, placing the decisions concerning employment of foreign labour exclusively on the individual employer. These and other current changes may in effect cause a heavy strain on the processes of multicultural consensus making that have prevailed for decades, and which have had equal access to citizenship and universal collective union–employer agreements as important basic social and institutional presuppositions.

FUTURE TRENDS

These brief comparisons do not imply that the road now lies open for the smooth liquidation of the Swedish welfare state or any of the other welfare states in the EU, or, for that matter, that the wholesale importation of the American model is just around the corner. Although there have been strong currents of convergence towards overall neoliberal hegemony, Europe's historical plurality of policies and regimes of citizenship has not come to an end. Nor has EU-Europe come to speak with one voice on today's increasingly complex and controversial issues of social welfare and migration.

Migration is becoming one of the EU's central policy areas, and an EU migration regime is emerging, in many aspects modelled on US policies. The positive side of this comprises a number of anti-discrimination directives and programmes, which require member states to combat discrimination and social exclusion. Yet EU policies also increasingly parallel those of the United States in terms of the propagation of temporary worker schemes, the criminalization of undocumented immigration, the securitization of migration, and the dismantling of formerly humanistic norms and practices concerning asylum. Increasingly unequal ethnic divisions of labour, discriminatory migration management, and unequal access to civil, political, and social rights are not compatible with measures for social inclusion of migrants and minorities. They are likely to create or exacerbate ambivalence towards the welfare state among racialized migrants and minorities (e.g. Ryner 2000) matched by welfare chauvinism and repudiation of diversity and multiculturalism among majority populations.

Ambiguity as to 'the social dimension' applies also to an EU that continues to pivot uneasily around a central contradiction between economic and political goals; between adjustment to the economic imperatives of global capitalism and the task of generating a new European identity based on a powerful notion of citizenship.

As we argue in Schierup et al. (2006), the intersection of transformations and conflicts around both diversity and welfare state restructuring represents a contemporary *dual crisis* of the welfare state and the nation: under the pressure of neoliberal globalization, both social citizenship and established national identities are challenged. The simultaneity of the cultural transformation through immigration and the economic transformation through the opening up of national economies to global competition has shaken the post-1945 class compromise that served as a basis for peace and economic expansion. The racialization of social citizenship has been an important part of the ideological apparatus developed to deal with this dual crisis. But the persistence of conflicts around immigration and welfare state restructuring—for instance through the simultaneous crisis of all the different integration models in Western European countries—shows that these issues remain as contentious and intractable as ever.

The agony of the neoliberal economic model that became manifest with the Crash of September 2008 will no doubt exacerbate this dual crisis. That is already evident in increasing hostility to migrant workers, as well as through increased pressure on unemployment insurance, pensions, and other welfare systems. At the time of writing it is too early to forecast directions of change. The widespread critique of the credit-fuelled and profit-oriented 'economic rationalist' model could open the way to a reassertion of the social functions of European states and the EU. Equally, current economic travails could lead to nationalism, protectionism, and even stronger trends to racialization and exclusion of minorities.

CHAPTER 20

....

EUROPEAN UNION

....

GERDA FALKNER

INTRODUCTION

....

THIS chapter discusses the European Union (EU) and its impact on welfare states in Europe. For decades, the individual European states and their welfare systems have been compared and categorized into different 'worlds of welfare' (Esping-Andersen 1990). At the same time, they themselves form part of a quasi-federalist quasi-state that has some features of a welfare state: the supra-national EU. To understand welfare developments in Europe it is therefore indispensable to take into consideration the joint promises and pressures that European integration represents.

The opening section looks at the ways in which European social policy has evolved, including

- regulation (in fields such as labour law and working conditions, health and safety at the workplace, gender equality, and anti-discrimination policies);
- redistribution (for example, via the European Social Fund) and the initiation of public debates on Europe's social dimension;
- mutual surveillance among national policymakers (the 'open method of coordination').

A second section summarizes the controversy over the 'social dimension of European integration', which has been ongoing since 1957, when the founding fathers of European integration agreed that economic issues—without social regulation to counterbalance liberalization effects—should be at the centre of the joint project. The third section presents criteria for evaluating the state of 'social Europe'. The final section will discuss how the EU impacts on different types of welfare states and creates conditions that promote more 'bounded varieties of welfare' in the EU, that is, a more restricted variety within limits that are directly or indirectly imposed or reinforced by European integration.

EVIDENCE ON THE DEVELOPMENT OF THE EU'S SOCIAL DIMENSION

EU social policy integration started rather slowly but later developed at a higher speed. During the early years of European integration, social policy consisted almost exclusively of efforts to secure the free movement of workers. National social security systems were co-ordinated with a view to improving the status of internationally mobile workers and their families. During the late 1960s, however, the political climate gradually became more favourable to a wider range of European social policy measures. At their 1972 Paris summit, the Community Heads of State and Government declared that economic expansion should not be an end in itself but should lead to improvements in more general living and working conditions. They agreed on a catalogue of EU social policy measures, which were later elaborated on by the European Commission (the institution that initiates EU policies) in the Social Action Programme of 1974. This was confirmation that governments now perceived social policy intervention as an integral part of European integration. Several of the legislative measures proposed in the Action Programme were adopted by the EU's Council of Ministers in the years that ensued, and further Social Action Programmes followed the first one. From the mid-1970s onwards, the development of EU social policy was rather impressive—at least, from a purely quantitative perspective.

EU Social Regulation

In 2009, approximately eighty binding norms existed in the three main fields of EU social regulation: health and safety, other working conditions, and equality at the workplace and beyond (Falkner 2010). Additionally, approximately ninety amendments and geographical extensions to these binding norms have been adopted (some of them for new member states). In addition to this hard law, there is soft law comprising approximately 120 non-binding policy outputs, including, for example, recommendations to the member states.

With regard to equality, matters such as equal pay for work of equal value, the equal treatment of men and women regarding working conditions and social security, and even the issue of burden of proof in discrimination law suits were, over time, regulated at the EU level (Hoskyns 1996; Ostner and Lewis 1995). Since the EU's 1997

Treaty of Amsterdam (new Article 13), a more general equality policy has been developed, targeting discrimination based on sex, racial or ethnic origin, religion or belief, disability, age or, sexual orientation (Bell 2004).

In the field of working conditions, a number of rules were adopted during the late 1970s, for example, on protection of workers in cases of collective redundancy, on the transfer of undertakings, and on employer insolvency. Many more followed during the 1990s and thereafter, including those on worker information, on conditions of work contracts, on the equal treatment of atypical (such as shift, temporary agency, or part-time) workers, and on parental leave.

With regard to health and safety at work, regulation was based on a number of specific Action Programmes. Directives (EU norms that must be turned into specific laws) include the protection of workers exposed to industrial emissions or pollutants, or responsible for heavy loads, as well as protection against risks associated with chemical, physical, and biological agents at work (such as lead or asbestos). These are the three main areas of regulative EU action.

The Distributive Dimension of EU Social Policy (in a Wider Sense)

The 1957 Treaty had already provided for a 'European Social Fund' (ESF). Its goal was to simplify the employment of workers, to increase their geographical and occupational mobility within the Community, and to facilitate their adaptation to change, particularly through vocational training and retraining. Initially, the ESF reimbursed member states for some of the costs involved in introducing and implementing such measures. The first major reform of the ESF in 1971 involved the definition of target groups and the co-funding of only those domestic projects considered appropriate from a Community perspective. After a number of further reforms, the ESF now co-finances projects for young people seeking employment, for the long-term unemployed, for disadvantaged groups, and for promoting gender equality on the labour market. The aim is to improve people's 'employability' through strategic long-term programmes (particularly in regions lagging behind), to upgrade and modernize workforce skills, and to foster entrepreneurial initiative.

In addition to the Social Fund, other EU Funds also seek to combat regional and social disparities (Allen 2005; Bache 2007). These are the European Regional Development Fund, the European Agricultural Guidance and Guarantee Fund (Guarantee Section), and the Financial Instrument for Fisheries Guidance. Additionally, the Cohesion Fund finances environmental projects and trans-European infrastructure networks in member states whose gross domestic product is less than 90 per cent of the EU average. Finally, the European Adjustment Fund for Globalization aims to help workers made redundant as a result of changing global trade patterns to find another job as quickly as possible. It became operational in 2007 with €500 million a year at its disposal, but at least during the initial period, the member states made fewer applications than expected.

In sum, the EU's social dimension is less regulatory than is often assumed. For 2006, finance for 'structural operations' claimed 31.6 per cent of the EU's general budget (European Commission 2006b: 8). The steering effect of the EU's labour market policy may be somewhat stronger than the ESF figures indicate. The latter display only the EU's part of the overall project budgets, but these projects are heavily co-funded by the national governments. Furthermore, the EU criteria for project selection may have indirect effects on national budgetary priorities. Add to this the 2009 economic recovery programmes, and the full scale of European social spending is apparent.

The Open Method of Coordination

In addition to the regulatory and redistributive levels of EU social policy, the last decade has also seen a new instrument being developed, the 'open method of coordination' (OMC). It is an explicitly non-regulatory strategy based on discourse and promotion of mutual learning, for example, via benchmarking. Although similar kinds of practices have existed in other supranational/international organizations (Schäfer 2006b), this development has produced a wave of political and academic statements in which it is assumed that harmonization of domestic policies will occur without the imperative of binding EU law.

The main features of the OMC were developed in the field of EU employment policy. This happened initially without a Treaty basis, as a follow-up to the Essen European Council of 1994. The 1997 Amsterdam Treaty's employment chapter later formalized these proceedings and the EU has since adopted employment policy guidelines on an annual basis. Their specification and implementation is left to national-level actors so that the domestic situation and party political preferences can be taken into consideration. The bottom line is that EU member states must regularly present reports on how they have dealt with the guidelines, and why they have chosen particular strategies in their 'National Action Plans'. They have to defend their decisions at the European level in regular debates, so that peer pressure comes into play and has, at least potentially, a harmonizing effect on social policies in Europe (for example, Porte and Pochet 2002). Over the years, the open method of coordination has been extended to new fields, including for example, health, pension reform, equal opportunities, and social inclusion.

Its success is still hard to judge due to the lack of reliable data on its practical effects in the member states (but see Zeitlin and Pochet 2005; Kröger 2009) and will always be difficult to measure since there is no counter-factual basis of comparison at the researchers' disposal. It seems plausible to expect that joint policy learning and mutual adaptation will have some effects on national policies, and that EU-level obligations, however loosely defined, will help governments to justify reforms domestically that they might otherwise not have dared to enforce for fear of electoral losses. Where national governments are not ready for policy change, however, the National Action Plans may do no more than either restate pre-existing domestic policies or perform a symbolic function (Scharpf 2002).

Debates on the 'Social Dimension of European Integration'

Ever since the inception of what later became the European Union, debates on whether or not a 'social dimension of European integration' was either present at all, or needed, were lively. The early writings focused on the weak legal foundations for EU social programmes (see in more detail Falkner 2007) and were mostly written by legal scholars (for later discussions on EU social policy from a mainly, though not exclusively, legal point of view, see the editions by Shaw 2000; De Búrca et al. 2005). Social policy competences were expected to remain a largely national affair in Europe, since the dominant philosophy of the 1957 Treaty was that improvements in welfare would stem from the economic growth caused by the liberalization of the European market, and not from regulatory and distributive forms of EU public policy. However, the Treaty contained a small number of concessions for the more 'interventionist' delegations (most importantly, the French). These were mainly the provisions on equal pay for both sexes and the establishment of the European Social Fund. This legal situation accounts for a number of features that make social policy unique among EU policies: for a long time the EU possessed no explicit competence provision empowering the European Commission to draft social legislation for adoption by the EU's Council of Ministers and the European Parliament (which would be the usual decision-making procedure). It was only due to the existence of so-called 'subsidiary competence provisions' that intervention in the social policy field was—implicitly—made possible, and then only if it was deemed necessary for market integration. It is crucial to note that from the 1970s onwards, these provisions were used to promote social policy harmonization at the EU level. However, they required unanimous approval by the Council of Ministers, which was very difficult to achieve. This state of affairs existed until the 1992 Treaty of Maastricht, and in some fields, unanimity will still be required even under the Lisbon Treaty.[1]

---

[1] The EC Treaty mandates for social legislation have evolved over time. The Single European Act introduced qualified majority voting for issues related to worker health and safety in 1986; in the Maastricht Treaty of 1992 the eleven member states agreed on far-reaching additional competences and procedural reforms, including significant extension of qualified majority voting, with a passing exception for the United Kingdom; the Amsterdam Treaty in 1997 ended the United Kingdom opt-out and inserted

In an oft-quoted article, Fritz Scharpf (1988) criticized this mode of decision making, claiming that it created a 'joint-decision trap' in federal and quasi-federal systems. Where the constituent governments' consent is needed for federal legislation, and decisions have to be unanimous or nearly unanimous, Scharpf noted, a 'pathology of interlocking politics' (ibid. 254) results. Competences are shared (not divided) but at the same time, the institutional self-interests of the lower level governments to preserve their veto position and hence their sovereignty are not filtered by a representation principle. Stalemate and sub-optimal outcomes can be expected from such systems (ibid.: 267).

When looking at the field of EU social policy, Scharpf's analysis was certainly accurate at the time of its publication. Nevertheless, a few counter-dynamics were detected in the ensuing years, and a proper debate on 'social Europe' began to flourish during the 1990s when an influential edited volume (Leibfried and P. Pierson 1995) provided the first comprehensive discussion on EU social policy, its development, and its relationship with national policy. The volume investigated the dynamics of social policy integration by examining and comparing the evolution of EU social policy in several areas. Summing up, Paul Pierson and Stephan Leibfried described an emerging 'system of shared political authority over social policy' (P. Pierson and Leibfried 1995a: 4). In this system, the power of the member states was not only pooled, but also increasingly constrained (ibid.: 7). 'What is emerging is a multileveled, highly fragmented system in which policy 'develops' but is beyond the firm control of any single political authority' (P. Pierson and Leibfried 1995b: 433).

Pierson and Leibfried also detected a specific dynamic that was bypassing the joint-decision trap. They noted that EU institutions were no longer simply tools of the member states, but that member state power was actually restrained by the autonomous activity of EU institutions and limited by three significant factors: the impact of previous policy commitments at the EU level; the growth of issue density; and the activity of non-state actors. Their book also showed that, at least in some fields, EU social policy initiatives had surpassed the lowest common denominator of member state preferences (P. Pierson and Leibfried 1995b: 458).

The multilevel system of shared political authority for social policy (Leibfried and Pierson 1995, 2000) created more social programmes and regulations on the supra-national level than previously expected, but whether or not these were sufficient to build an efficient counterweight to the ever stronger market forces, remains a matter of debate. A prominent example of this scholarly controversy was framed around the 'half-full glass' analogy (Ross 1994).

an employment co-ordination chapter into the EC Treaty; and the Nice Treaty of 2001 contained very minor reforms in the social realm, but it allowed the EU institutions to change the requirement of unanimous consent on some social issues to one of qualified majority.

EVALUATING EU ACTIVITIES
IN THE SOCIAL REALM

Most texts on EU social policy delimit their subject, though surprisingly few do this in a fully explicit manner, laying out the yardsticks, the operationalization, and the measurement methods. On the basis of an extensive literature review, it seems plausible that at least four different evaluation criteria are worth considering (Falkner 2000). First, a major task for EU social policy has been closing a number of legal gaps in labour law that were introduced or widened by the EU's Internal Market Programme and its liberalizing effect across national boundaries. New rules were needed, particularly with respect to the rights of workers assigned by their companies to work in a foreign member state (posted workers), and to European works councils that needed a trans-national setup in order to deal with the enlarged operational basis for their enterprises. In meeting these challenges, the EU performed better than most experts expected during the early 1990s, and all the important gaps discussed at the time have since been closed.[2] However, more recent further steps of liberalization in the EU's common market have created additional need for labour law clarification, most importantly in relation to the cross-border competition of service providers. With the benefit of hindsight, the closing of labour law gaps might be an issue of lasting concern because the European Union continues to instigate market-making projects that will eventually require re-regulation in the labour law and/or social spheres as well (Mabbett and Schelkle 2009).

Secondly, a somewhat more far-reaching criterion for judging EU social law is the differential between Commission proposals and Council legislation (note that the European Commission initiates all legislative projects on the EU-level, while the Council of Ministers is the major decision-taker, nowadays jointly with the European Parliament). There was a huge gap between what the Commission presented as potential EU social policy and what was actually adopted, during the late 1980s and early 1990s. However, this gap has almost completely disappeared. Even some of the most controversial projects, on, for example, sexual harassment in the workplace and on employee consultation in the European Company Statute, have been adopted.

A third indicator of the scope of the EU's social dimension is action taken to prevent reductions in national social standards, potentially induced by the increased competitive pressures (sometimes called 'social dumping') of the single market and the Economic and Monetary Union. One possibility of preventing this from happening could have been to agree on fluctuation margins, which would have stopped one country from gaining competitive advantages by lowering social standards. In any case, such proposals were only thought worthwhile by a handful of academics

---

[2] It should be mentioned that some recent judgements by the European Court of Justice have highlighted areas where even on the basis of EU directives explicitly designed to close such gaps, the effects of market integration on domestic labour laws might require further debate and further legal action (see concluding section 'The Impact of The EU on Different Families of Welfare States').

and politicians in a small number of member states, notably in Belgium, France, and Germany (Busch 2000; Dispersyn et al. 1990).

Finally, a fourth evaluation criterion might be the rather small extent to which the EU has forged a truly supranational social order. However, it should be noted that the EU as a quasi-federal system was set up when the member states already had fully-fledged welfare states. Therefore, policy pre-emption triumphed over supra-national ambition (Obinger et al. 2005*b*: 556) and the functional need to replace the domestic systems was neither indisputable nor widely accepted.

In short, it seems that while the EU's welfare activities perform not too badly compared with the rather low expectations, they clearly fall very short of the more far-reaching conceptions. What remains is the suspicion, shared by many authors, that 'member governments have lost more control over national welfare policies . . . than the EU has gained de facto in transferred authority' (Leibfried 2005: 243; see also Scharpf 1999; Ferrera 2005*a*). Beyond this evaluation of the status quo, however, it is hard to see an easy way out of the situation. To simply recreate the capabilities that have been lost from the national level at the EU level seems impractical. As a basis for this thought experiment, one needs to consider the various forms of EU activities in the field as shown in Table 20.1.

It seems that only fields (B) and (D) qualify for the argument that the EU should reunite the competences eroded on the domestic levels, since regulative competences

Table 20.1 Forms of EU social policy (in the very broadest sense)

	Issue areas	Member state / EU relations
(A) regulation of social rights and standards	Mainly: Labour law, health and safety at the workplace, equal treatment policies.	Both share competence, EU became of increasing importance 1970s–1990s.
(B) spending for social purposes	Mainly: European Social Fund, Globalization Fund, Agricultural Fund, Regional Fund.	EU expenditure minor if compared to national welfare systems, but within EU budget significant.
(C) coordination to stimulate voluntary harmonization in the social field	Mainly: Employment policy, pensions, social assistance, education.	EU impact depends on domestic willingness; hardly any information on de facto effects or proofs of causality.
(D) liberalization of public utilities in general, including 'social utilities' (a result of the EU's economic policy)	Mainly: Employment services, energy, transport, postal services, but also parts of the health industry. In fact, economic policies touch the 'outer ring' of social protection, in a wide sense, 'the welfare state's protective outer skins' (Leibfried 2005: 270).	Member states cannot discriminate private actors on the market or exclude them, outside a few narrowly defined and contentious core areas of public interest.

in the social chapter of the EC Treaty are shared between the member states and the EU, and the open method of coordination takes no competences away from the governments, in any case. The thought experiment would then result in (B) more significant spending for social programmes at the EU level, and (D) counterbalancing the liberalization of public utilities. The latter could lead up to, for example, a re-monopolization of employment services at the EU level. It is an interesting topic for debate, but a positive outcome in functional terms is far from certain. The effect of a potential EU monopoly for local public transport is also uncertain. An additional argument to be raised is that the liberalization of public utilities in general, in so far as it happened at all, was founded on the consideration that more competition would be beneficial overall. It seems doubtful that the EU-wide majority consensus in this direction has vanished. In other words: if there are broadly accepted arguments for liberalization at the level of the member states, these arguments will more often than not be valid at the European level as well. Therefore, the idea of allowing the EU to take on board whatever has been lost in terms of sovereignty at the national level is hardly viable. One may question the arguments underpinning the liberalization option (and one should discuss some obvious detrimental effects), but this would be an economic debate rather than one about appropriate levels of social policy.

Finally, with regard to more spending at the EU-level, the amount needed to counterbalance the pressures on the domestic level imposed by various European integration measures is hard to determine. Again, we can differentiate between forms of EU impact (see details in next section).

Table 20.2 again shows that simply taking on board at the EU level whatever now falls outside the full sovereignty (in the widest sense) of the nation states will hardly be an easy option. Technically, in the field of welfare expenditure, it would mean trying to establish the amount of welfare cuts that may have been enacted due to 'dumping' processes. However, the causality of any cuts in national welfare is hard to establish since there are, beyond inner-EU tax competition, also many other potential reasons for specific cuts that may have taken place. At the same time, it is hard to set up any EU regime to spend exactly this amount of money in such a way as to counter this consequence of European integration.

THE IMPACT OF THE EU ON DIFFERENT 'FAMILIES' OF WELFARE STATES

We have outlined how the EU's social dimension has been developed more strongly during the past forty years than originally anticipated by both politicians and

Table 20.2 Impact of European integration on national social spending

	Effect	EU policy	Evaluative arguments
Impact on expenditure	Direct	Opening borders and social security systems for citizens of other EU states: social transfers no longer restricted to 'own citizens' no longer consumed within state territory.	(a) From the member state perspective, this can be costly. But: Other countries' situations are similar, reciprocity is possible. If not: ECJ provides for (some) protection of financial stability of the social security systems. (b) From citizens' perspective, this offers new social rights.
Impact on budgetary resources	Direct	EMU, convergence criteria limit deficit spending.	(a) Short-term: restrictive effect on social expenses possible, although governments are in principle free to cut where they find useful, including outside the welfare area. (b) Long-term: not limiting the budgetary deficits might have had an even more negative effect on social budgets due to the danger of debt payment overload.
	Indirect	Only partial tax harmonization on EU level, hence room for tax competition between member states.	De facto pressure on nation states to lower their taxes (including social security contributions) on the mobile economic actors. But to be decided on national level.

academics. However, evaluations differ a great deal regarding the success of the 'social dimension' of European integration. This concluding section will discuss how the EU is impacting on welfare state policies overall, bringing about at least de facto significant pressures towards more bounded varieties of welfare. However, as the following two sections show, the methods are often indirect and the effects are different in different member states.

The Prominent Role of Unintended and Indirect Effects

It has already been shown that the domestic welfare states are restrained by European integration in the sense that they must now: guarantee free movement of labour within an integrated Europe and assure the related accumulation of trans-national social security entitlements as required by EU co-ordination rules; execute the anti-discrimination policies imposed by EU law aimed to support women and minorities with regard to age, racial and ethnic origin, religion and belief, sexual orientation, and disability; respect the minimum standards laid down in EU regulation for the fields of health and safety at the workplace and labour law; respect procedural rules of the open method of coordination by regularly reporting and justifying domestic choices in many other fields of social policies. These are all direct effects of European integration.

However, the impact of European integration on domestic welfare states and social policy regimes goes far beyond 'implementing' such EU social norms (as problematic as that may be in itself),[3] since many effects are 'indirect' ones, not triggered by explicit EU social policies but by *secondary effects of economic integration*, and/or by the European Court of Justice in Luxembourg interpreting EU law in an extensive and sometimes unexpected way.

As noted above, economic policies were given pre-eminent status in the 1957 Founding Treaty. To an extent that increased with the progress of liberalization over time, competition in the enlarged market imposed constraints on raising taxes and social security contributions from the mobile factors of production. During the second half of the 1980s, the 'Internal Market Programme' revived the European integration process, applying liberalization measures even in previously protected areas, such as state-owned infrastructures and services of public interest (energy, telecommunications, transport, employment agencies etc.). Slowly but surely and ever more extensively, the outer ring of welfare policies (Leibfried 2005) was affected (Scharpf 2002). The 1992 Maastricht Treaty, with its commitment to set up an Economic and Monetary Union, was a landmark in terms of its indirect effects on social spending. This eliminated national controls on monetary policy, while, in parallel, the Growth and Stability Pact imposed limits on budget deficits and hence created pressure for spending cuts (or tax rises, but see below), that affected social policy.

It is a broadly accepted economic view that all this triggered additional growth that can be expected to have allowed for a greater cake to be shared between all Europeans, but at the same time authors agree that the open borders reinforced the powers of the more mobile production factors and seem to have rather hampered the bargaining power of worker representatives. In principle, the size and much of the form of redistribution was still left to the member states to decide, but the

---

[3] It should be noted here that full evaluation of the success of existing European social law is restricted by the lack of knowledge about its practical effects in the member states. One comparative study of ninety cases of domestic adaptation performance across a range of EU social directives (Falkner et al. 2005) has revealed that there are major implementation failures and that, to date, the European Commission has not been able to perform its control function adequately. While all countries are occasional non-compliers, some usually take their EU-related duties seriously. Others frequently privilege their domestic political concerns over the requirements of EU law. A further group of countries neglect these EU obligations almost as a matter of course. Extending this kind of analysis to new member states from Central and Eastern Europe shows that EU standards all too often remain 'dead letter' (Falkner et al. 2008).

framework conditions of the decision were no longer the same. Welfare states, particularly in the EU, nowadays

> remain internationally viable only if their systems of taxation and regulation do not reduce the competitiveness of their economies in open product and capital markets—which implies that, by and large, redistribution must be achieved through public expenditures rather than through the regulation of employment relations, and that the costs of the welfare state have to be collected from the non-capital incomes and the consumption expenditures of the non-mobile population. (Scharpf and Schmidt 2000*b*: 336)

It is certainly difficult to establish the net effect of European integration on domestic social policy decisions. However, some accounts hold that the EU, if it was not the real source of change, has at least been used as an 'external justifier'. Particularly, but not only, in Southern Europe, the convergence criteria for EMU seem to have served as welcome justification for welfare state reforms (e.g. Martin and Ross 2004, with further references).

Next to indirect effects come *unexpected direct effects*. The EU's Court of Justice (ECJ) has the final say in the interpretation of EU law. Since the 1970s, it has been influential on a number of social policy issues and, at times, has significantly increased the practical impact of EU law by its jurisprudence. The equal treatment of women at the workplace and the protection of worker interests when enterprises change hands are two important examples (Leibfried and P. Pierson 2000). A recent case of 'spillover' from market integration to the realm of welfare is health care. Originally, this was a domestic competence and if a patient requested a publicly financed treatment in another EU country this needed advance authorization by the competent healthcare institution. In 1998, the ECJ ruled that healthcare was a service and hence subject to the competition law provisions under EU law. National health policies were affected by the market freedoms prevailing in the EU's so-called internal market more than politicians ever intended (Sindbjerg Martinsen 2009: 11). In fact, the European Commission has subsequently been using both the ECJ judgements and scientific evidence as authoritative inputs supporting its proposals to widen the regulatory competences of the EU in the field (ibid.).

Services provision in the EU's unified market has been a topic of much discussion, and, since 2004 when the Services Directive was first proposed, the cause of a number of mass demonstrations. The way that the Services Directive dealt with posted workers was particularly controversial: it created unequal conditions for resident and posted workers by making the latter subject to regulations in their home countries, which were often less worker-friendly than those of the host country (Schmidt 2009: 1). Most recently, further controversial ECJ cases, whose consequences will only be visible in the years to come, have touched the borderlines between market freedoms and basic social rights such as union action. A heated debate is ongoing as to their potential consequences in terms of domestic social and industrial relations, in particular what will happen to minimum wages and the right to strike if foreign companies that deliver services (e.g. in the building sector) do not need to apply the same rules as most employers in the host country (Scharpf 2009; Joerges and Rödl 2008).

The Differential Impact of European Integration

Just as 'globalization' has an uneven impact on the European welfare states (for example, Sykes et al. 2001), European integration affects the clusters of welfare states in Europe in different ways and to different degrees.

The original six EU founding states had welfare systems of the Bismarckian type of work-based social insurance. Differences were then much smaller not only in terms of structure but also of generosity. Therefore, harmonization at the EU-level would initially have been easier than at any time since—but this was 'a road not taken' (Scharpf 2002). After the first EU enlargement during the 1970s, Denmark, Britain, and Ireland had already increased the heterogeneity of the EU dramatically. Now one Scandinavian and two Anglo-Saxon types of welfare state were within the EU. Plurality increased even further later on, with Southern, further Scandinavian and Continental, and then Eastern European reform states becoming members.

The variety of welfare provision in terms of both funding (employer or/and employee contributions, direct/indirect taxes on various sources and groups) and expenditure (universal versus occupational, basic social benefits with means-testing and/or income-sustaining transfers and/or private service provision such as child-care), as well as divergent normative assumptions and values, made joint EU-level welfare policies much more difficult. At the same time, the feedback effects of European integration on the member states were ever more different. Large-scale comparative studies that systematically take into consideration all roots of EU impact outlined above, for all kinds of welfare systems and for all countries, are lacking and would be extremely difficult to coordinate. The basic mechanisms at play for pensions, health care, social assistance, and migration, however, have been illuminated in Ferrera's outstanding account of redrawing the boundaries of welfare in Europe (Ferrera 2005a).

In overall terms, it seems that the Continental systems are most adversely affected by the internationalization processes inside and outside the EU because their sources of income are in part no longer viable. When mobile production forces can easily migrate and avoid high employers' contributions to social security, shifting the burden elsewhere will be hard to prevent (Scharpf 2002). Tax-based systems seem less adversely affected, as long as citizens accept the immediate financial burden in exchange for more social security (ibid.). An exception may be Denmark with its largely VAT-based social system, which has also come under pressure via the EU's tax harmonization efforts (Leibfried 2005).

What is to be expected as a likely future trend? Will the EU's impact be such that all pre-existing differences will soon be eroded? This could, in principle, be the case, first, regarding expenditures and, second, concerning differences in the types of welfare system. However, empirical data suggest otherwise. Concerning the level of overall welfare spending, various empirical studies have concluded that a 'race to the bottom thesis' is supported neither by spending patterns nor by structural changes, be it at a global level or in Europe (e.g. Starke et al. 2008 with further references). These studies have revealed a 'blurring' of welfare regimes, which has resulted from similar policies being pursued everywhere—activation and workfare in labour market policy, enhanced co-payments in health insurance, more emphasis on family policy (see Obinger et al. 2005 for a study of four open economies). A similar situation characterizes healthcare systems, with a tendency of convergence from distinct types towards mixed types (Rothgang et al. 2005: 187).

A full convergence is neither functionally needed nor politically probable, for adaptation seems generally to happen 'in national colours' (Cowles and Risse 2001; Héritier et al. 2001). In the medium run, it seems therefore likely that the various direct and indirect effects of European integration will result in what can be called '*bounded varieties of welfare*' in Europe.

Regarding likely future trends in EU-level social policy, it seems that deep political and economic cleavages prevent a 'qualitative leap' towards 'major social transfer programmes that would enhance output legitimation and deepen social cohesion' (Obinger et al. 2005*b*: 546). Taken together with the dynamics of 'social Europe' outlined above, this probably means continued incremental change (Ferrera 2005*a*)—possibly with more judicial than regulatory action, especially after the enlargement and the Lisbon Treaty.

However, discontinuous development with even a breakdown and replacement of institutions is not impossible in times of abrupt change (Streeck and Thelen 2005*b*: 9), such as that witnessed in the financial market and economic crisis of 2008/9. The EU was not the main source of these problems, which proved so detrimental to societies and welfare systems worldwide (although it could probably have done much more to prevent them), but it is a crucial actor with at least the potential to win the struggle to contain the consequences of the crisis. At the time of writing, it is unclear what the dimensions and consequences of the crisis will be in the long run, but one insight from the development of social policy in national federal states comes to mind: 'major breakthroughs in the reallocation of powers were only achieved through severe external shocks' (Obinger et al. 2005*b*: 564).

CHAPTER 21

INTERGOVERNMENTAL ORGANIZATIONS

KLAUS ARMINGEON

INTRODUCTION

THIS survey reviews the role of Intergovernmental Organizations (IO) in domestic social policy. IOs we take to be those international organizations in which national governments are represented. Social policy denotes core welfare state activities such as social assistance, social security and social insurance plus labour market policy and education.

In recent years, the political left in the developed world and, in particular, members of 'anti-globalist' movements such as ATTAC (Association for the Taxation of Financial Transactions for the Aid of Citizens) have been enormously concerned about the impact IOs have had on the welfare state. Examples of their mobilization would include the demonstrations at the Seattle meeting of the World Trade Organization (WTO) in 1999 (which led to the World Social Forum) and the riots of January 2009 in Latvia, which were directed against the bourgeois government's implementation of the austerity policies demanded by the International Monetary Fund (IMF). These political activities notwithstanding, there is actually rather little systematic research in social sciences on the impact of IOs upon the national welfare state. This survey attempts to systematize the field by answering three questions: how do IOs influence social policy? What are major examples of IOs that have exercised some leverage on social policy? What do we know about the impact of IOs on national

Authors note: I am grateful to Jens Steffek and Stephan Leibfried for comments.

social policy and about the way nation states and IOs interact in the formulation and implementation of social policy?

Our review is focused on the welfare state in countries which are democratic and economically relatively developed. This includes the twenty-seven member states of the European Union plus the other established democracies of the OECD country groups, i.e. Canada, the United States, Japan, Australia, and New Zealand. This biases our description, since IOs such as the World Bank (WB) and the International Monetary Fund (IMF) have a global coverage and, in fact, place particular emphasis upon the behaviour of developing countries. But these organizations have major consequences for welfare states in developed countries. In a few cases, they actually transfer resources to these states, as in the case of Latvia. Perhaps more importantly, they diffuse ideas and standards that have a direct bearing on national political actors in the developed world, and they influence those IOs which do focus directly on developed countries, such as the Organization for Economic Co-operation and Development (OECD).

A focus on countries that are both democratic and developed makes sense when we consider that the impact of IO activity depends on how much political attention is dedicated to social policy, as well as on the amount of domestic resources available. In autocratic countries there is evidence that elites sometimes opt for more social security in order to stabilize their regime. This is the strategy widely said to have been deployed by the German chancellor Bismarck in the late nineteenth century (Alber 1982). But as long as they do not have major problems of legitimacy or face the pressures of (re-)election, elites in autocratic countries may also neglect social security. In fact, domestic politics and domestic political institutions condition the impact of IOs and, in its turn, this impact is a function of the strategic interaction of domestic elites with IOs. Less developed countries (which are frequently governed by autocratic elites) have far fewer domestic resources to commit to social policy. Most norms and suggestions for social policy reform are dependent on the level of available resources. Welfare state cuts may be necessary in one nation but not so in a much richer society. Reforms that can be financed in one country may be not feasible in another part of the world.

By contrast, governments in the rich countries are widely confronted with an electorate that has a strong interest in social benefits. As a rule of thumb, governing parties avoid massive welfare state retrenchment if they fear that they will be punished for this on election day. And these governments command far more abundant resources devoted to the public sector than are available in much poorer countries. Therefore conclusions about the role that IOs play in social policy in rich and democratic nations may not necessarily hold true for the poor and non-democratic nations. Stressing the interaction between domestic politics and international forces, Beth Simmons (Simmons 2009) has argued that international organizations may actually make the most difference when they seek to propagate human rights in moderately autocratic countries. In completely autocratic systems, rulers may not care about the norms of IOs, and in democratic regimes human rights are not contested but are already largely realized. However, if the regime is not yet democratic but still gives its population some political leeway, these citizens may use the norms and reputation of the IO in their struggle for more human rights. In this respect, IOs produce inputs which can be used by a mobilized citizenry in opposition to autocratic rulers.

The following overview is divided into three sections. The first describes those IOs which are most relevant for national welfare states in developed nations: the World Bank (WB), the International Monetary Fund, the World Trade Organization, the Organization for Economic Co-operation and Development, and the International Labour Organization (ILO) (the European Union is dealt with separately in Chapter 20). Due to space limitations two specialized agencies of the United Nations are not dealt with: the World Health Organization (WHO) and the United Nations Educational, Scientific and Cultural Organization (UNESCO). They rank well below organizations such as the World Bank in terms of their resources, and their impact on social policy development in economically advanced democracies is very limited. The descriptions of the five selected IOs will focus on their organizational structures and systems of decision-making, and on their official goals and tasks. These five IOs focus on different aspects of the welfare state. Interestingly, the core insurance programmes of the Western welfare state (for age, sickness, invalidity, unemployment) are dealt with only marginally by these IOs, with the possible exception of the World Bank and its suggestions for pension systems. Nevertheless, these IOs all influence welfare state policies either directly or indirectly. The OECD focuses on education, health and labour market policy. The ILO concentrates on employment and labour conditions. The IMF and WTO focus on increasing competitiveness in the liberalized world trading system and on promoting financial stability and growth. Their measures, exemplified by the IMF's call for debt and deficit reduction, have major implications for social policy in the sense that they often imply cuts in expenditures or taxes, thus limiting the room to manoeuvre.

The second section deals with the modes and means by which IOs attempt to have an impact on national welfare states. The final section looks into the impact of IOs on national welfare states, the strategic interactions between IOs and domestic political actors and the question of soft versus hard law.

MAJOR IOs IN THE FIELD OF SOCIAL POLICY

The World Bank was created in 1944 at the same time as the International Monetary Fund with which it has close ties (Marshall 2008; www.worldbank.org). Both institutions are specialized agencies of the United Nations but with substantive financial autonomy. The World Bank disburses about $25,000 million annually and thus dwarfs all the other international organizations that claim to improve the welfare of citizens. It is a cooperative made up of 185 member states which subscribe through financial contributions and have voting rights corresponding to the level of these contributions. Hence 'the governance structure is not designed to be democratic' (Marshall 2008: 2). Today, the World Bank is a group of five institutions: the International Bank for Reconstruction and Development (IBRD), the International Development Association (IDA), the International Finance Corporation (IFC), the Multilateral Investment Guarantee Agency (MIGA), and the International Center for the Settlement of Investment Disputes (ICSID). IBRD, IDA, and IFC are the principal institutions of the World Bank Group. The original aim of the World Bank was to promote the reconstruction of post-war Europe by loans to the war-torn countries. Later the focus moved to developing countries and the transition states of Eastern Europe. The Bank's major current official aim is the eradication of poverty. Its official policy is framed by the Millennium Development Goals of the UN of 2000, which lists the eradication of poverty and hunger, the achievement of universal primary education, the promotion of gender equality and the reduction of child mortality as major goals.

The ultimate authority of the Bank lies with the Board of Governors. Governors are usually the ministers of economy or finance of the member states. This board meets together with the IMF annually. Voting rights are a function of the level of national contributions. Day-to-day business is run by a Board of Directors. Five of the twenty-four members come from the most important contributing countries (the United States, Japan, Germany, France, the United Kingdom). Once again voting rights depend on the share of contribution. The Board strives for consensus and votes are rarely taken (Marshall 2008: 77). A powerful President chairs the organization. By tradition, Presidents come from the United States. The World Bank group has about 11,000 employees.

The major policy mechanisms of the bank are loans and grants to member governments for development projects (such as dams) or for structural adjustment. These loans are *conditional* upon criteria set by the bank. In addition, and this is what makes it important for the more developed democracies, it offers monitoring of social and economic policies in member states and comparative economic data. For example, the World Bank reports about labour market policies and this includes comparative data on hiring and firing rules (Employment Protection) around the world.

The International Monetary Fund (IMF) (Vreeland 2007; www.imf.org) was originally created to monitor and help maintain pegged but adjustable exchange rates in the post-war world. It has 186 member countries (2009). With the demise of the 'Bretton Woods' system, the Fund changed its role. It is now a lending organization mainly for developing countries. It aims to correct balance of payments difficulties, to provide temporary financing and to support policies aimed at correcting underlying problems. Although working closely together, the goals of IMF and the World Bank are different. First, the World Bank supports economic development; the IMF supports fiscal stabilization. Second, the IMF monitors economic and financial developments in all member countries—including the economically most developed democracies of the OECD group—and it provides policy advice, aimed especially at crisis prevention. Third, the IMF provides countries with technical assistance and training in its areas of its expertise. Supporting all three of these activities is IMF work in economic research and statistics.

The decision-making structure of the IMF resembles that of the World Bank. Member countries deposit an amount of money (called 'quotas') at the Fund, which defines their voting rights. In the IMF, all power comes from the Board of Governors, which meets together with the World Bank once a year. Each country is entitled to one governor who is typically the finance minister or the head of the central bank. Operational decisions are taken by an Executive Board of twenty-four members. Here again 'quotas' define voting shares. Whilst traditionally the World Bank President is from the US, the Managing Director of IMF is European. The IMF has about 2,700 employees.

The IMF's main goal is to provide loans to countries that have trouble meeting their international payments and which cannot otherwise find adequate funding on affordable terms. This financial assistance is designed to help countries restore macroeconomic stability by rebuilding their international reserves, stabilizing their currencies, and paying for imports. The IMF also provides concessional loans to low-income countries to help them develop their economies and reduce poverty.

Loans are conditional. Once countries do not comply with these conditions, loans are discontinued. The IMF has developed three modes of conditionality. Initially, this consisted of three main elements: reducing government budgets by cutting spending and raising taxes, reducing money supply, and sometimes devaluation of the currency. This 'macro'-conditionality was followed by more detailed conditions ('micro'-conditionality). At the turn of the Millennium, it became clear that 'micro'-conditionality was ineffective. It was replaced by conditionality based on 'policy ownership'. This refers to a commitment to a programme of policies by country officials who then have the responsibility to formulate and carry out these policies, based on their understanding that the programme is achievable and is in the country's best interest (see also Vreeland 2007: 127).

In contrast to the World Bank and IMF, the World Trade Organization is not a specialized agency of the UN. It does not claim to have any effects on social policy. In 1996 it rejected the idea of being responsible for labour standards. It argued that this is the task of the International Labour Organization (ILO) which is seen as a complementary organization. But the WTO does have social policy effects. Certain WTO decisions on patents for drugs of Western firms, for example, have enormous secondary effects on the health care system in poorer countries (Stiglitz 2002; Deacon 2007). In addition, liberalizing international trade increased the importance of competitiveness of national industries which in turn is also a function of the social policy system and its financing. Hence WTO trade policy has strong but indirect impacts on the room for manoeuvre of national welfare state policies (Hoekman and Mavroidis 2007, www.wto.org). Founded in 1995, WTO continues the former General Agreement on Tariffs and Trade (GATT) and adds a General Agreement on Trade in Services (GATS) and the Agreement on Trade-related Aspects of Intellectual Property Rights (TRIPs). As of 2009, 153 national governments were members of the WTO. The organization is governed by bi-annual meetings of member governments. The operative work is decided upon by the General Council. Based in Geneva, this is the WTO's highest level decision-making body. It has representatives (usually ambassadors or equivalent) from all member governments and has the authority to act on behalf of the ministerial conference. It is supported by a small secretariat. Decisions are usually made by consensus. Each member has one vote and each vote has equal weight, unlike in the IMF and the World Bank. Unanimity is required for amendments of core rules (such as the most favoured nation principle), a two-thirds majority is needed for other issues, and a simple majority is sufficient for all cases not specified and in case of failure to reach consensus (Hoekman and Mavroidis 2007: 26).

The Organization for Economic Development and Co-operation is based on a membership of thirty governments of the more economically developed countries which also claim to be democratic. (Sullivan 1997; www.oecd.org). The major decision-making body is the Council. It is made up of one representative per member country, plus a representative of the European Commission. The Council meets regularly at the level of permanent representatives to the OECD. Decisions are taken by consensus. The Council meets at ministerial level once a year to discuss key issues and set priorities for OECD work. The work mandated by the Council is carried out by the OECD Secretariat. It is a relatively small organization with 2,500 employees and an annual budget of €343 million. The main purpose of the OECD is to diffuse 'best practice' by information, consultation, and surveillance (Marcussen 2004). The OECD issues many types of reports and analyses; arguably the 'Economic Surveys' of the member countries are one of the cornerstones of its activity. Initially, the OECD focused on economic policies such as the business cycle or monetary policy, but it has increasingly become concerned with policies closely related to national welfare regimes. This applies to active and passive labour market policy, fiscal policy with its implications for social security schemes, and educational policy (Martens and Weymann 2007).

The International Labour Organization was founded in 1919 (www.ilo.org). It is a specialized UN agency, based on 182 national memberships. Its main official aims are to promote rights at work, encourage decent employment opportunities, enhance social protection, and strengthen dialogue in handling work-related issues. It has a tripartite structure representing national governments, trade unions, and employers' organizations. The major decision body is the International Labour Conference. It meets once a year. From each member country two representatives of the government and one representative from labour unions and employers' associations respectively are delegated to the conference. The International Labour Conference decides on Conventions and Recommendations. Each member state is required to submit them to the competent national authorities for a decision on action to be taken. In other words, an international organization has the right to put an issue on the social policy agenda of a national parliament. Once accepted, the ILO monitors the implementation of these national laws. The governing body is composed of twenty-eight government members, fourteen trade union members, and fourteen employer members. The work of the ILO is supported by a secretariat, the International Labour Office. 1,900 officials work for the ILO. In addition 600 experts work in projects of technical cooperation with countries. On average, US$130 million has been spent on these projects annually.

RESOURCES, STANDARDS, IDEAS,
AND INFORMATION

How do IOs attempt to influence national systems of welfare? At least three channels can be distinguished. IOs can give resources to nation states for welfare purposes or they may hinder nation states from using their resources for social policy schemes. A second mode is by setting standards and creating rules. This may result in more or fewer rules and standards than hitherto applied at the national level. And finally, IOs may diffuse ideas and information, thus helping to frame the outlook and options of national policymakers.

Social policies depend on resources. IOs may give resources to countries in order to support welfare states. This mode is of minor relevance for two reasons. First, most IOs have limited budgets that only provide for small, targeted programmes and the running of the organization. Major exceptions are the IMF, with annual resources of US$333,000 million in 2008, and the World Bank Group, which distributes annually about US$25,000 million to member countries and has an operating budget of US$2,100 million (Marshall 2008: 4). In contrast, the WHO's budget of 2008 amounted to US$4,227 million; the ILO spent US$146 million in FY 2002/3; the WTO disposed of 184 million Swiss Francs in 2008; and the OECD had a budget of €343 million in 2008.[1] Second, these expenditures are only marginally earmarked for social spending purposes. The expenditures and loans by the World Bank are not intended to support national welfare schemes, except for social security safety nets (means tested social assistance) and 'socially responsible investment', and IMF loans are intended to spur economic growth—with its alleged functions of poverty reduction—by promoting financial stability.

More important are the activities of IOs that hinder national governments from using domestic resources for social policy. The major example is IMF conditionality. The IMF makes loans to countries dependent on their making cuts in public expenditure, which often impact on education and social security. It is a major argument of critics of the World Bank and of the IMF that the use of their resources has increased rather than decreased social inequality (Marshall 2008: 145; Vreeland 2003; Toussaint 2008; Deacon 2007). Since IMF and World Bank resources are

---

[1] Sources: see websites of these organizations.

generally used in less developed countries, this effect is of minor importance for this review, which focuses on the richer and democratic nations. However, a few countries in the Western world have been subject to IMF conditionality; and Eastern European countries have experienced much IMF conditionality since the early 1990s (Stone 2002). According to Nooruddin and Simmons (2006), the effects of such conditionality are similar in autocratic and democratic nations. They argue that democracies tend to use more resources for social security than autocracies; however under IMF programmes the difference between democracies and non-democracies disappears.

For the richer democracies, resources for welfare state development from IOs are less important than the imposition of standards, which can require more social security effort. The ILO and its conventions and recommendations are the major examples of this type of policy steering (Senti 2001). The OECD may also require higher education spending and better education standards (Martens and Weymann 2007) or more active labour market policies (Armingeon 2007). But when IOs criticize national governments for excessive public expenditures for education, social security, or labour market regulations, and make recommendations for cuts, as the OECD, the IMF, and the World Bank often do, policies are steered in the opposite direction, social security standards are dismantled, and social standards are generally downgraded. It is in this sense that the IMF and World Bank are also important to rich and democratic nations. The IMF preaches lean states; the World Bank together with the OECD has warned against the continuation of generous and supposedly unsustainable pension schemes.

Finally, IOs may use ideas and information in order to influence national welfare state policy. The most typical case is the OECD, which lacks the resources (and the ensuing conditionality) of the IMF and World Bank and which also lacks the institutional means of standard setting and diffusion of the ILO. For the OECD, little is left but propagating ideas and supplying information. It has been described as a typical broker of ideas (Marcussen 2004; Kildal 2009). One category of ideas diffused by IOs has a strong normative bent, for example the ILO's insistence on 'decent work' or 'fair globalization'. Likewise, the IMF and World Bank were instrumental in developing the so called 'Washington Consensus' in the 1990s, articulating a kind of market fundamentalism and providing strong criticism of any state-led economic redistribution.

In a much less ideological way, ideas may develop as epistemic communities are created or supported by IOs. An epistemic community is 'a network of professionals with recognized expertise and competence in a particular domain and an authoritative claim to policy-relevant knowledge ... They have (1) a shared set of normative and principled beliefs ...; (2) shared causal beliefs, which are derived from their analysis of practices ... (3) shared notions of validity ... and (4) a common policy enterprise' (Haas 1992: 3). All the IOs under study have nurtured such epistemic communities. The clearest example may be found at the OECD which has built up international networks of economists working for national governments or the OECD (Armingeon and Beyeler 2004). Finally IOs generate, gather, and publish information that is essential for given policy fields. Examples are abundant. The World Bank publishes data for the comparison of public sector size and inequality; the OECD supplies high quality data in all fields of economic and social policies for their member states; and the ILO reports systematically about labour laws and standards around the globe. These data allow for more objective comparisons and evaluations of national welfare efforts, problems, and shortcomings. They are not only indispensable for scientific research, but also for political debate.

IMPACTS AND IMPLICATIONS

Given their enormous political and scientific impact, there is surprisingly little systematic research on the interaction between IOs and national welfare policies. In this section, we summarize some of the findings of the research that does exist.

One major concern has been the impact of IOs on domestic social policies. In particular, researchers have analysed whether the neoliberal turn in IOs since the 1980s—as exemplified by the idea of a 'Washington Consensus'—led to welfare retrenchment at the domestic level. Surprisingly, many empirical analyses have failed to identify any substantial influence. Castles and Obinger (Castles 2007a; Castles and Obinger 2008) have shown that there is no convergence between welfare regimes in the EU 27 and the established democracies of the non-European OECD country group. Comparing welfare states in Latin America, East Asia, and Eastern Europe, Haggard and Kaufman (2008: 350) could 'see very little evidence that international political forces ... are leading to a homogenization of social policy'. A project on the OECD's impact on national welfare reforms could not provide strong empirical evidence for a direct and powerful influence of OECD advice on national welfare reforms (Armingeon 2004). If a country adopts new social policy ideas, 'peer' countries seem to be more important than IOs (Brooks 2005, 2007). Finally, national political actors may use IOs recommendations and ideas in a pragmatic and incoherent way in order to legitimize their own political strategies; while other arguments by IOs are disregarded if they do not fit into the actual domestic strategy.

These findings are disputed. Supporting the political criticism of the 'anti-globalization' movement, Deacon (2007) argues that the IMF, World Bank, and ILO have become more involved in prescribing country policy. Trade liberalization, the core of the WTO's activities, tends to create a global private market in social provision and thereby undermines state-based national welfare regimes. Strang and Mei Ying Chan showed that countries that adopt ILO conventions increase their social security spending (Strang and Mei Yin Chang 1993). This fits with findings that, in general, international treaties and IO membership can make a difference for national policy (Simmons 2009; but see also the controversy between von Stein 2005 and Simmons and Hopkins 2005). In addition, national politicians tend not to give credit to IOs for reforms that prove successful and which they would like to claim as their own. In these cases, IOs are important brokers of ideas and information (Marcussen 2004), and pertinent to policy change, but they often go unnoticed because of the electoral imperatives which drive national political actors to claim all the credit. For example, Lindén argues that German family policy is strongly influenced by the OECD and EU, but politicians do not admit this openly (Lindén 2009).

Some of these differences in research findings on the impact of IOs on national social policy are the result of variable methodologies, case selection, and the type of empirical evidence. Some of the contradictory results can also be attributed to different conceptualizations of the ways in which IOs have an impact on national policies. There may be instances of direct impacts, where an IO has a clear norm and forces member states to adhere to this norm. But there may also be diffusion processes: a rule set by an IO is accepted in one country and diffused from there to other countries which are close in geographic or socio-economic terms (Jahn 2006; Simmons and Elkins 2004). There may also be endogeneity, good examples of which are countries that ratify ILO norms provided they already meet the standards before ratification (Senti 2001). In such cases, the correlation between international norms and domestic policies has not the assumed causal status since IO action has not caused the national reform.

Finally the impact of an organization can be indirect and hard to measure. If the IMF forces a country to cut its public expenditures, this may, but does not necessarily, lead to welfare retrenchment. Within the room for manoeuvre allowed by the Fund, one government will save on—say—agricultural subsidies and the other on pensions or public employment. This resembles the indirect and conditionally negative effects on welfare spending which researchers have identified for the case of the Maastricht Treaty in EU member states. There is pressure to reduce expenditures and in some countries this may result in welfare state retrenchment (Leibfried 2005). The influence of the WTO on social policy is mainly indirect, after attempts in 1996 to incorporate labour standards into the set of rules failed. The major social policy effects of the WTO, Deacon (2007) argues, are via the privatization of public services, the liberalization of social services, and the effects of the WTO treaty on intellectual property rights, which endanger the generic pharmaceutical industry in poor countries and hence raise the price of drugs in these countries.

Findings about impacts also reflect the different use of 'hard' versus 'soft' law. 'Hard' law is precise, rules are obligatory, and some functions of interpretation, monitoring, and implementation are delegated to a third party (Goldstein et al. 2000: 387). 'Soft' law does not fully meet at least one of these three criteria (Abbott and Snidal 2000: 422). Soft law can be more efficient than hard law, if the latter generates large costs, for example in terms of non-compliance or domestic conflicts. Soft law allows also for more flexible adaptation to country-specific needs. The Open Method of Coordination (OMC) of the European Union or the mixture of surveillance and persuasion by OECD are examples of extremely soft rules applied by IOs (Schäfer 2005; Schäfer 2006a). While soft law avoids many problems of hard law, by implication it can be so soft that it does not make a difference. Interestingly, in the cases of both the neoliberal IMF and the conservative-social ILO, hard law seems to be on the retreat. Both organizations learnt that their hard and very detailed law did not work as expected (Hassel 2008; Vreeland 2007) and have turned to soft regulation. In the case of the IMF, this generated the idea of 'policy ownership', which gives countries ample opportunity to adjust IMF norms to domestic needs and local practice. Reacting to an uneven pattern of ratifications of conventions—with poorer countries and the United States avoiding ratifications—and the criticism of 'too many standards, and too little effect' (Hassel 2008: 237), the ILO has recently focused on core labour standards, which are based around four rights (the freedom of association and the effective recognition of collective bargaining, elimination of all forms of forced or compulsory labour, abolition of child labour, elimination of (gender) discrimination regarding employment and occupation). These principles lack traditional enforcement mechanisms. The more such rules by IOs become 'soft', the more difficult it is to measure the extent to which member countries actually adhere to this now-malleable body of norms.

A related problem in pinning down the effects of IOs is the change of ideas held and propagated by IOs across time. The OECD developed from an organization which was strongly influenced by Keynesian ideas to a more liberal institution but has more recently stressed the contribution of social policy and social partnership to growth and competitiveness (Armingeon 2004; Deacon 2007: 57–61; Sullivan 1997). The World Bank contributed to the coining of the 'Washington Consensus', but then it retreated from this position by emphasizing social networks and equity for poorer nations (Marshall 2008: ch. 2; Ramesh 2007). Even the IMF has recently started to stress the goal of poverty prevention and watered down the 'Consensus' (Deacon 2007; Vetterlein 2007). Before turning into one of the major institutions of the Washington Consensus in the 1990s, IMF policy was based on Keynesian economics (Stiglitz 2002: ch. 1).

Social policy ideas do not only change within IOs due to internal debates. Rather IOs interact with each other, spreading ideas and norms. The international discourse on pensions policy took place between the World Bank, the OECD, and the ILO (Ervik 2009; Maier-Rigaud 2009). There is competition for ideational leadership. Schiller et al. (2009) show how the WHO has lost influence over health policies due to the increasing role of the WTO and the World Bank. Hence IO influence is sometimes mediated via other IOs.

Evaluating the effect of IOs on domestic welfare policies sometimes assumes a one-way influence from IOs to nation states. However there is strong empirical evidence of uneven 'uploading' from the national to the international level. Nation states try to establish their national standards as international standards. This may give them a competitive advantage or can help them to avoid the danger of dumping strategies by competitor economies with lower social standards. An instructive example is the emphasis on active labour market policy in the European Union which is linked to a Swedish initiative. Likewise, Senti (2001) argued that national actors support those ILO conventions that correspond to their own domestic standards. With regard to the IMF and World Bank, the United States has been accused of instrumentalizing these IOs for their domestic purposes. It is argued that the US unilaterally framed IMF and World Bank policy (Marshall 2008: 140; Stiglitz 2002: ch. 1). A recent statistical analysis of IMF loans found that, in the case of countries that are strategically important to the United States, it exerts some influence on defining the conditionality of IMF loans (Stone 2008).

The effect of IOs—and in particular the effects on welfare state retrenchment—may also be overestimated since national politicians pursue strategies of blame avoidance not only at the domestic level (P. Pierson 1994) but also in two-level games (Putnam 1993) in the interplay of IOs and nation states. For example, according to a well-known criticism of IMF loans, the Fund forces countries to change their social policies. However, every country is free to request or not to request IMF support in a critical economic situation. Vreeland (2003) argues that national politicians frequently just opt for the IMF loan in order to realize necessary social policy reform, which would be otherwise costly in electoral terms. Putting the blame on the IMF allows the government to pursue its reform policy without running the risk of electoral punishment. An illustration may be the austerity measures in Latvia in early 2009.

A final aspect of the interaction between IOs and national welfare states concerns the democratic deficit. Voting rights in the World Bank and the IMF are a function of national subscription, giving large countries—and in particular the United States—more power than small countries. In the ILO, the OECD, or the WTO, each country has the same voting rights irrespective of population size or economic power. Both rules are in conflict with democratic norms (cf. Zürn 2007). The welfare state has been a major field of domestic political contention. Assuming that IOs have some influence on national social policy, it is remarkable that a large and important segment of national democratic politics is shifted outside the realm of transparency and democracy. This is the more problematic since some of these policy decisions at the level of IOs have only indirect social policy effects and are legitimized on grounds of technical effectiveness or with regard to other goals (cf. Toussaint 2008). The democratic problem also becomes obvious if IOs develop a life of their own. In an analysis of the OECD, Martens and Weymann (2007) argued that governments turn to IOs since they can help in a particular situation—in their example, in education policy. But once given a mandate for a particular policy this may create a self-propelling dynamic and give to the IOs powers at the international level which originally the nation state had not intended (Martens and Weymann 2007).

CHAPTER 22

....

GLOBALIZATION

....

DUANE SWANK

INTRODUCTION
....

TODAY, it is clear that welfare states in rich democracies have not converged around an Anglo-liberal model of modest benefits, extensive means-testing, and significant private insurance and services (e.g. Starke et al. 2008; Scruggs and Allan 2008); welfare state trajectories in developing political economies also exhibit substantial variety (e.g. Haggard and Kaufman 2008). Yet, welfare states have been subject to market-oriented reforms: for social insurance, governments have periodically rolled back entitlement rights and income replacement rates, increased targeting of benefits, and encouraged private insurance; budget caps, internal markets, and other efficiency-oriented reforms have been commonplace in services (e.g. Castles 2004; Huber and Stephens 2001a; Swank 2002). New policy initiatives for labour market activation, 'flexicurity', and, in unequivocally neoliberal terms, 'workfare', have also been widespread (e.g. Martin 2004; Zeitlin and Trubek 2003). A fundamental question for social scientists has been—and continues to be—whether or not economic globalization has significantly influenced these reforms.

In the pages to follow, I offer a synopsis of the central theoretical arguments that link economic globalization (i.e. international market integration) to welfare state change and review the best research on the topic. The primary limitation on the scope of the chapter is that I will focus on empirical work that is explicitly comparative and quantitative in nature; a vast qualitative case-study literature on contemporary welfare states also addresses the impact of globalization. Any systematic

Author's note: I would like to acknowledge the exceptional research assistance of Craig Shockley and Jason Charrette.

inclusion of this literature would, however, far exceed space constraints.[1] On the other hand, this chapter seeks breadth by addressing a range of theories that link globalization to welfare state change, and by engaging scholarly work on the first (i.e. pre-World War I) wave of globalization and early welfare states as well as research on both contemporary developed and developing political economies. After an overview of the central theoretical issues and an assessment of empirical research, I will highlight a number of promising trends in the literature that should improve understanding of globalization's consequences for national systems of social protection.

THEORIES OF GLOBALIZATION
AND THE WELFARE STATE

....

Much of the burgeoning research on globalization and the welfare state in the 1990s was motivated by the familiar 'race to the bottom' thesis: economic globalization inexorably pressures developed nation policymakers to roll back generous and inclusive social protection; developing nation policymakers are similarly pressured to forego improvements in social insurance and services and adopt market-oriented systems of social protection. Yet, the absence of clear evidence of these sorts of policy effects led scholars by the late 1990s to resurrect a prominent theory of political economy from earlier decades: international market integration should actually generate demands for new insurance against heightened risks and compensation for losers of international competition. At the same time, scholars began advancing new theories about how domestic institutions should mediate the impacts of globalization on welfare-related preferences and political economic capacities of sectors and classes. Although familiar, a synopsis of theory is nevertheless important.

The Race to Market-Conforming Social Policy

Classic (e.g. Smith 1976 [1776]) as well as contemporary scholars (e.g. McKenzie and Lee 1991; Strange 1996; Scharpf 2000a) have famously argued that heightened internationalization of markets, especially international capital mobility, will constrain the ability of governments to sustain generous systems of pubic social protection.

---

[1] The qualitative literature parallels the large-N quantitative literature in the ways it frames the globalization question and in its empirical results. See, for representative examples, Bleses and Seeleib-Kaiser (2004), Hinnfors (2006), Rieger and Leibfried (2003), and, for detailed case studies in large-N quantitative analysis, Brooks (2009), Huber and Stephens (2001a), Rudra (2008), Segura-Ubiergo (2007), and Swank (2002).

In this theory, the impact of economic globalization on the welfare state is channelled through three basic mechanisms (Swank 2002; 2003; also see Garrett 1998*a*; 1998*b*; and Hay and Rosamond 2002). The first, what might be called the 'economic logic of globalization', entails the notion that increases in international capital mobility limit, through the consequences of economic choices by firms, an incumbent government's ability to manoeuvre to achieve social welfare goals. Technology-based reductions in transactions costs and the liberalization of national restrictions on capital movements enable mobile asset holders to pursue globally the highest rate of return on investment. If policymakers fail to achieve international coordination of economic and social policies (a highly likely outcome), they are confronted by a prisoner's dilemma: policymakers in each nation are faced with strong incentives to compete to secure mobile assets through reductions in social spending and the taxes that finance the welfare state. Trade openness also potentially pressures policymakers to roll back social insurance and services in order to reduce labour costs, public debt, and interest rates, and general disincentives to work and invest. In other words, economic globalization forces incumbent governments of all ideological stripes to pursue efficiency-oriented social policy reforms.

Alternatively, the 'political logic' of globalization stresses, first, that internationalization may lead to reductions in social protection through conventional democratic politics. Specifically, the credible threat of capital flight may significantly bolster the electoral and organizational resources of capital. For instance, enterprises and their interest associations often pressure policymakers for welfare retrenchment by arguing that the welfare state negatively affects profits, investment, and job creation and by citing the comparative advantages of foreign investment environments. Second, increases in trade and capital openness increase the rhetorical appeal of neoliberal economic orthodoxy. That is, liberal parties as well as business economists and interest group spokespersons commonly use the 'economic logic' of globalization when arguing for efficiency-enhancing policy reforms.

The Compensation Thesis

The major alternative to the conventional 'race to the bottom' argument consists of the 'compensation thesis', or what one might call a new theory of embedded liberalism (Polanyi 1944). As the study of contemporary international market integration intensified, scholars looked to earlier seminal work by David Cameron (1978) and Peter Katzenstein (1985), most notably, who argued that a large welfare state enables governments to lessen insecurities and risks attendant to internationalization, and otherwise pursue flexible adjustment to international openness.[2] Others such as John

---

[2] These scholars also pointed out that trade openness is often associated structurally with highly concentrated industrial sectors and, in turn, strong trade union and employer organizations, centralized wage bargaining, and electorally successful social democratic parties. These factors are strongly correlated with welfare state development (also see, among others, Stephens 1979).

Ruggie (1982) pointed out, contra conventional globalization theory, that a multi-national regime of embedded liberalism emerged in the post-World War II era in which a liberal international trade regime was bolstered by significant levels of government intervention in markets and social insurance. Taking their lead from this work, scholarship by Geoffrey Garrett (1998a, 1998b) and Dani Rodrik (1997, 1998) stressed that the welfare state continues to provide ample social insurance against international risks to employment and income as well as compensation to those who lose from global market competition. It is also interesting to note that while compensation may come from governments concerned with re-election or social stability, compensatory social transfers may also be the product of political exchange: workers in the tradable sector of the economy may agree to support social transfers, training, and similar policies for those in the non-tradable sectors in return for support of wage restraint that benefits internationally oriented production (e.g. Garrett and Lange 1995). The pre-World War I development of social protection may have been influenced by agreements between labour-oriented and liberal parties and groups where labour agreed to support tariff reduction in return for social compensation (Huberman and Lewchuck 2003; Huberman 2008).

Domestic Institutions and the Divergent Impacts of Globalization

A third major perspective on the welfare state impacts of globalization also developed in the mid- to late 1990s. Following Gourevitch (1986) and Rogowski (1989), most notably, Garrett and Lange (1995), in the most comprehensive sketch of this approach, argued that globalization should significantly influence in predictable ways the preferences and political economic capacities of sectors and classes in capitalist democracies. Yet, the extent to which, for example, producers in the tradeable sector emerge as a dominant actor in policy making, and the extent to which the state may still pursue its preferred policies, will fundamentally hinge on domestic political economic institutions. Garrett and Lange highlighted features of labour market institutions, electoral and representative systems, and formal institutional veto points as the central institutional conduits for the pressures unleashed by economic globalization.

A central example of this approach is Swank (2002). Drawing on international trade theory (Hecksher-Ohlin models) and 'new' and 'old' welfare state theory, Swank argued that the pressures for retrenchment generated by internationalization would produce a mobilization by a pro-welfare state coalition of 'losers' from globalization (e.g. semi- and unskilled workers), programmatic constituencies of mature programmes, and ideological proponents of generous and inclusive social protection (e.g. left and Christian democratic parties, trade union movements). The extent to which these actors, or a neoliberal coalition of internationally oriented producers and centre and right parties and groups, would prevail is a function of domestic political institutions. Where national institutions are characterized by corporatist interest representation, inclusive electoral systems, centralized polities and universal and conservative welfare states, long-term political biases, immediate opportunity structures, and mass value systems favour maintenance of the welfare state. Globalization-induced retrenchment should occur in pluralist, majoritarian, and fragmented polities with liberal welfare state structures.

A similar emphasis on the institutional mediation of globalization's impacts has also emerged in recent work on less developed political economies. For instance, Haggard and Kaufman (2008) and Segura-Ubiergo (2007) argue that the programmatic character of extant welfare regimes in developing nations fundamentally conditions contemporary welfare reforms under the pressure of domestic and international economic forces. Rudra (2008) draws on the literature on rich democracies to hypothesize that labour market institutions should interact with economic globalization to shape welfare reform in developing polities. Similarly, Mares (2005b) argues that external risk will generate compensatory policies only where institutions favour collective action by export-sector actors and where state capacity is high enough to make such policies possible.

Two additional arguments complement theory on political institutions. First, Burgoon (2001) suggests that globalization's welfare impacts should be differentiated by welfare programme type: openness may prompt continued compensation for workers while at the same time fostering rollbacks in areas most directly related to business costs and efficiency issues. Second, a generous welfare state is integral to the operation of coordinated market institutions (e.g. long-term product development of high-end consumer and industrial goods); it integrates labour into the political economy and promotes stable and cooperative employer–employee relations. Generous social insurance also fosters the acquisition of firm-specific skills by workers and, in turn, enhances the long-term employment commitments valued by workers and employers in coordinated market economies (Ebbinghaus and Manow 2001; Iversen 2005; also see contributions to Hall and Soskice 2001a). Thus, globalization should have muted impacts on functionally important and politically supported social protection in coordinated economies (Swank 2003).

A Note on the Indirect Welfare Consequences of Globalization

A number of additional theoretical arguments link globalization to welfare reform via indirect mechanisms. For instance, globalization has arguably eliminated some of the economic policy tools (e.g. domestic monetary policy autonomy) that allow large welfare states to maintain relatively low unemployment; subsequent rises in unemployment present challenges for generous welfare states (Huber and Stephens 2001a; Hicks and Zorn 2005). In addition, globalization may also undercut political institutions that favour pro-welfare state coalitions (Swank 2002: ch. 7). Perhaps the most important and well-researched of these theories highlights the consequences of economic internationalization for taxation. As commonly argued, globalization pressures policymakers to reduce tax burdens on mobile asset holders and high-income earners and, in turn, reduces tax revenues that fund social protection. I will return to this argument below.

DEVELOPED DEMOCRACIES: EVIDENCE FROM THE FIRST AND SECOND WAVES OF GLOBALIZATION

Research on globalization's impacts on the welfare state in the contemporary era is plentiful. Influential studies of early welfare state development, however, typically do not consider the impacts of the first wave of globalization (1860s to World War I) on social programme adoption (e.g. Hicks 1999). Yet, some work does exist. For some scholars, the first wave of globalization retarded domestic policy autonomy in most areas. For instance, Frieden (2006) emphasizes that the dictates of the gold standard heavily constrained macroeconomic and domestic policy autonomy. For others, such as Mosley (2003), the emergence of global capital markets had little bearing on domestic policies: Mosley's historical analyses suggest that the policy objectives of industrializing and democratizing nations were so meagre during the first wave, international capital markets played little attention to domestic social policies and thus, played little role in early welfare state development. On the other hand, some prominent studies (e.g. Lindert 2004) assert that expansion of social spending in the late nineteenth and early twentieth centuries explicitly offered a safety-net to workers facing new risks attendant upon international competition and capital flows.

The most direct evidence on the welfare impacts of globalization during the first wave comes from the work of economic historian Michael Huberman and collaborators. In fact, Huberman and Lewchuck (2003) provide a comprehensive empirical analysis of the impact of trade openness on labour market regulation and social insurance for seventeen European nations in 1870, 1900, and 1913. In models that control for important economic and political factors, Huberman and Lewchuck find that trade openness is significantly and positively associated with both labour market and social insurance protections. Huberman (2008) further elaborates theory and offers detailed empirical analysis of the first wave of globalization and labour protection in Belgium. In this work, Huberman suggests that while general compensation dynamics are operative, the bedrock of the positive association between globalization and welfare state development is political exchange: Belgian labour explicitly traded support for tariff reduction in return for support of increased labour market and social insurance protections by liberal parties.

Evidence on the welfare consequences of the second wave of globalization in capitalist democracies is much more abundant. Reinforcing the seminal findings of Cameron (1978), well-known studies of post-World War II welfare state expansion produced evidence of positive effects of openness on social welfare transfers as a share of GDP (e.g. Hicks and Swank 1992; Huber et al. 1993); the results from these studies, work that used increasingly sophisticated time-series cross-section (TSCS) estimators of the determinants of variation in welfare states, have been consistently reproduced in recent studies that focus on the era of welfare growth (e.g. Hicks 1999; Busemeyer 2009c). While Iversen and Cusack (2000) have offered theory and evidence that the general process of de-industrialization, and not trade openness, drove the post-World War II expansion of the welfare state, ample work continues to suggest that mechanisms highlighted by the compensation thesis were to some extent operative across industrialized democracies in the decades immediately after the war.

As the general debate on the impacts of post-1970s globalization intensified, new studies examined trajectories of the welfare state during the era of fiscal austerity (i.e. the 1980s to the 2000s). These works typically use TSCS, event history, or multiple cross-section analyses of 1980 to roughly 2000 data on social welfare policy and its determinants in 16–21 capitalist democracies. The principal focus of this work is to assess the direct effects of trade openness and capital mobility on spending or programmatic features of welfare states. While the specification of empirical models and measures of the welfare state, globalization, and other factors differ somewhat from study to study, analyses by Allan and Scruggs (2004), Brady et al. (2005), Castles (2007b), Garrett and Mitchell (1995), Hicks and Zorn (2005), Kittel and Obinger (2003), Mosley (2003), and Swank (2002), to name a large representative sample of extant studies, near universally find that the general welfare impacts of trade openness and capital mobility are substantively very weak, inconsistent in direction, or simply non-existent during the post-industrial era.

A parallel and complementary effort has assessed whether globalization forces policy convergence across social democratic and centre-right party governments. Surprising many scholars, Garrett's (1998a) seminal work revealed that the social policy differences between nations with high left-labour power and those with weak labour unions and left parties actually increased during the era of openness. The notion of persistent partisan government effects on the welfare state in the era of globalization is, nevertheless, controversial. Huber and Stephens (2001a), Kittel and Obinger (2003), and others have presented evidence that positive social democratic (and Christian democratic) party government impacts on social protection decline or disappear in the 1990s and beyond. Others scholars have emphatically rejected these claims. Influential work by Korpi and Palme (2003), analysis that uses precise measures of social citizenship entitlements, shows that the probability of significant 1980s and 1990s retrenchment of the welfare state is notably lower in periods of social democratic government than during centre-right party rule regardless of the level of globalization. Recent work by Cao et al. (2007) suggests right party governments increase industrial subsidies (but not social protection) under pressures of external risks; left governments distinctively respond to significant increases in openness with increases in social protection (but not industrial subsidies). Finally, Kwon and Pontusson (2008) offer a possible reconciliation of these diverse findings and bring the research back to political factors first stressed by Garrett. In a comprehensive analysis of partisan effects on welfare spending from 1962 to 2000, these authors find that left party government effects on the welfare state disappear under high globalization where labour power is in decline; where labour power is strong and stable, left parties continue to have a positive effect on social protection as globalization advances.

An additional set of studies anticipates the institutional mediation of globalization. Swank (2002) assesses the impact of five dimensions of international capital mobility on social policy in the 1980s and 1990s and finds that the explosion of capital markets is associated with welfare retrenchment in pluralist, majoritarian, and decentralized polities and liberal welfare state contexts; capital mobility is typically positively associated with social protection in universal and conservative welfare states as in polities characterized by corporatism, consensus democratic institutions and centralized states. Complementary results are reported by Swank (2003) on the importance of varieties of capitalism: globalization has positive or null effects on social protection in coordinated political economies, and negative impacts in liberal market economies. Other studies such as Ha (2008) also suggest that domestic institutions are important: positive effects of international capital mobility on social protection diminish as institutional veto points increase in strength. On the other hand, in a comprehensive analysis of welfare impacts of multiple dimensions of trade and capital openness, Brady et al. (2005) present findings that suggest there is little difference in the (generally null) effects of globalization on the welfare state across European and Anglophone nations and liberal and non-liberal welfare regimes.

Finally, a series of studies has suggested that the welfare state effects of globalization in post-industrial democracies have turned negative in recent years. Rodrik (1997), who generally finds evidence of compensation effects of globalization, reports that at high levels of capital mobility, the positive effect of trade openness on social provision turns negative in advanced democracies. Similarly, Hicks (1999) reports a curvilinear effect of capital openness where initially positive effects turn negative at high levels. In addition, Jahn (2006) provides clear evidence that welfare state impacts of greater trade openness are negative after a threshold of high globalization and economic turbulence are reached (i.e. roughly the mid-1990s on). Consistent with these findings, Busemeyer (2009c), who analyses five-year panels of developed nation data, reports the disappearance of compensation effects of openness by 1995 and after.

In sum, extant research on globalization and national systems of social protection in the developed democracies suggests the initial late nineteenth- and early twentieth-century development of the welfare state and the era of dramatic welfare expansion in the decades immediately after World War II were shaped to an extent by the impulse to offer insurance against risks and to compensate losers of international competition as well as by the dynamics of political exchange. The post-1970s explosion of international market integration did not, however, result in comparable expansions of social protection. On the other hand, neither did the notable economic globalization of this period produce a race to the bottom. While globalization has in all likelihood been associated with reductions in social protection in Anglo-liberal political economies, and while recent rises in openness may be related to contemporary declines in welfare provision, the small substantive magnitudes of the statistical effects and limited actual changes in programmatic features of welfare states indicate that cross-national differences among developed welfare states remain very prominent today. Moreover, as Brady et al. (2005) have recently put it (also see, among others, P. Pierson 2001b), whatever impacts globalization has had on national welfare states in recent years are dwarfed by the impact of domestic economic and political factors. Are these conclusions sustainable for the developing political economies?

LESS DEVELOPED NATIONS: EVIDENCE FROM DEVELOPING AND TRANSITION ECONOMIES

Scholars have typically approached the study of the welfare impacts of globalization in less developed countries (LDCs) with the expectation that openness would have more dire consequences for social protection than in rich democracies. This is so despite Rodrik's (1997, 1998) relatively early work that suggested external risks (trade openness weighted by the volatility of terms of trade) were positively associated with social security spending in LDCs. Yet, most scholars have followed the position articulated by, among others, Mosley (2003) and Wibbels (2006) that things should be different for LDCs. Mosley's argument, supported by extensive empirical analysis, is straightforward: the impact of international capital markets on domestic social and economic policies should be strong but narrow for developed democracies: with virtually no risk of default, international investors monitor, and respond to, a few primary economic indicators (i.e. inflation and budget balances); welfare states are not significantly affected. For LDCs, the risk of default is substantial and capital markets monitor and respond to a broad array of domestic policy signals, including social spending. Race-to-the-bottom pressures on LDC welfare states are quite real. Wibbels (2006) reinforces this line of reasoning by arguing that while the shocks and volatility associated with globalization can be absorbed by rich democracies, the fiscal, institutional, and political capacities of LDCs to do so are absent; globalization may well produce downward pressures on social protection.

Empirical research on the welfare state impacts of globalization in LDCs has increased in recent years. The seminal work of Kaufman and Segura-Ubiergo (2001) set the stage. Employing TSCS analysis of 1973 to 1997 data on Latin American welfare states, Kaufman and Segura-Ubiergo find that trade openness, and to a lesser degree capital mobility, depresses spending on social security and welfare; openness has no impacts, or small positive effects, on health and education spending. The later work of Segura-Ubiergo (2007) has reinforced these findings: using virtually identical methods but extending data to 2003, Segura-Ubiergo reports significant negative effects of trade openness on social security and positive (albeit insignificant) trade effects on health and education; capital mobility has substantively trivial positive associations with social security and no appreciable relationship with health and education.

These core findings have been replicated by Haggard and Kaufman (2008) and by Wibbels (2006). In the former study, however, the authors show that trade is actually positively associated with social security and welfare spending in Asia and unrelated to social protection in Eastern Europe.[3] In Wibbels's study, the business cycle and economic crises play important roles; trade openness has a depressing effect on social security and welfare during periods of positive and negative economic shocks; trade openness is, however, associated with reductions in human capital spending during negative shocks and is positively associated with human capital spending during 'good times'. Finally, a parallel and complementary analysis is offered by Rudra (2008). Contra Garrett (1998a), Rudra finds that for a sample of fifty-seven poor nations from 1972 to 1997, positive effects of labour power on social spending actually significantly decline (and disappear) as trade openness increases in LDCs.

On the other hand, two prominent studies have questioned the race-to-the-bottom effects of trade openness on social security and welfare in LDCs. Avelino, Brown, and Hunter (2005), utilizing TSCS analysis of 1980–99 data from nineteen Latin American nations and arguably better measures of trade (imports and export shares of GDP based on purchasing power parities) and capital openness (Quinn's (1997) index of restrictions on capital movements), find that trade is positively associated with social security and welfare as well as education spending; capital mobility is generally unrelated to social welfare. Similarly, Huber et al. (2008), in their study of 1970–2000 social spending in eighteen Latin American countries, find that trade, capital mobility, and IMF leverage are all generally unrelated to social security and welfare spending. In addition, Brooks (2009), in her study of pension privatization in Latin America, reports an absence of support for any clear version of the globalization thesis: exposure to capital flows is unrelated to the decision to privatize pensions and is actually negatively related to the magnitude of market-oriented structural change in pensions. The magnitude of World Bank loans is positively associated with the decision to privatize.

How do we reconcile these inconsistent findings? Virtually all the studies that produce support for the constraining impact of high trade openness employ Error Correction Models (ECM) where the change in social policy is modelled as a function of past social policy and past levels and changes of explanatory variables.

---

[3] In post-communist nations, Cook (2007a) illustrates that some features of internationalization such as global policy networks played a role in 1990s welfare state development. Yet, Cook makes clear that general economic globalization had only a minor if any role in welfare state change in transitional nations.

Avelino, Brown, and Hunter as well as Huber, Mustillo, and Stephens use simpler empirical specifications: the former use a simple lagged endogenous variable model while the latter models variations in levels of social policy as functions of levels of explanatory variables (by Prais-Winsten regression). The other difference is that Avelino, Brown, and Hunter utilize different measures of economic globalization and Huber, Mustillo, and Stephens use a more exhaustive set of political variables in the basic empirical model. Thus, to a degree, the current set of results will be interpreted through the lens of one's preference for particular measurement, model specification, and estimation strategies.

Two additional studies that highlight the institutional mediation of globalization pressures may shed light on these inconsistencies. First, Segura-Ubiergo (2007) finds that the negative effects of trade openness on social security and welfare are much more pronounced in 'welfare regimes', political economies characterized by statist legacies, than in 'non-welfare regimes', political economies more oriented to adjustment to market pressures. Rudra and Haggard (2005) find that negative trade effects on health, education, and social security and welfare spending in fifty-seven LDCs in the 1970s through the 1990s primarily occur in 'hard' authoritarian regimes. Trade openness is unrelated to major aggregates of social protection in relatively democratized LDCs. Thus, a tentative conclusion is that globalization may have depressed social security and welfare (although not human capital spending) in the LDCs from the 1970s primarily in authoritarian and statist regimes; in more democratic and market-oriented political economies, globalization has had little effect. The evidence certainly leans in this direction.

A Note on Globalization and the Funding Basis of the Welfare State

As discussed above, substantial research has been directed to the closely related question of whether or not economic globalization has produced a reduction of tax burdens on capital, or a general depression of tax revenues for welfare state funding. Swank (2002) and Swank and Steinmo (2002) have presented theory and evidence that while globalization has been associated with a shift of tax policy to a more market-conforming structure of lower statutory rates and broader tax bases, trade and capital openness are not related to effective tax rates on capital, labour and consumption (or total taxation). The vast majority of work in recent years reports substantively trivial, institutionally mediated, or null relationships between globalization and capital, labour, consumption, or total taxation (see Ganghof and Genschel 2008; Plümper et al. 2009; and Swank 2006 for reviews).[4]

---

[4] For reviews of work on globalization's welfare impacts via economic policy and labour market institutions, see Brady et al. (2007) and Swank (2002: ch. 7).

New Directions in Theory and Research
on Globalization and the Welfare State

....

Extant research offers significant insights into the limited, contingent, and, in many cases, null effects of economic globalization on the welfare state. Yet, two new areas of work stand out for their potential to improve our understanding of the welfare consequences of international economic integration. First, recent research has further developed the theoretical and empirical specification of the mechanisms through which globalization may shape national social policy choices. Scholars have increasingly distinguished the commonly experienced pressures from, say, past trade openness that some country 'i' independently assesses and responds to, from globalization-enhanced policy diffusion. As theory makes clear (e.g. Simmons et al. 2008; Brooks 2009), policy choices may not be independent responses to common pressures of globalization but highly interdependent responses by nations to commonly experienced phenomena. That is, social welfare reforms may diffuse. Moreover, past policy changes in nations that are internationally integrated with markets in some nation 'i' (e.g. high levels of bilateral trade) will be more important to social welfare policy choices in nation 'i' than recent policy reform in political economies that share few international flows with 'i'. Recent welfare state research by Franzese and Hays (2006) and Jahn (2006), among others, has theoretically highlighted the importance of separating general and diffusion-based impacts of globalization and have produced evidence that past social policy choices in internationally integrated partner-nations are important impulses for policy reform. Finally, scholars have further distinguished general and diffusion-based globalization effects on the one hand, from the potentially important interaction between levels of global integration and the degree of international market volatility for some country 'i' in the recent past. For example, as Wibbels (2006) has recently shown, social policy responses to globalization during periods of negative international shocks may well be different than in 'good times'. In sum, the scholarship that more precisely discriminates between the basic mechanisms that link international market integration to national social policy choices holds substantial promise.

Second, recent work has increasingly focused on the important yet under-studied question of how, precisely, economic globalization affects the social welfare preferences of individuals, specific sectors, classes, and the interest associations and political parties that represent them. This research has tended to support the compensation thesis. In an explicit study of the micro-foundations of compensation, Hays et al. (2005) utilize individual-level (and macro-level) data to assess the impact of social insurance on support for free trade and, in turn, trade-spending relationships. The authors report, for both micro- and macro-level analyses, strong evidence in favour of the embedded liberalism thesis. So too do Mayda et al. (2007): utilizing individual-level data from eighteen nations, these authors show that the positive association between risk aversion and anti-trade attitudes declines with greater levels of government spending. Relatedly, Hellwig et al. (2008) report the results of experiments that show support for free trade is grounded in the relatively widespread belief among citizens that governments have substantial room to manoeuvre to cushion themselves from threats to income and employment.

Recent research has also begun to explore whether and how globalization is manifest in new national cleavage dimensions (e.g. between winners and losers of internationalization) as well as coalitions and party alignments and programmatic orientations (see, among others, contributions to Kriesi et al. 2008). This work suggests that while globalization has created new coalitions and intensified conflicts that cross-cut traditional (e.g. class) cleavages, mainstream parties have not dramatically altered traditional programmatic orientations. Substantial opportunity exists in this line of research to gain new insights into the politics that undergird the contemporary impacts of globalization on welfare states and on broader patterns of social solidarity both in post-industrial democracies and in developing and transitional political economies around the world.

PART V

POLICIES

....

CHAPTER 23

SOCIAL EXPENDITURE AND REVENUES

....

HERBERT OBINGER

UWE WAGSCHAL

INTRODUCTION

....

THE budget is a sort of fingerprint of government. The innumerable figures listed therein not only tell us about a government's political priorities, but also reflect the preferences and demands of the population. Admittedly, politicians do not struggle for social spending per se, but most political conflicts in advanced democracies are related to the allocation of public resources to particular public policies. Tracing the budget composition over time illustrates the changing role played by the state in society. While at the beginning of the twentieth century a significant part of public spending was devoted to the military, more than 50 per cent of total public spending is today absorbed by the welfare state in the OECD area. The huge rise in social spending in the course of the twentieth century has not only contributed to a significant increase of the total outlays of government (Tanzi and Schuknecht 2000; Lindert 2004; Castles 2006) but has also been a major factor shaping the growth of the tax state in the post-war period.

This chapter focuses on both the expenditures and the revenues of the welfare state. Using the latest data available we depict and analyse major developments in social spending and public revenues in twenty-one advanced democracies since 1980. We discuss measurement issues and shed light on the determinants of cross-national differences in spending and revenue levels identified in the literature. Our argument is that spending and revenue figures, irrespective of shortcomings noted subsequently, provide important indicators of both the logic and pattern of welfare state development over the period.

Social Expenditure

Unlike other public policy areas, comparative welfare state research has benefited from the early availability of cross-national expenditure data compiled by international organizations such as the ILO and the OECD. Hence social spending has been widely utilized to map the size of the welfare state and to examine the factors accounting for the cross-national variance of welfare effort. However, the use of social expenditure as the dependent variable is not without its critics. Probably, the best known critique is that of Esping-Andersen (1990:19), who points out that spending levels provide little or no insight into the ways in which public monies are distributed. Given this, he and other scholars in the 'power resources' tradition have recommended a focus on the extent to which social rights are guaranteed by national welfare systems, with decommodification and social benefit generosity seen as offering better yardsticks of 'the theoretical substance of welfare states' than aggregate social expenditure.

However, since 1990, the time at which Esping-Andersen wrote, the quality of social expenditure data has improved remarkably. A milestone in this respect was the compilation of the Social Expenditure Data Set (SOCX) by the OECD in the mid-1990s. This database provides internationally comparable statistics on public and (mandatory and voluntary) private social expenditure. The latest version of the database (OECD 2008g) covers thirty OECD countries for the period 1980–2005 and breaks down social spending into nine programme categories. While older versions only included gross spending data, the most recent issue also contains estimates of net total social spending for twenty-six OECD countries in 2005. Given this remarkably improved data availability, we argue that social expenditure analysis offers important insights into the composition of the social budget and the public–private, social policy mix chosen by different countries. In a nutshell, social spending is valuable in helping us understand 'what welfare states do' (Castles 2009a) and how welfare states are organized. However, social expenditure is certainly 'not enough' (Castles 1994b) for mapping all relevant dimensions of the welfare state (Amenta 1993). Social expenditure is, therefore, just one, but as we shall argue, an important aspect of the dependent variable in comparative social policy research.

Trends and Patterns in Social Spending since 1980

Table 23.1 summarizes the main social expenditure indicators for twenty-one long-term OECD member states. With a view to identifying similarities and differences in social spending across welfare regimes, this table groups countries into four families of nations (Castles 1993). These families show a strong overlap with the three welfare regimes suggested by Esping-Andersen with the exception that a separate Southern country cluster is distinguished and that Japan and Switzerland, two classic welfare state hybrids, are not assigned to any of these families.

An examination of the figures for gross public social expenditure (columns 1–2) and the summary statistics reported in the last rows of Table 23.1 reveals that gross public social spending increased between 1980 and 2005 in all but two countries (Ireland and the Netherlands). The increase of almost five percentage points of GDP on average suggests anything but a race to the bottom. Even though cross-national differences in spending have declined since 1980, the contemporary variance is still impressive and fits the traditional league table notion of a Nordic and continental vanguard of big spenders and an English-speaking rearguard of countries with the lowest expenditure levels.

The most important reason for convergence in gross spending levels is a strong catch-up of the formerly low spending countries of southern Europe and disproportionately high spending growth in Japan and Switzerland. This picture of a continuous growth of the welfare state appears still more dramatic if social spending per capita (columns 6–7) and the share of social spending in total government spending (4–5) are examined. Whereas average social spending per head has more than doubled since 1980, the share of social spending in total government expenditure increased from 39 per cent in 1980 to well over 52 per cent in 2005.

Since total outlays of government have decreased in many countries over the last two decades (at least until the advent of the global financial crisis), the growing weight of social spending in the public budget implies that the welfare state has crowded out expenditure on other public policies. The welfare state has therefore proved much more immune to expenditure retrenchment than other public policy areas such as education, defence, and economic affairs (see Castles 2007a). It would, however, be entirely misleading to conclude that cutbacks of social benefits have not occurred. In fact, as Korpi and Palme (2003) have demonstrated, significant benefit cutbacks have taken place in numerous countries despite rising social expenditure. The reason is simply that needs have grown faster than spending levels (see Chapter 38).

In respect of private social expenditure, country coverage is sufficient to depict basic trends since 1990 (columns 8–11). The OECD distinguishes between voluntary and mandatory private social expenditure (see Chapter 8 for details). Voluntary social expenditure includes (1) benefits offered by privately operated programmes which involve redistributive effects and (2) tax-advantaged individual plans or collective support arrangements such as employment-related pension and health plans. Mandatory private spending includes social provision mandated by legislation but which is operated by private actors such as employers.

Table 23.1 Trends in social expenditure (1980–2005)

Country	(1) Gross public 1980	(2) Gross public 2005	(3) Net total 2005	(4) Gross public/total govt. spending 1980	(5) Gross public/total govt. spending 2005	(6) [a] Public expenditure per head 1980	(7) [a] Public expenditure per head 2005	(8) Vol. private 1990	(9) Vol. private 2005	(10) Mand. private 1990	(11) Mand. private 2005
Australia	10.6	17.1	19.3	31.4	49.2	1979	5154	0.9	2.6	0.0	1.1
Canada	13.7	16.5	20.7	32.7	56.8	2864	5117	3.3	5.5	na	na
Ireland	16.7	16.7	16.1	30.7	49.4	1891	5723	1.4	1.3	na	na
New Zealand	17.2	18.5	16.4	n.a	46.4	2737	4367	0.2	0.4	na	na
UK	16.7	21.3	25.9	35.9	64.2	2768	6093	4.8	6.3	0.3	0.8
USA	13.1	15.9	25.3	39	43.6	2894	5779	7.1	9.8	0.5	0.3
English family	14.7	17.7	20.6	33.9	51.6	2522	5372	2.9	4.3	0.3	0.7
Austria	22.5	27.2	23.5	45.2	54.7	4315	8285	1.1	1	1.2	0.9
Belgium	23.5	26.4	26.8	42	50.7	4458	7695	1.6	4.5	0	0
France	20.8	29.2	29	45.4	54.4	3744	7695	1.7	2.6	0.2	0.4
Germany	22.7	26.7	27	n.a	57.2	3580	7109	1.5	1.9	1.6	1.1
Netherlands	24.8	20.9	24.1	44.9	46.2	4764	6355	5.6	7.6	0.4	0.7
Continental family	22.9	26.1	26.1	44.4	52.6	4172	7428	2.3	3.5	0.7	0.6
Denmark	24.8	26.9	21.6	46.2	51	4685	8121	1.6	2.4	0.5	0.2
Finland	18	26.1	19.5	45	51.7	3059	7475	1.1	1.1	na	na
Norway	16.9	21.6	19.1	36.6	51.4	3623	8468	0.7	0.8	1.1	1.3
Sweden	27.1	29.4	24.8	42.7	53.2	5292	9081	1.2	2.4	na	0.4
Nordic family	21.7	26.0	21.2	42.6	51.8	4165	8286	1.1	1.7	0.8	0.6

Country	(1) Gross public 1980	(2) Gross public 2005	(3) Net total 2005	(4) Gross public/total govt. spending 1980	(5) Gross public/total govt. spending 2005	(6) [a] Public expenditure per head 1980	(7) [a] Public expenditure per head 2005	(8) Vol. private 1990	(9) Vol. private 2005	(10) Mand. private 1990	(11) Mand. private 2005
Greece	10.2	20.5	na	35	47.6	1553	4600	2.1	1.7	na	na
Italy	18	25	23.1	44.1	51.8	3123	6477	0.5	0.6	3.4	1.5
Portugal	10.2	23.1	21.4	29.8	49.7	988	3973	0.7	1.5	0.2	0.4
Spain	15.5	21.2	19.1	45.9	55.2	2011	4927	0.2	0.5	na	na
Southern family	13.5	22.4	21.2	38.7	51.1	1919	4994	0.9	1.1	1.8	0.9
Japan	10.6	18.6	20.7	30.4	64.7	1793	5053	n.a	3.3	0.3	0.5
Switzerland	13.5	20.3	na	na	57.4	3486	6549	1	1.1	4.3	7.3
Mean OECD21	17.5	22.35	22.3	39.0	52.7	3124	6385	1.9	2.8	1.0	1.1
Range	16.9	13.5	12.9	16.4	21.0	4303	5107	6.9	9.4	4.3	7.3
SD	5.3	4.3	3.6	6.2	5.4	1167	1489	1.9	2.5	1.3	1.8

Notes: All figures are expressed as percentage of GDP unless indicated otherwise.
[a] in constant prices and constant PPPs.

Source: OECD 2008g, data extracted on 11/02/2009.

As is the case for public spending, one can easily detect country clusters in terms of private spending which confirm the usual wisdom of comparative research. The English-speaking countries form the spending vanguard, whereas private spending is lowest in the Southern and Nordic families of nations. As in the case of public expenditure, private spending has increased over time. However, here there is no convergence. The increase in (voluntary) private spending has been most pronounced in those English-speaking countries where private spending had already played a prominent role in 1990. In contrast, levels of mandatory private spending decreased in the remaining families of nations. Moreover, the increase of voluntary spending in these latter countries was rather moderate despite low spending levels in 1990. We can therefore conclude that public spending was not substituted by private expenditure, with the Netherlands being the only obvious exception. Rather it seems that the increase in public social spending has been complemented by rising private expenditure, particularly in English-speaking countries.

Thanks to the massive effort of scholars like Willem Adema, the OECD now provides estimates of net social expenditure (cf. Chapter 8). The results are striking, especially if net spending is compared to gross public expenditure (columns 2 and 3 of Table 23.1). Countries such as the United States and the United Kingdom now appear in the spending vanguard, once taxes are netted out and private social expenditures are taken into account. In 2005, both countries even exceeded the Swedish *folkhemmet* in terms of social spending! Whereas the majority of English-speaking countries show higher spending levels in terms of total net social expenditure, the Nordic and Southern welfare states move downwards in the international net spending league. As a result, average levels of total net social spending are markedly more similar across the four families of nations than the levels of gross public expenditure.

The advantage of analysing net social spending is that these figures spotlight the 'hidden' (Howard 1997) or 'divided' (Hacker 2002) welfare state, which is based on 'social policies by other means' and includes tax breaks and private initiatives. In general, it seems that the major dividing line between different welfare state regimes is defined less by the extent of total welfare effort and more by differences in the public–private mix of benefit provision and the consequences thereof on distributional outcomes (see below).

As already mentioned, the SOCX-dataset breaks down total public social expenditure into nine programme categories, i.e. spending on old age, survivors, incapacity related benefits, health, family, active labour market programmes, unemployment, housing, and a residual category which includes spending on social assistance (Table 23.2). In addition, columns 10–11 of Table 23.2 show spending levels by programme type (cash vs. benefit in kind).

Disaggregated social spending provides much information about the structural make-up of welfare states and differences and similarities between the various families of nations. Spending data, for example, nicely reflect the reliance on cash transfers in Continental and Southern welfare states and their high spending levels for pensions. The main difference between the Continental and the Southern countries is

Table 23.2 Programme–related public spending in per cent of GDP (2005)

Country	(1) Old age	(2) Survivors	(3) Incapacity	(4) Health	(5) Family	(6) ALMP	(7) Unemployment	(8) Housing	(9) Others	(10) In kind	(11) Cash
Australia	4.4	0.2	2.4	5.9	2.8	0.4	0.5	0.3	0.1	8.7	8.1
Canada	3.7	0.4	0.9	6.8	1.0	0.3	0.6	0.4	2.2	9.4	6.8
Ireland	2.9	0.8	1.6	6.5	2.5	0.6	0.9	0.5	0.3	7.7	8.4
New Zealand	4.2	0.1	2.9	6.9	2.6	0.4	0.4	0.8	0.2	8.4	9.7
UK	6.1	0.2	2.4	7.0	3.2	0.5	0.3	1.4	0.2	10.5	10.3
USA	5.3	0.8	1.3	7.0	0.6	0.1	0.3	na	0.6	7.8	8.0
English family	*4.4*	*0.4*	*1.9*	*6.7*	*2.1*	*0.4*	*0.5*	*0.7*	*0.6*	*8.7*	*8.5*
Austria	12.6	0.4	2.4	6.8	2.8	0.6	1.1	0.1	0.3	8.2	18.4
Belgium	7.2	2.0	2.3	7.3	2.6	1.1	3.3	0.1	0.4	9.1	16.2
France	10.9	1.8	1.9	7.8	3.0	0.9	1.7	0.8	0.4	10.8	17.5
Germany	11.2	0.4	1.9	7.7	2.2	1.0	1.7	0.6	0.2	9.9	15.9
Netherlands	5.5	0.3	3.6	6.0	1.6	1.3	1.5	0.3	0.6	8.5	11.1
Continental family	*9.5*	*1.0*	*2.4*	*7.1*	*2.4*	*1.0*	*1.9*	*0.4*	*0.4*	*9.3*	*15.8*
Denmark	7.2	0.0	4.3	5.9	3.2	1.7	2.8	0.7	1.0	11.6	13.6
Finland	8.5	0.9	3.8	6.2	3.0	0.9	2.0	0.3	0.5	9.9	15.3
Norway	6.3	0.3	4.4	5.8	2.8	0.7	0.5	0.1	0.6	10.1	10.9
Sweden	9.6	0.6	5.6	6.8	3.2	1.3	1.2	0.5	0.6	13.6	14.5
Nordic family	*7.9*	*0.4*	*4.5*	*6.2*	*3.0*	*1.1*	*1.6*	*0.4*	*0.7*	*11.3*	*13.6*

(continued)

Table 23.2 Continued

Country	(1) Old age	(2) Survivors	(3) Incapacity	(4) Health	(5) Family	(6) ALMP	(7) Unemployment	(8) Housing	(9) Others	(10) In kind	(11) Cash
Greece	10.8	0.8	0.9	5.6	1.1	0.1	0.4	0.5	0.4	7.1	13.4
Italy	11.6	2.5	1.7	6.8	1.3	0.6	0.5	0.0	0.0	7.7	16.7
Portugal	8.7	1.6	2.3	7.2	1.2	0.7	1.2	0.0	0.2	7.8	14.6
Spain	7.9	0.5	2.5	5.8	1.1	0.8	2.2	0.2	0.2	7.4	13.1
Southern family	*9.7*	*1.3*	*1.8*	*6.3*	*1.2*	*0.5*	*1.1*	*0.2*	*0.2*	*7.5*	*14.4*
Japan	8.6	1.3	0.7	6.3	0.8	0.3	0.3	n.a	0.3	8.1	10.2
Switzerland	6.6	0.4	3.3	6.1	1.3	0.7	0.9	0.2	0.7	7.8	11.8
Mean OECD 21	*7.8*	*0.8*	*2.5*	*6.6*	*2.1*	*0.7*	*1.2*	*0.4*	*0.5*	*9.0*	*12.6*
Range	*9.7*	*2.5*	*4.9*	*2.2*	*2.6*	*1.6*	*3.0*	*1.4*	*2.2*	*6.5*	*11.6*
SD	*2.8*	*0.7*	*1.3*	*0.6*	*0.9*	*0.4*	*0.9*	*0.3*	*0.5*	*1.6*	*3.4*

Source: OECD 2008g, data extracted on 11/02/2009.

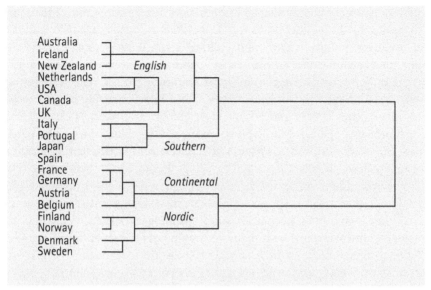

Figure 23.1 Patterns of social spending in 19 OECD countries (2005)

Note: This dendogram is based on the following spending items (z-transformed): Old age, survivors, incapacity, health, family, active labour market, unemployment, other contingencies, gross public, net total, benefits in kind, cash benefits, public expenditure as a percentage of total government spending, public spending per head, voluntary private; Distance measure: Squared Euclidean distance, Ward method. Greece and Switzerland are missing because of a lack of net spending data.

Source: OECD 2008g.

the extremely low level of resources directed to families in the latter. Spending data also reveal a distinct Nordic model where spending on families (mainly services), active labour market policy and incapacity benefits is higher than elsewhere in OECD world. Finally, Table 23.2 also shows up an English-speaking family in which spending on pensions is comparatively low and health expenditure constitutes the biggest single item of social spending. The fact that health expenditure is largely provided in-kind explains why spending on in-kind benefits outweighs cash benefit expenditure in the English-speaking countries. It therefore comes as no surprise that a cluster analysis of social expenditure data strongly supports the idea of the existence of distinct families of nations or welfare regimes (Figure 23.1).

Determinants of Cross-National Differences in Social Spending

Gross social expenditure has been widely used to assess the determinants of cross-national variation in welfare effort across the OECD world. The first generation of empirical studies emphasized the importance of wealth, economic growth, demographics, and the age of the social security system for explaining differences in social spending *levels* (Zöllner 1963; Wilensky 1975). The functionalist notion that social expenditure levels are mainly shaped by anonymous socio-economic developments was challenged by the 'politics do matter' school that emerged in the 1970s and 1980s. Power resources, political parties and political institutions were considered to be relevant for explaining the differences in spending between countries similar in socio-economic terms. A large number of empirical studies have demonstrated that left and Christian democratic parties spend more than liberal and secular-conservative parties (Hicks and Swank 1992; Huber et al. 1993; Hicks and Misra 1993; Schmidt 1997; Huber and Stephens 2001a; Castles 2004). Moreover, partisan competition, voter turn-out, contagion effects between parties, corporatism, and strong unions have also been identified as factors driving social spending up (Hicks and Swank 1992; Cameron 1978; Garrett 1998a; Hicks and Kenworthy 1998). Other studies found that small open economies manifest higher spending levels than relatively closed economies. In contrast, social spending is restricted in institutionally fragmented political systems with many veto-points (Huber et al. 1993). Significant institutional impediments to high spending levels are federalism (Wilensky 1975; Cameron 1978; Swank 2001) and referendums (Wagschal and Obinger 2000). In contrast to functionalist arguments, many studies failed to discern a significant linear effect of GDP on national welfare efforts. The problem here is that economic growth influences both the nominator and the denominator of the dependent variable. Once social spending per capita is analysed, however, economic affluence turns out to be an extremely powerful predictor for cross-national differences in social spending. Functionalist theories also gain significant explanatory power if net social spending is analysed. Economic wealth is by far the most important variable for explaining total net social expenditure levels. By contrast, political factors are either weak or statistically insignificant (Castles and Obinger 2007).

Inquiries focusing on social spending dynamics during the post-golden age period end up with somewhat different conclusions. Many studies analysing *changes* in social expenditure since 1980 have shown that the impact of political parties is weaker compared to the golden age or has disappeared altogether (Huber and Stephens 2001a; Swank 2001; Kittel and Obinger 2003; Potrafke 2007). In addition to the aforementioned strong catch-up of former spending laggards (Starke et al. 2008), many studies have shown that socio-economic problem pressure is the crucial factor for explaining social spending dynamics in hard times. Population ageing, low economic growth, unemployment, and deindustrialization are the main determinants that have fuelled social spending in the aftermath of the golden age (Castles 2004; Iversen and Cusack 2000; Kittel and Obinger 2003). In other words, increasing social needs are the main reason why social spending levels are higher in 2005 than in 1980. However, the fact that many countries have at the same time imposed significant benefit cutbacks suggests that increases in social spending have not been altogether sufficient to accommodate the social demands resulting from mounting socio-economic problem pressure (cf. Ch. 38). Findings concerning the impact of globalization on social spending are inconclusive. Most empirical studies neither confirm the compensation thesis nor support the notion of a race to the bottom (Castles 2004).

What all the studies mentioned have in common is that they focus on aggregate social spending. Using the rich information of the SOCX database at programme level, Francis G. Castles (2009a) has recently analysed the determinants of four broad (gross) spending categories, i.e. spending on (1) age-related cash benefits, (2) working age cash benefits, (3) health, and (4) other service expenditure. He convincingly demonstrates that the determinants of these four expenditure types differ quite significantly and do not coincide with those of total public spending.

Impact of Spending on Social Outcomes

Social spending is not an end in itself. However, financial resource availability is an essential prerequisite for social policy making, irrespective of whether one regards risk compensation or the fight against poverty and inequality as the core objective of the welfare state. Despite the critique of expenditure analysis discussed earlier, it is important to note that there is a strong correlation between public social expenditure and decommodification levels on the one hand, and replacement rates on the other. In addition, social spending also affects income inequality and poverty rates. Since these issues are broadly discussed in the entry on inequality and poverty (see Chapter 36), we restrict ourselves to the presentation of some stylized facts. First, gross public spending is more redistributive than all categories of net spending. One major reason is that gross spending measures entail a secondary redistribution mechanism since cash benefits are often subject to taxation. It is the better-off who are most likely to be affected by such tax claw-backs. Secondly, all categories of public spending (gross or net) have a stronger impact on the reduction of inequality and poverty than all categories of private spending (see Castles and Obinger 2007). The bulk of private social expenditure is made up of voluntary social spending. It is quite clear that it is mainly the middle-class and the core labour force which benefit from tax-advantaged individual or employer-based pension and health plans so that the redistributive effects of private social expenditure are necessarily rather limited. On the other hand, tax credits to families and the working poor, which are functionally equivalent to social cash transfers, are important redistributive instruments. That tax interventions of this type are reflected in net *public* spending explains, along with the 'tax churning' effect, why all measures of public spending outperform private spending indicators in terms of fighting poverty and inequality.

Once more, a disaggregated expenditure approach provides intriguing insights. Castles (2009a) shows that it is spending on cash benefits to the working-age population that is most strongly associated with redistribution (see also OECD 2008a). This effect is even stronger than the impact of decommodification—a measure deliberately developed to overcome the alleged shortcomings of social spending analysis. By contrast, neither health expenditure nor spending for the elderly is associated with significant vertical redistribution.

GOVERNMENT REVENUES

···

Inequality and Taxation

Major aims of welfare states such as the reduction of inequality and poverty can be achieved not only by spending on cash transfers and other benefits, but also by taxation (including social contributions). The latest available data from the OECD (2009*b*, 2008*i*) reveal a strong correlation between the Gini-coefficient and total tax revenues. However, it is not only the general level of taxation that affects equality. Other relevant characteristics include the presence or absence of negative income taxes, the type of taxation (joint versus individual taxation), tax exemptions, and the progressivity of taxation. The impact of these properties of the tax system in turn depends heavily on the level of income and individual characteristics.

A recent study by the OECD on the topic of income distribution (OECD 2008*a*), has shown that the reduction of inequality in disposable income attributable to taxes and transfers ranges from about 40 per cent in Sweden and Denmark to 5 per cent in Korea. This study further shows that the impact of taxation is significant in its own right and differs from earlier studies which pointed to only relatively minor taxation impacts (Messere 1993). With the notable exception of the United States, however, the effect of cash benefits is generally shown to be greater than that of taxation.

This analysis of redistribution effects does not, however, take into account possible distortionary impacts of high taxation on the labour market. Especially high marginal taxes may prevent low skilled workers from taking up a job (Layard et al. 2005), while an increase in the labour tax wedge may increase the level of unemployment. Moreover, many studies have found a significant relationship between greater equality and rising unemployment in the 1980s and 1990s, i.e. more 'unequal' countries experienced a better labour market performance (Feldstein 1998). More recent studies suggest—in addition to these findings—an interaction effect between labour taxation and the benefit replacement rate (Belot and van Ours 2004) on increases in unemployment.

Taxation also has a substantial impact on gender equality. It makes a difference whether individuals or families are taxed. In France, 'family splitting' (together with cash benefits) stimulates both the fertility rate and the inclusion of women in the labour market. By contrast, the joint taxation of couples in Germany with a different splitting system generates disincentives for married women to participate in the labour market (Dingeldey 2000). Today, individual taxation is the prevailing system of taxation, introduced in Scandinavia in the early 1970s and across much of the rest of continental Europe in the years thereafter, usually by social democratic or grand coalition governments. Overall, there is strong evidence that tax systems influence to a large extent the employment patterns of married women and mothers.

Two other and closely related attributes of the tax system affect inequality: tax credits and tax progressivity. Negative income taxes such as the 'Earned Income Tax Credit' (EITC), which was implemented in 1973 in the United States, and the

'Working Tax Credit' (WTC) in the United Kingdom, have become successful instruments for activating social policies with the aim of 'making work pay'. Studies generally report positive effects of such policies on reducing poverty because they are especially targeted at single parents. The main incentive derives from the requirement to take up a job in order to receive the tax credit, while the EITC has no effect on the eligibility to other welfare benefits (e.g. low income housing, food stamps). Negative income taxes also exist in other countries, but are of lesser importance.

A negative income tax increases tax progressivity. However, such taxes make the tax wedge for low incomes considerably lower. Tax progressivity means that the average tax rate increases with rising income. Adam Smith argued for progressive taxes in order to reduce inequality and poverty in the eighteenth century. However, their effects and how progressive they need to be are still hotly debated. According to the OECD (2008a: 106): 'Overall, there is less variation in the progressivity of taxes across countries than in the case of transfers. After the United States, the distribution of taxation tends to be most progressive in the English-speaking countries—Ireland, Australia, the United Kingdom, New Zealand and Canada—together with Italy, followed by the Netherlands, the Czech Republic and Germany. Taxes tend to be least progressive in the Nordic countries, France and Switzerland.' However, other indicators of progressivity lead to different rankings, e.g. effective tax rates or the tax wedge differ according to income, family status and number of children (OECD 2003d).

Funding the Welfare State: A Race to the Bottom?

The goods and services provided by the welfare state need sufficient funding. The general government's revenues come from different sources, namely tax revenues, social contributions, fees, fines, seignorage, income from economic activities, revenues from privatization, international budget contributions, and the public deficit. This last residual category balances the budget equation and has become a permanent source of income for some countries.

The main data source for government revenues is the OECD Revenue Statistics series (OECD 2008b). This publication distinguishes between six different revenue categories: (1) income, profits and capital gains, (2) social security contributions, (3) payroll taxes, (4) taxes on property, (5) taxes on goods and services, and (6) other taxes. The three main categories—taxes on income, profits, and capital gains, social security contributions, and taxes on goods and services—add up to 93 per cent of the total tax revenues in the OECD world. Table 23.3 shows levels of taxation for the most important tax categories for different families of nations. It shows a rather clear pattern with the highest levels of taxation in the Nordic countries, followed by the Continental and South European countries. The English-speaking countries display the lowest level of taxation (Peters 1991, see also below).

Table 23.3 Levels of taxation in 21 OECD countries (1990–2006)

Country	Total tax revenue 2006	Total tax revenue 1990	Taxes on corporate income 2006	Taxes on personal income 2006	Social security contributions 2006	Taxes on property 2006	Taxes on goods and services 2006
	(1)	(2)	(3)	(4)	(5)	(6)	(7)
Australia	30.6	28.5	6.6	11.4	–	2.8	8.3
Canada	33.3	35.9	3.7	12.1	4.9	3.4	8.1
Ireland	31.9	33.1	3.8	8.9	4.3	2.9	11.6
New Zealand	36.7	37.4	5.8	14.9	–	1.9	12.0
UK	37.1	36.1	4.0	10.8	6.9	4.6	10.8
USA	28.0	27.3	3.3	10.2	6.7	3.1	4.7
English family	*32.9*	*33.1*	*4.5*	*11.4*	*5.7*	*3.1*	*9.3*
Austria	41.7	39.6	2.2	9.3	14.4	0.6	11.5
Belgium	44.5	42.0	3.7	13.1	13.6	2.3	11.4
France	44.2	42.0	3.0	7.7	16.3	3.5	10.9
Germany	35.6	34.8	2.1	8.7	13.7	0.9	10.1
Netherlands	39.3	42.9	3.4	7.4	14.2	1.9	12.0
Continental family	*41.1*	*40.3*	*2.9*	*9.2*	*14.4*	*1.8*	*11.2*
Denmark	49.1	46.5	4.3	24.5	1.0	1.9	16.3
Finland	43.5	43.5	3.4	13.2	12.1	1.1	13.5
Norway	43.9	41.0	12.9	9.1	8.7	1.2	12.0
Sweden	49.1	52.2	3.7	15.7	12.5	1.4	12.8
Nordic family	*46.4*	*45.8*	*6.1*	*15.6*	*8.6*	*1.4*	*13.7*

Country	Total tax revenue 2006	Total tax revenue 1990	Taxes on corporate income 2006	Taxes on personal income 2006	Social security contributions 2006	Taxes on property 2006	Taxes on goods and services 2006
	(1)	(2)	(3)	(4)	(5)	(6)	(7)
Greece	31.3	26.2	2.7	4.7	11.1	1.4	11.3
Italy	42.1	37.8	3.4	10.8	12.6	2.1	10.8
Portugal	35.7	27.7	3.0	5.5	11.4	1.1	14.5
Spain	36.6	32.5	4.2	6.9	12.2	3.3	9.9
Southern family	*36.4*	*31.1*	*3.3*	*7.0*	*11.8*	*2.0*	*11.6*
Japan	27.9	29.1	4.7	5.1	10.2	2.5	5.2
Switzerland	29.6	25.8	3.0	10.5	6.9	2.4	6.8
Mean OECD 21	*37.7*	*36.3*	*4.1*	*10.5*	*10.2*	*2.2*	*10.7*
Range	*21.2*	*26.4*	*10.8*	*19.8*	*15.3*	*4*	*11.6*
SD	*6.4*	*7.1*	*2.2*	*4.3*	*4.0*	*1.0*	*2.8*

Note: All figures are expressed as percentage of GDP.

Source: OECD 2008i.

In light of economic globalization, economic theory predicts intensified tax competition leading to a downward adjustment of tax rates and tax revenues with arguably massive consequences for the welfare state. However, the development of tax revenues over time is not consonant with this 'race to the bottom' scenario (see Table 23.4). Currently (latest data for 2006), tax-to-GDP-ratios are on average at an all-time high and it is likely that the overall tax burden will increase in the wake of the present economic crisis. In contrast to the notion of a downward spiral in tax levels, revenues from taxes on corporate income have, in fact, increased relative to GDP over recent years (see column 2), while revenues from taxes on personal income have declined. In general, the greatest changes can be observed in the Nordic and Southern European families of nations.

This development stands in a sharp contrast to the fact that tax rates have been reduced since the early 1980s—especially for business and the top income group. Since tax rates are the most important signal of a country's economic attractiveness for business, governments are especially interested in lowering the tax burden to attract foreign direct investment and new settlements. At the same time, governments need sufficient tax revenues to finance expenditure. Therefore tax policies have often followed a *tax-cut-cum-base-broadening-strategy* in order to keep revenues at a high level. Data from the OECD (2008h), Eurostat (2008) and the World Tax Database (OTPR 1987 ff.) show a decline in top marginal rates for corporations as well as for individuals over time. In contrast, on average, minimum marginal rates have not decreased. Goods and services taxes have been reformed mainly due to harmonization within the European Union. However, rates have been raised—on average—by only by one percentage point since the early 1980s.

Families of Taxation and Welfare State Typologies

The significant variation in patterns of taxation illustrated in Table 23.3 raises the question whether it is possible to identify distinct country clusters. A cluster analysis for the selected twenty-one OECD countries on the basis of 144 tax indicators (e.g. tax structure, tax-to-GDP ratios, specific tax system features) reveals four 'families of taxation' (Wagschal 2005: 105; cf. Peters 1991) showing great similarities with the patterns of social expenditure in Figure 23.1. The four families of taxation are (1) an English-speaking family, (2) a Continental family, (3) a Nordic family, and (4) a peripheral or residual cluster.

1. The English-speaking family includes the United States, Canada, the United Kingdom, Australia, New Zealand plus Japan and Switzerland. The level of taxation is low compared to the other families. In line with the liberal ideology of taxation, the system is strongly based on the 'ability to pay' principle. Direct corporate, income taxes and property taxes (relative to GDP) exceed the OECD average (see Table 23.3).
2. The Continental family is committed to the 'benefits principle'. These nations rely heavily on social contributions and follow the benefit/insurance principle. Under such a system employees have stronger entitlements than under a tax financed welfare state, making welfare state reforms more difficult.

Table 23.4 Taxation trends in 21 OECD countries (1990–2006)

Country	Total tax revenue Δ 2006–1990	Taxes on corporate income Δ 2006–1990	Taxes on personal income Δ 2006–1990	Social security contributions Δ 2006–1990	Taxes on property Δ 2006–1990	Taxes on goods and services Δ 2006–1990
	(1)	(2)	(3)	(4)	(5)	(6)
Australia	2.1	2.6	-0.8	0.0	0.2	0.4
Canada	-2.6	1.1	-2.5	0.6	-0.2	-1.2
Ireland	-1.2	2.2	-1.7	-0.6	1.4	-2.4
New Zealand	-0.7	3.4	-3.0	0.0	-0.7	-0.5
UK	1.0	0.4	0.1	0.7	1.6	-0.5
USA	0.7	0.9	0.1	-0.2	0.0	0.0
English family	*-0.1*	*1.8*	*-1.3*	*0.1*	*0.4*	*-0.7*
Austria	2.1	0.8	1.0	1.4	-0.5	-0.9
Belgium	2.5	1.7	-0.4	-0.4	0.8	0.2
France	2.2	0.7	3.3	-2.2	0.9	-1.0
Germany	0.8	0.4	-0.9	0.6	-0.3	0.8
Netherlands	-3.6	0.1	-3.2	-1.8	0.3	0.7
Continental family	*0.8*	*0.7*	*0.0*	*-0.5*	*0.2*	*0.0*
Denmark	2.6	2.6	-0.3	0.1	-0.1	0.9
Finland	0.0	1.4	-1.9	1.0	0.0	-0.6
Norway	3.0	9.2	-1.7	-2.1	0.0	-2.6
Sweden	-3.1	2.1	-4.4	-1.7	-0.4	-0.2
Nordic family	*0.6*	*3.8*	*-2.1*	*-0.7*	*-0.1*	*-0.6*
Greece	5.1	1.2	1.0	3.2	0.2	-0.4
Italy	4.3	-0.4	0.9	0.1	1.3	0.2
Portugal	8.0	0.8	1.1	3.9	0.3	2.2
Spain	4.2	1.3	-0.1	0.7	1.5	0.7
Southern family	*5.4*	*0.7*	*0.7*	*2.0*	*0.8*	*0.7*
Japan	-1.2	-1.8	-2.9	2.5	-0.2	1.2
Switzerland	3.8	1.0	0.5	0.9	0.1	1.3
Mean OECD 21	*1.4*	*1.5*	*-0.8*	*0.3*	*0.3*	*-0.1*
Range	*11.6*	*11.0*	*7.7*	*6.1*	*2.3*	*4.8*
SD	*2.8*	*2.0*	*1.8*	*1.6*	*0.7*	*1.1*

Note: All figures are expressed as percentage point differences of the tax-to-GDP shares.

Source: OECD 2008*i*.

3. The Nordic family of taxation consists of Sweden, Denmark, and Finland. It is characterized by the highest levels of taxation (with a strong focus on income taxes), rather moderate business taxes and relatively low social security contributions. Moreover, taxes on goods and services exceed the OECD-average.

4. The peripheral cluster consists of the South European countries plus Norway and Ireland. The pattern of taxation in this cluster is similar to that in continental

Europe. Main properties are an overall level of taxation on a medium scale and high indirect taxes, mainly reflecting internal problems of tax collection.

A strong case can be made that 'families of taxation' can be accounted for by two variables which have been identified as important determinants of different welfare systems (van Kersbergen 1995: ch. 18), namely the partisan complexion of government and religious differences. Conservative and liberal parties are strong in the English-speaking family as well as in Japan and Switzerland. The Continental and Southern nations are dominated by Christian democratic and social democratic parties, i.e. two pro-welfare state party groupings. In the Nordic countries, the social democrats are traditionally the dominant party.

Taxation and Attitudes towards the Welfare State

Excessive taxation and political unrest are historically closely connected. However, the impact of taxation affects not only political stability, but also support for the welfare state in democratic societies. Given the steep increase in the size of the tax state during the course of the twentieth century, tax protest movements have appeared in a number countries. The Poujadists in the 1950s and later the Front National in France radically opposed the welfare state. In Denmark, the Progress Party ('Fremskridtspartiet') under Mogens Gilstrup became in 1973 the second largest party in Parliament on the basis of a platform demanding tax cuts and dismantling the welfare state. An even greater impact can be observed in countries with direct democracy. The American neo-con tax revolt of the 1980s onwards started with Proposition 13 reducing property tax in California by 50 per cent in 1978 and leading on to tax cutbacks in roughly the half of the states of the United States (Smith 1998).

In contrast to radical anti-welfare state parties, other parties support higher taxation. Such differences between parties can be identified in their programmatic positions. A long-lasting research project on party manifestos (Budge et al. 2001) has analysed the party manifestos for the 1945–98 period for most OECD countries. The data can be analysed in two ways: first, one can identify parties with strong preferences for 'high' or 'low' taxation and for 'pro-intervention' policies. Second, it is possible to compare differences between both variables and their change over time.

Apart from the radical anti-tax parties discussed above, Conservative and agrarian parties also put a strong emphasis on tax cuts. Surprisingly, liberal parties show lower preferences for tax reductions and relatively high pro-intervention scores. Parties in favour of taxation are the Communists, Social Democrats and the Greens. Christian Democrats and other religious parties are located in the middle of the spectrum. Communist and Social Democratic parties are those most in favour of intervention. Religious parties also embrace interventionist policies which led in the past to welfare state expansion.

Can we observe changes over time? The end of the golden era of the welfare state (i.e. the mid-1970s) marked a watershed in 'pro-intervention' attitudes. After the first oil crisis, bourgeois parties became less enthusiastic about interventionism. Moderate left and moderate right parties moved a bit in a 'pro-market and less taxation' direction. The biggest change can be observed for the ultra-right parties. In contrast, ultra-left parties became much more interventionist in the wake of the first oil crisis. From the mid-1970s onwards, most non-extremist party families are more inclined to pro-market attitudes with the exception of religious parties. Some parties dramatically changed their policy positions. The British Labour Party, for example, moved from being a very leftist party in 1945 (the party manifesto right–left score was −48.1) to a 'centre' party in 1997 (with a right–left score of +8.1).

To what extent does the electorate support the tax state? To answer this question one needs comparable data across countries and over time. One of the best data bases is the International Social Survey Programme (ISSP), especially the four ISSP surveys on the 'Role of Government' (1985, 1990, 1996, and 2006). 22 countries have participated in the last survey and for five countries data is available for all four waves. For the analysis which follows (see Table 23.5), four specific questions have been analysed relating to the tax preferences of the voters: (1) taxes on high income, (2) taxes on middle incomes, (3) taxes on low incomes, and (4) cuts in government spending.

Table 23.5 Attitudes towards taxation and the welfare state (1985–2006)

| | Taxes on high incomes | | | | |
	Much too high	Too high	About right	Too low	Much too low
ISSP (1996)	7.3%	16.0%	25.6%	36.1%	15.1%
ISSP (2006)	8.7%	17.7%	29.8%	31.9%	11.9%
	Taxes on middle incomes				
	Much too high	Too high	About right	Too low	Much too low
ISSP (1996)	14.2%	43.0%	39.8%	2.6%	0.3%
ISSP (2006)	15.3%	45.4%	37.1%	2.0%	0.2%
	Taxes on low incomes				
	Much too high	Too high	About right	Too low	Much too low
ISSP (1996)	33.5%	41.8%	22.9%	1.4%	0.5%
ISSP (2006)	31.4%	40.9%	25.2%	1.8%	0.7%
	Government and economy: cuts in government spending				
	Strongly in favour of	In favour of	Neither in favour of nor against	Against	Strongly against
ISSP (1985)	30.2%	35.2%	17.9%	13.5%	3.3%
ISSP (1990)	30.1%	40.8%	17.6%	9.3%	2.2%
ISSP (1996)	38.5%	37.3%	13.7%	8.4%	2.1%
ISSP (2006)	28.9%	31.1%	19.5%	14.7%	5.7%

Source: ISSP 1985–2006 cumulation; variables are weighted, number of respondents vary from 6112 to 21806 for each survey, data refers to fourteen OECD countries. Responses to each question measured on a 5-point scale.

Looking at attitudes towards taxation, we may observe a slight increase in discontent with taxation on high and middle incomes. Taxation of low incomes is seen as being too high. However, discontent decreased slightly. Asking respondents whether they prefer cuts in government spending, one can observe a peak in favour of expenditure cuts in the 1990s. Since then, resistance to spending cuts has increased, evidence supporting the increasing importance of the state.

Apart from cross-country variations, it is also possible to reveal relationships between the left–right placement of voters and their 'taxation' orientation. The 'voter ideology' variable used in the analysis is based on the left–right placement of the respondents classified into five categories ('far left', 'left', 'centre', 'liberal', 'right, conservative', 'far right'). The expectation is that the more rightist a respondent is, the stronger the disposition for lower taxation will be. This holds true for all countries for the first four categories. However, respondents classified as 'far right' have strong preferences for interventionist policies and smoother taxes for low incomes.

CONCLUSION

Social expenditure and tax revenues as percentages of GDP have increased since 1980. Despite some convergence, there still exist significant cross-national differences in levels and patterns of gross public social spending and taxation. Patterns of social spending and taxation strongly overlap and support the notion of distinct families of nations. Overall, this evidence is at odds with the idea that globalization triggers a race to the bottom. However, this does not imply that international competition is meaningless. Significant cuts in the top income tax rates and corporate taxes appear likely to have been influenced by a remarkably changed international political economy.

Despite the strong criticisms of comparisons based on aggregate spending, improved social expenditure data mapping programme-related spending, private expenditure and after-tax spending now provides important insights into what 'welfare states do' (Castles 2009a). Both revenue and spending data therefore are important tools for analysing mature welfare states, with particular scope for further research on disaggregated spending patterns. It should be nevertheless clear that spending and revenue data is not enough. Social spending neither tells us very much about levels of benefit provision nor does it capture the regulatory dimension of social policy.

CHAPTER 24

....

OLD-AGE PENSIONS

....

KARL HINRICHS

JULIA F. LYNCH

INVENTING PENSIONS

....

PENSION systems spread in Europe during the late nineteenth and early twentieth century as a political response to industrialization and the concomitant social risks of wage labourers. Prior to the first major pension initiatives, only select groups of elderly enjoyed regular pension payments after terminating employment: employees in the public sector (civil servants, veterans, municipal workers) and certain occupations (miners, railroad workers), and those whose employers voluntarily offered a private pension to their long-serving (white-collar) workforce. All other (blue-collar) labourers 'worked until death or disability' (Stearns 1975: 260). Limited pension coverage continues to be the norm in many African and Asian countries; and in these countries, pension privileges for policemen, military personnel, civil servants, and employees in state-owned enterprises are granted for motives similar to those at play in nineteenth-century Europe: namely, to ensure the loyalty of future beneficiaries while they are still at work.

Germany, by legislation of 1889, was the first country that compulsorily insured almost all employees against income loss due to disability and old age. That legislation was not only meant as a pre-emptive strategy to suppress potential working class unrest. It was also part of an unfinished state-building process (unburdening municipalities from poor relief payments) and, besides being supported by both Christian churches and early scholars of social policy, continued the tradition of patriarchal interventions by an authoritarian state. Subsequently, other nations also introduced public pension schemes that varied either slightly or more dramatically from the *Bismarckian* approach (see next section). During that period of maturing industrialization, the declining abilities of older workers were the main social problem and, thus, disability pensions predominated. A fixed retirement age (initially 70 in Germany, lower in other countries) served as a marker for generally assumed disability, but already embodied the concept of a work-free phase of 'retirement' within a tripartite life course. Benefits from newly implemented public schemes, however, were largely insufficient to ensure retirement as a universal social achievement before World War II. Rather, public old-age pensions supplemented other economic resources: (lower) earnings from continued employment, individual savings, family support or a private pension from the former employer. In a number of countries today, notably in Latin America and East Asia, one similarly finds broad public pension coverage but with benefit levels generally insufficient to ensure full economic independence at higher ages.

In contrast, welfare states within the traditional OECD area are considered 'developed' in part because after 1945 they arranged their pension systems so that complete exit from paid employment during an ever longer retirement period became a universal entitlement. Previously, the majority of men aged 65 and older remained members of the labour force—for example, in the United States three-quarters of them belonged to the labour force in 1890; by 1930 60 per cent still did so; but by 1970 only a quarter (25.7 per cent) of older men were active workers (Jacobs et al. 1991: 41). By the 1970s, declining employment rates after age 60 and, even more, after age 65, signalled that this entitlement had been for the most part achieved. In almost all of the advanced welfare states less than one quarter of the male population over age 65 participated in the labour force by 1970 (ILO 2009a). This institutionalization of retirement resulted from an expansion of pension systems in several dimensions: coverage was broadened to almost the entire (working) population, eligibility criteria for enjoying a pension became liberalized (e.g. flexible retirement), the range of benefits was expanded (e.g. survivors' pensions) and, most importantly, the generosity of benefits substantially increased.

In the remainder of this chapter we describe the origins, organization, and social consequences of mature pension systems in the developed welfare states; discuss the challenges posed to these systems by demographic, economic, and societal transformations occurring since the 1970s; and trace trajectories of reform, both actual and anticipated. Throughout, our focus is on the pension systems of the rich democracies of Western Europe, North America, and the Antipodes, with more selective attention to developments in Latin America, Asia, and Eastern Europe.

OLD-AGE PENSIONS IN DEVELOPED WELFARE STATES

Fully developed national pension systems perform different functions (cf. Barr and Diamond 2006, 2008): They aim to *smooth consumption* by transferring economic resources from the second (employment) to the third stage (retirement) of an institutionalized life course. Pensions as annuities *insure against biometric risks*—in particular, longevity—and thus protect retired individuals from outliving their savings. Pension systems also regularly insure against death and/or disability of the main earner (survivors' and disability benefits, the latter often through a separate scheme). Pension systems aim to *alleviate poverty* when flat-rate benefits are paid to all individuals above a certain age or are targeted at those with insufficient resources. Linked to that function, a final primary objective of pension systems is to *redistribute income*: pension systems may redistribute vertically (e.g. with progressive benefit formulae that replace a higher percentage of previous earnings for low-wage workers than for higher earners), or horizontally (e.g. towards families with a spouse supplement, as in the United States Social Security system; or between males and females when applying unisex mortality tables).

Welfare states differ as to whether the achievement of all four objectives is left to one single pension scheme or is allocated to several components of a 'multi-pillar' system. The distinction between *Bismarckian* and *Beveridgean* approaches to pension provision provides a helpful starting point for understanding how different national pension systems approach these objectives (Hinrichs 2001; Myles and P. Pierson 2001; Bonoli 2003). Both types of public pension provision emerged during the same time period, between 1889 and before World War II. The Bismarckian approach is centered on a main pillar or tier that is public and contribution-financed. This approach is employment-centred (occupational), with benefits derived from work, and implies a priority of status maintenance ('consumption smoothing') over poverty relief. In contrast, Beveridgean pension systems—named for the system that was proposed by the study commission chaired by British economist William Beveridge in 1942 and implemented in the United Kingdom with some modifications in 1946—focus on poverty alleviation via universal flat-rate pensions financed out of taxes or tax-like contributions. Beveridgean pension systems were generally means-tested when first introduced, with some, but not all, later developing into universal 'people's pensions.' In these systems, fully-funded supplementary pension schemes organized by private actors (employers and/or individuals) carry out the functions of status maintenance.

A large majority of countries on the European continent instituted Bismarckian pensions systems in the late nineteenth and early twentieth centuries. The United States joined the Bismarckian camp with a 'light' version introduced by the Social Security legislation of 1935 and 1939 (see Figure 24.1). In the mid-1960s to mid-1970s the countries of Southern Europe expanded their hitherto meagre public pension systems, which thereafter offered quite generous wage replacement for core workers and became more elderly-oriented as public spending on other items (notably unemployment and social services) lagged behind (Lynch 2006). At some stage during their development, all Bismarckian countries established a 'floor' of minimum protection for those elderly whose contribution records resulted in insufficient benefit entitlements. Minimum pensions were introduced either as part of general social assistance schemes or institutionalized as part of the social insurance system.

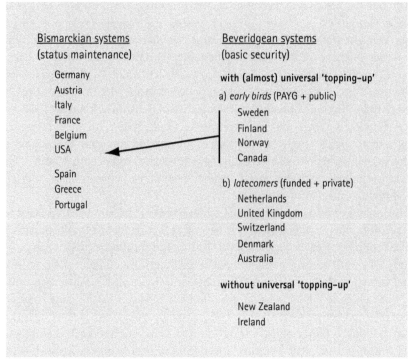

Figure 24.1 Typology of pension systems

The Anglo-Saxon nations (minus the United States) and all of the Nordic countries began as Beveridge-style systems—although in the case of the Nordic countries, Beveridge-style pension systems were introduced well before the Beveridge report. Subsequently this initially large group of countries has split, as different countries have supplemented their basic pension schemes in two main ways. Sweden (1959), Finland (1961), and, somewhat later, Canada (1965) and Norway (1966) were the *early birds*. In light of favourable economic and demographic conditions at that time, they topped up their flat-rate, universal 'people's pensions' with a second *public* pillar. This second pillar was contribution-based, unfunded (at least in principle), yielded an earnings-related supplementary pension, and included redistributive provisions in varying degrees. *De facto*, these countries joined the Bismarckian group during the course of the early 1960s.

The *latecomers*, i.e. Beveridgean countries that provided only a basic flat-rate pension as late as the early 1970s, took a different route to achieving status maintenance in old age on a large scale. An earnings-related topping-up and, hence, an expansion of the system, was accomplished via *occupational* pension schemes that were either mandated by law (Switzerland in 1985, Australia in 1992) or arose through collective agreements and eventually achieved almost universal coverage (Netherlands, Denmark). The United Kingdom, which introduced its State Earnings-Related Pension

Scheme (SERPS) in 1975, represents something of a unique 'hybrid' case.[1] Therefore, of the original Beveridgean camp, only Ireland and New Zealand retain systems in which provision for supplementary retirement income beyond public minimum pensions is left to voluntary action of private actors. They have not (yet) mandated occupational or personal pension schemes, but encourage broader coverage.

In the *latecomer* countries, the second pillar is private and fully funded. However, it is extensively regulated in order to protect employees' claims, and frequently enjoys tax privileges that extend the public's reach into these ostensibly private arrangements. Latecomer countries adopted a *multi-pillar approach*, i.e. a diversification of the structure, funding and administration of benefits, well before it was forcefully propagated by the World Bank (1994a). In these countries, 'third pillar' pensions resulting from voluntary individual provision regularly also play a substantial role in the retirement income mix.

The different pension systems described above have all facilitated the development of retirement as the third phase of an institutionalized life course by fostering the economic independence of those who are no longer in the workforce. In the advanced welfare states today, on average less than 7 per cent of men and 3 per cent of women over the age of 65 are active in the labour market (OECD 2009c), public pensions assure a net replacement rate vis-à-vis mean wages of 70 per cent (OECD 2007f: 35) but widely varying among countries (see Table 24.1), and only 12 per cent of the elderly are poor after taking into account taxes and transfers (OECD 2008d).

However, the diversity of pension system arrangements implies variation in both the means by which the economic independence of the elderly has been accomplished, and the precise contours of the resulting distribution of well-being among the elderly and in society at large. Public pension expenditure as a share of GDP varies from a low of 2.5 per cent in Ireland to a high of 12.4 per cent in Austria (see Figure 24.2). And while latecomer countries supplement relatively low levels of public spending on pensions with privately funded topping-up schemes, Bismarckian systems in general show markedly higher levels of public spending on pensions than do Beveridgean systems. Similar diversity across pension system types marks the weight of total social spending that is dedicated to pensions. Bismarckian systems on average spend more than half of their welfare resources on pensions, while in the Beveridgean countries generally less than one-third of social spending is devoted to pensions (Figure 24.3).

---

[1]   After introducing a national pension in 1946, the United Kingdom experienced a short 'Bismarckian' period, lasting from the mid-1970s until the late 1980s. During that period SERPS was legislated (1975), and the possibilities to 'contract out' were limited to employer-provided defined benefit occupational pensions. In 1988, SERPS was substantially cut back and contracting-out extended to include defined contribution occupational pensions and personal pension schemes. Since then, about three-quarters of all employees have left SERPS (which in 2002 was renamed the *State Second Pension*—S2P), so that the public scheme clearly plays a minor and decreasing role in providing earnings replacement for British pensioners. Because the latest pension reform (2007/8) will further enhance private provision through 'personal accounts', the United Kingdom now clearly belongs to the latecomer multi-pillar group.

Table 24.1 Net replacement rates[a] of public pensions at various earnings levels (2004)

	50% of mean earnings	Mean earnings	200% of mean earnings
United States	67	52	43
Germany	53	58	44
Belgium	77	63	41
France	78	63	55
Portugal	82	69	74
Italy	82	78	79
Spain	82	85	72
Austria	90	91	66
Greece	114	110	107
Bismarckian	81	74	65
Canada	89	57	31
Sweden	81	64	74
Finland	77	69	71
Norway	77	69	55
Early birds	81	65	58
United Kingdom	66	41	24
Australia	84	56	41
Switzerland	75	64	35
Denmark	133	87	72
Netherlands	97	97	95
Latecomers	91	69	53
Ireland	66	39	24
New Zealand	81	42	23
Beveridgean	74	40	23
Czech Republic	99	64	40
Poland	75	75	77
Hungary	95	102	99
Transition	89	81	72

Notes: [a]Pension entitlements as a share of net pre-retirement earnings, net of income taxes and social security contributions paid by workers and pensioners. The OECD figures cited here calculate pension benefits as a share of individual lifetime average earnings, accounting for economy-wide earnings growth, and assuming that workers earn the same percentage of economy-wide average earnings throughout their careers.

Source: OECD 2007f: 35.

Different pension systems imply divergent socioeconomic outcomes as well. Traditional Bismarckian systems tend to have higher rates of income inequality among the elderly, a natural consequence of their reliance on a main pillar whose primary goal is status maintenance rather than vertical redistribution (Lynch 2006) (Figure 24.4). In contrast, in countries that started from the Beveridgean approach, flat-rate basic pensions replace a higher proportion of former low-wage workers' earnings than they do for former high-wage employees (Table 24.1). This is most

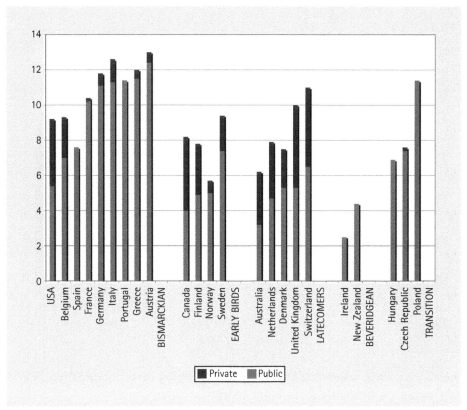

Figure 24.2 Public and private[a] pension spending as a percentage of gross domestic product (2003)

Note: [a]No data for private pension spending available for Spain, Portugal, New Zealand, Hungary, Poland. Private spending is near zero for Ireland, Czech Republic.

Source: Queisser et al. 2007.

obvious for the United Kingdom, Ireland, and New Zealand. The OECD includes spending on private quasi-mandatory occupational pension schemes in its calculation of net replacement ratios of *public* pensions, so for the Netherlands (and other countries with such arrangements) the replacement rate appears roughly the same for all earnings levels—much as in Italy, Spain, or Finland, where the public pillar is instead the backbone of the pension system (Table 24.1). The figures in Table 24.1 mainly relate to public pensions; the total replacement rate for pensioners with formerly high earnings is contingent on the extent of private components and the selective distribution of occupational and/or personal pensions. Thus, low/high public pension spending (Figure 24.2) is not a good predictor of (un)even replacement rates over the earnings spectrum or of the degree of income inequality among elderly households (Figure 24.4).

When very elevated public pension spending crowds out other social functions, Bismarckian systems may also see rates of poverty among the *non*-elderly comparable

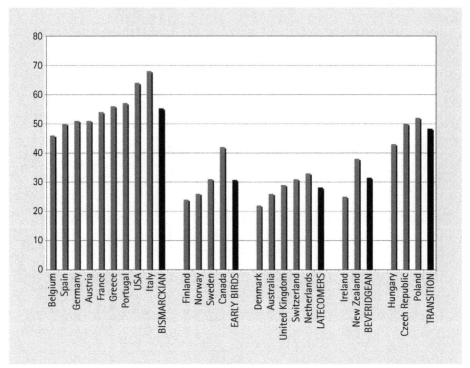

Figure 24.3 Pension spending[a] as a share of total non-health social expenditure (2003)

Note: [a] Public and mandatory private spending on old age and survivors pensions.
Source: OECD 2009*a*.

to countries with much lower levels of total social expenditure (OECD 2008*d*; Lynch 2006). While the political mobilization of a growing elderly population is sometimes cited as a cause of this discrepancy (Thomson 1989; Wilensky 1975), 'grey power' is by no means a deterministic force. The organization of socio-political institutions such as labour unions and the party system can dramatically alter both the policy demands and the political power of elderly voting blocs (Anderson and Lynch 2007; Lynch 2006; Williamson and Pampel 1993).

Challenges and Reforms

Some challenges to mature pension systems, such as the intergenerational inequities generated by pension-heavy welfare states discussed above, are closely linked to particular structural attributes of a given type of pension system. However, a number of challenges are more general. Even more than other welfare state domains, pension

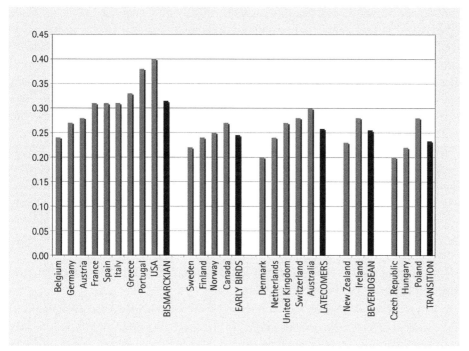

Figure 24.4 Household income inequality,[a] population aged 65+ (mid-2000s)

Note: [a] Gini coefficient, equivalized household income post-taxes and transfers.

Source: OECD 2009c.

systems are challenged by population aging. Below-replacement fertility in almost all developed welfare states and increasing longevity combine to increase old age dependency ratios and create problems of financial sustainability and intergenerational equity as more retirees will have to be supported by fewer people of working age. In the G7 countries the ratio of the inactive population aged 65 and over to the total labour force, which in 2005 ranged from 22.6 (Canada) to 45.9 (Italy), is projected to increase to between 50.3 (United States) and 98.5 (Italy) by 2050. This implies that in the absence of sharp increases in either immigration or birth rates, by the end of this century there will be roughly one elderly Italian for every member of the Italian labour force (OECD 2008d).

Further challenges to pension systems are posed by changes to labour markets. The prolonged period beginning in the 1970s of high unemployment and low activity rates has reduced the resources available to fund pensions, and in many countries has also heightened political pressure for additional spending on early retirement and disability pensions. Where labour markets have been liberalized in response to high unemployment and low growth, 'flexible' jobs may be delinked from social rights and in any case result in intermittent employment histories. This creates a 'new social risk' of ending up with insufficient pension entitlements when exiting employment (Hinrichs 2009).

In occupational pension systems in particular, high youth unemployment has made it difficult for young people to begin building eligibility for future pension rights.

Changing family structures also put stress on existing pension system arrangements, particularly where there is a substantial occupational pillar. Increases in both divorce rates and the number of women in full-time employment have challenged arrangements that linked women's pension rights to their husbands' employment. As women have entered as full participants into occupational pension schemes, however, there have also come calls to grant pension entitlements for time spent in child-rearing or elder-care.

Adjustments of pension systems to the challenges of population aging, labour market and family changes may be divided into *parametric* and *structural* reforms. The latter are systemic changes that move systems 'off path' (see below), while the former constitute incremental adjustments to elements of the basic equation linking contributions and benefits.[2] Parametric reforms aim to stabilize or contain a further rise of pension contribution rates by altering the worker/pensioner ratio, the wage replacement ratio, or by adding new sources of funding.

In countries with Bismarckian pension systems, five main types of parametric reforms have occurred beginning in about 1990.

(1) The *contribution/benefit link* has been tightened. Where previously a certain number of years in covered employment sufficed to attain a 'full' pension and the benefit level was determined by earnings achieved during a number of 'best years' or 'last years' prior to retirement, benefit formulae have been changed so that earnings over the entire employment career are taken into account. The strictest (and most transparent) link between lifetime contributions and benefits, which eliminates all internal redistribution, occurs in so called *notional defined contribution* (NDC) schemes, which mimic fully funded plans (with growth of covered wages defining the 'interest rate') but actually operate on a pay-as-you-go (PAYG) basis. Among others, Italy, Sweden, and Poland have shifted their public employment-related schemes to this almost actuarial mode of benefit calculation.

(2) The standard *retirement age* has been lifted from 65 to 67 in the United States and Germany, and made more uniform for the entire workforce in a number of countries, i.e. raised for women when it was lower than for men and for public sector employees if a lower eligibility age existed before. In addition to raising the statutory age of eligibility for full retirement, new or extended options for flexible retirement have been introduced in a number of countries. Individuals who decide to claim a public pension before reaching the standard retirement age incur permanent (and more or less actuarial) deductions from the standard benefit, while those who prolong their working lives beyond the standard age are rewarded with corresponding bonuses.

(3) In almost all countries *indexing formulae* have been modified. Past earnings, which determine the level of the first claimed pension entitlements, are less often

---

[2] Parametric reforms are related to the terms of the following equation: $c = (P : A) * (B : W) * (1—S)$ where: c = the required contribution rate, P = the number of pensioners, A = the number of active workers contributing to the scheme, B = the average pension benefit, W = the average wage subject to contribution payments, S = state subsidy from general taxation (also: withdrawal from accumulated funds).

valued in line with average earnings growth, and increasingly adjusted to match the inflation rate (e.g. in France). Elsewhere, demographic parameters—further life expectancy at retirement age, as in all the Nordic countries and Austria, or the changing contributor/pensioner ratio in Germany (Whitehouse 2009)—have been incorporated in the formula by which the benefit level is determined at the time of retirement. Finally, current pension benefits are increasingly adjusted to consumer prices instead of previous wage development.

(4) The only expansionary type of reform that has been visible in Bismarckian countries since the 1990s is the incorporation of *unpaid family work* into the benefit calculation, so that raising children and/or taking care of frail relatives may now result in (higher) pension entitlements. The procedures for crediting care work and the benefits that accrue to such work vary widely across countries. In most cases the costs of these expansions have been covered out of general tax revenues.

(5) Public pension schemes normally operate on a PAYG basis, holding reserve funds of varying amounts. In a number of countries these *reserves have been temporarily augmented* through a variety of means: by charging a higher contribution rate than is necessary to meet current expenditures (United States, Canada, and Finland), by incorporating revenues from privatizing public enterprises or state budget surpluses, often set aside in earmarked funds to be incorporated in the pension system at a later date (Belgium and France), or by drawing on other publicly owned funds (Norway).

Pressure from population ageing on public schemes that provide only basic pensions (among others, the latecomer countries) is less pronounced than in Bismarckian systems, since in the former the pension systems operate on a smaller scale. Nevertheless even the latecomer countries have undertaken reform measures similar to those seen in Bismarckian systems, for example raising the retirement age (United Kingdom, Denmark and New Zealand) or building up reserve funds (Netherlands, Ireland). Moreover, demographic change has also been utilized as an argument to cut back on basic pensions, e.g. by stricter testing against other (retirement) income (Denmark).

Beyond these incremental changes, *structural reforms* have been implemented in a number of countries that previously relied on earnings-related public schemes as the sole or predominant source of retirement income. International organizations, including the IMF, the OECD, and notably the World Bank, have pressed for such changes. The World Bank has even been directly involved in the reform process in some Latin American and Central and East European transition countries (Müller 2003; Orenstein 2005). In the 1994 publication *Averting the Old Age Crisis*, the World Bank argued that under current demographic and fiscal conditions, a three-pillar pension system was the soundest form of pension system for most polities and praised the Chilean pension reform of 1981 as a model. The type of system the World Bank envisioned would combine a small tax-funded basic pillar to assure a minimum income in old age, a mandatory employment-related funded pillar to provide more substantial benefits, and on top of those, personal pension savings plans to allow for increased consumption in retirement. Because of pre-funding, the latter two pillars were also meant to increase national savings as a vehicle for enhanced economic growth in emerging welfare states.

Therefore, the World Bank's advice was less directed towards welfare states with mature PAYG schemes but, nevertheless, contributed to weakening the prevailing pension policy paradigm in Bismarckian countries. Until about the 1990s, this paradigm had rested on cognitive and normative beliefs about the superiority of the social insurance approach vis-à-vis multi-pillar arrangements. This view was widely shared among political and social actors. The apparent exhaustion of this single-pillar approach in light of long-term financial problems, however, has allowed the competing multi-pillar approach to gain ground in these countries. Real path departure took place when private, funded pillars were introduced or substantially expanded in order to compensate for lower wage replacement that was caused by the first three reform trends mentioned above. Participation in those supplementary schemes is now either mandatory (Sweden, Poland) or voluntary but stimulated by tax advantages (Germany, Austria, France, Italy). By embracing the multi-pillar approach, pension systems in almost all Bismarckian countries have come closer to the structure implemented in *latecomer* countries.

Pension reforms in developed welfare states have followed a general trend of moving away from public (and private) defined benefit schemes towards those that are characterized by the defined contribution (DC) principle (see Table 24.2). This goes along with a 'risk shift' (Hacker 2006): future pensioners will bear as individuals the risks of exposure to financial markets and of increasing longevity.

Both parametric and paradigmatic pension reforms have proved to be difficult, and often involve serious political conflicts (Myles and P. Pierson 2001; Hinrichs 2001). Because pension systems bridge extended time spans—from the start of an earning career until the receipt of the final pension payout—and because the capacity of individuals to adjust to institutional changes decreases with proximity to retirement age, reforms regularly include long phasing-in periods. Nevertheless, public schemes have created large constituencies for whom pensions are of vital significance, and governments' reform efforts may be risky undertakings if they aim at cutbacks of vested rights of current and future pensioners. In order to mitigate the political risks of pension reform, governments have chosen a variety of strategies including forming coalitions with opposition parties to create oversized majorities in

Table 24.2 Funding and types of pension schemes

Pension funding/type	Defined benefit	Defined contribution
Pay as you go	Social insurance type public scheme	Notional defined pension scheme (e.g. Sweden, Italy)
Fully funded	Traditional employer sponsored private pensions	Individual retirement accounts—voluntary (e.g. United States, Germany) or mandatory (e.g. Poland, Chile)

parliament; seeking out cooperation with major stakeholders, notably labour unions and interest organizations of seniors; and/or forming expert commissions to furnish advice that can help legitimize painful decisions.

THE FUTURE OF OLD-AGE PENSIONS

At least three emerging trends in pension systems challenge existing arrangements for current pensioners, and even more for future beneficiaries. As mortality rates at higher ages decline further and, thus, longevity increases, finding a sustainable balance between the length of the working life and the length of retirement will demand an increase in the age of exit from the labour market. Most countries have already taken measures to increase the statutory retirement age, and that at least in theory should lead to a higher average age at retirement. The implementation of such reforms, however, has the potential to increase income inequality in old age because not all employees will be able to work up to age 65 or beyond. Workers in certain disproportionately low-paid occupations often have to terminate employment prematurely due to health reasons. There is a clear negative correlation between individual earnings, ill health, and the risk of forced exit from the labour force. Workers in low-paid occupations are thus penalized on two counts: they tend to have a shorter than 'normal' employment record, which results in lower pension benefits no matter the type or pillar of the pension system; and, on average, given the close relationship between income and life expectancy, they receive these benefits for a shorter period of time.

A second problematic development stems from changes in the labour market (see the previous section). Pension systems generally assume full-time jobs and a continuous employment career in order to guarantee a 'standard' replacement ratio. Women's employment trajectories have never mirrored these assumptions particularly well—so poorly did most women's working lives reflect the normal pattern necessary for a full pension, in fact, that earnings-related pension benefit systems have traditionally treated women as appendages of their working spouses. But factors such as trade internationalization, post-industrialization, labour market deregulation, permanent mass unemployment, and the growth of an informal sector in a number of countries—in addition to rising female participation in the paid labour force—mean that non-standard ('atypical') employment patterns are on the rise. Discontinuous employment careers may result in insufficient pension entitlements if public schemes do not contain redistributive features that ensure socially adequate benefits, and/or if non-redistributive, private DC schemes are prominent in the retirement income mix. The increasing reliance on private, funded pension schemes in the advanced as well as in the less developed welfare states thus increases the risk of insufficient retirement income for citizens with interrupted or otherwise atypical employment histories.

That shift to private, funded DC schemes is also related to a third problematic development. In such schemes, the risks of longevity, inflation, and financial (mis)management and market volatility are all borne by the future retiree. In the aftermath of the financial crisis beginning in the autumn of 2007, the results are painfully clear. Although no final figures are available yet, between January and October 2008, average real pension fund returns in the OECD area was *negative 22 per cent*. Pension funds in the United States lost about 27 per cent in real terms during the first nine month of 2008 (OECD 2009*b*). These financial losses have serious consequences for current and future pensioners, who may suffer dramatic income losses if they are unable to postpone retirement or receive tax-financed bailouts. Moreover, the objective of temporarily increasing the reserve funds of public pension schemes has been thwarted—at least for the time being, and depending on the share of equities in the portfolio (OECD 2009*b*).

Already before the onset of the financial crisis, optimism about funded pensions and the feasibility of the original World Bank strategy had declined in Latin America (Gill et al. 2004). In 2007, Chile put more emphasis on basic security by introducing a tax-funded 'solidarity pillar', and Argentina completely abolished the funded individual accounts that had been envisioned as the core component of the modernized pension arrangement. Nevertheless, and despite recent setbacks, the expanded role for private, funded pensions that has developed in recent decades seems unlikely to be undone. While many voters may demand the security that public schemes seem to offer, the underlying challenges that population ageing, slower growth, and declining employment pose to large, unfunded public pension schemes seem unlikely to abate.

··

CHAPTER 25

HEALTH

··

RICHARD FREEMAN

HEINZ ROTHGANG

Introduction

WE are concerned for our health and by everything which seems to put it at risk. We are alarmed by new diseases and hopeful about new cures for old ones. Our concerns for our health shape what we eat and the way we spend our leisure time even as we worry about the quality and availability of our health care.

Across the OECD, developed countries spend on average 9 per cent of their GDP on health care (OECD 2006c). Health and medicine are key areas of employment in service-based economies, as well as of innovation and investment in science and technology. Outside the OECD, health is a key factor in development. In turn, their social and economic importance mean that health issues are debated across the world, both in the formal arenas of politics and policy making—in parties, parliaments, and ministries—and more widely in the media.

Health, then, is a big deal: big in the sense that it is prominent if not paramount among contemporary social, economic, and political concerns; a deal in that promoting health and providing health care comprise multiple functions distributed among an array of individual, institutional and, organizational actors. Government responsibilities are invested in state agencies including ministries and regional and local health administrations, hospitals and related services as well as quasi-public agencies such as professional bodies and certain kinds of insurer. These interact with businesses small and large, including many doctors in local practice, pharmacists, some hospitals and insurers, and what are often multinational pharmaceutical firms, as well as an array of civil society organizations including trade unions, universities, and charities, associations of patients and users, and, not least, households and families.

In this chapter, we proceed from two macrosociological observations: the emergence and consolidation within societies of 'health systems' as distinct, observable domains of activity (Field 1973), and the construction of those systems as 'public' (Starr and Immergut 1987). Our focus is on the public aspects of health systems, on the ways in which concerns for health and health care are expressed in politics and policy. Consistent with most other cross-national, comparative analyses, we concentrate on OECD countries, partly because they have the most advanced health systems and partly because we draw on the most extensive and substantial comparative health data set available, that produced by the OECD.[1]

We begin by outlining the origins and development of health policy in the modern state, pointing to the different ways that development has been understood by welfare state scholars. We describe different standard forms of health system, discussing the ways health care is paid for, provided, and regulated in advanced industrial countries, and comment on the emergence of a new domain of international and global health.

Our conceptual point of orientation is Michael Moran's idea of the 'health care state', meaning simply 'that part of any state concerned with regulating access to, financing, and organizing the delivery of, health care to the population' (Moran 1992: 79). This thing, we might already expect, is something of a monster. It has three faces: it is at once a welfare state, charged with guaranteeing to deliver health care to its citizens; an industrial capitalist state, concerned to maintain a healthy workforce, yet not overburden employers with taxes and contributions, while even yet supporting its high-tech pharmaceutical and medical device industries; and a liberal democratic state, subject to pressure from parties and organized interests and obliged to a degree of openness and transparency in decision making (Moran 1995). It is the state, then, at least in advanced industrial countries and in many instances elsewhere, too, which processes competing, sometimes complementary, and sometimes contradictory demands for health and health care.

ORIGINS AND DEVELOPMENT

In the modern era, public responsibility for health was first expressed in church and charitable hospitals and foundations, complemented from the sixteenth and seventeenth centuries by statutory Poor Law institutions and then by local public health regulation, including sanitation and vaccination as well as quarantine (Porter 1999). The first national public health departments were often subsections of Ministries of

---

[1] *OECD Health Data*, a set of comparative statistics, is available at www.oecd.org. For detailed and up-to-date descriptions of different national systems in Europe, see WHO's *European Observatory on Health Systems* at www.euro.who.int/observatory. Textbook introductions to the field include Freeman (2000), Blank and Burau (2007), and Marmor et al. (2009).

the Interior or their equivalents: health policy, then, was a matter of policing. Much more recently, and in similar vein, the first European Union initiatives in health have been in respect of prevention, health promotion and public health, dealing variously with food standards, health and safety at work and smoking. In this way, questions about the relative powers and responsibilities of local and national—and supranational—authorities in health regulation are a key feature of state-building.

State licensing of physicians at court or in local guilds began in the late medieval period. The subsequent consolidation of their professional status gave doctors an effective monopoly of medical knowledge: this, in turn, has afforded them a central position in the provision of health care and, where they have been able to mobilize effectively, a veto position in the development of health systems. The institutional position of the medical profession is scarcely matched in any other field of public policy, and is what distinguishes health and health care from other domains of the welfare state. From this perspective, the development of the health care state has seemed a matter of pressure group politics (Eckstein 1960). Doctors are and have been differently organized in different countries, enabling them to assume different degrees of 'professional dominance' (Freidson 1970; Alford 1975). In the United States, for example, doctors only reluctantly came to accept patients with insurance cover, because funds sought to set fees at standard rates (Starr 1982); in the United Kingdom, clinical specialists only agreed to join the National Health Service in 1946 when it was clear how well they would be paid, while general practitioners carried on as independent contractors.

In other ways, the state regulation of health and health care has been understood as a problem of political economy (Korpi 1989; Navarro 1989). Germany's pioneering health insurance legislation of 1883 built on the model of the existing mutual funds set up among workers and by some firms to pay doctors fees and provide limited income maintenance, making such provision mandatory for certain groups of workers under new public schemes. Germany was then still a monarchy, but one which was rapidly industrializing: statutory health insurance represented a way of buying loyalty from an increasingly organized urban working class. In other countries, too, in the course of the twentieth century, schemes set up by bourgeois and conservative governments were subsequently extended and universalized by social democratic parties once in power. In many countries, health insurance expanded incrementally, step by step covering more people for more services, as in France or Germany. Where schemes ran into difficulty, and where labour and the state were both strong (as in the United Kingdom in the late 1940s, and Sweden in the 1960s), insurance-based systems were converted into publicly owned, tax-funded national health services. Where industrial development and democratization came late, as in Southern Europe, so did universal access to health care, in the 1980s.

The development of the health care state shows marked commonalities across countries (Mechanic and Rochefort 1996; Moran 1992): over the hundred years from the 1880s to the 1980s, almost all advanced industrial countries came to guarantee almost all necessary health services to almost all of their citizens under a public scheme. In the period of the long boom, health systems had been allowed to grow and expand, in what amounted to a win-win situation for doctors, patients, payers, and governments alike. Just at the point at which public commitments to health were greatest, however, economic growth slowed. Reinforced by critiques of medicine on one hand and government on the other, the need to control costs led to a period of retrenchment and reform of health care across countries (OECD 1992).

But different countries came to guarantee health care to their populations by different routes and in different ways, using different sorts of institutional apparatus (Anderson 1963). Following this line of thought, comparative investigation of the reform of health systems has been dominated by institutionalist analyses, including those of Immergut (1992*a*), Pierson (1994), Wilsford (1994), Tuohy (1999), and Hacker (2004*b*). In the United Kingdom, for example, a government with a majority in parliament, a unitary state, and a tax-based National Health Service found it easier to slow the growth of the health economy than did coalition governments responsible for stewarding much more pluralist insurance systems in federal or devolved administrations, as in Germany. And for similar reasons, the United States has long found it difficult to establish a guarantee of universal access to health care (at the time of writing, the measure of President Obama's 2010 legislation—though a landmark—is still to become clear).

In the era of expansion, the deal struck between states and professions had left health care systems an arena of 'private government', administered in routine ways and largely in the interests of doctors. But now, once health care costs were relatively contained, attention turned in the 1990s from the macro-management of the health economy to the micro-management of health labour. In both public and private sectors, the 'countervailing power' (Light 1995) of the 'corporate rationalizers' (Alford 1975) began to make itself felt in new forms of 'clinical governance', based on new regulatory instruments for audit and inspection.

HEALTH CARE SYSTEMS

Esping-Andersen's modelling of the 'worlds' of welfare capitalism (see Chapter 39) does not work well for health care systems. His core concept of 'decommodification' fails to discriminate among systems which nowadays provide universal coverage irrespective of labour market participation. It fails, too, to capture the element of service provision which is essential to health care (Moran 2000; Bambra 2005*b*).

Typologies of health care states tend to have been based on sources of financing and a dichotomy of public versus private ownership. The most commonly used distinction is still that between NHS systems, social insurance systems, and private systems though, like all such frameworks, it refers to ideal or typical patterns rather than actually existing arrangements. In national health services, hospitals are publicly owned; access to specialists may be by referral only, giving primary care doctors in local practice a gate-keeping function, and the system is tax-funded, doctors' income being derived principally from salary rather than fees. In social insurance systems, health care is provided either in hospitals owned by regional governments, non-profit organizations, or private firms, or by doctors in local practice, and funded through a patchwork of regional, industry-based, or occupational schemes. In private systems, health care is subject to the normal constraints of the market, provided by hospitals and doctors operating as entrepreneurs and paid for, usually on a fee-for-service basis, either directly ('out-of-pocket') by patients or by commercial insurers to whom they subscribe. In practice, most systems combine elements of more than one type.

National health services tend to predominate in Northern and Southern Europe (in the United Kingdom, Denmark, Sweden, Spain, Italy, and Greece) and social insurance systems in the West and Centre (France and Germany, the Benelux countries and Austria). Since 1990, most countries in the former Central and Eastern Europe have replaced integrated, state-led services with social insurance systems. The United States' health system is different, often mistakenly characterized as 'private'; it may be better described as a case than a type. It is not one system but many, its composition differing often markedly between states. While health insurance has been neither mandatory nor guaranteed, and so much less than universal, two-thirds of the population is covered by private or employer-based schemes, while those over 65 are covered by the federal Medicare programme (Marmor 2000). Hospitals are mostly private, non-profit foundations; most doctors are self-employed, though many are salaried members of group practices. Nevertheless, as a proportion of GDP, government spending on health is higher in the United States than in some European countries.

More recent attempts to classify health systems have focused on patterns of regulation, distinguishing broadly between markets, hierarchies, and networks (Wendt et al. 2009). They begin by identifying three types of stakeholder: service providers (doctors and hospitals), funding bodies (tax agencies and insurers), and beneficiaries (patients). These three, providers, payers, and patients, are party to a complicated triangular relationship. Payers and patients are concerned with who should be covered and on what terms. The relationship between payers and providers, meanwhile, is about remuneration mechanisms or the ways doctors and hospitals are paid, and about their operating conditions or access to markets. Providers and patients are concerned with entitlement to services and the content of the benefits package. At the same time, the regulation of these relationships might fall to three types of actor: the state, corporate bodies such as associations of sickness funds, and private agencies. In turn, therefore, three patterns of regulation can be distinguished: hierarchical control, collective negotiation, and competition.

FINANCE

Even since the end of the 'golden age' of the welfare state in the mid-1970s, health care expenditure has continued to rise across the OECD, not only in absolute terms per capita, but also as a percentage of GDP. This is true both for private and for public expenditure on health. As the share of public expenditure as a proportion of total spending has been declining slightly, however, we may speak in terms of a 'relative privatization' of the costs of health care (Rothgang et al. 2010). At the same time, too, patterns of spending across countries are becoming more alike. For the most part, this convergence is attributable to 'catch-up' effects among latecomers during the 1970s and 1980s (Hitris and Nixon 2001); it is especially pronounced in respect of the public share of total health spending (Rothgang et al. 2005).

How can these developments be explained? Fundamentally, health care spending has risen across advanced industrial countries because medical services are superior goods, which means that spending on them increases with increasing wealth. The share of national wealth spent on health care increases with the wealth of a nation (Arrow 1963; Gerdtham and Jönsson 2000; Docteur and Oxley 2003). This is also the reason why health expenditure as a percentage of GDP has become such a key indicator in international comparisons. There are, however, at least four other, additional explanations for increased spending on health care. First, medical services are personal services, which are much less subject to rationalization than industrial production. As a result, prices for medical services grow faster than the general price index: this 'cost disease of personal services' (Baumol and Oates 1972) produces medical inflation. Second, and related to this, technological progress in medicine tends to be a product rather than a process innovation, meaning that add-on technologies produce additional costs, not savings. Third, the success of health care itself creates future demand for it, as survivors of one treatment often need further therapy according to what has been described as a 'Sisyphus syndrome' (Zweifel et al. 2005). Finally, though there is now some consensus that demographic change has neither been the major driving force for rising health care expenditures in the past nor will it be so in the future, the 'greying of society' entails an increasing number of multi-morbid, chronically ill patients (see Chapter 26).

Meanwhile, what is interesting about the finding of convergence tendencies in public and private shares of health care spending is that it contradicts institutionalist ideas about the particularities and path dependency of health care systems, which would seem to preclude such a common pattern in health care financing. However, a middle way might be expected once universal access and efficient utilization are recognized as shared goals of health care systems. At the same time, some form of co-insurance or co-payment may be deemed necessary to prevent moral hazard. Thus, from an effectiveness and efficiency point of view, convergence tendencies in the public–private mix of financing are less surprising.

Nevertheless, while health financing is an issue everywhere, it is not always the same issue. Where insurance-based systems, which in principle promise 'all necessary services', have sought to limit spending, tax-based systems, which fund services according to what the country can afford, have looked for ways to raise additional resources or to use existing resources more efficiently. By the same token, the single-pipe financing of tax-based systems affords respective governments greater opportunity to control resource flows. Such distinct features of health care systems continue to be important in explaining levels of health care spending, if less so for the public–private mix.

DELIVERY

While pensions and employment benefits are granted in cash, health care systems provide benefits in kind: with social care, social work, and education, they represent the service intensive parts of the welfare state (Bambra 2005b). Across countries, notable trends in health service provision include a growth in health employment and a decline in inpatient beds.

In 1970, total health employment per 1,000 population ranged between 6.6 in Greece and 17.8 in Australia (OECD 2006c). By 2004, health employment density had grown to levels ranging from 13.5 in Portugal to 53.7 in Norway. This growth mirrors that in health spending and is a large part of the explanation for it: the factors which account for the rise in health spending do so because they make for correlative increases in health employment.

During the same period, the number of hospital beds has decreased. In 1970, the United States had 4.1 beds per 1,000 inhabitants and Switzerland 7.1. By 2004, these figures had declined to 2.8 and 3.8 respectively. Across the OECD, acute care bed density now ranges from 2.2 in Sweden to 8.4 in Japan (OECD 2006c). At the same time, the average length of stay in hospitals has been decreasing (Schmid and Wendt 2010). These figures point to more general trends in the relationship between public and private provision, and between primary and secondary care.

A shift from public to private provision of health services may take the form of material privatization, meaning a shift from public to private ownership; formal privatization, which refers to changes in the legal status of a public institution, or functional privatization, which means outsourcing activities which used to be carried by public institutions. Attempts to measure such changes have to take into account shifts between different types of care, which may end up in 'indirect privatization' if, for example, services migrate from the inpatient sector which tends to have a higher share of public service provision to the outpatient sector which has less. By and large, however, both direct and indirect privatization appear to have taken place since around 1990 in almost all OECD countries for which relevant data is available (Schmid and Wendt 2010). Direct material privatization has taken place particularly in the hospital sector, where it is also accompanied by formal privatization.

What are the consequences of this privatization of service providers? In the United States, Silverman et al. (1999) found higher prices and higher price increases over time in private for-profit hospitals as compared to both public and non-profit ones. Devereaux et al. (2002) conducted a systematic review and meta-analyses of fifteen studies and found mortality rates to be moderately but significantly higher in private hospitals, while a parallel study (Devereaux et al. 2004) also found significantly higher prices in private hospitals. As Eggleston et al. (2008) concluded from their systematic review of thirty-one United States-studies, ownership of hospitals is highly correlated with other factors which are responsible for variations in quality. Although the effects of privatization inevitably depend on the environment in which it takes place, this research raises some doubt as to whether it really leads to lower prices and better quality.

Meanwhile, developments in medicine and pharmacology, coupled to new financial and managerial incentives, make it possible for an increasing proportion of patients to be treated in ambulatory and primary care settings. The administrative functions of the general practitioner, such as commissioning and referral, tend to be more marked in NHS systems where the GP has a gatekeeping role. In social insurance systems, a shift to primary care remains more rhetorical than real, partly because patients there have immediate access to specialists in local practice. At the same time, across systems, some of the traditional functions of the family doctor are being lost or devolved to other, newer occupations: these include continuing care, counselling, and other kinds of information and advice-giving.

REGULATION

Health reform across the OECD has made for a blurring of the regulation patterns that go along with different kinds of health care state (Health Care Systems, above; and Rothgang et al. 2010). In this section, we take the United Kingdom, Germany, and the United States as archetypes of respective systems.

In Britain, the purchaser–provider split introduced in 1990 interrupted the vertical chain of command typical of hierarchical regulation. While hospital and primary care providers have become increasingly autonomous, many strategic decisions have been handed over by central government to regional and local bodies (Lewis et al. 2006). As hospitals now have to compete for contracts from primary care trusts, which administer the bulk of NHS care, competition—though the term itself has been replaced by 'commissioning'—has become a principal mechanism of regulation. Competition, decentralization, and other forms of new public management can also be found in other NHS systems.

Competition has also been introduced to Germany's social insurance schemes, initially among funds in order to attract members. In the mid-1990s, the right to choose among different sickness funds was extended from white to blue collar workers, while the introduction of a risk equalization scheme was meant to create the institutional framework needed for fair competition. Collective agreements between groups of funds and providers have been amended by selective contracts between single funds and providers in an increasingly competitive market. This enhanced role for competition has been accompanied by increased direct state interventions. Similar developments can be observed in other social insurance systems in the Netherlands, Belgium, Israel, and elsewhere.

In the United States, on the other hand, hierarchical regulation in the form of managed care has increased not only within the public schemes Medicare and

Medicaid but also and especially in the private sector. Since the 1990s, traditional forms of indemnity insurance have been marginalized while more than 90 per cent of private employer-sponsored programmes are now run by managed care organizations. Health Maintenance Organizations (HMOs) in particular have allowed for a considerable degree of control to be exerted on providers. Though there are significant differences between HMOs and softer forms of preferred provider organization, all managed care organizations are characterized by some degree of hierarchy in a previously unregulated area.

In general, health care systems have adopted 'alien' regulatory mechanisms designed to correct the perceived failings of their established types. This has made for a blurring of regimes that has been reinforced by some common regulatory trends, largely reflecting the emergence of a managerial function in health care systems. This is expressed as much in market-based as in hierarchical systems, in managed care in the United States as much as in new public management in the United Kingdom and the introduction of competition in Germany.

At both national and local levels, managers and policymakers have come increasingly to refer to evidence-based medicine, evidence-based health care, and health technology assessment in defining and redefining benefit packages (Sackett et al. 1996; Jost 2005). Evidence of cost-effectiveness, for example, has become particularly important in regulating access to drugs. One reason for the commonality of such trends is that managerial technologies, like medical technologies, diffuse quickly across countries. For example, the diagnosis-related groups (DRGs) developed to assess the costs of health care in the United States in the 1970s are now used for classifying patients and often for reimbursing hospitals all over the world. Reference pricing for drugs, developed in Germany in the early 1990s, has become similarly widespread.

INTERNATIONAL AND GLOBAL HEALTH

As in many other fields of public policy, health and health care are subject to processes of internationalization and globalization. As in those fields, too, this process is not new. The beginnings of the international regulation of infectious disease, for example, were marked by the International Sanitary Conference which brought doctors and diplomats to Paris in 1851 to discuss public health issues of common concern, notably cholera (Fidler 2003). The creation of the World Health Organization in 1948 gave organizational form to the management of health issues in the UN system, while in Europe, the more recent consolidation of the European Union has had significant implications for health policy.

The competence and autonomy of EU member states with respect to health care is jealously guarded, while the prospect of supranational regulation of health issues has probably been weakened rather than strengthened by the EU's eastward enlargement

(Mckee et al. 2004). The construction and regulation of the Single European Market has had inevitable effects on one of its biggest fields of economic activity, the health sector—though the EU has no specific competence in regulating health care (Randall 2000; Greer 2006). Health insurers, hospital chains, and, in particular, pharmaceutical firms operating across borders are necessarily subject to European legislation (Abraham and Lewis 2000). Most importantly, trans-border utilization of health services has become a gateway into health care systems for European law. Since 1998, a series of European Court of Justice decisions has effectively endorsed the right of citizens of one member state to use health services provided in another. Labour legislation such as the Working Time Directive has changed the way junior doctors work in some countries, while anti-discrimination directives have had major impact on private insurance markets. In the context of the more general development of the EU, that is to say, it is processes of negative rather than positive integration which are currently shaping national health care systems (Leibfried 2005).

Meanwhile, across the world, health issues associated with international social, economic, and political interdependence seem newly salient (Lee et al. 2002). These include the re-emergence of infectious diseases (AIDS, tuberculosis, BSE, and SARS, for example) as well as the perceived implications of disease and poverty in developing countries for international security (Ingram 2004). And while modern health care states remain dependent, for their very functioning, on skilled staff and specialist goods—on professionals and pharmaceuticals—the availability of these has become contingent on the international mobility of health labour and the operation and regulation of multinational firms.

Effective management of such issues is difficult in itself, but made more so by complicated and complex arrangements for international health governance (Kick-Busch 2000). This is a function of three related problems: the number and variety of relevant actors, the underdetermination of the issues with which they are concerned, and the underdevelopment of international institutions of health policy making. WHO has been displaced in international health in part by other UN agencies, such as the Global Program on AIDS (GPA), UNDP, and the World Bank; in part by the pre-eminence of the WTO in trade-related aspects of public health, as expressed in the GATS and TRIPS agreements, and in part by the sharp increase in number of international organizations of different types (IGOs and INGOs, associations, foundations, and corporations) and with different health-related concerns, from charitable missions and professional bodies to development and human rights agencies (Inoue and Drori 2006). This testifies to the way in which health problems can be— and are—readily reconstructed as problems of poverty, security, housing, education or the environment (and vice-versa), which testifies in turn to the nature of health as an essentially contested concept. Finally, health questions are articulated and debated not only by WHO and its Working Groups and Commissions but, as we have seen, in the OECD, in think tanks and other organizations—and not only within but in uncertain institutional spaces between them, in alliances and networks such as the World Economic Forum, in the 'invisible college' of academic seminars and conferences, in issue-based meetings of activists and others. What all this means, of course, is that health governance issues do not emerge in a vacuum somewhere above and beyond other concerns, but at the interface of local, national, regional, and global interests (Hein and Kohlmorgen 2003).

CONCLUSION

We conclude by noting the difference between the problems and pressures which health systems were designed to address and those which they currently face, including global economic competition, scientific and technological development, and demographic change. This gives us pause to wonder whether such changes should in turn prompt change not only in health policy, but in health policy analysis.

Changes in health and health care are compounded by questions about the continuing autonomy and capacity of states, individually and collectively, to regulate them (Reich 2002): to the extent that health regulation is a constituent of statehood (above), questions about health and health care are just as much questions about states. Some new comparative work on health policy takes cities, not countries, as its unit of analysis (Gusmano et al. 2006): major cities are at the cutting edge of health policy not least because they are more international than countries are.

We might ask again about the nature and extent of convergence between health systems across countries (Rothgang et al. 2010). But we might also wonder about the capacity of our standard typology of health care regimes to continue to capture significant difference (Freeman and Frisina 2009). How can we theorize the 'blurring' or 'hybridization' of health care regimes? Are there types of hybrid? Or is hybridity an artefact of our now outdated classification, itself always only a heuristic? Where and how would or should we begin again to describe and classify health systems?

International health issues are interesting not least because they cut across the logic of comparison. In some areas of health policy, Galton's problem has become inescapable: we can no longer treat countries as discrete, separate entities, comparing and contrasting between them. We have also to take interaction effects—flows between them of goods (pharmaceuticals and medical devices, accounting and regulatory instruments), people (doctors, nurses, and patients) and, not least, information—into account.

We should also recognize the extent to which comparison has become an instrument of policy, and not just of policy analysis. Within systems, individuals and agencies are measured against best practice and the behaviour of their peers. Something similar happens across systems, too: implicitly, as policymakers make sense of their own systems in terms of cross-national, comparative data (OECD *passim*), but also explicitly when systems as a whole or in part are subject to international benchmarking (WHO 2000). To understand contemporary health governance, then, we need not only to compare what governments and other actors do, but also to study the comparisons they themselves make.

CHAPTER 26

LONG-TERM CARE

AUGUST ÖSTERLE
HEINZ ROTHGANG

INTRODUCTION

FRAILTY, chronic illness, or disabilities can lead to limiting conditions in various spheres and activities of daily living. 'Long-term care' (LTC) has become an established term covering the heterogeneous range of 'care' provisions that can help and support people in these situations. Services can include nursing care, personal assistance, domestic help, and social support, but also supervision and care management. The emotional dimensions of care, such as personal relationships between carers and those cared for or the intimacy of care work, imply particular conditions and challenges for the understanding and the organization of care (Daly 2002).

From a welfare state perspective, LTC is a latecomer. For many decades, welfare states did not address LTC as a specific social risk. From the 1980s and 1990s, awareness of LTC and the need to ensure more systematic coverage has started to increase across the OECD. Countries have implemented novel or broadened earlier schemes. Others are currently considering more comprehensive LTC programmes. And the need for LTC will further increase because of demographic trends. Changes in the socio-economic context and in the understanding of individual, family, and public responsibility will have major implications for traditional care arrangements, while care policies themselves will feedback into perceptions.

The objective of this chapter is to outline and analyse the current state of LTC policies; the interconnectedness of welfare state, family, and other actors in the field; the challenges LTC systems face; and the major strands and perspectives for research. A lack of reliable comparative data and broad variations in terminology used are just one indication of the relative novelty of welfare state development and welfare state research in this area. Comparability and even availability of international data on LTC is still very limited as LTC is not well covered in international databases, but organizations such as WHO, OECD, or Eurostat and projects such as SHARE (Survey of Health, Ageing and Retirement in Europe) or HRS (US Health and Retirement Study) are working towards improved quality. Terminological differences in addressing, for example, care institutions (nursing home care, residential care, care homes, etc.) or caregivers (carers, care takers, care workers, etc.) and respective terms in other languages are an indication or accentuation of diverse understandings of roles and concepts but also a source of misunderstandings.

The chapter is organized in three main sections. In the next section, the role of the welfare state in LTC will be analysed. Following a brief historical outline and a view of LTC in comparative welfare state analysis, this section examines the ways in which LTC is defined and addressed in welfare state policies by looking at regulatory, financing and delivery structure. In the section following on from this, the relationship between welfare state, families, non-profit, and for-profit market sectors as well as novel arrangements between market and family are at the centre of the analysis. A final section focuses on selected future policy and research challenges including a discussion of future care needs and potential sources of provision. A brief summary concludes the chapter.

LONG-TERM CARE AND THE WELFARE STATE

Long-Term Care: A Latecomer in Welfare State Development

The need for LTC is not new, and indeed has always been a risk of human existence. However, unlike the welfare state giants of illness, unemployment, and old age (see Chapter 5), it has only quite recently been recognized as a specific social risk requiring welfare policy intervention. Care needs have traditionally been catered for within family networks and, historically, support from outside family or household networks came either from charitable sources or local social assistance. This provision was, however, extremely limited in coverage and extent, being mostly help for the very poorest. Apart from the Nordic countries, where more universalistic approaches began in the 1940s, LTC in many OECD countries was characterized by fragmentation and residualism into the 1980s and beyond. LTC was widely understood or even defined as a family responsibility with social assistance oriented public support. Residual welfare state support was found in health policies, pension policies, disability policies, or housing policies, but boundaries between policy sectors and the definition of LTC responsibilities often remained vague. And specific population groups in need of care such as frail elderly, disabled, or chronically ill, were addressed differently by different welfare sectors.

It is only in the past twenty years that welfare states have intensified efforts to address LTC as a specific social risk and have begun to search for more comprehensive policy approaches. The origins and drivers of these developments are manifold. Concepts of autonomy, normalization, or empowerment deriving from initiatives around disability needs (see Chapter 28) had an important impact on the understanding of LTC and ways to enable people to receive support. Traditional ways of covering LTC needs in hospitals or old age homes have been increasingly questioned for quality and for efficiency concerns, while traditional informal care provision is challenged by changes in socio-economic context, labour market, and migration characteristics, and the understanding of work and care or perceptions of individual, family, and public responsibilities. Finally, growing care needs, changes in the content of needs (e.g. dementia), and the implications for public funding drive LTC policies.

Welfare State Models and Long-Term Care

LTC and care work in general are characterized by particular, often interrelated, features. These include care as a good between work and love, the context of filial norms and family obligations, the gender dimension, the range of actors, and the mix of provisions (England 2005; Daly 2002). The mixed use of cash benefits, social services, and tax credits structures the organization of care, and is a reflection of underlying values and ideological principles. While levels of welfare state support follow roughly along the lines suggested by welfare state models, the actual mix and the organizational context of support emphasize particular objectives, principles, and traditions.

LTC has not been a key focus in the comparative welfare state models literature. Increasingly, however, the concept and the various facets of LTC, the organization of care at the boundaries of family, state, and market or the particular cash and service mix in LTC policies have been taken up in the literature. Attempts to cluster care regimes do not produce a very distinct picture compared to broader welfare state regime approaches, but they point at the diversity within social care (when comparing child care and LTC), at the diversity in the mix of cash and in-kind support and the different roles of actors involved. Anttonen and Sipilä (1996) identify two distinct social care models, the Scandinavian model of public services and the mostly Southern European family care model, and two more intermediary models, the Central European subsidiarity model and the British model of means-testing. Similarly, Bettio and Plantenga (2004) categorize the Southern European countries, scoring high for informal care and low for formal care, and the Northern European countries, with a universalistic approach and relatively high levels of formal care provision, as the two most clear-cut clusters. Timonen (2008) makes out three paradigms and three related care regimes, emphasizing the role of the state, the role of individuals and families, and the division between the funding role of the state and the providing role of the private sphere.

Other traditions and developments characterize the Asia Pacific Rim (Chi et al. 2001). Across the region, family and informal care make up the largest share of care provision, with filial norms being particularly strong in the Asian countries. There is also, however, an increasing recognition of LTC as a social risk leading to new paradigms in the organization of care. Japan was the first country to introduce a separate LTC insurance scheme in the Asian countries (Ikegami 2007), and South Korea is following that path (Kwon 2007). LTC systems in Australia, New Zealand, the United States, and Canada emphasize care services, but there is also a long tradition of paying family carers as in Australia and a recent trend towards more personalized care emphasizing consumer orientation as in the United States (OECD 2005a; Ungerson and Yeandle 2007). In developing countries, publicly funded LTC is, for the most part, narrowly focused on home health care or is not provided at all (Brodsky et al. 2008). In what follows, the regulatory structure, the financing structure, and the delivery structure (Alber 1995; Rothgang et al. 2005) are taken as cornerstones for examining the role of the welfare state in LTC in more detail.

Regulatory Structure

The regulatory structure of a welfare scheme entails the definition of state, societal, and private responsibilities, the allocation of public responsibilities to levels of government and welfare sectors as well as definitions of quality and quantity of the content of regulations. In terms of obligations, systems differ between countries with dominant state responsibilities in LTC and countries with legal or moral norms making care largely a responsibility of parents and children or the wider extended family. The (re-)definition of the extent of family and state responsibility and the definition of state and broader private sector roles is at the core of many recent LTC reform efforts. Major reforms in countries such as Germany, Japan, and France have substantially extended public responsibilities in recent years, but without abolishing the key role of family in care provision. At the same time, countries with traditionally strong state responsibility, such as Sweden, have rediscovered the role of family and explicitly or implicitly addressed the family's role in defining the degree of state support (Pavolini and Ranci 2008). In terms of regulatory roles, LTC is often characterized by strong local or regional competences and—at least as long as LTC is not addressed as a specific social risk—by regulatory competences in different welfare sectors (Daly 2002). Boundaries between health and social care are defined very rigidly in some countries (such as the United Kingdom) while they remain rather vague in others. Often an additional split is by the level of government, when health care is a federal and LTC a regional or local responsibility, or when LTC is administered at central, regional, or local levels (OECD 2005a).

The major objects of regulation are the definition of LTC as a social risk, the definition of support schemes (transfers, services, or tax credits), of target population and entitlement rules, quality and quantity of support as well as regulations concerning the organization of service provision and funding. While there is some broad consensus on the understanding of LTC as a social risk, explicit or implicit practical definitions vary widely across countries and even within countries. For the definition of target population and quality and quantity of support, a variety of eligibility criteria is applied. At the core of all these definitions is some concept of need (see Chapters 2 and 11). And need is interpreted quite differently in content and in the level of need that activates welfare state support. In some schemes needs assessment refers to limiting conditions in activities of daily living (ADLs) or instrumental activities of daily living (iADLs), in others the focus is on the requirements arising from these limitations. Some schemes emphasize a medical orientation in the assessment, while others are strictly social care oriented. The assessment can be undertaken for specific services or across potential provisions, by individual experts or interdisciplinary teams, with more or less involvement of users and potential informal carers. In addition to needs orientation, welfare state schemes often apply additional criteria such as age (e.g. when differentiating the provision made for younger disabled and frail elderly people), status (e.g. by considering the family context) or economic background (e.g. by applying means-testing) (Österle 2001). These different approaches in defining entitlement lead to substantial variations in personal and material coverage. For example, in Austria, LTC beneficiaries are 5 per cent of the population, while, in Germany, the figure is 2.5 per cent, in both cases, without age limit or means-testing.

Financing Structure

Levels of public expenditure on LTC vary more than in any other welfare state sector. According to OECD figures, spending levels range between 2.9 per cent of GDP in Sweden and less than 0.3 per cent in Korea, Hungary, or Mexico (OECD 2005a). Because of a lack of widely accepted definitions of LTC, differences in the boundaries between health care and LTC and alternative ways of collecting or modelling the data, the quality and comparability of the respective information is still a major concern. Different sources report quite different levels of public expenditure on LTC, again reflecting the relative novelty of this policy sector. Notwithstanding these quality concerns, spending levels confirm the different welfare state approaches to LTC, ranging from the most comprehensive policy schemes in Northern European countries (with spending levels above 1.5 per cent of GDP), to countries that have addressed LTC with novel schemes in the past two decades (with spending levels between 1 and 1.5 per cent of GDP) and countries where LTC is only a slowly emerging welfare sector or where LTC coverage is largely social assistance based (with spending levels below 0.5 per cent).

Overall, private provision is the major source of LTC funding. Private funding includes the use of unpaid care work provision from family members, income, or private savings, while the role of private insurance remains very limited (Norton

2000). With regard to public funding and pooling of funds for welfare state provision in LTC (Wittenberg et al. 2002), social insurance arrangements are less widespread than in health system funding (see Chapter 25). Major LTC insurance schemes exist in Germany, Luxembourg, the Netherlands, and Japan. In most other countries, public provision of LTC is largely tax-funded even though new social insurance arrangements are being discussed in Eastern Europe, Asia, and some Mediterranean countries.

The division of public and private responsibilities in funding LTC is an important characteristic of the welfare state approach in LTC. In the universal welfare states predominant in Northern Europe, care provisions are covered publicly, even though they entail private co-payments differentiating for income. More recent developments, such as the German or Japanese LTC insurance schemes, also apply a universality principle. But at the same time, benefit caps limit the range and quantity of services covered. Beyond these limits, LTC is defined as a private responsibility. Given the challenges arising from increasing care needs and declining family care potentials, many countries are currently searching for new strategies. Their objective is to ensure the availability of support beyond traditional social assistance programmes while at the same time containing public expenditure. Current debates include new ways of addressing assets in defining individual co-payments or models of reversed mortgage.

Delivery Structure

Current trends in the delivery structure of LTC are characterized by an extension of care in the community, a redefinition of residential care, the introduction of cash-for-care schemes and a slowly increasing recognition of informal carers as addressees of LTC policies. Care in the community is generally seen as a favourable approach enabling people to stay in their community and allowing a more adequate and more cost-effective response to needs. A considerable extension in this sector is accompanied by targeting of services towards high dependency, references to private resources (be it financial or in terms of informal caregiving), user orientation and choice, an emphasis of the role of the state as purchaser and the private sector as provider, and the increasing importance of quality monitoring (Doyle and Timonen 2007; Burau et al. 2007). The focus on high dependency and the purchaser/provider split also characterize developments in the nursing home sector. Increasingly, these institutions provide people with extended care needs where other provision is not adequate or not available. This has led to a reduction of beds in a few countries, while many countries—because of the original lack of services—are still extending care beds. According to the OECD (2008f), bed density in nursing homes in 2006 ranges between less than 20 beds per 1000 population aged 65+ in countries like Italy, Poland, or Korea, to more than 80 in Sweden and between 40 and 60 in many European countries, Australia, or the United States.

Historically, many welfare states provided some kind of cash benefit related to dependency. These benefits, however, were mostly designed and understood as subsidies to those on low levels of income. Recent cash-for-care developments more strictly designed for the support of dependent (elderly) people, either as personal budgets or as consumer directed cash allowances, have become a major new response to care needs in Europe and in the United States (Ungerson and Yeandle 2007; Glendinning and Kemp 2006; OECD 2005a). There are a variety of approaches: some focusing on the autonomy and choice for the person in need, others on financial support for service consumption or care employment, and still others on creating an impetus for market driven developments in the care sector. Variations in the options for using the benefit emphasize different underlying objectives: an emphasis on free choice for users, on regular employment of care work, or on the quality of services used. While the specific use of the benefit is not predetermined in systems in Austria, Italy, or Germany (in the latter case, when opting for the cash benefit), personal budgets in the Netherlands, direct payments in the United Kingdom or consumer-directed home care in the United States predefine potential uses.

WELFARE MIXES IN LONG-TERM CARE

Family Care

Despite a considerable extension of social services for dependent elderly people, close family members, in particular women, remain the major source of unpaid care. Except for the Nordic countries, it is estimated that about 70 to 80 per cent of care is provided within families. Among those providing long hours of care for heavily dependent elderly, the proportion of women in many countries exceeds 80 per cent. And it is also mainly women who confront the trade-offs related to informal caregiving and paid employment (Carmichael et al. 2008). The breadwinner model, the concept of defamilization, and the citizenship paradigm emphasize different ways of approaching these gender dimensions (Lewis 2007a; Knijn and Kremer 1997; Chapter 17, above). Filial norms and preferences for elder care within family networks remain strong, but vary considerably (Daatland and Herlofson 2003; Ikegami 2007). When asked about the best option for an elderly parent in need of regular help, 30 per cent of respondents in the EU27 regard cohabitation as the best option, followed by social services providing help in the home of the frail elderly person (27 per cent), and children regularly visiting and providing parents with help (24 per cent) (European Commission 2007a). But the survey reveals enormous variations across the continent. Cohabitation or support by children is the preferred option of more than half of the population in most Central-Eastern and Southern European countries, but less than 25 per cent in Sweden, Denmark, or the Netherlands. Similar patterns of family preference and variation across Europe can be found when Europeans are asked about preferences if they should need care themselves. Almost half (45 per cent) would prefer to be cared for by a relative in their own home.

The organization of care is embedded in and shaped by general welfare state policies and its underlying, potentially gendered principles (see Chapter 17). At the practical level, the decisions made by individuals and families on whether and how to provide and use informal care work within the family are a response to values, existing social protection rights in terms of availability and accessibility, but also the individual economic background that determines the ability and willingness to pay for alternative care arrangements. While the core focus in LTC policies is on those in need of care, there also is a slowly increasing recognition of informal family caregivers. Policies addressing caregivers as a resource attempt to lower the enormous burdens involved with informal caregiving, to recognize the work delivered but also to sustain this source of caregiving. Particular challenges arise for family carers of working age. Informal caregiving in these situations is associated with substantial costs of foregone labour market opportunities, partly because of foregone income, partly because of the need to adapt paid employment arrangements, and partly because of discrimination in social security rights, such as foregone pension insurance contributions (Carmichael et al. 2008; Bolin et al. 2008).

Policy measures directly addressing informal carers include cash benefits, services and the recognition of informal care work in social security regimes (Lamura et al. 2008). While most cash-for-care programmes direct benefits towards the person in need of care, many countries have also developed programmes providing payments to informal carers. Examples include carer payments and carer allowances in Australia, carer benefits in Ireland, or care leave programmes for those caring for a terminally ill relative as in Canada or in Ireland, (OECD 2005a). Additional services for family carers include advice and information or care work relief programmes as well as the recognition of care work periods in social protection schemes. Major indirect support for family care is provided with social services and benefits directed at the person in need of care.

The implications of these support measures for family carers and for the gendered division of care work depends again on the broader context of general welfare and more specific LTC policies, and the ways in which entitlements enter the processes and decisions in the family context. Given their size, many existing measures directly addressing informal carers will not make any fundamental change in the processes and decisions made in families. However, they can increase the recognition of the risks and burdens involved with family caregiving and, thus, impact on processes in the medium term. More importantly, whether potential caregivers have a choice to either provide or not to provide informal care work will be determined by the extent of available and affordable services from outside households. In particular, where public coverage of LTC needs is limited, the use of cheap labour in grey markets, mostly provided by migrants, has become more widespread, but again limited to those who have the necessary economic background. Where care work in the household is delivered by social services or by care workers employed in the household, family carers partly shift their roles towards that of care managers.

Non-Profit and For-Profit Actors

The private non-profit or voluntary sector has for long been an important initiator of services supporting people in need of care. From the early nursing home and social service initiatives in the nineteenth century, non-profits have been major providers of services. With the development of more comprehensive and publicly (co-)funded service structures, non-profits increasingly became contracted providers. In addition to the providing role, non-profit organizations also act as major lobbyists for the elderly or for family carers. The role of private for-profit providers is traditionally strong in the nursing home sector in the United States (Norton 2000) and, more recently, in countries like New Zealand and the United Kingdom. The role of such actors is increasingly important across OECD countries, both as contracted providers as well as in pure market sectors.

This growth in private sector initiatives is rooted in specific welfare state policies but also in the broader context of LTC. In terms of welfare state driven developments, the introduction of cash-for-care schemes and of a market orientation in the service sector are the main determinants. Explicitly or implicitly, and depending on the specific design, consumer-driven programmes (personal budgets or cash-for-care) emphasize autonomy and choice on the side of users, and competition on the side of potential providers. Additionally, the development of contractual relationships between public funders and private providers with accreditation and quality supervision is leading to quasi-markets in the care sector (Pavolini and Ranci 2008). This has opened up new opportunities for competitive private sector initiatives and has also led to privatization in countries with originally strong public service orientation. Connected with these trends, private sector developments are driven by shifts away from pure family care arrangements. Trends in employment participation, migration patterns, and changes in perceptions of family responsibility increasingly question traditional care arrangements where the entire care work is provided within the family network. To what extent this leads to marketization of care work, depends on the ability and willingness to pay for market services, which is largely co-determined by the extent of publicly funded schemes.

Migrant Care

The pressure on traditional family-centred care work arrangements together with increased but still limited welfare state programmes has in some countries led to a spreading of new care work arrangements between families and markets, between affective and contractual relationships. Cash-for-care schemes as 'routed wages' (Ungerson and Yeandle 2007) have created a particular drive for such arrangements, including migrant care and paid work of family members, in the latter case, novel cash-for-care schemes that have allowed for or even aimed at some commodification of family care work. For example, the French care system emphasizing care work employment explicitly supports the employment of family members (Morel 2007).

The development of migrant care markets has been particularly pronounced in Southern Europe and in some Central European countries (Da Roit et al. 2007). This development is driven by three interconnected factors. First, the arrangement offers an effective alternative to family care (e.g. when searching for a way to balance informal care obligations and paid employment) when social service provision is unavailable or too costly. Second, in many countries, cash-for-care schemes provide money without limiting use to some predefined options. Third, the arrangements often allow better incomes for those providing care compared to the income opportunities available in their home countries. However, these migrant care markets often exist as grey or even black care market arrangements outside labour and social security regulations. Apart from the lack of social protection rights, this undermines the development of social services and puts service quality and quality of employment relationships at risk. Regularization efforts in countries like Italy, Spain, or Austria have created new care work sectors with basic employment rights and relatively low pay that have helped preserve the relative cost-effectiveness of the approach. Apart from the issues of the social rights of carers and the organization of care work in the target country, particular challenges also arise for the home countries. On the macro level, migration of qualified carers can cause shortages in the care sector in the source countries and, on the micro level, adjustments are required in the families of migrant carers (Zechner 2008; Yeates 2008).

CHALLENGES AND PERSPECTIVES

Ageing and Future Long-Term Care Needs and Costs

The need for LTC is an age-related risk. As a result of the baby boom generation approaching retirement age, and as a consequence of an increase in life expectancy and low fertility rates, the number of elderly citizens will increase in absolute numbers and as a proportion of total population (OECD 2007*i*; Norton 2000; Jacobzone et al. 1998). According to OECD (2007*i*) estimates, the OECD population aged 65+ in relation to total population will grow from 13.8 per cent in 2005 to 20 per cent by 2030 and 25.2 per cent by 2050. Among the age group 85+ the increase will be of the order of 250 per cent (1.55 per cent of population in 2005 compared to 5.2 per cent in 2050). In order to project the future prevalence of LTC needs, demographic scenarios and dependency rates are combined (European Commission 2006*a*; Jacobzone et al. 1998). In the European Union, for example, assuming constant age- and sex-specific dependency rates, the number of people in need of LTC will more than double by 2050. According to OECD (2007*i*), between 2003 and 2030, considering only the population ageing effect, the number of people aged 65 and over with severe disability could more than double in countries like Australia, Canada, or Finland.

The results of such forecasts, however, are highly sensitive to changes in assumptions on mortality and dependency rates (Comas-Herrera et al. 2006). First, the need of LTC depends on age, but also on the proximity to death (Norton 2000). If life expectancy grows, age-specific prevalence rates, which can be conceived as the weighted mean of age-specific prevalence rates conditioned on the proximity to death, are going to decline. Second, age-specific prevalence rates decrease when a compression of morbidity is assumed (OECD 2007i). However, even assuming more moderate dependency levels, there will still be a very marked growth in the number of dependent people.

With regard to the welfare state costs involved, apart from trends in dependency, the future service structure, the extent of formal care use, price levels in the service sector and the macro-economic performance of the respective country have to be taken into account (Stearns et al. 2007; Oliveira Martins and De la Maisonneuve 2006; Comas-Herrera et al. 2006; European Commission 2006a). The European Commission study (2006a) concludes that LTC expenditure as proportion of GDP will almost double in a pure ageing scenario and increase by about two-thirds when assuming more moderate dependency levels. Assuming unchanged use profiles, increases are likely to be sharper in countries with well-developed publicly funded LTC systems. But while many of these countries are currently searching for cost containment approaches in LTC, other countries are still in the early stages of developing more comprehensive care systems. The range of current public expenditure on LTC between 0.3 per cent and 2.9 per cent of GDP in OECD countries, gives an indication of the implications of different welfare state approaches towards the risk of dependency on public expenditure.

Directions for Long-Term Care Policies

The ways in which societies respond to the need of LTC are developing in a complex interplay of demographic and socio-economic changes, perceptions and understandings of care and the organization of care work, but also the fiscal burdens involved. In most countries, informal caregiving is the backbone of LTC. But the ability and willingness for family caregiving is under substantial pressure. This is first, for demographic reasons as the number of children per dependent elderly is decreasing. Second, it is a consequence of changing patterns of family and household composition and migration. Third, it is a function of increasing labour market participation among women and postponing retirement age that increases opportunity costs of family caregiving. Fourth, the acknowledgment of LTC as a social risk reduces the perceived obligation for families to care. While most studies argue that relationships will remain strong despite these changes, the aforementioned challenges will affect the content of informal caregiving, require new care arrangements and a rethinking of concepts of intergenerational equity (Saraceno 2008).

From a welfare state perspective, two broad issues will dominate policy agendas: the provision of adequate and high quality care and the supply of sufficient and sustainable funding in an ageing society. In terms of LTC funding, and except for informal care work input, four potential sources can be identified: private financial means; (voluntary or mandatory) private insurance with risk-related premiums, with or without public subsidies or transfers; social insurance with income-related contributions and tax-based public systems with or without means-testing (Wittenberg et al. 2002). As individual expenditure in case of LTC needs would fast exceed the financial ability of large parts of the population, individual income or savings cannot work as the basis of sustainable funding. The private alternative of risk-related private insurance premiums would have far-reaching selectivity effects, excluding most of the older people, those in bad health and those with low income. The related concern of being uninsured can only be resolved if private insurance is mandatory and a system of premium caps and subsidization applies. With these regulations, a mandatory private insurance system comes close to a social insurance system. If there is a consensus on universal coverage, equal access, and sustainable funding as the major funding regime objectives, LTC systems need strong elements of some kind of public funding.

With regard to the actual provision of care, a projected increase in needs, pressures on informal caregiving, and potential shortages of care work labour in the formal sector challenge LTC policies. Strategies facing this development can address both the demand and the supply of care work. Healthier ageing with a compression of morbidity would definitely have a major impact on containing future care needs, but it is highly debatable to what extent this can be achieved. Moving from overall demand to demand for publicly funded professional care work from outside households, many countries have emphasized policy approaches that attempt to maintain or activate informal caregiving resources, be it by supporting family or other informal caregiving (through, e.g. financial incentives, social rights, or respite care) or by referring to family and household networks when defining eligibility criteria for social services. Turning to the supply-side of the care work sector, various attempts have been made to develop cost-effective approaches to the delivery of LTC. Most importantly, the emphasis on community care rather than institutional care is at least co-determined by efficiency concerns, where a combination of external paid support and informal support is provided in an already existing environment. A stricter differentiation in care work tasks and related competences is another efficiency approach. This, however, might heavily interfere with the more personal and emotional aspects of caregiving that to a considerable extent define quality of care and cannot be split from the more technical aspects of caregiving.

In the attempt to balance financial sustainability and the provision of adequate LTC, quality is moving towards the centre of debates on future LTC systems. Quality concerns are raised in recent consumer directed developments, when policymakers have to make a decision about the scope of choices. Choices, quality, and cost are also at the centre of quasi-market developments of publicly funded and privately provided services. Quality monitoring and accreditation procedures that adequately grasp user satisfaction and quality of care are indispensable to prevent cost containment at the expense of quality in increasingly competitive sectors. Finally, from a system perspective, integration is a key concern in LTC policies. Integration refers to ensuring a continuum of care. It refers to linking inputs in care arrangements that are based on both formal and informal care resources, and it refers to linking provisions where these are from different welfare sectors, most importantly from health and social care. While merging these two sectors in most countries is not seen as an adequate approach to integration, institutional linkages between separate subsystems, multidisciplinary approaches to LTC, and individual case and care management approaches are on the agenda in most advanced LTC, systems but developed to very different degrees.

Conclusions

LTC has come to the forefront of welfare state development after the end of the 'golden age' when welfare state policies became increasingly shaped by economic pressures and ideas of reconstruction or retrenchment. Many countries have implemented new LTC policies that move away from traditional characteristics of fragmentation and residualism. Other countries have proposed such policies, but implementation has been hindered above all for budgetary reasons. The novelty of LTC as a welfare state issue has encouraged thinking beyond traditional development paths, while at the same time developments remain deeply rooted in the traditional principles and ideas of particular welfare models.

In the past twenty years, welfare state developments in LTC have been characterized by a considerable degree of convergence. Starting from very different understandings of public and private responsibilities, there is a clear, even though often slow, trend towards recognizing a welfare state responsibility for the care of frail elderly people. At the same time, this responsibility is clearly limited in its extent, leading to some re-individualization or re-familialization of care in countries with originally extended levels of public support. The focus on institutional care for high dependency, the emphasis of mobile care services, the implementation of cash-for-care schemes, and some recognition of family care are other signs of convergence. At the same time, LTC policies are closely related to welfare state identities and traditions, which limit the aforementioned converging trends. Taken together, path dependency in LTC relates primarily to the general understanding of family, state and market relationships, while most countries do not look back to decades of comprehensive and strong sector specific policies in LTC. With increasing needs for LTC and changing contexts in which care is organized, LTC is a key concern of welfare state development in the twenty-first century. Given the relative novelty of LTC on the welfare state agenda, responding effectively to the challenges will require substantial investment in improving the information base and developing systematic research, reflection, and international exchange.

CHAPTER 27

WORK ACCIDENT AND SICKNESS BENEFITS

OLLI KANGAS

INTRODUCTION

THIS chapter traces past and present trends in the institutional development of work accident and sickness daily allowance schemes. The focus is mainly on OECD countries but in some instances references are made to a wider array of countries. The entry begins with a review of the history of work accident insurance, in most countries, the first social insurance programme legislated; its history highlights a number of factors behind the development of later programmes.

The latter part of the chapter focuses on sickness insurance. Again, we begin with historical developments, focusing, in particular, on the universalism and generosity of benefits. We then move on to discuss the extent to which sickness benefits have, in recent years, been targets for retrenchment. The final section tentatively discusses future trajectories of these two income maintenance programmes.

WHY DID WORK ACCIDENT COME FIRST?

The implementation of social insurance programmes followed a sequential pattern (Alber 1982). The order of the adoption of different programmes is depicted in Figure

27.1, which displays the time periods during which five main social insurance schemes were implemented (SSA 1999). The interpretation of the plots is straightforward. The upper boundary of the box is set at the 75th percentile and the bottom boundary represents the 25th percentile. Thus, half of the cases fall within the box. The median values for each scheme are indicated by the horizontal lines inside the boxes. The lines drawn from the upper and lower edge of the percentile box represent cases that are not outliers, e.g. cases with values of more than 1.5 box-lengths either from the upper or the lower boundary of the box. The minimum and maximum non-outliers are indicated by the short horizontal lines. Circles above or below these lines pertain to outliers. OECD-18 comprises Australia, Austria, Belgium, Canada, Denmark, Finland, France, Germany, Ireland, Italy, Japan, the Netherlands, New Zealand, Norway, Sweden, Switzerland, the United Kingdom, and the United States. OECD-18 countries have been excluded from their respective continent values. This diagram expands the sample of countries usually examined and seeks to avoid the OECD-bias from which the comparative social policy literature (including this entry) generally suffers.

In all continents, the first measure enacted was work injury insurance. Judging by the sequential order, work accident insurance enjoyed a greater legitimacy than the other schemes. The incidence of social security programmes throughout the world tells the same story. By the turn of the millennium, the majority of countries in the world were providing insurance against work accidents (167 countries), while only a minority (69 countries) provided unemployment allowances.

While early development of sickness benefits in OECD-18 and Europe kept pace with accident insurance, later developments in these programmes diverged. While the introductory period for accident insurance ranged from 1871 in Germany to 1918 in Canada, the range in sickness insurance is from 1883 in Germany to the latecomers Finland (1963), Canada (1972), and the United States, which introduced its first federal programme in 2010.

The United States case immediately highlights the issue of the timing of social programmes in federal states. In the United States, Australia, and Canada some states have adopted laws considerably earlier than others. The common procedure in macro-historical research has been to code the first laws according to the first state—e.g. in the United States the initial year for work accident is 1909 (the first law in Montana), whereas it was not until 1948 that Mississippi got workers' compensation (E. Berkowitz and M. Berkowitz 1984: 268). Why 1909 is the correct choice for United States programme adoption is not obvious. This problem is linked to the definition of research units in comparative studies. Generally, the standard unit of comparison is the nation state, but federal states challenge the appropriateness of such a focus. Nor is timing the only difficulty; policy making in federal states often has a rather different character to that in unitary and centralized states (Obinger et al. 2005a).

There have been a variety of explanations for the sequence in which these programmes were adopted. The earliest comparative studies emphasized structural

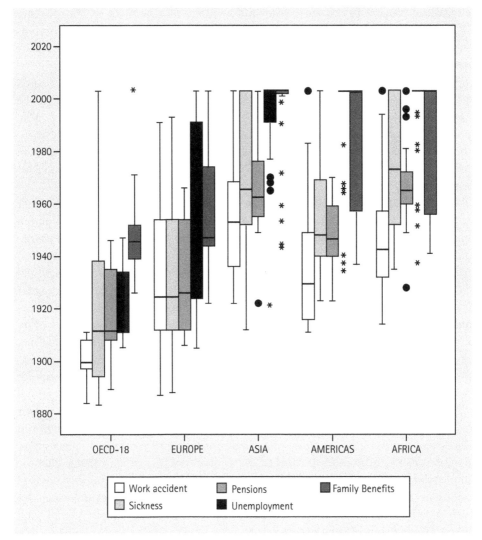

Figure 27.1 The sequential introduction of social insurance laws in different continents and in the OECD-18, with OECD-18 countries excluded from their continents (since the 1880s)

causes or the logic of industrialism (Kerr et al. 1960; Wilensky 1975, 2002). The rationale is easy to accept: work accidents were most closely related to industrial production and, as the number of workers involved in industrial production expanded, the risk of industrial accidents increased. Hence, the structural transformation created pressure to provide protection against the industrial hazards.

The second brand of explanation draws on the specific character of work accidents: the step from the old liberal idea of liabilities for individually caused damages to compulsory accident insurance was not a particularly big one, and represented a less radical break with the spirit of liberalism than other forms of social insurance (Flora and Alber 1981). Civil law liability was transformed into employers' compulsory payments to an insurance carrier who provided the damaged worker with legally defined benefits (Zöllner 1982).

The main body of comparative social policy literature is more conflict-oriented and emphasizes conflicts between employers and employees. According to the common wisdom, organized labour has been the driving force in statutory social policy, whereas organized capital has been the impediment to programme development. However, it has also been argued that employers have had a genuine interest in promoting social legislation (Swenson 2002), with work accident coverage a prominent instance.

Early work injury measures, whether resting on common law procedures or employers' liability legislation, were based on the fault principle and the injured had to sue the employer for damages (Berkowitz and Mcquaid 1980). As a consequence, the focus of conflict and litigation was on whether the injury in question really had occurred due to the negligence of the employer. Although employers frequently won litigated cases, they lost often enough to have good reasons to prefer insurance-based solutions (E. Berkowitz and M. Berkowitz 1984). Moreover, insurance helped employers anticipate the costs of accidents that were regarded as being intrinsic to the process of production in much the same way as the cost of repairing broken machines, inclining them to bear the total cost of the insurance. Finally, insurance companies favoured such solutions providing only that state insurance could be avoided (Lubove 1968: 62–3).

Economic interests apart, there were political reasons for promoting proper legislation. High levels of litigation poisoned relationships between employers and employees. Pavalko's (1989) study of accident insurance in the United States shows that, the greater the number of court cases (regardless of their result), the quicker the implementation of insurance. Thus, businesses benefited both economically and politically from accident insurance. In this sense, the programmes delivered not only greater security to injured workers, but also to the enterprises employing them (Friedman and Ladinsky 1978: 277).

The fear of extending the gulf between employers and the employees was presumably the most acute in monarchies with authoritarian regimes, as in Germany (Ritter 1986: 50–82) and Austria (Hofmeister 1982: 294–5), but the issue was present in many other countries as well.

In his analysis of the sequential timing of social insurance programmes, Väisänen (1992) further elaborates the conflict explanation. He argues that, while work accident legislation did not intrude into the employer–employee relationship, unemployment benefits, by providing a means of livelihood to the unemployed increased the employees' reservation wage, making these latter programmes unpopular with employers. Sickness insurance can be seen as falling between the unemployment and work accident schemes in its impact on employee–employer relations. This implied sequence gets support from the pattern of global adoption identified in Figure 27.1.

ADMINISTRATION PAVES THE WAY
TO WELFARE STATE REGIMES

The first accident Act adopted in Germany 1884 had huge unanticipated consequences. Bismarck rejected private insurance carriers and the centralized state-
administered model advocated by the social democrats in favour of compulsory
insurance run by the employers' corporatist associations (Rimlinger 1971; Zöllner
1982). Due to 'institutional learning', this administrative idea became the template of
other social insurance forms. Similarly, in Austria and Switzerland, the first organizational models utilized semi-public carriers for programme delivery and these
models remain to the present. Thus, the initial choices concerning the administrative
form of work accident insurance comprised the germ of the welfare state cluster that
later was labelled as the corporatist (Christian democratic) social policy regime
(Esping-Andersen 1990). The corporatist model has been long-lasting and deeply
resistant to change. However, there are now indications that even a 'frozen model'
may be melting (see Palier and Martin 2008).

The British work accident insurance legislation of 1897 departed most clearly from
the German model by adopting the principle of employers' liability. The Act suffered
from the standard problems of fault-based provision noted above and, after World
War II, the work injury scheme was merged into National Insurance (Gordon 1988).
The British scheme had a profound impact on subsequent developments in the
dominions (except for Canada with a statutory scheme) as well as in Ireland and
the United States. In the latter, provision was a state rather than a federal responsibility. Consequently, not only did timing vary from state to state, but also the choice
of insurance carriers (Friedman and Ladinsky 1978: 278). In Australia, this was also
the case. Initially, New Zealand followed the British lead, but, contrary to the
standard pattern, where work accident schemes have tended to be highly path
dependent, in New Zealand, provision has been subject to constant changes, with
the system moving back and forth between state monopoly and the more or less free
play of the market (Campbell 1996).

In the Netherlands, the initial corporatist system (from 1901) remained until 1966,
when the work accident scheme was merged with sickness insurance covering all
work incapacities, whether work-related or not. In 1996, the costs of sickness and
work accidents were levied on employers, who became responsible for wage continuation for the first 52 weeks of work incapacity. In practice, the scheme was totally
privatized opening up a new era for private insurance companies. Similar trends
towards employer's responsibility have occurred elsewhere and, it is arguable that we
have come full circle, with employers being left to organize protection against
employees' incapacity to work much as they were a hundred or so years ago.

Mixed models permitting employers to obtain insurance either from public or
private insurers were originally in use in Belgium (1903), Italy (1898), and Sweden
(1901). Belgium has preserved its initial model, while the other two countries

eventually chose to abandon the private option (Gordon 1963). In three European countries, Denmark (1898), Finland (1895), and France (1898), initial schemes relied on private insurance carriers. The original models continue in Denmark and Finland, but, after World War II, the French scheme was reformed in favour of a public agency (Saint-Jours 1982: 106).

It has been argued (Skocpol 1992) that the United States Supreme Court had a detrimental impact on early United States social policy development, with accident and sickness insurance a case in point, with much of the early legislation ruled unconstitutional by the Court. Interestingly, in recent years, the European Court of Justice (ECJ) has also ruled against certain aspects of national social legislation; for example, the Court reacted against the Belgian and Finnish work accident schemes run by private insurance companies, demanding that the insurance field should be opened to international competition. This raises the interesting question of whether the ECJ is gradually assuming a role similar to that of the United States Supreme Court and, in the process, becoming a constraint on the character of social policy development in Europe.

From Workmen's Compensation to Working Women's Insurance

In its early forms, the work accident scheme was limited to certain dangerous occupations and hazardous branches. The expansion of coverage took place via two main routes. The first was followed by Germany and the majority of the other continental European states, where accident insurance expanded by including new occupational groups in existing programmes or by instituting new programmes for the newly covered occupations (Gordon 1963: 195). The other route of including all occupations in the same scheme was followed by the United Kingdom and to a certain extent also the Scandinavian countries.

The evolution of coverage and generosity is shown in Figure 27.2. Universal coverage was achieved in some countries (Sweden, Germany, New Zealand) by the 1950s with Austria, Denmark, and Ireland joining the group subsequently. In the remaining countries, either specific categories of employees or, more often, some groups amongst the self-employed are excluded from coverage. These latter countries manifest high but not universal coverage. Overall, the coverage of work accident insurance (87 per cent of the labour force in the early 2000s) is higher than for unemployment (67 per cent) or sickness (65 per cent) insurance. The relatively high degree of legitimacy of work accident insurance is mirrored also in replacement rates (net work accident compensation as a percentage of net wage), which are, in some instances, relatively high compared to other social insurance schemes. Some countries provide compensation at close to 100 per cent, though others (e.g. Denmark, Ireland, and the United Kingdom) lag far behind. However, these apparent drastic differences in compensation levels are largely an artefact, having much more to do with the division of labour between compulsory insurance and private occupational arrangements than with any real differences in benefits (Dean and Taylor-Gooby 1989). Instead of legislated insurance that has been the benchmark in benefits calculations in the ostensibly more generous countries, in the latter countries, employees get compensation directly from the employers' occupational schemes.

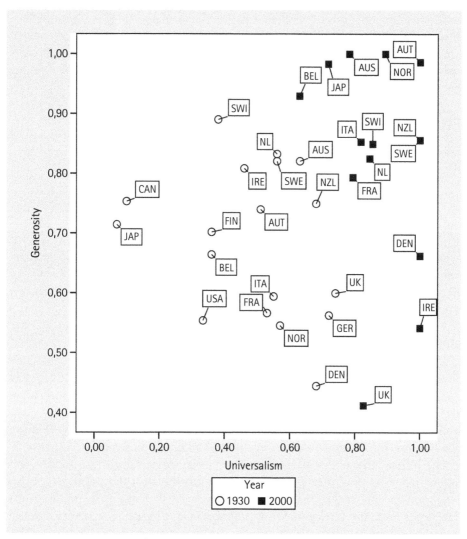

Figure 27.2 Generosity (net benefit/net wage) and universalism (insured/labour force) of work accident benefits in 18 OECD countries (1930, 2000)

Source: Korpi and Palme 2007.

Through more than a hundred years of gradual reform, the work accident insurance schemes of many countries provide nearly complete coverage of the labour force and nearly complete income loss compensation. In addition, narrow concepts of work injury defined as bodily injury or occupational diseases directly linked to work, such as black lung in the mining industry, have been widened to cover a wider variety of disabilities and diseases the aetiology of which need no longer be so directly related to the work-place. In tune with the reduction of industrial production and the expansion of white-collar employment, there has been a shift towards a growth in claims due to work-related mental symptoms such as stress, over-commitment, and burn-out. As a result, the line of demarcation between work injuries and other incapacities to work has been diluted and accident insurance schemes have been integrated into a broader context of social security and merged with sickness benefit schemes. This development has also meant that work accident insurance, originally planned to be working man's compensation, is gradually turning into working women's compensation as well.

SICKNESS BENEFITS

Early initiatives to secure the livelihood of the sick varied from support by kin and neighbourhood to various forms of charity. Later, Poor Laws began to provide some relief until gradually, following principles derived from the medieval guild system, voluntary sickness funds developed more formalized ways of giving protection to their members. The role of voluntary funds varied from country to country as did the state's involvement in fund activities. While, in some countries funds were totally run and financed by their members, in others the state also participated in financing and administration.

In addition to the primary function of guaranteeing help in case of illness, the early mutual sickness funds had important latent functions, which came to affect the strategies chosen by different political actors. Since the funds were often an organizational part of the activities of the emerging labour movement, they contributed to the formation of the working class and strengthened class solidarity (Ritter 1986: 71–82; Quadagno 1988a: 53). The early history of German sickness insurance is an excellent example.

The Bismarckian anti-socialist laws of 1873 banned socialist organizations, but mutual sickness funds offered socialists a legal substitute for the illegal party organizations. No wonder then that the labour movement preferred trade unions to the state as the insurance carrier. Statutory solutions and the state's governance in social insurance were met with suspicion—e.g. in 1893, the socialist leader Bebel warned his comrades that 'every new extension of state power is narrowing down the sphere of union activity' (Ritter 1986: 80). Bebel had some grounds for his fears. To undermine the support for the socialists, and to strengthen worker loyalty to the state, the government introduced compulsory sickness insurance with income-related benefits and separate schemes for different socio-economic categories (see Alber 1982; Hofmeister 1982; Ritter 1986; for Austria, see Tálos and Wörister 1984; for France, see Immergut 1992a). Whether or not the rationale of the political actors was a fully conscious one, the effect was to prevent the articulation of common employee interests and to emphasize status differences between them (Esping-Andersen 1990). History shows that social policy is not merely a distributional issue, but it also unifies and divides people, creates loyalties and social bonds.

Gradually, as the labour movement grew in political importance and obtained a meaningful representation in politics, the parliamentary path appeared as a realistic option for solving distributional conflicts (Korpi 1978; Przeworski 1985) and the working class movement abandoned its separatist ghetto strategies in favour of parliamentarianism and welfare statism. In some countries this had already happened by the end of the nineteenth century, but in others it occurred somewhat later, although usually prior to World War I.

To sum up, in Central Europe, labour movement pressure was just one of the factors pushing sickness insurance legislation. Just as often, the driving force behind the extension of statutory social policy was the urgency of authoritative regimes to legitimize their rule (Alber 1982: 195; Tálos and Wörister 1994). This meant that, in many cases, authoritarian regimes were ahead in the implementation of early social insurance, just because democratic regimes were obliged to seek consensus between different competing and sometimes conflicting social groups.

The results of historical case studies are supported by quantitative studies of the development of sickness and work accident benefits. It has been shown that, before World War I, left-wing parties had not that much impact on the generosity and universalism of schemes, while the role of Christian democracy was more significant (van Kersbergen 1995). In contrast, post-World War II improvements in benefits and extensions of coverage are more strongly associated with the strength of left-wing parties (Korpi 1989; Kangas 1991).

Japan has been a problematic case for regime analysis, with Esping-Andersen (1990) arguing that it is a kind of hybrid of conservative and liberal welfare state regimes (Esping-Andersen 1990). Early initiatives in statutory social policy in Japan were inspired by the German examples, introducing a strong corporatist flavour to the welfare mix. The first Japanese health insurance law, which became effective in 1927, was a case in point and was targeted towards the industrial elite, with subsequent expansion in coverage following the piecemeal corporatist route. The Japanese word *shakai seisaku* pertaining to social policy was translated directly from the German *Sozialpolitik* and, as in Germany, the scope of the term referred to the idea of reconciling relations between employers and employees. Subsequently, *shakai seisaku* came also to include also the British/Scandinavian notion of social policy as a means of safeguarding people's livelihoods (Takahashi 1995: 41–6). This latter and wider conception was channelled partially through statutory social policy and partially through employer provided social benefits whose role in Japan has been substantial (Campbell and Ikegami 1998; Peng 2005).

Precisely as in the sphere of work accidents, in sickness insurance, too, developments in the English-speaking world went in other directions from those in continental Europe. The British plan (passed in 1911) relied on uniform contributions and consequently on flat-rate benefits, while the Continental model relied on income-graduation both in social security contributions and daily allowances. These differences mirror the ideological and political underpinnings of social insurance development in these two groups of nations. In Britain and in its dominions, the scheme was planned to replace old Poor Laws and to give assistance to those who were worst off, while the German scheme was focused on meeting the needs of the more affluent sectors of the working class. To put it in more general terms, in the Central European countries, the emphasis was on horizontal redistribution between active and inactive periods in an individual's life, whereas the British, or the Anglo-American approach, emphasized vertical redistribution between the rich and the poor. The later approach has been especially strong in the Antipodean countries, heavily relying on means-tested rather than contribution-based or flat-rate universal benefits (Castles 1985; Castles and Mitchell 1990).

The first Nordic social policy programmes were amalgamations of peasant liberalism and nascent social democratic ideas and later a product of the emerging cross-class alliance between blue- and white-collar workers (Baldwin 1990; Olsson 1990). The emphasis and timing of these coalition-building efforts differs to some extent. In Denmark, the liberal tradition was strongest. In Sweden, from the 1930s onwards, Social democracy has been the dominant political force and essentially the same is true of Norway. In Finland, agrarian political interests were hegemonic up to the 1960s.

Denmark's liberalism was a force putting that country ahead of her northern neighbours in the development of voluntary sickness funds. Already, in 1892, the state began to subsidize voluntary sickness funds and, by the early 1930s, the funds covered 90 per cent of the labour force (Kolstrup 1996: 263; Figure 27.1). Together with the Swiss example, the Danish case demonstrates that, in some instances, it is possible to get extensive coverage even by voluntary measures. The fund-based system was in force until 1971 when it was superseded by a the public scheme (Nørby-Johansen 1986: 298–9).

In Sweden (the law on subsidies to voluntary funds in 1891) sick funds were part of the so-called Popular Movements (including the temperance movement and Free Church), attracting a much wider backing than from the working class alone, and so never as influential in developing class consciousness as in Germany (Immergut 1992a). The shift from a centralized voluntary fund-based system to a mandatory scheme (1955) was not a major political issue. The most vociferous opponent of obligatory membership was, as in the United States, organized medicine, but in the Swedish political system, doctors had no institutional veto points to prevent the bill as they did in the United States (Immergut 1992a).

In Norway and Finland, the voluntary sickness fund movement was never as important as in Denmark and Sweden and both countries went directly to obligatory insurance: Norway as early as 1909 and Finland as late as 1963 (Kuhnle 1981). The thesis of the importance of veto points gets support from the lateness of Finnish development. According to the Finnish constitution, support for reform required a two-thirds majority, allowing the opponents of sickness insurance a strong platform for resistance and making Finland the last country in Europe to legislate on sickness benefits (Kangas 1991).

By the end of the twentieth century, the United States was the only OECD country that had not (yet) instituted sickness insurance at a national level. Power resource scholars explain this by the lack of left-wing parties or strong trade unions. In their comparison of the United States and Europe, Orloff and Skocpol (1984) argue against such 'societal', politics-based explanations that rest on the assumption of a centralized state with well-organized bureaucracy and strong political parties. Instead, they emphasize the role of state institutions. Contrary to Europe, the United States did not have a state bureaucracy that was effective enough to carry out reforms and the success of social legislation heavily depended on public support. The proponents of health insurance have constantly failed to build enough support (Numbers 1978), whereas organized medicine has been successful in its campaign against federal insurance (Beland 2005; Quadagno 2005). A further institutional ally in this resistance has been the Supreme Court.

After unsuccessful attempts to implement sickness insurance, trade unionists drew their own conclusions and began to rely on collectively negotiated fringe benefits (Quadagno 2005: 52). Thus, American labour attitudes came close to Australian labour's notion of seeking social protection by 'other means' (see Castles 1985), i.e. through collective agreements (although in Australia such agreements were judicially sanctioned in a way they were not in the United States). Both the American and Australian cases suggest that, in federal states, national-level decisions are harder to carry through than in centralized states (Obinger et al. 2005a). In the United States, organized labour exercised its power more effectively at the state level and some of the states have, indeed, enacted compulsory health insurance (Skocpol 1992: 206).

Arguably, the conflicting explanations of American exceptionalism are more a matter of emphasis than of fundamentals. In her historical comparison of Canada and the United States, Maioni (1998) offers a compromise between the state-based and societal explanations: what mattered in Canada was the presence of a social democratic party that had influence in the debates on health insurance, while in the United States universal insurance was stymied by the medical lobby and the possibilities the American decision-making system gave for the representatives of particularistic interests.

COVERAGE AND GENEROSITY

In the categorization of welfare states or individual social policy programmes, the two most important dimensions have been the degree of universalism and generosity. Universalism pertains to the coverage of insurance, i.e. the ratio of those who are entitled to daily allowances. Usually coverage is expressed as a percentage of the total labour force. Generosity denotes the level of income loss replacement as a percentage of previous wage.[1] In principle, there are two main data sources that employ a similar strategy. The Social Citizenship Indicators Programme (SCIP; see Korpi and Palme 2007) and Scruggs's welfare data base (http://www.sp.uconn.edu/~scruggs/wp.htm). Both calculate benefits at average wage levels. In data for 2000, the correlation between net replacement rates in these two sources was very high (0.96). The SCIP provides figures also for minimums and maximums, qualifying conditions, and financing. While Scruggs's data are annual for the years 1960–2002, SCIP data are collected for every fifth year 1930–2000. Here we use both: scatterplots are based on the SCIP, whereas discussion on retrenchment is based on Scruggs's annual data.

From the citizen's point of view, one of the most central aspects of social insurance schemes is the level of economic security or the generosity the programme guarantees. As can be seen from Figure 27.3, there is a huge improvement in generosity 1930 to 2000. The mean for all the countries was 45 per cent in 1930 while it was 76 per cent in 2000. The coverage rate has doubled (from 32 to 74 per cent). There are some countries providing full income loss compensation, but there are also countries with scanty benefits, the Anglophone countries in particular. Australia and New Zealand also have low degree of universalism.

The low coverage of these latter countries is partially a technical artefact: in targeted, means-tested programmes, the coverage rate is set to 0 due to the fact that the sick person has no automatic right to claim benefit as in an insurance based-model. In fact, this zero-coding does no justice to the Australian and New Zealand systems, which are rather liberal in their means-testing. This is one obvious problem in both the SCIP and Scruggs's data. Moreover, in both Australia and New Zealand, occupational benefits have more or less completely taken over from sickness cash provision, and the role of legislated benefits is relatively minor. Indeed, the term 'targeted' is misleading, with a perhaps more appropriate label being 'labour market segmented system'. The low compensation level of the British system is explained in a similar way, with a clear shift from legislated benefits to labour market programmes taking place in recent years.

The importance of labour market based benefits has increased in a variety of forms almost everywhere. There are countries with employer's obligatory sick pay periods (that varies from a couple of weeks in most countries to two years in the Netherlands), and, in almost all countries, there are collective agreements that top up the legislated benefits. If we take into account collective non-legislated sick pay payments, countries are much more similar in the level and costs (see Adema 1999) of social protection than our data display. The social citizenship approach may capture some qualitative aspects of the state's responsibility, but, due to the trend towards labour

---

[1] The replacement rate as represented in Figure 27.3 is a compound index for four separate cases (replacement for two sickness spells: one week and 26 weeks and for two workers: a single person and a married worker with two children). The income level of the worker in question corresponds to the national average industrial wage in each country and each year in question.

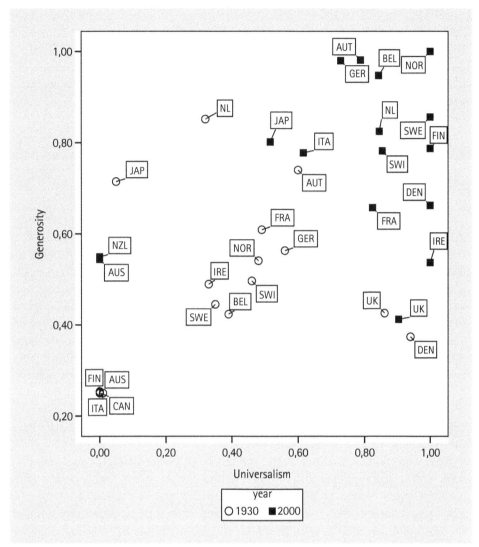

Figure 27.3 Generosity (net benefit/net wage) and universalism (insured/labour force) of sickness benefits in 17 OECD countries (1930, 2000)

Source: Korpi and Palme 2007.

market based programmes, the citizenship concept is becoming less and less adequate. Social citizenship is gradually being replaced by 'corporate citizenship'.

Calculations of the levels of social benefits can be criticized as being too one-dimensional: the 'standard worker' calculations the approach operates with are based on average income levels and on numerous assumptions on work-careers, etc. of a kind that may invalidate the indicator. First, the standard worker indicator may be unchanged over time and, while it may be the same for two countries, there may, nonetheless, be substantial differences at the upper and lower ends of the income ladder that the average measure neglects. Second, citizenship indicators measure what the legislation is supposed to do rather than how it actually works. Third, in post-industrial societies, the standard worker is a less and less common creature. All in all, there is a danger that social citizenship indicators are becoming empty slots, promising much but finally giving very little (van Gerven 2008: 48).

Retrenchment since the 1980s

If Esping-Andersen's *Three Worlds of Welfare Capitalism* initiated an avalanche of regime analyses, Paul Pierson's (1994) *Dismantling the Welfare State* launched a no less prolific debate on the retrenchment of social protection. When it comes to the generosity of sickness benefits, there is, indeed, a clear tendency towards lower benefit levels. The average for the seventeen countries featuring in Figure 27.3 was at the highest in the mid-1980s and, since that time, the improvement has levelled off and, in some countries, drastic cutbacks have taken place. As noted previously, some scholars argue that the institutional characteristics of welfare programmes matter and, due to institutional inertia, some schemes are more robust and others easier to reform. In most such accounts it is corporatist institutions, based on income-relatedness, social insurance contributions, and bi- or tripartite administration, that are seen as being most difficult to change, although some recent scholars have noticed an 'unfreezing' process even here.

The inspection of changes in the generosity of sickness programmes provides some *prima facie* support for the hypothesis that certain institutional arrangements are more prone to change than other programme types. In the liberal regime, the mean replacement level decreased by 21 percentage points between the high point of the 1980s and the turn of the millennium. In the Nordic hemisphere (social democratic regime), the cuts were more modest (a decline of 12 percentage points), while the average for the corporatist countries was much the same in 2000 as it was in the 1980s. The story of universalism is a bit different. The Scandinavian schemes have preserved their universality, whereas other groups have lost a bit in their coverage.

Conclusions

The evolution of work accident and sickness insurance schemes shows how insurance must be changed when the social problems for which the programme originally provided protection change in character. Work injury programmes are a good example. In early usage, work accident insurance was called workmen's compensation. Conceptually, a 'worker' was a male breadwinner responsible for his home-making wife and children. With increased female labour force participation, this concept became outdated. Similarly, the first laws dealt with broken arms and smashed legs; gradually, occupational diseases were also covered by insurance; still more recently, coverage has been expanded to more subtle hazards and the interpretation of direct causal connections has become yet more liberal. Nowadays, even a positional causation gives entitlement to benefits and various forms of rehabilitation and vocational training are available for the employee who for some reason is incapable of work. These developments have watered down the conceptual difference between work accident and sickness. In many countries, the two benefit systems have merged together and compensation is paid through the same programme irrespective of the cause of incapacity.

Another common trend, attached to cuts in legislated social policy, has been a shift towards collective and labour market based solutions. The lower the statutory allowance, the more important is the occupational element. This development interestingly demonstrates a shift in the character of the social contract inherent in social insurance. During the period of industrialization and the development of national states, social insurance was a national-level attempt to replace existing firm-level schemes and to homogenize benefits and contributions in order to create equal compensation for employees and competitive prerequisites for the employers. In a way, the circle has closed and, in the expanding occupational schemes, risk pooling takes place at industrial branch or even the enterprise level. Thus, the imaginary social contract is written between the employer and the employee and the role of the state as a producer of social security is withering away, with the state serving merely as a referee, ensuring that the rules of the contract are respected.

....

CHAPTER 28

DISABILITY

....

MARK PRIESTLEY

INTRODUCTION

....

THIS chapter is concerned with understanding the responses of modern welfare states to disability and disabled people. The topic is of particular interest in a handbook of this kind because disability has become an increasing concern for policymakers in recent years, both in Europe and internationally. There have been very significant developments, continuing to the present day, perhaps the most significant of which has been a reconceptualization of the needs of disabled people from models of care and compensation to models of social inclusion and human rights. Most recently, the enactment of a United Nations Convention on the Rights of Persons with Disabilities in 2008 marked a watershed in this story. The Convention places new obligations on states to protect and ensure the full participation and equality of disabled people in a comprehensive range of social policy areas, from employment and education to transport and incomes. But what of the realities? European countries, in particular, have sought to balance established welfare state histories with new rights-based claims from social movements of disabled people in civil society. To understand the significance of these tensions, and the challenges they pose to welfare states, it is first useful to understand more about the underlying paradigm shift that has taken place in understanding disability as a policy problem.

BACKGROUND AND CONCEPTS

....

There is an extensive literature within critical disability studies that expands on the implications of different models of disability. In particular, it is useful to distinguish broadly between 'individual' and 'social' models of disability (cf. Oliver 1983, 1990).

The traditional view, within an individual model paradigm, was to assume that people with impairments would inevitably find it difficult to perform 'normal' activities and, therefore, would have difficulty in fulfilling normal social roles (WHO 1981). If the root cause of the problem is presented as stemming from a person's impairment then it is all too easy to conclude that every aspect of that person's social situation can also be explained by their physical condition. From a policy perspective, it is then unsurprising that the disadvantage experienced by disabled people was often viewed within welfare states as a personal tragedy caused by impairment (Priestley 1999). From this perspective, the most appropriate policy responses were either to compensate disabled people for their perceived loss, to help them adjust through rehabilitation, or to provide alternative, less valued, social roles through segregated institutions. Whilst disability might commonly have been viewed as a deserving claim for welfare within this paradigm, it was less likely to be viewed as a legitimate claim for social inclusion.

By contrast, the social interpretation of disability turned this idea on its head, questioning the very idea of a necessary causal relationship between having an impairment and becoming 'disabled' (Oliver 1990). Crucially, the social model approach suggests that it is not cognitive, sensory, or physical impairments that cause disablement but the way in which societies fail to accommodate natural aspects of variation and difference between people (e.g. Zola 1989). A social interpretation of disability relocates the disability 'problem' from the individual to society. Disability is then viewed not as personal tragedy but as a social problem resulting from social processes (Priestley 2003). Viewed from this perspective, the most appropriate policy responses appear very differently. Rather than simply assessing an individual's functional limitation, for the purposes of adequate compensation or care, it becomes appropriate also to assess disabling barriers in society's infrastructure to increase its accessibility (e.g. to modify its workplaces, public attitudes, educational, and transport systems so they become more inclusive for a wider range of people).

This distinction between individual and social models was first articulated, in an academic context, by Oliver (1983). However, the impetus came from ideas and claims developed within the disabled peoples' movement in the 1970s (cf. Union of Physically Impaired Against Segregation/Disability Alliance 1976).

> Hence disability, according to the social model, is all the things that impose restrictions on disabled people; ranging from individual prejudice to institutional discrimination, from inaccessible buildings to unusable transport systems, from segregated education to excluding work arrangements, and so on. Further, the consequences of this failure do not simply and randomly fall on individuals but systematically upon disabled people as a group who experience this failure as discrimination institutionalized throughout society. (Oliver 1996: 33)

Social model approaches have been increasingly applied and adapted to explain the situation of people with diverse impairments, in diverse societies and at different points in the life course. The barriers facing people with physical, visual, hearing, cognitive, or psycho-emotional impairments may be different, and affect disabled children, adults, and older people in different ways (Priestley 2003). The social model provides a heuristic device for conceptualizing the commonality of these experiences as institutional discrimination or oppression.

Some social model writers have emphasized the role of culture and ideas in shaping disability labels and social roles (e.g. Ingstad and Reynolds Whyte 1995; Shakespeare 1994). Others have argued for a political economy of disability that explains the inequalities experienced by disabled people as a product of capitalism and modernity (Finkelstein 1991; Gleeson 1999; Oliver 1990). In this way, Oliver argued that the social relations of production and reproduction within capitalist political economy produced 'disabled' groups and created their enforced dependency on an emerging welfare state. This, Finkelstein (1991) argues, led to the growth of new institutional welfare arrangements to accommodate new needs for care and surveillance that were socially produced. Such argument is also reminiscent of Habermas's (1987) contention that welfare capitalism creates specifically new forms of domination and subordination as the 'life world' becomes increasingly 'colonized' under the control of rationalized bureaucracies. Disability may then be viewed as a significant welfare administration category—primarily a category of labour force exemption—arising in response to the needs of state and capital to control labour supply and legitimize the regulation of welfare (Finkelstein 1991; Priestley 1997; Stone 1984). Understanding this complex argument is crucial to understanding the contemporary dynamics of disability and welfare.

At least three key factors are significant to the underlying structural dependency of disabled people, and the challenge for welfare states. First, disability is a poverty issue—disabled people, and disabled women in particular, remain disproportionately unemployed, underemployed, and underpaid in contemporary societies. Up to 80 per cent of disabled people, in some countries, are unemployed, and the link between disability and poverty is evidenced throughout the world (Elwan 1999). Second, as a welfare category, disability is inextricably linked to participation in, and exemption from, work and employment. Indeed, national categorizations of disability, and entitlements to disability benefits, have frequently relied upon 'work able' definitions and work capability tests for adults of working age. Third, this construction is challenged by the fact that disability is experienced disproportionately amongst older people in economically developed welfare states, and increasingly compounded by demographic ageing trends (Eurolink Age 1995; Mclellan 1997).

The implication of the social model approach is that disability should not be viewed simply as a redistributive problem for contemporary welfare states (addressing disadvantage through care and compensation) but as a structural and relational problem of social exclusion. Viewing the problem in this way helps us to understand the recent expansion of disability policy and the shifts towards more holistic and rights-based approaches to social inclusion (illustrated later in this chapter). Advocates of social model approaches have argued, for instance, that structural investments in accessibility (e.g. in education, housing, transport, information and communication technologies, etc.), coupled with non-discrimination laws, might produce economic benefits for welfare states, as well as greater inclusion for individuals, by facilitating employment opportunities or reducing dependency on state-funded care and disability-related benefits. However, accessibility and inclusion for all disabled people also poses fundamental challenges to the markets and infrastructures of welfare states, which suggest needs for increasing rather than decreasing investment demands.

ORIGINS AND DEVELOPMENT

Analyses of early disability provision in the modern welfare state highlight the significance of different welfare traditions. In terms of historical development, the English example has received extensive attention within the social model literature and provides a useful starting point. In England, the earliest origins of a disability welfare category can be seen in Acts to control vagrancy, pauperism, and migration that were fundamental to the emergence of 'deserving' and 'undeserving' claims to public welfare even before the 1601 Poor Law (Priestley 1997). People with impairments figured prominently in subsequent accounts of those 'unable to work' and public welfare institutions sought a difficult balance between compassion and coercion—between 'carrot and stick'. The emergence of 'sick' categories can be seen more clearly in the nineteenth century, and the Poor Law Amendment Act of 1834 allowed concessions to sick people from the harsh constraints on outdoor relief imposed on the able poor. As Stone (1984: 43) notes, there was, nevertheless, some debate about whether sick and disabled people could also be 'healed' by the deterrence of the 'less eligibility' principle, and punitive implementation of means tested entitlement.

Over time, new forms of special provision (including medical wards within workhouses and specialist institutions) emerged. Within this context, the treatment of sick and disabled people was often seen to be more favourable than that for the able poor. Such distinctions also gave rise to power tensions between welfare officials and medical doctors, about who should exercise judgements of eligibility in different areas of welfare jurisdiction (a tension that is evident in a number of countries today). Medicine's separation of sick and disabled welfare recipients into different impairment categories was also a significant development, beginning with targeted interventions for 'lunatics' and the 'insane' (e.g. Borsay 2005). Yet, within the early public asylums and workhouses, there was little if any systematic distinction between people with pathological conditions and those whose needs arose from old age or criminality for example. Indeed, it was not until the twentieth century that disability emerged as a distinct category of welfare provision from general old age. Under the English Poor Law system then, welfare provision for disabled people was based primarily on inability to work, poverty, and a public provision of care that became increasingly institutionalized. Significantly, this model did not include the provision of disability pensions.

In Germany, by contrast, the Bismarck reforms of the 1880s laid foundations for a distinctive social insurance system in which 'invalidity' emerged as a key concept (notably in the 1889 Invalidity and Pension Law). These developments, and the concepts upon which they were based, established principles of welfare provision evident in the treatment of disabled people in many European countries today. As in England, rapid industrialization and nation building provided drivers for wealth creation and the emergence of new welfare challenges (although it could be argued that the legitimation of the state played a more central role in Germany). While the German response to disabled people in the late nineteenth century included elements of compulsion and conditionality, it developed within a more paternalistic welfare state model than the restrictive/punitive approach of the English Poor Law.

From Bismarck's reforms evolved a tripartite system of welfare finance in which contributions from employees and employers were complimented by active state funding of pensions and programmes. The German proto-system of public social insurance established an element of compulsion in contributions alongside a benevolent model of state responsibility for assistance. Importantly, the state assumed responsibility for the provision of invalidity pensions (as well as old-age pensions). Those unable to earn a living could, however, be required to work in alternative employment appropriate to their skills and experience. In common with the English model, 'ability to work' was central to the definition of eligibility for assistance (or, more specifically in the German case, the ability to earn a basic level of income specified as a percentage of average local earnings).

The introduction of invalidity pensions in Germany resulted in an explosion of claims for assistance by the turn of the twentieth century, underwritten by state subsidy, and driving the pension insurance system towards bankruptcy. This in turn, provided an incentive to tighten the eligibility criteria and to reinforce distinctions between two separate systems for sickness insurance and invalidity pensions. Subsequent developments then became increasingly characterized by complex and technocratic discussions about thresholds of eligibility, income, and work conditionality for different categories of worker (e.g. manual and white collar workers). The significance of the early German pension system, Stone (1984: 66) argues, was that it linked disability to income earning potential within the individual's accustomed 'sphere of activity' rather than to a specific medical condition or a total inability to work.

These early developments in England and Germany are useful examples, as they prefigure many of the concerns and debates that have emerged in other countries, although there are significant variations in the development, organization, and funding of national disability-related welfare provision. In Sweden, for example, both social insurance and health care benefits emerged in a publicly funded system for all (with welfare and support provided according to assessed need). This has had some positive benefits for disabled people since the risk of falling outside the scope of the social security system is significantly reduced (since there is little reliance on in-work contributions).

In contrast to European welfare models, there is little in the way of universal safety net protection in the United States and full entitlement to social security depends on in-work contributions made over time. Within this residual system, disability was acknowledged in the formative Social Security Program of the 1930s, but Social Security Disability Insurance was enacted relatively late (in 1956) and restricted only to those whose impairments made 'gainful employment' impossible for 'the rest of a person's life'. Initially, the limited cash benefits were also only paid to older workers (over 50 years old). Post-war developments in the United States thus echoed earlier debates in Europe, with great concern to strictly define and limit entitlements in order to prevent rapid or fraudulent expansion of disability claims on the state. However, in common with developments in other countries, rapid growth quickly ensued, placing increasing strain on public resources by the 1980s and 1990s (not least within the Supplemental Security Income system).

As this brief historical review illustrates, there is great variation in national systems of welfare provision but a number of common tensions and challenges can be identified, including: the problem of defining impairment and disability; the challenge of responding to partial work capacity; the appropriate balance between public and private funding; the degree of conditionality or compulsion in relation to work expectations; and state responses to the expansion of disability claims over time (particularly in periods of general economic downturn). Some of the key commonalities and differences between countries in meeting these core challenges are illustrated in the following section. The examples focus in particular on developments in European countries.

CONVERGENCE AND DIVERGENCE

Although there have been considerable developments towards the harmonization of disability policies (for example, via the development of a UN Convention and European Union legislation in recent times) there remains considerable scope for diversity at the national level. Even where there has been supra-national legislation, substantial subsidiarity exists. Thus, Waddington (2005) compares implementation of the European Framework Directive on Nondiscrimination in Occupation and Employment in Belgium and the Netherlands to illustrate the extensive scope for national discretion. While EU legislation demands non-discrimination in a common labour market, many prerequisites to this (such as policy investments in education, housing, social security and so on) rely on member states' own diverse policies (Machado and de Lorenzo 1997). Prior to EU enlargement, Hvinden (2003) questioned whether there was real evidence of convergence in disability policies amongst Western European countries (see Aarts et al. 1998; Prinz 2003; van Oorschot and Hvinden 2000, 2001). Hvinden further argued that key areas of policy concern for disabled people, like social security, were somewhat 'crowded' by existing national welfare regimes and traditions. By contrast, he noted that there was greater scope for

Europeanization in more 'vacant' areas (such as market regulation and antidiscrimination law).

In an enlarged European Union of twenty-seven countries harmonization of disability policy is further challenged by diverse national circumstances. Early European policies, advocating compensation and rehabilitation, may have raised concerns about welfare expenditure in the original member states but there was little to bind their compliance in the 1970s, 1980s, or even the mid-1990s. In contrast, states entering the EU in 2004 and 2007 confronted greater policy compliance challenges on disability and social inclusion, often with limited economic resources. Implementation of disability equality policies has thus raised significantly challenges for the transition economies of Central, Eastern, and Southern Europe (e.g. Ursic 1996; Walsh 1997) and highlighted some of the extreme challenges facing disabled people in Bulgaria and Romania. To understand more about national variation and comparison, both in Europe and beyond, it is relevant to return to some of the key challenges identified in the previous section and to illustrate examples in some specific areas.

Cash Payments and Expenditure

The OECD's Social Expenditure Database provides a baseline for comparing overall levels of expenditure (although, since disability, sickness, and accident benefits are all included within the category of 'incapacity related benefits', it is not always easy to disaggregate equivalent terms reliably between countries). Amongst the OECD countries, Norway, the United Kingdom, the Netherlands, Switzerland, and Sweden reported the largest proportions of public expenditure on incapacity-related disability pensions (cash benefits) in 2005, all of them at more than 4 per cent of total government expenditure. Reported trends vary, and it is clear that different countries have experienced different degrees of growth in expenditure. For example, while the overall number of working-age people in the United Kingdom receiving 'out of work' benefits fell from around 6 million in 1997 to less than 5 million in 2007, the number receiving sickness or disability related benefits within this group remained constant at around 2.7 million (although the number receiving such benefits for more than two years increased from 1.9 million to around 2.2 million in the same period). In Australia, reported public spending on disability pensions increased from 2.4 to 3.7 per cent between 1980 and 2005, but in the United Kingdom it increased threefold, from 1.8 to 5.5 per cent, while in the United States the proportion remained more constant (from 1.7 to 1.9 per cent).

The established welfare states of Northern and Western Europe continue to report relatively high levels of disability pension and cash benefit payments, with the Southern and Eastern European states remaining much lower. Using the same specific example of disability-related cash pensions from public expenditure, and in terms of the equivalent cost per head, Luxembourg and Norway reported the highest rates, with Hungary, Slovakia, Greece, and Italy reporting the lowest in the

EU. The five Nordic countries all ranked in the top seven (along with the Nether-lands). A broadly similar picture is obtained even when considering both public and mandatory private insurance schemes, with the five Nordic countries, Luxembourg, Switzerland, the Netherlands, the United States, Austria, and Belgium all above the OECD average (Australia being the only non-European country in this category). Germany and France fall well below the OECD average on this measure, at less than half the equivalent value per head of the Nordic–Netherlands–United Kingdom group. By contrast, figures for occupational injury and disease pensions show a very different pattern (e.g. with Canada topping the OECD table and Austria and Germany showing high levels of public spending).

However, trends vary. Using data from the national administrative registers of EU member states in the period 2000-2005, Shima and Rodrigues (2008) identify Finland, Denmark, and Iceland with a decline in the number of recipients of contributory and non-contributory disability benefits and an increase in expenditure (evidence of an increasing generosity of payments). Comparative data from Latvia, Poland, and the United Kingdom suggests a decline in numbers, relative benefit levels and share of GDP spent on disability pensions over the same period (see also, Applica et al. 2007). All of the EU27 countries show an increase in share of social expenditure on disability pension schemes in this period, except for the United Kingdom, Latvia, Poland, and Germany. Such comparisons should be treated with some caution and explaining reported differences requires a complex understanding of different types of benefit schemes in different countries and their eligibility criteria.

As an example, the United Kingdom exhibits a complex array of financial benefits and entitlements available to disabled people. In recent years, much attention has been focused on Incapacity Benefit, available to adults who could not work because of illness or disability (on condition that they had paid National Insurance contribu-tions, were not receiving Statutory Sick Pay, and were below retirement age when they became disabled). Claims were contingent on a Personal Capability Assessment undertaken by an approved Disability Analyst (who could recommend a medical assessment). In February 2008, some 2,659,650 people were receiving this benefit at an average weekly rate of £52.57. However, those requiring assistance and support in daily life could also claim additional income benefits via Disability Living Allowance, whether they were in or out of work and, usually, without a reference to medical examination or means testing of personal income. There are then additional disabil-ity premiums for those receiving Income Support (the basic income level of social security payments), Industrial Injuries Disablement Benefits, War Disablement Pen-sions and allowances, possible tax reductions, housing benefit supplements, and National Insurance credits.

Work-Centred Eligibility Definitions

Given the complexity of and variation between national systems of disability-related cash benefits, definitions and criteria for eligibility should be viewed as extremely important. As Bolderson and Mabbett (2001: 53) point out, 'Categorization is one of the basic techniques or practices of social policy' and their analyses highlight how key eligibility categories become established and contested. They highlight disability as a particularly significant and problematic example, arguing that it fails to function very successfully because, although it is viewed as a highly legitimate entitlement category, its identification and definition are difficult to operationalize. Despite these difficulties they find it hard to imagine a universal policy scenario in which the category of disability could be removed entirely.

Reporting on a comparative study of disability definitions used in cash benefit and employment schemes in the EU15 states, Mabbett (2005) identifies the difficulty of cross-national comparison between widely varying policy contexts, also highlighting the high level of discretion afforded to doctors and administrative officers in the authentication of welfare claims. Such work illustrates, for example, how: definitions for income maintenance and social insurance may change in response to rising costs and numbers of claimants; how population ageing challenges definitional criteria for assistance with daily living; and how the mainstreaming of disability policies has led to definitional changes (especially in employment). In this sense, the fitness for purpose of different disability definitions remains a significant concern for politicians and technocrats—and effective definitions for the administration of cash benefits do not necessarily function well for the wider protection of civil and social rights.

Many countries rely on some proportional measurement of an individual person's functional impairment to trigger minimum eligibility for certain disability benefits (e.g. 50 per cent in Austria, Belgium, Bulgaria, Cyprus, Iceland, and Romania; 66.6 per cent in the Czech Republic, Portugal, and Lithuania; 74 per cent in Italy, etc). For example, disability benefit can be claimed in Norway with a 50 per cent loss of income opportunity but in Denmark, Finland, and the United Kingdom eligibility relies on a qualitative or criterion-based assessment of work capability. The determination of functional impairment measurements is highly technocratic, sometimes complex, and often relying heavily on medical authority in gate keeping assessments. It is also open to considerable critique from a social model of disability perspective. Judgements of individual capacity to work, based on medical assessment of the body, may, for example, fail to consider the type of work available in the labour market, the availability of adaptive technology and supportive assistance, or the accessibility of the work environment.

The widespread reliance on work-able definitions of disability in welfare policies is significant and reinforces the underlying structural link between disability and historic exclusion from labour market participation—such definitions are a pervasive if not ubiquitous characteristic across diverse modern welfare states. Work-able definitions are problematic in failing to fully address the exclusion experienced by disabled children or older people. Yet, even for those of working age, it is clear that people judged 'unable to work' at times of low labour demand (e.g. during economic recession) have often been brought into the labour market at times of high demand (e.g. during wars or periods of economic growth). Definitions of 'ability to work' can and do change over time in response to political and economic circumstance (cf.

Stone 1984). In this sense, national disability definitions have been revealed as particularly 'elastic' (Gruber 2000). The social model of disability is therefore useful here in reminding us how capitalist market conditions and states' administrative definitions produce disability as a residual and flexible welfare category in modern states.

Within the adult-centred policy nexus of controlling labour supply and welfare expenditure there is a growing focus on more detailed functional assessments of work capacity for disability/incapacity benefit entitlement (including a growing emphasis on more medicalized assessments). However, as articulated in recent OECD opinion to Luxembourg, measures to assess work incapacity have sometimes achieved little more than the creation of a new category of 'unemployed disabled people' rather than a significant return to employment. Moreover, restrictive eligibility measures may have a new disincentive impact on adults who have already obtained disability status, making them more reluctant to seek employment (e.g. for fear of being unable to return to disability benefits).

This is significant because disability pensions have, in the past, been widely used to facilitate permanent exit from the labour force, both in Western European welfare states (during periods of high unemployment) and in the former Eastern bloc states. In both cases, concern that disability benefits have functioned as a path out of employment has become widespread. There has been a substantial policy reversal in recent years and active attention has turned to reforming such benefit pathways in several European countries (e.g. in Luxembourg, Romania, the United Kingdom, Malta, Hungary, the Netherlands, Romania, and Slovenia). This turnaround appears to be motivated primarily by concerns with welfare state expenditure (concerns that will quickly escalate in a period of economic downturn) rather than a benign concern with disabled people's inclusion. However, history may suggest that economic recession and higher unemployment may reverse this trend and revive the use of disability benefits to control labour supply.

Employment Measures

As outlined so far, the social model of disability, current welfare policy debates and technocratic gate-keeping mechanisms all draw attention to the fundamental connection between disability, work, and welfare. It is therefore relevant to consider some of the key features and developments in disability employment policies in contemporary welfare states. There is little doubt that employment has figured prominently, often dominantly, in the development of disability policies. Changes in employment policies for disabled people have also set the scene for subsequent changes in other policy areas.

There have been a number of comparative studies of policies for supporting and retaining disabled people in employment, focused predominantly on industrialized Western economies. For example, Thornton and Lunt (1997) studied disability employment policies in eighteen countries, building on earlier work in Europe,

North America, and Australia. Their review suggested an apparently universal commitment to the growing rhetoric of participation and equality for disabled people, with legislative approaches to this task becoming more widespread. This and other studies suggest some useful trend typologies. Thornton and Lunt identify two broad approaches at the national level: first, generic approaches to anti-discrimination disability legislation (in which employment is often a dominant theme), and second, the division of disability policy into separate departmental concerns (where employment may be seen as a single issue). Goss et al. (2000) also identify two policy traditions—what they define as a 'European' tradition based on protected employment quotas and state intervention, and an 'American' tradition, based on anti-discrimination measures and individual civil rights. Gooding (1996: 65) makes a similar distinction, equating employment quota systems with medical compensatory models of disability, and rights-based approaches with social models of disability. Such dichotomies are somewhat simplistic and open to question but they provide a helpful starting point in understanding recent policy developments.

There is no clear evidence of convergence on this example and Greve (2008) notes how different European countries have moved both towards and away from disability quota systems (e.g. with the introduction of a new quota system in Cyprus and the abolition of a previously unenforced quota in the United Kingdom). Indeed, the majority of European countries maintain some form of disability quota obligation on employers (these include Austria, Belgium, Bulgaria, Cyprus, The Czech Republic, France, Germany, Greece, Hungary, Ireland, Italy, Lithuania, Luxemborg, Malta, Poland, Portugal, Romania, Slovakia, Slovenia, and Spain). Typically, quota schemes legislate the minimum percentage of disabled people to be recruited and maintained by an employer (often applying only to large employers). In several countries (e.g. Poland, Austria, Germany, and France), financial levies derived from employers who do not fulfil their quotas are invested in a national fund to support training or employment opportunities for disabled people (e.g. National Rehabilitation Fund in Poland), but there is much diversity, not least in the level of enforcement. In Austria, for example, Zelderloo and Reynaert (2007) note that less than a third of companies complied with the 4 per cent quota norm in 2002 (compliance levels appear even lower in Spain). In addition, there is concern that employers' fulfilment of quota obligations often targets those disabled people who are closest to the labour market rather than those whose integration is more challenging (practically or financially).

Within the compensatory model, approaches to employment policy for disabled people also include 'sheltered' employment provision outside, or at the margins of, the mainstream labour market. Such provision has often been criticized for creating less-valued work roles that are either unpaid or low paid (e.g. Visier 1998). There has also been concern that the widespread placement of disabled people in work-related 'training centres' has had little impact on their subsequent labour market inclusion. From the 1980s there was a rapid growth in the use of 'supported' placements in mainstream settings, initially in North America (Wehman et al. 1997). The enactment of non-discrimination legislation in employment, including the Americans with Disabilities Act in the United States, the Disability Discrimination Act in the United

Kingdom, and European Directive (noted earlier) have all lent weight to this trend. However, significant elements of the compensatory model remain in national policies, particularly within European welfare states. However, supporting disabled people in ordinary jobs (as a legal right or as employment activation policy) may raise challenges to some of the historic concepts of disability welfare policy outlined earlier. In particular, some welfare systems have found it difficult to balance the realities of partial or temporary work capacity or flexible working needs with categorical definitions of disability and complex gateways to welfare entitlement.

Various approaches are evident in national polices as welfare states seek to accommodate new-found realizations that many 'disabled' people can and do work. For example, some countries have moved to implement wage subsidies for disabled employees and job seekers (e.g. in Belgium, Finland, Malta, the Netherlands, and Romania), yet most of these schemes are time-limited. Other financial incentives have included concessions on employer's tax or insurance costs (e.g. Czech Republic, Spain, Sweden). Other policy commitments include matching the skills of disabled people to available job opportunities (e.g. Belgium), policies focused on facilitating more 'severely disabled' people into jobs (e.g. Cyprus, Germany), efforts to better combine disability benefits with paid work (e.g. Denmark, United Kingdom), supporting disabled people's entrepreneurship and small business start-ups (e.g. Finland, Lithuania, Sweden), and counselling, information, and bespoke job seeking services (e.g. Luxembourg, Romania).

For those adults who find work there is some evidence of new policies to support more flexible and secure employment. These include incentives to create part-time jobs in the Czech Republic, the promotion of 'flexi-jobs' in Denmark, informing employers and employees about flexible working in Estonia, and legislation on partial work capacity in the Netherlands. Such policies have met with varying success and it remains to be seen how the implementation of recent proposals will fare in a period of economic recession. Such policies have also tended to favour individualized responses. Considering the scale of challenge that the social model poses—to eliminate structural barriers to inclusion—few countries have made any substantial and tangible policy connections between disabled people's welfare and the underlying accessibility of the social infrastructure that social inclusion outcomes require.

TRENDS AND FUTURE DIRECTIONS

As suggested in the preceding sections, contemporary concerns to reform welfare provision for disabled people have been driven by a combination of factors. Historic increases in the numbers of people identified as disabled, for the purposes of eligibility to disability-related benefits, have resulted in increased pressure on associated budgets. This tendency is evident in both the earliest schemes of the late nineteenth century and in recent comparative data on public expenditure. It has been most evident in the expansion of disability-related claims during periods of excess labour supply but is also a function of demographic ageing. Trends in increasing claims for disability-related benefits have been variously explained in terms of individual behaviour (assumed work avoidance behaviour) or declining job supply (particularly for older workers in longer-term unemployment). However, the concept of disability as a flexible administrative category has been clearly exemplified by the large-scale reclassification of unemployed workers onto 'incapacity' or 'invalidity' benefits in response to low labour demand during previous economic recessions. The use of disability-defined benefits to facilitate permanent early exit from the labour market has now become a prominent concern for welfare states, leading to substantial reform and tightening of eligibility assessments.

For example, recent modernization of United Kingdom policies has focused on streamlining a complex system towards a primary focus on employment activation programmes (projecting cost benefits for government if not necessarily for individual recipients). In 2008, Incapacity Benefit and Income Support paid for illness or disability were replaced by a new Employment and Support Allowance, with a new Work Capability Assessment and greater emphasis on medical authority in determining eligibility. The United Kingdom example is useful in indicating state concerns to maximize the employment contribution of disabled adults and older workers, to reinforce boundaries of eligibility, and to reduce public expenditure on disability-related benefits. Such themes are also clearly evident in recent developments elsewhere in Europe.

Recent labour and welfare policy developments in European countries include a shift away from a perception of total work disability (or incapacity) towards work ability, focusing assessments on what people could do, and targeting intervention based upon this evaluation. Such moves have seen an increased focus on partial work and job flexibility—including shorter working hours, possibilities for more flexible attendance (holidays, work-breaks, etc.). In Poland, as an example, legal rights were enacted to ensure the right to partial work opportunity, depending on the degree of impairment and in Norway part-time employment is more common among disabled people (48.3 per cent in 2007) than amongst all people employed (26.6 per cent in 2007). The OECD has taken a particular interest in initiatives based on partial work capacity, although whether such initiatives have so far improved the prospect of permanent labour market inclusion remains unclear (OECD 2003a, 2007d). It is relevant to note that the 'flexicurity' suggested by pressure towards part-time work amongst disabled people may also contribute to new forms of underemployment and poverty risk.

Against this background, there has also been the historic shift of emphasis from compensatory models of disability policy towards citizenship and rights-based models (legal models that may exist in parallel with, or distinct from, state welfare policies). The international policy agenda has been re-framed, both by rights-based claims from the disabled people's movement and the proliferation of new national laws targeting disability discrimination (Breslin and Yee 2004) to re-present the central policy challenge as one of human rights. The implementation of the 2008 UN Convention on the Rights of Persons with Disabilities is significant in this development. As individual countries ratify and legislate within its framework, new tensions and challenges to existing policies will emerge. Social model critics suggest that rights-based legislation alone is unlikely to resolve the deep structural basis of disability arising from capitalist markets.

Bolderson and Mabbett (2001) argue that social model and human rights concepts of disability do not sit comfortably with the welfare models and traditions of European states. They envisaged three possible policy scenarios: the unification of out-of-work benefits for disabled and non-disabled people with the abolition of incapacity type benefits; the emergence of benefits based on compensation for the real costs of disabling barriers rather than assessments of individual function; the abolition of disability categories; and the promotion of universal access through policy mainstreaming in all areas of social inclusion. Amongst these, they regard the first as the least radical scenario (at least in the United Kingdom)—an assessment that appears to be vindicated by the British government's 2008 welfare reforms. The second presents challenges for welfare states, because moves towards non-discrimination legislation (following the United States model) have conceptualized the responsibility for an individual's exclusion as a private rather than a public concern of the state, in the sense that an employer or service provider who unreasonably discriminates against a disabled person is held legally and financially liable for the consequences. The third option is partially evident in the rhetorical position of the European Commission to mainstream disability in all policy areas. What is clear is that current trends in disability policy have moved the topic well beyond the traditional boundaries of 'social policy' and welfare towards the wider concerns of social inclusion, equality, and citizenship for all.

CHAPTER 29

UNEMPLOYMENT INSURANCE

OLA SJÖBERG

JOAKIM PALME

EERO CARROLL

INTRODUCTION

UNEMPLOYMENT insurance has from time to time, and more, perhaps, than any other kind of social policy programme, evoked political conflict in industrial society. How the state responds to unemployment embodies conflicting values on work and the causes of unemployment, as well as on the role of states, markets, families, and the third sector. One sign of the controversial nature of unemployment insurance schemes is that such schemes have tended to be introduced last of the major social insurance schemes (Wennemo 1994).

This chapter describes the evolution of unemployment insurance schemes in a sample of eighteen long-standing welfare states since the enactment of the first laws. It also aims to discuss some of the effects that unemployment insurance schemes might have on the conditions, behaviour, and attitudes of individuals, and hence on society as a whole. This includes effects on labour supply, poverty, matching between firms and workers, the skill formation of individuals, and the role of unemployment insurance for maintaining demand during recessions.

Notwithstanding that there are many aspects of the unemployment insurance programmes that warrant our attention, in this chapter we focus on three central dimensions of these programmes by using data from the Social Citizenship Indicator

Program (SCIP; Korpi and Palme 2007): How many are covered? How much will an unemployed worker get? After what time and for how long will an unemployed person get the benefit? The comparability of these statistics over a broad range of time and space makes them well suited for generalizable findings on how the character of unemployment insurance schemes has developed. They also provide a fruitful starting point for our discussion of various effects of institutional variation.

THE INSTITUTIONAL DIVERSITY OF UNEMPLOYMENT INSURANCE PROGRAMMES[1]

By delineating ideal types of institutional forms, we can simplify a complex pattern of differences and similarities and, hence, structure comparisons of countries as well as analyses of changes over time. Before the advent of legislated unemployment insurance, labour unions and friendly societies offered mutual benefits within funds financed by membership contributions. In beginning to subsidize such funds from the turn of the century, a number of Scandinavian and Continental European states established the first institutional type of unemployment insurance, *voluntary state-subsidized insurance* (often also referred to as the 'Ghent system' after the Belgian town of Ghent, where it was first introduced). In 1905 France became the first country to introduce a subsidized voluntary unemployment insurance scheme at the national level. In this institutional form of unemployment insurance, benefit funds are a crucial instance of control and administration, with the state exercising a regulatory and supervising role. The basis on which the unemployed are entitled to benefits is membership in the funds. Historically, benefits have been paid as flat-rate daily benefits, but have increasingly been paid out also in earnings-related forms. The Ghent system is still operating in Sweden, Denmark, and Finland, but in the Finnish case extensive state subsidies were introduced as late as in the 1960s.

Targeted programmes, where entitlement is judged on the basis of assets held, need of support demonstrated at the time unemployment, or of income earned in/prior to unemployment, and where benefits are paid out at minimum levels, has historically also been an important institutional form of unemployment insurance. However, although a number of countries introduced such targeted schemes as their first scheme, or have introduced targeted schemes to complement existing non-targeted schemes, only in Australia and New Zealand have national programmes of means- or income-tested benefits been the sole form of state-legislated unemployment benefits.

Among the countries with compulsory unemployment insurance, it is useful to make a distinction between *state corporatist* and *comprehensive* schemes. The United

---

[1] This section is based on Carroll (1999) and later updates of the SCIP-data.

Kingdom introduced the world's first national compulsory insurance scheme in 1911 and, although benefits were close to minimum subsistence levels, this law represented a complete reversal of the principles of the old English Poor Laws. In the comprehensive form of unemployment insurance, payment of social insurance contributions is usually the basis of entitlement to benefits, though groups of job-seekers without a prior contribution record may also be granted benefit rights. Such programmes are neither differentiated for different groups in the labour market, nor limited to those voluntarily insured through funds. Benefits tend to be flat-rate in character, or to be so weakly graduated by income as to be flat-rate in practice for many groups of workers. In many countries on the continent of Europe, state corporatist insurance, (which may be seen as a variant of compulsory insurance) has prevailed. Its institutional characteristics include state insurance regimes differentiated along occupational lines, as well as these regimes' joint administration by employer and employee representatives. In partial accordance with its organization by the labour market partners in bi- or tripartite forms, occupational affiliation is central to benefit entitlement. Benefits are usually paid out in earnings-related forms.

Table 29.1 provides an overview of the institutional structure of the first laws of unemployment insurance among the eighteen OECD countries studied here as well

Table 29.1 Years of introduction of first laws providing for unemployment benefits at the national level in eighteen OECD countries

	Voluntary state-subsidized	Targeted programmes	Comprehensive insurance	Corporatist insurance
Australia	–	1944	–	–
Austria	–	1920	–	1949
Belgium	1920	–	–	1944
Canada	–	–	1940	–
Denmark	1907	–	–	–
Finland	1917	–	–	–
France	1905	1940	–	1967
Germany	–	–	–	1927
Ireland	–	–	1911	–
Italy	–	–	–	1919
Japan	–	–	–	1947
Netherlands	1916	1943	–	1949
New Zealand	–	1938	–	–
Norway	1906	–	1938	–
Sweden	1934	–	–	–
Switzerland	1924	–	1976	–
Great Britain	–	–	1911	–
United States	–	–	1935	–

Source: Carroll 1999: 127.

as subsequent institutional development. As observed by Alber (1981) in his pioneering study, the original cross-national diversities in the design of unemployment insurance schemes have, in important respects, persisted to the present day. These institutional forms seem to have had considerable consequences for the proportion of employees covered as well as the level of benefits.

The Early Development of Unemployment Benefit Schemes: The Great Depression and its Aftermath

The 1930s were a period of economic downturn, which (possibly until the first decade of the 2000s) was unprecedented in the history of the industrialized world and existing welfare state arrangements for the unemployed, therefore, became subject to considerable strain. However, this period is not exclusively characterized by retrenchment: in many countries, the development of unemployment insurance schemes was rather characterized by stability, and some countries even improved replacement rates and coverage, albeit from rather low levels.

Because of divergent political, economic, and not least institutional circumstances, labour market policy decision makers responded differently to the labour market slump of the 1930s. Some countries introduced means and income testing as a response to the crisis—for example, Germany and Great Britain respectively introduced means and income tests and discriminatory qualifying conditions, which in practice led to married women becoming ineligible for benefits. Austria retained its rather unique 1930s system of targeted benefits where access to benefits was tightened considerably through stricter means testing. However, in most countries with contributory financing (such as voluntary state-subsidized insurance schemes and the programmes in Great Britain and Ireland), the crisis did not lead to an increased use of means-testing.

Between 1930 and 1933, during the midst of the Depression, only two countries—Germany and Great Britain—reduced the duration of ordinary insurance benefits. In both of these countries, political controversy concerning unemployment insurance was apparent in the early 1930s—in Great Britain, it played a role in the split of the Labour Party and contributed to its electoral loss and, in Germany, it was a contributory cause of the fall of the Weimar Republic. Overall, we find the lowest benefit duration in countries with voluntary programmes, such as the Nordic countries, Belgium, and the Netherlands. During this period, a number of countries also introduced emergency benefit and relief programmes of extended or indefinite duration (not included here).

When it comes to *coverage*, we would expect countries with either form of compulsory insurance (i.e. comprehensive or corporatist) more easily to attain broader coverage than countries with voluntary insurance. In the 1930s, this expectation seems also to be largely supported by the data: coverage levels in the Nordic countries (except Denmark) as well as France were generally below average during this period (see Table 29.2). In the Nordic countries, it was far from evident that the state had the right or the capacity to assert a demand to regulate the nascent trade union movement's formerly autonomous programmes. The very low coverage of the French mutualist scheme, despite its status as the first unemployment scheme legislated on a national level, has been attributed to the fact that that those groups who long bore the brunt of unemployment—youth, aged, and migrants—also lacked the political representation necessary to force elites and core workers to recognize this as a salient social problem. However, that institutional structure alone cannot explain variation in coverage rates is demonstrated by the fact that in Belgium and Switzerland, countries with voluntary insurance in the inter-war period, coverage levels were well above the average especially in the second part of the 1930s. The countries where some variant of compulsory insurance had been introduced by 1930 (i.e. Germany, Ireland, Italy, and Great Britain) display comparatively higher coverage rates during this period. In Germany, duration

Table 29.2 Net replacement rates and coverage in labour force (in per cent) in eighteen countries (averages for 1930–39, 1947–70, and 1975–2005)

		Net replacement rates[a]			Coverage in labour force		
		1930–39	1947–70	1975–2005	1930–39	1947–70	1975–2005
Voluntary	Denmark	26	55	67	22	33	67
origins or	Finland	11	29	63	1	16	68
character in	Norway	19	32	69	5	55	86
Nordic	Sweden	9	59	75	2	43	92
countries							
Voluntary	Belgium	16	46	64	23	58	67
origins in	Netherlands	22	57	79	16	46	80
Continental–	France	29	29	61	1	10	60
European	Switzerland	35	35	70	24	24	79
countries							
Comprehensive	Canada	.	46	68	.	57	81
and targeted	Ireland	46	38	60	27	52	80
programmes	Great Britain	34	43	37	62	81	79
	United States	10	42	56	14	59	83
	Australia	.	25	43	.	.	.
	New Zealand	11	51	47	.	.	.
State	Austria	34	46	58	.	44	66
corporatist	Germany	23	60	74	40	56	71
Programmes	Italy	25	26	26	26	38	48
	Japan	.	59	72	.	28	48
Average		23	43	60	20	44	72

Note: [a] Net replacement rates are an average for (i) a single-person household and (ii) a family with a dependent spouse and two children of pre-school age. The duration of unemployment is assumed to be 26 weeks, with net benefits assessed as a share of the preceding half-year's net wage.

Source: SCIP 2009, see Korpi and Palme 2007.

cuts and means testing interacted with high unemployment rates to produce a substantial decline in coverage between 1930 and 1933.

It was also the case that *replacement rates* were comparatively low in the Nordic countries with voluntary programmes in the 1930s (once again with the exception of Denmark). However, again there is not a perfect fit between institutional structure and the outcome of interest—for example, France and Switzerland, both with a voluntary form of insurance, have rather high replacement rates in the 1930s. For the two nations which had a corporatist institutional structure in the 1930s, the picture is rather mixed. While the replacement rate in Germany decreased substantially in the interwar period (from nearly 50 per cent in 1930 to below 10 per cent in 1939), it actually improved in fascist Italy during the same period (from below 20 per cent in 1930 to above 30 per cent in 1939). Two of the countries that had instituted comprehensive unemployment insurance schemes before World War II—Ireland and Great Britain—had comparatively high replacement rates during this period. There was a significant increase in the replacement rate in Ireland between 1930 and 1933, not because of any increase in the flat-rate benefits but because of a deflationary wage decrease (the average production workers' wage decreased by around 40 per cent between 1930 and 1933). In the United States, federal unemployment insurance legislation was introduced and made part of the Social Security Act in 1935, and all states had joined by July 1937. In the late 1930s, this scheme provided replacement levels comparable to those in the voluntary schemes in the Nordic countries (i.e. below 20 per cent).

From Welfare State Expansion to Worldwide Economic Crisis and Retrenchment

As a number of commentators have pointed out, wartime experience with economic planning, national solidarity, and coordination of resources was carried over to welfare state extension in the post-war period. High economic growth in the wake of the rapid reconstruction of economies after the war entailed a growing revenue base, while low levels of unemployment sustained over longer periods of time reduced benefit expenditures. Of central importance for the development of unemployment insurance in this period was also a general move towards state interventionism in the economy. This golden age of welfare state expansion came to an end with the oil shocks in 1973 and 1979. Since unemployment benefits came to occupy an important place in explaining the rise and apparent persistence of unemployment rates in many countries, the legitimacy of providing cash benefits for the unemployed increasingly came into question.

In the post-war period, the average waiting time was remarkably stable. However, a few countries initiated significant increases in *waiting days*, the prime example being New Zealand which increased the number of waiting days substantially in association with the enactment of the so-called Economic and Social Initiative in

1990. Significant increases in waiting days also occurred in Canada in connection with the reform of unemployment insurance in 1971 as well as in France and Switzerland in the early 1990s. The only countries with no waiting days in their unemployment insurance schemes in 2005 were Austria, Belgium, Denmark, Germany, and the Netherlands. An interesting feature of the Canadian unemployment insurance scheme is that since the reform in 1971, eligibility (as well as benefits) is related to the unemployment rate of the region (i.e. high unemployment regions have less restrictive eligibility criteria).

A major increase in the *duration* of benefits is evident if we compare the immediate pre- and post-war years with each other. Some countries—Sweden, Finland, Great Britain, Denmark, and Norway—extended the duration of benefits within existing institutional structures. By 1947, a number of countries had also introduced targeted schemes with (at least theoretically) unlimited duration. In the Netherlands transitional targeted programmes were introduced in 1943, but in 1949 (fully implemented in 1952) this programme was replaced by a dual system of compulsory social and industrial insurance. This change to an essentially state corporatist institutional structure also entailed increasingly longer durations of unemployment benefits, from 13 weeks in 1950 to 182 weeks in 2000. Also in France, a post-war targeted programme succeeding its wartime predecessor was gradually complemented with collective industrially based provisions, and compulsory insurance was introduced in 1967. In 1944, Australia introduced a targeted scheme.

After World War II the average *coverage* rate in the eighteen countries discussed here increased monotonically up until 1985. The continental European countries which originally introduced voluntary state-subsidized insurance (Belgium, France, the Netherlands, and Switzerland) all experienced a substantial increase in coverage rates as they introduced compulsory insurance in the post-war period (Table 29.2). However, the Nordic countries are examples of the fact that voluntary insurance does not automatically lead to lower coverage rates: the Nordic countries with voluntary insurance (Sweden, Finland, and Denmark) had below-average coverage rates in the period 1947–70, but in the period 1975–2005 coverage rates in these countries were close to or well above (Sweden) the overall average. The increase in coverage rates in Sweden occurred mainly between 1965 and 1975, partly as a result of the fact that public sector unions began to join the system in 1970. Those countries which introduced a corporatist unemployment scheme from the beginning experienced, on average, a slower increase in coverage rates in the post-war period. Whereas these countries had coverage rates close to or above the average over the period 1947–70, their rates were below the overall average in the period after 1970. All the countries here defined as having a comprehensive unemployment insurance scheme have had coverage rates above the average throughout the post-war period. The coverage of the unemployment insurance system in Ireland was expanded considerably in 1974, when the earnings ceiling, which had disqualified higher paid employees from insurance, was removed. In Canada, unemployment insurance was thoroughly reformed in 1971, including a major extension of coverage.

During the post-war period of economic expansion, the increase in *replacement rates* in countries with voluntary state-subsidized insurance seems to have been somewhat more pronounced than the average increase. In Sweden, Denmark, and Finland, daily flat-rate benefits were also gradually replaced with income-related benefits, though with relatively low ceilings for maximum benefit-entitling incomes. Especially in the period after 1970, all the Nordic countries had replacement rates that, according to comparative standards, were relatively high. However, important reductions in replacement levels have also occurred in these countries. In Sweden and Finland, this is to a great extent the result of cut-backs during the recession in Sweden and Finland in the first half of the 1990s, cut-backs that have not been fully restored since then. In Norway and Denmark, this development is more a consequence of the fact that benefit ceilings have not kept pace with wage increases, which means that an increasing proportion of an average production worker's wage is not replaced in case of unemployment.

In those continental European countries where voluntarism was replaced by some variant of compulsory insurance (i.e. Belgium, France, the Netherlands, and Switzerland), the increase in benefit rates tended also to be above-average during the period of post-war economic expansion. In Belgium, the law introduced in 1949 provided, in principle, earnings-related benefits, but up until 1971 these benefits were in practice flat-rate. In the Netherlands, benefit rates increased substantially between 1950 and 1965 partly as a consequence of the fact that the income ceiling on earnings-related benefits was abolished in 1964 and partly because of an increase in gross replacement rates (to reach 80 per cent in 1964). In France, a major increase in replacement rates was obtained through a law on means-tested unemployment benefits passed in 1951. The increase in replacement rates in Switzerland in the 1970s was due to the abolition in 1973 of the depressive system that reduced the basic allowance rate by a certain percentage for each franc exceeding a certain limit of daily wage earnings, as well as the increase in the gross replacement rate for an average production worker.

Although countries here defined as having corporatist unemployment insurance followed the general expansion of replacement rates up until the 1970s, individual countries manifested somewhat divergent developments. In Germany, replacement rates increased dramatically after World War II as a result of the 1957 legislation from the Adenauer government, and have since then been rather stable. The implementation of the so-called Hartz IV Act in 2005 did not have any effect on replacement rates for the first 26 weeks of unemployment, but this reform meant that the unemployed received a flat-rate benefit (fixed at the level of former social assistance) after the first year of unemployment, as compared to the higher means-tested income-related benefit in the previous system (Kemmerling and Bruttel 2006). Although the development in Italy seems fairly stable, flat-rate benefits were gradually hollowed out in the post-war period up until 1985, largely through the results of political non-decisions. The replacement rate for ordinary unemployment benefits was increased in 2000 (from 30 to 40 per cent), and again in 2005 (to 50 per cent). Similarly, the increase in average net replacement rates in Austria between the periods 1947–70 and

1975–2005 hides a significant drop in these rates since 1985, mainly as a result of changes in the taxation system and in benefit ceilings.

In the post-war period up until 1970, all the countries here defined as having a comprehensive insurance tradition had, on average, replacement levels that were above or close to the overall average. However, in the period after the oil crisis in the 1970s and early 1980s, the growth in net replacement rates in these countries appears to have been slower than in many other countries. In fact, these average figures conceal important reductions in replacement rates in these countries. For example, there was a rather dramatic increase in replacement rates in Great Britain between 1960 and 1970 as a result of higher flat-rate benefits as well as the introduction of earnings-related benefits in 1966. However, the reduction and eventual abolition of these earnings-related benefits in 1982 meant that replacement rates have declined since the 1970s. In Ireland, an earnings-related supplement to the flat-rate benefit was introduced in 1974, payable with the basic flat-rate unemployment benefit from the fourth week of unemployment. The reduction of both flat-rate and earnings-related benefits, until the latter was abolished in 1994, meant a rather drastic reduction of replacement rates between 1980 and 1995. In Canada, unemployment insurance was thoroughly reformed in 1971, which (besides a major extension of coverage) also included increased replacement ratios. Since the 1971 reform, the system has experienced a series of subsequent fine-tunings and tightening-ups, which included decreased replacement rates in 1976 and 1979. The replacement rate in the United States has oscillated between 45 and 60 per cent in the post-war period. Finally, Australia and New Zealand, the two countries with targeted unemployment benefit schemes, have both experienced substantial decreases in benefit levels since the mid-1970s. As part of the so-called Economic and Social Initiative in New Zealand, benefit payments were rather dramatically reduced.

While we have observed an obvious political element behind the fact that unemployment insurance lagged behind other social insurance programmes in terms of first legislation, the picture is different regarding the post-war expansion period, when party-political factors only play a minor role in explaining the generosity of unemployment benefits (Carroll 1999). The contrast is striking as compared to the driving forces behind other social insurance programmes, where the strength of the political left figures prominently (e.g. Korpi 1989). Yet the class-political salience of unemployment insurance appears to have resurfaced during the era of retrenchment (Korpi and Palme 2003). Unemployment insurance not only appears to be particularly affected by cutbacks in all kinds of welfare states but it is also the case that party-political factors are of significant importance as 'risk' factors for retrenchment to occur. However, the politics of unemployment is not only about unemployment insurance but also about unemployment as such. The return of mass unemployment came to have major consequences for government fiscal balances. Government expenditures on unemployment insurance as well as on other social insurance programmes increased while the tax base shrunk. This had the effect that budgetary pressures increased. In the 'new politics' perspective, 'permanent austerity' defined in terms of government budgetary pressures is viewed as a largely exogenous factor driving welfare state retrenchment. It is however necessary to recognize that government budget imbalances during the period following the oil-crises were clearly associated with the return of high levels of unemployment. On average, during this period, levels of unemployment within countries can account for 42 per cent of variation in fiscal balances. Hence, to a significant extent, austerity appears to be endogenous to the retrenchment process rather than primarily an exogenous cause.

This means that the development of unemployment insurance has to be understood not only in terms of benefit entitlements but also in the context of expenditures and financing. What we have found as a general pattern for social insurance programmes is that the development in the size of 'needy' populations makes as great a contribution to cross-national differences in public social expenditures as has the expansion of social rights (Kangas and Palme 2007). However, the relative importance of needs vs. rights varies between the different branches of social insurance. In the case of unemployment insurance, unemployment levels have become increasingly important, but with substantial cross-national differences in levels. Denmark, for instance, spent as much as 3–6 per cent of GDP until the decline in unemployment after 2000. General levels, however, are modest compared with pensions and health care, and many OECD countries spend less than 1 per cent of GDP, with the average being somewhat above 1 per cent. Over the past two decades, it is also clear that expenditures have followed the business cycle and have fluctuated a great deal.

The financing of unemployment benefits takes different forms (Sjöberg 2000). Targeted programmes are tax financed whereas other kinds of programmes tend to split the burden between the insured person, the employers, and the state. The United States is an interesting exception with almost exclusively employer financing over the post-war period. The trend among all of the OECD countries we have studied is that, since 1980, employer financing has become somewhat more important. It should be noted that, even where there is a basic financial structure, this is often upset during periods of high unemployment, with the state typically covering temporary deficits from the general revenue.

UNEMPLOYMENT INSURANCE
AND LABOUR SUPPLY

An important factor underlying the controversies surrounding the introduction and subsequent reforms of unemployment benefit schemes is the belief that the generosity and duration of such benefits will have a detrimental effect on aggregate unemployment rates and labour supply. According to so-called job-search models, which have come to dominate the theoretical thinking on the incentive effects of unemployment benefits, unemployment benefits will raise the reservation wage of the unemployed and therefore allow them to be relatively more discriminating about job offers (Mortensen 1977). Unemployment benefits may also have an effect on unemployment through their effect on wages: since unemployment benefits may reduce the fear of unemployment, the existence of relatively generous benefits may increase the upward pressure on wages from unions and induce them to claim wage increases that are not consistent with full employment.

It is also argued that taxes imposed on employers to finance unemployment benefit schemes will increase labour costs and thereby reduce employment, a line of reasoning that applies to the total burden of social security financing. An increasing body of literature since the late 1980s has also been devoted to the potential macro-level implications of so-called 'duration effects' on unemployment (see e.g. Blanchard 1991; Layard et al. 2005; Darity and Goldsmith 1993). Duration effects usually refer to changes in the skills, motivation, or search behaviour of the unemployed as a function of the duration of their unemployment, and/or the perception by employers of such changes. According to this line of reasoning, the existence of unemployment benefits with long duration and little pressure to look for jobs might increase the proportion of long-term unemployed and act as a mechanism for the persistence or 'hysteresis' of unemployment (Layard et al. 2005; Blanchard and Katz 1997).

From a policy perspective, cross-national comparisons of countries with different benefit regimes over longer periods of time could be extremely valuable in evaluating these hypotheses. Moreover, such studies have also the potential to capture the general-equilibrium effects that are very difficult to include in studies based on micro-economic data (Holmlund 1998). However, no clear consensus over the empirical evidence seems to have been reached. For example, whereas Nickell et al. (2005) and Nunziata (2002) found a highly significant positive correlation between unemployment benefits and the unemployment rate, Baker et al. (2004) found no clear relationship. Belot and van Ours (2001, 2004) have even suggested that the generosity of unemployment benefits may be negatively correlated with unemployment.

In a seminal study by Atkinson and Micklewright (1991), the authors stress the complexity of unemployment insurance systems and the inadequacy of a simple story of unemployment insurance (dis)incentives. One important reason for this is the existence of a so-called entitlement effect of unemployment benefits, whereby more generous benefits will make it more attractive for both the unemployed and those outside the labour force, through work, to qualify for such benefits (Friedman 1977). Moreover, transitions on the labour market not only occur between work and unemployment, but also between other statuses—transitions to permanent jobs, transitions to a great number of different atypical jobs as well as transitions to permanent or temporary withdrawal from the labour force, for example in the form of schooling or training. These different transitions have different causes and different consequences, and are therefore likely to be influenced to differing degrees by the provisions (both incentive and administrative) of unemployment insurance schemes. Atkinson and Micklewright (1991) also argue that the summary measures of unemployment benefit generosity used in cross-national research are unable to capture many of the aspects of these schemes that may affect various transitions, such as whether individuals can collect benefits if 'reasonable' job offers are rejected.

Unemployment Insurance, Poverty, and the Macro-Economy

During the post-war expansion of the welfare state, social policies and full-employment policies were commonly regarded as complementary to and as supporting each other. Whereas high aggregate employment would finance the welfare state and hold back expenditures, social polices were also believed to contribute to full employment. The most obvious example of such a complementarity is the fact that unemployment benefits may reduce the volatility of households' disposable income relative to their market income, and therefore act as an automatic stabilizer over the business cycle (Chimerine et al. 1999).

The fact that unemployment benefit schemes may reduce the volatility of households' disposable income naturally evokes questions concerning the role of unemployment benefits in affecting cross-national variation in poverty rates among those of normal working age. Bäckman's (2005) study, using data from the Luxembourg Income Study (LIS) from the first wave (1980 and surrounding years) through the fifth wave (2000 and surrounding years), illustrates how comparative data on unemployment insurance of the kind used above for descriptive purposes can also be utilized for analytical purposes. In this study, a number of key institutional characteristics of unemployment insurance schemes are examined including coverage, replacement levels, and benefit duration. Bäckman's regression analysis also includes variables representing the general social policy model applied in a given country (targeted, basic security, state corporatist, and encompassing) and structural variables such as the unemployment rate and incidence of lone-parenthood, thereby making it possible to assess the relative importance of structural and policy factors shaping inequalities over time as well as between countries.

The analysis of trends over time suggests that, even if poverty rates have not converged or are in the process of converging, they have, on average, increased by two percentage points between 1980 and 2000. The replacement rate is the most important of the three institutional factors and it has effects on both temporal and cross-national variation in poverty rates. Alone, it explains a larger part of the overall variance than all the structural factors taken together. The duration of unemployment insurance also has an explanatory value for the overall variation. The period analysed is widely seen as one of welfare state retrenchment (Korpi and Palme 2003). The results of this study indicate that retrenchment in the form of cuts in unemployment cash benefits have had negative implications for poverty risks in contemporary welfare states. Cuts in replacement levels also explain part of the variation over time. The general conclusion that can be drawn from this analysis is that policy matters, not only for cross-country differences in poverty rates, but also, in the case of unemployment insurance, for changes in poverty rates across time.

From a political-economy perspective, the role of unemployment insurance as an automatic stabilizer over the business cycle is, however, rather complex. One reason is the well-known political problem of balancing the budget over the business cycle; another concerns the uncertainty on the part of households about the security of future unemployment benefit entitlements. If households cannot be certain that the level or duration of benefits will be maintained, they may refrain from consumption and save instead both during periods of work and unemployment. It is also important to note that unemployment benefits will become less sensitive to business-cycle fluctuations, and their efficiency as a macro-economic stabilizer therefore reduced, as the criteria for obtaining benefits tighten or the level of net benefits is reduced.

Even though the standard argument is that unemployment benefits will prolong the duration of an individual's unemployment spells, it is not evident that this will have a negative effect on individuals' human capital or on the overall efficiency of the economy. Generous unemployment benefits may also allow people to stay unemployed long enough to find a job that suits their skills and level of education. In fact, basic search-models predict that unemployment benefits (or indeed any non-work income source) will lower the alternative costs associated with continued job search. By subsidizing costly job searches, unemployment benefits may therefore allow the unemployed to sustain their search for relatively more adequate jobs over a longer period of time. Consequently, unemployment benefits may not only have the effect of stabilizing individual income in the short run, but also stabilizing workers' careers in the long run. This implies that unemployment benefits are a resource that can be used productively by the unemployed, by trading some additional search time for improvements in subsequent job quality (for a cross-national assessment, see Gangl 2006). This argument also implies that unemployment benefits may preserve workers' accumulated human capital through unemployment spells. It may be argued that there are overhead costs associated with maintaining labour's human capital stock, irrespective of whether labour is employed (Clark 1923). However, once labour is unemployed these costs are external to the firm. Unemployment insurance is a means of covering these costs, thus preventing the depletion of human capital stock which would represent a social cost.

The argument for the possible productivity-enhancing effects of unemployment insurance benefit broadly suggests that the institutions of the welfare state, of which unemployment benefit is, perhaps, the most controversial, exist not only to provide those who cannot perform on the market with economic resources, but may also serve as a prerequisite for market efficiency. In line with this perspective, it may be argued that relatively generous unemployment benefits can provide people with an important incentive to invest in various skills, since the presence of such benefits mean that this investment will also pay off during times of unemployment (Estévez-Abe et al. 2001). Depending on the broader institutional context of a country, generous unemployment benefits can therefore promote economic efficiency by helping actors to overcome market failures in skills formation. It has also been suggested that the existence of unemployment benefits increases labour productivity not only by encouraging workers to seek more productive jobs, but also by encouraging firms to create these jobs (Acemoglu and Shimer 2000).

CONCLUSIONS

Unemployment can be seen as one of the 'old risks' that the 'old' welfare states tried to address by instituting unemployment insurance. During the golden age of post-war capitalism, the hey-day of the welfare state development, the risk of unemployment was, interestingly enough, lower than ever. In 'post-oil-crises capitalism', however, waves of mass unemployment appear to be a recurrent phenomenon. The global financial crisis that started in 2008 indicates that the twenty-first century has not yet put an end to this. This, in turn, suggests that there are very good reasons to spend time and effort to develop good macro-economic policies to deal with the unemployment problem. In this endeavour, the role of unemployment insurance should not be forgotten. Macro-outcomes and their counter-cyclical effects may take centre stage for policymakers, but the often neglected inequality issue and micro-aspects influencing norms and behaviour are also of continuing importance.

In this chapter we have described developments over seven decades. Due to the fact that statistics production lags behind a number of years, we have as yet no comprehensive picture beyond 2005. Yet available information allows us to detect a number of interesting changes after 2005, even if these changes do not transform the general picture. We find, for example, that Sweden introduced a number of changes in its unemployment insurance programme following the election of a centre-right government in 2006. The changes include downward adjustments of benefit level, cutbacks in benefit duration and increased contributions from insured individuals. These changes may be seen as expressions of political preferences, but their explicit aim was to increase labour supply in a booming economy. As economic prospects change, policy-makers respond. In 2009, President Obama's economic stimulation package (presumably also aimed at improving protection of the unemployed) included an extension of the duration of unemployment insurance benefits from 26 to 39 weeks. However, as unemployment increases and public finances are squeezed by increased benefit expenditures and declining tax revenues, we may again expect pressure for retrenchment of entitlements. To judge from previous crises, decision making will be influenced by party-political as well as by institutional factors (Korpi and Palme 2003).

What we have tried to illustrate in this chapter is the insight that may be obtained from a programme-specific approach. The account here shows that unemployment insurance programmes deviate, in vital respects, from those assumed normal in the comparative social policy literature. This insight has been useful in analysing the consequences of cross-national variation in social insurance programme design. For example, information about the quality of unemployment insurance, together with other policy and structural factors, contributes significantly to explaining differences in poverty rates over time and among nations. The design of unemployment insurance also has the potential to affect norms and behaviour of individuals living under different policy regimes. In this context, unemployment insurance constitutes an important link between what in social science research has remained a fairly unexplored interrelationship between welfare state regimes and production regimes.

The chapter has dealt with the situation of the most advanced industrial nations but the political ramifications of unemployment insurance do not stop there. It is unlikely that economic globalization will be either politically acceptable or economically efficient without adequate unemployment insurance in the fast-growing economies of Asia and Latin America. Vietnam, one of the poorer countries in Asia, introduced unemployment insurance in 2009. This suggests that there might even be a future for unemployment insurance in what are currently the weakest areas of social insurance development such as the African continent, where social policy-related strategies of poverty reduction have so far been formulated primarily in terms of child benefits and pensions.

CHAPTER 30

LABOUR MARKET ACTIVATION

LANE KENWORTHY

INTRODUCTION

SOCIAL scientists and policymakers traditionally have viewed the welfare state as a means of achieving economic security and redistribution. Social programmes provide money and services to individuals and households; in doing so they insure against market-based risks and reduce market-generated inequality and poverty. In the past two decades, however, a third goal has become prominent: employment. Policy reforms and innovations have more and more aimed to increase paid work.

WHY ACTIVATION?

Activation is by no means novel. Policymakers in most countries have always considered employment to be an aim of policy. Particularly noteworthy is the set of active labour market programmes put in place in Sweden beginning in the 1950s, which included retraining, assistance with job placement, and public sector jobs as a last resort (Ohman 1974; Ginsburg 1983: ch. 6; Rehn 1985). What is new is the centrality of activation to modern welfare states. The activation turn has a number of causes.

Funding the welfare state. The most prominent cause, perhaps, is the financial strain imposed by the welfare state. Public services, social insurance, and redistributive programmes grew steadily in the 1950s, 1960s, and 1970s. This was facilitated by rapid economic growth. Moreover, governments were able to raise additional revenue beyond that produced by economic growth; they did so by increasing tax rates and by introducing new types of taxes, such as the value-added tax (VAT).

Several things have changed. A number of countries experienced sustained high rates of unemployment beginning in the late 1970s or early 1980s. Particularly in nations with unemployment benefits of unlimited duration and generous social assistance, this imposed large unexpected costs.

The populations of most rich countries are ageing. Initially this was a product of slowing birth rates. Now, as the post-World War II baby boom reaches retirement age, it is increasingly a function of a growing elderly population. Governments have made pension commitments, and those commitments will sap an expanding share of public revenues in coming decades, particularly if birth rates do not increase. The rise in immigration has helped and may continue to do so, but it is unlikely to fully solve the problem.

Health care is a 'luxury good'; as societies get richer, citizen demand for it tends to rise more rapidly than incomes. It is the fastest-growing category of social expenditures. And it is expensive; along with pensions, health care accounts for the largest share of social policy expenditures in most affluent nations. Particularly given the ageing of populations, rising demand for health care provision, and hence rising health care cost, is unlikely to reverse anytime soon.

Governments face not only growing expenditures but also new constraints on revenues. In the period since the mid-1970s economic growth has slowed, and while policymakers are ever hopeful that growth rates might return to those that obtained during the post-war golden age, thus far they have not. Nor is it any longer feasible to count on tax-rate increases to generate additional revenue. Capital mobility makes it difficult to raise tax rates at all. Indeed, policymakers have struggled to keep them at existing levels, often offsetting reductions in statutory rates with reductions in tax exemptions and deductions or with increases in payroll and/or consumption taxes.

A high employment rate is viewed by some as a key part of a potential solution to this bind (Esping-Andersen 1999; Ferrera et al. 2000; Scharpf and Schmidt 2000a; Esping-Andersen et al. 2002; Kok et al. 2003; Kenworthy 2004, 2008; OECD 2005b, 2006; Lindh and Palme 2006; Hemerijck 2010). More citizens in formal work means greater payroll and income tax revenue, without requiring an increase in tax rates. It also reduces expenditures on social assistance, unemployment compensation, and related programmes.

Fairness. Arguably, generous social programmes are sustainable over the long run only if they are perceived by citizens as fair. The chief goals of the postwar welfare state were insurance against risk and provision of financial assistance to those unable to support themselves. As programmes grew more generous, however, the incentive for cheating increased. In the 1970s a large share of the working-age population in the Netherlands received disability payments, and in the late 1980s Swedish employees averaged twenty-five sick days per year (Visser and Hemerijck 1997; Agell 1996). In a context of strong economic growth and quickly-rising living standards, this type of behaviour may be tolerated. But in a context of modest growth and slowly rising incomes, sentiment is more likely to favour a norm of reciprocity (Bowles and Gintis 1999).

Poverty reduction. Poverty alleviation has long been an implicit or explicit commitment in rich countries. Evidence suggests that employment is an effective way to reduce poverty (OECD 2008a).

Social inclusion. In many European countries, the initial response to high unemployment in the 1980s was to find ways to pull people out of the labour force in order to make room for the unemployed, with older workers and women among the chief targets (Ebbinghaus 2006). This was seen as a just and humane strategy, since pensions, special early retirement benefits, unemployment compensation, social assistance, and other types of supports would ensure that those without employment nevertheless maintained a good standard of living. But it turns out that non-employment is associated with feelings of social exclusion, discouragement, boredom, and unhappiness (Layard 2005).

Employment has other benefits (Jahoda 1982; Wilson 1996; Phelps 1997: ch. 1). Paid work can be a source of mental stimulation. It imposes regularity and discipline on people's lives. And with heightened geographic mobility, later marriage, and increased divorce, neighbourhood and family ties have been dissipating, making the office or factory an increasingly important site of social interaction. This had led to rethinking the merits of induced labour force withdrawal.

Women's independence and fulfilment. Steady increases in women's educational attainment and changes in gender norms have produced heightened preference by women for working careers. More and more women see employment as a means of realizing individual potential, boosting identity and self-esteem, achieving social integration, and ensuring financial independence. The turn toward activation among policymakers has in part been a response to these shifts (OECD 2007b; Kenworthy 2008: ch. 10).

External encouragement. The OECD's 1994 *Jobs Report* and its subsequent employment strategy pushed the activation turn forward in Europe. Despite considerable dispute about the specific recommendations in that report and in some of the OECD's follow-up studies, its highlighting of large-scale long-term unemployment and its argument in favor of institutional and policy reform altered, to some degree, the nature of policy discussions in a number of countries. The Lisbon Council's establishment of a European employment strategy with targets for 2010, the policy learning promoted via the open method of coordination, and a variety of policy reports from the European Commission arguably accelerated the move toward activation-oriented policy (Kok et al. 2003; European Commission 2007b; Viebrock and Clasen 2009).

How?

Discussion of labour market activation often focuses on particular policy tools. But it is helpful to think about it in terms of broad approaches as well. We can distinguish between three labour market activation strategies. They differ according to what is considered the aim of activation and according to the breadth of policies to be used in pursuing that goal.

One approach conceives of the aim as a high(er) employment rate and of the means as a relatively narrow set of government programmes typically referred to as 'active labour market policies' (ALMP). These include retraining, job placement, temporary financial assistance, and perhaps some subsidies or tax breaks to employers to encourage hiring. A second approach again focuses strictly on employment as the goal but features a much broader array of policy tools, from public employment to shifting taxes away from those that increase non-wage labour costs to fiscal policy. The third approach also takes this relatively wide view of policy tools, but it conceives the goal of activation to be not merely high employment but also labour market success. Here more attention is paid to skill development, to placement in appropriate jobs, to the payoff from employment, and to opportunity for upward mobility. One distinction sometimes made in this regard is between programmes that use negative incentives or punishments to force people into employment versus 'enabling' policies that improve people's ability to find good jobs and to advance in the labour market.

The specific policy tools used to pursue activation are wide-ranging. Some impose requirements while others provide incentives. Some work on the demand side, attempting to increase hiring by employers, while others seek to increase the supply of those seeking employment. Some are aimed broadly, at the entire working-age population, whereas others are targeted at particular groups for which the employment rate is low, such as women, those near retirement age, the young, persons with limited education and/or skills, immigrants, and people with physical, mental, or emotional disabilities.

Benefit limits, cuts, and conditions. Benefit programmes with easy eligibility conditions, generous payments, and lengthy duration discourage employment. One of the principal activation strategies countries have pursued is reductions in access to benefits and in the amount of benefits. Eligibility criteria have been tightened, benefit levels have been reduced, benefits have been made conditional on employment, and the duration of receipt has been shortened.

The United States welfare reform of 1996 is perhaps the most dramatic of these changes. Though the reform included money for supports such as child care, its fundamental thrust was in the direction of punitive activation. It imposed a maximum of two years in succession, and five years total over a lifetime, for receipt of cash social assistance. The aim is to increase employment by limiting cash and near-cash supports for able-bodied working-age persons who are outside the workforce. Put another way, the goal is to activate by reducing the extent to which government programmes 'decommodify' labour.

Another key component of American social assistance, though this varies across the states, is 'workfare', whereby receipt of benefits is conditional on participation in training or actual employment. The idea is to build human capital in the form of skills and/or work experience while providing income support. Critics tend to see this too as punitive, as it pushes recipients into the labour market while offering, in some instances, relatively little in the way of enabling supports.

A number of countries have moved in this direction, though not to the same degree. Denmark, one of the most generous countries in its benefit package, dramatically shortened the period of eligibility for unemployment benefit receipt in the 1990s. Germany's Hartz reforms in the early 2000s had a similar effect. Many other nations have made receipt of certain types of benefits conditional on training and/or employment.

An alternative is to provide benefits but to require recipients to accept a reasonable job if one becomes available. This condition has always applied to many unemployment compensation programmes, but caseworkers, through whom such rules are implemented, often did not know if in fact such jobs were available to benefit claimants. Now caseworkers tend to have better information about job opportunities and often are actively involved in securing this information.

Assistance with job search and placement. Public assistance with finding new employment has long been a key feature of Swedish active labour market policy. It has been utilized in other countries too, though to a much lesser extent. Since the mid-1990s its use has become more widespread. The trend in recent years has been toward individualized assistance. Clients are assigned an individual caseworker who evaluates their abilities and needs, helps with benefit receipt, oversees the search for new work and placement with the firm, and monitors employment outcomes.

Assistance with transportation. In areas where key sources of employment are not easily accessible via public transport, governments sometimes provide subsidies to defray the cost of transportation to and from work.

In-work subsidy. The Working Tax Credit in the United Kingdom and the Earned Income Tax Credit in the United States are the best-known instances of programmes that aim to encourage employment by subsidizing the incomes of low-earning households (Dilnot and Macrae 2000; Hotz and Scholz 2004). Earnings from employment (and in the United Kingdom also a minimum number of hours worked) are required for receipt, and the amount of the subsidy increases with earnings up to a point before it begins to decrease. At its maximum, the amount of the subsidy is substantial, around 40 per cent of earnings in the United States and higher in the United Kingdom. These subsidies have proven effective at encouraging labour market participation, and they are relatively inexpensive to administer. Several other countries—including Denmark, Finland, France, and the Netherlands—have similar programmes, but on a much smaller scale and with the subsidy given to individuals rather than households.

Despite their evident merits, most nations have thus far been reluctant to embrace a large-scale in-work subsidy along the lines of those in the United Kingdom and United States. One reason is that doing so is viewed as forgoing the opportunity to force employers to improve productivity (Bertola 2000). It also reduces the incentive for individuals in low-wage jobs to upgrade their skills in order to advance up the earnings ladder. More fundamentally, it signals a commitment by citizens and policymakers to a low-wage economy, which is viewed as a step backwards.

Another reason is that the chief obstacle to employment at the low end of the labour market is seen as being high non-wage labour costs, particularly payroll taxes, rather than low wages. Reducing the former by exempting certain types of employment from payroll taxes or by providing a subsidy to employers is therefore viewed as a better strategy. Mark Pearson and Stefano Scarpetta (2000: 19; see also Bargain and Orsini 2006; Marx and Verbist 2008) argue that an employer subsidy is a functional equivalent to an employment-conditional earnings subsidy, and one that is better suited to the conditions of many European countries.

> It seems that countries fall into two camps. In those with a low tax-benefit environment and relatively low minimum wages, the essential problem is to encourage labour supply and to provide higher incomes for those in poorly paid jobs. In these circumstances, it seems reasonable to place greater stress on in-work benefits. By contrast, in countries with high levels of taxes and benefits and relatively high wage floors, making work pay schemes are likely to have high fiscal costs and risk reinforcing disincentive effects related to higher marginal effective tax rates. As a result, policy interventions in the second group of countries should probably focus on wage subsidies, as the essential problem is one of increasing labour demand for low-skilled or inexperienced workers.

Indeed, up to this point countries such as France, Germany, and the Netherlands have pursued this latter route, with only very minor (if any) in-work subsidies to employees or their households.

Employer subsidy. As just noted, demand for labour can be enhanced via a targeted or general employer subsidy. Firms can be given a cash credit or tax reduction in return for hiring. This is particularly attractive in countries with high payroll taxes. Germany is an oft-cited example: employers and employees each pay 21 per cent of wages. This type of subsidy now accounts for a significant share of active labour market programme expenditures in a number of OECD countries (OECD 2003*b*, *c*; Marx and Verbist 2008).

Public employment. Public sector jobs can be used as a 'last resort' in providing employment for those unable to find work in the private sector. In the Nordic countries and France, the government typically has accounted for 25–30 per cent of total employment, making the public sector a likely source of employment whether as a last resort or a first option.

Promote part-time work and flexible work schedules. Part-time jobs are an attractive option for some, especially second earners in households. In a number of countries they now account for a quarter or more of all employment, and in the Netherlands a third. Some of this is due to inability to find a satisfactory full-time position, but surveys suggest much of it is by choice. The Dutch employment success story since the early 1980s is largely one of part-time employment growth, with three-quarters of new employment being part-time (Visser 2002: 25). The rapid growth of part-time work in the Netherlands has multiple causes, but in the 2000s it has been facilitated by legislation that ensures part-time employees the same wage and benefit status as full-time workers. Some other countries have followed suit (Gornick and Meyers 2003: ch. 6).

Flexible work schedules, for those employed either part-time or full-time, also tend to be attractive to potential employees, again especially in households with a second earner. Protections for such employees as well as financial incentives to employers to expand flexible work-time options can help to attract them.

Reduce tax disincentives to second earners. In some countries the tax system penalizes a couple with two earners relative to those with just one earner. (Plantenga and Hanson 1999; Sainsbury 1999; Daly 2000; Dingeldey 2001). An estimate for the year 2000, for instance, suggests that in Sweden and Finland, which have individualized taxation, there was no such penalty at all, whereas in Germany a two-earner couple faced a tax rate approximately 10 percentage points higher than a one-earner couple (Daly 2000: 496; Dingeldey 2001: 659). Reducing this disincentive should help to promote employment, particularly among women (Jaumotte 2003).

Reduce real wages. Wage moderation—specifically, reduction of real unit labour costs—has been among the most prominent suggestions by the OECD (1994*a*) and others favouring labour market activation. The argument is as follows: in jobs where productivity is low and difficult to increase, employers can afford to pay only minimal wages. If forced to pay more, they will hire fewer people. Hence, policy-makers and unions face a choice: allow low wages in such jobs and thereby get higher employment, or mandate higher wages and thereby get lower employment.

The difficulty from the perspective of policymakers is that they often have limited influence on wage levels and wage changes. A common response has been the formation of formal or informal social pacts, in which government encourages wage restraint in exchange for changes in certain social programmes, taxes, or active labour market programmes (Avdagic et al. 2010).

A more direct lever for policymakers is the statutory minimum wage. Only about half of the rich countries have a statutory minimum, however. In others, wages are set via collective bargaining with little or no government role. In the United States and the Netherlands, the inflation-adjusted value of the statutory minimum has been allowed to fall steadily since the early 1980s. In France, by contrast, it has tended to keep pace with price increases. Several countries, such as the United Kingdom and Ireland, first introduced a statutory minimum wage during this period.

Reduce non-wage labour costs. Earlier I mentioned that non-wage labour costs tend to be a source of concern, particularly in continental European countries such as Germany and France. In addition to exempting certain jobs from such taxes or providing a subsidy to employers to offset their impact, some governments have debated shifting the tax burden away from payroll taxes. The issue was part of the discussion in Germany's 'Alliance for Jobs' in the late 1990s, but no agreement to reform the tax system was reached (Streeck 2009). In 1990 France introduced a new tax on personal income (the CSG) in order to shift taxation away from payroll taxes. This was only a partial step, though, as payroll taxes still account for a large portion of the revenues that fund French social policy (Palier 2000).

Ease employment protection regulations. Employment protection regulations restrict employers' freedom to fire and hire. They can be instituted by the government as legal rules or negotiated by unions and employers in collective bargaining. For regular ('permanent') employees, regulations govern the justification employers are required to provide for dismissal, approval they may be required to secure from employee representatives, the length of notice they must give, the type and extent of compensation employees receive if dismissed, and the length of the trial period before employees are protected. For fixed-term ('temporary') employees, regulations limit the circumstances or tasks for which fixed-term contracts can be issued, the number of times or length of time a worker can be hired on such a contract, and the types of work for which temporary employment agencies can be utilized.

Strong employment protection regulations make it more difficult and/or costly for employers to fire employees. They may have little or no impact on unemployment, because they can reduce both hiring and firing. But even if they do not affect the unemployment rate, to the extent they reduce employer demand for new workers employment protection regulations may reduce growth of the *em*ployment rate (Nickell and Layard 1999; Kenworthy 2008). Since the mid-1990s, most of the continental European and Nordic countries have reduced the stiffness of employment protection regulations, mainly by easing restrictions on fixed-term employment (Kenworthy 2008: ch. 6).

Family-friendly policies. In the countries that have experienced employment growth since the 1970s, much of it has been among women. Differences in female employment also account for a large portion of the cross-country variation in employment rates. Family-friendly policies are commonly suggested to be a key contributor to growth of female employment (Sainsbury 1999; Daly 2000; Dingeldey 2001; Esping-Andersen et al. 2002: ch. 3; Orloff 2002; Gornick and Meyers 2003; Jaumotte 2003; Eliason et al. 2008).

One such policy is public provision or financing of child care. Lack of affordable child care can pose a significant obstacle to employment for women with pre-school-age children. Government-provided or -funded care for young children may therefore encourage female employment. In Denmark, for instance, 64 per cent of children aged 6 months to 2 years are in formal child care, commonly between seven and eight hours per day. Heavy public subsidies help limit the cost to parents to approximately 10 per cent to 20 per cent of an average production worker's earnings.

For women with school-age children (age 6 and older), school hours and the availability of extended-day or after-school services can potentially affect employment opportunities and decisions. Here some of the Continental countries have noteworthy roadblocks. For example, many German schools for 6-to-9-year-olds are open for only half days, and schools in France traditionally are closed on Wednesday afternoons.

A second policy often posited as conducive to women's employment is paid maternity/care leave. The expectation is that if women know they can take a reasonably long break from work without losing their job and without forgoing all of their earnings, more will choose to enter the labour market in the first place and more will return after having a child. Here too the Nordic countries have been at the forefront. Each of the four instituted a policy of paid maternity leave by the 1960s, and in the ensuing decades the length and financial generosity of these leaves have gradually been extended. On the other hand, Finland, France, and Norway each offer a two-to-three-year paid leave. There is reason to expect that leaves of this length reduce women's employment by encouraging extended breaks, which sometimes become permanent.

Human capital. In every rich country, employment rates are positively correlated with educational attainment; those with a college degree have a higher employment rate than those with only a secondary degree, who are more likely to be employed than persons without a secondary degree (OECD 2008a). This squares with the standard economic view that wages are determined by productivity, which in turn is a function of skills. A common strategy for increasing employment, then, is to improve educational attainment and/or the quality of schooling.

Policymakers have attempted to do this in a variety of ways: subsidizing early education; improving elementary and secondary schooling via increased funding, greater centralization or decentralization of decision making, heightened teacher accountability, school choice, and others; increasing opportunity for college attendance via reduced charges and/or increased access to loans. A variety of countries also have moved to improve opportunities for 'lifelong learning' via retraining, subsidies for return to schooling, access to online education, and others.

Career ladders. Skills are one key to upward mobility over the life course. Another is organized intra-firm and inter-firm career ladders. These are programmes that facilitate transitions from low-skill, low-paying jobs in an industry into higher-skill, better-paying ones. Joan Fitzgerald (2006) has examined organized career ladders in the United States in health care, child care, and a variety of other industries. In health care, for example, career ladder programmes provide training and classroom education at low cost and feasible schedules to help transitions from aide to nursing assistant to registered nurse. Many of these programmes, in the United States and elsewhere, are small in scale. But interest in them appears to be on the rise.

COUNTRY SIMILARITIES AND DIFFERENCES

Arguably there has been some convergence among affluent nations in policy strategies and in the use of particular policy tools to promote employment. Moreover, there is indication of convergence in administration, with governments moving towards centralized goal-setting with decentralized tactics and implementation (Eichhorst and Konle-Seidl 2008). Still, significant cross-country diversity remains, both in overall approach to activation and in the specific policy strategies and programmes countries utilize (Eichhorst and Konle-Seidl 2008; Kenworthy 2008).

Typologies abound in the comparative welfare state literature, and there have been several attempts to typologize activation approaches (Lødemel and Trickey 2000; van Berkel and Hornemann Møller 2002; Barbier 2004). The challenge for typologies is to identify the dimensions on which to base the country groupings. In the early stages of typologizing this decision typically is made on theoretical grounds. As data availability improves—that is, as more countries are scored on more components of the relevant policies or institutions—empirical techniques such as factor analysis and cluster analysis often take over. Labour market activation seems to have not yet reached this latter stage.

To my knowledge there have been no attempts to score or rank countries according to activation effort. The OECD (2009a) has data on public expenditures on active labour market programmes. The Nordic countries tend to be highest on this measure, followed by the continental nations, with the Anglo countries lowest. And there are various scores for other activation strategies, including the generosity of social assistance, the stiffness of employment protection regulations, public support for child care, and many others. But as the discussion in the 'How?' section above suggests, activation strategies encompass a large number of policies and programmes, which are combined in myriad ways.

DOES ACTIVATION WORK?

The chief aim of activation is to increase the employment rate. Has it succeeded? Numerous comparative empirical studies have examined the effect of particular labour market policies and institutions on employment (see the list and discussion in Kenworthy 2008: ch. 4). Many find a link between the two.

Figure 30.1 shows employment rates in twenty OECD countries in 1989 and 2007. Both years are business cycle peaks, so the comparison is a reasonable one. The rates are shown for four groups. One is all working-age (15–64) persons. The other three are groups whose employment rates traditionally have been relatively low. Policymakers have thus been especially keen to try to raise them. These are prime-working-age (25–54) women, the young (20–24), and the near-elderly (60–64).

In most countries the overall employment rate, as well as the rate for women of prime working age, has increased. The only notable exceptions are Sweden and Finland, both of which began this period with comparatively high employment rates and suffered very deep recessions in the early 1990s. If we accept that there has been a genuine activation turn in policy, the over-time trends in employment

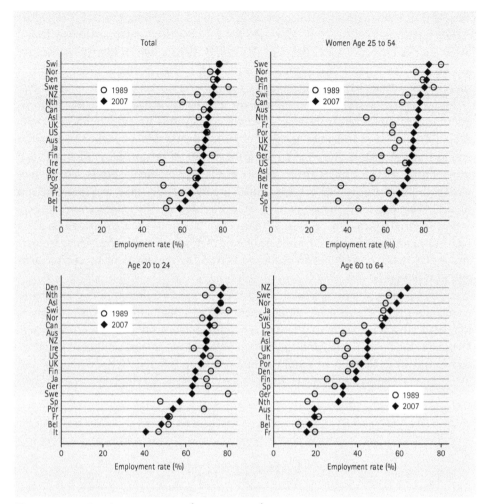

Figure 30.1 Employment rates (1989, 2007)

Note: Employment rate = employed persons in the relevant group as a share of all persons in the group. 1989 employment data are not available for Austria. First year for Switzerland is 1991 rather than 1989.

Source: Author's calculations from data in OECD 2009e.

support a conclusion that this shift has had an impact. But of course, many other things contributed to rising employment rates, including changes in cultural norms and increases in female educational attainment (Hicks and Kenworthy 2008). Moreover, in the Netherlands and Denmark, two oft-cited success stories, policy changes followed employment growth as much as they preceded it (Viebrock and Clasen 2009). It is thus difficult to know how much of the employment rise to attribute to policy shifts (Kenworthy 2008).

For the young and the near-elderly the picture is more mixed. Employment rates for the young (excluding 15-to-19-year-olds, who are most likely to still be in school) increased in some nations but decreased in others. Employment rates for the near-elderly increased in virtually all countries, but in some they remain extremely low—below 20 per cent in France, Belgium, Italy, and Austria. Given that these two age groups have been particular targets of activation efforts, perhaps a conclusion of success ought to be tempered.

Social scientists also have examined the impact of active labour market pro-grammes on employment outcomes. Here the conclusions are more divided (Martin 2000; Rønsen and Skarohamar 2009). Studies frequently find a beneficial impact on employment for at least some target groups. But it is not clear whether such programmes are cost effective in the sense that government spends less than it otherwise would on passive benefits. This is partly because these programmes tend to deal with the most difficult cases. When viewed in the larger context of an activation strategy, it can be argued that active labour market programmes are a vital component regardless of whether or not they are cost effective. They are part and parcel of a commitment to go beyond requiring employment by encouraging and facilitating it.

One conclusion that seems clear from the comparative literature is that there is more than one route to rising employment and to a high employment rate. There may be elective affinities among certain activation policies, but countries as diverse as Denmark, the Netherlands, and the United States have (at least until 2008) secured comparatively high rates of employment with very different sets of policies and institutions (Kenworthy 2008: ch. 11).

Conclusion

Is the activation turn real? A prevailing view of welfare states in affluent countries is that they have been remarkably stable over the past several decades. This image stems from studies that note the lack of reduction in tax revenues or social expenditures in the face of globalization and related pressures, as well as from descriptions of continental welfare states as incapable of adaptation to new risks and fiscal realities (Scharpf and Schmidt 2000a; Castles 2004). Drawing on this notion, a skeptical interpretation of the supposed turn toward labour market activation might suggest that what actually has happened is that the Anglo countries have cut some benefits, the Continental nations have done nothing at all, and the major activation develop-ments in the Nordic countries occurred mainly in the 1970s and 1980s.

I am more inclined to agree with the conclusion of recent comparative surveys by Werner Eichhorst and Regina Konle-Seidl (2008) and by Anton Hemerijck (2010), which suggest that most of the rich nations have undergone fairly extensive changes in policies related to activation. In part this is a shift in mindset—from an orienta-tion toward decommodification, or passive support to the non-employed and encouragement of labour market exit, to an orientation prioritizing employment. Shifts in actual policies have been somewhat far-reaching as well, including in some countries, such as Germany, where they were least expected. Case studies of country developments bear this out (Auer 2000; Madsen 2002; Visser 2002; Vail 2004; Eichhorst et al. 2008).

I write this chapter in the midst of the worst economic crisis since the 1930s. Will it have consequences for the activation turn? I suspect yes, in two ways. First, employment has fallen in virtually all of the rich countries, and may well continue to do so. This increases the pressure on governments to provide employment support on both the demand and supply sides. And large budget deficits incurred to try to stimulate the economy create additional incentives for governments to boost employment, in order to reduce expenditures on unemployment compensation, social assistance, early pension payments, and the like.

Second, the depth of this economic downturn may enhance support for an enabling orientation to activation. The notion that it is enough for government to simply force or induce work may increasingly lose its lustre. Then again, enormous budget deficits might lead governments to resist demands for a more enabling set of activation supports, and perhaps to cut back on existing efforts.

Whatever its form, I see no reason to expect the activation turn to reverse. And in spite of homogenizing pressures stemming from economic globalization, the European Union, enhanced knowledge about the programmes used in other countries, demographic trends, and the economic crisis, I expect a continuation of the extensive diversity we currently observe in activation strategies and policies.

....

CHAPTER 31

SOCIAL ASSISTANCE

....

THOMAS BAHLE

MICHAELA PFEIFER

CLAUS WENDT

INTRODUCTION

....

SOCIAL assistance provides social protection for people in need. The term is used primarily in Europe, while Americans refer to 'welfare'. In the global discourse, 'social safety-net' is most commonly used. These terms have specific connotations, but all focus on needy populations. Social assistance can have a broad and a specific meaning. Broadly, it delimits *means- or income-tested benefits* as distinguished from benefits based on membership rights or insurance claims. Notably, Anglophone countries have always relied on this approach extensively. More narrowly defined, social assistance provides a minimum income to all members of society (universal) or to selected groups (categorical) such as the elderly. This *minimum income protection* aims at securing an income of last resort. In this chapter social assistance is understood in both senses, as means-tested benefits and minimum income, but it does not include the concept of an unconditional *basic income* for all.

In advanced welfare states, social assistance is often regarded as a residual part of social security since expenditure and coverage rates are lower than for other areas. However, social assistance is of great significance for the welfare state. Historically, it was the first important public social policy that paved the way for welfare state development. Today, social assistance is crucial for the institutionalization of social rights (Leibfried 1992) because it provides the baseline of social security below which nobody should be allowed to fall.

Social assistance in the broad sense cannot be 'functionally' defined, because it does not cover a specific risk, purpose, or target group, whereas the function of minimum income is preventing poverty. Social assistance includes programmes for different needy groups, including the elderly, disabled persons, families (particularly lone parents), and the long-term unemployed. Low wage-earners also increasingly depend on means-tested top-ups or tax credits.

The number and composition of recipients depends on changes in labour markets and families. Moreover, differences in the 'inclusiveness' of other welfare institutions have a strong impact on cross-national variations. In this respect, functionally equivalent solutions should be considered. For example, income for elderly persons can be guaranteed by earnings-related insurance, universal flat-rate pensions, or means-tested assistance targeted at pensioners or covering the whole needy population. In some countries, particularly in the English-speaking world, tax credits for low-income earners provide additional means-tested income for large parts of the workforce (see further below). Cross-national differences in the mix of these instruments have a strong effect on social assistance schemes operating as the safety-net of last resort within the social security system.

The next section of this chapter provides an overview of social assistance programmes in the broad sense. It briefly describes their development and maps different types of assistance in OECD countries based on the seminal study by Eardley et al. (1996). The following section describes the salience and generosity of minimum income schemes, and the one after discusses political conflicts and debates. A further section outlines new policies that have changed the character of assistance programmes, most notably welfare-to-work. This analysis largely focuses on OECD countries. The final section takes a global perspective looking at social safety-nets in developing and transition countries.

SOCIAL ASSISTANCE IN OECD COUNTRIES

In Europe, poor relief is one of the oldest forms of public aid. Originally it was locally organized, often by private charities or churches. With industrialization and the development of national labour markets, these relief systems came under pressure, leading to state-intervention and centralization (Swaan 1988), but with significant international variations. The English Poor Law from 1834 and its Elizabethan predecessor from 1601 were probably the earliest examples of public involvement in which the workhouse occupied a major role (Fideler 2006). England was a pioneer, a consequence of early industrialization and the labour mobility that followed the land enclosures (Polanyi 1944). Poor relief was fairly unified and 'public' from early on, despite local variations in implementation. Revolutionary France first proclaimed a universal right to public assistance in 1793, but never realized it. Only a hundred years later, the Third Republic introduced various categorical assistance programmes that characterized the French system until recently. In Germany, as in other continental European countries, the principle of subsidiarity had a long-lasting impact on social welfare. It was especially prominent in the Catholic world and in religiously mixed countries where the church tried to preserve its realm against the nation state (see Chapter 18). Families, local communities, churches and charitable organizations were regarded as responsible for the poor. Only if they failed, did the state have the right to intervene. These 'intermediary' institutions have remained important especially in social services (Bahle 2007).

Despite differences, most relief systems distinguished between the deserving and undeserving poor and introduced strict tests of who was deserving and who was not. In the English Poor Law, welfare recipients lost civil rights and were often institutionalized in the workhouse. Yet nineteenth-century data suggest that British poor relief was the most extensive of the period, with much higher spending than the United States or any other European country (Lindert 2004: vol. 1, 46–7).

With the introduction of social insurance from the late nineteenth century onwards, the role of poor relief was transformed. More and more social groups were covered by other, more generous schemes. Employment-related insurance or universal benefits for pensioners, disabled persons, and the unemployed transformed social assistance into a residual safety-net. At the same time, harsh eligibility conditions and means tests were relaxed and social rights extended. The gradual extension of social rights (Therborn 1995a) together with occupationally specific social insurance meant that, in most countries, social assistance became a secondary form of provision.

The first comprehensive study on social assistance in OECD countries was undertaken by Eardley and colleagues (1996; see also Gough et al. 1997) and is still the major reference, even though it describes the situation in 1992. The authors used a broad definition of social assistance including means-tested benefits in different fields and also some services. They developed a taxonomy of benefits and introduced three major dimensions: (1) poverty-tested versus generally means-tested; (2) cash versus 'tied', i.e. benefits ear-marked for specific purposes like housing; (3) general versus categorical, i.e. targeted at specific groups. Subsequently they distinguished four benefit categories (Eardley et al. 1996: 3, 26–8): (a) *general assistance*: poverty-tested cash benefits provided to everybody in need (e.g. United Kingdom Income Support); (b) other *means-tested benefits* (e.g. family allowances); (c) *categorical assistance* for specific groups (e.g. minimum pensions); and (d) *tied assistance* for specific purposes (e.g. housing). Types (a) and (c) come close to minimum income benefits (see the discussion in the following section).

In most countries, various categories coexisted, but the mix differed. Gough et al. (1997: 36–7; see also Gough 2001: 165) identified eight social assistance types:

1. *Selective welfare systems*: most programmes are categorical and means-tested, but also relatively generous, rights-based and nationally integrated (Australia, New Zealand).

2. The *unique case of the United States*: extensive categorical but strongly stigmatizing low 'welfare' benefits and high work incentives.

3. *Welfare states with integrated safety-nets*: social assistance is institutionalized nationally, benefits are generous and social rights important (Ireland, Britain, Canada).

4. *Dual social assistance systems*: categorical programmes dominate, but are supplemented by a general safety-net of last resort for all (France, Belgium, Germany).

5. *Citizenship-based but residual systems*: a general scheme provides relatively generous benefits, but plays a marginal role within the well-developed social security system (the Netherlands, and Nordic countries, except Norway).

6. *Rudimentary social assistance systems*: a few categorical programmes beside localized and often non-publicly organized relief provide low benefits and limited coverage (Southern Europe, including Turkey).

7. *Decentralized, discretionary relief*: strong local discretion, above average benefits, but few beneficiaries (Norway, Austria, and Switzerland).

8. The *unique case of Japan*: a centralized but discretionary system.

Although this typology was built on multiple factors including institutional characteristics, the variations are also observable in quantitative indicators such as coverage rates and benefit levels (see Figure 31.1). In 1992 coverage varied from less than 1 per cent in Japan to 25 per cent in New Zealand. All Anglophone countries had quite extensive systems, but with variations. New Zealand's system, where most social benefits involve some form of means-testing and coverage often reaches into middle income strata, stands out as the most extensive. The exceptional position of the United States is confirmed by high coverage combined with low benefits. In this case, a food stamp programme provides extensive coverage, but it only covers a minor part of needs. In Southern Europe, both coverage and generosity were low due to rudimentary systems. Continental countries were characterized by moderate coverage and benefits, and both indicators are high for the Nordic countries. Hence, means-tested supplements assume a larger role in universal than in insurance-based systems. In the early 1990s, the Scandinavian countries faced a deep economic downturn, during which many people fell back on social assistance.

Compared to Esping-Andersen's (1990) typology of welfare regimes, which did not take assistance into account, the above analysis differentiates within the liberal and the conservative clusters. Within the Anglophone group distinctly different kinds of 'liberal' welfare states developed. There is a British–Irish variant in which the idea of social citizenship prevails and is institutionalized by a guaranteed minimum income. Secondly, there is a Pacific variant where generous means-tested benefits form the core of social security, reflecting the 'radical' welfare state tradition (Castles and Mitchell 1993). Finally, the North American variant seems to follow the 'classical' liberal approach of stigmatizing poor relief.

Southern European countries are distinct because of less-developed social security systems and the prominent role of the family (Leibfried 1992). Both factors have been detrimental to the establishment of comprehensive social assistance. Additionally,

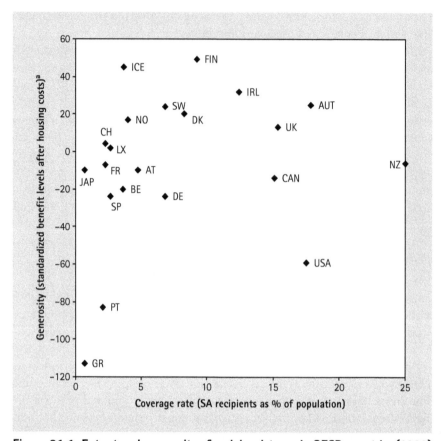

Figure 31.1 Extent and generosity of social assistance in OECD countries (1992)

Note: [a] Standardized benefit levels after housing costs for an average of 9 household types. In PPP expressed as a proportion of the mean for all OECD countries, standardized for GDP per capita in 1992.
Source: Gough et al. 1997: Table 2, column 1, p. 24; Table 6, column 4, p. 32.

strong shadow economies, limited administrative capacities and a widespread mistrust of public institutions (often permeated by clientelism) have hindered the development of general social assistance (Ferrera 2005b). The 'deviating' cases of Austria, Switzerland and Norway seemingly represent the survival of older local traditions of poor relief within decentralized polities.

GUARANTEED MINIMUM INCOME IN OECD COUNTRIES

This section focuses on the narrow meaning of social assistance, the guaranteed minimum income. In-kind benefits and services are not considered due to limited space, although they constitute a significant part of the overall benefit package for the poor in many countries. Cantillon et al. (2008: 219) follow the International Labour Organization (1942) in defining social assistance as 'benefits to persons of small means as of right in amounts sufficient to meet minimum standards of need and financed from taxation'. They distinguish four elements: the poverty-test; a social right; a minimum standard of need; and a non-contributory character. Furthermore, minimum income provisions can be divided into general schemes including the whole population (universal) and programmes for specific groups (categorical).

By 2006 most EU countries (19 of then 25 member states) had introduced universal social assistance, sometimes supplemented by categorical schemes. In a few countries only categorical schemes existed. Portugal introduced a scheme (in 1996) as have done all former Socialist new member states except Hungary. By 2006, Italy and Greece were the only two old members without general (nationwide) schemes; the Spanish system was institutionalized at the regional level. Among the other OECD countries (excluding Mexico), only the United States, New Zealand, and Australia did not have general systems. In the United States, general provisions cover only food stamps and public assistance is restricted to families (OECD 2007j).

The period since the early 1990s has been one of major social, economic, and political changes, including transition to EU member status in a number of countries. There was persistent high unemployment in many countries. Employment relations have become less protective for vulnerable groups, and low wages and atypical employment are common. At the same time, social benefits have been limited or reduced in some countries. Hence, social risks have grown while social security has been retrenched, both developments with the potential to give social assistance a greater significance.

Yet cross-national data on the salience of social assistance over time is limited, especially regarding expenditures and recipients. Data are available for nominal benefit rates, i.e. guaranteed minimum income levels.[1] Moreover, expenditure data are problematic, especially for minimum income, because benefits are calculated as the difference between recipients' own income and the guaranteed minimum. Thus aggregate spending does not reveal the real impact of social assistance on people's living conditions.

Updated data are available for some European countries,[2] covering at least four of the eight social assistance types identified by Eardley et al. (1996). The 2006 results broadly support the findings for 1992 (Table 31.1).[3] Within Europe, the United Kingdom and Ireland quite clearly form a separate family of nations with high expenditure and coverage. In Britain, more than a quarter of the population received a minimum

---

[1] Both OECD and Eurostat social expenditure statistics include social assistance programmes in the residual categories, making valid comparisons almost impossible. The number of beneficiaries is missing in international databases and even national figures covering all individual programmes are often lacking. For benefit rates comparable data are available thanks to two comparative studies (Nelson 2007; Cantillon et al. 2008) and the detailed OECD Benefits and Wages Database (from 2001 onwards). In addition, there is the SAMiP database developed by Nelson at the SOFI (Stockholm).

[2] Data from an ongoing research project on Social Assistance in Europe at the Mannheim Centre for European Social Research (MZES) funded by the Hans-Böckler-Foundation.

[3] It should be noted that the data presented here exclude many of the means-tested benefits included in the study by Eardley et al. (1996), because here the focus is on subsistence minimum income.

Table 31.1 Minimum income provisions in selected EU countries (1992–2006)

Type[a]	Country	Expenditure (as % of GDP)		Expenditure (as % of TSE)		Coverage rate[b]	
		1992	2006	1992	2006	1992	2006
3	UK	2.6	1.9	9.2	7.9	16.0	26.0[c]
	Ireland	3.6	2.6	23.0	16.3	22.3	19.0
4	France	1.1	1.1	3.5	3.5	10.1[d]	10.1[d]
	Germany	0.6	1.1	2.1	4.0	3.3	10.0
5	Denmark	1.7	1.2	5.3	4.2	7.9	5.5
	Sweden	0.6	0.3	1.5	1.1	2.5	2.1
6	Portugal	0.0	0.2	0.2	0.8	0.5	3.5

Notes: [a] Social assistance types defined by Eardley et al. (1996) and Gough et al. (1997).
[b] Beneficiaries (recipients of all schemes plus family members) as per cent of total population.
[c] Including recipients of working tax credit.
[d] Estimate.

Sources: Own calculations based on MZES Project on Minimum Income Policies in Europe, various national sources and EUROSTAT (2009a) reference data.

benefit (including working tax credits) in 2006. The Nordic countries and Portugal have the lowest percentages. In Denmark and Sweden, minimum income protection is well established but plays a limited role within these highly developed social security systems. Portugal's minimum income has a limited impact within the rudimentary welfare state. In the other Southern European countries, nationwide systems do not exist. France and Germany represent the traditional social insurance countries where social assistance plays a residual, but significant, role.

Concerning changes over time, there is no general trend. Considering the enormous changes in social and economic context, this is perhaps surprising. Generally, the salience of social assistance has not grown. Instead, the cross-national pattern shows great stability over time. Evidence from other developed countries suggests that Europe and the Anglophone world are still worldwide exceptions with respect to guaranteed minimum income. Elsewhere, the scope of systems is patchy and limited, also coverage rates are lower (see below). For example in 2004, about 1.1 per cent of the Japanese population was covered by public assistance (IPSS 2007: 30), whereas in Russia it was more than 11 per cent (World Bank 2006: 135).

The generosity of guaranteed minimums also varies cross-nationally, but the picture is more complex and the types do not align as neatly. Based on model calculations, Table 31.2 shows the guaranteed income levels in OECD countries for three different family types: a single person (1a), a single parent with two children (1a2c), and a couple with two children (2a2c). In all countries, guaranteed income levels are substantially lower than net incomes for the same family types with average earnings from work, but the gap is smaller for families with children. Here, the widely acknowledged less-eligibility principle and the need to support poor families and especially children are in conflict. Country differences are considerable, but not

Table 31.2 Guaranteed minimum income levels in OECD countries (2006)

Type[e]	Country	Minimum income replacement rate[a] One earner			Minimum income adequacy rate[b] Without housing[d]		With housing[d]	
		1a	1a2c	2a2c	2a2c	1a2c	2a2c	1a2c
1	Australia	31.7	53.3	63.0	n/a	n/a	n/a	n/a
	New Zealand	37.2	54.1	40.0	n/a	n/a	n/a	n/a
2	USA	6.1	30.6	36.4	n/a	n/a	n/a	n/a
3	UK	40.3	59.1	65.9	74.9	82.2	121.2	142.9
	Ireland	54.5	50.0	79.2	95.3	90.4	121.0	122.5
	Canada[f]	22.9	52.0	56.0	n/a	n/a	n/a	n/a
4	Belgium	34.3	52.4	48.4	77.7	102.0	77.7	102.0
	France	33.6	48.2	53.9	55.0	60.2	81.9	95.5
	Germany	35.4	64.2	65.8	88.9	102.1	128.5	146.6
5	Finland	46.5	55.5	76.0	74.0	75.2	102.0	111.9
	Denmark	59.5	69.3	76.7	90.2	102.2	109.9	128.0
	Sweden	47.2	52.1	69.3	55.8	66.0	100.8	111.5
	Iceland[f]	44.6	58.8	69.8	n/a	n/a	n/a	n/a
	Netherlands	56.4	59.5	69.8	88.5	105.7	106.8	129.7
6	Spain[f]	23.3	35.1	34.5	52.9	69.4	52.9	69.4
	Portugal	17.4	38.1	51.1	90.0	84.0	90.9	84.0
7	Austria	36.7	52.0	61.2	78.4	84.8	95.5	106.6
	Norway[f]	38.3	60.8	70.7	n/a	n/a	n/a	n/a
	Switzerland[f]	48.3	60.2	69.6	n/a	n/a	n/a	n/a
8	Japan[f]	28.9	56.9	60.3	n/a	n/a	n/a	n/a
X[g]	Korea	17.3	37.7	45.3	n/a	n/a	n/a	n/a
	Czech Republic	29.7	55.3	62.8	88.6	89.8	98.9	103.3
	Hungary	23.0	65.5	74.7	120.2	136.8	123.0	140.4
	Poland	27.9	55.8	49.4	47.5	70.9	82.9	117.3
	Slovak Republic	17.8	30.9	34.7	45.7	44.8	65.6	70.9

Notes: n/a = not available.

[a] Minimum income by family type as per cent of net income of the same family type with 1 earner at average wage (OECD 2007j).

[b] Minimum income by family type as per cent of national poverty line set at 50% of median net household income adjusted for household composition and size (new OECD equivalence scale).

[c] Number of adults (a) plus number of children (c); e.g. 2a2c = couple with 2 children.

[d] Benefit (minimum income) levels without and with the calculation of housing costs and housing supplements (if available).

[e] Social assistance types as defined by Eardley et al. (1996).

[f] Regional/local benefit rates: Canada (Ontario); Iceland (Reykjavik); Japan (Tokyo); Norway (Trondheim); Spain (Madrid); Switzerland (Zurich).

[g] Not included in study by Eardley et al. (1996; 1997).

Sources: Own calculations based on OECD 2007j and Eurostat 2009.

systematically related to social assistance types. Income replacement rates vary from just 6 per cent for a single person without children in the United States (relying only on Food Stamps) to almost 80 per cent for a couple with two children in Ireland. The Nordic countries and the Netherlands are on average the most generous, followed by Switzerland, Ireland, and Britain.

The gap between guaranteed incomes and the relative poverty line (50 per cent of median income) is smaller, but in many countries social assistance does not even lift families out of poverty. The adequacy rate is higher if housing costs are included in the calculations: Britain and Ireland remain among the most generous together with Germany, Denmark, and the Netherlands. Some Eastern European countries also provide benefits that lift recipients above national poverty lines, and the least generous are once again Spain and Portugal (with no extra housing benefits). Yet these model calculations should be interpreted with great caution, as housing benefits are based on highly problematic estimates of housing costs, which lead to an overestimation of benefit levels in many countries.

Social assistance schemes also differ in their effects. In the literature, the dominant position is that overall social spending is negatively related to poverty rates (see e.g. Kohl 2002). Though the welfare state thus makes a difference, the specific impact of social assistance is not as strong. Korpi and Palme (1998) identified a 'paradox of redistribution': the more social security targets the poor, the less redistribution actually occurs in favour of low income households. The major reason is (paraphrasing Titmuss) that services for poor people tend to be(come) poor services, mainly because the middle classes do not support them in the long run.

The weak impact of minimum income schemes on poverty in comparison to other benefits is confirmed by other studies. Sainsbury and Morrisens (2002: 314) show that means-tested benefits were insufficient to lift many people out of poverty in the mid-1990s: the reduction of the poverty rate ranged from 0.2 per cent in Italy to 8.5 per cent in the United Kingdom. Using institutional data, Nelson (2004) also finds that in most countries social assistance remains well below the relative poverty threshold. One reason for this limited effectiveness is the different poverty concepts used: social scientists tend to measure poverty in relative terms compared to average incomes in a society, while national governments set official poverty lines mostly at lower levels reflecting national political and financial considerations.

PUBLIC SUPPORT

Social assistance poses two crucial decisions: determining who is needy and how much is needed (Rothstein 1998). Defining a social minimum in a society is a contentious political and normative issue, posing central questions about the solidarity of those who pay with those in need. The most far-reaching idea of solidarity is to introduce a basic income for all citizens, ensuring an income independent of contributions, employment, or any other condition (for an overview see Widerquist et al. 2005). Thus far, there is no fully operative basic income scheme anywhere in the world. In advanced democracies, the politics of social assistance revolve around the definition of a means-tested minimum income and its conditions in a market economy. Setting the appropriate benefit levels implies finding some balance between benefits that are too high relative to low wages and create disincentives to work, and benefits that are so low they don't meet needs, thus prohibiting social participation. Social assistance and in particular selective schemes tend to stigmatize benefit recipients and often create doubts about their willingness to work and their deservingness (Oorschot 2006). The old question of the 'deserving' and 'non-deserving' poor is therefore still alive in developed welfare states.

Studies of welfare state attitudes in countries as different as the United States (Hetling et al. 2008), Denmark (Goul Andersen 1999), and Germany (Ullrich 2008) confirm the problems of achieving such a balance. Social assistance is generally less popular than pensions or healthcare (for an overview of research on welfare state attitudes see Chapter 16). For the United States, it has been argued that ethnic heterogeneity diminishes overall support for public 'welfare' (Alesina and Glaeser 2004). People in a good labour market position, the well educated and those with higher incomes, are less likely to support social assistance than the working classes and those with basic education. However, in the context of higher levels of unemployment, these differences tend to diminish (Pfeifer 2009).

In an 'age of permanent austerity' (P. Pierson 2001c) lower support levels on the part of influential groups make selective schemes more vulnerable to cutbacks than other programmes. Their constituencies are considerably smaller than those of either pension or healthcare systems and they tend to be less organized due to heterogeneous and 'weak' interests. Support for minimum income protection may increase as the middle classes face lower contributory benefits due to welfare retrenchment or face the likelihood of long-term unemployment in periods of economic distress.

NEW POLICY DEVELOPMENTS

Over the past three decades, mass unemployment and new social risks have redefined the role of social assistance. It is no longer a temporary minimum income of last resort, but has become a 'mass programme' (Aust and Ariba 2005), with financial support for long-term unemployed and incapacitated persons, in some cases on a more or less permanent basis. Furthermore, the individualization of life-courses and the growing instability of family lives have generated 'new' social risks (Bonoli 2005) that are insufficiently addressed by existing welfare programmes. The financial crisis of welfare states and persistent employment problems have led to the retrenchment of social security, and, hence, to greater reliance on the safety-net function of social assistance, as well as to considerable restructuring of social assistance programmes themselves.

This transformation of social assistance has to be understood in the context of a paradigm shift in policy goals from passive to active social policies. The increased emphasis on activation has led to a variety of policy changes affecting social assistance: introducing tax credits and income supplements for those with low earnings from work and new 'activation' requirements linked with social assistance benefits (see Chapter 30).

Earned income tax credits devised to 'make work pay' were first introduced in the United States in 1975, reformed several times after 1986 and are today's largest United States anti-poverty programme. The United Kingdom also established a working tax credit in 1986 and this was revised in 1999 and 2003 to provide a higher level of benefit than in the United States. Besides Canada's working income tax benefit, Ireland and New Zealand have similar schemes. Some form of tax credit also exists in some Nordic welfare states (Denmark, Finland) and in some continental European countries (Austria, Belgium, France, the Netherlands). Some systems (e.g. Germany) provide means-tested benefits to supplement earnings or unemployment benefits up to the minimum income level instead.

The politically charged American term 'workfare' ended 'welfare as we know it' under the Clinton administration in 1996. The existing welfare programme was replaced by Temporary Assistance for Needy Families (TANF), which limits public assistance to five years and applies a 'work first approach'. It includes three elements, 'that workfare is compulsory, that workfare is primarily about work, and that workfare is essentially about policies tied to the lowest tier of public income support' (Lødemel 2004: 202). 'Work first' programmes were at the heart of activation policies; most prominently the British Jobseekers' Act (1995), the Dutch Jobseekers Employment Act (1998), and the Danish Active Social Policy Act (1998). The OECD Job Study of 1994 and the EU Employment Strategy from 1997 onwards have propagated this paradigm shift towards 'activation'. Other passive labour market policies have also been changed to active policies; in particular early exit from work strategies have been reversed by reforms of unemployment insurance; pre-retirement benefits, and disability benefits for older people (Ebbinghaus 2006). Beyond punitive elements, proactive training policies and integrative measures are part of the carrot and stick strategy of activation. Thus social assistance is transformed from a social right to an 'offer you can't refuse' (Lødemel and Trickey 2000).

The term 'social inclusion' has been coined by the European Union, or rather, by its predecessor: the European Economic Community. In the 1960s, it was thought that poverty had ended due to high growth rates, full employment, and the expansion of the welfare state. During the 1970s, however, policymakers realized that poverty persisted and initiated the 'European Programme for the Fight Against Poverty I', also called 'Poverty I' which lasted from 1975 to 1980 and primarily financed research. 'Poverty II' followed from 1984 to 1989 and coined the term 'social exclusion', thus focusing on the societal dimension of poverty and its origins, and introduced the cross-national exchange of best practices. 'Poverty III' lasted from 1989 to 1994 and emphasized research, a multidimensional concept of poverty and social inclusion, partnership of actors and institutions, and participation of target groups in local projects. Explicit EU action on this front ceased in the late 1990s, but the member states profited from the experience gained, with a clear imprint on policy in a number of countries, e.g. on Portugal's national strategy of combating poverty (see ILO 2004*b* for a detailed description of Poverty programmes).

With the launch of the Lisbon strategy in 2000, the Open Method of Coordination (OMC) in the area of social exclusion was phased in. It incorporates elements of prior programmes: EU member states develop common objectives in combating social exclusion (Zeitlin et al. 2005). Within the OMC framework, member states produce national plans to enhance social inclusion, and they work together to develop indicators and report on outcomes, which also has the effect of putting the issue on national agendas. The European Commission then produces a Joint Report which highlights best practice and encourages member states to learn from one another.

Social inclusion policies, including enabling policies in activation differ widely. In Southern Europe in particular, the lack of nationwide social assistance programmes became the subject of considerable debate due to the growing need to complement other welfare arrangements. Countries like France and Spain that lacked general schemes of social assistance until the late 1980s have introduced tax-financed and means-tested schemes of 'last resort' for the first time. In most other countries, social inclusion became part of the activation agenda. Since the late 1990s, programmes for the integration of young jobseekers, immigrants and older workers were introduced as 'New Deals' (e.g. in the United Kingdom). Nevertheless, the most vulnerable still tend to be in danger of social exclusion (Handler 2003).

When introducing compulsory activation ('workfare') into social assistance, emphasis was given to younger persons. In the United Kingdom, New Labour improved benefits but combined these with strong compulsory activation initiatives, especially for those under 25 and the long-term unemployed. In 1997, Denmark introduced the rule that social assistance recipients below the age of 30 must be activated within thirteen weeks (Torfing 1999). Other Scandinavian countries followed suit. In Germany the need to improve the employment chances of younger persons also received greater attention. Since 2005 they have been obliged to accept any job-offer or training course (Aust and Arriba 2005).

SOCIAL SAFETY NETS IN GLOBAL PERSPECTIVE

In most developing countries, social assistance programmes are rudimentary, even though policies have developed since the late 1990s. International organizations have impacted strongly on the emerging social safety-nets: the United Nations' Millennium Goals combat global poverty, the World Bank promotes a programme on social safety-nets in developing nations, and the ILO emphasizes the global extension of social security (Barrientos and Holmes 2006; Barrientos and Hulme 2008; Gough et al. 2004; Leisering 2008).

In these societies, social safety-nets operate in a completely different environment than in developed welfare states. Poverty is not just a relative problem of inadequate income, but often a question of physical survival. Moreover, developing countries usually have pervasive subsistence economies, as well as widespread shadow economies. Since administrative capacities are often limited, major problems in implementing means-tested or targeted programmes emerge (Overbye 2005). Moreover, in many places social safety-nets are the only benefit available to large population groups, because other social programmes are lacking. These safety-nets are not a residual scheme of last resort but have to shoulder the full burden of poverty.

Leisering (2008) distinguishes four types of social cash benefits in developing nations (see also Barrientos and Holmes 2006): (1) non-contributory minimum pensions (few universal, mostly means-tested); (2) family-related social assistance; (3) other social assistance (categorical or universal); (4) conditional means-tested transfers (usually requiring participation in food-for-work or food-for-education programmes). Most widespread are minimum pensions, in particular for elderly and disabled persons: in 2006 at least twenty-eight developing and transition countries had such pension schemes, most of them means tested. These programmes are relatively easy to administer, because the target group is clearly delimited and work disincentives do not exist. Benefits are usually low, though some schemes are extensive. The Brazilian rural scheme as well as the Indian and South African schemes include significant parts of the elderly population. Conditional transfers existed in at least seventeen countries, with the Brazilian *Bolsa Escola* (since 2003 integrated into *Bolsa Familia*), which make benefits conditional upon regular school attendance, being the most prominent.

Other social assistance programmes of the kind existing in the OECD world are very limited in developing nations. A notable exception is the Chinese Minimum Living Standard Guarantee (MLSG) that started in 1993 in Shanghai and was soon extended to other cities. In 1997, the government assumed main financial responsibility and made the programme mandatory for urban areas (covering 4.2 per cent of the urban population) thus still excluding the vast majority of the Chinese population, also migrant workers (Leung 2006: 193–4). So far, the Chinese development has remained unique outside the OECD.

CONCLUSIONS

The wide variations in social assistance regimes discovered by Eardley et al. (1996) for the early 1990s still exist today. Against expectations, the overall salience of minimum income systems has not generally grown in spite of worsening labour market conditions and welfare retrenchment policies. Rather, the overall picture is one of surprising stability both over time and cross-nationally in the OECD world, though there are global developments towards extending social safety-nets due to international pressures and endogenous modernization processes.

In times of 'permanent austerity', social assistance schemes face higher risks of cutbacks than pensions or healthcare. Moreover, the international trend to activate welfare recipients has changed 'welfare as we know it'. Yet the extent and impact of these programmes vary considerably from punitive workfare to enabling activation measures. At the same time, in some countries, the number of working poor is growing. In fact, employment alone does not always effectively prevent people from falling into poverty.

The way in which social assistance schemes are institutionally embedded in overall social policies, education systems, and labour markets is highly important. In this respect, a broader concern for social inclusion is on the political agenda. For example, in most countries lone parents and therefore children are among the groups with the highest poverty risk. Many studies have shown that, for this group, participation in the labour force is the best means to effectively prevent poverty. Because that is so, family policy and social services, in particular child care, are more important than social transfers or work incentives.

CHAPTER 32

....

FAMILY BENEFITS
AND SERVICES

....

JONATHAN BRADSHAW
NAOMI FINCH

INTRODUCTION

....

FAMILY benefits and services fall under the umbrella of family policy. But, because family benefits and services are diverse and wide-ranging in their objectives, in many countries, family policy is not a distinct policy area. This potentially makes the task of cross-national comparison a difficult one. Generally, family benefits and services focus upon different aspects of family life and the different obligations and responsibilities which arise from different family relationships (Neyer 2003). These may be between partners, parents and children, and children and their elderly parents. The policy responses will be different depending upon the relationship in question. In this chapter, we shall concentrate upon policies that focus on families with children. Whilst the main relationship in question is the parental obligation towards the child, an extension of this relationship is the one between *parents*, and the role they each play in childrearing. Familial relationships, however, do not exist in a vacuum. Therefore, we shall also consider parenthood within a wider context, how it interacts with external factors, in particular the labour market, and the policy responses to these relationships. Indeed, it may be that the primary purpose of policy is not related to childrearing per se but to tackle wider issues such as population decline or to increase labour supply, to maintain gender relationships or to reduce poverty.

Recent global socio-economic and demographic trends have introduced new challenges to Western welfare states. The most important economic change has been the move to a post-industrial economy, with the decline of industrial employ-ment and expansion of the service sector as a result of technological innovation (Taylor-Gooby 2001). This has had two important effects on welfare states. On the one hand, the decline of the industrial sector has led in some countries to increased low-paid, insecure jobs, with full male employment no longer an assumption that the welfare state can base itself upon (Hudson and Lowe 2004). On the other hand, the growth in services has brought with it increased female, including maternal, employ-ment (Esping-Andersen 1999).

This has meant that the male breadwinner–female carer family that the post-war welfare state modelled itself on is no longer the norm (Taylor-Gooby 2001). This has important implications for gender equity but also demographically. One consequence is the increased pressure upon women in relation to balancing work and family life. The economic changes also mean that female employment is increasingly necessary to avoid poverty, with single earner families associated with higher poverty rates (Esping-Andersen 2002; Cantillon et al. 2001). When this is coupled with the change in family forms that Northern Europe has witnessed—notably the growing numbers of lone parent families—it brings significant challenges for welfare states because of the associated poverty risk.

This chapter is organized into three sections. In the first section we review the context of family policies: family change and changes in employment. Then we compare family policies, including the overall effort made by welfare states to support families with children; the measures that exist to reconcile work and family life; and the financial support provided by the state for families with children. Finally we examine outcomes of that effort focusing on fertility, employment, child poverty, and child well-being.

CONTEXT

Family Change

In comparative studies it is usually unwise to make generalizations about socio-economic processes, because there are usually countries that buck the general trend. However it is safe to claim that all industrial countries have seen profound changes in the form and function of their families in the last few decades. Perhaps the most dramatic has been the decline in fertility.

OECD data shows that among thirty-nine countries only Mexico and Turkey had fertility rates above replacement rate by 2006.[1] Apart from that there is a bunching of two 'families' of countries: Northern European and Anglophone countries (except

---

[1] http://www.oecd.org/dataoecd/37/59/40192107.pdf

Canada) having fertility rates above 1.7 and Southern, Central European (except Estonia but including Germany and Austria) and East Asian countries below 1.5.

This decline in fertility has been associated with other changes in most countries. These have included a decline in marriage, later marriage, marriage increasingly preceded by cohabitation, and an increase in remarriage almost invariably preceded by cohabitation. Associated with this have been later births and a sharp increase in births outside marriage, usually in cohabitations. Also associated has been relationship breakdown, divorce, and separation. Family demographers used to compare family instability by using divorce rates, but with the decline in marriage, divorce has become an increasingly useless indicator of changing family form. Now it is better to compare the prevalence of lone parent families. This is actually quite difficult to do comparatively, partly because of definitional differences, but also because in household surveys lone parent families can be hidden in multi-unit households and the prevalence of multi-unit households varies considerably between countries.

However using the EU Survey of Income and Living Conditions (SILC) in Figure 32.1 we compare the proportion of households which consist of lone parents living in a single unit lone parent family or there is 'at least one child under 18 with no resident father/mother or father/mother did not respond'. The proportion of lone parent families is still fairly low in Southern European countries. Nearly a quarter of all children live in lone parent families in Latvia and the United Kingdom.

The majority of lone parent families are headed by a mother—over 90 per cent in most EU countries, Sweden is an exception with only 70 per cent of lone parent

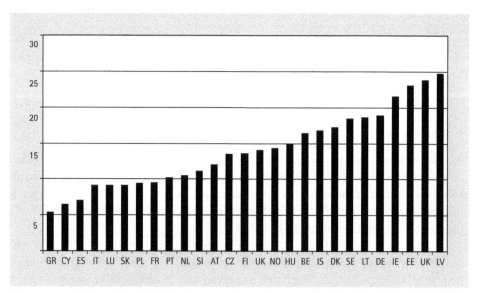

Figure 32.1 Per cent of children living in a lone parent family (2006)
Source: Own analysis of EU SILC 2006 data (EU-SILC 2008).

families headed by a mother (in EU SILC). As we shall see below, there is a higher risk of poverty for children living in a lone parent family in all countries.

These changes in family form have disrupted child rearing and have been one contributor to the decline in fertility. Also associated with the decline in fertility has been the increase in childlessness. Childlessness data is inevitably historical but, of the generation of women born in the mid-1960s, a fifth will remain childless in the Netherlands, the United Kingdom, and Finland and it is already a higher proportion than this in Germany.[2]

Changes to the pattern of families have meant that children's experience of them has changed. Parents are older than they were in the past and children are now less likely than in the past to have siblings. They are more likely to experience living in a lone parent family, to have step parents, absent parents, visiting parents and to have step siblings and half siblings. With all this change, intergenerational relationships are likely to prove more complicated for all concerned.

Mothers' Employment

Post-industrialization, and the growth in the service industry has increased female, and maternal employment across industrialized nations. This has had important implications for the family, indicating a move away from the norm of the male breadwinner–female carer model of the family, in which tasks are divided along gender lines. But nations can move away from the breadwinner model to different extents. Here we explore the extent to which nations have moved towards the dual earner model of the family by examining maternal employment patterns.

The male breadwinner model assumes that females restrict their labour market behaviour to focus on unpaid work. If there is an observed move away from this assumption towards dual earning, a high level of maternal employment would be observed. OECD data on maternal employment for 2005 shows a high level of variation, with the Nordic countries at one extreme and Eastern and Southern European (except Portugal) countries at the other.[3] Indeed, Iceland and Sweden have moved furthest towards dual earning with over 80 per cent of mothers in employment whereas under 50 per cent of mothers in the Slovak Republic, Italy, Poland, and Hungary undertake paid employment.

Overall employment rates do not, however, reflect hours worked. Mothers in countries with high employment levels may be working very short hours, and in fact spending most of their time undertaking unpaid work. OECD data shows that in all countries, women are disproportionately represented in part-time work.[4] Certain countries, such as the Netherlands and Switzerland, with a high proportion of mothers in employment, also have a high rate of part-time work amongst women.

[2] See www.oecd.org/els/social/family/database—SF7: Childlessness.
[3] http://www.oecd.org/dataoecd/29/61/38752721.pdf
[4] http://www.oecd.org/dataoecd/30/39/38752777.pdf

In these countries, the high overall employment rates hide a perpetuation of women spending more time in unpaid than paid employment.

The breadwinner–female carer model may be more accentuated when children are very young and caring needs are greatest. In countries which adhere more closely to the male breadwinner model, women are likely to take a complete break from the labour market to care for young children and return as children get older, go to school, and their care needs reduce. Generally, there is evidence of a decline in the male breadwinner model of the family for families with young children, falling from 53 to 35 per cent between 1985 and 2002 (OECD 2004*b*), based on data from the European Labour Force Survey, cited in Mayhew 2006). Indeed, the OECD found that the total hours that couples with one or more children under the age of 6 devoted to paid employment increased in this period, mainly due to mothers with young children moving into employment (OECD 2004*b*).

OECD data[5] show that there is wide national variation in maternal employment according to age of children. At one end are countries with high employment rates for mothers with very young children: In Denmark, Sweden, the Netherlands, and Portugal, 7 in 10 mothers with very young children are employed. In these countries, the gap between the employment rate for mothers with younger and older children is relatively small. Indeed, the employment rate for mothers with younger children is higher than older children in Sweden, Denmark, and Portugal, with virtually no difference in the Netherlands. In this sense, it appears that these countries have moved furthest towards the dual earner family.

At the other end of the spectrum, Hungary, the Czech Republic, Slovakia, Japan, and Germany have the lowest proportion of mothers with very young children who are employed. These countries also have a wide gap in employment levels between mothers with younger and older children—nearly 50 per cent difference in the cases of Hungary and the Czech Republic. Thus it seems that these countries adhere more strongly to the breadwinner model of the family when children are very young.

POLICIES

There are three methods we can use to assess the effort that states make to support families with children. Probably the best way is to compare outcomes, in particular outcomes for children, and we do that in the next section. This section is devoted to the other two methods: a comparison of overall spending on families with children; and a comparison of the welfare state institutions for families with children.

---

[5] http://www.oecd.org/dataoecd/29/61/38752721.pdf

Overall Welfare State Effort on behalf of Families

This requires the collection and analysis of national accounts and it is undertaken by both the EU in their ESPROSS series and the OECD in their public expenditure analysis. The most up to date analysis is for 2006 for the EU countries.[6] It shows an average of only 2 per cent of GDP is being devoted to these benefits for families with children and that the proportion ranges from 3.7 per cent in Denmark to only 0.8 per cent in Portugal.

The ESPROSS series includes cash and kind benefits but does not take account of tax expenditures on behalf of children, which are becoming an increasingly important part of the child benefit package in some countries. The OECD has produced an analysis of spending on families with children which does take account of tax expenditures. The most recent data are for 2005.[7] On average in 2005, the OECD countries spent 2.3 per cent of GDP on family benefits, services, and tax breaks and this proportion varied from 3.8 per cent in France to 0.02 per cent in Turkey. There were differences in how the expenditure was structured between countries between cash benefits, services, and tax breaks. But tax breaks were an important component of the package in a number of countries especially in France, Germany, the Netherlands, and the United States. In order to gauge welfare state effort on behalf of families with children they really need to be taken into account in a way that they are not in the current ESPROSS comparisons.

It is possible to use national accounts data to trace generational equity in spending over time. Figure 32.2 shows spending per child as a proportion of spending per pensioner between 1980 and 2003. All countries except Mexico spend more per older person than per child, but there is huge variation in spending per capita with Australia, Ireland, and Luxembourg spending more than 80 per cent per child of what they spend per pensioner, while Greece, Japan, and Italy spend only about 10 per cent. The only countries with more or less consistent downward trends on spending on children as a proportion of spending on the elderly are Japan, Sweden, and (over a shorter period) Slovakia. Australia, Denmark, and Ireland have shifted their comparative spending sharply in favour of children.

Reconciling Work and Care

We have seen that the male-breadwinner–female care model is weakening more in some countries than others, suggesting that policy may play a role in influencing employment patterns. This section will explore the extent to which nations support mothers to take up paid work.

Welfare states can encourage women's role in paid work via defamilializing care policies, with states and markets absorbing care responsibilities, thus reducing the

---

[6] http://nui.epp.eurostat.ec.europa.eu

[7] http://www.oecd.org/dataoecd/55/58/38968865.xls

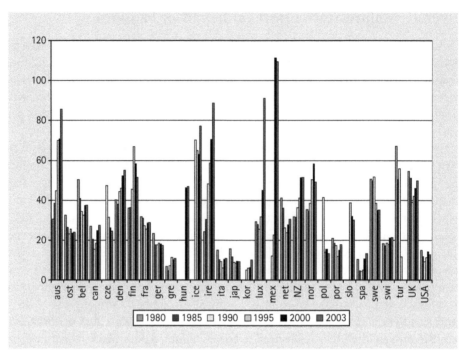

Figure 32.2 Spending per child in per cent of spending per older person (1980-2003)

Source: Own analysis of OECD 2009a.

care responsibilities of the main carer (usually the mother), and enabling their transition into paid work (Lister 1994; Esping-Andersen 1999). These include public provision of childcare and/or social services, or (the public subsidy of) care provision through the market.

There are various ways to assess the extent that welfare states defamilalize care. OECD data[8] show public expenditure on childcare and early educational services as a proportion of GDP, including all public financial support (in cash, in-kind or through the tax system) for families with children participating in formal day-care services (e.g. crèches, day care centres and family day care for children under 3), and pre-school institutions (including kindergartens and day-care centres which usually provide an educational content as well as traditional care for children aged from 3 to 5, inclusive).

It is apparent that Iceland and Denmark are leaders in overall spending, with two of their Nordic counterparts, Finland and Sweden, together with France not far behind. Norway lags a little behind its Nordic counterparts in this respect. The laggards in terms of overall spending are Switzerland, Korea, Canada, and Greece. Examining spending on formal day care services alone, spending is highest in Finland—closely followed by its Nordic counterparts. But spending is also relatively

---

[8] http://www.oecd.org/dataoecd/45/27/37864512.pdf

high in France, the United Kingdom, and Luxembourg. Many countries do not spend anything on formal day care services.

Support for childcare and early education is, however, fruitless without high enrolment rates. OECD data[9] show that there is great variation between nations in enrolment in childcare for children under three, which may partly be due to availability and partly due to the cost of childcare. The Nordic countries have relatively high enrolment rates, with the exception of Finland. This can be explained by the home childcare allowance in Finland, which acts as an alternative to childcare. It aims to provide parents (i.e. mothers) with children under 3 with the choice of whether or not to undertake paid work. Belgium's enrolment rate is also relatively high. At the other end are countries with an enrolment rate close to zero including the Czech Republic, Mexico, Poland, Switzerland, and Turkey.

To avoid a 'double burden' where mothers are undertaking both paid and unpaid work also requires support for familial care. This can enable mothers to balance work with family care when children are very young but with job protection to enable them to return to work. Without such protected leave, mothers are likely to take a complete break from the labour market. Because of their complexity, cross-national comparison of leave schemes is difficult. We will explore expenditure on leave systems as a proportion of GDP per child born. This will give us a picture of the different roles of lump-sum payments at birth and the number of parents (and children) that are actually entitled to paid parental leave benefits across countries (OECD 2008b).

OECD data[10] show spending on maternity and parental leave payments per child in 2003. Hungary is the leader in leave spending, with the Nordic countries together with Eastern European countries, following. At the opposite end, low spenders include Anglophone countries, the United Kingdom, Australia, and New Zealand together with Korea, Switzerland, and Greece.

Tax and Benefit Policies

Every welfare state has a package of policies that support families in the financial burdens of child rearing. These packages may consist of a variety of different elements including income tax concessions, income or non-income related cash benefits, housing benefits, the mitigation of charges for health, education or child-care, child support policies that ensure that lone mothers receive financial support from absent fathers, and other help in kind such as food stamps or free school meals. The objectives of the different elements of this package may vary. The structure certainly does. But the level of the package is a measure of the contribution that the state makes to mitigate the mainly private costs of child rearing.

---

[9] http://www.oecd.org/dataoecd/46/13/37864698.pdf
[10] http://www.oecd.org/dataoecd/45/26/37864482.pdf

One way this package has been compared is by exploring how it affects a set of standard families in different countries. This 'model family' method has been used in academic studies (Bradshaw and Piachaud 1980; Bradshaw et al. 1993; Bradshaw and Finch 2002; Bradshaw and Mayhew 2006; Bradshaw 2006). It is also the method used in the OECD (2008*b*) Taxing Wages series.

The advantage of the model family method is that it enables up to date comparisons of the structure and level of the packages. However the method can only compare the formal arrangements, entitlements, and not how they are actually experienced or taken up. Also it can only do it for model families, not representative families and a number of assumptions have to be made about the circumstances of the families, including importantly their housing costs. Nevertheless the method enables comparison of the structure and level and how this varies by employment status, earnings, the number of earners, the number and ages of children and family type.

Figure 32.3 shows the percentage extra that a couple with two children with one earner gets over what a childless couple on the same earnings would get. It can be seen that the rankings of countries change considerably with the level of earnings[11]. At low earnings Ireland and Australia have the most generous child benefit package. All countries except Greece and Korea have progressive child benefit packages—that is they are more generous to low-paid families. But some are more progressive than others. New Zealand does not pay any family benefits beyond a given income level.

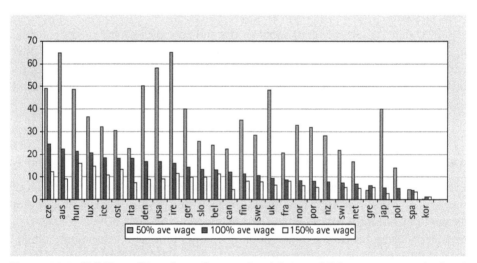

Figure 32.3 Child benefit package for couple with two children one earner by level of earnings (2005). Ranked by average earnings: Per cent extra over a childless couple on the same earnings

Source: Own analysis of OECD 2005*d.*

---

[11] This is 2005 data because (irritatingly) OECD changed the family types/income levels they publish data for in 2006 and 2007.

To find the Czech Republic and Hungary at the top of the league at average earnings may be quite unexpected—also the fact that the United States is not at the bottom of the league; Sweden and France are in the middle.

The OECD Benefits and Wages series only uses couples and singles with two children in its analysis. However in our work using more family types (Bradshaw 2006), we have found that, in addition to earnings and family type, the child benefit package varies with the number and ages of the children, the number of earners, and whether the comparisons are made before or after housing and childcare costs. Given all this variation it is quite difficult to produce an overall summary of the values of the packages. In Bradshaw (2007) we made an attempt using an illustrative sample of family types and earnings levels, selected from our model families, with a crude weighting on the more common types, and estimate an overall average child benefit package. We found that Austria was an outlier at the top of the league table—this is partly the result of its generous childcare subsidies which are not taken in to account in the OECD analysis. The Netherlands, Canada, and Japan were found among the laggards.

OUTCOMES OF FAMILY POLICIES

Fertility and Family Policy

Fertility rates are rather difficult to interpret and therefore to explain. One reason is that they have been extremely unstable over the last thirty years (and longer); or rather they have changed in different countries at different times. This is certainly partly because patterns of marriage and parenthood, female labour supply, contraceptive technology, and so on, have all been changing very rapidly, dramatically, and recently. We have no settled history. In seeking to explain fertility we have to cope with a moving target. It may be argued that recently fertility rates have stabilized and that it is a better time to make the examination. But France has certainly recovered very rapidly recently and some other countries may be following including the United Kingdom, the Netherlands, and Sweden. One problem now is that even if fertility rates are more stable, they have converged and there is not much variation to explain. Also national 'natural' fertility rates are being influenced (upwards) in some countries by the fertility of recent inward migrants. For example, 23 per cent of births in the United Kingdom in 2007 were to mothers born outside the United Kingdom and half of the recuperation in fertility from 1.68 in 2004 to 1.90 in 2007 is the result of births to migrants (UK ONS 2008).

If we had undertaken an analysis of the relationship between fertility and family policy before 1980 we would have concluded that there is a negative relationship— fertility had declined in the countries with strong family policies and been maintained in countries with weak family policies. But as Francis G. Castles (2002*b*) has pointed out, after 1980 the picture was transformed—the Northern welfare states either stopped their decline or had some recovery, whereas the Southern and East Asian welfare states' fertility plummeted. Now one might conclude that fertility was being maintained by strong family policies or that policy makes no difference.

In Figure 32.4 there is a fairly weak relationship between fertility (in 2006) and family spending as a proportion of GDP in 2005. It would be stronger if Turkey, Mexico and USA were excluded. Duensing (2006) found no relationship between changes in family spending and changes in fertility between 1980 and 2002. Of course even if there is an association, this relationship does not imply cause and effect. There is an endogeneity problem—the more children the higher the spending—and also the spending may be a function of the political power of parents.

It may be that policies that reconcile work and family life might have an impact on fertility. Sleebos (2003) found a positive relationship between an index of work/ family reconciliation and fertility and the *Babies and Bosses* series (OECD 2007*b*: 18) concluded that 'all policies which enhance female labour force participation may also help to avoid very low fertility rates'. Certainly those countries that have higher female participation rates have higher fertility levels. They may have higher female participation rates because of policies that enable women to reconcile work and

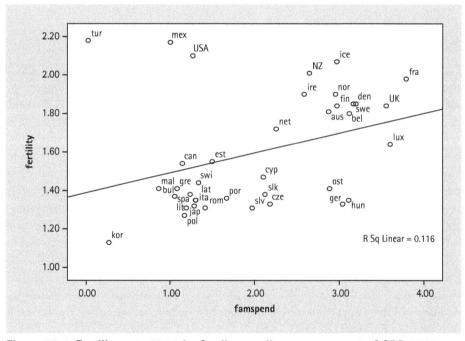

Figure 32.4 Fertility rate 2006 by family spending as a per cent of GDP 2005
Source: Own analysis of OECD 2009*h*.

family life. Thus those policies may enhance fertility. However, Bradshaw and Attar-Schwartz (2010) concluded that the level of female emancipation was probably an intervening variable—the greater the emancipation, the more women work, the more they work the more independent they are and the better off the family is and that is a securer base for child rearing. In that context policies reconciling work and family life are marginal.

The evidence now emerging is that it is the better educated and better off parents who are having the babies in the most advanced welfare states. Forssen and Ritakallio (2006: fig. 9.1) found that the proportion of 36 to 46-year-old women having no children was lower among the better educated in Denmark, Finland, Sweden, and Belgium and that the better educated also tended to have achieved more children. However, they found that this was not yet the case in Germany, the United Kingdom, France, Greece, Ireland, Italy, Portugal, and Spain. Similar results were found by Duensing (2006) modelling the number of children using LIS data. What this might indicate is that it is not family policy that matters now, it is human capital, a sense of security, power in the market place—in fact, possibly, that an independence from family policy is what matters to fertility.

Employment and Family Policy

Spending on and enrolment in childcare and preschool education does to some extent reflect maternal employment rates. The Nordic countries have high overall maternal employment rates and also are generous spenders on childcare. However, Finnish mothers with very young children have lower employment levels than other Nordic countries reflecting low enrolment rates in childcare. At the other end of the scale, the picture is not as clear—countries with low spending on childcare do not necessarily have lower maternal employment levels, even for mothers with very young children. For example, Switzerland has relatively low spending and enrolment, but its maternal employment rate is in the top half of the nations, even for very young children. Nevertheless, as we might expect with low state support for childcare, the employment data does provide some evidence that Swiss mothers have difficulties combining work and childcare—with a comparatively high part-time rate.

Spending on parental leave less overtly relates to maternal employment rates. Whilst high employment rates in the Nordic countries reflects high leave spending, Hungary, Slovakia, and Czech Republic are all generous spenders but with low employment levels. This is because motivations of leave spending differ between countries. High spending may reflect lengthy leaves, high replacement rates, high coverage, leave focused upon gender equity, etc., which will all impact differently upon maternal employment levels. Indeed, maternity/parental leave replacement rates rather than length are more important for achieving high maternal employment, given the documented associated negative consequences of lengthy leaves with maternal employment and the gender pay gap (see e.g. Ruhm 1998). So, due to the complexity of leave schemes, this suggests that expenditure is not a good indicator of the impact of leave schemes upon maternal employment.

Nevertheless, leave schemes may still account for the variability in maternal employment rates, not least because mothers on parental leave are often included in the employment statistics, whether the leave is paid or not. The OECD (2007b) *Babies and Bosses* report showed that if mothers on parental leave were excluded, national variation in employment rates for very young children is reduced, with Sweden and Denmark's high employment rates relative to other countries attributed to the high proportion of mothers taking up parental leave.

Family Policy and Child Poverty

The most common way that the outcomes of family benefits have been evaluated comparatively in the past has been by comparing child poverty rates. Relative child poverty rates are one of the 'Laeken' indicators used by the EU to monitor social inclusion (European Commission 2008) and the OECD publishes child poverty rates every five years or so. The Luxembourg Income Study is also used as a source of this data. At the time of writing, the LIS data are rather old so the two most up-to-date sources are EU and OECD. They use rather different methods. The EU now uses data derived from the EU Survey of Income and Living Conditions (SILC), a threshold of 60 per cent of the national median and the modified OECD equivalence scale. The OECD uses data supplied by national governments in a specified format. They use a threshold of 50 per cent of the median and the square root of the number of people in the household as the equivalence scale. OECD[12] shows that in most countries child poverty rates increased between the mid-1990s and the mid-2000s—the exceptions were Australia, Belgium, Hungary, Italy, Mexico, United Kingdom, and the United States.

Both the EU and OECD publish data on poverty gaps—how far below the poverty line families are, and the persistence of poverty—how many years children have been below the poverty threshold. They both also publish data on child poverty before and after transfers which is another useful means of comparing the relative effectiveness of family policies. Figure 32.5 shows that the league table of poverty rates in the EU would be very different if child poverty was measured before transfers—just on the basis of market incomes. The Nordic countries have much lower after transfer poverty rates than the southern and eastern European countries because their family policies are much more effective in reducing poverty.

There are problems with relative income poverty measures especially in comparative analysis. In particular the thresholds used are arbitrary and they are indicative of very different levels of living in different countries. For example, the 60 per cent of median poverty threshold in 2006 was 1,738 Euros per year in Romania and 27,397 Euros per year in Luxembourg. Using these thresholds we are hardly comparing like

---

12 http://dx.doi.org/10.1787/422456583733

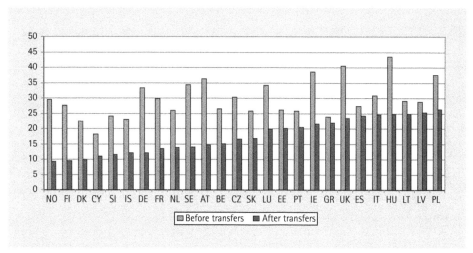

Figure 32.5 Child poverty rates before and after transfers (2006)
Source: Own analysis of EU SILC 2006 data (EU-SILC 2008).

with like. Both the OECD and EU have begun to recognize these problems by publishing data on deprivation alongside income poverty rates.

Family Policy and Child Well-Being

Neither relative income poverty nor a broader measure of material well-being are entirely satisfactory indicators of the outcomes for children. We developed an index of child well-being for the EU25 countries (Bradshaw et al. 2007). A similar index was published by UNICEF (2007) for OECD countries and for CEE/CIS countries (Richardson et al. 2008).

The idea behind these indices is that the well-being of children cannot be represented by a single dimension or indicator. Their lives are lived through multiple dimensions and each has an influence on their well-being (Ben-Arieh et al. 2001).

Table 32.1 provides a summary of a new comparison of child well-being in European countries with the rank order of countries overall and on each domain. The index was constructed by taking forty-three indicators from the most up-to-date survey and administrative sources and combines them to represent nineteen components, before combining them into the seven dimensions. Only the Netherlands comes in the top third of all countries on all dimensions and only Lithuania comes in the bottom third on all dimensions.

This kind of work is really only in its infancy and very little has been done to explain these differences in outcomes. However it does appear that policy matters. Figure 32.6 shows that there is a relationship between spending on family benefits and services as a proportion of GDP and overall well-being, albeit with some outliers.

Table 32.1 Child well-being in Europe by dimension (c. 2006)

Rank	Country	Child well-being in the EU 29	Health	Subjective	Relationships	Material	Risk	Education	Housing
1	Netherlands	117.3	2	1	1	7	4	4	9
2	Sweden	114.8	1	7	3	10	1	9	3
3	Norway	114.8	6	8	6	2	2	10	1
4	Iceland	112.7	4	9	4	1	3	14	8
5	Finland	111.0	12	6	9	4	7	7	4
6	Denmark	109.6	3	5	10	9	15	12	5
7	Slovenia	107.1	15	16	2	5	13	11	19
8	Germany	106.1	17	12	8	12	5	6	16
9	Ireland	105.3	14	10	14	20	12	5	2
10	Luxembourg	104.8	5	17	19	3	11	16	7
11	Austria	104.2	26	2	7	8	19	19	6
12	Cyprus	103.7	10			13			11
13	Spain	103.6	13	4	17	18	6	20	13
14	Belgium	103.0	18	13	18	15	21	1	12
15	France	100.9	20	14	28	11	10	13	10
16	Czech Republic	98.9	9	22	27	6	20	3	22
17	Slovakia	98.7	7	11	22	16	23	17	15
18	Estonia	96.9	11	20	12	14	25	2	25
19	Italy	96.1	19	18	20	17	8	23	20
20	Poland	94.6	8	26	16	26	17	8	23
21	Portugal	94.5	21	23	13	21	9	25	18
22	Hungary	94.3	23	25	11	23	16	15	21
23	Greece	94.0	29	3	23	19	22	21	14
24	United Kingdom	92.9	24	21	15	24	18	22	17
25	Romania	87.0	27	19	5		24	27	
26	Bulgaria	84.9	25	15	24		26	26	
27	Latvia	84.1	16	24	26	22	27	18	26
28	Lithuania	82.3	22	27	25	25	28	24	24
29	Malta	81.9	28	28	21		14		

Source: Bradshaw and Richardson 2009.

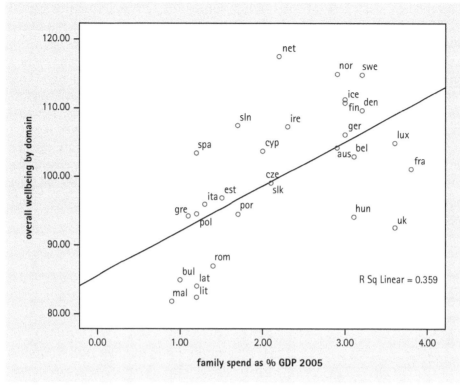

Figure 32.6 Overall child well-being by per cent GDP devoted to family benefits and services (2005)

Source: OECD 2009*h*.

CONCLUSIONS

There is a theory that because globalization has led to an eroding of the nation state both politically and economically, and increasingly operates across traditional geographic boundaries (Hudson and Lowe 2004), we can expect there to be increasing convergence in social policies. Also given that demographic and economic changes have created new social risks which are common to all welfare states, this will lead to common policy responses, either towards the 'ideal' of the universalist Nordic system of welfare or towards the minimalist American system (Gauthier 2002). The alternative view is that nations will develop distinctive social policies in response to common global policy challenges depending upon national histories, culture and politics.

In relation to family policy it is really difficult to come down clearly in favour of one or other of these theories. Certainly fertility levels have been converging below replacement rates. Female and maternal employment rates have been increasing though there are still big variations between countries. Public spending on families with children is still very variable. Most countries make efforts to assist parents to reconcile work and family life, but the structure and level of that effort and the financial support to families remains very different in different countries.

Very few countries have pursued explicit pro-natalist social policies and there is little evidence of association between family policy effort and fertility. Those countries that make more effort on childcare tend to have higher maternal employment rates, but this is not the case with parental leave. Child poverty increased in most countries between the mid-1990s and mid-2000s but the fact that it fell in United Kingdom and the United States from a very high base might have resulted in some convergence (OECD 2008a). It does appear that those countries with the strongest family policies have lower child poverty and higher child well-being. This leads us to conclude that, whether or not there is convergence or divergence, family policy matters.

CHAPTER 33

....

HOUSING

....

TONY FAHEY

MICHELLE NORRIS

INTRODUCTION

....

ASIDE from the rich and their servants, most of the population of Western countries in the late nineteenth century lived in private rented dwellings. Although an effective means of housing supply in many ways, this tenure produced significant social problems, especially in the form of dilapidated, overcrowded, barely affordable homes held on insecure terms by the poor in both city and countryside (Harloe 1985). In the background was a larger pattern of uneven distribution of housing capital which, in a *laissez faire* rental housing market, could put pressure on incomes and living standards even among the middle classes (Pooley 1992).

As the scope and interventionist ambitions of the state expanded in the twentieth century, housing increasingly came within the ambit of public policy and did so particularly in the phase of reconstruction and welfare state development that occurred after World War II. Public interest in housing often extended to issues such as macroeconomic management and spatial planning that went beyond the concerns of the welfare state. However, a welfare focus on housing would be hard to avoid given the significance of people's homes for their living standards and the large share of household expenditures that housing accounts for. This welfare focus, as we shall see below, was expressed in a wide range of ways, but looking back from the vantage point of today, many researchers have concluded that its achievements in housing compare poorly with many other elements of the welfare state. There is a common view that the impulse towards social solidarity and equality embodied in the welfare state has been less realized in housing than in any other area of social provision, a view captured in the widely used metaphor of housing as 'the wobbly pillar under the welfare state' (coined by Torgersen 1987). Harloe (1995), for example, concluded that in both Europe and America housing has remained the least decom-modified, most market determined sector of welfare provision and that even in countries where welfare systems are well developed, most housing services are provided by the market. Since the 1980s, a sizeable literature has emerged which argues that housing services have borne the brunt of retrenchment of public welfare spending (P. Pierson 1994).

In this chapter, we suggest that this view of the welfare state in housing markets as weak and declining rests on uncertain empirical and conceptual foundations and needs to be qualified, if not rejected. The empirical problem is that the role of the state in housing is so multiple and varied that neither its extent nor its distributive impact is open to the kind of quantification that would allow us to say confidently how great it is at any time or place or whether it has grown or declined over time. One of the key complexities here is that the housing market is not a single entity but is made up of a number of related sub-markets. Two of these reflect the dual nature of housing itself—one relating to dwellings as fixed, durable capital assets, which are traded in the purchase market for housing, and the other to accommodation conceived of as a service derived from dwellings, which is traded in the rental accommodation market. Two further sub-markets consist of a background enabling market in housing finance and an implicit parallel spatial market in neighbourhood (the forms of inequality in which are captured notions of socio-spatial segregation and neighbourhood disadvantage).

States in the developed world have tended to intervene in all these sub-markets at the same time, using a wide array of policy instruments. Some of these instruments are monetized and therefore measurable, as in the case of housing allowances for tenants or capital grants for housing construction (though even here there can be problems of measuring current and capital expenditure alongside each other). But others are hidden or non-monetized to varying degrees (rent controls in the private rented sector, rent subsidies built into below-market rents in social housing, interest rate setting that favours housing finance, tax biases in favour of particular tenures, etc.) so that even to recognize and list them, not to speak of measuring their value, is a challenge. Further problems arise if we try to distinguish between policies that enhance welfare by improving either equity or efficiency versus those that are regressive or wasteful. The result of this empirical complexity is that we need to be cautious in making assertions about how strong or weak the state's role in housing is or whether it is growing or receding over time.

While the empirical problem in measuring the state's role in housing is widely recognized, questions about the conceptual framework within which that should be done have attracted less attention. The usual approach, in housing as in other areas, is to adopt a two-sided model of state versus market and examine the fortunes of the welfare state as a matter of the shifting balance between these two sides. That traditional approach came under attack in the 1990s as being over-simplified because of its neglect of the third leg of the welfare system, the household, the importance of which was highlighted especially by feminists (Lewis 1992). The result was a new three-sided model of state, market, and household, in which welfare production in the household economy was given equal billing alongside welfare generation through the market and the state (Esping-Andersen 1999). However, this three-sided model has not been applied to the analysis of housing, even though major aspects of the evolution of modern housing, especially the rise of home ownership, would seem to embody the interaction of all three sides. While the rise of owner occupation can be partly understood by reference to the interaction between state and market (the usual approach in housing research), it can also be seen as a dimension of the household economy and as representing a major expansion of the household sector in developed societies in the twentieth century. A concern of the present chapter is to explore how this might be so and what it means for the way we think of the role of the welfare state in housing.

We turn in the next section to basic questions about the nature of housing provision in modern societies and follow that with a brief overview of the policy instruments that states have utilized to intervene in housing markets and sub-markets. That is followed by an assessment of the distributional impact of the state's role, keeping in mind the distinction between vertical and horizontal distribution at the household level and also the existence of a distinct axis of distribution that operates at the spatial level. Finally, we focus on the rise of owner occupation through the lens of the three-sided model of the welfare state and assess its significance in terms of the interaction between state, market and household.

HOUSING PROVISION

The term 'housing' has a double meaning in that it can refer to a service (the accommodation that housing provides) and a capital asset (the dwelling that pro-duces this service). Economists have long recognized this aspect of housing as fundamental and have sought to incorporate it into their models of housing markets (Henderson and Ioannides 1983; Smith et al. 1988), but this distinction is rarely recognized in the housing literature written from a social policy perspective.

A further key feature of housing capital is its capacity for deconcentration. Housing is the only major capital-based service which comes within the compass of the welfare state where households can purchase the capital themselves and use it to self-provision the service it produces (households cannot purchase their own hospitals or schools). Owner-occupation of housing means that accommodation, the service aspect of housing, may be removed from the market through incorporation into the self-provisioning household economy. One can think of households as purchasing a dwelling on the market and then purchasing accommodation from themselves through an implicit or shadow transaction captured in the concept of 'imputed rent'. This shadow non-monetized version of a market transaction echoes forms of self-provisioning in the household which carry a 'shadow wage' such as housework, childcare, and elder care (Zick et al. 2008). The latter services are labour intensive and thus differ from self-provisioning of accommodation, which requires only self-management of housing assets and their utilization. Yet the economic value of accommodation is large, as indicated by the size of rents in the marketed equivalents, so that its place in the household economy is real.

A consequence of the dual capital-cum-service nature of housing is that distributive public policy has the option of focusing either on the capital or the service in framing its distributive strategies. A capital distribution approach can be achieved by extending home ownership, while service distribution entails state intervention in the rental housing market.[1] Welfare states have often been classified from a housing point of view in terms of the priority they give to one or other of these strategies. English-speaking countries, along with developed South-East Asian states, are commonly regarded as 'home owner societies' where public policy affords this tenure type preferential treatment (Roland 2007). Following the mass privatization of former state-owned rented housing in the early 1990s, most of the former communist countries of Central and Eastern Europe are also in this category (Hegedüs and Tosics 1996). By contrast Northern European states generally favour state supports for rental accommodation (Kemeny 1995). However, shifts in individual countries over time and exceptional countries that deviate from type mean that this categorization is oversimplified. Thus for example, Norway, which is classified as a social democratic welfare regime in Esping-Andersen's (1990) typology, stands out for its extensive and long-standing state support for home ownership (Gulbrandsen 2004).

Furthermore, in the majority of developed countries, irrespective of welfare regime, home ownership has become the dominant tenure during the twentieth century. Table 33.1 demonstrates that it now the case in twenty-one of the twenty-five European Union member states. Denmark, Sweden, and the Czech Republic nominally are exceptions because of the high incidence of tenancies in cooperative housing in these countries but in fact such tenants have most of the rights associated with home ownership elsewhere. This leaves Germany as the only real exception. True, in Northern European states with large social housing sectors the growth in home ownership has been more restrained but they have not been immune. There is likely to be an upper limit to home ownership in well-functioning housing markets since there is always a mobile population for whom renting is more efficient and usually also a low-income population for whom investment in home purchase is not feasible. Instability on the housing market and the rise in family breakdown and job insecurity (the 'risk society')

---

[1] The concepts of 'owning' and 'renting' in this context refer to bundles of legal rights over residential property. The precise contents of these bundles are both highly complex within any legal regime and highly variable between regimes so that the two concepts have no standard detailed meaning. Sometimes, the boundary between the two becomes blurred, for example where renters have strong rights that give them long-term claims or are part-owners of their dwelling (as in the Swedish system of tenant ownership) or where owners have forms of title that are difficult to validate in court or are hedged around by restrictions through, for example, planning law. Yet, the distinction between long-term rights over housing as capital and shorter terms rights over housing as a service, which lies as the heart of the owner/renter distinction, does have some general applicability and is sufficiently meaningful in most legal regimes to be useful as an analytical shorthand.

Table 33.1 Occupied dwellings by tenure in European Union member states in per cent (1990, 2004)

Country	1990					2004				
	Private rented	Social rented	Owner Occupied	Co-operative	Other	Private Rented	Social rented	Owner Occupied	Co-operative	Other
Austria	19	22	55	0	4	18[a]	23[a]	52[a]	0[a]	7[a]
Belgium	27	6	67	0	0	23	7	68	0	2
Cyprus	13	0	64	0	23	14[a]	0	68[a]	0[a]	18[a]
Czech Republic	0	40[d]	38	19	3	9[a]	20[a]	47[a]	17[a]	7[a]
Denmark	23	17	54	5	1	19	19	49	7	6
Estonia	Nav	Nav	Nav	Nav	Nav	3	1	96	0	0
Finland	11	14	72	0	3	18	15	63	0	4
France	22	17	54	0	7	23	17	57	0	3
Germany	47[b]	10[b]	43[b]	0[b]	0[b]	51[c]	6[c]	43[c]	0[c]	0[c]
Ex GDR	0	74[d]	26	0	0					
Greece	20	0	76	0	4	20	0	74	0	6
Hungary	0	26	74	0	0	3	3	93	0	1
Ireland	8	10	79	0	3	13	8	79	0	0
Italy	20	6	68	0	6	14	4	73	0	9
Latvia	0	79[d]	21	0	0	18	1	77	4	0
Lithuania	Nav	Nav	Nav	Nav	Nav	7[e]		91[a]	0[a]	0[a]
Luxembourg	30		64	0	6	29[e]		68	0	3
Malta	Nav	Nav	Nav	Nav	Nav	26[e]		70	0	4
Netherlands	17	38	45	0	0	10	34	56	0	0

(continued)

Table 33.1 Continued

Country	1990					2004				
	Private rented	Social rented	Owner Occupied	Co-operative	Other	Private Rented	Social rented	Owner Occupied	Co-operative	Other
Poland	Nav	Nav	Nav	Nav	Nav	13	12	57	18	0
Portugal	21	7	67	0	5	17[a]	4[a]	75[a]	0[a]	4[a]
Slovak Republic	0	28[d]	49	22	1	1	4	85	7	3
Slovenia	0	0	61	0	39	3	6	84	0	7
Spain	13	2	78	0	7	11[e]		82	0	7
Sweden	22	22	39	17	0	27	18	38	17	0
United Kingdom	10	25	65	0	0	11	20	69	0	0

Source: Norris and Shields 2004 MOI and Federcasa 2006.

Notes: Nav = not available. GDR = German Democratic Republic. Data for Bulgaria and Romania are not available.
[a] Data refer to 2000.
[b] Data refer to 1995.
[c] Data refer to 2002.
[d] All rented housing is categorized as social housing, on the grounds that it was mostly state owned in 1990 and although the two sectors are not entirely equivalent, they share many key characteristics in common.
[e] Disaggregated data on households living in the private and social rented sectors are not available.

may also have an impact in this regard and some authors have suggested may precipitate a decline in home ownership rates in some countries (e.g. Doling and Ruonavaara 1996; Norris et al. 2007). Table 33.1 reveals that decline in home ownership occurred in five EU members between 1990 and 2004 and that home ownership rates remained static in two others. However, the exact location of the upper limit of home ownership in mature home ownership societies is likely to be country specific.

The stances of public policy towards owning and renting are often used to differentiate between a strong and weak welfare role for housing. Intervention in the rental market, particularly in the form of social housing, is usually thought of as giving a larger, more controlling role to the state and as representing a prominent presence for the welfare state in the housing field. Policies to support home ownership, by contrast, are identified with domination by the market and are seen as the antithesis of a public welfare approach (e.g. Harloe 1995; Kemeny 1995). However, if we replace the two-sided (state versus market) model of the welfare state on which this judgement rests with a three-sided (state, market, and household) model, we can nuance our understanding of owner occupied housing. Home ownership can be thought of as enabling housing as capital to be traded in the market, influenced to a greater or lesser degree by state regulation and intervention, while accommodation as a service is not traded at all since it is taken into the household sector. Home ownership thus entails a form of familialization of accommodation that echoes other forms of familial provision now routinely accepted as important elements of welfare regimes (Esping-Andersen 1999). Therefore public policies which support home ownership may indeed be thought of as enhancing the role of the market in regard to housing *capital* but as reducing the role of the market and extending the scope of the household in regard to accommodation as a *service*. (There are developed societies, mainly in Southern Europe, where the market even in housing as capital is underdeveloped and a high reliance is placed on self-build, inheritance, and intra-family supports for home acquisition—see Castles and Ferrera 1996—but this is a complication we do not have space to expand on here.) The task of following through on this way of thinking about home ownership is a major theoretical and empirical challenge for research on housing in the welfare state. Esping-Andersen (1999: 6) has identified the household economy as 'perhaps the single most important foundation of postindustrial economies'. The rise of home ownership attests that this may well be true of housing as much as any other area of welfare but it remains to be worked out precisely how this may be so, a question we will refer to further below in considering explanations for the dominance of home ownership in the tenure systems of present-day developed societies.

POLICY INSTRUMENTS

One of the complexities that arises in analyses of the state's welfare role in housing is the multiplicity of policy instruments that can be used across the various housing

Table 33.2 Government housing interventions in European Union member states (2004/5)

	Austria	Belgium	Cyprus	Czech Republic	Denmark	Estonia	Finland	France	Germany	Greece	Hungary	Ireland	Italy	Latvia	Lithuania	Luxembourg	Malta	Netherlands	Poland	Portugal	Slovak Republic	Slovenia	Spain	Sweden	United Kingdom
Direct Public Subsidies																									
Public Expenditure on Housing as % of GDP — 1990	0.1	0.1	0.4	0.0[a]	0.6		0.2	0.7	0.3[a]	0.5[a]		0.6[a]	0.0	0.1	0.1		0.3[a]	0.3[a]		0.0	0.0[a]		0.1	1.1[a]	1.3
Public Expenditure on Housing as % of GDP — 2004	0.1		0.4	0.1	0.7		0.3	0.8	0.4	0.5	0.4	0.4	0.0	0.1	0.1	0.2	0.3	0.3		0.0	0.0		0.2	0.6	1.4
Households Receiving Housing Allowances (%)					21		20	23	7	0.6		5.0	0.5	5.9				14	6.4		0.7	0.5	12	6.3	19
Social housing subsidies — For construction	Y	Y	Y	Y	Y	Y	Y	Y	Y	N	N	Y	Y	N	N	Y	Y	Y	Y	Y	Y	Y	Y	Y	
Social housing subsidies — For management	N	Y	Y	Y	N	N	N	N	N	N	N	Y	N	N	N	N	Y	N	N	N	N	N	N	N	N
Indirect Public Subsidies																									
Tax Relief on Mortgage Interest for Owner Occupiers	N	Y	Y	Y	Y	Y	Y	N	N	Y	Y	Y	Y	Y	Y	Y	Y	Y	Y	Y	N	N	Y	N	N
Taxes																									
Capital Gains Tax on the Sale of Owner Occupied Dwellings[b]	Y	N		N	N		Y	N	N	N	N	N	N	N	N	N	N	N	N	N	N	N	N	Y	N
Tax on Imputed Rent for Owner Occupiers	N	Y		N	Y		N	N	N	Y	N	N	Y	Y	Y	Y	N	Y	N	N	Y	N	N	N	N
Indirect Taxes (VAT) on New Dwellings (%)	10 – 12	21		5	25		22	19.6	16	11 – 13		13.5	4	18	18	3	0	19	7	0	19	7	7	25	0

	Austria	Belgium	Cyprus	Czech Republic	Denmark	Estonia	Finland	France	Germany	Greece	Hungary	Ireland	Italy	Latvia	Lithuania	Luxembourg	Malta	Netherlands	Poland	Portugal	Slovak Republic	Slovenia	Spain	Sweden	United Kingdom
Indirect Taxes on Refurbishment and Maintenance (%)	20			5	25		22	5.5				13.5	10			3			7		19			25	
House purchase tax (stamp duty) (%)[a]	6	5–12.5			1.5		4	2–3	3.5	11–13		0–9	3			7–10		6			0.8			1.5–3	1–4
Regulation																									
Rent control for new private rented tenancies[b]	Y	Y			Y	N	N	N	Y	N		N	N					Y					N	Y	N
Control of social housing rents	Y	Y		Y	Y	N	Y	Y	Y		Y	Y	Y	Y	N	Y	Y	Y	Y	Y	Y	Y	Y	Y	
Social housing is targeted at low income or vulnerable households	Y	Y		Y	Y	N	Y	Y	Y		Y	Y	Y	Y	N	Y	Y	Y	Y	Y	Y	Y	Y	Y	
Stronger legal protection for social tenants than private renters	N	Y		N	Y	Y	Y	Y	N		Y	Y	Y	Y	Y	N	Y	N	N	Y	N	N	N	N	
Privatization of social housing is permitted	Y	Y		Y	Y	N	Y	Y		N	Y	Y	Y	Y	Y	Y	Y	Y	Y	Y	Y	Y	Y	Y	Y

Notes: Y = intervention exists; N = intervention doesn't exist; blank field = information is not available. Data for Bulgaria and Romania are not available
[a] 1995 data.
[b] 2001 data.

Sources: ECB 2003; Eurostat 2009b; MOI and Federcasa 2006.

sub-markets and the difficulties this poses for recognizing them all, not to speak of trying to quantify their scale and impact. Table 33.2 lists a number of major instruments and identifies their presence or absence in twenty-five EU member states.

Some of the longest established and most intrusive policy instruments have to do with regulation of the private rented sector, at least in regard to building standards and tenancy conditions but often extending also into rent controls. Many of the countries in Table 33.2 apply rent controls but in recent decades rigid 'first generation' rent controls that were put in place after World War I, and fixed the rents charged for specific properties, have been abolished and replaced with a 'second generation' of more flexible controls which, for instance, limit the number of occasions on which rents can be reviewed or link increases to the market average. In some cases rent controls have been abolished for new tenancies (O'Sullivan and De Decker 2007). Rent controls entail no public expenditure but can seriously distort markets and lead to hidden wealth transfers. For example, in Stockholm the discounts on economic rents caused by rent controls are so great that the supply of apartments has been severely constrained and half of apartment exchanges in 2005 involved significant black market payments by prospective tenants (Hüfner and Lundsgaard 2007).

Explicit and Implicit Expenditures

Interventions that are costed in public expenditure accounts make up the estimates of public expenditure on housing normally used in international comparison, as shown for EU countries in Table 33.2 where the average public expenditure on housing for 2004 was around 0.5 per cent of GDP. However, when it comes to hidden expenditures of the types mentioned earlier, no standardized estimates of their value across countries are available.[2] It is evident that in many cases their value is large and may dwarf direct public expenditures on housing. In the United States, for example, a country widely assumed to have small public supports for housing, tax expenditures on mortgage interest deductions and non-taxation of imputed rent from owner occupation amounted to 0.85 per cent of GDP in 2007 (OECD 2007h). Thirteen of the twenty-one EU countries in Table 33.2 below for which information on this item is available provide tax relief on mortgage interest (see Table 33.2). Surprisingly, outside of the United States, some of the most generous schemes are found in Northern Europe where home ownership sectors are relatively small and there is a strong emphasis on social housing (the Netherlands and Denmark being cases in point). In general, however, the trend in Europe since the 1980s has been for tax relief on mortgage interest to be reduced (Scanlan and Whitehead 2004).

---

[2] The OECD has made an effort to estimate the value of 'tax breaks for a social purpose' in OECD countries and to include these in estimates of total social expenditures. However, only health and pension related tax breaks are included and no estimates are provided for tax expenditures relating to housing (Adema and Ladaique 2005).

Intervention in Credit Markets

Other even more opaque instruments also play a major role and many of these take the form of interventions in financial markets in order to affect the supply of credit to the housing sector. In fact, in most developed countries, credit is among the state's primary means of shaping the housing system and housing services are delivered by agents either inside or outside government who respond to these public policy driven credit incentives. The market failure which state intervention is designed to correct in these instances may have to do with either capital allocation (making sure that enough—but not too much—capital flows into the housing sector) or social distribution (making sure that housing is available to those who need it as well as those who can pay for it). Credit policy in much of post-war Europe was often more concerned with capital shortages and the consequent general under-supply of housing than with distributional issues—and in fact succeeded in producing a rapid, general and much-needed improvement in overall housing availability and standards (Harloe 1995).

Credit policies may be directed either at social or private housing and may seek to support either rental or ownership tenure. In recent years, especially in North-Western Europe, state subsidies for social house building and refurbishment increasingly take the form of credit supports (preferential state-backed interest rates, guarantees of borrowings by social landlords or borrowing on their behalf by state intermediary lenders) rather than direct government capital grant aid (Gibb 2002). In these instances, social housing can be thought of as the working face of the state's housing credit policies.

Government intervention in mortgage markets for home owners is another major type of support. In some instances, the state acted as direct lender, as in the case of the State Housing Bank in Norway (Gulbrandsen 2004) and the system of mortgage provision by local authorities in Ireland (Fahey and Maître 2004). However, state-backed loan guarantees for private lenders are now more common though the details vary greatly between countries as does the scale of coverage (Elsinga et al. 2009). The United States system of loan guarantees originated as part of the New Deal in the 1930s and matured after World War II, mainly under the aegis of government agencies such as Fannie Mae (Green and Wachter 2005). The US government's loan guarantee was for a long time self-supporting, while other major national schemes (of which that in the Netherlands was the largest) involved some element of subsidy (Elsinga et al. 2009). As credit became more abundant and cheaper in the United States in the 1990s, private lenders sought to emulate the effect of government guarantees by means of elaborate mortgage-backed securities where it seemed that private investors had devised effective means of risk mitigation even in dealing with sub-prime borrowers. This system won the United States mortgage market widespread approbation as the pinnacle of efficiency and good financial service to both home purchasers and investors (Green and Wachter 2005; OECD 2007h). However, it came crashing down in 2008 and sparked off the present financial crisis that has shaken the global economy to its foundations and caused enormous and general damage to human welfare (IMF 2009). It is now evident in hindsight that sub-prime lending is an effective instrument of housing policy only where it is treated as a dimension of welfare support (as was often the case in Europe), though even in Europe the record of governments in managing investment flows into housing has been patchy at best and has frequently generated cycles of boom and bust in housing markets that have prefigured the recent crisis.[3]

Relationship with the Welfare State

In recent years the comparative housing policy literature has been dominated by a debate about the convergence or divergence of housing systems (Kemeny and Lowe 1998). Among these viewpoints the former is currently dominant and a consensus is developing that housing systems in Western countries are converging around an 'Anglo-Saxon' model of minimal state intervention in housing (eg. Clapham 1995; Scanlon and Whitehead 2007). However, the policy instruments in this field are so numerous and complex and their development over time so varied that positions in this debate are strongly influenced by the subset of policies focused on. The view that housing systems are converging in the direction of an Anglo-Saxon model is pre-dicated largely on analysis of levels of social housing provision and subsidization. However as the preceding analysis demonstrates, the housing interventions em-ployed by governments are much wider than this. In addition, Dodson (2006) questions whether the contraction of the social rented sector in Australia, New Zealand, and the United Kingdom constitutes a withdrawal of state involvement, since it has been accompanied by much closer regulation of social landlords and tenants.

Distributive Impact

If it is difficult to quantify how much the state intervenes in housing markets, it is also difficult to measure the overall welfare impact of whatever intervention occurs. A complexity that arises here echoes that found in other areas of the welfare state,

---

[3] This recent experience is but an extreme example of a more general pattern of house price volatility which has been little noted in social policy research even though its welfare outcomes are likely to have been large. It is especially notable that this volatility has been pronounced in some of the Northern European states with strong welfare provision and reflects the dubious record of public policy in managing investment in housing. Even before the recent house price collapse, Finland, Sweden, and the Netherlands each had two housing slumps in the period 1970–2005, as did Switzerland, Italy, the United Kingdom, Spain, and France (a housing slump is defined as a real price fall of 15 per cent or more) (Ball 2009: 10). The maximum house price fall in these slumps reached 50 per cent in Finland, 38 per cent in Sweden, and 37 per cent in Denmark. The Netherlands and Norway each had one house price slump in this period, with a price fall of 50 per cent in the Netherlands and 40 per cent in Norway (Ball 2009: 10). The housing slump in Finland and Sweden in the early 1990s caused falls in GDP of 8–10 per cent and 5 per cent respectively (Hoeller and Rae 2007: 24).

namely, that distribution at household level can be either vertical or horizontal (and this is to set aside for the moment the issues of spatial distribution that arise at neighbourhood level). It has been suggested as a rule of thumb that the distributional impact of the welfare state is primarily horizontal (distributing resources from one stage of the life course to another, as is the central function of social insurance) and only secondarily vertical (taking from the rich and giving to the poor) (Esping-Andersen and Myles 2009: 640). However, assessment of distribution in housing policy tends to lean towards a vertical-only basis for judgement. That is one reason for the privileged position usually accorded to social housing in welfare terms—it can and often does place great emphasis on providing good housing for the least well off.

State promotion of owner occupation, on the other hand, is often thought to fare poorly in vertical distribution (perhaps wrongly in some cases, as for example in the highly progressive methods for promoting home ownership in Norway—Gulbrand-sen 2004). But even so, the claim of home ownership to consideration in welfare terms could also be asserted on the basis of possible horizontal distribution, particularly in the case of elderly households that enjoy economic security and savings on household expenditures by virtue of having invested in home purchase at an earlier stage in their lives (Castles 1998b). The argument could thus be advanced that state-supported home ownership has a quasi-social insurance function which complements the social assistance-type function of social housing, and even if the parallels are sometimes shaky, one needs to consider both before reaching conclusions on the distributive impact of housing policies (F. Castles 1998b; F. Castles and Ferrera 1996; Conley 2000; Fahey et al. 2004; Ritakallio 2003).

Explaining Home Ownership

The twentieth century converted the mass of the population in the Western world from renters into home owners. This was not a complete transformation since large blocks of renting remain in all societies but nevertheless it represents a more-or-less general trend. Amidst the mass of detailed change in housing policy and housing outcomes reviewed in the present chapter, this is the closest that we can observe to a single, central, universal development. It is also one that is difficult for research on the welfare state to come to terms with. It might be read as a consequence of the triumph of the market and the roll-back of the state following a temporary advance of social housing during the short golden age of welfare after World War II. Or one might be struck by how widely it is a product of public policy as much as of market forces—as if home ownership, as much as social housing or rent allowances, is a characteristic expression of the state's role in the housing field.

In order to sketch out how future research might seek to resolve this issue, it is necessary first to identify what home ownership is and how it fits into the welfare state. Here, as suggested earlier, two conceptual devices are helpful, first, the distinction between housing as capital and accommodation as a service, and second the three-sided framework of market, state, and household within which much recent thinking on the welfare state is couched. Home ownership means that housing as capital remains as capital—a form of wealth that is accumulated and distributed through the market, perhaps influenced to a greater or lesser degree by public policy but not directly controlled by the state. It also means that accommodation as a service is removed from the market into the self-provisioning household economy. It thereby becomes a non-monetized activity which in contrast to the rental systems it replaces is hard for both pure market forces and the taxing powers of the state to reach. Research on housing in the welfare state has said much about home ownership as wealth accumulation but little about its place in the household economy—and indeed the focus on the household as the third leg of welfare in recent theory of the welfare state has largely missed out on the significance of self-provisioned accommodation for that perspective. The growth of home ownership, then, could be interpreted as an instance of long-term expansion in the role of the household sector in welfare production and thus as something other than the advance of either market or state.

As we try to explain that outcome, we might seek to analyse the wealth accumulation represented by home ownership in the usual terms, that is, as a product of the forces of market and social class. However, such an approach might not suffice in explaining why *housing* rather than any other asset class is so widely selected by households as the form in which to hold their wealth, nor why they confine that wealth-holding to homes they live in themselves rather than housing in general. To deal with that question, we might draw on the notion advanced by Henderson and Ioannides (1983) in their seminal paper on the economics of housing tenure, namely, that ownership has certain competitive advantages over renting. They propose that renting is subject to a 'rental externality' arising from the incentive tenants have to over-utilize their dwelling and the response landlords make by building an appropriate premium into the rent. Home ownership enables householders to avoid that externality since they become their own landlords—and in most circumstances you can have no better landlord, or no better tenant, than yourself. The two major exceptions where self-renting is not advantageous are (*a*) where you are too mobile for it to be efficient for you to take on the contracting costs involved in home purchase, and (*b*) where you live in multi-household dwellings where there is an advantage in having a landlord manage the overall structure and common spaces in the building. Otherwise, it is in the home owners' interest to protect the asset value of the dwelling and there is no requirement for an external landlord to manage the asset or its use by the household, all of which leads to efficiencies in the provision of accommodation.

Acting as one's own landlord can give rise to certain inefficiencies also, mainly arising from the risk of under-utilization of dwellings, as in the case of empty-nest households that continue to live in homes that have become too large for their needs. Owner-occupiers do not ruthlessly treat their homes as capital assets from which they seek to extract maximum profit. In the absence of price signals in the form of rent they can be slow to adjust their residential space to their needs—they do not appreciate the opportunity cost of ownership of excess housing. The result is that they can short-change themselves on income, as frequently happens with households that are asset rich (in the form of housing) but income poor. On the other hand, gains can be made from the household's willingness to forego income from an under-used dwelling. These gains take the form of enhanced security and continuity in their homes. Once the dwelling is securely owned, the accommodation it provides, as a service generated within the household, is protected from market forces and from the risk and uncertainty that reliance on the market brings. It thus serves as a form of social insurance, not primarily as an asset that can generate income (though it can be drawn upon to play that role) but as a dwelling that guarantees accommodation, one of the most basic of household needs.

CONCLUSION

This chapter has sketched the multiple structure of the housing market, the many forms of intervention in that market that are possible and widely occur, and the consequent difficulty in summing all interventions together in order to assess either the extent of state involvement in housing or the net distributive impact of all interventions taken together. Nevertheless, it seems safe to draw two general conclusions. One is that the state role in housing continues to remain very large, especially if one takes into account its influence in the sub-markets of housing finance and the spatial or neighbourhood distribution of housing as well as its more direct engagement with the rental and home purchase sub-markets. It is difficult in that context to see signs of a roll-back of the state in the housing field, even if it is equally difficult to make judgements on how progressive or otherwise the state's impact is. The second conclusion is that in light of the general ascent of home ownership in the Western world in the twentieth century, the household economy must be recognized as having a particular significance for housing. The implication is that future research in this area should pay greater attention to the three-sided model of welfare state analysis, encompassing market, state, and household, in place of the simpler two-sided (market and state) model that has prevailed in this field up to now, and should treat housing, to use Malpass's (2008) term, as a cornerstone rather than a wobbly pillar of welfare systems.

CHAPTER 34

EDUCATION

MARIUS R. BUSEMEYER
RITA NIKOLAI

INTRODUCTION

In an early contribution to the comparative welfare state literature, Harold Wilensky (1975) argued that 'education is special'. Education, claimed Wilensky, should be seen and analysed separately from other parts of the welfare state. The reason is that social policies influence equality more directly than investments in education. Furthermore, education, especially higher education, is closely linked to and conditioned by the occupational structure, so that the move from elite to mass education in the postwar decades was not followed by a commensurate decline in inequality. Consequentially, argues Wilensky, these inherent differences between education and social policies would necessitate an analytical strategy that systematically distinguishes between the two.

Arguably, Wilensky's verdict contributed to the neglect of the study of education as an aspect of social policy. It is telling that seminal contributions to the literature of recent decades (Esping-Andersen 1990; Huber and Stephens 2001a) do not discuss the role of education systematically, although, as this chapter will show, there are obvious 'elective affinities' between welfare state and education regimes (Busemeyer 2009a; Estévez-Abe et al. 2001; Iversen and Stephens 2008). Moreover, the distinction between education and social policies is not just an analytical one, but has obvious empirical correlates. In some welfare state regimes, education is regarded as an integral part of the welfare state, whereas in others, the two spheres of policy making are much more separated in terms of politics and institutions (Allmendinger and Leibfried 2003). Hence what is required is a refocusing of the analytical perspective of the comparative welfare state literature in such a way that it systematically incorpo-rates the study of education. This chapter seeks to provide a step in this direction.

More specifically, we discuss the relationship between education and social policy from a comparative and historical perspective. We address the following questions: how can we make sense of the large diversity of education systems? Which institutional and political forces shaped their development? And where was education seen as an integral part of the welfare state rather than a separate sphere of policy making and why? In answering these questions, we rely on descriptive analyses of aggregate data for OECD countries and seek to identify distinct country clusters, i.e. worlds of 'human capital formation' (Iversen and Stephens 2008) that might be related to Esping-Andersen's typology of welfare state regimes. Subsequently, we present a tentative explanatory framework that may help to account for the observed variation.

But first, some conceptual groundwork is in order. Wilensky's verdict is appropriate in the sense that there are important differences between education and social policies. First, social insurance and similar welfare state policies need an encompassing infrastructure, often at the national level, that defines the boundaries of solidarity and redistribution. In contrast, education can be provided in a much more decentralized fashion, because it does not redistribute directly (Busemeyer 2008). Second, to a larger extent than other social policies, investments in education entail private benefits. Certainly, investments in education also create public benefits: a higher level of general education enhances productivity and the economic well-being of a society and can also be an important social policy instrument for promoting equality of opportunity and reducing social inequality (Allmendinger and Leibfried 2003). However, education is a basic element in the creation of individual human capital (Becker 1994), thereby affecting individual payoffs and employment opportunities in labour markets. Third and, perhaps, most importantly, education indirectly and prospectively affects the primary distribution of incomes in the labour market rather than compensating income inequalities *ex post* in the manner of most social insurance policies. To Wilensky (1975), this difference between education and other social policies is related to the different principles of social justice that the two kinds of policies serve, i.e. 'equality of opportunities' versus 'equality of outcomes'. Arguably, however, with the advent of the 'knowledge' economy and the enhanced importance of human capital, this picture seems increasingly incomplete. Given the strong relationship between educational achievements and family background, policy intervention in the field of education is a much more important determinant of equality than is implied by Wilensky (see Kaufmann 2003a for a similar assessment).

This makes the relationship between education and other welfare state policies worth investigating. We can identify three main accounts in the literature. First, education and social insurance policies may be seen as functionally equivalent. Analysing the long-term development of public policies in Europe and the United States, the rise of the welfare state and the expansion of new educational opportunities, Arnold Heidenheimer (1973, 1981) saw the difference in the focus on education and social policy between countries as 'alternative strategies pursued by emerging welfare states', i.e. the amelioration of social inequalities by different means. The relative timing of macro-social processes (industrialization, democratization) as well as cultural and political factors determined whether a country followed the 'education' (e.g. the United States) or the 'social insurance' (many European countries) route.

A second account of the relationship between education and other social policies sees education and social policy as complementary rather than as substitutes. For T. H. Marshall, the right to education is an important element in the catalogue of social rights: 'The right to education is a genuine social right of citizenship, because the aim of education during childhood is to shape the future adult. Fundamentally it should be regarded, not as the right of the child to go to school, but as the right of the adult citizen to have been educated' (Marshall 1964a: 81–2; see also Chapter 35). While Heidenheimer identifies a functional equivalence of education and welfare state regimes, Marshall emphasizes the fact that the full realization of social rights of citizenship necessarily entails the universal provision of a right to education (i.e. a right to being educated) in addition to other social rights.

Finally, the recent debate on the 'social investment state' (Giddens 1998) and 'activation' policies (see Chapter 30 above) implies a third perspective on the relationship between education and other social policies. From this perspective, economic and social change together with the fiscal constraints they produce necessitate the redrawing of boundaries between 'active' and 'passive' social policies. Viewing education as a *social* investment is seen as a way out of the key dilemma that policymakers face in a globalized knowledge economy. In an era when fiscal constraints seem to prevent the realization of universal rights of social citizenship that Marshall promoted, the notions of social investment and 'activation' go along with a new conception of social rights in which participation in labour markets is the prime motivation and goal.

As will become clear in the later parts of this chapter, these three accounts of the relationship between education and social policy are useful heuristic tools to describe changes over time as well as differences across countries. In the following section, we provide an overview of the variety of education regimes in advanced industrialized democracies. In the subsequent section, we offer an analytical framework locating the political and institutional foundations of diverse development paths that helps make sense of the observed variation of education regimes.

THE VARIETY OF EDUCATION REGIMES

OECD data on education spending and related measures reveal relatively robust patterns that mirror conventional groupings into families of nations (Castles 1993) or welfare state regimes (Esping-Andersen 1990; Iversen and Stephens 2008). As a starting point, we look at relativities of education vis-à-vis social spending, variations in total education spending as well as public expenditure on tertiary education,

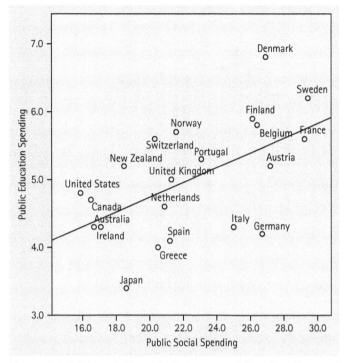

Figure 34.1 The relationship between public education and social spending in per cent of GDP (2005)

Sources: OECD 2008*c*; OECD 2009*d*: subsection social expenditure.

and, most importantly, the share of public relative to private spending. Figure 34.1 depicts the relationship between public social and education spending in OECD countries. In general, we find a positive association, i.e. higher public social spending is associated with higher education spending, indicating that Marshall's notion of a complementary relationship between the two is at least partly adequate.

However, by looking at the distance of countries or country groups from the regression line, we gain insights about the relative importance of education vs. social spending. For instance, Germany, Greece, Japan, Spain, and Italy exhibit far lower levels of education spending than one might expect on the basis of their levels of social spending. The United States as well as Switzerland and New Zealand, on the other hand, lie clearly above the regression line, indicating the relatively greater importance of education than of social policy in these countries. The Scandinavian countries exhibit high levels of social and education spending in general, but their positioning above the regression line shows that these countries spend even more on education than on social policies in relative terms.

In Figure 34.2, data on private and public education spending (as percentages of GDP) are presented. Several things can be seen from this graph: First, there is substantial variation in spending among OECD countries, with the Scandinavian

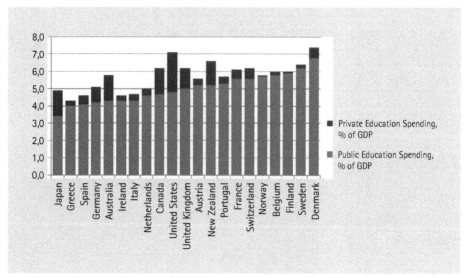

Figure 34.2 Variation of spending on education (2005)
Source: OECD 2008c.

countries spending the most, followed by Belgium, Switzerland, and France. Most other continental European countries (i.e. Germany, Italy, and the Netherlands) can be found in the lower middle field. Second, the English-speaking countries and Japan exhibit above average levels of private spending. Because of high levels of private spending, the United States vies with Denmark for the top position in this comparison of spending levels.

A more detailed analysis (Figure 34.3) reveals that the observed spending patterns are related to and driven by differences in public and private spending on tertiary education. Figure 34.3 shows that the variation between OECD countries in spending on tertiary education is even greater than in the case of spending on all levels of education. In addition, the variation in the relative importance of public and private spending is more pronounced. The special position of the United States with its high levels of private spending becomes even more obvious. However, Scandinavian countries still occupy top positions. This indicates that their high commitment to education is not restricted to primary and secondary education. However, in comparison to Figure 34.2, the lead of the United States and Canada in levels of spending is larger. In other words: Scandinavian countries are more willing to spend on high quality primary and secondary education in addition to tertiary education (see also Iversen and Stephens 2008). Countries like New Zealand and Portugal are different. They fall back in the ranking relative to their position in Figure 34.2, i.e. their emphasis is more on primary and secondary education than on tertiary education.

A way of examining clustering amongst these countries is by means of hierarchical cluster analysis. The raw data for the analysis is based on recent figures from the OECD's Education at a Glance series and relates to common indicators used in the

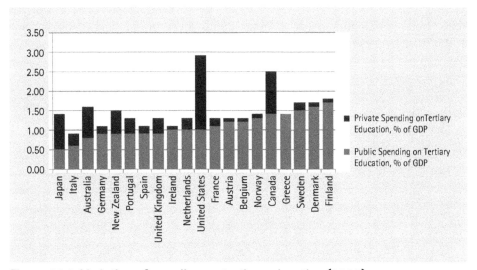

Figure 34.3 Variation of spending on tertiary education (2005)
Source: OECD 2008c.

comparative education science to distinguish and classify education systems (Hopper 1968; Müller et al. 1997):[1]

1. The division of labour between the state and private actors in the financing, administration, and provision of education.
2. The extent of public investment in education (across educational sectors as well as in relation to other public policies).
3. The organization of vocational training in schools and firms.
4. The distribution of students across and levels of enrolment in different educational sectors.
5. The degree of decentralization and the distribution of policy-making powers across levels of government.
6. The extent and forms of segregation of educational tracks (i.e. differentiation between separate academic and vocational tracks).
7. The degree of variation between schools and school forms with regard to curricula, exams, and quality of learning opportunities.

The cluster analysis in Figure 34.4 reveals three relatively robust groups of countries: Northern Europe, the Mediterranean countries, and the English-speaking countries (plus Japan).

---

[1] More specifically, we include data on public, private and total spending (for all levels of education, primary and secondary education as well as tertiary education), the public share of spending for all levels of education as well as for tertiary education, the share of the population (25–64 years old) with at least an upper secondary degree and the population share with tertiary education (all data are given in OECD 2008c). Because of missing data, Switzerland and Greece had to be excluded from the cluster analysis. Where available, the data for the year 2005 is used. In other cases, we rely on the most recently available data point.

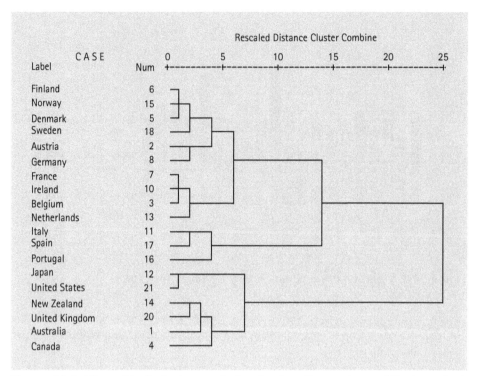

Figure 34.4 Hierarchical cluster analysis of education systems: Ward method, Euclidian distance measure (c. 2005)

Northern Europe

The first point to note is the existence of a broadly defined cluster of Northern European countries, which group into three quite distinct sub-clusters.

The Scandinavian countries. Within the Northern European grouping, Denmark, Finland, Norway, and Sweden have a quite distinct profile. The most important characteristics of this group are high levels of public education spending, low levels of private spending, and a high share of the population with at least upper secondary education. These are also countries which perform comparatively well in international comparisons of educational attainment, and exhibit an egalitarian distribution of competencies (Allmendinger and Leibfried 2003: 70). They are also strongly committed to vocational training, which is largely provided in vocational schools, with the exception of Denmark which retains a strong apprenticeship system.

The concept of a comprehensive education system is the foundation of what has been called the 'Nordic Model in Education' (Oftedal Telhaug et al. 2006). Historically, the Scandinavian countries started out with segmented education systems quite similar to those that still prevail in countries like Germany. Starting in Sweden in the late 1950s, however, the formerly elitist education systems were transformed into universal, comprehensive, and non-discriminatory regimes, in which access to higher education was opened up and vocational training was fully integrated into the general schooling system (Busemeyer 2009*a*; Erikson and Jonsson 1996). Thus, by the early 1980s, Sweden came very close to a citizenship-based model of comprehensive education (Oftedal Telhaug et al. 2006), the goal of which was to establish a national education system offering similar access and learning conditions to all pupils, level-ling out differences in educational achievements due to socio-economic background or geographical residence to the greatest extent possible. However, since the 1980s, the education systems of these countries has undergone significant changes. For example, Sweden has significantly deregulated its education system in the 1990s by introducing competition and expanding the role of private, albeit publicly funded (independent), schools (Lundahl 2002).

Germany and Austria form a separate sub-cluster in the broader Northern European cluster with some similarities to the Scandinavian grouping, but other quite distinct characteristics. In a manner similar to the Scandinavian countries, they are char-acterized by a low share of private spending on primary, secondary and tertiary education, by above average levels in the share of the population with at least upper secondary education, and a strong emphasis on vocational training. In contrast to the Scandinavian countries (with the partial exception of Denmark), vocational training is provided in the form of dual apprenticeship training, combining practical training in firms with theoretical training in vocational schools. As a consequence, private spending on primary, secondary, non-tertiary post-secondary education is above average in Germany, because spending of firms on apprenticeship training is counted as private education expenditure (Heidenheimer 1996; Schmidt 2002*b*). Another significant difference between Germany and Austria on the one hand and the Scandinavian countries on the other is that levels of public education spending on primary and secondary as well as on tertiary education are significantly lower in the German-speaking countries (see Figures 34.2 and 34.3).

In terms of educational institutions, the German-speaking countries remained committed to a segmented secondary school system, which channels pupils onto different educational tracks (vocational or academic) at an early stage in their education career with limited possibilities to 'change tracks' later on. To a certain extent, the segmented school system and firm-based vocational training are func-tionally dependent on each other. In a 'differentiated' skill regime (Busemeyer 2009*a*), the firms' willingness to invest in training hinges on the assurance that graduate apprentices remain with the training firm and do not wander off to higher education instead.

Segmented school systems produce and replicate educational inequalities across generations, which is why recent reforms have tried to expand access and enhance educational mobility. In Austria, the introduction of the *Berufsreifeprüfung* combining vocational qualifications with academic studies as well as the generally higher emphasis put on school-based vocational education result in easier transitions of students, apprentices and pupils across educational sectors. Reforms in Germany, however, remain more incremental, although some *Länder*, including Hamburg and Berlin, are transforming their three-track system into a less segmented two-track set-up.

The continental European countries of France, the Netherlands, Belgium, and, perhaps surprisingly, Ireland constitute a final Northern sub-cluster, related, but at a higher level, to the Scandinavian and Germanic sub-clusters. The characteristics of this sub-cluster are medium to somewhat above average levels of public spending on primary and secondary education, but little in the way of private spending. Public spending on tertiary education is low or average and private spending is also low. Moreover, the share of the population with at least upper secondary education is below average, and it is this factor which distinguishes these countries from the German-speaking nations and puts the latter closer to the Scandinavian cluster.

One conspicuous element that these countries have in common is a strong heritage of Catholicism (with the partial exception of the Netherlands). The importance of religious schooling in these countries is well-known, although it does not show up in above average levels of private spending as non-state education institutions receive generous public subsidies (Neave 1985). In Belgium, Ireland, and the Netherlands, the majority of pupils, primarily at the lower education levels, are enrolled in non-state institutions run by religious authorities (i.e. mostly the Catholic Church, except in the Netherlands). The share of pupils in non-state, i.e. government-dependent private schools in France is lower than in the other countries (between 15 and 30 per cent depending on the level of education; OECD 2008c: 436), but still significant. Italy also has a strong tradition of Catholicism, but there, the separation between state and church is more pronounced, resulting in much less direct subsidization of religious schools by the state (Neave 1985: 323, 334). In exchange for generous public subsidies, religious (i.e. 'free') schools are required to follow national standards and criteria in terms of the curriculum and examination standards in many areas (ibid.: 334).

The Mediterranean Countries

The Mediterranean countries (Italy, Spain, and Portugal) form a distinct cluster of their own. These countries are characterized by low levels of public and private spending—especially on tertiary education. The shares of the population with at least an upper secondary or tertiary degree lie well below the OECD average. Related to this, their positioning in rankings of educational performance is in the lower half, although variation of competencies within these countries seems to be less pronounced—as is argued by Allmendinger and Leibfried (2003: 70) for the case of Spain. These countries have many obvious cultural and historical commonalities: late industrialization, a late and interrupted course of democratic development, and a Catholic tradition if anything stronger and more conservative than in continental Europe.

The English-Speaking Countries (plus Japan)

Canada, the United States, Australia, New Zealand, and the United Kingdom (but not Ireland!) represent another homogeneous group. Its characteristics are medium levels of public spending, but high levels of private spending, associated with a low public share in education financing. This finding mirrors the importance of private social spending in the English-speaking countries (see Chapter 8). The share of the population with tertiary education is high (especially in the United States, Canada, and Australia), and variance in student performance is low, albeit higher than in the Scandinavian countries.

Japan also falls into this group, if only because the American occupation transferred important characteristics of the United States' education system (such as the comprehensive high school) to Japan in the wake of World War II. In comparison to the English-speaking countries, Japan exhibits very low levels of public education spending.

The United States stands slightly apart from the other English-speaking countries. Until the advent of World War II, the US occupied a pioneering position in the expansion of mass primary and secondary education (Heidenheimer and Layson 1982; Lindert 2004), when the British education system was still elitist in nature. Over time, other countries caught up: In 1960, Canada and New Zealand exhibited levels of tertiary enrolment similar to the United States, followed shortly afterwards by the Scandinavian countries (Castles 1998a: 179). In overcoming its elitist heritage, the British education system became more similar to that of its cousins, although it retains some peculiarities such as the public funding of formally independent higher education institutions and a stronger emphasis on vocational training than in the other English-speaking countries.

EDUCATION REGIMES AND WORLDS
OF WELFARE CAPITALISM

How do these clusters and sub-clusters of countries correspond to established typologies such as the three worlds of 'human capital formation' (Iversen and Stephens 2008), 'worlds of welfare capitalism' (Esping-Andersen 1990), or 'families of nations' (Castles 1993)? First, the fact that the Mediterranean countries constitute a clearly defined cluster fits with the view that there is a 'fourth' distinct world of welfare capitalism (Castles 1993, 1998; Ferrera 1996). The patchy coverage and dualism of the Southern European welfare states is mirrored in the selectiveness of their education systems, exemplified by low levels of spending and enrolment in higher education. At the other extreme are to be found the Scandinavian countries, where the universal social democratic welfare state corresponds with an education regime based on the notion of egalitarian citizenship education (Oftedal Telhaug et al. 2006). The comparison of the Scandinavian and the Mediterranean countries thus supports Marshall's (1964*b*) claim that education and social policy more conventionally defined stand in a complimentary relationship with each other rather than being substitutes.

The countries making up Esping-Andersen's conservative world of welfare capitalism are to be found in two of the sub-clusters constituting the broader Northern European grouping. In both the Germanic and continental European sub-types however there are clear resonances between welfare states regimes and education systems. The privileges granted to religious and free schools in the continental European countries correspond to the subsidiarity principle that van Kersbergen (1995) has identified as a central characteristic of Christian democratic social policy. The occupational stratification of social insurance institutions of a Bismarckian type is mirrored in the differentiation of separate educational tracks within the schooling system that lead to different 'places in society', which is equally reminiscent of Christian democratic ideology in social policy (Van Kersbergen 1995).

Finally, the reliance on markets in the liberal welfare state and the notion of social policy as a 'last resort' find their equivalents in the emphasis that English-speaking countries put on the provision of education as a 'first resort', i.e. the most effective insurance against labour market risks, an emphasis that the English-speaking world has recently been exporting to the wider world in the guise of activation strategies. It should also be underlined that, in the English-speaking countries, the division of labour between public and private in education is similar to that in social policy (Hacker 2002: ch. 8), with a much bigger role for private spending in both spheres than elsewhere in the OECD.

The Historical and Political Foundations of Education Systems

We conclude this analysis by offering a preliminary framework of analysis aimed at making sense of the observed variation of education regimes. Our overarching thesis is that the concrete manifestations of today's education regimes as well as their historical and contemporary development paths rest on historical foundations that should be understood in terms of the interaction between the relative timing of macro-social processes on the one hand and concrete political and institutional contexts on the other. The broad isomorphism of educational clusters and welfare regimes noted in the previous section arises because they share similar political and historical foundations.

Timing. Towards the end of the nineteenth century, industrialization increased the demand for more educated workers in Western countries. However, early democratization fuelled the demand for education instead of social insurance policies. In the

Bismarckian welfare state, the provision of social insurance was a tool in the hands of the ruling elite to protract democratization and stifle the rising power of labour. In contrast, early democratization in the United States promoted the expansion of educational opportunities, precisely because, in line with Marshall, education was seen as an important component of citizenship. Competition between local, state, private, and religious educational institutions in a context of a weak public bureaucracy contributed to the early expansion of education in the United States (Heidenheimer 1973, 1981). Where bureaucratization preceded democratization (e.g. Germany), education was used to systematize and restrict access to bureaucratic elites. Although Prussia was the first country to introduce compulsory schooling, educational expansion was protracted by a powerful bureaucratic elite restricting access to higher levels of education. In the cases of Portugal and Spain, late democratization has delayed the onset of educational expansion well into the second half of the twentieth century.

Religious heritage. The outcome of the state–church conflict over education significantly affected the overall commitment to education in relation to other social policies as well as the public–private division of labour (Wolf 2009). Generally speaking, Protestant countries (predominantly Scandinavia, North America) exhibit higher levels of total spending on education than countries with a Catholic heritage. However, the division of labour between the public and the private sphere varies in accordance with the type of Protestantism prevailing (see Chapter 18). Lutheran Protestantism (Scandinavia) goes along with a predominance of the public sphere in education, while Reformed Protestantism is associated with a strong role for private initiative (the United States, Canada). Most continental European countries have a strong heritage of Catholicism (France, Belgium, Italy, Spain, Portugal), which slowed down the expansion of educational opportunities in comparison to the expansion of the welfare state (Castles 1994a, 1998a).

   In part, this distinction is founded on ideological differences between Protestant denominations as well as between Catholicism and Protestantism. However, it can be speculated that the relative power position of religious institutions played a decisive role, shaping the severity of the state–church conflict over education and the structure of political cleavages (Swaan 1988; Manow and van Kersbergen 2009; Chapter 18 above). In the Scandinavian setting, the Lutheran church could pursue a 'maximalist' strategy (de Swaan 1988), employing the public school system to promote religious education. The Catholic Church, however, wanted to maintain the independence of religious education from the public school system, which generally meant that participation rates and spending had to catch up with other countries after World War II (Castles 1998a). In the United States, Reformed Protestantism and religious pluralism led to a strong separation between public and private providers of education (i.e. the state and the churches). Because no single denomination had a dominating position, but all remained committed to religious and general education, religious pluralism fuelled the expansion of secondary and higher education (Heidenheimer 1981).

The Balance of Power between Business and Labour

Historically, the position of the left (social democratic parties and trade unions) had an impact on the relative importance of education vis-à-vis social insurance policies. In the United States, unions regarded public welfare measures as potential competitors to their own bargains with employers (Heidenheimer 1973) and favoured the expansion of education instead. In contrast to the United States, where labour unions were active supporters of post-primary education, their counterparts in Europe did not become interested in education until the 1930s (Alber 1986; Heidenheimer 1973). Participation in the self-governance of social insurance institutions became an important power resource for unions in Bismarckian welfare states, and in countries like Germany, labour unions concentrated more on vocational education and the social protection of skilled workers. As a consequence, education and social policy have been institutionally and politically separated until today (Allmendinger et al. 2009).

   In the period after World War II, the government participation of leftist parties spurred the expansion of educational opportunities (Schmidt 2007) as well as the welfare state in general, which is in line with Marshall's notion on the progressive development of social citizenship. The long reign of social democrats in the Scandinavian countries was a crucial factor in the shaping of the comprehensive school system. The literature is still undecided, however, on the question of whether social democrats in government were more interested in expanding opportunities in higher education or general and vocational education (Ansell 2008b; Boix 1998; Busemeyer 2009b). Ansell (2008b) argues that social democrats initially opposed the expansion of higher education, because upper income classes benefit from this form of education to a larger extent than lower income classes. In contrast, Busemeyer (2009b) finds that government participation of social democrats is positively associated with increases in higher education spending, because leftist parties cater to new voter groups in the middle class.

Decentralization. A central finding of the welfare state literature (Obinger et al. 2005a) is that the extensive decentralization of power to lower levels of government has slowed down the expansion of welfare states. Federalism and fiscal decentralization can also be seen as playing a major role in education policy making (Archer 1989). Lower levels of government generally play a greater role in the provision of education than is the case of other public policies. Hence, in the case of education, extensive decentralization protects and possibly even promotes investment in education (Busemeyer 2008), because it enhances the competition between localities ('race to the top'). Here, it is important to distinguish between the decentralization of fiscal authority and federalism as a general principle of political decision making. Fiscal decentralization in federal (Canada, the United States, and Switzerland) as well as in non-federal countries (Denmark and Sweden) is likely to enhance the salience of education vis-à-vis social policy, whereas the predominance of joint decision making across levels of government or fiscal centralization (i.e. low levels of genuine decentralization of authority) hampers the expansion of education relative to social policy (e.g. Germany, Italy, France; see Figure 34.1).

Besides its impact on educational expansion and the importance of education relative to social policy, decentralization shapes the politics of education reform. Archer (1989), for example, argues that in centralized systems, education reformers are forced to pursue their agenda via the national arena of policy making. In contrast, decentralized systems are flexible enough to allow local innovation and variation. However, this implies that, from a systems perspective, decentralized systems are expected to resist encompassing reforms to a larger extent than centralized systems. The unequal success of social democratic reform efforts in Sweden and Germany in the 1970s plainly illustrates this mechanism.

CONCLUSIONS

Our chapter has reflected on resonances between the development of social and education policies across the OECD region. We find that conventional theses about the role of the relative timing of macro-social processes and the balance of power between business and labour have similar effects in both spheres. However, some factors such as the state–church conflict seem to be more important in the case of education, while others (decentralization and federalism) seem likely to affect the development of education in ways rather different from social policy.

How scholarship views the linkage between the spheres differs between clusters: in the English-speaking and Scandinavian countries education and social policy are viewed as related parts of wider strategies of societal intervention; however, in the states of continental Europe the study and practice of education and social policy are more separated (Allmendinger and Leibfried 2003; Heidenheimer 1981). The notion of the 'social investment state' (Giddens 1998) which has percolated from its English-speaking origins into a wider European and EU discourse may begin to change this. Indeed, the very fact of a wider Northern European grouping revealed in our cluster analysis might be taken as possible evidence of the beginnings of a convergence of education systems away from the English-speaking and Mediterranean peripheries. In general, the importance of early childhood education, lifelong learning, and further training—the longstanding pillars of the Scandinavian welfare state and education regime—are increasingly emphasized (Esping-Andersen et al. 2002), although reforms in countries such as Germany are still incremental rather than fundamental.

However, it should also be said that activation policies undertaken in the spirit of the 'social investment state' have often become discredited as fig leaves for welfare state retrenchment. Such strategies are perceived as weakening the decommodification of traditional social insurance policies while strengthening the commodification of education. In the words of Marshall (1964*b*), the social right to having been educated is incrementally transformed into a duty to stay educated in order to be able flexibly to meet the demands of changing economies and labour markets. It, therefore, remains an open question whether and to what extent the education regimes of OECD countries will converge on the Scandinavian or the British version of the social investment state. In any case, if education policy is supposed to step in for more traditional forms of social security, we need a better understanding of the limits of this approach as an effective tool for mitigating social inequality. Thus, future research in social policy needs to clarify the relationships between educational investment, educational institutions, and the distribution of life chances in different welfare state and education regimes.

A further topic for future research is the need to explore in greater depth the common political and historical foundations of welfare state and skill regimes. Within the confines of this chapter, we have explored the historical and contemporary variation of education regimes and presented an explanatory framework that may assist in understanding and explaining the observed variation. Clearly, this is only a first step. Future research should try to clarify the contribution of partisan and institutional factors to the historical and contemporary development of education regimes. In this, the analytical perspective should be broadened beyond the 'usual' suspects and include Eastern European and Asian countries—in particular countries such as Japan and South Korea.

PART VI

···

POLICY
OUTCOMES

···

CHAPTER 35

THE SOCIAL RIGHTS OF CITIZENSHIP

JOHN D. STEPHENS

INTRODUCTION

IN the literature on comparative welfare states, the dominant conception of the welfare state has been that it represents a transfer of allocation of goods and services from market determination to political determination. T. H. Marshall's formulation in his 1950 essay has undoubtedly been the most influential conceptualization of the welfare state. There he outlines three stage of the development of citizenship; civic, political, and social. Based on Marshall's conception, contemporary welfare state scholars generally view the best measure of the level of welfare state development historically and differences in welfare generosity across countries to be the degree to which welfare states substitute transfer payments and public services as 'social rights of citizenship' for income and services to be allocated by the market.

Marshall's conception was that social rights were citizenship rights exactly like (not simply analogous to) civil and political rights of citizenship, such as the right to vote or the right to assemble. Seemingly to be like political citizenship rights, social rights would have to be based on citizenship alone and accrue to all citizens equally. In fact, Marshall did not make this argument, and though contemporary scholars debate whether means- or income-tested benefits are 'social rights', they all consider earnings-related benefits to be social rights. These earnings-related benefits are not equal and they are not literally citizenship rights because they are usually contingent on a record of contribution.

Gendering the conception of social rights further muddies the picture. Precisely in the same way that feminists criticized the view that decommodification was inadequate as a master concept for the degree of welfare state generosity because for many women the goal was to be 'commodified' in the first place, that is, to enter the labour force (Orloff 1993*b*), it is arguable that the concept of social rights of citizenship should include the notion that all citizens should have the right to work, or even satisfying work. Such a conception of social rights would consider the activation policies that have been so commonplace across advanced welfare states in the past decade and a half to be an advance of social rights, whereas a more traditional conception might consider them to be 're-commodification' and to represent welfare regress.

I begin this chapter with a discussion of how Marshall and contemporary researchers have defined the social rights of citizenship. The second section reviews existing measures of social rights. The discussion of measurement issues necessarily revisits the previous section on the definition of social rights because how scholars measure social rights often clarifies how they define social rights. The final section examines the determinants of social rights and the impact of social rights on governmental redistribution, poverty reduction, employment, and gender equality.

SOCIAL RIGHTS DEFINED

Scholars often cite classic texts on the basis of secondary accounts of the classic and in the process the arguments of the classic are simplified and distorted. This has clearly been the case in the treatment of T. H. Marshall's 1950 essay *Social Class and Citizenship*. The strong contrast that Marshall (1964*b*: 15) did make between the Poor Law tradition in which recipients lost citizenship rights upon internment in the workhouse and modern social policy has led many scholars (e.g. Korpi 1989: 314) to regard means-tested benefits as not being social rights. Marshall's analysis which views social rights of the twentieth century as direct extensions of political rights of the nineteenth century has led some to view social benefits that are not based on citizenship with more or less equal benefits for all not to be true social rights. In fact, a close reading of Marshall (e.g. 1964*b*: 29–30, 32) reveals that he did not mean to exclude either means tested benefits or income- or contribution-related benefits. He cast his net very broadly (1964*b*: 8):

> By social element [of citizenship] I mean the whole range from the right to a modicum of economic welfare and security to the right to share to the full in the social heritage and to live the life of a civilized being according to the standards prevailing in the society.

As one can see, Marshall means much more than access to public transfers and publicly provided services. Rather he means to extend the concept to the right to active participation in society. This is the reason for his extensive discussion of public education, which is often not even considered part of the modern welfare state since it predated the Bismarckian sickness insurance law of 1883, which is widely considered to be the first piece of modern social legislation. The defining feature of the social rights of citizenship is that they entail a claim for public transfers, goods, and services 'which is not proportionate to the market value of the claimant' (Marshall 1964*b*: 28). This is the basis for his most often quoted assertion that 'in the twentieth century, citizenship and the capitalist class system have been at war' (Marshall 1964*b*: 18).

In fact most contemporary welfare state research on the social rights of citizenship does not spend very much time on the question of defining social rights. After a few brief comments on Marshall, they turn to the measurement of social rights and then in most cases to examining the determinants of social rights.[1] In the comparative social policy literature, Esping-Andersen (1990), Orloff (1993*b*), and Room (2000) stand out for their lengthy discussions of social citizenship and its twin concept decommodification.

Esping-Andersen (1990: 21) begins his discussion with the explicit statement that 'social rights . . . granted on the basis of citizenship . . . entail a decommodification of the status of individuals *vis-à-vis* the market'. He goes on to offer two different definitions of decommodification, which imply different operationalizations. Initially (1990: 23), he states that, in decommodifying welfare states, 'citizens can freely, and without potential loss of job, income, or general welfare, opt out of work when they consider it necessary'. Later (1990: 37), arguing that decommodification was not absolute but a matter of degree, he defines decommodification as 'the degree to which individuals, or families, can uphold a socially acceptable standard of living independent of market participation'. Both of these definitions are consistent with Marshall's notion of citizenship replacing the market as a distributive mechanism. Though not contradictory, they are not the same and would not be measured in the same way. The first assumes the person has a job (he/she is commodified) and can exit employment without income loss, thus high income replacement rates in transfer programmes would appear to be the sine qua non of decommodification. Generally, high income replacement rates are the product of earnings and contribution related transfer programmes and thus are not strictly speaking a right of *citizenship*. Nevertheless, they do substitute political allocation for market allocation, so they are consistent with Marshall's concept, and Marshall himself is explicit that such social insurance systems should be included as social rights. The second definition does not imply employment and thus would be measured by the benefits

---

[1] The most explicit discussion of the definition of social rights by a scholar of comparative social policy is Janoski (1998). However, this book is not a work on comparative social policy but rather on political theory, a field in which the topic of citizenship, including social citizenship, is frequently addressed.

provided on the basis of citizenship rather than employment or past social insurance contributions. To be consistent with this definition, transfers or services would have to be provided equally to each citizen or family or on the basis of need (e.g. larger families receive higher child allowances).

As we will see in the next section, Esping-Andersen's (1990) measure of decommodification taps the first of these two dimensions, which, since it assumes the person has a job, is gender biased, as Orloff (1993b) among others has pointed out. Orloff (1993b) argues that, for women, access to paid work (that is, the right to be commodified in the first place) is a fundamental social right. In addition, gendering the study of social rights would entail examining the extent to which the welfare state takes over some of the caring functions of the family (what Esping-Andersen (1999) in a later work calls de-familialization), the treatment of unpaid work, women's capacity to maintain autonomous households, and the extent to which citizenship (and not employment) is the basis for welfare state claims. I will discuss how some of these gendered dimensions have been and might be measured in the next section. Suffice it to note here that had Esping-Andersen also attempted to measure the second of his two definitions, it would have forced him directly to address Orloff's point about citizenship as a basis for welfare state claims.

Room (2000) argues that Esping-Andersen's conceptualization of decommodification as a fundamental cure for working class alienation in capitalism is insufficient because he only partially captures Marx and Polanyi's critique of the capitalist market society as labour commodifier. Marx argues that the commodification of labour results in working class alienation, not only because this limits workers' access to sustenance and consumption by making them reliant on selling labour, but also because commodification takes out the self-creation or self-development potential in work. Room suggests that Esping-Andersen pays sufficient attention to the consumption side, but not to the self-development side of labour commodification. In his reply to Room, Esping-Andersen (2000) acknowledges that human self-development is increasingly integrated with labour market participation and that this activation-based approach is also a key strategy in coping with emerging new social risks. Furthermore, he implies that this activation-based strategy of social protection cannot be effectively captured through the concept of decommodification.

Pulling Orloff's and Room's intervention and Esping-Andersen's reply together, one sees a common thread, namely that the conception of the social rights of citizenship should include a right to satisfying work and human self development and not just a 'a modicum of economic welfare and security'. Thus, social rights should include the whole range of public human capital investment policies from early childhood education to higher education, adult education, active labour market policy, and health care as well as work and family reconciliation policies such as public day care and maternity and parental leave.

Before moving on to measurement, it is necessary to address the issue of whether means-tested benefits can confer citizenship rights. It is commonplace in the comparative social policy literature to contrast modern welfare state legislation to legislation in the poor law tradition which involves means tests and is discretionary on the part of the authorities, and thus is not a 'social right'. However, in his writings on Antipodean transfer systems, Castles has questioned the assumption that income or means testing automatically indicates that no social right is granted by the legislation in question. He points out that (1) only well-to-do citizens are targeted out of the system, and (2) the authorities have very little discretionary latitude on whom to include and exclude from benefits. Thus, most citizens of these countries expect that they will receive a pension as a social right upon retirement. Similarly, the recent pension legislation of the Bachelet government in Chile guarantees a minimum pension to all Chileans of retirement age in the bottom 60 per cent of the income distribution. It is highly likely that these pensions will be considered a 'right' by the affected population. Similarly conditional cash transfers, such as Brazil's *Bolsa Familia*, should be considered a social right provided that the benefit is triggered more or less automatically by an income test and does provide authorities with much discretionary latitude.[2]

THE MEASUREMENT OF SOCIAL RIGHTS

Early quantitative analyses of cross-national variation in 'welfare state effort' followed the pioneering work of Wilensky (1975) and operationalized welfare state generosity as social spending (variously defined) as a percentage of GDP (see e.g Stephens 1979; Korpi 1983; Hicks and Swank 1984). From the outset, these researchers recognized that this was at best a proxy for what they were really interested in, which was welfare state redistribution or, following Marshall, some notion of social rights. Expenditure is pushed up by growth of the recipient populations; the aged and the unemployed, but also those on work injury insurance, early pensions, and in labour market programmes. Quantitative studies attempted to control for this by entering the proportions of the population aged and unemployed in the analysis as independent variables. Unfortunately, it was not possible to control for the other recipient populations. Even if it were possible, expenditure measures could not tap the different structuring of social expenditure in different countries.

The solution that gradually emerged in the field of comparative social policy was to measure social rights directly. An early attempt in this direction was Day's (1978) measure of pension rights. Myles (1984; see also DeVinney 1984) brought Day's work into the mainstream of comparative social policy research by setting it in a theoretical frame and carrying out a multivariate analysis of the determinants of his revised version of Day's index for fifteen OECD countries. Myles's index of pension quality scored each country's pension system on a 1–10 scale on eight items. Three items

---

[2] Inclusion of investments in education and income-tested benefits as social rights is consistent with Marshall's conception. His 1950 essay contains discussions of both matters.

measured the pension level, a quasi-replacement rate at different levels of income. The remaining five dimensions measured cost of living adjustments, means testing, coverage, retirement age flexibility, and degree of retirement test.

These early social rights measures concerned one programme at one point in time. In 1981, Korpi and Esping-Andersen undertook a much more ambitious research project, which later become known as the Social Citizenship Indicators Programme (SCIP),[3] the building of a dataset on social rights in five different welfare state programmes in eighteen OECD countries measured in roughly five year intervals from 1930 on. The countries are the universe of advanced capitalist democracies with populations over one million which have been continuously democratic since World War II: Australia, Austria, Belgium, Canada, Denmark, Finland, France, West Germany, Ireland, Italy, Japan, Netherlands, New Zealand, Norway, Sweden, Switzerland, the United Kingdom, and the United States. This same set of countries is included in virtually all of the quantitative analyses of comparative social policy and comparative political economy of advanced capitalist democracies (e.g. see Hicks 1999, Huber and Stephens 2001a; Swank 2002; Iversen 2005).

The programmes covered in SCIP are unemployment insurance, sickpay, disability insurance, pensions, and family benefits. For unemployment insurance, sickpay, and disability, SCIP collected data on replacement rates for an 'average production worker' in several categories of family types, coverage, waiting days, duration of benefits, and qualifying conditions. For pensions, SCIP collected data on replacement rates for different categories of family types and income levels, qualifying conditions, source of funding, and coverage. These data were put in the public domain in 2007 and are available at https://dspace.it.su.se/dspace/handle/10102/7 (Korpi and Palme 2007). The SCIP data on family benefits, which are not yet in the public domain, include data on child allowances, tax credits, and tax deductions, and a number of programme characteristics such as whether the mother or the father received the child allowance and whether the benefits were universal or employment based (Wennemo 1994). The first publication from the SCIP data was Korpi's 1989 *American Sociological Review* article on sick pay, which was followed by dissertation monographs on four of the five programmes: pensions (Palme 1990), sickpay (Kangas 1991), family benefits (Wennemo 1994), and unemployment (Carroll 1999) and by numerous journal articles and conference papers.

A 1980 cross-section of the SCIP data was the primary basis for Esping-Andersen's analysis in *The Three Worlds of Welfare Capitalism* (1990). The SCIP data were used to operationalize his master concept of decommodification, both dimensions of his measure of welfare state socialism and one of the two dimensions of his measure of welfare liberalism. The overall decommodification index is the sum of the sub-indices for pensions, sick pay, and unemployment insurance. The decommodification score for pensions is calculated from four dimensions: (1) minimum benefit level, (2) standard benefit level, (3) the length of the contribution period, and (4) the

---

[3] The original title of the project was Svensk Socialpolitik i International Belysning.

individual's share of pension financing. The decommodification scores for unemployment and sickness insurance are based on (1) benefit levels, (2) number of weeks of employment needed to qualify for benefits, (3) number of waiting days before receiving the benefit after becoming unemployed or sick, and (4) the number of weeks for which the benefit can be maintained. As I noted previously, the measure operationalizes the first of Esping-Andersen's two definitions of decommodification and thus assumes employment.

Though publications from SCIP began appearing in 1989, the data were not put in the public domain until almost twenty years later. This delay created an incentive for researchers to try to replicate the SCIP data collection, which was very laborious given the state of technology in the 1980s and early 1990s. The development of the internet and other advances in information technology changed the terrain radically and allowed a single scholar, Lyle Scruggs (2004), and a research assistant supported by a National Science Foundation grant to replicate the most important of the SCIP measures for three programmes; unemployment insurance, sick pay, and pensions on an annual basis for the period 1971–2002. The team began work on the data collection in 2001 and placed the data in the public domain in December 2004. The Comparative Welfare Entitlements Dataset (CWED) can be accessed at http://sp. uconn.edu/~scruggs/wp.htm.

The OECD Jobs Study (1994a) made sweeping claims that 'labor market rigidities' accounted for the high and persistent unemployment in Europe as compared to the United States on the basis of sparse empirical evidence. To its credit, over the next ten years, the organization conducted a massive effort to collect data relevant to the claims of the 1994 study. While most of these data were measures of employment and public expenditure, the OECD did collect measures of social rights in two welfare state arenas, unemployment insurance and employment protection laws (EPL). The unemployment insurance data are gross replacement rates in a number of different family types at two different income levels and three different durations, first year, second and third year, and fourth and fifth year. The data are biannual beginning in 1961 and are updated on a regular basis. The drawback is that they measure gross benefits, so if the benefits are taxed, they do not reflect the actual benefit to the unemployed worker. Bradley and Stephens (2007) have calculated a net replacement rate for a bout of unemployment one year long from CWED. The OECD one year gross and the CWED net replacement rate series are highly correlated (.85), so the OECD data may be useful, if a longer time series or different durations than are available in CWED data are needed. The OECD's (2004a) overall measure of EPL summarizes a number of sub-indices measuring the difficulty of layoff (notice, severance pay, etc.) and regulations restricting the use of temporary work. The data are annual and are available from 1985.

It is striking that all of the social rights measures discussed so far except the SCIP family policy measures (which are not in the public domain) share with Esping-Andersen's decommodification index that they are focused on the rights accorded an employed worker and thus are vulnerable to the criticism of such measures levelled by Orloff and Room. In the area of work and family reconciliation policies, Gornick et al. (1998) have developed a number of measures of social rights for most of the usual eighteen advanced capitalist democracies at one cross-section in the mid-1990s and this work has been greatly extended and updated by Gornick and Meyers (2003). Gauthier and Bortnik (2001) have assembled a pooled times-series dataset on parental leave and benefits with annual data from 1970 to 1999.[4] These can be accessed at http://www.soci.ucalgary.ca/FYPP/.

There are clear lacunae in the social rights data available to date. One is absence of pooled time-series data on gendered aspects of social policy, such as the work and family reconciliation policies covered in Gornick and Meyers (2003). The second is the striking absence of data on public services, given that arguably the most distinctive difference between the Nordic welfare states and the continental European welfare states is the public provision of a broad range of health, education, and welfare services in the Nordic countries. Third, the only data available on activation policies are data on spending on active labour market policies. Putting these three points together and returning to the critiques of Orloff and Room, we can observe that the available data on social rights (particularly, the pooled time-series data) almost completely neglect the right to satisfying work and human self-development. Thus, a very large part of what the welfare states do as measured by the volume of expenditure on education, health care, and social services is not tapped by the existing measures of social rights.

How do the social rights data available change our understanding of variations in welfare state generosity across countries and through time as compared to the public expenditure and employment data that have been used in most comparative welfare state studies? While Esping-Andersen's (1990) main argument for measuring welfare state effort with measures of social rights instead of social expenditure was that social rights and not expenditure was what comparative social policy scholars were actually interested in, he also criticizes social expenditure measures for being incapable of tapping the multidimensional nature of welfare state regimes. In truth, this apparent incapability was an artifact of the fact that all but a few analyses of welfare state effort to that point in time only employed one measure, mostly the ILO measure of social benefit expenditure which Wilensky used in his 1975 study. Using various measures of public expenditure on different programmes and employment, one can construct a multidimensional picture of welfare state regimes and their development through time which shows that while both continental European and Nordic welfare states are generous, continental European welfare states are transfer intensive while Nordic welfare states are service intensive and invest more in human capital and activation policies (Huber and Stephens 2001a; Iversen and Stephens 2008).

Nevertheless, there is no question that the social rights data now in the public domain allow the researcher to construct a much more nuanced description of the social policy regimes of different countries and their variation through time. Note

---

[4] Parental leave was later added to the SCIP data base (Ferrarini 2003). The SCIP parental leave data are considerably more detailed than the Gauthier and Bortnik data and allows the researcher to distinguish different types of family support.

that these data have not been in the public domain for a very long time and, in my view, it will be years before the community of comparative social policy scholars fully absorbs the information that is available in these data. Let me illustrate a few of the novel facts that emerge from examining the SCIP data for average replacement rates in three programmes for several different time points, a very small if crucial portion of the total data available from the sources outlined above (see Table 35.1). First, though social expenditure data show that the continental Christian democratic welfare states spend a greater proportion of GDP on transfer programmes than social democratic welfare states, this is not due to the fact that the transfer programmes are more generous, as one can see from the table. Rather expenditure is high because the recipient populations, the unemployed, the retired, and the disabled are large, partly as results of labour-shedding policies in the 1980s and 1990s, which placed many able bodied people under retirement age in early pensions or 'disability' pensions. Second, the 'three worlds of welfare capitalism' are not detectable in 1950. They were created in the post-war period. Third, while social expenditure data do not reveal a clear picture of welfare state retrenchment, it is very clear from the social rights data. One can see by comparing the peak year with 1995, the last year in the SCIP data now available, that retrenchment is pervasive. However, it does not lead to convergence. On the contrary, the cutbacks in sickpay and unemployment replacement rates are much more dramatic in the liberal welfare states, making these welfare states even more distinctively stingy.

As I pointed out above, the SCIP data that have been put in the public domain and the CWED tap social transfers aimed at the 'old social risks' faced by the average production worker in a male breadwinner family. Table 35.2 presents some data on services and gendered policies. Only the parental leave data are a true measure of social rights and only those data are available through time (Gauthier and Bortnik 2001). These parental leave data follow a different pattern from that shown in the old social risk data in Table 35.1. The Nordic countries are not distinctive until the mid-1980s and become much more clearly so by the late 1990s. Data on day care spending indicate that one would find the same thing for day care as the Nordic countries spent an average of 1.6 per cent of GDP on day care in the 1990s compared to 0.3 per cent of GDP in the other two regime types. If one had data on work and family reconciliation policies for several time points since 1970, such as the Gornick and Meyers data for the early 2000s in the first column of the table, one would certainly find a pattern of increasing Nordic distinctiveness. With regard to retrenchment of these work and family reconciliation policies, the patterns shown in the parental leave data indicate that cutbacks are much less common than in the case of the transfer programmes in Table 35.1, as only five countries experienced any cuts at all and only in Sweden, where the number of weeks of full pay fell from 57.6 to 40 in the late 1990s as a result of cuts in the replacement rate from 90 per cent to 67 per cent, were the cutbacks dramatic. Despite the cuts, Sweden still had the second most generous system in 1999.

We know even less about the cross-national differences and changes through time in the social rights to public services as no one has attempted to measure them in a

Table 35.1 Average replacement rates by welfare state regime (1950, 1995)

	Unemployment insurance				Sickpay				Pensions			
	1950	Peak	Peak year	1995	1950	Peak	Peak year	1995	1950	Peak	Peak year	1995
Social Democratic Welfare States												
Denmark	46.0	81.9	1975	57.2	7.2	78.8	1980	57.2	40.8	66.9	1985	62.2
Finland	5.0	76.1	1970	61.9	0.0	96.5	1990	86.1	29.4	91.0	1985	75.1
Norway	28.5	73.5	1975	63.5	37.5	100.0	1995	100.0	19.9	75.1	1990	70.4
Sweden	42.1	84.1	1990	76.8	18.9	90.1	1990	77.0	26.9	92.7	1985	81.6
Mean	*30.4*	*78.9*		*67.4*	*15.9*	*91.4*		*80.1*	*29.3*	*81.4*		*72.3*
Christian Democratic Welfare States												
Austria	47.4	67.5	1985	57.4	63.4	100.0	1985	95.4	59.6	76.9	1995	76.9
Belgium	42.5	77.1	1980	49.0	66.1	91.9	1975	82.6	36.4	78.0	1975	52.9
France	8.0	64.9	1985	58.0	44.1	55.7	1975	49.2	35.9	70.2	1980	68.0
Germany	40.6	79.2	1960	68.2	61.2	100.0	1995	100.0	37.7	55.4	1975	50.8
Italy	27.2	35.9	1960	34.3	60.3	83.4	1995	83.4	18.5	80.0	1990	72.5
Netherlands	41.8	83.2	1980	70.0	79.9	84.7	1975	70.0	51.7	68.4	1980	59.7
Switzerland	49.4	75.0	1995	75.0	31.8	77.4	1975	56.0	14.8	61.0	1975	43.2
Mean	*36.7*	*69.0*		*58.8*	*58.1*	*84.7*		*76.7*	*36.4*	*70.0*		*60.6*
Liberal Welfare States												
Australia	18.7	48.4	1975	38.3	18.7	48.4	1975	38.2	36.9	46.1	1995	46.1
Canada	37.7	69.6	1975	59.9	0.0	62.1	1975	49.5	30.3	54.5	1995	54.5
Ireland	36.1	72.1	1985	31.1	28.6	70.7	1984	31.1	32.3	60.7	1985	48.5
New Zealand	49.7	62.7	1985	33.2	49.7	70.5	1985	36.5	49.6	65.6	1985	50.5
UK	31.4	63.4	1975	23.4	31.5	63.4	1975	20.3	28.2	60.8	1985	57.9
USA	40.3	59.8	1975	47.0	0.0	0.0	1995	0.0	39.0	66.6	1980	65.5
Mean	*35.7*	*62.7*		*38.8*	*21.4*	*52.5*		*29.3*	*36.1*	*59.1*		*53.8*
Japan	67.3	72.6	1990	71.2	68.2	73.8	1995	73.8	18.6	74.2	1990	67.1
Grand Mean	*36.7*	*69.3*		*54.2*	*37.1*	*74.9*		*61.5*	*33.7*	*69.1*		*61.3*

Source: Korpi and Palme 2007.

Table 35.2 (Quasi-) social rights indicators of services and gendered policies (1970, 1985, 1999)

	Work & family reconciliation index	Parental leave—weeks of full pay			Skill acquistion index	Civilian government employment
		1970	1985	1999		
Social Democratic Welfare States						
Denmark	94	12.3	21.6	30.0	3.47	21
Finland	74	3.5	34.4	36.4	0.55	13
Norway	80	3.8	18.0	42.0	1.77	22
Sweden	89	16.6	27.7	40.0	1.52	22
Mean	84	9.1	25.4	37.1	1.83	19.5
Christian Democratic Welfare States						
Austria		12.0	16.0	16.0	0.27	13
Belgium	73	8.4	11.1	11.6	0.27	9
France	66	7.0	14.4	16.0	0.16	14
Germany	55	14.0	14.0	14.0	-0.13	8
Italy		13.6	17.2	17.2	0.03	8
Netherlands	65	12.0	12.0	16.0	0.47	6
Switzerland		0.0	0.0	0.0	-0.03	9
Mean	65	9.6	12.1	13.0	0.15	9.6
Liberal Welfare States						
Australia		0.0	0.0	0.0	-0.86	10
Canada	36	10.0	9.0	8.3	0.39	14
Ireland		4.1	9.8	9.8	-0.61	7
New Zealand		0.0	0.0	0.0	0.26	
UK	45	6.5	6.1	7.9	-0.29	9
USA	24	0.0	0.0	0.0	-0.42	10
Mean	35	3.4	4.2	4.3	-0.25	10.0
Japan		7.2	7.2	8.4	-0.92	6
Grand Mean	64	7.3	12.1	15.2	0.33	11.8

Sources: Gornick and Meyers 2003; Gauthier and Bortnik 2001; Nelson 2008; Huber et al. 2004.

systematic way. I include two measures of public service effort in Table 35.2, civilian government employment as a percentage of the working age population and Nelson's (2008) index of skill acquisition. The skills acquisition index attempts to measure the degree to which education and training systems provide broad access to basic and higher education as well as life long learning. It is constructed from numerous measures for states' financial investment in education as well as measures for the structure of educational institutions and formal regulation of firm-based training policies. As one can see, there is a marked difference between the social democratic regime and the other two regime types on these two measures.

Public health spending as a percentage of total health spending indicates that Nordic distinctiveness in health care emerged already by 1970. In terms of investment in human capital, data on spending on active labour market policy, higher education, and education at all levels show that a distinctive Nordic pattern of high spending did not emerge until the 1990s (Iversen and Stephens 2008). While Sweden was a pioneer in active labour market policy and in overall educational spending, Canada (8.5 per cent of GDP) and the United States (7.4 per cent) equalled or exceeded Sweden in education spending in 1970.

In his exchange with Room, Esping-Andersen notes that employment protection legislation, which clearly can be seen as a decommodifying social right, does not follow the same pattern as his measures of transfer payment decommodification as the continental European countries, and especially the Mediterranean countries, have stricter EPL than the Nordic countries. He also notes that EPL is somewhat of a zero sum game as stricter EPL makes it harder for outsiders, generally women and youth, to get jobs. Thus, if we consider the right to (satisfying) work to be a social right, extending some people's social rights can actually detract from those of others, something not envisioned in the Marshallian conception of social rights.

In the preceding paragraphs, I have noted that while one can see the same ordering of regimes in the 'old social rights' transfers shown in Table 35.1 that Esping-Andersen found for his decommodification index, one finds a different ordering for EPL, gendered social policies, and public health, education, and welfare services. Moreover, as originally noted by Palme (1990, also see Carroll 1999), the various components of Esping-Andersen's original measure (e.g. coverage, replacement rate, duration, qualifying conditions) do not co-vary that strongly, which suggests that one should analyse the determinants and effects of the components separately.

The Determinants and Outcomes of Variations in Social Rights

Myles's (1984) cross-sectional analysis and Korpi's (1989) pooled time-series analysis of determinants of social rights measures appeared to confirm straightforwardly the early power resources theory claims based on analyses of cross-national data on social spending (e.g. Stephens 1979; Korpi 1983), that measures of working class power, left government, and/or union strength were the best predictors of welfare state effort. Subsequent analyses present a more nuanced view (e.g. Esping-Andersen 1990; Palme 1990; Kangas 1991; Carroll 1999): consistent with the observation above that the various components of social rights were not that highly correlated, the determinants of social rights in these studies varied depending on what dimensions of social rights one measured. Esping-Andersen (1990) made the case for the existence of 'three worlds of welfare capitalism' by showing that different measures had different determinants. The core of Esping-Andersen's explanation is political: the dominance of social democracy, Christian democracy, and secular centre and right parties explained whether a country ended up in the social democratic, conservative, or liberal world.

Esping-Andersen's analysis is cross-sectional and given that there are more hypothesized determinants in the comparative welfare state literature than there are countries in such a cross-sectional analysis, one would have hoped that his arguments would have been tested in pooled time-series analysis. Unfortunately, no one has attempted to do this. Moreover, examining the results of existing pooled data analyses of the determinants of social rights does not yield a clear picture. Working with pooled data presents a number of methodological and measurement problems which are still being debated in political science and sociology. Chief among these are choice of levels or change as the dependent variable; inclusion of unit dummies or its equivalent, fixed effects; inclusion of a lagged dependent variable; and corrections for auto-regression.

My co-authors and I have carved out a clear position on these issues (Huber and Stephens 2001a; Huber et al. 2008; Huo et al. 2008): We use levels of the dependent variable, no unit dummies, no lagged dependent variables, and first order auto-regressive corrections (Prais Winsten regressions).[5] My co-authors and I have carried extensive analyses of the social rights data available from CWED and the OECD, some of it published (Huo et al. 2008) and some as yet unpublished.[6] The dependent variables are the various measures of social rights and the independent variables are Christian democratic government, social democratic government, and ten control variables operationalizing various other hypothesized determinants of welfare state effort. The results of these analyses for the partisanship variables are summarized in Table 35.3. The first four measures are Scruggs and Allan's (2006a) replication of Espring-Andersen's decommodification measures with the CWED data. As one would expect from Esping-Andersen's analysis, social democratic government and Christian democratic government are very strongly related to the overall index and the pension index. However, the political determinants of unemployment and sickpay decommodification are different and it is perhaps most surprising that social democratic government is not related to unemployment decommodification.[7] From the OECD data on unemployment replacement rates one can see that part of the reason for this is that social democracy and Christian democracy have different effects depending on the duration of benefits.

As I have noted, the SCIP and CWED social rights data on replacement rates show that retrenchment has been pervasive but only deep in some of the liberal

---

[5] See the cited publications for justifications of these methodological decisions.

[6] I have not systematically replicated these analyses on the SCIP data, but given the very high correlations between the SCIP data and Scruggs data on sick pay and unemployment insurance, I do not expect any differences on these measures. Differences on pension rights which are only moderately correlated in the two datasets are possible.

[7] This is consistent with Carroll's (1999) finding using SCIP data.

Table 35.3 Results of regression on social rights measures

	Left government	Christian Democratic government
Overall decommodification	+++	++
Pension decommodification	++	+++
Sickpay decommodification	+++	0
Unemployment decommodifcation	0	+
EPL	0	+++
Unemployment replacement rate (4th–5th year)[a]	0	+
Unemployment replacement rate (1st year)[a]	+	0
Parental Leave (weeks of full pay)	+	+

Notes: Level of significance: +++ = .001, ++ = .01, + = .05
[a] Workers with two thirds of median wage.

welfare states. With regard to the causes of retrenchment, the dominant view of welfare state retrenchment has been that demographic and economic factors have pushed partisanship aside as the main cause of welfare state change (P. Pierson 2001a). Social rights data have challenged this view as both Korpi and Palme (2003) and Allan and Scruggs (2004) have shown that left government does retard welfare state retrenchment.

More complete data on social rights would certainly considerably nuance the picture of pervasive retrenchment. We have already seen that the parental leave data do not show the same pattern as one sees in Table 35.1. I contend that the pattern shown in the parental leave data would be replicated by social rights data on a number of other policies which also tap the movement from addressing old social risks to new social risks, from passive welfare states to active welfare states. Other work and family reconciliation policies, such as day care; active labour market policies; basic, higher and continuing education would almost certainly show a general pattern of expansion with the Nordic countries in the lead. By contrast, EPL, the quintessential old welfare state policy aimed at protecting labour market insiders, shows a general pattern of decline, especially with regard to restrictions on temporary work.

Perhaps because the data have only been in the public domain for a few years, there are relatively few multivariate analyses of the impact of measures of social rights on other outcomes of interest to comparative welfare state researchers, such as poverty and redistribution.[8] Scruggs (2006, 2008) has examined the impact of his measures of social rights on absolute and relative poverty among various population groups and on government redistribution and poverty reduction. Controlling for a number of other possible determinants of the dependent variable, Scruggs finds the

---

[8] There are many studies by SCIP researchers which show bivariate relationships between SCIP measures and inequality and poverty (e.g. Korpi and Palme 1998; Ferrarini 2003).

social rights measures have a significant and large impact on all of these welfare state outcomes. My co-authors and I have examined the impact of the social rights measures on overall employment levels and women's employment (Bradley and Stephens 2007; Huo et al. 2008; Nelson and Stephens 2008). We find that high short-term unemployment replacement rates, sickpay generosity, and parental leave (the social democratic pattern shown in Table 35.3) have positive effects on both employment variables, while high long-term unemployment replacement rates and high EPL (the Christian democratic pattern) have a negative impact on both variables.

CHAPTER 36

INEQUALITY AND POVERTY

PETER SAUNDERS

INTRODUCTION

REDUCING inequality and combating poverty are goals that have driven the development of the welfare state. Most affluent democracies display what Myles (2006: 150) refers to as 'strong egalitarian sentiments' that find expression in community concern over inequality and political voice in support for redistribution. The extent of inequality and poverty, and the impact of policy on them, are important indicators of policy success; and although the fact that governments rarely announce their poverty or inequality reduction targets makes it difficult to assess performance against specified objectives, there have been recent attempts by governments in the United Kingdom (and Ireland) to set specific poverty reduction targets, using indicators informed by research (Department for Work and Pensions 2003). There are also many dimensions of inequality and alternative ways of conceptualizing poverty that further compound the task of measuring incidence and establishing the impact of policy. These conceptual and methodological issues must be addressed before it is possible to establish how much inequality and poverty exists, or to estimate the impact of policy.

These challenges have not prevented researchers from conducting studies of the impact of social policy on inequality and poverty, many of them with a comparative cross-national focus. In reviewing the main lessons to emerge from this literature, this chapter focuses on the experience of high-income OECD countries. Not only do these countries have the most developed (but varied) welfare states, they also produce the data needed to measure incidence and identify impacts. They also differ greatly in terms of inequality profiles and poverty rates, providing scope to explain observed differences and relate them to policy. This focus does not deny the important role that social policy plays in ameliorating inequality and poverty in middle-income and developing countries, a topic touched on in some of the later chapters discussing particular families of nations.

This chapter is organized as follows: the next section reviews the problems associated with estimating the impact of policy on inequality and poverty, while the one which follows describes the measures and data used to establish and compare cross-national impacts. There then follow two further sections which review the main findings produced by studies of outcomes and impacts in the areas of inequality and poverty, respectively. The final section summarizes the main conclusions.

OUTCOMES AND IMPACTS

The welfare state embodies a set of social programmes that establish as rights a set of entitlements (often conditioned by characteristics, events, or actions) for individuals facing vulnerability at different stages of the life cycle. Many of these programmes reduce inequality and combat poverty directly by raising the incomes of those at the bottom and by financing these transfers by imposing progressive taxes and contributions on those in the middle and at the top. Others operate indirectly, by providing access to services that those with low incomes would otherwise be unable to afford. The inequalities resulting from the free operation of market forces span many dimensions, but much of the policy focus—and the main focus of this discussion—is on inequality in *income*. Income is both a major determinant of the purchasing power that drives market forces and a signpost of success in the competitive economic struggles that take place in markets. It is not therefore surprising that state intervention in market processes would seek to influence how incomes are distributed. The comparative information on the distribution of wealth that has only recently become available through the Luxembourg Wealth Study (LWS), has provided a basis for researchers to begin examining national differences and relate them to social policy variations (see Sierminska et al. 2006, and Yates and Bradbury 2009).

The processes that shape these interventions can be analysed by distinguishing between: *market income* (MI), which reflects the return on market activity in the form of earnings, self-employment, and interest on investment; *gross income* (GI), which adds in the cash transfers (CT) received from the state (and from private sources); and *disposable income* (DI)—which deducts the state-imposed income taxes and income-related social contributions (TX). The identity $DI = GI - TX = MI + CT - TX$ links the different elements in the redistributional chain and provides a framework for estimating their impact. Information on these variables can be collected at both the macro (National Accounts) and micro (household income surveys) levels, making it possible to compare the different distributions and estimate the distributional impact of each link in the chain. Thus, a comparison of the distributions of MI and GI will reveal the redistributional impact of transfers, while a comparison of the distributions of GI and DI will indicate the redistributive impact of taxes.

Many studies have used this framework to examine the distributional impact of the welfare state, focusing on the relative strength of different policy instruments (e.g. transfers versus taxes; benefits to working-age versus pensions to older people) within and between countries (Atkinson et al. 1995; Förster and Vleminckx 2004; Hills 2004; OECD 2008a). However, measuring the *extent of inequality* in the income distribution is more straightforward than estimating the *distributional impact* of government policy because the latter involves comparing two situations, one of which (the 'non-government counterfactual') is not observable. Thus, when the distributions of DI and MI are used to estimate the impact of government transfers and taxes, the implicit assumption is that the distribution of MI is the situation that would prevail in the absence of these government programmes. But if those programmes did not exist, people's behavior would change in ways that would 'fill the gap' provided by government (e.g. individuals would have to work harder and save for their own retirement, or take out insurance against unemployment or disability) and this would lead to changes in MI, and in its distribution. By assuming the existing distribution of MI as the counterfactual, these behavioural changes are ignored—an assumption that is at odds with the literature on the (dis)incentive effects of transfers and taxes (Atkinson and Mogensen 1993). Although it is possible to model the behavioural impact of policy and build these marginal effects into the estimates of distributional impact, much of the comparative literature has focused on estimating the distributional impact of government as a whole, a task for which the modelling of marginal impacts provides little guidance.

These induced effects exert an important influence on how redistribution is measured, as has been highlighted in recent work by the OECD (2008a) on the redistributional impact of public pensions. If the initial (pre-pension) ranking of incomes is done on the basis of market income, then pensioners appear at the bottom of the pre-transfer distribution but much higher up in the post-transfer distribution, implying a strong redistributional effect. In contrast, if the ranking is based on post-transfer (disposable) incomes, pensioners fall just below the middle of the pre-transfer distribution, and just above the middle of the post-transfer distribution— implying a much weaker impact (OECD 2008a: 110). The first approach implicitly assumes that the existing distribution of market income is the counterfactual against which to assess the distributional impact of pensions, whereas the latter approach assumes that retiree incomes would adjust in the absence of pensions to 'fill the gap' completely. Thus while the first approach over-estimates the impact of pensions, the latter approach under-estimates it (because the income gap will not be completely filled). Each approach thus fulfils a different purpose by addressing a different aspect of the issue.

Further complications arise from the fact that social policies not only seek to redistribute incomes once they have been generated in the market, but also to influence the structure of market incomes themselves. The term welfare capitalism (Esping-Andersen 1990) captures the complex and intricate interconnections that exist between state and market in a welfare state, and this makes it difficult to unravel those effects that are a consequence of 'welfare' from those produced by 'capitalism'—yet this is what distributional impact studies seek to do. In countries like Australia and New Zealand, for example, institutional controls over wage outcomes have produced a more equal distribution of earnings (and hence market incomes) in what has been called a 'wage earners welfare state' (F. Castles 1985). Other countries set minimum wages and have introduced laws and regulations to affect market forces in ways that protect those at risk of disadvantage and thus affect the final distribution. Although many of these effects are captured in the statistics used to study income inequality and poverty, they often show up in market incomes and are thus not attributed to state intervention, or as a policy outcome.

Welfare states not only provide cash transfers to different groups, they also provide access to services that generate in-kind benefits to the recipients. Public healthcare systems provide healthcare services on the basis of assessed health need rather than ability to pay, and other services provide free or subsidized access to groups defined on the basis of their frailty (elder care services), disability (mental health services) or age (childcare services). These provisions affect the income distribution in two ways: first, they provide a platform from which individuals who might otherwise be prevented from participating in the labour market are able to do so, thus increasing their market incomes; second, the benefits themselves have an implicit value and can be viewed as contributing non-cash income to recipients (or beneficiaries) that will have distributional consequences. It is difficult to estimate the size of the former effects and few studies have attempted to do so, although the distributional impact of imputed non-cash benefits has attracted more attention (Smeeding et al. 1993). There are significant practical and methodological challenges that have to be resolved before non-cash benefits can be imputed to individuals as income. The benefits provided by most healthcare systems and other public schemes are a form of 'insurance against adversity' (Hills 2004: 184) and are thus received by all, not just those who become ill. Such benefits are often provided by employers and do not appear as part of state activity in the data, even if they are mandated by government fiat.

MEASURES AND DATA

Inequality and poverty are related but distinct issues. Community concern over the former is often expressed as concern over 'the (growing) gap between rich and poor' (Osberg and Smeeding 2006) illustrating that the two are closely related. Even when poverty is measured in relative terms, it captures only one element of the income distribution (the percentage below an income cut-off, or poverty line) and can thus move independently of inequality, defined across the whole distribution. However, the task of reducing relative poverty is made more difficult when there is more inequality, as many studies have observed (e.g. Bradbury and Jäntti 1999).

The two indicators of inequality most commonly employed in studies of policy impact are the Gini coefficient and the P90/P10 percentile ratio. The Gini captures the overall variation in incomes by measuring how far the actual distribution differs from one in which all incomes are distributed equally. The P90/P10 ratio better captures the impact of programmes that affect those with low or high incomes that are the targets of many social policies. The value of both indicators is affected by the choice between alternative units of analysis (e.g. the nuclear family vs. the household), by the equivalence scale used to adjust incomes for differences in need and by the weighting of different units (e.g. by households or individuals) (Atkinson 1998b). These technical issues of definition and measurement will affect conclusions drawn about the size of policy impacts.

Similar issues arise when measuring poverty, where further controversy exists over where to set the poverty line and, more fundamentally, whether income is capable of capturing deprivation, or whether an approach that captures living standards (or functioning) more directly is required (Ringen 1987; Sen 1985; Nolan and Whelan 1996). The latter approach seeks to establish that those identified as poor in income terms are experiencing the living conditions that are expected to be associated with it by focusing on *achieved outcomes* (at least as far as they are reported in surveys) as opposed to *available income.*

Many countries have only recently begun to apply the deprivation approach (Boarini and d'Ercole 2006; OECD 2008a: ch. 7), but it is not yet possible to draw any robust conclusions about the impact and effectiveness of social policy on deprivation, within or between countries.[1] Progress in addressing this issue will be constrained by the fact that, unlike studies of income poverty, it is not possible to estimate what deprivation would have been in the absence of existing policies and use this counterfactual to estimate the impact of policy.

Most comparative studies avoid the controversy surrounding where to set the poverty line by using an arbitrary but comparable measure set at a given percentage (most often 50 or 60 per cent) of median income. These poverty lines vary between countries, but represent the same point in each country's income distribution. The focus is primarily static—how much poverty exists at a particular point in time and how has policy affected it?—whereas there is also interest (particularly among policymakers) in understanding and influencing the persistence of poverty—how many of those who were poor last year remain poor today and what are the key pathways into and out of poverty? These questions can only be answered with the use

---

[1] The OECD has recently argued that the estimates it presents are not directly comparable, and argues that: 'Better comparative measures can be achieved only through greater ex ante standardization of surveys, so as to include a larger set of items that are comparable across countries' (OECD 2008a: 194).

of longitudinal (panel) data and an increasing array of countries are collecting the data required to estimate poverty persistence (OECD 2008a: chs. 6 and 8).

When estimating the impact of government programmes on inequality and poverty it is important to distinguish between the overall *size* of programmes (how much income is transferred) and how they are *structured* (the degree to which benefits are targeted). Heavily targeted (means-tested) schemes concentrate assistance on those with lowest incomes (or economic resources more generally), but they may not have as large a distributional impact as schemes that provide higher benefits on a more universal basis because the quantum of funds redistributed is then generally much larger. Universal systems tend to attract greater political support because the benefits provided are more widely spread (Le Grand 1982), whereas targeted schemes produce high effective marginal tax rates (as a consequence of means-testing) and are thus more likely to create disincentives to acquire income through market activity. This can create poverty traps for those with low income, generating more market inequality which state transfers are then shown to reduce (relative to the assumed counterfactual—see above).

In order to draw conclusions about the impact of policy on inequality and poverty, the data used must be comparable, otherwise the consequences of definitional differences between countries may be incorrectly identified as policy impacts. The use of national data that are not comparable can have major effects on empirical relationships. For example, Atkinson (2004) shows that the relationship between political structure and income distribution estimated by Birchfield and Crepaz (1998) is influenced by the authors' use of national income distribution figures. Once comparative estimates (derived from the Luxembourg Income Study—see below) are used, the political structure variable is no longer statistically significant, casting doubt on the authors' original claims about the role of political structure.

The demand for comparable microdata on economic well-being and inequality fuelled the establishment of the Luxembourg Income Study (LIS) in the early 1980s to develop a comparative household income microdata base by adjusting national data sets to conform to a standardized conceptual and definitional template (Smeeding 2004). The LIS project has set 'new standards for all comparative research' (Atkinson 2004: 166), and LIS data have been used in a major comparative study of income distribution produced by the OECD (Atkinson et al. 1995), have been widely cited by international agencies like the World Bank, the International Labour Organization (ILO) and the United Nations Development Programme (UNDP), and have formed the basis of a large number of independent academic studies (see Smeeding et al. 1990; Kenworthy 2004; Gottschalk and Smeeding 2000). The LIS project began in 1983 with seven countries but now includes five waves of data for twenty-five countries spanning two decades (further information can be found at www.lisproject.org).

Comparative data can also be generated by producing national statistics that conform to an internationally-agreed template that relates to a specific topic, e.g. inequality among families with children, or the impact of taxes and benefits on average production workers (Förster and Pearson 2002; OECD 2008j). This ('model family') approach has been widely used to compare child benefits packages and their impact on the well-being of children (Bradshaw and Finch 2002; Bradshaw et al. 2006). The approach has the advantage that because only a specific sub-set of variables needs to be rendered comparable, it can provide more up-to-date information. Against this, the figures do not provide the flexibility that the LIS unit record data provide, and data from both sources should ideally be combined.

REDISTRIBUTION AND INEQUALITY

Given that most government social programmes provide income transfers to those with low incomes and impose income-related taxes on those higher up the distribution, it would be surprising if they did not reduce income equality. These expectations are confirmed by the results from a large number of comparative (and national) studies conducted over many decades that have examined the distributional impact of government benefits and taxes (Reynolds and Smolensky 1977; Atkinson et al. 1995; Hills 2004; Kenworthy 2004; ILO 2008; OECD 2008a). However, analysts and policy-makers are not only interested in establishing whether redistribution takes place, but also how the degree of redistribution is related to the structure (progressivity) and size (spending level) of programmes. Research on this issue has generated a more diverse and contested set of findings about the relationships between programme size, structure of benefits and distributional impact.

The figures in Table 36.1 reveal large differences in the amount allocated to social spending in OECD countries, as well as in income inequality and poverty. The Gini coefficient varies from 0.23 in Denmark and Sweden to 0.38 in the United States—a difference of over 65 per cent, and the poverty rate in Turkey is well over three times higher than that in Denmark and Sweden. In Sweden, an individual at the 10th percentile of the distribution receives around 36 per cent of the income of an individual at the 90th percentile, whereas the corresponding figures are 23 per cent in Ireland and 17 per cent in the United States. If these two latter countries experienced the same degree of inequality as Sweden, the incomes of those at the 10th percentile could (ignoring second-round behavioural effects) increase by 35 per cent and 111 per cent, respectively. Even if these are overestimates, they still highlight the powerful effects of redistribution on individual incomes.

Table 36.1 also suggests that the relationship between social spending on cash benefits (expressed as a percentage of GDP) and income inequality across OECD countries is rather weak.[2] The average Gini coefficient in the three countries with the highest spending ratio (Austria, France, and Italy) is lower at 0.30 than in the three

[2] The ILO (2008: fig. 5.1) has shown that the relationship between social transfer spending and income inequality also exists across a broader range of countries, describing it as 'a relatively strong negative association' (ILO 2008: 129).

Table 36.1 Social expenditure, income inequality, and poverty rates in OECD countries (mid-2000s)

Country	Expenditure (percentage of GDP):		Gini Coefficient for disposable Income	P90/ P10 ratio	Poverty Rate (50% of median income)
	Cash benefits	Benefits in Kind			
Australia	8.1	6.7	0.30	3.95	12.4
Austria	18.4	8.2	0.27	3.27	6.6
Belgium	16.2	9.1	0.27	3.43	8.8
Canada	8.8	9.4	0.32	4.12	12.0
Czech Republic	11.4	7.8	0.27	3.20	5.8
Denmark	13.8	11.8	0.23	2.72	5.3
Finland	15.3	9.9	0.27	3.21	7.3
France	17.5	10.8	0.28	3.39	7.1
Germany	15.9	9.9	0.30	3.98	11.0
Greece	13.4	7.1	0.32	4.39	12.6
Hungary	13.8	8.7	0.29	3.36	7.1
Ireland	8.4	7.7	0.33	4.41	14.8
Italy	16.7	7.7	0.35	4.31	11.4
Japan	10.2	8.1	0.32	4.77	14.9
Luxembourg	13.9	8.8	0.26	3.25	8.1
Netherlands	11.1	8.5	0.27	3.23	7.7
New Zealand	9.7	8.4	0.34	4.27	10.6
Norway	10.9	10.1	0.28	2.83	6.8
Poland	15.7	4.9	0.37	5.63	14.6
Slovak Republic	10.2	6.1	0.27	3.26	8.1
Spain	13.1	7.4	0.32	4.59	14.1
Sweden	14.5	13.6	0.23	2.79	5.3
Switzerland	11.8	7.8	0.28	4.21	8.7
Turkey	8.1	5.6	0.43	6.49	17.5
United Kingdom	10.3	10.5	0.34	4.21	6.3
United States	8.0	7.8	0.38	5.91	17.1

Sources: OECD 2009*a* (accessed 19 Jan. 2009) and OECD 2008*a*: Tables 1.A2.2 and 5.A2.1.

lowest spending countries (Australia, Turkey, and the United States), where it averages 0.37. However, inequality is lower in low-spending Australia than in high-spending Italy, with the former closely resembling Austria and France and the latter performing similarly to the United States. This suggests that total transfer spending may not be the best measure of programme impact and that other factors play a role in influencing overall effects.

The evidence supports both propositions. For example, wage inequality has an important impact on overall income inequality, but is influenced by labour market institutions (ILO 2008: ch. 3), while many studies have shown that the employment rate is closely associated with income inequality, both directly and indirectly through its impact on earnings inequality (although this latter relationship is complicated by the different approaches used to study these two dimensions of inequality).[3] On balance, the comparative evidence indicates that:

- Cash benefits are more redistributive than the taxes/contributions that finance them (OECD 2008a; ILO 2008).
- Benefits paid to working-age individuals/households are more redistributive than benefits paid to older people (OECD 2008a; Castles 2009a).
- These patterns are broadly unchanged when the non-cash benefits derived from services provided free or subsidized by governments—although the method used to impute these benefits affects the results (Smeeding et al. 1993).

There is less agreement about the relative distributional impact of universal and selective (means-tested) systems, where issues relating to the disincentive effects produced by means-testing and the relationship between political support and universalism remain largely unresolved. These issues can only be answered within a causal (modeling) framework that seeks to explain differences in spending levels and outcomes, as opposed to the statistical (largely correlation-based) explanations that underpin the comparisons described above.

The impact of political forces on the shape, growth and distributional impact of the welfare state has generated a large number of comparative studies over the last three decades (Wilensky 1975; Korpi 1983; Castles and Obinger 2007). Many of these studies demonstrate that 'politics matters', as reflected in the following statement:

> Egalitarian capitalism is largely a product of strong unions and social democratic political parties. Sometimes separately but often in concert, these organizations put in place a set of institutions (collective bargaining, coordinated wage setting, corporatist policymaking) and policies (education, social welfare, active labour market, family, fiscal monetary) that reduce the degree of inequality produced by the market. (Kenworthy 2004: 171)

However, much of the empirical analysis that supports such claims is derived from rudimentary models that are incapable of identifying the subtle and complex relationships at work. Thus, Castles (2009a: 54) has recently claimed that the degree to which governments are left-leaning (measured by the number of cabinet seats held by left-wing parties) has exerted a 'hugely significant' effect on the level of social spending relative to GDP. This effect is shown to exist for social spending on working-age cash benefits and other services, but not on spending on cash benefits for older people, or health expenditure, and is stronger (i.e. statistically more significant) than the effects associated with economic variables such as economic growth and the unemployment rate. Expenditure on working-age programmes is also shown to be significantly inversely correlated with the Gini coefficient of inequality (and the poverty rate), which suggests that further disaggregation of the spending figures (e.g. by programme

---

[3] The most important of these is that studies of earnings inequality focus on the distribution of pre-tax (gross) individual earnings, whereas the focus of most income distribution studies is on post-tax (disposable) equivalized household income (Gottschalk and Smeeding 1997; OECD 2008a: ch. 3).

type or target group) should produce even stronger bi-variate correlations. If not, the observed correlations may not reflect causal mechanisms, casting doubt on the policy implications drawn from the analysis.

The above discussion has focused on how cross-sectional inequality is affected by social policies by examining vertical inequality and redistribution between rich and poor. Redistribution also takes place horizontally (i.e. between families with similar incomes who differ in other regards) and between groups defined on the basis of ethnicity or location, and many welfare state programmes seek to influence outcomes in these dimensions. Although these effects have not been identified in the discussion, their impacts are present in the data and this is another reason for caution when drawing conclusions about vertical impacts. When viewed through a life-cycle lens, those workers who contribute the taxes that pay for the pensions of retirees are the same person, viewed at different points in the life course. It follows that much of the vertical redistribution that talks place at a point in time is actually part of broader processes of intra-generational and intergenerational redistribution.

To assess the extent of life-cycle (intra-generational) redistribution, it is necessary to model the life-cycle patterns of earnings, incomes, and family circumstances of individuals over many generations, because the data are not available to observe changes over such a long period (and even if they were they would be of mainly historical interest). Such models reveal that much of the apparent redistribution *between* individuals that takes place at a point in time can be viewed as redistribution *within* the life-cycles of the same individuals. Studies conducted by Falkingham and Hills (1995) and Falkingham and Harding (1996) indicate, for the United Kingdom and Australia respectively, that the welfare state does redistribute income over the life-cycle—individuals do not simply get back in one phase what they contribute in another—but the effects are between one-quarter and one-third lower than that implied by cross-section studies.

REDISTRIBUTION AND POVERTY

Given that all welfare states spend large amounts on income transfers, it is not surprising that these transfers supplement the incomes of those who would otherwise be poor, raising them closer to or above the poverty line. Over the longer-term, many millions of older people have been assisted out of poverty by the welfare state and the poverty-reducing impact of pensions has recently been described by the Head of the OECD's Social Affairs Directorate as 'one of the triumphs of social policy in the second half of the twentieth century' (Martin and Whitehouse 2008: 21). There are, however, large country differences in relative poverty rates (see Table 36.1), raising questions about the role of differences in policy and other factors. Addressing this question requires the statistics to be disaggregated because the determinants of both poverty and benefit receipt vary greatly over the life cycle.

Most studies differentiate between the working-age and older-age (retired) populations, with the former further separated into families (or households) with and without children, and between couple and lone parent families. Pensions are the principal source of income for most retired people, so that estimating their impact on poverty is relatively straightforward. However, many pension systems seek to replace incomes earned whilst in work rather than provide an income safety net, so it cannot be presumed that systems that provide benefits to those who would not otherwise be poor are not achieving their stated objectives. For those of working age, the situation is more complex because other factors such as the overall extent of inequality and the level and structure of employment also affects the poverty profile, making the impact of welfare state benefits contingent, and thus harder to identify and quantify.

The complications that result from these subtleties are reflected in the evidence. The OECD *Growing Unequal* report found that, in the mid-2000s, government transfers and taxes reduced the poverty rate by between 12 per cent (in Korea) and 80 per cent (in Denmark and Sweden), with an average reduction of around 60 per cent. However, public pensions reduced poverty among older people by between 80 and 100 per cent, whereas the poverty-reducing impact of taxes and transfers was around two-thirds of that for people of working-age and smaller again, at around 57 per cent for children (more accurately, for households with children). Despite this, the cross-country relationship between the poverty rate and social spending (expressed as a percentage of GDP) is far stronger for people of working-age than it is for people of retirement age (OECD 2008a: fig. 5.13). This leads the OECD to argue that 'larger inroads into reducing poverty could be achieved by redirecting spending from pension programmes towards programmes targeted to people of working age and their children at the bottom of the income scale' (p. 144). The OECD figures also show that poverty rates are far higher in all countries in single adult households than in households with two or more adults, whether or not there are children present (OECD 2008a: fig. 5.7) and this would need to be taken into account in any proposal for sweeping change of benefit systems.

Given the attention being paid to the adverse consequences of child poverty for child development, considerable attention has been paid to understanding the determinants of child poverty as the basis for developing better policy (UNICEF 2000; OECD 2007e). The UNICEF study drew attention to the weak cross-country relationship between either unemployment or joblessness and child poverty, but also noted that there is a very strong relationship between the incidence of low wages and child poverty and (though not as strong), between social expenditure and child poverty. Similar findings are reported by Smeeding et al. (2001: figs. 5.2 and 5.3), who use them to raise concerns about the United States' reliance on employment and self-provision to combat poverty, 'regardless of the wages that workers must accept' (2001: 183). The link between low wages and child poverty serves to caution against policies that seek to address poverty *solely* by job creation: these policies can only work if the jobs created are taken up those who would otherwise be poor, and if they pay a wage that is sufficient to raise the incomes of working families above the poverty line.

The strong cross-country relationship that exists between the incidence of low wages and the child poverty rate has been observed in other studies. Although there is unlikely to be a direct causal link between these two variables, there are indirect linkages that operate through the functioning of the labour market and what this reveals about society's overall tolerance for inequality. Bradbury and Jäntti (1999: 71) show that the greater success of Nordic countries in addressing child poverty depends not so much on the generosity of family benefits, but on the higher *market incomes* of families with children. The authors argue that this may not necessarily reflect the impact of different labour market and family support policies, but may be partly a consequence of the different incentive structures imposed by different targeting regimes. However, it is difficult to dispute their view that understanding national differences in child poverty outcomes 'requires serious attention to be devoted to labour market environments and outcomes' (1999: 71).

These important messages have been reinforced by simulations reported by the (OECD 2007e) which involve comparing a 'redistribution strategy' with an 'employment strategy' in terms of their effects on child poverty. Two simple simulations are compared: in the first, each country is assumed to implement a tax and transfer regime that is as successful at reducing child poverty as that in the third most successful country in terms of its actual child poverty rate (Sweden). By applying Sweden's redistribution to the pre-market situations in other countries, this simulation reduces the average child poverty by almost half—from 11 per cent to 5.9 per cent—with no country having a poverty rate above 10 per cent. The 'employment strategy' involves simulating the effects of each country having the same number of jobless households as that existing in the country with the third-lowest rate of joblessness (Luxembourg). The estimated impact of this second simulation on child poverty varies greatly between countries (reducing it from around one to over 5 percentage points), but the overall effect is rather modest, with the poverty rate declining from 10.9 per cent to 9.4 per cent.

The report concludes that although a 'pure benefit strategy' is more effective at reducing child poverty than a 'pure work strategy', the cost of raising benefits to the required level (that achieved in Sweden) would be prohibitive in most countries. In contrast, the 'pure work strategy', though less effective, is also likely to be less costly, particularly if account is taken of induced effects on taxes received and social assistance benefits paid. The latter approach is also likely to be more ideologically appealing to those who favour market-based solutions over those that require greater reliance in state intervention. However, the key point is that more and better use of existing policy instruments would achieve better child poverty outcomes in most countries.

An alternative to the statistical approach generally favoured by international agencies involves specifying and estimating a structural model of causation to help identify the role of the various factors that contribute to observed poverty outcomes. This approach has been used in numerous academic studies (e.g. Korpi and Palme 1998; Smeeding et al. 2001). However, as Brady et al. (2008) have recently noted, these studies tend to adopt either a macro-level approach to examine the associations between poverty outcomes and variables of interest (e.g. welfare spending, GDP, demographic structure, and employment rates), or a micro-level approach to examine the role of transfers and taxes on the income structures of specific countries.

Using a model that captures both macro-level and micro-level effects, estimated using data for eighteen OECD countries from the LIS project, Brady et al. show that even after adjusting for individual level variables, the welfare state has a negative and statistically significant effect on overall poverty rates.[4] The size (and statistical significance) of the effect is unaffected when variables such as economic growth and unemployment rates are included in the model, and when alternative specifications are estimated. Once again, however, the use of highly aggregative measures of welfare state effort (in this case, spending aggregates) ignores the evidence showing that the structure of the benefit system is important as well as the amount spent, and that different age-focused programmes have different effects.

CONCLUSIONS

Reducing the inequality and poverty resulting from the unregulated functioning of market forces are central objectives of social policy in contemporary welfare states. Comparing inequality and poverty outcomes across countries with differing policy regimes and varying spending levels provides a basis for understanding observed differences and relating them to policy differences. This chapter has reviewed some of the problems—conceptual and practical, empirical and theoretical—involved in undertaking such comparisons and in drawing conclusions about the role and impact of social policy. It is apparent that there are a number of formidable issues that have to be addressed before one can draw any inferences about these complex and intersecting topics. Measurement alone requires some difficult choices to be made about how the issues themselves are formulated—equality of income or opportunity? Income poverty or material deprivation?—which have important implications for how to go about assessing the impact of policy.

Despite these challenges, considerable progress has been made over the last three decades in terms of formulating hypotheses, specifying models, and, most importantly, gathering the data needed to bring a comparative perspective to bear on these issues. Although we know a lot more about how to formulate and test different ideas, we are a long way from fully understanding the complex interactions between market and state, economy and polity, global forces and individual actions that are the drivers of inequality patterns and poverty rates. The importance of these issues seems set to grow as the forces of global development and state intervention evolve and intersect.

---

[4] Welfare state effort is measured by an index that covers four variables, government spending, social spending, and transfer spending as a percentage of GDP, and public health spending as a percentage of total health spending.

CHAPTER 37

MACROECONOMIC OUTCOMES

ISABELA MARES

INTRODUCTION

POLITICAL opponents of new social programmes have perennially invoked the spectre of the pernicious effect of such policies. These arguments go back a long time historically and are, in fact, as old as the welfare state itself. In 1846, a Dutch newspaper worried that 'doling out money and alms publicly is a bad habit . . . It is a disruptive activity that encourages sloth, idleness and inebriation' (cited in Lindert 2004: 55). Several decades later, German law-makers opposed the introduction of compulsory social insurance, alleging that these policies, financed by contributions of employers and employees would hurt the competitiveness of German firms vis-à-vis their foreign counterparts (Breger 1982; Mares 2003).

The steady growth of the size of social policy expenditures over the course of the twentieth century provided ample ammunition for critics of the welfare state. Around 1900, the level of social policy expenditures in European and North American economies was below 1 per cent of GNP. Even in Denmark, a country that was a welfare state leader at the time, social policy expenditures totalled only 1.41 per cent of GNP (Lindert 2004: 12). During the 1930s, the average level of social insurance expenditures in developed economies remained low, averaging 1.60 per cent of GNP. The decisive turning point in the rate of growth of social programmes took place in the aftermath of World War II. While in 1960, social insurance expenditures of

Author's note: The author gratefully acknowledges comments from Stephan Leibfried, Frank Castles, Jane Lewis, and Herbert Obinger on an earlier version of this draft.

advanced industrialized economies stood at 10 per cent of GNP, the ratio increased to 21.6 per cent by the year 2000 (Lindert 2004; OECD 2004d). Much of the popular discourse on the economic consequences of the welfare state has attempted to link this temporal trend of rising social policy expenditures to a variety of economic ills affecting advanced industrialized economies. Popular books, with wide readerships, such as Milton Friedman's *Capitalism and Freedom* and Bacon and Eltis's *Britain's Economic Problem* regarded the growth of the public sector as the main source of diverse economic problems, such as high inflation, low growth, or high unemployment (Bacon and Eltis 1978; Friedman 2003 [1962]).

In contrast to these popular writings, academic research on the economic consequences of the welfare state has followed a much more tortuous path. Initial studies shared the theoretical assumption that larger welfare states are inimical to growth and employment. Over and over again, empirical results failed to support these propositions. Empirical findings were fragile and not robust to changes in sample size or statistical specification or straightforwardly disconfirmed these propositions.

Academic scholarship has formulated two distinct attempts to reconcile this disjuncture between theoretical predictions and empirical findings. One set of studies has attempted to specify the positive economic externalities generated by the welfare state which can outweigh some of the costs imposed by social programmes on economic actors. In economics, endogenous growth theories made this analytical move, by exploring the positive economic externalities of education and health programmes. In political science, studies examining the employment consequences of the welfare state have attempted to specify different externalities of insurance and assistance programmes. Political scientists stressed that social insurance policies that raise the reservation wage of workers encourage both unions and firms to undertake higher investment in human capital (Mares 2001, 2003; Estévez-Abe et al. 2001). Social policies also facilitate moderation on the wage front of labour unions, which can offset the adverse effects of taxes and also lead to higher levels of growth (Esping-Andersen 1990; Mares 2005a).

A different attempt to resolve the contradiction between theoretical predictions and empirical findings has suggested that the effects of welfare states on economic outcomes are contingent on other policies and institutions. Economic agents—such as firms, individuals, or labour unions—operate in an environment that is densely populated by pre-existing institutions and policies. Actors' payoffs in response to changes in taxation or the introduction of new programmes depends on other institutions and policies that are present in this political environment. While this analysis was already present in the political economy literature of the 1970s, it became central to the 'varieties of capitalism' scholarship of the 1990s. This literature has been relatively successful in accounting for cross-national and temporal variation in economic outcomes across advanced industrialized economies and for the effects of differences in the size of the public sector on these outcomes (Hall and Gingrich 2005; Mares 2005a). So far, this literature has been less successful in accounting for the institutional determinants of variation in economic outcomes among developing countries.

This chapter surveys studies that have examined the consequence of larger welfare states on two macroeconomic outcomes: growth and employment. Mirroring the structure of the literature, the larger part of the chapter will review research on advanced industrialized economies. I also discuss a literature of more recent origin which examines the employment consequences of larger programmes in developing economies.

My survey of the literature focuses on growth and employment and leaves out other macroeconomic outcomes, such as inflation or public debt (for a survey of this literature, see Franzese 2002). I would like to note, however, that the literature examining the consequences of larger welfare states for inflation has experienced an intellectual trajectory similar to the one discussed above. Economists have approached these questions initially and advanced the conjecture that larger public sectors are inflationary. This occurs because governments will succumb to the temptation to print more money to finance existing policy commitments (rather than raise taxes) or because public sector employees will be more likely to set in motion wage price spirals (for the latter view, see Bacon and Eltis 1978). Empirical results have failed to confirm these predictions. Other studies have advanced an opposite hypothesis, suggesting that the welfare state can act as a substitute for a 'conservative' central bank because high unemployment benefits make the monetary authorities less concerned about the plight of the unemployed (Di Tella and MacCulloch 2004). The inconclusiveness of these initial findings motivated efforts to explore 'institutional interactions' between welfare states, macroeconomic authorities, and labour unions (Scharpf 1991; Scharpf and Schmidt, 2000a; Iversen 1999). These studies suggest that the effect of higher levels of spending on inflation can be offset by the strategic behaviour of labour unions and the interaction between the latter and monetary authorities. The effects of larger welfare states on inflation are nonlinear and depend on other institutions and policies.

The Impact of Larger Welfare States on Economic Growth

The literature on economic growth has provided the starting point for most analyses examining the relationship between larger welfare states and economic development. In its simplest form, this theoretical literature predicted that larger welfare states will have a negative impact on growth. Higher levels of taxes which are necessary to finance most social programmes are expected to distort and lower the incentives of private actors to invest and, thus, slow down growth. It is important to note, however, that disagreement exists about the magnitude and temporal persistence of this effect. In neoclassical growth models—such as the Solow model—the welfare state does not affect long-term rates of growth. The latter are influenced only by exogenous forces such as population changes and technological progress. Higher levels of taxes affect, however, the level of output during the transition to the steady state. A number of studies have argued that this transition stage to the steady state of growth can be quite long in duration. This observation implies that one can recover a prediction about a negative relationship between higher levels of taxes and lower rates of economic growth even in the framework of neoclassical growth models (Barro and Sala-i-Martin 1995).

Endogenous growth models relax the sharp distinction between long- and short-term rates of growth (Hammond and Rodriguez-Clare 1993; Agell et al. 1997). The long-term rate of growth is itself endogenous, determined by individual investment decisions and not just by demographic and technological shocks. Investment in knowledge and human capital are important determinants of the long-run growth rate (Lucas 1988). This allows endogenous growth theorists to consider the role of political institutions and economic policies as determinants of long-term rates of growth. Higher taxes are expected to decrease rates of investment and lead to a decline in the long-term rate of growth. By contrast, investment in public education and human capital is likely to enhance growth (Azariadis and Drazen 1990). In these models, the magnitude of the effect of larger and more encompassing welfare states on growth depends on a range of additional factors—such as the ability of technology to accumulate human capital. For certain values of these technology parameters, higher welfare states can be compatible with higher levels of economic growth. In practice, it is difficult to test the empirical predictions of endogenous growth models, due to difficulties in estimating many of the parameters whose values determine the magnitude of the relationship between higher taxes and the level of growth.

To explore the empirical relationship between the size of the welfare state and the level of economic development, one can begin by mapping out the broad historical trends in the co-evolution of these variables in advanced industrialized countries. In comparative terms, the period up to World War II combined relatively low rates of economic and productivity growth with relatively low levels of social policy expenditures. Across eighteen OECD economies, the average rate of economic growth was 1.4 per cent during the period between 1870 and 1913 and 1.2 per cent during the period between 1913 and 1950 (Maddison 1982). Until World War II both the size of the welfare state and its rate of growth were very low across all advanced industrialized countries. Social insurance expenditures as a percentage of GDP grew from an average of 0.29 per cent in 1880 to an average of 1.66 per cent in 1930 (Lindert 2004: 12). It thus makes very little sense to think of the welfare state as the primary factor accounting for the slow rates of economic growth of this period. The period between 1950 and 1973 stands in dramatic contrast to earlier developments. During that time OECD economies grew at an average rate of 3.7 per cent, a rate of growth that was three times higher than the economic growth of previous periods (Maddison 1982). At the same time, social insurance expenditures grew dramatically, reaching 15 per cent of GDP in 1970 (Lindert 2004). This combination of high levels of economic growth and high levels of growth in the public sector presents something of an anomaly to growth theories. It is only during recent years that high levels of social policy expenditure are associated with a slower rate of economic growth. Over the last three decades, social insurance expenditures as a percentage of GDP continued to climb, peaking at around 22 per cent of GDP in 1995 (OECD 2004d). Between 1973 and 1995, average growth rate of OECD economies stood at 2.2 per cent (Crafts 2003: 11).

Empirical studies examining the relationship between larger welfare states and economic growth have generally relied on multivariate statistical analysis. The results fail to confirm the predictions of neoclassical growth models. One set of studies that focused on the experience of advanced industrialized democracies during the post-war period found a positive relationship between the size of the public sector and economic growth. In an early econometric study, Walter Korpi explored the relationship between social security expenditures and GDP growth in seventeen OECD countries between 1950 and 1973 (Korpi 1985). After controlling for a number of labour market and economic differences between these countries and for the economic gap between these countries and the United States (which opens up room for 'catch up' growth), Korpi's study uncovered a positive and statistically significant relationship between the level of social security transfers and economic growth. The effect is also not small in magnitude. An increase in the level of social policy transfers by 5 per cent is expected to increase the level of economic growth by 0.9 per cent. In a subsequent study, McCallum and Blais have examined the impact of the level and changes in government spending on economic growth in seventeen OECD countries during the period 1960–83 (McCallum and Blais 1987). Their study also included various measures of the power and interest groups in the economy, such as the number of interest groups (adjusted for population) and unionization rates. McCallum and Blais found that various measures of the size of the government—the level and change in government outlays, government final consumption expenditures, or total taxation—have no impact on the level of economic growth. In agreement with Korpi's earlier finding, they also uncovered a positive relationship between the level of social security payments (adjusted for demographic differences across countries) and economic growth. In their own words this finding, 'comes as something of a surprise'. Their results for various models that test for the possibility of nonlinear relationship between social security transfers and economic growth are fragile, and not robust to the inclusion of various countries or periods in the sample.

By contrast, the findings of other econometric studies are inconclusive. Landau has analysed the impact of government expenditures on economic growth in 16 OECD countries during the period 1950–76 and did not find a statistically significant effect (Landau 1985). In a similar study, Castles and Dowrick also found that increases in the level of transfers do not affect economic growth in OECD economies between 1960 and 1985 (Castles and Dowrick 1990). Departing from earlier studies, Mendoza, Razin, and Tesar have developed reliable cross-national measures of the average tax burden in OECD economies. This allows them to test one of the underlying mechanisms postulated by growth theory, namely that high marginal tax rates on income slow down economic growth. Their econometric analysis found, however, no relationship between higher tax rates and economic growth in eighteen OECD economies during the period 1966–90 (Mendoza et al. 1994).

The results of quantitative studies examining the relationship between larger public sectors and economic growth in developing countries are also inconclusive. Kormendi and Meguire (1985) have examined the effect of changes in government consumption expenditure on average GDP growth rate in forty-seven countries during the period 1950–77. They do not find a robust statistical relationship between these variables. A different study of the relationship between government consumption and economic performance that includes observations from 132 countries between 1964 and 1993 found a negative relationship between these variables (Commander et al. 1997). Easterly and Rebelo (1993) have analysed the relationship between various indicators of fiscal policy—government surplus, government consumption and marginal tax rate on income and economic growth in various samples ranging from forty-three to seventy-four countries. As these authors summarize the results of their analysis, 'the link between most other fiscal variables and growth is statistically fragile. The statistical significance of these variables in a cross-section regression context depends heavily on what other control variables are included in the regression' (Easterly and Rebelo 1993: 419). The absence of a statistical relationship can be in part attributed to a high correlation between fiscal variables and the initial level of economic development. This makes it difficult—if not impossible—to disentangle the effect of fiscal policy on growth from the effect of convergence.

The ambiguity of these empirical findings raises a host of questions. As Peter Lindert has eloquently argued, 'the fact that most analyses fail to identify persistent negative consequences of larger public sectors on growth should give a pause to critics of the welfare state . . . The data refuse to confess that things work out that way. Across countries or over time, the coefficients linking growth to total government size are not negative, even in sophisticated multivariate analyses' (Lindert 2004). Why do the cross-national empirical findings fail to confirm the theoretical predictions of growth economists? One hypothesis points to the design of the tax system and suggests that governments have designed the latter in such a way as to minimize potential distortions arising from a larger public economy. The other hypothesis— already anticipated by growth economists—relates to differences in the economic externalities of social programmes. Social policies provide important positive externalities that outweigh their costs.

A range of studies that have examined the variation in the tax structure chosen by advanced industrialized economies suggests that economies with larger public sectors have financed these programmes, by relying on a more regressive tax structure (Kato 2003; Lindert 2004; Timmons 2006). Top marginal tax rates on dividends in Sweden are at 30 per cent, as compared to 46.6 per cent in the United States or 65 per cent in Japan, two countries with much smaller public sectors. Countries with larger public sectors also rely more heavily on regressive consumption taxes (Kato 2003; Timmons 2006). This choice of the tax mix has mitigated the potential of larger public sectors for distorting growth.

A second, complementary explanation for the absence of a negative relationship between larger welfare states and economic growth is that social programmes provide important economic externalities that outweigh the potential distortions resulting from higher taxes. For endogenous growth theorists, education programmes provide the strongest externalities. The initial level of human capital is expected to affect subsequent trajectories of growth and economic development. A number of studies have found support for this hypothesis. Easterly and Rebelo (1993) found that the level of primary and secondary enrolment in 1960 is positively correlated with the average growth rate of per capita GDP in 1970–1988. Azariadis and Drazen (1990), Barro and Sala-i-Martin (1995), and Hansson and Henrekson (1994) also report findings of positive effects on growth resulting from educational spending.

Other social programmes—in addition to education—can also create positive externalities to economic actors and affect long-term growth trajectories. Examining the historical evolution of welfare state development in European countries, several studies have shown that social insurance policies have affected the incentives of employees and employers to undertake long-term investments in skills (Mares 2003, 2006; Hall and Soskice 2001*a*). By providing benefits that are proportional to wages, these programmes raise the 'reservation wage' of high-skilled workers relative to low-skilled workers and provide some guarantees to these workers that their investments in skills will not be undermined in periods of temporary loss of work. Social insurance programmes also mitigate firms' reluctance to invest in firm- or industry-specific training to top up the general skills of their workers. The existence of high numbers of workers with firm- and industry-specific skills allows, in turn, firms in these economies to pursue a pattern of economic specialization premised on the production of high-quality, high value-added goods. The causal mechanism postulated by these studies differs from that of growth economists. In these explanations, the causal arrow runs from the existence of insurance programmes to investment by firms and employees in industry- and firm-specific skills, which influences, in turn, the growth trajectory of the economy.

In addition to education and to insurance programmes, other policies matter for economic development. A large number of studies have argued that targeted programmes can have important positive economic externalities. In early stages of economic development, even modest spending on healthcare can lead to significant reductions in infectious diseases and malnutrition. This, in turn, can have significant implications for the overall productivity level of the workforce. As Robert Fogel has shown, part of the huge increase in productivity in England during the later part of the nineteenth and early twentieth century came about 'when the bottom fifth of the population acquired enough calories to permit regular work. The principal way in which government policy contributed to that achievement was through its public health programmes. By reducing exposure to disease, more of the calories that the poor ingested were made available for work' (Fogel 2004: 42). Studies relying on cross-national statistical evidence have also found a positive correlation between higher levels of social sector spending and declines in infant mortality and increases in life expectancy, with consequences for the average productivity of workers (Commander et al. 1997).

THE EMPLOYMENT CONSEQUENCES
OF LARGER WELFARE STATES

Many scholars have argued that larger welfare states are not only inimical to growth, but also to employment. The neoclassical economic framework provides a simple formulation of these arguments. Social programmes and related labour market legislation, such as employment security regulations, raise the labour costs of firms. The resulting upward shift in labour demand is expected to lower employment. The magnitude of the effect of an increase in labour costs on employment depends, ultimately, on how these costs are distributed between firms and workers. There are two limit cases. If firms bear the entire costs of a new labour market regulation or of an increase in payroll taxes, this results in a perfectly elastic labour supply. In this case higher labour costs will have the strongest negative impact on employment. By contrast, workers can bear the entire costs of an increase in social security regulations in the form of lower wages. In this scenario, an increase in labour market regulations or labour taxes will have no impact on employment.

Empirical studies of the employment consequences of the welfare state have come in a variety of forms. One set of studies has examined the direct impact of a wide range of social policies on employment outcomes. For many years, empirical analysis was confined to the study of advanced industrialized countries only. More recently, a number of studies have expanded the universe of cases to include developing economies. Other studies have taken a different approach to this question. Their starting premise has been that the effect of social policies on employment is mediated through the wage-setting process. Workers and employers bargain not just over the level of wages, but also on the distribution of the costs associated with a new social policy. Labour market institutions, such as the level of centralization of the wage bargaining system, affect the relative bargaining power of unions and employers in the negotiation of wages and, thus, the distribution of the costs of a new social policy. The implication of these studies is that the employment consequences of different social policies differ in systematic ways across countries and that these differences can be traced to differences in wage bargaining institutions that are present in various economies.

As in the case of the literature examining the consequences of larger welfare states for growth, the results of empirical studies on the employment effects of larger welfare states are inconclusive. Consider the results of studies examining the effects of differences in unemployment benefits. A study by Layard et al. (2005) found support for the proposition that more generous unemployment policies are associated with higher levels of unemployment. A recent study by Allard and Lindert (2004: 108) has reported similar results. By examining a panel of fifteen advanced industrialized countries during the period between 1978 and 1995, they found that policies that 'raise the reservation wage from 5 per cent of the median wage to a sample average of 20 per cent raise unemployment by about 1.3 per cent of the labour force' (Allard and Lindert 2004: 110). The same study found however, that more generous unemployment compensation policies are associated with an increase in the productivity per worker (Allard and Lindert 2004: 101). Other studies have found that higher levels of unemployment benefits have had little impact on the overall labour supply. Given that labour market participation is a prerequisite for eligibility of these benefits, incentives for higher participation in the labour market might be higher in countries with more generous support during periods of loss of work. (Nickell 1997)

Other studies have examined the employment consequences of employment security regulations—in other words legislation that imposes restrictions on the ability of firms to lay off workers. The results are, again, inconclusive. Consider, for instance, the vast literature examining the effect of more stringent employment protection legislation on employment in advanced industrialized economies. Lazear has analysed the impact of severance pay regulations on employment and unemployment outcomes in twenty-two advanced industrialized countries over the period 1956–84 (Lazear 1990). He found a positive relationship between regulations mandating higher levels of pay during layoffs and the level of unemployment (Lazear 1990). Grubb and Wells have reported similar results (Grubb and Wells 1993). They found a negative relationship between measures of the stringency of employment protection legislation and employment ratios in OECD economies (Grubb and Wells 1993: 19). By contrast, other studies by Addison et al. (2000) concluded that high labour market standards adversely affect employment in OECD economies.

In a recent pioneering study, Carmen Pages and James Heckman (2004) have explored the employment effects of more generous social policies in a broader universe of cases, which includes both Latin American and OECD economies. This study has examined the consequences of three types of policies that raise the overall labour costs of firms and are thus expected to affect employment negatively. These include indemnity payments, seniority payments, and social security contributions. Their study uncovered a striking variation in the impact of these policies for employment outcomes. The first surprising finding is the existence of regional variation. If the sample of cases was restricted to advanced industrialized economies only, Heckman and Pages found that all three measures are positively associated with unemployment, a result that mirrors the results of Addison et al. (2000) discussed above. By contrast, in Latin American countries none of these policies has an impact on unemployment that is statistically different from zero (Heckman and Pages 2004: 74, Table 9). A second surprise is that in Latin American economies, different social policies have a different impact on aggregated levels of employment. Higher social security contributions are associated with lower employment rates, a finding that supports the predictions of neoclassical economists. By contrast, an increase in indemnity payments leads to increases in the level of employment (Heckman and Pages 2004: 73).

These findings raise a number of intriguing questions and need to be followed up by more careful analysis. One possible explanation for the differential impact of various social policies in Latin America is that workers assess the probability of receiving different social policy benefits in different ways. In the case of policies where the link between contributions and benefits is relatively tight—such as indemnity payments—an increase in the level of benefits has positive effects on the labour supply (Heckman and Pages 2004: 73). This is not necessarily the case for all social insurance programmes. In the case of some policies, weakness in the ability of the state to raise insurance contributions from different sectors decreases workers' perceptions of the likelihood of receiving social policy benefits (Mares 2005a). The consequence can be a decrease in the compliance with these policies and a reduction in labour supply. This, in turn, can heighten the adverse employment effect of some insurance programmes.

In contrast to this research that has attempted to identify direct effects of social policies on employment outcomes, other studies have attempted to open up the black box of the wage-setting process. In order to understand how the welfare state affects employment, these studies have argued that we need to specify the consequences of social policies on unions' incentives for moderation, on the one hand, and firms' employment responses to unions' wage demands, on the other hand (Mares 2005a). These studies add two important insights to previous research examining the employment consequences of larger welfare states. The first is that social policies affect employment outcomes not just through their direct effects on labour supply but also through their effects on the strategies pursued by unions during the wage bargaining process. From the perspective of unions, an expansion in the level of social policy benefits such as pensions, healthcare, or unemployment benefits is monetarily equivalent to higher wages. This implies that unions may voluntarily accept moderate wage settlements at moments when governments provide an expansion of services and transfers. This sustained moderation on the wage front can weaken the trade-off between larger welfare states and high levels of employment.

The second important contribution of this line of analysis is that labour market institutions, such as the level of centralization of the wage bargaining system, affect in systematic ways the incentives of unions and employers during the wage bargaining process and the resulting level of employment. Across OECD economies, we find three types of labour market institutions (Calmfors and Driffill 1988). In economies such as the United States or Canada, for example, wages are determined in individual negotiations between workers and firms. If competition in product markets is intense, individual firms will not be able to raise the relative prices in response to an increase in wage levels. Given that wage decreases are likely to result in steep decline in employment, unions are more likely to demand moderate wage increases. However, industry-level wage bargaining institutions encountered in countries like Italy or Belgium create different incentives for labour market actors. In these settings, unions set wages for all firms that produce similar products. Facing a lower level of competition in their product markets, firms can shift higher labour costs to consumers. In this institutional context, firms are less likely to resist higher wage increases and unions are more likely to demand higher wages. Finally, the case of highly centralized labour market institutions where wages are determined in negotiations between one peak association representing labour and employers, such as the wage bargaining institutions in Scandinavian political economies, is again distinct from the previous two cases. In this context, an increase in wages is likely to lead to a uniform price increase and to steep employment declines. This creates powerful incentives for wage moderation in economies with highly centralized wage-setting, resulting in overall lower levels of unemployment.

These studies have formulated precise predictions about the consequences of cross-national differences of labour market institutions on employment outcomes. But at the same time, they have generated important insights about different paths of employment adjustment in response to the growth in the fiscal burden of the welfare state. How can one explain the rise in unemployment experienced by many European economies during recent decades? If wage moderation was the critical instrument accounting for the presence of a virtuous cycle between high employment levels and a high provision of social benefits, what accounts for the decline in the effectiveness of this policy instrument? The critical factor that changed over time is the size of the fiscal burden of the welfare state (Daveri and Tabellini 2000; Mares 2005a, 2006). As a result, across OECD economies, the importance of wages as a proportion of total labour costs has declined. As unions and employers bargain now over a much smaller part of the total wage bill, the importance of wage moderation as a policy instrument is severely curtailed. Even strong levels of wage moderation have only a small impact on the level of employment (Mares 2003, 2006).

To sum up, one important result highlighted by this literature is that wage bargaining institutions mediate the effects of larger welfare states on employment. In other words, the effect of social spending on employment outcomes is non-linear and depends on pre-existing institutions and policies. If the overall fiscal burden is low, wage moderation can ensure high levels of employment, despite the growth of social policy transfers. Labour market institutions further amplify the effects of wage moderation on employment: the latter are higher in economies with either centralized or decentralized labour market institutions. Over time, the growth of the welfare state has constrained the effectiveness of this policy instrument—resulting in higher levels of unemployment. Table 37.1 provides preliminary support for these propositions. The measure of the centralization of the wage bargaining system is

Table 37.1 Average unemployment in advanced industrialized political economies: Cross-national and temporal trends (1960–75, 1976–95)

	Unemployment in economies with different wage bargaining institutions		
	Decentralized[a]	Intermediately centralized[b]	Highly centralized[c]
1960–75	3.04	3.135	1.49
1976–95	6.98	8.46	3.16

Notes: [a] Decentralized economies include Britain, the United States, and France.
[b] Intermediately centralized economies include: Belgium, Denmark, Finland, Germany, Italy, The Netherlands, and Switzerland.
[c] Highly centralized economies include Austria, Norway, Sweden.

For the construction of the centralization score see Mares 2005a: 65.
Source: OECD 1999.

constructed by averaging eight of the most widely used indicators of the literature constructed by Schmitter (1981), Cameron (1984), Calmfors and Driffill (1988), OECD (1997), Iversen (1999), Hall and Franzese (1998), Traxler and Kittel (2000), and Golden et al. (1998), respectively. (For details on the construction of this index, see Mares 2005*a*: 65.)

As Table 37.1 illustrates, these explanations can provide a persuasive account of both cross-national and temporal differences in employment outcomes in advanced industrialized economies. Table 37.1 classifies economies into those with centralized, intermediately centralized, and highly centralized labour markets. These descriptive patterns show economies with intermediate-level centralization of the wage bargaining system have an employment performance inferior to economies with either highly centralized or highly decentralized labour market institutions. While the employment performance of all economies has deteriorated over time, the change is least pronounced in economies with highly centralized labour market institutions.

While existing studies have made important contributions to our understanding of the institutional determinants of employment outcomes in advanced industrial economies, it is incumbent on future research to examine whether some of these results also 'travel' to other political contexts. Some of the tasks ahead are descriptive and exploratory in nature. We need a better understanding of the institutional design of labour market institutions in developing countries, which involves the collection of systematic information on the level of centralization of the wage bargaining system, the number of agents involved in the wage-setting process, the level of trade union density and membership in employers' associations, and so on. Secondly, we also know very little about the wage responses pursued by trade unions and whether unions were willing to pursue policies of wage moderation in exchange of the expansion of some social policy benefits and transfers. Do we find instances of a deliberate pursuit of moderation on the wage front in exchange for the expansion of benefits and transfers? How common was wage moderation? What were the social policy priorities for unions in these economies, and what kind of policies elicited a response in the form of wage moderation? In short, a better understanding of the strategic responses of trade unions and of differences in the structure of labour market institutions in developing countries will allow us to develop more nuanced predictions about the employment consequences of various social programmes in these economies.

CONCLUSIONS

This chapter has surveyed a vast literature examining the economic consequences of the welfare state. Neoclassical growth models have predicted that the relationship between larger welfare states and economic growth is unambiguously negative. By contrast, endogenous growth theorists have attributed an important role to educa-tion policies as determinants of economic growth. Empirical research has failed to confirm the stark predictions of neoclassical growth models and has found support for the proposition that investment in human capital can have a positive impact on economic growth. But a number of studies have shown that, in addition to education policies, other policies, such as health spending or social insurance programmes, also have positive effects on economic growth. In short, there is considerable evidence that social programmes provide a wide range of 'positive economic externalities' that outweigh the potential distortionary effects of higher taxes.

The evidence about the impact of larger welfare states on employment is also mixed. In the context of OECD economies, empirical research examining the con-sequences of more generous levels of benefits and more stringent labour protection laws for employment outcomes has generated rather inconclusive results. Studies examining these questions in developing economies have also reported a surprising variation across policies in their consequences for employment (Heckman and Pages 2004). A more promising line of theoretical and empirical analysis suggests that additional institutions mediate the impact of different social policies on employ-ment. The level of centralization of the wage bargaining system is of critical impor-tance in this respect. Highly centralized wage bargaining systems create powerful incentives for wage moderation for labour unions. This wage restraint, in turn, can mitigate the adverse effects of larger welfare states on employment.

These findings set an agenda for future theoretical work on the economic con-sequences of the welfare state. On the one hand, more theoretical work modelling the positive externalities of the welfare state is needed. On the other hand, the current findings call for additional mid-range theoretical work that identifies how other institutions—in addition to wage bargaining policies—mediate the impact of larger welfare states on employment. Simply stated, the consequences of a larger welfare state for growth and employment are not the same across countries and over time. The magnitude of these effects depends heavily on pre-existing institutions and policies.

CHAPTER 38

....

WELFARE RETRENCHMENT

....

JONAH D. LEVY

INTRODUCTION

....

THE three decades after World War II witnessed a dramatic expansion of social protection across Western Europe. This expansion was driven by a variety of factors, including rapid industrialization, which generated both new social tensions and the fiscal resources to address these tensions (Cutright 1965; Wilensky 1975); the so-called 'Keynesian compromise' between labour and capital, with the former acceding to private enterprise and the hegemony of management, while the latter accepted substantial social spending to protect employees against the harshest consequences of capitalist competition (Przeworski and Wallerstein 1984; Jessop 1994); and a widespread popular faith in the possibilities for state guidance and planning (Shonfield 1965). In addition, scholars pointed to two factors that seemed to differentiate welfare state development across countries. The first was the strength or 'power resources' of labour and left parties, who were presumed to be the chief advocates of welfare state expansion (Korpi 1983; Esping-Andersen and Korpi 1984; Esping-Andersen 1990). The second was the capacity of governments to translate their electoral victories into policy reform, unconstrained by so-called 'veto points' in the political system, that is, by constitutional provisions, such as divided government, federalism, and referenda, that provide opportunities to check government initiatives (Immergut 1992a and Chapter 15 above; Huber et al. 1993; Tsebelis 1995).

Beginning in the late 1970s, the overarching forces that had supported the development of the welfare state for decades shifted into reverse. Economic growth slowed, class conflict intensified, and state guidance was called into question. In this harsher context, scholars and pundits anticipated a general rollback of social programmes across the affluent democracies. Moreover, mirroring the arguments about cross-national variation in welfare expansion, retrenchment might have been expected to be most pronounced in countries where labour and the left were especially weak, and where constitutions provided few 'veto points' to block the cost-cutting initiatives of right-wing governments (see Chapter 14, for a discussion). Following the end of the Cold War, a growing literature suggested that international developments, such as globalization, European integration, and the neoliberal initiatives of institutions like the IMF and OECD, were intensifying the pressures for retrenchment (see Chapter 22, for a discussion). Yet in practice, welfare state cutbacks have fallen far short of doom-and-gloom forecasts. The surprising resilience of the welfare state (see also Chapter 47) has opened a debate about the politics of welfare retrenchment—the extent of retrenchment, the economic and political circumstances that permit retrenchment, and the forms that retrenchment may take.

This chapter provides an overview of the retrenchment debate. An initial section summarizes Paul Pierson's path-breaking 'new politics of the welfare state' thesis, which argues that the politics of welfare retrenchment operates according to fundamentally different rules from the politics of welfare expansion, making retrenchment exceedingly difficult. The following section lays out the various ways in which budget-cutters have sought to overcome these obstacles to retrenchment, according to Pierson. Two further sections describe subsequent revisions to Pierson's framework: one analyses claims that retrenchment may take different forms and be more extensive than Pierson initially acknowledged, while another presents arguments that retrenchment may occur via political processes different from those emphasized by Pierson. A final section offers brief concluding remarks.

OBSTACLES TO RETRENCHMENT

Paul Pierson framed the debate over welfare retrenchment with a book entitled *Dismantling the Welfare State? Reagan, Thatcher, and the Politics of Retrenchment* (P. Pierson 1994; see also P. Pierson 1996). As the title indicates, the book centres on two cases that appeared to be extremely favourable to retrenchment. Both Ronald Reagan in the United States and Margaret Thatcher in Britain were true neoliberal believers and highly effective politicians. During their years in office, Reagan and Thatcher presided over far-reaching market reforms across a number of areas, from industrial relations, to government regulation and industrial policy, to macroeconomic management.

Reagan and Thatcher made no secret of their desire to roll back the welfare state, blaming social programmes for driving up spending and taxes, discouraging work, and rewarding indolence and dependency. Moreover, the defence of the welfare state appeared exceedingly fragile. In the United States and the United Kingdom, labour's power resources had plummeted, with unions in full retreat and parties of the left in disarray. If the United States political system, with its checks and balances and Democratic-controlled Congress, offered some veto points for opponents of retrenchment, Britain's unitary, cabinet government and unwritten constitution provided Thatcher with an essentially free hand. Thus, a reasonable prediction would have been that the Reagan and Thatcher years would bring significant welfare retrenchment, just as there was significant reform in so many other economic policy areas, with perhaps somewhat more change in the British case, thanks to the relative paucity of veto points. Instead, in both countries, as Pierson shows, government social spending held steady or even increased (see Table 23.1 in Chapter 23). This is true no matter how government social spending is measured—whether in absolute terms, real terms (adjusted for inflation), or as a share of GDP. In other words, government social spending not only didn't decline; it grew at a somewhat faster rate than the economy as a whole.

Pierson offers three reasons for this surprising outcome. The first is a social-psychological reason. Pierson cites a variety of psychological studies suggesting that people are risk averse, that they respond more strongly to potential losses than to potential gains. Individuals will take a lot of chances and initiatives to prevent any worsening of their current situation. By contrast, they are much less likely to mobilize to achieve equivalent improvements in their situation. The implication for welfare retrenchment is that citizens will resist programme cuts, even if governments pledge to fully counterbalance these losses through lower taxes. In addition to psychological dynamics, resistance to such reforms may be fuelled by scepticism toward the promises of politicians. Many citizens fear that although politicians pledge to cut benefits and taxes in tandem, in practice, only the benefits will be cut (or, if taxes are cut, they will be 'somebody else's' taxes).

The second reason why welfare retrenchment is so difficult, according to Pierson, relates to the logic of collective action. Welfare retrenchment generally imposes immediate costs on specific groups in return for diffuse, long-term, and uncertain benefits to the population as a whole. As a result, opponents of programme cuts tend to have much stronger incentives to mobilize than supporters.

Opponents of proposed cuts have a lot to lose. Their pensions will shrink; their guarantee of affordable healthcare may be taken away. These are important issues. People will take to the streets over them. Many of the biggest demonstrations in Western Europe have occurred in response to proposed welfare state cuts, such as the Berlusconi pension reforms in Italy in 1994 and the Juppé Social Security Plan in France in 1995. In both of these instances, the government was forced to withdraw its proposed reforms; Berlusconi's coalition then collapsed, while Juppé's administration became essentially unable to govern. Even in the United States, the public pension system, Social Security, is commonly referred to as the 'third rail' of American politics—touch it, and you die. In contrast to targets of cutbacks, the average taxpayer has little to gain from social programme cuts. While the costs of retrenchment are concentrated on certain groups, the benefits are diffused throughout society. For the average citizen, welfare cuts may diminish taxes and social security charges a little bit, but not much. These kinds of small savings do not provide much incentive for mobilizing. Few people are going to take to the streets to cut their tax bills by a few dollars or euros per month.

The third and probably most important reason why it is so difficult to cut the welfare state, according to Pierson, relates to historical legacies, in particular, the 'policy feedback' or 'policy legacies' bequeathed by the welfare state itself. Budget-cutters do not confront a *tabula rasa*. On the contrary, welfare programmes have reshaped the terrain on which they operate in two critical ways. The first is through what Pierson calls 'lock-in'. Past policy commitments often narrow present options; they 'lock in' certain policies, regardless of the preferences of contemporary governments. Because governments are bound to honour the promises of their predecessors, they find that substantial welfare resources have been pre-committed by decisions taken decades ago.

Public pension systems offer a classic example of such lock-in. Governments have pledged that if citizens contribute to the public pension system during their working lives, there will be a pension waiting for them when they retire around age 60–65. In practice, it has proven all but impossible to renege on this commitment. The pension benefits are seen as a quasi-property right, as something that citizens have 'earned' by paying payroll taxes for many years. Moreover, people have built their retirement plans around the expectation of receiving their pensions. They don't have time, especially if they are already retired or even older workers, to adjust to sudden cuts in their benefits. Unless reformers are willing to endure charges of cheating senior citizens out of their hard-earned pensions, forcing the elderly into poverty without providing any means for them to build up substantial alternative sources of income, then governments are locked into paying the pension benefits promised by their predecessors as far back as forty years ago.

The other way in which the welfare state has reshaped the terrain for budget-cutters concerns the interest-group structure. The German sociologist, Claus Offe coined the phrase 'policy-takers' to denote political groups created by the existence of a policy, by their shared interest in the perpetuation and expansion of this policy (Offe 1981; 1985). Examples of policy-takers include veterans, senior citizens, and white-collar workers, who initially formed groups to lobby for better government benefits (Kocka 1981; Skocpol 1992). Pierson sees policy-takers as perhaps the single most significant bulwark of the welfare state against would-be programme cutters. Simply put, the welfare state has generated its own political support base. The dramatic expansion of social programmes in the post-war decades created an array of policy-takers, of powerful new constituencies with a stake in the perpetuation of generous social programmes. These groups stand ready to mobilize against proposed cuts in benefits. As a result, the defence of the welfare state is no longer left simply to labour and its dwindling power resources.

Beyond organized labour and left parties, the welfare state can count on the support of two sets of policy-takers. The first is the recipients of government services and transfer payments, such as pensioners, patients, the disabled, and the unemployed. These groups may tap additional support from family members, whose burden is lessened by social programmes, or from citizens who know that they too are likely to benefit some day from these programmes. For example, just about everyone expects to eventually retire and receive a pension. The second set of policy-takers is the providers of social services, such as physicians, nurses, childcare and elderly care workers, and assistants to the disabled. These service providers can be expected to resist retrenchment out of a combination of belief in their missions and defence of their budgets and incomes. Since many providers are highly skilled professionals, who are seen as committed to the public good, their views are often more credible with the electorate than those of the budget-cutters.

Taking a step back, the broader point suggested by Pierson is that when it comes to the defence of the welfare state, pensioners, patients, doctors, nurses, and social workers may be more important than left parties and trade unions. By a 'new politics of the welfare state', Pierson means that the political process surrounding welfare retrenchment is very different from the process surrounding welfare expansion. Reformers confront a much more complex political environment. Their decisions are constrained by the need to honour the pledges of previous governments (lock-in) and by the new interest groups that have arisen around existing social programmes (policy-takers). Although labour's power resources and constitutional veto points may have been decisive in the construction of the welfare state, in the era of retrenchment, Pierson argues, historical legacies like lock-in and policy-takers are proving to be more salient.

Pathways to Retrenchment

The 'new politics' thesis is not simply a claim that welfare retrenchment is difficult, let alone impossible. Pierson also seeks to specify the circumstances under which retrenchment may occur and the forms that it is likely to take. Pierson's starting point is the contention that cutting social programmes is unpopular. Even if the public supports lower social spending combined with lower taxes in the abstract, that support tends to evaporate as soon as specific programme cuts are suggested. As a result, governments must tread gingerly, seeking to avoid responsibility for retrenchment measures. According to Pierson, while welfare expansion was an exercise in credit claiming, with governments reaping political gains for extending social benefits, welfare retrenchment is an exercise in 'blame avoidance', in dodging or deflecting responsibility for unpopular programme cuts. Rather than a frontal assault on popular programmes, budget-cutters tend to try to confuse and divide the opposition through three main strategies.

The first is to lower the salience of negative consequences by diffusing these consequences over time, as opposed to delivering them in one shot. A classic example, which Pierson refers to as 'decrementalism', is to shift to a less generous indexation formula, such as indexing pensions to inflation instead of wages. Because pensions are still growing at the rate of inflation, governments can argue that they are still increasing pensions. Moreover, in any given year, the difference between the two indexation formulae is relatively small, on the order of one or two per cent. But over time, the cuts compound and become quite significant. Using such techniques, pension promises in EU countries have been reduced by about one-quarter during the past two decades (see Chapter 47). Pension spending is still rising, but by considerably less than it would have risen in the absence of reform.

A second blame avoidance strategy is to reduce traceability, that is, to blur the link between programme cuts and the public policies that caused them. A favourite tack, which Pierson labels 'burden sharing', is to transfer responsibilities from national to local actors without adequate funding, thereby forcing the locals to enact cuts. The 1996 welfare reform in the United States replaced federal payments to the fifty states for the costs of welfare claimants with block grants, and these block grants were not indexed to inflation. As a result, state officials had strong incentives to move as many people off welfare rolls as possible in order to avoid substantial financial liabilities. While the incentive structure was established by the federal government, the tough implementation measures fell to the fifty states, muddying the issue of who was to blame for austerity. Such uses and abuses of local governments are not confined to the United States. In the 1990s, Swedish authorities imposed a freeze on local tax rates for several years. Since most healthcare programmes are financed by local taxes, the effect was to force Swedish local governments to make cuts to the healthcare system. Once again, decisions at the national level made programme cuts inescapable, but it was local government officials who had to enact the unpopular changes.

A third strategy for managing the unpopularity of retrenchment is to divide and conquer. This strategy takes two main forms. The first is side-payments or compensation to potential opponents of reform. For example, the Thatcher government sold public housing at a steep discount to residents, while curtailing investment in new public housing, raising rents, and reducing housing allowances. As a result, the natural lobby for increased spending on housing policy was split, with those who had purchased their homes no longer so concerned about cuts to the government's housing budget. The second divide-and-conquer technique is delayed implementation of cuts ('lagged cutbacks', in Pierson's language), commonly referred to as 'grandfather clauses'. Under grandfather clauses, which are quite frequent in pension reform, existing claimants—and sometimes those who will become claimants in the next few years—continue to receive their benefits under the old generous formula, while the new, stricter rules apply only to future generations. Since current claimants are spared from austerity and future claimants are generally not represented at the bargaining table (indeed, they may not even be born!), opposition to the cuts tends to be muted.

Although the various techniques of blame avoidance may lessen the obstacles to retrenchment, they suffer two important drawbacks, according to Pierson. The first is that they do not necessarily achieve the intended budgetary savings. Small changes to indexation formulae are less likely to elicit resistance, but decrementalism yields most of its savings in the distant future, leaving open the possibility that future governments will reverse the planned benefit reductions. Offloading responsibility for austerity on other actors, such as local governments, reduces traceability. However, burden-shifting also reduces central government control, and local actors may find ways to avoid programme cuts. Finally, divide-and-conquer strategies, whether side payments or grandfather clauses, may divide the opposition, but these compensation measures tend to be quite costly, diluting overall savings.

Pierson is critical of blame avoidance strategies on normative as well as pragmatic grounds. By and large, governments are trying to enact cuts that do not have the support of the population. Moreover, in a number of instances, they are doing so in underhand ways. Techniques like decrementalism and burden sharing seek to hide the government's responsibility for retrenchment. They violate democratic norms of transparency and accountability. Divide-and-conquer techniques may be less opaque, but they are still objectionable. They amount to bribing the few in order to impose costs on the many. In addition, the many are generally excluded from the negotiations over cuts and compensation. Thus, in Pierson's depiction, retrenchment appears as a rather unsavoury process, with governments engaging in strategies of obfuscation and division to implement reforms that citizens do not support or even fully understand.

Pierson has clearly set the agenda for the study of welfare retrenchment. That said, his arguments have by no means gone unchallenged. The next section examines claims that there has been more retrenchment than *Dismantling the Welfare State* acknowledges. The ensuing section analyses arguments that retrenchment has taken place along distinct channels from those described by Pierson.

MORE RETRENCHMENT THAN MEETS THE EYE?

In *Dismantling the Welfare States*, Pierson shows that retrenchment is far more difficult and politically parlous than scholars had previously imagined. But difficult does not mean impossible. Some critics contend that Pierson has missed important cases of retrenchment. New Zealand, for example, is widely seen as having implemented dramatic cuts to the welfare state (Starke 2008). Even in the cases of the United States and Britain, it could be argued that Pierson's conclusions were premature (Clayton and Pontusson 1998; Korpi and Palme 2003). *Dismantling the Welfare State* was written in the early 1990s. At that point, the small changes to indexation introduced by Thatcher may not have amounted to much, but they continued to cumulate over ensuing years, resulting in significant reductions in programmes like pensions. Critics also note that the process of retrenchment did not end in the early 1990s (Clayton and Pontusson 1998). The United States 1996 welfare reform abolished the guarantee of support for single mothers, which arguably constituted a fundamental rollback in citizenship rights. More generally, a large body of scholarship (analysed in Chapter 22) suggests that international developments, most notably globalization and European integration, have intensified pressures for retrenchment in recent years. The implication is that if we extend Pierson's universe of cases across place and time, it is possible to identify instances of significant retrenchment. Still, in defence of Pierson's thesis, it should be noted that government social spending has continued to tick upward, even in those countries most closely associated with radical retrenchment, such as New Zealand, the United States, and the United Kingdom (see Table 23.1 in Chapter 23).

Notwithstanding these battles over government spending figures, the principal challenges to Pierson's characterization of retrenchment have been analytical or conceptual, rather than empirical. *Dismantling the Welfare State* offers a nuanced, sophisticated treatment of how to conceptualize retrenchment, but Pierson's main metric for determining whether retrenchment has indeed occurred in a particular country is government social spending as a share of GDP. If one had to pick a single metric for measuring retrenchment, this would almost surely be the one. However, like any single metric, government social spending as a share of GDP has its limitations. Those who believe that Pierson understates the extent of retrenchment tend to use one of four alternative metrics.

The first is government social spending relative to need (Clayton and Pontusson 1998). During the 1980s and early 1990s, unemployment increased significantly in many countries, while the wages of low-paid workers stagnated or even fell. As a result, citizens needed more help from their government than previously. Maintaining a constant level of social protection in the face of negative developments in the labour market would have required a big increase in social spending, not simply the same level of social spending. In short, governments needed to run faster just to stay in place. The fact that social spending as a share of GDP increased little, if at all, that it failed to keep pace with growing social need, could be read as a case of retrenchment. Instead of running faster to address growing social need, governments continued to jog at the old speed.

A second alternative metric of retrenchment incorporates private or employer-provided welfare benefits (Hacker 2002, 2005, 2006). Citizens receive part of their social protection through the work place, and in some countries, most notably the United States, these benefits can be quite important. Consequently, gauging retrenchment requires us to look at the evolution of private benefits as well as public benefits. In the United States, employers have curtailed healthcare coverage, reducing the options for healthcare plans, forcing workers to pay more, and sending the number of uninsured to ever-greater heights. Employers have also cut company pension programmes, generally replacing guaranteed defined-benefit pensions with less secure and cheaper defined-contribution pensions. Given that some two-thirds of Americans receive health insurance through the work place and roughly one-half receive private pensions, these changes amount to a significant retrenchment of social protection. Even if we concede that the public welfare state in the United States has remained largely intact, the private welfare state has eroded dramatically—and, with it, the coverage of millions of American citizens. A similar story could be told with respect to Australia and New Zealand, where once-significant benefits attached to labour market contracts have been rolled back or dismantled (Schwartz 2000).

A third alternative metric of retrenchment concerns the composition of spending and taxation. Although total spending levels have remained relatively constant, aggregate figures can mask significant cuts to individual programmes. Moreover, when it comes to preventing poverty or hardship, all social programmes are not created equal. Over the past two decades, pension and healthcare outlays have mostly continued to rise, in large part due to an aging population, while unemployment, anti-poverty, and disability benefits have been cut in many countries (Korpi and Palme 2003). The net effect is that government social spending has remained stable, but highly vulnerable groups like the poor and unemployed have lost resources and protections. The reduction of spending on unemployment and anti-poverty programmes has been especially painful, given that it has often taken place against a backdrop of growing unemployment and stagnant or falling real wages.

Changes in the composition of taxation in some countries have likewise produced dramatic transfers of resources from the poor to the wealthy. While Margaret Thatcher and her Conservative successors were unable to cut the overall level of British taxation, they made the system far more regressive (Adam and Brown 2000; Giles and Johnson 1995; Kato 2003). On the one hand, they slashed progressive taxes that increase with earnings or wealth. The top personal income tax rate was reduced from 83 to 40 per cent, the top corporate rate from 52 to 35 per cent, and the inheritance tax from 75 to 40 per cent. On the other hand, to make up for this lost revenue, the Conservatives boosted a series of regressive taxes that fall disproportionately on average- and low-income citizens. The national sales or value-added tax (VAT) more than doubled from 8 to 17.5 per cent, and employee payroll taxes jumped from 6.5 to 10 per cent. Taken together, this combination of tax cuts for the affluent counterbalanced by tax hikes for average- and low-income workers accounted for roughly one-third of the massive 40 per cent increase in inequality under the Tories.

A fourth alternative metric of retrenchment focuses on the government's commitment to maintain income streams (Schwartz 2001). During the post-war golden age, most governments not only tendered welfare benefits to those who were unable to work, but also intervened actively to provide jobs in the first place. At the macroeconomic level, so-called 'full employment policies' meant engaging in Keynesian demand management, that is, boosting spending in a recession in order to preserve high employment levels (often known as 'priming the pump'). At the microeconomic level, government ownership and regulation created large swathes of secure, well-paying jobs in the public sector, transportation, telecommunications, postal services, and utilities (gas, electricity, water). Since the late 1970s, governments have dramatically curtailed both kinds of intervention. In the macroeconomic arena, the fight against inflation has taken precedence over the fight against unemployment (at least until the recent financial crisis), while in the microeconomic arena, policies of privatization, trade liberalization, and deregulation scaled back the number of secure, sheltered jobs (Clayton and Pontusson 1998; Schwartz 2001; Korpi and Palme 2003). Although these changes have not reduced government social spending, they have reduced the government's commitment to maintaining the employment and incomes of millions of citizens.

The alternatives to the main metric of retrenchment in *Dismantling the Welfare State*, government social spending as a share of GDP, are just that—alternatives. They do not challenge Pierson's central assertion that governments have been largely unable to enact deep cuts in public social spending. Rather, they suggest that there are other sources of social protection, such as employer-provided benefits or government-guaranteed income streams, or that there are other ways of conceiving of social protection, such as social protection relative to need or social protection as the prevention of poverty. Put in academic language, scholars are offering a different kind of dependent variable, or outcome to be explained. In the next section, we will see that some are also advancing a different kind of independent variable, or determinant of retrenchment.

ALTERNATIVE PATHWAYS TO RETRENCHMENT

Pierson paints an unflattering picture of the politics of retrenchment, with governments manipulating and misleading the public in order to enact reforms that lack popular support. Certainly, many cases of retrenchment fit this image. That said, much recent literature suggests that retrenchment may take place by other means— more open, accountable, and participatory. Once again, the claim is not that Pierson's depiction is inaccurate, but rather that it is incomplete, that it does not cover the full universe of cases. The revisionist approach extends Pierson's depiction of the politics of retrenchment in three directions.

The first relates to the framing of retrenchment. Retrenchment is not always an exercise in blame avoidance. In some cases, it may offer opportunities for credit claiming. Much depends on how the reforms are justified. As Pierson notes, the public does not generally support cost cutting as an objective in and of itself. By contrast, politicians may be able to present retrenchment in a more positive light if it is hitched to higher objectives. For example, scholars observe that almost all cases of significant welfare retrenchment have occurred when countries have confronted deep economic crises and very large budget deficits (Korpi and Palme 2003; Starke 2008). In such contexts, politicians tend to argue that they are engaging in retrenchment not for its own sake, but in order to right public finances, recover economic sovereignty from foreign lenders and the IMF, reduce punitive interest payments on the national debt, and restore economic growth and employment. Likewise, during the 1990s, when countries needed to reduce their budget deficits below 3 per cent of GDP in order to qualify for European Monetary Union (EMU), retrenchment was justified as a means to advance European integration and create a common currency. Retrenchment can also be packaged as a sustainability issue. Governments often claim that they are reforming the welfare state in order to save the welfare state, for example, curbing pension benefits so that the system will be around 'for our children' (Baccaro and Locke 1996). Finally, retrenchment may be portrayed as part of an effort to improve fairness or social justice. Withdrawing benefits from 'undeserving' groups, such as the affluent, not only saves money, but also makes the welfare state more equitable, especially if some of the savings are redeployed on behalf of pressing social needs (Levy 1999).

Of course, governments' justifications should be taken with a grain of salt. While reformers may indeed be trying to save public finances from ruin, advance European integration, or make the welfare state more sustainable and just, in many instances, these are just convenient rationalizations to make retrenchment more palatable. The proof is in the pudding, in the details of reform, not just in the discourse.

A second modification to Pierson's depiction of how retrenchment takes place concerns the process and participants. Retrenchment is not always conducted in an opaque, exclusionary, and undemocratic manner. On the contrary, there can be significant advantages to enlarging the circle of participants. Because retrenchment is so politically contentious, governments find it both difficult and dangerous to pursue far-reaching reforms on the basis of a minimum winning coalition or 51 per cent majority. If they attempt to do so, the opposition has every incentive to throw in its lot with the protestors. Instead of avoiding blame, would-be budget-cutters become the epicentre of public wrath, with mammoth demonstrations often derailing the proposed retrenchment measures, as occurred in the cases of the Berlusconi and Juppé reforms.

The alternative to this top-down, go-it-alone approach is to open up the reform process, to pursue retrenchment through something closer to maximum winning coalitions. The 1983 Social Security reform in the United States was the product of a bipartisan agreement between Democrats and Republicans. Indeed, most major pension and healthcare reforms have been enacted by some kind of all-party deal or concertation between the government and opposition. In addition, where the social partners, especially the unions, are powerful or play a role in administering social programmes, they have often been brought into the negotiations—a process of reform that Martin Rhodes has dubbed 'competitive corporatism' (Rhodes 1998, 2001). The downside of this approach, from the government's perspective, is that negotiations can drag out the reform process for a very long time. The Swedish pension reform of 1998, admittedly a major overhaul, was some fifteen years in the making! In addition, in order to reach an agreement, governments must make concessions and compromises, diluting the effects of their reforms. But on the positive side, agreements with the opposition and social partners reduce the likelihood of protest, so that the announced reforms can indeed be implemented. They also spread the blame for unpopular retrenchment measures, providing political cover for reformers. Governments are far less likely to be punished at the polls by the opposition if the opposition is equally complicit in the painful changes. Finally, from a democratic perspective, negotiated reforms bring retrenchment into the open, making it less conspiratorial and more transparent and participatory.

A third extension of Pierson's understanding of the politics of retrenchment concerns traditional institutional factors. Pierson's 'new politics' framework places tremendous explanatory weight on policy legacies. Reforming pensions is very different from reforming healthcare because the policy legacies—the nature of government commitments and the interest group structure—are so different across the two sectors. Moreover, within a given sector, such as pensions, the prospects for retrenchment are profoundly shaped by various policy features. In the case of public pension programmes, these features include the age or maturity of the pension system; the percentage of the population that is enrolled; the availability of private-sector alternatives; and the benefit structure (flat-rate versus earnings-related). Pierson suggests that when it comes to retrenchment, programme structure and policy legacies matter more than conventional political science variables, such as labour's power resources or constitutional veto points.

A number of scholars take issue with this claim. It is not that policy features don't matter, but rather that conventional 'old politics' arguments also seem to carry significant weight. For example, the rare cases of radical retrenchment have been the product not only of deep economic crises, as described above, but also of secular right-wing governments, backed by large parliamentary majorities and presiding over political systems with few veto points (Korpi and Palme 2003; Starke 2008). In other words, retrenchment occurred only when both partisan and constitutional factors were strongly favourable. This logic has not been lost on the citizens of New Zealand. In 1992–3, following a decade of dramatic retrenchment, New Zealand voters approved two referenda that changed the electoral law from first-past-the-post to proportional representation, with the precise intent of reducing the government's capacity to pursue radical reform.

Another traditional political science explanation that has been deployed to explain welfare retrenchment is the distinction between pluralist and corporatist polities (Visser and Hemerijck 1997; Anderson 2001; Manow 2001). In a study of Swedish austerity measures in the 1990s, Karen Anderson argues that the centralized, encompassing character of Swedish interest groups provided opportunities for reform that are not available in fragmented, pluralist polities like the United States and United Kingdom. Pierson's claim that retrenchment entails imposing concentrated costs in return for diffuse benefits may be true in a pluralist environment, but not necessarily in a corporatist context. Because the Swedish employers' association enrols almost all of the country's companies, cutting social spending and the accompanying payroll taxes would provide concentrated benefits. Consequently, Swedish employers had an incentive to organize on behalf of retrenchment. Anderson also sees Swedish trade unions as having a stake in retrenchment. Echoing the corporatist literature on wage restraint, Anderson contends that encompassing unions may find it in their interest to accept welfare restraint in order to improve the health of the economy as a whole, since they represent essentially all workers and, therefore, do not confront a significant free-rider problem. Moreover, participation in the retrenchment process allowed Swedish unions to extract important concessions, such as better treatment of blue-collar workers relative to more affluent groups and continuing union involvement in the administration of unemployment benefits (the preservation of the so-called 'Ghent system' that facilitates union recruitment). Thus, the existence of encompassing organizations not only opened the door to austerity measures, but also took some of the harshest edges off those measures.

The revisions to Pierson's explanatory framework suggest that there are two basic approaches to retrenchment. The first, described by Pierson, is the preferred choice of secular right-wing governments, often within the 'liberal' welfare world. This approach relies primarily on stealth and 'blame avoidance', and the reforms tend to have strongly regressive consequences. The alternative approach, put forward in the subsequent literature, is generally deployed by Christian democratic or social democratic governments operating within a corporatist policy-making environment. This approach relies on negotiations between the government and the social partners and is more attuned to concerns about the vulnerable and disadvantaged. Once again, the revisionist literature constitutes an extension of the universe of possibilities described by Pierson, rather than a direct repudiation.

CONCLUSION

Paul Pierson's *Dismantling the Welfare State* has recast our collective understanding of welfare retrenchment. Pierson demonstrates that retrenchment is not simply the obverse of welfare expansion. Policy legacies, such as lock-in and policy-takers, have greatly bolstered the welfare state against would-be budget-cutters. For this reason, retrenchment is exceedingly difficult and politically contentious, often leading governments to try to hide what they are doing.

The revisionist literature has enriched Pierson's original interpretation in two ways. First, it has expanded the set of changes that may constitute retrenchment. Government inability or unwillingness to upgrade benefits to meet growing social risks or the reduction in private benefits may not show up in figures on government social spending as a share of GDP, but they represent significant rollbacks of social protection. Second, the revisionist literature has expanded the pathways for pursuing retrenchment. Retrenchment is not always unsavoury and conspiratorial. Governments can also enact spending cuts by taking their case to the public, hitching retrenchment to higher objectives, negotiating with the social partners, and addressing concerns about fairness.

Pierson's writings subsequent to *Dismantling the Welfare State* reflect this more variegated understanding of retrenchment (P. Pierson 2001*a*, 2001*c*). In the conclusion to an edited volume, Pierson notes that welfare restructuring is not confined to retrenchment. Beyond 'cost containment', governments may engage in what Pierson terms 're-commodification', increasing incentives for labour market participation, or 'recalibration', that is, efforts to repair or update the welfare state. Pierson also acknowledges that the politics of welfare restructuring may vary across place as well as policy. In particular, he emphasizes differences in the agenda and dynamics of reform across Esping-Andersen's three worlds of welfare capitalism.

In the end, the dialogue about retrenchment between Pierson and his critics has been more creative than destructive. The emerging academic consensus paints welfare retrenchment in a diverse light. Pierson's original work identified one channel of reform, while his critics have identified a second. The two channels are not mutually exclusive; rather, they point to different ways to cut, adapt, and modernize the welfare state.

PART VII

WORLDS
OF WELFARE

CHAPTER 39

MODELS OF THE WELFARE STATE

WIL A. ARTS
JOHN GELISSEN

INTRODUCTION

IT has long been recognized that to speak of *the* welfare state rather than of welfare states in the plural can be highly misleading. Welfare states come in different shapes and sizes and vary substantially in their political orientations and distributional outcomes. But this does not mean that every welfare state is 'unique'. We can identify patterns (or 'worlds' or 'regimes' or 'families') through which to identify groups of welfare states that share similar features persisting over time. Much of the work of comparative welfare state research has been concerned with establishing what these patterns are, how they emerged, why they persist, and why any of this might be important. This chapter builds on our earlier review of this debate (Arts and Gelissen 2002), bringing the story up to the present.

Although Esping-Andersen's (1990) *Three Worlds of Welfare Capitalism* was not the first contribution to this debate, it has had a defining influence upon the whole field of comparative welfare state research in the twenty years since its publication. We begin by discussing Esping-Andersen's paradigmatic typology of welfare states and consider why it has had such a major impact. Next we survey the debate that has resulted and consider the refinements of typology that this debate had generated. We then reach out from the 'established' to the 'emerging' welfare states. We ask further what has happened in the recent past and what will happen in the near future within (and between) the differing worlds of welfare capitalism, reflecting on the very varying hypotheses that have emerged in the critical literature. Finally, we discuss the theoretical and methodological adequacy of welfare state modelling.

THREE WORLDS OF WELFARE CAPITALISM

Esping-Andersen's *Three Worlds* (1990) began with a critique of contemporary comparative welfare state research in terms of both its research style and its under-theorization. The dominant research style of that time, the correlational approach, identified a straightforward relationship between levels of social expenditure and levels of 'welfare stateness'. But, in Esping-Andersen's view, expenditure in itself does not capture the 'theoretical substance of welfare states'. Welfare states can be compared in terms of 'more' or 'less' (spending, redistribution, progressive taxation), but, so Esping-Andersen argued, what we should be examining is not (just) how much welfare states spend but rather what they do and how they do it. In his judgement, there are three crucial dimensions to the 'what' and 'how' of welfare states: the degree to which a social service or social security benefit is rendered as a matter of right, enabling a person or family to maintain a livelihood without reliance on the market (the degree of decommodification); the manner in which the major institutions guaranteeing social security—state, market, and family—interact in the production of social welfare (the public–private mix); and the kind of stratification system promoted by social policy and upheld by the institutional mix of these institutions (the extent of status and class differentiation and inequality).

Three Worlds also took issue with prevailing theoretical models of the welfare state. Esping-Andersen's starting point was that 'history and politics matter'. Concerning politics, he argued that the balance of power in a society is decisive for what a welfare state will look like. In this he followed a *power resources* approach. The advocates of *power resources* hold that, in the post-war period—and under conditions of continuing economic growth—cross-national variation in welfare state development can be largely explained by the distribution of power resources in society between major interest groups, by the nature and the levels of power mobilization, the structuration of labour movements, and patterns of political coalition-formation. Class-based parties, including those operating in coalition with other religiously oriented parties, have used democratic politics in attempts to influence distributive processes through legislation and by institution building. This means that the historical legacy of regime institutionalization is also an important factor in explaining variation in worlds of welfare. In a follow-up book, Esping-Andersen (1999) concluded that the crystallization of welfare states into different worlds of welfare capitalism is best understood as the path-dependent outcome of political struggles and coalition formation at historically decisive turning-points.

Looking at the history of 'real' welfare states, Esping-Andersen concluded that one sees not so much a multitude of unique developmental pathways but rather a clustering around three ideal-typical developmental trajectories. Generally, welfare states with similar patterns of resource mobilization, dominant ideologies, and political coalitions will have relatively similar institutional structures. The tendency of welfare states' past history to influence their present institutional structure was strengthened by either the inability or lack of motivation of interest groups in these societies to change all their welfare institutions at once.

To test these theoretical conjectures empirically Esping-Andersen constructed three large cross-national data sets and he, indeed, found not merely variations of 'more' or 'less' around a common denominator but (three) quite distinct regime clusters. Clustering along the three dimensions was clear both on single indicators and when the different indicators were combined. The three regimes he identified were: (1) a social democratic or Scandinavian model manifesting high levels of decommodification, cross-class solidarity resulting in a system of generous universal benefits, and strong étatism; (2) a liberal or Anglo-Saxon model, with typically low levels of decommodification and a strong preference for private welfare spending; and (3) a conservative/Continental model manifesting a moderate degree of decommodification, a narrow sphere of solidarity related to occupational status, and a commitment to subsidiarity and the preservation of traditional family structures typical of the countries of continental Europe.

CRITICAL APPRECIATION

Why did *Three Worlds* become a modern classic? First, in contrast with much earlier work in the area which manifested strong normative and teleological overtones, Esping-Andersen's book was a sophisticated empirical-theoretical study without these undercurrents (Schubert et al. 2008). Secondly, many other contributions to the literature had explained the emergence and growth of welfare states in terms of a supposedly inherent unfolding of the logic of modernization or industrialization or else as a manifestation of the contradictions of capitalism. Such contributions to the literature suggested a process of welfare state convergence and, hence, failed to explain the persistent cross-national variation in welfare regimes, whereas Esping-Andersen's was focused precisely upon demonstrating and explaining why there was a continuing divergence in national experiences of welfare state development (Rudra 2007; van Kersbergen 2002). Thirdly, other researchers relied either on social policy programme characteristics that were not directly supported by systematic empirical data, or utilized generic spending data that eschewed institutional classification (Scruggs and Allan 2006a). By contrast, Esping-Andersen used social policy programme characteristics to construct a set of ideal-typical welfare state regimes and then sought to provide systematic empirical validation of his findings. He also performed a virtuoso slalom between the theoretical and the empirical. Finally, Esping-Andersen not only used his typology and power resources theory to study welfare states as dependent variables, but also set up the elements in the various welfare state regimes as independent variables which could explain internationally divergent outcomes.

Esping-Andersen's book elicited widespread comment, much of it favourable, some of it highly critical. Some of the more sympathetic critics recognized that his typology had merits, but insisted that it was neither exhaustive (there are more than three worlds of welfare capitalism) nor exclusive (there are more anomalous cases than presumed) and therefore required substantial modification or revision. Other critics referred to methodological shortcomings (incorrect criteria, inappropriate operationalizations, methods, variables). The more hostile critics were sceptical of the regime concept altogether as a tool for comparative analysis (Kasza 2002) or argued that typologies as such have no explanatory power (Baldwin 1996). Esping-Andersen has responded repeatedly to these criticisms, defending and elaborating upon his original thesis.

In our earlier review (Arts and Gelissen 2002), we discussed the epistemological implications of using ideal-types as a method for building welfare state models. There are two conditions for the legitimacy of such an approach: first, the typological method should be a valid and reliable instrument for classifying welfare states; secondly, it should be used not only for description but also for explanation. The question whether these conditions are met in this case is central to our discussion in the remainder of this chapter.

Alternative Typologies

Since the first publication of *Three Worlds* a voluminous literature focusing on the construction of welfare state models has emerged (Arts and Gelissen 2002; Esping-Andersen 2004). These alternative typologies incorporated four important criticisms of Esping-Andersen's classification: first, the neglect of the gender-dimension in social policy; secondly, the misspecification of the Mediterranean welfare, states; thirdly, the labelling of the Antipodean welfare states as 'liberal'; and, finally, the failure to recognize the major (but variable) contribution of employers to welfare state development.

Familialism and Late Female Mobilization

One of the most enduring criticisms of Esping-Andersen's classification is that it systematically neglects the gender dimension of welfare states. According to many feminist authors, the gendered division of paid and unpaid work—especially care and domestic labour—needs incorporation in the typology. There is also a more general question of whether the decommodification concept really fits in with a gendered discussion of welfare states, since a demand for employment is an important goal for women's citizenship rights. Indeed, gender cannot simply be 'added to' the existing categories, and the apparatus of classification may need to be more systematically re-tooled (Lewis 1992; O'Connor 1993; O'Connor et al. 1999; Orloff 1993*b*; Sainsbury 1996; see also the discussion in Chapter 35 above). Siaroff (1994) is one of those who have sought to build upon Esping-Andersen's work by examining a variety of indicators of gender equality and inequality in work and welfare. Although the labels he attaches to his types suggest otherwise, his typology shows a strong overlap with Esping-Andersen's classification. Only the one type—the Late Female Mobilization welfare regime—is an addition, effectively resembling a separate Mediterranean type.

The Mediterranean

Of the Mediterranean countries, Esping-Andersen only dealt with Italy and he classi-fied it as a conservative-corporatist welfare state. He thereafter wavered between questioning whether countries like Greece, Portugal, and Spain had genuine welfare states or whether they were 'conservative' welfare states at an early stage of develop-ment. Critics have, however, argued that they have at least 'budding' welfare states (Bonoli 1997; Ferrera 2005*b*, 1996; Leibfried 1992). Upon examining their combined arguments, it appears that a strong similarity exists among their first three types and those of Esping-Andersen. However, all three authors add a fourth—Mediterranean—patronage-based type of welfare state regime to Esping-Andersen's classification.

The Antipodes

Esping-Andersen classified the Antipodean countries (i.e. Australia and New Zealand) as liberal or Anglo-Saxon. According to Castles and Mitchell (1993) and Castles (1998*a*), a case can be made that these welfare states have a distinctive approach, one that is more inclusive than the standard liberal form. They contend that the Antipodes exhibit the world's most comprehensive systems of means-tested income support benefits, originally built on a substratum of 'social policy by other means', largely through the control of the earnings distribution. Other evidence for the exceptional position of the Antipodean countries, specifically Australia, is found when countries are classified according to the typology developed by Korpi and Palme (1998).

Varieties of Capitalism

Some of the heat went out of the regimes debate in the late 1990s. At the start of the new century, however, there was a revival of interest, though now its source lay with those who were interested in production instead of welfare regimes (Leibfried and Mau 2008*b*). Hall and Soskice (2001*a*) argued that production in market economies takes place in one of two ideal typical institutional settings: liberal or coordinated. They hypothesized that employers, because they needed specific skills, played a much more important role in welfare state development than Esping-Andersen had assumed. Liberal market economies fit liberal welfare states, because training systems focus on general skills, making a high level of social protection less necessary. Coordinated market economies rely on a highly specialized labour force and are vulnerable to the poaching of skilled labour (by one firm from another), and therefore require a high level of social protection of the kind to be found under conservative and social-democratic welfare regimes. They found, however, still another type of capitalism, marked by a large agrarian sector and recent histories of extensive state intervention, described as 'Mediterranean'. Their arguments gave rise to a profound debate on combining typologies of production regimes and welfare state regimes (Ebbinghaus and Manow 2001; Hicks and Kenworthy 2003; Mares 2003).

Ideal and Real Types

Does the overlap between typologies also show in the empirical clustering of countries? We can answer this question in the affirmative.[1] It appears that, even when one uses different indicators to classify welfare states, the same countries emerge as typical cases. The United States is the prototype of a liberal regime (with or without the suffix: Protestant, Anglo-Saxon, British, or basic security). Germany is the prototype of the conservative (Bismarckian, Christian-democratic, Continental, corporatist) regime and Sweden of the social-democratic (non-right hegemony, encompassing, Scandinavian/Nordic). Most other countries are less 'pure' cases, but there are few problems in classifying them. Finally, there are some difficult-to-classify hybrids.

Methodological Criticism and Empirical Tests

Several authors have pointed to methodological weaknesses in Esping-Andersen's empirical analyses. Bambra (2006) and Scruggs and Allan (2006*a*) have called in question the validity and reliability of parts of his analyses and criticized the fact that the data underlying his indices has not been publicly available, making replication difficult. Shalev (2007) has argued that Esping-Andersen's first technique (tabular analysis) was unnecessarily 'soft', while the second (regression) is fundamentally in conflict with its analytical premises. Others (Bambra 2006; Powell and Barrientos

---

[1] An overview of typologies of welfare state can be found in Table 39.1 and a classification of countries according to several of these typologies in Table 2 of Arts and Gelissen (2002).

2004; Saint Arnaud and Bernard 2003; Vrooman 2009) have noted that the regime typology rests exclusively on 1980 data and have wondered how the typology would fare if it were based on more recent data.

Because of the methodological points at issue, several authors have tested the goodness-of-fit of the welfare state models using statistically more sophisticated and robust methodologies. Some investigators have also generated new data sets to inquire into the robustness of the models over time. Table 39.1 presents an overview of these studies.

Table 39.1 Empirical robustness of welfare state models

	Number of types and classification assignment	Method of analysis
Kangas (1994)	1. Liberal: United States, Canada 2. Conservative: Austria, Germany, Italy, Japan, The Netherlands 3. Social-Democratic: Denmark, Finland, Norway, Sweden 4. Radical: Australia, Ireland, New Zealand, United Kingdom	Cluster-analysis
Ragin (1994)	1. Liberal: Australia, Canada, Switzerland, United States 2. Corporatist: Austria, Belgium, Finland, France, Italy 3. Social-democratic: Denmark, Norway, Sweden 4. Undefined: Germany, Ireland, Japan, The Netherlands, New Zealand, United Kingdom	Qualitative Comparative Analysis
Shalev (1996)	1. Liberal: United States, Canada, Switzerland, Japan 2. Conservative: Italy, France, Belgium, Austria, Ireland 3. Social-democratic: Sweden, Norway, Denmark, Finland 4. Undefined: Germany, The Netherlands, United Kingdom, Australia, New Zealand	Factor analysis
Obinger & Wagschal (1998)	1. Liberal: United States, Canada, Japan, Switzerland 2. European: Belgium, Germany, Finland, Ireland, United Kingdom, The Netherlands 3. Conservative: France, Italy, Austria 4. Social-Democratic: Denmark, Norway Sweden 5. Radical: Australia, New Zealand	Cluster-analysis
Saint-Arnaud & Bernard (2003)	1. Liberal: Canada, United States, United Kingdom, New Zealand, Australia, Ireland, Iceland 2. Conservative: Belgium, France, Germany, Austria, The Netherlands	Cluster analysis

(continued)

Table 39.1 Continued

	Number of types and classification assignment	Method of analysis
	3. Social-Democratic: Sweden, Finland, Norway, Denmark	
	4. Latin: Spain, Italy, Greece, Portugal	
Powell & Barrientos (2004)	1. Liberal: Austria, Ireland, United States, United Kingdom, Canada, Belgium	Cluster analysis
	2. Conservative: Greece, Germany, Australia, Portugal, France, Spain, New Zealand, Finland	
	3. Social-Democratic: Denmark, Sweden, Norway, The Netherlands	
Bambra (2006)	1. Liberal: Australia, United States, New Zealand, Canada, Japan	Face-value tabular analysis of descriptive statistics (replication of Esping-Andersen's procedure)
	2. Conservative: Ireland, United Kingdom, Italy, France, Germany, Finland, Switzerland	
	3. Social-Democratic: Austria, Belgium, The Netherlands, Denmark, Norway, Sweden	
Scruggs & Allan (2006a)	1. Liberal: United States, Australia, Japan, Italy, United kingdom, New Zealand	Face-value tabular analysis of descriptive statistics (replication of Esping-Andersen's procedure)
	2. Conservative: Ireland, canada, Italy, France, Austria, Germany, Finland	
	3. Social-Democratic: Belgium, The Netherlands, Switzerland, Denmark, Norway, Sweden	
Castles and Obinger (2008)	1. Liberal ('English'): United States, Australia, Canada, United Kingdom, Japan, Switzerland	Cluster analysis [Note: more than one cluster run for different dates and countries, so while groupings are clear, assignment sometimes differs]
	2. Conservative/continental: Australia, Belgium, France, Germany, Finland	
	3. Southern European: Italy, Greece, spain	
	4. Scandinavian: Sweden, Denmark, Norway	
	5. Post-communist (European): Estonia, Latvia, Lithuania, Hungary, Slovenia, Poland, Slovakia	
Schröder (2009)	1. Anglo-American: United States, Ireland, Canada, Australia, New Zealand, United Kingdom	Principal component analysis and cluster analysis
	2. Continental European: France, Austria, Belgium, The Netherlands, Portugal, Italy, Spain, Germany	
	3. Scandinavian: Sweden, Denmark, Finland, Norway	
	4. Undefined: Switzerland, Japan	
Vrooman (2009)	1. Liberal: United States, Canada, Australia, United Kingdom	Categorical principal component analysis
	2. Conservative: France, Germany, Belgium	
	3. Social-Democratic: Sweden, Denmark, Norway	
	4. Hybrid: The Netherlands	

The empirical evidence pertaining to Esping-Andersen's original three-worlds typology is mixed. We can perhaps safely say the following. First, his typology has at least some heuristic and descriptive value, but a case can be made for extending the number of welfare state regimes, perhaps to four or even five, with a Mediterranean grouping the most consistently suggested extension. Secondly, these analyses support Esping-Andersen's assumption that there are some cases which come close to his three ideal typical regimes, but that there are no pure cases. Some cases are (much) more impure than others, and some are clearly hybrids (the Netherlands and Switzerland, for example). Thirdly, if social programmes other than those included by Esping-Andersen are considered, it becomes clear that these do not conform so easily to his welfare regime patterns (Kasza 2002).

Emerging Welfare States

Esping-Andersen (1999) acknowledged that his typology was a snapshot of the world of welfare capitalism at one point in time (1980) and that it does not easily capture mutations or the birth of new species since then. Any static typology of welfare regimes can only remain valid as long as history stands still, which it has not. In the past decades, for example, welfare states have emerged or developed in Asia, Latin-America, and Eastern Europe (see relevant entries later in this Handbook for fuller discussions). It is important therefore to consider whether welfare regimes in the developing world also fall into distinct patterns (Gough et al. 2004; Rudra 2007).

Asia

Several authors have discussed the possibility that we can observe a distinct East Asian welfare regime (Goodman and Peng 1996; Goodman et al. 1998; Jones 1990; Walker and Wong 1996). Countries such as Hong Kong, Japan, Singapore, South Korea, and Taiwan may, arguably, be classified as belonging to a single Confucian, East-Asian communitarian model. Although many of the scholars cited have noted significant differences in the pattern of social welfare in these countries, they have also argued that these emerging welfare states have certain characteristics in common that differentiate them from Western types.

However, when comparative welfare states researchers added the second generation of Asian 'miracle' economies—in particular Malaysia and Thailand—and even a third group—comprising Indonesia and the Philippines—to their analyses, it became increasingly unconvincing to speak of a single 'Confucian' model: some of these countries are Confucian, but others are predominantly Muslim, Buddhist, or Catholic. This led to a return to the Esping-Andersen approach that focuses on institutional traits, political structures, and social outcomes (Croissant 2004). The basic argument is that, while East Asian countries are chronological latecomers, they have introduced social security legislation in much the same general sequence as that of the European pioneers, but that programme adoption has been at lower levels of economic development than in Europe (Croissant 2004; Hort and Kuhnle 2000).

Latin America

It is only recently that Latin American welfare states have received sustained and systematic attention from comparative welfare researchers. According to Seguar-Ubiergo (2007) there are three compelling reasons for studying Latin American welfare systems. First, some middle-income countries—such as Argentina, Chile, and Uruguay—have been pioneers in the early adoption of income security programmes, even preceding some OECD countries. Second, Latin America is the only developing region with at least some countries that have tried to create welfare systems similar to European welfare states. Third, these countries' recent experience of democratization and globalization allow us to explore the interplay between these two phenomena and welfare state development. The fact that the social security systems of most countries in this region have experienced a regime shift because of the economic crisis in the 1980s and early 1990s also makes them an interesting object of study (cf. Barrientos 2004).

Some consensus exists on the characterization of Latin American countries in terms of Esping-Andersen's typology. Several authors (Huber 1996; Seguar-Ubiergo 2007; Usami 2004) argue that some of the countries concerned (e.g. Argentina, Brazil, Chile) could tentatively be labelled conservative-corporatist, at least until the recent reforms. Barrientos (2004) sees some important similarities with the South European welfare states. Those employed in the informal sector have to rely on the family and the market for their welfare, because for them social assistance programmes are largely absent (see discussion in Chapter 41). He characterizes the Latin American regime after the 1990s as 'liberal-informal', because conservative elements of welfare provision have gradually disappeared. Most of the countries involved have cut back employment protection, have replaced social insurance with insurance schemes based on individual savings offered by private providers, have decentralized education and health provision, and have encouraged private provision and private financing.

Eastern Europe

During recent decades, with varying degrees of speed and conviction, almost all the former communist countries of Eastern Europe have entered the world of welfare capitalism. This has raised the question of whether these countries are merely copying the West or whether a new post-communist welfare regime is emerging.

Deacon (1993) tried to answer this question within Esping-Andersen's framework. He argued that the new welfare statism of Eastern Europe has some common characteristics: high levels of commodification, new inequalities, and great reliance on the market place for pension provision. As far as diversity is concerned, he boldly predicted that some Eastern European countries would gradually develop liberal welfare state regimes (e.g. Croatia, Hungary, Slovenia), that others (e.g. the Czech Republic) were most likely to emerge eventually as a social democratic regime type, whereas still others (e.g. East Germany) have already joined in a conservative-corporatist regime. In the case of Bulgaria, Romania, the former USSR (or at least parts of it), and Serbia his prediction was for the emergence, although probably only temporarily, of a new type. Subsequently, Deacon (2000) was in a position to take stock of a number of studies of social policy developments across the region. In this study, he was much more cautious, arguing that it is still premature to draw firm conclusions about the longer-term direction of social policy in each of the countries involved.

More recently, Castles and Obinger (2008) have concluded that the EU now contains a quite distinct post-communist family of nations, and Fenger (2007) has found that post-communist Eastern European countries can be distinguished from the Western and Southern European welfare states empirically in terms of less generous governmental programmes and a more delicate social situation.

WHAT IS NEXT?

In the 'old' worlds of welfare capitalism history also did not stand still. There is a debate about what has happened in the recent past or is likely to happen in the near future in the established welfare regimes as a consequence of globalization and European integration. Some locate and/or predict a retrenchment of the welfare state, while others observe welfare state resilience; some see a convergence of welfare state models, whereas others detect a process of growing diversification and even hybridization (Arts 2002). These are all hypotheses that are variously discussed throughout this Handbook.

There is an extensive literature regarding welfare state retrenchment (cf. Ferrera 2008; Korpi 2003; Starke 2006) and the convergence of welfare state regimes (cf. Rothgang et al. 2006; Swank 2002). Many theorists assume that retrenchment and convergence are inextricably intertwined, with globalization and Europeanization forcing welfare states to retrench radically and recommodify their social security systems for reasons of international competitiveness. In this view, retrenchment will even result, in a 'race to the bottom' or 'social dumping'. In this process, all welfare states will eventually be pushed toward residualism—an increasing reliance on means-tested benefits and privatization. Others, however, believe that convergence will be to the middle or mean rather than to the bottom.

Those who forecast divergence do not deny the challenges of globalization and European integration. They argue, however, that not only different welfare regimes but also specific welfare states will respond differently to these challenges. What they observe or predict is different problem-solving responses in different configurations. Kuhnle and Alestalo (2000), for example, have argued that there has been a 'natural' affinity between welfare state regimes and the pillars that support them. Some regimes sit more comfortably at the top of specific pillars than others. The liberal, Anglo-Saxon regime has an affinity with the market and the family; the Continental, conservative-corporatist regime with family, civil society, and the state; the Nordic social-democratic regime with the state; and the Southern European regime type with the family and civil society. There is, however, plenty of room for hybrid forms. Goodin and Rein (2001) also see much evidence of hybridization. They forecast a further proliferation of hybrid welfare states and an institutional persistence of only a few relatively pure cases.

Still others emphasize the institutional and ideological resilience of welfare regime types in virtue of path dependence (Castles and Obinger 2008) or enduring popular support (Brooks and Manza 2006). Path dependence is often most powerful at the macro-level of the interdependent web of an institutional matrix of complementary configurations and organizations (P. Pierson 2000). The length of the pedigree of such an institutional matrix or welfare state regime is one factor that may determine the degree of path dependence. Variations in path dependence also reflect differences in the extent to which welfare state regimes have been subject to external pressures for change and to their effectiveness and efficiency in the formation of citizen's interests and identities necessary for their continuation (Korpi 2001). What may we expect in the coming years, according to the adherents of this view? Their answer is a somewhat downsized continuation of the same three or more ideal typical worlds of welfare capitalism that we saw emerge in the course of the twentieth century. Mutations will occur, but the core institutions of the regimes will be preserved and they will continue following distinct social policy trajectories into the future.

Which of these possible futures is most likely to emerge? It is hard to tell. All of them concern the recent past and the near future and therefore appropriate data is scarce. Truth seems to lie, at least for the time being, to a considerable degree in the eye of the beholder.

CONCLUSION AND DISCUSSION

A key question we have addressed in this chapter is whether Esping-Andersen's typology of welfare regimes and kindred models are valid and reliable instruments for classifying 'real' welfare states. Abrahamson (1999a) concluded that, as an organizing principle for comparative welfare state research, Esping-Andersen's modified typology has proven to be a very robust and convincing tool. We are more cautious, arguing that the jury is still out. But from our review of empirical studies we conclude—in spite of all kinds of conceptual, operationalization,and data problems that must be solved—that his typology is promising enough for work to continue on welfare state models. That conclusion is reinforced by the fact that theory construction in the social sciences has in recent years moved increasingly towards model building.

In evaluating models of the welfare state, one has to realize that each model, however complex, is always a simplification of reality. Moreover, it is important to keep in mind that models have a dual function of explanation and description. Regarding explanation one should prefer highly simplified (and therefore often very unrealistic) models that have the advantage of great analytical power; concerning description one should prefer highly complex models that often have the advantage of realistic descriptiveness, but which are analytically less powerful. So there is a trade-off between analytical power and empirical accuracy. The guideline for model building is therefore: keep it as simple as possible and make it as complex as necessary. One has to keep this in mind when one reads the reply by Esping-Andersen (1999) to his critics that his typology concerns ideal-typical welfare regimes, not 'real' welfare states nor individual policies. Moreover, as he points out, extending the typology to five or more models would sacrifice the explanatory parsimony of his original thesis and that being so one might as well return to individual country comparisons. A principal value of Esping-Andersen's three ideal-types of welfare regimes is that it provides abstract models, so that deviations from the ideal types can be noted and explained. This could easily lead to rather atheoretical ways of accounting for departures from the ideal types. He and the other model builders mentioned in this chapter have, however, chosen the correct approach: They recast the ideal-types as models by reformulating the underlying dimensions as a set of interrelated variables, they pay attention to how they are causally interrelated and can be investigated in their own right.

A rule of model building is that a good model should contain an underlying explanatory mechanism. Baldwin (1996) has correctly argued that when asking about welfare regime typologies we must ask not just 'what' but also 'why'. It is the theory that creates the typology, not the typology the theory. Esping-Andersen used the power resources theory to explain why three different welfare state regime types have emerged. Korpi and Palme—and, for all that they come to somewhat different conclusions, some feminist authors—work in the same theoretical tradition. One problem is that this theory, as far as it is applied to welfare state variation, is more a narrative than a set of propositions (Schubert et al. 2008). It would be worthwhile theoretically to reconstruct and formalize the different contributions to this theory. Only then could the explanatory value of the typology really become apparent. A further problem is that the paradigm's scope is rather limited. Hicks and Misra (1993) and Korpi (2001), however, have successfully extended 'classical' power resources theory. A final problem is that the (modified) Esping-Andersen typology is static and the 'power resources' *cum* 'path dependency' paradigm has a propensity to overemphasize the worlds of welfare capitalism as 'frozen landscapes'. If different welfare states are changing differently, a systematic cross-national differentiation of how clusters of welfare states adjust their institutional matrix to these changes is needed (Palier 2003). To make the paradigm more dynamic, van Kersbergen (2002) has advanced propositions derived from the power resources paradigm that go beyond the issue of institutional resilience. These contributions promise well for the future.

As far as most of the alternative typologies are concerned, they lack a firm theoretical foundation. They seem to rely either on diffusion of institutional innovations and policy learning theories or else on 'culturalist' theories of family resemblances between nations. None of them has, however, yet been elaborated far enough to compete successfully with the power resources paradigm. More promising is the literature on models of the welfare state stemming from the varieties of capitalism approach. Authors working in this tradition react against what they view as an excessive concentration on unions and states in power resources theory. They assume that the political economy is a terrain populated by multiple actors, each of whom seeks to advance his interests in a rational way in strategic interaction with others. Therefore they can rely upon rational choice theories and especially the new political economics. They place firms in the centre of the analysis, assuming that companies are the crucial actors in a capitalist economy. According to Schröder (2009) the power resources and varieties of capitalism approaches are nested in each other and therefore typologies of modes of production and of welfare arrangements can be combined in a coherent way.

Two other rules of model building are that a good model enables the derivation of substantial and meaningful implications and that a model should be versatile in its applications. One of the important applications of welfare state modelling concerns the impact of welfare regimes on social attitudes. Comparative research has revealed that welfare regimes have had an impact on people's values with respect to welfare and care and their attitudes towards income-distribution (cf. Arts and Gelissen 2002). Within the power resources paradigm, it has been proposed that the type of welfare state regime is likely decisively to influence support for certain forms of social policy. A type that is characterized by universalism would generate the strongest support, whereas targeted institutional arrangements would not succeed in winning the support of majorities. Tests of this hypothesis have shown some empirical support, but the evidence is not really encouraging.[2]

Another important application has been the question of how variations in policy design affect welfare distributions. Esping-Andersen (2004), looking at the findings of several comparative research projects, comes to the conclusion that they lead to a surprisingly consensual view: the larger the welfare state, the greater the degree of

---

[2] For an overview of earlier tests and some new tests see Gelissen (2002). More recently Jæger (2009) has argued that limitations in operationalizing regimes might explain why previous studies show only limited empirical support.

equality in net disposable income and the lower the rates of poverty. This is, however, a subject bristling with methodological pitfalls. To solve the small-N problem, Vrooman (2009) performed a multilevel analysis. Regime types do have the postulated impact on the 'production of poverty', but the effects are modest and sometimes negligible in statistical terms. Only a small proportion of the variance in poverty incidence appears to be related to differences at the country level, the rest consists of differences between individual persons. Because welfare distributing effects are often described in terms of their intended social stratification, a tautological element easily sneaks into the explanations. Using panel-data to deal with this problem, Goodin et al. (1999) show that welfare states not only have intended results, but also generate unintended consequences. As intended and expected, the social-democratic regime succeeds best in realizing its fundamental value: minimizing inequality. But this regime is also at least as good in promoting the goals to which other regimes ostensibly attach most importance. Korpi and Palme (1998) find that institutional differences lead to a paradox of redistribution: The more benefits are targeted at the poor and the more the creation of equality through equal public transfers to all is a matter of priority, the less poverty and equality will be reduced. Thus, institutional arrangements characteristic of certain welfare regimes not only have unintended consequences, but even perverse effects.

All in all, these conclusions provide sufficient impetus to continue welfare state modelling. Elaboration of the theories on which the models are based deserves priority. What also seems to be necessary is the development of a set of empirical indicators—which is publicly and longitudinally available—and of a methodology for constructing decommodification, public-private mix and stratification indices based on the theory and enjoying the consensus of the community of comparative welfare states analysts. Then, predictions can be logically deduced—instead of impressionistically derived—from theory. Only then will a strict test of the theory be possible and only then will the heuristic and explanatory value of the respective models become apparent.

ESTABLISHED WELFARE STATES

CHAPTER 40

THE NORDIC COUNTRIES

MIKKO KAUTTO

INTRODUCTION

THE notion of a distinctive Nordic or Scandinavian welfare state was born long before Esping-Andersen (1990) advanced his general claim that advanced welfare states cluster around qualitatively different regime types. In the early post-war decades, at a time when Europe was divided by the Iron Curtain, the Scandinavian countries, and in particular Sweden, were frequently mentioned—both in domestic and international policy debates—as epitomizing a successful 'third-way' compromise between unregulated capitalism and state socialism. Within comparative welfare state research, the distinctive nature of Scandinavian social policies came increasingly into focus from the early 1980s as functionalist convergence theory was challenged by proponents of the power resources school (Korpi 1980; Stephens 1979) emphasizing the role of class politics as a driver of the institutional variation of welfare states. Today, the idea of a Nordic model still serves as an important reference category for comparative welfare state research and a yardstick for reflecting welfare state change in the Nordic countries themselves.

Debates about the Nordic welfare model tend to involve at least three fundamentally different sets of questions that are not always clearly distinguished: has the model ever existed as an empirical reality (and what are its defining characteristics), are its features and outcomes desirable, and, finally, does it still exist and can it survive?

In the analysis in Chapter 39, the existence of a distinctive Nordic type of welfare state appears to be the least controversial of all the model attributions. But while it may appear that the case for the existence of a Nordic model is strong, there is no consensus on the precise specification of the features that define the model. Traditionally the notion of a Nordic model simply (and somewhat vaguely) referred to an active state, a large public sector, and a broadly conceived public responsibility for the social welfare of citizens all within the framework of a market economy. But, as we shall see, in more recent debates, a range of other more specific aspects and attributes have been suggested as important, and even constitutive components of the Nordic model.

As already suggested, the idea of a distinctive Nordic welfare state has always had strong prescriptive overtones—most often as an example (model) to be followed by other countries, but also occasionally as a dystopia to be avoided. The appeal of the model stems from its alleged ability to produce desirable social outcomes, while at the same time maintaining economic competitiveness and full employment (Kangas and Palme 2005; Lundberg et al. 2008). While it tends to be generally accepted that the Nordic societies have been blessed with a range of beneficial social outcomes— such as a low degree of economic inequality, a relatively high degree of social mobility, gender equality, etc.—criticism of the model has mainly been focused on issues of economic efficiency and sustainability. High levels of public expenditure, the negative incentive effects of generous social protection, and above all high tax rates have been criticized as economically unsustainable and—in the long run— incompatible with economic growth (e.g. Lindbeck 1997; Andersen et al. 2007).

The popularity of the Nordic model—in academic as well as in policy oriented debates—has varied over time in close correspondence with fluctuations in the relative economic performance of the Nordic countries. It reached a climax in the 1980s as Sweden, Norway, and Finland were able to maintain full employment while the rest of Europe (including Denmark) continued to struggle with mass unemployment in the wake of the first and second oil crises. However, when Sweden and Finland and (on a smaller scale) Norway in the early 1990s themselves ran into severe macroeconomic problems, fiscal deficits, and record-high unemployment rates, confidence in the Nordic model faded, among both international and domestic observers. The concept has regained some of its former popularity in the period from the late 1990s onwards as all the Nordic countries experienced a return to fuller levels of employment. Even Denmark recovered from more than two decades of high unemployment combined with chronic balance of payment deficits to become a celebrated top performer in terms of macroeconomic stability and full employment.

In other words, the economic performance of the Nordic countries has once again become impressive, and—as a result of this—political and academic interest in the Nordic model has recovered. The question is, however, if and to what extent the model itself is still intact as an empirical reality in the Nordic countries.

In this chapter we concentrate on discussing the descriptive premises involved in the notion of a distinctive Nordic welfare model. We ask in what sense the Nordic welfare states constitute a distinctive type, and we discuss whether its core features have remained stable in recent decades. Although it should be emphasized that the existence of a Nordic model does not preclude the possibility of change over time in response to new social, economic, and demographic conditions and challenges, we shall argue that welfare state developments in the 1990s and 2000s have posed serious questions concerning both the continuity and the coherence of the model.

COMMON ROOTS AND HISTORICAL TRAJECTORIES

Certainly the concept of a Nordic 'model' is misleading if it is taken to suggest that the Nordic welfare states were created according to a common preconceived master-plan. The features of the developed Scandinavian welfare states have a long history and are the result of political bargaining, step-by-step reforms, and their imperfect implementation. They are, in other words, the result of processes of political evolution rather than intelligent design.

As elsewhere, early welfare state developments in the Nordic countries were related to industrialization, and the associated series of social, demographic, and political changes: urbanization and the birth of the working class, nation building, and the break through of political democracy (C. Pierson 1991). In many respects, the circumstances in which these developments occurred in Scandinavia marked them out from the rest of Europe and comparative historical accounts have pointed towards a specific Scandinavian route to the welfare state (see e.g. Baldwin 1990; Alestalo and Kuhnle 1987; Esping-Andersen and Korpi 1987; see also the special issue of the *Scandinavian Journal of History* 2001, vol. 26, no. 3; and Christiansen and Markkola 2006).

First, there is the role of religion and more specifically changes in the division of power between church and state as a result of the Reformation and conversion to Lutheranism. The responsibility for poor relief was transferred from church to state, and as centralized state power was weak, local civil authorities (municipalities) were delegated the task of taking care of those who could not support themselves. This laid the foundation for a strong role for local public authorities in the management of welfare policies, in close cooperation with the central authority. In time, these responsibilities and powers came to be increasingly funded from taxation (Christiansen and Markkola 2006).

Second, the pattern of land ownership in Scandinavia was distinctive, giving a relatively strong and autonomous position to the peasant population. Family-run small farms were the basic units of production. Due to the late onset of industrialization, farmers remained an important part of the population and a powerful political force in their own right in contrast both to Britain, where the peasantry had long been assimilated into the working class, and those other parts of Europe in which feudal arrangements still prevailed. Independent farmers became one cornerstone of the Scandinavian tri-polar class structure, together with the working and upper classes (Alestalo and Kuhnle 1987). This distinctive class structure, and its consequences in terms of party organization and support, underlines the importance in Scandinavia of building cross-class coalitions of political support for the welfare state project. It may also suggest why ideas of citizenship and equal rights found support amongst both farmers *and* workers, enabling cooperation and consensus. Social policy was not just a 'workers' question', but also included concern for the rural population, helping to pave the way for universalistic solutions.

Third, there is the distinctive role of (leftist) politics which was the leitmotif both of the classical power resources school and in Esping-Andersen's regime theory. In the 1930s social democratic parties came to power in all the three Scandinavian countries (Sweden, Denmark, and Norway) in alliance with agrarian and or social liberal parties, and they immediately implemented important reforms in social protection (most notably old-age pensions and unemployment insurance) that contrasted sharply with Bismarckian social insurance thinking and at the same time departed from the existing tradition of discretionary poor relief (Stjernø 2004). In the first decades after World War II the social democratic parties in Sweden and Norway achieved an almost hegemonic position from which they were able to effectively control the expansion of welfare policies—in close cooperation with a powerful trade union movement. Also in Denmark the social democratic party was comparatively strong, but more dependent on collaboration with a liberal coalition partner. In Finland and Iceland, however, social democratic parties were significantly weaker and hence arguably less pivotal in the design and implementation of welfare reforms (Christiansen and Markkola 2006).

Fourth, it can be argued that the Nordic countries share social structures and cultural values that are particularly conducive to gender equality, and that women have had a uniquely important place in Scandinavian welfare state developments. Women achieved suffrage relative early in all the Nordic countries and the active role of female reformers may help explain why even early social policy legislation reflected the interests of women to an extent that distinguishes the Nordic countries from other advanced countries at the time (an emphasis on individual entitlements, the early introduction of transfers to single mothers, child allowances paid to the mother, etc.).

Incorporating the role of ideas is a fifth candidate to include among the possible roots of Nordic distinctiveness. It has been argued that the Nordic societies are characterized by a particular passion for equality with cultural and historical roots (Graubart 1986). Recently a book edited by Kildal and Kuhnle (2005) has posed the question of whether it is the institutions or the moral commitments behind them that matter most. They argue that welfare programmes are essentially expressions of moral conceptions and values, in which ideas like 'universalism', 'public responsibility for welfare', and 'work for all' play an important role. More broadly, research based on World Value Surveys and European surveys also contributes to our understanding of what is distinctive about political and social policy attitudes in the Nordic region (e.g. Ervasti et al. 2008).

The relative weight of these factors—the timing of changes, the distribution of powers and cleavages in society, and the form that new responses took—was, of course, different in the various Nordic countries. While we can highlight historical similarities and shared practices, it is probably only after 1945 that the Scandinavian countries—operating in favourable economic and demographic conditions—started to emerge as a group with relatively similar social policy designs with Sweden as the forerunner, and Norway, Finland, Denmark, and Iceland as followers or partial outliers.

In summary, a number of structural factors point towards a common experience in the Scandinavian countries: reasonably similar structural conditions, parallels in political mobilization and class-based politics, the importance of public responsibility in the form of decision-making and administrative structures—at both central and local levels—and, rather later, a role for the social partners. Further, similarities between the countries favoured close contacts, diffusion of ideas, and mutual learning (see Petersen 2006). As a result, the Nordic countries bear some 'family resemblance', especially when viewed in a broader comparative framework (Castles 1993).

CHARACTERISTICS OF THE NORDIC MODEL

It has been said that the complexity of historical developments and causal dynamics require us to treat all cases as unique (e.g. Baldwin 1996). Adopting a critical tone towards typologies and regime analysis, Kasza (2002) argues that for various reasons—the cumulative nature of welfare policies, the diverse histories of policies in different welfare fields, the involvement of different sets of policy actors, variations in the policy-making process, and the influence of foreign models—national welfare systems fail to show the internal consistency that would be appropriate for the regime concept to have real explanatory power. Historical research has an eye for differences, and thus it is perhaps not surprising that the most recent historical reappraisal assessed the Nordic model as one with 'five exceptions' (Christiansen et al. 2006). It has also been argued that rather than a single uniform Nordic model, we have several Nordic models (Mjøset 1986), or different Nordic routes (for example, in relation to the development of pension schemes, Salminen 1993).

Whereas historical studies and detailed intra-Nordic comparisons point to differences, social policy research has tended to focus upon similarities in institutional design. By the mid-1980s, there was considerable evidence that the Nordic welfare states had developed a 'distinctive welfare state model' (see Erikson et al. 1987; Esping-Andersen and Korpi 1987; Esping-Andersen 1990; Kolberg 1991; Hansen et al. 1993). We have already referred to the role of the state and other structural factors as crucial for the Nordic model, but here we should also draw attention to the design of social insurance schemes, the role of services, and the functioning of the labour market.

The extensive role of the state and the wide scope of public policies, most generally evidenced in Sweden's high levels of social spending, were already widely commented on in the 1950s and 1960s. As the focus of research shifted in the 1970s and 1980s to consider how the welfare state operates, the scope and role of public policies was, in fact, further underlined as the power mobilization school showed that left power was related to the expansion of legislated social rights. In relation to social security benefits, most social insurance schemes across Scandinavia also had an earnings-related component which applied universally to all workers. In contrast to other groups of countries, where either only flat-rate basic security or occupational schemes dominated and where coverage criteria and social security patterns were different, this made these schemes stand out as being uniquely 'encompassing' (e.g. Korpi 1980; Palme 1990; Kangas 1991). Palme (1999) has argued that by establishing a model of social protection, in which uniform basic benefits and services based on residence were combined with earnings-related social insurance programmes, the Nordic countries took a distinctive path.

One of the aims in developing public solutions was to normalize the receipt of social security and to get away from the stigma associated with receiving public support. Cross-national comparisons of the institutional characteristics of welfare provision were offered as reasons why the Nordic welfare states achieved lower income inequality, lower poverty rates, smaller differences in standards of living, and more pronounced gender equality (e.g. Fritzell 2001).

One way to pinpoint the uniqueness of the Nordic model is to focus upon its combination or configuration of welfare state characteristics. Korpi and Palme (1998) set out to account for what they call 'the paradox of redistribution', arguing that social policies targeted at the poor turn out to be ineffective in abolishing poverty. Instead, their analysis shows that encompassing or inclusive welfare states achieve more equal income distribution and lower rates of poverty. These authors (2004) have further noted that the Nordic strategy of redistribution is constituted by generosity and broad coverage of transfers, combined with a strong emphasis on free or strongly subsidized service provision. Taken together, these necessitate higher social expenditure but also lead to a lower degree of income inequality. Abrahamson (1999b) argues similarly, that what matters in the Nordic case is not just the way that cash benefits have been designed, but the whole pattern of welfare provision (including services). The Nordic model can thus be seen as a combination or configuration of characteristics, some of which are not necessarily shared by all the Nordic countries.

In both Esping-Andersen's regime typology (see the discussion in Chapter 39) and other research based on the power resource perspective, the emphasis was placed upon social insurance and cash benefits, in terms of their coverage, financing shares, and compensation rates.

Assessing welfare state development in Scandinavia from women's perspective, Helga Hernes (1987) has pictured the Scandinavian welfare state as woman-friendly, giving women autonomy and allowing them the possibility of acting autonomously in politics, in the labour market, and as working mothers. While the role of caring services is often—and rightly so—highlighted as beneficial for gender equality, the woman-friendliness of the Nordic welfare states is not just a result of an extensive provision of child and elder care services. It also stems from the early introduction of individual taxation and choices that define the rights to participation, social insurance, and services. Citizenship as a core entitlement principle, combined with individual rights and personal needs assessment in practice, have helped to reduce the dependence of women upon their spouses. The Scandinavian welfare states have developed into dual-earner societies, in contrast to Continental and Southern European countries, where female labour force participation is significantly lower and the male-breadwinner family still relatively prevalent.

Kohl (1981) was one of the first scholars to point to the extent of the public provision of services as a distinguishing characteristic of the Nordic countries in expenditure-based comparisons. During the 1990s this insight has been deepened as cross-national comparisons of service provision have become more prominent in welfare research (Alber 1995; Anttonen and Sipilä 1996; Lehto et al. 1999; Daly and Lewis 2000; Kautto 2002). The most distinguishing feature of the Nordic welfare states to emerge is the prevalence of local and publicly funded and produced health and social service provision, aimed to cater for a wide variety of needs of the entire population (Sipilä 1997). The extraordinary powers of Nordic local authorities are underlined in comparative research; taxation rights, broad responsibility, and legislated autonomy especially emerge as distinctive.

Finally, we need to stress—with Scharpf (1991: 89–97), who relies on Meidner and Hedborg (1984)—the close relation between social policy and employment policy, and the importance of a positive interplay between the unique nature of industrial relations (with high union density and coordinated wage bargaining) in the Nordic countries and welfare state development (see Christiansen and Markkola 2006 and Barth and Moene 2009). Importantly, the Nordic countries have always had high employment rates, both for men and women, and also among older workers. Nordic social policies were designed as trampolines that would allow the unemployed to 'bounce back', favouring risk taking and job change in dynamic labour markets through active labour market policies. Investments in social policy were seen as worthwhile provided they led to a higher level and more egalitarian distribution of welfare, and contributed to the maintenance of full employment and economic growth. Arguably the generosity of social policy in the Nordic fashion is only fiscally sustainable provided that a large proportion of the population is mobilized in the labour market and that reliance on income transfers is short-lived among the working age population This helps to explain why publicly financed activation measures, understood as an investment in people's skills and employability, have been so prominent in the Scandinavian context.

Given this background, the notion of Scandinavian distinctiveness could hardly have been regarded as earth-shattering news when Esping-Andersen's *Three Worlds of Welfare Capitalism* was published in 1990. Given also what was already known about the Scandinavian model, it was the identification of Esping-Andersen's other two regime types and the theoretical insights arising from these that struck the research community and explain the continuing interest in welfare state typologies. For Scandinavian scholars at least, the corporatist-conservative and liberal regimes provided useful references for establishing what was distinctive about the Scandinavian policy package.

THE NORDIC MODEL: AN EMPIRICAL REAPPRAISAL

Esping-Andersen and other proponents of the power resource perspective have offered strong arguments for using institutional data to capture essential differences between modern welfare states. They have pointed out that many Continental welfare states resemble the Nordic ones in their high expenditure levels, but that policy design, coverage of schemes, and benefit rules in the two groups of nations are markedly different. Welfare regime analysis is based on the argument that it is the content of policies that matters more for outcomes than spending per se. Whilst this is true, we may note that the kind of social policy delivered in Nordic countries could hardly be achieved with low expenditure and that expenditure-based measures, if used in a sensitive manner (for instance, by disaggregating by type of programme: see Chapter 23), can be used as indicative measures.

Table 40.1 summarizes our account and highlights diversity in key indicators with OECD data for 1990, when *Three Worlds of Welfare Capitalism* was published. Levels of taxation, social policy spending, and public expenditure on welfare state services measured in proportion to GDP serve as proxies for the scope of the public sector. Gini coefficients measuring income inequality serve here as a relatively uncontested outcome indicator. The data are selected from two main OECD sources. Countries have been grouped according to the typology literature into what are seen as distinctive groups of nations. The Nordic countries are put at the top of the table to highlight their affinity on the selected indicators. Country rankings are intended to help the reader to judge each country's position in the OECD group, its proximity to other countries, and to assess intergroup similarity.

As can be seen from Table 40.1, in 1990, evidence of a grouping of Nordic welfare states was reasonably clear. Certainly, Sweden was the flagship with Denmark as her nearest companion. In terms of taxation, Finland and Norway came very close, but in terms of social spending these two countries could just as well feature in the company of Continental welfare states. However, spending figures for health and caring services distinguished the Nordic group very clearly from other groups, although France and Canada were also big spenders in this area. Spending on cash benefits (total expenditure minus service expenditure) did not reveal substantial differences. The strongest similarity amongst the Nordic countries is demonstrated in respect of the Gini coefficient that ranked these four countries as having the most equal income distribution in the OECD group. The table also shows reasons for treating Iceland

Table 40.1 Key OECD indicators of the role of the state in social policy (1990)

	Total tax revenue as % of GDP[a]		Public social expenditure as % of GDP[b]		Public expenditure for in-kind benefits as % of GDP[c]		Distribution of household disposable income among individuals[d]	
	1990	Rank	1990	Rank	1990	Rank	Mid–1980s	Rank
Sweden	52.7	1	30.5	1	12.5	1	19.9	1
Denmark	46.5	2	25.5	2	10.2	2	22.8	3
Finland	43.5	3	24.5	5	9.1	4	20.7	2
Norway	41.0	7	22.6	8	8.3	6	23.4	4
Iceland	30.9	17	14.0	19	8.3	6	..	
Nordic mean	42.9		23.4		9.7		21.7	
France	42.0	5	25.3	3	8.8	5	27.6	9
Netherlands	42.9	4	24.4	6	6.7	10	23.4	5
Belgium	42.0	6	25.0	4	6.7	10	..	
Austria	39.6	8	23.7	7	6.3	13	23.6	6
Germany	34.8	14	22.5	9	7.6	8	..	
Luxembourg	35.7	13	21.9	10	5.8	16	24.7	7
Switzerland	26.0	22	13.5	21	4.8	21	..	
Italy	37.8	9	19.9	13	6.5	12	30.6	13
Spain	32.5	16	20.0	12	5.6	17	36.7	18
Portugal	27.7	20	13.7	20	4.0	23	..	
Greece	22.8	23	18.6	14	4.5	22	33.6	16
United Kingdom	36.3	11	17.2	16	7.3	9	28.6	11
Ireland	33.1	15	15.5	17	5.2	19	33.1	15
United States	27.3	21	13.4	22	5.3	18	33.8	17
Canada	35.9	12	18.4	15	9.8	3	28.7	12
Australia	28.5	19	14.1	18	6.0	14	31.2	14
New Zealand	37.4	10	21.8	11	6.0	14	27.0	8
Japan	29.1	18	11.2	23	5.0	20	27.8	10
Korea	18.9	25	3.0	26	1.7	26	..	
Mexico	17.3	26	3.6	25	2.9	24	45.1	20
Turkey	20.0	24	7.6	24	2.3	25	43.5	19
OECD Ø	33.9		17.9		6.4		29.3	
OECD σ	8.9		6.9		2.5		6.9	

Notes:
[a] Indicates the share of a country's output that is collected by the government through taxes.
[b] Comprises cash benefits, direct 'in-kind' provision of goods and services, and tax breaks with social purposes.
[c] Public expenditure other than cash benefit expenditures, i.e. public consumption of goods and services plus capital investment in care infrastructure; primarily expenditure for residential care, health services, child day-care and home-help services.
[d] As measured by the Gini coefficients
.. = not available   Ø = average   σ = standard deviation
Sources: OECD 2009i, 2008d.

with special care. In assessing Norway's apparently lower spending than other countries in the group, it should, however, be kept in mind that GDP figures include Norway's oil revenues and that these comparisons necessarily underestimate that country's welfare effort.

Looking at the means and standard deviations in Table 40.1, it is clear that the Nordic countries stood out as a distinct group in all four dimensions covered in the table. Their average tax rate was 42.9 per cent, social spending 23.4 per cent, service spending 9.7 per cent and the Gini index 21.7. Moreover, if we relax our criteria and do not think it necessary to score high on all dimensions, but to score high on most dimensions, inter-group similarity and affinity to a Nordic ideal-type was even clearer.

The countries closest to the Nordic group can be found among the conservative Continental welfare states, where the status of Switzerland or Italy is debatable, but where their alternative positioning would not greatly affect the big picture. In the light of the figures here, the United Kingdom and Ireland could as well be grouped with the English-speaking countries overseas as systematically low spenders displaying high degrees of inequality. As can also be seen from Table 40.1, other OECD countries were a world apart, as were former CEE-countries at the time of their newly gained sovereignty.

A Nordic Model Forever?

There is obviously no one year that could mark a turning point in changing these welfare state clusters or their trajectories. If there were such a year, 1990 could be a feasible candidate, given that this is around the time at which concern about the fate of the Nordic model began to be voiced. At that time the bi-polar world order that had reigned since 1945 collapsed, the Soviet Union ceased to exist, and Central and Eastern European (CEE) countries gained a new independence and embraced a form of the market economy. The notion of a Third Way between capitalism and communism lost its appeal. Moreover, as already mentioned, the early 1990s marked a period of economic, employment, and fiscal crisis for Sweden and Finland, which resulted in serious reassessment of the role of public policy. These countries were forced to carry out savings measures to balance public budgets, while Norway and Denmark for somewhat different reasons enjoyed economic good fortune particularly through the latter half of the 1990s.

The early 1990s also marks a geopolitical watershed as Finland and Sweden abandoned EFTA and started their path towards integration in the EU, unlike Norway and Iceland which chose to stay out. Finland later adopted the euro as its currency while Denmark and Sweden retained their national currencies, a factor which inevitably further differentiated the mix of Nordic solutions. Moreover, global competition was increasing: the European Single Market underlined free movement in the EU, and deregulated capital sought lucrative investment opportunities, often guided by cheaper labour costs. Globalization, neoliberal ideas about deregulation and marketization, and worries concerning competitiveness made governments more capital-friendly and affected relationships between the social partners.

In this context, a large joint Nordic research endeavour was mounted to study the evolution of the model in the years since the 1980s (Kautto et al. 1999). A key conclusion was that the Nordic countries still formed a distinct group of nations in terms of welfare policies in the mid-1990s. Only limited convergence with the rest of the OECD countries could be observed. The obvious potential for restructuring coming from macroeconomic as well as demographic and political pressures had not led to fundamental changes in benefit or service provision. Most forms of cash benefit had been reduced, especially in Sweden and Finland, but not to a dramatically lower level in comparative terms. The existing safety net still offered universal coverage in the mid-1990s. When it came to services all the known Nordic hallmarks were still present: universalism, high quality, tax funding, and public provision. Other studies have confirmed this lack of evidence of a major welfare backlash—be it seen as 'retrenchment' or 'dismantling'—in the 1990s (Kuhnle 2001; Nordlund 2003; Castles 2002*b*).

Further research considered the Nordic cases in a larger European comparison (see Kautto et al. 2001; Kautto and Kvist 2002). Here the evidence for clustering was less strong, and no straightforward answer to the question of Nordic distinctiveness emerged from the findings. The Nordic countries as a group still tended to be different from other groups of Western European countries on key dimensions of policy and welfare. Taken together, there was more evidence for similarity than dissimilarity. Although convergence did seem to be occurring in some areas of the welfare state, overall developments tended to be characterized more by parallel trends. Sometimes even outright divergence was apparent as the empirical studies also demonstrated that a variety of policy responses to 'common pressures' existed. (Kautto et al. 2001)

So while Nordic welfare states had changed, in a broader comparison these changes were not of a kind to make scholars abandon the main lines of the regimes thesis. This is also the message of research by Kangas (2004), who considered the specificity of Nordic welfare in surveying state sickness insurance benefits in eighteen OECD countries. He showed that, while up until 1985 the Nordic programmes guaranteed better benefits than corporatist schemes, the situation had now changed. Nordic countries no longer provide higher compensation. In this respect, the two groups of countries have clearly converged, while simultaneously their distance from the countries with basic security or targeted schemes has increased. However, he also found that the Scandinavian schemes had largely preserved their universality, whereas the other country groupings had somewhat reduced their coverage. In another study, Abrahamson (2003) set out to evaluate whether recent major changes in welfare provision had merely modified the Nordic model or whether there had been convergence towards some kind of European social model. Abrahamson argued that there were many first order changes (such as reduced levels of benefits), but that a number of second and third order changes had also occurred; i.e. that the institutional setting and the objectives of the Nordic welfare states had, in certain respects, changed during the 1990s. His conclusion was that the Scandinavian welfare states were undergoing a process of Europeanization, but were still distinct, if decreasingly so.

To sum up, comparative analysis through the 1990s and into the early 2000s suggests that some sort of Nordic distinctiveness remained. However, evidence concerning even more recent change is more open to interpretation.

Part of this ongoing change may be captured by looking at the same aggregate indicators we presented earlier (Table 40.1), but this time for 2005/6 (Table 40.2). The first thing to note is that we do not detect any radical alteration in countries' relative positions. Even after a decade and a half, past budgets continued to be good predictors of the current year's expenditure. Secondly, inter-Nordic dispersion in mid-2000 was somewhat more pronounced than in 1990. Thirdly, the Nordic countries also appeared less exceptional than in 1990. The redistributive budgets in the Nordic countries showed striking continuity, with a Nordic average of 24.2 per cent of GDP for social expenditure and 11.3 per cent for services, while OECD averages as a whole had risen by close to three and two percentage points respectively. On average, the Nordic countries had a slightly heavier tax rate in 2006, but a somewhat less singular performance in respect of income distribution.

Some of the indicators might even suggest that it would be more accurate to speak of a large cluster of Northern European countries rather than distinct Nordic and Continental (or Southern) clusters of countries. The role of the state in France, Belgium, and Austria appeared no less significant than in the Nordic countries. Nordic similarity remained reasonably apparent in terms of taxation, yet here too we encounter other countries with a similar profile. Moreover, while an emphasis upon services was still common in Scandinavia, it was not an exclusively Nordic phenomenon. At the same time, the income inequality indicator revealed convergence. In fact, OECD data on income inequality show that inequality has grown fastest in Finland and Sweden over the past ten years, although from a low initial level. Overall, OECD means have risen and standard deviations have declined, while Nordic averages have remained rather stable giving a much more mixed picture of country differences and some grounds to speak of 'catch-up' convergence.

Farewell to Nordic Unity?

Clearly, two tables with crude indicators are not enough to justify bold generalizations about the fate of a regime. However, in the absence of a single systematic study covering all the crucial elements, this data together with the review provided, should give the reader a picture of change in the Nordic welfare states. But we also have studies at the national level and they tend to point to more significant changes.

Palme et al. (2002) carried out a massive welfare commission analysis on welfare trends in Sweden in the 1990s. This analysis was an overall stock-taking assessment of changes in different welfare policies with extensive data on welfare outcomes for different groups in the Swedish population. The analysis pointed to a number of changes in the system and to unwelcome developments in welfare outcomes, including

Table 40.2 Key OECD indicators of the role of the state in social policy (2005/6)

	Total tax revenue as % of GDP[a]		Public social expenditure as % of GDP[b]		Public expenditure for in-kind benefits as % of GDP[c]		Distribution of household disposable income among individuals[d]	
	2006	Rank	2005	Rank	2005	Rank	2000	Rank
Sweden	50.1	1	29.4	1	13.6	1	24.3	2
Denmark	49.0	2	26.9	4	11.6	2	22.5	1
Finland	43.5	6	26.1	7	9.9	7	26.1	6
Norway	43.6	5	21.6	11	10.1	6	26.1	7
Iceland[e]	41.4	9	16.9	20	11.1	3	..	..
Nordic mean	*45.5*		*24.2*		*11.3*		*24.8*	
France	44.5	4	29.2	2	10.8	4	27.3	10
Netherlands[g]	39.5	10	20.9	14	8.5	13	25.1	3
Belgium	44.8	3	26.4	6	9.1	10	..	..
Austria	41.9	8	27.2	3	8.2	15	25.2	4
Germany	35.7	15	26.7	5	9.9	7	27.7	11
Luxembourg	36.3	14	23.2	9	8.8	11	26.1	7
Switzerland	30.1	21	20.3	16	7.8	17	26.7	9
Italy	42.7	7	25.0	8	7.7	19	34.7	21
Spain	36.7	12	21.2	13	7.4	21	32.9	18
Portugal[f]	35.4	16	23.1	10	..	..	35.6	22
Greece	27.4	23	20.5	15	7.1	22	34.5	20
United Kingdom	37.4	11	21.3	12	10.5	5	32.6	17
Ireland	31.7	19	16.7	21	7.7	19	30.4	14
United States	28.2	22	15.9	23	7.8	17	35.7	23
Canada	33.4	17	16.5	22	9.4	9	30.1	13
Australia[e,g]	30.9	20	17.1	19	8.7	12	30.5	15
New Zealand	36.5	13	18.5	18	8.4	14	33.7	19
Japan[e,g]	27.4	23	18.6	17	8.1	16	31.4	16
Korea	26.8	25	6.9	26	3.8	25	..	..
Mexico	20.6	26	7.0	25	4.9	24	48.0	26
Turkey	32.5	18	13.7	24	5.6	23	43.9	25
Old OECD Ø	*36.5*		*20.6*		*8.7*		*30.9*	
Old OECD σ	*7.4*		*5.9*		*2.1*		*6.2*	
Czech Republic (1995)[i]	36.7		19.5		7.8		26.0	
Hungary (1995)[g,i]	37.1		22.5		8.7		29.3	
Poland (1996)[i]	34.3		21.0		4.9		36.7	

Notes:
[a] Indicates the share of a country's output that is collected by the government through taxes.
[b] Comprises cash benefits, direct 'in-kind' provision of goods and services, and tax breaks with social purposes.
[c] Public expenditure other than cash benefit expenditures, i.e. public consumption of goods and services plus capital investment in care infrastructure; primarily expenditure for residential care, health services, child day-care and home-help services.
[d] As measured by the Gini coefficients.
[e] Tax figures for Australia, Iceland, Japan, and Poland are from 2005.
[f] Social expenditure for Portugal is from 2004.
[g] Health expenditure for Australia, Hungary, and Japan are from 2004. For the Netherlands, the figure is from 2002.
[h] The OECD average is from 2005 and refers to the countries listed above.
[i] Data for countries joining the OECD after 1990 are included in the final rows of the table, but no rankings are provided, since this would limit direct comparability between Tables 40.1 and 40.2. The year of OECD membership is given after each new member.
.. = not available, Ø=average, σ=standard deviation

Sources: OECD 2009i, 2008d.

a rise in disadvantage, income inequality, poverty-risk, and increasing differences in levels of living. In the 1990s, single mothers, people born outside Sweden, families with children, and the young experienced more hardships than other groups and differences in incomes and living conditions had increased. Privatization of services and market-oriented management practices were also a new Swedish reality. The conclusion was that the Swedish welfare state was at a crossroads at the beginning of the twenty-first century.

Many of the social policy researchers who have analysed the development of the Finnish welfare state through the 1990s not only found changes in the system's characteristics, but also detected an ideological shift that can be seen in the revision of goals and changes in policy content (for references, see Kautto 2003). It is argued that Finland has grown away from a Nordic normative tradition with an emphasis on social rights, equity, and state responsibility. Several studies suggest that a real ideological shift occurred amongst policymakers in the early 1990s, with some arguing that Finland had taken a step towards more liberal policies, while others suggest that some of the changes point towards a conservative model.

Assessments are less gloomy for Denmark. Greve (2004) has examined the question of whether or not Denmark is still a universal welfare state. The initial basis for his assessment was a comparative-based analysis of the Nordic countries in respect of key welfare state parameters. The second element of his analysis was a case-based study of core areas of the Danish welfare state—pensions, unemployment, and early retirement benefit—to assess the distinctiveness of the Danish model. Greve concluded that the Danish model is more mixed today than it used to be, but that it continues to be distinctive in areas such as equality, full employment, spending on social security, and active labour market policy. Kvist (2003) in turn has underlined how Danish development in the 1990s was relatively favourable in contrast with a much poorer performance in the 1970s and 1980s. Activation, obligations, and targeting of benefits were part and parcel of Danish reforms, and local authorities were given even more say in activation measures and organizing services. Employment and the economy developed favourably, and close to the turn of the century, Denmark had encompassing welfare policies, progress in most aspects, with low unemployment and without significant increases in inequality.

In Norway, too, welfare state development seems more mixed. Here, welfare state reforms have put an increased emphasis on the responsibility to work. Obligations to work and qualifying conditions for unemployment benefits have been amended. On the other hand, the welfare state has been strengthened in other areas, especially in the area of family policy. In the health and social care sector, a focus on efficiency and market solutions has led to reforms inspired by New Public Management, but the primacy of public sector provision has not been challenged in any significant way. According to Botten et al. (2003) and Dølvik et al. (2007), the welfare state in Norway 'seems to be largely intact', although reform processes are complex and ambiguous.

As these short summaries show, Nordic welfare states do change, and they change in somewhat different directions. New policy lines have been adopted while some of the old ones have been abandoned or transformed. Moreover, core ideas of policies are shifting and being debated: Nordic universalism is being reconsidered and notions and practices of citizenship as a set of social duties as well as rights feature more prominently in policy rhetoric and agendas (Hvinden and Johansson 2007). Also, the introduction of new mechanisms may have wide-ranging effects and the underlying goals may have undergone a more radical transformation. For instance, the pension reforms that have been carried out in all Nordic countries will have far-reaching consequences in the future (see www.reassess.no for information on an ongoing collaborative research effort involving researchers from all the five Nordic countries to take stock of the Nordic Model).

CONCLUSION

At the most general level, the Nordic model can be understood in terms of broad, tax-financed public responsibility and legislated, collective, and universalistic solutions that respect employment interests yet aim at welfare and equity goals. The global interest in the Nordic model is best explained by Scandinavian countries' long record of good economic as well as social performance.

This chapter has argued that the concept of the 'Nordic model' can be and has been understood in different ways. Historical studies have pointed to similarities that may explain the emergence of welfare state institutions, but have also highlighted differences between Nordic countries. Sociologically oriented comparative research in turn has stressed underlying similarities, at least in the 1970s and 1980s, when Nordic exceptionalism was demonstrated in high welfare state spending and the design of social rights. In regime theorizing, these similarities were extended to encapsulate causal factors, welfare state institutions and their interplay with other social institutions, and also their outcomes. Differences from other regimes highlighted reasons to be interested in Nordic policies. The model arguably appeared to be fairly robust in the early 1990s, despite the fact that new winds of change were already blowing at that time.

More recent comparative research and national studies have called into question the uniformity of the Nordic countries and their continued path-dependence. Welfare state adjustment in the 1990s and 2000s along a number of the dimensions central to regime analysis show a degree of dilution of the Nordic distinctiveness that featured in earlier cross-national comparisons. Seen from afar, the Nordic welfare states still look rather similar, as suggested, for example, by their continuing good performance in cross-national economic and social indicator lists. However, a closer examination of reforms and institutional developments in the individual countries of the region suggests that Nordic distinctiveness is by no means as self-evident or as straightforward as it was two decades ago.

....

CHAPTER 41

CONTINENTAL WESTERN EUROPE

....

BRUNO PALIER

INTRODUCTION

....

THE welfare systems of continental European countries have usually been treated quite negatively by the comparative welfare state literature, been given pejorative names such as 'conservative corporatist' (Esping-Andersen 1990), been accused of performing relatively poorly from a social perspective, of currently confronting the deepest economic and social difficulties since the 1970s, and of being unable to change and adapt (Esping-Andersen 1996c; Scharpf and Schmidt 2000b; Huber and Stephens 2001a; P. Pierson 2001a). If this chapter does not deny the problems encountered by the welfare systems of Western continental Europe, it seeks, at least, to provide an account of the internal logic of these systems 'from within', as well as showing that they have changed very substantially during the past fifteen years.

The chapter will analyse the commonalities and transformations of a specific type of welfare system: one in which social insurance is the primary delivery mechanism, where access to benefits is mainly based on work and contribution records, where benefits are mainly in cash and calculated as a proportion of past earnings, where the biggest share of the financing comes from social contributions paid by employers and employees, and where the governance and management are neither directly run by the state nor by private companies, but by collective compulsory social insurance funds. These features dominate the welfare systems of Germany, France, Belgium, Austria, and to a lesser degree the Netherlands.[1]

The first part of this chapter will focus on the origins of these systems, the main goals they tried to achieve through their historical development and the specific principles on which they rely. The second part will show how they developed and functioned during their golden age, emphasizing their institutional traits and complementarities with certain forms of industrial capitalism. The third part will analyse the specificities of the crises these systems are facing. The last part will discuss the various sequences of welfare reform that have lead these systems to adopt structural reforms. The conclusion will focus on the dualization processes that characterize the main changes of Bismarckian welfare systems.

THE INDUSTRIAL ORIGINS OF 'BISMARCKIAN' WELFARE SYSTEMS

Using the notion of 'welfare state' to designate the welfare systems of continental Europe is probably misleading, since the state did not create the social insurance instruments, nor did it (and it still does not) totally finance or really run them. The state's initial primary role was to make social insurance compulsory (see Table 5.1 in Chapter 5 for the dates of the various legislative acts making social insurance in different fields compulsory). But before the state intervened, social insurance bodies had often been established at the firm or industry level, either by workers themselves or by their employers.

With the advent of industrialization, the conditions of life changed. Most industrial workers lived in urban areas, far from their extended families and other local providers of help in case of need. They were not self-sufficient. They had to sell their labour power to survive—in effect, as Marx and Polyani amongst others have suggested, they were transformed into commodities. This meant, of course, that they confronted huge problems if they could not work for reasons such as old age and incapacity, sickness, accidents at work—which were frequent in the early stage of industrialism—or simply because there were no jobs to be found.

To cope with these circumstances, during the nineteenth century, certain workers—usually the relatively politicized/educated/skilled ones—got organized (Zola 1885). They copied instruments used since the Middle Ages by the guilds and corporations of certain urban occupations, and created what were called 'friendly societies'

---

[1] Of course, the social insurance mechanism is also encountered elsewhere: in Switzerland, it is important, but not as prominent as in the countries mentioned; it is the usual although not invariable method for coping with the risk of unemployment in advanced societies and the preferred instrument of old age provision in Southern Europe, in Eastern Central Europe, and in Sweden before 1998.

(in England), '*Hilfskassen*' (in Germany), and '*Société de secours mutuelles*' (in France). These were solidaristic clubs whose members were supposed to belong to the same profession/occupation and to pay a contribution (a part of their wages). These societies also became places for political discussion; they could organize social movements and strikes, and also played a role in the development of trade unions. The more workers were organized, the more they could exert pressure on their employers and use that pressure to seek the improvement of members' working conditions and well-being.

Employers did not always seek to repress these organizations. On the contrary, some of them saw themselves as having an interest in developing or at least subsidizing these solidaristic societies. Isabella Mares (2003) has shown that employers had two main interests in social insurance for their workers. First, they could pool the risk that they themselves were running, i.e. of having to pay for the consequences of industrial injuries. Once workers were organized and could sue for negligence, it could make sense to admit a degree of responsibility and collectivize risk by creating work accident insurance systems (Ewald 1986). Second, confronted with the volatility of labour markets (work contracts were not common before the twentieth century), employers could not be certain of keeping their 'good' workers: those who were peaceful, worked well, and especially those in whom employers had invested heavily in terms of skills training. Offering higher wages was often not sufficient to retain the best workers and providing social protection to skilled workers to ensure their attachment to the company became a tool of workforce management (Mares 2003).

Of course, it was not just German, French, or Belgian employers who pursued their economic interests by promoting and financing social insurance schemes for their employees. Peter Swenson (2002) has shown that American and Swedish employers also supported social protection for their workers. What was specific to continental Europe though—especially in Germany, France, and Belgium, and, to a lesser degree, Austria and the Netherlands—was the type of social protection instruments chosen and the political context in which they were expanded thereafter.

While market solutions were chosen in the United States (where employers contracted with private pension funds or private health insurance schemes for their employees), and state solutions that established *national* insurance in the United Kingdom (starting with the 1911 National Insurance Act) and in Scandinavia (see Chapter 5), continental European countries preferred to rely on collective occupational social insurance funds (the German *Kassen* and the French *Caisses*). These social insurance funds were not run as private companies, but as not-for-profit bodies headed by representatives of the employees and employers (afterwards called the 'social partners'). However, the funds were not (nor are they now) public bodies: their representatives sought, as far as possible, to remain independent from the state. Hence when there was debate in mid-nineteenth-century France about whether the state should legislate to make social insurance compulsory, some workers' MPs opposed the idea of *l'Etat-providence* because of their resistance to state interference in the social protection domain. In the same vein, when Bismarck, after passing the three social insurance laws in 1883 (sickness), 1884 (accident), and 1889 (old age and invalidity), wanted to reinforce the role played by the state in the administration and the financing of the insurance bodies, he was opposed by the social partners who distrusted the authoritarian state and wanted to defend their autonomy of management (*Selbsverwaltung*) and the self-financing of the social insurance schemes they ran (social insurance contributions levied on wages rather than taxes on all income).

This distrust of state or market solutions was echoed in Catholic social doctrine as elaborated in the late nineteenth century as a reaction to the increased involvement of many European states in the traditional domains of church intervention, i.e. education and poor relief (on conflicts between church and state, see Chapter 18). This doctrine promoted subsidiarity as the main principle for distributing competences with respect to social issues, with the family coming first, religious charities and other communities (including working ones) second, and with the state playing a role only as a provider of last resort if the other institutions failed. As demonstrated by Kees van Kersbergen (1995), this social Catholic doctrine was crucial in shaping the approach to social issues of the emergent European Christian Democratic parties, which were to become one of the driving forces for the expansion of welfare systems in continental Europe over the course of the twentieth century (see also Huber and Stephens 2001a; van Kersbergen and Manow 2009).

This short historical account helps us better understand the main characteristics of the systems of social protection that survived after World War II. Born with industrial capitalism, these systems of collective social insurance are primarily focused on providing job and income security for male industrial workers. Based on the principle of subsidiarity, they distrust market or state solutions, favour occupational social insurance, and focus on the needs of families. Their primary goal is to provide income replacement to insured persons in the event of social risk. With separate insurance schemes in different industries or firms, they are highly fragmented and heterogeneous. In this framework, professional belonging is crucial in defining an individual's social identity; social rights are largely obtained through work and emphasis is given to collective protection and collectively negotiated rights. Social insurance schemes are less an arena of industrial conflict than an instrument of social partnership designed to address the issue of the social and political integration of industrial workers—*die Arbeiterfrage* in German, *la question sociale* in French—and a guarantee of social peace. As far as social justice is concerned, these schemes are less concerned with poverty or inequality than with ensuring the proportionality of benefits in respect of former wage levels and contribution records, i.e. reinforcing the so-called equivalence principle (*Äquivalenz-Prinzip*). As Richard Titmuss put it: 'the industrial achievement-performance model of social policy...incorporates a significant role for social welfare institutions as adjuncts of the economy. It holds that social needs should be met on the basis of merit, work performance and productivity' (1974a: 31).

THE SOCIAL INSURANCE WELFARE SYSTEMS
IN THEIR HEYDAY

The expansion of Bismarckian welfare systems was based on a specific post-war compromise. While all the governments of Western Europe shared the view that everybody should be protected against the main social risks, some decided to go for a state solution (the United Kingdom and later the Nordic countries), while the continental European governments, where Christian Democrats either dominated or played a significant role, chose to remain true to their own history and utilize 'Bismarckian means' to reach Beveridgean objectives. Instead of radically changing their inherited system of social insurance, they progressively extended these schemes to cover all employees and the self-employed (and their dependants), while supposing that it was mainly men who would form the workforce and that women would stay at home and care for the children and/or dependent elderly.

Instead of a major rupture, the story of these systems' expansion during the *Trente Glorieuses* (the golden era of the welfare state from 1945 to 1975) in continental Western Europe is, thus, one of progressive extension of both the coverage and the generosity of the various social insurance schemes already in existence. Very often, rather than be integrated into one universal scheme that covered the whole population, the different occupational groups wanted to preserve or create their own schemes. As a result, these systems had become 'quasi-universal' by the 1970s: that is, they provided social insurance to all workers and derived social rights to their dependants, although they remained fragmented and unequal, providing better benefits to some professions (core industrial workers, public servants) than to others (agricultural workers, for instance, or the self-employed). The strong fragmentation of these systems is one of their main characteristics. In the late 1980s, one could count 1,200 separate regional occupational or company-based health insurance funds in Germany, while pension provision was much more integrated, with two main schemes—one for blue-collar and one for white-collar workers—and special schemes for miners, civil servants, and the self-employed: in France, there were nineteen different health insurance schemes, over 600 basic pension schemes, and more than 6,000 complementary pension schemes. Belgium and Austria were also very fragmented. The Netherlands has a (Beveridgean) basic universal pension system, but it also has many separate complementary pension schemes and a number of health insurance providers. In general, unemployment insurance is much less fragmented, but still manifests a high degree of 'corporatism', being either run by both social partners or, in Belgium, by the trade unions. Social assistance schemes are not insurance-based, generally being locally run, tax financed, and managed by the public authorities. Family benefits are also generally not linked to previous contributions, but either given to all families or targeted to the poorest families.

In the early 1980s, the Bismarckian welfare systems of Germany, France, Austria, Belgium and the Netherlands shared the same basic *institutional features*:

- Old age, health, and work accident insurance were made compulsory for all dependent workers and the self-employed (with the richest being exempt from health care insurance in Germany and the Netherlands) and unemployment insurance was generalized.
- Access to social insurance was based mainly on prior contributions paid out of earnings.
- Benefits were provided in cash, proportional to past earnings, expressed in terms of replacement rate, and conditioned by the payment of social contributions—hence their name 'contributory benefits'. Even health care was partly conceived of as delivering cash benefits, with health insurance covering or reimbursing the cost of health services as well as replacing wages during sickness. The Bismarckian welfare systems were thus strongly cash oriented, leaving services (such as care) to women or to the third sector (in the name of the subsidiarity principle).
- Financing came mainly from social contributions—from two-thirds of all welfare system resources in Austria or Germany to 80 per cent in France.
- Administrative structures were quasi-public, involving the social partners in the management of the social insurance funds. Even if the state was involved, it had to share responsibility. In many instances, a state presence in the administration of schemes was wholly absent—as in old age and health insurance in Germany, or in unemployment and complementary occupational pension schemes in France.

In terms of *social outcomes*, these systems have long been characterized by medium levels of decommodification and a strong reproduction of social stratification (Esping-Andersen 1990), i.e. by quite significant levels of (income and gender) inequality. Because social insurance is work dependent, systems of social protection in continental Europe have relied on full employment to ensure universal social coverage.

In these systems, the level of social protection offered depends on employment situation, professional status, gender, and age of the individual. As a result of the relatively generous replacement rate of social benefits (around 70 per cent of net wages for old age pensions in France, Austria, or Germany and between 50 and 70 per cent for sick pay or unemployment insurance) in these systems, they guarantee insured individuals a certain level of independence from the market in the event of illness or job loss (hence the medium level of decommodification associated with this welfare regime by Gøsta Esping-Andersen 1990). Dependence on the market is indirect, in so far as the level of social benefits provided is itself related to prior employment (and family situation). But since benefits are proportional to earnings and contribution (in the name of the equivalence principle), high levels of inequality in the labour market (between blue and white collars, between skilled and unskilled workers) are simply reproduced by the social insurance schemes. Universality of coverage is dependent on the capacity of society to ensure full (male) employment.

Due to the weight of the male breadwinner model in most of these systems, with France and Belgium being to some degree exceptions (Lewis 1992), women obtained social protection mainly through derived mechanisms, as in their roles as spouses and/or as mothers (see Chapter 17). Children also obtained protection through derived benefits, and not as individuals (thus creating problems for young adults with no work record). Given that entitlements are heavily employment and contribution related, and given that women often do not have paid work but caring responsibilities instead, they receive far lower benefits throughout the pension, unemployment, accident, and disability insurance systems (Häusermann 2010). Although this strong gender bias and the inequalities in rights and benefits it creates have been strongly criticized by feminist scholars, it must be noted that many continental European feminist movements have themselves been long-time advocates of freedom of choice: that is, of programmes that offer financial support to women who choose to stay at home as caregivers, as well as support for those who enter the labour market (Nauman 2005).

From an *economic perspective*, the focus of social insurance on the 'standard employment relation' typical of industry and public service in these countries should be understood as consistent with the type of capitalist development characterizing continental Europe. The expansion of the Bismarckian welfare systems was linked to mass industrialization, and occurred largely in the context of the (post-war) heyday of Fordist, industrial capitalism. In this it differed both from the British welfare state, which was partly established earlier, and the social democratic welfare states, which only took off later, in a post-industrial context. Continental European welfare systems must also be understood in the context of the development of the specific forms of 'coordinated market economies' typical of continental Europe requiring patient capital, labour market stability, cooperation between employers and employees and high skill levels. As Bernhard Ebbinghaus notes (Ebbinghaus 2010: 259):

> Neo-corporatist theory saw the post-war expansion of continental welfare systems as part of an implicit social pact: social protection was expanded in exchange for the acceptance of the uncertainties of social market economies . . . In export-oriented economies, social protection became an important buffer against the cyclical proclivity of the international market, thereby helping to maintain the social consensus typical in corporatist, small European states such as Austria, the Netherlands and Switzerland . . . More recently [Estévez-Abe et al. 2001], the *Varieties of Capitalism* approach linked the development of coordinated market economies in Germany and its neighbours . . . to the emergence of social welfare institutions that were beneficial to maintaining a skilled labour force.

In sum, the Bismarckian welfare state in the post-war period assumed that men were working full time and that they had long and uninterrupted careers leading up to a relatively brief retirement. In most countries on the Continent, the concept of full employment involved primarily the male breadwinner. It was he who was supposed to provide support for the entire family; it was by virtue of his salary that social benefits were acquired. Steps were often taken to discourage women from working. This dependence by families on the income and social privileges of male family heads resulted in greater importance being given to job security and to guarantees of employment status (the seniority principle, regulation of hiring practices and employment termination) than to the development of employment for all (Esping-Andersen 1996c). As will be shown in the following section, all of these characteristics seem to have worsened the consequences of the economic problems besetting these countries from the late 1970s onwards.

EUROSCLEROSIS

Since the mid-1970s, social protection systems in affluent democracies have been exposed to new, but similar socio-economic challenges: increasing capital mobility, intensified competition between economies, de-industrialization, mass and structural unemployment, population ageing, and rising female labour market participation. However, certain systems seem to be more vulnerable to these changes than others. Indeed, these difficulties do not impact in the same way on all countries, because of the filtering effect of welfare institutions themselves.

The steps taken by the countries of continental Europe in response to the economic crisis of the 1970s and to the increase in unemployment that the crisis engendered differ radically from those of Nordic countries (a compensatory increase in the public service sector) or from the neoliberal strategies pursued by the English-speaking countries (retrenchment, deregulation, and the enhancement of labour market flexibility). Working within the context of the logic prevailing from 1950 to 1970, the countries of continental Europe wanted first of all to preserve the jobs of skilled male workers by excluding other workers (the unskilled, women, the young) from the labour market. Thus, these countries sought to resolve their employment problem by decreasing the supply of work, implementing a 'labour shedding' strategy, which led to what Esping-Andersen (1996a) called a 'welfare without work' syndrome.

Continental European countries favoured income guarantees, early retirement, and reductions in working hours in order to maintain the salaries and job security of highly skilled, highly productive, permanent (male) workers. Businesses themselves at first favoured a strategy based on high salaries and high quality production, both of which favoured permanent and highly qualified workers at the expense of less qualified or unqualified workers. Workforce reductions were often negotiated on the basis of income guarantees and early retirement, in the hope that the cost of massive retirement could be offset by proportionate gains in productivity (Kohli et al. 1991). These strategies were supported by the state, which, on the one hand, provided significant subsidies for early retirement arrangements and maintained a high level of unemployment compensation, and, on the other, created a variety of social security benefits designed to guarantee minimal incomes for individuals withdrawing from the labour force.

The strategies pursued during the 1980s and the beginning of the 1990s were closely linked to the social protection model based on the 'family wage': the man is the source of income from wages and transfers for the entire household—hence the income and social protection of this man should be protected first and foremost. This resulted both in very low levels of employment and a high degree of labour market polarization (Esping-Andersen 1996c) between a well integrated segment (skilled males between 25 and 55 years of age) and a marginalized or excluded one (poorly skilled or unskilled workers, the young, women, workers over 55 years of age, and migrants). While in the 1990s the rate of male labour force participation was comparable to that of Nordic countries (between 75 per cent and 80 per cent), the participation rate for persons between 55 and 64 years of age was clearly much lower: in 1992, 22.2 per cent in Belgium, 36.2 per cent in Germany, 29.8 per cent in France and 28.7 per cent in the Netherlands (Eurostat employment data series).

Despite the fact that the problems confronting these countries have been huge (very slow growth and extremely high rates of unemployment during the 1980s and 1990s in Belgium, France, and then Germany, with Austria and the Netherlands doing considerably better), it has been difficult until recently to implement change in the Bismarckian model. When he analysed 'national adaptation in global economies' and compared the capacity of different welfare regimes to face the new economic challenges, Esping-Andersen emphasized the rigidity of Continental welfare state arrangements, speaking of a 'frozen continental landscape' resulting from the 'frozen Fordism' of Germany, France, and Italy (Esping-Andersen 1996c). He concluded that 'the cards are very much stacked in favour of the welfare state "status quo" in these countries' (ibid. 267). Scharpf and Schmidt (2000b) have similarly argued that, even though all welfare states are in various ways vulnerable to increasingly open economies, welfare systems based on social insurance face the greatest difficulties of all, while Paul Pierson (2001c) has noted that significant welfare state reform has been rarest and most problematic in conservative corporatist regimes. These critiques, however, predate the major changes that have become highly visible in the continental European countries since the advent of the new millennium. During the 2000s, all continental European countries have implemented important structural reforms of their welfare systems. Even though these changes have only become fully apparent to most commentators over the past decade, they must be understood as the culmination of a longer reform trajectory.

A LONG GOODBYE TO BISMARCK?

Recent developments and researches have shown that instead of remaining frozen, continental welfare systems have been undergoing a substantial process of transformation: first, a relatively silent institutional transformation and then a relatively abrupt series of structural changes occurring during the 2000s. In order to present and understand these developments, one has to analyse the three successive phases following the first reactions to the crisis analysed above. One can find a detailed account of this sequential transformation of Bismarckian welfare systems in their various social policy fields in Palier and Martin (2008) and country by country in Palier (2010a).

Timid and Negotiated Retrenchments

The labour-shedding strategy adopted in the 1970s and 1980s had the consequence of decreasing the overall employment rate and increasing labour costs through the continuous increase in social contributions aimed at financing those who had lost their jobs: a much smaller number of workers had to pay more and more to preserve their social protection and to provide the inactive with income. This trend was in direct conflict with the new economic context of the early 1990s when the single market was implemented (1992) and the single currency was in preparation (Maastricht criteria adopted in 1993). The mid-1990s are characterized in the countries of continental Europe by a series of decisions aimed at stabilizing if not retrenching social expenditure.

These reforms were aimed at reducing levels of social benefits while preserving the logic of the system. One can refer here to the so-called 'consolidation' reforms of old-age pension and health insurance schemes in Germany at the end of the 1980s and in the early 1990s; to the multiple pension reforms in Austria; or to the French sectoral reforms, aimed at 'rescuing the social security system' (new medical agreements in healthcare in the early 1990s, a new benefit in unemployment insurance adopted in 1992, and new modes of calculating retirement pensions after 1993). These reforms share certain features, related to the specific institutional settings of social insurance welfare systems.

The main technique used for reducing welfare benefits was to strengthen the link between the amount of contribution and the volume of the benefits (through a change in the calculation formula and/or stricter entitlement rules). This of course relied on the existing logic of the schemes (the right to social benefits derives from paying social contributions), even though these reforms usually meant a shift away from redistributive (horizontal and vertical) towards actuarial principles. For instance, the pension reform adopted in 1989 in Germany planned the introduction of a permanent deduction for pensions claimed before the standard age of retirement, the phasing-out of subsidies for early retirement (by 2012), a shift in the indexation method from gross to net wages, and an increase in the federal subsidies paid into the scheme (Hinrichs 2010). In France, the 1993 pension reform, which was restricted to employees in the private sector, increased the number of contribution-years needed to qualify for a full pension of 50 per cent of the reference salary from 37.5 to 40. At the same time, the 'reference salary' was to be the average salary of the best 25 years (instead of 10 years). The indexation of benefits currently paid was to be shifted from gross wages to prices. In the same vein, there was an increase in the required period of contribution to access unemployment benefits in France in 1992 (Palier 2010*b*). In Austria, the assessment basis was extended stepwise from 5 to 15 contribution years; eligibility for early old-age pensions was restricted (1996), while the contribution rate for the self-employed and farmers was raised in 1995. Moreover, the Grand Coalition government enacted measures to harmonize the calculation of civil servants' pensions with that of general pensions, and it also changed the indexation method for benefits (adjustment based on net rather than gross wages) and introduced deductions in cases of early retirement (Obinger and Tálos 2010).

Such reforms often triggered considerable opposition and had to be negotiated with the social partners to gain acceptance. Since the systems are financed through social contributions levied on wages (and not through taxation), the representatives of those who contribute to and benefit from the systems are the key players in the political game concerning social policy reforms. They have a say in the process and have the power to eventually block proposals with which they do not agree. The acceptance of benefit cuts by the social partners was usually arrived at on a *quid pro quo* basis (Bonoli 2000*a*), linked to adjustments in financing formulas. Retrenchment in social insurance programmes has often been accompanied by a clarification of responsibility: the government proposes to the social partners that the state assume the financing of non-contributory benefits (flat-rate social minima for the elderly, the handicapped, the long-term unemployed; the crediting of contributions for periods out of work because of unemployment, child rearing, etc.) in exchange for their acceptance of cuts in social insurance benefits. Through these negotiations, the trade unions have managed to guarantee the position of current 'insiders' through a long phasing-in period for reforms in pension rights and a dual recalibration of unemployment insurance benefits, with greater benefits for those who worked full-time previously and less for those with more precarious careers (Clegg 2008). These negotiations started to introduce a new world of welfare for 'atypical' workers, through the development of tax-financed non-contributory benefits.

Institutional Changes, Meta-Reforms

These first retrenchment initiatives were extremely difficult to implement, triggering much discontent. They frequently required scaling down to gain acceptance. The political difficulties they caused and their failure to fully achieve the desired outcomes (social expenditure continued to increase and unemployment remained obstinately high) taught governments the lesson that the institutional setting of the systems had itself become a problem. Hence, governments concentrated more and more on 'institutional meta-reforms' aimed at transforming the very bases of these welfare systems: changes in financing mechanisms (toward less social contribution and more taxes) as well as in governance arrangements (weakening of the social partners, privatization or 'étatization').

Since the early 1990s, welfare systems based on social insurance have increasingly been perceived as exacerbating economic, social, and political difficulties. Before retrenchment, social insurance benefits were used as a support for the victims of economic crisis (compensation) and as a tool to counter it (reflation policies, welfare without work strategies). In the next period, when continuous increases in social spending appeared unaffordable, cutbacks were attempted, but essentially to rescue social insurance, which was itself perceived as a victim of the crisis (fewer resources, more expenses). In the new analyses, which support further and deeper reforms, these systems are seen as being part of a more general crisis. Social insurance is now accused of being in some degree a cause of a variety of economic, social, and political problems: by the sheer weight of social contributions, by creating high labour costs that hinder competitiveness and prevent job creation, and by weakening the state's capacity to control expenditure and implement reforms by giving undue influence to the social partners.

The basic pillars of Bismarckian social insurance, i.e. contribution-based financing and the involvement of the social partners in the management of social security, have come under close scrutiny. Some recent reforms have been aimed at modifying these institutional arrangements. This is certainly the case in France with the increase of exemptions for social contributions as well as the development of a new tax to finance non-contributory social benefits (CSG) and with the empowerment of parliament in the social policy-making process. In Germany, capping the level of social contributions was crucial in the reforms of the late 1990s and a new tax ('green tax') has been introduced to finance some social benefits, while the rise in VAT in the early 2000s replaced some part of the employers' contribution. Changes have also marked the governance of the system, usually at the expense of the social partners. Two trends can be seen: a reinforcement of state intervention in social policy making (highly visible in all Bismarckian welfare systems) and the privatization of some social protection functions (manifested in the increasing role of private complementary health insurance in France, of pension funds everywhere, and in the privatization of employment services in the Netherlands). Meanwhile, new types of benefits have been introduced to support the poorest, who do not have enough of a contribution record to be entitled to social insurance benefits: *Revenu minimum d'insertion* in France, minimum pension in Germany, and residualization of the unemployment benefit in Belgium. These institutional reforms introduced new instruments usually linked to a different logic of welfare (targeting, taxation, public or private management of the benefits). They have paved the way for the deeper structural changes that became visible during the 2000s.

The Structural Reforms of the 2000s

Since the early 2000s, a new wave of reforms has been developing in the countries of continental Europe.

• *In Germany*, in 2001, the Riester pension reform planned further restriction of the level of state pensions, but also created the possibility of complementary future pension rights through personal or occupational pension plans. During the early 2000s, the four so-called Hartz reforms deeply transformed German labour market and unemployment insurance, introducing activation and expanding low-cost jobs; between 2003 and 2007 healthcare reforms increased co-payments for patients and competition amongst heath insurance providers, and implemented new tax financing arrangements (Hinrichs 2010).

- *In France*, the 2001 unemployment reform meant activation for most of the unemployed while more and more in-work benefits have been developed (*Prime pour l'emploi, revenu de solidarité active*). The 2003 pension reforms expanded the scope of retrenchment to public sector workers, but also created pension saving plans, both individual and occupational. Throughout the 2000s, co-payments have been increased in the ambulatory healthcare sector giving private insurance a larger role, while the 2004 and 2008 health reforms increased the control of national and regional public authorities over the rest of the public healthcare system, in particular, over patient healthcare use and hospitals (Palier 2010*b*).

- *In Austria*, the various Pension Acts of the first half of the 2000s closed early exit options, harmonized the system by integrating civil servants into the general scheme, diminished the level of pay-as-you-go benefits, and progressively introduced a supplementary private pillar (financed through the conversion of the previous severance payments as earlier in Italy). Employment policies have also been characterized by tighter eligibility conditions for unemployment benefits and a stronger reliance on activation policies and increased efforts to create employment opportunities for the unskilled. In healthcare, due to ever-increasing co-payments and the application of new funding principles that decreased employers'contributions, the share of private health expenditure as a percentage of total health expenditure has increased continuously. At the same time, new state agencies have been created to better control the system (Obinger and Tálos 2010).

- *In Belgium*, after the reform of unemployment insurance to focus on minimum income protection, activation measures were adopted between 1999 and 2005, as well as a generation pact, aimed at diminishing early retirement; state pensions, provided through social security, have become so low that average to high earners have come to rely on occupational and private schemes to obtain a pension commensurate with their past earnings. The 2003 Law Vandenbroucke on supplementary pensions aimed to generalize access to such private provision (Hemerijck and Marx 2010).

- *In the Netherlands*, activation policies date back to the mid-1990s, with the so-called 'Melkert jobs' for low-skilled workers, women, younger workers, foreign nationals, and the long-term unemployed; the introduction in 1997 of cuts in employers' social security contributions for the long-term unemployed and low-pay workers; and the Jobseekers Employment Act (WIW) in 1998, which imposed an assessment interview on each new unemployment benefit. Competition between health insurance schemes became effective in 2005 (Hemerijck and Marx 2010).

In addition to these changes in traditional social insurance schemes, new 'care policies' are emerging. More childcare facilities will be provided to German families, while new policies were implemented in the late 1990s to cope with the new social risks of long-term care or the 'dependency of the elderly', including a new social insurance scheme in Germany (*Pflegeversicherung*), a tax-financed scheme (*Pflegegeld*) in Austria, and a new dependency benefit in France (*Allocation personnalisée à l'autonomie*). Most of these latter measures fall within a traditional social insurance framework, but they assume that women will be active in the labour market—thus adapting to the demise of the male breadwinner model—and have served as tools for creating lower-paid jobs (for women) in the service sectors (Morel 2007).

The accumulation of all these recent institutional and structural changes may signify a general paradigm change for the Continental welfare systems, evincing a shift away from systems aimed at income and status maintenance towards employment and market-friendly welfare systems. Both the objectives and instruments of reform are quite different from those typical of the traditional reaction of Bismarckian systems to social problems: the introduction of funded schemes for pensions, the reduction of early retirement pensions, the activation of the inactive population (including mothers, and even single mothers) and, hence, the defamilialization of care, and an increase of state control over public health expenditure in tandem with the introduction of competition and the rampant privatization of health insurance systems. In many fields, these reforms have also meant a weakening of the autonomy of the social partners. These structural changes are a mile away from the former 'labour-shedding strategy', with governments seeking ways of escaping the 'welfare without work' trap. In the long run, these developments may also force a structural transformation of the Bismarckian welfare systems themselves.

Such structural adaptations may appear marginal in the first instance. However, a study of the national cases shows that, however trivial they may appear when introduced, being usually presented as a mere complement to the still central social insurance systems, these policies can develop gradually to form the basis of a veritable 'second world' of welfare within one country (on these cumulative but transformative changes, in welfare systems, see Palier 2005). A dualization of welfare provision may, hence, be one of the main consequences of the recent reforms.

CONCLUSION: TOWARDS A NEO-BISMARCKIAN DUALISM

The recent reforms have resulted in multiple dualizations: the development of two worlds of welfare within the public system; the addition of a private component to the public one; and the division of the population between insured insiders and assisted or activated outsiders. Beside the remaining—but more individualized and partly privatized—social insurance schemes, a secondary world of work and welfare is developing, for outsiders, made up of secondary 'atypical' jobs, activation policies, and income-tested targeted benefits. This means that the whole population is no longer covered by the same principles and institutions: Bismarckian social insurance is no longer able to attain Beveridgean objectives!

Because of the progressive retrenchment of social insurance schemes through stricter eligibility criteria, fewer people are covered by social insurance and those covered are less well covered. This shrinking of social insurance leaves space both beneath the public system (for covering the poorest with minimum incomes) and above it (for private voluntary components, i.e. private pension funds and private health insurance). This is a new architecture for the Bismarckian welfare systems, with social insurance still central but no longer hegemonic.

This new architecture has created new forms of vertical dualism in society. The population itself seems to be increasingly divided into those whose employers or personal wealth afford them continued access to generous social insurance programmes and private complementary provision on the one hand, and those who have fallen out of that system and are dependent on minimum benefits on the other. To the latter group, one should probably add those being 'activated' into atypical contracts under which they benefit from second class labour and social protection (Clegg 2008). Social protection reforms have thus contributed to increase inequalities and divide society between insiders and outsiders (Palier and Thelen 2010).

One may argue that this dualistic mode of reform is the typical (conservative and corporatist) way of adapting to the new economic and social world (Bleses and Seeleib-Kaiser 2004) and hypothesise that this segmented pathway is quite robust and likely to shape the future of welfare provision in the countries of continental Europe. Even though these systems were already fragmented and inegalitarian, it is clear that recent trends are likely to deepen the divisions and create new social cleavages: a dual labour market, a dual welfare system, and a society even more divided between insiders and outsiders than it was before.

CHAPTER 42

THE SOUTH EUROPEAN COUNTRIES

MAURIZIO FERRERA

INTRODUCTION

THE idea that Italy, Spain, Portugal, and Greece should be considered as a distinct 'world of welfare', characterized by a number of common institutional traits, was launched in the first half of the 1990s in the context of three parallel strands of literature. The first was the typological debate prompted by Esping-Andersen's seminal work on welfare regimes. Italy was the only Southern European country included within Esping-Andersen's sample of countries and it had been assigned to the conservative corporatist cluster. With the extension of both the comparative and the analytical scope of regime theory, a number of scholars started however to suggest that it was empirically more accurate and conceptually more promising to group the four Southern European countries together in a separate cluster. Various labels were proposed to denote such cluster ('Latin Rim', 'Mediterranean', 'Catholic', and eventually just 'Southern European') and a rich strand of research developed throughout the 1990s with a view to capturing the specific organizational features, the overall functioning logic as well as the distributional consequences of the welfare regime in the four countries.

The second strand of literature was the debate on the 'new' Southern Europe as it emerged after the democratic consolidations of Greece, Portugal, and Spain (Gunther et al. 1995; O'Donnel et al. 1986). Though well aware of the peculiarities of each national experience, this debate had identified during the 1980s the commonalities of the modernization paths followed by the four countries (including Italy) along both the politico-institutional and socio-economic dimensions. In the early 1990s, some scholars of this literature discovered social policies as well (e.g. Castles 1995; Ferrera 1996; Petmesidou 1996) and started to highlight their 'family resemblance' across the area and to investigate the crucial role played by welfare state programmes in the anchoring of democratic institutions and in promoting social cohesion and economic growth.

The third strand of debate was, finally, prompted by the European Commission and centred on the issue of 'diversity and convergence'. In the wake of the two 'social' recommendations adopted in 1992, the Commission launched a number of seminars, expert studies, and reporting initiatives, the aim of which was to take stock of the existing variation in institutional adaptations across the member states in the social protection sphere, with a view to suggesting indicators of change and to eliciting reflections on how to foster convergence. This third debate gave two important spurs to the idea of a distinctive Southern European 'model' or 'type' of welfare: it provided a host of qualitative and quantitative data which could be used for detailed and contrasting characterizations; based on these characterizations, the European Commission itself officially endorsed, in various documents, a fourfold partition of 'Social Europe', thus legitimizing the existence of a typically 'Southern European' system of social protection alongside the 'Anglo-Saxon', 'Nordic', and 'Continental' ones (European Commission 1993 and 1995).

During the past fifteen years these three debates have intertwined with each other, but have also kept their own specific research agendas and analytic foci. Thus, within the regime debate a prime preoccupation has remained that of establishing the actual nature of the Southern European 'world': is it a fully fledged regime, clearly distinct from the other three? Is it an underdeveloped variant of the conservative corporatist regime? Or should it be considered as a mixed type, a *via media* between the corporatist and the liberal regime or possibly even the Nordic one? Different authors have provided different answers, depending on their choice of data, indicators, temporal frame, and analytical perspective.

The second debate has been less concerned with ontological questions and has instead tried to capture the flavour and direction of the Southern European road to welfare state formation in the wider European context. Italy, Spain, Portugal, and Greece have been essentially treated as a 'family of nations', displaying numerous affinities and thus experiencing similar developmental challenges in their journey towards modernity. In addition to identifying and describing common trends, historical sequences and critical junctures, this debate has always maintained a strong focus on intra-area variations, both along the East–West axis (e.g. contrasting the Iberian countries with Italy and Greece) and along the North–South axis (e.g. highlighting the persistence of backwardness in many 'Souths of the South'). Through a wealth of comparative-historical studies, the scholars of this literature have unveiled new aspects and new dimensions of Europe's 'fragmented modernity' at its Southern fringes, locating the specific position and role of social policies in the overall picture (Morlino 1998; Rhodes 1997).

The third debate has shared with the second an interest in the dynamics of change and modernization, but it has adopted a shorter temporal frame for analysis, essentially concentrating on the institutional profiles and spending commitments introduced during the 1990s and 2000s in response to changing needs and constraints. A main theme of this literature has been the growing 'Europeanization' of Southern welfare, i.e. the gradual overcoming of the gaps and distortions inherited from the past, which has allowed the four countries to catch up with the more developed systems of Continental and Northern Europe (Featherstone and Kazamias 2001; Ferrera 2005b).

Drawing freely on the three debates, this chapter will offer a characterization of the four Southern European welfare states and their developmental trajectory. The first section will sketch the main dynamics of political and socio-economic modernization. The second and third sections will briefly survey the take off, consolidation, and expansion of the most important welfare programmes. As will be seen, at the peak of the expansion parabola, *circa* 1990, the four countries did share a number of common traits which largely supported the claim of a typological distinctiveness.

The fourth section will reconstruct the process of reform undertaken in the last two decades. The reconstruction will be framed in terms of 'recalibration', i.e. a sequence of institutional changes aimed at gradually rebalancing social protection both across risks and across social categories.

The conclusion will offer a few summary remarks about the overall contribution that the literature(s) on Southern European welfare have given to the field of comparative welfare studies and about the policy 'lessons' which the South European experience can possibly offer to families of nations (or individual countries) in other parts of the world.

A DIFFICULT MODERNIZATION

The four nations of Southern Europe entered the epoch of modernity in conditions of socio-economic and political decline (Malefakis 1995; Sapelli 1995). Throughout the nineteenth century, their economies remained characterized by backward agricultures and vast pockets of underdevelopment. Particularistic cultural traits and patron–client relations survived much longer than in other parts of Europe (Eisenstadt and Roninger 1984) and nation building was accompanied by strong 'familism' and low 'stateness', owing also to religious factors and the encumbering role of the church (Castles 1994a). Industrialization took off between the nineteenth and twentieth centuries and was heavily supported by the state, giving rise to a distinctive form of 'assisted capitalism'. The compressed timing and internal differentiation of industrial take-off exacerbated social conflicts, provoking sharp working class radicalization. The transition to mass democracy was difficult and repeatedly challenged from both the radical right and the radical left. The twentieth century brought about long spells of authoritarianism: two decades of fascism in Italy; four decades of Francoism in Spain; half a century of dictatorship in Salazar's and then Caetanos' Portugal; and recurring periods of autocratic rule in Greece.

During the *Trentes Glorieuses*, modernization dynamics finally acquired momentum and a process of rapid and, again, highly compressed change unfolded, affecting not only the economy but also social, cultural, and political dimensions. Italy was the first country to leap forward, with an early consolidation of the new democratic regime and an economic miracle that more than doubled average per capita income between the 1950s and the 1970s. In the other three countries, economic development proceeded more slowly but, during the 1960s and early 1970s, both the Iberian countries and Greece became increasingly richer, more open, and more secularized. With the demise of the authoritarian regimes in the mid-1970s and the return of democracy, Southern Europe became 'new' from the Atlantic to the Aegean.

A late and compressed modernization however left a number of unresolved problems, especially in the labour market. Compared with their core Continental counterparts, the four South European countries lagged chronically behind in terms of employment levels and an adequate supply of 'good jobs'. This was largely due to a difference in starting conditions: in the 1940s and 1950s, these were predominantly countries of agriculture and of self-employment, in which the informal economy loomed large. The transition to industrial Fordism was much more complex than elsewhere and was still under way when the oil shocks hit the Western economies in the 1970s, increasing Southern Europe's vulnerabilities and undermining the viability of Fordist arrangements as such.

A number of policies introduced during the transition to industrialism gave rise to another peculiarity of South European labour markets: a pronounced insider/outsider cleavage. All four countries put in place highly protective employment regimes (especially in terms of job tenure) for those working in the core sectors of the economy (e.g. the public sector and large industrial enterprises). These regimes operated as differentiating devices, gradually segmenting the South European labour markets into three juxtaposed sectors, hugely different in terms of working conditions and job security: the 'core/regular', 'peripheral/irregular', and 'underground' sectors (Ferrera 1996; Moreno 2000; Peréz-Diaz and Rodriguez 1994). The core/regular sector was characterized by rigid rules regarding hiring and firing, high job stability, and 'family wages' with strong links to seniority. The peripheral/irregular sector (e.g. small enterprises, the building sector, etc.) was characterized by more flexible entry and exit rules, job instability (term-contracts, seasonal employment, and so on), and a much more differentiated wage structure. The underground sector was characterized (by definition) by marked fluidity, informal and differentiated rules, very high job instability, and performance-based (low) wages. The large size of the latter two sectors and the ensuing degree of polarization between guaranteed and non-guaranteed workers remained a hallmark of the South European labour markets, especially during the 1970s and 1980s.

South European labour markets shared with the other Continental labour markets a particular trait: the low level of female participation. Between the 1950s and the 1970s, female employment kept below 30 per cent in Spain, Italy, and Greece. In Portugal, female employment levels were already somewhat higher, because of the high incidence of military service among Portuguese males that pushed many women into paid jobs. Female workers had a more limited access to the core/regular sectors and were largely employed in the peripheral and underground sectors, especially in agriculture.

During the 1980s, the South European labour market witnessed a rapid process of change (Bermeo 2000): agriculture declined, tertiarization accelerated, the economy underwent massive productive restructurings, and employment flexibility started to increase. As in all other European countries, unemployment began to soar: by the mid-1980s, the unemployment rate was above 8 per cent in all four countries, with a peak of 20 per cent in Spain. The plague of unemployment (and 'precarious' employment) hit young people and women in particular: thus, during the 1980s, the insider/outsider cleavage acquired a marked generational and gender profile.

WELFARE STATE FORMATION: A DUALISTIC SOCIAL INSURANCE

The early origins of South European social insurance date back to the first two decades of the twentieth century (Ferrera 2007). Italy pioneered developments, introducing compulsory work injury insurance as early as 1898 and then establishing compulsory insurance for old age, invalidity, and unemployment in 1919. Greece introduced (limited) insurance against work injuries in 1915, but the real foundation of its social insurance system was the 1934 introduction of compulsory pension and sickness insurance. The Iberian countries took their first steps towards social insurance in 1919, but established fully fledged insurance systems only in the 1930s (Portugal) and early 1940s (Spain).

In Italy, the big wave of welfare expansion took place between the 1950s and 1970s, during which a series of ameliorative reforms were introduced, especially in the field of pensions. Social insurance schemes were consolidated in the 1960s and early 1970s in the other three countries as well, but here the big expansion came only after the transition to democracy, when incisive reforms were put in place, pushing up expenditures. During the 1980s, pensions grew by 94 per cent in real terms in Greece, by 27 per cent in Portugal and by 23 per cent in Spain (OECD 2004c).

Despite differences in timing, the formative path of social insurance in the four countries displayed certain similarities. To begin with, social insurance co-evolved with a segmented labour market, and thus acquired its own degree of internal polarization:

generous entitlements for core/regular workers, modest benefits for the peripheral/ irregulars, and only meagre subsidies (if anything at all) for those workers unable to establish a formal contact with the regular labour market (Gallie and Paugam 2000). In addition to this, in its expansionary phase, South European social insurance over-privileged the risk of old age and reserved only a marginal role for family benefits (Ferrera 1996). Thanks to extremely generous legal formulas, the replacement rate of contributory pension benefits in the four Southern countries was by far the highest among the EU member states in the early 1990s, while the value of benefits for the unemployed, family dependants, and the poor in general was by far the lowest (European Commission 1993). This dualism set the South European income mainte-nance systems apart not only from the highly homogeneous North European systems based on universal inclusion, but also from other continental 'corporatist' systems, characterized by a much smaller spread between 'high' and 'low' protection, on the one hand, and between old age and other social risks, on the other. It must be noted, however, that in the field of healthcare, the link with the corporatist tradition was broken in the direction of greater homogeneity rather than fragmentation and dualism (Ferrera 1996; Guillén 2002). Indeed, all four countries established universal national health services during the 1970s and 1980s: a rare but very significant instance of a fundamental 'path shift', which has worked to smooth the profile of the welfare state edifice and has contributed to an upgrading of the allocative and distributive efficiency of social expenditure in these countries—with significant implications also in terms of greater 'decommodification' and 'destratification' (Bambra 2005a).

How can we explain the peculiar institutional architecture of social insurance in Southern Europe? In addition to 'developmental' and socio-economic factors, the debate has highlighted the role of politico-institutional dynamics, emphasizing, in particular, ideological polarizations and the presence of a maximalist *and* divided left (Diamandouros 1994; Ferrera 1993; Watson 2008). Left parties fought hard (since the 1950s in Italy and since the 1970s in the other three nations) in order to promote broad welfare reforms in 'socialist' directions (wide ranging coverage, generous benefits, extensive redistributive role for the state). Owing precisely to such pres-sures, the Italian, Greek, Spanish, and Portuguese Constitutions included, for exam-ple, very ambitious prescriptions on the social duties of the state. In healthcare all the components of the left did pursue with great determination a universalistic project and the establishment of national health services can be largely seen as 'political victories' of the left over conservative-corporatist interests (including those of the Catholic Church) (Guillén 2002). In the field of transfer benefits, however (and pensions in particular), the 'workerist' inclinations of South European socialism and its internal divisions (communists v. socialist parties, maximalist v. reformist trade unions) operated in favour of corporatist fragmentation. Facing harsh compe-tition on the side of a strong conservative (and patronage oriented) bloc—but also competing against each other—the forces of the left opted for a dualist policy: a policy of amelioration of the benefits for core industrial workers, on the one hand, coupled with a policy of weak subsidization (occasionally of a particularistic nature) of marginal workers, on the other. The internal imbalances of South

European social insurance systems at the end of their expansive parabola can thus be partly seen as the by-product of the specific pattern of political competition.

WEAK SAFETY NETS AND STRONG FAMILIALISM

The promotion of social assistance and the fight against poverty have been the weakest front of policy achievement in the South European welfare states—at least up to the late 1980s (Matsaganis et al. 2003). The so-called safety-net evolved slowly, through a sequence of fragmented and mainly categorical additions (orphans, widows, disabled, poor elderly, etc.), with disparate rules, low integration between cash benefits, (generally underdeveloped) services, and wide holes. As a consequence of this, poverty levels have traditionally remained very high in Southern Europe (Atkinson 1998a; Petmesidou and Papatheodorou 2006; Saraceno 1997). Many poor households were (and still largely are) ineligible for social assistance, because they fail to fulfil the narrow conditions stipulated by the various categorical programmes. Needless to say, those affected by this syndrome include all the largest groups of outsiders: the long-term unemployed, new entrants into the labour markets, irregulars and underground workers, and, increasingly, immigrants.

Three factors help explain the marginal role of social assistance within South European systems of social protection: the role of the family, the incidence of the underground economy, and low administrative capacities.

The family has historically been the cornerstone of South European societies, functioning as an effective 'social shock absorber' and welfare broker for its members and responding to a wide range of risks and needs, from childcare to unemployment, from care for the elderly and the disabled to housing (Flaquer 2000; Naldini 2003; Castles and Ferrera 1996). The extended family, comprising three or more generations (and/or lateral kin), has survived for aeons, virtually to the present, backed by entrenched cultural norms (Moreno 2006). Even if actual cohabitation has been sharply declining in recent decades, the intensity of solidaristic ties among family members is still much stronger than in other parts of Europe, so that a peculiar 'care regime' is clearly visible in the whole area (Bettio and Plantenga 2004). South European familialism rests on the deep-rooted assumption that married women's place is at home as primary caregivers, an assumption traditionally promoted and emphasized by the church's social doctrine (Morgan 2006; Valiente 1997). The 'familialization' of social assistance functions has given rise to a distinct gender regime (with formal and informal rules), which has treated women principally on the basis of their family roles as regards their duties, while sending them unprotected into the market (especially in the irregular and underground sectors) in case of economic need (Saraceno 1994; Trifiletti 1999).

From a developmental perspective, the presence of strong extended families and of a familistic culture have played a blocking role, initially, in respect of public social assistance and family-oriented policies, keeping the demand for benefits and services in these fields low. In line with 'subsidiarity' precepts, families would meet the care needs of all their members and guarantee basic economic security; the state could refrain from intervening on this front and concentrate instead on other priorities (among which, typically, pensions had priority). This syndrome has undoubtedly had some positive results in terms of inclusion: the poor have remained more firmly integrated into the social fabric. But it has also generated some institutional traps (including the reproduction of the syndrome itself, in a process of circular causality: see Flaquer 2000) and various socio-economic pathologies: the low rates of female employment, especially in Spain, Italy, and Greece, and partly also the dramatic decline of fertility among women—sandwiched between heavy home duties and unfriendly labour markets—clearly indicate the high social strains present in the Southern model of welfare (Aasve et al. 2005; Del Boca and Wetzels 2008).

The irregular and informal economy represent the second factor that has worked to weaken both the functional need and the political demand for public anti-poverty and pro-family measures. The irregular economy has provided a substantial number of jobs for marginal workers (e.g. seasonal workers in agriculture, the building sector, or retail trade), offering low wages—with low contributions—but at least some anchor to the system of social protection (e.g. healthcare or minimum pensions). The black economy (estimated to produce between 15 and 30 per cent of total GDP) has added, in its turn, an equally substantial range of earning opportunities and has traditionally constituted an important source of income for all outsiders, especially women and young people. Poor families in Southern Europe are known to pool all possible crumbs of income to make ends meet: for instance, the social pension of a grandfather, the 'official' but modest seasonal earnings of the first spouse, the unemployment subsidy of the second spouse, topped by some undeclared income from the informal economy (Ahn and De la Rica 1997).

While strong familialism and an extended irregular/underground economy have operated on the demand side of social protection, the third factor has operated on the supply side: low state capacities have restrained innovation and reform, for fear of activating or exacerbating particularistic behaviours and syndromes of 'group pre-dation' (Arriba and Moreno 2005). As is well known, the delivery of means-tested benefits requires administrative competencies that have been slow to develop in Southern Europe. Owing in part to the legacy of authoritarianism, the administrative systems of this area have historically suffered from low autonomy, low implementa-tion effectiveness, and weak (or in any case, belated) incentives to develop those relational and pragmatic skills which are necessary to manage individualized social rights. Moreover, the low level of institutional autonomy of the administrative system in some parts of Southern Europe has made it difficult for officers in charge of benefit delivery to stand up to external pressures (Cazorla 1992; Ferrera 1996; Sotiropoulos 2004). As a result, the relationship between benefit administrators and beneficiaries has often come to be mediated by 'brokerage' structures between local and central authorities (and sometimes linked to political parties or the trade unions). The combination of extended households, high rates of (mainly traditional) self-employment, large informal economies, tax evasion, and an institutionally weak administrative apparatus has created peculiarly infertile grounds for the establishment and consolidation of social safety-nets based on universalistic criteria. In Italy and Greece particularly, fears of triggering or exacerbating 'welfare patronage' have been often evoked as politico-institutional justifications for limiting the scope of targeted schemes other than those based on relatively straightforward categorical criteria (such as old age or physical impairment) (Matsaganis et al. 2003).

REFORM AND 'RECALIBRATION'

South European welfare states entered the 1990s in a state of still incomplete maturation and laden with internal imbalances. The simplest way out of this syndrome would have been to complete the developmental parabola by gradually ironing out the imbalances with more institutional and quantitative growth. But this option was made more difficult by exogenous constraints. In 1993, when the Maastricht Treaty came into force, envisaging a maximum 3 per cent GDP/deficit ratio by 1998, the public deficit was 7.1 per cent in Portugal, 7.3 per cent in Spain, 9.5 per cent in Italy, and 16.3 per cent in Greece as compared to the then EU average of 6 per cent. South European welfare states were thus simultaneously forced to confront the politically perilous tasks of internal financial and institutional restructuring. Indeed, Southern Europe is the geo-social context in which the metaphor of welfare state 'recalibration' (Ferrera et al. 2000; Ferrera and Hemerijck 2003) appears most appropriate. It is, moreover, the context in which this metaphor has served most explicitly as the reference point for policy reform: both per se and in connection with the wider goal of 'catching up' with the other member states of the EU—perceived, precisely, as possessing a more balanced and solid array of social programmes (Guillén et al. 2001; Guillén and Matsaganis 2000).

The reform agenda has been focused on the following elements: attenuation of generous guarantees (especially in the field of pensions) for historically privileged occupational groups, accompanied by an improvement of minimum or 'social' benefits; introduction and consolidation of the so-called safety-net, especially through means-tested minimum income schemes; the expansion and amelioration of family benefits and social services—with explicit attention to gender equality and equity issues; measures against the black economy and tax evasion; the reform of labour market legislation with a view to promoting de-segmentation and modification of unemployment insurance benefits. Another distinctive element of South European recalibration has been politico-institutional: additional competencies have been assigned to regions and local governments and novel modes of concertation have been experimented with, promoting the involvement of social actors in the process of policy formulation and the formation of mixed partnerships in processes of policy implementation (Rhodes 2003; Guillén and Petmesidou 2008).

Italy can be regarded as an almost emblematic case of multidimensional recalibration (Ferrera and Gualmini 2004). Functionally, the country attempted to halt the expansion of its hypertrophic pension system, with a view to 'restoring to health' its battered public budget and to make room for some upgradings in family policy and social assistance. Pensions were reformed in 1992 and then again in 1995, 1997, 2004 and 2007. The so-called Dini reform of 1995 completely changed the pension formula, linking it closely to contributions in a quasi-actuarial fashion. A number of social pacts were signed between 1993 and the mid-2000s, family benefits were improved and a broad reform of social services and assistance was passed in 2000. Attempts have been made to introduce a minimum income guarantee against extreme poverty, but without success (Sacchi and Bastagli 2005).

From a distributive point of view, the reforms of the 1990s and 2000s worked in the direction of levelling off social rights and obligations across the various occupational groups. Within the pension system, for example, the privilege enjoyed by civil servants to retire after only twenty years of service regardless of age (which had created a mass of 'baby pensioners' since the 1960s and 1970s) was phased out; on the other hand, pension rights were accorded to atypical workers, and lower pensions were repeatedly upgraded. Outside the field of pensions, some traditional gaps in social coverage were eventually filled and new schemes were created for poor households. Little progress has been made, however, in de-segmenting the Italian labour market. Moreover, despite the proliferation of new 'atypical' contracts, the insider/outsider cleavage is still very pronounced, while the reform of a faulty system of unemployment insurance is still pending.

Between 1997 and 2008 substantial powers were transferred from the central government to the regions. While creating numerous problems of implementation and giving rise to new risks of inter-territorial inequities, this process of quasi-federalization of important sectors of Italy's social protection system constitutes a far-reaching experiment in politico-institutional recalibration.

Finally, the reform process has been accompanied by the appearance of a novel discourse on the current state and future prospects of the Italian social protection system, a discourse building on various notions of 'social equity', 'inter-generational justice', 'gender equality', 'productive efficiency', 'subsidiarity', and so on. The ideas that the Italian welfare state ought to give 'more to children, less to fathers' (Rossi 1997), that it should be aimed less at 'indemnifying' than at 'promoting' people's opportunities became the object of an articulated public debate. Measured against an historical background of harsh ideological confrontations between opposing visions of the world ('communism' vs. 'capitalism'), the new argumentative climate of the late 1990s and 2000s can be undoubtedly taken as a clear indicator of a significant 'normative' recalibration.

European integration has also played a prominent role in prompting recalibrating reforms in the Iberian countries (Guillén et al. 2001). In their effort to join the EMU by 1998, both Portugal and Spain engaged in restrictive pension reforms. Like Italy, however, they also proceeded during the 1990s and early 2000s to improve minimum benefits: in the field of old age, of family allowances, and of the basic safety-net. In respect of the latter, all Spanish regions introduced their own regional minimum income (RMI) schemes, embarking on a path originated by the Basque country in 1989 (Arriba and Moreno 2005). Portugal, in turn, introduced a pilot national minimum income scheme in 1996, which was adopted nationally in 1997 (Capucha et al. 2005).

During the 1990s, Spain witnessed—like Italy—a thoroughgoing process of de-centralization of competencies in healthcare and social services from the central government to the regions. But the major challenge that this country had to confront during the last two decades has been labour market reform. Several measures were introduced: flexible contracts, the rationalization of unemployment benefits, various activation measures, and a broad reform of employment services. Compared to Italy, Spain has made more progress in terms of labour market de-segmentation: in 1997, 2001, and 2006, labour laws were changed, relaxing the protection of 'core' employees and improving both the social security rights of irregular/temporary workers and their opportunities to access regular jobs.

Since the mid-2000s Spain has markedly accelerated the recalibration of its social model, clearly leapfrogging the other three countries of the area. The Zapatero governments have introduced incisive measures to promote the autono-mization of women and young people, in a discursive context emphasizing the notion of 'new equalities' and 'citizens' socialism'. A very progressive law on gender equality was passed in 2006, as well as laws to promote childcare and elderly care services and thus facilitate the reconciliation of work and family responsibilties. Female employment has rapidly increased, reaching 53.2 per cent in 2007 (1993 = 30.7 per cent)—a figure that puts Spain in the Southern Europe vanguard, still behind Portugal (62.0 per cent), but way ahead of Greece (47.4 per cent) and Italy (46.3 per cent) (Moreno 2006; Valiente 2006).

Portugal's employment performance remained remarkably good throughout the 1990s. The modernization of social protection was a prime objective of the Socialist government that ruled between 1995 and 2005, which placed particular emphasis on active labour market measures and, more generally, social inclusion policy (Guillén et al. 2001). Unemployment insurance was broadly reformed, occupational training and insertion programmes were expanded, and specific incentives were deployed in order to promote a 'social market for employment', based on insertion enterprises and local initiatives targeted at the most vulnerable groups of workers. In 1996, an innovative 'social pact for solidarity' was signed, with a view to mobilizing local potentials for employment creation. With its explicit reference—in official policy statements and public debates—to the principles of solidarity, social inclusion, but also for the need to fight against fraud and abuses and the need to rationalize pension protection, the Portuguese reforms of the 1990s and early 2000s can be interpreted as an interesting case of normative redefinition of the tasks and priorities of this country's social policy.

While Italy and the Iberian countries have clearly made significant steps forward in recalibrating their welfare systems, Greece has definitely lagged behind (Guillén and Petmesidou 2008). The 1990s did witness some movement towards reform in many sectors and a gradual reorientation of the overall discourse on social policy, reflecting the new EU guidelines and recommendations. But the pace of institutional innovation has been very slow. The hyper-fragmented character of Greek society and its mechanisms of interest representation have posed insurmountable obstacles to the formation of adequate social and political consensus concerning reform needs (Petmesidou and Mossialos 2006). The government did intervene more than once on the pension front, with a view to recalibrating an internally polarized and financially unsustainable system. However, none of these interventions has been able effectively to tackle the roots of the Greek pension crisis (Matsaganis 2004) and pension expenditure projections for Greece are the gloomiest of the whole EU. On the other hand, efforts to strengthen the safety-net, with a view to narrowing its relatively wide gaps in coverage, have not resulted in any substantial reform (Matsaganis 2005). Most of the items on the Greek-specific recalibration agenda still remain to be implemented.

CONCLUSION

During the second half of the twentieth century, the four nations of Southern Europe have gradually 'caught up' with the more advanced European countries and are now fully part of the group of rich and stable democracies. Total social expenditure as a percentage of GDP is still somewhat lower than the EU average, but the distance has been gradually decreasing. Welfare state building has followed a distinct path, characterized by weak Fordism, dualistic social insurance, and faulty and fragmented social assistance. However, under the spur of European integration, the 1990s and 2000s have witnessed substantial efforts to recalibrate and further modernize the welfare state, with a view to achieving more efficient and equitable labour markets, more sustainable and internally more homogeneous social insurance systems and a more effective and inclusive safety-net.

While political and social relations have become more secular and 'civilized', containing church influences and overcoming traditional polarizations and particularisms, the insider/outsider cleavage is still clearly visible and the recent economic crisis is likely to exacerbate it: Spanish unemployment has mounted again to more than 13 per cent at the end of 2008, hitting especially the young, immigrants, and women. It also remains to be seen whether South European familialism will be able to overcome its traditional 'ambivalence'. The crucial question on this front is whether the Southern family and its 'solidarity model' will gradually evolve into a socio-cultural asset fostering social integration, in virtuous combination with adequate, state-funded social policies (in cash and in kind). Alternatively, it might emphasize its perverse traits as a source of pronounced gender and generational inequities and inequalities in the context of persisting gaps in public provision. For the moment there are signs pointing in both directions (as well as of increasing intra-national territorial variations), and it is, thus, too early to suggest a definitive 'balance sheet' of the critical nexus between family and welfare in these countries or to make predictions about the future. Other critical fronts are education and skills formation more generally: the importance of investing in these areas for a successful performance in the global knowledge economy is not sufficiently recognized in Southern Europe.

To what extent might the study of South European developments and recent innovations be relevant for other regions of the world? A debate has recently begun on the potential relevance of the experience of Portugal, Spain, Italy, and Greece for Eastern and in particular South-Eastern European countries (i.e. Romania, Bulgaria, Albania, Croatia, Macedonia, and even Turkey). As argued for example by Sotiropoulos (2005), there are a number of features that make a comparison between the two groups of nations worth pursuing: (1) the dominance of agriculture and the ensuing presence of a pronounced urban–rural divide; (2) a widespread informal economy and concomitant tax evasion; (3) the persistence of extended and traditional household forms, with all the ensuing implications in terms of gender; (4) limited administrative capacity, both on the revenue side (low capacity to raise taxes) and on the spending side (low capacity to manage means-tested schemes). Given these similarities, it can be suggested that South-Eastern Europe is likely to embark upon a path to welfare state building which will bear many resemblances with that followed in the past by Greece, Italy, Spain, and Portugal (probably in this order). The labour market, social insurance, and social assistance systems of these countries have high probabilities of evolving towards segmented, functionally and distributionally unbalanced conditions—with the additional challenge of much more disadvantaged starting points and a much more turbulent international economic environment. Another region of the world where family resemblances can be noted is Latin America (see Chapter 44): in addition to the above mentioned socio-economic elements, the countries of this area are characterized by a legacy of ideological polarizations and Catholic influence on social policy that is not too distant from that described in earlier sections of this chapter.

Can Southern Europe 'teach' anything to other regions and nations? Policy transfer is a tricky institutional operation and it seldom works. There are, however, weaker forms of cross-national policy links that might play a positive 'bridging' role: let us think of benchmarking, of initiatives for studying and taking inspiration from good practices (but also from other countries' failures), initiatives for promoting the formation of epistemic communities that can facilitate and channel innovation from one national context to the next. Southern Europe is not used to considering itself as a social policy 'model': but, as the last section of this chapter has suggested, some promising lights have started to glow in the South during the last two decades. And besides, everything is relative, including social policy models. For Eastern European and Latin American reformers in search of ideas and inspiration, the Greek, Italian, and Iberian experiences could be a promising point of reference in their own difficult journey towards modernization.

CHAPTER 43

....

THE ENGLISH-
SPEAKING
COUNTRIES

....

FRANCIS G. CASTLES

INTRODUCTION

....

COMPARISON is about identifying patterns of similarity and difference, but the features of the landscape located as significant depend on the focus of the comparison. A mapping analogy helps to make the point. Looked at from afar, the only contrast possible may be of gross features of the landscape: of the presence of light or shadow, landmass or ocean, mountains or plains. Closer up, the contrast resolves into sets of regularities: areas with particular types of vegetation or patterns of settlement. Closer still, patterns reveal themselves as constituted by sub-patterns, so that apparent similarities are revealed as only skin-deep, with fields of grain shown in some places to be of wheat, sometimes of barley, and with towns differing in their layout depending on their origins as centres of commerce or of industry. Finally, through the closest of close-up lenses, we perceive the uniqueness of every geographic feature, but only at the cost of making comparison almost impossible because our lens allows us only to look at one thing at a time.

An important theme of this chapter is that accounts of the similarity or difference of the policy profiles of the English-speaking nations of advanced capitalism (Australia, Canada, Ireland, New Zealand, the United Kingdom, and the United States) similarly depend on the focus of the comparison in question. From atop 'a peak in Darien', as it were, the gross contrast may be between a single prominent instance of a particular policy profile and all the rest. From the time of De Tocqueville's *Democracy in America*, scholars have argued about whether society and politics in the United States are in some sense exceptional, a debate that, as we shall see, is alive and well in contemporary analyses of differences between the American and European social models. Viewed from the middle distance, the patterns most apparent are the regime structures and family resemblances that constitute the substance of what has been described as 'the welfare modelling business' (Abrahamson 1999*a*), with the countries we are here examining variously labelled as typical instances of a 'liberal' world of welfare capitalism or identified as members of an English-speaking family of nations. Finally, when the focus of the analysis is more narrowly on the particularities of some or all of these nations or is on the variation of particular policies across many nations, we may notice differences and incongruities that challenge some of the assumptions commonly made on the basis of patterns perceived in the middle distance.

This chapter is organized as follows. We begin with a middle-distance focus, looking at the literature that has identified strong policy similarities between the English-speaking countries of a kind distinguishing them from other groups of nations. These similarities, including low levels of public spending on welfare and the weak development of social citizenship rights, are generally taken as evidence of the poverty of social policy in the English-speaking world. We then look more closely at the strategies of redistribution adopted in these countries and show that, despite belonging to a common world of welfare, there remain significant differences between them and ones which make blanket assumptions about these countries' commitment to welfare quite inappropriate. Finally, we devote some attention to the big divide between European and American social policy, asking whether apparent American exceptionalism arises simply from a failure to identify that country as a typical member of an English-speaking world of welfare. We show that in some instances this does indeed seem to be the case, but that, in others, public policy priorities in the United States really do appear to march to the beat of a different drum.

DISCOVERING A NEW WORLD

It is important to recognize from the start that the emergence of a literature on the social policy commonalities of the English-speaking nations is both relatively new and relatively underdeveloped. It is new because the phenomenon it describes is quite new: the emergence in these countries in the quarter century following World War II of a set of patterns of policy outcomes that were distinctive compared to those of other advanced welfare states. As late as the mid-1970s, it might well have seemed absurd for social policy commentators to classify the United States and Britain together as typical members of an English-speaking cluster, when the former was widely seen as the foremost instance of a 'residual', 'last resort', approach to social intervention and the latter remained, in the literature of British social administration at least, a welfare state pioneer and an exemplar, if a somewhat tarnished one, of an 'institutional' and comprehensive approach to social policy (Titmuss 1974*a*).

The underdevelopment of the literature—the fact that, whilst an English-speaking cluster of nations now features frequently in cross-national research findings and has been theorized as a core element in two important paradigms of cross-national policy variation, there is almost no scholarship focused centrally on these countries' social policy experience in the manner of, say, the literature on the 'Scandinavian model' or on emergent social policy similarities in Southern Europe—can be accounted for in a number of ways. One is the huge disparity in the size and scholarly salience of the countries making up the cluster. For scholars in both Britain and the United States (as similarly in Germany and France within the continental European cluster) the temptation is strong to remain within the bounds of extensive and developed national debates rather than to delve into the details of, or to generalize from, the experience of distant lands and of far less developed literatures.

Another reason the literature is undeveloped is that the resemblances becoming only too apparent amongst the English-speaking countries in the decades after 1970 were ones that could easily be seen as more suitable for individual than collective diagnosis and treatment. The emergence of a social democratic model in Scandinavia or of the rapid, if uneven, development of the welfare state in Southern Europe after 1980 could legitimately be the occasion of both scholarly and national pride in the countries concerned. In stark contrast, the story of the English-speaking world—of social policy retreat in some countries and of a gradual clustering of all these nations towards the bottom of a wide variety of social and economic policy distributions—has undoubtedly been a source of dismay to many policy commentators in these nations. Dismay and the critique it occasions are expressed most tellingly where their object is close and familiar rather than diffuse and distant. A focus on the common deficiencies of social policy across the English-speaking world may be rare; books and articles on what is wrong with social and public policy in the individual countries constituting that world are an academic and popular publishing staple.

Although, as we shall see, the 1980s were a period in which more and more studies were being published demonstrating strong affinities in policy outcomes and ante-cedents in the English-speaking nations, undoubtedly the credit for first identifying a set of welfare state characteristics clearly distinguishing these countries from others must go to Gøsta Esping-Andersen's work on the nature and origins of distributional regimes in contemporary capitalism. His initial treatment, deriving from 'power resources' theory and ideal typical in its delineation of regime characteristics, iden-tifies a 'liberal' regime configuration, the key features of which are weak rights of social citizenship or decommodification, a tax and transfer system that does little to promote equality, a welfare system with a poor relief orientation, a preference for private provision, and a labour market without effective corporatist mechanisms or full employment guarantees (Esping-Andersen 1985*b*: 248). This regime, he notes, exhibits a 'surprising synonymity' with the 'Anglo-Saxon "New World" nations, where the bourgeois impulse was especially powerful, such as Britain, the United States, Canada and Australia' (Ibid. 233). This curious elision by which Britain becomes literally part of the 'New World' has, perhaps, a more profound significance than a mere slip of the pen. In this account, Britain, homeland of the post-war 'institutional' welfare state, is now seen as imbued with the same 'hallmark' liberal characteristics as the English-speaking world overseas: 'its residualism, its stress on private market provision, the conspicuous role played by targeted means testing and its self-reliant individualism' (Ibid.).

In successive iterations of the argument, these characteristics do not change a great deal, but the countries highlighted as exemplars do. 'The three political economies of the welfare state' published in 1989 distinguishes between 'archetypical examples' of the liberal regime type (the United States, Canada, and Australia) and countries 'that approximate the model', including, somewhat surprisingly, Denmark, which is also seen as a candidate member of the 'social democratic' regime type, as well as Switzerland and Great Britain (Esping-Andersen 1989: 25). In *The Three Worlds of Welfare Capitalism* published a year later, with the explicit inclusion of Ireland and New Zealand and the identification of the six English-speaking nations as the six advanced capitalist states with the lowest scores on the decommodification index, the liberal regime finally becomes coterminous with the English-speaking world (Esping-Andersen 1990). However, Esping-Andersen now explicitly recognizes Britain as a borderline case, noting that, in 1950, after five years of 'breakthrough' Labour government, it had been 'in the top decommodification group' (1990: 53). He fails to point out that one of the two new entrants to his English-speaking 'liberal' club, New Zealand, was, already by late 1930s widely regarded as one of the world's leading welfare states (see Briggs 1961). Truly then, Esping-Andersen's liberal world of welfare capitalism depicts not just a new world, but a world turned upside down.

Esping-Andersen's route to this new world is via theory, but a similar destination could also be arrived at by more empirical methods. In the 1980s, more and more papers and datasets reported cross-national distributions of variables measuring aspects of economic performance and social protection that were indicative of generally inferior outcomes in English-speaking nations. These variables included economic growth rates (Dowrick and Nguyen 1987), rates of unemployment and days lost in strikes (Cameron 1984), increased rates of inflation (OECD 1986*a*), spending on welfare transfers (Varley 1986), total tax receipts (OECD 1986*b*), and child poverty rates (Smeeding et al. 1988). In 1989, a paper by Castles and Merrill used the evidence provided by these studies to rehearse a possible argument for 'the awfulness of the English' or, less evaluatively, for the existence of a 'distinct syndrome of policy attributes' significantly associated 'with English national attributes' (Castles and Merrill 1989: 183).

This focus on shared national attributes derived from work then being undertaken by a group of scholars, amongst whom Manfred Schmidt, Göran Therborn, and Francis G. Castles were prominent, which was to result in an edited volume published in 1993 with the title *Families of Nations* that explored the possibility that 'shared geographical, linguistic, cultural and /or historical attributes' may lead to 'distinctive patterns of policy outcomes' (Castles 1993: xiii). The family of nations and the regimes concepts are not necessarily contradictory, but they do have different emphases (see Castles and Obinger 2008). The regimes concept focuses on the way policy is determined by social structure, and in Esping-Andersen's rendering, in particular, how it is shaped by the political articulation of the class struggle, but the families' notion supplies the cultural linkages that explain why particular structures tend to be grouped along the territorial axis in the manner they are. The regimes concept is more policy specific, pointing to the institutional logic underlying policy variation in particular fields, while the families' notion supplies a basis for understanding why different policy regimes are frequently superimposed. Finally, the families' notion is, in some ways, less rigid than its counterpart, allowing for the possibility that a common ancestry is compatible with divergences in some areas of behaviour whilst simultaneously supplying a cultural transmission mechanism for the subsequent reassertion of affinity (on this and other aspects of family patterning, see Therborn 1993). That Britain and New Zealand temporarily became welfare state leaders in the 1930s and 1940s, but then reverted to type, becoming in the process leaders of an initially largely English-speaking push towards dismantling the welfare state, makes perfect sense in terms of a family of nations approach.

Exploring the Hinterland

Since the original elaboration of these accounts of somewhat differently accented worlds of English-speaking social and public policy outcomes, research in both traditions has proceeded further. In the regimes literature, much of the energy has been devoted to debates on what is the correct number of welfare regimes, but, for the most part, there has been little questioning of the existence of what by the early 1990s was already beginning to be called the 'Anglo-Saxon' regime type (Leibfried 1992). There are, however, a few exceptions. Scruggs and Allan (2006a) have noted that the exclusively English-speaking identity of the liberal type is actually the result of a mathematical error in the construction of Esping-Andersen's decommodification index. Britain is not just a borderline case; it is not a member of the liberal world at all. Castles and Mitchell (1993) have pointed to systematic differences in the egalitarian thrust of social spending in the English-speaking countries of a kind that might suggest the existence of more than one kind of English-speaking world of welfare and this possibility is further explored in the next section of this chapter. Finally, Gough (2001) has undertaken work on the poor relief dimension of the liberal syndrome which demonstrates clearly the point made earlier, that everything depends on the lens through which patterns of similarity and difference are viewed. Using a cluster analysis methodology, he notes that a two cluster solution produces an outcome which 'separates out the English-speaking world according to higher expenditure, more people receiving social assistance and lower social exclusion scores' (Gough 2001: 166). However, selecting for an optimally homogeneous seven cluster solution, whilst it does produce moderately coherent Scandinavian and continental Western European social assistance regimes, does so at the cost of creating three separate and distinctive English-speaking clusters as well as two Southern European clusters.

Apart from the debate on the number of regimes, the main preoccupation of this literature has been identifying the presence of regimes in new policy areas. Some of these analyses locate distinctively English-speaking characteristics and others do not. The coverage here of myriad contributions to the literature is necessarily selective and designed only to be indicative of the kind of topics examined. Anttonen and Sipilä (1996) argue that the provision of care services is not patterned in the same way as income transfers, with the European English-speaking countries falling some- where between Scandinavian and continental European models. Esping-Andersen in his review of the robustness of the *Three Worlds* typology in light of a further decade of research (1999) supports this finding. Lynch (2001) notes that social policy in modern welfare states is more or less strongly oriented to the needs of the elderly, but that the countries of the English-speaking world do not cluster together on this dimension, with the United States strongly age oriented, but Canada and Ireland much less so. In contrast, Wagschal (2001) notices a much closer correspondence between patterns of taxation and the classical *Three Worlds* patterns.

The way in which gender maps onto welfare regimes has received special attention (see Orloff 1996, for a review of this literature, and O'Connor et al. 1999, for a comparative analysis of gender policy in the English-speaking countries), with the thrust of the debate more on how gender considerations can be incorporated into a regimes typology framework than on the appropriateness of the classification as such. Lewis (1992), the first scholar to identify the gender dimension of regime difference, distinguishes between 'strong male breadwinner' welfare states in liberal countries such as Ireland and Britain, a 'modified male breadwinner' state in conser- vative France, and a 'weak male breadwinner' state in social democratic Sweden. She does note, however, that there are important variations in the strength of these orientations amongst countries of ostensibly the same regime type. She also notes the paradox that, whilst the English-speaking countries have been women unfriendly in many respects, feminism has been stronger in Britain than in continental Europe or Scandinavia. Arguably the dimension of gender difference she identifies here is that which Weldon sees as shaping policy responsiveness to violence against women, an area in which she argues 'Canada, Australia and the United States have had the most developed social policies, while policy development in Sweden and Finland has remained stunted' because policy in the latter has been shaped by class rather than by gender considerations (Weldon 2002: 32).

Regimes analysis has also proliferated into the cognate area of political economy, with the main focus of attention on differences in types of capitalist economic organization or 'production regimes' (Soskice 1999; Hall and Soskice 2001a). This is an arena in which a two rather than a three regime model reigns supreme, with marked differences between an almost entirely English-speaking club of 'liberal market economies' and the 'coordinated market' regimes of Japan, continental Europe, and Scandinavia being reflected in a wide range of policy differences in the areas of education and training, wage-setting, and microeconomic management (Soskice 1999). Although the policy foci of the social policy and political economy literatures differ, the ultimate source of the distinctiveness of the English-speaking countries in both domains is seen as stemming from the same source: policies that seek to accommodate market imperatives.

The treatment of the English-speaking world in the families' literature has also moved on. The original discussion in *Families of Nations* was largely illustrative, identifying English-speaking resemblances amongst these countries in terms of economic performance, patterns of social expenditure, and levels of marital instability. Subsequent treatments have been more systematic. In particular, *Comparative Public Policy* (Castles 1998a) seeks to identify and explain family differences between English-speaking, Scandinavian, continental European, and Southern European families of nations across an extremely wide range of policy outcomes over the post-war period. In summary, the analysis suggests that the countries of the English-speaking world have exhibited significantly lower total spending, total taxation and social security spending than other groupings in the 1990s and a significant decline in all three measures of public finances over time. Moreover, these countries differ from others in policies relating to the personal sphere, with persistently higher levels of private home ownership, higher levels of fertility and higher divorce rates (Ibid. 317). Svallfors (1997: 295) also identifies 'rather clear-cut configurations' of attitudes to the welfare state conforming to a four family pattern. A recent collaborative research project on patterns of expenditure retrenchment in areas others other than social policy (Castles 2007a) has variously noted that, in recent decades, the English-speaking countries have manifested a greater decline in educational spending than other OECD countries (Schmidt 2007), a significantly more aggressive stance in cutting total economy subsidies (Obinger and Zohlnhöfer 2007) and highly distinctive patterns of product market and employment regulation (Siegel 2007).

There have been various attempts to replicate or validate the regimes and families of nations' typologies. Both Scruggs and Allan (2006a) and Bambra (2006) question whether updated decommodification data manifest a clear *Three Worlds* pattern. However, a study by Powell and Barrientos (2004), focusing on different dimensions and measures of welfare, confirms the existence of just such a pattern and one that is persistent over time. A validation study of Castles' 1998 analysis concludes not only that 'the hypothesized families of nations can be shown to exist', but also that 'they are quite robust and stable over time' (Obinger and Wagschal 2001: 99). A more recent study has attempted to validate the same pattern for the period 2000–2004 and argues that 'the boundaries between the distinct worlds of public policy have become even more clear-cut over time, with convergence exceeding that of the sample as a whole' (Castles and Obinger 2008: 330–1). This study also seeks to identify factors that might account for the patterning of outcomes in these distinct worlds and finds that a range of socio-economic, institutional and party political attributes cluster in a very similar way to policy outcomes. This isomorphism of structural and policy attributes does not distinguish between families of nations and regimes accounts, since prior territorial affinities often shape structural attributes. An illustration of seemingly direct relevance to the issues under discussion here is to be found in recent work by Iversen and Soskice (2006) which argues that the majoritarian election systems of the English-speaking world favour the emergence of centre-right governments with weak redistributive ambitions.

The validation exercise in the Castles and Obinger study seeks to identify which outcomes variables make a statistically significant contribution to families of nations' patterns. Table 43.1 reports values of these variables for the English-speaking nations along with Esping-Andersen's most recent (1999) rendering of liberal regime characteristics. This table may be regarded as a summary statement of the most important policy resemblances of the English-speaking nations as identified by these two approaches. Despite the fact that one is an ideal type and the other a set of empirical findings, the policy profiles identified are in many respects broadly compatible, with the centrality of the market translated into lower levels of public spending, a lower total tax burden, and high to moderately high levels of labour force participation. An apparent paradox, however, is the fact that market-based societies with low tax and transfer profiles are the ones that exact the highest levels of taxes on incomes and profits. This is a paradox addressed in the next section of this chapter which reconsiders the nature of 'English awfulness' in light of evidence relating to these countries' strategies of redistribution.

Table 43.1 Liberal regime characteristics according to Esping–Andersen and English–speaking family of nation characteristics according to Castles and Obinger

	Liberal regime		English-speaking family of nations
Role of:		Significant variables:	
Family	Marginal	Fertility rate	Highest
Market	Central	Education spending	Lowest
State	Marginal	Total tax burden	Lowest
Welfare state:		Taxes on income and profits	Highest
Dominant mode of solidarity	Individual	Total disbursements	Lowest
		Female labour force	Middle
Dominant locus of solidarity	Market	Male labour force	Highest
		Government employment	Lowest
Degree of decommodification	Minimal	Social security transfers	Lowest

Sources: Liberal regime characteristics from Esping-Andersen (1999: 85); significant family of nations characteristics from Castles and Obinger (2008: 332).

ENGLISH AWFULNESS RECONSIDERED

The labelling of social policy in the English-speaking countries as 'residual' or 'last resort' suggests a policy profile in which state intervention of a redistributive nature is weak or, at least, muted compared with other advanced nations. The case for 'English awfulness' or for the ranking of the 'liberal' regime as weakest in conferring social rights is that the English-speaking countries from about the end of the third quarter of the twentieth century have typically scored lower than other countries in the extent to which they have employed certain social policy instruments for ameliorating the income inequalities of Western capitalist societies: namely, high levels of taxation, public spending, and benefit generosity. There are, however, other policy instruments available for tackling inequality and poverty and, when we consider these, the case for non-interventionism, English-speaking commonality, and 'English awfulness' has to be reconsidered. In principle, there are three ways of modifying the distribution of income from employment: through the quantum of taxing and spending, through the progressivity of taxation and spending, and through direct measures to reduce the dispersion of earnings. All modern welfare states combine these instruments to differing degrees, but what has distinguished the strategy of redistribution favoured in the English-speaking countries, both historically and at the present time, has been a preference for progressivity and direct measures over taxing and spending.

When one focuses on mechanisms of redistribution, differences amongst the English-speaking countries begin to be apparent. It has been argued, for instance, that Australia and New Zealand used direct state control of the wages system from early on in the twentieth century to create a unique kind of welfare state delivering 'social protection by other means' (Castles 1985). Direct state control was exercised by courts or quasi-judicial bodies with the authority to arbitrate industrial disputes by setting wages and conditions of work and, from an early date, interpreted their remit as using the wages system to establish a social policy minimum or 'living wage' judicially defined as one providing for 'the normal needs of the average employee, regarded as a human being living in a civilized community' (Higgins 1968: 3) and more practically as a wage level capable of supporting a worker, his wife, and two or three children. Arguably, this 'wage-earners' welfare state' (Castles 1985) pre-empted much of the need (or demand) for substantial redistribution through an extensive mechanism of taxing and spending and explains the weak development of social expenditure programmes in these countries in the 1950s and 1960s. Arguably, too, the dismantling of the arbitration system as part of these countries' neo-liberal response to the forces promoting economic globalization from the mid-1980s onwards helps account for a marked increase in inequality in both countries since that time.

Compulsory wage fixing by governments has been experimented with in many countries (e.g. in wartime), but nowhere else so extensively or with so explicit a social policy aim. Another strategy, however, has been more general across the English-speaking world, although again most strenuously pursued in the Antipodes, with the idea being that whatever taxation and spending was required for welfare amelioration purposes should be maximally effective in delivering redistributive bang for the taxpayer's buck. Benefit targeting, means-testing, and tax progressivity have been the instruments of this strategy, on the tax side explaining the paradox that it is has been the low taxing English-speaking liberal welfare states that most favour progressive taxes on incomes and profits. Esping-Andersen, of course, notices the targeted nature of benefits in the English-speaking world, but fails to notice that, along with tax progressivity, this makes a genuine difference to the capacity of at least some of these countries' to achieve redistributive goals.

Unlike the 'wage earners' welfare state' and New Zealand's and Britain's status as pioneers of institutional welfare reform in the 1930s and 1940s, the greater progressivity of taxing and spending and its redistributive effects are very much with us to the present day. Table 43.2, derived from a recent OECD (2008b) report shows this very clearly indeed. Exactly as the conventional account tells us, the share of cash benefits and taxes in household incomes in the English-speaking countries is substantially lower than in the OECD countries in general or in comparison countries chosen from other families of nations. However, in all six English-speaking countries tax progressivity exceeds the OECD norm and, with the exception of the United States, the same applies to the progressivity of cash transfers, with Australia, New Zealand, and the United Kingdom the three top countries in the OECD distribution. The redistributive bias of these three countries was prominent amongst the reasons

Table 43.2 Shares and progressivity of cash benefits and household taxes in household disposable income in English-speaking and selected other OECD countries (mid–2000s)

	Public Cash Benefits		Household Taxes	
	Share	Progressivity	Share	Progressivity
Australia	14.3	−0.400	23.4	0.533
Canada	13.6	−0.152	25.8	0.492
Ireland	17.7	−0.214	19.4	0.57
New Zealand	13.0	−0.345	29.0	0.498
UK	14.5	−0.275	24.1	0.533
USA	9.4	−0.089	25.6	0.586
Germany	28.2	0.013	35.5	0.468
Italy	29.2	0.135	30.2	0.546
Sweden	32.7	−0.145	43.2	0.337
English-speaking Average	13.7	−0.248	24.6	0.535
OECD Average	21.9	−0.099	29.3	0.428

Source: OECD 2008a: Tables 4.2 and 4.3. Progressivity measures are concentration coefficients with high progressivity indicated by negative scores for cash benefits and positive scores for household taxes. The OECD average reported here is not merely for the countries reported in Table 43.2, but for the 24 countries featuring in the OECD analysis.

that Castles and Mitchell (1993) distinguished between two English-speaking worlds of welfare: a 'radical' world focusing on redistributive ends and a 'liberal' one in which that emphasis is lacking, although it is worth noting that the impact of the Earned Income Tax Credit (EITC) in the United States has now given that country the distinction of having the most progressive tax system in the OECD.

The OECD report argues that 'the combined effect of transfers and taxes in reducing inequality is similar in Ireland and Australia to that achieved in Sweden and Denmark, whilst the redistribution in the United Kingdom and New Zealand is similar to the levels achieved in Germany and the Netherlands' (OECD 2008b: 112). This conclusion leaves us with the puzzle of why, as the awfulness thesis suggests and many other studies have shown, levels of inequality are appreciably higher in the English-speaking countries than in continental Europe and Scandinavia. The OECD report suggests that the answer to this puzzle is not that the welfare states of the English-speaking countries are less effective than in these other countries, but that their levels of market-income inequality are greater, a conclusion identical to that of another quite recent study of the causes of high child poverty in the English-speaking countries (Mickelwright 2003). Reconsidering English awfulness suggests therefore that, for the non-North American English-speaking countries, awfulness is to be found less in the realm of social policy than of the unconstrained functioning of capitalist labour markets. This is a phenomenon which is, arguably, quite recent and attributable largely to the victory of neo-liberalism in an English-speaking world, which, in the immediate aftermath of World War II through to the late 1960s, manifested a lower degree of inequality in household incomes than either Scandinavia or continental Europe (see Mann and Riley 2007).

Is America Different?

We have argued that there is strong case for identifying commonalities amongst the English-speaking countries in respect of taxing, spending, and benefit levels, but have suggested that, in respect of redistributive strategy, there may be some important differences amongst them. We conclude our discussion by examining evidence relevant to the frequently made assertion that there is a significant divide between the European social policy model and an American model which is essentially unique. This argument is relevant to our topic since it seems to imply, although often by the inadvertence of failing to mention English-speaking countries other than the United States, that the American social policy experience is set apart not only from that of most European countries, but also from that of the other English-speaking countries.

A strategy for establishing the depth of the divide between Europe and America is to determine whether differences amongst European nations—or, at least, those seen as conforming to the European social model—exceed those between Europe and America or, more simply, whether the American experience falls somewhere within a given European policy distribution and, if it does not, how far outside it falls (see Castles 2002a; Alber 2006; Baldwin 2009). The same strategy can be used to establish whether the United States is a typical English-speaking nation in respect of some particular dimension of policy or whether, in this respect, at least, the notion of a coherent family pattern breaks down.

In Table 43.3, we present data from eighteen OECD countries relevant to answering these questions in respect of a variety of components of social expenditure and two measures of redistributive outcomes. The expenditure components are those involved in moving from the standard measure of gross public social expenditure to net total expenditure (i.e. the sum of resources expended in a given country on welfare provision), which involves deducting taxes incident on social expenditure and contributions and adding in net private expenditures for social purposes (for more on these expenditure concepts, see Chapters 8 and 23 in this volume). The measures of redistributive outcomes are the Gini index of inequality and child poverty headcount. A simple measure of the coherence of country groupings is provided by the coefficient of variation (CV) and of the distinctiveness of groupings/countries by the standard deviation (SD) of the entire sample of eighteen countries (for an extended discussion, see Castles 2009b).

The evidence provided by Table 43.3 is decidedly mixed. A case for American exceptionalism could easily be built around the fact that for four of the six variables located here, the United States is the lowest or highest case in the distribution, with

Table 43.3 Measures of the dispersion of components of social expenditure, child poverty, and inequality in 18 OECD countries (mid-2000s)

	European		English-speaking		USA		Standard Deviation
	Mean	CV	Mean	CV	Value	Rank	
Gross Public Expenditure	26.0	21.5	19.8	12.3	17.1	Lowest	5.6
Tax Incidence	3.3	81.0	0.9	171.1	-1.4	Lowest	2.7
Net Private Expenditure	3.1	84.7	4.6	73.7	10.1	Highest	2.6
Net Total Expenditure	25.7	16.4	23.0	19.6	27.2	6th	4.2
Child Poverty	9.8	57.6	14.8	25.3	21.0	Lowest	5.5
Gini Index	0.288	15.6	0.333	8.1	0.381	17th	0.045

Notes: Countries compared: Australia, Austria, Belgium, Canada, Denmark, Finland, France, Germany, Ireland, Italy, Netherlands, New Zealand, Norway, Portugal, Spain, Sweden, the United Kingdom, and the United States. The UK and Ireland are not included in the European measures.
Sources: Social expenditure measures for 2005 calculated from OECD (2009a); measures of poverty (Table 5.2) and inequality (Table 1.A2.4) c. mid-2000s from OECD (2008a).

the expected findings of low public spending and high inequality complemented by the lowest tax incidence in the OECD (a corollary of that country's extremely high tax progressivity discussed above) and much the highest level of private expenditure in the OECD. That case could be further bolstered by pointing to the fact, with the single exception of net total expenditure, United States values are set apart by one and a half to two standard deviations from the European mean. There are, however, some real surprises of a kind which suggest either that the divide between Europe and America is less real than supposed or that the European model is less than fully consolidated. Among them is the fact that Portugal has a higher Gini index score than the United States, that the Netherlands come second to the United States in terms of private spending and that, in respect of child poverty, there is a sizeable group of European nations that cluster around one standard deviation away from the United States, including not only a number of Southern European nations, but also Germany.

A case for a divide between Europe and an English-speaking world including America can also be made in respect of the dimensions in which it is usually made. Profiles for levels of household inequality are both distinct and reasonably coherent; profiles for total spending are distinct, although more coherent in the English-speaking world than in Europe. That said, there is also clear evidence that the American experience is consistently at one end of the English-speaking spectrum and often by some considerable distance and exceeding one standard deviation in respect of private spending, child poverty, and household inequality. There are also outcome dimensions on which these countries clearly do not cluster at all, with Ireland and New Zealand amongst those with the lowest private social expenditure and, hence also, of net total spending, a dimension of spending on which the United States actually scores sixth highest in the OECD.

These findings bring us round once again to the theme of the introduction to this chapter: that everything depends on the focus of the comparison we are seeking to make. A distinct English-speaking world of welfare is apparent in respect of spending patterns and redistributive outcomes as well as of policy outcomes in the realm of the personal, which space considerations have precluded us from discussing here. Once we consider strategies of redistribution, however, differences become apparent and ones which potentially influence our evaluation of at least some of these countries' commitment to welfare. Finally, looking at the divide between Europe and America helps us to identify other differences, both between the European and American social models and between social policy provision in the United States and in the other English-speaking countries. Strident debates on the existence of worlds of welfare need to give way to empirical accounts of the dimensions on which countries cluster and those on which they do not.

EMERGING WELFARE STATES

....

CHAPTER 44

LATIN AMERICA

....

EVELYNE HUBER
JUAN BOGLIACCINI

Introduction

....

THIS chapter is organized into three sections. The first discusses the origins and development of Latin American welfare states before moving on to outline more recent reforms of social policy regimes in the area. A second section examines reasons why some policy regimes are more effective than others and discusses evidence concerning the impact of programmes in the different countries. The chapter concludes by discussing future directions for research on Latin American policy regimes.

DEVELOPMENT AND REFORMS OF LATIN AMERICAN WELFARE STATES

....

Origins of the Welfare State

The concept of the Welfare State (*Estado de Bienestar*) has come into widespread use relatively recently in the Latin American literature. Traditionally, studies of social security dominated the literature. This reflected reality in so far as states—to the extent that they began to take responsibility for the welfare of their citizens—emphasized employment based social insurance, that is, social security, over non-contributory social assistance. In healthcare, the dominant model was social security coverage for the employed population and dependents. Public health services in charge of preventive care and provision of care for the uninsured tended to be severely underfunded.

More recent authors have developed the concept of social policy regimes or models of social policy to denote the totality of social programmes.[1] Typically, these authors are concerned with the distributive effects of the structure and generosity of social programmes and therefore include not only transfers and health services but also education in their analyses. The distribution of access to quality education is an important determinant of poverty and inequality in Latin American societies. It is worth noting that price controls and subsidies constituted an important instrument of social protection for the poorer sectors of the population before the debt crisis of the 1980s and the subsequent opening and deregulation of the Latin American economies. However, the general welfare state/social policy literature did not include systematic analyses of price controls and subsidies.

The theoretical perspective offered by the pioneering works that sought to explain the formation of social security regimes was a combination of economic development and pressure group politics (Mesa-Lago 1978; Malloy 1979; Isuani 1985). Social stratification came to be reflected in the social security systems of Latin American countries because the most important pressure groups over time managed to extract from the state their own schemes of social protection. Typically, the military received the earliest and best social protection, accompanied or followed by the judiciary and other high-ranking civil servants, then professionals and other white-collar sectors, and finally unionized blue-collar workers in the urban sector and on rural plantations (Mesa-Lago 1978). Only later and only in some countries did the bulk of the rural population become incorporated into social security. Extensions of social security protection were not always a response to direct pressure from organized groups; the alternative consisted of state incorporation attempts of groups that elites perceived to be potential threats or power bases, or concerns with state building and modernization (Mesa-Lago 1978; Spalding 1978; Papadópulos 1992).

The uneven pace of industrialization led to uneven development of social security schemes. In the pioneer countries (Argentina, Brazil, Chile, Uruguay, and Cuba), the main social security schemes were established in the 1920s and grew in a gradual and fragmented manner. In the second group (Colombia, Costa Rica, Mexico, Paraguay, Peru, and Venezuela), the main schemes were installed in the 1940s and tended to grow in a less fragmented manner. In the remaining countries, the least economically developed ones, social security schemes appeared even later (Mesa-Lago 1989: 3–6). The pioneer countries plus Costa Rica had achieved the highest levels of social security health coverage by 1980, over 60 per cent of the population; Colombia, Guatemala, Mexico, Panama, Peru, and Venezuela covered between 30 and 60 per cent of their populations; in the rest of the countries coverage was below 30 per cent. The

---

[1] The literature on advanced industrial societies distinguishes between three or more welfare state regime types (e.g. Esping-Andersen 1990); the literature on Latin America uses the concept of regimes simply to denote the total configuration of social policies.

English-speaking Caribbean was an important exception, with coverage of 80 per cent or higher, despite the low level of economic development. The figures for pension coverage of the economically active population showed a similar pattern (Mesa-Lago 1994: 22).

More recently authors have used a power constellations perspective, developing their analyses in dialogue with welfare state theories formulated for advanced industrial countries, and focusing on structural changes (industrialization and urbanization) leading to changes in political regimes (democratization) and/or power distributions (strength of labour and the left) and political alignments or coalitions (Dion 2005; Filgueira and Filgueira 2002; Haggard and Kaufman 2008; Huber et al. 2008; Pribble 2008; Segura-Ubiergo 2007). In particular, they have emphasized the political economy of Import Substitution Industrialization (ISI), which on the one hand fostered growth of urban labour and unionization and enabled employers to pass on high social security taxes to consumers behind high tariff walls, but on the other hand developed only a limited capacity to absorb the swelling ranks of the urban labour force and thus left a rapidly growing urban informal sector and the still large rural sector without coverage. These authors have also identified different paths to extensive social security coverage, through either high industrialization and strength of labour and left-of-centre parties, with or without long records of democracy, or in the absence of high industrialization through long records of democracy and strength of left-of-centre parties (Huber and Stephens 2009; Haggard and Kaufman 2008; Pribble 2008; Segura-Ubiergo 2007; Martínez Franzoni 2008).

Reforms of Social Policy Regimes

The literature here is quite voluminous. The studies of the deficiencies of the social security systems as they had developed by the early 1980s emphasize the large fiscal deficits faced by the social security schemes in the more advanced countries. These schemes had matured and the ratio of active to inactive affiliates had deteriorated; the surpluses in the social security funds had been poorly invested or spent on other purposes altogether; life expectancy rose; expenses for costly curative healthcare escalated; employers evaded or greatly delayed contributions, particularly during periods of high inflation; and administrative costs were exorbitant (Mesa-Lago 1994). The debt crisis and the ensuing austerity and structural adjustment policies aggravated these problems. Rising unemployment and growing informalization caused declines in social security contributions; the fiscal crisis of the state reduced state subsidies; high inflation eroded the value of benefits or put great strain on the systems and created a debt to beneficiaries. The deficits of the social security systems aggravated the general fiscal crisis of the state and attracted the attention of the International Financial Institutions (IFIs), particularly the International Monetary Fund (IMF).

The policy prescriptions issued by the IFIs and the United States Agency for International Development (US AID) applied neoliberal principles to both economic and social policies. Essentially, these agencies pushed for cuts in government expenditures, liberalization of trade and capital flows, privatization of state enterprises, relaxation of economic regulations, and incentives for foreign direct investment, along with a reduction of the role of the state in financing social policy and in providing social services in favour of greater involvement of the private sector in financing and providing social insurance and social services (Williamson 1990; World Bank 1994*b*). These prescriptions, however, were differentially implemented, dependent on the balance of power between the IFIs and internal advocates of neoliberalism on the one hand, and stake holders in the existing systems and advocates of more state-oriented reforms on the other hand (Huber 2005).

Alternative prescriptions of a more social democratic nature were offered, increasingly so by left-leaning think tanks in Latin America, but they lacked political and financial backing. The International Labour Office emphasized the principles of equity and solidarity in labour market and social policy (Bertranou et al. 2002), but it also lacked the financial clout to be able to compete with the IFIs. In the late 1990s, some forces in the IFIs engaged in important re-examinations of the reforms and their shortcomings (Holzmann and Stiglitz 2001; De Ferranti et al. 2004; both volumes published by the World Bank). Finally, after two decades of disappointment with the effects of neoliberal social policy reforms, the Inter-American Development Bank gave exposure to an alternative vision by supporting a project on *Universalismo Básico* (Basic Universalism) (Molina 2006). The coming to power of left-of-centre governments in the first decade of the twenty-first century reinforced interest in comprehensive and equity-oriented social policy.

Pension privatization was at the forefront of neoliberal policy recommendations, but in reality the reforms ranged all the way from putting existing public systems on firmer financial footing, as in Brazil, to full privatization and a closing down of the public system, as in Chile (Müller 2003). Other countries, like Argentina and Uruguay, kept a basic public tier and privatized supplementary pensions or pensions for higher income earners. Madrid (2003: 16) developed a useful index of degree of pension privatization based on the percentage of total contributions going to the public system and the percentage of total members belonging to the private system, which showed Bolivia, Nicaragua, and Chile scoring highest, followed by El Salvador, the Dominican Republic, and Mexico. He explains pension privatization with the economic burden of pension spending, domestic capital shortages, influence of the World Bank and of economists, and the extent of party discipline in the President's party and his control over the legislature (2003: 59).

Other authors agree on the importance of World Bank influence and of the networks of domestic technocrats in close contact with the Bank (Huber 2005; Teichman 2001) but also emphasize domestic power constellations and constitutional structures, such as the existence of the referendum in Uruguay (Castiglioni 2005; Hernández 2000, 2003; Huber and Stephens 2009). Finally, Weyland (2006) emphasizes cognitive processes of decision-makers, arguing that policy diffusion happened because technocrats and politicians working under time and financial pressures took cognitive shortcuts to process lessons from the Chilean example.

Reforms in other social policy areas, particularly health and education, were more varied than in pensions. There was no neoliberal blueprint out there similar to the pension privatization model, though the World Bank exerted general pressures towards decentralization of service delivery and greater involvement of the private sector. As Kaufman and Nelson (2004) and the various contributors to their volume argue, reforms in health and education had to deal with more stakeholders than pension reforms, particularly among the providers of the services. Typically, these stakeholders were well organized, from doctors and hospital associations to teachers' unions, and thus had the capacity to exercise effective resistance. Administratively, it is more difficult to design functioning systems to deliver quality health and education than transfers. Accordingly, reforms and their implementation were heavily shaped by the interaction between coalitional alignments, executive involvement and follow-up, and policy legacies that manifested themselves in domestic institutional arrangements and interest groups.

Studies of the outcomes of pension reforms found that they were disappointing in terms of the expected expansion of coverage, the burden of administrative costs, and competition among pension funds, along with equity, solidarity, and gendered impacts (Cruz-Saco and Mesa-Lago 1998; Ewig 2008; Dion 2006; Huber and Stephens 2000b; Kay and SinHa 2008 and contributors to their volume). The report commissioned by President Bachelet in Chile highlighted these shortcomings and gave rise to a significant re-reform of the Chilean pension system, expanding coverage for those not covered or having accumulated insufficient funds in the private system (Consejo de Reforma Previsional 2006). Useful review essays are Dion (2008) and Mesa-Lago (2008).

Some studies have looked specifically at social policy reforms and evaluated their gendered impact. In general, they have found that greater reliance on the market and the private sector intensified the disadvantage of women. Women in general are in a weaker position in the market because they have more breaks in their work lives, they are more likely to work in the informal sector, and they are earning less than men in both the formal and informal sectors. Accordingly, contribution-based social insurance leaves them with less protection. In addition, their reproductive role and their social role as caregivers means that they require more healthcare both for themselves and their children and more support services to be able to combine family responsibilities and paid work (Castiglioni 2005; Dion 2006; Ewig and Bello 2009; Martínez Franzoni, 2008).

ORIGINS AND CURRENT IMPACT OF SOCIAL POLICY REGIMES: THE EVIDENCE

Origins of Effective Social Policy Regimes

Effective social policy regimes should result in low levels of poverty and inequality and high levels of human capital, or at least in significant and sustained movement towards lowering levels of poverty and inequality and improving the human capital base. Of course, the policy regimes should demonstrate their contribution to such an outcome in the form of social spending as a percentage of GDP and the allocation of spending in a progressive manner. By these standards, there are no fully successful social policy regimes in Latin America. To begin with, social expenditures are comparatively low. Total social expenditures (for social security and welfare, health, and education) in 2002–3 surpassed 15 per cent of GDP only in Argentina, Brazil, Costa Rica, Panama, and Uruguay; Chile, Bolivia, Colombia, Venezuela, and Mexico spent between 11 and 15 per cent; the remaining countries spent less than 10 per cent of GDP.

Low spending is intimately related to the weakness of the tax base. As a consequence of trade liberalization, revenue from trade taxes fell; the share of total tax revenue coming from taxes on foreign trade fell from 18 per cent in 1980 to 14 per cent in the mid-1990s. Tax reforms reduced marginal tax rates on personal income and taxes on corporate profits, and they increased reliance on value added taxes. However, collection rates have remained lower than the statutory rates (Lora 2001), and average tax revenue has remained low compared not only to OECD countries but also to East Asian countries at similar levels of development. Average tax revenue in Latin America, including social security contributions, in 2002 was 16 per cent of GDP, compared to 36 per cent for OECD countries in general and 26 per cent for the US and Japan, the two advanced industrial countries with the lowest tax burdens (Centrángolo and Gómez Sabaini 2007: 53). There are major differences between Latin American countries, Brazil being at the top end with a tax burden that had surpassed 30 per cent of GDP by 2005, but Chile, for instance, remaining at only 18 per cent of GDP.

Correspondingly, outcome indicators of social policy leave much to be desired. All countries have rather large groups that live in poverty, with Uruguay being the only country in the 1990s where less than 10 per cent of households were below the poverty level defined either by a basket of basic necessities (Economic Commission for Latin America and the Caribbean (ECLAC)) or by the $2 per day in purchasing power parity (World Bank). The economic crisis of the early 2000s in Argentina and Uruguay saw poverty rates shoot up to 26 per cent in Argentina and 19 per cent in Uruguay in 2005. In that year, Uruguay and Chile had the lowest poverty rates in Latin America with 19 per cent, thus leaving close to a fifth of their populations in poverty. Moreover, almost all countries have rather large groups with access to poor quality education and healthcare only.

Compared to the rest of Latin America though, Argentina, Chile, Costa Rica, and Uruguay have clearly developed the most effective social policy regimes. Brazil is high on social spending but low on the outcome indicators (Huber and Stephens 2009). The four comparatively successful countries exemplify three paths to effective social policy regimes: significant industrialization under populist-authoritarian auspices (Argentina), or democratization with (Chile, Uruguay) or without (Costa Rica) significant industrialization, but with the presence of a powerful left-of-centre party or coalition (Pribble 2008; Segura-Ubiergo 2007). Quantitative studies have confirmed that length of the democratic record and left strength in the legislature are significantly associated with lower poverty and inequality in Latin America (Huber et al. 2006).

Reforms and Distributive Outcomes of Social Policy Regimes

A large number of studies have looked at the distributive impact of specific social policies (e.g. De Ferranti et al. 2004; CEPAL: Social Panorama, various years) and a few studies have tried to construct a synthetic view of the distributive impact of the totality of transfer policies in several countries (Lindert et al. 2006). They have uniformly found that social security is highly regressive and social assistance highly progressive, but that social security by far outweighs social assistance and thus gives a highly regressive profile to the totality of social transfers, in stark contrast to the impact of transfers in advanced industrial countries. In education and health, programmes focusing on basic education and primary and preventive healthcare are progressive, whereas expenditures for tertiary education and expensive curative medicine are regressive. Overall and on average, health expenditures are distributively neutral and education expenditures slightly progressive. However, there is considerable variation between countries.

As noted quantitative studies have found that length of the democratic record and long-term strength of left-of-centre parties depress both poverty and inequality, but they have also found that these variables do not significantly influence social security expenditures. Rather, social security schemes are hard to modify once put into place, be it by authoritarian or democratic regimes, and they push up expenditures with an ageing population. There is no conclusive evidence about the resilience of different types of social spending in the face of budget deficits. While Huber et al. (2008) find that social security expenditures are comparatively more resilient than health and education expenditures, Kaufman and Segura-Ubiergo (2001) contrarily suggest that the area of social security transfers (mainly pensions) is the most vulnerable, while health and education expenditures are far less so. Another important finding in terms of social expenditures in the region (and the developing world) is its countercyclical nature (Wibbels 2006). Wibbels found that given the patterns of integration into global markets, where shocks associated with international markets are profound and access to capital markets in difficult times is limited (in comparison with developed nations), Latin American governments have more incentives to balance budgets by cutting social spending, and so are unable to smooth consumption across the business cycle.

Government spending in a democratic context does reduce income inequality; this is true in a worldwide sample (Lee 2005) as well as for social transfer expenditures in Latin America (Huber et al. 2006). In Latin America, length of the democratic record is highly correlated with strength of left-wing parties. This is due to the fact that the main alternative to democracy was authoritarianism of the right, not the left. Right-wing authoritarian regimes repressed organized labour and left-wing parties, whereas unions and parties of all stripes were allowed to form and consolidate under democratic regimes. Left-of-centre parties produced redistribution not by overall higher expenditures (no statistical effect on social expenditures) but by the allocation of these expenditures. Of particular importance is spending on non-contributory programmes for those outside the formal labour market. This includes non-contributory pensions as well as income support for working-age families, such as family allowances and conditional cash transfer programmes.

Conditional cash transfer programmes (CCTs) have become popular in Latin America. As of 2005, at least nine Latin American countries had introduced a programme that provides cash to poor families (preferably the mother) in exchange for keeping the children in school and under regular medical supervision for vaccinations and other preventive care (Lindert et al. 2006). Not all of these programmes were introduced by left governments; one of the best known is 'Oportunidades' in Mexico introduced by President Fox in 2002.[2] However, the largest of these programmes was developed under President Lula da Silva of Brazil; by 2006, *Bolsa Familia* had grown to reach 11 million families, or over 20 per cent of the Brazilian population, and it was credited with playing an important role in Lula's re-election that year (Hunter and Power 2007). Early evaluations of these programmes show that they are not only effective in reducing poverty but also in improving school attendance and health outcomes (Rawlings and Rubio 2005).

Emergency employment programmes introduced in the wake of economic crises constitute another important kind of anti-poverty programme. Argentine employment programmes, in their latest incarnation known as *Plan Jefes y Jefas de Hogar Desocupados*, grew dramatically from 1993 to 2002 to cover 1.5 million heads of household, and they survived into the recovery phase. On the one hand, these programmes did play an important role in poverty alleviation, but, on the other, they also became a political tool in the hands of the central government to build alliances with provincial politicians and placate areas with strong protest movements (Giraudy 2007).

The left-wing *Frente Amplio* (FA) government in Uruguay launched a particularly comprehensive anti-poverty programme in 2007, to replace the two-year emergency social programme it had launched upon taking office in 2005. The new *Plan Equidad* is available to all low-income households and includes family allowances contingent on children's school attendance, non-contributory social assistance pensions for individuals from 65 years of age, incentives for attendance in secondary schools, expansion of preschool education, support for employment, nutrition cards, and subsidies for electricity and water costs (Cuenca 2007). Estimates put potential beneficiaries at up to one million citizens, or about one third of the population (Campodónico 2007). The Chilean government under Socialist President Lagos launched a similarly comprehensive programme, *Chile Solidario*, but on a much smaller scale, directed only at households in extreme poverty, or less than 6 per cent of the population. President Bachelet then attempted to extend the programme by incorporating new groups into the programme, primarily the homeless.

Universal pre-school education has been on the agenda of progressive governments, both for reasons of preparing children from poorer backgrounds to succeed in school and of enabling mothers to enter gainful employment. Thus, free high quality

---

[2] The programme was based on a previous one, PROGRESA, initiated in 1997.

public pre-school education is a means to combat poverty and inequality both in this generation and the next. Latin America has significantly improved pre-school coverage during the last two decades. In 2005, more than 84 per cent of children in the region attended the last year of pre-school education (ECLAC 2007). In Uruguay, pre-school education coverage of 5-year-old children from the lowest quintile increased from 64 per cent in 1991 to 94 per cent in 2007, and coverage of 4-year-old children increased from 27 per cent to 72 per cent in the same period (Cardozo 2008). The gap between the lowest and highest income quintile narrowed from 62 to 23 points for 4-year-old children and from 33 to 5 points for 5-year-olds. This improvement is mainly a consequence of the expansion of public coverage by the 1995 reform. In Chile, while pre-school education experienced no significant improvements in coverage during the 1990s (ECLAC 2002), the Bachelet government announced a major expansion, setting the goal of incorporating 180,000 children at the 4-year-old level into pre-school education for 2010, the equivalent of 37 per cent of non-matriculated children in 2008 (OAS 2008).

Healthcare reforms have varied widely, heavily contingent on policy legacies. All of the more advanced Latin American countries have been facing growing elderly populations requiring more healthcare services. The cutbacks in public expenditures in the wake of the debt crisis had left public systems with severely underpaid personnel, outdated equipment, and facilities in dire need of repair. Significant growth in public health expenditures from the early 1990s on remedied some of these deficiencies but was unable to close the quality gap between the public and private systems. Those who could afford it continued to resort to private alternatives.

The most recent round of Costa Rican and Uruguayan reforms arguably went furthest towards providing high quality healthcare for the entire population. The Chilean reform aimed in the same direction but encountered stronger private sector opposition. Under the previous reform implemented by the Pinochet regime, formal sector employees could choose to have their mandatory health insurance contributions go to the public system or a for-profit private provider that could charge additional premiums and discriminate on the basis of risk. Both the Costa Rican and the Uruguayan systems were insurance-based and covered virtually the entire economically active population; contributions in Costa Rica were subsidized for low-income earners in the informal sector. The non-insured poor in all three countries had a right to free care in public facilities. The Costa Rican system had been a unified public one since the 1970s, which means that the poor were served by the same facilities as the insured population, whereas the insured in Uruguay relied mostly on not-for-profit private insurers and providers.

The Costa Rican reform expanded primary care centres throughout the country in order to improve access to healthcare for all. The Uruguayan reform introduced centralized financing, with public and private providers alike receiving a per capita payment for patients under their care, and those making the mandatory contributions having a choice of providers. The reform also strengthened the network of primary care clinics (Pribble 2008). The Chilean reform under President Lagos guaranteed universal coverage of fifty-six common illnesses, with co-payments being capped in a progressive manner according to family income, and time limits set within which treatment has to be provided. If the public sector is unable to provide care, treatment in the private sector will be covered. In Uruguay and Chile, the groups that are left out of these reformed systems are the non-poor informal sector workers; in Costa Rica, strong efforts have been made to include them through subsidies for their contributions. In sum, the Costa Rican and Uruguayan reforms go far towards basic universalism, whereas the universalism of the Chilean reform remains confined to the specified set of illnesses.

Brazil's health system illustrates the gap between constitutional rights to universal free healthcare and the practice of accessibility of services. The Brazilian constitution of 1988 granted this right to all citizens and established a unified public health system like the Costa Rican one, but implementation was left up to the legislature and the Ministry of Health. Little progress was made before the administration of President Cardoso who gave backing to a strong Minister of Health to push forward with improvements in universal basic healthcare. As a result, indicators like infant mortality, vaccination, and maternal health improved significantly (PNUD 2005). However, despite the fact that they and their employers are required to pay into the public system (in contrast to Chile), higher income earners heavily use private insurers and providers and rely on the public system for the most expensive kinds of care. Moreover, gaps in access to complicated care remain huge across classes and gaps in access even to primary care remain great across regions (Arretche 2006).

The effects that democracy and the strength of left parties have on reducing poverty and income inequality work not only through allocation of social expenditures but also through other legislation, such as the level of minimum wages and support for unions and coordinated wage setting policies. In Chile and Costa Rica the minimum wage is an important instrument that can keep a small household above the poverty line. The ratio of median wage for all wage and salary earners to the minimum wage in 2002 was roughly 2.8:1 in Chile (Marinakis 2006: 6) and 2.2:1 in Costa Rica (Estado de la Nación 2004: 409–10). Since 1990, the real minimum wage has stayed roughly constant, with a slight upward trend in Costa Rica, whereas it has increased steeply in Chile; in Argentina it deteriorated dramatically after 2001. In Uruguay, the national minimum wage is not a relevant floor; it deteriorated consistently and strongly from 1985 to 2005, when the FA government doubled it. More important have historically been tripartite wage setting councils, from which the state withdrew under National Party President Lacalle in 1992, but which were re-established quickly by the FA government (Rodriguez et al. 2007). Under the FA government, rural and public sector workers were included for the first time in collective negotiations, and salaries improved in real terms.

Globalization and Social Policy

The debate about globalization and social policy has overcome initial extreme positions, both with regard to advanced industrial and developing countries. As a result of much research, an intermediate position has gained ground which holds that globalization has no direct effects, either negative or positive, on social spending, but rather that domestic forces and institutions serve as mediating factors (see e.g. the contributions to Glatzer and Rueschemeyer 2005).

In statistical analyses, Garrett (2001) in a sample of developed and developing countries, and Kaufman and Segura-Ubiergo (2001) in a set of Latin American countries find negative effects of trade integration (i.e. changes in trade openness) on changes in general government consumption and in social spending, respectively. Kaufman and Segura-Ubiergo also find negative effects of the level of trade openness and of the interaction of trade and capital market openness on changes in social spending. Avelino et al. (2005) find a negative effect of trade openness but a positive effect of financial openness on levels of social spending in 19 Latin American countries between 1980 and 1999. Kaufman and Segura-Ubiergo (2001) find unstable effects of levels of capital controls on changes in social expenditures and weakly positive effects of changes in capital controls. Rudra (2004) finds a positive effect of capital flows on the level of social expenditures in a worldwide sample, and Garrett (2001) finds no significant effect of levels and changes in capital flows on levels of government consumption.

The inconsistency of the findings has various explanations, such as the particular cases and time periods examined, different sets of control variables, different operationalizations of the dependent variables, and different analytic techniques. Arguably the most serious reason is the use of different control variables, in particular the omission of domestic political variables. Results of statistical analyses that include urbanization, democracy, and long-term strength of different political tendencies in the legislature or the executive, indicate that trade openness and foreign direct investment have no effects on social expenditures, neither social security and welfare nor health and education expenditures (Huber et al. 2008).

FUTURE DIRECTIONS IN RESEARCH ON LATIN AMERICAN SOCIAL POLICY REGIMES

The distributive impact of social policy. So far, comparative studies of the distributive impact of social policies have been hampered by the lack of comparability of the data. There are excellent country case studies based on analyses of national household surveys, and some attempts to compare the results of these analyses across countries, but these national surveys use different concepts and/or equivalency scales for household size, which makes strict comparison essentially impossible. Now the Luxembourg Income Study is adding several Latin American countries to their data base, which will be a huge step forward. It will allow systematic comparative examination of the distributive impact of social policies on different social groups (by income level, gender, level of education, geographic location, etc.).

Nexus to labour market policy. It is clear that overcoming poverty requires employment, both at the individual and the societal level. At the societal level, the transition from ISI to the neoliberal model caused deindustrialization, a loss of jobs in the formal sector, and rapid growth of informal employment. Even in the post-adjustment period, job growth was concentrated in the informal sector, with low productivity and therefore low wages (Tokman 2002). The commodities boom starting in 2004 stimulated growth in the Latin American economies, but it did little to improve the structural weaknesses of Latin American economies. Most governments remained reluctant to engage in industrial policy, and private sector initiatives for productivity increases are few and far between. Research into options for job creation linked to active labour market policies to make qualified workers available will be an essential component of the entire welfare state research programme in Latin America.

In the area of labour market policy, governments have had great difficulty making the transition from traditional forms of employment protection to more flexible labour markets and policies that would still protect workers from falling into poverty with their families. Unemployment insurance is a new feature and has been introduced in only some Latin American social policy regimes, and even where it exists, coverage and benefits are very small. Active labour market policies in the form of job training and support for job placement are few and far between. Some pilot programmes have linked conditional cash transfer programmes with labour market training and jobs in the public sector. This is clearly an important direction both for practical policy experiments and for research.

The politics of social policy. Another major area of developing research is the comparative analysis of political struggles over specific policy initiatives. Understanding these struggles is important both theoretically, to help scholars build better models of welfare state development in Latin America, and practically, to help governments committed to welfare state construction build the most effective political alliances. As more materials, such as legislative debates, party positions, and newspaper archives become available on line, the details of the politics of policy will become more amenable to systematic comparative analysis. These kinds of data sources will never substitute for interviews with those directly involved in the struggles, but they will constitute the basis for triangulation of information and for systematic testing of generalizations.

CHAPTER 45

··

EAST ASIA

··

ITO PENG

JOSEPH WONG

INTRODUCTION

··

RESEARCH interest in the evolution of social policy regimes in East Asia has grown considerably over the past two decades, particularly as scholars have begun to consider the distributive implications of the region's economic 'miracle'. We know that economic growth in post-war East Asia was among the fastest in the world. Until recently, however, we knew much less about the parallel development, or lack thereof, of social policies. There are those who contend that rapid industrialization in East Asia came at the expense of a more broadly encompassing social compact. The welfare state, they argue, was sacrificed for the sake of aggregate growth (Holliday 2000). There are also those, on the other hand, who see the longer term trajectory of social policy development in the region more favourably, especially when compared to other late developers in Latin America and the former Soviet Union (Gough and Wood, 2004, with their collaborators; Kasza 2006; Haggard and Kaufman 2008). They see social policy deepening, despite global trends towards welfare state retrenchment. Despite these disagreements, most scholars of social policy in the region agree that it offers a rich source of cases to be considered within, as opposed to outside of, the conventional welfare state literature. Indeed, the region's differences from the experiences of the Anglo-European welfare state 'worlds' should inform more global debates about the past, present and future of the welfare state. This chapter endeavours to do this, integrating East Asia into the larger welfare state canon and situating our analysis in terms of common global challenges.

EAST ASIAN EXCEPTIONALISM?

Debates about the direction of welfare state reform in East Asia notwithstanding, most scholars of the region will agree that the state has tended to play a much smaller and leaner fiscal role in providing and financing welfare and social security. Japan is the regional leader in terms of social spending at 18.6 per cent of GDP (in 2005). Even then, Japan is a laggard spender when compared to averages in social spending among OECD and EU countries of 20.5 per cent and 27 per cent respectively. Other East Asian countries have lagged far behind. During the mid 2000s, Taiwan and Hong Kong spent close to 10 per cent of GDP on social programmes, while social spending in Korea, China, and Singapore accounted for less than 7 per cent of gross national product (OECD 2008e; ADB 2008; Taiwan Executive Yuan 2008). But as we know, social spending is only one indicator of social welfare commitment. Observers thus also note that the institutional persistence of social insurance schemes rather than more universal programmes in many of these cases has precluded more redistributive implications. In these respects, the East Asian variant of the welfare state stands apart from—and behind—its Western comparators.

Explaining East Asia's 'exceptionalism' resulted in a first wave of comparative social policy analysis of the region during the 1990s. Three complementary explanations emerged. Together they constituted a relatively distinctive and regionally-based 'East Asian approach' to welfare state evolution. As such, scholars of the region smoothed out national distinctions—and in the case of China, excluded it from consideration altogether—and inductively generated a set of hypotheses regarding the distinctiveness of the East Asian welfare state.

First, tremendous emphasis was placed on a 'common' Confucian heritage shared among East Asian societies. Scholars asserted that distinctly 'Asian' values—such as the respect for education, filial piety, deference to authority, patriarchy, and above all the centrality of the family and kinship ties in social organization—constrained the development of more 'Western' conceptions of the welfare state (Jones 1993; Goodman et al. 1998). The evidence pointed to extraordinarily high levels of household savings, a preponderance of three-generation households and low labour market participation rates among women, all of which suggested that the family or household was responsible for social protection, and not the state. Where the state did matter was in education, for which East Asian governments allocated high levels of public resources. Even in the labour market, the family motif was juxtaposed onto the firm. Asian-style 'company welfare' reflected paternalistic-filial norms which were transposed from the prototypical male breadwinner family. Simply put, East Asia's exceptionalism was explained, in part, by constructed notions of Asian or Confucian values.

Second, the underdeveloped welfare state in industrial Asia was also explained by the absence of a strong political 'left' in mainstream politics (Wong 2004). The exception of course was China, though again, the Chinese case was disregarded in conceptualizations of the 'capitalist' welfare state in Asia. Inspired by the dominant power resources theory derived from the Anglo-European experience (Esping-Andersen 1990), it was argued that the absence in East Asia of leftist parties, the presence of weak unions, and low unionization rates among workers constrained the growth of the welfare state. In Japan, for instance, the Socialist Party was decimated early on, a move encouraged by the American Occupation forces at the time. Labour was also excluded from the policy process (Pempel and Tsunekawa 1979; Kume 1998). The Cold War logic of the post-war period likewise marginalized the political left in other places such as Korea, Singapore, and Taiwan. Labour movements in industrializing Asia were crushed and co-opted into the state apparatus. In other words, leftist forces failed to play any significant policy role.

Third, the 'productivist' approach articulated by Holliday (2000) offered a compelling account of social policy evolution in East Asia. This approach contended that social policy reform among Asia's newly industrialized countries (NICS) was not intended for social protection or redistribution, but rather to promote economic productivity. Selective social policy provisions (health, education, housing, skills training) were subordinated to the imperatives of labour production (and reproduction), human capital investment and sustained economic growth. As such, social policies were initiated by economic rather than social policymakers. Productivism also reinforced the nation-building aspirations of the post-war Asian developmental state. According to Goodman and Peng (1996), for instance, welfare state development in Japan was driven by a nation-building project which began during the nineteenth century Meiji Restoration and which strengthened after the devastation of World War II. In other words, proponents of the productivist approach argued that economic productivity (i.e. growth) reflected national power and social policy 'investments' toward those ends were understood as part of broader economic nationalist narratives.

These three complementary perspectives—Confucian values, the absence of leftist power resources, and the primacy of productivism—provided important scholarly insight into the uniqueness of the East Asian experience in social policy development. As an exercise in 'exceptionalism', they offered a compelling starting point from which to understand social policy reform in the region. However, we contend that they reflected important efforts to demarcate East Asia's regionally bounded *differences* from the Anglo-European experience. Our point is that upon examining the cases more specifically—to effectively de-essentialize the prevailing exceptionalist point of view—one can find significant variations among these cases and considerable dynamism and change over time. In other words, we argue against an exceptionalist East Asian experience.

Indeed, we identify two broad patterns of social policy regime evolution in East Asia. The first is a more inclusive social insurance model which has, over time, evolved into a set of programmes based on social solidarity, universality and with redistributive implications. The exemplary cases in the region are Japan, Korea, and Taiwan. Meanwhile, the second pattern of regime evolution centres on a more individualistic and market-based model, where workers and citizens more generally live without relatively encompassing social safety nets. This pattern is most prevalent, we argue, in Singapore, Hong Kong and ironically, communist China. The remainder of this chapter analyzes these two patterns of social policy development. We both describe and explain these divergent pathways by identifying the political economic mechanisms which led to certain social policy decisions and outcomes. In other words, we elaborate on the different *choices* made by social policy reformers across a range of cases.

INCLUSIVE SOCIAL INSURANCE: JAPAN, KOREA, AND TAIWAN

The pattern of social policy development in Japan, Korea, and Taiwan shares three key characteristics. First, rapid economic growth among these cases during the post-war period was accompanied by a relatively egalitarian distribution of income. Despite near 10 per cent annual growth and continual industrial upgrading, Gini coefficients in Japan, Korea, and Taiwan hovered between 0.3 and 0.4, which were comparable to levels in other egalitarian industrial economies of the west. A focus on export-oriented industrialization in the region created employment opportunities, generated high levels of upward labour mobility, and encouraged the growth of small and medium sized enterprises. Even today, Gini coefficients in Japan, Korea, and Taiwan have continued to be below 0.4, which stands in stark contrast to Hong Kong (0.514), Singapore (0.481), and China (0.473) where levels of inequality are widening (OECD 2008e; ADB 2008).

Second, the legacy of post-war growth with equity has entrenched high levels of public support for solidaristic values. World Values Survey data, for instance, show that respondents in Japan, Korea, and Taiwan are far less tolerant of income inequality than those surveyed in Singapore and China (which includes Hong Kong). While the majority of people living in Korea, Japan, and Taiwan believe that their governments are not doing enough for people living in conditions of poverty, only a minority of Chinese share this view (World Values Survey 2008). To be sure, current mainstream debates in Japan, Korea, and Taiwan reveal serious concerns and anxieties over problems of social inequality (Hara and Seiyama 2005; Koo 2007; Tai 2006). In short, people there have come to expect a fair degree of socio-economic equity to accompany growth.

Third, the governments in Japan, Korea, and Taiwan have actively deepened their commitment to creating more redistributive social insurance institutions. In all three cases, social policy deepening has been driven by the continued expansion in eligibility to pre-existing social insurance schemes. Health and pension schemes were created in the pre- and immediate post-World War II eras, but they were far from universal, being limited in scope and occupationally specific in terms of eligibility.

Universality was achieved over time, with the gradual expansion of existing schemes to include workers in other employment sectors and eventually self-employed workers as well. In addition to universalizing coverage, governments sought to enhance the redistributive capacity of social insurance by cross-subsidizing occupationally organized funds (for example, Japan) or by eliminating occupational differentiations altogether by integrating disparate funds into a single pipe mechanism in order to maximize risk- and financial-pooling (Korea and Taiwan). Furthermore, since the 1990s, Japan, Korea, and Taiwan have also introduced new publicly administered social insurance (long-term care) and tax-based child care programmes to address the problems of population ageing and fertility decline. These have not only led to dramatic increases in social spending, but they also represent further efforts to socialize through the state the costs of family care (Boling 2008; Peng 2008; Peng and Wong 2008; Kwon 2007). In sum, the governments in Japan, Korea, and Taiwan have both deepened existing social insurance programmes and added new schemes intended to remove and socialize the burden of care away from the family to the state.

We offer three reasons as to why these paragons of what Chalmers Johnson refers to as 'capitalist' developmental states chose the pathway of inclusive social insurance. The first relates to democracy. Governments in Japan, Korea, and Taiwan were, we argue, compelled to enlarge social welfare provision throughout the post-war period because of bottom-up democratic political pressure. Second, these countries were more inclined to choose the option of welfare state deepening because the political and economic costs of universalism and redistribution were lower in what were already relatively egalitarian societies. And third, Japan, Korea, and Taiwan were able to draw on a deeper sense of social solidarity because the real or imagined social 'distance' amongst the population was in fact relatively limited. More specifically, we argue that these states were able to gain support for solidaristic solutions to social risks because of a deeply entrenched narrative of national population homogeneity, a deeper sense of national 'we-ness' around which social policymakers could more easily sell the idea of a universal and inclusive social insurance state.

DEMOCRACY, DEVELOPMENT, AND NATIONAL IDENTITY

Social policy reform in Japan was initiated in the immediate post-war period. Rebuilding the Japanese economy, especially the growth of large industrial firms, resulted in increasing levels of inequality during the 1950s. The dominant and conservative Liberal Democratic Party (LDP) pre-empted social instability, however, by legislating comprehensive health insurance and pensions in 1958 and 1959 respectively. A year later, the government initiated its 'income doubling plan', a macro-economic policy to achieve full employment and industrial diversification. The LDP government later legislated an employment insurance programme to provide income security for unemployed industrial workers to address labour concerns after the 1974 oil shock and the subsequent economic crisis. Early efforts to address the challenges of income inequality and rapid growth in Japan thus comprised specific universal social insurance schemes and broader economic policies aimed at continual industrial upgrading (Campbell 1992; Milly 1999).

Social policy reform led by the LDP was not a function of the party's ideological commitments, however. Rather, policy reform in post-war Japan was prompted by political pressures on the governing LDP to secure broad-based electoral support. The LDP was a conservative catch-all party, meaning it looked to fashion broad socio-economic coalitions of support (Calder 1986). Political pressure for the LDP to initiate some social policy reform came from the bottom-up, specifically, the electorate. The Japanese Socialist Party, never a significant challenger to the LDP, nonetheless compelled the government to attend to issues of socio-economic inequality. Meanwhile, the American Occupation administration, despite its opposition to the socialist party and its ideologies, encouraged the LDP to address growing levels of inequality in order to prevent a tide of popular support for left-leaning parties and the still nascent labour union movement. Perhaps most important, the LDP included in its power base the electoral support of (and the generous seat bonus associated with) rural voters and small business entrepreneurs. To mitigate a concentration of social policy benefits among the labour aristocracy (i.e. those employed in large firms), the LDP universalized social insurance programmes early on. In Japan, the impetus for early social policy expansion was therefore political; in order to maintain its political dominance, the governing LDP needed to facilitate both growth and a relatively equitable distribution of income in cities and the countryside. Its strategy was to pre-empt political instability which might stem from growing levels of socio-economic inequality.

This political logic of 'compensation' exchanged for support (Calder 1986) was evident in post-war Korea and Taiwan as well. During the authoritarian period in both places, the non-democratic state provided some social insurance protection to its citizens, though the scope of coverage was extremely limited. In Korea, voluntary health insurance was first introduced in 1963, and then made compulsory in 1976. The scope of coverage was limited to only those workers employed in large firms, while government workers and military service personnel were included in separate insurance schemes. By the early 1980s, still less than one-fifth of workers enjoyed any medical insurance coverage. The extent of insurance coverage in Taiwan was similarly exclusionary during the authoritarian period. The Kuomintang (KMT) government first introduced a labour insurance programme (which included medical care) in 1953. As in Korea, government and military employees in Taiwan were covered by separate social insurance schemes. Labour insurance in Taiwan was only gradually expanded. Similar to the Korean experience, less than one-fifth of workers were eligible for labour insurance coverage by the 1980s (Wong 2004).

In both places, the introduction of social insurance was from the start non-universal in coverage, and expansion was gradual and piecemeal. There was also very little socio-economic redistribution among households and social classes. Most importantly, the authoritarian state in South Korea and Taiwan selectively compensated those strata deemed politically and economically important to the state: specifically the labour aristocracy, civil servants and the military. As authoritarian regimes, the government in Korea and KMT in Taiwan could politically and economically afford to exclude significant portions of the population. In fact, the exclusionary social insurance programmes initiated during the authoritarian period in both places stratified society further, exacerbating rather than ameliorating social class and status differences.

The process of democratization, which was initiated in Korea and Taiwan during the late 1980s with the introduction of national elections, shaped the course of social policy reform in the post-authoritarian era. The introduction of political competition altered the political incentives for the then ruling parties, compelling them to legislate significant social policy changes. In Korea, the authoritarian-turned-democratic ruling party extended health insurance to rural self-employed workers (farmers) in 1988, timed to occur with founding presidential and legislative elections. A year later, in 1989, the ruling party again expanded the scope of healthcare insurance to urban-based self-employed workers. It was also during this time that the government introduced a national pensions programme to appeal to labour. Winning the support of labour was critical for the Korean state as workers had been a main source of opposition to the authoritarian regime during the mid to late 1980s. The KMT in Taiwan reacted to the introduction of democratization in similarly strategic ways. Though the ruling party there had historically eschewed demands for universal health insurance, it did an about-face when it initiated reform discussions during the late 1980s and legislated a comprehensive national health insurance (NHI) system in 1994. The NHI was implemented in the spring of 1995, on the eve of founding presidential elections. In both places, democratic reform and the political incentives of electoral competition prompted the universalization of what were formerly limited social insurance schemes (Wong 2004). Democratic transition in Korea and Taiwan essentially 'de-aligned' the political party system, with the introduction of new opposition parties. De-alignment was then followed by a process of party 'realignment', whereby nominally conservative parties turned to social policy reform as winning electoral platforms.

Japan, though democratic since the beginning of the post-war period, experienced a similar process of party de-alignment and realignment during the early 1990s, which prompted a renewed round of social policy reform. Throughout the 1980s and when policymakers began to feel the pressures of the increasingly globalized economy, the LDP government initiated a policy discourse about a 'Japanese-style welfare society', essentially a plan for welfare retrenchment. This idea resulted in new waves of bottom-up societal mobilization around social policy deepening rather than government efforts at retrenchment. Civil society groups emerged, especially those which pushed for more not less comprehensive social policy reform in the 1990s. The mainstreaming of social policy reform became even more pronounced after the LDP lost power for the first time in 1993 (Pempel 1997). The 'Japanese-style welfare society' idea failed to resonate.

Multi-party competition in Japan turned the prospect of social policy reform into a highly contested, and increasingly winning, political issue. Contending parties built new electoral coalitions around social policy reform. Though the LDP remained the dominant party throughout the 1990s, it was still forced to co-opt policy ideas from opposition parties such as the Social Democratic Party, as well as newly formed splinter parties and prospective coalition partners such as the populist New Komeito (Clean Party) and Liberal Party. The LDP thus initiated new social care programmes for the elderly and children, expanding government outlays, organizing insurance schemes, and subsidizing care facilities. Functionally, these programmes were intended to address Japan's rapid demographic shift and greying society. Politically, however, these initiatives proved popular among voters and vital for the LDP's political survival.

A similar political-economic logic played out in Korea and Taiwan during the late 1990s, especially after the 1997 Asian Financial Crisis. The election of former dissident and populist-leaning Kim Dae-Jung in 1997 deepened the state's commitment to social welfare in Korea. The precariousness of the labour situation and threats of social unrest prompted the Kim government to quickly implement the national pensions programme, to centralize the national health insurance system and to launch new reform efforts in socialized care for the elderly and children (Peng 2004). In Taiwan, the electoral defeat of the KMT in 2000 created new social policy promises, specifically in old-age income security and gender-sensitive labour market and workplace policies. Wong (2003) argues that electoral competition during the late 1990s resulted in a 'race to the top' and a 'ratcheting up' of social policy reform promises among political entrepreneurs. Indeed, the continued mobilization of civil society groups and the integration of activist social movements into the political arena ensured that social policy reform remained a key policy agenda item in democratizing Korea and Taiwan.

The political logic of the inclusive social insurance model in Japan, Korea, and Taiwan is rooted in democratic processes in which bottom-up demands for welfare deepening were mobilized through civil society activism and electoral politics. Still, the democratic state in these cases proved relatively receptive to such welfare reform demands in part because of the legacies of post-war growth with equity. The gap between the haves and have-nots was relatively narrow, meaning the economic costs of redistribution were lower. Growth with equity also ensured the social distance between social classes was relatively close, thus legitimating a more solidaristic approach to mitigating social risk. Politically, the experience of growth with equity in Japan, Korea, and Taiwan, also meant that the political system was not *a priori* structured along class lines. A left–right cleavage was not deeply entrenched in mainstream democratic politics, which we see elsewhere in the developing world, which provided the ideological flexibility for political entrepreneurs to legitimately advocate positions for social policy deepening. Thus, it was nominally conservative parties such as the LDP, the Grand National Party in Korea, and the KMT which initiated the universalization of social insurance.

Social solidarity and the normative basis of universal social insurance were also afforded by narratives of national population homogeneity. In Japan, Korea, and Taiwan, this narrative served as a powerful galvanizing force in the post-war nation-building process. For example, the idea of a Japanese-style welfare society, which attributed Japan's low levels of public welfare spending to its deep socio-cultural norms of family and community solidarity, was premised on the 'theory of Japaneseness' (*Nihonjinron*), a deeply ingrained discourse which asserted that Japan was historically and remains a culturally, ethnically, and racially homogeneous society. Though the *Nihonjinron* narrative no longer resonates as strongly in a globalized Japan, the idea of 'the Japanese' as a uniquely homogeneous society remains strong. Similarly powerful national narratives structured the development of identity politics in Korea and Taiwan which in turn inculcated a sort of solidaristic base for legitimating the politics of welfare state deepening.

Tensions surrounding this intensely nationalist narrative have recently emerged, however, particularly with respect to increased immigration. The inability of the Japanese government, for example, to reform its immigration policies to address the problems of demographic ageing, fertility decline, and chronic labour shortages has largely been the result of strong resistance among Japanese to opening the country to foreign newcomers. Public policy debates about foreign care workers have been terribly negative and bordering on xenophobic, revealing concerns about the cultural inappropriateness of having foreigners caring for elderly Japanese. Similar anxieties about population diversity have obstructed more general policy debates over immigration policy reforms (Shipper 2008; Shinkawa 2008). A similar narrative of population homogeneity, and thus resistance to the idea of multiculturalism, is evident in Korea. Like Japan, debate in Korea regarding allowing non-Koreans to immigrate (and claim citizenship) has been intensely conflictual (Lee et al. 2006). Even in Taiwan, where tensions between Taiwanese and Chinese mainlanders (who arrived in 1949) have already existed for half a century, the prospects of opening Taiwan to other foreigners increasingly have been met with social and political opposition. Policy conflicts about more open immigration policies, specifically those related to foreign workers from South-East Asia and to the growing number of foreign brides have revealed ardent resistance in democratic Taiwan to the idea of population diversity. In sum, rapid flows of in-migration have begun to challenge the social bases of the welfare state in Japan, Korea, and Taiwan.

INDIVIDUALISTIC SOCIAL PROTECTION: HONG KONG, SINGAPORE, AND CHINA

Income inequality in Hong Kong, Singapore, and China was much higher than in Japan, Korea, and Taiwan during the 1990s and 2000s. And in the case of China, levels of inequality have continued to widen rapidly. Though the aggregate economic growth rate in China has been the fastest in world for nearly a generation now, nearly 40 per cent of Chinese have continued to live on less than $2 purchasing power parity (PPP) per day (ABD 2008). Levels of economic disparity between the over 800 million people living in the countryside and city dwellers have been particularly acute. Economic reform in China, which was initiated during the 1970s, prioritized the industrial development of coastal cities, which skewed the distribution of economic gains away from China's inland provinces. Beyond descriptive economic measures of inequality, however, the social 'distance' between those living in Chinese cities and the countryside is also vast and disparate, which has undermined notions of social solidarity. To be sure, unlike in Japan, Korea, and Taiwan, attitudinal support for 'competitiveness' in Hong Kong, Singapore, and China is much higher than popular support for more 'egalitarianism'. And despite recent efforts by the Chinese state to address issues of socio-economic inequality, popular attitudes there have continued to be more tolerant of income inequality (World Values Survey 2008). The same can be said of prevailing attitudes in Hong Kong and Singapore.

Whereas growth with equity allowed places such as Japan, Korea, and Taiwan to pursue greater social policy deepening, the absence of such a development—measured in terms of income distribution or popular attitudes regarding the normative place of egalitarianism—has made it more difficult for governments in Hong Kong, Singapore, and China to pursue sweeping social policy reforms. Indeed, the preferred mode of social protection in the latter three continues to rest with the individual's capacity to mitigate social risk, which in fact maintains and even exacerbates, rather than ameliorates, socio-economic stratification. Singapore's Central Provident Fund (CPF), for instance, was first introduced by the British colonial administration in 1955 as a compulsory savings scheme for individual old age income security. Comprising both employee and employer contributions, the CPF was gradually extended to other social protection needs such as housing (in 1968) and medical care (in 1984) and later to education. Following the Singaporean example, Hong Kong adopted in 2000 the Mandatory Provident Fund scheme for retirement income security. China also introduced a similar savings-based model. The Housing Provident Fund was introduced in Shanghai during the early 1990s and eventually became a national programme a few years later in an effort increase home ownership among China's growing city-dwelling middle class. The move towards individualized savings mechanisms in China marks a change in emphasis in social protection, a move from the collective to the individual and from the public provision of welfare to protection through private means. In all three places, social protection has been individualized through incentivized private savings. Such programmes are not redistributive.

CONSTRAINED CHOICES

There are several reasons why we see this alternative pattern of social policy development in East Asia, or more specifically why social policymakers have been constrained in their choices about new directions and innovations in social policy reform. First, unlike in Japan, Korea, and Taiwan, where the pressures of electoral competition and the strategic imperatives of political entrepreneurship compelled policymakers and activists there to push for welfare state deepening, the absence of democracy in China, Singapore, and Hong Kong has precluded both this political logic and the incentives for radical social policy change. For instance, despite a vocal civil society and one which has historically leaned towards a social democratic ideal, Hong Kong has never actually enjoyed a fully fledged democratic system of government. Likewise, there is little political competition in Singapore, a political reality which has allowed the ruling People's Action Party great latitude in designing social policy with little opposition. China's political system is non-democratic, without either viable opposition parties or an independent civil society or media to instigate bottom-up pressures for change. In all three places, therefore, social policy reform has been motivated neither by a broader normative commitment of the state to promote greater equity nor a political imperative or incentive to have to appeal to voters.

Second, Hong Kong, Singapore, and China are without the central fiscal capacity to increase the state's role in social protection. Hong Kong, for instance, known as one of the world's 'freest' market economies, has a negligible tax (individual or corporate) base from which to accumulate fiscal resources. Firms there are also resistant to paying employer contributions to social insurance. Singapore is the same. After gaining independence from the Malayan Federation in 1965, the city-state embarked on a development strategy that was underpinned by a discourse of mere 'economic survivalism'. As such, full employment, rather than socio-economic redistribution, was the main priority for economic policymakers. Social policy advocates were marginalized. Without natural resources to exploit, Singapore, not unlike Hong Kong, was forced to leverage its locational advantages to attract foreign investment and multinational corporations. One such advantage was, and continues to be, a low tax burden for foreign firms. The state's fiscal base is therefore uniquely small, believed to be among the smallest in the industrial world (Ramesh 1995). Both Hong Kong and Singapore are fiscally lean states. Furthermore, to impose social insurance contributions onto employers, a *de facto* payroll tax, would be economically inconceivable. That they currently face greater economic competition from challengers in South-East Asia and from China has only made the prospects of sharing the costs of social insurance with industry even less tenable.

Though China continues to insist that its economy remains nominally socialist, its government has similarly come under increasing fiscal constraint. Demands on the central state for more social protection have arisen because of demographic pressures (i.e. an ageing society), increasing numbers of migrant workers without a social safety net, and overall growing levels of socio-economic inequality, especially among those living in the rural areas vis-à-vis relatively well-off city dwellers. In response, the Chinese state has offloaded its fiscal responsibilities in the provision of social insurance benefits for the already limited few who are eligible. For instance, state-owned enterprises (SOEs), and later non-SOEs, have increasingly been made responsible for contributing to workers' social insurance and benefits rather than the government. The central state has also decentralized the management of labour and social insurance to county and city-level governments, with the expectation that sub-national administrations can more effectively tailor social programmes to meet local needs. Indeed, it was also rationalized by the central state that local governments would create insurance 'pools' to mitigate risk and socialize the costs and benefits to those eligible (Selden and You 1997). However, this process of administrative decentralization, especially after the 1994 fiscal reforms which earmarked tax flows upwards, has failed to provide local governments with the resources required to pay-out pensions and other social benefits. The problem of local corruption and the realities of China's 'leaky' fiscal federalism have compounded the challenges of ensuring adequate resources to sustain the provision of social protection at the local level.

Even more notable is the fact that the Chinese state has increasingly offloaded its prior social welfare responsibilities onto individuals. Citing the influence of the World Bank and other international economic institutions, Chinese social policy-makers have gradually replaced pre-existing pay-as-you-go pension schemes with personal retirement accounts. This reform has minimized intergenerational transfers in old age income security (Frazier 2006; Hurst 2009). Furthermore, despite recent efforts to overhaul the rural healthcare system, new insurance benefits are to cover only catastrophic illnesses and the government's share in covering the costs of healthcare has remained miniscule. The vast majority of China's healthcare bill is paid directly out-of-pocket by patients. In other words, because of fiscal constraints on the central government, China's former social welfare system based on the socialist ideal of a single pillar of support (the central state) has evolved towards what analysts call a 'three pillar' model comprising the firm, resource-poor local government and individual savings. It needs to be emphasized, however, that those living in the countryside are virtually without any form of social protection at all (Davis 1989; Wong 1993; Frazier 2004).

Third, in addition to the absence of democracy and the realities of fiscal constraint, Hong Kong, Singapore, and China have had to opt for a more individualistic and market-based approach to social policy because of a much shallower normative base from which to draw a sense of social solidarity: the realities of the Chinese countryside are so disparate from the realities of those living in the coastal cities; the experiences of Hong Kong's wealthy have little resonance with the city's underclass. In other words, these societies have not benefited from the social legacies of growth with equity experienced in Japan, Korea, and Taiwan. But even deeper than that, Hong Kong, Singaporean, and Chinese societies are without the same sort of national homogeneity and ethnic solidarity that have formed the basis of inclusive social citizenship in Japan, Korea, and Taiwan.

Hong Kong and Singapore are former British colonies, and both have had a historically large foreigner presence. Singapore is home to South Asians, Chinese, Muslim Malays, and a large community of Western ex-pats. Both Hong Kong and Singapore have also historically utilized migrant workers from neighbouring countries to take-up low-wage and low-skill jobs in precarious employment sectors, making up a significant part of the population (Athukorala and Manning 1999). For example, nearly 30 per cent of all employed workers in Singapore are foreigners, with a large proportion of immigrant workers in the domestic care sector. China's vast geography and ethnic diversity have similarly undermined the construction of a singular national ethnic narrative, the central government's efforts to impose a uniform national identity notwithstanding. Our point is that the absence of any deeply felt national identity and the contestation over the presence of 'others' have weakened the social basis and thus public support for solidaristic solutions for mitigating social risk. In other words, such attitudes have legitimated individual efforts at social protection rather than collective or solidaristic means.

CONCLUSION AND LOOKING FORWARD

The emergence of a uniquely East Asian model of welfare state development, as documented by the first generation of scholars interested in social policy reform in the region, was tremendously helpful in clarifying, in broad strokes, the empirical realities of what was then a relatively understudied region in the welfare state main. It furthermore provided a useful lens through which to view canonical welfare state theories, even if the exceptionalist view seemed to suggest that Asia fell outside existing theories. This chapter contends that contrary to the exceptionalist thesis, two broad patterns or pathways of welfare development have emerged in the region: the universal social insurance model, with Japan, Korea, and Taiwan as exemplars, contrasted with a more individualistic approach to social protection evidenced in Hong Kong, Singapore, and China. These broad patterns are just that: broad. As such, universalism in Japan, Korea, and Taiwan is not without its blind spots in terms of coverage or redistributive impact, just as individual savings programmes implemented in other places do not preclude some experimentation with more inclusive social insurance. Our point, rather, is that though social policy regimes in Asia are dynamic, the evidence nonetheless suggests trending among key cases along these divergent evolutionary trajectories.

This short chapter has also endeavoured to offer some explanations for these divergent pathways. Distilling from the different country experiences, we find three factors that were most influential in shaping policymakers' choices and social policy decisions. First, democratic reform and specifically the imperatives of electoral competition and political entrepreneurship created a set of incentives to deepen welfare state reform and to effect greater coverage and redistribution; the absence of such political incentives afforded non-democratic states the policy latitude to pursue other options. Second, the experience of growth with equity, particularly in Japan, Korea, and Taiwan, reduced the structural costs of greater redistributive social policy. The legacy of rapid though equitable growth helped foster a deeper sense of social solidarity—aided also by relatively homogeneous populations—among citizens. The absence of growth with equity in the other cases highlights how socio-economic equity was not a priority and how the eventual social, political, and economic costs of promoting equity became considerably (or even prohibitively) higher. And finally, we have argued that policy choices favouring either social insurance or individual-based social protection are a function of a state's fiscal capacity; i.e. the state's willingness to expend its fiscal resources, on the one hand, as opposed to a strategy of offloading its responsibilities onto other levels of government, actors or institutions, on the other.

Looking forward, the East Asian welfare state, similar to all social policy regimes around the world, is currently facing new challenges associated with the process of post-industrialism. Modernization in Asia has been very rapid, characterized as a 'compressed modernity' (Chang 1999). Economies have been transformed, from agriculture to manufacturing to value-added technology to services, in just over a half-century. As a result, labour markets have been in flux. Workers are mobile, and employment needs demand constant retraining. Gone, for instance, are the company welfare model in capitalist Asia and the 'iron rice bowl' in socialist China. Economic modernization into the current post-industrial era has also ushered in new social configurations due to rapid de-familialization and changes in gender relations. The number of three-generational households in East Asia has dropped dramatically, with increases in divorce rates, the number of single parent households, and an overall decline in fertility rates. Gender relations in the family and the labour market have also evolved. Attitudes in Asia have shifted towards greater gender equality in both public and private spheres, even if they are not yet reflected in actual experience. Female participation rates in the formal (as opposed to the casual or informal) labour market have increased, thus progressively eroding the male breadwinner household. In addition, East Asia's ageing society, which is the most rapid in the world, has placed greater stress on the welfare state, particularly in terms of old age income security, long-term care, and health. At the other end of the demographic profile, the shrinking proportion of young 'productive' people has translated into fewer resources saved or injected into the welfare state system.

One of the most urgent challenges confronting social policymakers in the six East Asian countries discussed here stems from the increasingly globalized and transformed labour market situation. New labour demands resulting from continual economic upgrading and rapid population ageing have begun to reshape patterns of intra-regional migration. This is especially pronounced in low-wage employment sectors such as domestic care, low-skill manufacturing, and other forms of casual work. There has been a growth in the number of migrant workers from developing and industrializing South-East Asian countries to industrial East Asia. The evidence suggests that in-migration has begun to threaten prevailing norms of social solidarity, particularly in what had been relatively homogenous societies such as Japan and Korea. 'Outsiders' are perceived to be a strain on local social policy regimes, especially those migrant workers employed in informal labour sectors and thus less likely to be paying-in to social protection schemes. In-migration in places like Japan and Korea has also exposed the shallowness of the basis of social citizenship, forcing us to reconsider the sort of 'inclusiveness' their social policy regimes strive for.

Policymakers are keenly aware of these emerging challenges to their existing social policy regimes. Demographic pressures, reduced fiscal capacity and labour migration are shaping domestic debates about the future of social policy reform. At the risk of engaging in uncertain futurology, the evidence seems to suggest that there might eventually be some long-term convergence in the two broad patterns of social policy development discussed in this chapter. The universal social insurance approach, for instance, is under threat, as pensions fail to pay-out, health insurance runs chronic fiscal deficits, and as the social bases of solidarity begin to erode. We should expect that democratic political institutions in Japan, Korea, and Taiwan will resist systematic retrenchment, and indeed, recent evidence—such as the legislation of long-term care in Korea or the continued public management of health insurance in Taiwan— suggests that this might be the case (Peng and Wong 2008). However, over the long term, efforts to rethink and reform the current social insurance model more radically may prevail. Yet, just as the challenges of post-industrialism may compel relatively generous social insurance states to become less generous, these same challenges may force states like China, Hong Kong, and Singapore to consider more solidaristic approaches to social protection. Hong Kong's government, for instance, has considered comprehensive healthcare reform. Meanwhile, the Chinese state has initiated new efforts to reintroduce minimal social insurance schemes in the countryside as well as to strengthen the social safety net for a growing number of unemployed workers. In sum, as different countries face similar challenges, it is not inconceivable that we may begin to see some retrenchment in the universal social insurance model, while at the same time, some deepening of socialized protection among adherents to the individual, market-based approach to mitigating risk.

CHAPTER 46

....

EASTERN EUROPE AND RUSSIA

....

LINDA J. COOK

INTRODUCTION

....

EAST EUROPE's welfare states have undergone enormous changes in the twenty years since the collapse of communism. After inhabiting a distinctive communist political economy for four decades, they have 'diversified into some countries that are already close to the circumstances of existing EU members and some which are in a desperately disintegrated state' (Manning 2004: 211). Retrenchment and restructuring have reshaped statist welfare systems in market-conforming directions, redefining the boundaries between public and private responsibility for societal well-being. The present chapter maps the trajectories of welfare state change, and considers scholarly debates about the agents of reform, the extent of transformation, and the typology of the region's contemporary welfare regimes. The story involves communist legacies and strong elements of path-dependency as well as innovation and path-departing change. It exposes conflicting pressures between radical liberalization and European-ization, and the unprecedented influence of transnational actors in shaping post-communist welfare institutions. It finds complex patterns of convergence and divergence of welfare regimes across the region, as well as ongoing changes in the mix of welfare policies and an uncertain future.

A major theme of the chapter is the divergent trajectories of Central and Eastern Europe (CEE, focusing on Poland, Hungary, the Czech Republic, Slovenia, and the three Baltic states, Estonia, Latvia, and Lithuania) and the states of the Former Soviet Union (FSU, focusing on the Russian Federation, Belarus, and Kazakhstan). CEE states made rapid economic recoveries, consolidated democracy, and acceded to the European Union (EU). Welfare state restructuring here involved complex negotiations among domestic, European, and transnational actors. The outcome shows a 'layering' of inherited communist, revived Bismarckian, and market-oriented elements that has eroded, but by no means eliminated, the solidaristic and redistributive features of CEE welfare regimes. Scholars see these regimes as broadly convergent, though there is much dispute over whether they fit into existing typologies, and where they stand in relation to Europe. Both economic and political factors produced much deeper collapse of FSU welfare states, social sector reforms proved more erratic, and *de facto* privatization and state withdrawal have been much more extensive. FSU welfare states are treated rarely and for the most part separately in the literature, which finds elements of radical retrenchment, re-traditionalization, and, in Russia, a recent revival of a more expansive statist welfare role under semi-authoritarian auspices.

The chapter proceeds as follows: the communist welfare state model is presented briefly as a common starting point and source of persistent legacies, both institutional and normative. Debates over the agents and the depth of post-communist transformation are covered next. Key questions concern the pressures of transitional recessions, domestic politics, and solidaristic legacies, interventions of international financial institutions (IFIs), and the potential influence of a 'European Social Model'. The institutions and performance of contemporary CEE welfare states are then compared with both the more comprehensive and generous European welfare states and the more deeply retrenched and residualized cases of the FSU. Finally, we consider the divergent conclusions of scholars who seek to 'fit' the CEE regimes into established, Eurocentric welfare 'worlds' and 'families,' and those who compare the regions' welfare states with a broader range of middle-income countries. Attention will also be focused on how gender maps onto post-communist welfare regimes.

COMMUNIST LEGACIES

Communist welfare states formed part of a distinctive developmental model based on state planning and bureaucratic allocation of most human and material resources. The model entailed much more comprehensive and intrusive labour and income policies than are found in other regions, mobilizing very high levels of both male and female labour force participation, repressing wage and income differentials, and excluding almost all market activity. A broad, state-controlled, budget-financed system of welfare provision emerged in rudimentary form during the 1930s Stalinist industrialization, within highly repressive political and labour regimes. As communism spread across CEE states after World War II, the Soviet system was grafted onto established Bismarckian social insurance systems (Inglot 2008). While never entirely uniform, communist welfare states converged around a single model in organization, financing, and programmatic features. They expanded rapidly from the 1950s, reaching their peak of development in the 1970s, providing basic healthcare and education, pensions and social insurance, family benefits, housing, and food subsidies to broad populations at low standards of provision (Haggard and Kaufman 2008). The strength of the communist welfare state was in its breadth of coverage and provision for basic needs.

While the comparative literature has paid limited attention to communist welfare states, the specialist literature proposes several explanations. In a variant of the 'logic of industrialism', some argue that Soviet planners constructed welfare to meet the industrializing states' expansive needs for human capital and labour force planning. A second view sees the welfare state as the outcome of a bureaucratic planning process that prioritized heavy industry and defence sectors, funding welfare on the 'residual principle'. Other explanations focus on politics. Some see the welfare state as a central mechanism for state construction and societal stratification, with provision differentiated for elite, industrial, and rural sectors; privileges attaching to party, state, military, security forces, and workers in key industries; and rural populations included last and least. Others stress the use of social policy to divide and discipline labour, or as part of an implicit social contract that contributed to political stability, labour quiescence, and ideological legitimacy, or, especially in CEE, as a response to political protest and crises. (For reviews of these arguments see Cook 1993; Haggard and Kaufman 2008; Inglot 2008.)

Communist welfare states do not fit standard Western typologies, and are most aptly characterized as authoritarian-paternalist. Broadly inclusive and stratified, they featured elements of both Esping-Andersen's (1990) status-reinforcing conservative and redistributive-universalist models. Adequacy and generosity of benefits varied, lower in the Soviet Union, higher in CEE, especially Hungary and Czechoslovakia; the best available estimates place average welfare effort at 15–20 per cent of GDP (Kornai 1992: 314). Overall, social provision was high relative to resources and fiscal capacities, leading Janos Kornai to characterize them famously as 'premature' welfare states (Kornai 1992, 1996). Haggard and Kaufman's (2008) broad comparative study found CEE welfare states to be generous in comparison with those of both Latin America and East Asia. However, benefits fell in real value over time, the bureaucratic planning process built in rigidities and inefficiencies, social sectors were underfunded, technologically lagging, and plagued by chronic shortages. As the political economies in which they were embedded collapsed in the late 1980s, these welfare states left legacies of institutions and programmes, fiscal obligations, social sector infrastructure, providers and beneficiaries, popular attachments and expectations, and an absence of alternative private social security markets or services.

Communist welfare states were distinctive in their treatment of women, featuring what might be characterized as 'dual breadwinner, double burden' systems. They early built in accommodations for women's employment, including extended maternity leaves, subsidized child care, and, especially in Hungary and Czechoslovakia, generous family benefits. These policies led some analysts to label Communist welfare states as women-friendly. At the same time, the state supported women's unpaid care work without transforming the extremely unequal domestic division of labour, rendering women's dual role as worker and homemaker a heavy 'double burden' (Pascall and Lewis 2004). Family policies (as all others) were crafted by the authoritarian state in the absence of societal voice, and served statist interests in increasing birth rates and mobilizing labour. Inglot captures well their multiple purposes, describing family policies as a 'hybrid combination of social insurance traditions, pronatalist tendencies, labour market incentives, and even remnants of old-fashioned poverty relief' (Inglot 2008: 188).

TRAJECTORIES OF WELFARE STATE TRANSFORMATION

Between 1989 and 1991 communist regimes and economies were transformed across Eastern Europe and the Soviet Union, marking a new stage in the development of their welfare states. Most governments adopted macroeconomic reform policies of liberalization, privatization, and stabilization, and suffered deep transitional recessions, inflation, and fiscal crises. The literature initially stressed the dramatic welfare losses resulting from the transition to market economies and global integration. Some analysts feared that a popular backlash would end reforms or result in repression. In the event, though, democratizing CEE states responded to initial hardships by increasing welfare effort in the short term, then initiating structural reforms of their welfare states. In the FSU, where recessions were much longer and deeper and polities more dysfunctional, welfare effort collapsed to a much greater extent and reforms generally lagged. In the war-torn states of Central Asia, the Caucasus, and South-Eastern Europe, the collapse was nearly complete (Manning 2004).

Much scholarly analysis has focused on the patterns and agents of change in CEE welfare states, with attention devoted especially to Poland, Hungary, and the Czech Republic. Debates concentrate on the extent of welfare state transformation and the relative influence of domestic versus international actors. The dominant view, for example in the work of Haggard and Kaufman (2008) and Inglot (2008), sees CEE welfare state reform as heavily constrained and 'path dependent'. Scholars point variously to domestic political, institutional, historical, and/or normative factors to account for substantial continuity in patterns of social provision, as well as some divergence among states. Others, for example Orenstein (2008a and b), Müller (2003), and Ferge (2001), place more emphasis on retrenchment and path-departing structural change, and stress the influence of globalization and international financial institutions (IFIs) in transforming welfare states, especially pension systems, social assistance and labour regimes. Much less attention has been devoted to the FSU, where patterns of change have been more erratic and varied, and less constrained by democratic politics, ranging from radical liberalization to preserved statism (Cook 2007*a* and *b*).

TRAJECTORIES IN CEE

The welfare losses imposed on CEE populations by the shock of transition should not be understated. In the initial period, across the region, wages declined, unemployment surged, and poverty and inequality grew rapidly (Manning 2004). Many middle-aged workers were pushed out of labour forces permanently, and life expectancy and birth rates declined. Only the Czech Republic proved largely an exception to these trends. Beginning in the early 1990s, however, CEE governments implemented targeted 'safety nets' and compensatory policies, including expanded pension entitlement, unemployment and family benefits. These policies had an *ad hoc* or crisis-driven quality. Variously seen as responses to perceived need or to mobilized constituencies with protest potential (i.e., workers in Solidarity's Poland) or as an anticipatory elite strategy to avoid social unrest, compensatory benefits strained fiscal capacities and crowded out other social expenditures, but effectively limited poverty and distress in the early transition years (Vanhuysse 2006).

As the 1990s progressed, CEE governments restructured their welfare states in liberalizing and market-conforming directions. Reforms ended state monopolies in welfare provision and legalized private medical practices and educational services. Universal subsidies and family benefits were partially replaced by means-tested benefits targeted on the poor. In a return to pre-communist Bismarckian traditions, financing of pensions and other social insurance was moved from state budgets to payroll taxes. More complex 'second stage' institutional reforms transformed health and pension provision: tax-based health insurance funds replaced state-guaranteed universal care, and mandatory capitalized pillars were added to inherited pay-as-you-go (PAYG) pension systems. Rigid and protective communist-era labour market institutions were deregulated. The timing and specifics of these reforms varied from case to case, but the overall trend toward less statist and solidaristic, more liberal and market-oriented welfare institutions held across the region. Some analysts saw a process of welfare state residualization (e.g. Ferge 2001).

Many analysts were struck, though, by the limitations of these reforms, their bounded nature and path dependency, in light of the fundamental transformation of communist political economies, fiscal constraints, and the accumulation of entitlements in overburdened social sectors. Reforms typically began with proposals for radical retrenchment and restructuring by technocratic reform teams and IFIs, but in the event legislated changes built on or left in place substantial parts of inherited systems and welfare commitments, including predominantly public financing and state subsidies. Moreover, reforms were sometimes reversed when fiscal pressures eased or governing coalitions changed. (Inglot 2008; Golinowska et al. 2009) Scholars puzzled over the persistence of welfare provision in CEE; Haggard and Kaufman (2008), for example, contrasted it with the much deeper welfare cuts that accompanied macro economic reforms in Latin America.

Analysts pointed to various sources of path dependence. Inglot's (2008) major study emphasized institutional and policy legacies in CEE: inherited organizations, laws and norms that formed the basis of pre-transition welfare systems proved resistant to radical change; while an established reservoir of expertise and repertoire of policy choices shaped decisions. Some studies pointed to political constraints, arguing that welfare provision could not be radically cut in CEE democratic polities because of electoral and other feedback mechanisms, political bargaining over reforms, and/or overwhelming popular expectations that held governments responsible for broad social provision. These factors, it was argued, constrained policymakers' options (Offe 1993; Kornai 1996; Lipsmeyer 2003). Orenstein's (2008b) study of post-communist welfare states found a strong correlation between democracy and levels of social spending, with CEE democracies consistently higher spenders than more authoritarian FSU states, leading Orenstein to argue strongly for the positive impact of democracy on welfare. At the same time, civil society, suppressed under communism, was broadly seen as weak; parties as pragmatic and programmatically flexible; social and class structures as amorphous; union density, averaging below 25 per cent, as low. The mechanisms of constraint seemed weakly specified, their effectiveness partial (Crowley and Ost 2001).

Another group of scholars saw CEE welfare state change as deeper and more transformative, and assigned a major role to the economic pressures of globalization and the influence of IFIs in shaping reforms across postcommunist states. Most CEE governments depended on International Monetary Fund (IMF) stabilization agreements for some part of the 1990s, and loan conditionalities included social and labour policies. The World Bank intruded deeply into domestic policy processes, funding think tanks and governmental reform teams and building alliances with finance ministries and liberal policy elites, promoting welfare reforms based on 'fiscal stabilization, regulative liberalization and organizational privatization' (Wagener 2002: 163). The need to attract foreign investment produced pressures for more flexible labour markets. In the view of Deacon (1997) and his collaborators, during this period the social policies of transition states were made at the headquarters of the IFIs (see also Chapter 21 above).

In the end, trajectories of welfare state reform must be seen as resulting from a mix of domestic and international pressures. The IFIs put a 'liberal imprint' on policy, promoting a new pension orthodoxy that reduced intergenerational solidarity, redistribution, and government responsibility, and contributing to fiscal pressures to cut entitlements and restrict eligibility. Healthcare and benefit reforms proved more partial and remain contested. In sum, international pressures met countervailing domestic ones. The mix is well captured by Gans-Morse and Orenstein (2007: 14): 'CEE politicians and policymakers were caught in a double crossfire: first, between the exigencies of market transition and the social legacies of the communist past, and second, between domestic political demands and pressures from international institutions.' These conflicting pressures produced welfare states that were characterized by compromise solutions and hybrid arrangements, rather than by any radical breakthrough.

The CEE states began the transition at somewhat different starting points, and both the decline of welfare and the extent of liberalization varied. The Czech Republic and Slovenia maintained the strongest and most solidaristic welfare provision, avoiding significant poverty and unemployment, and largely rejecting liberal reforms (see Table 46.1, which includes social expenditure as per cent of GDP, poverty rates, and ratios of public vs. private healthcare expenditure as an indicator of extent of liberalization). Hungary and Poland constitute intermediate cases in terms of both poverty rates and liberalizing institutional change. The Baltic States (along with Bulgaria, Romania, and Slovakia), poorer and recovering more slowly, generally suffered greater welfare declines, lagged in adopting reforms, and in the end implemented more radical changes. Overall, similarity outweighed diversity; most CEE states continue to be seen as a single 'regime type' or as part of the same 'world of welfare' by analysts.

Table 46.1 Selected welfare indicators (2005)

	Social Benefits, General and Central Government[a] (% GDP)	Labour Force Participation Rate[b] (%)		Poverty Rate (% below PPP US $ 4.00/ day)[c]	Ratio of Public v. Private Healthcare Expenditure[d]
		Male	Female		
Poland	17.34	63.0	47.7	20.6	69.3
Hungary	18.52	71.3	60.7	15.9	70.8
Czech Republic	16.82	78.4	62.4	1.0	88.6
Slovenia	17.6	66.0	52.0	–	72.4
Estonia	10.63	67.9	56.0	33.2	76.9
Latvia	8.24	69.1	56.8	26.3	60.5
Lithuania	10.86	63.4	51.2	36.0	67.3
Russian Federation	9.37	70.3[e]		45.3	62.0
Kazakhstan	3.93	73.3		56.7	64.2
Belarus	13.04	67.1		15.9	75.8

Sources: [a] IMF 2007, data for 2006.
[b] ILO 2009a.
[c] UNDP 2008: Country Tables, 2007/08, 1990 PPP US $ 2000–2004.
[d] WHO 2009.
[e] UNICEF 2008.

TRAJECTORIES IN THE FSU

Literature on post-communist welfare states outside the CEE is comparatively sparse (for exceptions see Cook 2007*a* and *b*; Manning 2004; World Bank 2005) and shows sharp divergence from CEE patterns as well as a much greater degree of welfare contraction (see Table 46.1). This development has been well captured in the summary statement that welfare expenditure in the post-communist space 'tapered off to the East and South' (Gans-Morse and Orenstein 2007). In the FSU states of Russia, Belarus and Kazakhstan, during the 1990s, contraction was abetted by both worse economic conditions and more political conflict and instability than in CEE states. All three developed semi-authoritarian polities in which societal pressures were weak and institutional capacity for reform was limited. Governments failed to create even minimally effective safety nets. Despite these similarities, the three states followed different trajectories of welfare state change.

In Russia during the 1990s, inherited communist parliamentary factions and resistant bureaucrats kept old structures and entitlements in place despite collapsing revenues. As the economy contracted by an estimated 40 per cent, hyperinflation emerged and large numbers of workers remained nominally employed with no or sporadic pay. Average pensions and the majority of public-sector salaries fell below the subsistence minimum and were often in arrears, and one-quarter to one-third of the population lived in poverty through most of the decade. The Gini index rose to approximate the highest recorded world levels, male life expectancy experienced declines not before seen in an industrialized state during peacetime, infectious diseases re-emerged, and the Human Development Index fell dramatically. Liberalizing welfare reforms, encouraged by the World Bank, were initiated but proved abortive. Instead, health and educational sectors underwent processes of 'spontaneous privatization,' informalization and corruption that increased disparities and restricted access for lower-income groups (Cook 2007*a*).

By contrast, Kazakhstan's autocratic ruler adopted an IFI-promoted policy of radical liberalization that privatized the pension and healthcare systems and deeply retrenched social assistance, slashing welfare expenditures, and worsening hardships. Belarus followed yet another pattern. Here transition to the market proved abortive, and inherited statist structures remained in welfare as in other areas. Provision deteriorated because of economic recession and inherited problems of over-centralization and inefficiency, but welfare was better preserved than elsewhere in the FSU. By the end of the decade, FSU states overall showed greater declines in welfare effort, and higher levels of privatization and exclusion from access to basic services than their CEE counterparts. In sum, the trajectories of CEE and FSU welfare states diverged from the beginning of post-communist transition and were clearly differentiated by key measures of expenditure, structure, and performance (see Table 46.1).

EU INTEGRATION AND THE QUESTION
OF EUROPEANIZATION

In the mid-1990s, CEE successor states initiated the process of accession to the European Union; by 2007, all had achieved membership. The EU is associated with a 'European Social Model' that, though nowhere codified, is broadly understood to emphasize solidarity, social cohesion, social rights and inclusion, and policy bargaining among the social partners. It contrasts sharply with IFI-promoted welfare state residualism, privatization, and weakening of state responsibility. Accession raised the question of whether CEE social policy making would become 'Europeanized', i.e. pulled toward more solidaristic norms and practices. Per capita GDP in the new accession states was only about one-third of that in the EU-15 and comparatively weaker CEE welfare regimes raised concerns that enlargement would produce a 'race to the bottom', or massive labour migration from East to West, or, conversely, that the diversity of social security systems would prove an obstacle to labour mobility (Wagener 2002).

Scholars generally agree that the EU's influence on social policy in accession states has been modest and ambiguous (e.g. Cerami 2006; Sissenich 2002; Iankova 2002). The EU has a broad commitment to social security and protection, but very limited leverage on social policy. Most relevant competencies remain with member governments, which in practice implement a great variety of welfare systems, varying from liberal to social-democratic. The Social Chapter of the *acquis communitaire* covers a restricted set of issues, mainly workplace safety, conditions, and gender equality. Few conditions relate to public or state responsibility for well-being. Solidaristic policies of 'social inclusion' are promoted at the rhetorical level, but legal provisions or enforcement of social policy were largely absent in the accession process. Accession states were required to build legal and institutional frameworks for social dialogue and national tripartite bargaining, but the EU focused mainly on transposing institutions and legislation, rather than on effectiveness. These institutions often had little life after accession. Moreover, EU demands for budgetary stringency reinforced pressures for retrenchment and restructuring in CEE, and monitoring reports endorsed liberal reforms.

Some scholars argue that accession has nevertheless had indirect effects favouring social protection in CEE, particularly the strengthening of democratic institutions that enable interest groups to lobby more effectively for high levels of welfare provision (Orenstein and Haas 2005). Economic opportunities offered by integration also facilitated the rapid recovery of CEE economies, thereby supporting maintenance of welfare. Since the 2000 Nice Treaty and adoption of the Lisbon Strategy, harmonization of national social policies, especially efforts to address poverty and social exclusion, has received more attention, but efforts continue to rely on 'soft law' and the 'Open Method of Coordination', making implementation effectively dependent on the political will of member states (Golinowska et al. 2009). In sum, the EU has exerted limited effort to pull CEE states in a more social democratic direction. On the contrary, some argue that CEE reforms should be taken as models for change in the overburdened, 'Eurosclerotic' welfare states further West, and that the future is more likely to bring convergence in a liberal than a social democratic direction.

INSTITUTIONS AND PERFORMANCE OF CONTEMPORARY WELFARE STATES: EAST-CENTRAL EUROPE

The most comprehensive descriptions of CEE welfare states are provided by OECD country studies: Cerami (2006) and Haggard and Kaufman (2008). International Monetary Fund (IMF) estimates of total social expenditure are given in Table 46.1. Welfare state performance is affected by low per capita GDP relative to European averages, the shocks of transition to incomes and labour markets, and demographic factors, especially ageing populations and low fertility. Institutions and performance across policy areas are briefly assessed below.

Contributory social insurance systems have replaced budget financing through most of the region. CEE pension systems now rely on a mix of PAYG and private funding. The major distinctions fall in the size of the funded tier and whether it is compulsory; in the more solidaristic systems, for example in the Czech Republic and Slovenia, funding remains voluntary, and in all cases it is being phased in gradually (Orenstein 2008a). Social insurance coverage has declined significantly. Pensions now cover about three-quarters of the labour force and two-thirds of the working-age population, well below the virtually universal coverage in the pre-transition systems and below average European levels. Unemployment insurance is provided in all states, though eligibility has been restricted. Wage replacement rates and duration of benefits fall well below European averages and most systems are severely strained by continuing high levels of unemployment, which in 2005 ranged from 6.5 per cent in Slovenia to almost 18 per cent in Poland (Cerami 2006: 129, table 1.6; Gans-Morse and Orenstein 2007: 38).

All CEE states inherited well-developed, state-financed systems of family and maternity benefits, including birth grants, parental leave, and family allowances. Policy battles have been waged around whether to maintain universalism or move to means-testing, with most systems now mixed. Hungary has famously generous family benefits, spending 2.7 per cent of GDP, while other CEE states provide more modest assistance. All states guarantee a subsistence minimum and fund at least some social assistance from general tax revenues. Continuing substantial rates of poverty—sixteen million remained at risk of poverty in the region in 2006—attest to the limited effectiveness of these income supports. At the same time, analysis by Cerami (2006: 206, fig. 3.1) shows that total social transfers reduced poverty to less than half pre-transfer levels in CEE states during the 1990s.

Healthcare is partially privatized and provided on various insurance models funded by mandatory wage taxes. Despite major institutional reforms, however, state responsibility remains the norm. Insurance covers more than 90 per cent of populations throughout the region, and access is nearly universal both *de jure* and *de facto* (Cerami 2006: 123, citing multiple studies). Federal and local governments commonly pay for those outside the labour force and cover shortfalls to ensure solvency of the new insurance funds. The scope of covered services is typically broad, though not comprehensive. According to World Health Organization (WHO) data, private financing has increased to various degrees across CEE states, while public funding remains predominant (see Table 46.1). Basic public education remains free and almost universally accessible, though segregation and low completion rates are common for Roma children throughout the region. Publicly financed childcare services have been significantly reduced, and post-secondary education is substantially privatized and fee-based.

The most dramatic changes have affected labour market institutions and performance. The ILO's Employment Protection Legislation Index (EPL) shows increased flexibility, reduced restrictions and protections, in all areas of employment, labour contracts, and wage setting, though Morse-Gans and Orenstein (2007: 41, table 4) find that CEE labour markets remain more restrictive than those in states conforming to the liberal model. Real wages remain depressed, and labour market stratification has increased. Investment has flowed into the region, but economic recovery has not brought proportional job creation. Labour force participation rates, below 70 per cent overall (see Table 46.1), remain low among all demographic groups, while collective bargaining institutions cover less than 40 per cent of the labour force in most cases.

Low labour force participation and demographic trends present the greatest challenges to CEE welfare states. Depressed employment rates among the working-age population weakens tax bases, worsens dependency ratios throughout social security systems, and excludes parts of populations from coverage by the work and earnings-dependent benefits that have increasingly characterized social insurance provision. Ageing of populations and below-replacement fertility contribute to the problems. CEE states have tended towards regressive tax structures, with high payroll tax rates, declining corporate rates, and flat income taxes introduced in several states. Welfare systems overall have become less redistributive, more stratified, and favourable to middle- and upper-income groups, while strong popular support for state provision and universal entitlements maintain influence for solidaristic legacies. Since EU accession, out-migration of labour and remittances have become important factors in the income/stratification/welfare mix.

INSTITUTIONS AND PERFORMANCE OF CONTEMPORARY WELFARE STATES: FORMER SOVIET STATES

In the FSU, welfare recovered much more slowly and unevenly than in CEE. Contemporary institutions range from radical liberalization in Kazakhstan to largely preserved statism in Belarus, with Russia a more complex mix. The most comprehensive descriptions of current welfare systems are provided by OECD studies and World Bank reports (see especially World Bank 2005). With the exception of Belarus, welfare effort remains well below CEE levels and private expenditure has replaced public to a substantially larger degree (see Table 46.1) Poorly regulated social insurance markets and weak state administrative capacities contribute to frequent welfare policy failures, as well as to continuing large-scale informality and corruption in social sectors.

Kazakhstan has transformed its welfare state to a liberal model, with privatized social security, deregulated labour markets, and means-tested social benefits characterized by highly restricted eligibility. Public welfare provision has been deeply retrenched and residualized; almost 36 per cent of healthcare expenditure is private and effective pension coverage extends to less than half of the labour force. Especially among the ethnic Kazakh population, welfare has returned to traditional forms with a greater reliance on family provision. Belarus, by contrast, has maintained an overwhelmingly public, state-administered welfare sector, with more than 75 per cent of healthcare expenditure public and near-universal social insurance coverage. While the government has experimented with liberalizing reforms, Belarus maintains an essentially Soviet-era welfare system.

Russia's welfare state underwent substantial liberalization in the years after 2000. Reforms introduced a private pension tier, de-regulated labour markets, and expanded health insurance and private education, though changes often remained partial. Massive public protests against an attempt to rationalize and monetize social benefits in 2005 set the limits to liberalization. Subsequently welfare policy (as policy in other areas) has turned in a more statist direction, with a pro-natalist agenda at its core. The government launched a set of 'Priority

National Projects' in healthcare, education and housing that entail deep interventions into markets and a selective revival of state planning. Neo-familialist policies serve the state's interest in rebuilding its depleted population to provide for national security and economic development. The contemporary welfare state, financed by the inflow of abundant energy revenues, constitutes a mix of liberal and revived statist models.

THE GENDER DIMENSION

How does gender map onto contemporary post-communist welfare regimes? Pascall and Lewis (2004) and Pascall and Manning (2000) conclude that high unemployment and economic insecurity have rendered women more economically dependent on families and men's incomes, undermining the communist-era 'dual breadwinner' model throughout the region. Women's labour market participation rates have fallen to below 60 per cent in several cases (see Table 46.1); reformed social security systems that rely more on individuals' earnings increase gender disparities. Labour market liberalization has eroded protections around pregnancy and child-bearing, and availability of socialized child care remains limited. Though CEE states have retained many family benefits and services, declining public provision has led to a refamilialization of health and education that increases women's care work and reliance on informal networks. Birth rates have fallen, domestic violence and sex trafficking have increased. Politics throughout the region is male-dominated, limiting voice and representation of women's issues (Rueschemeyer and Wolchik 2009).

The literature shows two divergent trends in policy toward women and families. Governments in Poland and Russia have increased statist benefits and protections, restricted abortion rights, and promoted women's domestic and maternal roles. These policies, animated by pro-natalism and championed by rightist and nationalist parties, mark a return to traditional gender roles. The broader revival of nationalism has also revived patriarchal gender ideologies (Chandler 2008). At the same time, the EU promotes gender equality and reconciliation of work and family life. Accession states are supposed to comply with EU directives on equal employment opportunities, pay, treatment in the workplace, social security, maternity and parental leaves, and sex discrimination, as well as recommendations to increase representation of women in decision-making positions. Pascall and Lewis (2004) find limited evidence of improving gender equality in CEE, but many analysts stress the limits of the EU's commitment to enforce incorporation of equality in domestic legislation, and failures of CEE national-level governments to follow through (for a review, see van der Molen and Novikova 2005).

REGIME TYPOLOGIES, MODELS, CLUSTERING, AND CONVERGENCE

There have been a number of efforts to determine whether CEE cases 'fit' existing welfare state typologies, including Esping-Andersen's (1990) regimes, Castles' (1993) families, and Bonoli's (1997) two-dimensional Bismarckian–Bevridgian model. All ask whether CEE states cluster or converge to produce a distinctive model, and where they stand in relation to Europe. None of these efforts includes the FSU states, largely because of data limitations; reliable, comparable data on welfare are largely limited to members of the EU or OECD. Studies cover varying subsets of the CEE cases, limiting their generalizability and comparability. Below I discuss the somewhat divergent conclusions of several studies, i.e. that CEE welfare states comprise a distinctive 'post-communist' cluster below the other European 'families', that they constitute a hybrid of Esping-Andersen's conservative and liberal regimes, or that they qualify as low-expenditure Bismarckian systems. Finally, I consider where CEE welfare regimes stand in relation to European norms, and to those of other middle-income countries.

In a recent inclusive and sophisticated study, Castles and Obinger (2008: 336) analyse the EU25 from 2000 to 2005 and find a distinctive post-communist welfare state family, excluding the Czech Republic, with Baltic and CEE sub-types. The authors apply a hierarchical cluster analysis to a combination of social policy, labour market, and tax policy indicators. They conclude that the post-communist family stands below the European families—North and South Continental, English-speaking, and Scandinavian—in both welfare provision and outcomes, with 'extreme values on nearly all variables shaping the clustering of EU-25 policy patterns' (Castles and Obinger, 2008: 337). A sub-group of post-communist welfare states is distinguished on the input side by low social outlays, transfers, subsidies, and taxes, and on the outcomes side by low male labour force participation, high inflation, massive unemployment, and low fertility. The authors conclude that, in the EU25, the 'awfulness of the English' has been replaced by post-communist exceptionalism and malaise (Castles and Obinger, 2008: 338), though CEE states also exhibited the highest rates of economic growth.

In an impressive study that examines fewer cases but more detailed dimensions of their regime structures and performance, Gans-Morse and Orenstein (2007) apply Esping-Andersen's 'Worlds' framework and conclude that a continental-liberal hybrid has emerged in four CEE states, Poland, Hungary, Slovakia, and the Czech Republic. Their study shows that, on virtually all dimensions of welfare state structure and indicators of provision—social expenditures, benefit levels, generosity, and financing, extent of redistribution—the average post-communist welfare state is slightly more generous than the average liberal state, but less generous than the average continental one. The authors see this hybrid as the outcome of policy-makers' response to the cross-pressures of economic reform, globalization, and the legacy of popular expectations of extensive welfare provision. They argue that these conflicting pressures prevented the emergence of a 'pure' social policy model, instead producing convergence on a hybrid model that falls between liberal and conservative and shares little with the social-democratic world. In Bonoli's two-dimensional Bismarckian–Beveridgian scheme, by contrast, post-communist states are placed in a single classification, low-expenditure Bismarckian, i.e. devoting less than 24 per cent of GDP to social expenditures and financing at least 50 per cent of social insurance through contributions (Bonoli 1997).

In a recent anthology edited by Cerami and Vanhuysse (2009), a group of prominent experts seeks to sort out the patterns and causes of post-communist welfare transformation in CEE, focusing on questions of unity and diversity, path-dependence and path-departure. The authors agree that emerging welfare models are likely to be hybrids, shaped by both history and politics, and not corresponding to existing typologies. In Claus Offe's terms, they are a 'joint outcome of "the past" and "the West"' (2009: 1). The anthology provides a complex account of causal factors and institutional mechanisms for divergent welfare state pathways, adding to the usual domestic and international causes the roles of social learning and of elites' political and distributive strategies, including elites' use of early pensions to de-mobilize labour. The editors end by speculating that the 2008–9 global economic crisis is likely to affect CEE welfare states by leading to 'path-departures, institutional ruptures, permanent emergencies, and zero-sum distributive conflict' (Cerami and Vanhuysse 2009: 19).

Finally, scholars' basis for comparison matters for judgments about post-communist welfare states. Many comparisons are Eurocentric, emphasizing low levels of CEE and FSU welfare provision versus the EU15 or OECD. By contrast, in a recent study (Golinowska et al. 2009), a group of CEE scholars argue that regional welfare states are impressively close to their European counterparts in comparison to their overall levels of economic development. The authors point out that all new EU member states have higher international rankings on the Human Development Index than in GDP rankings, and are closer to the EU average in human development than in economic development (Golinowska et al. 2009: 17). Haggard and Kaufman (2008), comparing CEE welfare states with other middle-income countries of Latin America and East Asia, are impressed by the relatively high levels of welfare effort, public provision, and preservation of welfare states in CEE. Orenstein echoes this broader comparative view for the FSU states, pointing out that, while public welfare provision is lower here than in CEE states, 'overall welfare state spending remains higher and more significant than in most developing countries in Latin America and Asia. While some countries such as Georgia and Kazakhstan have cut back considerably, most FSU countries retain large public health and pension systems, and provide other cash benefits' (Orenstein 2008b: 90).

CONCLUSION

During the past twenty years, post-communist welfare states have been transformed. Their trajectories show strong elements of path-dependency but they are not 'locked in', and have also implemented highly innovative reforms. CEE welfare states have been shaped by the layering of egalitarian legacies of communism, conservative Bismarckian social insurance revivals, and the liberal imprint of the IFIs and other globalizing influences. They have retrenched and liberalized, becoming less solidaristic and redistributive, but still retain large elements of public responsibility for societal well-being and affinities to Europe. Within the FSU, trajectories of welfare state change have diverged sharply, from extreme liberalization to preserved statism. Welfare has suffered from sharp economic contractions, and reform from weak state capacities. Predominant welfare state patterns include poorly administered liberalization, deep retrenchment, and informalization of social sectors. Broad social indicators show continuing depressed levels of welfare, while energy-rich Russia shows signs of reverting to more generous statist, paternalist, and neo-traditionalist patterns of provision. The impact of the 2008–9 global financial crisis welfare throughout the post-communist region remains to be seen.

PART VIII

PROSPECTS

....

CHAPTER 47

THE SUSTAINABILITY OF WESTERN WELFARE STATES

....

HOWARD GLENNERSTER

INTRODUCTION

....

How sustainable are the older established welfare states discussed in this Handbook, as distinct from the fate of the newer ones discussed by Ian Gough and Göran Therborn in the final chapter? I think this question contains at least three linked sub-questions:

- Will their populations continue to vote the higher taxes required to support older and more demanding populations? This is a question of fiscal sustainability.
- Are their present bureaucratic structures capable of adapting to fast changing consumer expectations? Will other political priorities overtake social policy—climate change, population movement or responding to global economic crises? These are questions of political sustainability.
- In trying to respond to such concerns, will these institutions retain a commitment to the needs of the poorest and to enhancing social solidarity? This is a question of moral sustainability.

At the time of writing the economic world has been turned upside down by a banking and credit crisis. Yet forty years ago the world was in the grips of a global oil crisis followed by rising global competition. Dire predictions were then made about the sustainability of Western welfare states and it is important to critically appraise this reasoning and the lessons that were drawn from it before attempting any more predictions.

REFLECTIONS ON PAST PREDICTIONS

The Prophets of Doom

Baumol concluded that there were fundamental reasons why labour intensive public services would suffer fiscal difficulty (Baumol 1967). The productivity gains achieved in private sector enterprises, and captured in part by the workers in those industries, would force up labour costs. A comparable analysis by the Marxist left predicted a 'fiscal crisis' (O'Connor 1973; Gough 1979) and to a fiscal crisis would be added a crisis of legitimacy as these services failed to meet the expectations put upon them (Offe 1984).

Public choice theory became an influential contributor to traditional economic theory and public policy. Particularly influential was its challenge to the supposedly benign motivations of public servants and professionals working for the state (Niskanen 1971; Mueller 1989). Growing public budgets were the result of self interested 'rent seeking' public bureaucrats who controlled the supply of public knowledge in their own interests creating supposed 'needs'.

The Swedish economist Assar Lindbeck (1995) argued that the 'good behaviour' and social norms of populations were being undermined, over the long run, by social policy. Welfare was changing people's attitudes to work. Since the penalties for not working were low, a long-term shift in attitudes to work had taken place. Persistent unemployment in Europe and the social evils associated with it could be blamed, in large part, on welfare states. Similar conclusions were drawn in the United States in relation to its narrower notion of 'welfare' (Murray 1984; Ellwood 1988).

This set of writings constituted the most fundamental intellectual critique welfare states had faced since World War II (see Chapter 4 above). The Danish inventor of comparative 'welfare regimes', Esping-Andersen (1990, 1996a) questioned whether any of these 'regimes' could survive international economic competition from the Third World without significant change. Most at risk, he concluded were the welfare systems of the United States, Canada, and the United Kingdom which depended on 'the loyalties of a numerically weak, and often politically residual, social stratum' (1990: 38).

Doom Avoided

As previous chapters have shown none of these 'decline and fall' scenarios came about. The 'Anglo-Saxon' and other low spenders increased their social spending share of GDP by about a fifth between 1980 and 2005. The Scandinavian countries did roughly the same from a higher base. Japan increased its social spending share by an extraordinary 75 per cent, as its population aged. Nor is it true that the higher spending was merely a response to growing demographic pressure. Services have been extended in many places. The most rapidly growing welfare states were those of the Mediterranean countries who sought to catch up with the established welfare states of Europe. Greece, Spain, Portugal, and Italy increased their welfare effort by two-thirds. It was only in the middle European welfare states—Belgium, the Netherlands, Germany, and France—that spending has grown more modestly (OECD 2009a).

So why were the prophets of doom wrong? Were they wrong? Have such prophecies only been delayed? Or have adaptations been made to modern welfare states that meet many of the criticisms then levelled at them? In responding to neoconservative critiques have governments damaged the moral basis and appeal of their welfare states (Ellison 2006; Streeck and Thelen 2005a; Clasen 2005; Taylor-Gooby 2008)?

THE REASONS FOR RESILIENCE

Politics

One of the earliest authors to ask the question 'why resilience?' was Paul Pierson (for a fuller discussion, see Chapter 38 above). He first compared social policy changes in the United Kingdom and the United States under Reagan and Thatcher (Pierson 1994). Both Thatcher and Reagan had powerful electoral support. They had committed themselves to rolling back the state. Why had they not, in the main, succeeded? His answer was that such retrenchment was politically difficult where a large proportion of the population was dependent on welfare services— pensions, schooling, and healthcare—and where so many jobs depended on them. The client groups affected had mobilized effectively –'programme-based interest networks' as he called them. Where a poor minority was involved, public housing tenants in the United Kingdom or welfare mothers in the United States, retrench-ment was relatively easier but overall the welfare state had not been rolled back because it was just too important to voters as users and employees. The next decades would nevertheless be about the politics of retrenchment and adaptation (P. Pierson 2001c). In the event, they have been concerned with adaptation but not decline.

The politics of the next few decades may not be as benign. As we shall later argue other priorities may claim public attention and support.

Economics

Helpful though this approach was, however, it failed to consider the fundamental economic reasons that made scaling back difficult. Looking back at the literature of the 1980s, it is revealing to see that the problems identified were only seen to impact *public services*. No attention was given to the funding problems that might face private insurers, for example. Market failure and its growing importance for an ageing population were never mentioned.

Market failure is not just an abstract academic idea. The United Kingdom's Pension Commission (2004) set out in a devastating analysis just how market failure adversely affected the pension incomes of a whole generation. When occupational pension schemes began to fail, a rapid consensus was reached that the state had to intervene in ways we discuss later. The prime private model, held up by the World Bank to the emerging economies, was that of Chile. There, too, it has failed in a primary duty all states have—to support the elderly poor (Barr and Diamond 2008). Chile is now introducing what is, effectively, a basic citizen's pension on which reformed private schemes can be built. In the poorest economies, insurance market failures were compounded by the weakness of their capital markets. A devastating review of its own advice and errors was undertaken by the World Bank's Independent Evaluation Group in 2006. In the diplomatic words of its summary—'the Bank did not always fully consider the country's underlying economic and financial structure'!

We now understand much better why individuals systematically under-save and under-insure for retirement and long-term care (Choi et al. 2004; Pensions Commission 2004: ch. 6). Individuals find information about future financial options difficult to grasp. Even when they do grasp it they do not act on it. It is always rational at any given point to defer action if you are making a difficult decision about the distant future. This is exactly what individuals do when considering investing in a pension scheme—there is always tomorrow. For firms, the cost of company pension schemes grew and led them to abandon defined benefit schemes.

In short, when growing longevity was seized upon by those forecasting a decline in welfare states, they completely ignored evidence that private alternatives were equally, if not more, prone to funding difficulties. That was true even when private capital markets were booming.

A similar blind spot applied to the argument that their labour-intensive character would cause difficulties for public sector human services. What private human services typically sell is *more* intensive staffing by *higher* qualified more expensive staff. Private schools sell small classes and good staffing quality. In the United Kingdom between 1996/7 and 2001/2 school fees rose by 34 per cent. From 2001/2 to 2006/7 they rose by 39 per cent. This not only outstripped general inflation but was more than *twice* the increase in earnings of those in professional and managerial jobs. The private sector has thus barely grown. Health cost inflation is similarly a problem for private health insurance companies and employers worldwide.

There were, in short, some economic fundamentals underpinning the resilience political scientists had noted in welfare spending. Yet many of the points the pessimists had raised were correct. What they underestimated was the political will to surmount the difficulties and the feasibility of doing so. That politicians did succeed, at least to some extent, suggests that they may do so again.

FISCAL SUSTAINABILITY

A range of fiscal responses taken by governments can be distinguished.

More priority given to social policy spending. Social policy came to take a higher share of public spending across the Western world after the Cold War ended. A lower share went to defence spending and, with the privatization of major basic industries in most countries, less tax revenue has been devoted to industrial subsidies. Neither trick can be played again. Other demands, like that of environmental policy, and international terrorism may make life more difficult for social policy budgets. But electorates will be older too and their votes will matter. Recent collapses in the value of individual private pension schemes will have alerted people to the risks of that route.

Charges. Introducing or increasing service charges or co-payments has been a major strategy in many, but not all, healthcare systems. However, the exceptions that are made, not to overburden the long-term sick or the elderly, mean that there is limited room to extend this strategy.

Reduced pension promises. Governments gradually scaled back unrealistic pension promises. The Swedish pension scheme, as it was in the 1990s, would have required contributions equivalent to 20 per cent of the average person's lifetime earnings (Fenge and Werding 2004). The cross-party reform agreed in 1998 stabilized this lifetime contribution at 12 per cent of lifetime earnings. In Italy, the 1995 reforms reduced the equivalent projected lifetime tax rate from about a quarter to 18 per cent. German pension promises have been reduced over a fifteen-year period of reform (Börsch-Supan et al. 2007). Over the whole of the EU, pension promises have been reduced by a quarter in the past two decades (European Commission 2006a).

Longer working lives. Longer life is only a major fiscal problem if pension ages remain unchanged while life expectancy grows. Attempts to lengthen working life are beginning to pay off. A century-long decline in the age of retirement was reversed in the United States in the 1980s, in the United Kingdom about 1995, and slightly later in other OECD countries. Across the Western world, governments have been getting a difficult message across with increasing success. Both the Swedish and German pension reforms have built in automatic reviews of pension levels to bring them in line with rising life expectancy. Italy has steadily reduced its very early retirement rights. France has done so in the private sector and is trying to do so in the public. In the United Kingdom, the Pension Commission persuasively argued that the portion of adult life spent in retirement could not reasonably and fairly continue to go on *growing*. In 1950 the average male spent 17 per cent of his adult life in retirement. By 2000, it was 31 per cent. That could not continue, they argued. 'Let's keep retirement at about 30 per cent of adult life and raise the full state pension age as life expectancy increases.' That case gained cross-party support. Voters may be less irrational than many supposed. It will be necessary to protect those with shorter life expectancy but the equity of placing growing burdens on young families to fund longer retirement for the healthy elderly is difficult to accept.

Sustainable additional spending? On average members of the European Union will have to devote another 4 per cent of their GDP to welfare spending by 2050 to sustain current policies and promised benefit levels. Widening the definition of 'Western' to most OECD countries increases the estimate to between 5 and 6 per cent. (See Table 47.1). These figures are tentative but this kind of transition is surely politically

Table 47.1 Additional spending driven by demography, assuming present policies in per cent of expected GDP, excluding education (2004–2050)

Anglo Saxon	
Australia	5.6
Canada	8.7
New Zealand	8.4
USA	5.5
UK	5.0
Ireland	8.8
Middle continental Europe	
Belgium	7.0
France	3.4
Germany	3.6
Netherlands	5.2
Southern Europe	
Greece	–
Italy	2.4
Spain	9.1
Portugal	10.1
Scandinavia	
Denmark	5.1
Finland	5.9
Norway	13.4
Sweden	3.1
New Europe	
Czech	7.9
Slovak	4.1
Poland	−4.8
Hungary	1.1

Sources: EU Economic Policy Committee 2006; OECD 2001; OECD 2007c; Glennerster 2009.

feasible especially given the costs of alternative private solutions. There are wide variations around the average because some countries have still to adapt to the implications of their demographic future.

'Quasi-taxation'. As an alternative to raising taxes the state has intervened to encourage or require individuals to fund their own provision. A whole range of new mixed modes of funding have developed (Glennerster 2009).

- In Sweden, 2.5 per cent of a worker's earnings have to be invested in private funded pensions. In Germany, a voluntary top up contribution attracts government matching money. In the United Kingdom, people will have to take active measures to opt out of a national savings scheme which will take 4 per cent of their income and must be matched by employer and government funding.
- Australia, followed by New Zealand and more recently Hungary and the United Kingdom, has developed a version of the graduate tax as a way of funding universities. Universities can charge fees for courses and receive the cash up front when the student enters but students only pay these fees as an addition to their tax bill after they graduate.
- In the Netherlands, all citizens have been required, under recent reforms, to take out private health insurance that covers a full range of health risks. They must pay a small premium towards the cost of that cover but most is funded out of taxation and varies according to the age and health status of the individual.
- Perhaps the most surprising example of this new funding model is health care in the United States. Both Massachusetts and California have introduced 'universal health care' coverage by making it compulsory for individuals to take out health insurance. President Obama promised near-universal cover achieved through subsidized private health cover that could not exclude bad health risks and with enhanced access to Medicare and Medicaid.

We are likely to see more variants of such mixed funding models emerging. They may ease the fiscal problems states face but the downside of 'quasi-taxes' is that they may reduce people's willingness to pay 'real' taxes. Whether such moves are fiscally redistributive depends critically on how the poorest are treated. Mixed funding need not necessarily lead to less equity, but it may well. Here is an important future research agenda.

Most states in the West have also taken steps to remedy perceived incentives not to work. There has been 'an internationalization of labour market policy in these respects' (Banks et al. 2005; Lødemel and Trickey 2000). Few countries in Europe have taken really radical or draconian steps. 'A radical change from welfare to workfare is supported only in Ireland and moderately in Denmark' (Vis 2007: 105). The United Kingdom's attempt to make work pay with weak penalties had relatively little impact in getting single parents into work but did reduce child poverty (Waldfogel 2007). The current recession will make tougher 'workfare' policies difficult to take forward in the short run. When it is over, however, as it surely will be, governments will return to the objective. There will be more pressure on those who do not actively seek work, positive help for those who do return, and higher subsidies for lower-paid jobs (Lindbeck 2008). Work and longer years of paid work are likely to remain a central part of social welfare policy in my view.

POLITICAL SUSTAINABILITY

Faced with increasingly demanding electorates, governments have tried to improve service standards in a variety of ways. Public sector management reforms (notably measuring outcomes and setting targets) have been adopted in most Western nations. These have been complemented by the use of competition and choice between providers designed to drive up efficiency and responsiveness. The British dubbed this latter strategy 'quasi markets'. It had its counterparts in Swedish health and education reforms and in the Netherlands and German health care reforms. The jury is still out on how far this strategy has either improved efficiency or public support for social provision.

- In selling these changes politicians have emphasized service deficiencies to win public approval against the opposition of public service unions. This may have had the net result of reducing public confidence in these services. In the United Kingdom, there has been a marked decline in the public's belief that government is capable of spending its money to good effect (Sefton 2009).
- Hard evidence that these reforms have had an impact on efficiency is mixed. One reason may be that there has been little in the way of new entrants to the welfare market beyond social care. Governments have not been willing to see poor providers go bankrupt—in short, to make welfare markets work.
- Sweden has been prepared to permit new private schools funded by the state to enter the education market on a significant scale (15 per cent of school places in 2007 compared to hardly any a decade before). It is an example the Conservative Party in England wish to emulate. But in most countries there has been no big appetite to extend the scope of private education to challenge state schools.

Nevertheless, an increasingly educated electorate with wide choice in the rest of its life is going to be more demanding than ever of public services. Raising their quality is going to be a continuing theme of welfare politics. How this is done through more 'voice' (a say in local service administration), how much by more competition and consumer 'exit' power, and how much by a mixture of the two will become a distinguishing feature of welfare politics.

   If ageing is an economic problem it carries a political benefit. Welfare spending is very heavily loaded towards old age. But as electorates age so the electoral weight of the older population will grow. What happens to the long-term care of older people, their medical care, or their pensions will not be things politicians will be able to forget.

There is another side to this relatively optimistic picture, however. For much of the twentieth century 'the condition of the people' question dominated domestic political concern. The pressure exerted by labour unions, the labour left, and middle class moral endeavour was directed to extending social rights of various kinds.

In the twenty-first century the big claim on political attention may shift to climate change and to the plight of the Third World. Indeed, it is already doing so. If the future of life as we know it on the planet is in danger, if those who are to be most adversely affected are the poorest in the less developed countries, then political and moral concern should appropriately turn to these issues. That is what seems to be happening in the younger generation. This may take away political interest and hard cash from traditional social policy.

Yet, this may not be a zero-sum game. Climate change presents the biggest collective action problem the world has ever faced as Nicholas Stern (2007) has argued. But a mindset that can come to terms with such a problem may well be one that is more sympathetic to state action in the welfare field too. In the nineteenth century, the public health movement raised public awareness of the health risks of uninhibited private actions and pioneered collective action solutions. Perhaps the environmental movement may have a similar collateral political impact.

The world banking crisis is another example of a worldwide collective action problem. Here was an example of government failure to regulate. Markets require powerful states to regulate them. But individual states are powerless in the face of worldwide financial markets. International collective action is needed. This too may help change the political climate in favour of more collective welfare action. But it may not.

Perhaps there is a limited reservoir of moral and political concern for others. World scale problems may make us turn inwards to things we can grasp and risks that face us. Young people may worry about the environment and not about the poor on their doorstep. The costs of the banking crisis may be so great that they crowd out welfare spending.

MORAL SUSTAINABILITY

A Slide into a Neoliberal Future?

One more negative way of viewing the economic adaptation that welfare states have made in order to survive is to see that process as a betrayal of the moral purpose that should underpin them. Can the process of adaptation described earlier therefore be seen as a 'slide into a neo-liberal future'? Ellison (2006) cites with approval Ferge (1997), who sees some of the kinds of trends I have described as 'the individualization of the social', and Klein and Millar (1995) say 'social policy is becoming a branch of the do it yourself industry'.

I disagree. I do not accept that increasing choice and individual agency in education or health, social care, or pensions undermines social solidarity. On the contrary both are good in themselves—the necessary means to gaining greater human freedom. Moreover, without these changes the state may lose the support necessary to bind in the middle-class voter on whose taxes and support as users the welfare state depends. But it is a legitimate debate.

A related but different claim is that Western societies are less and less aware of what binds them. Post-war national collective sentiments are being overtaken by narrow individual concerns. Belonging to voluntary organizations and mutual self-help activities has declined (Putnam 2000). We 'bowl alone' and hence the very glue that binds us is disappearing. I am no sociologist but I find this unconvincing. Traditional and national forms of belonging, such as trade union membership, are indeed declining but less formal groups (of users, sufferers, and carers, for example) seem to be on the increase—not least because communication is so much easier. They may well mobilize to produce new kinds of mutual help groups which will interact with more local and responsive welfare institutions.

Where most welfare states have struggled is in coping with the sharply rising inequalities in original market incomes (Brandolini and Smeeding 2007; OECD 2008a). In nearly all countries, inequalities in original market incomes have risen. In Canada, Finland, Germany, Sweden, and the United Kingdom, the equalizing effect of taxes and benefits has had to grow to mitigate those inequalities. The Swedish economy has generated a similar level of original inequality to the United Kingdom economy and inequality has grown there too a since the 1960s. But Sweden has managed to reduce its market-driven inequality by much more than the United Kingdom or other welfare states (by 45 per cent compared to the United Kingdom's 33 per cent, for example). If we include benefits in-kind in the calculation the scale of redistribution is even greater and has grown in nearly all OECD countries (OECD 2008a; Garfinkel et al. 2006). This experience does not suggest to me that populations have abandoned their support for redistribution though it has been under strain in some countries (Sefton 2009). There is growing evidence, persuasively marshalled by Richard Wilkinson (Wilkinson and Pickett 2009), that unequal societies are dysfunctional in a whole variety of ways that affect not just the poor but the rich within them. This applies to individuals' health, their happiness, their fears for their safety, their hopes for their children, and much more. We cannot escape the contagion of inequality and gross unfairness any more than the Victorians could escape the contagion of cholera.

The Global Economic Crisis

In the 1980s it was plausible to blame an excessively burdensome state for the inflationary ills of the day. Today the appeal of unrestrained capitalism has taken a serious knock. If the banking crisis has done any good it may be that it has called into question the belief that unrestrained individual greed can somehow result in collective welfare. The moral claims that dominated political and academic debate on social welfare in the advanced economies during the later twentieth century tended to be couched in terms of the nation state. 'Solidarity' was the solidarity associated with national collective action or social action by institutions, unions or not for profit associations. These had national or sub-national allegiances. Citizenship claims were national. Increasingly morally based claims have become international—world poverty, world hunger, the global environment.

New Challenges and Possible Futures

So the challenges the world will face in the next half century are going to be partly the same but partly very different from the past five decades. These new challenges may include:

- A faster shift towards an older population and sustained low fertility. Some respected demographers consider that we are seriously underestimating the potential for life expectancy to grow (Oeppen and Vaupel 2002).
- Rapid technological change, growing international trade, and the rewards for innovation could all provoke even wider inequalities of income and wealth (Helpman et al. 2008).
- Major climate change will produce food shortages, rising sea levels, and displace people in large numbers (Stern 2007).
- Financial crises may well become more common as it proves impossible to erect effective international regulatory regimes that police international banking irresponsibility. This may undermine the stability and growth of modern economies and sap their fiscal capacity. The public debt interest costs of the current crisis will cast a long shadow and may crowd out other public spending as we have suggested earlier.
- Large population movement into the advanced economies may overwhelm the capacity of host nations to absorb immigrants tolerantly (see Chapter 19 above). Two American authors (Alesina and Glaeser 2004) have suggested that one of the reasons for American relative reluctance to develop European-type welfare states lies in the past homogeneity of Europe's nation states and in America's diversity. The more newcomers there are the less willing will Europe's population be to support the poor. Others argue this is a misplaced fear. It is the organized labour traditions in Europe that have sustained welfare traditions and their absence in the United States (Taylor-Gooby 2005b). I suspect that this view underestimates the scale of the challenge.
- Legal family structures may continue to become less secure and more varied, while the sense of obligation becomes more complex as does the state's complementary role in the care of children (Finch 1989).

- Superstates or federations may emerge in Europe, North America, South America, and Asia. There may be growing intervention by international agencies into the field of social policy. The notion of the collective may change.

These suggest a wider set of scenarios for welfare futures than we have seen in the past.

Market Dominance

It is possible to envisage, as market optimists have always done, the growing capacity of the market to solve the problems of poor information and individual decision making about the long term. This may be helped by state rules that require individuals to take out private health, long-term care, and pension provision. Along with improved individual action to adopt healthy life styles this will lead individuals to take the finance of their health, education, and old age into their own hands with no more than a 'nudge' from the state (Thaler and Sunstein 2008). The political demand to do so may grow as the fiscal burdens of the banking crisis turn voters against governments.

Those who are human capital rich and internationally mobile, can safely ignore the problems of those who are left behind in the race for higher incomes, many of whom will be immigrants from the increasingly arid lands of Africa and the flooded deltas of India. Their presence as newcomers is increasingly resented in the 'West'. The social cohesion necessary for state-level welfare institutions to exist evaporates.

Social institutions, including marriage and family, no longer inspire confidence. People recognize that personal partnerships are less secure and will make temporary partner contracts that recognize this. The law gives those who break with their partners' rights to assets and pensions that reflect 'joint production'. Individuals and the market adapt to these new lifestyle arrangements and fluid institutions (Eekelaar 2000).

State organizations remain slow to incorporate choice and flexibility and exhibit poor productivity. Private providers gradually take over both the provision and finance of most basic services. This remains a possible if, on previous analysis, unlikely scenario.

A Basic Citizenship Model

There is growing interest in the idea of a basic unconditional income for all—a Citizen's Income (www.citizensincome.org). Some may see this as a compromise with the market model. The state could provide a secure platform on which individuals can build their own varied mix of provision. This could take the form of a basic citizen's pension as in the Netherlands, a minimum income for those with children, the right to a voucher that is transferable but gives all children access to a given standard of education. The same model could give risk-adjusted levels of state support to help individuals pay for membership of either private or collective insurance. A basic housing voucher would go with this model, perhaps varied by income and region.

As people come to move between the old nation states these basic citizenship rights may become transferable for citizens of the new federations—across Europe, Northern Asia, or Southern America. This is not an impossible future.

But who is a citizen? The rights could be narrow and targeted on long-standing indigenous people. The definition of citizenship, a long period of residence, could become the justification for narrowing rights to welfare—exclusive not inclusive. Citizenship and what it means may return as the key political debate of the early twenty-first century.

Inclusive but Adaptive

The strong traditions of inclusive welfare states may prove resistant to major change and adapt to the demographic and economic changes we have outlined as they have done in the past three decades. Supplementary private additions to basic state pension schemes and health insurance will remain small in many countries. Divergent historical pathways to social welfare will remain too. Welfare provision will gradually adapt to new family forms. Childcare will become a major public service integrated with schooling. Parents will be given more incentives to stay at home to care for children during their early years. These opportunity costs of family life become, at least partially, met. The state will invest in the heightened human capital needs of children. Higher education will be funded jointly by the state and by individuals investing in their own human capital with state assistance in borrowing to do so.

Schooling, healthcare, and social housing all come to involve users in local service management and offer choice and variety. Big investments in human capital throughout life become a top priority. The state may have to come to the rescue as private pensions and long-term care fail. An older electorate forces higher pension spending and higher standards of care. Voters recognize that this can only be achieved through a longer working life and somewhat higher taxation. Populations adjust to this.

Global environmental policy becomes a central part of a wider collective action policy agenda. Concern with poverty and human rights broadens in scope. 'Welfare' is not merely seen as a goal confined to a nation state's citizens but as a worldwide goal. Development aid is not seen as a separate activity from domestic social policy but as a part of a common human rights agenda.

Family Friendly

Perhaps one of the most striking changes in recent decades has been the decline in fertility rates in some countries and the general change in family forms. In Germany, Italy, and Spain, this is seen as a major social policy issue. Support for families, extra funds for larger families and free childcare become politically viable. But so too may policies to restore the 'traditional family'. Debates about family forms and gender rights become central.

Welfare states have responded at different speeds and in different ways to changing family forms. As Lewis (2007*b*) has argued, governments find this an extremely difficult area in which to move. When they do, they can be contradictory. At one extreme some have been penal, seeking to deter single parenthood, and subsidize the traditional family. At the other they have been accommodating to new family forms or they have faltered between the two—'Janus-faced' (Lewis 2000). But in the end legal unions of lesbians and gay couples have been legislated across Europe in some very unlikely countries such as Spain. Pension and property rights of women, and indeed both partners, in broken partnerships have been extended either by statute or judges' rulings in many countries (Maclean 2005). These trends will continue.

'Super-Nationalization'

Increased labour and capital mobility, climate change, the spread of contagious diseases, all these require wider international regulation, rules about rights to protection, to safety nets, to refugee status. Little by little specific agreements to tackle each will be worked out. Yet despite facing similar problems European countries may be reluctant to adopt overarching EU reforms (Clasen 2005). But in the end this will come.

However, the most likely future is one we cannot know. The world will be hit by events we cannot now foresee or dimly foresee and fear. But the experience of the past half century through which I have lived and studied and taught social policy leaves me optimistic. Ordinary people have shown a more generous humanity and growing capacity to reach out to others in need as their global horizons have widened. Political systems have shown themselves capable of learning and adapting. Welfare institutions have grown smarter. It is a long slow process but this is not a time to despair.

CHAPTER 48

....

THE GLOBAL
FUTURE OF
WELFARE STATES

....

IAN GOUGH
GÖRAN THERBORN

INTRODUCTION

....

THE title 'The Global Future of Welfare States' suggests two separate but equally big questions. First, will Western forms of welfare state be reproduced elsewhere in the world? Second, is the Western welfare state globally sustainable in the face of a series of unprecedented challenges, notably climate change and the emerging crisis of financial capitalism? Given the confines of word length and the scope of these two questions, we have decided to focus on the first; but will return to the second question at the end.

THE WELFARE STATE IN A GLOBAL
HISTORICAL CONTEXT

....

A global approach to social policy, welfare states, and their futures cannot be simply an add-on to the conventional Euro- or OECD-centric approach with its particular

Authors' note: Ian Gough gratefully acknowledges the support of the Economic and Social Research Council. Much of his contribution was undertaken as part of the programme of the ESRC Research Group on Wellbeing in Developing Countries at the University of Bath.

institutional gaze and incessantly researched repertoire of models and variations. Without here being able to dig into history, we need to establish a historical and global perspective.

A political responsibility for the well-being of a state's population is not a European invention. It is found in all the major ethico-religious traditions of Asia, for instance, from the Rig-Veda and Confucius to Islam (see e.g. Mabbett 1985). Relief from hunger and indigence, dispensation of justice, protection of comfort, and prosperity were normatively expected. Crop failures and other national disasters were often interpreted as indicators of misrule. Institutions of charity, food buffer stocks, quarantines, flood control, and so on developed long before modern times.

Nevertheless, it remains true, of course, that the welfare state in its recent meaning is a European invention, which exists outside Europe only to a limited extent, less extensive even in the European offshoot settlements. The very concept emerged in World War II Britain and gained international currency, to begin with in academic circles, only in the 1970s. Why was that the case, and, above all, what does that imply for the future?

Europe's world conquest in the sixteenth through nineteenth centuries took place in a context of decay and division in virtually all the great extra-European states, from the Amerindian Aztecs and Incas, to the Mughal and Ottoman empires, from Qing China to the savannah states of Africa. In that period of decline and disintegration the classical extra-European political precepts of the well-being of the population lost their material bearings and supports.

There was virtually nothing indicating a special European welfare state development in 1500, 1600, 1700, or in 1800. But in retrospect it is possible to identify at least two significant facilitating factors, though these are by no means sufficient. One was the unique Western European family system, with a nuclear, neo-local household as its core, which meant weaker kinship ties and responsibilities than in other parts of the world, and which gave more space and importance to occupational associations as well to territorial organizations, villages, cities, and states (Therborn 2004). The other was the conception of rights, coming out of Roman law and reinforced by the canonical law of the Catholic Christian Church, from which notions of natural law developed in early modernity. Rights took concerns with the well-being of the population out of lordly benevolence or religious charity, and the administration of justice into areas of popular claims and of new institutions.

The subsequent development of Western welfare states has spawned an immense scholarly apparatus, ably synthesized in this volume. Gough has summarized this work in terms of five drivers of modern welfare states, the 'five I's': Industrialization, Interests, Institutions, Ideas/Ideologies, and International Influences (see Gough 2008 for detailed arguments and citations). Let us briefly recap these.

The bases of European welfare state development were two: new social challenges and new resources to meet them. *Industrial capitalism* produced both. It tore apart the social patterns of minimal protection of the subsistence family, the village, and the guilds, and it brought together large numbers of men and women outside traditional tutelage, in factories and new cities, creating and incessantly increasing the challenges of social disintegration and of social protest. At the same time, industrial economic growth, and the new medical and scientific knowledge associated with it in European modernity, provided novel resources to deal with poverty, disease, and death.

In the new societies of industrial capitalism, two powerful and opposite *interests* converged in generating public social policies. There was the interest of the industrial proletariat in at least some minimally adequate housing and social amenities in the new industrial cities, and in acquiring some kind of security in cases of injury, sickness, unemployment, old age. That interest was soon organized, in trade unions, mutual aid societies, and labour-based parties. On the other side of the fence, there was the interest of political elites in social order and the quality of the population, more often out of concern with soldier material than for productivity. The French revolutions of 1789, 1830, 1848, and 1870–1 meant that elite interest in making efforts to prevent disorder and rebellion was quite rational. The immediate background to the landmark German social insurance legislation of the 1880s was the Paris Commune of 1871, which a key adviser of Bismarck witnessed close by, with the invading Prussian troops.

Institutions turned challenges, resources, and interests into consolidated, self-reproducing realities. The welfare state is part of a longer-term process by which power is accumulated in nation states by building state capacities, collecting taxes and constructing citizenship. The French Revolution was the first to launch a major programme of social rights and policy, but it was never institutionalized. The European welfare state emerged out of the coalescence of the bureaucratic *Rechtsstaat* (state of public law) and insurance, prompted by the fear of workers' rebellion and with a view to nation-state strengthening and development. This happened in recently unified Germany, setting an example for the rest of Europe, as a trigger of initiative rather than as a model to copy exactly.

In addition *ideas* influence public policies as human practices (putting to one side whether they are considered major autonomous forces or as derivable from large social processes and the interests generated by these). Formative ideas behind the emergence and development of European welfare states included the European rights tradition, the ancient civic republican tradition modernized into two major branches, British social liberalism and French post-revolutionary republicanism, social democracy, and social Catholicism. Later inputs have come from Keynesian economics and post-Keynesian economic theories of 'human capital' and 'productive social policy'.

Finally, the *international environment* must be considered. European welfare state development first got a push from the fact that its institutional pioneer, Germany, was the strongest, most dynamic, fastest growing country on the continent. The early period was also one of war, never far from the horizon, between national mass conscript armies. No serious big power politician in Europe could afford to be indifferent to the lives and loyalties of his future soldiers. The outcome of World War II popularized the 'welfare state' idea, of British wartime coinage, and the Beveridge Report became for a short while a new European model. But British influence soon dwindled, along with empire and big power status. Though the United States was the new lodestar, admiration for and dependence on America never significantly affected European welfare state development (until perhaps the Clinton attack on social assistance). The immediate reason was institutionalization and policy path dependence. The European social mould had been set. For fear of communism, United States leaders refrained from trying to impose their own model of capitalism on Western Europe; rather they were supportive of attempts at European integration and at sustaining Western European institutions. Marshall Aid had none of the conditionalities of the later IMF-World Bank 'structural adjustment programmes'. Western welfare states flourished in a supportive international environment: of a West-dominated capitalism, with little low-wage competition and nationally governed currencies and capital flows.

What clinched the rise of the European welfare state to its present size was the post-war boom. The question raised in the 1950s—does an emerging 'affluent society' need a welfare state, or is it only now that we can really afford the extensive social policy we need?—was definitely answered in the latter way. Again Germany was the leader, installing a new dynamic pension system, as a support of a policy of Western alliance rearmament.

LESSONS FROM THE EMERGENCE OF EUROPEAN WELFARE STATES

Will European forms of welfare state be reproduced elsewhere in the world? Will individual risks continue to be collectively managed, or left to lie where they fall? If the former, will the forms of collective management of risk follow Western models, or develop in quite novel ways? We tackle these questions in two parts. First, we use the above five-part model to ask what lessons, if any, it has for the likely emergence of welfare states in the developing world. Second, we recognize the immense variety within the 'global South' and distinguish distinctive patterns of risk management within it.

Industrialization and Post-Industrialism: Economic and Social Conditions and Change

Is the new tide of global industrialization and growth in the late twentieth and early twenty-first century fostering new state social programmes? Industrialization explanations are likely to remain relevant in the newly emerging 'workshops of the world', particularly in Asia. But even in these successful industrializers the growing secondary sector is combined with far larger tertiary and primary sectors than were European societies in the late nineteenth and early twentieth centuries—with implications for growth, taxation, labour market security, and the applicability of the European social insurance model.

In fact, the European experience of post-agrarian societies dominated, at least relatively, by industrial employment was never repeated outside Europe, not in the United States, not in Japan, nor in the British White Dominions. Third World urban employment today is largely in the so-called informal sector—overwhelming in South Asia and Africa, big and growing in Latin America—of self-employment and tiny enterprises below the radar of the state and of social entitlements. Under these circumstances, big industry employment became enclaves of particularistic social rights, once rather extensive in urban Maoist China, but still islands in a rural sea, of basic social services—largely eroded during the capitalist turn—but without pension rights, for instance.

And most of the non-Western world has never experienced the long post-war booms interspersed, until now, with only mild recessions. Plummeting commodity markets, financial crises, and demographically overburdened stagnations have haunted it most of the time. The more successful exceptions, like Japan and later South Korea, have witnessed burgeoning social policies, but still far from European levels, even in Japan. It is true that an unprecedented demographic transition is underway across much of the world, which suggests dramatic new 'requirements' for schools, pensions and health services. Yet the role of families and households in attempting to mitigate risk and secure welfare is also far more extensive in the developing than in the developed world. All these factors complicate any simple transposition of lessons from European industrialization to the developing world.

Interests

Both the interests of social rights and the interests of social fear are weaker outside Europe. The interests of rights are weaker because societies are much more fragmented: between urban and rural areas, within large agrarian sectors (between labourers and peasants), and within urban areas, between formal and informal employment. On some exceptional occasions progressive coalitions may arise, as in the making of the far-reaching constitutions of Brazil and South Africa, in 1988 and 1994, respectively, or in the late 1980s democratic movement in South Korea. But such coalescence of interests has been difficult, more or less impossible, to sustain in consistent policies and institutions.

In the zones of global accumulation, notably East Asia and now South Asia, proletarianization proceeds at breakneck speed, and has fostered unofficial trade unions and militant class struggle in uneven ways. In such countries, one might predict growing class pressures for minimal economic security and an improved 'social wage'. One might further expect the classic European 'social insurance dynamic' (Hort and Kuhnle 2000): social insurance beginning with groups of manual and factory workers in large industrial firms, gradually rippling outwards to include medium and small enterprises, agricultural, white-collar and other workers. However, this lesson is not applicable where capitalist development is not accompanied by proletarianization, and not necessarily where it is. The labour movement is weak almost everywhere in the developing world, squeezed between repression and deregulation. The growing structural power of capital and its willingness to exert agency power also contributes a bias against comprehensive welfare systems.

The interests of social fear have naturally also been weaker, partly because of fragmented rights. The distinctive features of the non-European roads to modernity also have to be kept in mind. Modern Europe was never threatened by non-European powers, never driven by a desire to catch up with the non-European world. European developers never had to bother with peoples close by who were not part of the people-nation, such as slaves and ex-slaves in the Americas and South Africa. Outside Europe, the major threats to ruling elites have come from without—from superior states and economies—not from within.

Institutions

Institutions have travelled across the world, including the nation state and social insurance, but nowhere is there a European-type, European-size welfare state in sight outside the old colonialist continent, although the old dominions of the British empire are not that far behind. However, the role of welfare systems in extending citizenship as a later phase of state and nation building in Europe has some parallels in the global South: from the development of social protection policies in the face of the 1930s depression in the Southern Cone of Latin America, to the ambitious plans for welfare states in newly independent ex-colonies such as Sri Lanka and Ghana, to concessionary social programmes to stem revolutionary pressures such as the 1953 Social Insurance Act in the Philippines. There is a need for a more comparative study of these paths, of their very different antecedents, such as Therborn's (1995*b*) 'four roads to modernity'—pioneers, 'settler' countries, colonies, and independent-but-constrained nation states—and of the forms of social citizenship on offer. However, all these cases presuppose state institutions with certain minimal capacities and legitimacy: a welfare state presupposes a reasonably functioning Weberian state. Where states are failed, 'shadow', or collapsed, this cannot happen.

A related question concerns the export of Western-style democracy across the world and its impact on pressures for social programmes. During the Cold War, democracy always took second place to loyalty to the United States in zones of the world deemed critical to Western interests, but since 1990 there has been a substantial spread of at least formal democratic processes. However, research on European social insurance suggests that democratic representation of subordinate classes was not a precondition for state welfare—rather the opposite: it was authoritarian regimes that pioneered social insurance. The Bismarckian strategy has clear parallels, for example, in East Asia where authoritarian leaders have introduced social policies to strengthen national solidarity, secure the loyalty of elites and legitimize undemocratic regimes. The lesson from early European welfare developments is that specific state social policies can be initiated by authoritarian regimes, but that healthy democratization is perhaps a necessary condition to transform these into generous social rights.

Democracy also fostered the clientelistic political machine, initially in the United States—deals whereby citizens trade votes for access to employment and transfers. It was imported into Latin America by Vargas in Brazil and Perón in Argentina, and has taken 'tribal' forms in independent Africa and caste forms in India. Since the democratization in Bangladesh in 1991, new gatekeepers have appeared regulating access to government food aid and other programmes. Villagers must maintain good links with *mastaans* (mafia-style gangs) and/or local party representatives in order to receive essential benefits, but at a price of loyalty, votes and other *quid pro quos* (Devine 2007). There is no simple link between the spread of 'democracy' and the emergence of real social rights.

Ideas

Outside Europe, and its American, Oceanian, and South African offshoots, there is no tradition of civic or popular rights to draw upon. But there are powerful ideas of social justice within Islamic, African, and Gandhian cultures, for instance. The emergence of proto-welfare states in East Asia has also prompted the study of the 'Confucian welfare state': a 'fundamentally different orientation to social policy' to the West and 'an independent path of welfare state evolution in East Asia' (Rieger and Leibfried 2003: 261). In late twentieth-century Latin America, an indigenous trans-plant of social Catholicism, the Theology of Liberation, has played a significant role, in Brazil above all.

Many countries have pursued roads to modernity different from T. H. Marshall's idea of social citizenship following upon political citizenship. Rather, they have followed a much more central idea of national development, recognized in recent research on the developmental state. This was pioneered by Japan under pressure to catch up with Europe whilst maintaining national cohesion. The Japanese project presupposed a strong, externally threatened but not defeated national culture, capable of overwhelming class conflict.

There have been times when ideas of European social policy have been imported, such as in Uruguay at the time of President Battle in the late 1910s and early 1920s. But the most effective ideological imports have occurred under the auspices of late twentieth-century neoliberalism, not very conducive to policies of social rights. Since the Pinochet coup in Chile, neoliberal ideas have dominated social policy thinking, though since Jeffrey Sachs' ephemerally successful expedition into Bolivia in the mid-1980s there has been enough of the old social fear to preach a 'social safety net'. The World Bank pushed in the 1990s for private pensions schemes, successfully in Latin America and in post-Communist Europe, although being reversed in both regions. Another World Bank and IMF idea in the 1980s was to introduce fees for primary education and basic health care in poor countries, but its impact, pushing enrolment and uptake rates down, soon appalled even the Washington economists who had come up with the idea, which is now abandoned.

Crucially, many highly indebted low-income countries in the South lack the power and institutional capacities to adapt international policy models to their contexts. Policy transfer imposed by fiat or threat of heavy penalties or conditionality is very different from policy learning—indeed, they can be mutually exclusive. Many developing countries have experienced 'dependent learning' (something no Western country ever faced). This is a novel barrier to the emergence of autonomous social policy in much of the South.

International Environment

When considering the impact of international factors, the ability of European history to offer any useful lessons is severely tested. The developing world today is enmeshed in a network of economic relationships with powerful financial and corporate actors, is part of a world society of intergovernmental institutions with powers to constrain and sometimes control Southern governments, and is subject to ruling ideas and ideologies promulgated by powerful epistemic communities, notably that of economists. The roles of supra-national structures, interests, institutions, and ideas were not insignificant in the twentieth century during the emergence of Western welfare states—above all, the two World Wars had an immense shaping role. But in the last quarter of the twentieth and into the new century, all four of the national factors considered above have become profoundly internationalized.

Contrary to naïve interpretations of globalization, the world's most generous welfare states have developed in societies wide open to and heavily dependent on the world market, such as Belgium, the Netherlands, and Scandinavia. These welfare states, in particular the Scandinavian ones, always come at the top in managerial rankings of 'world competitiveness' (e.g. Schwab and Porter 2007). But they compete in the world market as niche players, on the basis of high skills. Unlike in the West, where social protection emerged early on as the only alternative to trade protection, in much of the developing world international exposure has occurred before mechanisms of social protection have been set up.

The East Asian national development states faced much stiffer cost constraints, arriving later and without old trading networks to build upon. East Asia benefited enormously from American largesse, but in ways very different from Europe after World War II—via access to United States consumer markets, off-shore military ones as well as mainland. Nevertheless, they provide the only successful model outside the West of indigenous capitalist development, only briefly interrupted by the 1997 Asian economic crisis. It remains to be seen to what extent they can accommodate the far more threatening and systemic global financial crisis of 2008.

The tide within intergovernmental institutions may now be turning. International organizations have been very important conveyers of ideas of different kinds. The

ILO has importantly inspired formal sector labour rights. The UN, from its 1974 Women's Conference in Mexico has spread ideas of gender equality, and the UN Convention of the Rights of the Child and its permanent child-focused organization UNICEF are highlighting children's well-being. Deacon (2007) provides a detailed account of the debates and contests between inter-governmental organizations, including between the UN family and the more powerful Bretton Woods institutions. There is some evidence that crass anti-welfare stances are being modified in the light of experience, but no evidence to date of an emerging 'progressive programme of global social policy'. Indeed, a rising chorus of voices in the global South questions the desirability of such a programme.

From all this, three conclusions seem warranted: first, the developmental paths of European welfare states are not likely to be repeated. Second, an array of social programmes already exists in the global South, but they do not yet coalesce into an alternative 'social policy model'. Third, these programmes are likely to expand in favoured locations, but they will move forward along their own paths. To chart this variegated pattern, we summarize a recent cluster analysis of broader 'welfare regimes' across the global South in 2000 and then indicate some social policy innovations in the South.

Mapping Social Policies across the Global South

Though there have been many attempts to apply Esping-Andersen's welfare state regime framework to other parts of the world, including Central and Eastern Europe, Latin America, and East Asia, these all adopt the original conceptual framework developed to understand the OECD world. This approach is rejected by Gough and Wood (Gough and Wood 2004, and their collaborators; Wood and Gough 2006). To apply this paradigm to the nations and peoples of the global South requires, they argue, a *radical* reconceptualization in order to recognize the very different realities described above. To do this Abu Sharkh and Gough (2010) include a wider range of variables and use cluster analysis to map the welfare regimes of sixty-five non-OECD countries in 2000.

This analysis generates eight country clusters which can be ordered according to the distances of their final cluster centres from the OECD welfare states (see Table 48.1). The cluster with the highest scores for public expenditure, public provision, and welfare outcomes is labelled *A*. Most remote from this cluster are clusters *G* and *H*.

Countries in cluster *A*, and only these, exhibit some characteristics of Western welfare states and may be labelled *proto-welfare states*. These countries share in common relatively extensive state commitments to welfare provision and relatively

Table 48.1 Cluster analysis and mean values for welfare regimes of 65 non–OECD countries (2000)

Cluster identifier	A	B	C	D	E	F	G	H
No of countries	14	16	7	5	5	7	5	4
Aid per capita/ GNI	0.81	2.08	2.98	2.59	6.22	3.96	12.05	27.19
Workers' remittances/GNI	0.64	0.66	9.2	0.03	0.34	1.54	2.3	0.99
Public spend. health + education/ GDP	9.35	6.77	5.77	8.63	4.35	4.8	5.44	5.17
Social contributions/ total revenue	29.46	7.06	6.78	1.05	1.72	1.19	1.29	0.43
School enrolment, secondary, fem. (%ogross)	91.99	76.05	63.64	59.7	29.7	28.27	12.39	14.0
Immunization, measles (% of children u. 12m.)	90.5	89.19	92.86	76.4	62.8	65.14	58.4	78.75
Life expectancy at birth, total (years)	72.32	69.57	70.3	44.17	53.74	56.9	46.32	41.3
Illiteracy rate, youth total (% ages 15–24)	1.28	2.2	13.39	7.29	6.65	35.57	48.21	27.42
	Argentina	Bolivia	Dominican Rep.	Botswana	Cameroon	Bangladesh	Benin	Mozambique
	Belarus	Chile	Ecuador	Kenya	Congo, Rep.	Côte d'Ivoire	Burundi	Guinea–Bissau
	Brazil	China	El Salvador	Namibia	Ghana	India	Ethiopia	Rwanda
	Bulgaria	Colombia	Jamaica	South Africa	Indonesia	Nepal	Mali	Zambia
	Costa Rica	Iran, Islamic Rep	Morocco	Zimbabwe	Tanzania	Pakistan	Senegal	
	Croatia	Kazakhstan	Nicaragua			Papua New Guinea		
	Estonia	Korea, Rep.	Sri Lanka			Togo		
	Israel	Malaysia						
	Lithuania	Mexico						
	Poland	Moldova						
	Romania	Paraguay						
	Tunisia	Peru						
	Ukraine	Philippines						
	Uruguay	Tajikistan						
		Thailand						
		Turkey						

Source: Abu Sharkh and Gough 2010.

effective delivery of services plus moderately extensive social security programmes and superior welfare outcomes (by, it must be stressed, the standards of the non-OECD world). Apart from Israel and Costa Rica, this cluster comprises two distinct geographical zones and historical antecedents: the countries of the former Soviet Union and its bloc members and the relatively industrialized countries of southern South America. Both developed European-style forms of social protection policies in the middle of the twentieth century, and both suffered degradation of these in the late twentieth century through the external imposition of neo-liberal programmes. The imposition of robber capitalism in the former Soviet Union has cut male life expectancy in Russia and Ukraine to 59 and 62 years respectively, though the central European countries admitted to the EU have fared much better (Unfpa 2008: 86 ff.).

Cluster B exhibits the second-best level of welfare outcomes and social service outputs yet with low levels of state social spending (and low reliance on external flows of aid and remittances). This interesting combination suggests that security and illfare are mitigated by fast-growing average incomes and/or by other domestic, non-state institutions. This combination is found in three major world regions: (1) China and most countries in East Asia from Korea to Malaysia (except Indonesia, which dropped out of this group in 2000 having suffered most from the 1997 crisis); (2) the remaining countries of South and Central America not in cluster A; and (3) some countries in Western Asia (Iran, Turkey and Tajikistan).

Countries in this group are mainly but not always low-middle income, with high growth rates, but are relatively undemocratic and unequal. This group includes some countries that have achieved historic reductions in poverty levels (living under $1 a day PPP at 2005 prices): China's economic take off has cut its proportion of the global poverty population from 41 per cent in 1981 to 16 per cent in 2005 (Chen and Ravaillon 2008: 31). One notable finding is that this cluster includes most countries of externally induced, reactive modernization (Therborn's fourth route to modernity), where states have been forced over longer periods to adjust to outside developmental pressures. This may indicate the presence of 'developmental states' with considerable infrastructure capacity but which have not prioritized traditional social policies. Here one might expect to see new forms of collective management of risk emerge.

Cluster C is similar to the above group but is distinguished by great reliance on remittances from abroad which account for 9 per cent of gross national income on average and which constitute an informal functional alternative to public transfers. It comprises small countries in the Caribbean and Central America, plus Ecuador, Morocco and Sri Lanka.

In southern and east Africa (South Africa, Namibia, Botswana, Zimbabwe, and Kenya) a distinct cluster D exhibited in 2000 relatively extensive public social policy (in both tax, expenditures and outreach and literacy levels), but these improvements were swamped by rising mortality and morbidity due mainly to the HIV-AIDS pandemic.

Cluster F, centred on the countries of the Indian sub-continent—India, Pakistan, Bangladesh, and Nepal—exhibits modest expenditure and social programmes alongside high levels of youth illiteracy and low numbers of females in secondary education. South Asia is always differentiated from East and South-East Asia most notably due to its illiteracy and poor education of women. These are by no means 'failed states': India is proclaimed as a future economic giant. Moreover, they boast a plethora of targeted social programmes and informal security mechanisms. However, the absence of effective schooling, health, and social protection policies coupled with highly gendered outcomes, according to such indicators as the population sex ratio, betokens high levels of insecurity among the mass of the population.

Clusters *G* and *H* comprise a chronic insecurity regime with high poverty and morbidity. These countries in sub-Saharan Africa exhibit low and in some cases falling life expectancy alongside relatively weak states with low levels of public responsibility, indicated both by spending levels and social outputs, and higher dependence on overseas aid. The prevalence of poverty is also high and persistent—the change in the proportion in poverty in sub-Saharan Africa over the last quarter century is within the margin of error, a decline from 43 to 40 per cent.

Thus we find a highly variegated pattern of welfare and illfare systems across the global South. We conclude that different groups of countries in the developing world face divergent threats to human well-being and divergent potentials for social policies to mitigate these. In Central and parts of Eastern Europe and parts of South America, despite serious erosion of their traditional welfare systems, we see a potential for new forms of social citizenship. In much of East and South-East Asia, much of Latin America, Iran, Turkey, and possibly other parts of the MENA region, we find distinctive, different yet moderately effective informal welfare systems alongside small state sectors. In the Indian subcontinent, there is a plethora of formal and informal programmes but with little realization in terms of spending, delivery or welfare outcomes. In much of sub-Saharan Africa, what social programmes there are have been eroded and submerged beneath a rising tide of human need; this remains a zone of high insecurity and illfare.

CHALLENGES TO 'THE REST': SOCIAL ISSUES AND POLICIES OUTSIDE THE OECD

We conclude this part by noting profound challenges to people's well-being outside the OECD and by identifying some innovative policy solutions now emerging. The most egregious threats to well-being include the following.

- Disease and ill-health: most acutely, the ravages of AIDS in sub-Saharan Africa and elsewhere.
- Malnutrition, a major plague in South Asia and sub-Saharan Africa with enduring effects on children.
- Poverty: notably extreme poverty—the 'bottom billion'—centred again in sub-Saharan Africa.

- Unsustainable population growth. In the last decades of the twentieth century this was brought under control in most parts of the poor world, with one major exception, sub-Saharan Africa. By the end of the past century, if Africa since 1960 had had the same population growth as China, its GDP per capita would have been more than forty per cent higher than it was (Therborn 2003). Though it has gone down somewhat, high fertility remains a major challenge to the well-being of Africans.
- Urban amenities: the explosion of cities across the global South, out of proportion to urban services and employment, poses acute problems. Amazing human ingenuity has come up with makeshift shelters, hijacked electricity, hawking, scavenging, and other 'informal' activities. But sanitation and a reliable safe water supply are elementary social services, which are largely missing.
- Existential inequalities: girls and women are still systematically discriminated against in large parts of the South, especially in South Asia and most parts of Africa, but also in the Chinese interior, in Central Asia, and the Middle East. Despite constitutional rights and affirmative action, caste still has its specific weight upon poverty in India. Amerindian communities along the Andean ridge have been victims of long social exclusion, only now beginning to break up under contestation, as in Bolivia.
- Old age: huge rises in the proportion of elderly populations are emerging notably in China and East Asia. Nowhere in the South, outside parts of South America, is there an adequate pension system in place, although there are some pension schemes in urban China, and in some Indian states.
- Finance: economic development will aid tax collection and social insurance in some favoured enclaves, but across much of the South taxes remain coercive and rent-based and tax capacity has been damaged by IMF policies (Moore 2008).
- Climate change: finally the damage caused by global warming to environments and livelihoods notably in tropical and subtropical areas poses a long-term and cumulative threat to well-being (briefly and inadequately discussed below).

However, this pessimistic picture ignores the limitless inventiveness of human communities. The South has also witnessed the emergence of novel policy solutions to social problems, of variable range (see ILO 2004a: ch. 14, for a full review and evaluation). These include:

- Conditional cash transfers. The payment of a monthly income to mothers conditional on their children attending school is a broadly successful new programme, pioneered in Mexico but developed most extensively in the *bolsa escola* and *bolsa familia* programmes in Brazil. It is now being emulated in other Latin American countries.
- Provident funds. These are forms of social insurance account, financed by individual and employer contributions, which the individual can draw upon for different purposes, including medical care and housing. They developed under British colonial administrations and are notable in Singapore and Malaysia.
- Affirmative action programmes. In independent India these target a number of discriminated or 'backward' castes, becoming 'scheduled castes' and tribes, with

certain quotas of education and public employment. It has been so successful that more castes are demanding to be scheduled as backward. More socially dubious is the Nigerian system of state quotas of higher education and of public employment.

- Price subsidies. Though anathema to neo-liberals and with many unwanted side-effects, many people still rely on large schemes of subsidized food, energy, and other essentials, such as the Indian Public Distribution System.
- Micro-credit. Providing small sums of credit to poor people, mainly women, without collateral, this was developed in Bangladesh by the Grameen Bank and others. Similar programmes have spread across the South, but with mixed results.
- Social pensions. The South African social pension programme is nominally means-tested but in practice provides near-universal pensions to citizens over 70 years. It is being extended in Namibia as a universal unconditional cash transfer programme.

This incomplete list demonstrates that constructing social policy is a continually creative process, not a list of practices to be learned from Beveridge or other Western models. The challenges facing the South are formidable, but their very different character and contexts will stimulate new forms of social policies as yet unimagined, as well as the adaptation of proven programmes from Europe and the West.

CLIMATE CHANGE: A NEW AND UNPRECEDENTED CHALLENGE

Livelihoods and well-being across the planet now face a formidable new long-term challenge: climate change. But while the economics and politics of this challenge are the object of energetic enquiry (e.g. IPCC 2007; Stern 2007; Giddens 2009), its implications for social policy are unstudied (see Gough et al. 2008, for arguments and references).

What are the implications of climate change for social policies and welfare states? Social policy is often defined as the public management of social risks. These policies usually address *idiosyncratic* risks: individually unpredictable but collectively predictable. But climate change is a *systemic* risk: 'novel, big, global, long-term, persistent and uncertain' (Stern 2007: 25). Moreover, unlike the consequences of early industrialization, which were visible and directly felt by many people, and which generated new social forces fostering collective mobilizations to correct or prevent them, the 'externalities' of climate change are distant in time and global in space; the material bases for collective mobilizations are far weaker. The climate challenge more resembles a wartime emergency mobilization.

The direct harmful impacts on human livelihoods and well-being are predicted to be most dire in the tropics and subtropics. The fact that the adverse effects will fall disproportionately on poor peoples with no responsibility for the past accumulation of greenhouse gases raises profound issues of social justice, which we cannot address here. Instead we return to the implications for social policies in Europe and the West, the home of welfare states. According to Gough et al. (2008), these fall into four categories:

1. *Direct* risks to well-being. Though more modest than in the global South, these will still be real and adverse, especially in coastal areas and Mediterranean regions. This poses new challenges for traditional social programmes, for example, new housing and settlement patterns, new insurance costs, health demands of extreme climatic events, the management of natural disasters and their dislocations and traumas.

2. *Indirect* risks to well-being. Perhaps the most significant in Europe would be climate migration from the developing world: the report of Javier Solana and Benita Ferrero-Waldner has told the EU to prepare for 'a flood of climate change migrants'.

3. Implications of climate *adaptation* policies. There will be an opportunity cost in making settlements, infrastructure, and buildings more resilient to climate change. Thus there is potential fiscal competition between welfare and environmental demands, unless synergies are exploited.

4. Implications for 'traditional' social policy of climate *mitigation* policies. These are the most significant for European welfare states. Much will depend on the policies implemented to reduce carbon emissions and their redistributive effects.

After decades of market solutions, climate change brings back centre stage the role of *public governance*. The comparative evidence is clear: social democratic welfare states and some continental welfare states have been pioneers in developing comprehensive environmental policies, including climate change mitigation. Thus the novelty and scale of climate change risks is driving a new governance agenda. This may benefit strong welfare states as suggested above. But on the other hand it may threaten them. Climate change might displace social policy issues, by providing a new focus of countervailing governance in the twenty-first century, by capturing the political imagination and weakening the traditional concerns of social justice.

More profound still is the potential challenge of climate change to economic growth and thus to welfare states' past dependence on economic growth. The key issue is whether we can move to a sustainable low carbon world whilst still maintaining growth in the West. Here there is at present a dominant consensus that sufficient investment in alternative technologies can achieve growing production and consumption whilst massively cutting carbon emissions—the two can be 'decoupled'. If so, the material base of Western welfare states can persist. But there are strong and growing reasons to doubt this optimistic scenario, as argued by Jackson in the United Kingdom Sustainable Development Commission (UK SDC 2009).

The key issue is that, even if the required huge reductions in carbon emissions per unit of output were achieved, it would allow for no greater catch-up by the developing world. The world in 2050 would be one of similarly egregious inequalities and suffering to the present; indeed absolute inequalities would be greater. And it would be a world of continuing cumulative income growth in the West, with average incomes more than doubling again. To achieve a world where the entire population enjoyed an income comparable with EU citizens *today*, the world economy would need to grow 6 times between now and 2050, implying a technical shift of still higher orders of magnitude if climatic disaster is to be avoided.

At this point the climate change debate intersects with the ethics and politics of human well-being. There is now growing evidence that excessive economic growth beyond some point (that has been exceeded in most OECD countries) can harm objective well-being and subjective well-being (Kasser 2002), as well as environmental sustainability. The strong implication is that to preserve the planet and its fundamental resource system, and to improve global social justice, growth in the West must be curbed, probably ended, and perhaps reversed.

This is a very different political and economic scenario from the environmental concerns of early social policy, such as sanitation, sewage, urban industrial pollution, and, in the conquered colonial areas, tropical diseases. Dealing with them was not cost-free, but it did not involve holding back the opulent lifestyle of the privileged. On the contrary, those local environmental policies were a boon also to the latter. Similarly, the huge post-war welfare state provides obvious benefits as well as costs to major constituencies. But if the growth state on which the welfare state was built is quite simply unsustainable in the West, the welfare state will have to transform.

THE CURRENT CRISIS OF FINANCIALIZED CAPITALISM

This links to the second systemic challenge to Western welfare states, which have flourished in an era of persistent economic growth. Does an effective welfare state therefore *require* a growth state? If so, the current economic and financial crisis poses another fundamental challenge to existing welfare states.

The expansionary period 1950–75 certainly recorded fast absolute growth in the value of social spending and a rising share of GDP. This was driven by several 'automatic factors', notably demographic change and the 'relative price effect'. But it also reflected the emergence and labelling of 'new needs' and pressures for higher standards and greater coverage coming from a resurgent labour movement and a plethora of new social movements. By 1980 predictions of a crisis of the welfare state were common. But as Glennerster shows in the previous chapter, national

welfare systems have displayed great ingenuity in confronting many of these problems. In addition, the opportunity cost of private market alternatives has been high,
sometimes ruinously so. As a result social expenditure continued to climb, both
absolutely and relatively, in the neoliberal and Third Way dominated decades following 1980.

The term 'crisis' has certainly been overused in the past, but following 2008 it is
surely appropriate. It reflects not simply the global recession of 2009, but the collapse
of a global model of financialized capitalism, ushered in by Thatcher and Reagan in
1980. This model comprised inter alia financial liberalization, new forms of corporate
governance and a huge rise in credit/debt; for example, mortgage borrowing exceeds
100 per cent of GDP in the United Kingdom. One immediate effect of this is that
public spending to deal with defaults and the banking crisis have been huge (20 per
cent of GDP in the United Kingdom, 7 per cent of GDP in the United States) and will
compete with the welfare state for public funds.

More significant still in the longer run is the end of personal consumption as the
driver of capital accumulation in the West. Since 1980, profit shares have risen, wage
shares have fallen, and the wage share has become skewed towards the rich. The
corollary was that mass consumption spending was supported more and more by
borrowing (Glyn 2007). This model has been exposed as unsustainable and also very
risky, especially for highly-indebted English-speaking liberal market economies.
Alongside climate change, the restructuring of capitalism provides a second reason
why the share of consumption in the economy may have to decline.

Thus the scenario is for feeble growth rates, the repayment of debt, and very likely
falling levels of personal consumption. In fiscal terms the challenge of climate change
will require very substantial public investment as argued above. Environmental
spending plus climbing debt interest would thus narrow the scope for expenditure
on traditional social programmes. Yet politically, a need for greater redistribution
would emerge in a less benign world of contracting incomes and still faster contracting
consumption.

Outside the North Atlantic region the perspectives are different. The crisis from
2008 has brought home the importance of a public social safety net for the whole
population. Pensions cannot be left as an appendix to the financial market, as the
World Bank taught in the 1990s. The Chinese government has recognized the role of
an expansive social policy in boosting domestic demand, and the public health
service which was left to fall apart in the 1980s–1990s will now be put together
again. But in the South too, though in different ways, social prospects will very
much depend on what happens to economic growth. By early 2009 the crisis had
spawned no major socio-political realignments, neither in the South nor in the
North, with the possible exception of the Obama election in the United States, the
social reach of which is still undecided.

The implications of the challenges of climate change and the new crisis of capitalism
are still unclear. There is a growing consensus on the 'Green New Deal' as a way of
tackling both. But beyond that we need to consider new forms of de-commodification
that transcend those of the welfare state. If both market and state threaten planetary

resources, we need to reconsider the 'core economy' and the role that it can play in enhancing human well-being. This would point to such policies as prioritizing preventive health, constructing sustainable public services, and creating local support networks. The systemic nature of the current crisis may provide an opportunity for a radical rethinking of the future of Western welfare states.

The developed welfare state was a response to the social challenges of industrial capitalism, particularly in the class-structured European road to modernity. It was a response made fully possible by the unprecedented economic growth in the decades after World War II. It has proved itself a resilient institution under neoliberal attack. As capitalism and proletarianization spread across the world, demands for social insurance and social rights will grow in the new century, but the forms in which such demands are realized will likely differ from existing models. However, in both North and South, policies for security, justice, and well-being will have to factor in the challenges to all three posed by global threats of environmental disasters. The twentieth-century formula of economic growth and social security/justice will no longer be adequate.

References

Notes on the Bibliography: All Web sources were verified between 7 and 10 September 2009; links are provided in a complete Word version of the bibliography at http://www.state.uni-bremen.de/handbook-welfare-state. When article, chapter or book titles are cited in a foreign language, the English translation is given in brackets. Databases are indicated as such by the addition of 'Database:' before the title. If an acronym like OECD is cited as such in the text, then it will be found in the bibliography under the acronym rather than the full name (which is shown in parentheses under the first listing). Reprints of much of the theoretical literature can be found in Leibfried and Mau (2008a); this is indicated in parentheses after the citation for the original publication. Leibfried and Mau (2008b: xxxviii f.) also present an overview of the Anglo-American journals with good social policy coverage; for an international list of such journals see the links at http://www.z-sozialreform.de.

AARTS, LEO J. M., BURKHAUSER, RICHARD V., and DE YONG, PHILIP R., 1998. Convergence: A comparison of European and United States disability policy, in *New Approaches to Disability in the Work Place*, ed. Terry Thomason, John F. Burton, and Douglas Hyatt, Ithaca, NY: Cornell University Press, 299–338.

AASVE, ARNSTEIN, MAZZUCO, STEFANO, and MENARINI, LETIZIA, 2005. Childbearing and well-being: A comparative analysis of European welfare regimes. *Journal of European Social Policy*, 15 (4): 283–99.

ABBOTT, KENNETH W., and SNIDAL, DUNCAN, 2000. Hard and soft law in international governance. *International Organization*, 54 (3): 421–56.

ABRAHAM, JOHN, and LEWIS, GRAHAM, 2000. *Regulating Medicines in Europe. Competition, Expertise and Public Health*. London: Routledge.

ABRAHAMSON, PETER, 1999a. The welfare modelling business. *Social Policy & Administration*, 33 (4): 394–415.

—— 1999b. The Scandinavian model of welfare, in *Comparing Social Welfare Systems in Europe*, Vol. 4: *Copenhagen Conference. France–Nordic Europe*, ed. Dennis Bouget and Bruno Palier, Paris: Service de l'Information et de la Communication (SICOM) for the Mission Interministérielle Recherche-Expérimentation (MIRE) under DREES (Ministère des affaires sociales, du travail et de la solidarité, Direction de la recherche, des études, de l'évaluation et des statistiques), 31–60.

—— 2003. The end of the Scandinavian model? Welfare reform in the Nordic countries. *Journal of Societal and Social Policy*, 2 (2): 19–36.

ABU SHARKH, MIRIAM, and GOUGH, IAN, 2010. Global welfare regimes: A cluster analysis. *Global Social Policy* 10 (1): 1–32.

ACEMOGLU, DARON, and ROBINSON, JAMES A., 2005. *Political Origins of Dictatorship and Democracy*. Cambridge: Cambridge University Press.

ACEMOGLU, DARON, and SHIMER, ROBERT, 2000. Productivity gains from unemployment insurance. *European Economic Review*, 44 (7): 1195–224.

ACKERMAN, BRUCE, and ALSTOTT, ANNE, 1999. *The Stakeholder Society.* New Haven, CT: Yale University Press.

ADAM, STUART, and BROWN, JAMES, 2000. *A Survey of the UK Tax System.* London: Institute for Fiscal Studies, Briefing Note No. 9. Available at http://www.ifs.org.uk/bns/bn09.pdf.

ADAMS, JULIA, CLEMENS, ELISABETH S., and ORLOFF, ANN SHOLA, 2005. *Remaking Modernity: Politics, History, and Sociology.* Durham, NC: Duke University Press.

ADB (ASIAN DEVELOPMENT BANK), 2008. *Key Indicators, 2008.* Manila, Philippines: ADB.

ADDISON, JOHN T., TEIXEIRA, PAULINO, and GROSSO, JEAN-LUC, 2000. The effect of dismissals protection on employment: More on a vexed theme. *Southern Economic Journal*, 67 (1): 105–22.

ADEMA, WILLEM, 1999. 'Net social expenditures' (OECD Labour Market and Social Policy Occasional Papers, 39). Paris: OECD. Available at http://ideas.repec.org/p/oec/elsaaa/39-en.html.

ADEMA, WILLEM, and EINERHAND, MARCEL, 1998. 'The growing role of private social benefits' (Labour Market and Social Policy Occasional Papers, 32). Paris: OECD. Available at http://www.olis.oecd.org/olis/1998doc.nsf/LinkTo/NT000008FA/$FILE/04E81564.PDF.

ADEMA, WILLEM, and LADAIQUE, MAXIME, 2005. 'Net social expenditure, 2005 Edition: More comprehensive measures of social support and a selection of charts & tables' (OECD Social, Employment and Migration Working Papers, 29). Paris: OECD. Available at http://www.oecd.org/dataoecd/56/2/35632106.pdf.

—— —— 2009. How expensive is the welfare state? Gross and net indicators in the OECD Social Expenditure Database (SOCX) (OECD Social Employment and Migration Working Papers, 92). Paris: OECD. Available at www.oecd.org/els/workingpapers.

AGELL, JONAS, 1996. Why Sweden's welfare state needed reform. *Economic Journal*, 106 (439): 1760–71.

AGELL, JONAS, LINDH, THOMAS, and OHLSSON, HENRY, 1997. Growth and the public sector: A critical review essay. *European Journal of Political Economy*, 13 (1): 33–52.

AHN, NAMKEE, and DE LA RICA, SARA, 1997. The underground economy in Spain: An alternative to unemployment. *Applied Economics*, 29 (6): 733–43.

AKALIN, AYSE, 2007. Hired as a caregiver, demanded as a housewife: Becoming a migrant domestic worker in Turkey. *European Journal of Women's Studies*, 14 (3): 209–25.

ALBER, JENS, 1979. The growth of social insurance in Western Europe: Has social democracy made a difference? Paper presented at IPSA World Congress. Moscow, 12–18 August (unpubl. MS).

—— 1981. Government responses to the challenge of unemployment: The development of unemployment insurance in Western Europe, in *The Development of Welfare States in Europe and America*, ed. Peter Flora and Arnold J. Heidenheimer, New Brunswick, NJ: Transaction Press, 151–83.

—— 1982. *Vom Armenhaus zum Wohlfahrtsstaat. Analysen zur Entwicklung der Sozialversicherung in Westeuropa [From Poorhouse to Welfare State: Analyses on the Development of Social Insurance in Western Europe].* Frankfurt a.M.: Campus.

—— 1983. Einige Grundlagen und Begleiterscheinungen der Entwicklung der Sozialausgaben in Westeuropa [Some basics for and consequences of the development of welfare state expenditure in Western Europe]. *Zeitschrift für Soziologie*, 12 (2): 93–118.

—— 1986. Germany, in *Growth to Limits. The Western European Welfare States Since World War II*. Vol. 2: *Germany, United Kingdom, Ireland, Italy*, ed. Peter Flora. Berlin: Walter de Gruyter, 1–154.

—— 1989. *Der Sozialstaat in der Bundesrepublik: 1950–1983 [The Welfare State in the Federal Republic of Germany 1950–1983]*. Frankfurt a.M.: Campus.

—— 1995. A framework for the comparative study of social services. *Journal of European Social Policy*, 5 (2): 131–49.

—— 2006. The European Social Model and the United States. *European Union Politics*, 7 (3): 393–419.

ALBER, JENS, and STANDING, GUY, 2000. Social dumping, catch-up, or convergence? Europe in a comparative global context. *Journal of European Social Policy*, 10 (2): 99–119.

ALBERTINI, MARCO, KOHLI, MARTIN, and VOGEL, CLAUDIA, 2006. Intergenerational transfers of time and money in European families: Common patterns–different regimes? *Journal of European Social Policy*, 17 (4): 319–34.

ALESINA, ALBERTO, and GLAESER, EDWARD L., 2004. *Fighting Poverty in the US and Europe. A World of Difference*. Oxford: Oxford University Press.

ALESINA, ALBERTO, GLAESER, EDWARD L., and SACERDOTE, BRUCE, 2001. Why doesn't the United States have a European-style welfare state? *Brookings Papers on Economic Activity*, 2001 (2): 187–254.

ALESTALO, MATTI, and KUHNLE, STEIN, 1987. The Scandinavian route: Economic, social, and political developments in Denmark, Finland, Norway, and Sweden, in *The Scandinavian Model. Welfare States and Welfare Research*, ed. Robert Erikson, Erick Jørgen Hansen, Stein Ringen, and Hannu Uusitalo, Armonk, NY: M. E. Sharpe, 3–38.

ALFORD, ROBERT R., 1975. *Health Care Politics. Ideological and Interest Group Barriers to Reform*. Chicago: University of Chicago Press.

ALKIRE, SABINA, 2002. Dimensions of human development. *World Development*, 30 (2): 181–205.

ALLAN, JAMES P., and SCRUGGS, LYLE A., 2004. Political partisanship and welfare state reform in advanced industrial societies. *American Journal of Political Science*, 48 (3): 496–512.

ALLARD, GAYLE, and LINDERT, PETER H., 2004. Reconciling unemployment and growth in the OECD, in *Growing Public: Social Spending and Economic Growth since the Eighteenth Century*, ed. Peter H. Lindert, 5th edn, Cambridge: Cambridge University Press, 100–21.

ALLEN, DAVID, 2005. Cohesion and Structural Funds, in *Policy-Making in the European Union* (5th edn.), ed. Helen Wallace, William Wallace and Mark A. Pollack, Oxford: Oxford University Press, 213–41.

ALLISON, PAUL D., 1974. *Event History Modeling: A Guide for Social Scientists*. Beverly Hills: Sage.

ALLMENDINGER, JUTTA, EBNER, CHRISTIAN, and NIKOLAI, RITA, 2009. Soziologische Bildungsforschung [Education research in Sociology], in *Handbuch Bildungsforschung*, ed. Rudolf Tippelt and Bernhard Schmidt, Wiesbaden: VS-Verlag, 47–70.

ALLMENDINGER, JUTTA, and LEIBFRIED, STEPHAN, 2003. Education and the welfare state: The four worlds of competence production. *European Journal of Social Policy*, 13 (1): 63–81.

ÅLUND, ALEKSANDRA, and SCHIERUP, CARL-ULRIK, 1991. *Paradoxes of Multiculturalism. Essays on Swedish Society*. Aldershot: Avebury.

ALY, GÖTZ, 2008. *Hitler's Beneficiaries: Plunder, Racial War and the Nazi Welfare State*. New York: Metropolitan.

AMENTA, EDWIN, 1993. The state of the art in welfare state research on social spending efforts in capitalist democracies since 1960. *American Journal of Sociology*, 99 (3): 750–63.

AMENTA, EDWIN, 1998. *Bold Relief: Institutional Politics and the Origins of Modern American Social Policy*. Princeton, NJ: Princeton University Press.

—— 2003. What we know about the development of social policy: Comparative and historical research in comparative and historical perspective, in *Comparative Historical Analysis in the Social Sciences*, ed. James Mahoney and Dietrich Rueschemeyer, Cambridge: Cambridge University Press, 91–130 (reprint in Leibfried and Mau 2008*a*: vol. 1, 22–61).

AMENTA, EDWIN, CAREN, NEAL, and OLASKY, SHEERA JOY, 2005. Age for leisure? Political mediation and the impact of the pension movement on U.S. old-age policy. *American Sociological Review*, 70 (3): 516–38.

AMENTA, EDWIN, CAREN, NEAL, OLASKY, SHEERA JOY, and STOBAUGH, JAMES E., 2009. All the movements fit to print: Who, what, when, where, and why SMOs appeared in the New York Times in the twentieth century. *American Sociological Review*, 74 (4), 636–56.

AMENTA, EDWIN, and HALFMAN, DREW, 2000. Wage wars: Institutional politics, the WPA, and the struggle for U.S. social policy. *American Sociological Review*, 65 (4): 506–28.

ANDALL, JACQUELINE, 2003. Hierarchy and interdependence: The emergence of a service caste in Europe, in *Gender and Ethnicity in Contemporary Europe*, ed. Jacqueline Andall, Oxford: Berg, 39–60.

ANDERSEN, TORBEN M., HOLMSTRÖM, BENGT, HONKAPOHJA, SEPPO, KORKMAN, SIXTEN, SÖDERSTRÖM, HANS TSON, and VARTIAINEN, JUHANA, 2007. *The Nordic Model: Embracing Globalization and Sharing Risks*. Helsinki: The Research Institute of the Finnish Economy (ETLA). Available at http://www.etla.fi/files/1892_the_nordic_model_complete.pdf.

ANDERSON, BRIDGET, 2000. *Doing the Dirty Work: The Global Politics of Domestic Labour*. London: Zed Books.

—— 2007. A very private business: Exploring the demand for migrant domestic workers. *European Journal of Women's Studies*, 14 (3): 247–64.

ANDERSON, ELIZABETH, 1999. What is the point of equality? *Ethics*, 109 (2): 287–337.

ANDERSON, KAREN M., 2001. The politics of retrenchment in a social democratic welfare state: Reform of Swedish pensions and unemployment insurance. *Comparative Political Studies*, 34 (9): 1063–91.

ANDERSON, KAREN M., and LYNCH, JULIA, 2007. Reconsidering seniority bias: Ageing, internal institutions, and union support for pension reform. *Comparative Politics*, 39 (2): 189–208.

ANDERSON, ODIN W., 1963. Medical care: Its social and organizational aspects: Health services systems in the United States and other countries. *New England Journal of Medicine*, 269 (16, October 17): 839–43.

ANDRESS, HANS-JÜRGEN, and HEIEN, THORSTEN, 2001. Four worlds of welfare state attitudes? A comparison of Germany, Norway, and the United States. *European Sociological Review*, 17 (4): 337–56.

ANDRESS, HANS-JÜRGEN, HEIEN, THORSTEN, and HOFÄCKER, DIRK, 2001. *Wozu brauchen wir noch den Sozialstaat? Der deutsche Sozialstaat im Urteil seiner Bürger [Do we still need a welfare state? The German Welfare State as Judged by its Citizens]*. Wiesbaden: Westdeutscher Verlag.

ANSELL, BENJAMIN W., 2008*a*. Traders, teachers, and tyrants: Democracy, globalization, and public investment in education. *International Organization*, 62 (2): 289–322.

—— 2008*b*. University challenges: Explaining institutional change in higher education. *World Politics*, 60 (2): 189–230.

ANTHIAS, FLOYA, and LAZARIDIS, GABRIELLA (eds.), 1999. *Into the Margins: Migration and Exclusion in Southern Europe*. Aldershot: Ashgate.

ANTONNEN, ANNELI, and SIPILÄ, JORMA, 1996. European social care services: Is it possible to identify models? *Journal of European Social Policy*, 6 (2): 87–100.

APPLICA, CESEP, and European Centre, 2007. Study of compilation of disability statistical data from the administrative registers of the member states: Study financed by DG Employment, Social Affairs, and Equal Opportunities (contract no. VC/2006/0229) Brussels etc.: APPLICA, CESEP, and European Centre. Available at http://ec.europa.eu/employment_social/index/comp_disb_final_en.pdf.

ARCHER, MARGARET S., 1989. Cross-national research and the analysis of educational systems, in *Cross-National Research in Sociology*, ed. Melvin L. Kohn, Newbury Park etc.: Sage, 243–62.

ARMINGEON, KLAUS, 2002. The effects of negotiation democracy: A comparative analysis. *European Journal of Political Research*, 41 (1): 81–105.

—— 2004. OECD and national welfare state development, in *The OECD and European Welfare States*, ed. Klaus Armingeon and Michelle Beyeler, Cheltenham: Edward Elgar, 226–41.

—— 2007. Active labour market policy, international organizations and domestic politics. *Journal of European Public Policy*, 14 (6): 905–32. Available at http://www.informaworld.com/10.1080/13501760701497923.

ARMINGEON, KLAUS, and BEYELER, MICHELLE (eds.), 2004. *The OECD and European Welfare States*. Cheltenham: Edward Elgar.

ARMINGEON, KLAUS, and BONOLI, GIULIANO (eds.), 2006. *The Politics of Post-Industrial Welfare States: Adapting Post-War Social Policies to New Social Risks*. London: Routledge.

ARRETCHE, MARTA, 2006. Toward a unified and more equitable system: Health reform in Brazil, in *Crucial Needs, Weak Incentives: Social Sector Reform, Democratization, and Globalization in Latin America*, ed. Robert R. Kaufman and Joan M. Nelson, Baltimore, MD: Johns Hopkins University Press, 155–88.

ARRIBA, ANA, CALZADA, INÉS, and DEL PINO, ELOÍSA, 2006. *Los ciudadanos y el Estado de Bienestar en España (1985–2005) [The Citizens and the Welfare State in Spain (1985–2005)]*. Madrid: Centro de Investigaciones Sociológicas.

ARRIBA, ANA, and MORENO, LUIS, 2005. Spain: Poverty, social exclusion and safety nets, in *Welfare State Reform in Southern Europe. Fighting Poverty and Social Exclusion in Italy, Spain, Portugal and Greece*, ed. Maurizio Ferrara, London: Routledge, 141–203.

ARROW, KENNETH J., 1963. Uncertainty and the welfare economics of medical care. *American Economic Review*, 53 (5): 941–73.

ARTS, WIL [also WIL A. or WILHELMUS ANTONIUS], 2002. Pathways to the future of the welfare state: Institutional persistence, hybridization, reflexive modernization, or what?, in *Social Security in Transition*, ed. Jos Berghman, Ad Nagelkerke, Monica Boos, Reinoud Doeschot and Gijsbert Vonk, The Hague: Kluwer Law International, 21–34.

ARTS, WIL A., and GELISSEN, JOHN, 2001. Welfare states, solidarity and justice principles: Does the type really matter? *Acta Sociologica*, 44 (4): 283–99.

—— —— 2002. Three worlds of welfare capitalism or more? A state-of-the-art report. *Journal of European Social Policy*, 12 (2): 137–58.

ASHFORD, DOUGLAS E., 1993. Advantages of complexity: Social insurance in France, in *The French Welfare State: Surviving Social and Ideological Change*, ed. John S. Ambler, New York: New York University Press, 32–57.

ATHUKORALA, PREMA-CHANDRA, and MANNING, CHRIS, 1999. Hong Kong and Singapore: City states shaped by migrants, in *Structural Change and International Migration in East Asia: Adjusting to Labour Scarcity*, ed. Prema-Chandra Athukorala and Chris Manning, Oxford: Oxford University Press, 122–48.

ATKINSON, ANTHONY B., 1998a. *Poverty in Europe*. Oxford: Blackwell.

—— 1998b. Political arithmetic: Financial poverty in the European Union—The measurement of poverty: Two cautionary tales, in *Poverty in Europe*, ed. Anthony B. Atkinson, Oxford: Blackwell, 10–17.

—— 2004. The Luxembourg Income Study (LIS): Past, present and future. *Socio-Economic Review*, 2 (4): 165–90.

ATKINSON, ANTHONY B., and BOURGUIGNON, FRANÇOIS, 2000. Introduction: Income distribution and economics, in *Handbook of Income Distribution*. Vol. 1, ed. Anthony B. Atkinson and François Bourguignon, Amsterdam: Elsevier, 1–58.

ATKINSON, ANTHONY B., and MICKLEWRIGHT, JOHN, 1991. Unemployment compensation and labor market transitions: A critical review. *Journal of Economic Literature*, 29 (4): 1679–727.

ATKINSON, ANTHONY B., and MOGENSEN, GUNNAR V. (eds.), 1993. *Welfare and Work Incentives: A North-European Perspective*. Oxford: The Clarendon Press of Oxford University Press.

ATKINSON, ANTHONY B., RAINWATER, LEE, and SMEEDING, TIMOTHY M., 1995. *Income Distribution in OECD Countries: The Evidence from the Luxembourg Income Study (LIS)*. Paris: OECD.

ATKINSON, ROB, and DAVOUDI, SIMIN, 2000. The concept of social exclusion in the European Union: Context, development and possibilities. *Journal of Common Market Studies*, 38 (3): 427–48.

AUER, PETER, 2000. *Employment Revival in Europe: Labour Market Success in Austria, Denmark, Ireland, and the Netherlands*. Geneva: International Labour Organization. Available at http://econpapers.repec.org/bookchap/iloesbook/ebook1.htm.

AUST, ANDREAS, and ARRIBA, ANA, 2005. Towards activation? Social assistance reforms and discourses, in *Ideas and Welfare State Reform in Western Europe*, ed. Peter Taylor-Gooby, Basingstoke: Palgrave Macmillan, 100–23.

AUSTEN-SMITH, DAVID, and WALLERSTEIN, MICHAEL, 2006. Redistribution and affirmative action. *Journal of Public Economics*, 90 (10/11): 1789–823.

AVDAGIC, SABINA, 2005. State-labour relations in East Central Europe: Explaining variations in union effectiveness. *Socio-Economic Review*, 3 (1): 25–53.

AVDAGIC, SABINA, RHODES, MARTIN, and VISSER, JELLE (eds.), 2010. *Social Pacts in Europe: Emergence, Evolution, and Institutionalization*. (forthcoming; for a summary, see http://www.connex-network.org/eurogov/pdf/egp-newgov-N-05-01.pdf).

AVELINO, GEORGE, BROWN, DAVID S., and HUNTER, WENDY, 2005. The effects of capital mobility, trade openness, and democracy on social spending in Latin America, 1980–1999. *American Journal of Political Science*, 49 (3): 625–41.

AZARIADIS, COSTAS, and DRAZEN, ALLEN, 1990. Threshold externalities in development economics. *Quarterly Journal of Economics*, 105 (2): 501–26.

BACCARO, LUCIO, 2002. Negotiating the Italian pension reform with the unions: Lessons for corporatist theory. *Industrial and Labor Relations Review*, 55 (3): 413–31.

BACCARO, LUCIO, and LOCKE, RICHARD M., 1996. Public sector reform and union participation: The case of the Italian pension reform. Paper presented at Annual meeting of the

American Political Science Association. San Francisco, 29 August–1 September. Available at http://ideas.repec.org/p/mit/sloanp/2633.html.

BACHE, IAN, 2007. The politics of redistribution, in *Handbook of European Union Politics*, ed. Knud Erik Jørgensen, Mark A. Pollack, and Ben Rosamond, London: Sage, 395–412.

BÄCKMAN, OLOF, 2005. 'Welfare states, social structure and the dynamics of poverty rates: A comparative study of 16 countries, 1980–2000' (Institute for Future Studies Working Paper Series, 7). Stockholm: Institute for Future Studies. Available at http://ideas.repec.org/p/hhs/ifswps/2005_007.html.

BÄCKSTRÖM, AANDERS, and DAVIE, GRACE (with Ninna Edgardh and Per Pettersson) (eds.), 2009. *Welfare and Religion in 21st Century Europe*, 2 vols. Aldershot: Ashgate.

BACON, ROBERT W., and ELTIS, WALTER, 1978. *Britain's Economic Problem: Too few Producers*. London: Macmillan.

BAHLE, THOMAS, 2007. *Wege zum Dienstleistungsstaat. Deutschland, Frankreich und Großbritannien im Vergleich [En Route to the Service State: Germany, France and Great Britain Compared]*. Wiesbaden: VS-Verlag.

—— 2008. Family policy patterns in the enlarged EU, in *Handbook of Quality of Life in the Enlarged European Union*, ed. Jens Alber, Tony Fahey, and Chiara Saraceno, London: Routledge, 100–25.

—— 2009. Public child care in Europe: Historical trajectories and new directions, in *Child Care and Preschool Development in Europe–Institutional Perspectives*, ed. Kirsten Scheiwe and Harry Willekens, Basingstoke: Palgrave Macmillan, 23–42.

BAKER, DEAN, GLYN, ANDREW, HOWELL, DAVID, and SCHMITT, JOHN, 2004. 'Unemployment and labour market institutions: The failure of the empirical case for deregulation' (Working Paper, 43). Geneva: ILO. Available at http://www.ilo.org/integration/resources/papers/lang--en/docName--WCMS_079135/index.htm.

BALDWIN, PETER, 1990. *The Politics of Social Solidarity: Class Bases of the European Welfare State 1875–1975*. Cambridge: Cambridge University Press (Introduction in Leibfried and Mau 2008a: vol. 1, 423–76).

—— 1996. Can we define a European welfare state model?, in *Comparative Welfare Systems: The Scandinavian Model in a Period of Change*, ed. Bent Greve, Basingstoke: Macmillan, 29–44.

—— 1999. *Contagion and the State in Europe: 1830–1930*. Cambridge: Cambridge University Press.

—— 2009. *The Narcissism of Minor Differences: How America and Europe are Alike*. Oxford: Oxford University Press.

BALL, MICHAEL, 2009. *RICS European Housing Review 2009*. Brussels: RICS (The Royal Institute of Chartered Surveyors). Available at http://www.iut.nu/Facts%20and%20figures/RICS/2009EuropeanHousingReviewl.pdf.

BALZAC, HONORÉ DE, 1896–1898. *La comédie humaine*, ed. George Saintsbury. London: J. M. Dent, 37 vols. (first publ. in French 1829 ff.).

BAMBRA, CLARE, 2005a. Worlds of Welfare and the health care discrepancy. *Social Policy and Society*, 4 (1): 31–41.

—— 2005b. Cash versus services: 'Worlds of Welfare' and the decommodification of cash benefits and health care services. *Journal of Social Policy*, 34 (2): 195–213.

—— 2006. Decommodification and the worlds of welfare revisited. *Journal of European Social Policy*, 16 (1): 73–80.

BANKS, JAMES, DISNEY, RICHARD, DUNCAN, ALAN S., and VAN REENAN, JOHN, 2005. The internationalisation of public welfare policy. *The Economic Journal*, 115 (502): C62–81.

BANTING, KEITH G., 2000. Looking in three directions: Migration and the European welfare state in comparative perspective, in *Immigration and Welfare: Challenging the Borders of the Welfare State*, ed. Michael Bommes and Andrew Geddes, London: Routledge, 13–33 (reprint in Leibfried and Mau 2008a: vol. 3, 410–34).

BANTING, KEITH G., JOHNSTON, RICHARD, KYMLICKA, WILL, and SOROKA, STUART, 2006. Do multiculturalism policies erode the welfare state? An empirical analysis, in *Multiculturalism and the Welfare State: Recognition and Redistribution in Contemporary Democracies*, ed. Keith G. Banting and Will Kymlicka, Oxford: Oxford University Press, 49–91 (reprint in Leibfried and Mau 2008a: vol. 3, 435–92).

BANTING, KEITH G., and KYMLICKA, WILL (eds.), 2006a. *Multiculturalism and the Welfare State: Recognition and Redistribution in Contemporary Democracies*. Oxford: Oxford University Press.

——— ——— 2006b. Introduction: Multiculturalism and the welfare state: Setting the context, in *Multiculturalism and the Welfare State: Recognition and Redistribution in Contemporary Democracies*, ed. Keith G. Banting and Will Kymlicka, Oxford: Oxford University Press, 1–45.

BARBIER, JEAN-CLAUDE, 2004. Systems of social protection in Europe: Two contrasted paths to activation, and maybe a third, in *Labour and Employment Regulation in Europe*, ed. Jens Lind, Herman Knudsen, and Henning Jørgensen, Brussels: Peter Lang, 233–54.

BARGAIN, OLIVER, and ORSINI, KRISTIAN, 2006. Beans for breakfast? How exportable is the British workfare model? *Research in Labour Economics*, 25: 165–98. Available at http://www.emeraldinsight.com/10.1016/S0147–9121(06)25007–6.

BARR, NICHOLAS A., 1992. Economic theory and the welfare state. *Journal of Economic Literature*, 30 (2): 741–803.

BARR, NICHOLAS A., and DIAMOND, PETER A., 2006. The economics of pensions. *Oxford Review of Economic Policy*, 22 (1): 15–39.

——— ——— 2008. *Reforming Pensions: Principles and Policy Choices*. Oxford: Oxford University Press.

BARRIENTOS, ARMANDO, 2004. Latin America: Towards a liberal-informal welfare regime, in *Insecurity and Welfare Regimes in Asia, Africa and Latin America: Social Policy in Development Contexts*, ed. Ian Gough, Geoffrey D. Wood, Armando Barrientos, Philippa Bevan, Peter Davis, and Graham Room, Cambridge: Cambridge University Press, 121–68.

BARRIENTOS, ARMANDO, and HOLMES, REBECCA, 2006. Database: Social Assistance in Developing Countries Database. Version 2.0. London: DFID (UK Department for International Development). Available at http://www.chronicpoverty.org/publications/details/social-assistance-in-developing-countries-database-version-2-0.

BARRIENTOS, ARMANDO, and HULME, DAVID (eds.), 2008. *Social Protection for the Poor and the Poorest. Concepts, Policies and Politics*. Basingstoke: Palgrave Macmillan.

BARRO, ROBERT J., and SALA-I-MARTIN, XAVIER, 1995. *Economic Growth*. New York: McGraw Hill.

BARRY, BRIAN M., 1991. Justice between generations, in *Liberty and Justice*, ed. Brian Barry, Oxford: Oxford University Press, 242–58.

——— 2005. *Why Social Justice Matters*. Cambridge: Polity.

BARRY, BRIAN M., and GOODIN, ROBERT E., 1992. *Free Movement*. London: Harvester Wheatsheaf.

BARRY, NORMAN, 1997. Conservative thought and the welfare state. *Political Studies*, 45 (2): 331–45.

BARTELS, LARRY, 2008. *Unequal Democracy: The Political Economy of the New Gilded Age.* Princeton, NJ: Princeton University Press.

BARTH, ERLING, and MOENE, KARL O., 2009. The equality multiplier. Oslo: Department of Economics, University of Oslo. Available at http://papers.ssrn.com/sol3/papers.cfm?abstract_id=1418934.

BAUMOL, WILLIAM J., 1967. Macroeconomics of unbalanced growth: The anatomy of urban crisis. *American Economic Review*, 57 (3): 415–26.

BAUMOL, WILLIAM J., and OATES, WALLACE E., 1972. The cost disease of the personal services and the quality of life. *Skandinaviska Enskilda Banken Quarterly Review*, 1 (2): 44–54.

BAWN, KATHLEEN, and ROSENBLUTH, FRANCES MCCALL, 2006. Short and long coalitions: Electoral accountability and the size of the public sector. *American Journal of Political Science*, 50 (2): 251–65.

BAYLY, CHRISTOPHER A., 2004. *The Birth of the Modern World, 1780–1914: Global Connections and Comparisons.* Oxford: Blackwell.

BEAN, CLIVE, and PAPADAKIS, ELIM, 1998. A comparison of mass attitudes towards the welfare state in different institutional regimes, 1985–1990. *International Journal of Public Opinion Research*, 10 (3): 211–36.

BECK, NATHANIEL, 2007. From statistical nuisance to serious modeling: Changing how we think about the analysis of time-series-cross-section data. *Political Analysis*, 15 (2): 97–100.

BECK, ULRICH, 1992. *Risk Society: Towards a New Modernity.* London: Sage.

—— 1999. *World Risk Society.* Cambridge: Polity.

BECKER, GARY S., 1981. *A Treatise on the Family.* Cambridge, MA: Harvard University Press.

—— 1994. *Human Capital: A Theoretical and Empirical Analysis with Special Reference to Education.* Chicago: University of Chicago Press.

BELAND, DANIEL, 2005. *Social Security: History and Politics from the New Deal to the Privatization Debate.* Lawrence, KS: University Press of Kansas.

BELAND, DANIEL, and HACKER, JACOB S., 2004. Ideas, private institutions and American welfare state exceptionalism: The case of health and old-age insurance, 1915–1965. *International Journal of Social Welfare*, 13 (1): 42–54.

BELL, MARK, 2004. A patchwork of protection: The new anti-discrimination law framework. *Modern Law Review*, 67 (3): 465–77.

BELOT, MICHÈLE, and OURS, JAN C. VAN, 2001. Unemployment and labor market institutions: An empirical analysis. *Journal of the Japanese and International Economies*, 15 (4): 403–18.

—— —— 2004. Does the recent success of some OECD countries in lowering their unemployment rates lie in the clever design of their labor market reforms? *Oxford Economic Papers*, 56 (4): 621–42.

BEN-ARIEH, ASHER, KAUFMAN, NATALIE H., ANDREWS, ARLENE B., GOERGE, ROBERT M., LEE, BONG JOO, and ABER, J. LAWRENCE, 2001. *Measuring and Monitoring Children's Well Being.* Dordrecht, Netherlands: Kluwer Academic Press.

BENEDICT XVI., 2009. *Charity in Truth (Caritas in Veritate).* Ft. Collins, CO: Ignatius.

BENOIT, KENNETH, and LAVER, MICHAEL, 2006. *Party Policy in Modern Democracies.* London: Routledge.

BENSON, JOHN, and ZHU, YING (eds.), 2008. *Trade Unions in Asia: An Economic and Sociological Analysis.* London: Routledge.

BERGER, SUZANNE, 1987. Religious transformations and the future of politics, in *Changing Boundaries of the Political: Essays on the Evolving Balance between the State and Society, Public and Private in Europe,* ed. Charles S. Maier, Cambridge: Cambridge University Press, 107–49.

BERGER, STEFAN, and COMPSTON, HUGH (eds.), 2002. *Policy Concertation and Social Partnership in Western Europe: Lessons for the 21st Century.* New York: Berghahn.

BERGQVIST, CHRISTINA, BORCHORST, ANNETTE, CHRISTENSEN, ANN-DORTE, RAMSTEDT-SILÉN, VIVECA, RAAUM, NINA C., and STYRKÁRSDÓTTIR, AUUR, 1999. *Equal Democracies? Gender and Politics in the Nordic Countries.* Oslo: Scandinavian University Press.

BERKEL, RIK VAN, and HORNEMANN MØLLER, IVER, 2002. *Active Social Policies in the EU. Inclusion through Participation?* Bristol: Policy Press.

BERKOWITZ, EDWARD, and BERKOWITZ, MONROE, 1984. The survival of workers' compensation. *Social Service Review,* 58 (2): 259–80.

BERKOWITZ, EDWARD, and MCQUAID, KIM, 1980. *Creating the Welfare State: The Political Economy of Twentieth-Century Reform.* New York: Praeger.

BERLIN, ISAIAH, 1969. Two concepts of liberty, in *Four Essays on Liberty,* ed. Isaiah Berlin, Oxford: Oxford University Press, 118–72.

BERMEO, NANCY G. (ed.), 2000. *Unemployment in Southern Europe: Coping with the Consequences.* London: Frank Cass.

BERTOLA, GIUSEPPE, 2000. Policy choices and interactions with existing instruments. *OECD Economic Studies,* 31 (2): 185–98.

BERTRANOU, FABIO M., SOLORIO, CARMEN, and GINNEKEN, WOUTER VAN (eds.), 2002. *Pensiones no contributivas y asistenciales: Argentina, Brasil, Chile, Costa Rica y Uruguay [Non-contributory pensions and social assistance: Argentina, Brazil, Costa Rica and Uruguay].* Santiago de Chile: Oficina Internacional del Trabajo (ILO). Available at http://www.oitchile.cl/pdf/publicaciones/pro/pro012.pdf.

BETTIO, FRANCESCA, and PLANTENGA, JANNEKE, 2004. Comparing care regimes in Europe. *Feminist Economics,* 10 (1): 85–113.

BEVERIDGE, WILLIAM H., 1942. *Social Insurance and Allied Services, Presented to Parliament as Command Paper 6404. Report by Sir William Beveridge [The Beveridge Report].* London: HMSO.

BEYME, KLAUS VON, 1985. *Political Parties in Western Democracies.* Aldershot: Gower.

BIEBACK, KARL-JÜRGEN, 1992. Family benefits: The new legal structures of subsidizing the family. *Journal of European Social Policy,* 2 (4): 239–54.

BIRCHFIELD, VICKI, and CREPAZ, MARKUS L., 1998. The impact of constitutional structures and collective and competitive veto points on income inequality in industrialized democracies. *European Journal of Political Research,* 34 (2): 175–200.

BLAIR, TONY, and SCHRÖDER, GERHARD, 1999. Europe: The Third Way. Available at http://www.fcpp.org/main/publication_detail.php?PubID=349.

BLANCHARD, OLIVER, 1991. Wage bargaining and unemployment persistence. *Journal of Money, Credit and Banking,* 23 (3): 277–92.

BLANCHARD, OLIVER, and KATZ, LAWRENCE F., 1997. What we know and do not know about the natural rate of unemployment. *Journal of Economic Perspectives,* 11 (1): 51–71.

BLANK, ROBERT H., and BURAU, VIOLA, 2007. *Comparative Health Policy.* Basingstoke: Palgrave Macmillan (2nd edn.).

BLEKESAUNE, MORTEN, and QUADAGNO, JILL S., 2003. Public attitudes toward welfare state policies: A comparative analysis of 24 nations. *European Sociological Review*, 19 (5): 415–27.

BLESES, PETER, and SEELEIB-KAISER, MARTIN, 2004. *The Dual Transformation of the German Welfare State*. Basingstoke: Palgrave Macmillan.

BLOCK, FRED, 1984. The ruling class does not rule: Notes on the Marxist theory of the state, in *The Political Economy*, ed. Thomas Ferguson and Joel Rogers, Armonk, NY: M. E. Sharpe (1st edn. 1977), 32–46.

BLOMBERG-KROLL, HELENA, 1999. *Kosta vad det kosta vill? Attitydmönster och attitydförändringar hos befolkning och eliter beträffande välfärdsservicen i nedskärningarnas tid [At Any Cost? Attitude Patterns and Attitude Changes Regarding Welfare Services among the Population and Elite Groups in Times of Cuts]*. Vasa: Institutionen för socialpolitik, Samhälls- och vårdvetenskapliga fakulteten, Åbo akademi.

BLYTH, MARK, 2001. The transformation of the Swedish model: Economic ideas, distributional conflict, and institutional change. *World Politics*, 54 (1): 1–26.

BMA (BUNDESMINISTERIUM FÜR ARBEIT UND SOZIALORDNUNG) and BA (BUNDESARCHIV), 2001–9. *Geschichte der Sozialpolitik in Deutschland seit 1945 [History of Social Policy in Germany since 1945]*, 11 vols. & 10 vols. documentation. Baden-Baden: Nomos.

BOARINI, ROMINA, and MIRA D'ERCOLE, MARCO, 2006. Measures of material deprivation in OECD countries (OECD Social, Employment and Migration Working Paper, 37). Paris: OECD Directorate for Employment, Labour and Social Affairs. Available at http://www.oecd.org/dataoecd/52/5/37223552.pdf.

BOCK, GISELA, and THANE, PAT (eds.), 1991. *Maternity and Gender Policies: Women and the Rise of the European Welfare States, 1880s–1950s*. London: Routledge.

BOIX, CARLES, 1998. *Political Parties, Growth and Equality: Conservative and Social Democratic Economic Strategies in the World Economy*. Cambridge: Cambridge University Press.

—— 1999. Setting the rules of the game: The choice of electoral systems in advanced democracies. *American Political Science Review*, 93 (3): 609–24.

—— 2003. *Democracy and Redistribution*. Cambridge: Cambridge University Press.

BOLDERSON, HELEN, and MABBETT, DEBORAH, 2001. Non-discriminating social policy? Policy scenarios for meeting needs without categorisation, in *What Future Social Security? Debates and reforms in national and cross-national perspective*, ed. Jochen Clasen, The Hague & Bristol: Kluwer Law International & Policy, 53–67.

BOLIN, KRISTIAN, LINDGREN, BJÖRN, and LUNDBORG, PETTER, 2008. Your next of kin or your own career? Caring and working among the 50+ of Europe. *Journal of Health Economics*, 27 (3): 718–38.

BOLING, PATRICIA, 2008. Demography, culture and policy: Understanding Japan's low fertility. *Population and Development Review*, 34 (2): 307–26.

BOLZENDAHL, CATHERINE, 2009. Making the implicit explicit: Gender influences on social spending in twelve industrialized democracies, 1980–99. *Social Politics*, 16 (1): 40–81.

BOMMES, MICHAEL, and HALFMANN, JOST, 1998. *Migration in nationalen Wohlfahrtstaaten: Theoretische und vergleichende Untersuchungen [Migration in National Welfare States: Theoretical and Comparative Inquiries]*. Osnabrück: Universitätsverlag Rasch.

BONASTIA, CHRIS, 2000. Why did affirmative action in housing fail during the Nixon era? Exploring the 'institutional homes' of social policies. *Social Problems*, 47 (4): 523–42.

BONNETT, ALASTAIR, 2006. The Americanisation of anti-racism? Global power and hegemony in ethnic equity. *Journal of Ethnic and Migration Studies*, 32 (7): 1083–103.

BONOLI, GIULIANO, 1997. Classifying welfare states: A two-dimensional approach. *Journal of Social Policy*, 26 (3): 351–72 (reprint in Leibfried and Mau 2008*a*: vol. 2, 78–99).

—— 2000*a*. *The Politics of Pension Reform: Institutions and Policy Change in Western Europe.* Cambridge: Cambridge University Press.

—— 2000*b*. Public attitudes to social protection and political economy traditions in Western Europe. *European Societies*, 2 (4): 431–52.

—— 2003. The two worlds of pension reform in Western Europe. *Comparative Politics*, 35 (4): 399–416.

—— 2005. The politics of the New Social Policies. Providing coverage against new social risks in mature welfare states. *Policy & Politics*, 33 (3): 431–49 (reprint in Leibfried and Mau 2008*a*: vol. 1, 497–516).

—— 2006*a*. The politics of the New Social Policies. Providing coverage against social risks in mature welfare states, in *The Politics of Postindustrial Welfare States*, ed. Klaus Armingeon and Giuliano Bonoli, London: Routledge, 3–26.

—— 2006*b*. Providing coverage against new social risks in mature welfare states, in *The Welfare State Reader*, ed. Christopher Pierson and Francis G. Castles, Cambridge: Polity, 389–407.

—— 2007. Time matters: Postindustrialization, new social risks, and welfare state adaptation in advanced industrial democracies. *Comparative Political Studies*, 40 (5): 495–520.

BONOLI, GIULIANO, and POWELL, MARTIN, 2002. Third Ways in Europe? *Social Policy and Society*, 1 (1): 59–66.

BOREUS, KRISTINA, 1997. The shift to the right: Neo-liberalism in argumentation and language in the Swedish public debate since 1969. *European Journal of Political Research*, 31 (3): 257–86.

BORRE, OLE, and SCARBROUGH, ELINOR, 1995. *The Scope of Government.* Oxford: Oxford University Press.

BORSAY, ANNE, 2005. *Disability and Social Policy in Britain since 1750: A History of Exclusion.* Basingstoke: Palgrave Macmillan.

BÖRSCH-SUPAN, AXEL H., REIL-HELD, ANETTE, and WILKE, CHRISTINA BENITA, 2007. How an unfunded pension system looks like defined benefits but works like defined contributions: The German Pension Reform, in *Estado de bienestar y competitividad. La experiencia europea*, ed. Alvaro Espina, Madrid: Fundación Carolina, 319–47.

BOTTEN, GRETE, ELVBAKKEN, KARI TORE, and KILDAL, NANNA, 2003. The Norwegian welfare state on the threshold of a new century. *Scandinavian Journal of Public Health*, 31 (2): 81–84.

BOWLES, SAMUEL, and GINTIS, HERBERT, 1999. Is equality passé? Homo reciprocans and the future of egalitarian politics. *Boston Review*, 23 (6): 4–10. Available at http://www.umass.edu/preferen/gintis/isinequa.pdf.

BOX-STEFFENSMEIER, JANET M., and JONES, BRADFORD S., 2004. *Event History Modeling: A Guide for Social Scientists.* New York: Kindle Books.

BRADBURY, BRUCE, and JÄNTTI, MARKUS, 1999. Child poverty across industrialized nations' (Innocenti Occasional Paper, 71). Florence: UNICEF International Child Development Centre. Available at http://www.unicef-irc.org/publications/pdf/eps71.pdf.

BRADLEY, DAVID, HUBER, EVELYN, MOLLER, STEPHANIE, NIELSEN, FRANÇOIS O., and STEPHENS, JOHN D., 2003. Distribution and redistribution in postindustrial democracies. *World Politics*, 55 (2): 193–228.

BRADLEY, DAVID, and STEPHENS, JOHN D., 2007. Employment performance in OECD countries. *Comparative Political Studies*, 40 (12): 1486–510.

BRADSHAW, JONATHAN R., 2006. Child benefit packages in 15 countries in 2004, in *Children, Changing Families and the Welfare State*, ed. Jane Lewis, Cheltenham: Edward Elgar, 69–89.

BRADSHAW, JONATHAN R., and ATTAR-SCHWARTZ, SHALHEVET, 2010. Fertility and social policy, in *Fertility and Public Policy: How to Reverse the Fertility Decline*, ed. Martin Werding and Noriyuki Takayama, Cambridge, MA: MIT Press (forthcoming).

BRADSHAW, JONATHAN R., DITCH, JOHN, HOLMES, HILARY, and WHITEFORD, PETER, 1993. A comparative study of child support in fifteen countries. *Journal of European Social Policy*, 3 (4): 255–71.

BRADSHAW, JONATHAN R., and FINCH, NAOMI, 2002. 'A comparison of child benefit packages in 22 countries' (Department for Work and Pensions Research Report, 174). Leeds: Corporate Document Services. Available at http://research.dwp.gov.uk/asd/asd5/rrep174.pdf.

BRADSHAW, JONATHAN R., HOELSCHER, PETRA, and RICHARDSON, DOMINIC, 2006. Comparing child well-being in OECD countries: Concepts and methods (Innocenti Working Papers, IWP-2006–03). Florence: Innocenti Research Centre. Available at http://www.unicef-irc.org/publications/pdf/iwp2006_03_eng.pdf.

—— —— 2007. An index of child well-being in the European Union. *Social Indicators Research*, 80 (1): 133–77.

BRADSHAW, JONATHAN R., and MAYHEW, EMESE, 2006. Family benefit packages, in *Social Policy, Family Change and Employment in Comparative Perspective*, ed. Jonathan Bradshaw and Aksel Hatland, Cheltenham: Edward Elgar, 97–117.

BRADSHAW, JONATHAN R., and PIACHAUD, DAVID, 1980. Child support in the European Community (Occasional Paper in Social Administration, 66). London: Bedford Square Press.

BRADSHAW, JONATHAN R., and RICHARDSON, DOMINIC, 2009. Child well-being in Europe, *Journal of Child Indicators Research*, 2 (3): 319–50.

BRADY, DAVID, BECKFIELD, JASON, and SEELEIB-KAISER, MARTIN, 2005. Economic globalization and the welfare state in affluent democracies, 1975–2001. *American Sociological Review*, 70 (6): 921–48.

BRADY, DAVID, BECKFIELD, JASON, and ZHAO, WEI, 2007. The consequences of economic globalization for affluent democracies. *Annual Review of Sociology*, 33: 313–34.

BRADY, DAVID, FULLERTON, ANDREW, and CROSS, JENNIFER M., 2008. Putting poverty in political context: A multi-level analysis of working-aged poverty across 18 affluent democracies (Working Paper, 487). Luxembourg: Luxembourg Income Study. Available at http://www.lisproject.org/publications/liswps/487.pdf.

BRANDOLINI, ANDREA, and SMEEDING, TIMOTHY M., 2007. Inequality patterns in western-type democracies: Cross-country differences and time changes (Luxembourg Income Study Working Paper Series, 458). Luxembourg: Luxemburg Income Study. Available at http://www.lisproject.org/publications/liswps/458.pdf.

BREGER, MONIKA, 1982. *Die Haltung der industriellen Unternehmer zur staatlichen Sozialpolitik in den Jahren 1878–1891 [The Approach of Industrial Entrepreneurs to Public Social Policy between 1878 and 1891]*. Frankfurt a.M.: Haag + Herchen.

BRENNAN, DEBORAH, 2007. Babies, budgets, and birthrates: Work/family policy in Australia 1996–2006. *Social Politics*, 14 (1): 31–57.

BRENNAN, GEOFFREY, and BUCHANAN, JAMES M., 1980. *The Power to Tax: Analytical Foundations of a Fiscal Constitution*. Cambridge: Cambridge University Press.

BRESLIN, MARY LOU, and YEE, SILVIA (eds.), 2004. *Disability Rights Law and Policy: International and National Perspectives.* Washington, DC: Disability Rights Education and Defense Fund. Available at http://www.dredf.org/international/book.shtml.

BRIDGEN, PAUL, and HARRIS, BERNARD (eds.), 2007. *Charity and Mutual Aid in Europe and North America since 1800.* London: Routledge.

BRIGGS, ASA, 1961. The welfare state in historical perspective. *Archives Européennes de Sociologie,* 2 (2): 221–58.

BRIGHOUSE, HARRY, 2000. *School Choice and Social Justice.* Oxford: Oxford University Press.

BRINKLEY, ALAN, 1996. *The End of Reform: New Deal Liberalism in Recession and War.* New York: Vintage.

BRODSKY, JENNY, HABIB, JACK, and HIRSCHFELD, MIRIAM (eds.), 2008. *Long-term Care in Developing Countries. Ten Case Studies.* Geneva: World Health Organization. Available at http://www.who.int/chp/knowledge/publications/Case_studies/en/index.html.

BROOKS, CLEM, and MANZA, JEFF, 2006. Why do welfare states persist? *Journal of Politics,* 68 (4): 816–27.

—— —— 2007. *Why Welfare States Persist: The Importance of Public Opinion in Democracies.* Chicago: University of Chicago Press.

BROOKS, SARAH M., 2002. Social protection and economic integration: The politics of pension reform in an era of capital mobility. *Comparative Political Studies,* 35 (5): 491–523.

—— 2005. Interdependent and domestic foundations of policy change: The diffusion of pension privatization around the world. *International Studies Quarterly,* 49 (2): 273–94.

—— 2007. When does diffusion matter? Explaining the spread of structural pension reforms across nations. *Journal of Politics,* 69 (3): 701–15. Available at http://ssrn.com/abstract=1065984.

—— 2009. *Social Protection and the Market in Latin America: The Transformation of Social Security Institutions.* Cambridge: Cambridge University Press.

BROWNING, EDGAR K., 1975. Why the social insurance budget is too large in a democracy. *Economic Inquiry,* 13 (3): 373–87.

BRUCE, MAURICE, 1968. *The Coming of the Welfare State.* London: Batsford (4th edn.).

BRUIJN, HANS DE, 2007. *Managing Performance in the Public Sector.* London: Routledge.

BRUSH, LISA D., 2002. Changing the subject: Gender and welfare regime studies. *Social Politics: International Studies in Gender State and Society,* 9 (2): 161–86.

BUCHAN, JAMES, 2006. The impact of global nursing migration on health services delivery. *Policy, Politics, & Nursing Practice,* 7 (3): 16S–25S.

BUDGE, IAN, and KEMAN, HANS, 1993. *Parties and Democracies: Coalition Formation and Government Functioning in Twenty States.* Oxford: Oxford University Press.

BUDGE, IAN, KLINGEMANN, HANS-DIETER, VOLKENS, ANDREA, BARA, JUDITH, and TANENBAUM, ERIC, 2001. *Mapping Policy Preferences: Estimates for Parties, Electors, and Governments 1945–1998.* Oxford: Oxford University Press.

BURAU, VIOLA D., THEOBALD, HILDEGARD, and BLANK, ROBERT H., 2007. *Governing Home Care: A Cross-national Comparison.* Cheltenham: Edward Elgar.

BURGOON, BRIAN, 2001. Globalization and welfare compensation: Disentangling the ties that bind. *International Organization,* 55 (3): 509–51.

BUSCH, KLAUS, 2000. Economic integration and the welfare state: The corridor model as a strategy for an European social policy, in *The Role of the Social Sciences in the Making of the European Union,* ed. Max Haller, Berlin: Springer, 25–42.

BUSEMEYER, MARIUS R., 2007. Bildungspolitik in den USA: Eine historisch-institutionalistische Perspektive auf das Verhältnis von öffentlichen und privaten Bildungsinstitutionen [Education policy in the USA: A historical-institutionalist perspective on the relationship between public and private education institutions]. *Zeitschrift für Sozialreform*, 53 (1): 57–78.

—— 2008. The impact of fiscal decentralization on education and other types of spending. *Swiss Political Science Review*, 14 (3): 451–81.

—— 2009a. Asset specificity, institutional complementarities and the variety of skill regimes in coordinated market economies. *Socio-Economic Review*, 7 (3): 375–406.

—— 2009b. Social democrats and the new partisan politics of public investment in education. *Journal of European Public Policy*, 16 (1): 107–26.

—— 2009c. From myth to reality: Globalization and public spending in OECD countries revisited. *European Journal of Political Research*, 48 (4): 455–82.

BUTLER, JUDITH, 1990. *Gender Trouble: Feminism and the Subversion of Identity*. London: Routledge.

—— 2004. *Undoing Gender*. London: Routledge.

BUTLER, JUDITH, and SCOTT, JOAN W., 1992. *Feminists Theorize the Political*. London: Routledge.

CALAVITA, KITTY, 2005. *Immigrants at the Margins: Law, Race, and Exclusion in Southern Europe*. Cambridge: Cambridge University Press.

CALDER, KITTY, 1986. *Crisis and Compensation: Public Policy and Stability in Japan*. Princeton, NJ: Princeton University Press.

CALMFORS, LARS, and DRIFFILL, JOHN, 1988. Coordination of wage bargaining. *Economic Policy*, 6 (1): 14–61.

CAMERON, DAVID R., 1978. The expansion of the public economy: A comparative analysis. *American Political Science Review*, 72 (4): 1243–61.

—— 1984. Social Democracy, corporatism, labour quiescence, and the representation of economic interest in advanced capitalist society, in *Order and Conflict in Contemporary Capitalism*, ed. John H. Goldthorpe, Oxford: Oxford University Press, 143–78.

CAMINADA, KOEN, and GOUDSWAARD, KEES PIETER, 2005. Are public and private social expenditures complementary? *International Advances in Economic Research*, 11 (2): 175–89.

CAMPBELL, ANGUS, CONVERSE, PHILIP E., MILLER, WARREN E., and STOKES, DONALD E., 1960. *The American Voter*. Chicago: University of Chicago Press.

CAMPBELL, IAN, 1996. *Compensation for Personal Injury in New Zealand*. Auckland: Auckland University Press.

CAMPBELL, JOHN C., 1992. *How Policies Change: The Japanese Government and the Aging Society*. Princeton, NJ: Princeton University Press.

CAMPBELL, JOHN C., and IKEGAMI, NAOKI, 1998. *The Art of Balance in Health Policy*. Cambridge: Cambridge University Press.

CAMPBELL, MARY, 2008. Labour's policy on money for parents: Combining care with paid work. *Social Policy and Society*, 7 (4): 457–70.

CAMPODÓNICO, M., 2007. Bajan edad para cobro de pensión a la vejez [Lower age limit for old age pension payments]. *Diario el Observador*, 6 December 2007.

CANTILLON, BEA, GHYSELS, JORIS, MUSSCHE, NINKE, and VAN DAM, RUDI, 2001. Female employment differences, poverty and care provisions. *European Societies*, 3 (4): 447–69.

CANTILLON, BEA, VAN MECHELEN, NATASCHA, and SCHULTE, BERND, 2008. Minimum income policies in old and new member states, in *Handbook of Quality of Life in the*

Enlarged European Union, ed. Jens Alber, Tony Fahey, and Chiara Saraceno, London: Routledge, 218–34.

CAO, XUN, PRAKASH, ASEEM, and WARD, MICHAEL D., 2007. Protecting jobs in the age of globalization: Examining the relative salience of social welfare and industrial subsidies in OECD countries. *International Studies Quarterly*, 51 (2): 301–27.

CAPUCHA, LUIS, BOMBA, TERESA, FERNÁNDEZ, RITA, and MATOS, GISELA, 2005. Portugal: A virtuous path towards minimum income?, in *Welfare State Reform in Southern Europe: Fighting Poverty and Social Exclusion in Italy, Spain, Portugal and Greece*, ed. Maurizio Ferrera, London: Routledge, 204–65.

CARDOZO, SANTIAGO, 2008. 'Políticas de educación: Políticas educativas, logros y desafíos del sector en Uruguay 1990–2008 [Politics of education: Education politics—Accomplishments and challenges in the area of education politics in Uruguay 1990–2008]' (Cuadernos de ENIA). Montevideo: Comité de Coordinación Estratégica Nacional para la Infancia y la Adolescencia (CCE). Available at http://www.enia.org.uy/pdf/Politicas_educativas.pdf.

CAREN, NEAL, and PANOFSKY, AARON, 2005. TQCA: A technique for adding temporality to qualitative comparative analysis. *Sociological Methods & Research*, 34 (2): 147–72.

CARLSON, ALLAN C., 1990. *The Swedish Experiment in Family Politics*. Edison, NJ: Transaction.

CARMICHAEL, FIONA, HULME, CLAIRE, SHEPPARD, SALLY, and CONNELL, GEMMA, 2008. Work-life imbalance: Informal care and paid employment in the UK. *Feminist Economics*, 14 (2): 3–35.

CARROLL, EERO, 1999. *Emergence and Structuring of Social Insurance Institutions*. Edsbruk: Akademitryck.

CASTELLS, MANUEL, 1996. *The Rise of the Network Society*. Oxford: Blackwell.

CASTIGLIONI, ROSSANA, 2005. *The Politics of Social Policy Change in Chile and Uruguay: Retrenchment versus Maintenance, 1973–1998*. London: Routledge.

CASTLES, FRANCIS G. (ed.), 1982a. *The Impact of Parties: Politics and Policies in Democratic Capitalist States*. London: Sage.

—— 1982b. The impact of parties on public expenditure, in *The Impact of Parties: Politics and Policies in Democratic Capitalist States*, ed. Francis G. Castles, London: Sage, 21–96.

—— 1985. *The Working Class and Welfare: Reflections on the Political Development of the Welfare State in Australia and New Zealand 1890–1980*. Wellington: Allen & Unwin.

—— 1988. *Australian Public Policy and Economic Vulnerability*. Sydney: Allen & Unwin.

—— 1989. *The Comparative History of Public Policy*. Oxford: Oxford University Press.

—— (ed.), 1993. *Families of Nations: Patterns of Public Policy in Western Democracies*. Aldershot: Dartmouth.

—— 1994a. On religion and public policy: Does catholicism make a difference? *European Journal of Political Research*, 25 (1): 19–40.

—— 1994b. Is expenditure enough? On the nature of the dependent variable in comparative public policy analysis. *Journal of Commonwealth and Comparative Politics*, 32 (3): 349–63.

—— 1995. Welfare state development in Southern Europe. *West European Politics*, 18 (2): 291–313.

—— 1997. Needs-based strategies of social protection in Australia and New Zealand, in *Welfare States in Transition: National Adaptations in Global Economies*, ed. Gøsta Esping-Andersen, London: Sage, 88–110.

—— 1998a. *Comparative Public Policy: Patterns of Post-war Transformation*. Cheltenham: Edward Elgar.

—— 1998*b*. The really big trade-off: Home ownership and the welfare state in the New World and the Old. *Acta Politica*, 33 (1): 5–19.

—— 2002*a*. The European Social Model: Progress since the early 1980s. *European Journal of Social Security*, 4 (1): 7–21.

—— 2002*b*. The world turned upside down: Below replacement fertility, changing preferences and family friendly public policy in 21 OECD countries. *Journal of European Social Policy*, 13 (3): 209–27.

—— 2002*c*. Developing new measures of welfare state change and reform. *European Journal of Political Research*, 41 (5): 613–41.

—— 2004. *The Future of the Welfare State: Crisis Myths and Crisis Realities*. Oxford: Oxford University Press.

—— 2006. The growth of the post-war public expenditure state. Long-term trajectories and recent trends (Transtate Working Paper, 35). Bremen: University of Bremen, Sonderforschungsbereich 597. Available at http://www.sfb597.uni-bremen.de/pages/pubApBeschreibung.php?SPRACHE=en&ID=38.

—— (ed.), 2007*a*. *The Disappearing State? Retrenchment Realities in an Age of Globalisation*. Cheltenham: Edward Elgar.

—— 2007*b*. Testing the retrenchment hypothesis: An aggregate overview, in *The Disappearing State? Retrenchment Realities in an Age of Globalization*, ed. Francis G. Castles, Cheltenham: Edward Elgar, 19–43.

—— 2009*a*. What welfare states do: A disaggregated expenditure analysis. *Journal of Social Policy*, 38 (1): 45–62.

—— 2009*b*. Patterns of state expenditure in Europe and America, in *United in Diversity? Comparing Social Models in Europe and America*, ed. Jens Alber and Neil Gilbert, Oxford: Oxford University Press, 109–32.

CASTLES, FRANCIS G., and DOWRICK, STEVE, 1990. The impact of government spending levels on medium-term economic growth in the OECD 1960–1985. *Journal of Theoretical Politics*, 2 (2): 173–204.

CASTLES, FRANCIS G., and FERRERA, MAURIZIO, 1996. Home ownership and the welfare state: Is Southern Europe different? *South European Politics and Society*, 1 (2): 163–84.

CASTLES, FRANCIS G., and MERRILL, VANCE, 1989. Towards a general model of public policy outcomes. *Journal of Theoretical Politics*, 1 (2): 177–212.

CASTLES, FRANCIS G., and MITCHELL, DEBORAH, 1990. Three worlds of welfare capitalism or four? (Discussion Paper, 21). Canberra: The Australian National University, Graduate Program in Public Policy.

—— —— 1992. Identifying welfare state regimes: The links between politics, instruments and outcomes. *Governance*, 5 (1): 1–26.

—— —— 1993. Worlds of welfare and families of nations, in *Families of Nations: Patterns of Public Policy in Western Democracies*, ed. Francis G. Castles, Aldershot: Dartmouth, 93–128.

CASTLES, FRANCIS G., and OBINGER, HERBERT, 2007. Social expenditure and the politics of redistribution. *Journal of European Social Policy*, 17 (3): 206–22.

—— —— 2008. Worlds, families, regimes: Country clusters in European and OECD area public policy. *West European Politics*, 31 (1/2): 321–44.

CASTLES, FRANCIS G., OBINGER, HERBERT, and LEIBFRIED, STEPHAN, 2005. Bremst der Föderalismus den Leviathan? Bundesstaat und Sozialstaat im internationalen Vergleich, 1880–2005 [Reining in the Leviathan? Federalism and the welfare state, 1880–2005]. *Politische Vierteljahresschrift*, 46 (2): 215–37.

CASTLES, FRANCIS G., and UHR, JOHN, 2005. Australia: Federal constraints and institutional innovations, in *Federalism and the Welfare State. New World and European Experiences*, ed. Herbert Obinger, Stephan Leibfried, and Francis G. Castles, Cambridge: Cambridge University Press, 51–88.

CASTLES, STEPHEN, and MILLER, MARK J., 2009. *The Age of Migration: International Population Movements in the Modern World*. Basingstoke: Palgrave Macmillan (4th edn.).

CENTRÁNGOLO, OSCAR, and GÓMEZ SABAINI, JUAN CARLOS, 2007. *La tributación directa en América Latina y los desafíos a la imposición sobre la renta [Direct taxation in Latin America and the challenges of imposing taxes on income]*. Santiago de Chile: United Nations, Economic Commission for Latin America and the Caribbean. Available at http://www.pmcgp.opp.gub.uy/evento-04–2008/documentos/oscar-cetrangolo/lcl2838_p.pdf.

CERAMI, ALFIO, 2006. *Social Policy in Central and Eastern Europe: The Emergence of a New European Welfare Regime*. Berlin: LIT.

CERAMI, ALFIO, and VANHUYSSE, PIETER (eds.), 2009. *Postcommunist Welfare Pathways: Theorizing Social Policy Transformations in Central and Eastern Europe*. Basingstoke: Palgrave Macmillan.

CHANDLER, ANDREA, 2008. The truant society: Gender, nationalism, and social welfare in Russia. Ottawa: Carleton University (unpubl. MS).

CHARLES, MARIA, and GRUSKY, DAVID B., 2004. *Occupational Ghettos: The Worldwide Segregation of Women and Men*. Stanford, CA: Stanford University Press.

CHEN, SHAOHUA, and RAVAILLON, MARTIN, 2008. The developing world is poorer than we thought, but no less successful in the fight against poverty (Policy Research Paper, 4703). Washington, DC: World Bank. Available at http://ideas.repec.org/p/wbk/wbrwps/4703.html.

CHENG, TUN-JEN, 1990. Political regimes and development strategies: South Korea and Taiwan, in *Manufacturing Miracles*, ed. Gary Gereffi and Donald L. Wyman, Princeton, NJ: Princeton University Press, 139–78.

CHERUBINI, ARNALDO, and PIVA, ITALO, 1998. *Dalla libertà all'obbligo: La previdenza sociale fra Giolitti e Mussolini [From Freedom to Obligation: Social Security from Giolitti to Mussolini]*. Milan: Franco Angeli.

CHI, IRIS, MEHTA, KALYANI M., and HOWE, ANNA L. (eds.), 2001. *Long-Term Care in the Twenty-first Century. Perspectives from around the Asia Pacific Rim*. New York: Haworth.

CHILD, JACK, 2008. *Miniature Messages: The Semiotics and Politics of Latin American Postage Stamps*. Durham, NC: Duke University Press.

CHIMERINE, LAWRENCE, BLACK, THEODORE, and COFFEY, LESTER, 1999. Unemployment insurance as an automatic stabilizer: Evidence of effectiveness over three decades (Unemployment Insurance Occasional Paper, 99–8). Washington, DC: U.S. Department of Labor. Available at http://wdr.doleta.gov/owsdrr/99–8/99–8.pdf.

CHOI, JAMES J., LAIBSON, DAVID, MADRIAN, BRIGITTE C., and METRICK, ANDREW, 2004. For better or for worse: Default effects and 401(k) savings behaviour, in *Perspectives in the Economics of Ageing*, ed. David Wise, Chicago: Chicago University Press, 81–126.

CHRISTIANSEN, NIELS FINN, and MARKKOLA, PIRJO, 2006. Introduction, in *The Nordic Model of Welfare: A Historical Reappraisal*, ed. Niels Finn Christiansen, Klaus Petersen, Nils Edling, and Per Haave, Copenhagen: Museum Tusculanum Press, 9–29.

CHRISTIANSEN, NIELS FINN, PETERSEN, KLAUS, EDLING, NIELS, and HAAVE, PER (eds.), 2006. *The Nordic Model of Welfare. A Historical Reappraisal*. Copenhagen: Museum Tusculanum Press.

CHRISTENSEN, TORN, and LAEGREID, PER, 2007. The whole-of-government approach to public sector reforms. *Public Administration Review,* 67 (6): 1059–66.

CHRISTOPHER, KAREN, 2002. Welfare state regimes and mothers' poverty. *Social Politics,* 9 (1): 60–86.

CLAPHAM, DAVID, 1995. Privatisation and the East European housing model. *Urban Studies,* 32 (4/5): 679–94.

CLARK, JANINE A., 2005. *Islam, Charity, and Activism: Middle-Class Networks and Social Welfare in Egypt, Jordan, and Yemen.* Bloomington: Indiana University Press.

CLARK, JOHN M., 1923. Overhead costs in modern industry. *Journal of Political Economy,* 31 (5): 606–36.

CLASEN, JOCHEN, 2005. *Reforming European Welfare States.* Oxford: Oxford University Press.

CLASEN, JOCHEN, and CLEGG, DANIEL, 2004. Does the Third Way work? The left and labour market policy reform in Britain, France, and Germany, in *Welfare State Change: Towards a Third Way?,* ed. Jane Lewis and Rebecca Surender, Oxford: Oxford University Press, 89–110.

CLASEN, JOCHEN, and SIEGEL, NICO A.. (eds.), 2007. *Investigating Welfare State Change: The 'Dependent Variable Problem' in Comparative Analysis.* Cheltenham: Edward Elgar.

CLAYTON, RICHARD, and PONTUSSON, JONAS, 1998. Welfare state retrenchment revisited: Entitlement cuts, public sector restructuring, and inegalitarian trends in advanced capitalist societies. *World Politics,* 51 (1): 67–98.

CLEGG, DANIEL, 2008. Continental drift on unemployment policy: Change in Bismarckian welfare states, in *Reforming the Bismarckian Welfare Systems: Broadening Perspectives in Social Policy,* ed. Bruno Palier and Claude Martin, Oxford: Blackwell, 62–81.

CNEL (CONSIGLIO NAZIONALE DELL'ECONOMIA E DEL LAVORO), 1963. Sintesi storica della previdenza sociale in Italia e dei suoi progetti di riforma, appendice A [Synthesis of the history of the Italian welfare state and its reform projects], in *Relazione preliminare sulla riforma della previdenza sociale,* ed. CNEL (Consiglio nazionale dell'economia e del lavoro), Rome: Instituto Poligrafico dello Stato, 265–345.

COCKETT, RICHARD, 1995. *Thinking the Unthinkable: Think Tanks and the Economic Counter-Revolution, 1931–1983.* London: Fontana.

COHEN, GERALD A., 1988. Freedom, justice, and capitalism, in *History, Labour and Freedom,* ed. Gerald A. Cohen, Oxford: Oxford University Press, 286–304.

—— 1989. On the currency of egalitarian justice. *Ethics,* 99 (4): 912–44.

—— 1997. Back to socialist basics (appendix: On money and liberty), in *Equality,* ed. Jane Franklin, London: Institute for Public Policy Research, 29–47.

COLLIER, DAVID, and MESSICK, RICHARD, 1975. Prerequisites versus diffusion: Testing alternative explanations of social security adoption. *American Political Science Review,* 69 (4): 1299–315.

COLLINI, STEFAN, 1991. *Public Moralists: Political Thought and Intellectual Life in Britain, 1850–1930.* Oxford: The Clarendon Press of Oxford University Press.

COMAS-HERRERA, ADELINA, WITTENBERG, RAPHAEL, COSTA-FONT, JOAN, GORI, CHRISTIANO, DIMAIO, ALESSANDRA, PATXOT, CONCEPCIÓ, PICKARD, LINDA, POZZI, ALESSANDRO, and ROTHGANG, HEINZ, 2006. Future long-term care expenditure in Germany, Spain, Italy and the United Kingdom. *Ageing & Society,* 26 (2): 285–302.

COMMANDER, SIMON, DAVOODI, HAMID R., and LEE, UNE J., 1997. The causes of government and the consequences for growth and well-being (World Bank Policy Research

Working Paper, 1785). Washington, DC: World Bank. Available at http://papers.ssrn.com/sol3/papers.cfm?abstract_id=597205.

CONLEY, DALTON, 2000. Home ownership, social insurance, and rightist response. Paper presented at Conference Proceedings on Saving, Intergenerational Transfers, and the Distribution of Wealth. Annandale-on-Hudson, NY, June 7–9. Available at http://www.levy.org/pubs/saving00.pdf.

CONLEY, DALTON, and GIFFORD, BRIAN, 2006. Home ownership, social insurance, and the welfare state. *Sociological Forum*, 21 (1): 55–82.

CONNELL, RAEWYN, 1987. *Gender and Power: Society, the Person and Sexual Politics.* Stanford, CA: Stanford University Press.

CONSEJO DE REFORMA PREVISIONAL (CONSEJO ASESOR PRESIDENCIAL PARA LA REFORMA PREVISIONAL, CHILE [PRESIDENTIAL ADVISORY COMMITTEE ON THE REFORM OF SOCIAL PROVISION, CHILE]), 2006. El derecho a una vida digna en la vejez. Informe del Consejo Asesor Presidencial para la Reforma del Sistema Previsional. Resumen Ejecutivo [The right to a dignified life in old age]. Santiago de Chile. Available at http://www.consejor-eformaprevisional.cl/documentos/InformeFinal/Resumen-Ejecutivo.pdf.

COOK, FAY L., and BARRETT, EDITH J., 1992. *Support for the American Welfare State: The Views of Congress and the Public.* New York: Columbia University Press.

COOK, LINDA J., 1993. *The Soviet Social Contract and Why It Failed: Welfare Policy and Workers' Politics from Brezhnev to Yeltsin.* Cambridge, MA: Harvard University Press.

—— 2007a. *Postcommunist Welfare States: Reform Politics in Russia and Eastern Europe.* Ithaca, NY: Cornell University Press.

—— 2007b. Negotiating welfare in postcommunist states. *Comparative Politics*, 40 (1): 41–62.

CORNIA, GIOVANNI ANDREA., 2004. *Inequality, Growth, and Poverty in an Era of Liberalization and Globalization.* Oxford: Oxford University Press.

COUGHLIN, RICHARD M., 1979. Social policy and ideology: Public opinion in eight rich nations. *Comparative Social Research*, 2: 3–40.

—— 1980. *Ideology, public opinion & welfare policy: Attitudes toward taxes and spending in industrialized societies.* Berkeley: University of California, Institute of International Studies (Research Series, 42).

COUSINS, MEL, 1997. Ireland's place in the worlds of welfare capitalism. *Journal of European Social Policy*, 7 (3): 223–35.

COWLES, MARIA GREEN, and RISSE, THOMAS, 2001. Transforming Europe: Conclusions, in *Transforming Europe: Europeanization and Domestic Change*, ed. Maria Green Cowles, James A. Caporaso, and Thomas Risse, Ithaca, NY: Cornell University Press, 217–37.

COX, ROSIE, 2006. *The Servant Problem: Domestic Employment in a Global Economy.* London: Tauris.

COX, ROSIE, and WATT, PAUL, 2002. Globalization, polarization and the informal sector: The case of paid domestic workers in London. *Area*, 34 (1): 39–47.

COX, ROBERT H., 2001. The social construction of an imperative: Why welfare reform happened in Denmark and the Netherlands, but not in Germany. *World Politics*, 53 (3): 463–98.

CRAFTS, NICHOLAS, 2003. Fifty years of economic growth in Western Europe: No longer catching up, but falling behind? (SIEPR Discussion Paper, 03–21). Stanford:: Stanford University, Stanford Institute for Economic Policy Research (SIEPR). Available at http://siepr.stanford.edu/publicationsprofile/373.

CREPAZ, MARCUS M. L., 1998. Inclusion versus exclusion: Political institutions and welfare expenditures. *Comparative Politics*, 31 (1): 61–80.

—— 2006. 'If you are my brother, I may give you a dime!' Public opinion on multicultur-alism, trust, and the welfare state, in *Multiculturalism and the Welfare State: Recognition and Redistribution in Contemporary Democracies*, ed. Keith Banting and Will Kymlicka, Oxford: Oxford University Press, 92–117.

CROISSANT, AUREL, 2004. Changing welfare regimes in East and Southeast Asia: Crisis, change and challenge. *Social Policy & Administration*, 38 (5): 504–24.

CROMPTON, ROSEMARY, 1999. *Restructuring Gender Relations and Employment: The Decline of the Male Breadwinner*. Oxford: Oxford University Press.

CROSLAND, ANTHONY, 1964. *The Future of Socialism*. London: Cape (first publ. 1956).

CROUCH, COLIN, 1993. *Industrial Relations and European State Traditions*. Oxford: The Clarendon Press of Oxford University Press.

—— 1999. *Social Change in Western Europe*. Oxford: Oxford University Press.

CROWLEY, STEPHEN, and OST, DAVID, 2001. *Workers after the Workers' State: Labour and Politics in Postcommunist Eastern Europe*. Lanham, MD: Rowman & Littlefield.

CROZIER, MICHEL, HUNTINGTON, SAMUEL P., and WATANUKI, JŌJI, 1975. *The Crisis of Democracy: Report on the Governability of Democracies to the Trilateral Commission*. New York: New York University Press.

CRUZ-SACO, MAÑA AMPARO, and MESA-LAGO, CARMELO (eds.), 1998. *Do Options Exist? The Reform of Pension and Health Care Systems in Latin America*. Pittsburgh, PA: University of Pittsburgh Press.

CUENCA, A., 2007. Plan de Equidad subsidiará agua y luz de hogares pobres [Equity Plan will subsidize water and electricity for poor homes]. *Diario el Observador*, 13 December 2007.

CUSACK, THOMAS R., 1997. Partisan politics and public finance: Changes in public spending in the industrialized democracies, 1955–1989. *Public Choice*, 91 (3/4): 375–95.

—— 2007. Sinking budgets and ballooning prices: Recent developments connected to military spending, in *The Disappearing State? Retrenchment Realities in an Age of Globa-lisation*, ed. Francis G. Castles, Cheltenham: Edward Elgar, 103–32.

CUSACK, THOMAS R., IVERSEN, TORBEN, and REHM, PHILIPP, 2006. Risks at work: The demand and supply sides of government redistribution. *Oxford Review of Economic Policy*, 22 (3): 365–89.

CUSACK, THOMAS R., IVERSEN, TORBEN, and SOSKICE, DAVID, 2007. Economic interests and the origins of electoral systems. *American Political Science Review*, 101 (3): 373–91.

CUTRIGHT, PHILLIPS, 1965. Political structure, economic development, and national social security programmes. *American Journal of Sociology*, 70 (5): 537–50.

DA ROIT, BARBARA, LE BIHAN, BLANCHE, and ÖSTERLE, AUGUST, 2007. Long-term care policies in Italy, Austria and France: Variations in cash-for-care schemes. *Social Policy & Administration*, 41 (6): 653–71.

DAATLAND, SVEIN O., and HERLOFSON, KATHARINA, 2003. 'Lost solidarity' or 'changed solidarity': A comparative European view of normative family solidarity. *Ageing & Society*, 23 (5): 537–60.

D'ADDIO, ANNA CRISTINA, and MIRA D'ERCOLE, MARCO, 2005. Trends and determinants of fertility rates in OECD countries: The role of policies (OECD Social, Employment, and Migration Working Paper, 27). Paris: OECD. Available at http://www.oecd.org/dataoecd/7/33/35304751.pdf.

DAHRENDORF, RALF, 1999. The Third Way and liberty: An authoritarian streak in Europe's new center. *Foreign Affairs*, 78 (5): 13–17.

DALY, MARY, 2000. 'A fine balance?' Women's labour market participation patterns in international comparison, in *From Vulnerability to Competitiveness: Welfare and Work in the Open Economy*, vol. II: *Diverse Responses to Common Challenges*, ed. Fritz W. Scharpf and Vivien A. Schmidt, Oxford: Oxford University Press, 467–510.

—— 2002. Care as a good for social policy. *Journal of Social Policy*, 31 (2): 251–70.

—— 2004. Changing conceptions of family and gender relations in European states and the Third Way, in *Welfare State Change Towards a Third Way?*, eds. Jane Lewis and Rebecca Surender, Oxford: Oxford University Press, 135–54.

DALY, MARY, and LEWIS, JANE, 2000. The concept of social care and the analysis of contemporary welfare states. *British Journal of Sociology*, 51 (2): 281–98.

DALY, MARY, and RAKE, KATHERINE, 2003. *Gender and the Welfare State: Care, Work and Welfare in Europe and the USA*. Cambridge: Polity.

DARITY, WILLIAM, and GOLDSMITH, ARTHUR H., 1993. Unemployment, social psychology, and unemployment hysteresis. *Journal of Post Keynesian Economics*, 16 (1): 55–71.

DAUNTON, MARTIN J., 2001. *Trusting Leviathan: The Politics of Taxation in Britain, 1799–1914*. Cambridge: Cambridge University Press.

—— 2002. *Just Taxes: The Politics of Taxation in Britain 1914–79*. Cambridge: Cambridge University Press.

DAVERI, FRANCESCO, and TABELLINI, GUIDO E., 2000. Unemployment and taxes: Do taxes affect the rates of unemployment? *Economic Policy*, 15 (30): 47–104.

DAVIS, DEBORAH S., 1989. Chinese social welfare: Policies and outcomes. *The China Quarterly*, 119 (September): 577–97.

DAY, LINCOLN, 1978. Government pensions for the aged in 19 industrialized countries, in *Comparative Studies in Sociology*, ed. Richard F. Tomasson, Greenwich, CT: JAI Press, 217–34.

DEACON, ALAN, 2000. Learning from the US? The influence of American ideas upon 'new labour' thinking on welfare reform. *Policy & Politics*, 28 (1): 5–18.

DEACON, BOB, 1993. Developments in East European social policy, in *New Perspectives on the Welfare State in Europe*, ed. Catherine Jones, London: Routledge, 177–97.

—— 2000. Eastern European welfare states: The impact of the politics of globalization. *Journal of European Social Policy*, 10 (2): 146–61.

—— 2007. *Global Social Policy and Governance*. London: Sage.

DEACON, BOB, HULSE, MICHELLE, and STUBBS, PAUL, 1997. *Global Social Policy: International Organizations and the Future of Welfare*. London: Sage (chapter 6 reprinted in Leibfried and Mau 2008a: vol. 2, 629–57).

DEAN, HARTLEY, 2003. Re-conceptualising welfare-to-work for people with multiple problems and needs. *Journal of Social Policy*, 32 (3): 441–59.

DEAN, HARTLEY, and TAYLOR-GOOBY, PETER, 1989. Statutory sick pay and the control of sickness absence. *Journal of Social Policy*, 19 (1): 47–67.

DE BÚRCA, GRÁINNE, DE WITTE, BRUNO, and OGERTSCHNIG, LARISSA (eds.), 2005. *Social Rights in Europe*. Oxford: Oxford University Press.

DE FERRANTI, DAVID, PERRY, GUILLERMO E., FERREIRA, FANCISCO H. G., and WALTON, MICHAEL, 2004. *Inequality in Latin America: Breaking with History?* Washington, DC: World Bank. Available at http://go.worldbank.org/4EYOLY9851.

DE GRAZIA, VICTORIA, 1992. *How Fascism Ruled Women: Italy, 1920–1945*. Berkeley: University of California Press.

DEL BOCA, DANIELA, and WETZELS, CÉCILE (eds.), 2008. *Social Policies, Labour Market and Motherhood*. Cambridge: Cambridge University Press.

DEVEREAUX, P.J., CHOI, PETER T. L., LACCHETTI, CHRISTINA, WEAVER, BRUCE, SCHÜNE-MANN, HOLGER J., HAINES, TED, LAVIS, JOHN D., GRANT, BRYDON J.B., HASLAM, DAVID R.S., BHANDARI, MOHIT, SULLIVAN, TERRENCE, COOK, DEBORAH J., WALTER, STEPHEN D., MEADE, MAUREEN, KHAN, HUMAIRA, BHATNAGAR, NEERA, and GUYATT, GORDON H., 2002. A systematic review and meta-analysis of studies comparing mortality rates of private for-profit and private not-for-profit hospitals. *Canadian Medical Association Journal*, 166 (11): 1399–406.

DEVEREAUX, P.J., HEELS-ANSDELL, DIANE, LACCHETTI, CHRISTINA, HAINES, TED, BURNS, KAREN E.A., COOK, DEBORAH J., RAVINDRAN, NIKILA, WALTER, S.D., MCDONALD, HEATHER, STONE, SAMUEL B., PATEL, RAKESH, BHANDARI, MOHIT, SCHÜNEMANN, HOL-GER J., CHOI, PETER T.-L., BAYOUMI, AHMED M., LAVIS, JOHN N., SULLIVAN, TERRENCE, STODDART, GREG, and GUYATT, GORDON H., 2004. Payments for care at private for-profit and private not-for-profit hospitals: A systematic review and meta-analysis. *Canadian Medical Association Journal*, 170 (12): 1817–24.

DEVINE, JOE, 2007. Governance, democracy and the politics of wellbeing (WeD (Wellbeing in Developing Countries) Working paper, 36). Bath: University of Bath—Wellbeing in Developing Countries Research Group. Available at http://www.welldev.org.uk/research/working.htm#wed36.

DEVINEY, STANLEY, 1984. The political economy of public pensions. *Journal of Political and Military Sociology*, 12 (Fall): 295–310.

DIAMANDOUROS, NIKIFOROS P., 1994. Cultural dualism and political change in post-authoritarian Greece (Working Paper, 1994/50). Madrid: Juan March Institute. Available at http://www.march.es/ceacs/ingles/publicaciones/working/archivos/1994_50.pdf.

DICKENS, CHARLES, 1849/50. *The Adventures of Oliver Twist etc*. London: Chapman & Hall (last, 2006 with Oxford University Press).

—— 1861. *Great Expectations*. London: Chapman & Hall (republished London: Folio Society 2004; Oxford: Oxford University Press, 1999).

DILNOT, ANDREW, and MCCRAE, JULIAN, 2000. The family credit system and the Working Families Tax Credit in the United Kingdom. *OECD Economic Studies*, 31 (2): 69–84. Available at http://www.oecd.org/dataoecd/6/38/2724186.pdf.

DINGELDEY, IRENE, 2000. *Erwerbstätigkeit und Familie in Steuer- und Sozialversicherungs-systemen [Employment and the Family in Tax and Social Insurance Systems]*. Opladen: Leske und Budrich.

—— 2001. European tax systems and their impact on family employment patterns. *Journal of Social Policy*, 30 (4): 653–72.

DION, MICHELLE, 2005. The origins of Mexican social security policy during the Cárdenas and Ávila Camacho administrations. *Mexican Studies*, 21 (1): 59–95.

—— 2006. Women's welfare and social security reform in Mexico. *Social Politics*, 13 (3): 400–26.

—— 2008. Pension reform and gender inequality, in *Lessons from Pension Reform in the Americas*, ed. Stephen Kay and Tapen Sinha, Oxford: Oxford University Press, 143–63.

DISNEY, RICHARD, 2004. Are contributions to public pension programmes a tax on em-ployment? *Economic Policy*, 19 (39): 267–311.

DISPERSYN, MICHEL, VAN DER VORST, PIERRE, DE FALLEUR, M., GUILLAUME, Y., HECQ, C. H., LANGE, M., and MEULDERS, DANIÈLE, 1990. La construction d'un serpent social européen [On the construction of a European 'social queue']. *Revue Belge de Sécurité Sociale*, 1990 (12): 889–980.

DI TELLA, RAFAEL, and MACCULLOCH, ROBERT, 2004. Unemployment benefits as a substitute for a conservative central banker. *The Review of Economics and Statistics* 86 (4): 911–23.

DIXIT, AVINASH K., and LONDREGAN, JOHN, 1996. The determinants of success of special interests in redistributive politics. *Journal of Politics*, 58 (4): 1132–55.

DOCTEUR, ELIZABETH, and OXLEY, HOWARD, 2003. 'Health-care systems: Lessons from the reform experience' (Economics Department working papers, 374). Paris: OECD. Available at http://www.oecd.org/dataoecd/5/53/22364122.pdf.

DODSON, JAGO, 2006. The 'roll' of the state: Government, neoliberalism and housing assistance in four advanced economies. *Housing Theory and Society*, 23 (4): 224–44.

DOLING, JOHN, and RUONAVAARA, HANNU, 1996. Home ownership undermined? An analysis of the Finnish case in the light of British experience. *Journal of Housing and the Built Environment*, 11 (1): 31–46.

DØLVIK, JON ARNE, FLÖTTEN, TONE, HERNES, GUDMUND, and HIPPE, JON (eds.), 2007. *Hamskifte: Den norske modellen i endring [Shedding Skins: The Nordic Model under Transformation]*. Oslo: Universitetsforlaget.

DONSELAAR, GIJS VAN, 2008. *The Right to Exploit: Parasitism, Scarcity, Basic Income*. Oxford: Oxford University Press.

DORWART, REINHOLD A., 1971. *The Prussian Welfare State Before 1740*. Cambridge, MA: Harvard University Press.

DOWRICK, STEVE, and NGUYEN, DUC-THO, 1987. Australia's post war economic growth: Measurement and international comparison (Paper, 160). Canberra: The Australian National University, Centre for Economic Policy Research.

DOYAL, LEN, and GOUGH, IAN, 1991. *A Theory of Human Need*. Basingstoke: Macmillan.

DOYLE, MARTHA, and TIMONEN, VIRPI, 2007. *Home Care for Ageing Populations: A Comparative Analysis of Domiciliary Care in Denmark, the United States and Germany*. Cheltenham: Edward Elgar.

DUENSING, MARTIN, 2006. Raising fertility: Lessons for Germany from cross country comparisons? (Luxembourg Income Study Working Paper, 453). Luxembourg: Luxembourg Income Study. Available at http://www.lisproject.org/publications/liswps/453.pdf.

DUNLEAVY, PATRICK, 1980. The political implications of sectional cleavages and the growth of state employment. Part 1: The analysis of production cleavages. *Political Studies*, 28 (3): 364–83.

DURKHEIM, ÉMILE, 1984. *The Division of Labour in Society*. London: Macmillan (first publ. 1893; 2nd edn. 1902, with a preface on professional organizations).

—— 1992. *Suicide. A Study in Sociology*. London: Routledge (first publ. 1897).

DÜVELL, FRANCK (ed.), 2005. *Illegal Immigration in Europe: Beyond Control*. Basingstoke: Palgrave Macmillan.

DWORK, DEBÓRAH, 1987. *War is Good for Babies and Other Young Children: A History of the Infant and Child Welfare Movement in England, 1898–1918*. London: Tavistock.

DWORKIN, GERALD, 1971. Paternalism, in *Morality and the Law*, ed. Richard A. Wasserstrom, Belmont, CA: Wadsworth, 107–26.

DWORKIN, RONALD, 2000. *Sovereign Virtue*. Cambridge, MA: Harvard University Press.

DWP (DEPARTMENT FOR WORK AND PENSIONS), 2003. *Measuring Child Poverty*. London: DWP. Available at http://www.dwp.gov.uk/docs/final-conclusions.pdf.

EARDLEY, TONY, BRADSHAW, JONATHAN R., DITCH, JOHN, GOUGH, IAN, and WHITEFORD, PETER, 1996. 'Social Assistance in OECD Countries: Synthesis Report' (Research Report,

46). London: HMSO. Department of Social Security. Available at http://research.dwp. gov.uk/asd/asd5/rrep046.pdf.

EASTERLY, WILLIAM, and REBELO, SERGIO, 1993. Fiscal policy and economic growth. *Journal of Monetary Economics*, 32 (3): 417–58.

EBBINGHAUS, BERNHARD, 2006. *Reforming Early Retirement in Europe, Japan and the USA*. Oxford: Oxford University Press.

—— 2010. Reforming Bismarckian corporatism: The changing role of social partnership in Continental Europe, in *A Long Goodbye to Bismarck? The Politics of Welfare Reforms in Continental Europe*, ed. Bruno Palier, Amsterdam: Amsterdam University Press, 250–278.

EBBINGHAUS, BERNHARD, and HASSEL, ANKE, 2000. Striking deals: Concertation in the reform of Continental European welfare states. *Journal of European Public Policy*, 7 (1): 44–62.

EBBINGHAUS, BERNHARD, and MANOW, PHILIP (eds.), 2001. *Comparing Welfare Capitalism. Social Policy and Political Economy in Europe, Japan and the USA*. London: Routledge.

EBBINGHAUS, BERNHARD, and VISSER, JELLE, 2000. *Trade Unions in Western Europe since 1945*. London: Macmillan.

ECB (EUROPEAN CENTRAL BANK), 2003. *Structural Factors in the EU Housing Markets*. Frankfurt a.M.: European Central Bank. Available at http://www.ecb.b.int/pub/pdf/ other/euhousingmarketsen.pdf.

ECKSTEIN, HARRY, 1960. *Pressure Group Politics: The Case of the British Medical Association*. London: Allen & Unwin.

—— 1975. Case Study and Theory in Political Science, in *Handbook of Political Science*, vol. 7: *Strategies of Inquiry*, ed. Fred I. Greenstein and Nelson W. Polsby, Reading, MA: Addison-Wesley, 79–137.

ECLAC (UNITED NATIONS ECONOMIC COMMISSION FOR LATIN AMERICA AND THE CARIB-BEAN) (ed.), 2002. *Social Panorama of Latin America 2001–2002*. Santiago: ECLAC. Available at http://www.eclac.org/cgi-bin/getProd.asp?xml=/dds/agrupadores_xml/ aes31.xml&xsl=/agrupadores_xml/agrupa_listado.xsl.

—— (ed.), 2007. *Social Panorama of Latin America 2007*. Santiago: ECLAC. Available at http://www.eclac.org/publicaciones/xml/9/30309/PSI2007_Sintesis_Lanzamiento.pdf.

EDLUND, JONAS, 1999a. Progressive taxation farewell? Attitudes to income redistribution and taxation in Sweden, Great Britain and the United States, in *The End of the Welfare State? Responses to State Retrenchment*, ed. Stefan Svallfors and Peter Taylor-Gooby, London: Routledge, 106–34.

—— 1999b. Trust in government and welfare regimes: Attitudes to redistribution and financial cheating in the USA and Norway. *European, Journal of Political Research*, 35 (3): 341–70.

EEKELAAR, JOHN, 2000. The end of an era?, in *Cross Currents: Family Law and Policy in the US and England*, ed. Sanford N. Katz, John Eekelaar, and Maris Maclean, Oxford: Oxford University Press, 637–55.

EGGLESTON, KAREN, SHEN, YU-CHU, LAU, JOSEPH, SCHMI, CHRISTOPER H., and CHAN, JIA, 2008. Hospital ownership and quality of care: What explains the different results in the literature? *Health Economics*, 17 (12): 1345–62.

EHRENREICH, BARBARA, and HOCHSCHILD, ARLIE R. (eds.), 2004. *Global Woman: Nannies, Maids, and Sex Workers in the New Economy*. New York: Henry Holt.

EICHHORST, WERNER, KAUFMAN, OTHON, and KONLE-SEIDL, REGINA, 2008. *Bringing the Jobless into Work? Experiences with Activation Schemes in Europe and the US.* Berlin: Springer.

EICHHORST, WERNER, and KONLE-SEIDL, REGINA, 2008. Contingent convergence: A comparative analysis of activation policies (Discussion Paper, 3905). Bonn: Institute for the Study of Labour (IZA). Available at http://ftp.iza.org/dp3905.pdf.

EISENSTADT, SHMUEL, and RONINGER, LUIS, 1984. *Patrons, Clients and Friends.* Cambridge: Cambridge University Press.

ELIASON, SCOTT, STRYKER, ROBIN, and TRANBY, ERIC., 2008. The welfare state, family policies, and women's labour market participation: Combining fuzzy-set and statistical methods to assess causal relations and estimate causal effects, in *Method and Substance in Macrocomparative Analysis*, ed. Lane Kenworthy and Alexander M. Hicks, Basingstoke: Palgrave Macmillan, 135–95.

ELLINGSÆTER, ANNE L., and LEIRA, ARNLAUG, 2006. *Politicising Parenthood in Scandinavia: Gender Relations in Welfare States.* Bristol: Policy Press.

ELLISON, NICHOLAS, 2006. *The Transformation of Welfare States?* London: Routledge.

ELLWOOD, DAVID T., 1988. *Poor Support: Poverty in the American Family.* New York: Basic Books.

ELSINGA, MARJA, PRIEMUS, HUGO, and CAO, LIOU, 2009. The government mortgage guarantee as an instrument in housing policy: Self-supporting instrument or subsidy? *Housing Studies*, 24 (1): 67–80.

ELWAN, ANN, 1999. *Poverty and Disability: A Survey of the Literature.* Washington, DC: World Bank, Social Protection Unit. Available at http://siteresources.worldbank.org/DISABILITY/Resources/280658–1172608138489/PovertyDisabElwan.pdf.

ENGELS, FRIEDRICH, 1975. The condition of the working class in England, in *Collected Works*, Vol. 4, *1844–45*, ed. Karl Marx and Friedrich Engels, New York: International Publishers, 295–596.

ENGLAND, PAULA, 2005. Emerging theories of care work. *Annual Review of Sociology*, 31: 381–99.

EPSTEIN, JESSICA, DUERR, DANIEL, KENWORTHY, LANE, and RAGIN, CHARLES, 2008. Comparative employment performance: A fuzzy-set analysis, in *Method and Substance in Macrocomparative Analysis*, ed. Lane Kenworthy and Alexander M. Hicks, Basingstoke: Palgrave Macmillan, 67–90.

ERIKSON, ROBERT, HANSEN, ERIK JØRGEN, RINGEN, STEIN, and UUSITALO, HANNU (eds.), 1987. *The Scandinavian Model. Welfare States and Welfare Research.* Armonk, NY: M. E. Sharpe.

ERIKSON, ROBERT, and JONSSON, JAN O., 1996. Introduction: Explaining class inequality in education: The Swedish test case, in *Can Education Be Equalized? The Swedish Case in Comparative Perspective*, ed. Robert Erikson and Jan O. Jonsson, Boulder, CO: Westview, 1–63.

ERVASTI, HEIKKI, FRIDBERG, TORBEN, HJERM, MIKAEL, and RINGDAL, KRISTEN, 2008. *Nordic Social Attitudes in a European Perspective.* Cheltenham: Edward Elgar.

ERVIK, RUNE, 2009. Policy actors, ideas and power: EU and OECD pension policy recommendations and national policies, in *The Role of International Organizations in Social Policy. Ideas, Actors and Impact*, ed. Rune Ervik, Nanna Kildal, and Even Nilssen, Cheltenham: Edward Elgar, 138–64.

ESPING-ANDERSEN, GØSTA, 1985a. *Politics Against Markets. The Social Democratic Road to Power.* Princeton, NJ: Princeton University Press.

—— 1985b. Power and distributional regimes. *Politics & Society*, 14 (2): 223–56.

—— 1989. The three political economies of the welfare state. *Canadian Review of Sociology and Anthropology*, 26 (1): 10–36.

—— 1990. *The Three Worlds of Welfare Capitalism*. Cambridge & Princeton, NJ: Polity & Princeton University Press (chapters 1–3 reprinted in Leibfried and Mau 2008a: vol. 2, 3–77).

—— (ed.), 1996a. *Welfare States in Transition: National Adaptations in Global Economies*. London: Sage.

—— 1996b. After the golden age? Welfare state dilemmas in a global economy, in *Welfare States in Transition: National Adaptations in Global Economies*, ed. Gøsta Esping-Andersen, London: Sage, 1–31.

—— 1996c. Welfare states without work: The impasse of labour shedding and familialism in Continental European social policy, in *Welfare States in Transition: National Adaptations in Global Economies*, ed. Gøsta Esping-Andersen, London: Sage, 66–87.

—— 1999. *Social Foundations of Postindustrial Economies*. Oxford: Oxford University Press (chapter 6 reprinted in Leibfried and Mau 2008a: vol. 2, 485–506).

—— 2000. Multi-dimensional decommodification. *Policy & Politics*, 28 (3): 353–59.

—— 2002. A child-centred social investment strategy, in *Why We Need a New Welfare State*, ed. Gøsta Esping-Andersen, Duncan Gallie, Anton Hemerijk, and John Myles, Oxford: Oxford University Press, 26–67.

—— 2003. Towards the good society, once again? Paper presented at 4th International Research Conference on Social Security of the International Social Security Association (ISSA, Geneva). Antwerpen, May 5–7. Available at http://www.ingentaconnect.com/content/oso/658357/2002/00000001/00000001/art00001.

—— 2004. Social welfare policy, comparisons, in *International Encyclopedia of the Social and Behavioural Sciences*, ed. Neil J. Smelser and Paul B. Baltes, Amsterdam: Elsevier, 14481–85.

ESPING-ANDERSEN, GØSTA, GALLIE, DUNCAN, HEMERIJCK, ANTON, and MYLES, JOHN, 2002. *Why we Need a New Welfare State*. Oxford: Oxford University Press.

ESPING-ANDERSEN, GØSTA, and KORPI, WALTER, 1984. Social policy as class politics in post-war capitalism: Scandinavia, Austria, and Germany, in *Order and Conflict in Contemporary Capitalism*, ed. John H. Goldthorpe, Oxford: The Clarendon Press of Oxford University Press, 179–208.

—— —— 1987. From Poor Relief to institutional welfare states: The development of Scandinavian social policy, in *The Scandinavian Model: Welfare States and Welfare Research*, ed. Robert Erikson, Erik J. Hanson, Stein Ringen, and Hannu Uusitalo, Armonk, NY: M. E. Sharpe, 39–74.

ESPING-ANDERSEN, GØSTA, and MYLES, JOHN, 2009. Economic inequality and the welfare state, in *Oxford Handbook of Economic Inequality*, ed. Wiemer Salverda, Brian Nolan, and Timothy M. Smeeding, Oxford: Oxford University Press, 639–64.

ESTADO DE LA NACIÓN [STATE OF THE NATION], 2004. Estado de la nación en desarrollo sostenible [State of the nation in sustainable development]. San José, Costa Rica: Programmea Estado de la Nación.

ESTÉVEZ-ABE, MARGARITA, 2005. Gender bias in skills and social policies: The Varieties of Capitalism perspective on sex segregation. *Social Politics*, 12 (2): 180–215.

ESTÉVEZ-ABE, MARGARITA, IVERSEN, TORBEN, and SOSKICE, DAVID, 2001. Social protection and the formation of skills: A reinterpretation of the welfare state, in *Varieties of Capitalism: The Institutional Foundations of Comparative Advantage*, ed. David Soskice and Peter A. Hall, Oxford: Oxford University Press, 145–83.

EUROLINK AGE, 1995. *The European Union and Older Disabled People.* London: Eurolink Age.
EUROPEAN COMMISSION, 1993. Social protection in Europe. *Document:* COM (93) 531 fin.
—— 1995. Social protection in Europe. *Document:* COM (95) 457 fin.
—— 1999. *Employment in Europe.* Brussels: Commission of the European Communities.
—— 2005. Communication from the commission: Policy plan on legal migration. *Document:* COM (2005) 669 fin.
—— 2006a. *The Impact of Ageing on Public Expenditure: Projections for the EU25 Member States on Pensions, Health Care, Long-Term Care, Education and Unemployment Transfers (2004–2050). Special Report 1/2006.* Brussels: Commission of the European Communities, Directorate-General for Economic and Financial Affairs. Available at http://ec.europa.eu/economy_finance/publications/publication6654_en.pdf.
—— 2006b. General budget of the European Union for the financial year 2006: The figures. *Document:* SEC (2006) 50.
—— 2007a. Health and long-term care in the European Union (Special Eurobarometer Report, 238). Brussels: Commission of the European Communities. Available at http://ec.europa.eu/public_opinion/archives/ebs/ebs_283_en.pdf.
—— 2007b. Towards common principles of flexicurity: More and better jobs through flexibility and security. *Document:* COM (2007) 359 fin. Available at http://ec.europa.eu/social/BlobServlet?docId=2756&langId=en.
EUROPEAN COMMISSION—SOCIAL PROTECTION COMMITTEE, 2008. Child poverty and well-being in the EU: Current status and way forward. Luxembourg: Office for Official Publications of the European Communities. Available at http://www.libertysecurity.org/IMG/pdf_ke3008251_en.pdf.
EUROSTAT, 1996. *ESSPROS Manual 1996.* Luxembourg: Office for Official Publications of the European Communities.
—— 2008. *Taxation Trends in the European Union. Data for the EU Member States and Norway. 2008 Edition.* Luxembourg: Office for Official Publications of the European Communities.
—— 2009a. Living conditions and social protection [data set]. Luxembourg: Office for Official Publications of the European Communities. Available at http://ec.europa.eu/eurostat/.
—— 2009b. Statistics by themes: Population and social conditions. Available at http://epp.eurostat.ec.europa.eu/portal/page/portal/statistics/themes.
EU-SILC, 2006. Database: European Union Statistics on Income and Living Conditions (EU-SILC). Available as cross-sectional and longitudinal data at http://epp.eurostat.ec.europa.eu/portal/page/portal/microdata/eu_silc (EU-SILC 2007 also available; see also http://www.eui.eu/Research/Library/ResearchGuides/Economics/Statistics/DataPortal/EU-SILC.aspx.
EVANS, GEOFFREY, 1998. Britain and Europe: Separate worlds of welfare? *Government and Opposition,* 33 (2): 183–98.
EWALD, FRANÇOIS, 1986. *L'État Providence [The Providential State].* Paris: Grasset.
EWIG, CHRISTINA, 2008. Reproduction, re-reform and the reconfigured state. Feminists and neoliberal health reforms in Chile, in *Beyond States and Markets: The Challenges of Social Reproduction,* ed. Isabella Bakker and Rachel Silvey, New York: Routledge 143–58.
EWIG, CHRISTINA, and BELLO, AMPARO H., 2009. Gender equity and health sector reform in Colombia: Mixed state-market model yields mixed results. *Social Science & Medicine,* 68 (6): 1145–52.
FAHEY, TONY, and MAÎTRE, BERTRAND, 2004. Housing and social inequality in Ireland, in *Housing and Social Inequality in Comparative Perspective,* ed. Karin Kurz and Hans-Peter Blossfeld, Stanford, CA: Stanford University Press, 281–303.

FAHEY, TONY, NOLAN, BRIAN, and MAÎTRE, BERTRAND, 2004. Housing expenditures and income poverty in EU countries. *Journal of Social Policy*, 33 (3): 437–54.

FAIST, THOMAS, 1995. *Social Citizenship for Whom?* Aldershot: Avebury.

FALKINGHAM, JANE, and HARDING, ANN, 1996. Poverty alleviation versus social insurance: A comparison of lifetime redistribution (Discussion Paper, 12). Canberra: National Centre for Social and Economic Modeling, University of Canberra. Available at https://guard.canberra.edu.au/natsem/index.php?mode=download&file_id=539.

FALKINGHAM, JANE, and HILLS, JOHN (eds.), 1995. *The Dynamics of Welfare: The Welfare State and the Life Cycle*. Hemel Hempstead: Harvester Wheatsheaf.

FALKNER, GERDA, 2000. EG-Sozialpolitik nach Verflechtungsfalle und Entscheidungslücke: Bewertungsmaßstäbe und Entwicklungstrends [EC social policy beyond the 'joint-decision trap' and the 'decision gap': Evaluation benchmarks and developmental trends]. *Politische Vierteljahresschrift*, 41 (2): 279–301.

—— 2007. Europeanization and social policy, in *Europeanization: New Research Agendas*, ed. Paolo Graziano and Maarten Vink, Basingstoke: Palgrave Macmillan, 253–65.

—— 2010. The EU's social dimension, in *European Union Politics*, ed. Michelle Cini, Oxford: Oxford University Press, 276–290.

FALKNER, GERDA, TREIB, OLIVER, HARTLAPP, MIRIAM, and LEIBER, SIMONE, 2005. *Complying with Europe. EU Harmonisation and Soft Law in the Member States*. Cambridge: Cambridge University Press.

FALKNER, GERDA, TREIB, OLIVER, and HOLZLEITHNER, ELISABETH (eds.), 2008. *Compliance in the Enlarged European Union: Living Rights or Dead Letters?* Aldershot: Ashgate.

FEATHERSTONE, KEVIN, and KAZAMIAS, GEORGE (eds.), 2001. *Europeanization and the Southern Periphery*. London: Frank Cass.

FELDSTEIN, MARTIN S., 1998. Income inequality and poverty (NBER Working Papers, 6670). Cambridge, MA: National Bureau of Economic Research. Available at http://www.nber.org/papers/w6770.pdf?new_window=1.

FENGE, ROBERT, and WERDING, MARTIN, 2004. Ageing and the tax implied in public pension schemes: Simulations for selected OECD countries. *Fiscal Studies*, 25 (2): 159–200.

FENGER, H.J.M., 2007. Welfare regimes in Central and Eastern Europe: Incorporating post-communist countries in a welfare regime typology. *Contemporary Issues and Ideas in Social Sciences*, 3 (2): 1–30.

FERGE, ZSUZSA, 1997. The changed welfare paradigm: The individualisation of the social. *Social Policy & Administration*, 31 (1): 20–44.

—— 2001. Welfare and 'ill-fare' systems in Central-Eastern Europe, in *Globalization and European Welfare States: Challenges and Change*, ed. Robert Stykes, Bruno Palier, and Pauline M. Prior, Basingstoke: Palgrave Macmillan, 127–52.

FERRARINI, TOMMY, 2003. *Parental Leave Institutions in Eighteen Post-War Welfare States*. Stockholm: Stockholm University, Swedish Institute for Social Research (Edsbruk: Aka-demitryck).

FERRERA, MAURIZIO, 1986. Italy, in *Growth to Limits: The Western European Welfare States since World War II*, vol. 2: *Germany, United Kingdom, Ireland, Italy*, ed. Peter Flora, Berlin: Walter de Gruyter, 385–500.

—— 1993. *Modelli di solidarietà [Models of Solidarity]*. Bologna: Il Mulino.

—— 1996. The 'Southern model' of welfare in Social Europe. *Journal of European Social Policy*, 6 (1): 17–37.

FERRERA, MAURIZIO, 2005a. *The Boundaries of Welfare: European Integration and the New Spatial Politics of Social Protection.* Oxford: Oxford University Press.

—— (ed.), 2005b. *Welfare State Reform in Southern Europe: Fighting Poverty and Social Exclusion In Italy, Spain, Portugal and Greece.* London: Routledge.

—— 2007. Democratisation and social policy in Southern Europe: From expansion to 'recalibration', in *Democracy and Social Policy,* ed. Yusuf Bangura, Basingstoke: Palgrave Macmillan, 90–113.

—— 2008. The European welfare state: Golden achievements, silver prospects. *West European Politics,* 31 (1/2): 82–107.

FERRERA, MAURIZIO, and GUALMINI, ELISABETTA, 2004. *Rescue by Europe? Social and Labour Market Reforms from Maastricht to Berlusconi.* Amsterdam: Amsterdam University Press.

FERRERA, MAURIZIO, and HEMERIJCK, ANTON, 2003. Recalibrating European welfare regimes, in *Governing Work and Welfare in a New Economy: European and American Experiments,* ed. Jonathan Zeitlin and David M. Trubek, Oxford: Oxford University Press, 88–128.

FERRERA, MAURIZIO, HEMERIJCK, ANTON, and RHODES, MARTIN, 2000. *The Future of Social Europe: Recasting Work and Welfare in the New Economy. Report Prepared for the Portuguese Presidency of the EU.* Oeiras: Celta Editora.

FESER, EDWARD S., 2006. Introduction, in *The Cambridge Companion to Hayek,* ed. Edward S. Feser, Cambridge: Cambridge University Press, 1–12.

FIDELER, PAUL A., 2006. *Social Welfare in Pre-Industrial England: The Old Poor Law Tradition.* Basingstoke: Palgrave Macmillan.

FIDLER, DAVID P., 2003. Emerging trends in international law concerning global infectious disease control. *Emerging Infectious Diseases,* 9 (3): 285–90.

FIELD, MARK G., 1973. The concept of the 'health system' at the macrosociological level. *Social Science & Medicine,* 7 (10): 763–85.

FILGUERIA, CARLOS H., and FILGUERIA, FERNANDO, 2002. Models of welfare and models of capitalism: The limits of transferability, in *Models of Capitalism: Lessons for Latin America,* ed. Evelyne Huber, University Park, PA: Pennsylvania State University Press, 127–57.

FINCH, JANET, 1989. *Family Obligations and Social Change.* London: Routledge.

FINKELSTEIN, VIC, 1991. Disability: An administrative challenge? The health and welfare heritage, in *Social Work: Disabled People and Disabling Environments,* ed. Michael Oliver, London: Jessica Kingsley, 19–38.

FITZGERALD, JOAN, 2006. *Moving Up in the New Economy: Career Ladders for U.S. Workers.* Ithaca, NY: Cornell University Press.

FITZPATRICK, TONY, 2003. *After the New Social Democracy: Social Welfare for the Twenty-First Century.* Manchester: Manchester University Press.

FLAQUER, LLUÍS, 2000. 'Family policy and welfare state in Southern Europe' (Working Paper, 185). Barcelona: Institut de Ciencies Politiques i Socials. Available at http://www.recercat.net/bitstream/2072/1280/1/ICPS185.pdf.

FLIGSTEIN, NEIL, 2002. Globalization or Europeanization? Evidence on the European economy since 1980. *Acta Sociologica,* 45 (1): 7–22.

FLORA, PETER, 1983. *State, Economy, and Society in Western Europe, 1815–1975: A Data Handbook in Two Volumes.* Chicago: St. James.

—— (ed.), 1986–7. *Growth to Limits: The Western European Welfare States since World War II;* vol 1: *Sweden, Norway, Finland, Denmark* (1986); vol. 2: *Germany, United Kingdom, Ireland, Italy* (1986); vol. 4: *Appendix: Synopses, Bibliographies* (1987). Berlin: Walter de Gruyter.

FLORA, PETER, and ALBER, JENS, 1981. Modernization, democratization, and the development of welfare states in Western Europe, in *The Development of Welfare States in Europe and America*, ed. Peter Flora and Arnold J. Heidenheimer, New Brunswick, NJ: Transaction Books, 37–80 (reprint in Leibfried and Mau 2008a: vol. 1, 167–210).

FLORA, PETER, and HEIDENHEIMER, ARNOLD J., 1981. The historical core and changing boundaries of the welfare state, in *The Development of Welfare States in Europe and America*, ed. Peter Flora and Arnold J. Heidenheimer, New Brunswick, NJ: Transaction Books, 17–34.

FOGEL, ROBERT W., 2004. *The Escape from Hunger and Premature Death 1700–2100. Europe, America and the Third World*. Cambridge: Cambridge University Press.

FORSSEN, KATJA, and RITAKALLIO, VELI-MATTI, 2006. First births: A comparative study of transition to parenthood in Europe, in *Social Policy, Family Change and Employment in Comparative Perspective*, ed. Jonathan R. Bradshaw and Aksel Hatland, Cheltenham: Edward Elgar, 161–77.

FÖRSTER, MICHAEL F., and MIRA D'ERCOLE, MARCO, 2005. Income distribution and poverty in OECD countries in the second half of the 1990s (OECD Social, Employment and Migration Working Paper, 22). Paris: OECD. Available at http://ssrn.com/abstract=671783.

FÖRSTER, MICHAEL F., and PEARSON, MARK, 2002. Income distribution and poverty in the OECD area: Trends and driving forces. *OECD Economic Studies*, 34 (1): 7–40.

FÖRSTER, MICHAEL F., and VLEMINCKX, KOEN, 2004. International comparisons of income inequality and poverty: Findings from the Luxembourg Income Study. *Socio-Economic Review*, 2 (2): 191–212.

FRANZESE, ROBERT J., 2002. *Macroeconomic Policies of Developed Democracies*. Cambridge: Cambridge University Press.

FRANZESE, ROBERT J., and HAYS, JUDE, 2006. Strategic interaction among EU governments in active-labour-market policymaking: Subsidiarity and policy coordination under the European Employment Strategy. *Europe Union Politics*, 7 (2): 167–89.

FRASER, NANCY, 1989a. *Unruly Practices: Power, Discourse and Gender in Contemporary Social Theory*. Minneapolis: University of Minnesota Press.

—— 1989b. Women, welfare, and the politics of need intepretation, in *Unruly Practices: Power, Discourse and Gender in Contemporary Social Theory*, ed. Nancy Fraser, Minneapolis: University of Minnesota Press, 144–60.

—— 1994a. After the family wage: Gender equity and the welfare state. *Political Theory*, 22 (4): 591–618 (also in a 1997 version in Leibfried and Mau 2008a: vol. 3, 41–63).

—— 1994b. Talking about needs: Interpretative contests as political conflicts in welfare state societies, in *Feminism and Political Theory*, ed. Cass R. Sunstein, Chicago: University of Chicago Press, 159–81.

FRAZIER, MARK W., 2004. After pension reform: Navigating the 'third rail' in China. *Studies in Comparative International Development*, 39 (2): 43–68.

—— 2006. Pensions, public opinion and the graying of China. *Asia Policy*, 1 (1): 43–68.

FREEDEN, MICHAEL, 1978. *The New Liberalism: An Ideology of Social Reform*, Oxford: Clarendon Press.

—— 2003. The coming of the welfare state, in *The Cambridge History of Twentieth Century Political Thought*, ed. Terence Ball and Richard Bellamy, Cambridge: Cambridge University Press, 7–44.

FREEMAN, RICHARD, 2000. *The Politics of Health in Europe.* Manchester: Manchester University Press.

FREEMAN, RICHARD, and FRISINA, LORRAINE, 2009. Health care systems and the problem of classification. *Journal of Comparative Policy Analysis* (Special Issue, forthcoming).

FREIDSON, ELIOT, 1970. *Professional Dominance: The Social Structure of Medical Care.* New York: Atherton.

FRIEDEN, JEFFRY A., 2006. *Global Capitalism: Its Fall and Rise in the Twentieth Century.* New York: W. W. Norton.

FRIEDMAN, LAWRENCE M., and LADINSKY, JACK, 1978. Social change and the law of industrial accidents, in *American Law and the Constitutional Order,* ed. Lawrence M. Friedman and Harry N. Scheiber, Cambridge, MA: Harvard University Press, 269–82.

FRIEDMAN, MILTON, 1977. Nobel lecture: Inflation and unemployment. *Journal of Political Economy,* 85 (3): 451–72.

—— (with the assistance of ROSE D. FRIEDMAN), 2003. *Capitalism and Freedom.* Chicago: University of Chicago Press (first published 1962; with a new preface 1982).

FRITZELL, JOHAN, 2001. Still different? Income distribution in the Nordic countries in a European comparison, in *Nordic Welfare States in the European Context,* ed. Mikko Kautto, Johan Fritzell, Björn Hvinden, Jon Kvist, and Hannu Uusitalo, London: Routledge, 18–41.

GALLIE, DUNCAN, and PAUGAM, SERGE, 2000. *Welfare Regimes and the Experience of Unemployment in Europe.* Oxford: Oxford University Press.

GAMBLE, ANDREW, 1994. *The Free Economy and the Strong State: The Politics of Thatcherism.* Basingstoke: Macmillan.

GANGHOF, STEFFEN, and GENSCHEL, PHILIPP, 2008. Taxation and democracy in the EU. *Journal of European Public Policy,* 15 (1): 58–77.

GANGL, MARKUS, 2006. Scar effects of unemployment: An assessment of institutional complementarities. *American Sociological Review,* 71 (6): 986–1013.

GANS-MORSE, JORDAN, and ORENSTEIN, MITCHELL, 2007. The emergence of continental-liberal welfare regimes in postcommunist Europe (draft paper, 17 August).

GARFINKEL, IRWIN, RAINWATER, LEE, and SMEEDING, TIMOTHY M., 2006. A re-examination of welfare state and inequality in rich nations: How in-kind transfers and indirect taxes change the story. *Journal of Policy Analysis and Management,* 25 (4): 855–919.

GARRETT, GEOFFREY, 1998a. *Partisan Politics in a Global Economy.* Cambridge: Cambridge University Press.

—— 1998b. Global markets and national policies: Collision course or virtuous circle. *International Organization,* 52 (4): 787–824 (reprint in Leibfried and Mau 2008a: vol. 2, 389–430).

—— 2001. Globalization and government spending around the world. *Studies in Comparative International Development,* 35 (1): 3–29.

GARRETT, GEOFFREY, and LANGE, PETER, 1995. Internationalization, institutions and political change, in *Internationalization and Domestic Politics,* ed. Robert O. Keohane and Helen V. Milner, Cambridge: Cambridge University Press, 48–75.

GARRETT, GEOFFREY, and MITCHELL, DEBORAH, 1995. 'Globalization and the welfare state: Income transfers in the advanced industrialized democracies, 1965–1990' (Discussion Papers, 320). Canberra: Australian National University, Centre for Economic Policy Research. Available at http://econpapers.repec.org/paper/auudpaper/330.htm.

—— —— 2001. Globalization, government spending and taxation in the OECD. *European Journal of Political Research*, 39 (2): 145–77.

GAUTHIER, ANNE H., 1996. *The State and the Family: A Comparative Analysis of Family Policies in Industrialized Countries.* Oxford: The Clarendon Press of Oxford University Press.

—— 2002. Family policies in industrialized countries: Is there a convergence? *Population*, 57 (3): 447–74.

GAUTHIER, ANNE H., and BORTNIK, ANITA, 2001. Database: Comparative Maternity, Parental, and Childcare Database. Version 2. Calgary: University of Calgary. Available at http://soci.ucalgary.ca/fypp/home/research-lab.

GELISSEN, JOHN, 2000. Popular support for institutionalised solidarity: A comparison between European welfare states. *International Journal of Social Welfare*, 9 (4): 285–300.

—— 2002. *Worlds of Welfare, Worlds of Consent? Public Opinion on the Welfare State.* Leiden: Brill.

GEORGE, ALEXANDER L., and BENNETT, ANDREW, 2005. *Case Studies and Theory Development in the Social Sciences.* Cambridge, MA: MIT Press.

GERDTHAM, ULF-G., and BENGT, JÖNSSON, 2000. International comparisons of health expenditure: Theory, data and econometric analysis, in *Handbook of Health Economics*, vol. 1A, ed. Anthony J. Culyer and Joseph P. Newhouse, Amsterdam: Elsevier, 11–53.

GERRING, JOHN, 2007. *Case Study Research: Principles and Practices.* Cambridge: Cambridge University Press.

GERVEN, MINNA VAN, 2008. *The Broad Tracks of Path Dependent Benefit Reforms.* Helsinki: Kela.

GIAIMO, SUSAN, and MANOW, PHILIP, 1999. Adapting the welfare state: The case of health care reform in Britain, Germany, and the United States. *Comparative Political Studies*, 32 (8): 967–1000.

GIBB, KENNETH, 2002. Trends and change in social housing finance and provision within the European Union. *Housing Studies*, 17 (2): 325–36.

GIDDENS, ANTHONY, 1994. *Beyond Left and Right: The Future of Radical Politics.* Cambridge: Polity.

—— 1998. *The Third Way: The Renewal of Social Democracy.* Cambridge: Polity.

—— 2000. *The Third Way and its Critics.* Cambridge: Polity.

—— (ed.), 2001. *The Global Third Way Debate.* Cambridge: Polity.

—— 2009. *The Politics of Climate Change.* Cambridge: Polity.

GILBERT, NEIL, 2005. The 'enabling state'? From public to private responsibilities for social protection. Pathways and pitfalls (OECD Social, Employment and Migration Working Paper, 26). Paris: OECD. Available at http://www.oecd.org/dataoecd/7/34/35304720.pdf.

—— 2008. *A Mother's Work: How Feminism, the Market, and Policy Shape Family Life.* New Haven, CT: Yale University Press.

GILES, CHRISTOPHER, and JOHNSON, PAUL 1995. Tax Reform in the UK and Changes in the Progressivity of the Tax System, 1985–1995. *Fiscal Studies*, 15 (3): 64–86.

GILL, ANTHONY, 1998. *Rendering Unto Caesar: The Catholic Church and the State in Latin America.* Chicago: University of Chicago Press.

GILL, ANTHONY, and LUNDSGAARDE, ERIK, 2004. State welfare spending and religiosity: A cross-national analysis. *Rationality and Society*, 16 (4): 399–437.

GILL, INDERMIT SINGH, TRUMAN, G. PACKARD, and YERMO, JUAN, 2004. *Keeping the Promise of Social Security in Latin America.* Stanford, CA: Stanford University Press.

GINNEKEN, WOUTER VAN, 2003. Extending social security: Policies for developing countries (Extension of Social Security Papers, 13). Geneva: ILO, Social Security and Development branch. Available at http://ssrn.com/abstract=673121.

GINSBURG, HELEN, 1983. *Full Employment and Public Policy: The United States and Sweden.* Lexington, MA: D. C. Heath.

GINTIS, HERBERT, BOWLES, SAMUEL, BOYD, ROBERT, and FEHR, ERNST (eds.), 2004. *Moral Sentiments and Material Interests: The Foundations of Cooperation in Economic Life.* Cambridge, MA: MIT Press.

GIRAUDY, AGUSTINA, 2007. The distributive politics of emergency employment programmes in Argentina (1993–2002). *Latin American Research Review,* 42 (2): 33–55.

GLATZER, MIGUEL, and RUESCHEMEYER, DIETRICH (eds.), 2005. *Globalization and the Future of the Welfare State.* Pittsburgh, PA: University of Pittsburgh Press.

GLAZER, NATHAN, 1998. The American welfare state: Exceptional no longer?, in *Challenges to the Welfare State: Internal and External Dynamics for Change,* ed. Henry Cavanna, Cheltenham: Edward Elgar, 7–20.

GLEESON, BRENDAN, 1999. *Geographies of Disability.* London: Routledge.

GLENDINNING, CAROLINE, and KEMP, PETER A. (eds.), 2006. *Cash and Care: Policy Challenges in the Welfare State.* Bristol: Policy Press.

GLENN, EVELYN N., 1992. From servitude to service work: Historical continuities in the racial division of paid reproductive labor. *Signs,* 18 (1): 1–43.

GLENNERSTER, HOWARD, 2009. *Understanding the Finance of Welfare: What It Costs and How to Pay for It.* Bristol: Policy Press.

GLYN, ANDREW, 2007. *Capitalism Unleashed: Finance, Globalization, and Welfare.* Oxford: Oxford University Press.

GOFFMAN, ERVING, 1990. *Stigma: Notes on on the Management of Spoiled Identity.* London: Penguin (1st edn. 1963).

GOLDEN, MIRIAM, LANGE, PETER, and WALLERSTEIN, MICHAEL, 1998. Database: Union Centralization among Advanced Industrial Societies: An Empirical Study. Los Angeles: University of California Los Angeles. Available at http://www.shelley.polisci.ucla.edu/data.

GOLDSTEIN, JUDITH L., KAHLER, MILES, KEOHANE, ROBERT O., and SLAUGHTER, ANNE-MARIE, 2000. Introduction: Legalization and world politics. *International Organization,* 54 (3): 385–99.

GOLINOWSKA, STANISŁAWA, HENGSTENBERG, PETER, and ZUKOWSKI, MADEJ (eds.), 2009. *Diversity and Commonality in European Social Policies: The Forging of a European Social Model.* Warsaw: Friedrich-Ebert Stiftung.

GOODHART, DAVID, 2004. Too diverse? *Prospect,* 95. Available at http://www.prospectmagazine.co.uk/2004/02/toodiverse/.

GOODIN, ROBERT E., 1985. The priority of needs. *Philosophy and Phenomenological Research,* 45 (4): 615–25.

—— 1986. *Protecting the Vulnerable.* Chicago: University of Chicago Press.

—— 1988. *Reasons for Welfare: The Political Theory of the Welfare State.* Princeton, NJ: Princeton University Press (Introduction in Leibfried and Mau 2008a: vol. 3, 19–40).

—— 1990a. Stabilizing expectations: The role of earnings-related benefits in social welfare policy. *Ethics,* 100 (3): 530–53.

—— 1990b. Relative needs, in *Needs and Welfare,* ed. Alan Ware and Robert E. Goodin, London: Sage, 12–33.

Goodin, Robert E., and Dryzek, John S., 1995. Justice deferred: Wartime rationing and postwar welfare policy. *Politics & Society*, 23 (1): 49–73.

Goodin, Robert E., Headey, Bruce, Muffels, Ruud, and Dirven, Henk-Jan, 1999. *The Real Worlds of Welfare Capitalism.* Cambridge: Cambridge University Press.

Goodin, Robert E., and Klingemann, Hans-Dieter (eds.), 1998. *A New Handbook of Political Science.* Oxford: Oxford University Press.

Goodin, Robert E., and Le Grand, Julian (eds.), 1987. *Not only the Poor: The Middle Classes and the Welfare State.* London: Allen & Unwin.

Goodin, Robert E., and Rein, Martin, 2001. Regimes on pillars: Alternative welfare state logics and dynamics. *Public Administration*, 79 (4): 769–801.

Gooding, Caroline, 1996. Employment and disabled people: Equal rights or positive action, in *Removing Disabling Barriers*, ed. Gerry Zarb, London: Policy Studies Institute, 64–76.

Goodman, Roger, and Peng, Ito, 1996. The East Asian welfare states: Peripatetic learning, adaptive change, and nation-building, in *Welfare States in Transition: National Adaptations in Global Economies*, ed. Gøsta Esping-Andersen, London: Sage, 192–224.

Goodman, Roger, White, Gordon, and Kwon, Huck-Ju (eds.), 1998. *The East Asian Welfare Model: Welfare Orientalism and the State.* London: Routledge.

Gordon, Margaret, 1963. Industrial injuries in Europe and the British Commonwealth before World War II, in *Occupational Disability*, ed. Earl Cheit and Margaret Gordon, New York: John Wiley, 191–220.

—— 1988. *Social Security in Industrial Countries.* Cambridge: Cambridge University Press.

Gornick, Janet, and Meyers, Marcia K., 2003. *Families that Work: Policies for Reconciling Parenthood and Employment.* New York: Russell Sage Foundation.

—— —— (eds.), 2009. *Gender Equality: Transforming Family Divisions of Labor.* London: Verso.

Gornick, Janet, Meyers, Marcia K., and Ross, Katherin E., 1998. Public policies and the employment of mothers. *Social Science Quarterly*, 79 (1): 35–54.

Gorski, Philip S., 2003. *The Disciplinary Revolution. Calvinism and the Rise of the State in Early Modern Europe.* Chicago: University of Chicago Press.

Goss, David, Goss, Fiona, and Adam-Smith, Derek, 2000. Disability and employment: A comparative critique of UK legislation. *International Journal of Human Resource Management*, 11 (4): 807–21.

Gottschalk, Peter, and Smeeding, Timothy M., 1997. Cross-national comparisons of earnings and income inequality. *Journal of Economic Literature*, 35 (2): 633–87.

—— —— 2000. Empirical analysis on income inequality in industrialized countries, in *Handbook of Income Distribution*, ed. Anthony B. Atkinson and François Bourguignon, New York: Elsevier-North Holland, 261–307.

Gough, Ian, 1979. *The Political Economy of the Welfare State.* London: Macmillan.

—— 2001. Social assistance regimes: A cluster analysis. *Journal of European Social Policy*, 11 (2): 165–70.

—— 2008. European welfare states: Explanations and lessons for developing countries, in *Inclusive States: Social Policy and Structural Inequalities*, ed. Anis A. Dani and Arjan de Haan, Washington, DC: World Bank, 39–72.

Gough, Ian, Bradshaw, Jonathan R., Ditch, John, Eardley, Tony, and Whiteford, Peter, 1997. Social assistance in OECD countries. *Journal of European Social Policy*, 7 (1): 17–43.

GOUGH, IAN, MEADOWCROFT, JAMES, DRYZEK, JOHN S., GERHARDS, JÜRGEN, LENGFELD, HOLGER, MARKANDYA, ANIL, and ORTIZ, RAMON, 2008. Climate change and social policy. *Journal of European Social Policy*, 18 (4): 325–44.

GOUGH, IAN, and WOOD, GEOFFREY D., with BARRIENTOS, ARMANDO, BEVAN, PHILIPPA, DAVIS, PETER, and ROOM, GRAHAM, 2004. *Insecurity and Welfare Regimes in Asia, Africa and Latin America. Social Policy in Development Contexts.* Cambridge: Cambridge University Press.

GOUL ANDERSEN, JØRGEN, 1999. Changing labour markets, new social divisions and welfare state support, in *The End of the Welfare State? Responses to State Retrenchment*, ed. Stefan Svallfors and Peter Taylor-Gooby, London: Routledge, 13–33.

—— 2000. Welfare crisis and beyond: Danish welfare policies in the 1980s and 1990s, in *Survival of the European Welfare State*, ed. Stein Kuhnle, London: Routledge, 60–87.

GOULD, ANDREW C., 1999. *Origins of Liberal Dominance: State, Church and Party in Nineteenth-Century Europe.* Ann Arbor: University of Michigan Press.

GOUREVITCH, PETER, 1986. *Politics in Hard Times: Comparative Responses to International Economic Crises.* Ithaca, NY: Cornell University Press.

GRAUBART, STEPHEN RICHARDS, 1986. *Norden: The Passion for Equality.* Oslo: Scandinavian University Press.

GREEN, RICHARD K., and WACHTER, SUSAN M., 2005. The American mortgage in historical and international context. *Journal of Economic Perspectives*, 19 (4): 93–114.

GREEN, THOMAS H., 1991. Liberal legislation and freedom of contract, in *Liberty*, ed. David Miller, Oxford: Oxford University Press, 21–32.

GREENE, WILLIAM H., 2000. *Econometric Analysis.* Upper Saddle River, NJ: Prentice Hall.

GREEN-PEDERSEN, CHRISTOFFER, KERSBERGEN, KEES VAN, and HEMERIJCK, ANTON, 2001. Neo-liberalism, the 'Third Way' or what? Recent Social Democratic welfare politics in Denmark and the Netherlands. *Journal of European Public Policy*, 8 (2): 307–25.

GREER, SCOTT L., 2006. Uninvited Europeanization: Neofunctionalism and the EU in health policy. *Journal of European Public Policy*, 13 (1): 134–52.

GREGORY, ROBERT, 1998. The changing face of the state in New Zealand: Rolling back the public service. Paper presented at Annual Meeting of the American Political Science Association. Boston, September 3–6.

GREVE, BENT, 2004. Denmark: Universal or not so universal welfare state. *Social Policy & Administration*, 38 (2): 156–69.

—— 2008. The labour market situation of disabled people in European countries and implementation of employment policies: A summary of evidence from country reports and research studies. Utrecht: Academic Network of European Disability experts. Available at http://www.disability-europe.net/content/pdf/ANED%20Task%206%20final%20report%20-%20final%20version%2017-04-09.pdf (last consulted September 10, 2009).

GRIFFIN, LARRY J., 1993. Narrative, event-structure analysis, and causal interpretation in historical sociology. *American Journal of Sociology*, 98 (5): 1094–120.

GRIMMER-SOLEM, ERIK, 2003. *The Rise of Historical Economics and Social Reform in Germany, 1864–1894.* Oxford: Oxford University Press.

GRUBB, DAVID, and WELLS, WILLIAM, 1993. Employment regulation and patterns of work in EC countries. *OECD Economic Studies*, 21 (Winter): 7–58.

GRUBER, JONATHAN, 2000. Disability insurance benefits and labor supply. *Journal of Political Economy*, 108 (6): 1162–83.

GRUBER, JONATHAN, and HUNGERMAN, DANIEL M., 2007. Faith-based charity and crowd out during the Great Depression. *Journal of Public Economics*, 91 (5/6): 1043–69.

GUILLÉN, ANNA M., 2002. The politics of universalisation: Establishing national health services in Souhern Europe. *West European Politics*, 25 (4): 49–68.

GUILLÉN, ANNA M., ALVAREZ, SANTIAGO, and ADAO E SILVA, PEDRO, 2001. Redesigning the Spanish and Portuguese welfare states: The impact of accession into the European Union (Working paper, 85). Cambridge, MA: Harvard University, Center for European Studies. Available at http://www.ces.fas.harvard.edu/publications/docs/pdfs/guillen.pdf.

GUILLÉN, ANNA M., and MATSAGANIS, MANOS, 2000. Testing the 'social dumping' hypothesis in Southern Europe: Welfare policies in Greece and Spain during the last 20 years. *Journal of European Social Policy*, 10 (2): 120–45.

GUILLÉN, ANNA M., and PETMESIDOU, MARIA, 2008. The public–private mix in Southern Europe, in *Welfare State Transformations. Comparative Perspectives*, ed. Martin Seeleib-Kaiser, Basingstoke: Palgrave Macmillan, 56–78.

GUIRAUDON, VIRGINIE, 1998. The Marshallian triptych re-ordered? The role of courts and bureaucracies in furthering migrants' social rights, in *Immigration and Welfare. Challenging the Borders of the Welfare State*, ed. Michael Bommes and Andrew Geddes, London: Routledge, 72–89.

GUJARATI, DAMODAR, 2003. *Basic Econometrics*. New York: McGraw-Hill.

GULBRANDSEN, LARS, 2004. Home ownership and social inequality: Norway, in *Home Ownership and Social Inequality in Comparative Perspective*, ed. Karin Kurz and Hans-Peter Blossfeld, Stanford, CA: Stanford University Press, 166–86.

GUNTHER, RICHARD, DIAMANDOUROS, P. NIKIFOIOS, and PUHLE, HANS-JÜRGEN (eds.), 1995. *The Politics of Democratic Consolidation: Southern Europe in Comparative Perspective*. Baltimore: Johns Hopkins University Press.

GUSMANO, MICHAEL K., RODWIN, VICTOR G., and WEISZ, DANIEL, 2006. A new way to compare health systems: Avoidable hospital conditions in Manhattan and Paris. *Health Affairs*, 25 (2): 510–20.

HA, EUNYOUNG, 2008. Globalization, veto players, and welfare spending. *Comparative Political Studies*, 41 (6): 783–813.

HAAS, PETER M., 1992. Introduction: Epistemic communities and international policy coordination. *International Organization*, 46 (1): 1–35.

HABERMAS, JÜRGEN, 1987. *The Theory of Communicative Competence*. Vol. 2: *Lifeworld and System*. Boston: Beacon Press.

HACKER, JACOB S., 1998. The historical logic of national health insurance: Structure and sequence in the development of British, Canadian, and U.S. medical policy. *Studies in American Political Development*, 12 (1): 57–130.

—— 2002. *The Divided Welfare State: The Battle over Public and Private Social Benefits in the United States*. Cambridge: Cambridge University Press (chapter 1 reprinted in Leibfried and Mau 2008a: vol. 1, 609–59).

—— 2004a. Privatizing risk without privatizing the welfare state: The hidden politics of social policy entrenchment in the United States. *American Political Science Review*, 98 (2): 243–60.

—— 2004b. Dismantling the health care state? Political institutions, public policies and the comparative politics of health reform. *British Journal of Political Science*, 34 (4): 693–724.

—— 2005. Policy drift: The hidden politics of US welfare state retrenchment, in *Beyond Continuity: Institutional Change in Advanced Political Economies*, ed. Wolfgang Streeck and Kathleen Thelen, Oxford: Oxford University Press, 40–82.

HACKER, JACOB S., 2006. *The Great Risk Shift: The Assault on American Jobs, Family, Health Care, and Retirement—And How You Can Fight Back.* Oxford: Oxford University Press.

—— 2008. *The Great Risk Shift: The New Economic Insecurity and the Decline of the American Dream.* Oxford: Oxford University Press (rev., exp. & retitled edn. of the 1st edn. 2006).

HAGGARD, STEPHAN, and KAUFMAN, ROBERT R., 2008. *Development, Democracy, and Welfare States: Latin America, East Asia, and Eastern Europe.* Princeton, NJ: Princeton University Press.

HAKIM, CATHERINE, 2000. *Work-Lifestyle Choices in the 21st Century: Preference Theory.* Oxford: Oxford University Press.

HALL, PETER A., 1986. *Governing the Economy: The Politics of State Intervention in Britain and France.* Cambridge: Polity.

—— 1993. Policy paradigms, social learning, and the state: The case of economic policy-making in Britain. *Comparative Politics,* 25 (3): 275–96.

HALL, PETER A., and FRANZESE, ROBERT J., 1998. Central bank independence, coordinated wage bargaining and European Monetary Union. *International Organization,* 52 (2): 505–35.

HALL, PETER A., and GINGERICH, DANIEL W., 2005. Varieties of Capitalism and institutional complementarities in the macroeconomy (Discussion Paper, 04/05). Cologne: Max Planck Institute for the Study of Soceities. Available at http://www.mpifg.de/pu/mpifg_dp/dp04-5.pdf.

HALL, PETER A., and SOSKICE, DAVID (eds.), 2001a. *Varieties of Capitalism: The Institutional Foundations of Comparative Advantage.* Oxford: Oxford University Press.

—— —— 2001b. An introduction to Varieties of Capitalism, in *Varieties of Capitalism: The Institutional Foundations of Comparative Advantage,* ed. Peter A. Hall and David Soskice, Oxford: Oxford University Press, 1–68 (reprint in Leibfried and Mau 2008a: vol. 2, 159–235).

HAMMOND, PETER, and RODRIGUEZ-CLARE, ANDRES, 1993. On endogenizing long-run growth. *Scandinavian Journal of Economics,* 95 (4): 391–425.

HANDLER, JOEL F., 2003. Social citizenship and workfare in the US and Western Europe: From status to contract. *Journal of European Social Policy,* 13 (3): 229–43.

HANEY, LYNNE A., 2002. *Inventing the Needy: Gender and the Politics of Welfare in Hungary.* Berkeley: University of California Press.

HANSEN, ERIK J., RINGEN, STEIN, UUSITALO, HANNU, and ERIKSON, ROBERT (eds.), 1993. *Welfare Trends in the Scandinavian Countries.* Armonk, NY: M. E. Sharpe.

HANSSON, PÄR, and HENREKSON, MAGNUS, 1994. A new framework for testing the effect of government spending on growth and productivity. *Public Choice,* 81 (3/4): 381–401.

HARA, JUNSUKE, and SEIYAMA, KAZUO, 2005. *Inequality amid Affluence: Social Stratification in Japan.* Melbourne: Trans Pacific Press.

HARAWAY, DONNA J., 1991. *Simians, Cyborgs, and Women.* London: Routledge.

HARLOE, MICHAEL, 1985. *Private Rented Housing in the United States and Europe.* London: Croom Helm.

—— 1995. *The People's Home? Social Rented Housing in Europe and America.* Oxford: Wiley Blackwell.

HARRIS, BERNARD, 2004. *The Origins of the British Welfare State: Society, State and Social Welfare in England and Wales, 1800–1945.* Basingstoke: Palgrave Macmillan.

HARRIS, JOSÉ, 1981. Some aspects of social policy in Britain during the Second World War, in *The Emergence of the Welfare State in Britain and Germany,* ed. Wolfgang J. Mommsen, London: Croom Helm, 247–62.

HASSEL, ANKE, 2008. The evolution of a global labor governance regime. *Governance*, 21 (2): 231–51. Available at http://www.blackwell-synergy.com/doi/abs/10.1111/j.1468–0491 .2008.00397.x.

HÄUSERMANN, SILJA, 2010. *The Politics of Welfare State Reform in Continental Europe: Modernization in Hard Times*. Cambridge: Cambridge University Press (forthcoming).

HAY, COLIN, and ROSAMOND, BEN, 2002. Globalization, European integration, and the discursive construction of economic imperatives. *Journal of European Public Policy*, 9 (2): 147–67.

HAY, COLIN, and WATSON, MATTHEW, 2003. The discourse of globalisation and the logic of no alternative: Rendering the contingent necessary in the political economy of New Labour. *Policy & Politics*, 31 (3): 289–305.

HAYEK, FRIEDRICH AUGUST VON, 1944. *The Road to Serfdom*. Chicago: University of Chicago Press.

—— 1960. *The Constitution of Liberty*. London: Routledge and Kegan Paul.

—— 1980. Free enterprise and competitive order, in *Individualism and Economic Order*, ed. Friedrich August von Hayek, Chicago: University of Chicago Press, 107–18 (first publ. 1947).

HAYS, JUDE C., EHRLICH, SEAN D., and PEINHARDT, CLINT, 2005. Government spending and public support for trade in the OECD: An empirical test of the embedded liberalism thesis. *International Organization*, 59 (2): 473–94.

HECKMAN, JAMES J., and PAGES, CARMEN, 2004. *Law and Employment: Lessons from Latin America and the Caribbean*. Chicago: University of Chicago Press.

HECLO, HUGH, 1974. *Modern Social Politics in Britain and Sweden: From Relief to Income Maintenance*. New Haven, CT: Yale University Press.

—— 1981. Toward a new welfare state?, in *The Development of Welfare States in Europe and America*, ed. Peter Flora and Arnold J. Heidenheimer, New Brunswick, NJ: Transaction Books, 383–406.

HEGA, GUNTHER M., and HOKENMAIER, KARL G., 2002. The welfare state and education: A comparison of social and educational policy in advanced industrial societies. *German Policy Studies*, 2 (1): 1–29.

HEGEDÜS, JÓZSEF, and TOSICS, IVAN, 1996. The disintegration of the East European housing model, in *Housing Privatization in Eastern Europe*, ed. David Clapham, Jozsef Hegedüs, Keith Kintrea and Ivan Tosics, London: Greenwood, 15–40.

HEIDENHEIMER, ARNOLD J., 1973. The politics of public education, health and welfare in the USA and Western Europe: How growth and reform potentials have differed. *British Journal of Political Science*, 3 (3): 315–40.

—— 1981. Education and social security entitlements in Europe and America, in *The Development of Welfare States in Europe and America*, ed. Peter Flora and Arnold J. Heidenheimer, New Brunswick, NJ: Transaction Books, 269–306.

—— 1983. Secularization patterns and the westward spread of the welfare state, 1883–1983: Two Dialogues about how and why Britain, the Netherlands, and the United States have differed, in *The Welfare State 1883-1983* (*Comparative Social Research*, vol. 6), ed. Richard F. Tomasson, London: JAI Press Inc., 3–38.

—— 1996. Throwing money and heaving bodies: Heuristic callisthenics for comparative policy buffs, in *Comparing Government Activity*, ed. Louis M. Imbeau and Robert D. McKinlay, Basingstoke: Macmillan, 13–25.

HEIDENHEIMER, ARNOLD J., 2004. Educational policy: Comparative perspective, in *International Encyclopedia of the Social & Behavioral Sciences*, ed. Neil J. Smelser and Paul B. Baltes, Amsterdam: Elsevier, 4296–302.

HEIDENHEIMER, ARNOLD J., and LAYSON, JOHN, 1982. Social policy development in Europe and America: A longer view on selectivity and income testing, in *Income-tested Transfer Programs: The Case for and against*, ed. Irwin Garfinkel, New York: Academic Press, 97–131.

HEIN, WOLFGANG, and KOHLMORGEN, LARS (eds.), 2003. *Globalisation, Global Health Governance and National Health Politics in Developing Countries: An Exploration into the Dynamics of Interfaces*. Hamburg: Deutsches Übersee-Institut.

HEISE, DAVID R., 1989. Modeling event structures. *Journal of Mathematical Sociology*, 14 (2/3): 139–69.

HELLWIG, MARTIN F., 2009. Systemic risk in the financial sector: An analysis of the subprime-mortgage financial crisis. *De Economist*, 157 (2): 129–207.

HELLWIG, TIMOTHY T., RINGSMUTH, EVE M., and FREEMAN, JOHN R., 2008. The American public and the room to maneuver: Responsibility attributions and policy efficacy in an era of globalization. *International Studies Quarterly*, 52 (4): 855–80.

HELPMAN, ELHANAN, ITSKHOKI, OLEG, and REDDING, STEPHEN, 2008. Inequality and unemployment in a global economy (NBER Working Paper, 14478). Cambridge, MA: National Bureau of Economic Research. Available at http://www.nber.org/papers/w14478.pdf.

HEMERIJCK, ANTON, 2010. *In Search of a New Welfare State*. Oxford: Oxford University Press (forthcoming).

HEMERIJCK, ANTON, and MARX, IVE, 2010. Continental welfare at a crossroads: The choice between activation and minimum income protection in Belgium and the Netherlands, in *A Long Goodbye to Bismarck? The Politics of Welfare Reforms in Continental Europe*, ed. Bruno Palier, Amsterdam: Amsterdam University Press, 129–155.

HENDERSON, J. VERNON, and IOANNIDES, YANNIS M., 1983. A model of housing tenure choice. *The American Economic Review*, 73 (1): 98–113.

HENNOCK, ERNEST P., 1987. *British Social Reform and German Precedents: The Case of Social Insurance, 1880–1914*. Oxford: Clarendon Press.

—— 2007. *The Origin of the Welfare State in England and Germany, 1850–1914: Social Policies Compared*. Cambridge: Cambridge University Press.

HÉRITIER, ADRIENNE, KERWER, DIETER, KNILL, CHRISTOPH, LEHMKUHL, DIRK, TEUTSCH, MICHAEL, and DOUILLET, ANNE-CÉCILE, 2001. *Differential Europe: The European Union Impact on National Policymaking*. Lanham, MD: Rowman & Littlefield.

HERNÁNDEZ, DIEGO, 2000. *Acerca del aprendizaje democrático. Seguridad social en el Uruguay, una perspectiva comparada. Informe final del concurso: Democracia, derechos sociales y equidad; y Estado, política y conflictos sociales [On learning democracy: Social security in Uruguay, a comparative perspective: Final report of the conference Democracy, social rights and equity; and State, politics and social conflict]*. Buenos Aires: Programmea Regional de Becas CLACSO [Consejo Latinoamericano de Ciencias Sociales—Latin American Council of Social Sciences]. Available at http://bibliotecavirtual.clacso.org.ar/ar/libros/becas/1999/hernandez.pdf.

—— 2003. Pension reform in Uruguay. Chapel Hill, NC: Department of Political Science, University of North Carolina at Chapel Hill, MA Thesis.

HERNES, HELGA M., 1987. *Welfare State and Woman Power: Essays in State Feminism*. Oslo: Norwegian University Press.

HERREN, MADELEINE, 1992. La formation d'une politque du travail internationale avant la première guerre mondiale [The evolution of an international labour policy before World War One], in *Histoire de l'Office du Travail*, ed. Jean Luciani, Paris: Syros, 409–26.

HERREN-OESCH, MADELEINE, 2009. *Internationale Organisationen seit 1865: Eine Global-geschichte der internationalen Ordnung [International Organizations since 1865: A Global History of International Order]*. Darmstadt: Wissenschaftliche Buchgesellschaft.

HERTNER, PETER, 2003. Autarkiepolitik im faschistischen Italien. Zu einigen neueren Forschungsergebnissen [Policies for autarchy in fascist Italy: On some new resarch], in *Wirtschaftsordnung, Staat und Unternehmen. Neue Forschungen zur Wirtschaftsgeschichte des Nationalsozialismus. Festschrift für Dietmar Petzina zum 65. Geburtstag*, ed. Werner Abelshauser, Jan-Otmar Hesse and Werner Plumpe, Essen: Klartext, 139–49.

HETLING, ANDREA, McDERMOTT, MONIKA L., and MAPPS, MINGUS, 2008. Symbolism versus policy learning. Public opinion of the 1996 U.S. welfare reforms. *American Politics Research*, 36 (3): 335–57.

HIBBS, DOUGLAS A., 1977. Political parties and macroeconomic policy. *American Political Science Review*, 71 (4): 1467–87.

—— 1987. *The Political Economy of Industrial Democracies*. Cambridge, MA: Harvard University Press.

—— 1992. Partisan theory after fifteen years. *European Journal of Political Economy*, 8 (3): 361–73.

HICKS, ALEXANDER, 1993. Introduction to pooling, in *The Comparative Political Economy of the Welfare State: New Methodologies and Approaches*, ed. Thomas Janoski and Alexander M. Hicks, Cambridge: Cambridge University Press, 169–88.

—— 1999. *Social Democracy and Welfare Capitalism*. Ithaca, NY: Cornell University Press.

HICKS, ALEXANDER, and ESPING-ANDERSEN, GØSTA, 2005. Comparative and historical studies of social policy and the welfare state, in *Handbook of Political Sociology*, ed. Thomas Janoski, Robert R. Alford, Alexander M. Hicks, and Mildred A. Schwartz, Cambridge: Cambridge University Press, 509–25.

HICKS, ALEXANDER, and FREEMAN, KENDRALIN, 2009. Pension income replacement: Permanent and transitory determinants. *Journal of European Public Policy*, 16 (1): 127–43.

HICKS, ALEXANDER, and KENWORTHY, LANE, 1998. Cooperation and political economic performance in affluent democratic capitalism. *American Journal of Sociology*, 103 (6): 1631–72.

—— —— 2003. Varieties of welfare capitalism. *Socio-Economic Review*, 1 (1): 27–61.

—— —— 2008. Family policies and women's employment: A regression analysis, in *Method and Substance in Macrocomparative Analysis*, ed. Lane Kenworthy and Alexander M. Hicks, Basingstoke: Palgrave Macmillan, 196–220.

HICKS, ALEXANDER, and MISRA, JOYA, 1993. Political resources and the growth of welfare in affluent capitalist democracies, 1960–1982. *American Journal of Sociology*, 99 (3): 668–710.

HICKS, ALEXANDER, MISRA, JOYA, and NG, TANG NAH, 1995. The programmatic emergence of the welfare state. *American Sociological Review*, 60 (3): 329–49.

HICKS, ALEXANDER, and SWANK, DUANE, 1984. On the political economy of welfare expansion: A comparative analysis of 18 advanced capitalist democracies 1960–1971. *Comparative Political Studies*, 17 (1): 81–119.

—— —— 1992. Politics, institutions, and welfare spending in industrialized democracies, 1960–1982. *American Political Science Review*, 86 (3): 658–74.

HICKS, ALEXANDER, and ZORN, CHRISTOPHER, 2005. Economic globalization, the macro economy, and reversals of welfare expansion in affluent democracies, 1978–1994. *International Organization*, 59 (3): 631–62.

HIGGINS, HENRY B., 1968. *A New Province for Law and Order: Being a Review by its Late President for Fourteen Years, of the Australian Court of Conciliation and Arbitration.* London: Dawsons of Pall Mall (first publ. 1922).

HILLS, JOHN, 2004. *Inequality and the State.* Oxford: Oxford University Press.

HILLS, JOHN, LE GRAND, JULIAN, and PIACHAUD, DAVID (eds.), 2002. *Understanding Social Exclusion.* Oxford: Oxford University Press.

HIMMELWEIT, SUSAN, 2007. The prospects for caring. *Cambridge Journal of Economics*, 31 (4): 581–99.

HINNFORS, JONAS, 2006. *Reinterpreting Social Democracy.* Manchester: Manchester University Press.

HINRICHS, KARL, 2001. Elephants on the move: Patterns of public pension reform in OECD countries, in *Welfare State Futures*, ed. Stephan Leibfried, Cambridge: Cambridge University Press, 77–102 (= *European Review* 2000, 8 (3): 353–78; reprint in Leibfried and Mau 2008a: vol. 3, 583–608).

—— 2009. When political risks and new social risks coincide: Will pension reforms and increasing labor market flexibility bring back old age poverty in Germany? (Working Papers, 2009: X). Helsinki: Finnish Centre for Pensions (Eläketurvakeskus). Available at http://www.etk.fi/Page.aspx?Section=42909&Item=16009.

—— 2010. A social insurance state withers away. Welfare state reforms in Germany—or: Attempts to turn around in a cul-de-sac, in *A Long Goodbye to Bismarck? The Politics of Welfare Reforms in Continental Europe*, ed. Bruno Palier, Amsterdam: Amsterdam University Press (forthcoming).

HIRST, PAUL Q., 1994. *Associative Democracy: New Forms of Economic and Social Governance.* Cambridge: Polity.

HITRIS, THEO, and NIXON, JOHN, 2001. Convergence of health care expenditure in the EU countries. *Applied Economics Letters*, 8 (4): 223–28.

HOBSBAWM, ERIC J., 1994. *Age of Extremes 1914–1991: The Short Twentieth Century.* New York: Vintage.

HOBSON, BARBARA, 1990. No exit, no voice: Women's economic dependency and the welfare state. *Acta sociologica*, 33 (3): 235–50.

—— 2002. *Making Men into Fathers: Men, Masculinities, and the Social Politics of Fatherhood.* Cambridge: Cambridge University Press.

HOBSON, BARBARA, and LINDHOLM, MARIKA, 1997. Collective identities, women's power resources, and the making of welfare states. *Theory and Society*, 26 (4): 475–508.

HOCKERTS, HANS GÜNTER, 1980. *Sozialpolitische Entscheidungen im Nachkriegsdeutschland. Alliierte und deutsche Sozialversicherungspolitik 1945 bis 1957 [Social Policy Decisions in Postwar Germany: Allied and German Social Insurance Politics 1945–1947].* Stuttgart: Klett-Cotta.

—— (ed.), 2006. *Geschichte der Sozialpolitik in Deutschland seit 1945. Eine Zeit vielfältigen Aufbruchs [History of Social Policy in Germany since 1945: A Time of Many New Beginnings].* Baden-Baden: Nomos Verlag.

HOCKERTS, HANS GÜNTER, and WENGST, UDO (eds.), 2006. *Bundesrepublik Deutschland 1966–1974. Eine Zeit vielfältigen Aufbruchs [Federal Republic of Germany: A Time of Many*

New Beginnings]. Baden-Baden: Nomos Verlag (*Geschichte der Sozialpolitik in Deutschland seit 1945*, vol. 5).

HOEKMAN, BERNARD M., and MAVROIDIS, PETROS C., 2007. *The World Trade Organization: Law, Economics, and Politics*. London: Routledge.

HOELLER, PETER, and RAE, DAVID, 2007. Housing markets and adjustment in monetary union (OECD Economics Department Working Papers 550) Paris: OECD.

HOFMEISTER, HERBERT, 1982. Austria, in *The Evolution of Social Insurance 1881–1981: Studies of Germany, France, Great Britain, Austria and Switzerland*, ed. Peter A. Köhler and Hans F. Zacher, London: Frances Pinter, 265–383.

HOLLIDAY, IAN, 2000. Productivist welfare capitalism: Social policy in East Asia. *Political Studies*, 48 (4): 708–23.

HOLMLUND, BERTIL, 1998. Unemployment insurance in theory and practice. *Scandinavian Journal of Economics*, 100 (1): 113–41.

HOLZMAN, ROBERT, and STIGLITZ, JOSEPH E. (eds.), 2001. *New Ideas about Old Age Security: Toward Sustainable Pension Systems in the 21st Century*. Washington, DC: World Bank.

HOPPER, EARL I., 1968. A typology for the classification of educational systems. *Sociology*, 2 (1): 29–46.

HORT, SVEN E. O., and KUHNLE, STEIN, 2000. The coming of East and South-East Asian welfare states. *Journal of European Social Policy*, 10 (2): 162–84 (reprint in Leibfried and Mau 2008*a*: vol. 2, 136–58).

HOSKYNS, CATHERINE, 1996. *Integrating Gender: Women, Law and Politics in the European Union*. London: Verso.

HOTZ, V. JOSEPH, and SCHOLZ, JOHN KARL, 2004. The earned income tax credit, in *Means-Tested Transfer Programs in the United States*, ed. Robert Moffitt, Chicago: University of Chicago Press, 141–97.

HOWARD, CHRISTOPHER, 1997. *The Hidden Welfare State: Tax Expenditures and Social Policy in the United States*. Princeton, NJ: Princeton University Press.

—— 2003. Is the American welfare state unusually small? *PS: Political Science and Politics*, 36 (3): 411–16.

HUBER, EVELYNE, 1996. Options for social policy in Latin America: Neoliberal versus social democratic models, in *Welfare States in Transition: National Adaptations in Global Economies*, ed. Gøsta Esping-Andersen, London: Sage, 141–91.

—— 2005. Globalization and social policy developments in Latin America, in *Globalization and the Future of the Welfare State*, ed. Miguel Glatzer and Dietrich Rueschemeyer, Pittsburgh: University of Pittsburgh Press, 75–105.

HUBER, EVELYNE, MUSTILLO, THOMAS, and STEPHENS, JOHN D., 2008. Politics and social spending in Latin America. *Journal of Politics*, 70 (2): 420–36.

HUBER, EVELYNE, NIELSEN, FRANÇOIS, PRIBBLE, JENNY, and STEPHENS, JOHN D., 2006. Politics and inequality in Latin America and the Caribbean. *American Sociological Review*, 71 (6): 943–63.

HUBER, EVELYNE, RAGIN, CHARLES, and STEPHENS, JOHN D., 1993. Social Democracy, Christian Democracy, constitutional structure, and the welfare state. *American Journal of Sociology*, 99 (3): 711–49.

HUBER, EVELYNE, RAGIN, CHARLES, STEPHENS, JOHN D., BRADY, DANA, and BECKFIELD, JASON 2004. Database: Comparative Welfare States Data Set. Northwestern University, University of North Carolina, Duke University, Indiana University. Available at http://www.lisproject.org/publications/welfaredata/welfareaccess.htm.

HUBER, EVELYNE, and STEPHENS, JOHN D., 1998. Internationalization and the Social Democratic model. *Comparative Political Studies*, 31 (3): 353–97.

—— —— 2000*a*. Partisan governance, women's employment, and the Social Democratic service state. *American Sociological Review*, 65 (3): 323–42.

—— —— 2000*b*. The political economy of pension reform: Latin America in comparative perspective (Occasional Paper, 7). Geneva: United Nations Research Institute for Social Development. Available at http://www.unrisd.org/80256B3C005BB128/(httpProjects)/AB848CABCB1F893380256B61003A1EB5?OpenDocument.

—— —— 2001*a*. *Development and Crisis of the Welfare State: Parties and Policies in Global Markets*. Chicago: University of Chicago Press.

—— —— 2001*b*. Welfare state and production regimes in the era of retrenchment, in *The New Politics of the Welfare State*, ed. Paul Pierson, Oxford: Oxford University Press, 107–45.

—— —— 2010. Successful social policy regimes? Political economy, politics, and the structure of social policy in Argentina, Chile, Uruguay, and Costa Rica, in *Successful Democratic Governance*, ed. Scott Mainwaring and Tim Scully, Stanford: Stanford University Press, 159–213 (forthcoming).

HUBERMAN, MICHAEL, 2008. Ticket to trade: Belgian labour and globalization before 1914. *Economic History Review*, 61 (2): 326–59.

HUBERMAN, MICHAEL, and LEWCHUCK, WAYNE, 2003. European economic integration and the Labour Compact, 1850–1913. *European Review of Economic History*, 7 (1): 3–41.

HUDSON, JOHN, and LOWE, STUART, 2004. *Understanding the Policy Process: Analysing Welfare Policy and Practice*. Bristol: Policy Press.

HÜFNER, FELIX, and LUNDSGAARD, JENS, 2007. The Swedish housing market: Better allocation via less regulation (OECD Economics Department Working Papers, 559). Paris: OECD. Available at http://dx.doi.org/10.1787/175230504175.

HUGO, VICTOR, 2008. *Les miserables*. Translated by Julie Rose, with an introduction by Adam Thirlwell; annotated by James Madden. London: Vintage Books (first publ. 1882).

HUNGERMAN, DANIEL M., 2005. Are church and state substitutes? Evidence from the 1996 Welfare Reform. *Journal of Public Economics*, 89 (11/12): 2245–67.

HUNTER, WENDY, and POWER, TIMOTHY, 2007. Rewarding Lula: Executive power, social policy, and the Brazilian elections of 2006. *Latin American Politics and Society*, 49 (1): 1–30.

HUNTINGTON, SAMUEL P., 1971. The change to change: Modernization, development and politics. *Comparative Politics*, 3 (3): 283–322.

HUO, JINGJING, NELSON, MOIRA L., and STEPHENS, JOHN D., 2008. Decommodification and activation in social democratic policy. *Journal of European Social Policy*, 18 (1): 5–20.

HURRELMANN, ACHIM, LEIBFRIED, STEPHAN, MARTENS, KERSTIN, and MAYER, PETER (eds.), 2008. *Transforming the Golden-Age Nation State*. Basingstoke: Palgrave Macmillan.

HURST, WILLIAM, 2009. *The Chinese Worker after Socialism*. Cambridge: Cambridge University Press.

HUTTON, WILL, 1995. *The State We're In*. London: Jonathan Cape.

HVINDEN, BJÖRN, 2003. The uncertain convergence of disability policies in Western Europe. *Social Policy & Administration*, 37 (6): 609–24.

HVINDEN, BJÖRN, and JOHANSSON, HÅKAN, 2007. *Citizenship in Nordic Welfare States: Dynamics of Choice, Duties and Participation in a Changing Europe*. London: Routledge.

IANKOVA, ELENA A., 2002. Transformation, accession to the European Union, and institutional design: The fate of tripartism, in *Norms and Nannies. The Impact of International*

Organizations on Central and East European States, ed. Ronald H. Linden, Lanham, MD: Rowman & Littlefield, 205–26.

IKEGAMI, NAOKI, 2007. Rationale, design and sustainability of long-term care insurance in Japan—In retrospect. *Social Policy and Society*, 6 (3): 423–34.

ILO (INTERNATIONAL LABOUR ORGANIZATION), 1942. *Approaches to Social Security: An International Survey*. Montreal: ILO.

—— 1949. *Systems of Social Security: New Zealand*. Geneva: ILO.

—— 2004a. *Economic Security for a Better World: ILO Socio-Economic Security Programme*. Geneva: ILO.

—— 2004b. *The Fight Against Poverty and Social Exclusion in Portugal: Experiences from the National Programme of Fight against Poverty*. Geneva: ILO. Available at http://www.ilo.org/public/english/protection/socsec/step/download/99p1.pdf.

—— 2005. ILO Social Security Inquiry: First Inquiry 2005. Manual. Geneva: ILO. Available at http://www.ilo.org/public/english/protection/secsoc/downloads/stat/ssimane.pdf.

—— 2008. *World of Work Report 2008: Income Inequalities in the Age of Financial Globalization*. Geneva: International Labour Office. Available at http://www.ilo.org/public/english/bureau/inst/download/world08.pdf

—— 2009a. Database: Laborsta. Geneva: ILO. Available at http://laborsta.ilo.org.

—— 2009b ff. Global Extension of Social Security (GESS). Geneva: ILO. Available at http://www.socialsecurityextension.org.

IMF (INTERNATIONAL MONETARY FUND), 2007. *Government Finance Statistics Yearbook*, vol. 31. Washington, D.C.: IMF. Available at https://www.imf.org/ and as CD Rom.

—— 2009. *Global Economic Policies and Prospects. Note by the Staff of the International Monetary Fund for the G20 Meeting of Ministers and Central Bank Governors, March 13–14, London*. Washington, DC: International Monetary Fund. Available at http://www.imf.org/external/np/g20/pdf/031909a.pdf.

IMMERGUT, ELLEN M., 1990. Institutions, veto points, and policy results: A comparative analysis of health care. *Journal of Public Policy*, 10 (4): 391–416 (reprint in Leibfried and Mau 2008a: vol. 1, 583–608).

—— 1992a. *Health Politics: Interests and Institutions in Western Europe*. Cambridge: Cambridge University Press.

—— 1992b. The rules of the game: The logic of health policy-making in France, Switzerland and Sweden, in *Structuring Politics: Historical Institutionalism in Comparative Analysis*, ed. Sven Steinmo, Kathleen Thelen, and Frank Longstreth, Cambridge: Cambridge University Press, 57–89.

—— 2005. Paradigms of change in political science: Historical-institutionalism and the problem of change, in *Understanding Change: Models, Methodologies and Metaphors*, ed. Andreas Wimmer and Reinhart Kössler, Basingstoke: Palgrave Macmillan, 282–310.

IMMERGUT, ELLEN M., ANDERSON, KAREN M., and SCHULZE, ISABELLA, 2007. *The Handbook of West European Pension Politics*. Oxford: Oxford University Press.

INGLOT, TOMASZ, 2008. *Welfare States in East Central Europe. 1919–2004*. Cambridge: Cambridge University Press.

INGRAM, ALAN, 2004. Health, foreign policy and security: Towards a conceptual framework for research and policy (UK Global Health Programme Working Paper, 2). London: Nuffield Trust. Available at http://www.nuffieldtrust.org.uk/research/index.aspx?id=136.

INGSTAD, BENEDICTE, and REYNOLDS WHYTE, SUSAN (eds.), 1995. *Disability and Culture*. Berkeley: University of California Press.

INOUE, KEIKO, and DRORI, GILI S., 2006. The global institutionalization of health as a social concern: Organizational and discursive trends. *International Sociology*, 21 (2): 199–219.

IPCC (INTERGOVERNMENTAL PANEL ON CLIMATE CHANGE), 2007. *Climate Change 2007: Mitigation of Climate Change: Fourth Assessment Report*. Cambridge: Cambridge University Press.

IPSS (NATIONAL INSTITUTE OF POPULATION AND SOCIAL SECURITY RESEARCH), 2007. *Social Security in Japan*. Tokyo: IPSS. Available at http://www.ipss.go.jp/s-info/e/Jasos2007/SS2007.pdf.

ISAAC, LARRY W., and GRIFFIN, LARRY J., 1989. Ahistoricism in time-series analysis of historical process: Critique, redirection, and illustrations from U.S. labour history. *American Sociological Review*, 54 (6): 873–90.

ISAAC, LARRY W., STREET, DEBRA A., and KNAPP, STAN J., 1994. Analyzing historical contingency with formal methods: The case of the relief explosion. *Sociological Methods & Research*, 23 (1): 114–24.

ISSP [INTERNATIONAL SOCIAL SURVEY PROGRAMME], 1985–2006. Database: Role of Government. Survey I (1985), II (1990), III (1996). IV (2006). Version 1.0. Available at http://www.issp.org.

ISUANI, ERNESTO ALDO, 1985. Social security and public assistance, in *The Crisis of Social Security and Health Care: Latin American Experiences and Lessons*, ed. Carmelo Mesa-Lago, Pittsburgh: University of Pittsburgh, Center for Latin American Studies, 89–102 (Latin American Monograph Series, 9).

IVERSEN, TORBEN, 1999. *Contested Economic Institutions: The Politics of Macroeconomics and Wage Bargaining in Advanced Democracies*. Cambridge: Cambridge University Press.

—— 2005. *Capitalism, Democracy, and Welfare*. Cambridge: Cambridge University Press.

—— 2006. Capitalism and democracy, in *Oxford Handbook of Political Economy*, ed. Donald A. Wittman and Barry R. Weingast, Oxford: Oxford University Press, 601–23.

IVERSEN, TORBEN, and CUSACK, THOMAS R., 2000. The causes of welfare state expansion: Deindustrialization or globalization. *World Politics*, 52 (3): 313–49.

IVERSEN, TORBEN, and SOSKICE, DAVID, 2001. An asset theory of social policy preferences. *American Political Science Review*, 95 (4): 875–93.

—— —— 2006. Electoral institutions, parties, and the politics of coalitions: Why some democracies redistribute more than others. *American Political Science Review*, 100 (2): 165–81.

—— —— 2009. Distribution and redistribution: The shadow from the Nineteenth Century. *World Politics*, 61 (3): 438–86.

IVERSEN, TORBEN, and STEPHENS, JOHN D., 2008. Partisan politics, the welfare state, and three worlds of human capital formation. *Comparative Political Studies*, 41 (4/5): 600–37.

IVERSEN, TORBEN, and WREN, ANNE, 1998. Equality, employment, and budgetary restraint: The trilemma of the service economy. *World Politics*, 50 (4): 507–46.

JACOBS, KLAUS, KOHLI, MARTIN, and REIN, MARTIN, 1991. The evolution of early exit: A comparative analysis of labor force participation patterns, in *Time for Retirement: Comparative Studies of Early Exit from the Labor Force*, ed. Martin Kohli, Martin Rein, Anne-Marie Guillemard, and Herman van Gunsteren, Cambridge: Cambridge University Press, 36–66.

JACOBZONE, STEPHANE, CAMBOIS, EMMANUELLE, CHAPLAIN, EMMANUEL, and ROBINE, JEAN-MARIE, 1998. The health of older persons in OECD countries: Is it improving fast enough to compensate for population ageing? (Labour Market and Social Policy Occasional Papers, 37). Paris: OECD. Available at http://ideas.repec.org/p/oec/elsaaa/37-en.html.

JÆGER, MADS MEIER, 2009. United but divided: Welfare regimes and the level and variance in public support for redistribution. *European Sociological Review*, 25 (6): 723–37.

JÆGER, MADS MEIER, and KVIST, JON, 2003. Pressures on state welfare in post-industrial societies: Is more or less better? *Social Policy & Administration*, 37 (6): 555–72.

JAHN, DETLEF, 2006. Globalization as 'Galton's problem': The missing link in the analysis of diffusion patterns in welfare state development. *International Organization*, 60 (2): 401–31.

JAHODA, MARIE, 1982. *Employment and Unemployment: A Social Psychological Analysis*. Cambridge: Cambridge University Press.

JAMES, HAROLD. 1996. *International Monetary Cooperation Since Bretton Woods*. Washington, DC: IMF/Oxford: Oxford University Press.

JANOSKI, THOMAS, 1992. *The Political Economy of Unemployment: Active Labour Market Policy in West Germany and the United States*. Berkeley: University of California Press.

—— 1998. *Citizenship and Civil Society*. Cambridge: Cambridge University Press.

JAUMOTTE, FLORENCE, 2003. Female labour force participation: Past trends and main determinants in OECD countries (OECD Economics Department Working Papers, 376). Paris: OECD. Available at http://ideas.repec.org/p/oec/ecoaaa/376-en.html.

JENSEN, LAURA, 1996. The early American origins of entitlements. *Studies in American Political Development*, 10 (2): 360–404.

—— 2003. *Patriots, Settlers, and the Origins of American Social Policy*. Cambridge: Cambridge University Press.

JENSON, JANE, 1997. Who cares? Gender and welfare regimes. *Social Politics*, 4 (2): 182–7.

—— 2006. The LEGO™ paradigm and new social risks: Consequences for children, in *Children, Changing Families and Welfare States*, ed. Jane Lewis, Cheltenham: Edward Elgar, 27–50.

JENSSEN, ANDERS T., and MARTINUSSEN, WILLY, 1994. *Velferdsstaten i våre hjerter [The Welfare State in Our Hearts]*. Oslo: Ad notam Gyldendal.

JESSOP, BOB, 1994. The transition to Post-Fordism and the Schumpeterian workfare state, in *Towards a Post-Fordist Welfare State?*, ed. Roger Burrows and Brian Loader, London: Routledge, 13–37.

JOERGES, CHRISTIAN, and RÖDL, FLORIAN, 2008. On the 'Social Deficit' of the European integration project and its perpetuation through the ECJ-judgements in Viking and Laval (RECON Online Working Papers, 2008/06). Oslo: ARENA. Available at http://www.reconproject.eu/main.php/RECON_wp_0806.pdf?fileitem=5456225.

JOHNSON, LOUISE C., and YANCA, STEPHEN J., 2004. *Social Work Practice: A Generalist Approach*. Boston: Pearson (8th edn.; 1st edn. 1983 by L.C. Johnson alone).

JONES, CATHERINE, 1990. Hong Kong, Singapore, South Korea and Taiwan: Economic welfare states. *Government and Opposition*, 25 (4): 446–62.

—— (ed.), 1993. *New Perspectives on the Welfare State in Europe*. London: Routledge.

JORDAN, BILL, and DÜVELL, FRANCK, 2002. *Irregular Migration: The Dilemmas of Transnational Mobility*. Cheltenham: Edward Elgar.

JOSHI, HEATHER, PACI, PIERELLA, and WALDFOGEL, JANE, 1999. The wages of motherhood: Better or worse? *Cambridge Journal of Economics*, 23 (5): 543–64.

JOST, TIMOTHY STOLZFUS (ed.), 2005. *Health Care Coverage Determinations. An International Comparative Study*. Maidenhead: Open University Press.

JOWELL, ROGER, 1998. How comparative is comparative research? *American Behavioral Scientist*, 42 (2): 168–77.

JUDIS, JOHN B., 1988. Conservatism and the price of success, in *The Reagan Legacy*, ed. Sidney Blumenthal and Thomas B. Edsall, New York: Pantheon, 135–71.

JUDT, TONY, 2005. *Postwar. A History of Europe since 1945*. London: Penguin Group.

KAASE, MAX, and NEWTON, KENNETH, 1995. *Beliefs in Government*. Oxford: Oxford University Press.

KALLEBERG, ARNE L., 2006. Nonstandard employment relations and labour market inequality: Cross-national patterns, in *Inequalities of the World*, ed. Göran Therborn, London: Verso, 136–61.

KALYVAS, STATHIS, 1996. *The Rise of Christian Democracy in Europe*. Ithaca, NY: Cornell University Press.

KAMERMAN, SHEILA B., and KAHN, ALFRED J., 1978. *Family Policy: Government and Families in Fourteen Countries*. New York: Columbia University Press.

KANGAS, OLLI E., 1991. *The Politics of Social Rights: Studies on the Dimensions of Sickness Insurance in OECD Countries*. Stockholm: Stockholm University, Swedish Institute for Social Research (Edsbruk: Akademitryck).

—— 1994. The politics of social security: On regressions, qualitative comparisons, and cluster analysis, in *The Comparative Political Economy of the Welfare State*, ed. Thomas Janoski and Alexander M. Hicks, Cambridge: Cambridge University Press, 346–64.

—— 2004. Institutional development of sickness cash-benefit programmes in 18 OECD countries. *Social Policy & Administration*, 38 (2): 190–203.

KANGAS, OLLI E., and PALME, JOAKIM, 2005. *Social Policy and Economic Development in the Nordic Countries*. Basingstoke: Palgrave Macmillan.

—— —— 2007. Social rights, structural needs and social expenditures, in *Investigating Welfare State Change: The 'Dependent Variable Problem' in Comparative Analysis*, ed. Jochen Clasen and Nico A. Siegel, Cheltenham: Edward Elgar, 106–29.

KASSER, TIM, 2002. *The High Price of Materialism*. Cambridge, MA: MIT Press.

KASZA, GREGORY J., 2002. The illusion of welfare 'regimes'. *Journal of Social Policy*, 31 (2): 271–87.

—— 2006. *One World of Welfare: Japan in Comparative Perspective*. Ithaca, NY: Cornell University Press.

KATO, JUNKO, 2003. *Regressive Taxation and the Welfare State: Path Dependence and Policy Diffusion*. Cambridge: Cambridge University Press.

KATZENSTEIN, PETER J., 1985. *Small States in World Markets: Industrial Policy in Europe*. Ithaca, NY: Cornell University Press.

KAUFMAN, ROBERT R., and NELSON, JOAN M. (eds.), 2004. *Crucial Needs, Weak Incentives. Social Sectors Reform, Democratization, and Globalization in Latin America*. Washington, DC: Woodrow Wilson Center Press.

KAUFMAN, ROBERT R., and SEGURA-UBIERGO, ALEX, 2001. Globalization, domestic politics, and social spending in Latin America: A time-series cross-section analysis, 1973–97. *World Politics*, 53 (4): 553–87.

KAUFMANN, FRANZ-XAVER, 1988. Christentum und Wohlfahrtsstaat [Christianity and the welfare state]. *Zeitschrift für Sozialreform*, 34 (2): 65–89.

—— 1990. *Zukunft der Familie. Stabilität, Stabilitätsrisiken und Wandel der familialen Lebensformen sowie ihre gesellschaftlichen und politischen Bedingungen [On the Future of the Family: Stability, Risks in Stability and Change of Family Forms and their Social and Political Backgrounds]*. Munich: C. H. Beck.

—— 1997. *Herausforderungen des Sozialstaates [Challenges to the Welfare State]*. Frankfurt a.M.: Suhrkamp.

—— 2001. Towards a theory of the welfare state, in *Welfare State Futures*, ed. Stephan Leibfried, Cambridge: Cambridge University Press, 15–36.

—— 2003*a*. *Varianten des Wohlfahrtsstaats. Der deutsche Sozialstaat im internationalen Vergleich [Varieties of Welfare States. The German Welfare State in International Comparison]*. Frankfurt a.M.: Suhrkamp.

—— 2003*b*. *Sozialpolitisches Denken: Die deutsche Tradition [Social Policy Thinking: The German Tradition]*. Frankfurt a.M.: Suhrkamp.

—— 2003*c*. *Die Entstehung sozialer Grundrechte und die wohlfahrtsstaatliche Entwicklung [The Origins of Constitutional Social Rights and Welfare State Development]*. Paderborn: Schöningh (Nordrhein-Westfälische Akademie der Wissenschaften, Lectures, G 387).

—— 2010. *The Foundations of European Social Policy. Essays.* (forthcoming).

KAUFMANN, FRANZ-XAVER, KUIJSTEN, ANTON, SCHULZE, HANS-JOACHIM, and STROHMEIER, KLAUS PETER (eds.), 2002. *Family Life and Family Policies in Europe, vol 2: Problems and Issues in Comparative Perspective*. Oxford: Oxford University Press.

KAUTTO, MIKKO, 2002. Investing in services in West European welfare states. *Journal of European Social Policy*, 12 (1): 53–65.

—— 2003. Welfare in Finland in the 1990s. *Scandinavian Journal of Public Health*, 31 (1): 1–4.

KAUTTO, MIKKO, FRITZELL, JOHAN, HVINDEN, BJÖRN, KVIST, JON, and UUSITALO, HANNU. (eds.), 2001. *Nordic Welfare States in the European Context.* London: Routledge.

KAUTTO, MIKKO, HEIKKILÄ, MATTI, HVINDEN, BJÖRN, MARKLUND, STAFFAN, and PLOUG, NIELS (eds.), 1999. *Nordic Social Policy. Changing Welfare States.* London: Routledge.

KAUTTO, MIKKO, and KVIST, JON, 2002. Parallel trends, persistent diversity: Nordic welfare states in the European and global context. *Global Social Policy*, 2 (2): 189–208.

KAY, STEPHEN J., 1999. Unexpected privatizations: Politics and social security reform in the Southern cone. *Comparative Politics*, 31 (4): 403–22.

KAY, STEPHEN J., and SINHA, TAPEN (eds.), 2008. *Lessons from Pension Reform in the Americas.* Oxford: Oxford University Press.

KEMENY, JIM, 1995. *From Public Housing to the Social Market.* London: Routledge.

KEMENY, JIM, and LOWE, STUART, 1998. Schools of comparative housing research: From convergence to divergence. *Housing Studies*, 13 (2): 161–76.

KEMMERLING, ACHIM, and BRUTTEL, OLIVER, 2006. 'New Politics' in German labour market policy? The implications of the recent Hartz Reforms for the German welfare state. *West European Politics*, 29 (1): 90–112.

KENWORTHY, LANE, 2003. Do affluent countries face an incomes–jobs trade-off? *Comparative Political Studies*, 36 (10): 1180–209 (reprint in Leibfried and Mau 2008*a*: vol. 3, 147–76).

—— 2004. *Egalitarian Capitalism: Jobs, Incomes and Growth in Affluent Countries.* New York: Russell Sage Foundation.

—— 2008. *Jobs with Equality.* Oxford: Oxford University Press.

KERR, CLARK, DUNLOP, JOHN T., HARBISON, FREDERICK H., and MYERS, CHARLES A., 1960. *Industrialism and Industrial Man: The Problems of Labor and Management in Economic Growth.* Cambridge, MA: Harvard University Press.

KERSBERGEN, KEES VAN, 1995. *Social Capitalism: A Study of Christian Democracy and the Welfare State.* London: Routledge.

—— 2000. The declining resistance of welfare states to change, in *The Survival of the Welfare State*, ed. Stein Kuhnle, London: Routledge, 19–36.

—— 2002. The politics of welfare state reform. *Swiss Political Science Review*, 8 (2): 1–20.

KERSBERGEN, KEES VAN, and MANOW, PHILLIP, 2008. The welfare state, in *Comparative Politics*, ed. Daniele Caramani, Oxford: Oxford University Press, 520–45.

—— —— eds., 2009. *Religion, Class Coalitions and Welfare States*. Cambridge: Cambridge University Press.

KICKBUSCH, ILONA, 2000. The development of international health policies—accountability intact? *Social Science & Medicine*, 51 (6): 979–89.

KILDAL, NANNA, 2001. *Workfare Tendencies in Scandinavian Welfare Policies*. Geneva: International Labour Office.

—— 2009. Comparing social policy ideas within the EU and the OECD, in *The Role of International Organizations in Social Policy. Ideas, Actors and Impact*, ed. Rune Ervik, Nanna Kildal, and Even Nilssen, Cheltenham: Edward Elgar, 20–48.

KILDAL, NANNA, and KUHNLE, STEIN (eds.), 2005. *Normative Foundations of the Welfare State: The Nordic Experience*. London: Routledge.

KILKEY, MAJELLA, and BRADSHAW, JONATHAN R. (eds.), 1999. *Lone Mothers, Economic Well-Being and Policies*. Oxford: Oxford University Press.

KING, DESMOND, 1987. *The New Right: Politics, Markets and Citizenship*. Basingstoke: Macmillan.

—— 1995. *Actively Seeking Work? The Politics of Unemployment and Welfare Policy in the United States and Great Britain*. Chicago: University of Chicago Press.

—— 1999. *In the Name of Liberalism: Illiberal Social Policy in the United States and Britain*. Oxford: Oxford University Press.

KING, DESMOND, and RUEDA, DAVID, 2008. Cheap labor: The new politics of 'Bread and Roses' in industrial democracies. *Perspectives on Politics*, 6 (2): 279–97.

KING, DESMOND, and WICKHAM-JONES, MARK, 1999. From Clinton to Blair: The Democratic (Party) origins of welfare to work. *Political Quarterly*, 70 (4): 62–74.

KING, GARY, KEOHANE, ROBERT O., and VERBA, SIDNEY, 1994. *Designing Social Inquiry: Scientific Inference in Qualitative Research*. Princeton, NJ: Princeton University Press.

KING, RUSSELL, LAZARIDIS, GABRIELLA, and TSARDANIDIS, CHARALAMBOS (eds.), 2000. *Eldorado or Fortress? Migration in Southern Europe*. London: Macmillan.

KINGMA, MIREILLE, 2007. Nurses on the move: A global overview. *Health Research and Educational Trust*, 42 (3): 1281–98.

KITSCHELT, HERBERT, 1999. European Social Democracy between political economy and electoral competition, in *Continuity and Change in Contemporary Capitalism*, ed. Herbert Kitschelt, Peter Lange, Gary Marks, and John D. Stephens, Cambridge: Cambridge University Press, 317–45.

KITSCHELT, HERBERT, and REHM, PHILIPP, 2006. New social risk and political preferences, in *The Politics of Post-Industrial Welfare States: Adapting Postwar Social Policies to New Social Risks*, ed. Klaus Armingeon and Giuliano Bonoli, London: Routledge, 52–82.

KITTEL, BERNHARD, and OBINGER, HERBERT, 2003. Political parties, institutions, and the dynamics of social expenditure in times of austerity. *Journal of European Public Policy*, 10 (1): 20–45.

KJOENSTAD, ASBJØRN, and SYSE, ASLAK, 2008. *Velferdsrett I and II [Welfare Law I and II]*. Oslo: Gyldendal Akademisk.

KLEIN, RUDOLF, 1993. O'Goffe's tale: Or what can we learn from the sucess of the capitalist welfare states?, in *New Perspectives on the Welfare State in Europe*, ed. Catherine Jones, London: Routledge, 7–17.

KLEIN, RUDOLF, and MILLAR, JANE, 1995. Do it yourself social policy: Searching for a new paradigm. *Social Policy & Administration*, 29 (4): 303–16.

KLEINBAUM, DAVID G., and KLEIN, MITCHEL, 2005a. *Logistic Regression: A Self Learning Text*. New York: Springer.

—— —— 2005b. *Survival Analysis: A Self Learning Text*. New York: Springer.

KLINE, DONNA S., 2003. Push and pull factors in international nurse migration. *Journal of Nursing Scholarship*, 35 (2): 107–11.

KLINGEMANN, HANS-DIETER, VOLKENS, ANDREA, BARA, JUDITH L., BUDGE, IAN, and MCDONALD, MICHAEL D., 2006. *Mapping Policy Preferences II: Estimates for Parties, Electors and Governments in Central and Eastern Europe, European Union and OECD 1990–2003*. Oxford: Oxford University Press.

KLOOSTERMAN, ROBERT C., 1999. The institutional context: Theoretical exploration, in *Immigrant Businesses: The Economic, Political and Social Environment*, ed. Jan Rath, Basingstoke: Macmillan, 90–106.

KNIJN, TRUDIE, and KREMER, MONIQUE, 1997. Gender and the caring dimension of welfare states: Towards inclusive citizenship. *Social Politics*, 4 (3): 328–61.

KOCKA, JÜRGEN, 1981. Class formation, interest articulation, and public policy: The origins of the German white-collar class in the late Nineteenth and early Twentieth Centuries, in *Organizing Interests in Western Europe: Pluralism, Corporatism, and the Transformation of Politics*, ed. Suzanne Berger, Cambridge: Cambridge University Press, 63–82.

—— 1990. 'Bürgertum' and professions in the Nineteenth Century: Two alternative approaches, in *Professions in Theory and History: Rethinking the Study of the Professions*, ed. Michael Burrage and Rolf Torstendahl, London: Sage, 62–74.

KOHL, JÜRGEN, 1981. Trends and problems in postwar public expenditure development in Western Europe and North America, in *The Development of Welfare States in Europe and America*, ed. Peter Flora and Arnold J. Heidenheimer, New Brunswick, NJ: Transaction Books, 307–44.

—— 2002. Armut und Armutsforschung in der Europäischen Union [Poverty and Poverty Research in the European Union], in *Sozialer Wandel und gesellschaftliche Dauerbeobachtung*, ed. Wolfgang Glatzer, Roland Habich, and Karl Ulrich Mayer, Opladen: Leske + Budrich, 163–79.

KOHLI, MARTIN, 1987. Retirement and the moral economy: An historical interpretation of the German case. *Journal of Aging Studies*, 1 (2): 125–44.

—— 2007. The institutionalization of the life course: Looking back to look ahead. *Research in Human Development*, 4 (3/4): 253–71.

KOHLI, MARTIN, ALBERTINI, MARCO, and KÜNEMUND, HARALD, 2010. Linkages among adult family generations. Evidence from comparative survey research, in *Family, Kinship and State in Contemporary Europe*. Vol. 3: *Perspectives on Theory and Policy*, ed. Patrick Heady and Martin Kohli, Frankfurt a.M.: Campus (forthcoming).

KOHLI, MARTIN, REIN, MARTIN, GUILLEMARD, ANNE-MARIE, and GUNSTEREN, HERMAN VAN, 1991. *Time for Retirement: Comparative Studies of Early Exit from the Labor Force*. Cambridge: Cambridge University Press.

KOK, WIM, DELL'ARINGA, CARLO, LOPEZ, FEDERICO DURAN, ECKSTRÖM, ANNA, RODRIGUES, MARIA JOÃO, ROUX, ANNETTE, and SCHMID, GÜNTHER, 2003. *Jobs, Jobs, Jobs: Creating More Employment in Europe: Report of the European Commission's Employment Taskforce*. Brussels: European Commission.

KOLBERG, JON EIVIND (ed.), 1991. *The Welfare State as Employer*. Armonk, NY: M. E. Sharpe.

KOLSTRUP, SØREN, 1996. Velfœrds statens rødder. Fra kommune-socialisme til folke-pension [The roots of the welfare state: From communal socialism to peoples' pensions] (skrifts-erie, 38). Viborg: Selskabet til Forskning i Arbejderbevaegelsens Historie (SFAH).

KOO, HAGEN, 2007. *Korean Society: Civil Society, Democracy and the State*. London: Routledge.

KOOPMANS, RUUD, 2003. Good intentions sometimes make bad policy: A comparison of Dutch and German integration policies, in *The Challenge of Diversity: European Social Democracy Facing Migration, Integration, and Multiculturalism*, ed. René Cuperus, Karl A. Duffek, and Johannes Kandel, Innsbruck: Studien Verlag, 163–8.

KORMENDI, ROGER C., and MEGUIRE, PHILIP G., 1985. Macroeconomic determinants of growth. *Journal of Monetary Economics*, 16 (2): 141–63.

KORNAI, JÀNOS, 1992. *The Socialist System: The Political Economy of Communism*. Princeton, NJ: Princeton University Press.

—— 1996. Paying the bill for goulash communism: Hungarian development and macro stabilization in a political-economy perspective. *Social Research*, 63 (4): 943–1040.

KORPI, WALTER, 1978. *Working Class in Welfare Capitalism: Work, Unions and Politics in Sweden*. London: Routledge & Kegan Paul.

—— 1980. Social policy and distributional conflict in the capitalist democracies. *West European Politics*, 3 (3): 296–316.

—— 1983. *The Democratic Class Struggle: Swedish Politics in a Comparative Perspective*. London: Routledge & Kegan Paul (chapters 'The democratic class struggle' and 'Social policy' reprinted in Leibfried and Mau 2008a: vol. 1, 347–98).

—— 1985. Economic growth and the welfare state: Leaky bucket or irrigation system? *European Sociological Review*, 1 (2): 97–118.

—— 1989. Power, politics and state autonomy in the development of social citizenship: Social rights during sickness in Eighteen OECD Countries since 1930. *American Sociological Review*, 54 (3): 309–28.

—— 2000. Faces of inequality: Gender, class, and patterns of inequalities in different types of welfare states. *Social Politics*, 7 (2): 127–91.

—— 2001. Contentious institutions: An augmented rational-action analysis of the origins and path dependence of welfare state institutions in western countries. *Rationality and Society*, 13 (2): 235–83.

—— 2003. Welfare-state regress in Western Europe: Politics, institutions, globalization, and Europeanization. *Annual Review of Sociology*, 29: 589–609.

—— 2006. Power resources and employer-centered approaches in explanations of welfare state and varieties of capitalism: Protagonists, consenters, and antagonists. *World Politics*, 58 (2): 167–206.

KORPI, WALTER, and PALME, JOAKIM, 1998. The paradox of redistribution and the strategy of equality: Welfare state institutions, inequality and poverty in the Western countries. *American Sociological Review*, 63 (5): 661–87 (reprint in Leibfried and Mau 2008a: vol. 3, 67–93).

—— —— 2003. New politics and class politics in the context of austerity and globalization: Welfare state regress in 18 countries, 1975–1995. *American Political Science Review*, 97 (3): 425–46 (reprint in Leibfried and Mau 2008a: vol. 1, 399–420).

—— —— 2004. Robin Hood, St. Matthew, or simple egalitarianism? Strategies of equality in welfare states, in *A Handbook of Comparative Social Policy*, ed. Patricia Kennet, Cheltenham: Edward Elgar, 153–79.

———— ———— 2007. The Social Citizenship Indicators Program (SCIP). Stockholm: Stockholm University, Swedish Institute for Social Research. Available at https://dspace.it.su.se/dspace/handle/10102/7.

KOVEN, SETH, and MICHEL, SONYA, 1993. *Mothers of a New World: Maternalist Politics and the Origins of Welfare States.* London: Routledge.

KREMER, MONIQUE, 2007. *How Welfare States Care: Culture, Gender and Parenting in Europe.* Amsterdam: Amsterdam University Press.

KRIESI, HANSPETER, GRANDE, EDGAR, LACHAT, ROMAIN, DOLEZAL, MARTIN, BORNSCHIER, SIMON, and FREY, TIMOTHEOS (eds.), 2008. *West European Politics in the Age of Globalization.* Cambridge: Cambridge University Press.

KRÖGER, SANDRA (ed.), 2009. What we have learnt: Advances, pitfalls and remaining questions of OMC research. European Integration Online Papers, special issue 1(13), forthcoming at http://eiop.or.at/eiop/.

KUHNLE, STEIN, 1981. The growth of social insurance programs in Scandinavia: Outside influences and internal forces, in *The Development of Welfare States in Europe and America,* ed. Peter Flora and Arnold J. Heidenheimer, New Brunswick, NJ: Transaction Books, 125–50.

———— 1996. International modeling, states, and statistics: Scandinavian social security solutions in the 1890s, in *States, Social Knowledge, and the Origins of Modern Social Policies,* ed. Dietrich Rueschemeyer and Theda Skocpol, Princeton, NJ: Princeton University Press, 3–14.

———— (ed.), 2001. *Survival of the European Welfare State.* London: Routledge.

KUHNLE, STEIN, and ALESTALO, MATTI, 2000. Growth, adjustments and survival of European welfare states, in *Survival of the European welfare state,* ed. Stein Kuhnle, London: Routledge, 3–18.

KUISMA, MIKKO, 2007. Social democratic internationalism and the welfare state: After the 'golden age'. *Cooperation and Conflict,* 42 (1): 9–26.

KUME, IKUO, 1998. *Disparaged Success: Labor Politics in Postwar Japan.* Ithaca, NY: Cornell University Press.

KUMLIN, STAFFAN, 2004. *The Personal and the Political: How Personal Welfare State Experiences Affect Political Trust and Ideology.* Basingstoke: Palgrave Macmillan.

———— 2007. The welfare state: Values, policy preferences, and performance evaluations, in *The Oxford Handbook of Political Behavior,* ed. Russell J. Dalton and Hans-Dieter Klingemann, Oxford: Oxford University Press, 362–82.

KUMLIN, STAFFAN, and SVALLFORS, STEFAN, 2007. Social stratification and political articulation: Why attitudinal class differences vary across countries, in *Social justice, legitimacy and the welfare state,* ed. Steffen Mau and Benjamin Veghte, Aldershot: Ashgate, 19–46.

KVIST, JON, 2003. A Danish welfare miracle? Policies and outcomes in the 1990s. *Scandinavian Journal of Public Health,* 31 (4): 241–5.

KWON, HYEOK YONG, and PONTUSSON, JONAS, 2008. *Unions, globalization, and the politics of social spending growth in OECD countries, 1962–2000.* Princeton, NJ: Princeton University, Department of Politics (unpubl. MS).

KWON, SOONMAN, 2007. Future of long-term care financing for the elderly in Korea. *Journal of Aging & Social Policy,* 20 (1): 119–36.

LAMURA, GIOVANNI, DÖHNER, HANNELI, and KOFAHL, CHRISTOPHER (eds.), 2008. *Family Carers of Older People in Europe. A Six-Country Comparative Study.* Münster: LIT.

LANDAU, DANIEL L., 1985. Government expenditure and economic growth in the developed countries. *Public Choice*, 47 (3): 459–78.

LANDES, DAVID S., 1972. Statistics as a source for the history of economic development in Western Europe, in *The Dimensions of the Past: Materials, Problems, and Opportunities for Quantitative Work in History*, ed. Val R. Lorwin and Jacob M. Price, New Haven, CT: Yale University Press, 53–92.

LANGE, PETER, and GARRETT, GEOFFREY, 1985. The politics of growth: Strategic interaction and economic performance, 1974–1980. *Journal of Politics*, 47 (4): 792–827.

LARSEN, CHRISTIAN A., 2006. *The Institutional Logic of Welfare Attitudes: How Welfare Regimes Influence Public Support*. Aldershot: Ashgate.

—— 2008. The institutional logic of welfare attitudes: How welfare regimes influence public support. *Comparative Political Studies*, 41 (2): 145–68.

LARSEN, CHRISTIAN A., and GOUL ANDERSEN, JORGEN, 2009. How new economic ideas changed integration and globalization: A perspective for the next century. *Social Policy & Administration*, 34 (1): 44–63.

LASH, SCOTT, and URRY, JOHN, 1987. *The End of Organized Capitalism*. Cambridge: Polity.

LAVER, MICHAEL, and HUNT, W. BEN, 1992. *Policy and Party Competition*. London: Routledge.

LAVER, MICHAEL, and SCHOFIELD, NORMAN, 1990. *Multiparty Government: The Politics of Coalition in Western Europe*. Oxford: Oxford University Press.

LAYARD, RICHARD, 2005. *Happiness. Lessons from a New Science*. London: Penguin.

LAYARD, RICHARD, NICKELL, STEPHEN J., and JACKMAN, RICHARD, 2005. *Unemployment: Macroeconomic Performance and the Labour Market*. Oxford: Oxford University Press (2nd edn.; 1st edn. 1991).

LAZEAR, EDWARD P., 1990. Job security provisions and employment. *Quarterly Journal of Economics*, 55 (3): 699–726.

LEE, CHEOL-SUNG, 2005. Income inequality, democracy, and public sector size. *American Sociological Review*, 70 (1): 158–81.

LEE, EDDY, 1994. The Declaration of Philadelphia: Retrospect and prospect. *International Labour Review*, 133 (4): 467–84.

LEE, KELLEY, BUSE, KENT, and FUSTUKIAN, SUZANNE (eds.), 2002. *Health Policy in a Globalising World*. Cambridge: Cambridge University Press.

LEE, YEAN-JU, SEOL, DONG-HOON, and CHO, SUNG-NAM, 2006. International marriages in South Korea: The significance of nationality and ethnicity. *Journal of Population Research*, 23 (2): 165–82.

LE GRAND, JULIAN, 1982. *The Strategy of Equality: Redistribution and the Social Services*. London: Allen & Unwin.

—— 1997. Knights, knaves or pawns? Human behaviour and social policy. *Journal of Social Policy*, 26 (2): 149–69.

—— (ed.), 1999. *Quasi-Markets and Social Policy*. Basingstoke: Macmillan (1st publ. 1993).

—— 2003. *Motivation, Agency and Public Policy: Of Knights and Knaves, Pawns and Queens*. Oxford: Oxford University Press.

—— 2007. *The Other Invisible Hand: Delivering Public Services through Choice and Competition*. Princeton, NJ: Princeton University Press.

LEHTO, JUHANI, MOSS, NINA, and ROSTGAARD, TINE, 1999. Universal public social care and health services?, in *Nordic Social Policy. Changing Welfare States*, ed. Mikko Kautto, Matti Heikkilä, Björn Hvinden, Staffan Marklund, and Niels Ploug, London: Routledge, 104–32.

LEIBFRIED, STEPHAN, 1992. Towards a European welfare state? On integrating poverty regimes into the European Community, in *Social Policy in a Changing Europe*, ed. Zsuzsa Ferge and Jon Eivind Kolberg, Frankfurt a.M.: Campus, 245–79.

—— 2000. National welfare states, European integration and globalization: A perspective for the next century. *Social Policy and Administration*, 34 (1): 44–63.

—— (ed.), 2001. *Welfare State Futures*. Cambridge: Cambridge University Press.

—— 2005. Social policy—Left to judges and the markets?, in *Policy-making in the European Union* (5th edn.), ed. Helen Wallace, William Wallace, and Mark A. Pollack, Oxford: Oxford University Press, 243–78.

—— 2010. Social policy: Left to the judges and the markets? in *Policy-Making in the European Union* (6th edn.), ed. Helen Wallace, Mark A. Pollack, and Alasdair R. Young, Oxford: Oxford University Press, 250–78.

LEIBFRIED, STEPHAN, and MAU, STEFFEN (eds.), 2008*a*. *Welfare States: Construction, Deconstruction, Reconstruction*. Vol. 1: *Analytical Approaches;* vol. 2: *Varieties and Transformations;* vol. 3: *Legitimation, Achievement and Integration*. Cheltenham: Edward Elgar.

—— 2008*b*. Introduction: Welfare States: Construction, Deconstruction, Reconstruction, in *Welfare States: Construction, Deconstruction, Reconstruction. Vol 1: Analytical Approaches*, ed. Stephan Leibfried and Steffen Mau, Cheltenham: Edward Elgar, xi–lxiv.

LEIBFRIED, STEPHAN, and PIERSON, PAUL (eds.), 1995. *European Social Policy: Between Fragmentation and Integration*. Washington, DC: Brookings Institution Press.

—— —— 2000. Social policy: Left to court and markets?, in *Policy-Making in the European Union* (4th edn.), ed. Helen Wallace and William Wallace, Oxford: Oxford University Press, 267–92.

LEIBFRIED, STEPHAN, and RIEGER, ELMAR, 1997. Limits to Globalization: Welfare State Reasons for Economic Openness or Closure. Stanford, CA & Mannheim: European Forum, Stanford University & MZES, Mannheim University (reproduced MS).

LEIBFRIED, STEPHAN, and ZÜRN, MICHAEL (eds.), 2005. *Transformations of the State?* Cambridge: Cambridge University Press.

LEIRA, ARNLAU, 1992. *Welfare States and Working Mothers: The Scandinavian Experience*. Cambridge: Cambridge University Press.

LEISERING, LUTZ, 2008. Social assistance in the global south: A survey and analysis. *Zeitschrift für ausländisches und internationales Arbeits- und Sozialrecht*, 22 (1/2): 74–103.

LEITNER, SIGRID, 2003. Varieties of familialism. *European Societies*, 5 (4): 353–75.

LEITNER, SIGRID, and LESSENICH, STEPHAN, 2007. (In)Dependence as dependent variable: Conceptualizing and measuring 'de-familization', in *Investigating Welfare State Change: The 'Dependent Variable Problem' in Comparative Analysis*, ed. Jochen Clasen and Nico A. Siegel, Cheltenham: Edward Elgar, 244–60.

LENOIR, RÉMI, 1991. Family policy in France since 1938, in *The French Welfare State: Surviving Social and Ideological Change*, ed. John S. Ambler, New York: New York University Press, 144–86.

LESSENICH, STEPHAN (ed.), 2003. *Wohlfahrtsstaatliche Grundbegriffe [Basic Welfare State Concepts]*. Frankfurt a.M.: Campus.

LEUNG, JOE C. B., 2006. The emergence of social assistance in China. *International Journal of Social Welfare*, 15 (3): 188–98.

LEUZE, KATRIN, MARTENS, KERSTIN, and RUSCONI, ALESSANDRA, 2007. New arenas of education governance: The impact of international organizations and markets on education policy making, in *New Arenas of Education Governance: The Impact of*

International Organizations and Markets on Educational Policy Making, ed. Kerstin Martens, Alessandra Rusconi and Katrin Leuze, Basingstoke: Palgrave Macmillan, 152–72.

LEVY, JONAH, 1999. Vice into virtue? Progressive politics and welfare reform in Continental Europe. *Politics & Society*, 27 (2): 239–73.

LEWIS, JANE, 1992. Gender and the development of welfare regimes. *Journal of European Social Policy*, 2 (3): 159–73.

—— 2000. Family policy in the post-war period, in *Cross Currents: Family Law and Policy in the US and England*, ed. Sanford N. Katz, John Eekelaar, and Mavis Maclean, Oxford: Oxford University Press, 81–100.

—— 2001. The decline of the male breadwinner model: Implications for work and care. *Social Politics*, 8 (2): 152–69.

—— 2006a. Work/family reconciliation, equal opportunities and social policies: The interpretation of policy trajectories at the EU level and the meaning of gender equality. *Journal of European Public Policy*, 13 (3): 420–37.

—— 2006b. Employment and care: The policy problem, gender equality and the issue of choice. *Journal of Comparative Policy Analysis*, 8 (2): 103–14.

—— 2007a. Gender, ageing and the 'new social settlement': The importance of developing a holistic approach to care policies. *Current Sociology*, 55 (2): 271–86.

—— 2007b. Families, individuals and the state, in *Making Social Policy Work*, ed. John Hills, Julian Le Grand, and David Piachaud, Bristol: Policy Press, 59–84.

LEWIS, JANE, and CAMPBELL, MARY, 2007. Work/Family balance policies in the UK since 1997. *Journal of Social Policy*, 36 (3): 365–81.

LEWIS, JANE, and HUERTA, CARMEN, 2008. Patterns of paid and unpaid work in Western Europe: Gender, commodification, preferences and the implications for policy. *Journal of European Social Policy*, 18 (1): 21–37.

LEWIS, JANE, and SURENDER, REBECCA (eds.), 2004. *Welfare State Change: Towards a Third Way?* Oxford: Oxford University Press.

LEWIS, RICHARD, ALVAREZ ROSETE, ARTURO, and MAYS, NICHOLAS, 2006. *How to Regulate Health Care in England? An International Perspective*. London: King's Fund.

LEWIS-BECK, MICHAEL S., NORPOTH, HELMUT, JACOBY, WILLIAM G., and WEISBERG, HERBERT F., 2008. *The American Voter Revisited*. Ann Arbor: University of Michigan Press.

LIEBERMAN, ROBERT C., 2005. *Race, State, and Policy: American Race Politics in Comparative Perspective*. Princeton, NJ: Princeton University Press.

LIGHT, DONALD W., 1995. Countervailing powers: A framework for professions in transition, in *Health Professions and the State in Europe*, ed. Terry Johnson, Gerald Larkin, and Mike Saks, London: Routledge, 7–24.

LIJPHART, AREND, 1999. *Patterns of Democracy: Government Forms and Performance in Thirty-Six Countries*. New Haven, CT: Yale University Press.

LINDBECK, ASSAR, 1995. Welfare state disincentives with endogenous habits and norms. *Scandinavian Journal of Economics*, 97 (4): 477–94.

—— 1997. *The Swedish Experiment*. Stockholm: SNS Förlag.

—— 2008. *Prospects for the welfare state*. Stockholm: Stockholm University, Institute for International Economic Studies.

LINDBOM, ANDERS, 2008. The Swedish Conservative Party and the welfare state: Institutional change and adapting preferences. *Government and Opposition*, 43 (4): 539–60.

LINDÉN, TORD SKOGEDAL, 2009. EU and OECD policy advice and changes in national family policy: Can reforms be attributed to participation in learning processes?, in *The Role of International Organizations in Social Policy: Ideas, Actors and Impact*, ed. Rune Ervik, Nanna Kildal, and Even Nilssen, Cheltenham: Edward Elgar, 111–37.

LINDERT, KATHY, SKOUFIAS, EMMANUEL, and SHAPIRO, JOSEPH, 2006. Redistributing income to the poor and the rich: Public transfers in Latin America and the Caribbean (Social Protection Discussion Paper, 0605). Washington, DC: World Bank. Available at http://siteresources.worldbank.org/SOCIALPROTECTION/Resources/SP-Discussion-papers/Safety-Nets-DP/0605.pdf.

LINDERT, PETER H., 1996. What limits social spending? *Explorations in Economic History*, 33 (1): 1–34.

—— 2004. *Growing Public. Social Spending and Economic Growth Since the Eighteenth Century*, 2 vols. Cambridge: Cambridge University Press.

—— 2005. Growing public: Is the welfare state mortal or exportable? (Working Paper, 25). Paris: American University of Paris. Available at http://www.international.ucla.edu/media/files/PERG.Lindert.pdf.

LINDH, THOMAS, and PALME, JOAKIM (eds.), 2006. *Sustainable Policies in an Ageing Europe: A Human Capital Response*. Stockholm: Institute for Future Studies. Available at http://www.framtidsstudier.se/sv/redirect.asp?p=2144.

LINGSOM, SUSAN, 1997. The substitution issue: Care policies and their consequences for family care (NOVA Report, 6/97). Oslo: Norwegian Social Research (NOVA).

LINNA, VÄINÖ, 2001–3. *Under the North Star*, 3 vols. Beaverton, Ont.: Aspasia Books, (first publ. 1959–1962).

LIPSMEYER, CHRISTINE S., 2003. Welfare and the discriminating public: Evaluating entitlement attitudes in post-Communist Europe. *Policy Studies Journal*, 31 (4): 545–64.

LISTER, RUTH, 1994. 'She has other duties': Women, citizenship and social security, in *Social Security and Social Change: New Challenges to the Beveridge Model*, ed. Sally Baldwin and Jane Falkingham, New York: Harvester Wheatsheaf, 31–44.

—— 2003a. *Citizenship: Feminist Perspectives*. New York: New York University Press.

—— 2003b. Investing in the citizen-workers of the future: Transformations in citizenship and the state under New Labour. *Social Policy & Administration*, 37 (5): 427–43.

—— 2004. The Third Way's social investment state, in *Welfare State Change. Towards a Third Way*, ed. Jane Lewis and Rebecca Surender, Oxford: Oxford University Press, 157–81.

LØDEMEL, IVAR, 2004. The development of workfare within social activation policies, in *Resisting Marginalization: Unemployment Experience and Social Policy in the European Union*, ed. Duncan Gallie and Serge Paugam, Oxford: Oxford University Press, 197–222.

LØDEMEL, IVAR, and TRICKEY, HEATHER (eds.), 2000. *An Offer you Can't Refuse: Workfare in International Perspective*. Bristol: Policy Press.

LONGEST, KYLE, and VAISEY, STEPHEN, 2008. Fuzzy: A program for performing qualitative comparative analyses (QCA) in STATA. *The Stata Journal*, 8 (1): 79–104.

LORA, EDUARDO, 2001. Structural reforms in Latin America: What has been reformed and how to measure it (Research department working paper, 466). Washington, DC: Inter-American Development Bank. Available at http://papers.ssrn.com/sol3/papers.cfm?abstract_id=909562.

LUBOVE, ROY, 1968. *The Struggle for Social Security 1900–1935*. Cambridge, MA: Harvard University Press.

LUCAS, ROBERT E., 1988. On the mechanics of economic development. *Journal of Monetary Economics*, 22 (1): 3–42.

LUHMANN, NIKLAS, 1981. *Politische Theorie im Wohlfahrtsstaat [Political Theory in the Welfare State]*. Munich: Olzog.

LUNDAHL, LISBETH, 2002. Sweden: Decentralization, deregulation, quasi-markets—and then what? *Journal of Education Policy*, 17 (6): 687–97.

LUNDBERG, OLLE, ÅBERG YNGWE, MONICA, KÖLEGÅRD STJÄRNE, MARIA, BJÖRK, LISA, and FRITZELL, JOHAN, 2008. *The Nordic Experience: Welfare States and Public Health (NEWS)*. Stockholm: Center for Health Equity Studies (CHESS) and Karolinska Institutet. Available at http://www.chess.su.se/content/1/c6/04/65/23/NEWS_Rapport_080819.pdf.

LUSTICK, IAN, 1996. History, historiography, and political science: Historical records and selection bias. *American Political Science Review*, 90 (2): 605–18.

LUTZ, HELMA (ed.), 2008. *Migration and Domestic Work: A European Perspective on a Global Theme*. Aldershot: Ashgate.

LYNCH, JULIA, 2001. The age-orientation of social policy regimes in OECD countries. *Journal of Social Policy*, 30 (3): 411–36.

—— 2006. *Age in the Welfare State: The Origins of Social Spending on Pensioners, Workers, and Children*. Cambridge: Cambridge University Press.

—— 2009. Italy: A Christian Democratic or Clientelist Welfare State?, in *Religion, Class-Coalitions and Welfare State Regimes*, ed. Kees van Kersbergen and Philip Manow, Cambridge: Cambridge University Press, 91–118.

MABBETT, DEBORAH, 2005. Some are more equal than others: Definitions of disability in social policy and discrimination law in Europe. *Journal of Social Policy*, 43 (2): 215–33.

MABBETT, DEBORAH, and SCHELKLE, WALTRAUD, 2009. The politics of conflict management in EU regulation. *West European Politics*, 32 (4, Special Issue): 699–718.

MABBETT, IAN (ed.), 1985. *Patterns of Kingship and Authority in Traditional Asia*. London: Croom Helm.

MACHADO, SANTIAGO M., and LORENZO, RAFAEL DE (eds.), 1997. *European Disability Law*. Madrid: Escuela Libre Editorial.

MACLEAN, MAVIS (ed.), 2005. *Family Law and Family Values*. Oxford: Hart.

MADDISON, ANGUS, 1982. *Phases of Capitalist Development*. Oxford: Oxford University Press.

MADRID, RAÚL L., 2003. *Retiring the State: The Politics of Pension Privatization in Latin America and Beyond*. Stanford, CA: Stanford University Press.

MADSEN, PER K., 2002. Security and flexibility: Friends or foes? Some observations from the case of Denmark. Paper presented at Lyon Conference (ILO) on the Future of Work and Social Protection, January 16–18. Not available on the web any more.

MAHON, RIANNE, 2002. Child care: Toward what kind of 'Social Europe'? *Social Politics*, 9 (3): 343–79.

—— 2006. The OECD and the work/family reconciliation agenda: Competing frames, in *Children, Changing Families and Welfare States*, ed. Jane Lewis, Cheltenham: Edward Elgar, 173–97.

MAHONEY, JAMES, 2000. Path dependence in historical sociology. *Theory and Society*, 29 (4): 507–48.

MAIER-RIGAUD, REMI, 2009. Pension policy of the International Labour Office, in *The Role of International Organizations in Social Policy. Ideas, Actors and Impact*, ed. Rune Ervik, Nanna Kildal, and Even Nilssen, Cheltenham: Edward Elgar, 165–89.

MAIONI, ANTONIA, 1998. *Parting at the Crossroads: The Emergence of Health Insurance in the United States and Canada.* Princeton, NJ: Princeton University Press.

MALEFAKIS, EDWARD, 1995. The political and socioeconomic contours of Southern European history, in *The Politics of Democratic Consolidation,* ed. Richard Gunther, P. Nikiforas Diamandouros, and Hans-Jürgen Puhle, Baltimore, MD: Johns Hopkins University Press, 33–76.

MALLOY, JAMES M., 1979. *The Politics of Social Security in Brazil.* Pittsburgh, PA: University of Pittsburgh Press.

MANDEL, HADAS, and SEMYONOV, MOSHE, 2006. A welfare state paradox: State interventions and women's employment opportunities in 22 countries. *American Journal of Sociology,* 111 (6): 1910–49.

MANN, MICHAEL, and RILEY, DYLAN, 2007. Explaining macro-regional trends in global income inequalities. *Socio-Economic Review,* 5 (1): 81–115.

MANNING, NICK, 2004. Diversity and change in pre-accession Central and Eastern Europe since 1989. *Journal of European Social Policy,* 14 (3): 211–32.

MANOW, PHILIP, 2001. Comparative institutional advantages of welfare state regimes and new coalitions in welfare state reforms, in *The New Politics of the Welfare State,* ed. Paul Pierson, Oxford: Oxford University Press, 146–64.

—— 2004. The good, the bad, and the ugly: Esping-Andersen's regime typology and the religious roots of the Western welfare state (Working Paper, 04/3). Cologne: Max Planck Institute for the Study of Societies. Available at http://www.ciaonet.org/wps/mpifg10723/mpifg10723.pdf.

—— 2005. Germany: Cooperative federalism and the overgrazing of the fiscal commons, in *Federalism and the Welfare State: New World and European Experiences,* ed. Herbert Obinger, Stephan Leibfried, and Francis G. Castles, Cambridge: Cambridge University Press, 222–62.

—— 2007. Wahlregeln, Klassenkoalitionen und Wohlfahrtsstaatsregime—oder: wie man Esping-Andersen mit Stein Rokkan erklären kann [Election rules, class coalitions and welfare state regimes: Or how Esping-Andersen can be explained via Stein Rokkan]. *Zeitschrift für Soziologie,* 36 (6): 414–30.

MANOW, PHILIP, and KERSBERGEN, KEES VAN, 2006. The impact of class coalitions, cleavage structures and church-state conflicts on welfare state development (Working Papers Political Science, 2006/03). Amsterdam: Vrije Universiteit Amsterdam, Department of Political Science. Available at http://hdl.handle.net/1871/10634.

—— —— 2009. Religion and the Western welfare state: The theoretical context, in *Religion, Class Coalitions and the Welfare State,* ed. Kees van Kersbergen and Philip Manow, Cambridge: Cambridge University Press, 1–38.

MANOW, PHILIP, and PALIER, BRUNO, 2009. A conservative welfare state regime without Christian Democracy? The French état-providence, 1880–1960, in *Religion, Class-Coalitions and Welfare States,* ed. Kees van Kersbergen and Philip Manow, Cambridge: Cambridge University Press, 146–74.

MARCH, JAMES G., and OLSEN, JOHAN P., 1984. The New Institutionalism: Organizational factors in political life. *American Political Science Review,* 78 (3): 734–49.

MARCUSSEN, MARTIN, 2004. Multilateral surveillance and the OECD: Playing the idea game, in *The OECD and European Welfare States,* ed. Klaus Armingeon and Michelle Beyeler, Cheltenham: Edward Elgar, 13–31.

MARES, ISABELA, 2001. Firms and the welfare state: When, why and how does social policy matter to employers, in *Varieties of Capitalism: The institutional Foundations of Comparative Advantage*, ed. Peter A. Hall and David Soskice, Oxford: Oxford University Press, 184–213.

—— 2003. *The Politics of Social Risk: Business and Welfare State Development*. Cambridge: Cambridge University Press.

—— 2005*a*. Wage bargaining in the presence of social services and transfers. *World Politics*, 57 (1): 99–142.

—— 2005*b*. Social protection around the world: External insecurity, state capacity, and domestic political cleavages. *Comparative Political Studies*, 38 (6): 623–52.

—— 2006. *Taxation, Wage Bargaining and Unemployment*. Cambridge: Cambridge University Press.

MARES, ISABELA, and CARNES, MATTHEW E., 2009. Social policy in developing countries. *Annual Review of Political Science*, 12: 93–113.

MARINAKIS, ANDRÉS, 2006. Desempolvando el salario mínimo: Reflexiones a partir de la experiencia en el Cono Sur [Dusting off the minimum wage: Reflections based on experiences in the Southern Cone], in *¿Para Qué Sirve el Salario Mínimo? Elementos Para su Determinación en los Países del Cono Sur*, ed. Andrés. Marinakis and Juan J. Velasco, Santiago de Chile: Oficina Internacional del Trabajo (ILO), 2–20.

MARMOR, THEODORE. R., 2000. *The Politics of Medicare*. New York: Aldine de Gruyter (2nd edn.; 1st edn. 1970).

MARMOR, THEODORE R., FREEMAN, RICHARD, and OKMA, KIEKE (eds.), 2009. *Comparative Studies and the Politics of Modern Medical Care*. New Haven, CT: Yale University Press.

MARMOR, THEODORE R., and OBERLANDER, JONATHAN, 2009. Health Reform: The Fateful Moment. *The New York Review of Books*, 56 (13): 69–73. Available at http://www.nybooks.com/articles/22931.

MARSH, DAVID C., 1980. *The Welfare State*. London: Longman.

MARSHALL, KATHERINE, 2008. *The World Bank. From Reconstruction to Development to Equity*. London: Routledge.

MARSHALL, THOMAS H., 1963. *Sociology at the Crossroads and Other Essays*. London: Heinemann.

—— 1964*a*. *Class, Citizenship and Social Development*. Garden City, NY: Doubleday.

—— 1964*b*. Citizenship and social class, in *Class, Citizenship and Social Development*, ed. Thomas H. Marshall, Garden City, NY: Doubleday, 65–122 (first published 1950; reprinted in Leibfried and Mau 2008*a*: vol. 1, 3–60).

—— 1964*c*. International comprehension in and through social science, in *Class, Citizenship, and Social Development*, ed. Thomas H. Marshall, Garden City, NY: Doubleday, 42–61 (first published 1962).

MARTENS, KERSTIN, and WEYMANN, ANSGAR, 2007. The internationalization of education policy: Towards convergence of national paths?, in *Transforming the Golden-Age Nation State*, ed. Achim Hurrelmann, Stephan Leibfried, Kerstin Martens, and Peter Mayer, Basingstoke: Palgrave Macmillan, 152–72.

MARTIN, ANDREW, and ROSS, GEORGE (eds.), 2004. *Euros and Europeans. Monetary Integration and the European Model of Society*. Cambridge: Cambridge University Press.

MARTIN, CLAUDE, and LE BIHAN, BLANCHE, 2009. Public childcare and preschools in France: New policy paradigm and path dependency, in *Child Care and Preschool*

Development in Europe: Institutional Perspectives, ed. Kerstin Scheiwe and Harry Willekens, Basingstoke: Palgrave Macmillan, 57–71.

MARTIN, CATHIE JO, 2000. *Stuck in Neutral: Business and the Politics of Human Capital Investment Policy*. Princeton, NJ: Princeton University Press.

—— 2004. Reinventing welfare regimes: Employers and the implementation of active social policy. *World Politics*, 57 (1): 39–69.

MARTIN, CATHIE JO, and SWANK, DUANE, 2008. The political origins of coordinated capitalism: Business organizations, party systems, and state structure in the age of innocence. *American Political Science Review*, 102 (2): 181–98.

MARTIN, CATHIE JO, and THELEN, KATHLEEN, 2007. The state and coordinated capitalism: Contributions of the public sector to social solidarity in postindustrial societies. *World Politics*, 60 (1): 1–36.

MARTIN, DAVID, 1978. The religious condition of Europe, in *Contemporary Europe. Social Structures and Cultural Patterns*, ed. Salvador Giner and Margaret S. Archer, London: Routledge & Kegan, 228–87.

MARTIN, JOHN P., 2000. What works among active labour market policies: Evidence from OECD countries' experiences. *OECD Economic Studies*, 30 (1): 79–113.

MARTIN, JOHN P., and WHITEHOUSE, EDWARD, 2008. Reforming retirement-income systems: Lessons from the recent experiences of OECD countries (OECD Social, Employment and Migration Working Paper, 66). Paris: OECD Directorate for Employment, Labour and Social Affairs. Available at http://econpapers.repec.org/paper/oecelsaab/66-en.htm.

MARTÍNEZ FRANZONI, JULIANA, 2008. *Domesticar la incertidumbre: Mercado laboral, política social y familia en América Latina [Domesticating Uncertainty: Labor Market, Social Policy, and Family in Latin America]*. San José: Editorial UCR.

MARX, IVE, and VERBIST, GERLINDE, 2008. Combating in-work poverty in Europe: The policy options assessed, in *The Working Poor in Europe*, ed. Hans-Jürgen Andress and Henning Lohmann, London: Edward Elgar, 273–92.

MASON, TIMOTHY W., 1993. *Social Policy in the Third Reich: The Working Class and the National Community*. Providence, RI: Berg.

—— 1995. *Nazism, Fascism and the Working Class [Essays]*, ed. Jane Caplan, Cambridge: Cambridge University Press.

MATHESON, GEORGE, and WEARING, MICHAEL, 1999. Within and without: Labour force status and political views in four welfare states, in *The End of the Welfare State? Responses to State Retrenchment*, ed. Stefan Svallfors and Peter Taylor-Gooby, London: Routledge, 135–60.

MATSAGANIS, MANOS, 2004. 'A tale of recurrent policy failure? Tackling retirement pensions in Greece' (URGE Policy Paper). Torino: URGE [L' Unità die Recerca sulla Governance Europea], Collegio Carlo Alberto, Moncalieri]. Available at http://www.urge.it/files/papers/2_2_wp_3_2004.pdf.

—— 2005. Greece—Fighting with hands tied behind the back: Anti-poverty policy without a minimum income, in *Welfare State Reform in Southern Europe*, ed. Maurizio Ferrera, London: Routledge, 33–83.

MATSAGANIS, MANOS, CAPUCHA, LUIS, FERRERA, MAURIZIO, and MORENO, LUIS, 2003. Mending nets in the South: Anti-poverty policies in Greece, Italy, Portugal and Spain. *Social Policy & Administration*, 37 (6): 639–55.

MAU, STEFFEN, 2003. *The Moral Economy of Welfare States: Britain and Germany Compared.* London: Routledge.

—— 2004. Welfare regimes and the norms of social exchange. *Current Sociology,* 52 (1): 53–74.

MAYDA, ANNA M., O'ROURKE, KEVIN H., and SINNOTT, RICHARD, 2007. Risk, government and globalization: International survey evidence (NBER Working Paper, 13037). Cambridge, MA: National Bureau of Economic Research. Available at http://www.nber.org/papers/w13037.

MAYER, KARL ULRICH, 2001. The paradox of global social change and national path dependencies: Life course patterns in advanced societies, in *Inclusions and Exclusions in European Societies,* ed. Alison Woodward and Martin Kohli, London: Routledge, 89–110.

MAYHEW, DAVID R., 1986. *Placing Parties in American Politics: Organizations, Electoral Settings, and Government Activity in the Twentieth Century.* Princeton, NJ: Princeton University Press.

MCCALLUM, JOHN, and BLAIS, ANDRE, 1987. Government, special interest groups and economic growth. *Public Choice,* 54 (1): 3–18.

MCKEE, MARTIN, MACLEHOSE, LAURA, and NOLTE, ELLEN (eds.), 2004. *Health policy and European enlargement.* Maidenhead: Open University Press.

MCKENZIE, RICHARD B., and LEE, DWIGHT R., 1991. *Quicksilver Capital: How the Rapid Movement of Wealth Has Changed the World.* New York: Free Press.

MCLELLAN, D. LINDSAY, 1997. *Framework for the Qualitative and Quantitative Analysis of Data on the Ageing of People with Disabilities.* Strasbourg: Council of Europe.

MEAD, LAWRENCE M., 1986. *Beyond Entitlement: The Social Obligations of Citizenship.* New York: Free Press.

—— 1992. *The New Politics of Poverty: The Nonworking Poor in America.* New York: Basic Books.

—— 1996. Welfare Policy: The Administrative Frontier. *Journal of Policy Analysis and Management,* 15 (4): 587–600.

—— 1997a. Optimizing JOBS: Evaluation versus administration. *Public Administration Review,* 57 (2): 113–23.

—— 1997b. Citizenship and social policy: T. H. Marshall and poverty. *Social Philosophy and Policy,* 14 (2): 197–230.

MECHANIC, DAVID, and ROCHEFORT, DAVID A., 1996. Comparative medical systems. *Annual Review of Sociology,* 22: 239–70.

MEIDNER, RUDOLF, and HEDBORG, ANNA, 1984. *Modell Schweden: Erfahrungen einer Wohlfahrtsgesellschaft [The Swedish Model: Experiences of a Welfare Society].* Frankfurt a.M: Campus.

MELTZER, ALLAN H., and RICHARD, SCOTT F., 1981. A rational theory of the size of government. *Journal of Political Economy,* 89 (5): 914–27.

MENDOZA, ENRIQUE G., ASSAF, RAZIN, and TESAR, LINDA L., 1994. Effective tax rates in macroeconomics: Cross country estimates of tax rates on factor incomes and consumption. *Journal of Monetary Economics,* 34 (3): 297–323.

MERKEL, WOLFGANG, 1993. *Ende der Sozialdemokratie? Machtressourcen und Regierungspolitik im westeuropäischen Vergleich [The End of Social Democracy? Power Resources and Government Policies in West European Comparison].* Frankfurt a.M.: Campus.

MESA-LAGO, CARMELO, 1978. *Social Security in Latin America: Pressure Groups, Stratification, and Inequality.* Pittsburgh: University of Pittsburgh Press.

—— 1989. *Ascent to Bankruptcy: Financing Social Security in Latin America*. Pittsburgh: University of Pittsburgh Press.

—— 1994. *Changing Social Security in Latin America: Toward Alleviating the Social Costs of Economic Reform*. Boulder, CO: Lynne Rienner.

—— 2008. *Reassembling Social Security: A Survey of Pensions and Health Care Reforms in Latin America*. Oxford: Oxford University Press.

MESSERE, KEN C., 1993. *Tax Policy in OECD Countries: Choices and Conflicts*. Amsterdam: IBFD Publications.

METTLER, SUZANNE, and SOSS, JOE, 2004. The consequences of public policy for democratic citizenship: Bridging policy studies and mass politics. *Perspectives on Politics*, 2 (1): 55–73.

MEYER, THOMAS, 2007. *The Theory of Social Democracy*. Cambridge: Cambridge University Press.

MICKELWRIGHT, JOHN, 2003. Child poverty in English-speaking countries (Innocenti Working Papers, 94). Florence: UNICEF Innocenti Research Centre. Available at http://www.unicef-irc.org/publications/pdf/iwp94.pdf.

MILESI-FERRETTI, GIAN M., PEROTTI, ROBERTO, and ROSTAGNO, MASSIMO, 2002. Electoral systems and public spending. *Quarterly Journal of Economics*, 117 (2): 609–57.

MILLY, DEBORAH J., 1999. *Poverty, Equality and Growth: The Politics of Economic Need in Postwar Japan*. Cambridge, MA: Harvard University Press.

MINGIONE, ENZO, 1996. Conclusion, in *Urban Poverty and the Underclass: A Reader*, ed. Enzo Mingione, Oxford: Blackwell, 372–83.

MINOGUE, MARTIN, 1998. Changing the state: Concepts and practice in the reform of the public sector, in *Beyond the New Public Management: Changing Ideas and Practices in Governance*, ed. Martin Minogue, Charles Polidano, and David Hulme, Cheltenham: Edward Elgar, 17–37.

MISRA, JOYA, BUDIG, MICHELLE J., and MOLLER, STEPHANIE, 2007. Reconciliation policies and the effects of motherhood on employment, earnings and poverty. *Journal of Comparative Policy Analysis: Research and Practice*, 9 (2): 135–55.

MITCHELL, DEBORAH, 1991. *Income Transfers in Ten Welfare States*. Aldershot: Avebury.

MJØSET, LARS (ed.), 1986. *Norden dagen derpå: De nordiske ekonomisk-politiske modellene og deres problemer på 70–80-tallet [The Nordic Countries the Morning After: The Nordic Economic-Political Models and their Problems in the 70s and 80s]*. Oslo: Universitetsforlaget.

MOENE, KARL OVE, and WALLERSTEIN, MICHAEL, 2001. Inequality, social insurance and redistribution. *American Political Science Review*, 95 (4): 859–74.

MOI and FEDERCASA (MINISTRY OF INFRASTRUCTURE OF THE ITALIAN REPUBLIC AND ITALIAN HOUSING FEDERATION, I.E. FEDERAZIONE ITALIANA PER LA CASA), 2006. *Housing Statistics in the European Union 2005/2006*. Rome: Federcasa.

MOLEN, IRINA VAN DER, and NOVIKOVA, IRINA, 2005. Mainstreaming gender in the EU-accession process: The case of the Baltic Republics. *Journal of European Social Policy*, 15 (2): 139–56.

MOLINA, CARLOS GERARDO (ed.), 2006. *Universalismo básico. Una nueva política social para América Latina [Basic Universalism: A New Social Policy for Latin America]*. Washington, DC: Inter-American Development Bank.

MOMMSEN, WOLFGANG J. (ed.), 1981. *The Emergence of the Welfare State in Britain and Germany*. London: Croom Helm.

MOORE, MICK, 2008. Between coercion and contract: Competing narratives on taxation and governance, in *Taxation and State-Building in Developing Countries*, ed. Deborah A.

Bräutigam, Odd-Helge Fjelstad, and Mick Moore, Cambridge: Cambridge University Press, 34–63.

MORAN, MICHAEL, 1992. The health-care state in Europe: Convergence or divergence. *Environment and Planning C: Government and Policy*, 10 (1): 77–90.

—— 1995. Three faces of the health care state. *Journal of Health Politics, Policy and Law*, 20 (3): 767–81.

—— 2000. Understanding the welfare state: The case of health care. *British Journal of Politics and International Relations*, 2 (2): 135–60.

MOREL, NATHALIE, 2007. From subsidiarity to 'free choice': Child- and elder-care policy reforms in France, Belgium, Germany and the Netherlands. *Social Policy & Administration*, 41 (6): 618–37. (Repr. in *Reforming the Bismarckian Welfare Systems. Broadening Perspectives in Social Policy*, ed. Bruno Palier and Claude Martin, Oxford: Blackwell, 2008, 82–101).

MORENO, LUIS, 2000. The Spanish development of Southern welfare, in *Survival of the Welfare State*, ed. Stein Kuhnle, London: Routledge, 146–65.

—— 2002. Mediterranean welfare and 'superwomen' (UPC Working Paper, 02/02). Madrid: Spanish National Research Council (CSIC), Unit on Comparative Politics and Policy (UPC). Available at http://www.iesam.csic.es/doctrab2/dt-0202.pdf.

—— 2004. Spain's transition to New Risks: A farewell to 'superwomen', in *New Risks and New Welfare in Europe: The Transformation of the European Welfare State*, ed. Peter Taylor-Gooby, Oxford: Oxford University Press, 133–56.

—— 2006. The model of social protection in Southern Europe: Enduring characteristics? *Revue Française des Affaires Sociales*, 60 (1): 73–95. Available at http://www.iesam.csic.es/proyecto/grupo/ficheros/morenorfas12006A.pdf.

MORGAN, KIMBERLY J., 2005. The 'production' of child care: How labor markets shape social policy and vice versa. *Social Politics*, 12 (2): 243–63.

—— 2006. *Working Mothers and the Welfare State: Religion and the Politics of Work-Family Policies in Western Europe and the United States*. Stanford, CA: Stanford University Press.

—— 2009. The religious foundations of work-family policies in Western Europe, in *Religion, Class-Coalitions and Welfare States*, ed. Kees van Kersbergen and Philip Manow, Cambridge: Cambridge University Press, 56–90.

MORLINO, LEONHARDO, 1998. *Democracy Between Consolidation and Crisis: Parties, Groups and Citizens in Southern Europe*. Oxford: Oxford University Press.

MORTENSEN, DALE T., 1977. Unemployment insurance and job search decisions. *Industrial and Labor Relations Review*, 30 (4): 505–17.

MOSLEY, LAYNA, 2003. *Global Capital and National Governments*. Cambridge: Cambridge University Press.

MOSS, DAVID A., 1996. *Socializing Security: Progressive-era Economists and the Origins of American Social Policy*. Cambridge, MA: Harvard University Press.

MUELLER, DENNIS C., 1989. *Public Choice II: A Revised Edition of Public Choice*. Cambridge: Cambridge University Press (presently 'III' 2009; 1st edn. 1979).

MÜLLER, KATHARINA, 2003. *Privatising Old-Age Security: Latin America and Eastern Europe Compared*. Cheltenham: Edward Elgar.

MÜLLER, WALTER, STEINMANN, SUSANNE, and SCHNEIDER, REINHART, 1997. Bildung in Europa [Education in Europe], in *Die westeuropäischen Gesellschaften im Vergleich*, ed. Stefan Hradil and Stefan Immerfall, Opladen: Leske+Budrich, 177–245.

MURJI, KARIN, and SOLOMOS, JOHN (eds.), 2005. *Racialization: Studies in Theory and Practice.* Oxford: Oxford University Press.

MURRAY, CHARLES A., 1984. *Losing Ground. American Social Policy 1950–1980.* New York: Basic Books.

MUTARI, ELLEN, and FIGART, DEBORAH M., 2001. Europe at a crossroads: Harmonization, liberalization, and the gender of work time. *Social Politics,* 8 (1): 36–64.

MYLES, JOHN, 1984. *Old Age and the Welfare State: The Political Economy of Public Pensions.* Boston: Little Brown (2nd edn. Lawrence, KS: University Press of Kansas 1989).

—— 2006. Do egalitarians have a future? *Review of Income and Wealth,* 52 (1): 145–51.

MYLES, JOHN, and PIERSON, PAUL, 2001. The comparative political economy of pension reform, in *The New Politics of the Welfare State,* ed. Paul Pierson, Oxford: Oxford University Press, 305–33.

MYLES, JOHN, and QUADAGNO, JILL S., 2002. Political theory of the welfare state. *Social Service Review,* 76 (1): 34–57 (reprint in Leibfried and Mau 2008a: vol. 1, 62–85).

MYLES, JOHN, and SAINT-ARNAUD, SÉBASTIEN, 2006. Population diversity, multiculturalism, and the welfare state: Should welfare theory be revisited?, in *Multiculturalism and the Welfare State: Recognition and Redistribution in Contemporary Democracies,* ed. Keith Banting and Will Kymlicka, Oxford: Oxford University Press, 339–54.

MYRDAL, GUNNAR, 1957. Economic nationalism and internationalism. *Australian Outlook,* 11 (1): 3–50.

NALDINI, MANUELA, 2003. *The Family in the Mediterranean Welfare State.* London: Frank Cass.

NASH, GEORGE H., 1976. *The Conservative Intellectual Movement in America: Since 1945.* New York: Basic Books.

—— 2004. Hayek and the American Conservative Movement. Paper presented at Intercollegiate Studies Institute (ISI), April 3. Available at http://www.isi.org/lectures/text/pdf/ hayek4–3–04.pdf.

NATALI, DAVID, and RHODES, MARTIN, 2004. Trade-offs and veto players: Reforming pensions in France and Italy. *French Politics,* 2 (1): 1–23.

NAUMANN, INGELA K., 2005. Child care and feminism in West Germany and Sweden in the 1960s and 1970s. *Journal of European Social Policy,* 15 (1): 47–63.

NAVARRO, VICENTE, 1989. Why some countries have national health insurance, others have national health services, and the United States has neither. *International Journal of Health Services,* 19 (3): 383–404.

NEAVE, GUY, 1985. The non-state sector in education in Europe: A conceptual and historical analysis. *European Journal of Education,* 20 (4): 312–37.

NELSON, KENNETH, 2004. Mechanisms of poverty alleviation: Anti-poverty effects of non-means-tested and means-tested benefits in five welfare states. *Journal of European Social Policy,* 14 (4): 371–90.

—— 2007. Universalism versus targeting: The vulnerability of social insurance and means-tested minimum income protection in 18 countries 1990–2002. *International Social Security Review,* 60 (1): 33–58.

NELSON, MOIRA L., 2008. 'Education policy and the consequences for labour market integration in Denmark, Germany, and the Netherlands'. Chapel Hill, NC: University of North Carolina, Chapel Hill, Ph.D. Dissertation.

NELSON, MOIRA L., and STEPHENS, JOHN D., 2008. Welfare state regimes and women's employment. Paper presented at The Political Economy of the Service Transition. Institute for International Integration Studies, Trinity College, Dublin, May 16–17.

NEYER, GERDA, 2003. Family policies and low fertility in Western Europe (MPIDR Working Paper, 2003/021). Rostock: Max Planck Institute for Demographic Research (MPIDR). Available at http://www.iesf.es/fot/Fertility-western-Europe-2003.pdf.

NICKELL, STEPHEN J., 1997. Unemployment and labor market rigidities: Europe versus North America. *Journal of Economic Perspectives*, 11 (3): 55–74.

NICKELL, STEPHEN J., and LAYARD, RICHARD, 1999. Labour market institutions and economic performance, in *Handbook of Labour Economics*, vol. 3C, ed. Orley Ashenfelter and David Card, Amsterdam: Elsevier, 3029–84.

NICKELL, STEPHEN J., NUNZIATA, LUCA, and OCHEL, WOLFGANG, 2005. Unemployment in the OECD since the 1960s. What do we know? *Economic Journal*, 115 (500): 1–27.

NISKANEN, WILLIAM A., 1971. *Bureaucracy and Representative Government*. Chicago: Aldine Atherton.

NOLAN, BRIAN, and WHELAN, CHRISTOPHER T., 1996. *Resources, Deprivation and Poverty*. Oxford: The Clarendon Press of Oxford University Press.

NOORUDDIN, IRFAN, and SIMMONS, JOEL W., 2006. The politics of hard choices: IMF programs and government spending. *International Organization*, 60 (4): 1001–33.

NØRBY-JOHANSEN, LARS, 1986. Denmark, in *Growth to Limits: The Western European Welfare States Since World War II. Vol. 1: Sweden, Norway, Finland, Denmark*, ed. Peter Flora, Berlin: de Gruyter, 293–381.

NORDLUND, ANDERS, 2003. Persistence and change: Nordic social policy in the 1980s and 1990s. *European Societies*, 5 (1): 69–90.

NORRIS, MICHELLE, COATES, DERMOT, and KANE, FIONA, 2007. Breaching the limits of owner occupation? Supporting low-income buyers in the inflated Irish housing market. *European Journal of Housing Policy*, 7 (3): 337–56.

NORRIS, MICHELLE, and SHIELDS, PATRICK, 2004. Regular national report on housing developments in European countries. Dublin: Stationery Office. Available at http://www.iut.nu/EU/2005.pdf.

NORRIS, PIPPA, and INGLEHART, RONALD, 2004. *Sacred and Secular: Religion and Politics Worldwide*. Cambridge: Cambridge University Press.

NORTH, DOUGLAS C., 1990. *Institutions, Institutional Change and Economic Performance*. Cambridge: Cambridge University Press.

NORTON, EDWARD C., 2000. Long-term care, in *Handbook of Health Economics*, vol. 1B, ed. Anthony J. Culyer and Joseph P. Newhouse, Amsterdam: Elsevier, 955–94.

NOZICK, ROBERT, 1974. *Anarchy, State, and Utopia*. Oxford: Blackwell.

NULLMEIER, FRANK, KÖPPE, STEPHAN, and FRIEDRICH, JONAS, 2009. Legitimationen der Sozialpolitik [Legitimations of social policy], in *Wohlfahrtsstaatlichkeit in entwickelten Demokratien. Herausforderungen, Reformen und Perspektiven*, ed. Herbert Obinger and Elmar Rieger, Frankfurt a.M.: Campus, 151–89.

NUMBERS, RONALD, 1978. *Almost Persuaded: American Physicians and Compulsory Health Insurance, 1912–1920*. Baltimore, MD: Johns Hopkins University Press.

NUNZIATA, LUCA, 2002. Unemployment, labour market institutions and shocks (Economics Papers from the Economics Group, 2002/W 16). Oxford: Nuffield College, University of Oxford. Available at http://www.nuffield.ox.ac.uk/Economics/papers/2002/w16/p4unemploymentWP.pdf.

NUSSBAUM, MARTHA C., 1990. Aristotelian social democracy, in *Liberalism and the Good*, ed. R. Bruce Douglas, Gerald M. Mara, and Henry S. Richardson, London: Routledge, 203–52.

—— 2000. *Women and Human Development: The Capabilities Approach.* Cambridge: Cambridge University Press.

NYGARD, MICHAEL, 2006. Welfare-ideological change in Scandinavia: A comparative analysis of partisan welfare state positions in four Nordic countries, 1970–2003. *Scandinavian Political Studies*, 29 (4): 356–85.

OAS (ORGANISATION OF AMERICAN STATES), 2008. *Chile: Lineamientos y Acciones sobre educación parvularia 2008 [Chile: Guidelines and actions on early childhood education 2008]*. Washington, DC: OAS. Available at http://www.oei.es/noticias/spip.php?article2418&debut_5ultimasOEI=20.

OBINGER, HERBERT, 1998. Federalism, direct democracy, and welfare state development in Switzerland. *Journal of Public Policy*, 18 (3): 241–63.

OBINGER, HERBERT, LEIBFRIED, STEPHAN, BOGEDAN, CLAUDIA, GINDULIS, EDITH, MOSER, JULIA, and STARKE, PETER 2005. The intervention state: The shifting welfare component: Welfare state transformation in small open economies, in *Tansformations of the State?*, ed. Stephan Leibfried and Michael Zürn, Cambridge: Cambridge University Press, 161–85.

OBINGER, HERBERT, LEIBFRIED, STEPHAN, and CASTLES, FRANCIS G. (eds.), 2005a. *Federalism and the Welfare State: New World and European Experiences*. Cambridge: Cambridge University Press.

—— —— —— 2005b. Bypasses to a social Europe? Lessons from federal experience. *Journal of European Public Policy*, 12 (3): 545–71 (reprint in Leibfried and Mau 2008a: vol. 3, 599–625).

OBINGER, HERBERT, STARKE, PETER, BOGEDAN, CLAUDIA, MOSER, JULIA, OBINGER-GINDULIS, EDITH, and LEIBFRIED, STEPHAN, 2010. *Transformations of the Welfare State: Small States—Big Lessons*. Oxford: Oxford University Press.

OBINGER, HERBERT, and TÁLOS, EMMERICH, 2006. *Sozialstaat Österreich zwischen Kontinuität und Umbau. Eine Bilanz der ÖVP/FPÖ/BZÖ-Koalition [Welfare State Austria between Continuity and Transformation: Taking Stock of the ÖVP/FPÖ/BZÖ Party-Coalition Government]*. Wiesbaden: VS-Verlag.

—— —— 2010. Janus-faced developments in a prototypical Bismarckian welfare state: Welfare reforms in Austria since the 1970s, in *A Long Goodbye to Bismarck? The Politics of Welfare Reforms in Continental Europe*, ed. Bruno Palier, Amsterdam: Amsterdam University Press, 101–128.

OBINGER, HERBERT, and WAGSCHAL, UWE, 1998. Das Stratifizierungskonzept in der Clusteranalytischen Überprüfung [The stratification concept tested via cluster analysis], in *Welten des Wohlfahrtskapitalismus: Der Sozialstaat in vergleichender Perspektive*, ed. Stephan Lessenich and Ilona Ostner, Frankfurt a.M.: Campus, 109–35.

—— —— (eds.), 2000. *Der gezügelte Wohlfahrtsstaat. Sozialpolitik in reichen Industrienationen [The Restrained Welfare State: Social Policy in Rich Industrial Nations]*. Frankfurt a.M.: Campus.

—— —— 2001. Families of nations and public policy. *West European Politics*, 24 (1): 99–114.

OBINGER, HERBERT, WAGSCHAL, UWE, and KITTEL, BERNHARD (eds.), 2003. *Politische Ökonomie: Demokratie und wirtschaftliche Leistungsfähigkeit [Political Economy: Democracy and Economic Capability]*. Opladen: Leske+Budrich.

OBINGER, HERBERT, and ZOHLNHÖFER, REIMUT, 2007. The real race to the bottom: What happened to economic affairs expenditure after 1980?, in *The Disappearing State:*

Retrenchment Realities in an Age of Globalisation, ed. Francis G. Castles, Cheltenham: Edward Elgar, 184–214.

O'CONNOR, JAMES, 1973. *The Fiscal Crisis of the State.* New York: St. Martin's Press.

O'CONNOR, JULIA S., 1993. Gender, class and citizenship in the comparative analysis of welfare state regimes: Theoretical and methodological issues. *The British Journal of Sociology,* 44 (3): 501–18.

—— 1996. From women in the welfare state to gendering welfare state regimes. *Current Sociology,* 44 (2): 1–124.

O'CONNOR, JULIA S., ORLOFF, ANN SHOLA, and SHAVER, SHELIA, 1999. *States, Markets, Families: Gender, Liberalism, and Social Policy in Australia, Canada, Great Britain, and the United States.* Cambridge: Cambridge University Press.

O'DONNEL, GUILLERMO, SCHMITTER, PHILIPPE C., and WHITEHEAD, LAURENCE (eds.), 1986. *Transitions from Authoritarian Rule: Southern Europe.* Baltimore, MD: Johns Hopkins University Press.

OECD (ORGANIZATION FOR ECONOMIC COOPERATION AND DEVELOPMENT), 1986a. *Historical Statistics 1960–83.* Paris: OECD.

—— 1986b. *Revenue Statistics of OECD Member Nations.* Paris: OECD.

—— 1992. *Reform of Health Care: A Comparative Analysis of Seven OECD Countries.* Paris: OECD.

—— 1994a. *The OECD Jobs Study.* Paris: OECD.

—— 1994b. Education at a Glance. Paris: OECD. Available at http://www.oecd.org/dataoecd/36/4/40701218.pdf.

—— 1997. *Employment Outlook.* Paris: OECD.

—— 1999. *Economic Outlook.* Paris: OECD.

—— 2001. Fiscal implications of ageing: Projections of age-related spending. *OECD Outlook* 69: 145–67.

—— 2002a. Society at a Glance Paris: OECD. Available at http://www.oecd.org/els/social/indicators/SAG.

—— 2002b. *Employment Outlook.* Paris: OECD.

—— 2003a. *Transforming Disability into Ability: Policies to Promote Work and Income Security for Disabled People.* Paris: OECD.

—— 2003b. Benefits and employment, friend or foe? Interactions between passive and active social programmes. *OECD Employment Outlook:* 171–235.

—— 2003c. Making work pay, making work possible. *OECD Employment Outlook:* 113–70.

—— 2003d. *Taxing Wages 2002–2003.* Paris: OECD.

—— 2004a. Employment protection regulation and labour market performance. *OECD Employment Outlook:* 61–126.

—— 2004b. Clocking in and Clocking out: Recent trends in working hours (Policy Brief, October). Paris: OECD. Available at http://www.oecd.org/dataoecd/42/49/33821328.pdf.

—— 2004c. *Social Protection Expenditure and Receipts: 1980–2001.* Paris: OECD.

—— 2004d. Database: Social Expenditure Database. 1980–2001 (SOCX 2001). Paris: OECD. Available at http://www.oecd.org/els/social/expenditure.

—— 2005a. *The OECD Health Project. Long-term Care for Older People.* Paris: OECD.

—— 2005b. *Extending Opportunities: How Active Social Policy Can Benefit Us All.* Paris: OECD.

—— 2005c. Education at a glance. Paris: OECD. Available at http://www.oecd.org/dataoecd/36/4/40701218.pdf.

—— 2005d. Database: Benefits and Wages Data Base. Available at http://www.oecd.org/els/ social/family/database (new version June 2009).

—— 2006a. *OECD Taxing Wages 2004–2005*. Paris: OECD.

—— 2006b. *OECD Employment Outlook: Boosting Jobs and Incomes*. Paris: OECD.

—— 2006c. *OECD Health Data 2006, 2nd Version, October 2006 (CD-ROM)*. Paris: OECD.

—— 2007a. *Jobs for Immigrants*. Vol 1: *Labour Market Integration in Australia, Denmark, Germany and Sweden;* vol 2: *Labour Market Integration in Belgium, France, the Netherlands and Portugal*. Paris: OECD.

—— 2007b. *Babies and Bosses: Reconciling Work and Family Life: A Synthesis of Findings for OECD Countries*. Paris: OECD.

—— 2007c. *Economic Survey of France 2007: Coping with Demographic Ageing*. Paris: OECD.

—— 2007d. 'New ways of addressing partial work capacity: OECD thematic review on sickness, disability and work. Issues paper and progress report'. Paris: OECD. Available at http://www.oecd.org/dataoecd/6/6/38509814.pdf.

—— 2007e. Child poverty in OECD countries: Trends, causes and policy responses, document DELSA/ELSA/WP1(2007)17. Paris: OECD (internal OECD-document, forthcoming in the OECD Social, Employment and Migration Working Papers).

—— 2007f. *Pensions at a glance: Public policies across OECD countries*. 2007 edn. Paris: OECD.

—— 2007g. International migration outlook: Annual report 2007. Paris: OECD. Available at http://www.oecd.org/els/migration/imo.

—— 2007h. *Economic survey of the United States, May 2007*. Paris: OECD.

—— 2007i. Trends in severe disability among elderly people: Assessing the evidence in 12 OECD countries and the future implications (OECD Health Working Papers, 26). Paris: OECD. Available at http://www.oecd.org/dataoecd/13/8/38343783.pdf.

—— 2007j. Database: Benefits and Wages: OECD Indicators (Database, latest version). Paris: OECD. Available at http://www.oecd.org/els/social/workincentives.

—— 2007k. Database: Social Expenditure Database (Annex: An interpretative guide SOCX 1980–2003 (SOCX 2007)). Paris: OECD. Available at http://www.oecd.org/els/social/ expenditure.

—— 2008a. *Growing Unequal? Income Distribution and Poverty in OECD Countries*. Paris: OECD.

—— 2008b. *Key characteristics of parental leave systems. Definitions and methodology*. Paris: OECD. Available at http://www.oecd.org/dataoecd/45/26/37864482.pdf.

—— 2008c. *Education at a glance*. Paris: OECD. Available at http://www.oecd.org/edu/ eag2008.

—— 2008d. *OECD Factbook 2008: Economic, Environmental and Social Statistics*. Paris: OECD.

—— 2008e. OECD Statistics. Paris: OECD. Available at http://www.oecd.org.

—— 2008f. Database: OECD Health Data 2008. Statistics and Indicators for 30 Countries (CD-Rom). Paris: OECD (update 2009 available). Available at http://www.oecd.org/ health/healthdata.

—— 2008g. Database: The OECD Social Expenditure Database 1980–2005 (SOCX 2008). Paris: OECD. Available at http://www.oecd.org/els/social/expenditure.

—— 2008h. Database: Tax Database. Paris: OECD. Available at http://www.oecd.org/ctp/ taxdatabase.

—— 2008i. *Revenue Statistics 1965–2006*. Paris: OECD.

OECD (Organization for Economic Cooperation and Development), 2008j. *Taxing Wages 2006–2007, 2007 Edition Special Feature: Tax Reforms and Tax Burdens, 2000–2006.* Paris: OECD.

—— 2009a. Database: Social Expenditure Database (SOCX 2009). Paris: OECD. Available at http://www.oecd.org/els/social/expenditure.

—— 2009b. *OECD Private Pensions Outlook 2008.* Paris: OECD.

—— 2009c. OECD Statistical Extracts. Paris: OECD. Available at http://stats.oecd.org/index.aspx.

—— 2009d. *OECD Factbook 2009: Economic, Environmental and Social Statistics.* Paris: OECD. Available at http:// www.oecd.org/publications/factbook

—— 2009e. Database: Labour Force Statistics Online Database. Paris: OECD. Available at http://stats.oecd.org/index.aspx.

—— 2009f. Database: OECD Main Economic Indicators Online Database. Paris: OECD. Available at http://stats.oecd.org\WBOS\index.aspx.

—— 2009g. *Complementary and Private Pensions throughout the World 2008.* Paris: OECD (a report of OECD, International Social Security Association [ISSA], International Organisation of Pensions Supervisors [IOPS]).

—— 2009h. Database: OECD Family Database. Available at http://www.oecd.org/els/social/family/database.

—— 2009i. Social Expenditure: Aggregated Data. Available at http://stats.oecd.org.

Oeppen, Jim, and Vaupel, James W., 2002. Broken limits to life expectancy. *Science,* 296 (5570): 1029–31.

Offe, Claus, 1981. The attribution of public status to interest groups: Observations on the West German case, in *Organizing Interests in Western Europe: Pluralism, Corporatism, and the Transformation of Politics,* ed. Suzanne Berger, Cambridge: Cambridge University Press, 123–58.

—— 1984. *Contradictions of the Welfare State.* Cambridge, MA: MIT Press.

—— 1985. *Disorganized Capitalism: Contemporary Transformations of Work and Politics.* Cambridge, MA: MIT Press.

—— 1993. The politics of social policy in East European transitions. *Social Research* 60 (4): 649–84.

—— 2009. Epilogue: Lessons learnt and open questions, in *Postcommunist Welfare Pathways: Theorizing Social Policy Transformations in Central and Eastern Europe,* ed. Alfio Cerami and Pieter Vanhuysse, Basingstoke: Palgrave Macmillan, 237–47.

Offe, Claus, and Wiesenthal, Helmut, 1980. Two logics of collective action: Theoretical notes on social class and organisational form, in *Political Power and Social Theory,* ed. Maurice Zeitlin, Greenwich, CT: JAI Press, 67–115.

Oftedal Telhaug, Alfred, Asbjørn Mediås, Odd, and Aasen, Petter, 2006. The Nordic model in education: Education as part of the political system in the last 50 years. *Scandinavian Journal of Educational Research,* 50 (3): 245–83.

Ohman, Berndt, 1974. *LO and Labour Market Policy Since the Second World War.* Stockholm: Bokforlaget Prisma.

Oliveira Martins, Joaquim, and De la Maisonneuve, Christine, 2006. *The Drivers of Public Expenditure on Health and Long-term Care: An Integrated Approach.* Paris: OECD.

Oliver, Michael, 1983. *Social Work with Disabled People.* London: Macmillan.

—— 1990. *The Politics of Disablement: Critical Texts in Social Work and the Welfare State.* Basingstoke: Palgrave Macmillan.

—— 1996. *Understanding Disability: From Theory to Practice.* Basingstoke: Macmillan.

OLSON, MANCUR, 1965. *The Logic of Collective Action: Public Goods and the Theory of Groups* Cambridge, MA: Harvard University Press.

—— 1982. *The Rise and Decline of Nations.* New Haven, CT: Yale University Press.

OLSSON, SVEN. E., 1990. *Social Policy and Welfare State in Sweden.* Lund: Arkiv.

OORSCHOT, WIM VAN, 1998. Dutch public opinion on social security (CRSP Series, 315). Loughborough: Centre for Research in Social Policy, Loughborough University. Available at http://arno.uvt.nl/show.cgi?fid=94170.

—— 2006. Making the difference in social Europe: Deservingness perceptions among citizens of European welfare states. *Journal of European Social Policy,* 16 (1): 23–42.

OORSCHOT, WIM VAN, and HVINDEN, BJÖRN, 2000. Introduction: Towards convergence? Disability policies in Europe. *European Journal of Social Security,* 2 (4): 293–302.

—— —— 2001. *Disability Policies in European Countries.* The Hague: Kluwer Law International.

OORSCHOT, WIM VAN, OPIELKA, MICHAEL, and PFAU-EFFINGER, BIRGIT (eds.), 2008. *Culture and the Welfare State. Values and Social Policy in Comparative Perspective.* Cheltenham: Edward Elgar.

ORENSTEIN, MITCHELL A., 2005. The New Pension Reform as Global Policy. *Global Social Policy,* 5 (2): 175–202.

—— 2008*a.* *Privatizing Pensions: The Transnational Campaign for Social Security Reform.* Princeton, NJ: Princeton University Press.

—— 2008*b.* Postcommunist welfare states. *Journal of Democracy,* 19 (4): 81–94.

ORENSTEIN, MITCHELL. A., and HAAS, MARTINE R., 2005. Globalization and the future of welfare states in Post-Communist East-Central European Countries, in *Globalization and the Future of the Welfare State,* ed. Miguel Glatzer and Dietrich Rueschemeyer, Pittsburgh, PA: University of Pittsburgh Press, 130–52.

ORLOFF, ANN SHOLA, 1993*a.* *The Politics of Pensions: A Comparative Analysis of Britain, Canada, and the United States, 1880–1940.* Madison: University of Wisconsin Press.

—— 1993*b.* Gender and the social rights of citizenship: The comparative analysis of state policies and gender relations. *American Sociological Review,* 58 (3): 303–28 (reprint in Leibfried and Mau 2008*a:* vol. 3, 495–522).

—— 1996. Gender in the welfare state. *Annual Review of Sociology,* 22: 51–78.

—— 2002. Women's employment and welfare regimes: Globalization, export orientation and social policy in Europe and North America (Social Policy and Development Programme Paper, 12). New York: United Nations Research Institute for Social Development (UNRISD). Available at http://www.unrisd.org/80256B3C005BCCF9/(http Publications)/58EC1361F09195F7C1256C080044FC77?OpenDocument.

—— 2005*a.* *Remaking Modernity: Politics, History and Sociology.* Durham, NC: Duke University Press.

—— 2005*b.* Farewell to maternalism? State policies and mothers' employment (Working Paper Series, WP-05–10). Chicago: Northwestern University. Available at http://www. northwestern.edu/ipr/publications/papers/2005/WP-05–10.pdf.

—— 2006. From maternalism to 'Employment for All': State policies to promote women's employment across the affluent democracies, in *The State after Statism: New State Activities in the Age of Liberalisation,* ed. Jonah D. Levy, Cambridge, MA: Harvard University Press, 230–68.

ORLOFF, ANN SHOLA, 2009. Should feminists aim for gender symmetry? Why a dual-earner/ dual-caregiver society is not every feminist's utopia, in *Gender Equality: Transforming Family Divisions of Labour*, ed. Janet Gornick, Marcia K. Meyers, and Erik Olin Wright (Real Utopia Project, 6), New York: Verso, 129–60.

ORLOFF, ANN SHOLA, and SKOCPOL, THEDA, 1984. Why not equal protection? Explaining the politics of public social spending in Britain, 1900–1911, and the United States, 1880s– 1920. *American Sociological Review*, 49 (6): 726–50 (reprint in Leibfried and Mau 2008*a*: vol. 1, 519–43).

OSBERG, LARS, and SMEEDING, TIMOTHY M., 2006. 'Fair' inequality? Attitudes toward pay differentials: The United States in comparative perspective. *American Sociological Review*, 71 (3): 450–73.

OSTERHAMMEL, JÜRGEN, 2009. *Die Verwandlung der Welt. Eine Geschichte des 19. Jahrhunderts [The Transformation of the World: A History of the Nineteenth Century]*. Munich: Beck.

ÖSTERLE, AUGUST, 2001. *Equity Choices and Long-term Care Policies in Europe: Allocating Resources and Burdens in Austria, Italy, the Netherlands, and the United Kingdom*. Aldershot: Ashgate.

OSTNER, ILONA, and LEWIS, JANE, 1995. Gender and the evolution of European social policies, in *European Social Policy: Between Fragmentation and Integration*, ed. Stephan Leibfried and Paul Pierson, Washington, DC: Brookings Institution Press, 159–94.

OSTROM, CHARLES W., 1978. *Time-series Analysis: Regression Techniques*. Beverly Hills: Sage.

O'SULLIVAN, EOIN, and DE DECKER, PASCAL, 2007. Regulating the private rental housing market in Europe. *European Journal of Homelessness*, 1 (December): 95–117.

OTPR (OFFICE OF TAX POLICY RESEARCH), 1987 ff. Database: World Tax Database. Ann Arbor, MI: Michigan Ross School of Business. Available at http://www.bus.umich.edu/ OTPR/otpr/introduction.htm.

OVERBYE, EINAR, 2005. Extending social security in developing countries: A review of three main strategies. *International Journal of Social Welfare*, 14 (4): 305–14.

—— 2008. How do politicians get away with path-breaking pension reforms?, in *Pension Reform in Europe: Politics, Policies, and Outcomes*, ed. Camila Arza and Martin Kohli, London: Routledge 70–86.

PAINE, THOMAS, 1987. Agrarian justice (first publ. 1797), in *The Thomas Paine Reader*, ed. Michael Foot and Isaac Kramnick, Harmondsworth: Penguin, 471–89.

PALIER, BRUNO, 2000. 'Defrosting' the French welfare state. *West European Politics*, 23 (2): 113–36.

—— 2002. *Gouverner la sécurité sociale. Les réformes du système français de protection sociale depuis 1945 [Governing Social Security: The Reforms of the French Social Protection System since 1945]*. Paris: Presses Universitaires de France.

—— 2003. Beyond retrenchment: Four problems in current welfare state research and one suggestion on how to overcome them, in *What future for social security? Debates and reforms in national and cross-national perspective*, ed. Jochen Clasen, The Hague: Kluwer Law International, 105–20.

—— 2005. Ambiguous agreement, cumulative change: French social policy in the 1990s, in *Beyond Continuity: Institutional Change in Advanced Political Economies*, ed. Kathleen A. Thelen and Wolfgang Streeck, Oxford: Oxford University Press, 127–44.

—— (ed.), 2010*a*. *A Long Goodbye to Bismarck? The Politics of Welfare Reforms in Continental Europe*. Amsterdam: Amsterdam University Press (forthcoming).

—— 2010b. The Dualisations of the French Welfare System, in *A Long Goodbye to Bismarck? The Politics of Welfare Reforms in Continental Europe*, ed. Bruno Palier, Amsterdam: Amsterdam University Press, 73–99.

PALIER, BRUNO, and MARTIN, CLAUDE (eds.), 2008. *Reforming the Bismarckian Welfare Systems: Broadening Perspectives in Social Policy*. Oxford: Blackwell.

PALIER, BRUNO, and THELEN, KATHLEEN, 2010. Institutionalizing dualism: Complementarities and change in France and Germany. *Politics and Society*, 38 (1): 119–48.

PALME, JOAKIM, 1990. *Pension Rights in Welfare Capitalism: The Development of Old-Age Pensions in 18 OECD Countries 1930 to 1985*. Stockholm: Stockholm University, Swedish Institute for Social Research (Edsbruk: Akademitryck).

—— 1999. *The Nordic Model and the Modernisation of Social Protection in Europe*. Copenhagen: The Nordic Council of Ministers.

—— 2006. Welfare states and inequality: Institutional designs and distributive outcomes. *Research in Social Stratification and Mobility*, 25 (4): 387–403.

PALME, JOAKIM, BERGMARK, ÅKE, BÄCKMAN, OLOF, ESTRADA, FELIPE, FRITZELL, JOHAN, LUNDBERG, OLLE, SJÖBERG, OLA, SOMMESTAD, LENA, and SZEBEHELY, MARTA, 2002. Welfare in Sweden: The balance sheet for the 1990s (Ministry Publication Series, 2002/32). Stockholm: Ministry of Health and Social Affairs, Sweden. Available at http://www.regeringen.se/sb/d/574/a/17480.

PAMPEL, FRED C., and WILLIAMSON, JOHN B., 1988. Welfare spending in advanced industrial democracies, 1950–1980. *American Journal of Sociology*, 93 (6): 1424–56.

—— —— 1989. *Age, Class, Politics, and the Welfare State*. Cambridge: Cambridge University Press.

PAPADÓPULOS, JORGE, 1992. *Seguridad social y política en el Uruguay. Orígenes, evolución y mediación de intereses en la restauración democrática [Social Security Politics in Uruguay: Origins, Evolution and Interest Mediation in the Restoring of Democracy]*. Montevideo: CIESU.

PARIJS, PHILIPPE VAN, 1995. *Real Freedom for All: What (if Anything) Can Justify Capitalism?* Oxford: Oxford University Press.

PARREÑAS, RHACEL SALAZAR, 2005. *Children of Global Migration: Transnational Families and Gendered Woes*. Stanford, CA: Stanford University Press.

PARSONS, TALCOTT, 1967. *Sociological Theory and Modern Society*. New York: Free Press.

—— 1971. *The System of Modern Societies*. Englewood Cliffs, NJ: Prentice-Hall.

PASCALL, GILLIAN, and LEWIS, JANE, 2004. Emerging gender regimes and policies for gender equality in a wider Europe. *Journal of Social Policy*, 33 (3): 372–94.

PASCALL, GILLIAN, and MANNING, NICK, 2000. Gender and social policy: Comparing welfare states in Central and Eastern Europe and the former Soviet Union. *Journal of European Social Policy*, 10 (3): 240–66.

PATEMAN, CAROLE, 1989. *The Disorder of Women: Democracy, Feminism, and Political Theory*. Cambridge: Polity.

PAVALKO, ELIZA, 1989. State timing of policy action: Workmen's compensation in the United States, 1909–1929. *American Journal of Sociology*, 95 (3): 592–615.

PAVOLINI, EMMANUELE, and RANCI, COSTANZO, 2008. Restructuring the welfare state: Reforms in long-term care in Western European countries. *Journal of European Social Policy*, 18 (3): 246–59.

PEACOCK, ALAN T., and WISEMAN, JOHN (with VEVERKA, JINDRICH), 1961. *The Growth of Public Expenditure in the United Kingdom*. Princeton, NJ: Princeton University Press.

PEARSON, MARK, and MARTIN, JOHN P., 2005. Should we extend the role of private social expenditure? (OECD Social, Employment and Migration Working Papers, 23). Paris: OECD. Available at http://www.oecd.org/dataoecd/59/22/34621653.pdf.

PEARSON, MARK, and SCARPETTA, STEPHANO, 2000. What do we know about policies to make work pay? *OECD Economic Studies*, 31 (2): 11–24.

PEDERSEN, SUSAN, 1993. *Family, Dependence, and the Origins of the Welfare State: Britain and France, 1914–1945*. Cambridge: Cambridge University Press.

PEMPEL, T. J., 1997. Regime shift: Japanese politics in a changing world economy. *Journal of Japanese Studies*, 23 (2): 333–61.

PEMPEL, T. J., and TSUNEKAWA, KEIICHI, 1979. Corporatism without Labor? The Japanese anomaly, in *Trends Towards Corporatist Intermediation*, ed. Philippe C. Schmitter and Gerhard Lehmbruch, Beverly Hills: Sage, 231–70.

PENG, ITO, 2004. Postindustrial pressures, political regime shifts, and social policy reforms in Japan and South Korea. *Journal of East Asian Studies*, 4 (3): 389–425.

—— 2005. The new politics of the welfare state in a developmental context: Explaining the 1990s social care expansion in Japan, in *Transforming the Developmental Welfare State in East-Asia*, ed. Kwon Huck-Ju, Basingstoke: Palgrave Macmillan, 73–97.

—— 2008. The political and social economy of care: South Korea research report 3. Geneva: United Nations Research Institute for Social Development (UNRISD). Available at http://www.unrisd.org/80256B3C005BCCF9/(httpPublications)/1EF2AE4F5E388259C125756100541F68?OpenDocument.

PENG, ITO, and WONG, JOSEPH, 2008. Institutions and institutional purpose: Continuity and change in East Asian social policy. *Politics & Society*, 36 (1): 61–88.

PENSIONS COMMISSION, 2004. *Pensions: Challenges and Choices. The First Report of the Pensions Commission*. Norwich, UK: The Stationery Office (TSO). Available at http://www.fsa.gov.uk/pubs/pensions/pensions_report1.pdf.

PEREZ DIAZ, VICTOR, and RODRIGUEZ, JUAN C., 1994. Inertial choices: Spanish human resources policies and practices (Analistas Socio-Politicos Research Paper, 2b). Madrid: Analistas Socio Políticos Research Center.

PERRIN, GUY, 1969. Reflections on fifty years of social security. *International Labour Review*, 99 (3): 249–92.

PERSSON, TORSTEN, and TABELLINI, GUIDO E., 1999. The size and scope of government: Comparative politics with rational politicians. *European Economic Review*, 43 (4/6): 699–735.

—— —— 2003. *The Economic Effects of Constitutions*. Cambridge, MA: MIT Press.

PETERS, B. GUY, 1991. *The Politics of Taxation: A Comparative Perspective*. Oxford: Blackwell.

PETERSEN, KLAUS, 2006. Constructing Nordic welfare: Nordic social political cooperation 1919–1955, in *The Nordic Model of Welfare: A Historical Reappraisal*, ed. Niels Finn Christiansen, Klaus Petersen, Nils Edling, and Per Haave, Copenhagen: Museum Tusculanum Press, 67–98.

PETMESIDOU, MARIA, 1996. Social protection in Southern Europe: Trends and problems. *Journal of Area Studies*, 4 (9): 95–125.

PETMESIDOU, MARIA, and MOSSIALOS, ELIAS, 2006. *Social Policy Developments in Greece*. Aldershot: Ashgate.

PETMESIDOU, MARIA, and PAPATHEODOROU, CHRISTOS (eds.), 2006. *Poverty and Social Deprivation in the Mediterranean: Trends, Policies and Welfare Prospects in the New Millennium*. London: Zed Books.

PETTIT, PHILIPP, 1997. *Republicanism: A Theory of Freedom and Government*. Oxford: Oxford University Press.

PFEIFER, MICHAELA, 2009. Public opinion on state responsibility for minimum income protection: A comparison of 14 European countries. *Acta Sociologica*, 52 (2): 117–34.

PHELPS, EDMUND S., 1997. *Rewarding Work: How to Restore Participation and Self-Support to Free Enterprise*. Cambridge, MA: Harvard University Press.

PIERSON, CHRISTOPHER, 1991. *Beyond the Welfare State? The New Political Economy of Welfare*. Cambridge: Polity (1998 2nd rev. edn.; 2006 3rd rev. edn.).

PIERSON, CHRISTOPHER, and CASTLES, FRANCIS G. (eds.), 2006. *The Welfare State: A Reader*. Cambridge: Polity.

PIERSON, PAUL, 1993. When effect becomes cause: Policy feedback and political change. *World Politics*, 45 (4): 595–628.

—— 1994. *Dismantling the Welfare State? Reagan, Thatcher, and the Politics of Retrenchment*. Cambridge: Cambridge University Press.

—— 1995. Fragmented welfare states: Federal institutions and the development of social policy. *Governance*, 8 (4): 449–78.

—— 1996. The new politics of the welfare state. *World Politics*, 48 (2): 143–79 (reprint in Leibfried and Mau 2008a: vol. 2, 239–75).

—— 1998. Irresistible forces, immovable objects: Post-industrial welfare states confront permanent austerity. *Journal of European Public Policy*, 5 (4): 539–60.

—— 2000. Increasing returns, path dependence, and the study of politics. *American Political Science Review*, 94 (2): 251–67.

—— (ed.), 2001a. *The New Politics of the Welfare State*. Oxford: Oxford University Press.

—— 2001b. Post-industrial pressures in mature welfare states, in *The New Politics of the Welfare State*, ed. Paul Pierson, Oxford: Oxford University Press, 80–106.

—— 2001c. Coping with permanent austerity: Welfare state restructuring in affluent democracies, in *The New Politics of the Welfare State*, ed. Paul Pierson, Oxford: Oxford University Press, 410–56.

—— 2004. *Politics in Time: History, Institutions, and Social Analysis*. Princeton, NJ: Princeton University Press.

—— 2006. Public policies as institutions, in *Rethinking Political Institutions*, ed. Ian Shapiro, Stephen Skowronek, and Daniel Galvin, New York: New York University Press, 114–31.

—— 2007. The costs of marginalization: Qualitative methods in the study of American politics. *Comparative Political Studies*, 40 (2): 145–69.

PIERSON, PAUL, and LEIBFRIED, STEPHAN, 1995a. Multitiered institutions and the making of social policy [Introduction], in *European Social Policy: Between Fragmentation and Integration*, ed. Paul Pierson and Stephan Leibfried, Washington, DC: Brookings Institution Press, 1–40.

—— —— 1995b. The dynamics of social policy integration [Conclusion], in *European Social Policy: Between Fragmentation and Integration*, ed. Paul Pierson and Stephan Leibfried, Washington, DC: Brookings Institution Press, 432–66.

PIERSON, PAUL, and SKOCPOL, THEDA, 2002. Historical institutionalism in contemporary political science, in *Political Science: The State of the Discipline*, ed. Ira Katznelson and Helen V. Milner, New York: Norton, 693–721.

PINKER, ROBERT A, 1971. *Social Theory and Social Policy*. London: Heinemann.

PIOPPI, DANIELA, 2004. From religious charity to the welfare state and back. The case of islamic endowments (waqfs) revival in Egypt (EUI Working Papers RSCAS, 2004/34).

Fiesole (Florence): European University Institute. Available at http://www.eui.eu/RSCAS/WP-Texts/04_34.pdf.

PIVEN, FRANCES FOX, and CLOWARD, RICHARD A., 1993. *Regulating the Poor: The Functions of Public Welfare.* New York: Vintage.

—— —— 1997. *The Breaking of the American Social Compact.* New York: The New Press.

PLANTENGA, JANNEKE, and HANSEN, JOHAN, 1999. Assessing equal opportunities in the European Union. *International Labour Review,* 138 (4): 351–79.

PLICKERT, PHILIP, 2008. *Wandlungen des Neoliberalismus. Eine Studie zu Entwicklung und Ausstrahlung der 'Mont Pèlerin Society' [Mutations of Neoliberalism. A Study on the Development and the Influence of the 'Mont Pèlerin Society'].* Stuttgart: Lucius & Lucius.

PLÜMPER, THOMAS, and TRÖGER, VERA E., 2004. Panel data in comparative politics: Linking method to theory. *European Journal of Political Research,* 44 (2): 327–54.

PLÜMPER, THOMAS, TROEGER, VERA E., and WINNER, HANNES, 2009. Why is there no race to the bottom in capital taxation? Tax competition among countries of unequal size, different levels of budget rigidities, and heterogeneous fairness norms. *International Studies Quarterly,* 53 (3): 761–86.

PNUD (UNITED NATIONS DEVELOPMENT PROGRAMME), 2005. *Informe sobre Desarrollo Humano [Report on Human Development].* La Paz: PNUD. Available at http://hdr.undp.org/en/media/HDR05_sp_complete.pdf.

POLANYI, KARL, 1957 [1944]. *The Great Transformation: The Political and Economic Origins of Our Time.* Boston MA: Beacon Press [orig. New York: Farrar and Rinehart].

PONTUSSON, JONAS, 2005. *Inequality and Prosperity: Social Europe Versus Liberal America.* Ithaca, NY: Cornell University Press.

—— 2010. Once again a model: Nordic Social Democracy in a globalized world, in *Futures of the Left,* ed. James Cronin, George Ross and James Shoch, Durham, NC: Duke University Press (forthcoming).

PONTUSSON, JONAS, and CLAYTON, RICHARD, 1998. Welfare-state retrenchment revisited: Entitlement cuts, public sector restructuring, and inegalitarian trends in advanced capitalist societies. *World Politics,* 51 (1): 67–98.

POOLEY, COLIN G. (ed.), 1992. *Housing Strategies in Europe, 1880–1930.* Leicester: Leicester University Press.

PORTE, CAROLINE DE LA, and POCHET, PHILIPPE (eds.), 2002. *Building Social Europe through the Open Method of Co-ordination.* Brussels: Peter Lang.

PORTER, DOROTHY, 1999. *Health, Civilization, and the State: A History of Public Health from Ancient to Modern Times.* London: Routledge.

POTRAFKE, NIKLAS, 2007. Social expenditure as a political cue ball? OECD countries under examination (Discussion Papers, 676). Berlin: German Institute for Economic Research (DIW). Available at http://www.diw.de/documents/publikationen/73/55856/dp676.pdf.

POWELL, BINGHAM, 2002. PR, the median voter, and economic policy: An exploration. Paper presented at the 2002 Meetings of the American Political Science Association, Boston.

POWELL, MARTIN, and BARRIENTOS, ARMANDO, 2004. Welfare regimes and the welfare mix. *European Journal of Political Research,* 43 (1): 83–105.

POWELL, WALTER W., and DIMAGGIO, PAUL J., 1991. *The New Institutionalism in Organizational Analysis.* Chicago: University of Chicago Press.

PRABHAKAR, RAJIV, 2008. *The Assets Agenda: Principles and Policy.* Basingstoke: Palgrave Macmillan.

PRIBBLE, JENNIFER, 2008. 'Protecting the poor: Welfare politics in Latin America's free market era'. Chapel Hill, NC: Department of Political Science, University of North Carolina, Ph.D. Dissertation.

PRIBBLE, JENNIFER, HUBER, EVELYNE, and STEPHENS, JOHN D., 2009. The politics of poverty in Latin America. *Comparative Politics*, 41 (4, forthcoming).

PRIESTLEY, MARK, 1997. The origins of a legislative disability category in England: A speculative history. *Disability Studies Quarterly*, 17 (2): 87–94.

—— 1999. *Disability Politics and Community Care*. London: Jessica Kingsley.

—— 2003. *Disability: A Life Course Approach*. Cambridge: Polity.

PRINZ, CHRISTOPHER (ed.), 2003. *European Disability Pension Policies: 11 Country Trends; 1970–2002*. Aldershot: Ashgate.

PRZEWORSKI, ADAM, 1985. *Capitalism and Social Democracy*. Cambridge: Cambridge University Press.

PRZEWORSKI, ADAM, and TEUNE, HENRY, 1970. *The Logic of Comparative Social Inquiry*. New York: Wiley-Interscience.

PRZEWORSKI, ADAM, and WALLERSTEIN, MICHAEL, 1984. Democratic capitalism at the crossroads, in *The Political Economy: Readings in the Politics and Economics of American Public Policy*, ed. Thomas Ferguson and Joel Rogers, Armonk, NY: M. E. Sharpe, 335–48.

PUTNAM, ROBERT D., 1993. Diplomacy and domestic politics. The logic of two-level games, in *Double-Edged Diplomacy. International Bargaining and Domestic Politics*, ed. Peter B. Evans, Harold K. Jacobson and Robert D. Putnam, Berkeley: University of California Press, 431–68.

—— 2000. *Bowling Alone: The Collapse and Revival of American Community*. New York: Simon and Schuster.

QUADAGNO, JILL S., 1988a. *The Transformation of Old Age Security: Class and Politics in the American Welfare State*. Chicago: University of Chicago Press.

—— 1988b. From old-age assistance to supplementary security income: The political economy of relief in the South, 1935–1972, in *The Politics of Social Policy in the United States*, ed. Margaret Weir, Ann Shola Orloff and Theda Skocpol, Princeton, NJ: Princeton University Press, 235–64.

—— 2005. *One Nation Uninsured: Why the U.S. has no National Health Insurance*. Oxford: Oxford University Press.

QUEISSER, MONIKA, WHITEHOUSE, EDWARD, and WHITEFORD, PETER, 2007. The public–private pension mix in OECD countries. *Industrial Relations Journal*, 38 (6): 542–68.

QUINE, MARIA S., 2002. *Italy's Social Revolution: Charity and Welfare from Liberalism to Fascism*. Basingstoke: Palgrave Macmillan.

QUINN, DENNIS, 1997. The correlates of change in international financial regulation. *American Political Science Review*, 91 (3): 531–52.

RAGIN, CHARLES, 1987. *The Comparative Method: Moving Beyond Qualitative and Quantitative Strategies*. Berkeley: University of California Press.

—— 1994. A qualitative comparative analysis of pension systems, in *The Comparative Political Economy of the Welfare State*, ed. Thomas Janoski and Alexander M. Hicks, Cambridge: Cambridge University Press, 320–45.

—— 2008. *Redesigning Social Inquiry: Fuzzy Sets and Beyond*. Chicago: University of Chicago Press.

RAMESH, MISHRA, 1995. Social security in South Korea and Singapore: Explaining the differences. *Social Policy & Administration*, 29 (3): 228–40.

RAMESH, MISHRA, 2007. The World Bank and pension reforms, in *The World Bank and Governance: A Decade of Reform and Reaction*, ed. Diane Stone and Christopher Wright, London: Routledge, 109–24.

RANDALL, ED, 2000. *The European Union and Health Policy*. Basingstoke: Palgrave Macmillan.

RAVENTÓS, DANIEL, 2007. *Basic Income: The Material Conditions of Freedom*. London: Pluto.

RAWLINGS, LAURA B., and RUBIO, GLORIA M., 2005. Evaluating the impact of conditional cash transfer programmes. *World Bank Research Observer*, 20 (1): 29–55.

RAWLS, JOHN, 1999. *A Theory of Justice: Revised Edition*. Cambridge, MA: Harvard University Press (1st edn. 1971).

—— 2001. *Justice as Fairness. A Restatement*. Cambridge, MA: Harvard University Press.

RECKER, MARIE-LUISE, 1985. *Nationalsozialistische Sozialpolitik im Zweiten Weltkrieg [National-Socialist Social Policy in World War II]*. Munich: Oldenbourg.

REHN, GÖSTA, 1985. Swedish active labour market policy: Retrospect and prospect. *Industrial Relations*, 24 (1): 62–89.

REICH, MICHAEL R., 2002. Reshaping the state from above, from within, from below: Implications for public health. *Social Science & Medicine*, 54 (11): 1669–75.

REIN, MARTIN, and RAINWATER, LEE (eds.), 1986. *Public/Private Interplay in Social Protection: A Comparative Study*. Armonk, NY: M. E. Sharpe.

REVILLARD, ANNE, 2006. Work/family policy in France: From state familialism to state feminism? *International Journal of Law, Policy and the Family*, 20 (2): 135–50.

REYNOLDS, MORGAN, and SMOLENSKY, EUGENE, 1977. *Public Expenditure, Taxes and the Redistribution of Income: The USA, 1950, 1961, 1970*. New York: Academic Press.

RHODES, MARTIN (ed.), 1997. *Southern European Welfare States: Between Crisis and Reform*. London: Frank Cass.

—— 1998. Globalisation, labour markets and welfare states: A future of 'competitive corporatism'?, in *The Future of the European Welfare State: A New Social Contract?*, ed. Martin Rhodes and Yves Mény, London: Macmillan, 178–203.

—— 2001. The political economy of social pacts: 'Competitive corporatism' and European welfare reform, in *The New Politics of the Welfare State*, ed. Paul Pierson, Oxford: Oxford University Press, 165–94.

—— 2003. National 'pacts' and EU governance in social policy and the labour market, in *Governing Work and Welfare in a New Economy: European and American Experiments*, ed. Jonathan Zeitlin and David M. Trubek, Oxford: Oxford University Press, 129–57.

RICHARDSON, DOMININC, HOELSCHER, PETRA, and BRADSHAW, JONATHAN R., 2008. Child well-being in Central and Eastern European countries (CEE) and the Commonwealth of Independent States (CIS). *Child Indicators Research*, 1 (3): 211–50.

RIEGER, ELMAR, and LEIBFRIED, STEPHAN, 2003. *Limits to Globalization: Welfare States and the World Economy*. Cambridge: Polity.

RIKER, WILLIAM H., 1986. *The Art of Political Manipulation*. New Haven, CT: Yale University Press.

RIMLINGER, GASTON V., 1971. *Welfare Policy and Industrialization in Europe, America and Russia*. New York: Wiley & Sons.

RINGEN, STEIN, 1987. *The Possibility of Politics: A Study in the Political Economy of the Welfare State*. Oxford: The Clarendon Press of Oxford University Press.

RITAKALLIO, VELLI-MATTI, 2003. The importance of housing costs in cross-national comparisons of welfare (state) outcomes. *International Social Security Review*, 56 (2): 81–101.

RITTER, GERHARD A., 1986. *Social Welfare in Germany and Britain: Origins and Development*. Leamington Spa: Berg (1st German edn. 1983).

—— 2006. *Der Preis der deutschen Einheit. Die Wiedervereinigung und die Krise des Sozialstaates [The Price of German Unity: Reunification and the Crisis of the Welfare State]*. Munich: C. H. Beck.

ROBERTSON, ANN, 1998. Critical reflections on the politics of need: Implications for public health. *Social Science & Medicine*, 47 (10): 1419–30.

RODDEN, JONATHAN A., 2003. Reviving Leviathan: Fiscal federalism and the growth of government. *International Organization*, 57 (4): 695–729.

—— 2006. *Hamilton's Paradox: The Promise and Peril of Fiscal Federalism*. Cambridge: Cambridge University Press.

RODGERS, DANIEL T., 1998. *Atlantic Crossings: Social Politics in a Progressive Age*. Cambridge, MA: The Belknap Press of Harvard University Press.

RODGERS, GERRY, LEE, EDDY, SWEPSTON, LEE, and VAN DAELE, JASMIEN, 2009. *The ILO and the Quest for Social Justice, 1919–2009*. Geneva: ILO.

RODRÍGUEZ, JUAN MANUEL, COZZANO, BEATRIZ, and MAZZUCHI, GRACIELA, 2007. *Relaciones laborales y modelo de desarrollo [Labor Relations and the Model for Development]*. Montevideo: Universidad Católica del Uruguay.

RODRIK, DANI, 1997. *Has Globalization Gone too Far?* Washington, DC: Institute for International Economics.

—— 1998. Why do more open economies have bigger governments? *Journal of Political Economy*, 106 (5): 997–1032.

—— 1999. Democracies pay higher wages. *Quarterly Journal of Economics*, 114 (3): 707–38.

ROEMER, JOHN E., 1993. A pragmatic theory of responsibility for the egalitarian planner. *Philosophy and Public Affairs*, 22 (2): 146–66.

—— 1998. Why the poor do not expropriate the rich: An old argument in new garb. *Journal of Public Economics*, 70 (3): 399–424.

ROGERS, JOEL, and STREECK, WOLFGANG (eds.), 1995. *Works Councils: Consultation, Representation, and Cooperation in Industrial Relations*. Chicago: University of Chicago Press.

ROGOWSKI, RONALD, 1989. *Commerce and Coalitions: How Trade Affects Domestic Political Alignments*. Princeton, NJ: Princeton University Press.

ROGOWSKI, RONALD, and MACRAY, DUNCAN, 2008. Inequality and institutions: What theory, history, and (some) data tell us, in *Democracy, Inequality and Representation: A Comparative Perspective*, ed. Pablo Beramendi and Christopher J. Anderson, New York: Russell Sage Foundation, 354-86.

ROKKAN, STEIN, 1999. *State Formation, Nation-building, and Mass Politics in Europe: The Theory of Stein Rokkan, Based on his Collected Works, edited by Peter Flora with Stein Kuhnle and Derek Urwin*. Oxford: Oxford University Press.

ROLAND, RICHARD, 2007. Comparing homeowner societies: Can we construct an East-West model? *Housing Studies*, 22 (4): 473–93.

ROLLER, EDELTRAUT, 1992. *Einstellungen der Bürger zum Wohlfahrtsstaat der Bundesrepublik Deutschland [The Citizens' Attitudes to the (West-)German Welfare State]*. Opladen: Westdeutscher Verlag.

RØNSEN, MARIT, and SKARØHAMAR, TORBJØRN, 2009. Do welfare-to-work initiatives work? Evidence from an activation programme targeted at Social Assistance recipients in Norway. *Journal of European Social Policy*, 19 (1): 61–77.

ROOM, GRAHAM (ed.), 1995. *Beyond the Threshold: The Measurement and Analysis of Social Exclusion*. Bristol: Policy Press.

—— 2000. Commodification and decommodification. *Policy & Politics*, 28 (3): 331–51.

ROSE, HILARY, 1981. Rereading Titmuss: The sexual division of welfare. *Journal of Social Policy*, 10 (4): 477–502.

ROSE, RICHARD, 1984. *Do Parties Make a Difference?* London: Macmillan.

ROSS, ARTHUR M., and HARTMAN, PAUL T., 1960. *Changing Patterns of Industrial Conflict*. New York: Wiley.

ROSS, FIONA, 2008. The politics of path-breaking change: The transformation of the welfare state in Britain and Germany. *Journal of Comparative Policy Analysis*, 10 (4): 365–84.

ROSS, GEORGE, 1994. On half-full glasses, Europe and the left: Comments on Wolfgang Streeck's 'European Social Policy after Maastricht'. *Economic and Industrial Democracy*, 15 (3): 486–96.

ROSS, MICHAEL, 2006. Is democracy good for the poor? *American Journal of Political Science*, 50 (4): 860–74.

ROSSI, NICOLA DI, 1997. *Meno ai padri più ai figli. Stato sociale e modernizzazione dell'Italia [Less for the Fathers, more for the Children: The Welfare State and the Modernization of Italy]*. Bologna: Il Mulino.

ROTHGANG, HEINZ, CACACE, MIRELLA, GRIMMEISEN, SIMONE, and WENDT, CLAUS, 2005. The changing role of the state in OECD health care systems, in *Transformations of the State?*, ed. Stephan Leibfried and Michael Zürn, Cambridge: Cambridge University Press, 187–212.

—— —— —— —— 2010. *The Changing Role of the State in OECD Health Care Systems. From Heterogeneity to Homogeneity?* Basingstoke: Palgrave Macmillan (forthcoming).

ROTHGANG, HEINZ, OBINGER, HERBERT, and LEIBFRIED, STEPHAN, 2006. The state and its welfare state: How do welfare state changes affect the make-up of the nation state? *Social Policy & Administration*, 40 (3): 250–66.

ROTHSCHILD, EMMA, 1995. Social security and laissez faire in 18th century political economy. *Population and Development Review*, 21 (4): 711–44.

ROTHSTEIN, BO, 1992. Labor-market institutions and working-class strength, in *Structuring Politics: Historical Institutionalism in Comparative Analysis*, ed. Sven Steinmo, Kathleen Thelen, and Frank Longstreth, Cambridge: Cambridge University Press, 33–56.

—— 1998. *Just Institutions Matter: The Moral and Political Logic of the Universal Welfare State*. Cambridge: Cambridge University Press (chapter 6, 'The political and moral logic of the universal welfare state' reprinted in Leibfried and Mau 2008a: vol. 1, 660–88).

—— 2001. Social capital in the social democratic welfare state. *Politics & Society*, 29 (2): 206–40.

ROTHSTEIN, BO, and STOLLE, DIETLIND (eds.), 2003. *Social Capital, Impartiality and the Welfare State: An Institutional Approach*. Basingstoke: Palgrave Macmillan.

RUDRA, NITA, 2004. Openness, welfare spending and inequality in the developing world. *International Studies Quarterly*, 48 (3): 683–709.

—— 2007. Welfare states in developing countries: Unique or universal? *Journal of Politics*, 69 (2): 378–96.

—— 2008. *Globalization and the Race to the Bottom in Developing Countries: Who Really Gets Hurt?* Cambridge: Cambridge University Press.

RUDRA, NITA, and HAGGARD, STEPHAN, 2005. Globalization, democracy, and effective welfare spending in the developing world. *Comparative Political Studies*, 38 (9): 1015–49.

RUEDA, DAVID, 2008. *Social Democracy Inside Out: Partisanship and Labor Market Policy in Advanced Industrial Democracies.* Oxford: Oxford University Press.

RUESCHEMEYER, DIETRICH, 2003. Can one or a few cases yield theoretical gains?, in *Comparative Historical Analysis in the Social Sciences,* ed. James Mahoney and Dietrich Rueschemeyer, Cambridge: Cambridge University Press, 305–36.

RUESCHEMEYER, DIETRICH, and SKOCPOL, THEDA (eds.), 1996. *States, Social Knowledge, and the Origins of Modern Social Policies.* Princeton, NJ: Princeton University Press.

RUESCHEMEYER, MARILYN, and WOLCHIK, SHARON (eds.), 2009. *Women in Power in Post-Communist Parliaments.* Washington, DC: Woodrow Wilson Center; Bloomington IN: Indiana University Press.

RUGGIE, JOHN GERALD, 1982. International regimes, transactions, and change: Embedded liberalism in the postwar economic order. *International Organization,* 36 (2): 379–415.

RUHM, CHRISTOPHER J, 1998. The economic consequences of parental leave mandates: Lessons from Europe. *Quarterly Journal of Economics,* 113 (1): 285–317. Available at http://ideas.repec.org/a/tpr/qjecon/v113y1998i1p285–317.html.

RYNER, MAGNUS, 2000. European welfare state transformation and migration, in *Immigration and Welfare: Challenging the Borders of the Welfare State,* ed. Michael Bommes and Andrew Geddes, London: Routledge, 51–71.

SACCHI, STEFANO, and BASTAGLI, FRANCESCA, 2005. Italy—Striving uphill but stopping halfway: The troubled journey of the experimental minimum insertion income, in *Welfare State Reform in Southern Europe: Fighting Poverty and Social Exclusion in Italy, Spain, Portugal, and Greece,* ed. Maurizio Ferrera, London: Routledge, 84–140.

SACKETT, DAVID L., ROSENBERG, WILLIAM M. C., GRAY, J. A. MUIR, HAYNES, R. BRIAN, and RICHARDSON, W. SCOTT, 1996. Evidence based medicine: What it is and what it isn't. *British Medical Journal,* 312 (7023), January 13): 71–72. Available at http://www.bmj.com/cgi/content/full/312/7023/71.

SAINSBURY, DIANE, 1996. *Gender, Equality, and Welfare States.* Cambridge: Cambridge University Press.

——— 1999. Taxation, family responsibilities, and employment, in *Gender and Welfare State Regimes,* ed. Diane Sainsbury, Oxford: Oxford University Press, 185–209.

——— 2006. Immigrants' social rights in comparative perspective: Welfare regimes, forms in immigration and immigration policy regimes. *Journal of European Social Policy,* 16 (3): 229–44.

SAINSBURY, DIANE, and MORISSENS, ANN, 2002. Poverty in Europe in the mid-1990s: The effectiveness of means-tested benefits. *Journal of European Social Policy,* 12 (4): 307–27.

SAINT-ARNAUD, SÉBASTIEN, and BERNARD, PAUL, 2003. Convergence or resilience? A hierarchical cluster analysis of the welfare regimes in advanced countries. *Current Sociology,* 51 (4): 499–527.

SAINT-JOURS, YVES, 1982. France, in *The Evolution of Social Insurance 1881–1981. Studies of Germany, France, Great Britain, Austria and Switzerland,* ed. Peter A. Köhler and Hans F. Zacher, London: Frances Pinter, 93–149.

SALMINEN, KARI, 1993. *Pension Schemes in the Making: A Comparative Study of the Scandinavian Countries* (The Central Pension Security Institute, Studies, 1993/2). Helsinki: The Central Pension Security Institute.

SAPELLI, GIULIO, 1995. *Southern Europe since 1945: Tradition and Modernity in Portugal, Spain, Italy and Greece.* London: Longman.

SARACENO, CHIARA, 1994. The ambivalent familism of the Italian welfare state. *Social Politics,* 1 (1): 60–82.

——— 1997. Family change, family policies and the restructuring of welfare, in *Family, Market and Community: Equity and Efficiency in Social Policy,* ed. Patrick Hennessy and Mark Pearson, Paris: OECD, 63–80.

SARACENO, CHIARA, (ed.), 2008. *Families, Ageing and Social Policy: Intergenerational Solidarity in European Welfare States.* Cheltenham: Edward Elgar.

SAUNDERS, PETER (CIS), 1986. *Social Theory and the Urban Question.* London: Hutchinson Education.

—— 1990. *A Nation of Home Owners.* London: Unwin Hyman.

SAUNIER, PIERRE-YVES, 2008. Les régimes circulatoires du domaine social 1800–1940: projets et ingénierie de la convergence et de la différence [The exchange regimes of the social domain 1800–1940: Projects and engineering of convergence and difference]. *Genèses,* 71 (2): 4–25.

SAWER, MARIAN, 2003 *The Ethical State? Social Liberalism in Australia.* Carleton, Australia: University of Melbourne Press.

SCANLON, KATHLEEN, and WHITEHEAD, CHRISTINE M. E., 2004. 'International trends in housing tenure and mortgage finance'. London: Council of Mortgage Lenders. Available at http://www.cml.org.uk/cml/media/press/94.

—— ——, 2007. Social housing in Europe, in *Social Housing in Europe,* ed. Kathleen Scanlon and Christine M. E. Whitehead, London: London School of Economics and Political Science, 8–33.

SCARBROUGH, ELINOR, 2000. West European welfare states: The old politics of retrenchment. *European Journal of Political Research,* 38 (2): 225–59.

SCHÄFER, ARMIN, 2005. *Die neue Unverbindlichkeit. Wirtschaftspolitische Koordinierung in Europa [The New Non-Binding Quality of Economic Policy Coordination in Europe].* Frankfurt a.M.: Campus.

—— 2006a. A new form of governance? Comparing the open method of co-ordination to multilateral surveillance by the IMF and the OECD. *Journal of European Public Policy,* 13 (1): 70–88.

—— 2006b. Resolving deadlock: Why international organisations introduce soft law. *European Law Journal,* 12 (2): 194–208.

SCHARPF, FRITZ W., 1988. The joint-decision trap: Lessons from German federalism and European integration. *Public Administration,* 66 (3): 239–78.

—— 1991. *Crisis and Choice in European Social Democracy.* Ithaca, NY: Cornell University Press.

—— 1994. Community and autonomy: Multi-level policy-making in the European Union. *Journal of European Public Policy,* 1 (2): 219–42.

—— 1999. *Governing in Europe: Effective and Democratic?* Oxford: Oxford University Press.

—— 2000a. Economic changes, vulnerabilities, and institutional capabilities, in *Work and Welfare in the Open Economy.* Vol. 1: *From Vulnerability to Competitiveness in Comparative Perspective,* ed. Fritz W. Scharpf and Vivien A. Schmidt, Oxford: Oxford University Press, 21–124.

—— 2000b. The viability of advanced welfare states in the international economy: Vulnerabilities and options. *European Journal of Public Policy,* 7 (2): 190–228.

—— 2002. The European Social Model: Coping with the challenges of diversity. *Journal of Common Market Studies,* 40 (4): 645–70.

—— 2009. Legitimacy in the multilevel European polity. *European Political Science,* 1 (2): 173–228.

SCHARPF, FRITZ W., and SCHMIDT, VIVIEN A. (eds.), 2000a. *Welfare and Work in the Open Economy,* vol. 1: *From Vulnerability to Competitiveness in Comparative Perspective;* vol. 2: *Diverse Responses to Common Challenges in Twelve Countries.* Oxford: Oxford University Press.

—— —— 2000b. Conclusions, in *Welfare and Work in the Open Economy*, vol. 1: *From Vulnerability to Competitiveness in Comparative Perspective*, ed. Fritz W. Scharpf and Vivien A. Schmidt, Oxford: Oxford University Press, 310–36.

SCHEFFLER, SAMUEL, 2003. What is egalitarianism? *Philosophy and Public Affairs*, 31 (1): 5–39.

SCHEVE, KENNETH, and STASAVAGE, DAVID, 2006. Religion and preferences for social insurance. *Quarterly Journal of Political Science*, 1 (3): 255–86.

SCHIERUP, CARL-ULRIK, HANSEN, PEO, and CASTLES, STEPHEN, 2006. *Migration, Citizenship and the European Welfare State: A European Dilemma*. Oxford: Oxford University Press.

SCHILLER, CHRISTOF, HENSEN, HENNI, and KUHNLE, STEIN, 2009. Health policy—A global dimension?, in *The Role of International Organizations in Social Policy. Ideas, Actors and Impact*, ed. Rune Ervik, Nanna Kildal, and Even Nilssen, Cheltenham: Edward Elgar, 212–45.

SCHLUDI, MARTIN, 2005. *The Reform of Bismarckian Pension Systems: A Comparison of Pension Politics in Austria, France, Germany, Italy and Sweden*. Amsterdam: Amsterdam University Press.

SCHMID, ACHIM, and WENDT, CLAUS, 2010. The service provision dimension, in *The Changing Role of the State in OECD Health Care Systems. From Heterogeneity to Homogeneity?*, ed. Heinz Rothgang, Mirella Cacace, Simone Grimmeisen, and Claus Wendt, Basingstoke: Palgrave Macmillan (forthcoming).

SCHMIDT, MANFRED G., 1982a. *Wohlfahrtsstaatliche Politik unter bürgerlichen und sozialdemokratischen Regierungen. Ein internationaler Vergleich [Welfare State Politics under Bourgeois and Social-democratic Governments]*. Frankfurt a.M.: Campus.

—— 1982b. The role of the parties in shaping macroeconomic policy, in *The Impact of Parties. Politics and Policies in Democratic Capitalist States*, ed. Francis G. Castles, London: Sage, 97–176.

—— 1995. The parties-do-matter hypothesis and the case of the Federal Republic of Germany. *German Politics*, 4 (3): 1–21.

—— 1996. When parties matter: A review of the possibilities and limits of partisan influence on public policy. *European Journal of Political Research*, 30 (2): 155–83.

—— 1997. Determinants of social expenditure in liberal democracies: The post World War II experience. *Acta Politica*, 32 (2): 153–73.

—— 2001. Ursachen und Folgen wohlfahrtsstaatlicher Politik. Ein internationaler Vergleich [Causes and consequences of welfare state policies: An international comparison], in *Wohlfahrtsstaatliche Politik. Institutionen, politischer Prozess und Leistungsprofil*, ed. Manfred G. Schmidt, Opladen: Leske+Budrich, 33–53.

—— 2002a. The impact of political parties, constitutional structures and veto players on public policy, in *Comparative Democratic Politics: A Guide to Contemporary Theory and Research*, ed. Hans Keman, London: Sage, 166–84.

—— 2002b. Warum Mittelmaß? Deutschlands Bildungsausgaben im internationalen Vergleich [Why only mediocre? Germany's education expenditures internationally compared]. *Politische Vierteljahresschrift*, 43 (1): 3–19.

—— 2005. *Sozialpolitik in Deutschland. Historische Entwicklung und internationaler Vergleich [Social Policy in Germany: Historical Development and International Comparison]*. Wiesbaden: VS-Verlag.

—— 2007. Testing the retrenchment hypothesis: Educational spending, 1962–2002, in *The Disappearing State: Retrenchment Realities in an Age of Globalisation*, ed. Francis G. Castles, Cheltenham: Edward Elgar, 159–83.

SCHMIDT, MANFRED G., 2008. Database: Die parteipolitische Zusammensetzung der OECD-Demokratien, 1945 bis 2007 [The party-political composition of OECD democracies, 1945–2007]. Heidelberg: Universität Heidelberg, Institut für Politikwissenschaft (SPSS file).

SCHMIDT, MANFRED G., OSTHEIM, TOBIAS, SIEGEL, NICO A., and ZOHLNHÖFER, REIMUND (eds.), 2007. Der Wohlfahrtsstaat. Eine Einführung in den historischen und internationalen Vergleich [The Welfare State: An Introduction to Historical and International Comparison]. Wiesbaden: VS-Verlag.

SCHMIDT, SUSANNE K., 2009. When efficiency results in redistribution: The conflict over the Single Services Market. West European Politics, 32 (4, Special Issue): 847–65.

SCHMITTER, PHILIPPE C., 1981. Interest intermediation and regime governability in contemporary Western Europe and North America, in Organizing Interests in Western Europe: Pluralism, Corporatism, and the Transformation of Politics, ed. Suzanne Berger, Cambridge: Cambridge University Press, 287–330.

SCHMITTER, PHILIPPE C., and LEHMBRUCH, GERHARD (eds.), 1981. Trends toward Corporatist Intermediation. Beverly Hills: Sage.

SCHMITTER, PHILIPPE C., and STREECK, WOLFGANG, 1999. 'The organization of business interests: Studying the associative action of business in advanced industrial societies' (Discussion Paper, 99/1). Cologne: Max-Planck-Institute for the Study of Societies. Available at http://www.mpifg.de/pu/mpifg_dp/dp99–1.pdf.

SCHNEIDER, REINHART, 1982. Die Bildungsentwicklung in den westeuropäischen Staaten 1870–1975 [The development of education in West European States 1870–1975]. Zeitschrift für Soziologie, 11 (3): 207–26.

SCHRÖDER, MARTIN, 2009. Integrating welfare and production typologies: How refinements of the varieties of capitalism approach call for a combination of welfare typologies. Journal of Social Policy, 38 (1): 19–43.

SCHUBERT, KLAUS, HEGELICH, SIMON, and BAZANT, URSULA, 2008. Europäische Wohlfahrtssysteme: Stand der Forschung—theoretisch-methodische Überlegungen [European Welfare Systems: State of Research—Reflections on Theory and Methodology], in Europäische Wohlfahrtssysteme, ed. Klaus Schubert, Simon Hegelich, and Ursula Bazant, Wiesbaden: VS-Verlag, 13–43.

SCHUKNECHT, LUDGER, and TANZI, VITO, 2005. Reforming public expenditure in industrialised countries: Are there trade-offs? (Working Paper, 435). Frankfurt a.M.: European Central Bank. Available at http://www.ecb.int/pub/pdf/scpwps/ecbwp435.pdf.

SCHUMPETER, JOSEPH A., 1942. Capitalism, Socialism, and Democracy. New York: Harper.

SCHWAB, KLAUS, and PORTER, MICHAEL E., 2007. The Global Competitiveness Report 2007–2008. Geneva: World Economic Forum.

SCHWARTZ, HERMAN, 2000. Internationalization and two welfare states: Australia and New Zealand, in Welfare and Work in the Open Economy, vol. 2: Diverse Responses to Common Challenges in Twelve Countries, ed. Fritz W. Scharpf and Vivien A. Schmidt, Oxford: Oxford University Press, 69–130.

—— 2001. Round up the usual suspects! Globalization, domestic politics, and welfare state change, in The New Politics of the Welfare State, ed. Paul Pierson, Oxford: Oxford University Press, 17–44.

SCOTT, JOAN W., 1988. Deconstructing equality-versus-difference: Or, the uses of poststructuralist theory for feminism. Feminist Studies, 14 (1): 32–50.

SCRUGGS, LYLE A., 2004. <u>Database</u>: Comparative Welfare Entitlements Data Set 1960–2002. Storrs, CT: University of Conneticut, Department of Political Science. Available at http://sp.uconn.edu/~scruggs/wp.htm.

—— 2006. The generosity of social insurance, 1971–2002. *Oxford Review of Economic Policy*, 22 (3): 349–64.

—— 2008. Social rights, welfare generosity, and inequality, in *Democracy, Inequality, and Representation: A Comparative Perspective*, ed. Pablo Beramendi and Christopher J. Andersen, New York: Russell Sage Foundation, 62–90.

SCRUGGS, LYLE A., and ALLAN, JAMES P., 2006a. Welfare-state decommodification in 18 OECD countries: A replication and revision. *Journal of European Social Policy*, 16 (1): 55–72.

—— —— 2006b. The material consequences of welfare states: Benefit generosity and absolute poverty in 16 OECD Countries. *Comparative Political Studies*, 39 (7): 880–904.

—— —— 2008. Social stratification and welfare regimes for the twenty-first century: Revisiting The Three Worlds of Welfare Capitalism. *World Politics*, 60 (4): 642–64.

SEELEIB-KAISER, MARTIN, 2001. *Globalisierung und Sozialpolitik. Ein Vergleich ihrer Diskurse und Wohlfahrtssysteme in Deutschland, Japan und in den USA [Globalization and Social Policy. A Comparison of Discourses and Welfare States in Germany, Japan and the USA]*. Frankfurt a.M.: Campus.

SEELEIB-KAISER, MARTIN, DYK, SILKE VAN, and ROGGENKAMP, MARTIN (eds.), 2008. *Party Politics and Social Welfare: Comparing Christian Democracy in Austria, Germany and the Netherlands*. Cheltenham: Edgar Elgar.

SEFTON, TOM, 2009. Moving in the right direction? Public attitudes to poverty, inequality and redistribution, in *Towards a More Equal Society? Poverty, Inequality and Policy Since 1997*, ed. John Hills, Tom Sefton and Kitty Stewart, Bristol: Policy Press, 223–44.

SEGURA-UBIERGO, ALEX, 2007. *The Political Economy of the Welfare State in Latin America: Globalization, Democracy, and Development*. Cambridge: Cambridge University Press.

SELDEN, MARK, and YOU, LAIYIN, 1997. The reform of social welfare in China. *World Development*, 25 (10): 1657–68.

SEN, AMARTYA KUMAR, 1983. Poor, relatively speaking. *Oxford Economic Papers*, 35 (2): 153–69.

—— 1985. *Commodities and Capabilities*. Amsterdam: North-Holland.

—— 1987. *The Standard of Living: The Tanner Lectures, Clare Hall, Cambridge, 1985*. Cambridge: Cambridge University Press.

—— 1992. *Inequality Reexamined*. New York & Cambridge, MA: Russell Sage Foundation & Harvard University Press.

—— 2000. Social justice and the distribution of income, in *Handbook of Income Distribution*, vol. 1, ed. Anthony B. Atkinson and François Bourguignon, Amsterdam: Elsevier, 59–85.

SENTI, MARTIN, 2001. *Internationale Regime und nationale Politik: Die Effektivität der Internationalen Arbeitsorganisation (ILO) im Industrieländervergleich [International Regimes and National Policy: A Comparson of the Effectiveness of the International Labour Organisation in Industrial Countries]*. Bern: Paul Haupt.

SHAKESPEARE, TOM, 1994. Cultural representation of disabled people: Dustbins for disavowal? *Disability & Society*, 9 (3): 283–99.

SHALEV, MICHAEL (ed.), 1996. *The Privatization of Social Policy? Occupational Welfare and the Welfare State in America, Scandinavia and Japan*. Basingstoke: Macmillan.

SHALEV, MICHAEL (ed.), 2007. Limits and alternatives to multiple regression in comparative research, in *Capitalisms Compared*, ed. Lars Mjøset and Tommy H. Clausen, Amsterdam: Elsevier 261–308 (Comparative Social Research, 24).

—— 2008. Class divisions among women. *Politics & Society*, 36 (3): 403–20.

SHAVER, SHEILA, 1994. Body rights, social rights and the liberal welfare state. *Critical Social Policy*, 13 (9): 66–93.

SHAW, JO (ed.), 2000. *Social Law and Policy in an Evolving European Union*. Oxford: Hart.

SHIMA, ISILDA, and RODRIGUES, RICARDO, 2008. The implementation of EU social inclusion and social protection strategies in European countries with reference to equality for disabled people. Utrecht: Academic Network of European Disability Experts. Available at http://www.disability-europe.net/content/pdf/ANED%20Task%207%20report%20So cial%20Inclusion%20final%2020–05–09.pdf.

SHINKAWA, TOSHIMITSU (ed.), 2008. *Social Integration and National Identity in Multi-Cultural Societies*. Kyoto: Minerva Shobo.

SHIPPER, APICHAI W., 2008. *Fighting for Foreigners: Immigration and Its Impact on Japanese Democracy*. Ithaca, NY: Cornell University Press.

SHONFIELD, ANDREW, 1965. *Modern Capitalism: The Changing Balance of Public and Private Power*. Oxford: Oxford University Press.

SIAROFF, ALAN, 1994. Work, welfare and gender equality: A new typology, in *Gendering Welfare States*, ed. Diane Sainsbury, London: Sage, 82–100.

SIEGEL, NICO A., 2002. *Baustelle Sozialpolitik. Konsolidierung und Rückbau im internationalen Vergleich [The Welfare State as a Construction Site: Consolidation and Retrenchment Internationally Compared]*. Frankfurt a.M.: Campus.

—— 2005. Social Pacts revisited: 'Competitive concertation' and complex causality in negotiated welfare state reforms. *European Journal of Industrial Relations*, 11 (1): 107–26.

—— 2007. Moving beyond expenditure accounts: The changing contours of the regulatory state, 1980–2003, in *The Disappearing State? Retrenchment Realities in an Age of Globalisation*, ed. Francis G. Castles, Cheltenham: Edward Elgar.

SIERMINSKA, EVA, BRANDOLINI, ANDREAS, and SMEEDING, TIMOTHY M., 2006. Comparing wealth distribution across rich countries: First results from the Luxembourg Wealth Study' (LWS [Luxembourg Wealth Study] Working Paper No. 1). Luxembourg: Luxembourg Income Study. Available at http://www.lisproject.org/publications/lwswpapers.htm.

SILVERMAN, ELAINE M., SKINNER, JONATHAN S., and FISHER, ELLIOTT S., 1999. The association between for-profit hospital ownership and increased Medicare spending. *The New England Journal of Medicine*, 341 (6): 420–26.

SIMMONS, BETH A., 2009. *Mobilizing for Human Rights: International Law in Domestic Politics*. Cambridge: Cambridge University Press.

SIMMONS, BETH A., DOBBIN, FRANK, and GARRETT, GEOFFREY (eds.), 2008. *The Global Diffusion of Markets and Democracy*. Cambridge: Cambridge University Press.

SIMMONS, BETH A., and ELKINS, ZACHARY, 2004. The globalization of liberalization: Policy diffusion in the international political economy. *American Political Science Review*, 98 (1): 171–89.

SIMMONS, BETH A., and HOPKINS, DANIEL J., 2005. The constraining power of international treaties: Theory and methods. *American Political Science Review*, 99 (4): 623–31.

SIMONAZZI, ANNAMARIA, 2009. Care regimes and national employment models. *Cambridge Journal of Economics*, 33 (2): 211–32.

SINDBJERG MARTINSEN, DORTE, 2009. Conflict and conflict management in the cross-border provision of healthcare services. *West European Politics*, 32 (4, Special Issue): 792–809.

SINFIELD, ADRIAN, 1978. Analyses in the social division of welfare. *Journal of Social Policy*, 7 (2): 129–56.

SIPILÄ, JORMA, 1997. *Social Care Services: The Key to the Scandinavian Welfare Model.* Aldershot: Avebury.

SISSENICH, BEATE, 2002. The diffusion of EU social and employment legislation in Poland and Hungary, in *Norms and Nannies: The Impact of International Organizations on Central and East European States*, ed. Ronald H. Linden, Lanham, MD: Rowman & Littlefield, 287–316.

SJÖBERG, OLA, 2000. *Duties in the Welfare State. Working and Paying for Social Rights*, Edsbruk: Akademitryck.

SKINNER, QUENTIN, 1998. *Liberty Before Liberalism.* Cambridge: Cambridge University Press.

SKOCPOL, THEDA, 1985. Bringing the state back in: Strategies of analysis in current research, in *Bringing the State Back in*, ed. Peter B. Evans, Dietrich Rueschemeyer, and Theda Skocpol, Cambridge: Cambridge University Press, 3–37.

—— 1992. *Protecting Soldiers and Mothers: The Political Origins of Social Policy in the United States.* Cambridge, MA: The Belknap Press of Harvard University Press.

—— 1995. *Social Policy in the United States: Future Possibilities in Historical Perspective.* Princeton, NJ: Princeton University Press.

SKOCPOL, THEDA, ABEND-WEIN, MARJORIE, HOWARD, CHRISTOPHER, and LEHMANN, SUSAN G., 1993. Women's associations and the enactment of Mothers' Pensions in the United States. *American Political Science Review*, 87 (3): 686–701.

SKOCPOL, THEDA, and SOMERS, MARGARET, 1980. The uses of comparative history in macrosocial inquiry. *Comparative Studies in Society and History*, 22 (2): 174–97.

SLAVNIC, ZORAN, and URBAN, SUSANNE, 2008. Socio-economic trends in the Swedish taxi sector: Deregulation, recommodification, ethnification. *International Journal on Multi-cultural Societies*, 10 (1): 76–94.

SLEEBOS, JOËLLE, 2003. Low fertility rates in the OECD Countries: Facts and policy responses (OECD Social, Employment and Migration Working papers, 15). Paris: OECD. Available at http://www.oecd.org/dataoecd/13/38/16587241.pdf.

SMEEDING, TIMOTHY M., 2002. Globalization, inequality and the rich countries of the G-20. Evidence from the Luxembourg Income Study (LIS) (SPRC Discussion Paper, 122). Sydney: University of New South Wales. Available at http://www.sprc.unsw.edu.au/dp/DP122pdf.

—— 2004. Twenty years of research on income inequality—Poverty and redistribution in the developed world: Introduction and overview. *Socio-Economic Review*, 2 (2): 149–63.

SMEEDING, TIMOTHY M., O'HIGGINS, MICHAEL, and RAINWATER, LEE (eds.), 1990. *Poverty, Inequality, und the Distribution of Income in a Comparative Perspective: The Luxembourg Income Study (LIS)*, with an introduction by Anthony B. Atkinson. London: Wheatsheaf Books.

SMEEDING, TIMOTHY M., RAINWATER, LEE, and BURTLESS, GARY, 2001. U.S. poverty in a cross-national context, in *Understanding Poverty*, ed. Sheldon H. Danzinger and Robert H. Haveman, New York: Russell Sage Foundation, 162–89.

SMEEDING, TIMOTHY M., SAUNDERS, PETER (UNSW), CODER, JOHN, JENKINS, STEPHEN P., FRITZELL, JOHAN S., HAGENAARS, ALEIDA J. M., HAUSER, RICHARD, and WOLFSON, MICHAEL, 1993. Poverty, inequality and family living standards impacts across seven nations: The effect of noncash subsidies for health, education and housing. *Review of Income and Wealth*, 39 (3): 229–56.

SMEEDING, TIMOTHY M., TORREY, BARBARA B., and REIN, MARTIN, 1988. Patterns of income and poverty: The economic status of the young and old in eight countries, in *The Vulnerable*, ed. John L. Palmer, Timothy M. Smeeding, and Barbara B. Torrey, Washington, DC: Urban Institute Press, 89–119.

SMITH, ADAM, 1976. *An Inquiry into the Nature and Causes of the Wealth of Nations*. Oxford: The Clarendon Press of Oxford University Press (first publ. 1776).

SMITH, DANIEL A., 1998. *Tax Crusaders and the Politics of Direct Democracy*. London: Routledge.

SMITH, LAWRENCE B., ROSEN, KENNETH T., and FALLIS, GEORGE, 1988. Recent developments in economic models of housing markets. *Journal of Economic Literature*, 26 (1): 29–64.

SNA (SYSTEM OF NATIONAL ACCOUNTS), 1993. System of National Accounts 1993. New York: United Nations, United Nations Statistics Division. Available at http://unstats.un.org/unsd/sna1993/introduction.asp.

SNYDER, JAMES M., and KRAMER, GERALD H., 1988. Fairness, self-interest, and the politics of the progressive income tax. *Journal of Public Economics*, 36 (2): 197–230.

SOPER, KATE, 1993. The thick and thin of human needing, in *New Approaches to Welfare Theory*, ed. Glenn Drover and Patrick Kerans, Cheltenham: Edward Elgar, 69–81.

SOSKICE, DAVID, 1999. Divergent production regimes: Coordinated and uncoordinated market economies in the 1980s and 1990s, in *Continuity and Change in Contemporary Capitalism*, ed. Herbert Kitschelt, Peter Lange, Gary Marks, and John D. Stephens, Cambridge: Cambridge University Press, 101–34.

SOSKICE, DAVID, and IVERSEN, TORBEN, 2006. Electoral institutions and the politics of coalitions: Why some democracies redistribute more than others. *American Political Science Review*, 100 (2): 165–81.

SOSS, JOE, 1999. Lessons of welfare: Policy design, political learning, and political action. *American Political Science Review*, 93 (2): 363–80.

—— 2005. Making clients and citizens: Welfare policy as a source of status, belief and action, in *Deserving and Entitled: Social Constructions and Public Policy*, ed. Anne L. Schneider and Helen M. Ingram, Stony Brook: State University of New York Press, 291–328.

SOSS, JOE, HACKER, JACOB S., and METTLER, SUZANNE (eds.), 2007. *Remaking America: Democracy and Public Policy in an Age of Inequality*. New York: Russell Sage Foundation.

SOSS, JOE, and SCHRAM, SANFORD F., 2007. A public transformed? Welfare reform as policy feedback. *American Political Science Review*, 101 (1): 111–27.

SOTIROPOULOS, DIMITRI, 2004. Southern European public bureaucracies in comparative perspective. *West European Politics*, 27 (3): 405–22.

—— 2005. Poverty and the safety net in Eastern and South Eastern Europe in the Post-Communist Era, in *Welfare State Reform in Southern Europe. Fighting Poverty and Social Exclusion in Italy, Spain, Portugal and Greece*, ed. Maurizio Ferrera, London: Routledge, 266–96.

SPALDING, ROSE J., 1978. *Social Security Policy Making: The Formation and Evolution of the Mexican Social Security Institute*. Chapel Hill: University of North Carolina at Chapel Hill, Ph.D. Dissertation.

SSA (SOCIAL SECURITY ADMINISTRATION, US DEPARTMENT OF HEALTH AND HUMAN SERVICES), 1999. *Social Security Programs Throughout the World*. Washington, DC:

USGPO, Social Security Administration. Available at http://www.ssa.gov/policy/docs/progdesc/ssptw/.

STAERKLÉ, CHRISTIAN, DELAY, CHRISTOPHE, GIANETTONI, LAVINIA, and ROUX, PATRICIA, 2007. *Qui a droit à quoi? Représentations et légitimation de l'ordre social. [Who has a Right to What? Representations and Legitimation of Social Order].* Grenoble: Presses Universitaires de Grenoble.

STARKE, PETER, 2006. The politics of welfare state retrenchment: A literature review. *Social Policy & Administration*, 40 (1): 104–20.

—— 2008. *Radical Welfare State Retrenchment: A Comparative Analysis.* Basingstoke: Palgrave Macmillan.

STARKE, PETER, OBINGER, HERBERT, and CASTLES, FRANCIS G., 2008. Convergence towards where: In what ways, if any, are welfare states becoming more similar? *Journal of European Public Policy*, 15 (7): 975–1000.

STARR, PETER, 1982. *The Social Transformation of American Medicine.* New York: Basic Books.

STARR, PETER, and IMMERGUT, ELLEN M., 1987. Health care and the boundaries of politics, in *Changing Boundaries of the Political: Essays on the Evolving Balance Between State and Society, Public and Private in Europe*, ed. Charles S. Maier, Cambridge: Cambridge University Press, 221–54.

STATISTICS CANADA, 2007. Immigration and citizenship: Highlight tables, 2001 Census. Ottawa: Statistics Canada. Available at http://www.census2006.ca/english/census01/.

STEARNS, PETER N., 1975. *Lives of Labour: Work in a Maturing Industrial Society.* London: Croom Helm.

STEARNS, SALLY C., NORTON, EDWARD C., and YANG, ZHOU, 2007. How age and disability affect long-term care expenditures in the United States. *Social Policy and Society*, 6 (3): 367–78.

STEELE, GERALD R., 2007. *The Economics of Friedrich Hayek.* Basingstoke: Palgrave Macmillan.

STEIN, JANA VON, 2005. Do treaties constrain or screen? Selection bias and treaty compliance. *American Political Science Review*, 99 (4): 611–22.

STEINER, HILLEL, 1994. *An Essay on Rights.* Oxford: Blackwell.

STEINMO, SVEN, 1993. *Taxation and Democracy: Swedish, British and American Approaches to Financing the Modern State.* New Haven, CT: Yale University Press.

STEPHENS, JOHN D., 1979. *The Transition from Capitalism to Socialism.* London: Macmillan (also Urbana, IL: University of Illinois Press 1986).

STERN, NICHOLAS H., 2007. *The Economics of Climate Change: The Stern Review.* Cambridge: Cambridge University Press.

STIGLITZ, JOSEPH E., 2002. *Globalization and its Discontents.* New York: W. W. Norton.

STINCHCOMBE, ARTHUR L., 1985. The functional theory of social insurance. *Politics & Society*, 14 (4): 411–30.

STJERNØ, STEINAR, 2004. *Solidarity in Europe: The History of an Idea.* Cambridge: Cambridge University Press.

STONE, DEBORAH A., 1984. *The Disabled State.* Philadelphia: Temple University Press.

—— 2002. *Policy Paradox: The Art of Political Decision Making.* New York: W.W. Norton (1st edn. 1988).

STONE, JUDITH F., 1985. *The Search for Social Peace: Reform Legislation in France, 1890–1914.* Albany: State University of New York Press.

STONE, RANDALL W., 2002. *Lending Credibility: The International Monetary Fund and the Post-Communist Transition.* Princeton, NJ: Princeton University Press.

—— 2008. The scope of IMF conditionality. *International Organization,* 62 (4): 589–620.

STRANG, DAVID, and CHANG, PATRICIA M.Y., 1993. The International Labour Organisation and the welfare state: Institutional effects on national welfare spending, 1960–80. *International Organization,* 47 (2): 235–62.

STRANGE, SUSAN, 1996. *The Retreat of the State: The Diffusion of Power in the World Economy.* Cambridge: Cambridge University Press.

STRAUSS, ANSELM L., 1987. *Qualitative Analysis for Social Scientists.* Cambridge: Cambridge University Press.

STREECK, WOLFGANG, 1991. Interest heterogeneity and organizing capacity: Two logics of collective action?, in *Political Choice, Institutions, Rules, and the Limits of Rationality,* ed. Roland M. Czada and Adrienne Windhoff-Héritier, Frankfurt a.M.: Campus, 76–104.

—— 2009. *Re-Forming Capitalism: Institutional Change in the German Political Economy.* Oxford: Oxford University Press.

STREECK, WOLFGANG, and THELEN, KATHLEEN A. (eds.), 2005a. *Beyond Continuity: Institutional Change in Advanced Political Economies.* Oxford: Oxford University Press.

—— —— 2005b. Introduction: Institutional change in advanced political economies, in *Beyond Continuity. Institutional Change in Advanced Political Economies,* ed. Wolfgang Streeck and Kathleen A. Thelen, Oxford: Oxford University Press, 1–39.

STREECK, WOLFGANG, and YAMAMURA, KŌZŌ (eds.), 2002. *The Origins of Nonliberal Capitalism: Germany and Japan in Comparison.* Ithaca, NY: Cornell University Press.

STREMMEL, RALF, TENNSTEDT, FLORIAN, and FLECKENSTEIN, GISELA (eds.), 2006. *Quellensammlung zur Geschichte der deutschen Sozialpolitik 1867 bis 1914,* vol. 1: *Grundfragen der Sozialpolitik in der öffentlichen Diskussion: Kirchen, Parteien, Vereine und Verbände [A Collection of Sources on the History of German Social Policy 1867–1914,* vol. 1: *Fundamental Issues of Social Policy in the Public Discourse: Churches, Parties, Associations and Lobbies].* Darmstadt: Wissenschaftliche Buchgesellschaft.

SULLIVAN, SCOTT, 1997. *From War to Wealth: 50 Years of Innovation.* Paris: OECD.

SVALLFORS, STEFAN, 1989. *Vem älskar välfärdsstaten? Attityder, organiserade intressen och svensk välfärdspolitik [Who Loves the Welfare State? Attitudes, Organized Interests and Swedish Welfare Policies].* Lund: Arkiv.

—— 1993. Policy regimes and attitudes to inequality: A comparison of three European nations, in *Scandinavia in a New Europe,* ed. Thomas P. Boje and Sven E. Olsson Hort, Oslo: Scandinavian University Press, 87–133.

—— 1996. *Välfärdsstatens moraliska ekonomi: välfärdsopinionen i 90-talets Sverige [The Moral Economy of the Welfare State: Welfare Opinions in Sweden of the 1990s].* Umeå: Boréa.

—— 1997. Worlds of welfare and attitudes to redistribution: A comparison of eight Western nations. *European Sociological Review,* 13 (3): 283–304 (reprint in Leibfried and Mau 2008a: vol. 3, 331–52).

—— 2003. Welfare regimes and welfare opinions: A comparison of eight Western countries. *Social Indicators Research,* 64 (3): 495–520.

—— 2004. Class, attitudes and the welfare state: Sweden in comparative perspective. *Social Policy & Administration,* 38 (2): 119–38.

—— 2006. *The Moral Economy of Class: Class and Attitudes in Comparative Perspective.* Stanford, CA: Stanford University Press.

—— (ed.), 2007. *The Political Sociology of the Welfare State: Institutions, Social Cleavages, and Orientations*. Stanford, CA: Stanford University Press.

SVALLFORS, STEFAN, and TAYLOR-GOOBY, PETER, 1999. *The End of the Welfare State? Responses to State Retrenchment*. London: Routledge.

SWAAN, ABRAM DE, 1988. *In Care of the State: Health Care, Education and Welfare in Europe and the USA in the Modern Era*. Cambridge: Polity.

SWANK, DUANE, 2001. Political institutions and welfare state restructuring, in *The New Politics of the Welfare State*, ed. Paul Pierson, Oxford: Oxford University Press, 197–237.

—— 2002. *Global Capital, Political Institutions, and Policy Change in Developed Welfare States*. Cambridge: Cambridge University Press.

—— 2003. Whither welfare? Globalization, political institutions, and contemporary welfare states, in *States in the Global Economy: Bringing Domestic Institutions Back In*, ed. Linda Weiss, Cambridge: Cambridge University Press, 58–82.

—— 2006. Tax policy in the era of internationalization: Explaining the spread of neoliberalism. *International Organization*, 60 (4): 847–82.

SWANK, DUANE, and STEINMO, SVEN, 2002. The new political economy of taxation in advanced capitalist democracies. *American Journal of Political Science*, 46 (3): 642–55.

SWENSON, PETER A., 2002. *Capitalists Against Markets: The Making of Labor Markets and Welfare States in the United States and Sweden*. Oxford: Oxford University Press.

SWIFT, ADAM, 2001. *Political Philosophy. A Beginners' Guide for Students and Politicians*. Cambridge: Polity.

SYKES, ROBERT, PALIER, BRUNO, and PRIOR, PAULINE M. (eds.), 2001. *Globalization and European Welfare States: Challenges and Change*. Basingstoke: Palgrave Macmillan.

TÅHLIN, MICHAEL, 2008. Asset specificity, labor market outcomes, and policy preferences. Paper presented at SOFI SWS Seminar [Swedish Institute for Social Research, Stockholm University]. Stockholm, March.

TAI, PO-FEN, 2006. Social Polarisation: Comparing Singapore, Hong Kong and Taipei. *Urban Studies*, 43 (1): 1737–56.

TAIWAN EXECUTIVE YUAN, 2008. *Statistical Yearbook—2008*. Taipei: Executive Yuan.

TAKAHASHI, MUTSUKO, 1995. Japanese Welfare Society: Analyzing the Japanese Welfare Discourses. Tampere: University of Tampere, Ph.D. Dissertation.

TÁLOS, EMMERICH, 1981. *Staatliche Sozialpolitik in Österreich [The Welfare State in Austria]*. Vienna: Verlag für Gesellschaftskritik.

TÁLOS, EMMERICH, and WÖRISTER, KARL, 1994. *Soziale Sicherung im Sozialstaat Österreich: Entwicklung, Herausforderungen, Strukturen [Social Security in Welfare State Austria: Development, Challenges, Structures]*. Baden-Baden: Nomos.

TANZI, VITO, and SCHUKNECHT, LUDGER, 2000. *Public Spending in the 20th Century: A Global Perspective*. Cambridge: Cambridge University Press.

TAYLOR, GARY, 2007. *Ideology and Welfare*. Basingstoke: Palgrave Macmillan.

TAYLOR-GOOBY, PETER, 1982. Two cheers for the welfare state: Public opinion and private welfare. *Journal of Public Policy*, 2 (4): 319–46.

—— 1983. Legitimation deficit, public opinion and the welfare state. *Sociology*, 17 (2): 165–82.

—— 1985. *Public Opinion, Ideology, and State Welfare*. London: Routledge & Kegan Paul.

—— 2001. The politics of welfare in Europe, in *Welfare States Under Pressure*, ed. Peter Taylor-Gooby, London: Sage, 1–28.

—— 2002. The silver age of the welfare state: Perspectives on resilience. *Journal of Social Policy*, 31 (4): 597–621.

Taylor-Gooby, Peter, (ed.), 2004. *New Risks, New Welfare: The Transformation of the European Welfare State*. Oxford: Oxford University Press.

—— 2005a. *Ideas and Welfare State Reform in Western Europe*. Basingstoke: Palgrave Macmillan.

—— 2005b. Is the future American? Or, can left politics preserve European welfare states from erosion through growing 'racial' diversity? *Journal of Social Policy*, 34 (4): 661–72.

—— 2006. Social and public policy: Reflexive individualization and regulatory governance, in *Risk in Social Science*, ed. Peter Taylor-Gooby and Jens O. Zinn, Oxford: Oxford University Press, 271–87.

—— 2008. *Reframing Social Citizenship*. Oxford: Oxford University Press.

Teichman, Judith, 2001. *The Politics of Freeing Markets in Latin America: Chile, Argentina, and Mexico*. Chapel Hill, NC: University of North Carolina Press.

Tennstedt, Florian, Henning, Hansjoachim, Born, Karl Erich, Winter, Heidi, Ayass, Wolfgang, and Rassow, Peter, 1978 ff. *Quellensammlung zur Geschichte der deutschen Sozialpolitik: 1867 bis 1914. Editionsprojekt der Historischen Kommission der Akademie der Wissenschaften und der Literatur in Mainz [A Collection of Sources on the History of German Social Policy 1867–1914: A Project undertaken by the Committe on History of the Academy of Sciences in Mainz]*. Overview available at http://www.uni-kassel.de/fb4/akademie.

Tennstedt, Florian, and Winter, Heidi (eds.), 1994. *Quellensammlung zur Geschichte der deutschen Sozialpolitik 1867 bis 1914. Vol. 1: Grundfragen staatlicher Sozialpolitik [Collection of Sources on the History of German Social Policy 1867 to 1914. Vol. 1: Fundamental Questions of Social Policy]*. Darmstadt: Wissenschaftliche Buchgesellschaft.

Thaler, Richard H., and Sunstein, Cass R., 2008. *Nudge: Improving Decisions about Health, Wealth and Happiness*. New Haven, CT: Yale University Press.

Thane, Pat, 1996. *Foundations of the Welfare State*. London: Longman.

Thelen, Kathleen A., 1999. Historical institutionalism in comparative politics. *Annual Review of Political Science*, 2: 369–404.

—— 2004. *How Institutions Evolve: The Political Economy of Skills in Germany, Britain, the United States and Japan*. Cambridge: Cambridge University Press.

Therborn, Göran, 1993. Beyond the lonely nation-state, in *Families of Nations: Patterns of Public Policy in Western Democracies*, ed. Francis G. Castles, Aldershot: Dartmouth, 329–40.

—— 1995a. *European Modernity and Beyond: The Trajectory of European Societies, 1945–2000*. London: Sage.

—— 1995b. Routes to/through modernity, in *Global Modernities*, ed. Mike Featherstone, Scott Lash and Roland Robertson, London: Sage, 124–39.

—— 2003. Dimensions and processes of global inequalities, in *The Moral Fabric in Contemporary Societies*, ed. Grażyna Skapska and Annamaria Orla-Bukovska, Leiden: Brill, 119–40.

—— 2004. *Between Sex and Power. Family in the World, 1900–2000*. London: Routledge.

Thomas, John C., 1976. *The Decline of Ideology in Western Political Parties: A Study of Changing Policy Orientations*. London: Sage.

Thomson, David, 1989. The welfare state and generation conflict: Winners and losers, in *Workers Versus Pensioners: Intergenerational Justice in an Ageing World*, ed. Paul Johnson, Christoph Conrad and David Thomson, Manchester: Manchester University Press, 33–56.

THORNTON, PATRICIA, and LUNT, NEIL, 1997. *Employment Policies for Disabled People in Eighteen Countries: A Review*. York: Social Policy Research Unit, University of York. Available at http://digitalcommons.ilr.cornell.edu/cgi/viewcontent.cgi?article=1158&context=gladnetcollect.

TILLY, CHARLES, 1984. *Big Structures, Large Processes, Huge Comparisons*. New York: Russell Sage Foundation.

TILTON, TIMOTHY A., 1990. *The Political Theory of Swedish Social Democracy: Through the Welfare State to Socialism*. Oxford: Oxford University Press.

TIMMONS, JEFFREY F., 2006. The fiscal contract: States, taxes and public services. *World Politics*, 57 (4): 530–67.

TIMONEN, VIRPI, 2008. *Ageing Societies. A Comparative Introduction*. Maidenhead: Open University Press.

TITMUSS, RICHARD M., 1950. *Problems of Social Policy (History of the Second World War: United Kingdom Civil Series)*. London: HMSO/Longmans.

—— 1974a. *Social Policy: An Introduction*. London: Allen & Unwin.

—— 1974b. What is social policy?, in *Social Policy: An Introduction*, ed. Brian Abel-Smith and Richard M. Titmuss, New York: Pantheon, 23–32 (reprint in Leibfried and Mau 2008a: vol. 1, 138–47).

—— 1976a. War and social policy, in *Essays on 'The Welfare State'*, ed. Richard M. Titmuss, London: Allen & Unwin, 76–87 (3rd. edn.).

—— 1976b. The social division of welfare, in *Essays on 'The Welfare State'*, ed. Richard M. Titmuss, London: Allen & Unwin, 34–55 (3rd edn.; originally published in 1955).

TOKMAN, VÍCTOR E., 2002. Jobs and solidarity: Challenges for labor market policy in Latin America, in *Models of Capitalism: Lessons for Latin America*, ed. Evelyne Huber, University Park, PA: Pennsylvania State University Press, 159–94.

TORFING, JACOB, 1999. Workfare with welfare: Recent reforms of the Danish welfare state. *Journal of European Social Policy*, 9 (1): 5–28.

TORGERSEN, ULF, 1987. Housing: The wobbly pillar under the welfare state, in *Between State and Market: Housing in the Post-industrial Era*, ed. Bengt Turner, Jim Kemeny, and Lennart Lundqvist, Gavle: Almqvist and Wiksell International, 116–27.

TOUSSAINT, ERIC, 2008. *The World Bank: A Critical Primer*. London: Pluto.

TOWNSEND, PETER, 1979. *Poverty in the United Kingdom: A Survey of Household Resources*. London: Penguin.

TRAMPUSCH, CHRISTINE, 2007. Industrial relations as a source of solidarity in times of welfare state retrenchment. *Journal of Social Policy*, 36 (2): 197–215.

TRAXLER, FRANZ, 1993. Business associations and labor unions in comparison: Theoretical perspectives and empirical findings on social class, collective action and associational organizability. *British Journal of Sociology*, 44 (4): 673–91.

—— 1999. The state in industrial relations: A cross-national analysis of developments and socioeconomic effects. *European Journal of Political Research*, 36 (1): 55–85.

TRAXLER, FRANZ, and KITTEL, BERNHARD, 2000. The bargaining system and performance: A comparison of 18 OECD countries. *Comparative Political Studies*, 33 (9): 1154–90.

TRIFILETTI, ROSSANA, 1999. Southern European welfare regimes and the worsening position of women. *Journal of European Social Policy*, 9 (1): 49–64.

TROELTSCH, ERNST, 1931. *The Social Teaching of the Christian Churches*. London: Allen & Unwin (first publ. in German 1912 as *Die Soziallehren der christlichen Kirchen und Gruppen*; republ. in English 1950 und 1956).

TSEBELIS, GEORGE, 1995. Decision making in political systems: Veto players in presidentialism, parliamentarism, multicameralism and multipartyism. *British Journal of Political Science*, 25 (3): 289–325.

—— 2002. *Veto Players: How Political Institutions Work*. Princeton, NJ: Princeton University Press.

TUFTE, EDWARD R., 1978. *Political Control of the Economy*. Princeton, NJ: Princeton University Press.

TULLOCK, GORDON, 1983. *Economics of Income Redistribution*. Boston: Kluwer Nijhoff.

TUOHY, CAROLYN J., 1999. *Accidental Logics: The Dynamics of Change in the Health Care Arena in the United States, Britain and Canada*. Oxford: Oxford University Press.

UK ONS (OFFICE OF NATIONAL STATISTICS), 2008. *Annual Update: Births in England and Wales, 2007, Population Trends 134, Winter 2008*. London: ONS.

UK SDC (UK SUSTAINABLE DEVELOPMENT COMMISSION), 2009. *Prosperity without Growth? The Transition to a Sustainable Economy*. London: Sustainable Development Commission. Available at http://www.sd-commission.org.uk/publications/downloads/prosperity_without_growth_report.pdf.

ULLRICH, CARSTEN G., 2008. *Die Akzeptanz des Wohlfahrtsstaates. Präferenzen, Konflikte, Deutungsmuster [The Acceptance of the Welfare State. Preferences, Conflicts and Patterns of Interpretation]*. Wiesbaden: VS-Verlag.

UNDP (UNITED NATIONS DEVELOPMENT PROGRAMME), 2008. Human Development Report 2007/08. New York: UNDP. Available at http://worldbank/org.

UNFPA (UNITED NATIONS POPULATION FUND), 2008. *State of the World Population 2008: Reaching Common Ground: Culture, Gender and Human Rights*. New York: UNFPA. Available at http://www.unfpa.org/swp.

UNGERSON, CLARE, and YEANDLE, SUSAN (eds.), 2007. *Cash for Care in Developed Welfare States*. Basingstoke: Palgrave Macmillan.

UNICEF (UNITED NATIONS CHILDREN'S FUND), 2000. A League Table of Child Poverty in Rich Nations. Florence: UNICEF, Innocenti Research Centre. Available at http://www.unicef-irc.org/publications/pdf/repcard1e.pdf.

—— 2007. Child poverty in perspective: An overview of child well-being in rich countries (Innocenti Report Card). Florence: UNICEF, Innocenti Research Center. Available at http://www.unicef.org.uk/publications/pdf/rc7_eng.pdf.

—— 2008. Database: TransMONEE Database 2008. Paris: UNICEF. Available at http://www.unicef-irc.org/databases/transmonee/.

UPIAS (UNION OF PHYSICALLY IMPAIRED AGAINST SEGREGATION/DISABILITY ALLIANCE), 1976. *Fundamental Principles of Disability*. London: UPIAS/Disability Alliance. Available at http://www.leeds.ac.uk/disability-studies/archiveuk/UPIAS/fundamental%20principles.pdf.

URSIC, CVETO, 1996. Social (and disability) policy in the new democracies of Europe (Slovenia by way of example). *Disability & Society*, 11 (1): 91–105.

USAMI, KOICHI, 2004. Introduction: Comparative study of social security systems in Asia and Latin America—A contribution to the study of emerging welfare states. *The Developing Economies*, 42 (2): 125–45.

U.S. CENSUS BUREAU, 2005. 2005 American Community Survey. Washington, DC: US Census Bureau. Available at http://factfinder.census.gov/home/saff/main.html?_lang=en.

USUI, CHIKAKO, 1994. Welfare state development in a world system context: Event history analysis of first social insurance legislation among 60 countries, 1880–1960, in *The*

Comparative Political Economy of the Welfare State, ed. Thomas Janoski and Alexander M. Hicks, Cambridge: Cambridge University Press, 254–74.

Vail, Mark I., 2004. The myth of the frozen welfare state and the dynamics of contemporary French and German social-protection reform. *French Politics*, 2 (2): 151–83.

Väisänen, Ilkka, 1992. Conflict and consensus in social policy development: A comparative study of social insurance in 18 OECD countries, 1930–1985. *European Journal of Political Research*, 22 (3): 307–27.

Valiente, Celia, 2006. Spanish gender equality policy: At the vanguard of Europe? Paper presented at Women and Politics Annual Conference 2006 (United Kingdom Political Studies Association). University of Edinburgh, Feburary 11. Available at http://www.sps.ed.ac.uk/gradschool/psafem/pdf/Spanishgenderequality.pdf.

Vanhuysse, Pieter, 2006. *Divide and Pacify: Strategic Social Policies and Political Protests in Post-Communist Democracies*. Budapest: Central European University Press.

Varley, Rita, 1986. Database: The Government Household Data Base, 1960–1984. (OECD Department of Economics and Statistics Working Papers, 36). Paris: OECD. Available at http://econpapers.repec.org/RePEC:oec:ecoaaa:36-en.

Vetterlein, Antje, 2007. Change in international organizations: Innovation or adaptation? A comparison of the World Bank and the International Monetary Fund, in *The World Bank and Governance: A Decade of Reform and Reaction*, ed. Diane Stone and Christopher Wright, London: Routledge, 125–44.

Viebrock, Elke, and Clasen, Jochen, 2009. Flexicurity and welfare reform: A review. *Socio-Economic Review*, 7 (2): 305–31.

Villandsen, Kaspar, 2007. Magt og selv-teknologi: Foucaults aktualitet for velfærdsforskningen [Power and the technology of the self: Foucault's relevance for welfare research]. *Tidsskrift for Velferdsforskning*, 10 (3): 156–67.

Vis, Barbara, 2007. States of welfare or states of workfare? Welfare state restructuring in 16 capitalist democracies, 1985–2002. *Policy & Politics*, 35 (1): 105–22.

Visier, Lauren, 1998. Sheltered employment for persons with disabilities. *International Labour Review*, 137 (3): 347–65.

Visser, Jelle, 2002. The first part-time economy in the world: A model to be followed? *Journal of European Social Policy*, 12 (1): 23–42.

—— 2003. Unions and unionism around the world, in *International Handbook of Trade Unions*, ed. John T. Addison and Claus Schnabel, Cheltenham: Edward Elgar, 366–414.

Visser, Jelle, and Hemerijck, Anton, 1997. 'A Dutch Miracle': Job Growth, Welfare Reform, and Corporatism in the Netherlands. Amsterdam: Amsterdam University Press.

Volkens, Andrea, McDonald, Michael D., and Klingemann, Hans-Dieter, 2007. *Mapping Policy Preferences II. Estimates for Parties, Electors, and Governments in Central and Eastern Europe, European Union, and OECD 1990–2003*. Oxford: Oxford University Press.

Võrk, Andres, Kallaste, Epp, and Priinits, Marit, 2004. *Migration Intentions of Health Care Professionals: The Case of Estonia*. Budapest: Central European University Press. Available at http://pdc.ceu.hu/archive/00003402/.

Vreeland, James Raymond, 2003. *The IMF and Economic Development*. Cambridge: Cambridge University Press.

—— 2007. *The International Monetary Fund: Politics of Conditional Lending*. London: Routledge.

VROOMAN, J. COK, 2009. *Rules of Relief: Institutions of Social Security, and their Impact*. The Hague: The Netherlands Institute of Social Research (SCP).

WAARDEN, FRANS VAN, 1995. Employers and employers' associations, in *Comparative Industrial and Employment Relations*, ed. Joris Van Ruysseveldt, Rien Huiskamp, and Jacques van Hoof, London: Sage, 68–108.

WADDINGTON, LISA, 2005. Implementing the disability provisions of the Framework Employment Directive: Room for exercising national discretion, in *Disability Rights in Europe: From Theory to Practice*, ed. Anna Lawson and Caroline Gooding, Oxford: Hart, 107–34.

WAGENER, HANS-JÜRGEN, 2002. The welfare state in transition economies and accession to the EU. *West European Politics*, 25 (2): 152–74.

WAGNER, ADOLPH, 1893. *Grundlegung der politischen Ökonomie. Erster Theil: Grundlagen der Volkswirtschaft [Foundations of Political Economy. Part I: Foundations of National Economy]*. Leipzig: Winter.

—— 1911. Staat (in nationalökonomischer Sicht) [The State (in an economic perspective)], in *Handwörterbuch der Staatswissenschaften*, vol. 7, ed. Johannes Conrad, Ludwig Elster, Wilhelm Lexis and Edgar Loening, Jena: Gustav Fischer, 727–39.

WAGSCHAL, UWE, 2001. Deutschlands Steuerstaat and die vier Welten der Besteuerung [Germany's tax state and the four worlds of taxation], in *Wohlfahrtsstaatliche Politik: Institutionen, politische Prozess und Leistungsprofil*, ed. Manfred G. Schmidt, Opladen: Leske + Budrich, 124–60.

—— 2005. *Steuerpolitik und Steuerreformen im internationalen Vergleich. Eine Analyse der Ursachen und Blockaden [Tax Policies and Tax Reforms in International Comparison. An Analysis of Driving Forces and Blockades]*. Münster: LIT.

WAGSCHAL, UWE, and OBINGER, HERBERT, 2000. Der Einfluss der Direktdemokratie auf die Sozialpolitik [The impact of direct democracy on social policy]. *Politische Vierteljahresschrift*, 41 (3): 466–97.

WAGSCHAL, UWE, and WENZELBURGER, GEORG, 2008. Roads to success: Budget consolidations in OECD countries. *Journal of Public Policy*, 28 (3): 309–39.

WALBY, SYLVIA, 2004. The European Union and gender equality: Emergent varieties of gender regimes. *Social Politics*, 11 (1): 4–29.

WALDFOGEL, JANE, 1997. The effect of children on women's wages. *American Sociological Review*, 62 (2): 209–17.

—— 2007. Welfare reforms and child well-being in the US and UK (Working Paper Series, CASE Paper, 126). London: London School of Economics and Political Science. Available at http://sticerd.lse.ac.uk/dps/case/cp/CASEpaper126.pdf.

WALDRON, JEREMY, 1993. Homelessness and the issue of freedom, in *Liberal Rights. Collected Papers 1981–1991*, ed. Jeremy Waldron, Cambridge: Cambridge University Press, 309–38.

—— 2006. Mr. Morgan's yacht, in *The Egalitarian Conscience: Essays in Honour of G. A. Cohen*, ed. Christine Sypnowich, Oxford: Oxford University Press, 154–76.

WALKER, ALAN, and WONG, CHACK-KIE, 1996. Rethinking the western construction of the welfare state. *International Journal of Health Services*, 26 (1): 67–92.

WALSH, PATRICK N., 1997. Old world—new territory: European perspectives on intellectual disability. *Journal of Intellectual Disability Research*, 41 (2): 112–19.

WARNER, CAROLYN M., 2000. *Confessions of an Interest Group: The Catholic Church and Political Parties in Europe*. Princeton, NJ: Princeton University Press.

WATSON, SARA E., 2008. The left divided: Parties, unions and the resolutions of Southern Spain's agrarian social question. *Politics & Society*, 36 (4): 451–77.

WEBER, MAX, 2001. *The Protestant Ethic and the Spirit of Capitalism.* Cary: Roxbury Publishing (first publ, 1904/05, revised 1920).

WEHLER, HANS-ULRICH, 1985. *The German Empire, 1871–1918.* New York: Berg.

WEHMAN, PAUL, REVELL, GRANT, and KREGEL, JOHN, 1997. Supported employment: A decade of rapid growth and impact, in *Supported Employment Research: Expanding Competitive Employment Opportunities for Persons with Significant Disabilities,* ed. Paul Wehman, Grant Revell, John Kregel and Michael West, Richmond: Virginia Commonwealth University Press, 1–18.

WEINGAST, BARRY R., 1995. The economic role of political institutions: Market-preserving federalism and economic development. *Journal of Law, Economics, and Organization,* 11 (1): 1–31.

WEIR, MARGARET, 1992. *Politics and Jobs: The Boundaries of Employment Policy in the United States.* Princeton, NJ: Princeton University Press.

WEIR, MARGARET, and SKOCPOL, THEDA, 1985. State structures and the possibilities for 'Keynesian' responses to the Great Depression in Sweden, Britain, and the United States, in *Bringing the State Back in,* ed. Peter B. Evans, Dietrich Rueschemeyer, and Theda Skocpol, Cambridge: Cambridge University Press, 107–63.

WELDON, S. LAUREL, 2002. *Protest, Policy and the Problem of Violence against Women.* Pittsburgh, PA: University of Pittsburgh Press.

WELSHMAN, JOHN, 1998. Evacuation and social policy during the Second World War: Myth and reality. *Twentieth Century British History,* 9 (1): 28–53.

WENDT, CLAUS, FRISINA, LORRAINE, and ROTHGANG, HEINZ, 2009. Healthcare system types—A conceptual framework for comparison. *Social Policy & Administration,* 75 (1): 70–90.

WENNEMO, IRENE, 1994. *Sharing the Cost of Children: Studies on the Development of Family Support in the OECD Countries.* Edsbruk: Akademitryck.

WEST, CANDACE, and ZIMMERMAN, DON H., 1987. Doing gender. *Gender and Society,* 1 (2): 125–51.

WESTERN, BRUCE, 1998. Causal heterogeneity in comparative research: A Bayesian hierarchical modeling approach. *American Journal of Political Science,* 42 (4): 1233–59.

WESTNEY, D. ELEANOR, 1987. *Imitation and Innovation: The Transfer of Western Organizational Patterns to Meiji-Japan.* Cambridge, MA: Harvard University Press.

WEYLAND, KURT, 2006. *Bounded Rationality and Policy Diffusion: Social Sector Reform in Latin America.* Princeton, NJ: Princeton University Press.

WHITE, JENNY B., 2002. *Islamist Mobilization in Turkey: A Study in Vernacular Politics.* Seattle: University of Washington Press.

WHITE, STUART, 2000. Social rights and the social contract: Political theory and the New Welfare Politics. *British Journal of Political Science,* 30 (3): 507–32.

—— 2003. *The Civic Minimum: On the Rights and Obligations of Economic Citizenship.* Oxford: Oxford University Press.

—— 2004a. What's wrong with workfare? *Journal of Applied Philosophy,* 21 (3): 271–84.

—— 2004b. Welfare philosophy and the Third Way, in *Welfare State Change. Towards a Third Way,* ed. Jane Lewis and Rebecca Surender, Oxford: Oxford University Press, 25–46.

—— 2006. *Equality.* Cambridge: Polity.

WHITEHOUSE, EDWARD R., 2009. Pensions, purchasing-power risk, inflation and indexation (OECD Social, Employment and Migration Papers, 77). Paris: OECD. Available at http://econpapers.repec.org/paper/oecelsaab/77-en.htm.

WHO (WORLD HEALTH ORGANISATION), 1981. *International Classification of Impairments, Disabilities and Handicaps.* Geneva: World Health Organisation. Recent Classification available at http://www.who.int/classifications/icf/en/.

—— 2000. *World Health Report 2000: Health Systems: Improving Performance.* Geneva: WHO. Available at http://www.who.int/whr/2000/en/whr00_en.pdf.

—— 2009. Database: Health for All Database. Available at http://www.euro.who.int/HFADB.

WIBBELS, ERIK, 2003. Bailouts, budget constraints, and Leviathans—Comparative federalism and lessons from the early United States. *Comparative Political Studies*, 36 (5): 475–508.

—— 2006. Dependency revisited: International markets, business cycles and social spending in the developing world. *International Organization*, 60 (2): 433–68.

WICHTERICH, CHRISTA, 2002. *The Globalized Woman: Reports from a Future of Inequality.* London: Zed.

WICKHAM-JONES, MARK, 2003. From reformism to resignation and remedialism? Labour's trajectory through British politics. *Journal of Policy History*, 15 (1): 26–45.

WIDERQUIST, KARL, LEWIS, MICHAEL A., and PRESSMAN, STEVEN, 2005. *The Ethics and Economics of the Basic Income Guarantee.* Aldershot: Ashgate.

WILENSKY, HAROLD L., 1975. *The Welfare State and Equality: Structural and Ideological Roots of Public Expenditures.* Berkeley: University of California Press.

—— 1981. Leftism, catholicism, and democratic corporatism: The role of political parties in recent welfare state development, in *The Development of Welfare States in Europe and America*, ed. Peter Flora and Arnold J. Heidenheimer, New Brunswick, NJ: Transaction Books, 345–82.

—— 2002. *Rich Democracies: Political Economy, Public Policy and Performance.* Berkeley: University of California Press.

WILENSKY, HAROLD L., and LEBEAUX, CHARLES N., 1958. *Industrial Society and Social Welfare.* New York: Free Press.

WILKINSON, RICHARD, and PICKETT, KATE, 2009. *The Spirit Level: Why More Equal Societies Almost Always Do Better.* London: Allen Lane.

WILLETTS, DAVID, 2003. Conservatism and Christian Democracy: Three principles of public service reform. Available at http://www.guardian.co.uk/politics/2003/dec/10/conservatives.uk.

WILLIAMS, FIONA, 1995. Race/ethnicity, gender, and class in welfare states: A framework for comparative analysis. *Social Politics*, 2 (2): 127–59.

WILLIAMS, FIONA, and GAVANAS, ANNA, 2008. The intersection of childcare regimes and migration regimes: A three-country study, in *Migration and Domestic Work: A European Perspective on a Global Theme*, ed. Helma Lutz, Aldershot: Ashgate, 13–28.

WILLIAMSON, JOHN (ed.), 1990. *Latin American Adjustment: How Much Has Happened?* Washington, DC: Institute for International Economics.

WILLIAMSON, JOHN B., and PAMPEL, FRED C., 1993. *Old-Age Security in Comparative Perspective.* Oxford: Oxford University Press.

WILLIAMSON, OLIVER E., 1985. *The Economic Institutions of Capitalism: Firms, Markets, Relational Contracting.* New York: Free Press.

WILSFORD, DAVID, 1994. Path dependency, or why history makes it difficult but not impossible to reform health care systems in a big way. *Journal of Public Policy*, 14 (3): 285–309.

WILSON, WILLIAM JULIUS, 1987. *The Truly Disadvantaged: The Inner City, the Underclass and Public Policy*. Chicago: University of Chicago Press.

—— 1996. *When Work Disappears: The World of the New Urban Poor*. New York: Knopf.

—— 1999. *The Bridge over the Racial Divide*. Berkeley: University of California Press.

WIMMER, ANDREAS, and GLICK SCHILLER, NINA, 2003. Methodological nationalism, the social sciences and the study of migration: An essay in historical epistemology. *International Migration Review*, 37 (3): 576–610.

WINCOTT, DANIEL, 2003. Slippery concepts, shifting context: (National) States and welfare in the Veit-Wilson/Atherton debate. *Social Policy & Administration*, 37 (3): 305–15.

WINGEN, MAX, 1997. *Familienpolitik. Grundlagen und aktuelle Probleme [Family Policy: Foundations and Current Problems]*. Stuttgart: Lucius & Lucius.

WITTENBERG, RAPHAEL, SANDHU, BECKY, and KNAPP, MARTIN, 2002. Funding long-term care: The public and private options, in *Funding Health Care: Options for Europe*, ed. Elias Mossialos, Anna Dixon, Joseph Figueras, and Joe Kutzin, Buckingham: Open University Press, 226–49.

WOLF, FRIEDER, 2009. The division of labour in education funding: A cross-national comparison of public and private education expenditure in 28 OECD countries. *Acta Politica*, 44 (1): 50–73.

WONG, JOSEPH, 2003. Deepening democracy in Taiwan. *Pacific Affairs*, 76 (2): 235–56.

—— 2004. *Healthy Democracies: Welfare Politics in Taiwan and South Korea*. Ithaca, NY: Cornell University Press.

WONG, LINDA, 1994. Privatization of social welfare in post-Mao China. *Asian Survey*, 3 (4): 307–25.

WOOD, GEOFFREY D., and GOUGH, IAN, 2006. A comparative welfare regime approach to global social policy. *World Development*, 34 (10): 1696–712.

WORLD BANK (ed.), 1994a. *Averting the Old Age Crisis: Policies to Protect the Old and Promote Growth*. Oxford: Oxford University Press.

—— 1994b. *World Development Report*. Washington, DC: World Bank. Available at http://go.worldbank.org/KMHUE61CU0.

—— 2005. *Growth, Poverty and Inequality: Eastern Europe and the Former Soviet Union*. Washington, DC: World Bank. Available at http://go.worldbank.org/8TLGYMRRX1.

—— (ed.), 2006. *Reducing Poverty through Growth and Social Policy Reform in Russia*. Washington, DC: World Bank.

—— 2009. *Global Safety Nets*. Washington, DC: World Bank. Available at http://web.worldbank.org.

WORLD BANK INDEPENDENT EVALUATION GROUP, 2006. *Pension Reform: How to Strengthen World Bank Assistance*. Washington, DC: World Bank. Available at http://lnweb90.worldbank.org/OED/OEDDocLib.nsf/OEDSearch?OpenForm.

YATES, JUDITH, and BRADBURY, BRUCE, 2009. Home Ownership as a (Crumbling) Fourth Pillar of Social Insurance in Australia (LWS [Luxembourg Wealth Study] Working Paper No. 8 Luxembourg: Luxembourg Income Study. Available at http://www.lisproject.org/publications/lwswpapers.htm.

YEATES, NICOLA, 2008. *Globalizing Care Economies and Migrant Workers: Explorations in Global Care Chains*. Basingstoke: Palgrave Macmillan.

YOUNG, IRIS M., 1990. *Justice and the Politics of Difference*. Princeton, NJ: Princeton University Press.

ZECHNER, MINNA, 2008. Care of older persons in transnational settings. *Journal of Aging Studies*, 22 (1): 32–44.

ZEITLIN, JONATHAN, and POCHET, PHILIPPE (with MAGNUSSON, LARS) (eds.), 2005. *The Open Method of Co-ordination in Action: The European Employment and Social Inclusion Strategies*. Brussels: P.I.E.-Peter Lang.

ZEITLIN, JONATHAN, and TRUBEK, DAVID M. (eds.), 2003. *Governing Work and Welfare in a New Economy: European and American Experiments*. Oxford: Oxford University Press.

ZELDERLOO, LUK, and REYNAERT, JELLE, 2007. An International comparison of methods of financing employment for disadvantaged people. Brussels: European Association of Service Providers for Persons with Disabilities (EASPD). Available at http://www.easpd. eu/LinkClick.aspx?fileticket=30633366354C4D6E6C66553D&tabid=4954&stats=false.

ZERILLI, LINDA M. G., 2005. *Feminism and the Abyss of Freedom*. Chicago: University of Chicago Press.

ZICK, CATHLEEN D., BRYANT, WILFRIED.K., and SRISUKHUMBOWORNCHAI, SIVITHEE, 2008. Does housework matter anymore? The shifting impact of housework on economic inequality. *Review of Economics of the Household*, 6 (1): 1–28.

ZINN, JENS (ed.), 2008. *Social Theories of Risk and Uncertainty: An Introduction*. Oxford: Blackwell.

ZOHLNHÖFER, REIMUT, 2009. *Globalisierung der Wirtschaft und finanzpolitische Anpassungs-reaktionen in Westeuropa [Globalization of the Economy and Adaptive Reactions of Fiscal Policy in Western Europe]*. Baden-Baden: Nomos.

ZOLA, ÉMILE, 1885. *Germinal*. Paris: Charpentier (part of the 20-volume series Les Rougon-Marcquart; for an English version of *Germinal*: Oxford University Press, 1998).

ZOLA, IRVING KENNETH, 1989. Towards a necessary universalizing of disability policy. *Millbank Memorial Quarterly*, 67 (2): 401–28.

ZÖLLNER, DETLEV, 1963. *Öffentliche Sozialleistungen und wirtschaftliche Entwicklung. Ein zeitlicher und internationaler Vergleich [Public Social Expenditures and Economic Develop-ment: A Chronological and International Comparison]*. Berlin: Duncker & Humblot.

—— 1982. Germany: Characteristics and special features of social legislation in Germany, in *The Evolution of Social Insurance 1881–1981: Studies of Germany, France, Great Britain, Austria and Switzerland*, ed. Peter A. Köhler and Hans F. Zacher, London: Frances Pinter, 1–92.

ZÜRN, MICHAEL, 2007. Institutionalisierte Ungleichheit in der Weltpolitik. Jenseits der Alternativen 'Global Governance' versus 'American Empire' [Institutionalized inequality in global politics: Going beyond the alternatives of 'global governance' and 'American empire']. *Politische Vierteljahresschrift*, 48 (4): 680–704.

ZWEIFEL, PETER, STEINMANN, LUKAS, and EUGSTER, PATRICK, 2005. The Sisyphus syn-drome in health revisited. *International Journal of Health Care Finance and Economics*, 5 (2): 127–45.

accident benefits 391
  and development of 395–6, 603
    expanded concept of work injury
      398, 405
    expansion of coverage 396–8
    as first social insurance programme
      391–4
    conflict explanation 394
    employers' role 394
    extension of civil law liability 393–4
    political motivations 394
    structural explanation 392–3
  and sequence of social insurance
      programme introduction 391–3
activation, see labour market activation
affirmative action programmes 716
Africa:
  and trade unions 209
  and unemployment insurance 434
AIDS, and developing countries 714
Aid to Families with Dependent Children
    (AFDC, USA) 46, 50, 51
alienation, and commodification 514
American Association for Labor
    Legislation 39
American Enterprise Institute (AEI) 47
Americans with Disabilities Act 416
Amsterdam, Treaty of (1997) 294, 295
Argentina 578
  and employment programmes 651
  and minimum wage 653
  and pension reform 647
  and poverty 649
  and social expenditure 649
  see also Latin American welfare states
Asia, and welfare regimes 577–8
  see also East Asia; South-East Asia
associational welfarism 30

Association for the Taxation of Financial
    Transactions for the Aid of Citizens
    (ATTAC) 306
Atlantic Charter (1941) 7, 41, 84–5
Atlas Economic Research Foundation 47
Australia:
  and accident benefits 395
  and child benefits 470
  and disability provision 412
  and education 503
  and employment-related risk 179
  and ethnic diversity 279
  and family policy 143
    political philosophy, influence
      of 148
    reform of 146–7
  and female employment 176
  and fertility 176
  and income inequality 533
  and long-term care 381, 385
  and origins of welfare state 38
    old age pensions 68
  and pension policy 134–5
  and service sector 176
  and sickness benefits 402
  and social assistance 450
  and social expenditure 126, 133
  and taxation 348
    of benefits 128–129
  and unemployment insurance
      421, 428
  see also English-speaking countries
Austria:
  and accident benefits 395, 396
  and child benefits 471
  and disability provision 413, 416
  and education 501–2
  and health care 371

Austria (*cont.*)
  and income inequality 532
  and long-term care 382
  and pension reform 610, 611, 613
  and social assistance 451
  and social expenditure 126, 130
  and taxation of benefits 129
  and structural reforms 613
  and unemployment insurance 423, 426,
    427–8
  see also Western Europe welfare states
authoritarianism and the welfare
    state 228–9, 239, 619, 623
  and the developing world 328
  and East Asia 661–2, 708–9
  and Eastern Europe 662, 673–4, 676, 678
  and European monarchies 4, 62, 64, 353,
    394, 399, 604, 708
  and Latin America 209, 239, 649–50
  neoliberal view of 46
  and state-centred theories 198
  and the Third Way 54

banking crisis 697, 698–9
  see also global economic crisis (2008–9)
basic income 456–7, 700–1
basic needs 20–21, 23–25, 28, 171–172, 673
Belarus, and welfare state change 678, 682
  see also Former Soviet Union (FSU)
Belgium:
  and accident benefits 395–6
  and childcare 469
  and disability provision 413, 417
  and education 498, 502
  and postage stamps with welfare
    motifs xxii
  and social assistance 451
  and social expenditure, net levels of 130
  and structural reforms 613
  and unemployment insurance 423, 424,
    426, 427
  see also Western European welfare states
Beliefs in Government (BiG) project 244–5
benefits system:
  and activation policy 438–9
  and benefit levels 94–5
  and child benefits 469–71

and conservative criticism of 50–1
and Third Way 54
see also accident benefits; sickness benefits;
  unemployment insurance
Beveridge Report (1942) 42,
  79, 705
bibliography, citation analysis 2–3
Bismarckian welfare states
  origins of 35–6, 64–5, 602–4
    autonomy of social insurance
    funds 603–4
    Catholic social doctrine 604
    distrust of state and market solutions
     603–4
    employers' role 603
    friendly societies 602–3
    ideological compromise 158
    industrialization 64, 602
    protraction of democratization 505
  and post-war period 42–3, 83–84, 605–8
    characteristics of 607–8
    children 607
    economic perspective 607
    expansion and extension 605
    fragmentation 605
    inequality 606
    institutional features 605–6
    social outcomes 606
    women 607
  see also Western European welfare
    states
Blair-Schroeder Document (1999) 53
Bolivia:
  and pension reform 647
  and social expenditure 649
  see also Latin American welfare states
Brazil 578
  and conditional cash transfer
    programme 651
  and health care 653
  and pension reform 647
  and social assistance 460
  and social expenditure 649
  see also Latin American welfare states
Bretton Woods financial system 97
  collapse of 10
Bulgaria 579

and welfare state change 677
see also Central and Eastern Europe
(CEE)

Canada:
and child benefits 471
and childcare 468
and education 498, 503
and ethnic diversity 279
and long-term care 381, 385
and social assistance 451
and social expenditure 133
and taxation 348
of benefits 128–129
and unemployment insurance 426, 428
see also English-speaking countries
capabilities:
and positive liberty 28
and satisfaction of basic needs 20–1
capitalism:
crisis of 718–20
and democracy 183–4
and distributive politics, *see under*
redistribution
see also varieties of capitalism
career ladders, and activation policy 443
care in the community, and long-term
care 383
care work:
and defamilialization 467–8
features of 380
and gender 256–9, 260–1
and migrant labour 260, 282–3
and pension entitlements 363
and social policies 260–1
see also long-term care
cash-for-care schemes, and long-term care
383–4, 385
Catholicism 268–9, 271, 272
and corporatism 268
and education 502, 504–505
and family policy 146, 272
as impediment to welfare state
development 271, 273, 621
and Latin America 628
and Pentecostalism 266
and political parties 269, 271, 274–5

and postage stamps with welfare state
motifs xxvi–vii
encyclicals xxix
and social doctrine 271, 275, 604, 704, 709
and social rights, the genesis of 704
and subsidiarity 36, 269, 450
as type of welfare state 616
and unions 269, 282
and welfare state origin and expansion
4, 66, 110–11, 269
Central and Eastern Europe (CEE):
and challenges facing 681
and communist welfare states 672–4
and European Union accession 679–80
and family benefits 680–1
and gender issues 683
and health care 681
and labour market reform 681
and pension reform 680
and poverty 681
and social assistance 681
and social insurance 680
and transitional welfare losses 675
and unemployment insurance 680
and welfare regimes 684–5
relationship to European norms 685
and welfare state change 671–2, 674,
675–7, 686
characteristics of 681–2
conflicting international and domestic
pressures 676–7
impact of globalization 676
international financial institutions 676
liberalization 676, 677
limitations of reforms 675–6
path dependence 676
transition period 675
see also individual countries
Centre for Business and Policy Studies
(Sweden) 48
Centre for Policy Studies (CPS, UK) 48
Charity Organization Societies 38
child benefits 469–71
childcare:
and activation policy 442
and enrolment rates 469
and family policy 143, 145, 146, 147, 148, 151

childcare: (*cont.*)
  public expenditure on 468–9
  and women's employment 258
children:
  and child poverty 474–5, 536–7
    employment strategy 537
    redistribution strategy 537
  and child well-being 475–7
  and experience of families 465
  and politicization of childhood 148
Children's Bureau (USA) 39
Chile 578
  and anti-poverty programme 651
  and education 652
  and health care 652–3
  and minimum wage 653
  and pension reform 363, 515, 647, 648, 692
  and poverty 649
  and social expenditure 649
  see also Latin American welfare states
China:
  and constraints on social policy development
    absence of democracy 666
    lack of fiscal capacity 666–7
    lack of social solidarity 667–8
  and economic reform 665
  and health care 667
  and Housing Provident Fund 665
  and individualistic social protection
    664–5
  and inequality 664–5
  and Minimum Living Standard
    Guarantee 460
  and pension reform 667
  and postage stamps with welfare
    motifs xxvii
  and poverty 664–5
  and social assistance 460
  and social expenditure 657
  and trade unions 209
  and welfare state development 89
  see also East Asia
Christian democracy 265, 269–70, 276
  and Catholic social doctrine 604
Christianity:
  and philanthropy 37
  and welfare state development 265

  impact of denominational
    differences 267–8, 268–9
  see also religion
citizenship:
  and basic citizenship model 700–1
  and conservative approaches to welfare
    state 52
  definition of 701
  and gender 263
  and immigrants 281
  and intellectual roots of welfare state 33–4
  and social citizenship 42
  and social rights 511
  and welfare state 21
citizen's income 21, 22–3, 700
civil servants, and origins of welfare state 33
class:
  and conflict theory 229
  and electoral systems 272–3
  and political-class coalitions 272–4
  and welfare attitudes 244
climate change 697
  and developing countries 715
  implications of 716–18
coalitional politics, and distributive
    politics 184, 187–9
cognitive turn 158
Cohesion Fund (EU) 294
Cold War, and development of welfare
    state 7–8
collective bargaining 206
Colombia, and social expenditure 649
  see also Latin American welfare states
commodification:
  and alienation 514
  and education 507–8
  and family care work 386
  and United States 287
communism, collapse of 10, 86
communist welfare states 672–4
Comparative Welfare Entitlements Dataset
    (CWED) 517, 519
compensation thesis, and globalization
    320–1, 329–30
concertation, and social governance 205
conditional cash transfer programmes
    (CCTs)

and developing countries 715
and Latin America 651
conditionality:
  fairness argument for 22
  and International Monetary Fund loans
      310, 312–13
  paternalist argument for 21
  and reciprocity 22
  and Third Way 54
  and welfare state programmes 21
  and workfare 50–1, 695–6
conflict theory 229
conservatism:
  and attitude towards welfare state 49
  and contrasted with neoliberalism 49
  and critique of welfare state 45–6, 49–52
    citizenship 52
    difficulty in attributing 49–50
    impact on civil society and private
        sector 50
    influence of 51–2
    restructuring of benefit systems 50
    social consequences 50
    workfare 50–1
conservative welfare state 571
  and luck egalitarianism 25
consultation, and social governance 205
convergence:
  and disability provision 411, 412
  and economics 156–7
  and European Commission 617
  and globalization 324, 477
  and health care 372, 377
  and housing policy 490
  and long-term care 390
  and social expenditure 335
  and sociology 155
  and welfare regimes 579–80
convergence theory 228
coordination, and social
      administration 162–3
corporatist theory:
  and retrenchment 563–4
  and union and employer impact 198
Costa Rica:
  and health care 652, 653
  and minimum wage 653

and social expenditure 649
  see also Latin American welfare states
credit policy, and housing 489–90
crisp-set qualitative comparative analysis,
      and research methodology 110
Croatia 579
Cyprus, and disability provision 417
Czech Republic 579
  and child benefits 471
  and disability provision 417
  and social expenditure, effects of tax
      system 129
  and welfare state change 677
  see also Central and Eastern Europe (CEE)

decentralization 162
  and education 506–7
  and Italy 625
  and Spain 626
decommodification 253
  feminist view of 512
  measurement of 516–17
  and social rights 513–14
democracy:
  and capitalism 183
    varieties of 184
  and distributive politics see under
      redistribution
democratization 708, 709
  and origins of welfare state 6
demographic changes 12–13
  and long-term care 387–8
  and old age pensions 360–1
Denmark:
  and accident benefits 396, 397
  and activation policy 439, 442, 458, 459
  and changes in welfare system 599
  and childcare 468
  and disability provision 413, 417
  and education 500–1
    spending on 498
  and employment-related risk 178
  and health care 371
  and income inequality 532
  and origins of welfare state 68
    early extensive coverage 69
    old age pensions 68

Denmark: (*cont.*)
   risk prioritization 70
  and poverty reduction 536
  and service sector 176
  and sickness benefits 400
  and social assistance 456, 457
   minimum income 454
  and taxation 349
   of benefits 128–129
   tax protests 350
  and unemployment insurance 421, 425,
   426, 427, 429
  see also Nordic countries
dependency culture, and conservative
   criticism of welfare state 50
dependent learning, and developing
   countries 710
deregulation 10–11
  and capital markets 595
  and Eastern Europe 86, 675, 682
  and education systems 501, 681
  and employer associations 210
  and labour markets 203, 207, 364, 561,
   608, 708
  and Latin America 645
  See also privatization, retrenchment
developing countries:
  and challenges to well-being 714–15
   novel policy solutions 715–16
  and climate change 717, 718
  and cluster analysis of welfare
    regimes 711–14
   proto-welfare states 711–13
  and lessons from European welfare states
   international environment 710–11
   nature of industrialization 706–7
   nature of interests 707–8
   role of ideas 709–10
   role of institutions 708–9
  and long-term care 381
  and social safety nets 460
  and unions and employer associa-
    tions 208–10
  and welfare effects of globalization 326–8
developmental state 709
Director's Law hypothesis 161
Disability Discrimination Act (UK) 416–17

disability provision 406
  convergence of 411, 412
  diversity of 411
  and employment measures 415–17
   activation programmes 418
   financial incentives 417
   flexible work 417, 440–441
   quota systems 416
   sheltered employment 416
   supported placements 416–17
   training centres 416
   work capacity 415, 417–418
  and European Union 411–12
  and future of 419
  and models of disability 406
   capitalism 408
   individual model 407
   social model 407–9
  and origins and development of 409–11
   England 409
   Germany 410
   Sweden 410
   United States 410–11
  and public expenditure on 412–13
   pressures on budgets 417–18
  and reforms of, budgetary pressures 417–18
  and rights-based approach 418–19
  and social exclusion 408
  and social inclusion 408–9
  and structural dependency of disabled
    people 408
  and United Nations Convention on the
    Rights of Persons with Disabilities
    (2008) 406, 419
  and work-centred eligibility
    definitions 413–15
domestic service, and migrant labour 282–3
Dominican Republic, and pension
   reform 647
  see also Latin American welfare states
duration effects, and unemployment 430

Earned Income Tax Credit (USA) 344–5,
  439, 458, 640
East Asia:
  and challenges facing:
   changes in gender relations 669

de-familialization 669
demographic changes 669
labour market changes 669
transition to post-industrialism 669
and constraints on social policy
    development 665–8
and dynamic nature of policy regimes 668
and East Asian exceptionalism 657–9
    arguments against 658–9, 668
    Asian/Confucian values 657
    economic aims of social policy 658
    weakness of political left 657–8
and future of social policy reform 670
and inclusive social insurance model 659–60
    democratic pressures 660–3
    economic development 663
    national identity 663–4
and individualistic social protection 664–5
    absence of democracy 666
    lack of fiscal capacity 666–7
    lack of social solidarity 667–8
and industrial relations 209–10
research interest in 656
and public pension coverage 354
and social capital investment 96
and social expenditure 657
and social investment strategy 95–6
and social policy expansion, factors
    affecting
    democratic reform 662, 668
    economic growth with equity 659, 663,
        665, 667, 668
    fiscal capacity 666, 669, 670
and welfare regimes 577–8
and welfare state expansion 88–9
Eastern Europe:
and collapse of communism
    (1989) 86
and communist welfare states 672–4
and health care 371
and trade unions 209
and welfare regimes 578–9
see also Central and Eastern Europe
    (CEE); Former Soviet Union (FSU);
    individual countries
economic crises, and retrenchment 561–2
see also global economic crisis (2008–9)

economic growth:
and climate change 717–18
and impact of global economic crisis
    718–19
and impact of welfare state 541–5, 550–1
    econometric analyses 543–4
    economic externalities of social
        programmes 540, 544–5, 551
    endogenous growth theory 540,
        542, 545
    historical trends 542–3
    inconclusiveness of studies of 543–4
    negative impact 541
    neoclassical growth models 541–2
    quantitative studies 544
    tax structure effects 544
and welfare state expansion 155
and wellbeing 718
economics:
and sociology 157
and welfare state 156–7
education:
and activation policy 443, 496
and decentralization 506–7
and economic growth 542, 545, 551
and education regimes:
    Belgium, France, Ireland and
        Netherlands 502
    English-speaking countries and
        Japan 503
    expenditure 496–8
    Germany and Austria 501–2
    hierarchical cluster analysis 498–500
    Mediterranean countries 502
    Northern Europe cluster 500
    relationship with welfare regimes 503–4
    Scandinavia 500–1
and equality 495
and expenditure on 496–7
    net levels of 497–8
    relationship with social spending 497
    tertiary education 498–9
and future research on 508
and historical foundations of systems 504
    business-labour balance of power 506
    religious heritage 505
    timing 504–5

education: (*cont.*)
  and income distribution 495
  and comparative welfare literature
      494–5
  and Latin America 651–2
  and private benefits 495
  and social citizenship 496
  as social investment 496, 507
  and social policy, relationship with
      494, 495–6
  as social right 496, 508
  and state-church conflict 271, 505
efficiency, and economic perspectives on
      welfare state 156
electoral system:
  and distributive politics 190–1
  and middle class 272–3
  and political institutions 231
  and welfare state outcomes 238
El Salvador, and pension reform 647
  see also Latin American welfare states
embedded liberalism 320–1
employer associations:
  and developing countries 208–10
  and industrial relations, cross-national
      variations 203
  and influence in social policy areas:
    collective bargaining 206
    health care 208
    labour market policy 206–7
    pension policy 207–8
  organization of 200, 201
    free-rider problem 200
  research on 196
  role of 196, 197, 210
  and social governance, forms of 205
  and theories of impact of:
    corporatist theory 198
    Europeanization thesis 199
    globalization thesis 199
    institutional theories 199
    modernization theory 197
    power resource theory 197–8
    state-centred theories 198–9
    varieties of capitalism approach 198
    veto player theorem 199
  see also industrial relations

employment:
  flexibility *see* flexible work
  and impact of welfare state 546–50, 551
    direct effects of social policies 547–8
    empirical studies 546
    employment protection
        regulations 547
    future research on 550
    inconclusiveness of studies of 546–7
    labour market institutions 548–9
    Latin America 547–8
    neoclassical economic framework 546
    regional variations 547
    unemployment benefits 546–7
    wage bargaining institutions 546, 548–50
  and women: *see* women, and labour
      market participation
  see also labour market activation; labour
      markets; unemployment
employment policy:
  and disability provision: *see* disability
      provision, and employment
      measures
  and family policy 142, 143, 144, 145–6, 147,
      150, 151
    maternal employment 473–4
  see also labour market activation; labour
      markets
employment protection 522
  and activation policy 442
  and employment consequences of 547
employment rates 12, 182, 445
  and activation 438, 444–6
  and age of children 466
  and childcare 147, 473–4
  and education 443
  and employment protection 442
  and full employment 87
  and income inequality 533–4
  of older adults 354, 446
  high, roads to 446
  and social security contribution level,
      effects of 547
  of women 257–8, 438, 442, 477–8
    equal to men 592
  and work hours 465–6
  of young people 445–6

endogenous growth theory 540, 542, 545
English-speaking countries:
  and American exceptionalism 640–2
  and cluster analyses 634–5
  comparisons between 630–1
  differences from Europe 640–2
  and family of nations perspective on
    633–4, 636–7
  and identification as cluster:
    empirical evidence for 633
    Esping-Andersen's influence 632–3
    family of nations perspective 633–4,
      636–7
    as recent development 631–2
    regime perspective 632–3, 634
    shared national attributes 633–4
    underdevelopment of literature 632
  and inequality 640
  and policy resemblances 637
  and redistribution 638–40
  and regimes analysis 634
    gender 635
    policy differences 634–5
    political economy 635–6
  and residual social policy 638
  and social rights 638
  and taxation 639–40
  see also individual countries
epistemic communities 313
equality:
  and education 495
  and European Union social policy 293–4
  and family policy 142–3
  and immigration policy 31
  and luck egalitarianism 24–6
  and power relations 26–7
  and relational equality 26–7
  and social expenditure 135–8
  and strong meritocracy 24
  and taxation 344–5
  and welfare state 23–7
  see also inequality; redistribution; gender
equal opportunity
  comprehensiveness 591–2
  and distinctiveness, loss of 172
  as egalitarian objective 24
  and liberal parties/liberalism 225, 262

Estonia:
  and disability provision 417
  and welfare state change 677
  see also Central and Eastern Europe (CEE)
ethics, and the welfare state 19–20
  and equality 23–7
    immigration policy 31
    luck egalitarianism 24–6
    relational equality 26–7
    strong meritocracy 24
  and intergenerational justice 31
  and liberty 27–31
    capabilities 28
    choice and diversity 30–1
    moralized conception of 29–30
    negative liberty 27–9
    paternalism 30
    positive liberty 28
  and needs 20–3
    capabilities 20–1
    conditionality 21–2
    means testing 23
    reciprocity 22
    right to satisfaction of 21
    satisfaction of basic needs 20–1
ethnic diversity 13, 278–9
  and extent of 279
  and impact on welfare states 285–7
    growth of extreme-right parties 286
    hostility to transfers to
      immigrants 285–6
  and multicultural policies 283–4, 285
  and racialization of welfare 287–90
    Italy 289
    Sweden 289–90
    United Kingdom 288–9
    United States 287–8
  and social spending 284–5
  and weakening of welfare state 285
ethnic minorities:
  definition of 279
  deprivation among 280
  and inclusion/exclusion 280–1
  and migrant labour in welfare sector
    282–3
  and racialized exclusion 281–2
  and racialized working poor 281–2

ETHNO programme 114
eugenics 38
Eurobarometer 244
European Adjustment Fund for
    Globalization 294–5
European Agricultural Guidance and
    Guarantee Fund 294
European Commission:
    and convergence 617
    and disability provision 419
    and health care 303
    and long-term care costs 388
    and social policy 293, 296, 298
    and Third Way 54
European Court of Justice 302, 376
    and social policy 303, 396
European integration 8, 10–11
    and bounded varieties of welfare 305
    and Central and Eastern Europe 679–80
    and differential impact of 304–5
    and partisan effects on welfare state 222
    and social dimension of 296–7
    and Southern European reforms 624,
        625–6
    and union and employer impact 199
    and welfare regimes 579–80
European Monetary Union 11
European Regional Development Fund 294
European Round Table 201
European Social and Economic Council 205
European Social Fund 294, 296
European Social Survey 244, 249
European Trade Union Confederation
    (ETUC) 201
European Union 292–3
    and activation policy 437, 458
    and Central and Eastern Europe
        679–80
    and disability provision 411–12
    eastern enlargement of 11
    and family policy, features of 143–4
    and global economic crisis 305
    and Growth and Stability Pact 302
    and health care 303, 369, 375–6
    and labour law 298
    and migration 290
    and national welfare state policies 301–4

bounded varieties of welfare 305
conservation critiques, influence on 51
differential impact 304–5
direct effects 301–2
European Court of Justice rulings
    303–4, 376, 396
indirect effects 302–3
secondary effects of economic
    integration 302–3
unintended effects 303–4
and social dimension of European
    integration 290, 292, 296–8, 300–1
and social expenditure:
    private sector 128
    public expenditure 126–7
and social inclusion 458–9
and social policy 97
    distributive dimension of 294–5
    equality 293–4
    evaluation of 298–9
    forms of 299–300
    future trends 305
    health and safety 294
    integration of 293
    Open Method of Coordination 295–6
    Social Action Programmes 293
    social regulation 293–4
    working conditions 294
and transnational expertise 41
European Values Surveys 244
event history analysis 119
event structure analysis, and research
    methodology 114–15
Fabian Society 65
fairness:
    and activation policy 436–7
    and conditionality 22
familialism 142, 146, 572
    and Southern Europe 622–3, 627–8
families, and long-term care provision 384–5
    support measures for carers 385
family policy 462
    and activation policy 442–3
    and attitudes towards family 139
    and Australia 143
    political philosophy 148
    reform of 146–7

and communist welfare states 674
and conceptualization of family:
  economic 141, 150–1
  ideological 141
  political 141
  as social institution 150–1
  sociological 141
contexts of:
  children's experience of families 465
  decline in fertility 463–4
  expansion of service economy 140–1
  family change 139, 463–5
  industrialization and
    nation-building 140
  lone parent families 464–5
  male breadwinner model 140, 463,
    465, 466
  mothers' employment 465–6
European Union approach to 143–4
and factors affecting:
  international organizations 148
  labour market developments 147
  new social risks 148–9
  political philosophy 147–8
  social integration 149, 151
and familial relationships 462
and family, state and market relations,
  axes of 151
and family change 139, 463–5
and France 142
  reforms 145–6
and future of welfare states 701–2
and gender 257
and Germany 142
  labour market effects 147
  reforms 145
and lone parent families 464–5
and mothers' employment:
  childcare 468–9
  maternity leave 469
  support for 467–9
and OECD 143–4
outcomes of:
  child poverty 474–5
  child well-being 475–7
  fertility 471–3
  maternal employment 473–4

public expenditure on:
  childcare 468–9
  children 467
  families with children 467
  parental leave 469, 473–4
purpose of 462
reforms of 144
  Australia 146–7
  factors encouraging 150
  France 145–6
  Germany 145
  Sweden 144–5
  United Kingdom 145
and religion 147, 262, 272
and risks of family transformation 176,
  179, 181
and Scandinavia 142–3
scholarship on 141
  development of 141–2
  narrow focus of 141
and state engagement with family:
  egalitarian model 142–3
  male breadwinner/female homemaker
    model 142
  non-interventionist 143
  pro-family and pro-natalist 142
and Sweden, reforms 144–5
and tax and benefit policies 469–71
and tax system 129–30
third age of, features of 150
and United Kingdom 143
  labour market effects 147
  reforms 145
  Third Way 148
and United States 143, 144
Fascism, and welfare state 7 n5, 27, 85, 87,
  425, 619
  see also authoritarianism
federalism:
  and distributive politics 191–2
  and education 506
  and timing of social programmes 392
  and welfare state outcomes 237–8
feminism:
  and critique of welfare state 10, 52
  and decommodification 512
  and family policy 141–2

feminism: (*cont.*)
  and gender studies 252–3
  incorporation into mainstream
     scholarship 254, 264
  and regimes analysis 253–4
  see also gender
fertility:
  decrease in 176, 463–4
  and family policy outcomes 471–3
Financial Instrument for Fisheries Guidance
    (EU) 294
Finland:
  and accident benefits 396
  and activation policy 439, 441, 443
  and changes in welfare system 599
  and childcare 468, 469
  and disability provision 413, 417
  and education 500–1
  and origins of welfare state 66, 70, 76
  and postage stamps with welfare
    motifs xxvii
  and sickness benefits 400–1
  and taxation 349
  and unemployment insurance 421, 426, 427
  see also Nordic countries
fiscal welfare 121
flexible work 12, 145, 418, 620, 681
  and activation policy 440–1
  and disability provision 417
Former Soviet Union (FSU):
  and communist welfare states 672–4
  and gender issues 683
  and welfare state change 672, 674–5, 678,
    682–3, 686
  see also individual countries
France:
  and accident benefits 396
  and activation policy 439, 440, 441–2, 443
  and child benefits 471
  and childcare 468, 469
  and disability provision 413, 416
  and education 502
    spending on 498
  and employment-related risk 179
  and ethnic minority policies 283–4
  and family policy 142, 176
    reform of 145–6

  and fertility rates 471
  and health care 371
  and income inequality 532
  and long-term care 381, 386
  and origins of welfare state 36–7, 602–3
    post-1945 developments 43
  and pension reform 610, 613
  and *Plan de Sécurité Sociale* 43
  and poor relief 63, 450
  and religion 275
  and social assistance 451, 454, 459
  and social expenditure 126, 130, 133
  and structural reforms 613
  and taxation of benefits 129–30
  and tax protests 350
  and unemployment insurance 69, 421,
    424, 425, 426, 427
  see also Western European welfare states
free-rider problem, and organization of
    capital and labour 200
French Revolution 705
friendly societies 67, 602–3
functionalism:
  and social policies 173
  and welfare state development 92–3, 228
fuzzy-set qualitative comparative analysis,
    and research methodology 110–11

gender:
  and care work 256–9
    economic vulnerability of women 259
    long-term care 384
    social policies 260–1
  and communist welfare states 673–4
  concept of 252–3, 254–6
  and employment 257–8
    childcare availability 258
    occupational segregation 259
  and English-speaking countries 635
  equality, politics of 262–4, 282, 292, 294,
    309, 344, 512
    East Asia 669
    Eastern Europe 679, 683
    Nordic model 587, 589, 591
    Southern Europe 624, 625, 626
  and family models 257
  and gendered division of labour 256, 257, 259

and incorporation into mainstream
  scholarship 254, 264
and Nordic model 589
and politics of welfare states 261–4
  anti-feminism 264
  citizenship 263
  gendered actors 263
  left-right differences 261–2
  regimes analysis 261
  women's impact on 263–4
and post-communist welfare
  regimes 683
and social rights 512, 514
and taxation 344
and welfare regimes 253–4, 261–2, 572–3
General Agreement on Tariffs and Trade
  (GATT) 310
General Agreement on Trade in Services
  (GATS) 310
Germany:
  and accident benefits 395, 396
  and activation policy 439, 440, 441, 459
  and disability provision 413, 416, 417
    development of 410
  and education 501–2
    spending on 497
  and employment-related risk 179
  and family policy 142
    labour market effects 147
    reform of 145
  and female employment 176
  and health care 371
    regulation of 374
  and long-term care 381, 382, 383
  and old age pensions 353
    pension reform 610, 611, 693
  and origins of welfare state 35–6, 602–3
    post-1945 developments 42–3
  and poor relief 63, 450
  and racialized exclusion 281
  and sickness benefits 398–9
  and social assistance 451, 454, 456, 457
  and social expenditure 126, 130, 133
  and social insurance:
    Bismarck's reforms 64
    international influence of 66
    motives for implementing 65

reasons for leading role in
  developing 66–7
and social market economy 42
and structural reforms 612–13
and taxation of benefits 129–30
and unemployment insurance 423, 425,
  426, 427
and welfare reform 610
see also Western Europe welfare states
Gini coefficient 530
global economic crisis (2008–9) 698–9
  and activation policy 447
  and European Union 305
  and impact of 14–15, 100–1, 719–20
globalization:
  and convergence 324, 477
  and emergence of global economy 10–11
  first era of 5
    welfare consequences of 323
  and health care 376
  and impact on social democrats 52
  indirect welfare consequences of
    322–3
  and Latin America 653–4
  and less developed countries (LDCs)
    326–8
  and national cleavage dimensions 330
  and partisan effects on welfare state 222,
    324–5
  and recent research on welfare effects
    of 329–30
  and social expenditure 342
  and social policy 477
  and tax competition 348
  and tax system 323, 328
  and union and employer impact 199
  and welfare regimes 579–80
  and welfare state change 318–19
    compensation thesis 320–1,
      329–30
    evidence for impact on 324–6
    first era of globalization 323
    institutional mediation 321–2, 325
    race to the bottom thesis 319–20
  and welfare state development 93
Global Program on AIDS (GPA) 376
global South, see developing countries

governance:
    and climate change 717
    and social administration 163
    see also social governance
government overload hypothesis 244–5
graduate tax 695
grandfather clauses, and retrenchment 557
Great Depression 6
    and impact of 77
    and unemployment insurance 423–5
        coverage 423–5
        replacement rates 425
Greece:
    and child benefits 470
    and childcare 468
    and disability provision 412
    and education, spending on 497
    and health care 371
    and social expenditure 126
    and social insurance 620
    and welfare reform 627
    see also Southern European welfare states
Green New Deal 719
Guatemala, see also Latin American
        welfare states

Hamas 276
Hartz IV Act (Germany, 2005) 427
Health and Retirement Study (HRS,
        USA) 379
health and safety, and European Union social
        policy 294
health care:
    and Central and Eastern Europe 681
    and challenges facing 377
    and comparison as policy instrument 377
    and economic growth 545
    and European Union 303,
        369, 375–6
    and expenditure on 367
        convergence of 372
        growth of 371–2
        partial privatization 372
        reasons for growth of 372
    and globalization 376
    and health care state 368
        development of 369–70

and health care systems 370–1
    convergence 377
    national health services 370, 371
    patterns of regulation 371
    private systems 371
    social insurance systems 370–1
    stakeholders 371
and international health governance
        376–7
and international health issues 377
international regulation of 375
and Latin America 645, 652–3
and medical profession 369
and origins and development of health
        policy 368–70
regulation of 374–5
    Germany 374
    United Kingdom 374
    United States 374–5
and role of states 377
and significance of health issues 367
and Southern Europe 621
trends in provision of 373–4
    decline in hospital beds 373
    growth in health employment 373
    privatization 373–4
    role of primary care 374
and union and employer association
        influence 208
    see also long-term care
Health Maintenance Organizations
        (HMOs, USA) 375
Heritage Foundation 47
Hizbullah 276
Hong Kong 577
    and constraints on social policy
        development:
        absence of democracy 666
        lack of fiscal capacity 666
        lack of social solidarity 667–8
    and individualistic social protection
        664–5
    and inequality 664
    and Mandatory Provident Fund 665
    and social expenditure 657
    see also East Asia
housing 479–81

conceptual framework for 480–1
double meaning of 481
and dual capital-cum-service nature
    of 481–2, 491, 492
and global economic crisis 15
and home ownership 482
    competitive advantages over
        renting 492
    decline in 485
    explanation of 491–3
    familialization of accommodation 485
    growth of 491
    household economy 492
    public policy towards 485
    social insurance function 491, 493
    upper limit on 482–5
    wealth accumulation 492
and market complexity 480
and policy instruments 485–8
    convergence 490
    credit market intervention 489–90
    distributive impact 490–1
    public expenditure 488
    regulation of private rented
        sector 488
    rent controls 488
provision of 481–5
public interest in 479
and rental accommodation 482
    public policy towards 485
and rented housing 479
state's role in 480
    difficulty in assessing 480
welfare focus on 479
    disappointing outcome of 479–80
human capital:
    and activation policy 443
    and economic growth 545
Human Development Index 171
human rights, and disability provision
        418–19
Hungary 579
    and child benefits 471
    and disability provision 412
    and family benefits 680–1
    and welfare state change 677
    see also Central and Eastern Europe (CEE)

Iceland 68
    and childcare 468
    and disability provision 413
    and social expenditure 126
    see also Nordic countries
ideas:
    and developing countries 709–10
    and institutional change 47, 56
    and Nordic model 589
    and origins of welfare state 705
    role of 55–7
    and welfare state development 99–100
immigrants and immigration:
    and citizenship 281
    definition of 279
    and deprivation among 280
    and East Asian attitudes 664
    and equality 31
    and impact on welfare states 285–7
        growth of extreme-right parties 286
        hostility to transfers to 285–6
    and inclusion/exclusion 280–1
    and migrant labour in welfare sector 282–3
        long-term care 386–7
    and multicultural policies 283–4
    and racialization of welfare 287–90
        Italy 289
        Sweden 289–90
        United Kingdom 288–9
        United States 287–8
    and racialized exclusion 281–2
    and racialized working poor 281–2
    scholarly neglect of 278
    and significance for welfare systems 279
    and United Kingdom 288–9
    see also ethnic diversity
impact studies 98
Import Substitution Industrialization (ISI),
        and Latin America 646
Incapacity Benefit (UK) 413
incentives:
    and economic perspectives on welfare
        state 156
    and effects of welfare provision 134
    and pension programme design 134–5
income distribution:
    and education 495

income distribution: (*cont.*)
  and impact of social policy:
    inequality 532–5
    poverty 535–8
  and measurement of 527–8
  and outcomes of programmes 98
  and provision of access to services 529
  and social expenditure 135–8, 343
    private provision 136–8
  and taxation 344–5
  see also inequality; redistribution
India:
  and social assistance 460
  and trade unions 209
Indonesia 577
industrialization:
  and developing countries 706–7
  and family policy 140
  and origins of welfare state 3, 4, 5, 35, 63,
    175, 602–3, 704–5
industrial relations and social
    governance 204–5
  and concertation 205
  and consultation 205
  and self-administration 205
  and self-regulation 205
  and unilateral state intervention 204–5
  see also employer associations; trade unions
inequality 526
  and developing countries 715
  and English-speaking countries 640
  and impact of social policy on 526–7, 538
    data requirements 531–2
    difficulties in measuring 528–9
    income measurement 527–8
    programme size 531
    programme structure 531
    redistribution 532–5
  and measures of:
    Gini coefficient 530
    P90-P10 percentile ratio 530
  and old age pensions 365
  and poverty 529–30
  and redistribution 532–5
  reduction of 526, 538
  and social expenditure 343
  and sustainability of welfare states 698

  and taxation 344–5
  see also equality; income distribution;
    poverty; redistribution
inflation, and impact of welfare state 541
insider-outsider theory 48
  and social policy 161–2
  and Southern Europe 162, 619, 627
Institute for Economic Affairs (IEA, UK) 47
Institute for Public Policy Research (UK) 54
institutional change, and ideas 47, 56
institutionalism, and union and employer
    impact 199
institutions:
  and developing countries 708–9
  and origins of welfare state 705
intellectual roots of the welfare state 32–5
  and Australia 38
  and changes across time 34
  and citizenship 33–4
  and complexity of 32, 34–5
  and France 36–7, 43
  and Germany 35–6, 42–3
  and knowledge sharing 33
  and meaning of welfare state 32–3
  and modern nation state 33
  and New Zealand 38
  and post-1945 developments 41–4
    features of post-war welfare state 43–4
    Keynesian welfare state 43, 552
    political consensus 43, 44
    as project of social democracy 43
    re-moralization of welfare 44
  pre-existing traditions of amelioration 33
  and Sweden 39–40
  and transnational policy
    development 40–1
  and United Kingdom 37–8
    post-1945 developments 41–2
  and United States 38–9
  and welfare creep 33
Inter-American Development Bank 647
interest groups:
  and pluralist theories of politics 228
  and retrenchment of welfare state 221–2
    as obstacles to 555–6
  see also employer associations; trade
    unions

interests:
  and developing countries 707–8
  and origins of welfare state 705
intergenerational justice 31
Intergovernmental Organizations (IO):
  definition of 306
  and democratic deficit 317
  and impact on social policy 306–7,
    314–17
    changes in ideas 316, 710–11
    hard vs soft law 315–16
    ideas and information 313–14
    overestimation of 317
    political context 307–8
    resources 312
    standard setting 312–13
    upward national influences 316–17
  and International Labour Organiza-
    tion 311–12
    budget of 312
    governance structure 311
    policy focus 311
  and International Monetary Fund 309–10
    budget of 312
    changes in ideas of 316
    conditional loans 310, 312–13
    democratic deficit 317
    governance structure 310
    role of 309–10
  and OECD 311
    budget of 312
    changes in ideas of 316
    governance structure 311
    policy focus 311
  protests against 306
  and World Bank 308–9
    budget of 312
    changes in ideas of 316
    components of 309
    democratic deficit 317
    governance structure 308–9
    policy focus 309
    policy mechanisms 309
  and World Trade Organization 310–11
    governance structure 310–11
    social policy effects 310
internal markets 30–1

International Association for Labour
    Legislation 41
International Bank for Reconstruction and
    Development (IBRD) 309
International Center for the Settlement of
    Investment Disputes (ICSID) 309
International Development Association
    (IDA) 309
international environment:
  and developing countries 705–6
  and origins of welfare state 705–6
International Finance Corporation
    (IFC) 309
International Labour Organization
    (ILO) 10, 311–12
  budget of 312
  and collective bargaining 206
  and establishment of 6
  and governance structure 311
  and internationalization of social
    security 78–9
  and Philadelphia Declaration (1944)
    41, 85
  policy focus of 308, 311
  and postage stamps with welfare
    motifs xxvi
  and social safety nets 460
  and transnational policy development 41
international law, and post-war development
    of 85
International Monetary Fund (IMF) 10, 97,
    307, 309–10
  budget of 312
  and Central and Eastern Europe 676
  and changes in ideas of 316
  and conditional loans 310, 312–13
  and democratic deficit 317
  and governance structure 310
  and policy focus of 308
  role of 309–10
international organizations, and welfare
    governance 97
  see also Intergovernmental
    Organizations (IO)
international political economy, and
    transformation of 10–11
International Sanitary Conference 375

International Social Survey Programme
     (ISSP) 248, 351
International Survey Program 244
Ireland:
  and accident benefits 395, 396, 397
  and child benefits 470
  and education 502
  and long-term care 385
  and old age pensions 357, 358
  and religion 275
  and social assistance 451
     minimum income 453, 456
  and social expenditure 126, 133
  and taxation 349
     of benefits 129
  and unemployment insurance 425, 428
  see also English-speaking countries
Islam 276–7
Italy:
  and accident benefits 395
  and disability provision 412
  and education 502
     spending on 497
  and family policy 176
  and fertility 176
  and health care 371
  and immigration 289
  and income inequality 532, 533
  and migrant labour 282
  and pension reform 134, 625, 693
     impact of ageing population 361
  and religion 267
  and social expenditure, net levels of 130
  and social insurance 620
  and unemployment insurance 425, 427
  and welfare expansion 620
  and welfare reform 625
  see also Southern European welfare states
Japan 577
  and child benefits 471
  and developmental state 709
  and education 503
     spending on 497, 498
  and family policy 176
  and fertility 176
  and immigration, opposition to 664
  and inclusive social insurance model

  democratic pressures 660–1, 662–3
  economic development 663
  national identity 663–4
  and long-term care 381, 383
  and sickness benefits 399
  and social assistance 451, 454
  and social expenditure 657
  and social policy development 659–60
  and taxation 348
     of benefits 129
  see also East Asia
journals, welfare state research in 2

Kazakhstan, and welfare state change 678,
     682
  see also Former Soviet Union (FSU)
Keynesian consensus 8, 552
  and Keynesian welfare state 43, 44
Keynesianism:
  and collapse of 46
  and neoliberal challenge 49
Korea 577
  and child benefits 470
  and childcare 468
  and immigration, opposition to 664
  and inclusive social insurance model:
     democratic pressures 662, 663
     economic development 663
     national identity 663–4
  and poverty reduction 536
  and social expenditure 126, 657
  and social policy development 659–60
     under authoritarian regimes 661–2
  and taxation of benefits 129
  see also East Asia

labour market activation:
  and aims of 438
  and cross-national convergence 443–4
  and cross-national diversity 444
  and disability provision 418
  and education 496
  and effectiveness of:
     employment outcomes 446
     employment rates 444–6
  and global economic crisis 447
  and legal environment 164

and means of 163–4
and policy change 446–7
and policy tools:
  benefits system 438–9
  career ladders 443
  ease employment protection
    regulations 442
  educational attainment 443
  employer subsidy 440
  family-friendly policies 442–3
  flexible working 441
  in-work subsidies 439–40
  job search assistance 439
  part-time work 440–1
  public sector employment 440
  reduce non-wage labour costs 441–2
  reduce tax disincentives to second
    earners 441
  transportation assistance 439
  workfare 439, 695–6
reasons for 435
  external encouragement of 437
  fairness 436–7
  financial pressures 436
  poverty reduction 437
  social inclusion 437
  women's independence 437
and reduction of real wages 441
and social assistance 458
and social rights 512
and typologies of approaches to 444
labour markets:
  and Central and Eastern Europe 681
  and changes in 12
  and East Asia 669
  and family policy 147
  and migrant labour in welfare sector
    282–3
  and Nordic countries 592
  and old age pensions 361–2
  and risk profiles 178–9, 180
  and Southern Europe 619, 620
  and union and employer association
    influence 206–7
  women's participation in: *see under*
    women
Labour Party (UK) 67

Latin American welfare states:
  and distributive impact of policies 650
    anti-poverty programmes 651
    conditional cash transfer programmes
      (CCTs) 651
    education 651–2
    employment programmes 651
    health care 652–3
    non-contributory programmes 650–1
  and education 651–2
  and effectiveness of social policy
    regimes 648–9
  and employer associations 209
  future research on 654–5
    distributive impact of social
      policy 654–5
    labour market policy 655
    politics of social policy 655
  and globalization 653–4
  and health care 645, 652–3
  and impact of social policies on
    employment 547–8
  and Import Substitution
    Industrialization 646
  origins of 89, 644–6
    power constellations perspective 646
    pressure groups 645
  and poverty 649
  and public pension coverage 354
  reforms of 646–8
    Basic Universalism 647
    gendered impact 648
    health and education 647–8
    international financial
      institutions 646–7
    outcomes 648
    pensions 647, 648
  and social expenditure 649, 650
  and taxation 649
  and trade unions 209
  and welfare regimes 578
  see also individual countries
Latvia 317
  and disability provision 413
  and welfare state change 677
  see also Central and Eastern Europe (CEE)
legal studies, and welfare state 153, 164–6

rule of law 164–5
legal welfare 121
less developed countries (LDCs), and welfare
    effects of globalization 326–8
liberalism, and origins of welfare state 4
liberal welfare state 571
  and luck egalitarianism 25
  and needs 174–5
  see also English-speaking countries
liberty 27–31
  and diversity and choice 30–1
  and moralized conception of 29–30
  and negative liberty 27–9
  and new liberalism 37
  and paternalism 30
  and positive liberty 28
    capabilities 28
  and Third Way 54
life-cycle, and redistribution 535
lifelong learning, and activation policy 443
Lisbon strategy (2000) 459, 679
Lithuania:
  and disability provision 417
  and welfare state change 677
  see also Central and Eastern Europe (CEE)
lone parent families 464–5
long-term care 390
  and challenges facing:
    funding sources 388–9
    integration of care 389–90
    provision of care 389
    quality concerns 389
  and delivery structure 383–4
    care in the community 383
    cash-for-care schemes 383–4
    residential care 383
  and developing countries 381
  and development of 378, 379–80
    convergence 390
  and family care 384–5
    commodification of 386
    support measures for carers 385
  and features of 380
  and financing structure 382–3
    future costs 388
    private provision 382–3
    public expenditure 382, 383

and impact of ageing population 387–8
and increasing need for 378
and lack of comparative data 378–9
and migrant care 386–7
and needs assessment 382
and private provision:
  for-profit sector 386
  non-profit sector 386
and regulatory structure 381–2
and scope of 378
as social risk 381, 382
and variations in coverage 382
and welfare state models 380–1
luck egalitarianism 24–6
  and personal responsibility 26
Lutheranism 268, 588
  and education 505
  see also religion
Luxembourg:
  and childcare 469
  and disability provision 412,
    413, 417
  and long-term care 383
Luxembourg Income Study 98,
    431, 474
Luxembourg Wealth Study (LWS) 527

Maastricht, Treaty of (1992) 296, 302, 624
macroeconomic outcomes:
  and impact of larger welfare states:
    economic growth 541–5, 550–1
    employment 546–50, 551
  and impact of welfare state 540–1
  and unemployment insurance 432–3
  see also economic growth; employment
majoritarian democracies, and middle
    class 272–3
Malaysia 577
malnutrition, and developing countries 715
Malta, and disability provision 417
market failure 692
market mechanisms, and primacy of 55
Marshall Aid 706
Marxism:
  and critique of welfare state 10
  and Marxist functionalism 228
maternity leave 469, 473–4

and activation policy 443
means testing 23
  and social assistance 448
  and social rights 514–15
median voter theorem 185, 186
Medicaid (USA) 87
medical profession, and health
    care 369
Medicare (USA) 87, 371
Meltzer-Richard hypothesis
    161, 185
meritocracy, and equality 24
methodology 105–6, 119–20
  and causal research 106
    approaches to 106–7
    causality 107
  and comparative and historical
    research 116
    analysis of pooled cross-sections and
      time-series 118–19
    classical comparative and historical
      research 116–18
    event history analysis 119
  and comparative studies 109
    crisp-set qualitative comparative
      analysis 110
    cross-country statistical analyses 112
    definition 107
    fuzzy-set qualitative comparative
      analysis 110–11
    qualitative comparative analysis
      (QCA) 110–12
    regression analysis 112
    systematic comparison 109–10
  and diversity of approaches 105
  and employment of multiple
    approaches 120
  and historical studies 113
    definition 107
    event structure analysis 114–15
    historical narrative work 113–14
    process tracing 113
    time-series analysis 115
  and topics tackled 105–6
  and within-country analyses 108–9
    advantages of 108
    disadvantages of 108–9

Mexico:
  and conditional cash transfer
    programme 651
  and pension reform 647
  and social expenditure:
    effects of tax system 129
    private sector 128
    public expenditure 126
  see also Latin American welfare states
micro-credit, and developing countries 716
middle class, and electoral systems 272–3
Middle East, and trade unions 209
migration, and impact on welfare states
    13, 285–7
  growth of extreme-right parties 286
  hostility to transfers to immigrants
    285–6
  see also ethnic diversity; ethnic minorities;
    immigrants
Millennium Development Goals 309, 460
minimum income:
  in OECD countries 452–6
    categorical schemes 453
    levels of 454–6
    universal schemes 453
  and social assistance 448
minimum wage, and activation policy 441
modernization theory, and union and
    employer impact 197
Mont Pelerin Society 47
multiculturalism 283–4, 285
Multilateral Investment Guarantee Agency
    (MIGA) 309

National Insurance Act (UK, 1911) 68
nationalism, and methodological
    nationalism 278
Nazism, and social policy 7, 7 n5, 42, 79
needs 20–3, 166, 169
  and acceptance as community members:
    differentiation 172
    participation 172
  and capabilities 20–1
  and conceptions of 171–3
    absolute 171
    analytical problems 172–3
    relative 171

needs (*cont.*)
  and conditionality:
    fairness argument for 22
    paternalist argument for 21
    reciprocity 22
  and effectiveness in addressing 169
  and emergence of new:
    risk groups 179–82
    socio-economic causes 176–8
  and empirical perspective 170, 171
  and identification of 169
  and means testing 23
  and normative perspective 169–70, 171
  and rational evaluation of 170–1
  and relevance of 170
  and satisfaction of 20–1
    reference groups 171–2
    right to 21
  and universal standards of 171
  and welfare state theory 173–5
    functionalism 173, 228
    institutional approaches 174
    political approaches 173–4
    regime variations 174–5
neo-institutionalism 158–9
neoliberalism:
  and conservatism 49
  and critique of welfare state 9–10, 45, 48–9
    challenge to Keynesianism 49
    Friedman 47
    Hayek 46–7
    impact of ideas 48, 56
  institutional support of 47–8
  and recovery of individual liberty 27
  and sustainability of welfare states 697–8
  and Third Way 54
neomarxists, and critique of welfare state 52
neo-republicanism, and
    non-domination 27, 29
Netherlands:
  and accident benefits 395
  and activation policy 439, 440–1, 458
  and child benefits 471
  and disability provision 413, 417
  and education 502
  and employment-related risk 179
  and family policy 176

and female employment 176
and fertility rates 471
and housing, finance 489
and long-term care 383
and service sector 176
and social assistance 451
and social expenditure 128, 130
and structural reforms 613
and unemployment insurance 423, 426, 427
  see also Western Europe welfare states
neutrality, and liberal principle of 22
New Deal (USA) 230
new institutionalism,
  see political institutions
New Labour (UK) 459
  and family policy 145
  and Third Way 53
  and work-to-welfare 51
new liberalism 37
New Public Management 162
New Right:
  and critique of welfare state 9–10
  and Friedman's influence 47
  and Hayek's influence 47
  institutional support of 47–8
  see also neoliberalism
new structuralism 194–5
New Zealand:
  and accident benefits 395, 396
  and child benefits 470
  and education 503
    spending on 497, 498
  and long-term care 381, 386
  and old age pensions 357, 358
  and origins of welfare state 38
    interwar period 77
    old age pensions 68
  and retrenchment 558
  and sickness benefits 402
  and social assistance 450
  and social expenditure 133
  and taxation 348
  and unemployment insurance 421,
    425–6, 428
  see also English-speaking countries
Nicaragua, and pension reform 647
  see also Latin American welfare states

non-profit sector, and long-term care 386
Nordic countries:
  and activation policy 440, 443, 444
  and appeal of Nordic model 587
  and changes in Nordic model 595–7
    country comparisons 597–600
    research findings 596–7
  and characteristics of Nordic model
    590–3, 600
    labour markets 592
    public service provision 592
    redistribution 591
    social insurance schemes 591
    woman-friendliness 591–2
  and childcare 258, 469
  and child poverty 537
  and common roots of Nordic model 590
    class structure 588–9
    gender equality 589
    land ownership patterns 588–9
    religion 588
    role of (leftist) politics 589
    role of ideas 589
  and criticisms of Nordic model 587
  and debates about Nordic model 586
  and disability provision 413
  and distinctiveness of social policies 586
  and economic performance of 587
  and education 500–1
    spending on 497–8
  and empirical reappraisal of Nordic
    model 593–5
  and family policy 142–3
  and influence of conservative approaches 51
  and old age pensions 356
  and origins of welfare state 39–40
  and political-class coalitions 273, 274
  and popularity of Nordic model 587
  and religion 267
  and sickness benefits 400–1
  and social assistance 451
    minimum income 454, 456
  and taxation 349
  and traditional understanding of Nordic
    model 587
  and unemployment insurance 423–4,
    425, 427

  and welfare state development 9
  see also individual countries
Nordic model, concept of 39, 588–90
Norway:
  and activation policy 443
  and changes in welfare system 599
  and childcare 468
  and disability provision 412, 418
  and education 500–1
  and influence of conservative
    approaches 51
  and origins of welfare state:
    German influence 69
    impact of World War II 80
    risk prioritization 70
  and sickness benefits 400
  and social assistance 451
  and taxation 349
  and unemployment insurance 426, 427
  see also Nordic countries
nudge behaviouralism 50
nurses, and migration of 283

occupational welfare 121
oil price shocks 10
Old Age Pension Act (UK, 1908) 67, 68
old age pensions:
  and Beveridgean systems 355, 356
    socio-economic outcomes 357–8
  and Bismarckian systems 355
    multi-pillar approach 364
    origins of 602–3
    parametric reforms 362–3
    socio-economic outcomes 357
    weakening of 364
  challenges facing:
    changing family structures 362
    labour market changes 361–2
    population ageing 360–1
  and coverage limitations 353
  and defined contribution principle 364
  and extending working life 693–4
  functions of 354–5
  funding of 364
  future of 365–6
    income inequality in old age 365
    interrupted employment history 365–6

old age pensions: (*cont.*)
    private funded schemes 366
    and indexing formulae 362–3
    and intergenerational justice 31
    and market failure 692
    and minimum pensions 355
    and notional defined contribution
        schemes 362
    origins of 353–4, 355
        Australia 68
        Denmark 68
        Germany 64, 353
        New Zealand 68
        Sweden 69
        United Kingdom 67–8
    and pay as you go (PAYG) schemes 363
    and pension types 356–7
    and post-war development of 354
    and programme design, incentive
        effects 134–5
    and public expenditure on 357
        poverty among non-elderly 359–60
    and reducing pension promises 693
    reforms of 122–3
        parametric reforms 362–3
        problems with 364–5
        structural reforms 363–4
        veto points 236
        World Bank proposals 363–4
    and replacement rates 358–9
    and retirement period 354, 357
        raising retirement age 362
    and social pensions 716
    and socio-economic outcomes 357–8
    and supplementing basic pensions
        356–7, 364
    and union and employer association
        influence 207–8
    and unpaid family work 363
Open Method of Coordination (EU) 97,
    295–6, 459
Organization for Economic Co-operation
    and Development (OECD) 307, 311
    and activation policy 437, 444, 458
    budget of 312
    and family policy 143–4
    and governance structure 311

and *Growing Unequal* report 536
and influence of conservative approaches 51
and measurement of social rights 517
philosophy of 316
and policy focus of 308, 311
and social expenditure:
    effects of tax system 129
    net levels of 130
    private sector 128
    public expenditure 126–7
and Social Expenditure Data Set
    (SOCX) 334
and social spending, definition of 123
and transnational expertise 41
origins of the welfare state 3–7
    and Australia 38
    and changes in patterns of public
        expenditure 5–6
    and changing role of the state 64–5
    and democratization 6
    diversity in development of 4–5
    and early collective solutions to social
        problems 62–3
    and expansion of risks and groups
        covered 76–7
    and first era of globalization 5
    and France 36–7
        post-1945 developments 43
    and Germany 35–6
        international influence of 66
        post-1945 developments 42–3
        reasons for leading role 66–7
        social insurance 64, 65
    and global historical context 703–4
        conception of rights 704
        European invention 704
        extra-European precursors 704
        family structure 704
        ideas 705
        industrialization 704–5
        institutions 705
        interests 705
        international environment 705–6
    and growth in state capacity 65
    and ideas 705
    and industrialization 3, 4, 5, 35, 63, 175,
        602–3, 704–5

and institutions 705
and interest groups 705
and international diffusion of social
    security schemes 70–5, 78–9
and international environment 705–6
and Latin America 644–6
and the 'liberal break' 64
and New Zealand 38
and religion 66
and risk prioritization 69–70
and role of small nations 68–9
and sequence of programme
    introduction 391–3
and social, economic and political
    change 3–4
and social citizenship 78
and social insurance 61–2
   Bismarck's reforms 64
   changing role of state 64–5
   international diffusion of schemes 70–5
   international influence of German
     example 66
   motives for implementing 65
   as new concept 64
   reasons for Germany's leading role 66–7
and spread of social security
    principles 75–6
   unequal development 76
and Sweden 39–40
and transnational policy
    development 40–1
and United Kingdom 37–8, 67–8
   post-1945 developments 41–2
and United States 38–9, 67
   as laggard 76
and urbanization 3, 35
and World War II, impact of 7, 8, 79–80
see also Bismarckian welfare states;
    individual countries; periodization of
    post-war welfare state development
outsourcing 162

Panama, and social expenditure 649
  see also Latin American welfare states
parental leave 144–5, 260, 469, 473–4
  and family policy 146
partisan theory, *see* political parties

part-time work:
  and activation policy 440–1
  and women 465
Party Manifesto Project 100
paternalism:
  and conditionality 21
  and conservative welfare agenda 50
  and liberty 30
  and state-building 51
paternity leave 144–5
pensions, *see* old age pensions
performance measurement 162
periodization of post-war welfare state
    development 81–2
  and 1945 as starting point 83–5
  and assumptions behind 82–3
  and benefit levels 94–6
  and collapse of communism (1989) 86
  and contextual factors 92–3
  and diversity in policy-specific
    developments 89–90
  and East Asia 88–9, 95–6
  and Eastern Europe 86
  and exemplary reforms as markers of
    development 90–1
  and expansion phase 81, 86, 552
   contextual factors 92–3
   social expenditure levels 93
   sub-periods 87
   welfare production forms 96
  and future trends 100–1
  and ideational approach to 99–100
  and lack of congruence with historians'
    periodization 83
  and Latin America 89
  and outcomes of programmes 97–9
  and political uses of 83
  and region-specific approaches 88–9
  and retrenchment phase 81, 82, 86
   benefit levels 94–5
   contextual factors 93
   impact of ideas 99–100
   outcomes of programmes 98
   social expenditure levels 93–4
   sub-periods 87–8
   welfare production forms 96
  and social expenditure levels 93–4

periodization of post-war welfare state
        development (*cont.*)
    and South-East Asia 88–9
    and sub-periods 87–8
    terminology of 82
    and welfare governance 97
    and welfare production forms 96–7
personal responsibility, and luck
        egalitarianism 26
Philadelphia Declaration (ILO, 1944) 41, 85
philanthropy, and poor relief 63
Philippines 577
pluralist theories of politics 228
Poland:
    and disability provision 413, 416, 418
    and social expenditure 126
    and welfare state change 677
    see also Central and Eastern Europe (CEE)
policy change, typology of 91
policy learning, and developing
        countries 710
policy-takers 555–6
policy transfer, and developing
        countries 710
political economy, and welfare state 157
political institutions, and the welfare
        state 227, 240
    and broader view of institutional
        effects 239–40
    and consensus democracies 231
    and electoral system 231, 238
    and federalism 237–8
    and feedback effects 239
    and globalization 321–2
    as ideal types 231
    and impact on outcomes 236–7
    and majoritarian democracies 231
    and multivariate analysis 236–7
    and new institutionalism 230–1
    and parliamentary systems 231
    as political configurations 232–6
        veto players 232
        veto points 232–6
    and presidential systems 231, 239
    and state-centred approach 228–30
        conflict theory 229
        Marxist functionalism 228

pluralist politics 228
    role of states 229–30
political parties
    and adaptation to external change 222
    and co-governing parties 220
    and contagion processes 220
    and Europeanization 222
    and gender 261–2
    and globalization 222, 324–5
    and partisan effects on welfare state 215–20
        party composition of government 217–20
        West European/non-European
            differences 215–16
    and partisan theory 211
        criticisms of 212–13
        democratic markets 211
        empirical support for 213
        key propositions of 212
        limitations of 220–1
        majoritarian democracies 221
        non-majoritarian democracies 221
        predictions of 211–12
    and policy positions of parties 213–15
        expansion vs retrenchment 214–15
        party families framework 213–15,
            223–6
    and religion 269–70
    and retrenchment 221–3
    and social expenditure 342
    and Southern Europe 621–2
    and taxation 350–1
political science:
    and retrenchment:
        corporatist polities 563–4
        institutional factors 563
    and welfare state 153–4, 157–9
        neo-institutionalism 158–9
        retrenchment 159
poor laws 63, 449–50
population growth:
    and developing countries 715
    and origins of welfare state 3
Portugal:
    and education 502
        spending on 498
    and social assistance 456
        minimum income 453, 454

and social expenditure 126
  effects of tax system 129
and social insurance 620
and welfare reform 625–6
see also Southern European welfare states
post-industrial economy:
  and challenges facing 182
  and emergence of new risks and needs:
    risk groups 179–82
    socio-economic causes 176–8
  and impact on social democrats 52
  transition to 11–12, 462–3
  and welfare state development 93
post-materialism, and critique
    of welfare state 10
Poujadists 350
poverty 526
  and activation policy 437
  and basic needs 20–1
  and Central and Eastern Europe 681
  and child poverty 474–5, 536–7
    employment strategy 537
    redistribution strategy 537
  and deserving/undeserving poor
      distinction 62–3
  and developing countries 715
  and disability 408
  and early collective solutions to social
      problems 62–3
  growth of 98
  impact of social policy on 526–7, 538
    data requirements 531–2
    difficulties in measuring 528–9
    income measurement 527–8
    programme size 531
    programme structure 531
    redistribution 535–8
  and inequality 529–30
  and Latin America 649
  measures of:
    deprivation 530
    living standards 530
    poverty line 530–1
  and minimum income 456
  in nineteenth century 63
  and poverty traps 531
  and racialized working poor 281–2

and redistribution 535–8
reduction of 526, 538
and social exclusion 458–9
and social expenditure 343, 536
  old age pensions 359–60
and Southern Europe 622
and tax credits 345
and unemployment insurance 431–2
and women 259
see also income distribution; inequality;
    redistribution
power relations, and equality 26–7
power resource theory 156
  and distributive politics 185–6
  and religion 266–7
  and union and employer impact 197–8
  and welfare state development 570
preference theory, and gender 255
private sector:
  and long-term care 382–3, 386
  and social expenditure 122, 335–8
    distributive effects 136–8
    encouragement through tax system 130
    government influence on 125
    international comparisons 128, 130–2
    mandatory social benefits 124
    steady increase in 128
    voluntary expenditure 125
  as welfare state substitute in U.S. 96–7
privatization 89, 96, 561, 579, 611–12, 614, 679
  of basic industries 693
  of care work 184, 386
  and charities, increased welfare role 268
  and Eastern Europe 672, 674
  and education 681
  forms of 373, 678
  and global economic crisis 14–5
  government revenues from 324, 363
  of health care costs 207, 362, 395, 614,
      677, 681–2
  of health service providers 372
  of housing 482, 487
  and Latin America 327, 646–7
  of old age security 89, 236, 327, 646–8,
      677, 682
  of risk 54, 56, 239
  of services 599, 677

privatization (*cont.*)
  and World Bank 326
  and WTO effects 314, 676
      See also retrenchment; deregulation
process tracing 113
proportional representation 231, 237, 238
  and middle class 272–3
  and political-class coalitions 273–4
Protestantism 268–9, 270–1
  and education 505
  as impediment to welfare state
      development 269
  see also religion
provident funds 665, 715–16
public attitudes:
  and challenges of researching 249
    data availability 249
    methods 249–50
    theory and analysis 250
  and comparative approach 242, 244–7
    Beliefs in Government (BiG)
      project 244–5
    broadening regime concept 247
    data availability 244, 245
    development of 251
    effects on policy development 248–9
    feedback effects 247–8
    hierarchical modelling 248
    measurement of welfare state
      support 246
    norms of reciprocity 246
      political economy approach 249
    political-sociological approach 249
    quantification 248
    recent developments in 247–9
    risk profiles 247
    skill specificity 247
    welfare regimes 245–7
  and data availability 242
  and distinguishing from elite opinion 241
  effects of public policy on 241–2
  future research on 250
  national surveys of 242–3
    common key findings 243–4
  and policy change 241
  reasons for study of 241
  and social assistance 456–7

  and taxation 351–2
  and welfare regimes 582
public choice theory 690
public deficit 345
public expenditure, *see* social expenditure
public-private partnerships, and social
    administration 163
public sector employment, and activation
    policy 440
public sector management reforms 696
purchaser-provider models 162

qualitative comparative analysis (QCA), and
    research methodology 110–12

race:
  and distributive politics 188
  and racialization of welfare 287–90
    Italy 289
    Sweden 289–90
    United Kingdom 288–9
    United States 287–8
  and racialized exclusion 281–2
race to the bottom thesis:
  and globalization 319–20
  and taxation 348
rational choice theory 10
reciprocity:
  and conditionality 22
  and public attitudes 246
redistribution:
  and Director's Law hypothesis 161
  and distributive politics 183–4
    coalitional politics 184, 187–9
    electoral system 190–1
    federalism 191–2
    left-right structure 184
    Meltzer-Richard hypothesis 185
    new structuralism 194–5
    partisanship 185–6
    power resource theory 185–6
    Robin Hood paradox 185
    role of institutions 184, 189–92
    varieties of capitalism 184, 192–4
    voter preferences 186
  and English-speaking countries 638–40
  and housing policy 490–1

and inequality 532–5
and measurement difficulties 528–9
and Meltzer-Richard hypothesis 161, 185
and Nordic model 591
paradox of 135, 591
and pension systems 355
and poverty 535–8
and social expenditure 125, 135–8, 343
   private provision 136–8
and social policy 160–1
and taxation 344–5
types of 121–2
see also equality; income distribution;
      inequality; poverty
regression analysis, and research
      methodology 112
relational equality 26–7
religion and the welfare state:
   and Christian democracy 265, 269–70, 276
   and education 505
   and family policy 147, 262, 272
   and future research on 275–7
   and gender 262
   and impact of denominational
      differences 99, 267–8, 268–9
   and Lutheranism 268
   and non-Christian religions 578, 276–7
   and Nordic model 588
   and political-class coalitions 273–4
   and links between 265–6, 266–7, 270–2
   scholarly neglect of 266, 274–5
   and state-church conflict 271–2
   as substitutes for each other 268
   and taxation 350
   and welfare state development 66, 99, 265
   see also Catholicism; Protestantism
research methods, see methodology
residential care, and long-term care 383
retirement:
   and extending working life 693–4
   and the life course 354, 357
   see also old age pensions
retrenchment 81, 82, 552–3
   and benefit levels 94–5, 404
   causes of 524
   and contextual factors 93
   and economic crises 561–2
extent of 558–9
framing of 561–2
and impact of ideas 99–100
measures of:
   composition of spending and taxation 560
   maintenance of income streams 560–1
   private and employer-provided
      benefits 559–60
   social spending as share of GDP 559
   social spending relative to need 559
and negotiated reforms 562–3
obstacles to:
   historical legacies 555
   interest groups and policy-takers 555–6
   logic of collective action 554–5
   policy legacies 555, 563
   policy 'lock-in' 555
   programme structures 563
   psychological dynamics 554
and outcomes of programmes 98
overcoming obstacles to 556–8
   blame avoidance 556
   broadening support 562–3
   burden sharing 557
      decrementalism 557
   delayed implementation 557
   diffusing consequences over time 557
   divide and conquer 557
   drawbacks to blame avoidance
      strategies 558
   reducing traceability 557
and partisan effects 221–3
and Pierson's 'new politics of the welfare
      state' thesis 553–6, 564
   overcoming obstacles to
      retrenchment 556–8
political science explanation of 159
   corporatist polities 563–4
   institutional factors 563
and protests against 554
and resilience of the welfare state:
   economic factors 692–3
   political factors 691
and social expenditure levels 93–4
and social rights 523–4
and sub-periods of 87–8
and unemployment insurance 428–9

retrenchment (*cont.*)
  and unpopularity of 556
  and welfare production forms 96
  and welfare regimes 579
  and Western European welfare regime 610–11
revenues, *see* taxation
rights, and origins of welfare state 704
risks:
  definition of 169
  and emergence of new 175–6
    risk groups 179–82
    socio-economic causes 176–8
  and employment-related 178–9, 180
  and family transformation 179, 181
  privatization of 56
  protection from 169
  relevance of 170
  and risk groups 179–82
  and Third Way 53–4
  and welfare state theory 173–5
    functionalism 173
    institutional approaches 174
    political approaches 173–4
Robin Hood paradox 185
Romania 579
  and disability provision 417
  and welfare state change 677
  see also Central and Eastern Europe (CEE)
rule of law 164–5
Russia:
  and social assistance 454
  and welfare state change 678, 682–3
  see also Former Soviet Union (FSU)
Scandinavia, *see* Nordic countries
self-administration, and social
    governance 205
self-regulation, and social governance 205
Serbia 579
service sector:
  growth of 176, 463
  and migrant labour 282–3
  and risks associated with 178
Settlement Houses 38
sickness benefits 391
  generosity of 402–4
  and historical development of 398–401
    Central Europe 400

    Germany 398–9
    Japan 399
    labour movement pressure 398–9
    Nordic countries 400–1
    United Kingdom 400
    United States 401
    voluntary funds 398
  and retrenchment of 404
  and universalism, degree of 401–4
Singapore 577
  and Central Provident Fund (CPF) 665
  and constraints on social policy
    development
    absence of democracy 666
    lack of fiscal capacity 666
    lack of social solidarity 667–8
  and individualistic social protection
    664–5
  and inequality 664
  and social expenditure 657
  see also East Asia
Slovak Republic:
  and disability provision 412
  and social expenditure, effects of tax
    system 129
  and welfare state change
    see also Central and Eastern Europe (CEE)
Slovenia 579
  and welfare state change 677
    see also Central and Eastern Europe (CEE)
Social Action Programmes (EU) 293
social administration, and welfare state
    162–3
  coordination 162–3
  New Public Management 162
social assistance 460–1
  and Central and Eastern Europe 681
  and definition of 448, 449, 453
  and developing countries 460
  and global perspective 459–60
  and guaranteed minimum income in
    OECD countries 452–6
    categorical schemes 453
    effects of 456
    levels of 454–6, 457
    universal schemes 453
  and means testing 448

and minimum income support 448
and new policy developments 457–9
   activation policy 458
   social inclusion 458–9
   workfare 458
politics of 457
and poverty reduction 456
and programmes in OECD
      countries 449–52
   benefit categories 450
   coverage rates 451
   diversity of 451–2
   evolution of 449–50
   taxonomy of benefits 450
   types of assistance 450–1
   welfare regimes 451–2
public support for 456–7
significance of 448–9
and Southern Europe 622
transformation of 457–8
social capital, and Asian investment in 96
social citizenship 42, 62
development of 78
and education 496
Social Citizenship Indicators Programme
      (SCIP) 90, 94, 402, 420–1
and measurement of social rights 516, 517, 519
social democracy:
and critique of welfare state 46
   impact of post-industrialism and
      globalization 52
   Third Way 52–5
and welfare state as project of 43
social democratic welfare state 571
and luck egalitarianism 25
Social Democratic Workers' Party of Ger-
      many 67
social exclusion:
and disability 408
and poverty 458–9
social expenditure 352
areas covered by 124
changes in patterns of 5–6
and data availability 334
definition of 123–5
and determinants of cross-national
      differences 341–3

economic affluence 342
globalization 342
institutions 342
partisan effects 342
socio-economic causes 342
and disability provision 412–13
   pressures on budgets 417–18
economic impact of 540
and education spending:
   net levels of 497–8
   relationship between 497
   tertiary education 498–9
and effects of welfare provision 133
   distributional outcomes 135–8
      incentives 134–5
and ethnic diversity 284–5
and family policy:
   childcare 468–9
   children 467
   families with children 467
   parental leave 469, 473–4
growth of 539–40
and health care 367, 371–2
and housing 488
and impact on social outcomes 343
and income inequality 532–4
and international comparisons:
   items excluded from 125–6
   net levels of 130–2
   private sector 128
   public expenditure 126–7
and Latin America 649, 650
and limitations as explanatory factor 334
and long-term care 382–3
   funding sources 388–9
   future costs 388
measurement of 122
as measure of welfare state size 122
net (public and private) levels of 122–3
   international comparisons 130–2
   trends in 338
and old age pensions 357
and political conflict 333
and poverty rate 536
pressures on 436
and private provision 122–3, 335–8
   distributive effects 136–8

social expenditure (*cont.*)
  government influence on 125
  mandatory social benefits 124
  steady increase in 128
  voluntary expenditure 125
  and public provision 124
  redistributive effects 125
  and redistribution 125, 135–8, 343
  resilience of:
    economic reasons 692–3
    political reasons 692
  rise in 333
  and Social Expenditure Data Set
      (SOCX) 334
  and tax system:
    effects on social effort 128–30
    encouragement of private
        provision 130
    family support 129–30
    indirect taxation 129
    taxation of transfer payments 128–9
  trends and patterns since 1980
      335–41
    convergence in 335
    country clusters 335, 338
    growth of 335
    net levels of 338
    private sector 335–8
    programme types 338–41
  and underestimation by conventional
      measures 123
  and welfare state development 93–4
Social Expenditure Data Set (SOCX) 334
social governance:
  and concertation 205
  and consultation 205
  and self-administration 205
  and self-regulation 205
  and unilateral state intervention 204–5
social inclusion:
  and activation policy 437
  and disability 408–9
  and social assistance 458–9
  and Third Way 54
social insurance:
  and Bismarckian welfare systems:
    industrial origins of 602–4

  in post-war period 605–8
  response to problems facing 608–9
  transformation of 609–14
and economic growth 545
and Germany:
  Bismarck's reforms 64
  motives for implementing 65
  reasons for leading role 66–7
international diffusion of 70–5
and Nordic model 591
origins of 61–2
  changing role of state 64–5
  expansion of risks and groups
      covered 76–7
  international influence of German
      example 66
  internationalization of social security 78–9
  as new concept 64
  risk prioritization 69–70
  role of small nations 68–9
  sequence of programme
      introduction 391–3
and Southern Europe 620–2
  common features 620–1
  dualistic nature of 621
  origins of 620
  political influences on 621–2
and spread of social security
    principles 75–6
  unequal development 76
social integration:
  and family policy 149, 151
  and sociological perspectives on
      welfare state 154–6
social investment state 44
  and East Asia 95–6
  and education 496, 507
social justice, and welfare state 19, 78
social market economy 42
social pensions, and developing
    countries 716
social policy:
  components of 89
  and insider/outsider schism 161–2
  and post-war paradigm shift 85
  and redistribution 160–1
  and welfare state 160–2

social problems, and early collective
    solutions 62–3
social rights:
  and acceptance as universal rights 84–5
  and activation policy 512
  as citizenship rights 511
  and decommodification 513–14
    measurement of 516–17
  definition of 512–15
    breadth of policies encompassed by 514
    Esping-Andersen 513–14
    Marshall's conception 512–13
    means tested benefits 514–15
    Orloff 514
    Room 514
  determinants of variations in 522–3
  and education 496, 508
  emergence of 63, 78, 84
  and English-speaking countries 638
  and gender 512, 514
  measurement of 515–22
    activation policy 522
    Comparative Welfare Entitlements
      Dataset 517, 519
    data gaps 518
    decommodification 516–17
    education 521, 522
    expenditure measures 515
    impact of data availability 518–19
    OECD data 517
    parental leave 519
    public health 522
    public service effort 519–21
    replacement rates by regime 519
    single programmes 515–16
    Social Citizenship Indicators
      Programme (SCIP) 516, 517, 519
  and outcomes of variations in 524–5
  and retrenchment 523–4
  and Universal Declaration of Human
    Rights (1948) 85
  and welfare state 21
social science, growth of 65
Social Security Act (New Zealand, 1938) 77
Social Security Act (USA, 1935) 39, 76, 425
social stratification 98, 239–40
social welfare 121

social work, and welfare state 163–4
sociology:
  and economics 157
  and welfare state 154–6
    debates over 155–6
    social integration 154–6
solidarity, and social assistance 456–7
South Africa, and social assistance 460
South-East Asia:
  and industrial relations 209–10
  and welfare state development 88–9
South-Eastern Europe, and comparison with
    Southern Europe 628
Southern European welfare states:
  common features of 620–1
  and comparison with South-Eastern
    Europe 628
  development of 627
  dualistic nature of 621
  and Europeanization of welfare 618
  and familialism 622–3, 627–8
  and gender regime 622
  and health care 621
  and identification as welfare regime 616
    debate over 617
    by European Commission 617
  and insider/outsider schism 162, 619, 627
  and labour markets:
    characteristics of 619
    women's participation 620
  and low state capacity 623–4
  and modernization 616–17, 618–20
    democratization 618–19
    economic development 619
    industrialization 618
    labour markets 619–20
  origins of 620
  political influences on 621–2
  and poverty 622
  reform of:
    elements of 624–5
    external constraints 624
    Greece 627
    Italy 625
    Portugal 625–6
    Spain 625–6
  and relevance for other regions 628–9

Southern European welfare states: (*cont.*)
 Latin America 628
 South-Eastern Europe 628
 and social assistance, marginal role of 622
 and underground economy 623
 and unemployment 620
  see also individual countries
Soviet Union, and welfare state 672–4
Spain:
 and disability provision 417
 and education 502
  spending on 497
 and employment-related risk 179
 and female employment 176, 626
 and fertility 176
 and health care 371
 and labour market reform 626
 and social assistance 456, 459
  minimum income 453
 and social insurance 620
 and welfare reform 625–6
 see also Southern European welfare states
stamps with welfare motifs xxvi–xxx
standard setting, and Intergovernmental
  Organizations 313
state, the:
 and change from 'warfare' to 'welfare'
  state 5–6
 and health care 377
 and origins of welfare state 64–5
 and social policy activism in nineteenth
  century 34
state-building, and paternalism 51
State Earnings-Related Pension Scheme
  (UK) 356–7
state intervention, and social governance 204–5
state structures 227, 240
 and policy development 229–30
 and state-centred approach 228–30
  conflict theory 229
  Marxist functionalism 228
  pluralist politics 228
  role of states 229–30
 see also political institutions
Stockholm School 40
structuralism, and new structuralism 194–5
sub-prime lending 489–90

subsidiarity:
 and family policy 142, 145
 and France 36
subsidies, and activation policy 439–40
substitution issue 155–6
Survey of Health, Ageing and Retirement in
  Europe (SHARE) 379
sustainability of Western welfare states 689
 challenges facing 699–700
 and fiscal sustainability 693
  extending working lives 693–4
  higher priority for social policy
   spending 693
  increased spending 694–5
  introducing charges 693
  new funding methods 695
  quasi-taxation 695
  reducing pensions promises 693
  workfare 695–6
 and future of welfare states:
  basic citizenship model 700–1
  family friendly 701–2
  inclusive and adaptive 701
  international regulation 702
  market dominance 700
 and moral sustainability:
  forms of belonging 698
  global economic crisis 698–9
  individualism 698
  inequality 698
  neoliberalism 697–8
 and past predictions 690
  predictions confounded 690–1
 and political sustainability 696–7
 and reasons for resilience:
  economic factors 692–3
  political factors 691
Sweden:
 and accident benefits 395, 396
 and activation policy 439, 441
 and changes in welfare system 597–9
 and child benefits 471
 and childcare 468
 and child poverty 537
 and disability provision 410, 417
 and education 500–1, 696
 and employment-related risk 178

and family policy, reform of 144–5
and fertility rates 471
and health care 371
and immigration and welfare 289–90
and impact of neoliberalism 48
and income inequality 532
and inequality 698
and influence of conservative approaches 51
and origins of welfare state 39–40
    old age pensions 69
and pension reform 134, 693
and poverty reduction 536
and retrenchment
    corporatist polity 563–4
    putting responsibility on local
        government 557
and Saltsjöbaden agreement (1938) 40
and service sector 176
and sickness benefits 400
and social assistance, minimum income 454
and social expenditure 126, 130
and taxation 349
    of benefits 129
and unemployment insurance 421, 426,
    427, 433
see also Nordic countries
Switzerland:
and accident benefits 395
and childcare 468
and disability provision 413
and education, spending on 497, 498
and social assistance 451
    minimum income 456
and social expenditure, private sector 128
and taxation 348
and unemployment insurance 424, 425,
    426, 427
systematic comparison, and research
    methodology 109–10

Taiwan 577
and immigration, opposition to 664
and inclusive social insurance model
    democratic pressures 662, 663
    economic development 663
    national identity 663–4
and social expenditure 657

and social policy development 659–60
    under authoritarian regimes 661–2
see also East Asia
targets 162
taxation 352
and activation policy 441–2
and attitudes towards welfare state 350–2
    changes in 350–1
and developing countries 715
and economic growth 544
and effects on social effort 128–30
    encouragement of private provision 130
    family support 129–30
    indirect taxation 129
    taxation of transfer payments 128–9
and English-speaking countries 639–40
and family policy 469–71
and gender equality 344
and globalization 323, 328
    tax competition 348
and inequality 344–5
and Latin America 649
levels of 345–8
and national 'families' of taxation 348–50
and negative income tax 344–5
and partisan effects 350–1
progressivity of 345
and protests movements 350
and public attitudes towards 351–2
and race to the bottom thesis 348
and rate reductions 348
and religion 350
and retrenchment 560
role of 122
and tax competition 348
and tax credits 344–5
Temporary Assistance for Needy Families
    (TANF, USA) 46, 51, 458
tertiary education, and spending on 498–9
Thailand 577
see also East Asia
Third Way 44, 46, 52–5
and authoritarianism 54
and conditionality 54
and contrasted with neoliberalism 54
emergence of:
    United Kingdom 53

Third Way (*cont.*)
    United States 52–3
    and family policy 148
    and Giddens 53–4
    and influence of 54–5
    and liberty 54
    and risk 53–4
    and role of the state 54
    and social inclusion 54
    and triumph of market
        orthodoxy 55
    and undesirability of traditional welfare
        state 53
Timbro (Sweden) 48
time-series analysis, and research
        methodology 115
trade liberalization 10
Trade-Related Aspects of Intellectual
        Property Rights (TRIPS) 310
trade unions:
    and developing countries 208–10
    and education 506
    and industrial relations, cross-national
        variations 203
    and influence in social policy areas:
        collective bargaining 206
        health care 208
        labour market policy 206–7
        pension policy 207–8
    organization of 200–1, 201–3
        free-rider problem 200
    research on 196
    role of 196, 197, 210
    and social policy as alternative to
        socialism 34
    theories of impact of:
        corporatist theory 198
        Europeanization thesis 199
        globalization thesis 199
        institutional theories 199
        modernization theory 197
        power resource theory 197–8
        state-centred theories 198–9
        varieties of capitalism approach 198
        veto player theorem 199
    see also industrial relations, and social
        governance

transition economies, and welfare effects
        of globalization 326–8
    see also Central and Eastern Europe
        (CEE); Former Soviet Union (FSU)
transnational policy development,
        and origins of welfare state 40–1
Turkey:
    and income inequality 533
    and social assistance 451
    and social expenditure:
        private sector 128
        public expenditure 126
twentieth century, nature of 1
typologies of welfare states 19–20
    criticism of 89–90
    see also welfare regimes

underclass, and immigrants 281
undeserving poor 37, 62–3
unemployment:
    and duration effects 430
    and effects of unemployment
        insurance 429–30
    and unemployment rates 425–431, 534,
        587, 610, 620, 681
unemployment insurance 420–1
    and Central and Eastern Europe 680
    and coverage rates:
        Great Depression 423–5
        post-war period 426
    and duration of benefits 426
    and economic efficiency 432–3
    and employment levels 546–7
    and financing of 429
    and Great Depression 423–5
    and institutional diversity of 421–3
        comprehensive schemes 421–2
        Ghent system 421
        state corporatist schemes 422
        targeted programmes 421
        voluntary state-subsidized insurance 421
    and labour supply 429–31, 432
        detrimental effects on 429–30
        entitlement effect 430
        unemployment rate 430
    legitimacy of 425
    and macroeconomic impact 432–3

politics of 428
and poverty 431–2
and productivity-enhancing effects 432–3
and replacement rates:
  Great Depression 425
  post-war period 427–8
and retrenchment 428–9
and waiting times 425–6
unions, see trade unions
United Kingdom:
and accident benefits 395, 396, 397
and activation policy 439, 458, 459
and childcare 258, 469
and disability provision 417
  development of 409
  expenditure on 412, 413
  Incapacity Benefit 413
  reform of 418
and education 503
and employment-related risk 178–9
and ethnic diversity 288–9
and family policy 143, 176
  labour market effects 147
  reform of 145
  Third Way 148
and fertility rates 471
and health care 371
  regulation of 374
and immigration policy 288–9
and inequality 698
and influence of conservative
    approaches 51
and influence of neoliberalism 47–8
and long-term care 381, 386
and old age pensions 358
  State Earnings-Related Pension
    Scheme 356–7
and origins of welfare state 37–8, 67–8
  impact of World War II 79
  post-1945 developments 41–2
  risk prioritization 70
and poor laws 63, 449–50
and poverty reduction 526
and retrenchment 553–4, 558–9
and service sector 176
and sickness benefits 400
and social assistance 451

minimum income 453–4
and social expenditure:
  effects of tax system 129
  net levels of 130, 338
  private sector 128
and taxation 348
  regressiveness of 560
  Working Tax Credit 344–5
and Third Way 53
and unemployment insurance 421–2,
    423, 425, 426, 428
and work-to-welfare 51
see also English-speaking countries
United Kingdom Sustainable Development
    Commission 718
United Nations:
and Economic and Social Council of 85
and postage stamps xxvi
and Universal Declaration of Human
    Rights (1948) 41, 85
and World Social Summits 10
United Nations Children's Fund (UNICEF),
    and child poverty 536
United Nations Convention on the Rights of
    Persons with Disabilities (2008)
    406, 419
United Nations Development Programme
    (UNDP) 376
United Nations Educational, Scientific and
    Cultural Organization
    (UNESCO) 308
United States:
and accident benefits 395
and activation policy 438–9, 443, 458
and American exceptionalism 640–2
and child benefits 471
and childcare 258
and conservative criticism of welfare
    state 50–1
and disability provision 410–11
  expenditure on 412, 413
and education 503
  spending on 497, 498
and effects of tax system on social
    expenditure 129, 130
and employment-related risk 178
and ethnic diversity 279

United States (*cont.*)
  and extent of welfare state 96–7
  and family policy 143, 144, 176
  and health care 371, 695
    regulation of 374–5
  and housing 15
    finance 489
    sub-prime lending 489–90
  and income inequality 532, 533
  and influence of neoliberalism 47–8
  and Intergovernmental Organizations,
    instrumentalizing of 316–17
  and long-term care 381, 386
  and old age pensions 355
  and origins of welfare state 38–9, 67
    as laggard 76
  and private welfare sector 96–7
    increase in spending on 128
    social expenditure 128
  and race and welfare 284, 287–8
  and racialized exclusion 281
  and retrenchment 553–4, 558–9
    private benefits 559–60
    putting responsibility on local
      government 557
  and service sector 176
  and sickness benefits 401
  and social assistance 451, 453, 456, 457
  and social expenditure, net levels of
    130, 338
  and taxation 348
    Earned Income Tax Credit 344–5
    tax protests 350
  and Third Way 52–3
  and unemployment insurance 425,
    428, 433
  and welfare state development 8–9
  and workfare 50–1, 458
  see also English-speaking countries
United States Agency for International
    Development (USAID) 646
United States Supreme Court, and impact
    on social policy 396
urbanization:
  and developing countries 715
  and origins of welfare state 3, 35
Uruguay 578

and anti-poverty programme 651
and education 652
and European social policy 709
and health care 652, 653
and minimum wage 653
and pension reform 647
and postage stamps with welfare motifs
    xxvii–xxviii
and poverty 649
and social expenditure 649
see also Latin American welfare states

varieties of capitalism:
  and distributive politics 184, 192–4
  and union and employer impact 198
  and welfare regimes 573–4
Venezuela, and social expenditure 649
  see also Latin American welfare states
Verein für Socialpolitik 35, 65
Versailles, Treaty of (1919) 6 n4, 78
veto players, and political institutions 232
veto player theorem, and union and
    employer impact 199
veto points, and political institutions 232–6
Vietnam, and unemployment insurance 434
vouchers 30–1

wage bargaining institutions, and
    employment effects 546, 548–50
wage levels:
  and activation policy 441
  and child poverty 536–7
war:
  as locomotive of change 7
  and welfare state development 79–80
Washington Consensus 97, 313, 314, 316
welfare capitalism 529
welfare creep 33
Welfare Internationalism 85
welfare regimes 569–70
  and Asia 577–8
  and Christian democracy 270
  and cluster analysis of non-OECD
    countries 711–14
  and convergence 579–80
  and developing countries 711–14
    proto-welfare states 711–13

and divergence 580
and Eastern Europe 578–9
and education regimes 503–4
and Esping-Andersen's typology of welfare
    states 570–1
  critical appreciation of 571–2
  criticisms of 572
  empirical tests of 575–7
  labelling of Antipodes countries 573
  methodological criticisms 574–5
  misspecification of Mediterranean
    welfare states 573
  neglect of employers' role 573–4
  neglect of gender 572–3
  theoretical weakness of alternative
    typologies 582
  usefulness of 580–1
and European integration 579–80
and evaluating models 581
  derivation of implications 582–3
  explanatory power 581–2
  versatility in application 582–3
and globalization 579–80
and hybrid forms 580
and ideal and real types 574
and influence on gendered study
    of welfare states 253–4
and Latin America 578
and long-term care 380–1
and measurement of welfare state
    support 246
and norms of reciprocity 246
and path dependence 580
and problems with concept of 246
and public attitudes 245–7
resilience of 580
  economic 692–3
  political 691
and retrenchment 579
and social assistance 451–2
and social attitudes 582
and social expenditure, net levels
    of 338
and varieties of capitalism 573–4
see also Central and Eastern Europe
    (CEE); East Asia; English-speaking
    countries; Latin American

welfare states; Nordic countries; Southern
    European welfare states; Western
    Europe welfare states
welfare state:
  and ambiguity of concept 153
  and challenges facing 13–14, 699–700
    changes in international political
      economy 10–11
    climate change 716–18
    crisis of capitalism 718–20
    demographic changes 12–13
    diverse responses to 13
    ethnic heterogeneity 13
    labour markets 12
    transition to post-industrial
      economy 11–12, 462–3
  as commitment device 156
  components of 89
  and critiques of 9–10
    role of ideas 55–7
  see also conservatism; neoliberalism;
    Third Way
  and disciplinary perspectives on 152, 166
    core debates 153
    cross-cutting questions 152–3
    economics 156–7
    legal studies 153, 164–6
    political science 153–4, 157–9
    social administration 162–3
    social policy 160–2
    social work 163–4
    sociology 154–6
  economic impact of 540–1, 551
    economic growth 541–5, 550–1
    employment 546–50, 551
  future development of 14–15
  and future of:
    basic citizenship model 700–1
    family friendly 701–2
    inclusive and adaptive 701
    international regulation 702
    market dominance 700
  and incentive effects 134–5
  Marshall's conceptualization of 511
  meaning of 32–3
  post-war development of 7–9, 41–4
    cross-national differences 8–9

welfare state: (*cont.*)
    features of post-war welfare state 43–4
    Keynesian welfare state 43, 552
    political consensus 43, 44
    as project of social democracy 43
    re-moralization of welfare 44
  public perceptions of 90–1
  and social division of welfare 121–2
  and socio-economic transformations
    175–8
  see also ethics, and the welfare state;
    intellectual roots of the welfare state;
    origins of the welfare state;
  periodization of post-war welfare state
    development; sustainability of
    Western welfare states
welfare-to-work 50–1
  and origins of 9
  see also labour market activation; workfare
wellbeing, and economic growth 718
Western European welfare states:
  and characteristics of 601, 604
  and dual nature of 614–15
  and paradigm change 614
  responses to challenges facing 608–9
    difficulties in changing 609
    labour shedding 608 .
    protection of male income 609
  rigidities in 609
  transformation of 609–10
    care policies 613–14
    institutional meta-reforms 611–12
    retrenchment 610–11
    structural reforms 612–14 *see also*
    individual countries
  see also Bismarckian welfare states
Widows, Orphans and Old Age Contributory
    Pensions Act (UK, 1925) 68
women:
  and activation policy 437, 442–3
  and care work 178, 256–9
    long-term care 384
    social policies 260–1
  and communist welfare states 673–4
  and impact on social policy 263–4
  and labour market participation 12, 140,
    176, 257–8, 465–6

    childcare 151, 258, 467–9, 473–4
    maternal employment 260, 473–4
    occupational segregation 259
    part-time work 465
  and migrant labour 282–3
  and Nordic model 591–2
  and poverty 259
  see also feminism; gender
Women's Bureau (USA) 39
work accident benefits,
  see accident benefits
workfare 50–1, 458, 695–6
  and activation policy 439
working conditions, and European Union
    social policy 294
Working Tax Credit (UK) 344–5, 439, 458
work-life balance:
  and family policy 150, 151
  and family policy reform 143, 145
World Bank 10, 97, 307, 308–9, 376
  budget of 312
  and Central and Eastern Europe 676
  and components of 309
  and democratic deficit 317
  and governance structure 308–9
  and pension reform 363–4
  philosophy of 316
  and policy focus of 309
  and policy mechanisms 309
  and social safety nets 460
  and transnational expertise 41
World Economic Forum 376
World Health Organization (WHO) 10, 308,
    375, 376
  and postage stamps xxvi
World Social Forum 306
World Trade Organization (WTO)
    310–11, 376
  and governance structure 310–11
  and policy focus of 308
  and Seattle protest 306
  and social policy effects 310
World Values Surveys 244
World War I, and radicalizing
    effect 70
World War II, and development of welfare
    state 7, 8, 79–80

Name Index

Includes all referenced authors.

Aarts, Leo J M 411
Aasve, Arnstein 623
Abbott, Kenneth W 315
Abraham, John 376
Abrahamson, Peter 580–1, 591, 596, 631
Abu Sharkh, Miriam 711
Acemoglu, Daron 194
Ackerman, Bruce 24
Adam, Stuart 560
Adams, Julia 253, 255
Addison, John T 547
Adema, Willem 122, 128 n4, 130, 133,
    338, 402, 488 n2
Adenauer, Konrad xxvi
Agell, Jonas 437, 542
Ahn, Namkee 623
Akalin, Ayse 283
Alber, Jens 61, 65, 66, 67, 69, 70, 77, 78, 84, 93,
    198, 199, 216, 217, 229, 307, 381, 391, 394, 399,
    423, 506, 592, 641
Albertini, Marco 178
Alesina, Alberto 13, 188, 284, 457, 699
Alestalo, Matti 580, 588
Alford, Robert R 369, 370
Alkire, Sabina 171
Allan, James P 89, 98, 105, 106, 186, 222, 246,
    318, 324, 523, 524, 571, 574, 576, 634, 636
Allard, Gayle 546–7
Allen, David 294
Allison, Paul D 119
Allmendinger, Jutta 494, 495, 500,
    502, 506, 507
Alstott, Anne 24
Ålund, Aleksandra 289
Aly, Götz 7 n4
Amenta, Edwin 1, 76, 106, 107, 108, 109, 111,
    114, 115, 116, 117, 118, 119, 120, 334

Andall, Jacqueline 282
Andersen, Torben M 587
Anderson, Bridget 282
Anderson, Elizabeth 24, 26–7
Anderson, Karen M 360, 563–4
Anderson, Odin W 370
Andress, Hans Jürgen 244 n2, 245, 246
Ansell, Benjamin W 185, 506
Anthias, Floya 281
Antonnen, Anneli 258, 380, 592, 635
Archer, Margaret S 506, 507
Armingeon, Klaus 13, 182, 237, 313, 316
Arretche, Marta 653
Arriba, Ana 244 n2, 457, 459, 623, 626
Arrow, Kenneth J 372
Arts, Wil A 245, 569, 572, 574 n1, 579, 582
Ashford, Douglas E 36
Athukorala, Prema-Chandra 667
Atkinson, Anthony B 172, 430, 527, 530,
    531, 532, 622
Attar-Schwartz, Shalhevet 473
Auer, Peter 447
Aust, Andreas 457, 459
Austen-Smith, David 188
Avdagic, Sabina 209, 441
Avelino, George 327, 328, 654
Azariadis, Costas 542, 545

Baccaro, Lucio 236, 562
Bache, Ian 294
Bäckman, Olof 431
Bäckström, Aanders 268
Bacon, Robert W 540, 541
Bahle, Thomas 140, 146, 147, 148, 149, 150, 450
Baker, Dean 430
Baldwin, Peter 4–5, 33, 75, 78, 116, 161, 198,
    273, 400, 572, 581, 588, 590, 641

Balzac, Honoré de 3
Bambra, Clare 370, 373, 574, 576, 621, 636
Banks, James 695
Banting, Keith G 13, 284, 285, 286, 287, 288
Barbier, Jean-Claude 444
Bargain, Oliver 440
Barr, Nicholas A 89, 91, 153, 157, 354, 692
Barrett, Edith J 243
Barrientos, Armando 460, 574–5, 576, 578
Barro, Robert J 542, 545
Barry, Brian M 24, 31
Barry, Norman 49, 50
Bartels, Larry 186
Barth, Erling 592
Bastagli, Francesca 625
Batlle y Ordoñez, José xxvi
Baumol, William J 372, 690
Bawn, Kathleen 190
Bayly, Christopher A 5
Bean, Clive 245
Beck, Nathaniel 118
Beck, Ulrich 10, 53
Becker, Gary S 141, 495
Beland, Daniel 56, 401
Bell, Mark 294
Bello, Amparo H 648
Belot, Michèle 344, 430
Ben-Arieh, Asher 475
Benedict XVI, Pope 15
Bennett, Andrew 106, 113
Benoit, Kenneth 213, 215, 226
Benson, John 209
Berger, Stefan 198
Berger, Suzanne 267
Bergqvist, Christina 261
Berkel, Rik van 444
Berkowitz, Edward 392, 394
Berkowitz, Monroe 392, 394
Berlin, Isaiah 27, 28
Bermeo, Nancy G 620
Bernard, Paul 575
Bertola, Giuseppe 440
Bertranou, Fabio M 647
Bettio, Francesca 380, 622
Bevan, Aneurin xxviii
Beveridge, William xxiii, xxvii, xxviii, 32, 33, 42, 83, 355

Beyme, Klaus von 217
Bieback, Karl-Jürgen 141
Birchfield, Vicki 237, 531
Bismarck, Otto von xxvi, 32, 35, 36, 64, 65, 395, 604
Blair, Tony 53
Blais, Andre 543
Blanchard, Oliver 430
Blank, Robert H 368 n1
Blekesaune, Morten 248
Bleses, Peter 319 n1, 615
Block, Fred 228
Blomberg-Kroll, Helena 244 n2
Blyth, Mark 47, 48, 49, 52, 54, 56
Boarini, Romina 172, 530
Bock, Gisela 34
Boix, Carles 194, 222, 506
Bolderson, Helen 414, 419
Bolin, Kristian 385
Boling, Patricia 660
Bolzendahl, Catherine 264
Bommes, Michael 280
Bonastia, Chris 117
Bonnett, Alastair 287
Bonoli, Giuliano 13, 53, 148, 178, 179, 182, 208, 236, 245, 355, 457, 573, 611, 684, 685
Boreus, Kristina 51
Borre, Ole 244
Borsay, Anne 409
Börsch-Supan, Axel H 693
Bortnik, Anita 518, 519
Botten, Grete 599
Bourgeois, Léon 37
Bourguignon, François 172
Bowles, Samuel 437
Box-Steffensmeier, Janet M 119
Bradbury, Bruce 527, 530, 537
Bradley, David 186, 517, 525
Bradshaw, Jonathan 259, 470, 471, 473, 532
Brady, David 324, 325, 326, 328 n4, 537
Brandolini, Andrea 698
Breger, Monika 539
Brennan, Deborah 146
Brennan, Geoffrey 191
Breslin, Mary Lou 418
Bridgen, Paul 33
Briggs, Asa 63, 68, 75, 158, 633

Brighouse, Harry 31
Brinkley, Alan 80
Brodsky, Jenny 381
Brooks, Clem 248, 249, 580
Brooks, Sarah M 119, 236, 314, 319 n1, 327, 329
Brown, David S 327, 328
Brown, Gordon 54
Brown, James 560
Browning, Edgar K 157
Bruce, Maurice 37
Bruijn, Hans de 162
Brush, Lisa D 256 n2
Bruttel, Oliver 427
Buchanan, James M 191, 283
Budge, Ian 100, 211, 350
Burau, Viola 368 n1, 383
Burgoon, Brian 322
Busch, Klaus 299
Busemeyer, Marius R 324, 325, 494, 495, 501, 506
Bush, George W 47
Butler, Judith 253, 255, 256

Calder, Kitty 661
Calmfors, Lars 548, 550
Cameron, David R 112, 191, 229, 320, 324, 342, 550, 633
Caminada, Koen 136
Campbell, Angus 186
Campbell, Ian 395
Campbell, John C 399, 661
Campbell, Mary 145, 151
Campodónico, M 651
Cantillon, Bea 453, 463
Cao, Xun 324
Capucha, Luis 626
Cardozo, Santiago 652
Caren, Neal 109
Carlson, Allan C 40
Carmichael, Fiona 384, 385
Carnes, Matthew 209
Carroll, Eero 421 n1, 428, 516, 522, 523 n7
Castiglioni, Rossana 647, 648
Castles, Francis G 6, 8, 38, 77, 94, 105, 106, 112, 113, 116, 117, 120, 136, 153, 160, 186, 187, 191, 194, 211, 216, 222, 228, 246, 266, 269, 314, 318, 324, 333, 334, 335, 342, 343, 352, 400,

401, 451, 472, 485, 491, 496, 503, 505, 515, 529, 534, 543, 573, 576, 579, 580, 590, 596, 617, 618, 622, 633–4, 636, 637, 638, 640, 641, 684
Castles, Stephen 279, 280, 284
Centrángolo, Oscar 649
Cerami, Alfio 679, 680, 681, 685
Chandler, Andrea 683
Chang, Patricia 106, 314
Charles, Maria 259
Chen, Shaohua 713
Cherubini, Arnaldo 7 n4
Chi, Iris 381
Chimerine, Lawrence 431
Choi, James J 692
Christensen, Torn 162
Christiansen, Niels Finn 588, 589, 590, 592
Christopher, Karen 259
Churchill, Winston 7, 84
Clapham, David 490
Clark, Janine A 276
Clark, John M 432
Clasen, Jochen 54, 213, 437, 445, 691, 702
Clayton, Richard 558, 559, 561
Clegg, Daniel 54, 611, 615
Clinton, Bill 53
Cloward, Richard A 287
Cockett, Richard 47, 48
Cohen, Gerald A 24, 26, 28, 29
Collier, David 105, 112, 119
Collini, Stefan 4 n3
Comas-Herrera, Adelina 388
Commander, Simon 544, 545
Compston, Hugh 198
Condorcet, Marquis de 38
Conley, Dalton 491
Connell, Raewyn 253, 255, 256
Cook, Fay L 243
Cook, Linda J 327 n3, 673, 675, 678
Cornia, Giovanni Andrea 1
Coughlin, Richard 243
Cousins, Mel 275
Cowles, Maria Green 305
Cox, Robert H 47, 56
Cox, Rosie 282
Crafts, Nicholas 543
Crepaz, Marcus M L 190, 237, 285–6, 286, 531

Croissant, Aurel 578
Crompton, Rosemary 260
Crosland, Anthony 43
Crouch, Colin 140, 198, 203
Crowley, Stephen 676
Crozier, Michael 9
Cruz-Saco, Maria Amparo 648
Cuenca, A 651
Cusack, Thomas R 6, 12, 118, 178, 186, 193, 194, 238, 247, 249, 324, 342
Cutright, Phillips 112, 552

Daatland, Svein O 384
Dahrendorf, Ralf 54
Daly, Mary 141, 148, 257, 258, 378, 380, 381, 441, 442, 592
Darity, William 430
Da Roit, Barbara 387
Daunton, Martin J 4 n3
Daveri, Francesco 549
Davie, Grace 268
Davis, Deborah S 667
Davoudi, Simin 172
Day, Lincoln 515
Deacon, Alan 51, 53
Deacon, Bob 10, 97, 310, 312, 314, 315, 316, 579, 676, 711
Dean, Hartley 182, 397
De Búrca, Gráinne 296
De Decker, Pascal 488
De Ferranti, David 647, 650
De Grazia, Victoria 7 n4
De la Maisonneuve, Christine 388
De la Rica, Sara 623
Del Boca, Daniela 623
d'Ercole, Mira 172, 530
Devereaux, P J 373
Devine, Joe 709
Deviney Stanley 515
Diamandouros, Nikiforos P 621
Diamond, Peter A 89, 91, 354, 692
Dickens, Charles 3
Dilnot, Andrew 439
Dimaggio, Paul J 158
Dingeldey, Irene 344, 441, 442
Dion, Michelle 646, 648
Disney, Richard 123, 134–5, 138

Dispersyn, Michel 299
Di Tella, Rafael 541
Dixit, Avinash K 187 n1
Docteur, Elizabeth 372
Dodson, Jago 490
Doling, John 485
Dølvik, Jon Arne 599
Donselaar, Gijs van 22
Dorwart, Reinhold A 63
Douglas, Roger 46
Douglas, Tommy xxvii
Dowrick, Steve 543, 633
Doyal, Len 171
Doyle, Martha 383
Drazen, Allen 542, 545
Driffill, John 548, 550
Dryzek, John S 7, 79
Duensing, Martin 472, 473
Dunleavy, Patrick 244
Durkheim, Émile 154–5
Dworkin, Gerald 21, 30
Dworkin, Ronald 24, 25

Eardley, Tony 450, 453, 460
Easterly, William 544, 545
Ebbinghaus, Bernhard 198, 199, 200, 201, 203, 205, 206, 207, 208, 236–7, 322, 437, 458, 574, 607
Eckstein, Harry 113, 369
Edlund, Jonas 245
Eekelaar, John 700
Eggleston, Karen 373
Eichhorst, Werner 444, 446, 447
Einerhand, Marcel 122, 130, 133
Eisenstadt, Shmuel 618
Eliason, Scott 442
Elkins, Zachary 315
Ellingsaeter, Anne L 142–3, 257, 260
Ellison, Nicholas 691, 697
Ellwood, David T 690
Elsinga, Marja 489
Eltis, Walter 540, 541
Elwan, Ann 408
Engels, Karl 3
England, Paula 257, 258, 380
Epstein, Jessica 111
Erhard, Ludwig 42

Erikson, Robert 501, 590

Ervasti, Heikki 589

Ervik, Rune 316

Esping-Andersen, Gøsta 9, 13, 19–20, 23, 44, 76, 82, 89, 90, 94, 96, 98, 105, 106, 116, 117, 120, 141, 142, 153, 160, 174–5, 178, 185, 187, 188, 197–8, 216, 220, 223, 229, 245, 253, 254, 255, 269–70, 272, 273 276, 282, 292, 334, 395, 399, 404, 436, 442, 451, 463, 468, 481, 482, 485, 491, 494, 496, 503, 507, 513, 514, 516, 518, 522–3, 529, 540, 552, 569, 570–2, 573, 577, 581, 582–3, 586, 588, 590, 592, 593, 601, 606, 608, 609, 632–3, 635, 637, 645 n1, 658, 673, 684, 690

Estévez-Abe, Margarita 193, 198, 238, 258, 259, 432, 494, 540

Eucken, Walter 42

Evans, Geoffrey 245

Ewald, François 33, 603

Ewig, Christina 648

Fahey, Tom 489, 491

Faist, Thomas 281

Falkingham, Jane 535

Falkner, Gerda 293, 296, 298, 302 n3

Featherstone, Kevin 618

Feldstein, Martin S 344

Fenge, Robert 693

Fenger, H J M 579

Ferge, Zsuzsa 674, 675, 697

Ferrarini, Tommy 518 n4, 524 n8

Ferrera, Maurizio 82, 97, 217, 299, 304, 305, 436, 452, 485, 491, 503, 573, 579, 617, 618, 619, 620, 621, 622, 623, 624, 625

Ferrero-Waldner, Benita 717

Feser, Edward S 46, 47

Fideler, Paul A 449

Fidler, David P 375

Field, Mark G 368

Figart, Deborah M 260

Filgueria, Carlos H 646

Filgueria, Fernando 646

Finch, Janet 699

Finch, Naomi 470, 532

Finkelstein, Vic 408

Fisher, Anthony 47

Fitzgerald, Joan 443

Fitzpatrick, Tony 56

Flaquer, Lluís 622, 623

Fligstein, Neil 199

Flora, Peter 2, 61, 66, 67, 69, 70, 78, 84, 93, 94, 198, 207, 216, 229, 270–1, 394

Fogel, Robert 545

Forssen, Katja 473

Förster, Michael F 172, 528, 531

Franzese, Robert J 185, 329, 541, 550

Fraser, Nancy 10, 21, 171, 174, 262

Frazier, Mark W 667

Freeden, Michael 34, 37

Freeman, Kendralin 118

Freeman, Richard 368 n1, 377

Freidson, Eliot 369

Frieden, Jeffry A 323

Friedman, Lawrence M 394, 395

Friedman, Milton 9, 45, 46, 47, 430, 540

Frisina, Lorraine 377

Fritzell, Johan 591

Gallie, Duncan 621

Gamble, Andrew 49

Ganghof, Steffen 328

Gangl, Markus 432

Gans-Morse, Jordan 676–7, 678, 680, 681, 684

Garfinkel, Irwin 698

Garrett, Geoffrey 193, 199, 320, 321, 324, 327, 342, 654

Gauthier, Anne H 141, 142, 477, 518, 519

Gavanas, Anna 283

Gelissen, John 245, 569, 572, 574 n1, 582

Genschel, Philipp 328

George, Alexander L 106, 113

Gerdtham, Ulf-G 372

Gerhardsen, Einar xxvii

Gerring, John 106, 113, 116

Gerven, Minna van 404

Giaimo, Susan 208

Gibb, Kenneth 489

Giddens, Anthony 44, 53–4, 96, 496, 507, 716

Gilbert, Neil 122, 255

Giles, Christopher 560

Gill, Anthony 266, 268

Gill, Indermit Singh 366

Gingrich, Daniel W 540

Ginneken, Wouter van 161, 162
Ginsburg, Helen 435
Gintis, Herbert 248 n3, 437
Giraudy, Agustina 651
Glaeser, Edward L 13, 188, 284, 457, 699
Glatzer, Miguel 654
Glazer, Nathan 8
Gleeson, Brendan 408
Glendinning, Caroline 384
Glenn, Evelyn N 260
Glennerster, Howard 695
Glick Schiller, Nina 278
Glyn, Andrew 719
Goffman, Erving 163
Golden, Miriam 550
Goldsmith, Arthur 430
Goldstein, Judith L 315
Goldwater, Barry 47
Golinowska, Stanislaw 676, 680, 685
Gómez Sabaini, Juan Carlos 649
Gompers, Samuel xxvii
Goodhart, David 284
Goodin, Robert E 2, 7, 10, 24, 27, 31, 79,
    108, 161, 171, 172, 176, 580, 583
Gooding, Caroline 416
Goodman, Roger 577, 657, 659
Gordon, Margaret 395, 396
Gornick, Janet 260, 441, 442, 517–18
Gorski, Philip S 267, 268
Goss, David 416
Gottschalk, Peter 531, 534 n3
Goudswaard, Kees Pieter 136
Gough, Ian 10, 52, 171, 228, 450, 460, 577,
    634–5, 656, 689, 690, 704, 711, 717
Goul Andersen, Jorgen 48, 51, 54, 56, 457
Gould, Andrew C 267
Gourevitch, Peter 321
Green, Richard K 489
Green, Thomas H 28, 37, 38
Greene, William H 115
Green-Pedersen, Christoffer 54, 55
Greer, Scott L 376
Gregory, Robert 46
Greve, Bent 416, 599
Griffin, Larry J 113, 114, 115
Grimmer-Solem, Erik 35
Grubb, David 547

Gruber, Jonathan 268, 415
Grusky, David B 259
Gualmini, Elisabetta 625
Guillén, Anna M 621, 624, 625, 626, 627
Guiraudon, Virginie 280
Gujarati, Damodar 115
Gulbrandsen, Lars 482, 489, 491
Gunther, Richard 616
Gusmano, Michael K 377

Ha, Eunyoung 325
Haas, Martine R 679
Haas, Peter M 313
Hacker, Jacob S 39, 56, 87, 96, 97, 98, 122, 198,
    236, 238, 239, 338, 364, 370, 504, 559
Haggard, Stephan 88, 89, 96, 119, 209, 314,
    318, 322, 327, 328, 646, 656, 673, 674, 676,
    680, 685
Hakim, Catherine 178, 255
Halfmann, Drew 108, 119, 120
Halfmann, Jost 280
Hall, Peter 91, 117, 192, 198, 226, 322, 540, 545,
    550, 574, 635
Hammond, Peter 542
Handler, Joel F 459
Haney, Lynne A 255
Hansen, Erik 590
Hansen, Johan 441
Hansson, Pär 545
Hansson, Per Albin 39, 40
Hanusch, Ferdinand xxvii
Hara, Junsuke 659
Haraway, Donna J 252
Harding, Ann 535
Harloe, Michael 479, 480, 485, 489
Harris, Bernard 33, 38
Harris, José 80
Hartman, Paul T 197
Hassel, Anke 199, 205, 206, 208, 236–7, 316
Häusermann, Silja 607
Hay, Colin 53, 320
Hayek, Friedrich August von 9, 27, 44, 45,
    46–7, 49
Hays, Jude 329
Heckman, James J 547, 548, 551
Heclo, Hugh 33, 45, 116, 198, 230
Hedborg, Anna 592

Hega, Gunther M 4
Hegedüs, József 482
Heidenheimer, Arnold J 4, 117, 207, 266, 495, 501, 503, 505, 506, 507
Heien, Thorsten 245, 246
Hein, Wolfgang 377
Heise, David R 114
Hellwig, Martin F 15
Hellwig, Timothy T 330
Helpman, Elhanan 699
Hemerijck, Anton 436, 437, 446, 563, 613, 624
Henderson, J Vernon 481, 492
Hennock, Ernest P 5, 36, 41, 64, 67
Henrekson, Magnus 545
Herlofson, Katharina 384
Hernández, Diego 647
Hernes, Helga M 591
Herren, Madeleine 6 n4
Hetling, Andrea 457
Hibbs, Douglas A 211
Hicks, Alexander 105, 106, 109, 112, 117, 118, 119, 120, 186, 216, 220, 236, 322, 323, 324, 325, 342, 445, 515, 516, 574, 581
Higgins, Henry B 638
Hills, John 172, 528, 529, 532, 535
Himmelweit, Susan 260
Hinnfors, Jonas 319 n1
Hinrichs, Karl 355, 361, 364, 610, 613
Hirst, Paul 30
Hitris, Theo 372
Hobsbawm, Eric J 1, 83
Hobson, Barbara 258, 259, 260, 261
Hockerts, Hans Günter 217, 220
Hoekman, Bernard M 310, 311
Hoeller, Peter 490 n3
Hofmeister, Herbert 394, 399
Hokenmaier, Karl G 4
Holliday, Ian 656, 659
Holmes, Rebecca 460
Holmlund, Bertil 430
Holzman, Robert 647
Hopkins, Daniel J 314
Hopper, Earl I 499
Hornemann Møller, Iver 444
Hort, Sven E O 578, 707
Hoskyns, Catherine 294
Hotz, V Joseph 439

Howard, Christopher 96, 122, 338
Huber, Evelyne 54, 55, 88, 95, 106, 116, 117, 118, 119, 120, 174, 185, 191, 198, 211, 215, 217, 236, 238, 239, 246, 254, 261, 269, 270, 318, 319 n1, 322, 324, 327, 328, 342, 494, 516, 518, 523, 552, 578, 601, 604, 647, 648, 649, 650, 654
Huberman, Michael 321, 323
Hudson, John 463, 477
Huerta, Carmen 178
Hüfner, Felix 488
Hugo, Victor 4
Hulme, David 460
Hungerman, Daniel M 268
Hunt, W Ben 215, 226, 275
Hunter, Wendy 327, 328, 651
Huntington, Samuel P 230
Huo, Jingjing 523, 525
Hurst, William 667
Hutton, Will 54
Hvinden, Björn 411, 600

Iankova, Elena A 679
Ikegami, Naoki 381, 384, 399
Immergut, Ellen M 116, 199, 204, 231, 232, 236, 368, 370, 399, 400, 552
Inglehart, Ronald 268
Inglot, Tomasz 672, 673, 674, 676
Ingram, Alan 376
Ingstad, Benedicte 408
Ioannides, Yannis M 481, 492
Isaac, Larry W 113, 114, 115
Isuani, Ernesto Aldo 645
Iversen, Torben 12, 55, 118, 120, 178, 186, 191, 193, 194, 238, 247, 249, 271, 272, 273, 322, 324, 342, 494, 495, 496, 498, 503, 516, 518, 522, 541, 550, 637

Jacobzone, Stephane 387
Jaeger, Mads Meier 45, 245, 248, 582 n2
Jahn, Detlef 315, 325, 329
Jahoda, Marie 437
James, Harold 5
Janoski, Thomas 115, 513 n1
Jäntti, Markus 530, 537
Jaumotte, Florence 442
Jensen, Laura 15, 38

Jenson, Jane 148, 257
Jenssen, Anders T 244 n2
Jessop, Bob 56, 552
Joerges, Christian 304
Johansson, Håkan 600
Johnson, Chalmers 660
Johnson, Louise C 163
Johnson, Paul 560
Jones, Bradford S 119
Jones, Catherine 577, 657
Jönsson, Bengt 372
Jonsson, Jan O 501
Joseph, Keith 48
Joshi, Heather 258
Jost, Timothy Stolzfus 375
Jowell, Roger 250
Judis, John B 47, 48
Judt, Tony 15

Kaase, Max 244
Kahn, Alfred J 141
Kalyvas, Stathis 274
Kamerman, Sheila B 141
Kangas, Olli E 76, 399, 401, 429, 516,
    522, 575, 587, 591, 596
Kasser, Tim 718
Kasza, Gregory J 572, 577, 590, 656
Kato, Junko 544, 560
Katz, Lawrence 430
Katzenstein, Peter J 193, 198, 320
Kaufman, Robert R 88, 89, 96, 119,
    209, 314, 318, 322, 326, 327, 646,
    648, 650, 654, 656, 673, 674,
    676, 680, 685
Kaufmann, Franz-Xaver 3 n2, 5, 6, 7, 11,
    84, 90, 96, 141, 149, 266, 495
Kautto, Mikko 592, 596, 599
Kay, Stephen J 236, 648
Kazamias, George 618
Keman, Hans 211
Kemeny, Jim 482, 485, 490
Kemmerling, Achim 427
Kemp, Peter A 384
Kenworthy, Lane 112, 178, 342, 436,
    437, 442, 444, 445, 446, 531, 532,
    534, 574
Kerr, Clark 197, 393

Kersbergen, Kees van 36, 45, 66, 76, 99, 189,
    217, 238, 267, 270, 272 n1, 350, 399, 504, 505,
    571, 582, 604
Keynes, John Maynard 34, 40
Kickbusch, Ilona 376
Kildal, Nanna 51, 52, 100, 313, 589
Kilkey, Majella 259
King, Desmond 45, 46, 47, 50–1, 52–3, 54, 57
King, Gary 113, 114
Kingma, Mireille 283
Kitschelt, Herbert 52, 247
Kittel, Bernhard 324, 342, 550
Kjoenstad, Asbjørn 165
Klein, Mitchel 119
Klein, Rudolf 10, 697
Kleinbaum, David G 119
Kline, Donna S 283
Klingemann, Hans-Dieter 2, 100
Kloosterman, Robert C 281
Knijn, Trudie 257, 260, 263, 384
Kocka, Jürgen 240, 555
Kohl, Jürgen 456, 592
Kohli, Martin 175, 178, 248 n3, 608
Kohlmorgen, Lars 377
Kok, Wim 436, 437
Kolberg, Jon Eivind 590
Kolstrup, Søren 400
Konle-Seidl, Regina 444, 446
Koo, Hagen 659
Koopmans, Ruud 284
Kormendi, Roger C 544
Kornai, Jànos 673, 676
Korpi, Walter 40, 49, 76, 87, 90, 94, 106, 123,
    135, 156, 161, 174, 185, 197, 216, 222, 229, 246,
    254, 259, 261, 262, 269, 324, 335, 369, 399,
    402, 421, 428, 431, 433, 456, 512, 515, 516, 522,
    524, 534, 537, 543, 552, 558, 560, 561, 563, 573,
    579, 580, 581, 583, 586, 588, 590, 591
Koven, Seth 263
Kramer, Gerald H 187
Kremer, Monique 257, 260, 263, 384
Kriesi, Hanspeter 330
Kristol, Irving 47–8
Kröger, Sandra 295
Kuhnle, Stein 65, 66, 68, 69, 100, 400, 578,
    580, 588, 589, 596, 707
Kume, Ikuo 659

Kumlin, Staffan 242 n1, 248
Kuyper, Abraham 36
Kvist, Jon 45, 596, 599
Kwon, Hyeok Yong 325
Kwon, Soonman 660
Kymlicka, Will 13, 284, 285, 288

Ladaique, Maxime 122, 128 n4, 133, 488 n2
Ladinsky, Jack 394, 395
Laegereid, Per 162
Lamura, Giovanni 385
Landau, Daniel L 543
Landes, David S 65
Lange, Peter 193, 321
Laroque, Pierre 33, 43
Larsen, Christian A 48, 51, 54, 56, 245
Lash, Scott 198
Laver, Michael 186, 213, 215, 226, 275
Layard, Richard 344, 430, 437,
    442, 546
Layson, John 503
Lazaridis, Gabriella 281
Lazear, Edward P 547
Lebeaux, Charles N 197
Le Bihan, Blanche 146
Lee, Cheol-Sung 650
Lee, Dwight R 319
Lee, Eddy 85
Lee, Kelley 376
Lee, Yean-Ju 664
Le Grand, Julian 10, 30–1, 161, 162, 531
Lehmbruch, Gerhard 200
Lehto, Juhani 592
Leibfried, Stephan xxiii, xxviii, 3, 5, 11, 15,
    99, 162, 199, 221, 266, 267, 297, 299, 302,
    303, 304, 315, 319 n1, 376, 449, 451,
    494, 495, 500, 502, 507, 573, 574,
    634, 709
Leira, Arnlaug 142–3, 257, 260, 261
Leisering, Lutz 460
Leitner, Sigrid 142, 182
Lenoir, Rémi 142
Lessenich, Stephan 182
Leung, Joe C 460
Levy, Jonah 562
Lewchuck, Wayne 321, 323
Lewis, Graham 376

Lewis, Jane 51, 53, 54, 141, 144, 145, 178, 254,
    257, 260, 261, 294, 384, 480, 573, 592, 607,
    635, 674, 683, 702
Lewis, Richard 374
Lewis-Beck, Michael S 186
Lieberman, Robert C 240
Light, Donald W 370
Lijphart, Arend 231
Lindbeck, Assar 48, 54, 587, 690, 696
Lindbom, Anders 52
Lindén, Tord Skogedal 315
Lindert, Peter H 5–6, 34, 134, 135, 185, 193,
    323, 333, 450, 503, 539, 540, 542, 544,
    546–7, 650, 651
Lindh, Thomas 436
Lindholm, Marika 261
Lingsom, Susan 155–6
Linna, Väinö xxvii
Lipsmeyer, Christine S 676
Lister, Ruth 54, 96, 263, 468
Lloyd George, David xxviii
Locke, Richard 562
Lødemel, Ivar 163, 444, 458, 695
Lohmann, Theodor 33, 36
Londregan, John 187 n1
Lora, Eduardo 649
Lorenzo, Rafael de 411
Lowe, Stuart 463, 477, 490
Lubove, Roy 394
Lucas, Robert E 542
Luhmann, Niklas 213
Lundahl, Lisbeth 501
Lundberg, Olle 587
Lundsgaard, Jens 488
Lundsgaarde, Erik 268
Lunt, Neil 415
Lustick, Ian 114, 117
Lutz, Helma 260, 282
Lynch, Julia 238, 271, 355, 358, 360, 635

Mabbett, Deborah 298, 414, 419, 704
McCallum, John 543
McCrae, Julian 439
MacCulloch, Robert 541
Machado, Santiago M 411
McKee, Martin 375–6
McKenzie, Richard B 319

Maclean, Mavis 702
McLellan, D Lindsay 408
McQuaid, Kim 394
Macray, Duncan 194
Maddison, Angus 542
Madrid, Raúl L 647
Madsen, Per K 447
Mahon, Rianne 143, 260
Mahoney, James 114
Maier-Rigaud, Remi 316
Maioni, Antonia 236, 238, 401
Maître, Bertrand 489
Malefakis, Edward 618
Malloy, James M 645
Mandel, Hadas 259
Mann, Michael 640
Manning, Chris 667
Manning, Nick 671, 674, 675, 678, 683
Manow, Philip 36, 65, 66, 99, 189, 198, 208,
    217, 226, 238, 267, 269, 271, 272 n1, 275, 322,
    505, 563, 574, 604
Manza, Jeff 248, 249, 580
March, James G 230
Marcussen, Martin 311, 313, 315
Mares, Isabela 193, 194, 198, 209, 322, 539,
    540, 545, 548, 549, 550, 574, 603
Marinakis, Andrés 653
Markkola, Pirjo 588, 589, 592
Marmor, Theodore R 9, 368 n1, 371
Marsh, David C 62, 63
Marshall, Katherine 308, 309, 312, 316, 317
Marshall, T H xxv, 21, 42, 64, 78, 85,
    153, 198–9, 496, 504, 508, 511, 512–13,
    709
Martens, Kerstin 311, 313, 317
Martin, Andrew 303
Martin, Cathie Jo 194, 198, 238, 239, 318
Martin, Claude 98, 146, 395, 610
Martin, David 275
Martin, John 122, 446, 535
Martínez Franzoni, Juliana 646, 648
Martinussen, Willy 244 n2
Marx, Ive 440, 613
Marx, Karl 514, 602
Mason, Timothy W 7 n4
Matheson, George 245
Matsaganis, Manos 622, 624, 627

Mau, Steffan xxiii, 3, 15, 221, 246, 248 n3,
    249, 574
Mavroidis, Petros C 310, 311
Mayda, Anna M 329
Mayer, Karl Ulrich 175
Mayhew, David R 108
Mayhew, Emese 466, 470
Mead, Lawrence 9, 21, 45, 50, 51, 76
Mechanic, David 369
Meguire, Philip G 544
Meidner, Rudolf 592
Meltzer, Allan H 185
Mendoza, Enrique G 543–4
Merkel, Wolfgang 216
Merrill, Vance 633
Mesa-Lago, Carmelo 645, 646, 648
Messere, Ken C 344
Messick, Richard 105, 112, 119
Mettler, Suzanne 247–8
Meyer, Thomas 220
Meyers, Marcia 260, 441, 442, 518
Michel, Sonya 263
Mickelwright, John 430, 640
Milesi-Ferretti, Gian M 190
Millar, Jane 697
Miller, Mark J 279, 280, 284
Milly, Deborah J 661
Mingione, Enzo 282
Minogue, Martin 162
Misra, Joya 258, 342, 581
Mitchell, Deborah 137, 199, 246, 324, 400,
    451, 573, 634, 640
Mjøset, Lars 590
Moene, Karl Ove 185, 592
Mogensen, Gunnar V 528
Molen, Irina van der 683
Molina, Carlos Gerardo 647
Mommsen, Wolfgang 80
Moore, Mick 715
Moran, Michael 368, 369, 370
Morel, Nathalie 386, 614
Moreno, Luis 619, 622, 623, 626
Morgan, Kimberly J 147, 255, 260, 272, 622
Morissens, Ann 456
Morlino, Leonhardo 617
Mortensen, Dale T 430
Mosley, Layna 323, 324, 326

Moss, David A 39
Mossialos, Elias 627
Mueller, Dennis C 161, 690
Müller, Katharina 91, 363, 647, 674
Müller, Walter 499
Müller-Armack, Alfred 42
Murray, Charles A 9, 45, 50, 51, 156, 690
Mustillo, Thomas 328
Mutari, Ellen 260
Myles, John 112, 173, 229, 278, 286, 355,
    364, 491, 515, 522, 526
Myrdal, Gunnar 9 n6, 40, 44, 47

Naldini, Manuela 622
Napoleon III 65
Nash, George H 46
Natali, David 236
Naumann, Ingela K 240, 607
Navarro, Vicente 369
Neave, Guy 502
Nelson, Joan M 648
Nelson, Kenneth 453 n1, 456
Nelson, Moira L 521, 525
Newton, Kenneth 244
Neyer, Gerda 462
Nguyen, Duc-Tho 633
Nickell, Stephen J 430, 442, 547
Niskanen, William A 690
Nixon, John 372
Nixon, Richard M 47
Nolan, Brian 530
Nooruddin, Irfan 313
Nørby-Johansen, Lars 400
Nordlund, Anders 596
Norris, Michelle 485
Norris, Pippa 268
North, Douglas C 189 n3, 192
Norton, Edward C 382–3, 386,
    387, 388
Novikova, Irina 683
Nozick, Robert 27, 29
Nunziata, Luca 430
Nussbaum, Martha 28, 171
Nygard, Michael 222

Oates, Wallace E 372
Oberlander, Jonathan 9

Obinger, Herbert 5, 119, 136, 186, 187, 191, 192,
    195, 216, 221, 222, 236, 237, 238, 299, 305, 314,
    324, 342, 343, 392, 401, 506, 534, 575, 576,
    579, 580, 611, 613, 634, 636, 637, 684
O'Connor, James 10, 690
O'Connor, Julia S 117–18, 141, 143, 253, 254,
    256, 258, 261, 264, 573, 635
O'Donnel, Guillermo 616
Oeppen, Jim 699
Offe, Claus 10, 52, 200, 228, 555, 676, 685, 690
Oftedal Telhaug, Alfred 500, 501, 504
Ohman, Berndt 435
Oliveira Martins, Joaquim 388
Oliver, Michael 406, 407, 408
Olsen, Johan P 230
Olson, Mancur 157, 200
Olsson, Sven E 400
Oorschot, Wim van 244 n2, 268, 285, 411, 457
Orenstein, Mitchell A 363, 674, 676–7, 678,
    679, 680, 681, 684, 685
Orloff, Ann Shola 67, 106, 116, 144, 230, 253,
    254, 256, 257, 258, 259, 260, 261, 262, 263,
    264, 401, 442, 512, 513, 514, 573, 635
Orsini, Kristian 440
Osberg, Lars 529
Ost, David 676
Osterhammel, Jürgen 83
Österle, August 382
Ostner, Ilona 294
Ostrom, Charles W 115
O'Sullivan, Eoin 488
Ours, Jan C van 344, 430
Overbye, Einar 159, 460
Oxley, Howard 372

Pages, Carmen 547, 548, 551
Paine, Thomas 22
Palier, Bruno 43, 98, 271, 275, 395, 442, 582,
    610, 611, 613, 614, 615
Palme, Joakim 49, 69, 87, 90, 94, 123, 135, 161,
    222, 246, 324, 335, 402, 421, 428, 429, 431,
    433, 436, 456, 516, 522, 524, 537, 558, 560,
    561, 563, 573, 581, 583, 587, 591, 597
Pampel, Fred C 106, 112, 120, 236, 360
Panofsky, Aaron 109
Papadakis, Elim 245
Papadópulos, Jorge 645

Papatheodorou, Christos 622
Parijs, Philippe Van xxix, 21, 22
Parreñas, Rhacel Salazar 260
Parsons, Talcott 141, 155
Pascall, Gillian 674, 683
Pateman, Carole 34
Paugam, Serge 621
Pavalko, Eliza 394
Pavolini, Emmanuele 381, 386
Peacock, Alan T 7, 79
Pearson, Mark 122, 440, 531
Pedersen, Susan 36, 142, 263
Pempel, T J 659, 662
Peng, Ito 399, 577, 659, 660, 663, 670
Peréz-Diaz, Victor 619
Perkins, Frances xxvi
Perrin, Guy 65, 75, 78
Persson, Torsten 190, 231
Peters, B Guy 345, 348
Petersen, Klaus 590
Petmesidou, Maria 617, 622, 625, 627
Pettit, Philipp 27, 29
Pfeifer, Michaela 457
Phelps, Edmund S 437
Piachaud, David 470
Pickett, Kate 698
Pierson, Christopher 34, 40, 42, 44, 82,
    84, 87, 173, 588
Pierson, Paul 11, 14, 82, 99, 106, 109, 114, 116,
    117, 119, 159, 174, 191, 194, 221, 239, 247, 297,
    303, 317, 326, 355, 364, 370, 404, 457, 480,
    524, 553, 554, 556, 557, 558, 559, 561, 563, 564,
    565, 580, 601, 609, 691
Pinker, Robert A 164
Pioppi, Daniela 276
Piva, Italo 7 n4
Piven, Frances Fox 287
Plantenga, Janneke 380, 441, 622
Play, Frederic le 36
Plickert, Philip 9
Plümper, Thomas 118, 328
Pochet, Philippe 295
Polanyi, Karl 3, 4, 5, 192 n5, 320, 449, 514, 602
Pontusson, Jonas 52, 105, 186, 193, 325, 558,
    559, 561
Pooley, Colin G 479
Porte, Caroline de la 295

Porter, Dorothy 368
Porter, Michael E 710
Potrafke, Niklas 342
Powell, Bingham 186
Powell, Martin 53, 574–5, 576
Powell, Walter W 158
Power, Timothy 651
Pribble, Jennifer 646, 649, 652
Priestley, Mark 407, 408, 409
Prinz, Christopher 411
Przeworski, Adam 116, 399, 552
Putnam, Robert D 317, 698

Quadagno, Jill S 155, 173, 248, 398, 401
Queisser, Monika 123
Quine, Maria S 7 n4
Quinn, Dennis 327

Rae, David 490 n3
Ragin, Charles 109, 110, 112, 114, 236, 575
Rainwater, Lee 122
Rake, Katherine 141
Ramesh, Mishra 316, 666
Ranci, Costanzo 381, 386
Randall, Ed 376
Ravaillon, Martin 713
Raventós, Daniel 21, 27
Rawlings, Laura B 651
Rawls, John 22, 24
Razin, Assaf 543–4
Reagan, Ronald 45, 47, 82, 262, 553, 691
Rebelo, Sergio 544, 545
Recker, Marie-Luise 7
Rehm, Philipp 247
Rehn, Gösta 435
Reich, Michael R 377
Rein, Martin 122, 580
Revillard, Anne 142
Reynaert, Jelle 416
Reynolds, Morgan 532
Reynolds White, Susan 408
Rhodes, Martin 198, 236, 562, 617, 625
Richard, Scott F 185
Richardson, Dominic 475
Rieger, Elmar xxviii, 5, 99, 199, 266, 267,
    319 n1, 709
Riker, William H 188

Riley, Dylan 640
Rimlinger, Gaston V 4, 6, 63, 64, 65, 67, 68, 93, 120, 395
Ringen, Stein 530
Risse, Thomas 305
Ritakallio, Veli-Matti 473, 491
Ritter, Gerhard A 35, 220, 394, 398, 399
Robertson, Ann 174
Robinson, James A 194
Rochefort, David A 369
Rodden, Jonathan A 191, 237
Rodgers, Daniel T 1, 33, 39, 41
Rödl, Florian 304
Rodrigues, Ricardo 413
Rodriguez, Juan C 619
Rodríguez, Juan Manuel 653
Rodriguez-Clare, Andres 542
Rodrik, Dani 156, 185, 321, 325, 326
Roemer, John E 26, 188
Rogers, Joel 201
Rogowski, Ronald 194, 321
Rokkan, Stein 4
Roland, Richard 482
Roller, Edeltraut 243
Roninger, Luis 618
Rønsen, Marit 446
Room, Graham 155, 513, 514
Roosevelt, Franklin D xxvi, 7, 41, 84, 85, 230
Rosamond, Ben 320
Rose, Hilary 121
Rose, Richard 211
Rosenbluth, Frances McCall 190
Ross, Arthur M 197
Ross, Fiona 53, 54
Ross, George 297, 303
Ross, Michael 185
Rossi, Nicola di 625
Rothgang, Heinz 208, 305, 372, 374, 377, 381, 579
Rothschild, Emma 38
Rothstein, Bo 23, 156, 186, 207, 239, 456
Rubio, Gloria M 651
Rudra, Nita 319 n1, 322, 327, 328, 571, 577, 654
Rueda, David 57, 222
Rueschemeyer, Dietrich 65, 107, 113, 117, 654
Rueschemeyer, Marilyn 683
Ruggie, John 320–1

Ruhm, Christopher J 473
Ruonavaara, Hannu 485
Ryner, Magnus 290

Sacchi, Stefano 625
Sackett, David L 375
Sainsbury, Diane 260, 261, 262, 281, 441, 442, 456, 573
Saint-Arnaud, Sébastien 278, 286, 575
Saint-Jours, Yves 396
Sala-I-Martin, Xavier 542, 545
Salminen, Karl 590
Sapelli, Giulio 618
Saraceno, Chiara 262, 388, 622
Saunders, Peter 243, 244
Saunier, Pierre-Yves 41
Savage, Michael Joseph xxvii
Sawer, Marian 38
Scanlon, Kathleen 488, 490
Scarbrough, Elinor 179, 244
Scarpetta, Stefano 440
Schäfer, Armin 295, 315
Scharpf, Fritz W 10, 11, 12, 13, 191, 296, 297, 299, 302, 303, 304, 319, 436, 446, 541, 592, 601, 609
Schelkle, Waltraud 298
Scheve, Kenneth 268
Schierup, Carl-Ulrik 279, 282, 286–7, 288, 289, 290
Schludi, Martin 199, 236
Schmid, Achim 373
Schmidt, Manfred G 211, 215, 216, 217, 220, 221, 228, 236, 269, 342, 501, 506, 633, 636
Schmidt, Susanne K 303
Schmidt, Vivien A 303, 436, 446, 541, 601, 609
Schmitter, Philippe C 200, 201, 550
Schofield, Norman 186
Scholz, John Karl 439
Schram, Sanford F 248
Schröder, Martin 576, 582
Schubert, Klaus 571, 581
Schuknecht, Ludger 134, 333
Schumpeter, Joseph A 241
Schwab, Klaus 710
Schwartz, Herman 560, 561
Scott, Joan W 253

Scruggs, Lyle A 89, 98, 105, 106, 186, 220, 222, 246, 318, 324, 402, 517, 523, 524, 571, 574, 576, 634, 636

Seeleib-Kaiser, Martin 213, 217, 220, 319 n1, 615

Sefton, Tom 696, 698

Segura-Ubiergo, Alex 89, 209, 319 n1, 322, 326–7, 328, 578, 646, 649, 650, 654

Seiyama, Kazuo 659

Selden, Mark 667

Semyonov, Moshe 259

Sen, Amartya Kumar 20, 28, 171, 172, 530

Senti, Martin 313, 315, 316

Shakespeare, Tom 408

Shalev, Michael 205, 259, 574, 575

Shaver, Sheila 263

Shaw, Jo 296

Shima, Isilda 413

Shinkawa, Toshimitsu 664

Shipper, Apichai W 664

Shonfield, Andrew 552

Siaroff, Alan 573

Siegel, Nico A 205, 213, 222, 223, 636

Sierminska, Eva 527

Silverman, Elaine M 373

Simmons, Beth A 307, 314, 315, 329

Simmons, Joel W 313

Simonazzi, Annamaria 283

Sindbjerg Martinsen, Dorte 303

Sinfield, Adrian 122

Sinha, Tapen 648

Sipilä, Jorma 258, 380, 592, 635

Sissenich, Beate 679

Sjöberg, Ola 429

Skarohamar, Torbjørn 446

Skinner, Quentin 27, 29

Skocpol, Theda 38, 39, 65, 67, 76, 106, 108, 109, 113, 114, 117, 120, 229–30, 263, 396, 401, 555

Sleebos, Joëlle 472

Smeeding, Timothy M 529, 531, 534, 537, 633, 698

Smith, Adam 20, 319, 345

Smith, Daniel A 350

Smith, Lawrence B 481

Smolensky, Eugene 532

Snidal, Duncan 315

Snyder, James M 187

Solana, Javier 717

Somers, Margaret 108, 109

Soper, Kate 171

Soskice, David 185, 186, 191, 192, 193, 194, 198, 226, 238, 247, 249, 272, 273, 322, 545, 574, 635, 636, 637

Soss, Joe 247–8

Sotiropoulos, Dimitri 623, 628

Spalding, Rose J 645

Staerklé, Christian 244 n2

Standing, Guy 199

Starke, Peter 94, 223, 305, 318, 342, 558, 561, 563, 579

Starr, Peter 368, 369

Stasavage, David 268

Stearns, Peter N 353

Stearns, Sally C 388

Steele, Gerald R 46

Steiner, Hillel 22

Steinmo, Sven 116, 117, 328

Stephens, John 54, 55, 88, 95, 106, 116, 117, 118, 120, 174, 185, 191, 198, 211, 215, 217, 229, 236, 239, 246, 254, 261, 269, 270, 318, 319 n1, 320 n2, 322, 328, 342, 494, 495, 496, 498, 503, 515, 516, 517, 518, 522, 523, 525, 586, 601, 604, 647, 648, 649

Stern, Nicholas 697, 699, 716

Stiglitz, Joseph E 310, 316, 317, 647

Stinchcombe, Arthur L 157

Stolle, Dietlind 186

Stone, Deborah A 408, 409, 410, 414–15

Stone, Judith F 37

Stone, Randall W 174, 313, 317

Strang, David 106, 314

Strange, Susan 319

Strauss, Anselm L 113

Streeck, Wolfgang 41, 200, 201, 305, 441, 691

Stremmel, Ralf 36

Sullivan, Scott 311, 316

Sunstein, Cass R 30, 50, 700

Surender, Rebecca 53, 54

Svallfors, Stefan 243, 244 n2, 245, 246, 247, 248, 249, 636

Swaan, Abram de 449, 505

Swank, Duane 106, 112, 117, 118, 120, 186, 194, 216, 220, 236, 237, 238, 318, 319 n1, 320, 321, 322, 324, 325, 328, 342, 515, 516, 579
Swenson, Peter A 194, 198, 207, 394, 603
Swift, Adam 28
Sykes, Robert 304
Syse, Aslak 165

Tabellini, Guido E 190, 231, 549
Tåhlin, Michael 247
Tai, Po-Fen 659
Takahashi, Mutsuko 399
Tálos, Emmerich 217, 222, 399, 611, 613
Tandler, Julius xxvii
Tanzi, Vito 134, 333
Taylor, Gary 47, 48, 49, 50, 52, 54
Taylor-Gooby, Peter 9, 82, 88, 93, 100, 178, 182, 243, 244 n2, 284, 397, 463, 691, 699
Teichman, Judith 647
Temple, Archbishop William 41–2
Tennstedt, Florian 3 n2, 36
Tesar, Linda L 543–4
Teune, Henry 116
Thaler, Richard H 30, 50, 700
Thane, Pat 34, 37
Thatcher, Margaret 45, 47, 48, 49, 82, 262, 553, 560, 691
Thelen, Kathleen A 194, 201, 239, 305, 615, 691
Therborn, Göran 8, 13, 450, 633, 634, 689, 704, 708, 715
Theresa, Mother xxvii
Thomas, John C 213
Thomson, David 360
Thornton, Patricia 415
Tilly, Charles 108
Tilton, Timothy A 40
Timmons, Jeffrey F 544
Timonen, Virpi 380, 383
Titmuss, Richard M 7, 79–80, 121, 160, 604, 632
Tocqueville, Alexis De 631
Tokman, Víctor E 655
Torfing, Jacob 55, 459
Torgersen, Ulf 480
Tosics, Ivan 482
Toussaint, Eric 312, 317

Townsend, Peter 172
Trampusch, Christine 205
Traxler, Franz 200, 206, 550
Trickey, Heather 163, 444, 458, 695
Trifiletti, Rossana 622
Troeltsch, Ernst 266
Tröger, Vera E 118
Trubek, David M 318
Tsebelis, George 199, 232, 552
Tsunekawa, Keiichi 659
Tufte, Edward R 211
Tullock, Gordon 161
Tuohy, Carolyn J 236, 370

Uhr, John 77
Ullrich, Carsten G 457
Ungerson, Clare 381, 384, 386
Urry, John 198
Ursic, Cveto 412
Usami, Koichi 578
Usui, Chikako 119

Vail, Mark I 447
Väisänen, Ilkka 394
Valiente, Celia 622, 626
Vanhuysse, Pieter 675, 685
Varley, Rita 633
Vaupel, James W 699
Verbist, Gerlinde 440
Vetterlein, Antje 316
Viebrock, Elke 437, 445
Villandsen, Kaspar 164
Vis, Barbara 695
Visier, Lauren 416
Visser, Jelle 200, 201, 202, 203, 209, 210, 437, 441, 447, 563
Vleminckx, Koen 528
Vogelsang, Karl Freiherr von xxvii
Volkens, Andrea 213
Võrk, Andres 283
Vreeland, James Raymond 309, 310, 312, 316, 317
Vrooman, J Cok 575, 576, 583

Waarden, Frans van 201, 205
Wachter, Susan M 489
Wagener, Hans-Jürgen 676, 679

Wagner, Adolph 5
Wagschal, Uwe 216, 223, 342, 348, 575, 635, 636
Walby, Sylvia 263
Waldfogel, Jane 258, 695
Waldron, Jeremy 28, 29
Walker, Alan 577
Wallerstein, Michael 185, 188, 552
Walsh, Patrick N 412
Warner, Carolyn M 265
Watson, Matthew 53
Watson, Sara E 621
Watt, Paul 282
Wearing, Michael 245
Weber, Max 266
Wehler, Hans-Ulrich 65
Wehman, Paul 416
Weingast, Barry M 191
Weir, Margaret 117, 230
Weldon, S Laurel 256 n2, 635
Wells, William 547
Welshman, John 80
Wendt, Claus 371, 373
Wennemo, Irene 141, 142, 420, 516
Wenzelburger, Georg 223
Werding, Martin 693
West, Candace 256
Western, Bruce 115
Westney, D Eleanor 33
Wetzels, Cécile 623
Weyland, Kurt 647
Weymann, Ansgar 311, 313, 317
Whelan, Christopher 530
White, Jenny B 276, 277
White, Stuart 21, 22, 24, 26, 100
Whitehead, Christine M E 488, 490
Whitehouse, Edward R 363, 535
Wibbels, Erik 192, 194, 326, 327, 329, 650
Wichern, Johann Hinrich xxvii
Wichterich, Christa 282
Wickham-Jones, Mark 51, 52–3, 54
Wiesenthal, Helmut 200
Wigforss, Ernst 34, 40
Wilensky, Harold L 93, 94, 105, 106, 112, 155, 173, 197, 213, 228, 229, 236, 269, 341, 342, 360, 393, 494, 495, 515, 534, 552
Wilkinson, Richard 698

Willetts, David 49
Williams, Fiona 254, 283
Williamson, John B 106, 112, 120, 236, 360, 647
Williamson, Oliver E 192
Wilsford, David 370
Wilson, William Julius 287, 437
Wimmer, Andreas 278
Wincott, Daniel 56
Wingen, Max 141
Winter, Heidi 36
Wiseman, John 7, 79
Witte, Edwin 33
Wittenberg, Raphael 383, 389
Wolchik, Sharon 683
Wolf, Frieder 505
Wong, Chack-Kie 577
Wong, Joseph 657, 660, 661, 662, 663, 670
Wong, Linda 667
Wood, Geoffrey D 656, 711
Wörister, Karl 399
Wren, Anne 12, 178

Yamamura, K 41
Yanca, Stephen J 163
Yates, Judith 527
Yeandle, Susan 381, 384, 386
Yeates, Nicola 387
Yee, Silvia 418
Ylppö, Arvo xxvii
You, Laiyin 667
Young, Iris M 21, 26

Zechner, Minna 387
Zeitlin, Jonathan 295, 318, 459
Zelderloo, Luk 416
Zerilli, Linda M G 255, 256, 262
Zhu, Ying 209
Zick, Cathleen D 481
Zimmerman, Don H 256
Zinn, Jens 169
Zohlnhöfer, Reimut 211, 222, 636
Zola, Émile 3, 602
Zola, Irving Kenneth 407
Zöllner, Detlev 341, 394, 395
Zorn, Christopher 119, 322, 324
Zürn, Michael 317
Zweifel, Peter 372